THE MUELLER REPORT

Report On the Investigation Into Russian Interference in the 2016 Presidental Election

Volume I of II

Special Counsel Robert S. Mueller, III

Submitted Pursuant to 28 C.F.R. §
600.B(c)

Washington, D.C.

March 2019

PROSECUTION AND DECLINATION DECISIONS 216

VOLUME II OF II 245

INTRODUCTION TO VOLUME II 246

EXECUTIVE SUMMARY TO VOLUME II 250

I. BACKGROUND LEGAL AND EVIDENTIARY PRINCIPLES 261

II. FACTUAL RESULTS OF THE OBSTRUCTION INVESTIGATION 272

INTRODUCTION TO VOLUME I

This report is submitted to the Attorney General pursuant to 28 C.F.R. § 600.8(c), which states that, "[a]t the conclusion of the Special Counsel's work, he ... shall provide the Attorney General a confidential report explaining the prosecution or declination decisions [the Special Counsel] reached."

The Russian government interfered in the 2016 presidential election in sweeping and systematic fashion. Evidence of Russian government operations began to surface in mid-2016. In June, the Democratic National Committee and its cyber response team publicly announced that Russian hackers had compromised its computer network. Releases of hacked materials — hacks that public reporting soon attributed to the Russian government — began that same month. Additional releases followed in July through the organization WikiLeaks, with further releases in October and November.

In late July 2016, soon after WikiLeaks's first release of stolen documents, a foreign government contacted the FBI about a May 2016 encounter with Trump Campaign foreign policy advisor George Papadopoulos. Papadopoulos had suggested to a representative of that foreign government that the Trump Campaign had received indications from the Russian government that it could assist the Campaign through the anonymous release of information damaging to Democratic presidential candidate Hillary Clinton. That information prompted the FBI on July 31, 2016, to open an investigation into whether individuals associated with the Trump Campaign were coordinating with the Russian government in its interference activities.

That fall, two federal agencies jointly announced that the Russian government "directed recent compromises of e-mails from US persons and institutions, including US political organizations," and, "[t]hese thefts and disclosures are intended to interfere with the US election process." After the election, in late December 2016, the United States imposed sanctions on Russia for having interfered in the election. By early 2017, several congressional committees were examining Russia's interference in the election

Within the Executive Branch, these investigatory efforts ultimately led to the May 2017 appointment of Special Counsel Robert S. Mueller, III. The order appointing the Special Counsel authorized him to investigate "the Russian government's efforts to interfere in the 2016 presidential election," including any links or coordination between the Russian government and individuals associated with the Trump Campaign.

As set forth in detail in this report, the Special Counsel's investigation established that Russia interfered in the 2016 presidential election principally through two operations. First, a Russian entity carried out a social media campaign that favored presidential candidate Donald J. Trump and disparaged presidential candidate Hillary Clinton. Second, a Russian intelligence service conducted computer-intrusion operations against entities, employees, and volunteers working on the Clinton Campaign and then released stolen documents. The investigation also identified numerous links between the Russian government and the Trump Campaign. Although the investigation established that the Russian government perceived it would benefit from a Trump presidency and worked to secure that outcome, and that the Campaign expected it would benefit electorally from information stolen and released through Russian efforts, the investigation did not establish that members of the Trump Campaign conspired or coordinated with the Russian government in its election interference activities.

*   *   *

Below we describe the evidentiary considerations underpinning statements about the results of our investigation and the Special Counsel's charging decisions, and we then provide an overview of the two volumes of our report, The report describes actions and events that the Special Counsel's Office found to be supported by the evidence collected in our investigation. In some instances, the report points out the absence of evidence or conflicts in the evidence about a particular fact or event. In other instances, when substantial, credible evidence enabled the Office to reach a conclusion with confidence, the report states that the investigation established that certain actions or events occurred. A statement that the investigation did not establish particular facts does not mean there was no evidence of those facts.

In evaluating whether evidence about collective action of multiple individuals constituted a crime, we applied the framework of conspiracy law, not the concept of "collusion." In so doing, the Office recognized that the word "collud]e]" was used in communications with the Acting Attorney General confirming certain aspects of the investigation's scope and that the term has frequently been invoked in public reporting about the investigation. But collusion is not a specific offense or theory of liability found in the United States Code, nor is it a term of art in federal criminal law. For those reasons, the Office's focus in analyzing questions of joint criminal liability was on conspiracy as defined in federal law. In connection with that analysis, we addressed the factual question whether members of the Trump Campaign "coordinat[ed]"-a term that appears in the appointment order-with Russian election interference activities. Like collusion, "coordination" does not have a settled definition in federal criminal law. We understood coordination to require an agreement-tacit or express-between the Trump Campaign and the Russian government on election interference. That requires more than the two parties taking actions that were informed by or responsive to the other's actions or interests. We applied the term coordination in that sense when stating in the report that the investigation did not establish that the Trump Campaign coordinated with the Russian government in its election interference activities.

*   *   *

The report on our investigation consists of two volumes:

Volume I describes the factual results of the Special Counsel's investigation of Russia's interference in the 2016 presidential election and its interactions with the Trump Campaign. Section I describes the scope of the investigation. Sections II and III describe the principal ways Russia interfered in the 2016 presidential election.
Section IV describes links between the Russian government and individuals associated with the Trump Campaign. Section V sets forth the Special Counsel's charging decisions.

Volume II addresses the President's actions towards the FBI's investigation into Russia's interference in the 2016 presidential election and related matters, and his actions towards the Special Counsel's investigation.
Volume II separately states its framework and the considerations that guided that investigation.

EXECUTIVE SUMMARY TO VOLUME I

RUSSIAN SOCIAL MEDIA CAMPAIGN

The Internet Research Agency (IRA) carried out the earliest Russian interference operations identified by the investigation-a social media campaign designed to provoke and amplify political and social discord in the United States. The IRA was based in St. Petersburg, Russia, and received funding from Russian oligarch Yevgeniy Prigozhin and companies he controlled. Prigozhin is wide! rep████████████████████████████████████
████ Harm to Ongoing Matter ████████████████

In mid-2014, the IRA sent employees to the United States on an intelligence-gathering mission with instructions Harm to Ongoing Matter ███

The IRA later used social media accounts and interest groups to sow discord in the U.S. political system through what it termed "information warfare." The campaign evolved from a generalized program designed in 2014 and 2015 to undermine the U.S. electoral system, to a targeted operation that by early 2016 favored candidate Trump and disparaged candidate Clinton. The IRA's operation also included the purchase of political advertisements on social media in the names of U.S. persons and entities, as well as the staging of political rallies inside the United States. To organize those rallies, IRA employees posed as U.S. grassroots entities and persons and made contact with Trump supporters and Trump Campaign officials in the United States. The investigation did not identify evidence that any U.S. persons conspired or coordinated with the IRA. Section II of this report details the Office's investigation of the Russian social media campaign.

RUSSIAN HACKING OPERATIONS

At the same time that the IRA operation began to focus on supporting candidate Trump in early 2016, the Russian government employed a second form of interference: cyber intrusions (hacking) and releases of hacked materials damaging to the Clinton Campaign. The Russian intelligence service known as the Main Intelligence Directorate of the General Staff of the Russian Army (GRU) carried out these operations.

In March 2016, the GRU began hacking the email accounts of Clinton Campaign volunteers and employees, including campaign chairman John Podesta. In April 2016, the GRU hacked into the computer networks of the Democratic Congressional Campaign Committee (DCCC) and the Democratic National Committee (DNC). The GRU stole hundreds of thousands of documents from the compromised email accounts and networks. Around the time that the DNC announced in mid-June 2016 the Russian government's role in hacking its network, the GRU began disseminating stolen materials through the fictitious online personas "DCLeaks" and "Guccifer 2.0."

The GRU later released additional materials through the organization WikiLeak

The presidential campaign of Donald J. Trump ("Trump Campaign" or "Campaign") showed interest in WikiLeaks's releases of documents and welcomed their potential to damage candidate Clinton. Beginning in June 2016, forecast to senior Campaign officials that WikiLeaks would release information damaging to candidate Clinton. WikiLeaks's first release came in July 2016. Around the same time, candidate Trump announced that he hoped Russia would recover emails described as missing from a private server used by Clinton when she was Secretary of State he later said that he was speaking sarcastically .

WikiLeaks began releasing Podesta's stolen emails on October 7, 2016, less than one hour after a U.S. media outlet released video considered damaging to candidate Trump. Section lil of this Report details the Office's investigation into the Russian hacking operations, as well as other efforts by Trump Campaign supporters to obtain Clinton-related emails.

RUSSIAN CONTACTS WITH THE CAMPAIGN

The social media campaign and the GRU hacking operations coincided with a series of contacts between Trump Campaign officials and individuals with ties to the Russian government. The Office investigated whether those contacts reflected or resulted in the Campaign conspiring or coordinating with Russia in its election-interference activities. Although the investigation established that the Russian government perceived it would benefit from a Trump presidency and worked to secure that outcome, and that the Campaign expected it would benefit electorally from information stolen and released through Russian efforts, the investigation did not establish that members of the Trump Campaign conspired or coordinated with the Russian government in its election interference activities.

The Russian contacts consisted of business connections, offers of assistance to the Campaign, invitations for candidate Trump and Putin to meet in person, invitations for Campaign officials and representatives of the Russian government to meet, and policy positions seeking improved U.S.-Russian relations. Section IV of this Report details the contacts between Russia and the Trump Campaign during the campaign and transition periods, the most salient of which are summarized below in chronological order.

2015. Some of the earliest contacts were made in connection with a Trump Organization real-estate project in Russia known as Trump Tower Moscow. Candidate Trump signed a Letter of intent for Trump Tower Moscow by November 2015, and in January 2016 Trump Organization executive Michael Cohen emailed and spoke about the project with the office of Russian government press secretary Dmitry Peskov. The Trump

Organization pursued the project through at least June 2016, including by considering travel to Russia by Cohen and candidate Trump.

Spring 2016. Campaign foreign policy advisor George Papadopoulos made early contact with Joseph Mifsud, a London-based professor who had connections to Russia and traveled to Moscow in April 2016. Immediately upon his return to London from that trip, Mifsud told Papadopoulos that the Russian government had "dirt" on Hillary Clinton in the form of thousands of emails. One week later, in the first week of May 2016, Papadopoulos suggested to a representative of a foreign government that the Trump Campaign had received indications from the Russian government that it could assist the Campaign through the anonymous release of information damaging to candidate Clinton. Throughout that period of time and for several months thereafter, Papadopoulos worked with Mifsud and two Russian nationals to arrange a meeting between the Campaign and the Russian government. No meeting took place.

Summer 2016. Russian outreach to the Trump Campaign continued into the summer of 2016, as candidate Trump was becoming the presumptive Republican nominee for President. On June 9, 2016, for example, a Russian lawyer met with senior Trump Campaign officials Donald Trump Jr., Jared Kushner, and campaign chairman Paul Manafort to deliver what the email proposing the meeting had described as "official documents and information that would incriminate Hillary." The materials were offered to Trump Jr. as "part of Russia and its government's support for Mr. Trump." The written communications setting up the meeting showed that the Campaign anticipated receiving information from Russia that could assist candidate Trump's electoral prospects, but the Russian lawyer's presentation did not provide such information.

Days after the June 9 meeting, on June 14, 2016, a cybersecurity firm and the DNC announced that Russian government hackers had infiltrated the DNC and obtained access to opposition research on candidate Trump, among other documents.

In July 2016, Campaign foreign policy advisor Carter Page traveled in his personal capacity to Moscow and gave the keynote address at the New Economic School. Page had lived and worked in Russia between 2003 and 2007. After returning to the United States, Page became acquainted with at least two Russian intelligence officers, one of whom was later charged in 2015 with conspiracy to act as an unregistered agent of Russia. Page's July 2016 trip to Moscow and his advocacy for pro-Russian foreign policy drew media attention. The Campaign then distanced itself from Page and, by late September 2016, removed him from the Campaign.

July 2016 was also the month WikiLeaks first released emails stolen by the GRU from the DNC. On July 22, 2016, WikiLeaks posted thousands of internal DNC documents revealing information about the Clinton Campaign. Within days, there was public reporting that U.S. intelligence agencies had "high confidence" that the Russian government was behind the theft of emails and documents from the DNC. And within a week of the release, a foreign government informed the FBI about its May 2016 interaction with Papadopoulos and his statement that the Russian government could assist the Trump Campaign. On July 31, 2016, based on the foreign government reporting, the FBI opened an investigation into potential coordination between the Russian government and individuals associated with the Trump Campaign.

Separately, on August 2, 2016, Trump campaign chairman Paul Manafort met in New York City with his long-time business associate Konstantin Kilimnik, who the FBI assesses to have ties to Russian intelligence. Kilimnik requested the meeting to deliver in person a peace plan for Ukraine that Manafort acknowledged to the Special Counsel's Office was a "backdoor" way for Russia to control part of eastern Ukraine; both men believed the plan would require candidate Trump's assent to succeed (were he to be elected President). They also discussed the status of the Trump Campaign and Manafort's strategy for winning Democratic votes in Midwestern states. Months before that meeting, Manafort had caused internal polling data to be shared with Kilimnik, and the sharing continued for some period of time after their August meeting.

Fall 2016. On October 7, 2016, the media released video of candidate Trump speaking in graphic terms about women years earlier, which was considered damaging to his candidacy. Less than an hour later, WikiLeaks made its second release: thousands of John Podesta's emails that had been stolen by the GRU in late March 2016. The FBI and other U.S. government institutions were at the time continuing their investigation of suspected Russian government efforts to interfere in the presidential election. That same day, October 7, the Department of Homeland Security and the Office of the Director of National Intelligence issued a joint public statement "that the Russian Government directed the recent compromises of e-mails from US persons and institutions, including from US political organizations." Those "thefts" and the "disclosures" of the hacked materials through online platforms such as WikiLeaks, the statement continued, "are intended to interfere with the US election process."

Post-2016 Election. Immediately after the November 8 election, Russian government officials and prominent Russian businessmen began trying to make inroads into the new administration. The most senior levels of the Russian government encouraged these efforts. The Russian Embassy made contact hours after the election to congratulate the President-Elect and to arrange a call with President Putin. Several Russian businessmen picked up the effort from there.

Kirill Dmitriev, the chief executive officer of Russia's sovereign wealth fund, was among the Russians who tried to make contact with the incoming administration. In early December, a business associate steered Dmitriev to Erik Prince, a supporter of the Trump Campaign and an associate of senior Trump advisor Steve Bannon. Dmitriev and Prince later met face-to-face in January 2017 in the Seychelles and discussed U.S.-Russia relations. During the same period, another business associate introduced Dmitriev to a friend of Jared Kushner who had not served on the Campaign or the Transition Team. Dmitriev and Kushner's friend collaborated on a short written reconciliation plan for the United States and Russia, which Dmitriev implied had been cleared through Putin. The friend gave that proposal to Kushner before the inauguration, and Kushner later gave copies to Bannon and incoming Secretary of State Rex Tillerson.

On December 29, 2016, then-President Obama imposed sanctions on Russia for having interfered in the election. Incoming National Security Advisor Michael Flynn called Russian Ambassador Sergey Kislyak and asked Russia not to escalate the situation in response to the sanctions. The following day, Putin announced that Russia would not take retaliatory measures in response to the sanctions at that time. Hours later, President-Elect Trump tweeted, "Great move on delay (by V. Putin)." The next day, on December 31, 2016, Kislyak called Flynn and told him the request had been received at the highest levels and Russia had chosen not to retaliate as a result of Flynn's request.

On January 6, 2017, members ofthe intelligence community briefed President-Elect Trump on a joint assessment-drafted and coordinated among the Central Intelligence Agency, FBI, and National Security Agency-that concluded with high confidence that Russia had intervened in the election through a variety of means to assist Trump's candidacy and harm Clinton's. A declassified version of the assessment was publicly released that same day.

Between mid-January 2017 and early February 2017, three congressional committees-the House Permanent Select Committee on Intelligence (HPSCI), the Senate Select Committee on Intelligence (SSCI), and the Senate Judiciary Committee (SJC)-announced that they would conduct inquiries, or had already been conducting inquiries, into Russian interference in the election. Then-FBI Director James Corney later confirmed to Congress the existence of the FBI's investigation into Russian interference that had begun before the election. On March 20, 2017, in open-session testimony before HPSCI, Corney stated:

> I have been authorized by the Department of Justice to confirm that the FBI, as part of our counterintelligence mission, is investigating the Russian government's efforts to

interfere in the 2016 presidential election, and that includes investigating the nature of any links between individuals associated with the Trump campaign and the Russian government and whether there was any coordination between the campaign and Russia's efforts.... As with any counterintelligence investigation, this will also include an assessment of whether any crimes were committed.

The investigation continued under then-Director Corney for the next seven weeks until May 9, 2017, when President Trump fired Corney as FBI Director-an action which is analyzed in Volume II of the report.

On May 17, 2017, Acting Attorney General Rod Rosenstein appointed the Special Counsel and authorized him to conduct the investigation that Corney had confirmed in his congressional testimony, as well as matters arising directly from the investigation, and any other matters within the scope of 28 C.F.R. § 600.4(a), which generally covers efforts to interfere with or obstruct the investigation.

President Trump reacted negatively to the Special Counsel's appointment. He told advisors that it was the end of his presidency, sought to have Attorney General Jefferson (Jeff) Sessions recuse from the Russia investigation and to have the Special Counsel removed, and engaged in efforts to curtail the Special Counsel's investigation and prevent the disclosure of evidence to it, including through public and private contacts with potential witnesses. Those and related actions are described and analyzed in Volume II of the report.

* * *

THE SPECIAL COUNSEL'S CHARGING DECISIONS

In reaching the charging decisions described in Volume I of the report, the Office determined whether the conduct it found amounted to a violation of federal criminal law chargeable under the Principles of Federal Prosecution. See Justice Manual § 9-27.000 et seq. (2018). The standard set forth in the Justice Manual is whether the conduct constitutes a crime; if so, whether admissible evidence would probably be sufficient to obtain and sustain a conviction; and whether prosecution would serve a substantial federal interest that could not be adequately served by prosecution elsewhere or through non-criminal alternatives. See Justice Manual § 9 27.220

Section V of the report provides detailed explanations of the Office's charging decisions, which contain three main components.

First, the Office determined that Russia's two principal interference operations in the 2016 U.S. presidential election-the social media campaign and the hacking-and-dumping operations• violated U.S. criminal law. Many of the individuals and entities involved in the social media campaign have been charged with participating in a conspiracy to defraud the United States by undermining through deceptive acts the work of federal agencies charged with regulating foreign influence in U.S. elections, as well as related counts of identity theft. See United States v. Internet Research Agency, et al., No. 18-cr-32 (D.D.C.). Separately, Russian intelligence officers who carried out the hacking into Democratic Party computers and the personal email accounts of individuals affiliated with the Clinton Campaign conspired to violate, among other federal laws, the federal computer-intrusion statute, and the have been so char ed. See United States v. Ne ksho, et al. No.

18-cr-215 D.D.C..

Second, while the investigation identified numerous links between individuals with ties to the Russian government and individuals associated with the Trump Campaign, the evidence was not sufficient to support criminal charges. Among other things, the evidence was not sufficient to charge any Campaign official as an unregistered agent of the Russian government or other Russian principal. And our evidence about the June 9, 2016 meeting and WikiLeaks's releases of hacked materials was not sufficient to charge a criminal campaign-finance violation. Further, the evidence was not sufficient to charge that any member of the Trump Campaign conspired with representatives of the Russian government to interfere in the 2016 election.

Third, the investigation established that several individuals affiliated with the Trump Campaign lied to the Office, and to Congress, about their interactions with Russian-affiliated individuals and related matters. Those lies materially impaired the investigation of Russian election interference. The Office charged some of those lies as violations of the federal false• statements statute. Former National Security Advisor Michael Flynn pleaded guilty to lying about his interactions with Russian Ambassador Kislyak during the transition period. George Papadopoulos, a foreign policy advisor during the campaign period, pleaded guilty to lying to investigators about, inter alia, the nature and timing of his interactions with Joseph Mifsud, the professor who told Papadopoulos that the Russians had dirt on candidate Clinton in the form of thousands of emails. Former Trump Organization attorney Michael Cohen leaded uil to making false statements to Congress about the Trump Moscow project.

Harm to Ongoing
Matter

And in February 2019, the U.S. District Court for the District of Columbia found that Manafort lied to the Office and the grand jury concerning his interactions and communications with Konstantin Kilimnik about Trump Campaign polling data and a peace plan for Ukraine

* * *

The Office investigated several other events that have been publicly reported to involve potential Russia-related contacts. For example, the investigation established that interactions between Russian Ambassador Kislyak and Trump Campaign officials both at the candidate's April 2016 foreign policy speech in Washington, D.C., and during the week of the Republican National Convention were brief, public, and non-substantive. And the investigation did not establish that one Campaign official's efforts to dilute a portion of the Republican Party platform on providing assistance to Ukraine were undertaken at the behest of candidate Trump or Russia. The investigation also did not establish that a meeting between Kislyak and Sessions in September 2016 at Sessions's Senate office included any more than a passing mention of the presidential campaign.

The investigation did not always yield admissible information or testimony, or a complete picture of the activities undertaken by subjects of the investigation. Some individuals invoked their Fifth Amendment right against compelled self-incrimination and were not, in the Office's judgment, appropriate candidates for grants of immunity. The Office limited its pursuit of other witnesses and information-such as information known to attorneys or individuals claiming to be members of the media-in light of internal Department of Justice policies. See, e.g., Justice Manual§§ 9-13.400, 13.410. Some of the information obtained via court process, moreover, was presumptively covered by legal privilege and was screened from investigators by a filter (or "taint") team. Even when individuals testified or agreed to be interviewed, they sometimes provided information that was false or incomplete, leading to some of the false-statements charges described above. And the Office faced practical limits on its ability to access relevant evidence as well-numerous witnesses and subjects lived abroad, and documents were held outside the United States.

Further, the Office learned that some of the individuals we interviewed or whose conduct we investigated-including some associated with the Trump Campaign-deleted relevant communications or communicated during the relevant period using applications that feature encryption or that do not provide for long-term retention of data or communications records. In such cases, the Office was not able to corroborate witness statements through comparison to contemporaneous communications or fully question witnesses about statements that appeared inconsistent with other known facts.

Accordingly, while this report embodies factual and legal determinations that the Office believes to be accurate and complete to the greatest extent possible, given these identified gaps, the Office cannot rule out the possibility that the unavailable information would shed additional light on (or cast in a new light) the events described in the report

I. THE SPECIAL COUNSEL'S INVESTIGATION

On May 17, 2017, Deputy Attorney General Rod J. Rosenstein-then serving as Acting Attorney General for the Russia investigation following the recusal of former Attorney General Jeff Sessions on March 2, 2016-appointed the Special Counsel "to investigate Russian interference with the 2016 presidential election and related matters." Office of the Deputy Att'y Gen., Order No. 3915-2017, Appointment of Special Counsel to Investigate Russian Interference with the 2016 Presidential Election and Related Matters, May 17, 2017) ("Appointment Order"). Relying on "the authority vested" in the Acting Attorney General, "including 28 U.S.C. §§ 509, 510, and 515," the Acting Attorney General ordered the appointment of a Special Counsel "inorder to discharge [the Acting Attorney General's] responsibility to provide supervision and management of the Department of Justice, and to ensure a full and thorough investigation of the Russian government's efforts to interfere in the 2016 presidential election." Appointment Order (introduction). "The Special Counsel," the Order stated, "is authorized to conduct the investigation confirmed by then-FBI Director James B. Corney in testimony before the House Permanent Select Committee on Intelligence on March 20, 2017," including:

(i) any links and/or coordination between the Russian government and individuals associated with the campaign of President Donald Trump; and

(ii) any matters that arose or may arise directly from the investigation; and

(iii) any other matters within the scope of 28 C.F.R. § 600.4(a).

Appointment Order ,r (b). Section 600.4 affords the Special Counsel "the authority to investigate and prosecute federal crimes committed in the course of, and with intent to interfere with, the Special Counsel's investigation, such as perjury, obstruction of justice, destruction of evidence, and intimidation of witnesses." 28 C.F.R. § 600.4(a). The authority to investigate "any matters that arose ... directly from the investigation," Appointment Order ,r (b)(ii), covers similar crimes that may have occurred during the course of the FBI's confirmed investigation before the Special Counsel's appointment. "If the Special Counsel believes it is necessary and appropriate," the Order further provided, "the Special Counsel is authorized to prosecute federal crimes arising from the investigation of these matters." Id. ,r (c). Finally, the Acting Attorney General made applicable "Sections 600.4 through 600.10 of Title 28 of the Code of Federal Regulations." Id. ,r (d).

The Acting Attorney General further clarified the scope of the Special Counsel's investigatory authority in two subsequent memoranda. A memorandum dated August 2, 2017, explained that the Appointment Order had been "worded categorically in order to permit its public release without confirming specific investigations involving specific individuals." It then confirmed that the Special Counsel had been authorized since his appointment to investigate allegations that three Trump campaign officials-Carter Page, Paul Manafort, and George Papadopoulos-"committed a crime or crimes by colluding with Russian government officials with respect to the Russian government's efforts to interfere with the 2016 presidential election." The memorandum also confirmed the Special Counsel's authority to investigate certain other matters, including two additional sets of allegations involving Manafort (crimes arising from payments he received from the Ukrainian government and crimes arising from his receipt of loans from a bank whose CEO was then seeking a position in the Trump Administration); allegations that Papadopoulos committed a crime or crimes by acting as an unregistered agent of the Israeli government; and four sets of allegations involving Michael Flynn, the former National Security Advisor to President Trump.

On October 20, 2017, the Acting Attorney General confirmed in a memorandum the Special Counsel's investigative authority as to several individuals and entities. First, "as part of a full and thorough investigation of the Russian government's efforts to interfere in the 2016 presidential election," the Special Counsel was authorized to investigate "the pertinent activities ofMichael Cohen, Richard Gates, ███████████████████████ , Roger Stone, and"Confirmation of the authorization to investigate such individuals," the memorandum stressed, "does not suggest that the Special Counsel has made a determination that any of them has committed a crime." Second, with respect to Michael Cohen, the memorandum recognized the Special Counsel's authority to investigate "leads relate[d] to Cohen's establishment and use of Essential Consultants LLC to, inter alia, receive funds from Russian-backed entities." Third, the memorandum memorialized the Special Counsel's authority to investigate individuals and entities who were possibly engaged in "jointly undertaken activity" with existing subjects of the investigation, including Paul Manafort. Finally, the memorandum described an FBI investigation opened before the Special Counsel's appointment into "allegations that [then-Attorney General Jeff Sessions] made false statements to the United States Senate[,]" and confirmed the Special Counsel's authority to investigate that matter.

The Special Counsel structured the investigation in view of his power and authority "to exercise all investigative and prosecutorial functions of any United States Attorney." 28 C.F.R:§ 600.6. Like a U.S. Attorney's Office, the Special Counsel's Office considered a range of classified and unclassified information available to the FBI in the course of the Office's Russia investigation, and the Office structured that work around evidence for possible use in prosecutions of federal crimes (assuming that one or more crimes were identified that warranted prosecution). There was substantial evidence immediately available to the Special Counsel at the inception of the investigation in May 2017 because the FBI had, by that time, already investigated Russian election interference for nearly 10 months. The Special Counsel's Office exercised its judgment regarding what to investigate and did not, for instance, investigate every public report of a contact between the Trump Campaign and Russian-affiliated individuals and entities.

The Office has concluded its investigation into links and coordination between the Russian government and individuals associated with the Trump Campaign. Certain proceedings associated with the Office's work remain ongoing.

After consultation with the Office of the Deputy Attorney General, the Office has transferred responsibility for those remaining issues to other components of the Department of Justice and FBI. Appendix D lists those transfers.

Two district courts confirmed the breadth of the Special Counsel's authority to investigate Russia election interference and links and/or coordination with the Trump Campaign. *See United States v. Manafort*, 312 F. Supp. 3d 60, 79-83 (D.D.C. 2018); *United States v. Manafort*, 321 F. Supp. 3d 640, 650-655 (E.D. Va. 2018). In the course of conducting that investigation, the Office periodically identified evidence of potential criminal activity that was outside the scope of the Special Counsel's authority established by the Acting Attorney General. After consultation with the Office of the Deputy Attorney General, the Office referred that evidence to appropriate law enforcement authorities, principally other components of the Department of Justice and to the FBI. Appendix D summarizes those referrals.

* * *

To carry out the investigation and prosecution of the matters assigned to him, the Special Counsel assembled a team that at its high point included 19 attorneys-five of whom joined the Office from private practice and 14 on detail or assigned from other Department of Justice components. These attorneys were assisted by a filter team of Department lawyers and FBI personnel who screened materials obtained via court process for privileged information before turning those materials over to investigators; a support staff of three paralegals on detail from the Department's Antitrust Division; and an administrative staff of nine responsible for budget, finance, purchasing, human resources, records, facilities, security, information technology, and administrative support. The Special Counsel attorneys and support staff were co-located with and worked alongside approximately 40 FBI agents, intelligence analysts, forensic accountants, a paralegal, and professional staff assigned by the FBI to assist the Special Counsel's investigation. Those "assigned" FBI employees remained under FBI supervision at all times; the matters on which they assisted were supervised by the Special Counsel.'

During its investigation the Office issued more than 2,800 subpoenas under the auspices of a grand jury sitting in the District of Columbia; executed nearly 500 search-and-seizure warrants; obtained more than 230 orders for communications records under 18 U.S.C. § 2703(d); obtained almost 50 orders authorizing use of pen registers; made 13 requests to foreign governments pursuant to Mutual Legal Assistance Treaties; and interviewed approximately 500 witnesses, including almost 80 before a grand jury.

* * *

From its inception, the Office recognized that its investigation could identify foreign intelligence and counterintelligence information relevant to the FBI's broader national security mission. FBI personnel who assisted the Office established procedures to identify and convey such information to the FBI. The FBI's Counterintelligence Division met with the Office regularly for that purpose for most of the Office's tenure. For more than the past year, the FBI also embedded personnel at the Office who did not work on the Special Counsel's investigation, but whose purpose was to review the results of the investigation and to send-in writing-summaries of foreign intelligence and counterintelligence information to FBIHQ and FBI Field Offices. Those communications and other correspondence between the Office and the FBI contain information derived from the investigation, not all of which is contained in this Volume. This Volume is a summary. It contains, in the Office's judgment, that information necessary to account for the Special Counsel's prosecution and declination decisions and to describe the investigation's main factual results.

---

1 FBI personnel assigned to the Special Counsel's Office were required to adhere to all applicable federal law and all Department and FBI regulations, guidelines, and policies. An FBI attorney worked on FBI-related matters for the Office, such as FBI compliance with all FBI policies and procedures, including the FBI's Domestic Investigations and Operations Guide (DIOG). That FBI attorney worked under FBI legal supervision, not the Special Counsel's supervision

II. RUSSIAN "ACTIVE MEASURES" SOCIAL MEDIA CAMPAIGN

The first form of Russian election influence came principally from the Internet Research Agency, LLC (IRA), a Russian organization funded by Yevgeniy Viktorovich Prigozhin and companies he controlled, including Concord Management and Consulting LLC and Concord Catering (collectively "Concord").[2] The IRA conducted social media operations targeted at large U.S. audiences with the goal of sowing discord in the U.S. political system.[3] These operations constituted "active measures" (aKTHBHbJe MeponplD1Tml), a term that typically refers to operations conducted by Russian security services aimed at influencing the course of international affairs.[4]

The IRA and its employees began operations targeting the United States as early as 2014. Using fictitious U.S. personas, IRA employees operated social media accounts and group pages designed to attract U.S. audiences. These groups and accounts, which addressed divisive U.S. political and social issues, falsely claimed to be controlled by U.S. activists. Over time, these social media accounts became a means to reach large U.S. audiences. IRA employees travelled to the United States in mid-2014 on an intelligence-gathering mission to obtain information and photographs for use in their social media posts.

IRA employees posted derogatory information about a number of candidates in the 2016 U.S. presidential election. By early to mid-2016, IRA operations included supporting the Trump Campaign and disparaging candidate Hillary Clinton. The IRA made various expenditures to carry out those activities, including buying political advertisements on social media in the names of U.S. persons and entities. Some IRA employees, posing as

U.S. persons and without revealing their Russian association, communicated electronically with individuals associated with the Trump Campaign and with other political activists to seek to coordinate political activities, including the staging of political rallies.[5] The investigation did not identify evidence that any U.S. persons knowingly or intentionally coordinated with the IRA's interference operation.

By the end of the 2016 U.S. election, the IRA had the ability to reach millions of U.S. persons through their social media accounts. Multiple IRA-controlled Facebook groups and Instagram accounts had hundreds of thousands of U.S. partrcipants. IRA-controlled Twitter accounts separately had tens of thousands of followers, including multiple U.S. political figures who retweeted IRA-created content. In November 2017, a Facebook representative testified that Facebook had identified 470 IRA-controlled Facebook accounts that collectively made 80,000 posts between January 2015 and August 2017. Facebook estimated the IRA reached as many as 126 million persons through its Facebook accounts.[6] In January 2018, Twitter announced that It had identified 3,814 IRA-controlled Twitter accounts and notified approximately 1.4 million people Twitter believed may have been in contact with an iRA-controlled account.[7]

A. Structure of the Internet Research Agency

The organization quickly grew. Harm to Ongoing Matter

Harm to Ongoing Matter
[11]

[12]

The growth of the organization also led to a more detailed organizational structure.
Harm to Ongoing Matter

Harm to Ongoing Matter

[3]

Two individuals headed the IRA's management: its general director, Mikhail Bystrov, and its executive director, Mikhail Burchik. Harm to Ongoing Matter

[14] Harm to Ongoing Matter
[15]

As early as the spring of 2014, the IRA began to hide its funding and activities.
Harm to Ongoing Matter

[16]

The IRA's U.S. operations are part of a larger set of interlocking operations known as "Project Lakhta,"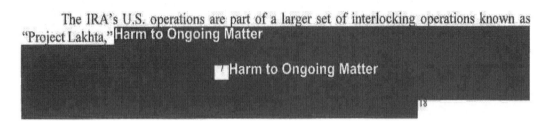

Numerous media sources   have reported on Prigozhin's ties to Putin, and the two   have appeared together in public photographs.[22]

IRA employees were aware that Prigozhin was involved in the IRA's U.S. operations,
Harm to Ongoing Matter

[29]

Harm to Ongoing Matter

[30] In May
2016, IRA employees, claiming to be U.S. social activists and administrators of Facebook groups,
recruited U.S. persons to hold signs (including one in front of the White House) that read "Happy
55th Birthday Dear Boss," as an homage to Prigozhin (whose 55th birthday was on June 1, 2016).[31]
Harm to Ongoing Matter

[32]

Harm to Ongoing Matter

C. The IRA Targets U.S. Elections

1. The IRA Ramps Up U.S. Operations As Early As 2014

The IRA's U.S. operations sought to influence public opinion through online media and forums. By the spring of 2014, the IRA began to consolidate U.S. operations within a single subdivided department, known internally as the "Translator" (Переводчик) department Harm to Ongoing Matter

IRA

Harm to Ongoing Matter

Harm to Ongoing Matter

Harm to Ongoing Matter

Harm to Ongoing Matter

IRA employees also traveled to the United States on intelligence-gathering missions. In June 2014, four IRA employees applied to the U.S. Department of State to enter the United States, while lying about the purpose of their trip and claiming to be four friends who had met at a party.38 Ultimately, two IRA employees—Anna Bogacheva and Aleksandra Krylova—

received visas and entered the United States on June 4, 2014. Prior to traveling, Krylova and Bogacheva compiled itineraries and instructions for the trip.

Harm to Ongoing Matter

Harm to Ongoing Matter

Harm to Ongoing Matter

Harm to Ongoing Matter

40

41

2. U.S. Operations Thrbugh IRA-Controlled Social Media Accounts

Dozens of IRA employees were responsible for operating accounts and personas on different U.S. social media platforms. The IRA referred to employees assigned to operate the social media accounts as "specialists."[42] Starting as early as 2014, the IRA's U.S. operations included social media specialists focusing on Facebook, YouTube, and Twitter.[43] The IRA later added specialists who operated on Tumblr and Instagram accounts.[44]

Initially, the IRA created social media accounts that pretended to be the personal accounts of U.S. persons.[45] By early 20 I 5, the IRA began to create larger social media groups or public social media pages that claimed (falsely) to be affiliated with U.S. political and grassroots organizations. In certain cases, the IRA created accounts that mimicked real U.S. organizations.

For example, one IRA-controlled Twitter account,@TEN_GOP, purported to be connected to the Tennessee Republican Party.46 More commonly, the IRA created accounts in the names of fictitious U.S. organizations and grassroots groups and used these accounts to pose as anti• immigration groups, Tea Party activists, Black Lives Matter protestors, and other U.S. social and political activists.

Harm to Ongoing Matter

Harm to Ongoing Matter

Harm to Ongoing Matter

By February 2016, internal IRA documents referred to support for the Trump Campaign and opposition to candidate Clinton.[49] For example, HOM directions to IRA operators Harm to Ongoing Matter

"Main idea: Use any opportunity to criticize Hillary [Clinton] and the rest (except Sanders and Trump - we support them)."[50] Harm to Ongoing Matter

The focus on the U.S. presidential campaign continued throughout 2016. In il 2016 internal ▇▇▇▇▇ reviewing the IRA-controlled Facebook group "Secured Borders," the author criticized the "lower number of posts dedicated to criticizing Hillary Clinton" and reminded the Facebook specialist "it is imperative to intensify criticizing Hillary Clinton."51

IRA employees also acknowledged that their work focused on influencing the U.S. presidential election. Harm to Ongoing Matter

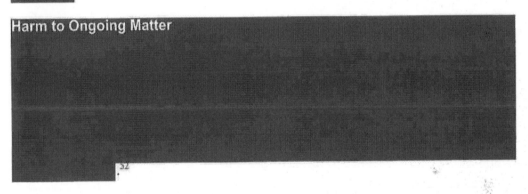

Harm to Ongoing Matter

3. U.S. Operations Through Facebook

Many IRA operations used Facebook accounts created and operated by its specialists. Harm to Ongoing Matter

53

during the 2016 campaign covered a range of political issues and included purported conservative groups (with names such as "Being Patriotic," "Stop All Immigrants," "Secured Borders," and "Tea Party News"), purported Black social justice groups ("Black Matters," "Blacktivist," and "Don't Shoot Us"), LGBTQ groups ("LGBT United"), and religious groups ("United Muslims of America").

Throughout 2016, IRA accounts published an increasing number of materials supporting the Trump Campaign and opposing the Clinton Campaign. For example, on May 31, 2016, the operational account "Matt Skiber" began to privately message dozens of pro-Trump Facebook groups asking them to help plan a "pro-Trump rally near Trump Tower.[55]

To reach larger U.S. audiences, the IRA purchased advertisements from Facebook that promoted the IRA groups on the newsfeeds of U.S. audience members. According to Facebook, the IRA purchased over 3,500 advertisements, and the expenditures totaled approximately $100,000

During the U.S. presidential campaign, many IRA-purchased advertisements explicitly supported or opposed a presidential candidate or promoted U.S. rallies organized by the IRA (discussed below). As early as March 2016, the IRA purchased advertisements that overtly opposed the Clinton Campaign. For example, on March 18, 2016, the IRA purchased an advertisement depicting candidate Clinton and a caption that read in part, "If one day God lets this liar enter the White House as a president – that day would be a real national tragedy."[57] Similarly, on April 6, 2016, the IRA purchased advertisements for its account "Black Matters" calling for a "flashrnob" of U.S. persons to "take a photo with #HillaryClintonForPrison2016 or #nohillary2016." IRA-purchased advertisements featuring Clinton were, with very few exceptions, negative.[59]

IRA-purchased advertisements referencing candidate Trump largely supported his campaign. The first known IRA advertisement explicitly endorsing the Trump Campaign was purchased on April 19, 2016. The IRA bought an advertisement for its Instagram account "Tea Party News" asking U.S. persons to help them "make a patriotic team of young Trump supporters" by uploading photos with the hashtag "#KIDS4TRUMP."[60] In subsequent months, the IRA purchased dozens of advertisements supporting the Trump Campaign, predominantly through the Facebook groups "Being Patriotic," "Stop All Invaders," and "Secured Borders."

Collectively, the IRA's social media accounts reached tens of millions of U.S. persons. Individual IRA social media accounts attracted hundreds of thousands of followers. For example, at the time they were deactivated by Facebook in mid-2017, the IRA's "United Muslims of America" Facebook group had over 300,000 followers, the "Don't Shoot Us" Facebook group had over 250,000 followers, the "Being Patriotic" Facebook group had over 200,000 followers, and the "Secured Borders" Facebook group had over 130,000 followers.[61] According to Facebook, in total the IRA-controlled accounts made over 80,000 posts before their deactivation in August 2017, and these posts reached at least 29 million U.S persons and "may have reached an estimated 126 million people."[62]

4. U.S. Operations Through Twitter

A number of IRA employees assigned to the Translator Department served as Twitter specialists. Harm to Ongoing Matter

[63]

The IRA's Twitter operations involved two strategies. First, IRA specialists operated certain Twitter accounts to create individual U.S. personas, Harm to Ongoing Matter

[4] Separately, the IRA operated a network of automated Twitter accounts (commonly referred to as a bot network) that enabled the IRA to amplify existing content on Twitter.

a. Individualized Accounts

Harm to Ongoing Matter
[66]
The   of its Facebook IRA operated individuaized Twitter accounts similar to the operation accounts, by continuously posting original content to the accounts while also communicating with U.S. Twitter users directly (through public tweeting or Twitter's private messaging).

The IRA used many of these accounts to attempt to influence U.S. audiences on the election.   Individualized accounts used to influence the U.S. presidential election   included @TEN_GOP (described above); @jenn_abrams (claiming to be a Virginian Trump supporter with 70,000 followers); @Pamela_Moore13 (claiming to be a Texan Trump supporter with 70,000 followers); and @America_1st_ (an anti-immigration persona with 24,000 followers).[67] In May 2016, the IRA created the Twitter account @march_for_trurnp, which promoted IRA-organized rallies in support of the Trump Campaign (described below).[68]

Using these accounts and others, the IRA provoked reactions from users and the media. Multiple IRA-posted tweets gained popularity." U.S. media outlets also quoted tweets from IRA-controlled accounts and attributed them to the reactions of real U.S. persons.71 Similarly, numerous high-profile U.S. persons, including former Ambassador Michael McFaul,72 Roger Stone,73 Sean Hannity,74 and Michael Flynn Jr.,75 retweeted or responded to tweets posted to these IRA• controlled accounts. Multiple individuals affiliated with the Trump Campaign also promoted IRA tweets (discussed below).

b. IRA Botnet Activities

Harm to Ongoing Matter

Harm to Ongoing Matter

In January 2018, Twitter publicly identified 3,814 Twitter accounts associated with the IRA.79 According to Twitter, in the ten weeks before the 2016 U.S. presidential election, these accounts posted approximately

175,993 tweets, "approximately 8.4% of which were election- related.[80]" Twitter also announced that it had notified approximately 1.4 million people who Twitter believed may have been in contact with an IRA-controlled account.[81]

5. U.S. Operations Involving Political Rallies

The IRA organized and promoted political rallies inside the United States while posing as U.S. grassroots activists. First, the IRA used one of its preexisting social media personas (Facebook groups and Twitter accounts, for example) to announce and promote the event. The IRA then sent a large number of direct messages to followers of its social media account asking them to attend the event. From those who responded with interest in attending, the IRA then sought a U.S. person to serve as the event's coordinator. In most cases, the IRA account operator would tell the U.S. person that they personally could not attend the event due to some preexisting conflict or because they were somewhere else in the United States.[82] The IRA then further promoted the event by contacting U.S. media about the event and directing them to speak with the coordinator.[83] After the event, the IRA posted videos and photographs of the event to the IRA's social media accounts.[84]

The Office identified dozens of U.S. rallies organized by the IRA. The earliest evidence of a rally was a "confederate rally" in November 2015.[85] The IRA continued to organize rallies even after the 2016 U.S. presidential election. The attendance at rallies varied. Some rallies appear to ~~Harm to Ongoing Matter~~ have drawn few (if any) participants while others

o

From June 2016 until the end of the presidential campaign, almost all of the U.S. rallies organized by the IRA focused on the U.S. election, often promoting the Trump Campaign and opposing the Clinton Campaign. Pro-Trump rallies included three in New York; a series of pro-Trump rallies in Florida in August 2016; and a series of pro-Trump rallies in October 2016 in Pennsylvania. The Florida rallies drew the attention of the Trump Campaign, which posted about the Miami rally. Harm to Ongoing Matter

me IRA employees who oversaw the IRA's social media accounts also conducted the day-to-da recruitin for olitical rallies inside the United States.

IRA Poster for Pennsylvania
Rallies organized by the IRA

6. Targeting and Recruitment of U.S. Persons

As early as 2014, the IRA instructed its employees to target U.S. persons who could be used to advance its operational goals. Initially, recruitment focused on U.S. persons who could amplify the content posted by the IRA. Harm to Ongoing Matter

IRA employees frequently used Investigative Technique Twitter, Facebook, and Instagram to contact and recruit U.S. persons who followed the group. The IRA recruited U.S. persons from across the political spectrum. For example, the IRA targeted the family of_ and a number of black social justice activists while posing as a grassroots group called "Black Matters US."89 In February 2017, the persona "Black Fist" (purporting to want to teach African-Americans to protect themselves when contacted by law enforcement) hired a self-defense instructor in New York to offer classes sponsored by Black Fist. The IRA also recruited moderators of conservative social media groups to promote IRA-generated content." as well as recruited individuals to perform political acts (such as walking around New York City dressed up as Santa Claus with a Trump mask).[91]

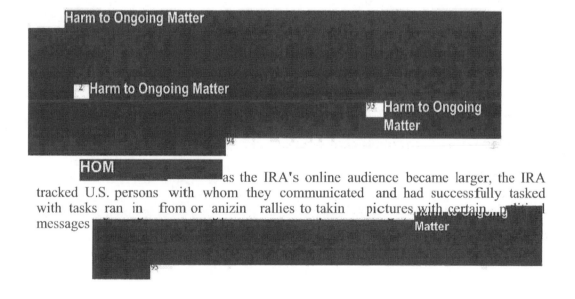

Harm to Ongoing Matter

Harm to Ongoing Matter

Harm to Ongoing Matter

[94]

HOM as the IRA's online audience became larger, the IRA tracked U.S. persons with whom they communicated and had successfully tasked with tasks ran in from or anizin rallies to takin pictures with certain political messages [Harm to Ongoing Matter]

[95]

47

7. **Interactions and Contacts with the Trump Campaign**

The investigation identified two different forms of connections between the IRA and members of the Trump Campaign. (The investigation identified no similar connections between the IRA and the Clinton Campaign.) First, on multiple occasions, members and surrogates of the Trump Campaign promoted—typically by linking, retweeting, or similar methods of reposting ➡ pro-Trump or anti-Clinton content published by the IRA through IRA-controlled social media accounts. Additionally, in a few instances, IRA employees represented themselves as U.S. persons to communicate with members of the Trump Campaign in an effort to seek assistance and coordination on IRA-organized political rallies inside the United States.

a. *Trump Campaign Promotion of IRA Political Materials*

Among the U.S. "leaders of public opinion" targeted by the IRA were various members and surrogates of the Trump Campaign. In total, Trump Campaign affiliates promoted dozens of tweets, posts, and other political content created by the IRA. Posts from the IRA-controlled Twitter account @TEN_GOP were cited or retweeted by multiple Trump Campaign officials and surrogates, including Donald J. Trump Jr.,[96] Eric Trump,[97] Kellyanne Conway,[98] Brad Parscale,[99] and Michael T. Flynn.[100] These posts included allegations of voter fraud,101 [101] as well as allegations that Secretary Clinton had mishandled classified information.P"

A November 7, 2016 post from the IRA-controlled Twitter account @Pamela_Moore13 was retweeted by Donald J. Trump Jr.[103]

On September 19, 2017, President Trump's personal account @realDonaldTrump responded to a tweet from the IRA-controlled account @10_gop (the backup account of @TEN_GOP, which had already been deactivated by Twitter). The tweet read: "We love you, Mr. President!'t'P'

IRA employees monitored the reaction of the Trump Campaign and, later, Trump Administration officials to their tweets. For example, on August 23, 2016, the IRA• controlled persona "Matt Skiber" Facebook account sent a message to a U.S. Tea Party activist, writing that "Mr. Trump posted about our event in Miami! This is great![105] The IRA employee included a screenshot of candidate Trump's Facebook account, which included a post about the August 20, 2016 political rallies organized by the IRA.

b. Contact with Trump Campaigno officials in Connection to Rallies

Starting in June 2016, the IRA contacted different U.S. persons affiliated with the Trump Campaign in an effort to coordinate pro-Trump IRA-organized rallies inside the United States. In all cases, the IRA contacted the Campaign while claiming to be U.S. political activists working on behalf of a conservative grassroots organization. The IRA's contacts included requests for signs and other materials to use at rallies,[107] as well as requests to promote the rallies and help coordinate logistics.I'" While certain campaign volunteers agreed to provide the requested support (for example, agreeing to set aside a number of signs), the investigation has not identified evidence that any Trump Campaign official understood the requests were coming from foreign nationals.

* * *

In sum, the investigation established that Russia interfered in the 2016 presidential election through the "active measures" social media campaign carried out by the IRA, an organization funded by Prigozhin and companies that he controlled. As explained further in Volume I, Section V.A, infra, the Office concluded (and a grand jury has alleged) that Prigozhin, his companies, and IRA employees violated U.S. law through these operations, principally by undermining through deceptive acts the work of federal agencies charged with regulating foreign influence in U.S. elections.

****

[2] The Office is aware of reports that other Russian entities engaged in similar active measures operations targeting the United States. Some evidence collected by the Office corroborates those reports, and the Office has shared that evidence with other offices in the Department of Justice and FBI. *see also* SM-2230634, serial 44 (analysis). The FBI case number cited here, and other FBI case numbers identified in the report, should be treated as law enforcement sensitive given the context. The report contains additional law enforcement sensitive information.

[4] As discussed in Part V below, the active measures investigation has resulted in criminal charges against 13 individual Russian nationals and three Russian entities, principally for conspiracy to defraud the United States, in violation of 18 U.S.C. § 371. *See* Volume I, Section V.A, *infra;* Indictment, *United States v. Internet Research Agency, et al.,* 1:18-cr-32 (D.D.C. Feb. 16, 2018), Doc. 1 *("Internet Research Agency* Indictment").

[5] *Internet Research Agency* Indictment ¶¶ 52, 54, 55(a), 56, 74; Harm to Ongoing Matter

[6] *Social Media Influence in the 2016 US. Election, Hearing Before the Senate Select Committee on Intelligence,* 11 5th Cong. 13 (11/1/17) (testimony of Colin Stretch, General Counsel of Facebook) ("We estimate that roughly 29 million people were served content in their News Feeds directly from the IRA's 80,000 posts over the two years. Posts from these Pages were also shared, liked, and followed by people on Facebook, and, as a result, three times more people may have been exposed to a story that originated from the Russian operation. Our best estimate is that approximately 126 million people may have been served content from a Page associated with the IRA at some point during the two-year period."). The Facebook representative also testified that Facebook had identified 170 Instagram accounts that posted approximately 120,000 pieces of content during that time. Facebook did not offer an estimate of the audience reached via Instagram.

7. Twitter, Update on Twitter's Review of the 2016 US Election (Jan. 31, 2018).

[20] Harm to Ongoing Matter

22 See, e.g., Neil MacFarquhar, Yevgeny Prigozhin, Russian Oligarch Indicted by U.S., Is Known as "Putin's Cook", New York Times (Feb. 16, 2018).

24 Harm to Ongoing Matter see also SM

26 Harm to Ongoing Matter

28 The term "troll" refers to internet users-in this context, paid operatives-who post inflammatory or otherwise disruptive content on social media or other websites.

[29] Investigative Technique   *See* SM-2230634, serials 131 & 204.

[30] *See* SM-2230634, serial 156.

[31] *Internet Research Agency* Indictment ,¶ 12 b); *see also* 5/26/16 Facebook Messages, ID 1479936895656747 (United Muslims of Ame Personal Privacy

[32] Harm to Ongoing Matter
see also SM-2230634, serial 189. Harm to Ongoing Matter

35 Harm to Ongoing Matter
37 Harm to Ongoing Matter

[4][5] *See, e.g.,* Facebook ID l00011390466802 (Alex Anderson); Facebook ID l00009626173204 (Andrea Hansen); Facebook ID l00009728618427 (Gary Williams); Facebook ID l00013640043337 (Lakisha Richardson).

[46] The account claimed to be the "Unofficial Twitter of Tennessee Republicans" and made posts that appeared to be endorsements of the state political party. *See, e.g.,* @TEN_GOP, 4/3/16 Tweet ("Tennessee GOP backs @realDonaldTrump period #makeAmericagreatagain #tngop #tennessee #gop").

47 Harm to Ongoing Matter

48 See, e.g., SM-2230634 serial 131

49 The IRA posted content about the Clinton candidacy before Clinton officially announced her presidential campaign. IRA-controlled social media accounts criticized Clinton's record as Secretary of State and promoted various critics use of her candidacy. The IRA also used other techno

55 5/31/16 Facebook Message, ID 100009922908461 (Matt Skiber) to ID ....
5/31/16 Facebook Message, ID 100009922908461 (

56 Social Media Influence in the 2016 U.S. Election, Hearing Before the Senate Select Committee on Intelligence, 115th Cong. 13 (11/1/17) (testimony of Colin Stretch, General Counsel of Facebook).

57 3/18/16 Facebook Advertisement ID 6045505152575.

58 4/6/16 Facebook Advertisement ID 6043740225319.

59 See SM-2230634, serial 213 (documenting politically-oriented advertisements from the larger set provided by Facebook).

60 4/19/16 Facebook Advertisement ID 6045151094235.

61 See Facebook ID 1479936895656747 (United Muslims of America); Facebook ID 1157233400960126 (Don't Shoot); Facebook ID 1601685693432389 Bein Patriotic ; Facebook ID 757183957716200 Secured Borders).Harm to Ongoing Matter

62 Social Media Influence in the 2016 US. Election, Hearing Before the Senate Select Committee on Intelligence, 115th Cong. 13 (11/1/17) (testimony of Colin Stretch, General Counsel of Facebook).

63 Harm to Ongoing Matter

64 Harm to Ongoing Matter

65 Harm to Ongoing Matter

66 Harm to Ongoing Matter

67 Other individualized accounts included @MissouriNewsUS (an account with 3,800 followers that posted pro-Sanders and anti-Clinton material).

68 See @march_for_trump, 5/30/16 Tweet (first post from account). 7° For example, one IRA account tweeted, "To those people, who hate the Confederate flag. Did you know that the flag and the war wasn't about slavery, it was all about money." The tweet received over 40,000 responses. @Jenn_Abrams 4/24/17 (2:37 p.m.) Tweet.

71 Josephine Lukito & Chris Wells, Most Major Outlets Have Used Russian Tweets as Sourcesfor Partisan Opinion: Study, Columbia Journalism Review (Mar. 8, 2018); see also Twitter Steps Up to Explain #NewYorkValues to Ted Cruz, Washington Post (Jan. 15, 2016) (citing IRA tweet); People Are Slamming the CIA/or Claiming Russia Tried to Help Donald Trump, U.S. News & World Report (Dec. 12, 2016).

72@McFaul 4/30/16 Tweet (responding to tweet by @Jenn_Abrams).

73 @RogerJStoneJr 5/30/16 Tweet (retweeting @Pamela_Moorel3); @RogerJStoneJr 4/26/16 Tweet (same).

74 @seanhannity 6/21/17 Tweet (retweeting @Pamela_Moore 13).

75 @mflynnJR 6/22/17 Tweet ("RT @Jenn_Abrams: This is what happens when you add the voice over of an old documentary about mental illness onto video of SJWs...").

76 A botnet refers to a network of private computers or accounts controlled as a group to send specific automated messages. On the Twitter network, botnets can be used to promote and republish ("retweet") specific tweets or hashtags in order for them to gain larger audiences.

77 Harm to Ongoing Matter

78 Harm to Ongoing Matter

79 Eli Rosenberg, Twitter to Tell 677, 000 Users they Were Had by the Russians. Some Signs Show the Problem Continues, Washington Post (Jan. 19, 2019).

80 Twitter, "Update on Twitter's Review ofthe 2016 US Election" (updated Jan. 31, 2018). Twitter also reported identifying 50,258 automated accounts connected to the Russian government, which tweeted more than a million times in the ten weeks before the election.

81 Twitter, "Update on Twitter's Review of the 2016 US Election" (updated Jan. 31, 2018).

82 8/20/16 Facebook Message, ID 100000992290846 1 (Matt Skiber) to ID

83 See, e.g., 7/21/16gmail.com to ; 7/21/16 Email, joshmilton024@gmail.com to-

84 @march_for_trump 6/25/16 Tweet (posting photos from rally outside Trump Tower).

85 Instagram ID 2228012168 (Stand For Freedom) 11/3/15 Post ("Good evening buds! Well I am planning to organize a confederate rally[...] in Houston on the 14 of November and I want more people to attend.").

86 The pro-Trump rallies were organized through multiple Facebook, Twitter, and email accounts. See, e.g., Facebook ID 100009922908461 (Matt Skiber); Facebook ID 1601685693432389 (Being Patriotic); Twitter Account @march_for_trump; beingpatriotic@gmail.com. (Rallies were organized in New York on June 25, 2016; Florida on August 20, 2016; and Pennsylvania on October 2, 2016.)

87 Harm to Ongoing Matter

88 Harm to Ongoing Matt

er89 3/11/16 Facebook Advertisement ID 6045078289928, 5/6/16 Facebook Advertisement ID 6051652423528 10/26/16 Facebook Advertisement ID 6055238604687; 10/27/16 Facebook Message, ID & ID 100011698576461 (Taylor Brooks).

90 8/19/16 Facebook Message, ID 100009922908461 (Matt Skiber) to ID

91 12/8/16 Email, robot@craigslist.org to beingpatriotic@gmail.com (confirming Craigslist advertisement).

92 8/18-19/16 Twitter DMs, @march_for_trump & bull horn). ID 100011698576461 (Taylor Brooks) & (arranging to pay for plane tickets and for a Facebook Message, ID 100009922908461 (Matt Skiber) & (discussing payment

for rally supplies); 8/18/16 Twitter DM, (discussing payment for construction materials).

96 See, e.g., @DonaldJTrumpJr 10/26/16 Tweet ("RT @TEN_GOP: BREAKING Thousands of names changed on voter rolls in Indiana. Police investigating #VoterFraud. #DrainTheSwamp."); @DonaldJTrumpJr 11/2/16 Tweet ("RT @TEN_GOP: BREAKING: #VoterFraud by counting tens of thousands of ineligible mail in Hillary votes being reported in Broward County, Florida."); @DonaldJTrumpJr 11/8/16 Tweet ("RT @TEN_GOP: This vet passed away last month before he could vote for Trump. Here he is in his #MAGA hat. #voted #ElectionDay."). Trump Jr. retweeted additional @TEN_GOP content subsequent to the election.

97 @EricTrump 10/20/16 Tweet ("RT @TEN_GOP: BREAKING Hillary shuts down press conference when asked about DNC Operatives corruption & #VoterFraud #debatenight #TrumpB").

98 @KellyannePolls 11/6/16 Tweet ("RT @TEN_GOP: Mother of jailed sailor: 'Hold Hillary to same standards as my son on Classified info' #hillarysemail #WeinerGate.").

99 @parscale 10/15/16 Tweet ("Thousands of deplorables chanting to the media: 'Tell The Truth!' RT if you are also done w/ biased Media! #FridayFeeling").

100 @GenFlynn 11/7/16 (retweeting @TEN_GOP post that included in part "@realDonaldTrump & @mike_pence will be our next POTUS & VPOTUS.").

101 @TEN_GOP 10/11/16 Tweet ("North Carolina finds 2,214 voters over the age of 110! !").

102 @TEN_GOP 11/6/16 Tweet ("Mother of jailed sailor: 'Hold Hillary to same standards as my son on classified info #hillaryemail #WeinerGate.'").

103 @DonaldJTrumpJr 11/7/16 Tweet ("RT@Pamela_Moore 13: Detroit residents speak out against the failed policies of Obama, Hillary & democrats ....").

104 @rea!DonaldTrump 9/19/17 (7:33 p.m.) Tweet ("THANK YOU for your support Miami! My team just shared photos from your TRUMP SIGN WAYING DAY, yesterday! I love you - and there is no question - TOGETHER, WE WILL MAKE AMERICA GREAT AGAIN!").

105 8/23/16 Facebook Message, ID 100009922908461 (Matt Skiber) to 1

107 See, e.g., 8/16/16 Email, joshmilton024@gmail.com to.@donaldtrump.com (asking for /Pence signs for Florida rally); 8/18/16 Email, joshmilton024@gmail.com to @donaldtrump.com (for Trump/Pence signs for Florida rally); 8/12/16 Email, joshmilton024@gmail.com to - @donaldtrump.com (asking for "contact phone numbers for Trump -Campaign affiliates" in various Florida cities and signs).

108 8/15/16 Email, to joshrnilton024 locations to the "Florida Goes Trump," list); 8 16/16 Email, to joshmilton024@gmail.com (volunteering to send an email blast to followers

III.RUSSIAN HACKING AND DUMPING OPERATIONS

Beginning in March 2016, units of the Russian Federation's Main Intelligence Directorate of the General Staff(GRU) hacked the computers and email accounts of organizations, employees, and volunteers supporting the Clinton Campaign, including the email account of campaign chairman John Podesta. Starting in April 2016, the GRU hacked into the computer networks of the Democratic Congressional Campaign Committee (DCCC) and the Democratic National Committee (DNC). The GRU targeted hundreds of email accounts used by Clinton Campaign employees, advisors, and volunteers. In total, the GRU stole hundreds of thousands of documents from the compromised email accounts and networks.1''? The GRU later released stolen Clinton Campaign and DNC documents through online personas, "DCLeaks" and "Guccifer 2.0," and later through the organization WikiLeaks. The release of the documents was designed and timed to interfere with the 2016 U.S. presidential election and undermine the Clinton Campaign.

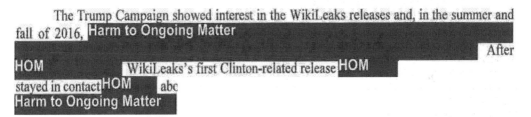

WikiLeaks's release of the stolen Podesta emails on October 7,2016, the same day a video from years earlier was published of Trump using graphic language about women.

A. GRU Hacking Directed at the Clinton Campaign

1. GRU Units Target the Clinton Campaign

Two military units of the GRU carried out the computer intrusions into the Clinton Campaign, DNC, and DCCC: Military Units 26165 and 74455.[110] Military Unit 26165 is a GRU cyber unit dedicated to targeting military, political, governmental, and non-governmental organizations outside of Russia, including in the United States.[111] The unit was sub-divided into departments with different specialties. One department, for example, developed specialized malicious software "malware" while another de artment conducted large-scale spear phishing campaigns.[112]

A bitcoin mining operation to Military Unit 74455 is a related GRU unit with multiple departments that engaged in cyber operations. Unit 74455 assisted in the release of documents stolen by Unit 26165, the promotion of those releases, and the publication of anti-Clinton content on social media accounts operated by the GRU. Officers from Unit 74455 separately hacked computers belonging to state boards of elections, secretaries of state, and U.S. companies that supplied software and other technology related to the administration of U.S. elections.[114]

Beginning in mid-March 2016, Unit 26165 had primary responsibility for hacking the DCCC and DNC, as well as email accounts of individuals affiliated with the Clinton Campaign:[115] IT ▮▮▮▮▮▮▮▮ to learn about different Democratic websites, including democrats.org, hillaryclinton.com, dnc.org, and dccc.org. Investigative Technique ▮▮▮▮▮▮▮▮▮▮▮▮▮▮▮▮▮▮▮

began before the GRU had obtained any credentials or gained access to t ese networks, indicating that the later DCCC and DNC intrusions were not crimes of opportunity but rather the result of targeting.[116]

GRU officers also sent hundreds of spearphishing emails to the work and personal email accounts ofClinton Campaign employees and volunteers. Between March 10, 2016 and March 15, 2016, Unit 26165 appears to have sent approximately 90 spearphishing emails to email accounts at hillaryclinton.com. Starting on March 15, 2016, the GRU began targeting Google email accounts used by Clinton Campaign employees, along with a smaller number of dnc.org email accounts.[117]

The GRU spearphishing operation enabled it to gain access to numerous email accounts of Clinton Campaign employees and volunteers, including campaign chairman John Podesta, junior volunteers assigned to the Clinton Campaign's advance team, informal Clinton Campaign advisors, and a DNC employee.[118] GRU officers stole tens of thousands of emails from spear phishing victims, including various Clinton Campaign-related communications.

2. Intrusions into the DCCC and DNC Networks

a. Initial Access

By no later than April 12, 2016, the GRU had gained access to the DCCC computer network using the credentials stolen from a DCCC employee who had been successfully spearphished the week before. Over the ensuing weeks, the GRU traversed the network, identifying different computers connected to the DCCC network. By stealing network access credentials along the way (including those of IT administrators with unrestricted access to the system), the GRU compromised approximately 29 different computers on the DCCC network.[119]

Approximately six days after first hacking into the DCCC network, on April 18, 2016, GRU officers gained access to the DNC network via a virtual private network (VPN) connection 'P' between the DCCC and DNC networks.[121] Between April 18, 2016 and June 8, 2016,

Unit 26165 compromised more than 30 computers on the DNC network, including the DNC mail server and shared file server.[122]

b. *Implantation of Malware on DCCC and DNC Networks*

Unit 26165 implanted on the DCCC and DNC networks two types of customized malware,[123] known as "X-Agent" and "X-Tunnel"; Mimikatz, a credential-harvesting tool; and rar.exe, a tool used in these intrusions to compile and compress materials for exfiltration. X-Agent was a multi-function hacking tool that allowed Unit 26165 to log keystrokes, take screenshots, an gather other data about the infected computers (*e.g.,* file directories, operating systems).[124] X•Tunnel was a hacking tool that created an encrypted connection between the victim DCCC/DNC computers and GRU-controlled computers outside the DCCC and DNC networks that was capable of large-scale data transfers.[125] GRU officers then used X-Tunnel to exfiltrate stolen data from the victim computers.

To operate X-Agent and X-Tunnel on the DCCC and DNC networks, Unit 26165 officers set up a group of computers outside those networks to communicate with the implanted malware.[126] The first set of GRU-controlled computers, known by the GRU as "middle servers," sent and received messages to and from malware on the DNC/DCCC networks. The middle servers, in tum, relayed messages to a second set of GRU-controlled com;p,ters, labeled internally by the GRU as an "AMS Panel." The AMS Panel served as a nerve center through which GRU officers monitored and directed the malware's operations on the DNC/DCCC networks.[127]

The AMS Panel used to control X-Agent during the DCCC and DNC intrusions was housed on a leased computer located near [1] Arizona.[128] Investigative Technique

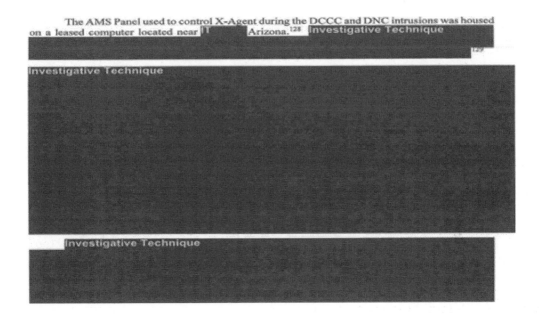

Investigative Technique

Investigative Technique

The Arizona-based AMS Panel also stored thousands of files containing keylogging sessions captured through X-Agent. These sessions were captured as GRU officers monitored DCCC and DNC employees' work on infected computers regularly between April 2016 and June 2016. Data captured in these keylogging sessions included passwords, internal communications between employees, banking information, and sensitive personal information.

c. Theft of Documents from DNC and DCCC Networks

Officers from Unit 26165 stole thousands of documents from the DCCC and DNC networks, including significant amounts of data pertaining to the 2016 U.S. federal elections. Stolen documents included internal strategy documents, fundraising data, opposition research, and emails from the work inboxes of DNC employees.P?

The GRU began stealing DCCC data shortly after it gained access to the network. On April 14, 2016 (approximately three days after the initial intrusion) GRU officers downloaded rar.exe onto the DCCC's document server. The following day, the GRU searched one compromised DCCC computer for files containing search terms that included "Hillary," "DNC," "Cruz," and"Trump."!" On April 25, 2016, the GRU collected and compressed PDF and Microsoft documents from folders on the DCCC's shared file server that pertained to the 2016 election.[132] The GRU appears to have compressed and exfiltrated over 70 gigabytes of data from this file server.[133]

The GRU also stole documents from the DNC network shortly after gaining access. On April 22, 2016, the GRU copied files from the DNC network to GRU-controlled computers. Stolen documents included the DNC's opposition research into candidate Trump.[134] Between approximately May 25, 2016 and June 1, 2016, GRU officers accessed the DNC's mail server from a GRU-controlled computer leased inside the United States.1" During these connections, Unit 26165 officers appear to have stolen thousands of emails and attachments, which were later released by WikiLeaks in July 2016.[136]

B. **Dissemination of the Hacked Materials**

The GRU's operations extended beyond stealing materials, and included releasing documents stolen from the Clinton Campaign and its supporters. The GRU carried out the anonymous release through two fictitious online personas that it created—DCLeaks and Guccifer 2.0—and later through the organization WikiLeaks.

1. **DCLeaks**

The GRU began planning the releases at least as early as April 19, 2016, when Unit 26165 registered the domain dcleaks.com through a service that anonymized the registrant.[137] Unit 26165 paid for the registration using a pool of bitcoin that it had rnined.!" The dcleaks.com landing page pointed to different tranches of stolen documents, arranged by victim or subject matter. Other dcleaks.com pages contained indexes of the stolen emails that were being released (bearing the sender, recipient, and date of the email). To control access and the timing of releases, pages were sometimes password-protected for a period of time and later made unrestricted to the public.

Starting in June 2016, the GRU posted stolen documents onto the website dcleaks.com, including documents stolen from a number of individuals associated with the Clinton Campaign. These documents appeared to have originated from personal email accounts (in particular, Google and Microsoft accounts), rather than the DNC and DCCC computer networks. DCLeaks victims included an advisor to the Clinton Campaign, a former DNC employee and Clinton Campaign employee, and four other campaign volunteers.[139] The GRU released through dcleaks.com thousands of documents, including personal identifying and financial information, internal correspondence related to the Clinton Campaign and prior political jobs, and fundraising files and information.r'?

GRU officers operated a Facebook page under the DCLeaks moniker, which they primarily used to promote releases of materials.[141] The Facebook page was administered through a small number of preexisting GRU-controlled Facebook accounts.[142]

GRU officers also used the DCLeaks Facebook account, the Twitter account @dcleaks_, and the email account dcleaksproject@gmail.com to communicate privately with reporters and other U.S. persons. GRU officers using the DCLeaks persona gave certain reporters early access to archives of leaked files by sending them links and passwords to pages on the dcleaks.com website that had not yet become public. For example, on July 14, 2016, GRU officers operating under the DCLeaks persona sent a link and password for a non-public DCLeaks webpage to a U.S. reporter via the Facebook account.[143] Similarly, on September 14, 2016, GRU officers sent reporters Twitter direct messages from @dcleaks_, with a password to another non-public part of the dcleaks.com website.[142] The DCLeaks.com website remained operational and public until March 2017.

2. Guccifer 2.0

On June 14, 2016, the DNC and its cyber-response team announced the breach of the DNC network and suspected theft of DNC documents. In the statements, the cyber-response team alleged that Russian state-sponsored actors (which they referred to as "Fancy Bear") were responsible for the breach.[145] Apparently in response to that announcement, on June 15, 2016, GRU officers using the persona Guccifer 2.0 created a WordPress blog. In the hours leading up to the launch of that WordPress blog, GRU officers logged into a Moscow-based server used and managed by Unit 74455 and searched for a number of specific words and phrases in English, including "some hundred sheets," "illuminati," and "worldwide known." Approximately two hours after the last of those searches, Guccifer 2.0 published its first post, attributing the DNC server hack to a lone Romanian hacker and using several of the unique English words and phrases that the GRU officers had searched for that day.[146]

Tennessee-based web-hosting company, called Smartech Corporation. William Bastone, *RNC E-Mail Was, In Fact, Hacked By Russians,* The Smoking Gun (Dec. 13, 2016). That same day, June 15, 2016, the GRU also used the Guccifer 2.0 WordPress blog to begin releasing to the public documents stolen from the DNC and DCCC computer networks. The Guccifer 2.0 persona ultimately released thousands of documents stolen from the DNC and DCCC in a series of blog posts between June 15, 2016 and October 18, 2016.[147] Released document included opposition research performed by the DNC (including a memorandum analyzing potential criticisms of candidate Trump), internal policy documents (such as recommendations on how to address politically sensitive issues), analyses of specific congressional races, and fundraising documents. Releases were organized around thematic issues, such as specific states (*e.g.,* Florida and Pennsylvania) that were perceived as competitive in the 2016 U.S. presidential election.

Beginning in late June 2016, the GRU also used the Guccifer 2.0 persona to release documents directly to reporters and other interested individuals. Specifically, on June 27, 2016, Guccifer 2.0 sent an email to the news outlet The Smoking Gun offering to provide "exclusive access to some leaked emails linked [to] Hillary Clinton's staff."[148] The GRU later sent the reporter a password and link to a locked portion of the dcleaks.com website that contained an archive of emails stolen by Unit 26165 from a Clinton Campaign volunteer in March 2016.[149] That the Guccifer 2.0 persona provided reporters access to a restricted portion of the DCLeaks website tends to indicate that both personas were operated by the same or a closely-related group of people.P?

The GRU continued its release efforts through Guccifer 2.0 into August 2016. For example, on August 15, 2016, the Guccifer 2.0 persona sent a candidate for the U.S. Congress documents related to the candidate's opponent.[151] On August 22, 2016, the Guccifer 2.0 persona transferred approximately 2.5 gigabytes of Florida-related data stolen from the DCCC to a U.S. blogger covering Florida politics.[152] On August 22, 2016, the Guccifer 2.0 persona sent a U.S. reporter documents stolen from the DCCC pertaining to the Black Lives Matter movement.[153]

The GRU was also in contact through the Guccifer 2.0 persona with HOM a former Trump Campaign member Harm to Ongoing Matter

[154]

In early August 2016,   Twitter's suspension of the Guccifer 2.0
Twitter account. After it was reinstated, GRU officers posing as Guccifer 2.0 wrote via
private message, "thank u for writing back ... do u find anyt[h]ing interesting in the added,
"please tell me if i can help u anyhow ... docs i posted?" On August 17, 2016, the GRU it
would be a great pleasure to me." On September 9, 2016, the GRUi;tfwf posing as
Guccifer 2.0-referred to a stolen DCCC document posted online and asked   1   "what
do u think of the info on the turnout model for the democrats   entire presidential
campaign." responded, "pretty standard."155   The investigation did not identify
evidence of other communications between- and Guccifer 2.0.

3. Use of WikiLeaks

In order to expand its interference in the 2016 U.S. presidential
election, the GRU units transferred many of the documents they stole from
the DNC and the chairman of the Clinton Campaign to WikiLeaks. GRU
officers used both the DCLeaks and Guccifer 2.0 personas to communicate
with WikiLeaks through Twitter private messaging and through encrypted
channels, including possibly through WikiLeaks's private communication
system.

a. WikiLeaks's Expressed Opposition Toward the Clinton Campaign

WikiLeaks, and particularly its founder Julian Assange, privately
expressed opposition to candidate Clinton well before the first release of
stolen documents. In November 2015, Assange wrote to other members and
associates of WikiLeaks that "[w]e believe it would be much better for GOP
to win ... Dems+Media+liberals woudl [sic] then form a block to reign in
their worst qualities. . . .   With Hillary in charge, GOP will be
pushing   for   her   worst   qualities., dems+media+neoliberals will be
mute.... She's a bright, well connected, sadisitic sociopath."156

In March 2016, WikiLeaks released a searchable archive of approximately 30,000 Clinton emails that had been obtained through FOIA litigation.[157] While designing the archive, one WikiLeaks member explained the reason for building the archive to another associate:

> [W]e want this repository to become "the place" to search for background on hillary's plotting at the state department during 2009-2013. . . . Firstly because its useful and will annoy Hillary, but secondly because we want to be seen to be a resource/player in the US election, because eit [sic] may en[]courage people to send us even more important leaks.[158]

b. WikiLeaks's First Contact with Guccifer 2.0 and DCLeaks

Shortly after the GRU's first release of stolen documents through dcleaks.corn in June 2016, GRU officers also used the DCLeaks persona to contact WikiLeaks about possible coordination in the future release of stolen emails. On June 14, 2016, @dcleaks_ sent a direct message to @WikiLeaks, noting, "You announced your organization was preparing to publish more Hillary's emails. We are ready to support you. We have some sensitive information too, in particular, her financial documents. Let's do it to ether. What do ou think about ublishin our info at the same moment? Thank ou."[159]

Around the same time, WikiLeaks initiated communications with the GRU persona Guccifer 2.0 shortly after it was used to release documents stolen from the DNC. On June 22, 2016, seven days after Guccifer 2.0's first releases of stolen DNC documents, WikiLeaks used Twitter's direct message function to contact the Guccifer 2.0 Twitter account and suggest that Guccifer 2.0 "[s]end any new material [stolen from the DNC] here for us to review and it will have a much higher impact than what you are doing."[160]

On July 6, 2016, WikiLeaks again contacted Guccifer 2.0 through Twitter's private messaging function, writing, "if you have anything biliary related we want it in the next tweo [sic] days prefable [sic] because the DNC is approaching and she will solidify bernie supporters behind her after." The Guccifer 2.0 persona responded, "ok ... i see." WikiLeaks also explained, "we think trump has only a 25% chance of winning against biliary ... so conflict between bernie and hillary is interesting."[161]

c. The GRU's Transfer of Stolen Materials to WikiLeaks

Both the GRU and WikiLeaks sought to hide their communications, which has limited the Office's ability to collect all of the communications between them. Thus, although it is clear that the stolen DNC and Podesta documents were transferred from the GRU to WikiLeaks, The Office was able to identify when the GRU (operating through its personas Guccifer 2.0 and DCLeaks) transferred some of the stolen documents to WikiLeaks through online archives set up by the GRU. Assan e had access to the internet from the Ecu▇▇▇▇▇▇▇▇▇▇▇▇▇▇▇ land.

[62]

On July 14, 2016, GRU officers used a Guccifer 2.0 email account to send WikiLeaks an email bearing the subject "big archive" and the message "a new attempt."[163] The email contained an encrypted attachment with the name "wk dnc linkl .txt.gpg."[164] Using the Guccifer 2.0 Twitter account, GRU officers sent WikiLeaks an encrypted file and instructions on how to open it.[165] On July 18, 2016, WikiLeaks confirmed in a direct message to the Guccifer 2.0 account that it had "the lGb or so archive" and would make a release of the stolen documents "this week."[166] On July 22, 2016, WikiLeaks released over 20,000 emails and other documents stolen from the DNC computer networks.[167] The Democratic National Convention began three days later.

Similar communications occurred between WikiLeaks and the GRU-operated persona DCLeaks. On September 15, 2016, @dcleaks wrote to @WikiLeaks, "hi there! I'm from DC Leaks. How could we discuss some submission-related issues? Am trying to reach out to you via your secured chat but getting no response. I've got something that might interest you. You won't be disappointed, I promise."[168]   The WikiLeaks account responded, "Hi there," without further elaboration. The @dcleaks_ account did not respond immediately.

The same day, the Twitter account@guccifer_2 sent @dcleaks_ a direct message, which is the first known contact between the personas.[169] During subsequent communications, the Guccifer 2.0 persona informed DCLeaks that WikiLeaks was trying to contact DCLeaks and arrange for a way to speak through encrypted emails.'?"

An analysis of the metadata collected from the WikiLeaks site revealed that the stolen Podesta emails show a creation date of September 19, 2016. [171]   Based on information about Assange's computer and its possible operating system, this date may be when the GRU staged the stolen Podesta emails for transfer to WikiLeaks (as the GRU had previously done in July 2016 for the DNC emails).[172]   The WikiLeaks site also released PDFs and other documents taken from Podesta that were attachments to emails in his account; these documents had a creation date of October 2, 2016, which appears to be the date the attachments were separately staged by WikiLeaks on its site.[173]

Beginning on September 20, 2016, WikiLeaks and DCLeaks resumed communications in a brief exchange. On September 22, 2016, a DCLeaks email account dcleaksproject@gmail.com sent an email to a WikiLeaks account with the subject "Submission" and the message "Hi from D@Leaks." The email contained ▮▮▮▮▮▮▮▮▮▮▮▮▮▮▮▮▮▮▮▮▮▮▮▮▮▮e "▮▮▮▮▮▮▮▮▮▮▮▮▮▮▮▮▮▮▮▮▮▮▮▮▮▮▮▮▮▮▮ n▮▮▮▮▮▮▮▮▮▮▮▮ to the July 14, 2016 email in which GRU officers used the Guccifer 2.0 persona to give WikiLeaks access to the archive of DNC files. On September 22, 2016 (the same day of DCLeaks' email to WikiLeaks), the Twitter account   dcleaks   sent a sin le messa e to
The Office cannot rule out that stolen documents were transferred to WikiLeaks through intermediaries who visited during the summer of 2016. For example, public reporting identified

On October 7, 2016, WikiLeaks released the first emails stolen from the Podesta email account. In total, WikiLeaks released 33 tranches of stolen emails between October 7, 2016 and November 7, 2016. The releases included private speeches given by Clinton.!"? internal communications between Podesta and other high-ranking members of the Clinton Campaign;[178] and correspondence related to the Clinton Foundation.[179] In total, WikiLeaks released over 50,000 documents stolen from Podesta's personal email account. The last-in-time email released from Podesta's account was dated March 21, 2016, two days after Podesta received a spearphishing email sent by the GRU.

d. WikiLeaks Statements Dissembling About the Source of Stolen Materials

As reports attributing the DNC and DCCC hacks to the Russian government emerged, WikiLeaks and Assange made several public statements apparently designed to obscure the source of the materials that WikiLeaks was releasing. The file-transfer evidence described above and other information uncovered during the investigation discredit WikiLeaks's claims about the source of material that it posted.

Beginning in the summer of 2016, Assange and WikiLeaks made a number of statements about Seth Rich, a former DNC staff member who was killed in July 2016. The statements about Rich implied falsely that he had been the source of the stolen DNC emails. On August 9, 2016, the @WikiLeaks Twitter account posted: "ANNOUNCE: WikiLeaks has decided to issue a US$20k reward for information leading to conviction for the murder of DNC staffer Seth Rich."[180]

Likewise, on August 25, 2016, Assange was asked in an interview, "Why are you so interested in Seth Rich's killer?" and responded, "We're very interested in anything that might be a threat to alleged Wikileaks sources." The interviewer responded to Assange's statement by commenting, "I know you don't want to reveal your source, but it certainly sounds like you're suggesting a man who leaked information to WikiLeaks was then murdered." Assange replied, "If there's someone who's potentially connected to our publication, and that person has been murdered in suspicious circumstances, it doesn't necessarily mean that the two are connected. But it is a very serious matter... that type of allegation is very serious, as it's taken very seriously by us."[181]

After the U.S. intelligence community publicly announced its assessment that Russia was behind the hacking operation, Assange continued to deny that the Clinton materials released by WikiLeaks had come from Russian hacking. According to media reports, Assange told a U.S. congressman that the DNC hack was an "inside job," and purported to have "physical proof" that Russians did not give materials to Assange.[182]

C. Additional GRU Cyber Operations

While releasing the stolen emails and documents through DCLeaks, Guccifer 2.0, and WikiLeaks, GRU officers continued to target and hack victims linked to the Democratic campaign and, eventually, to target entities responsible for election administration in several states.

1. Summer and Fall 2016 Operations Targeting Democrat-Linked Victims

On July 27 2016 Unit 26165 targeted email accounts connected to candidate Clinton's personal office Earlier that day, candidate Trump made public statements that included the following: "Russia, if you're listening, I hope you're able to find the 30,000 emails that are missing. I think you will probably be rewarded mightily by our press."[183] The "30,000 emails" were apparently a reference to emails described in media accounts as having been stored on a personal server that candidate Clinton had used while serving as Secretary of State.

Within approximately five hours of Trump's statement, GRU officers targeted for the first time Clinton's personal office. After candidate Trump's remarks Unit 26165 created and sent malicious links targeting 15 email accounts at the domain including an email account belonging to Clinton aide —— The investigation did not find evidence of earlier GRU attempts to compromise a con this domain. It is unclear how the GRU was able to identify these email accounts, which were not public.[184]

Unit 26165 officers also hacked into a DNC account hosted on a cloud-computing service On September 20, 2016, the GRU began to generate copies of the DNC data u ·databases (referred to function designed to allow users to produce backups of as "snapshots"). The GRU then stole those snapshots by moving them to - account that they controlled; from there, the copies were moved to GRU• controlled computers. The GRU stole approximately 300 gigabytes of data from the DNC cloud• based account.[185]

2. Intrusions Targeting the Administration of U.S. Elections

In addition to targeting individuals involved in the Clinton Campaign, GRU officers also targeted individuals and entities involved in the administration of the elections. Victims included U.S. state and local entities, such as state boards of elections (SBOEs), secretaries of state, and county governments, as well as individuals who worked for those entities.[186] The GRU also targeted private technology firms responsible for manufacturing and administering election-related software and hardware, such as voter registration software and electronic polling stations. [187] The GRU continued to target these victims through the elections in November 2016. While the investigation identified evidence that the GRU targeted these individuals and entities, the Office did not investigate further. The Office did not, for instance, obtain or examine servers or other relevant items belonging to these victims. The Office understands that the FBI, the U.S. Department of Homeland Security, and the states have separately investigated that activity.

By at least the summer of 2016, GRU officers sought access to state and local computer networks by exploiting known software vulnerabilities on websites of state and local governmental entities. GRU officers, for example, targeted state and local databases of registered voters using a technique known as "SQL injection," by which malicious code was sent to the state or local website in order to run commands (such as exfiltrating the database contents).[188] In one instance in approximately June 2016, the GRU compromised the computer network of the Illinois State Board of Elections by exploiting a vulnerability in the SBOE's website. The GRU then gained access to a database containing information on millions of registered Illinois voters,[189] and extracted data related to thousands of U.S. voters before the malicious activity was identified.[1'']

GRU officers Investigative Technique   scanned state and local websites vulnerabilities. For example, over a two-day p Investigative Technique two dozen states. Investigative Technique

Unit 74455 also sent spear phishing emails to public officials involved in election administration and personnel ◄ ? ► involved in voting technology. In August 2016, GRU officers targeted employees of —— , a voting technology company that developed software used by numerous U.S.

Investigative Technique

Similarly   used by Florida county officials responsible for administering the 20   S. election.[191] The spear phishing emails contained an attached Word document coded with malicious software (commonly referred to as a Trojan) that permitted the GRU to access the infected computer.[1'?] The FBI was separately responsible for this investigation. We understand the FBI believes that this operation enabled the GRU to gain access to the network of at least one Florida county government. The Office did not independently verify that belief and, as explained above, did not undertake the investigative steps that would have been necessary to do so.

D. Trump Campaign and the Dissemination of Hacked Materials

The Trump Campaign showed interest in WikiLeaks's releases of hacked materials throughout the summer and fall of 2016. Harm to Ongoing Matter

1. HOM

a. Background

Harm to Ongoing Matter

b. Contacts with the Campaign about WikiLeaks

Harm to Ongoing Matter

Harm to Ongoing Matter

on June 12, 2016, Assange c aimed in a televised interview to "have emails relating to Hillary Clinton which are pending publication,"[194] but provided no additional context.

In debriefings with the Office, former deputy campaign chairman Rick Gates said that,

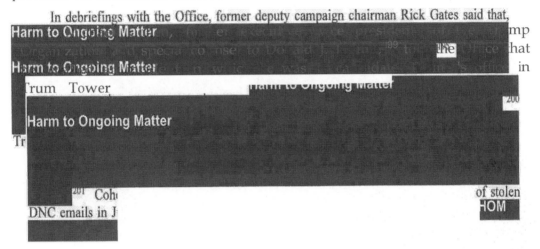

According to Gates, by the late summer of 2016, the Trump Campaign was planning a press strategy, a communications cam   n, and messa in based on the   possible release of Clinton emails   b   WikiLeaks. 1! Mr.lll!l5.MfiMIIII
208

According to Malloch, Corsi asked him to put Corsi in touch with Assange, whom Corsi wished to interview. Malloch recalled that Corsi also suggested that individuals in the "orbit" of U.K. politician Nigel Farage might be able to contact Assange and asked if Malloch knew them. Malloch told Corsi that he would think about the request but made no actual attempt to connect Corsi with Assange.[218]

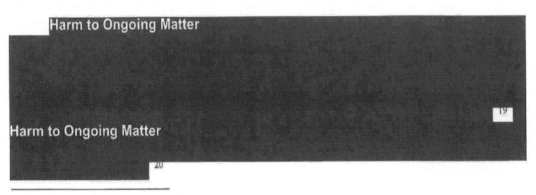

Harm to Ongoing Matter

Harm to Ongoing Matter

[19]

[20]

Malloch stated to investigators that beginning or about August 2016 he and Corsi had multiple FaceTime discussions about WikiLeaks■■■■■■■illi■■■■■ [   ] had made a connection to Assange and that the hacked emails of John Podesta would be released prior to Election Day and would be helpful to the Trump Campaign. In one conversation in or around August or September 2016, Corsi told Malloch that the release of the Podesta emails was coming, after which "we" were going to be in the driver's seat.[221]

Harm to Ongoing Matter

[222] Harm to Ongoing Matter

[23] Harm to Ongoing Matter

[24] Harm to Ongoing Matter

[225]

d. WikiLeaks's October 7, 2016 Release of Stolen Podesta Emails

On October 7 2016 four days after the Assange press conference

███████████████████████

the Washington Post published an *Access Hollywood* video that captured comments by candidate Trump some years earlier and that was expected to adversely affect the Campaign.[239] Less than an hour after the video's publication, WikiLeaks released the first set of emails stolen by the GRU from the account of Clinton Campaign chairman John Podesta.

Harm to Ongoing Matter
[24] **Harm to Ongoing Matter**

███████████████████████████

he had no direct means o communicating with WikiLeaks, he told members of the news site WND–who were participating on a conference call with him that day—to reach Assange immediately.[244] Corsi claimed that the pressure was enormous and recalled telling the conference call the *Access Hollywood* tape was coming.[245] Corsi stated that he was convinced that his efforts had caused WikiLeaks to release the emails when they did.[246] In a later November 2018 interview, Corsi stated that he thought that he had told people on a WNO conference call about the forthcoming tape and had sent out a tweet asking whether anyone could contact Assange, but then said that maybe he had done nothing.[247]

The Office investigated Corsi's allegations about the ████████ , 2016 but found events of October 7 little corroboration for his all████████ Harm to Ongoing Matter
[249] **Harm to Ongoing Matter**

h█████████████████████████████ so ████████████████ ███████████████████████████ versation.

However, the Office has not identified any conference call participant, or anyone who spoke to Corsi that day, who says that they received non-public information about the tape from Corsi or acknowledged having contacted a member of WikiLeaks on October 7, 2016 after a conversation with Corsi.

e. *Donald Trump Jr. Interaction with WikiLeaks*

Donald Trump Jr. had direct electronic communications with WikiLeaks during the campaign period. On September 20, 2016, an individual named Jason Fishbein sent WikiLeaks the password for an unlaunched website focused on Trump's "unprecedented and dangerous" ties to Russia, PutinTrump.org.[252] WikiLeaks publicly tweeted: "'Let's bomb Iraq' Progress for America PAC to launch "PutinTrump.org' at 9:30am. Oops pw is 'putintrump' putintrump.org." Several hours later, WikiLeaks sent a Twitter direct message to Donald Trump Jr., "A PAC run anti-Trump site putintrump.org is about to launch. The PAC is a recycled pro-Iraq war PAC. We have guessed the password. It is 'putintrump.' See 'About' for who is behind it. Any comments?"[253]

> Several hours later, Trump Jr. emailed a variety of senior campaign staff:
>
> Guys I got a weird Twitter OM from wikileaks. See below. I tried the password and it works and the about section they reference contains the next pie in terms of who is behind it. Not sure if this is anything but it seems like it's really wikileaks asking me as I follow them and it is a DM. Do you know the people mentioned and what the conspiracy they are looking for could be? These are just screen shots but it's a fully built out page claiming to be a PAC let me know your thoughts and if we want to look into it.[254]

Trump Jr. attached a screenshot of the "About" page for the unlaunched site PutinTrump.org. The next day (after the website had launched publicly), Trump Jr. sent a direct message to WikiLeaks: "Off the record, I don't know who that is but I'll ask around. Thanks."[255]

On October 3, 2016, WikiLeaks sent another direct message to Trump Jr., asking "you guys" to help disseminate a link alleging candidate Clinton had advocated using a drone to target Julian Assange. Trump Jr. responded that he already "had done so," and asked, "what's behind this Wednesday leak I keep reading about?"[256] WikiLeaks did not respond.

On October 12, 2016, WikiLeaks wrote again that it was "great to see you and your dad talking about our publications. Strongly suggest your dad tweets this link if he mentions us wlsearch.tk."[257] WikiLeaks wrote that the link would help Trump in "digging through" leaked emails and stated, "we just released Podesta emails Part 4."[258] Two days later, Trump Jr. publicly tweeted the wlsearch.tk link.[259]

2. Other Potential Campaign Interest in Russian Hacked Materials

Throughout 2016, the Trump Campaign expressed interest in Hillary Clinton's private email server and whether approximately 30,000 emails from that server had in fact been permanently destroyed, as reported by the media. Several individuals associated with the Campaign were contacted in 2016 about various efforts to obtain the missing Clinton emails and other stolen material in support of the Trump Campaign. Some of these contacts were met with skepticism, and nothing came of them; others were pursued to some degree. The investigation did not find evidence that the Trump Campaign recovered any stich Clinton emails, or that these contacts were part of a coordinated effort between Russia and the Trump Campaign.

a. Henry Oknyansky (a/k/a Henry Greenberg)

In the spring of 2016, Trump Campaign advisor Michael Caputo learned through a Florida• based Russian business partner that another Florida-based Russian, Henry Oknyansky (who also went by the name Henry Greenberg), claimed to have information pertaining to Hillary Clinton.

Caputo notified Roger Stone and brokered communication between Stone and Oknyansky. Oknyansky and Stone set up a May 2016 in-person meeting.[i'"]

Oknyansky was accompanied to the meeting by Alexei Rasin, a Ukrainian associate involved in Florida real estate. At the meeting, Rasin offered to sell Stone derogatory information on Clinton that Rasin claimed to have obtained while working for Clinton. Rasin claimed to possess financial statements demonstrating Clinton's involvement in money laundering with Rasin's companies. According to Oknyansky, Stone asked if the amounts in question totaled millions of dollars but was told it was closer to hundreds of thousands. Stone refused the offer, stating that Trump would not pay for opposition research.[261]

Oknyansky claimed to the Office that Rasin's motivation was financial. According to Oknyansky, Rasin had tried unsuccessfully to shop the Clinton information around to other interested parties, and Oknyansky would receive a cut if the information was sold.[262] Rasin is noted in public source documents as the director and/or registered agent for a number of Florida companies, none of which appears to be connected to Clinton. The Office found no other evidence that Rasin worked for Clinton or any Clinton-related entities.

In their statements to investigators, Oknyansky and Caputo had contradictory recollections about the meeting. Oknyansky claimed that Caputo accompanied Stone to the meeting and provided an introduction, whereas Caputo did not tell us that he had attended and claimed that he was never told what information Oknyansky offered. Caputo also stated that he was unaware Oknyansky sought to be paid for the information until Stone informed him after the fact.[263]

The Office did not locate Rasin in the United States, although the Office confirmed Rasin had been issued a Florida driver's license. The Office otherwise was unable to determine the content and origin of the information he purportedly offered to Stone. Finally, the investigation did not identify evidence of a connection between the outreach or the meeting and Russian interference efforts.

b. Campaign Efforts to Obtain Deleted Clinton Emails

After candidate Trump stated on July 27, 2016, that he hoped Russia would "find the 30,000 emails that are missing," Trump asked individuals affiliated with his Campaign to find the deleted Clinton emails.[264] Michael Flynn—who would later serve as National Security Advisor in the Trump Administration—recalled that Trump made this request repeatedly, and Flynn subsequently contacted multiple people in an effort to obtain the emails.[265]

Barbara Ledeen and Peter Smith were among the people contacted by Flynn. Ledeen, a long-time Senate staffer who had previously sought the Clinton emails, provided updates to Flynn about her efforts throughout the summer of 2016.[266] Smith, an investment advisor who was active in Republican politics, also attempted to locate and obtain the deleted Clinton emails.[267]

Ledeen began her efforts to obtain the Clinton emails before Flynn's request, as early as December 2015.[268] On December 3, 2015, she emailed Smith a proposal to obtain the emails, stating, "Here is the proposal I briefly mentioned to you. The person I described to you would be happy to talk with you either in person or over the phone. The person can get the emails which 1. Were classified and 2. Were purloined by our enemies. That would demonstrate what needs to be demonstrated."[269]

Attached to the email was a 25-page proposal stating that the "Clinton email server was, in all likelihood, breached long ago," and that the Chinese, Russian, and Iranian intelligence services could "re-assemble the server's email content."[270] The proposal called for a three-phase approach. The first two phases consisted of open-source analysis. The third phase consisted of checking with certain intelligence sources "that have access through liaison work with various foreign services" to determine if any of those services had gotten to the server. The proposal noted, "Even if a single email was recovered and the providence [sic] of that email was a foreign service, it would be catastrophic to the Clinton campaign[.]" Smith forwarded the email to two colleagues and wrote, "we can discuss to whom it should be referred."[271] On

December 16, 2015, Smith informed Ledeen that he declined to participate in her "initiative." According to one of Smith's business associates, Smith believed Ledeen's initiative was not viable at that time.[272]

Just weeks after Trump's July 2016 request to find the Clinton emails, however, Smith tried to locate and obtain the emails himself. He created a company, raised tens of thousands of dollars, and recruited security experts and business associates. Smith made claims to others involved in the effort (and those from whom he sought funding) that he was in contact with hackers with "ties and affiliations to Russia" who had access to the emails, and that his efforts were coordinated with the Trump Campaign.[273]

On August 28, 2016, Smith sent an email from an encrypted account with the subject "Sec. Clinton's unsecured private email server" to an undisclosed list of recipients, including Campaign co-chairman Sam Clovis. The email stated that Smith was "[j]ust finishing two days of sensitive meetings here in DC with involved groups to poke and probe on the above. It is clear that the Clinton's home-based, unprotected server was hacked with ease by both State-related players, and private mercenaries. Parties with varying interests, are circling to release ahead of the election."[274]

On September 2, 2016, Smith directed a business associate to establish KLS Research LLC in furtherance of his search for the deleted Clinton emails.[275] One of the purposes of KLS Research was to manage the funds Smith raised in support of his initiative.[276] KLS Research received over $30,000 during the presidential campaign, although Smith represented that he raised even more money.F?

Smith recruited multiple people for his initiative, including security experts to search for and authenticate the emails.[278] In early September 2016, as part of his recruitment and fundraising effort, Smith circulated a document stating that his initiative was "in coordination" with the Trump Campaign, "to the extent permitted as an independent expenditure organization."[279] The document listed multiple individuals affiliated with the Trump Campaign, including Flynn, Clovis, Bannon, and Kellyanne Conway.P? The investigation established that Smith communicated with at least Flynn and Clovis about his search for the deleted Clinton emails,[281] but the Office did not identify evidence that any of the listed individuals initiated or directed Smith's efforts.

In September 2016, Smith and Ledeen got back in touch with each other about their respective efforts. Ledeen wrote to Smith, "wondering if you had some more detailed reports or memos or other data you could share because we have come a long way in our efforts since we last visited.___ We would need as much technical discussion as possible so we could marry it against the new data we have found and then could share it back to you 'your eyes only.'"[282]

Ledeen claimed to have obtained a trove of emails (from what she described as the "dark web") that purported to be the deleted Clinton emails. Ledeen wanted to authenticate the emails and solicited contributions to fund that effort. Erik Prince provided funding to hire a tech advisor to ascertain the authenticity of the emails. According to Prince, the tech advisor determined that the emails were not authentic.[283]

A backup of Smith's computer contained two files that had been downloaded from WikiLeaks and that were originally attached to emails received by John Podesta. The files on Smith's computer had creation dates of October 2, 2016, which was prior to the date of their release by WikiLeaks. Forensic examination, however, established that the creation date did not reflect when the files were downloaded to Smith's computer. (It appears the creation date was when WikiLeaks staged the document for release, as discussed in Volume I, Section III.B.3.c, *supra*.[284] The investigation did not otherwise identify evidence that Smith obtained the files before their release by WikiLeaks. Smith continued to send emails to an undisclosed recipient list about Clinton's deleted emails until shortly before the election. For example, on October 28, 2016, Smith wrote that there was a "tug-of-war going on within WikiLeaks over its planned releases in the next few days," and that WikiLeaks "has maintained that it will save its best revelations for last, under the theory this allows little time for response prior to the U.S. election November 8."[285] An attachment to the email claimed that WikiLeaks would release "All 33k deleted Emails" by "November 1st." No emails obtained from Clinton's server were subsequently released.

Smith drafted multiple emails stating or intimating that he was in contact with Russian hackers. For example, in one such email, Smith claimed that, in August 2016, KLS Research had organized meetings with parties who had access to the deleted Clinton emails, including parties with "ties and affiliations to Russia."[286] The investigation did not identify evidence that any such meetings occurred. Associates and security experts who worked with Smith on the initiative did not believe that Smith was in contact with Russian hackers and were aware of no such connection.[287] The investigation did not establish that Smith was in contact with Russian hackers or that Smith, Ledeen, or other individuals in touch with the Trump Campaign ultimately obtained the deleted Clinton emails.

In sum, the investigation established that the GRU hacked into email accounts of persons affiliated with the Clinton Campaign, as well as the computers of the DNC and DCCC. The GRU then exfiltrated data related to the 2016 election from these accounts and computers, and disseminated that data through fictitious online personas (DCLeaks and Guccifer 2.0) and later through WikiLeaks. The investigation also established that the Trump Campaign ~~Harm to Ongoing Matter~~ As explained in Volume I, Section V.B, *infra*, the evidence was sufficient to support computer-intrusion (and other) charges against GRU officers for their role in election-related hacking. Harm to Ongoing Matter

---

[109] As discussed in Section V below, our Office charged 12 GRU officers for crimes arising from the hacking of these computers, principally with conspiring to commit computer intrusions, in violation of 18 U.S.C. §§1030 and 371. *See* Volume I, Section V.B, *infra;* Indictment, *United States v. Netyksho,* No. 1:18-cr-215 (D.D.C. July 13, 2018), Doc. 1 *("Netyksho* Indictment").

[110] *Netyksho* Indictment ¶ 1.

[111] Separate from this Office's indictment of GRU officers, in October 2018 a grand jury sitting in the Western District of Pennsylvania returned an indictment charging certain members of Unit 26165 with hacking the U.S. Anti-Doping Agency, the World Anti-Doping Agency, and other international sport associations. *United States v. Aleksei Sergeyevich Morenets,* No. 18-263 (W.D. Pa.).

[112] A spearphishing email is designed to appear as though it originates from a trusted source, and solicits information to enable the sender to gain access to an account or network, or causes the recipient to secure bitcoins used to purchase computer infrastructure used in hacking operations.

[113] Bitcoin mining consists of unlocking new bitcoins by solving computational problems. Ill kept its newly mined coins in an account on the bitcoin exchange platform CEX.io. To make purchases, the GRU routed funds into other accounts through transactions designed to obscure the source of funds. Netyksho Indictment ¶ 62.

[114] Netyksho Indictment ¶ 69.

[115] Netyksho Indictment ¶ 9.

[116] See SM-2589105, serials 144 &

[120] A VPN extends a private network, allowing users to send and receive data across public networks (such as the internet) as if the connecting computer was directly connected to the private network. The VPN in this case had been

created to give a small number of DCCC employees access to certain databases housed on the DNC network. Therefore, while the DCCC employees were outside the DNC's private network, they could access parts of the DNC network from their DCCC computers.

123 "Malware" is short for malicious software, and here refers to software designed to allow a third party to infiltrate a computer without the consent or knowledge of the computer's user or operator.

124 Investigative Technique

126 In connection with these intrusions, the GRU used computers (virtual private networks, dedicated servers operated by hosting companies, etc.) that it leased from third-patty providers located all over the world. The investigation identified rental a reements and payments for computers located in, inter alia, all of which were used in the operations targeting the U.S. election.

127 Netyksho Indictment ,r 25.

128 Netyksho Indictment ,r 24(c).

129 Netyksho Indictment ,r 24(b).

130 Netyksho Indictment ,i,i 27-29; Investigative Technique

131 Investigative Technique

135 Investigative Technique

• See SM-2589105-GJ, serial 649. As part of its investigation, the FBI later received images of DNC servers and copies of relevant traffic logs. Netyksho Indictment ,i,i 28-29.

136 Netyksho Indictment ,i 29. The last-in-time DNC email released by WikiLeaks was dated May 25, 2016, the same period of time during which the GRU gained access to the DNC's email server. Netyksho Indictment ,i 45.

137 Netyksho Indictment ,i 35. Approximately a week before the registration of dcleaks.com, the same actors attem ted to re ister the website electionleaks.com using the same domain registration service.

138 See SM-2589105, serial 181; Netyksho Indictment ,i 21(a).

140 See, e.g., Internet Archive, "htt s://dcleaks.com/" archive date Nov. 10, 2016). Additionally, DCLeaks released documents relating t , emails belonging to-, and emails from 2015 reating to Republican Party employees (under the portfolio name "The United States Republican Party"). "The United States Republican Party" portfolio contained approximately 300 emails from a variety of GOP members, PACs, campaigns, state parties, and businesses dated between May and October 2015. According to open-source reporting, these victims shared the same

141 Netyksho Indictment ,i 38.

142 See, e.g., Facebook Account 100008825623541 (Alice Donovan).

143 7/14/16 Facebook Message, ID 793058100795341 (DC Leaks) to ID

144 See, e.., 9/14/16 Twitter DM @dcleaks_ to KvFsg%* 14@gPgu& enjoy;)." dcleaks_ to ; 9/14/16 Twitter DM,The messages read: "Hi https://t.co/QTvKUjQcOx pass:

145 Dmitri Alperovitch, Bears in the Midst: Intrusion into the Democratic National Committee, CrowdStrike Blog (June 14, 2016). CrowdStrike updated its post after the June 15, 2016 post by Guccifer 2.0 claiming responsibility for the intrusion

146 Netyksho Indictment ,i,i 41-42.

147 Releases of documents on the Guccifer 2.0 blog occurred on June 15, 2016; June 20, 2016; June

21, 2016; July 6, 2016; July 14, 2016; August 12, 2016; August 15, 2016; August 21, 2016; August 31,

2016; September 15, 2016; September 23, 2016; October 4, 2016; and October 18, 2016. ccifer20@aol.fr to (subject "leaked emails");.

149 6/27/16 Email, uccifer20@aol.fr to; see also 6/27/16 (subject "leaked emails");project").(sub· ect "leaked emails" ; cc·fer20@aol.fr to (claiming DCLeaks was a "Wikileaks sub

150 Before sending the reporter the link and password to the closed DCLeaks website, and in an apparent effort to deflect attention from the fact that DCLeaks and Guccifer 2.0 were operated by the same organization, the Guccifer 2.0 persona sent the reporter an email stating that DCLeaks was a "Wikileaks sub project" and that Guccifer 2.0 had asked DCLeaks to release the leaked emails with "closed access" to give reporters a preview of them.

151 Netyksho Indictment ,r 43(a).

152 Netyksho Indictment ,r 43(b).

153 Netyksho Indictment ,r 43(c).

154

ISS Harm to Ongoing Matter

156 11/19/15 Twitter Group Chat, Group ID 594242937858486276, @WikiLeaks et al. Assange also wrote that, "GOP will generate a lot oposition [sic], including through dumb moves. Hillary will do the same thing, but co-opt the liberal opposition and the GOP opposition. Hence hillary has greater freedom to start wars than the GOP and has the will to do so." Id.

157 WikiLeaks, "Hillary Clinton Email Archive," available at https://wikileaks.org/clinton-emails/.

158 3/14/16 Twitter DM, @WikiLeaks to   Less than two weeks earlier, the same account had been used to send a private message opposing the idea of Clinton "in white house with her bloodlutt and amitions [sic] of empire with hawkish liberal-interventionist appointees." 11/19/15 Twitter Group Chat, Group ID 594242937858486276, @WikiLeaks et al.

159 6/14/16 Twitter DM, @dcleaks_ to @WikiLeaks.

160 Netyksho Indictment ,r 47(a).

161 7/6/16 Twitter DMs, @WikiLeaks & @guccifer_2.

163 This was not the GRU's first attempt at transferring data to WikiLeaks. On June 29, 2016, the GRU used a Guccifer 2.0 email accouted file to a WikiLeaks email account.

6/29/16 Email, guccifer2@mail.com llmllllllllllll (The email appears to have been undelivered.)

164 See SM-2589105-DCLEAKS, serial 28 (analysis).

165 6/27/16 Twitter DM, @Guccifer_2 to @WikiLeaks.

166 7/18/16 Twitter DM, @Guccifer_2 & @WikiLeaks.

167 "DNC Email Archive," WikiLeaks (Jul. 22, 2016), available athttps://wikileaks.org/dnc-emails.

168 9/15/16 Twitter DM, @dcleaks_ to @WikiLeaks.

169 9/15/16 Twitter DM, @guccifer_2 to @dcleaks_

. 170 See SM-2589105-DCLEAKS, serial 28; 9/15/16 Twitter DM, @Guccifer_2 & @WikiLeaks.

171 See SM-2284941, serials 63 & 64 Investigative Technique

At t e time, certain Apple operating systems use a setting that left a downloaded file's creation date the same as the creation date shown on the host computer. This would explain why the creation date on WikiLeaks's version of the files was still September 19, 2016. See SM-2284941, serial 62 Investigative Technique

173 When WikiLeaks saved attachments separately from the stolen emails, its computer system appears to have treated each attachment as a new file and given it a new creation date. See SM-2284941, serials 63 & 64.

174 See 9/22/16 Email, dcleaksproject@gmail.com

175 Ellen Nakashima et al., A German Hacker Offers a Rare Look Inside the Secretive World of Julian Assange and Wikil.eaks, Washington Post (Jan. 17, 2018).

181 See Assange: "MurderedDNC Staffer Was 'Potential' Wikil.eaks Source," Fox News (Aug. 25,

2016)(containing video of Assange interview by Megyn Kelly).

182 M. Raju & Z. Cohen, A GOP Congressman's Lonely Quest Defending Julian Assange, CNN (May 23, 2018).

183 "Donald Trump on Russian & Missing Hillary Clinton Emails," YouTube Channel C-SPAN, Posted 7/27/16, available at https://www.youtube.com/watch?v=3kxG8uJUsWU (starting at 0:41).

185 Netyksho Indictment ,i 34; see also SM-2589105-HACK, serial 29 Investigative Technique

186 Netyksho Indictment 169.

-188 Investigative Technique

194 See Mahita Gajanan, Julian Assange Timed DNC Email Release for Democratic Convention,

Time (July 27, 2016) (quoting the June 12, 2016 television interview).

195 In February 2018, Gates pleaded guilty, pursuant to a plea agreement, to a superseding criminal information charging him with conspiring to defraud and commit multiple offenses (i.e., tax fraud, failure to report foreign bank accounts, and acting as an unregistered agent of a foreign principal) against the United States, as well as making false statements to our Office. Superseding Criminal Information, United States v. Richard W. Gates III, 1: 1 7-cr-201 (D.D.C. Feb. 23, 2018), Doc. 195 ("Gates Superseding Criminal Information"); Plea Agreement, United States v. Richard W. Gates III, 1: 17-cr-201 (D.D.C. Feb. 23, 2018), Doc. 205 ("Gates Plea Agreement"). Gates has provided information and in-court testimony that the Office has deemed to be reliable.

196 Gates 10/25/18 302, at 1-2.

197 As explained further in Volume I, Section IV.A.8, infra, Manafort entered into a plea agreement with our Office. We determined that he breached the agreement by being untruthful in proffer sessions and before the grand jury. We have generally recounted his version of events in this report only when his statements are sufficiently corroborated to be trustworthy; to identify issues on which Manafort's untruthful responses may themselves be ofevidentiary value; or to provide Manafort's explanations for certain events, even when we were unable to determine whether that explanation was credible. His account appears here principally because it aligns with those of other witnesses.

198

199 In November 2018, Cohen pleaded guilty pursuant to a plea agreement to a single-count information charging him with making false statements to Congress, in violation of 18 U.S.C. § 100 l(a) & (c). He had previously pleaded guilty to several other criminal charges brought by the U.S. Attorney's Office in the Southern District ofNew York, after a referral from this Office. In the months leading up to his false-statements guilty plea, Cohen met with our

Office on multiple occasions for interviews and provided information that the Office has generally assessed to be reliable and that is included in this report.

202 Cohen 9/18/18 302, at 10.

203 Gates 10/25/18 302 (serial 241), at 4.

204

207 Gates 4/10/18 302, at 3; Gates 4/11/18 302, at 1-2 (SM-2180998); Gates 10/25/18 302, at 2.

208

209 Gates 10/25/18 302 (serial 241), at 4.

210 ,HOM

211

212 Corsi first rose to public prominence in August 2004 when he published his book Unfit for Command: Swift Boat Veterans Speak Out Against John Kerry. In the 2008 election cycle, Corsi gained prominence for being a leading proponent of the allegation that Barack Obama was not born in the United States. Corsi told the Office that Donald Trump expressed interest in his writings, and that he spoke with Trump on the phone on at least six occasions. Corsi 9/6/18 302, at 3.213 Corsi 10/31/18 302, at 2;   Corsi was first interviewed on September 6, 2018 at the Special Counsel's o fices in Washington, D.C. He was accompanied by counsel throughout the interview. Corsi was subsequently interviewed on September 17,

2018; September 21, 2018; October 31, 2018; November I, 2018; and November 2, 2018. Counsel was

215 Corsi 10/31/18 302, at 4.

218.Malloch denied ever communicating with Assange r uest to contact Assange because he believed he had no

244 In a later November 2018 interview, Corsi stated Harm to Ongoing Matter that he believed Malloch was on the call but then focused on other individuals who were on the call-mvitation, which Malloch was not. (Separate travel records show that at the time of the call, Malloch was aboard a transatlantic flight). Corsi at one point stated that after WikiLeaks's release of stolen emails on October 7, 2016, he concluded Malloch had gotten in contact with Assange. Corsi 11/1/18 302, at 6.

245 During the same interview, Corsi also suggested that he may have sent out public tweets because he knew Assange was reading his tweets. Our Office was unable to find evidence of any such tweets.

246 Corsi 9/21/18 302, at 6-7.

247 Corsi 11/1/18 302, at 6.

252 9/20/16 Twitter OM, asonFishbein to @WikiLeaks; see JF00587 (9/21/16 Messages,

-@jabber.cryptoparty.is   @jabber.cryptoparty.is); Fishbein 9/5/18 302, at 4. When interviewed by our Office, Fishbein pro uce what he claimed to be logs from a chatroom in which the participants discussed U.S. politics; one of the other participants had posted the website and password that Fishbein sent to WikiLeaks.

253 9/20/16 Twitter OM, @WikiLeaks to @OonaldJTrumpJr.

254   TRUMPORG_28_000629-33 (9/21/16 Email, Trump Jr. to Conway et al. (subject"Wikileaks")).

255   9/21/16 Twitter OM,@OonaldJTrumpJr to@WikiLeaks.

256   10/3/16 Twitter OMs,@OonaldJTrumpJr & @WikiLeaks.

257 At the time, the link took users to a WikiLeaks archive of stolen Clinton Campaign documents.

258   10/12/16 Twitter DM,@WikiLeaks to@DonaldJTrumpJr.

259   @OonaldJTrumpJr 10/14/16 (6:34 a.m.) Tweet.

26° Caputo 5/2/18 302, at 4; Oknyansky 7/13/18 302, at 1.

261 Oknyansky 7/13/18 302, at 1-2.

262 Oknyansky 7/13/18 302, at 2.

263 Caputo 5/2/18 302, at 4; Oknyansky 7/13/18 302, at 1

. 264 Flynn4/25/18 302, at 5-6; Flynn 5/1/18 302, at 1-3.

265 Flynn 5/1/18 302, at 1-3.

266 Flynn 4/25/18 302, at 7; Flynn 5/4/18 302, at 1-2; Flynn 11/29/17 302, at 7-8.

267 Flynn 11/29/17 302, at 7.

268 Szobocsan 3/29/17 302, at 1.

269   12/3/15 Email, Ledeen to Smith.

270   12/3/15 Email, Ledeen to Smith (attachment).

271   12/3/15 Email, Smith to Szobocsan & Safron.

272 Szobocsan 3/29/18 302, at I.

273   8/31/16 Email, Smith to Smith.

274   8/28/16 Email, Smith to Smith.

275   Incorporation papers of KLS Research LLC, 7/26/17 Szobocsan 3/29/18 302, at 2.

276   Szobocsan 3/29/18 302, at 3.

277   Financial Institution Record of Peter Smith and KLS Research LLC, 10/31 /17 -   10/11/16 Email, Smith to

278 Tait 8/22/17 302, at 3; York 7/12/17 302, at 1-2; York 11/22/17 302, at 1.

279 York 7/13/17 302 (attachment KLS Research, LLC, "Clinton Email Reconnaissance Initiative," Sept. 9, 2016).

280   The same recruitment document listed Jerome Corsi under "Independent Groups/Organizations/Individuals," and described him as an "established author and writer from the right on President Obama and Sec. Clinton."

281   Flynn 11/29/17 302, at 7-8; I 0/15/ 16 Email, Smith to Flynn et al.; 8/28/16 Email, Smith to Smith (bee: Clovis et al.).

282 9/16/16 Email, Ledeen to Smith.

283   Prince 4/4/18 302, at 4-5.

284   The forensic analysis of Smith's computer devices found that Smith used an older Apple operating system that would have preserved that October 2, 2016 creation date when it was downloaded (no matter what day it was in fact downloaded by Smith). See Volume I, Section III.B.3.c, supra. The Office tested this theory in March 2019 by downloading the two files found on Smith's computer from WikiLeaks's site using the same Apple operating system on Smith's computer; both files were successfully downloaded and retained the October 2, 2016 creation date. See SM-2284941, serial 62.

285   10/28/16 Email, Smith to Smith.

286   8/31/16 Email, Smith to Smith.

287   Safron 3/20/18 302, at 3; Szobocsan 3/29/18 302, at 6.

IV. RUSSIAN GOVERNMENT LINKS To AND CONTACTS WITH THE TRUMP CAMPAIGN

The Office identified multiple contacts — "links," in the words of the Appointment Order ➤ between Trump Campaign officials and individuals with ties to the Russian government. The Office investigated whether those contacts constituted a third avenue of attempted Russian interference with or influence on the 2016 presidential election. In particular, the investigation examined whether these contacts involved or resulted in coordination or a conspiracy with the Trump Campaign and Russia, including with respect to Russia providing assistance to the Campaign in exchange for any sort of favorable treatment in the future. Based on the available information, the investigation did not establish such coordination.

This Section describes the principal links between the Trump Campaign and individuals with ties to the Russian government, including some contacts with Campaign officials or associates that have been publicly reported to involve Russian contacts. Each subsection begins with an overview of the Russian contact at issue and then describes in detail the relevant facts, which are generally presented in chronological order, beginning with the early months of the Campaign and extending through the post-election, transition period.

A. Campaign Period (September 2015 – November 8, 2016)

Russian-government-connected individuals and media entities began showing interest in Trump's campaign in the months after he announced his candidacy in June 2015.[288] Because Trump's status as a public figure at the time was attributable in large part to his prior business and entertainment dealings, this Office investigated whether a business contact with Russia-linked individuals and entities during the campaign period — the Trump Tower Moscow project, *see* Volume I, Section IV.A. I, *infra* —led to or involved coordination of election assistance.

Outreach from individuals with ties to Russia continued in the spring and summer of 2016, when Trump was moving toward — and eventually becoming — the Republican nominee for President. As set forth below, the Office also evaluated a series of links during this period: outreach to two of Trump's then-recently named foreign policy advisors, including a representation that Russia had "dirt" on Clinton in the form of thousands of emails (Volume I, Sections IV.A.2 & IV.A.3); dealings with a D.C.-based think tank that specializes in Russia and has connections with its government (Volume I, Section IV.A.4); a meeting at Trump Tower between the Campaign and a Russian lawyer promising dirt on candidate Clinton that was "part of . Russia and its government's support for [Trump]" (Volume I, Section IV.A.5); events at the Republican National Convention (Volume I, Section IV.A.6); post-Convention contacts between Trump Campaign officials and Russia's ambassador to the United States (Volume I, Section IV.A.7); and contacts through campaign chairman Paul Manafort, who had previously worked for a Russian oligarch and a pro-Russian political party in Ukraine (Volume I, Section IV.A.8).

1. **Trump Tower Moscow Project**

The Trump Organization has pursued and completed projects outside the United States as part of its real estate portfolio. Some projects have involved the acquisition and ownership (through subsidiary corporate structures) of property. In other cases, the Trump Organization has executed licensing deals with real estate developers and management companies, often local to the country where the project was located.[289]

Between at least 2013 and 2016, the Trump Organization explored a similar licensing deal in Russia involving the construction of a Trump-branded property in Moscow. The project, commonly referred to as a "Trump Tower Moscow" or "Trump Moscow" project, anticipated a combination of commercial, hotel, and residential properties all within the same building. Between 2013 and June 2016, several employees of the Trump Organization, including then• president of the organization Donald J. Trump, pursued a Moscow deal with several Russian counterparties. From the fall of 2015 until the middle of 2016, Michael Cohen spearheaded the Trump Organization's pursuit of a Trump Tower Moscow project, including by reporting on the project's status to candidate Trump and other executives in the Trump Organization. P?

a. *Trump Tower Moscow Venture with the Crocus Group (2013-2014)*

The Trump Organization and the Crocus Group, a Russian real estate conglomerate owned and controlled by Aras Agalarov, began discussing a Russia-based real estate project shortly after the conclusion of the 2013 Miss Universe pageant in Moscow.[291] Donald J. Trump Jr. served as the primary negotiator on behalf of the Trump Organization; Emin Agalarov (son of Aras Agalarov) and Irakli "Ike"

Kaveladze represented the Crocus Group during negotiations,[292] with the occasional assistance of Robert Goldstone.[293]

In December 2013, Kaveladze and Trump Jr. negotiated and signed preliminary terms of an agreement for the Trump Tower Moscow project.[294] On December 23, 2013, after discussions with Donald J. Trump, the Trump Organization agreed to accept an arrangement whereby the organization received a flat 3.5% commission on all sales, with no licensing fees or incentives.[295] The parties negotiated a letter of intent during January and February 2014.[296]

From January 2014 through November 2014, the Trump Organization and Crocus Group discussed development plans for the Moscow project. Some time before January 24, 2014, the Crocus Group sent the Trump Organization a proposal for a 800-unit, 194-meter building to be constructed at an Agalarov-owned site in Moscow called "Crocus City," which had also been the site of the Miss Universe pageant.[297] In February 2014, Ivanka Trump met with Emin Agalarov and toured the Crocus City site during a visit to Moscow.[298] From March 2014 through July 2014, the groups discussed "design standards" and other architectural elements.[299] For example, in July 2014, members of the Trump Organization sent Crocus Group counterparties questions about the "demographics of these prospective buyers" in the Crocus City area, the development of neighboring parcels in Crocus City, and concepts for redesigning portions of the building.P? In August 2014, the Trump Organization requested specifications for a competing Marriott-branded tower being built in Crocus City.[301]

Beginning in September 2014, the Trump Organization stopped responding in a timely fashion to correspondence and proposals from the Crocus Group.[302] Communications between the two groups continued through November 2014 with decreasing frequency; what appears to be the last communication is dated November 24, 2014.[303] The project appears not to have developed past the planning stage, and no construction occurred.

b. Communications with JC. Expert Investment Company and Giorgi Rtskhiladze (Summer and Fall 2015)

In the late summer of 2015, the Trump Organization received a new inquiry about pursuing a Trump Tower project in Moscow. In approximately September 2015, Felix Sater, a New York• based real estate advisor, contacted Michael Cohen, then-executive vice president of the Trump Organization and special counsel to Donald J. Trump.[304] Sater had previously worked with the Trump Organization and advised it on a number of domestic and international projects. Sater had explored the possibility of a Trump Tower project in Moscow while working with the Trump Organization and therefore knew of the organization's general interest in completing a deal there.[305] Sater had also served as an informal agent of the Trump Organization in Moscow previously and had accompanied Ivanka Trump and Donald Trump Jr. to Moscow in the mid-2000s.[306]

Sater contacted Cohen on behalf of LC. Expert Investment Company (I.C. Expert), a Russian real-estate development corporation controlled by Andrei Vladimirovich Rozov.[P?] Sater had known Rozov since approximately 2007 and, in 2014, had served as an agent on behalf of Rozov during Rozov's purchase of a building in New York City.[308] Sater later contacted Rozov and proposed that I.C. Expert pursue a Trump Tower Moscow project in which I.C. Expert would license the name and brand from the Trump Organization but construct the building on its own. Sater worked on the deal with Rozov and another employee of l.C. Expert.[P?]

Cohen was the only Trump Organization representative to negotiate directly with I.C. Expert or its agents. In approximately September 2015, Cohen obtained approval to negotiate with LC. Expert from candidate Trump, who was then president of the Trump Organization. Cohen provided updates directly to Trump about the project throughout 2015 and into 2016, assuring him the project was continuing.[310] Cohen also discussed the Trump Moscow project with Ivanka Trump as to design elements (such as possible architects to use for the project'!') and Donald Trump Jr. (about his experience in Moscow and possible involvement in the project[312] during fall of 2015.

Also during the fall of 2015, Cohen communicated about the Trump Moscow proposal with Giorgi Rtskhiladze, a business executive who previously had been involved in a development deal with the Trump Organization in Batumi, Georgia.[313] Cohen stated that he spoke to Rtskhiladze in part because Rtskhiladze had pursued business ventures in Moscow, including a licensing deal with the Agalarov-owned Crocus Group.[314] On September 22, 2015, Cohen forwarded a preliminary design study for the Trump Moscow project to Rtskhiladze, adding "I look forward to your reply about this spectacular project in Moscow." Rtskhiladze forwarded Cohen's email to an associate and wrote, "[i]f we could organize the meeting in New York at the highest level of the Russian Government and Mr. Trump this project would definitely receive the worldwide attention."[315]

On September 24, 2015, Rtskhiladze sent Cohen an attachment that he described as a proposed "[!]etter to the Mayor of Moscow from Trump org," explaining that "[w]e need to send this letter to the Mayor of Moscow (second guy in Russia) he is aware of the potential project and will pledge his support."[316] In a second email to Cohen sent the same day, Rtskhiladze provided a translation of the letter, which described the Trump Moscow project as a "symbol of stronger economic, business and cultural relationships between New York and Moscow and therefore United States and the Russian Federation."[317] On September 27, 2015, Rtskhiladze sent another email to Cohen, proposing that the Trump Organization partner on the Trump Moscow project with "Global Development Group LLC," which he described as being controlled by Michail Posikhin, a Russian architect, and Simon Nizharadze.[318] Cohen told the Office that he ultimately declined the proposal and instead continued to work with I.C. Expert, the company represented by Felix Sater.[319]

c. Letter of Intent and Contacts to Russian Government (October 2015-January 2016)

i. Trump Signs the Letter of Intent on behalf of the Trump Organization

Between approximately October 13, 2015 and November 2, 2015, the Trump Organization (through its subsidiary Trump Acquisition, LLC) and I.C. Expert completed a letter of intent (LOI) for a Trump Moscow property. The LOI, signed by Trump for the Trump Organization and Rozov on behalf of I.C. Expert, was "intended to facilitate further discussions" in order to "attempt to enter into a mutually acceptable agreement" related to the Trump-branded project in Moscow.P" The LOI contemplated a development with residential, hotel, commercial, and office components, and called for "[a]pproximately 250 first class, luxury residential condominiums," as well as "[o]ne first class, luxury hotel consisting of approximately 15 floors and containing not fewer than 150 hotel rooms." [321]

For the residential and commercial portions of the project, the Trump Organization would receive between 1% and 5% of all condominium sales,[322] plus 3% of all rental and other revenue.[323] For the project's hotel portion, the Trump Organization would receive a base fee of 3% of gross operating revenues for the first five years and 4% thereafter, plus a separate incentive fee of 20% of operating profit. [324] Under the LOI, the Trump Organization also would receive a $4 million "up-front fee" prior to groundbreaking.[325] Under these terms, the Trump Organization stood to earn substantial sums over the lifetime of the project, without assuming significant liabilities or financing commitments.[326]

On November 3, 2015, the day after the Trump Organization transmitted the LOI, Sater emailed Cohen suggesting that the Trump Moscow project could be used to increase candidate Trump's chances at being elected, writing:

> Buddy our boy can become President of the USA and we can engineer it. I will get all of Putins team to buy in on this, I will manage this process. . . . Michael, Putin gets on stage with Donald for a ribbon cutting for Trump Moscow, and Donald owns the republican nomination. And possibly beats Hillary and our boy is in. _ _ _ We will manage this process better than anyone. You and I will get Donald and Vladimir on a stage together very shortly. That the game changer.[327]

Later that day, Sater followed up:

> Donald doesn't stare down, he negotiates and understands the economic issues and Putin only want to deal with a pragmatic leader, and a successful business man is a good candidate for someone who knows how to negotiate. "Business, politics, whatever it all is the same for someone who knows how to deal"

> I think I can get Putin to say that at the Trump Moscow press conference.
> If he says it we own this election. Americas most difficult adversary agreeing that Donald is a good guy to negotiate.. . .
> We can own this election.
> Michael my next steps are very sensitive with Putins very close people, we can pull this off.
> Michael lets go. 2 boys from Brooklyn getting a USA president elected. This is good really good.328

According to Cohen, he did not consider the political import of the Trump Moscow project to the 2016 U.S. presidential election at the time. Cohen also did not recall candidate Trump or anyone affiliated with the Trump Campaign discussing the political implications of the Trump Moscow project with him. However, Cohen recalled conversations with Trump in which the candidate suggested that his campaign would be a significant "infomercial" for Trump-branded properties.329

ii. Post-LOI Contacts with Individuals in Russia

Given the size of the Trump Moscow project, Sater and Cohen believed the project required approval (whether express or implicit) from the Russian national government, including from the Presidential Administration of Russia.P? Sater stated that he therefore began to contact the Presidential Administration through another Russian business contact.33 In early negotiations with the Trump Organization,

Sater had alluded to the need for government approval and his attempts to set up meetings with Russian officials. On October 12, 2015, for example, Sater wrote to Cohen that "all we need is Putin on board and we are golden " and that a "meeting with Putin and top deputy is tentatively set for the 14th [of October]."[332] this meeting was being coordinated by associates in Russia and that he had no direct interaction with the Russian government.[333]

Approximately a month later, after the LOI had been signed, Lana Erchova emailed Ivanka Trump on behalf of Erchova's then-husband Dmitry Klokov, to offer Klokov's assistance to the Trump Campaign.[334] Klokov was at that time Director of External Communications for PJSC Federal Grid Company of Unified Energy System, a large Russian electricity transmission company, and had been previously employed as an aide and press secretary to Russia's energy minister. Ivanka Trump forwarded the email to Cohen.[335] He told the Office that, after receiving this inquiry, he had conducted an internet search for Klokov's name and concluded (incorrectly) that Klokov was a former Olympic weightlifter.[336]

Between November 18 and 19, 2015; Klokov and Cohen had at least one telephone call and exchanged several emails. Describing himself in emails to Cohen as a "trusted person" who could offer the Campaign "political synergy" and "synergy on a government level," Klokov recommended that Cohen travel to Russia to speak with him and an unidentified intermediary. Klokov said that those conversations could facilitate a later meeting in Russia between the candidate and an individual Klokov described as "our person of interest."[337] In an email to the Office, Erchova later identified the "person of interest" as Russian President Vladimir Putin.[338]

In the telephone call and follow-on emails with Klokov, Cohen discussed his desire to use a near-term trip to Russia to do site surveys and talk over the Trump Moscow project with local developers. Cohen registered his willingness also to meet with Klokov and the unidentified intermediary, but was emphatic that all meetings in Russia involving him or candidate

Trump-• including a possible meeting between candidate Trump and Putin — would need to be "in conjunction with the development and an official visit" with the Trump Organization receiving a formal invitation to visit.[339] (Klokov had written previously that "the visit [by candidate Trump to Russia] has to be informal.")[340]

Klokov had also previously recommended to Cohen that he separate their negotiations over a possible meeting between Trump and "the person of interest" from any existing business track.[341]

Re-emphasizing that his outreach was not done on behalf of any business, Klokov added in second email to Cohen that, if publicized well, such a meeting could have "phenomenal" impact "in a business dimension" and that the "person of interest['s]" "most important support" could have significant ramifications for the "level of projects and their capacity." Klokov concluded by telling Cohen that there was "no bigger warranty in any project than [the] consent of the person of interest."[342] Cohen rejected the proposal, saying that "[c]urrently our LOI developer is in talks with VP's Chief of Staff and arranging a formal invite for the two to meet."[343] This email appears to be their final exchange, and the investigation did not identify evidence that Cohen brought Klokov's initial offer of assistance to the Campaign's attention or that anyone associated with the Trump Organization or the Campaign dealt with Klokov at a later date. Cohen explained that he did not pursue the proposed meeting because he was already working on the Moscow Project with Sater, who Cohen understood to have his own connections to the Russian government.[344]

By late December 2015, however, Cohen was complaining that Sater had not been able to use those connections to set up the promised meeting with Russian government officials. Cohen told Sater that he was "setting up the meeting myself."[345] On January 11, 2016, Cohen emailed the office of Dmitry Peskov, the Russian government's press secretary, indicating that he desired contact with Sergei Ivanov, Putin's chief of staff. Cohen erroneously used the email address "Pr_peskova@prpress.gof.ru" instead of "Pr_peskova@prpress.gov.ru," so the email apparently did not go through.[346] On January 14, 2016, Cohen emailed a different address (info@prpress.gov.ru) with the following message:

Dear Mr. Peskov,

Over the past few months, I have been working with a company based in Russia regarding the development of a Trump Tower-Moscow project in Moscow City.

Without getting into lengthy specifics, the communication between our two sides has

stalled. As this project is too important, I am hereby requesting your assistance.

I respectfully request someone, preferably you; contact me so that I might discuss the specifics as well as arranging meetings with the appropriate individuals.

I thank you in advance for your assistance and look forward to hearing from you soon.[347]

Two days later, Cohen sent an email to Pr_peskova@prpress.gov.ru, repeating his request to speak with Sergei Ivanov.[348]

Cohen testified to Congress, and initially told the Office, that he did not recall receiving a response to this email inquiry and that he decided to terminate any further work on the Trump Moscow project as of January 2016. Cohen later admitted that these statements were false. In fact, Cohen had received (and recalled receiving) a response to his inquiry, and he continued to work on and update candidate Trump on the project through as late as June 2016.[349]

On January 20, 2016, Cohen received an email from Elena Poliakova, Peskov's personal assistant. Writing from her personal email account, Poliakova stated that she had been trying to reach Cohen and asked that he call her on the personal number that she provided.P? Shortly after receiving Poliakova's email, Cohen called and spoke to her for 20 minutes.[351] Cohen described to Poliakova his position at the Trump Organization and outlined the proposed Trump Moscow project, including information about the Russian counterparty with which the Trump Organization had partnered. Cohen requested assistance in moving the project forward, both in securing land to build the project and with financing. According to Cohen, Poliakova asked detailed questions and took notes, stating that she would need to follow up with others in Russia.[352]

Cohen could not recall any direct follow-up from Poliakova or from any other representative of the Russian government, nor did the Office identify any evidence of direct follow-up. However, the day after Cohen's call with Poliakova, Sater texted Cohen, asking him to "[c]all me when you have a few minutes to chat ... It's about Putin they called today."[353] Sater then sent a draft invitation for Cohen to visit Moscow to discuss the Trump Moscow project,[354] along with a note to "[t]ell me if the letter is good as amended by me or make whatever changes you want and send it back to me."[355] After a further round of edits, on January 25, 2016, Sater sent Cohen an invitation — signed by Andrey Ryabinskiy of the company MHJ — to travel to "Moscow for a working visit" about the "prospects of development and the construction business in Russia," "the various land plots available suited for construction of this enormous Tower," and "the opportunity to co-ordinate a follow up visit to Moscow by Mr. Donald Trump."[356] According to Cohen, he elected not to travel at the time because of concerns about the Jack of concrete proposals about land plots that could be considered as options for the project.[357]

d. Discussions about Russia Travel by Michael Cohen or Candidate Trump (December 2015-June 2016)

i. Sater 's Overtures to Cohen to Travel to Russia

The late January communication was neither the first nor the last time that Cohen contemplated visiting Russia in pursuit of the Trump Moscow project. Beginning in late 2015, Sater repeatedly tried to arrange for Cohen and candidate Trump, as representatives of the Trump Organization, to travel to Russia to meet with Russian government officials and possible financing partners. In December 2015, Sater sent Cohen a number of emails about logistics for traveling to Russia for meetings.[358] On December 19, 2015, Sater wrote:

> Please call me I have Evgeney [Dvoskin] on the other line.[[359]] He needs a copy of your and Donald's passports they need a scan of every page of the passports. Invitations & Visas will be issued this week by VTB Bank to discuss financing for Trump Tower Moscow. Politically neither Putins office nor Ministry of Foreign Affairs cannot issue invite, so they are inviting commercially/ business. VTB is Russia's 2 biggest bank and VTB Bank CEO Andrey Kostin, will be at all meetings with Putin so that it is a business meeting not political. We will be invited to Russian consulate this week to receive invite & have visa issued.[360]

In response, Cohen texted Sater an image of his own passport.[361] Cohen told the Office that at one point he requested a copy of candidate Trump's passport from Rhona Graff, Trump's executive assistant at the Trump Organization, and that Graff later brought Trump's passport to Cohen's office.[362] The investigation did not, however, establish that the passport was forwarded to Sater.[363]

Into the spring of 2016, Sater and Cohen continued to discuss a trip to Moscow in connection with the Trump Moscow project. On April 20, 2016, Sater wrote Cohen, "[t]he People wanted to know when you are coming?"[364] On May 4, 2016, Sater followed up:

> I had a chat with Moscow. ASSUMING the trip does happen the question is before or after the convention. I said I believe, but don't know for sure, that's it's probably after the convention. Obviously the pre-meeting trip (you only) can happen anytime you want but the 2 big guys where [sic] the question. I said I would confirm and revert. . . . Let me know about If I was right by saying I believe after Cleveland and also when you want to speak to them and possibly fly over.[365]

Cohen responded, "My trip before Cleveland. Trump once he becomes the nominee after the convention."[366]

The day after this exchange, Sater tied Cohen's travel to Russia to the St. Petersburg International Economic Forum ("Forum"), an annual event attended by prominent Russian politicians and businessmen. Sater told the Office that he was informed by a business associate that Peskov wanted to invite Cohen to the Forum.[367] On May 5, 2016, Sater wrote to Cohen:

> Peskov would like to invite you as his guest to the St. Petersburg Forum which is Russia's Davos it's June 16-19. He wants to meet there with you and possibly introduce you to either Putin or Medvedev, as they are not sure if 1 or both will be there.
> This is perfect. The entire business class of Russia will be there as well.
> He said anything you want to discuss including dates and subjects are on the table to discuss[.368]

The following day, Sater asked Cohen to confirm those dates would work for him to travel; Cohen wrote back, "[w]orks for me."[369] On June 9, 2016, Sater sent Cohen a notice that he (Sater) was completing the badges for the Forum, adding, "Putin is there on the 17th very strong chance you will meet him as well."[370]

On June 13, 2016, Sater forwarded Cohen an invitation to the Forum signed by the Director of the Roscongress Foundation, the Russian entity organizing the Forum.[371] Sater also sent Cohen a Russian visa application and asked him to send two passport photos.[372] According to Cohen, the invitation gave no indication that Peskov had been involved in inviting him. Cohen was concerned that Russian officials were not actually involved or were not interested in meeting with him (as Sater had alleged), and so he decided not to go to the Forum.[373] On June 14, 2016, Cohen met Sater in the lobby of the Trump Tower in New York and informed him that he would not be traveling at that time.[374]

ii. Candidate Trump's Opportunities to Travel to Russia

The investigation identified evidence that, during the period the Trump Moscow project was under consideration, the possibility of candidate Trump visiting Russia arose in two contexts.

First, in interviews with the Office, Cohen stated that he discussed the subject of traveling to Russia with Trump twice: once in late 2015; and again in spring 2016.[375] According to Cohen, Trump indicated a willingness to travel if it would assist the project significantly. On one occasion, Trump told Cohen to speak with then-campaign manager Corey Lewandowski to coordinate the candidate's schedule. Cohen recalled that he spoke with Lewandowski, who suggested that they speak again when Cohen had actual dates to evaluate. Cohen indicated, however, that he knew that travel prior to the Republican National Convention would be impossible given the candidate's preexisting commitments to the Campaign.[376]

Second, like Cohen, Trump received and turned down an invitation to the St. Petersburg International Economic Forum. In late December 2015, Mira Duma—a contact of Ivanka Trump's from the fashion industry—first passed along invitations for Ivanka Trump and candidate Trump from Sergei Prikhodko, a Deputy Prime Minister of the Russian Federation.[377] On January 14, 2016, Rhona Graff sent an email to Duma stating that Trump was "honored to be asked to participate in the highly prestigious" Forum event, but that he would "have to decline" the invitation given his "very grueling and full travel schedule" as a presidential candidate.[378] Graff asked Duma whether she recommended that Graff "send a formal note to the Deputy Prime Minister" declining his invitation; Duma replied that a formal note would be "great."[379]

It does not appear that Graff prepared that note immediately. According to written answers from President Trump,[380] Graff received an email from Deputy Prime Minister Prikhodko on March 17, 2016, again inviting Trump to participate in the 2016 Forum in St. Petersburg.[381] Two weeks later, on March 31, 2016, Graff prepared for Trump's signature a two-paragraph letter declining the invitation.[382] The letter stated that Trump's "schedule has become extremely demanding" because of the presidential campaign, that he "already ha[d] several commitments in the United States" for the time of the Forum, but that he otherwise "would have gladly given every consideration to attending such an important event."[383] Graff forwarded the letter to another executive assistant at the Trump Organization with instructions to print the document on letterhead for Trump to sign.[384]

At approximately the same time that the letter was being prepared, Robert Foresman—a New York-based investment banker—began reaching out to Graff to secure an in-person meeting with candidate Trump. According to Foresman, he had been asked by Anton Kobyakov, a Russian presidential aide involved with the Roscongress Foundation, to see if Trump could speak at the Forum.[385] Foresman first emailed Graff on March 31, 2016, following a phone introduction brokered through Trump business associate Mark Burnett (who produced the television show *The Apprentice*). In his email, Foresman referenced his long-standing personal and professional expertise in Russia and Ukraine, his work setting up an early "private channel" between Vladimir Putin and former U.S. President George W. Bush, and an "approach" he had received from "senior Kremlin officials" about the candidate. Foresman asked Graff for a meeting with the candidate, Corey Lewandowski, or "another relevant person" to discuss this and other "concrete things" Foresman felt uncomfortable discussing over "unsecure email."[386] On April 4, 2016, Graff forwarded Foresman's meeting request to Jessica Macchia, another executive assistant to Trump.[387]

With no response forthcoming, Foresman twice sent reminders to Graff—first on April 26 and again on April 30, 2016.[388] Graff sent an apology to Foresman and forwarded his April 26 email (as well as his initial March 2016 email) to Lewandowski.[389] On May 2, 2016, Graff forwarded Foresman's April 30 email—which suggested an alternative meeting with Donald Trump Jr. or Eric Trump so that Foresman could convey to them information that "should be conveyed to [the candidate] personally or [to] someone [the candidate] absolutely trusts" — to policy advisor Stephen Miller.[390]

No communications or other evidence obtained by the Office indicate that the Trump Campaign learned that Foresman was reaching out to invite the candidate to the Forum or that the Campaign otherwise followed up with Foresman until after the election, when he interacted with the Transition Team as he pursued a possible position in the incoming Administration.[391] When interviewed by the Office, Foresman denied that the specific "approach" from "senior Kremlin officials" noted in his March 31, 2016 email was anything other than Kobyakov's invitation to Roscongress. According to Foresman, the "concrete things" he referenced in the same email were a combination of the invitation itself, Foresman's personal perspectives on the invitation and Russia policy in general, and details of a Ukraine plan supported by a U.S. think tank (EastWest Institute). Foresman told the Office that Kobyakov had extended similar invitations through him to another Republican presidential candidate and one other politician. Foresman also said that Kobyakov had asked Foresman to invite Trump to speak after that other presidential candidate withdrew from the race and the other politician's participation did not work out.[392] Finally, Foresman claimed to have no plans to establish a back channel involving Trump, stating the reference to his involvement in the Bush-Putin back channel was meant to burnish his credentials to the Campaign. Foresman commented that he had not recognized any of the experts announced as Trump's foreign policy team in March 2016, and wanted to secure an in-person meeting with the candidate to share his professional background and policy views, including that Trump should decline Kobyakov's invitation to speak at the Forum.[393]

2. George Papadopoulos

George Papadopoulos was a foreign policy advisor to the Trump Campaign from March2016 to early October 2016. [394] In late April 2016, Papadopoulos was told by London-based professor Joseph Mifsud, immediately after Mifsud's return from a trip to Moscow, that the Russian government had obtained "dirt" on candidate Clinton in the form of thousands of emails. One week later, on May 6, 2016, Papadopoulos suggested to a representative of a foreign government that the Trump Campaign had received indications from the Russian government that it could assist the Campaign through the anonymous release of information that would be damaging to candidate Clinton.

Papadopoulos shared information about Russian "dirt" with people outside of the Campaign, and the Office investigated whether he also provided it to a Campaign official. Papadopoulos and the Campaign officials with whom he interacted told the Office that they did not recall that Papadopoulos passed them the information. Throughout the relevant period of time and for several months thereafter, Papadopoulos worked with Mifsud and two Russian nationals to arrange a meeting between the Campaign and the Russian government. That meeting never came to pass.

a. *Origins of Campaign Work*

In March 2016, Papadopoulos became a foreign policy advisor to the Trump Campaign. [395] As early as the summer of 2015, he had sought a role as a policy advisor to the Campaign but, in a September 30, 2015 email, he was told that the Campaign was not hiring policy advisors.[396] In late 2015, Papadopoulos obtained a paid position on the campaign of Republican presidential candidate Ben Carson. [397]

Although Carson remained in the presidential race until early March 2016, Papadopoulos had stopped actively working for his campaign by early February 2016.[398] At that time, Papadopoulos reached out to a contact at the London Centre of International Law Practice (LCILP), which billed itself as a "unique institution ... comprising high-level professional international law practitioners, dedicated to the advancement of global legal knowledge and the practice of international law."[399] Papadopoulos said that he had finished his role with the Carson campaign and asked if LCILP was hiring.[400] In early February, Papadopoulos agreed to join LCILP and arrived in London to begin work.t?'

As he was taking his position at LCILP, Papadopoulos contacted Trump campaign manager Corey Lewandowski via LinkedIn and emailed campaign official Michael Glassner about his interest in joining the Trump Campaign.t'"

On March 2, 2016, Papadopoulos sent Glassner another message reiterating his interest.t'" Glassner passed along word of Papadopoulos's interest to another campaign official, Joy Lutes, who notified Papadopoulos by email that she had been told by Glassner to introduce Papadopoulos to Sam Clovis, the Trump Campaign's national co• chair and chief policy advisor.i'"

At the time of Papadopoulos's March 2 email, the media was criticizing the Trump Campaign for lack of experienced foreign policy or national security advisors within its ranks.[405]

To address that issue, senior Campaign officials asked Clovis to put a foreign policy team together on short notice.[406] After receiving Papadopoulos's name from Lutes, Clovis performed a Google search on Papadopoulos, learned that he had worked at the Hudson Institute, and believed that he had credibility on energy issues.i'" On March 3, 2016, Clovis arranged to speak with Papadopoulos by phone to discuss Papadopoulos joining the Campaign as a foreign policy advisor, and on March 6, 2016, the two spoke.f' Papadopoulos recalled that Russia was mentioned as a topic, and he understood from the conversation that Russia would be an important aspect of the Campaign's foreign policy.[409] At the end of the conversation, Clovis offered Papadopoulos a role as a foreign policy advisor to the Campaign, and Papadopoulos accepted the offer.t'?

b. Initial Russia-Related Contacts

Approximately a week after signing on as a foreign policy advisor, Papadopoulos traveled to Rome, Italy, as part of his duties with LCILP.[411] The purpose of the trip was to meet officials affiliated with Link Campus University, a for-profit institution headed by a former Italian government official.[412] During the visit, Papadopoulos was introduced to Joseph Mifsud.

Mifsud is a Maltese national who worked as a professor at the London Academy of Diplomacy in London, England.[413] Although Mifsud worked out of London and was also affiliated with LCILP, the encounter in Rome was the first time that Papadopoulos met him.[414] Mifsud maintained various Russian contacts while living in London, as described further below. Among his contacts was ,[415] a one-time employee of the IRA, the entity that carried out the Russian social media campaign *(see* Volume I Section II, *supra).* In January and February 2016, Mifsud and —— discussed possibly meeting in Russia. The investigation did not identi evidence of —— meeting. Later, in the spring of 2016, —— was also in contact that was linked to an employee of the Russian Ministry of Defense, and that account had overlapping contacts with a group of Russian military• controlled Facebook accounts that included accounts used to promote the DCLeaks releases in the course of the GRU's hack-and-release operations *(see* Volume I, Section III.B.1, *supra).*

According to Papadopoulos, Mifsud at first seemed uninterested in Papadopoulos when they met in Rome.[416] After Papadopoulos informed Mifsud about his role in the Trump Campaign, however, Mifsud appeared to take greater interest in Papadopoulos.[417] The two discussed Mifsud's European and

Russian contacts and had a general discussion about Russia; Mifsud also offered to introduce Papadopoulos to European leaders and others with contacts to the Russian government.[418] Papadopoulos told the Office that Mifsud's claim of substantial connections with Russian government officials interested Papadopoulos, who thought that such connections could increase his importance as a policy advisor to the Trump Campaign.[419]

On March 17, 2016, Papadopoulos returned to London.[420] Four days later, candidate Trump publicly named him as a member of the foreign policy and national security advisory team chaired by Senator Jeff Sessions, describing Papadopoulos as "an oil and energy consultant" and an "[e]xcellent guy."[421]

On March 24, 2016, Papadopoulos met with Mifsud in London.[422] Mifsud was accompanied by a Russian female named Olga Polonskaya. Mifsud introduced Polonskaya as a former student of his who had connections to Vladimir Putin.[423] Papadopoulos understood at the time that Polonskaya may have been Putin's niece but later learned that this was not true.[424] During the meeting, Polonskaya offered to help Papadopoulos establish contacts in Russia and stated that the Russian ambassador in London was a friend of hers.[425] Based on this interaction, Papadopoulos expected Mifsud and Polonskaya to introduce him to the Russian ambassador in London, but that did not occur.[426]

Following his meeting with Mifsud, Papadopoulos sent an email to members of the Trump Campaign's foreign policy advisory team. The subject line of the message was "Meeting with Russian leadership=including Putin."[427] The message stated in pertinent part:

> I just finished a very productive lunch with a good friend of mine, Joseph Mifsud, the director of the London Academy of Diplomacy-who introduced me to both Putin's niece and the Russian Ambassador in London=who also acts as the Deputy Foreign Minister.[428]

The topic of the lunch was to arrange a meeting between us and the Russian leadership to discuss U.S.-Russia ties under President Trump. They are keen to host us in a "neutral" city, or directly in Moscow. They said the leadership, including Putin, is ready to meet with us and Mr. Trump should there be interest. Waiting for everyone's thoughts on moving forward with this very important issue.[429]

Papadopoulos's message came at a time when Clovis perceived a shift in the Campaign's approach toward Russia — from one of engaging with Russia throu h the NATO framework and takin a stron stance on Russian a ression in Ukraine [redacted] Grand Jury [redacted][430]

Clovis's response to Papadopoulos, however, did not reflect that shift. Replying to Papadopoulos and the other members of the foreign policy advisory team copied on the initial email, Clovis wrote:

This is most informative. Let me work it through the campaign. No commitments until we see how this plays out. My thought is that we probably should not go forward with any meetings with the Russians until we have had occasion to sit with our NATO allies, especially France, Germany and Great Britain. We need to reassure our allies that we are not going to advance anything with Russia until we have everyone on the same page.
More thoughts later today.
Great work.[431]

c. March 31 Foreign Policy Team Meeting

The Campaign held a meeting of the foreign policy advisory team with Senator Sessions and candidate Trump approximately one week later, on March 31, 2016, in Washington, D.C.[432] The meeting—which was intended to generate press coverage for the Campaign[433]—took place at the Trump International Hotel.[434] Papadopoulos flew to Washington for the event. At the meeting, Senator Sessions sat at one end of an oval table, while Trump sat at the other. As reflected in the photograph below (which was posted to Trump's Instagram account), Papadopoulos sat between the two, two seats to Sessions's left:

March 31, 2016 Meeting of Foreign Policy Team, with Papadopoulos (Fourth from Right of Candidate Trump

During the meeting, each of the newly announced foreign policy advisors introduced themselves and briefly described their areas of experience or expertise.v" Papadopoulos spoke about his previous work in the energy sector and then brought up a potential meeting with Russian officials.[436] Specifically, Papadopoulos told the group that he had learned through his contacts in London that Putin wanted to meet with candidate Trump and that these connections could help arrange that meeting.[437]

Trump and Sessions both reacted to Papadopoulos's statement. Papadopoulos and Campaign advisor J.D. Gordon—who told investigators in an interview that he had a "crystal clear" recollection of the meeting—

have stated that Trump was interested in and receptive to the idea of a meeting with Putin.[438] Papadopoulos understood Sessions to be similarly supportive of his efforts to arrange a meeting.[439] Gordon and two other attendees, however, recall that Sessions generally opposed the proposal, though they differ in their accounts of the concerns he voiced or the strength of the opposition he expressed."?

d. George Papadopoulos Learns That Russia Has "Dirt" in the Form of Clinton Emails

Whatever Sessions'.s precise words at the March 31 meeting, Papadopoulos did not understand Sessions or anyone else in the Trump Campaign to have directed that he refrain from making further efforts to arrange a meeting between the Campaign and the Russian government. To the contrary, Papadopoulos told the Office that he understood the Campaign to be supportive of his efforts to arrange such a meeting.[441] Accordingly, when he returned to London, Papadopoulos resumed those efforts.[442]

Throughout April 2016, Papadopoulos continued to correspond with, meet with, and seek Russia contacts through Mifsud and, at times, Polonskaya.[443] For example, within a week of her initial March 24 meeting with him, Polonskaya attempted to send Papadopoulos a text message — which email exchanges show to have been drafted or edited by Mifsud — addressing Papadopoulos's "wish to engage with the Russian Federation."[444] When Papadopoulos learned from Mifsud that Polonskaya had tried to message him, he sent her an email seeking another meeting.[445] Polonskaya responded the next day that she was "back in St. Petersburg" but "would be very pleased to support [Papadopoulos's] initiatives between our two countries" and "to meet [him] again."[446] Papadopoulos stated in reply that he thought "a good step" would be to introduce him to "the Russian Ambassador in London," and that he would like to talk to the ambassador, "or anyone else you recommend, about a potential foreign policy trip to Russia."[447]

Mifsud, who had been copied on the email exchanges, replied on the morning of April 11, 2016. He wrote, "This is already been agreed. I am flying to Moscow on the 18th for a Yaldai meeting, plus other meetings at the Duma. We will talk tomorrow."[448] The two bodies referenced by Mifsud are part of or associated with the Russian government: the Duma is a Russian legislative assembly,[449] while "Valdai" refers to the Valdai Discussion Club, a Moscow-based group that "is close to Russia's foreign-policy establishment.t'P" Papadopoulos thanked Mifsud and said that he would see him "tomorrow."[451] For her part, Polonskaya responded that she had "already alerted my personal links to our conversation and your request," that "we are all very excited the possibility of a good relationship with Mr. Trump," and that "[t]he Russian Federation would love to welcome him once his candidature would be officially announced."[452]

Papadopoulos's and Mifsud's mentions of seeing each other "tomorrow" referenced a meeting that the two had scheduled for the next morning, April 12, 2016, at the Andaz Hotel in London. Papadopoulos acknowledged the meeting during interviews with the Office,[453] and records from Papadopoulos's UK cellphone and his internet-search history all indicate that the meeting took place.[454]

Following the meeting, Mifsud traveled as planned to Moscow.[455] On April 18, 2016, while in Russia, Mifsud introduced Papadopoulos over email to Ivan Timofeev, a member of the Russian International Affairs Council (RIAC).[456] Mifsud had described Timofeev as having connections with the Russian Ministry of Foreign Affairs (MFA),[457] the executive entity in Russia responsible for Russian foreign relations.[458] Over the next several weeks, Papadopoulos and Timofeev had multiple conversations over Skype and email about setting "the groundwork" for a "potential" meeting between the Campaign and Russian government officials.[459] Papadopoulos told the Office that, on one Skype call, he believed that his conversation with Timofeev was being monitored or supervised by an unknown third party, because Timofeev spoke in an official manner and Papadopoulos heard odd noises on the line.[460] Timofeev also told Papadopoulos in an April 25, 2016 email that he had just spoken "to Igor Ivanov[,] the President ofRIAC and former Foreign Minister of Russia," and conveyed Ivanov's advice about how best to arrange a "Moscow visit."'"[461]

After a stop in Rome, Mifsud returned to England on April 25, 2016.[462] The next day, Papadopoulos met Mifsud for breakfast at the Andaz Hotel (the same location as their last meeting).[463] During that meeting, Mifsud told Papadopoulos that he had met with high-level Russian government officials during his recent trip to Moscow. Mifsud also said that, on the trip, he learned that the Russians had obtained "dirt" on candidate Hillary Clinton. As Papadopoulos later stated to the FBI, Mifsud said that the "dirt" was in the form of "emails of Clinton," and that they "have thousands of emails."[464] On May 6, 2016, 10 days after that meeting with Mifsud, Papadopoulos suggested to a representative of a foreign government that the Trump Campaign had received indications from the Russian government that it could assist the Campaign through the anonymous release of information that would be damaging to Hillary Clinton.[465]

e. Russia-Related Communications With The Campaign

While he was discussing with his foreign contacts a potential meeting of campaign officials with Russian government officials, Papadopoulos kept campaign officials apprised of his efforts. On April 25, 2016, the day before Mifsud told Papadopoulos about the emails, Papadopoulos wrote to senior policy advisor Stephen Miller that "[t]he Russian government has an open invitation by Putin for Mr. Trump to meet him when he is ready," and that "[t]he advantage of being in London is that these governments tend to speak a bit more openly in 'neutral' cities."[466] On April 27, 2016, after his meeting with Mifsud, Papadopoulos wrote a second message to Miller stating that "some interesting messages [were] coming in from Moscow about a trip when the time is right."[467] The same day, Papadopoulos sent a similar email to campaign manager Corey Lewandowski, telling Lewandowski that Papadopoulos had "been receiving a lot of calls over the last month about Putin wanting to host [Trump] and the team when the time is right."[468]

Papadopoulos's Russia-related communications with Campaign officials continued throughout the spring and summer of 2016. On May 4, 2016, he forwarded to Lewandowski an email from Timofeev raising the possibility of a meeting in Moscow, asking Lewandowski whether that was "something we want to move forward with."[469] The next day, Papadopoulos forwarded the same Timofeev email to Sam Clovis, adding to the top of the email "Russia update."[470] He included the same email in a May 21, 2016 message to senior Campaign official Paul Manafort, under the subject line "Request from Russia to meet Mr. Trump," stating that "Russia has been eager to meet Mr. Trump for quite sometime and have been reaching out to me to discuss."!" Manafort forwarded the message to another Campaign official, without including Papadopoulos, and stated: "Let[']s discuss. We need someone to communicate that [Trump] is not doing these trips. It should be someone low level in the Campaign so as not to send any signal."[472]

On June 1, 2016, Papadopoulos replied to an earlier email chain with Lewandowski about a Russia visit, asking if Lewandowski "want[ed] to have a call about this topic" and whether "we were following up with it."[473] After Lewandowski told Papadopoulos to "connect with" Clovis because he was "running point," Papadopoulos emailed Clovis that "the Russian MFA" was asking him "if Mr. Trump is interested in visiting Russia at some point."[474] Papadopoulos wrote in an email that he "[w]anted to pass this info along to you for you to decide what's best to do with it and what message I should send (or to ignore)."[475]

After several email and Skype exchanges with Timofeev,[476] Papadopoulos sent one more email to Lewandowski on June 19, 2016, Lewandowski's last day as campaign manager.[477] The email stated that "[t]he Russian ministry of foreign affairs" had contacted him and asked whether, if Mr. Trump could not travel to Russia, a campaign representative such as Papadopoulos could attend meetings.[478] Papadopoulos told Lewandowski that he was "willing to make the trip off the record if it's in the interest of Mr. Trump and the campaign to meet specific people."[479]

Following Lewandowski's departure from the Campaign, Papadopoulos communicated with Clovis and Walid Phares, another member of the foreign policy advisory team, about an off• the-record meeting between the Campaign and Russian government officials or with Papadopoulos's other Russia connections, Mifsud and Timofeev.P? Papadopoulos also interacted directly with Clovis and Phares in connection with the summit of the Transatlantic Parliamentary Group on Counterterrorism (TAG), a group for which Phares was co-secretary general."! On July 16, 2016, Papadopoulos attended the TAG summit in Washington, D.C., where he sat next to Clovis (as reflected in the photograph below).[482]

George Papadopoulos (far right) and Sam Clovis
(second from right)

Although Clovis claimed to have no recollection of attending the TAG summit,[483] Papadopoulos remembered discussing Russia and a foreign policy trip with Clovis and Phares during the event.[484] Papadopoulos's recollection is consistent with emails sent before and after the TAG summit. The pre-summit messages included a July 11, 2016 email in which Phares suggested meeting Papadopoulos the day after the summit to chat,[485] and a July 12 message in the same chain in which Phares advised Papadopoulos that other summit attendees "are very nervous about Russia. So be aware."[486] Ten days after the summit, Papadopoulos sent an email to Mifsud listing Phares and Clovis as other "participants" in a potential meeting at the London Academy of Diplomacy.[487]

Finally, Papadopoulos's recollection is also consistent with handwritten notes from a journal that he kept at the time.[488] Those notes, which are reprinted in part below, appear to refer to potential September 2016 meetings in London with representatives of the "office of Putin," and suggest that Phares, Clovis, and Papadopoulos ("Wal id/Sam me") would attend without the official backing of the Campaign ("no official letter/no message from Trump").[489]

September:

Have an exploratory meeting te or lose. In September – if allowed they will blast Mr. Trump.

We want the meeting in London/England

Walid/Sam me

No official letter/no message from Trump

They are talking to us.
-It is a lot of risk.
Office of Putin.

-Explore: we are a campaign

off Israel! EGYPT Willingness to meet the FM sp with Walid/Sam

-FM coming

-Useful to have a session with him.

Later communications indicate that Clovis determined that he (Clovis) could not travel. On August 15, 2016, Papadopoulos emailed Clovis that he had received requests from multiple foreign governments, "even Russia[]," for "closed door workshops/consultations abroad," and asked whether there was still interest for Clovis, Phares, and Papadopoulos "to go on that trip."[490] Clovis copied Phares on his response, which said that he could not "travel before the election" but that he "would encourage [Papadopoulos] and Walid to make the trips, if it is feasible."[491]

Papadopoulos was dismissed from the Trump Campaign in early October 2016, after an interview he gave to the Russian news agency *Interfax* generated adverse publicity.[492]

f. Trump Campaign Knowledge of "Dirt"

Papadopoulos admitted telling at least one individual outside of the Campaign — specifically, the then-Greek foreign minister—about Russia's obtaining Clinton-related emails.[493]

In addition, a different foreign government informed the FBI that, 10 days after meeting with Mifsud in late April 2016, Papadopoulos suggested that the Trump Campaign had received indications from the Russian government that it could assist the Campaign through the anonymous release of information that would be damaging to Hillary Clinton.[494] (This conversation occurred after the GRU spearphished Clinton Campaign chairman John Podesta and stole his emails, and the GRU hacked into the DCCC and DNC, *see* Volume I, Sections III.A & III.B, *supra.*) Such disclosures raised questions about whether Papadopoulos informed any Trump Campaign official about the emails.

When interviewed, Papadopoulos and the Campaign officials who interacted with him told the Office that they could not recall Papadopoulos's sharing the information that Russia had obtained "dirt" on candidate Clinton in the form of emails or that Russia could assist the Campaign through the anonymous release of information about Clinton. Papadopoulos stated that he could not clearly recall having told anyone on the Campaign and wavered about whether he accurately remembered an incident in which Clovis had been upset after hearing Papadopoulos tell Clovis that Papadopoulos thought "they have her emails."[495] The Campaign officials who interacted or corresponded with Papadopoulos have similarly stated, with varying degrees of certainty, that he did not tell them. Senior policy advisor Stephen Miller, for example, did not remember hearing anything from Papadopoulos or Clovis about Russia having emails of or dirt on candidate Clinton.[496] Clovis stated that he did not recall anyone, including Papadopoulos, having given him non-public information that a forei n overnment mi ht be in ossession of material dama in to Hillar Clinton.[497]

g. Additional George Papadopoulos Contact

The Office investigated another Russia-related contact with Papadopoulos. The Office was not fully able to explore the contact because the individual at issue — Sergei Millian — remained out of the country since the inception of our investigation and declined to meet with members of the Office despite our repeated efforts to obtain an interview.

Papadopoulos first connected with Millian via LinkedIn on July 15, 2016, shortly after Papadopoulos had attended the TAG Summit with Clovis.[500] Millian, an American citizen who is a native of Belarus, introduced himself "as president of [the] New York-based Russian American Chamber of Commerce," and claimed that through that position he had "insider knowledge and direct access to the top hierarchy in Russian politics."[501] Papadopoulos asked Timofeev whether he had heard of Millian.[502] Although Timofeev said no,[503] Papadopoulos met Millian in New York City.[504] The meetings took place on July 30 and August 1, 2016.[505] Afterwards, Millian invited Papadopoulos to attend — and potentially speak at — two international energy conferences, including one that was to be held in Moscow in September 2016.[506] Papadopoulos ultimately did not attend either conference.

On July 31, 2016, following his first in-person meeting with Millian, Papadopoulos emailed Trump Campaign official Bo Denysyk to say that he had been contacted "by some leaders of Russian-American voters here in the US about their interest in voting for Mr. Trump," and to ask whether he should "put you in touch with their group (US-Russia chamber of commerce)."[507] Denysyk thanked Papadopoulos "for taking the initiative," but asked him to "hold off with outreach to Russian-Americans" because "too many articles" had already portrayed the Campaign, then-campaign chairman Paul Manafort, and candidate Trump as "being pro-Russian.t'f"

On August 23, 2016, Millian sent a Facebook message to Papadopoulos promising that he would "share with you a disruptive technology that might be instrumental in your political work for the campaign."[509] Papadopoulos claimed to have no recollection of this matter.t'"

On November 9, 2016, shortly after the election, Papadopoulos arranged to meet Millian in Chicago to discuss business opportunities, including potential work with Russian "billionaires who are not under sanctions."[511] The meeting took place on November 14, 2016, at the Trump Hotel and Tower in Chicago.[512] According to Papadopoulos, the two men discussed partnering on business deals, but Papadopoulos perceived that Millian's attitude toward him changed when Papadopoulos stated that he was only pursuing private-sector opportunities and was not interested in a job in the Administration.[513] The two remained in contact, however, and had extended online discussions about possible business opportunities in Russia.[514] The two also arranged to meet at a Washington, D.C. bar when both attended Trump's inauguration in late January 2017.[515]

3. Carter Page

Carter Page worked for the Trump Campaign from January 2016 to September 2016. He was formally and publicly announced as a foreign policy advisor by the candidate in March 2016.[516] Page had lived and worked in Russia, and he had been approached by Russian intelligence officers several years before he volunteered for the Trump Campaign. During his time with the Campaign, Page advocated pro-Russia foreign policy positions and traveled to Moscow in his personal capacity. Russian intelligence officials had formed relationships with Page in 2008 and 2013 and Russian officials may have focused on Page in 2016 because of his affiliation with the Campaign. However, the investigation did not establish that Page coordinated with the Russian government in its efforts to interfere with the 2016 presidential election.

a. Background

Before he began working for the Campaign in January 2016, Page had substantial prior experience studying Russian policy issues and living and working in Moscow. From 2004 to 2007, Page was the deputy branch manager of Merrill Lynch's Moscow office.[517] There, he worked on transactions involving the Russian energy company Gazprom and came to know Gazprom's deputy chief financial officer, Sergey Yatsenko.[518]

In 2008, Page founded Global Energy Capital LLC (GEC), an in ▬ advisor firm focused on the ener___ sector in emerging markets.[519] ▬

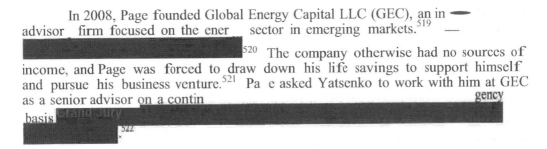

[520] The company otherwise had no sources of income, and Page was forced to draw down his life savings to support himself and pursue his business venture.[521] Pa e asked Yatsenko to work with him at GEC as a senior advisor on a contin_____gency basis_____.[522]

In 2008, Page met Alexander Bulatov, a Russian government official who worked at the Russian Consulate in New York.[523] Pa e later learned that Bulatov was a Russian intelli ence officer,[524]

In 2013, Victor Podobnyy, another Russian intelligence officer working covertly in the United States under diplomatic cover, formed a relationship with Page.[525] Podobnyy met Page at an energy symposium in New York City and began exchanging emails with him.[526] Podobnyy and Page also met in person on multiple occasions, during which Page offered his outlook on the future of the energy industry and provided documents to Podobnyy about the energy business.[527]

In a recorded conversation on April 8, 2013, Podobnyy told another intelligence officer that Page was interested in business opportunities in Russia.[528] In Podobnyy's words, Page "got hooked on Gazprom thinking that if they have a project, he could ... rise up. Maybe he can.... [I]t's obvious that he wants to earn lots of money."[529] Podobnyy said that he had led Page on by "feed[ing] him empty promises" that Podobnyy would use his Russian business connections to help Page.[530]

Podobnyy told the other intelligence officer that his method of recruiting foreign sources was to promise them favors and then discard them once he obtained relevant information from them.[531]

In 2015, Podobnyy and two other Russian intelligence officers were charged with conspiracy to act as an unregistered agent of a foreign government.[532] The criminal complaint detailed Podobnyy's interactions with and conversations about Page, who was identified only as "Male-1."[533] Based on the criminal complaint's description of the interactions, Page was aware that he was the individual described as "Male-I."[534] Page later spoke with a Russian government official at the United Nations General Assembly and identified himself so that the official would understand he was "Male-I" from the Podobn laint.[535] Page told the official that he "didn't do anything"[536]

In interviews with the FBI before the Office's opening, Page acknowledged that he understood that the individuals he had associated with were members of the Russian intelligence services, but he stated that he had only provided immaterial non-public information to them and that he did not view this relationship as a backchannel.[537] Page told investigating agents that "the more immaterial non-public information I give them, the better for this country."[538]

b. Origins of and Early Campaign Work

In January 2016, Page began volunteering on an informal, unpaid basis for the Trump Campaign after Ed Cox, a state Republican Party official, introduced Page to Trump Campaign officials.[539]   Page told the Office that his goal in working on the Campaign was to help candidate Trump improve relations with Russia.[540]   To that end, Page emailed Campaign officials offering his thoughts on U.S.-Russia relations, prepared talking points and briefing memos on Russia, and proposed that candidate Trump meet with President Vladimir Putin in Moscow.[541]

In communications with Campaign officials, Page also repeatedly touted his high-level contacts in Russia and his ability to forge connections between candidate Trump and senior Russian governmental officials.   For example, on January 30, 2016, Page sent an email to senior Campaign officials stating that he had "spent the past week in Europe and ha[d] been in discussions with some individuals with close ties to the Kremlin" who recognized that Trump could have a "game-changing effect . . . in bringing the end of the new Cold War."[542]   The email stated that "[t]hrough [his] discussions with these high level contacts," Page believed that "a direct meeting in Moscow between Mr[.] Trump and Putin could be arran ed."[543]   Pa e closed the email b criticizin U.S. sanctions on Russia.[544]

On March 21, 2016, candidate Trump formally and publicly identified Page as a member of his foreign policy team to advise on Russia and the energy sector.[546]   Over the next several months, Page continued providing policy-related work product to Campaign officials.   For example, in April 2016, Page provided feedback on an outline for a foreign policy speech that the candidate gave at the Mayflower Hotei,[547] *see* Volume I, Section IV.A.4, *infra.* In May 2016, Page prepared an outline of an energy policy speech for the Campaign and then traveled to Bismarck, North Dakota, to watch the candidate deliver the speech.[548]   Chief policy advisor Sam Clovis expressed appreciation for Page's work and praised his work to other Campaign officials.[549]

c. *Carter Page's July 2016 Trip To Moscow*

Page's affiliation with the Trump Campaign took on a higher profile and drew the attention of Russian officials after the candidate named him a foreign policy advisor. As a result, in late April 2016, Page was invited to give a speech at the July 2016 commencement ceremony at the New Economic School (NES) in Moscow.P? The NES commencement ceremony generally featured high-profile speakers; for example, President Barack Obama delivered a commencement address at the school in 2009.[551] NES officials told the Office that the interest in inviting Page to speak at NES was based entirely on his status as a Trump Campaign advisor who served as the candidate's Russia expert.[552] Andrej Krickovic, an associate of Page's and assistant professor at the Higher School of Economics in Russia, recommended that NES rector Shlomo Weber invite Page to give the commencement address based on his connection to the Trump Campaign.[553]

Denis Klimentov, an employee of NES, said that when Russians learned of Page's involvement in the Trump Campaign in March 2016, the excitement was palpable.[554] Weber recalled that in summer 2016 there was substantial interest in the Trump Campaign in Moscow, and he felt that bringing a member of the Campaign to the school would be beneficial.[555]

Page was eager to accept the invitation to speak at NES, and he sought approval from Trump Campaign officials to make the trip to Russia.[556] On May 16, 2016, while that request was still under consideration, Page emailed Clovis, J.D. Gordon, and Walid Phares and suggested that candidate Trump take his place speaking at the commencement ceremony in Moscow.[557] On June 19, 2016, Page followed up again to request approval to speak at the NES event and to reiterate that NES "would love to have Mr. Trump speak at this annual celebration" in Page's place.[558] Campaign manager Corey Lewandowski responded the same day, saying, "If you want to do this, it would be out side [sic] of your role with the DJT for President campaign. I am certain Mr. Trump will not be able to attend."[559]

In early July 2016, Page traveled to Russia for the NES events. On July 5, 2016, Denis Klimentov, copying his brother, Dmitri Klimentov.P? emailed Maria Zakharova, the Director of the Russian Ministry of Foreign Affairs' Information and Press Department, about Page's visit and his connection to the Trump Campaign.[561] Denis Klimentov said in the email that he wanted to draw the Russian government's attention to Page's visit in Moscow.[562] His message to Zakharova continued: "Page is Trump's adviser on foreign policy. He is a known businessman; he used to work in Russia. _ _ _ If you have any questions, I will be happy to help contact him."[563] Dmitri Klimentov then contacted Russian Press Secretary Dmitry Peskov about Page's visit to see if Peskov wanted to introduce Page to any Russian government officials.[564] The following day, Peskov responded to what appears to have been the same Denis Klimentov-Zakharova email thread. Peskov wrote, "I have read about [Page]. Specialists say that he is far from being the main one. So I better not initiate a meeting in the Kremlin."[565]

On July 7, 2016, Page delivered the first of his two speeches in Moscow at NES.[566] In the speech, Page criticized the U.S. government's foreign policy toward Russia, stating that "Washington and other Western capitals have impeded potential progress through their often hypocritical focus on ideas such as democratization, inequality, corruption and regime change."[567]

On July 8, 2016, Page delivered a speech during the NES commencement.[568] After Page delivered his commencement address, Russian Deputy Prime Minister and NES board member Arkady Dvorkovich spoke at the ceremony and stated that the sanctions the United States had imposed on Russia had hurt the NES.[569] Page and Dvorkovich shook hands at the commencement ceremony, and Weber recalled that Dvorkovich made statements to Pa e about workin to ether in the

Page said that, during his time in Moscow, he met with friends and associates he knew from when he lived in Russia, including Andrey Baranov, a former Gazprom employee who had become the head of investor relations at Rosneft, a Russian energy cornpany.F? Page stated that he and Baranov talked about "immaterial non-public" information.[573] Page believed he and Baranov discussed Rosneft president Igor Sechin, and he thought Baranov might have mentioned the possibility of a sale of a stake in Rosneft in passing.[574] Page recalled mentioning his involvement in the Trump Campaign with Baranov, although he did not remember details of the conversation.[575] Page also met with individuals from Tatneft, a Russian energy company, to discuss possible business deals, including having Page work as a consultant.[576]

On July 8, 2016, while he was in Moscow, Page emailed several Campaign officials and stated he would send "a readout soon regarding some incredible insights and outreach I've received from a few Russian legislators and senior members of the Presidential Administration here."[577]

On July 9, 2016, Page emailed Clovis, writing in pertinent part:

The Office was unable to obtain additional evidence or testimony about who Page may have met or communicated with in Moscow; thus, Page's activities in Russia—as described in his emails with the Campaign—were not fully explained.

d. Later Campaign Work and Removal from the Campaign

In July 2016, after returning from Russia, Page traveled to the Republican National Convention in Cleveland.[583] While there, Page met Russian Ambassador to the United States Sergey Kislyak; that interaction is described in Volume I, Section IV.A.6.a, *infra*.[584] Page later emailed Campaign officials with feedback he said he received from ambassadors he had met at the Convention, and he wrote that Ambassador Kisl ak was ver worried about candidate Clinton's world views.[585]

Following the Convention, Page's trip to Moscow and his advocacy for pro-Russia foreign policy drew the media's attention and began to generate substantial press coverage. The Campaign responded by distancing itself from Page, describing him as an "informal foreign policy advisor" who did "not speak for Mr. Trump or the campaign."[587] On September 23, 2016, Yahoo! News reported that U.S. intelligence officials were investigating whether Page had opened private communications with senior Russian officials to discuss U.S. sanctions policy under a possible Trump Administration.[588] A Campaign spokesman told Yahoo! News that Page had "no role" in the Campaign and that the Campaign was "not aware of any of his activities, past or present."[589]
On September 24, 2016, Page was formally removed from the Campaign.V"

Although Page had been removed from the Campaign, after the election he sought a position in the Trump Administration.[591] On November 14, 2016, he submitted an application to the Transition Team that inflated his credentials and experiences, stating that in his capacity as a Trump Campaign foreign policy advisor he had met with "top world leaders" and "effectively responded to diplomatic outreach efforts from senior government officials in Asia, Europe, the Middle East, Africa, [and] the Americas."[592] Page received no response from the Transition Team. When Page took a personal trip to Moscow in December 2016, he met again with at least one Russian government official. That interaction and a discussion of the December trip are set forth in Volume I, Section IV.8.6, *infra.*

4. Dimitri Simes and the Center for the National Interest

Members of the Trump Campaign interacted on several occasions with the Center for the National Interest (CNI), principally through its President and Chief Executive Officer, Dimitri Simes. CNI is a think tank with expertise in and connections to the Russian government. Simes was born in the former Soviet Union and immigrated to the United States in the 1970s. In April 2016, candidate Trump delivered his first speech on foreign policy and national security at an event hosted by the *National Interest,* a publication affiliated with CNI. Then-Senator Jeff Sessions and Russian Ambassador Kislyak both attended the event and, as a result, it gained some attention in relation to Sessions's confirmation hearings to become Attorney General. Sessions had various other contacts with CNI during the campaign period on foreign-policy matters, including Russia. Jared Kushner also interacted with Simes about Russian issues during the campaign. The investigation did not identify evidence that the Campaign passed or received any messages to or from the Russian government through CNI or Simes.

a. CNI and Dimitri Simes Connect with the Trump Campaign

CNI is a Washington-based non-profit organization that grew out of a center founded by former President Richard Nixon.[593] CNI describes itself "as a voice for strategic realism in U.S. foreign policy," and publishes a bi-monthly foreign policy magazine, the *National Interest.*[594] CNI is overseen by a board of directors and an advisory council that is largely honorary and whose members at the relevant time included Sessions, who served as an advisor to candidate Trump on national security and foreign policy issues.[595]

Dimitri Simes is president and CEO of CNI and the publisher and CEO of the *National Interest.*[596] Simes was born in the former Soviet Union, emigrated to the United States in the early 1970s, and joined CNI's predecessor after working at the Carnegie Endowment for International Peace.[597] Simes personally has many contacts with current and former Russian government officials,[598] as does CNI collectively. As CNI stated when seeking a grant from the Carnegie Corporation in 2015, CNI has "unparalleled access to Russian officials and politicians among Washington think tanks,"[599] in part because CNI has arranged for U.S. delegations to visit Russia and for Russian delegations to visit the United States as part of so-called "Track II" diplomatic effort.

On March 14, 2016, CNI board member Richard Plepler organized a luncheon for CNI and its honorary chairman, Henry Kissinger, at the Time Warner Building in New York.[601] The idea behind the event was to generate interest in CNI's work and recruit new board members for CNI.[602] Along with Simes, attendees at the event included Jared Kushner, son-in-law of candidate Trump.[603] Kushner told the Office that the event came at a time when the Trump Campaign was having trouble securing support from experienced foreign policy professionals and that, as a result, he decided to seek Simes's assistance during the March 14 event.[604]

Simes and Kushner spoke again on a March 24, 2016 telephone call,[605] three days after Trump had publicly named the team of foreign policy advisors that had been put together on short notice.[606] On March 31, 2016, Simes and Kushner had an in-person, one-on-one meeting in Kushner's New York office.[607] During that meeting, Simes told Kushner that the best way to handle foreign-policy issues for the Trump Campaign would be to organize an advisory group of experts to meet with candidate Trump and develop a foreign policy approach that was

consistent with Trump's voice.[608]   Simes believed   that Kushner   was
receptive to that suggestion.P'?

Simes also had contact with other individuals associated with
the Trump   Campaign regarding the Campaign's foreign policy positions.
For example, on June 17, 2016, Simes sent J.D. Gordon an email with a
"memo to Senator Sessions that we discussed at our recent meeting" and
asked   Gordon to both read it and share it with Sessions.   The
memorandum proposed building a "small and carefully selected group of
experts"   to assist Sessions   with the Campaign, operating under   the
assumption "that Hillary Clinton is very vulnerable on national security
and foreign policy issues."   The memorandum outlined key issues for
the Campaign, including a "new beginning with Russia."[610]

b. *National Interest Hosts a Foreign Policy Speech at the*
Mayflower Hotel

During   both their March   24 phone   call and their March   31 in-person
meeting,   Simes and Kushner discussed the possibility of CNI hosting   a
foreign policy   speech   by candidate Trump.[611]   Following   those
conversations, Simes agreed that he and others associated with CNI
would provide behind-the-scenes input on the substance   of the foreign-
policy speech and that CNI officials   would   coordinate   the logistics of
the   speech   with   Sessions   and his   staff, including Sessions's chief of
staff, Rick Dearborn.[612]

In mid-April 2016, Kushner put Simes in contact with senior policy
advisor Stephen Miller and forwarded to Simes an outline of the foreign-
policy speech that Miller had prepared.[613]   Simes sent   back to the
Campaign bullet points   with ideas for the speech   that he had drafted
with CNI Executive Director Paul Saunders   and board member Richard
Burt.[614]   Simes received subsequent draft outlines from Miller, and he
and Saunders spoke to Miller by phone about substantive changes to
the speech.[615]   It is not clear, however, whether CNI officials received
an actual draft of the speech for comment; while Saunders recalled having
received an actual draft, Simes did not, and the emails that CNI produced
to this Office do not contain   such a draft.[616]

After board members expressed concern to Simes that CNI's hosting the speech could be perceived as an endorsement of a particular candidate, CNI decided to have its publication, the *National Interest*, serve as the host and to have the event at the National Press Club.[617] Kushner later requested that the event be moved to the Mayflower Hotel, which was another venue that Simes had mentioned during initial discussions with the Campaign, in order to address concerns about security and capacity.[618]

On April 25, 2016, Saunders booked event rooms at the Mayflower to host both the speech and a VIP reception that was to be held beforehand.[619] Saunders understood that the reception — at which invitees would have the chance to meet candidate Trump—would be a small event.[620] Saunders decided who would attend by looking at the list of CNI's invitees to the speech itself and then choosing a subset for the reception.[621] CNI's invitees to the reception included Sessions and Kislyak.[622] The week before the speech Simes had informed Kislyak that he would be invited to the speech, and that he would have the opportunity to meet Trump.[623]

When the pre-speech reception began on April 27, a receiving line was quickly organized so that attendees could meet Trump.[624] Sessions first stood next to Trump to introduce him to the members of Congress who were in attendance.[625] After those members had been introduced, Simes stood next to Trump and introduced him to the CNI invitees in attendance, including Kislyak.[626] Simes perceived the introduction to be positive and friendly, but thought it clear that Kislyak and Trump had just met for the first time.[627] Kislyak also met Kushner during the pre-speech reception. The two shook hands and chatted for a minute or two, during which Kushner recalled Kislyak saying, "we like what your candidate is saying ... it's refreshing."[628]

Several public reports state that, in addition to speaking to Kushner at the pre-speech reception, Kislyak also met or conversed with Sessions at that time.[629] Sessions stated to investigators, however, that he did not remember any such conversation.P? Nor did anyone else affiliated with CNI or the *National Interest* specifically recall a conversation or meeting between Sessions and Kislyak at the pre-speech reception.[631] It appears that, if a conversation occurred at the pre-speech reception, it was a brief one conducted in public view, similar to the exchange between Kushner and Kislyak.

The Office found no evidence that Kislyak conversed with either Trump or Sessions after the speech, or would have had the opportunity to do so. Simes, for example, did not recall seeing Kislyak at the post-speech luncheon,[632] and the only witness who accounted for Sessions's whereabouts stated that Sessions may have spoken to the press after the event but then departed for Capitol Hill.[633] Saunders recalled, based in part on a food-related request he received from a Campaign staff member, that Trump left the hotel a few minutes after the speech to go to the airport.[634]

c. *Jeff Sessions 's Post-Speech Interactions with CNI*

In the wake of Sessions's confirmation hearings as Attorney General, questions arose about whether Sessions's campaign-period interactions with CNI apart from the Mayflower speech included any additional meetings with Ambassador Kislyak or involved Russian-related matters. With respect to Kislyak contacts, on May 23, 2016, Sessions attended CNI's Distinguished Service Award dinner at the Four Seasons Hotel in Washington, D.C.[635] Sessions attended a pre-dinner reception and was seated at one of two head tables for the event.[636] A seating chart prepared by Saunders indicates that Sessions was scheduled to be seated next to Kislyak, who appears to have responded to the invitation by indicating he would attend the event.[637] Sessions, however, did not remember seeing, speaking with, or sitting next to Kislyak at the dinner.[638] Although CNI board member Charles Boyd said he may have seen Kislyak at the dinner,[639] Simes, Saunders, and Jacob Heilbrunn-- editor of the *National Interest* —all had no recollection of seeing Kislyak at the May 23 event.[640] Kislyak also does not appear in any of the photos from the event that the Office obtained.

In the summer of 2016, CNI organized at least two dinners in Washington, D.C. for Sessions to meet with experienced foreign policy professionals.[641] The dinners included CNI• affiliated individuals, such as Richard Burt and Zalmay Khalilzad, a former U.S. ambassador to Afghanistan and Iraq and the person who had introduced Trump before the April 27, 2016 foreign- policy speech.[642] Khalilzad also met with Sessions one-on-one separately from the dinners.P" At the dinners and in the meetings, the participants addressed U.S. relations with Russia, including how U.S. relations with NATO and European countries affected U.S. policy toward Russia.[644] But the discussions were not exclusively focused on Russia.[645] Khalilzad, for example, recalled discussing "nation-building" and violent extremism with Sessions.[646] In addition, Sessions asked Saunders (of CNI) to draft two memoranda not specific to Russia: one on Hillary Clinton's foreign policy shortcomings and another on Egypt.[647]

d. Jared Kushner's Continuing Contacts with Simes

Between the April 2016 speech at the Mayflower Hotel and the presidential election, Jared Kushner had periodic contacts with Simes.[648] Those contacts consisted of both in-person meetings and phone conversations, which concerned how to address issues relating to Russia in the Campaign and how to move forward with the advisory group of foreign policy experts that Simes had proposed.P" Simes recalled that he, not Kushner, initiated all conversations about Russia, and that Kushner never asked him to set up back-channel conversations with Russians.v" According to Simes, after the Mayflower speech in late April, Simes raised the issue of Russian contacts with Kushner, advised that it was bad optics for the Campaign to develop hidden Russian contacts, and told Kushner both that the Campaign should not highlight Russia as an issue and should handle any contacts with Russians with care.[651] Kushner generally provided a similar account of his interactions with Simes.[652]

Among the Kushner-Simes meetings was one held on August 17, 2016, at Simes's request, in Kushner's New York office. The meeting was to address foreign policy advice that CNI was providing and how to respond to the Clinton Campaign's Russia-related attacks on candidate Trump.[653]   In advance of the meeting, Simes sent Kushner a "Russia Policy Memo" laying out "what Mr. Trump may want to say about Russia."[654] In a cover email transmitting that memo and a phone call to set up the meeting, Simes mentioned "a well-documented story of highly questionable connections between Bill Clinton" and the Russian government, "parts of [which]" (according to Simes) had even been "discussed with the CIA and the FBI in the late 1990s and shared with the [Independent Counsel] at the end of the Clinton presidency."[655] Kushner forwarded the email to senior Trump Campaign officials Stephen Miller, Paul Manafort, and Rick Gates, with the note "suggestion only."[656] Manafort subsequently forwarded the email to his assistant and scheduled a meeting with Simes.[657] (Manafort was on the verge of leaving the Campaign by the time of the scheduled meeting with Simes, and Simes ended up meeting only with Kushner).

During the August 17 meeting, Sime████████████████████████████Personal Privacy████████████████████████
in██████████████████████████[658]██
██
[659]   Simes claimed that he had received this information from former CIA and Reagan White House official Fritz Ermarth, who claimed to have learned it from U.S. intelligence sources, not from Russians.[?][660]

Simes perceived that Kushner did not find the information to be of interest or use to the Campaign because it was, in Simes's words, "old news."[661] When interviewed by the Office, Kushner stated that he believed that there was little chance of something new being revealed about the Clintons given their long career as public figures, and that he never received from Simes information that could be "operationalized" for the Trump Campaign.[662] Despite Kushner's reaction, Simes believed that he provided the same information at a small group meeting of foreign policy experts that CNI organized for Sessions.[663]

5. June 9, 2016 Meeting at Trump Tower

On June 9, 2016, senior representatives of the Trump Campaign met in Trump Tower with a Russian attorney expecting to receive derogatory information about Hillary Clinton from the Russian government. The meeting was proposed to Donald Trump Jr. in an email from Robert Goldstone, at the request of his then-client Emin Agalarov, the son of Russian real-estate developer Aras Agalarov. Goldstone relayed to Trump Jr. that the "Crown prosecutor of Russia ... offered to provide the Trump Campaign with some official documents and information that would incriminate Hillary and her dealings with Russia" as "part of Russia and its government's support for Mr. Trump." Trump Jr. immediately responded that "if it's what you say I love it," and arranged the meeting through a series of emails and telephone calls.

Trump Jr. invited campaign chairman Paul Manafort and senior advisor Jared Kushner to attend the meeting, and both attended. Members of the Campaign discussed the meeting before it occurred, and Michael Cohen recalled that Trump Jr. may have told candidate Trump about an upcoming meeting to receive adverse information about Clinton, without linking the meeting to Russia. According to written answers submitted by President Trump, he has no recollection of learning of the meeting at the time, and the Office found no documentary evidence showing that he was made aware of the meeting--or its Russian connection—before it occurred.

The Russian attorney who spoke at the meeting, Natalia Veselnitskaya, had previously worked for the Russian government and maintained a relationship with that government throughout this period of time. She claimed that funds derived from illegal activities in Russia were provided to Hillary Clinton and other Democrats. Trump Jr. requested evidence to support those claims, but Veselnitskaya did not provide such information. She and her associates then turned to a critique of the origins of the Magnitsky Act, a 2012 statute that imposed financial and travel sanctions on Russian officials and that resulted in a retaliatory ban on

135

adoptions of Russian children. Trump Jr. suggested that the issue could be revisited when and if candidate Trump was elected. After the election, Veselnitskaya made additional efforts to follow up on the meeting, but the Trump Transition Team did not engage.

a. Setting Up the June 9 Meeting

i. Outreach to Donald Trump Jr.

Aras Agalarov is a Russian real-estate developer with ties to Putin and other members of the Russian government, including Russia's Prosecutor General, Yuri Chaika.[664] Aras Agalarov is the president of the Crocus Group, a Russian enterprise that holds worked with Trump in connection with the 2013 Miss Universe pageant in Moscow and a potential Trump Moscow real-estate project.[665] The relationship continued over time, as the parties pursued the Trump Moscow project in 2013-2014 and exchanged gifts and letters in 2016.[666]
For example, in April 2016, Trump responded to a letter from Aras Agalarov with a handwritten note.[667] Aras Agalarov expressed interest in Trump's campaign, passed on "congratulations" for winning in the primary and—according to one email drafted by Goldstone—an "offer" of his "support and that of many of his important Russian friends and colleagues[,] especially with reference to U.S./Russian relations."[668]

On June 3, 2016, Emin Agalarov called Goldstone, Emin's then-publicist.[669] Goldstone is a music and events promoter who represented Emin Agalarov from approximately late 2012 until late 2016.[670] While representing Emin Agalarov, Goldstone facilitated the ongoing contact between the Trumps and the Agalarovs—includin an invitation that Trum sent to Putin to attend the 2013 Miss Universe Pa eant in Moscow.[671]

The mentioned by Emin Agalarov was Natalia Veselnitskaya. From approximately 1998 until 2001, Veselnitskaya worked as a prosecutor for the Central Administrative District of the Russian Prosecutor's Office,[677] and she continued to perform government-related work and maintain ties to the Russian government following her departure.[678] She lobbied and testified about the Magnitsky Act, which imposed financial sanctions and travel restrictions on

Russian officials and which was named for a Russian tax specialist who exposed a fraud and later died in a Russian prison.[679] Putin called the statute "a purely political, unfriendly act," and Russia responded by barring a list of current and former U.S. officials from entering Russia and by halting the adoption of Russian children by U.S. citizens.[680]

Veselnitskaya performed legal work for Denis Katsyv,[681] the son of Russian businessman Peter Katsyv, and for his company Prevezon Holdings Ltd., which was a defendant in a civil-forfeiture action alleging the laundering of proceeds from the fraud exposed by Magnitsky.[682] She also appears to have been involved in an April 2016 approach to a U.S. congressional delegation in Moscow offering "confidential information" from "the Prosecutor General of Russia" about "interactions between certain political forces in our two countries."[683]

Shortly after his June 3 call with Emin Agalarov, Goldstone emailed Trump Jr.[684] The email stated:

> Good morning
> . Emin just called and asked me to contact you with something very Interesting.
> The Crown prosecutor of Russia met with his father Aras this morning and in their meeting offered to provide the Trump campaign with
> some official documents and information that would incriminate Hillary and her dealings with Russia and would be very useful to your father. This is obviously very high level and sensitive information but Is part of Russia and Its government's support for Mr. Trump • helped along by Aras and Emin.
> What do you think is the best way to handle this information and would you be able to speak to Emin about ii directly?
> I can also send this Info to your rather via Rhona, but it Is ultra sensitive so wanted to send to you first.

Within minutes of this email, Trump Jr. responded, emailing back: "Thanks Rob I appreciate that. I am on the road at the moment but perhaps I just speak to Emin first. Seems we have some time and if it's what you say I love it especially later in the summer. Could we do a call first thing next week when I am back?"[685] Goldstone conveyed Trump Jr.'s interest to Emin Agalarov, emailing that Trump Jr. "wants to speak personally on the issue."[686]

On June 6, 2016, Emin Agalarov asked Goldstone if there was "[a]ny news," and Goldstone explained that Trump Jr. was likely still traveling for the "final elections ... where [T]rump will be 'crowned' the official nominee."[687] On the same day, Goldstone again emailed Trump Jr. and asked when Trump Jr. was "free to talk with Emin about this Hillary info."[688] Trump Jr. asked if they could "speak now," and Goldstone arranged a call between Trump Jr. and Emin Agalarov.[689] On June 6 and June 7, Trump Jr. and Emin Agalarov had multiple brief calls.[690]

Also on June 6, 2016, Aras Agalarov called Ike Kaveladze and asked him to attend a meeting in New York with the Trump Organization.[691] Kaveladze is a Georgia-born, naturalized U.S. citizen who worked in the United States for the Crocus Group and reported to Aras Agalarov.[692] Kaveladze told the Office that, in a second phone call on June 6, 2016, Aras Agalarov asked Kaveladze if he knew anything about the Magnitsky Act, and Aras sent him a short synopsis for the meeting and Veselnitskaya's business card. According to Kaveladze, Aras Agalarov said the purpose of the meeting was to discuss the Magnitsky Act, and he asked Kaveladze to translate.[693]

ii. Awareness of the Meeting Within the Campaign

On June 7, Goldstone emailed Trump Jr. and said that "Emin asked that I schedule a meeting with you and [t]he Russian government attorney who is flying over from Moscow."[694] Trump Jr. replied that Manafort (identified as the "campaign boss"), Jared Kushner, and Trump Jr. would likely attend.[695] God to learn that Trump Jr., Manafort, and Kushner would attend.[696] Kaveladze —— "puzzled" by the list of attendees and that he checked with one of Emin Agalarov's assistants, Roman Beniaminov, who said that the purpose of the meeting was for Veselnitskaya to convey "negative information on Hillary Clinton."[697] Beniaminov, however, stated that he did not recall having known or said that.[698]

Early on June 8, 2016 Kushner emailed his assistant, asking her to discuss a 3:00 p.m. meeting the following day with Trump Jr.[699]

Later that day, Trump Jr. forwarded the entirety of his email correspondence regarding the meeting with Goldstone to Manafort and Kushner, under the subject line "FW: Russia– Clinton– private and confidential," adding a note that the "[m]eeting got moved to 4 tomorrow at my offices."[700] Kushner then sent his assistant a second email, informing her that the "[m]eeting with don jr is 4pm now."[701] Manafort responded, "See you then. P."[702]

Rick Gates, who was the deputy campaign chairman, stated during interviews with the Office that in the days before June 9, 2016 Trump Jr. announced at a regular morning meeting of senior campaign staff and Trump family members that he had a lead on negative information about the Clinton Foundation.[703] Gates believed that Trump Jr. said the information was coming from a group in Kyrgyzstan and that he was introduced to the group by a friend.[704] Gates recalled that the meeting was attended by Trump Jr., Eric Trump, Paul Manafort, Hope Hicks, and, joining late, Ivanka Trump and Jared Kushner. According to Gates, Manafort warned the group that the meeting likely would not yield vital information and they should be careful.[705] Hicks denied any knowledge of the June 9 meeting before 2017,[706] and Kushner did not recall if the planned June 9 meeting came up at all earlier that week.[707]

Michael Cohen recalled being in Donald J. Trump's office on June 6 or 7 when Trump Jr. told his father that a meeting to obtain adverse information about Clinton was going forward.[708] Cohen did not recall Trump Jr. stating that the meeting was connected to Russia.[709] From the tenor of the conversation, Cohen believed that Trump Jr. had previously discussed the meeting with his father, although Cohen was not involved in any such conversation.[710]

In an interview with the Senate Judiciary Committee, however, Trump Jr. stated that he did not inform his father about the emails or the upcoming meeting.[711] Similarly, neither Manafort nor Kushner recalled anyone informing candidate Trump of the meeting, including Trump Jr.[712] President Trump has stated to this Office, in written answers to questions, that he has "no recollection of learning at the time" that his son, Manafort, or "Kushner was considering participating in a meeting in June 2016 concerning potentially negative information about Hillary Clinton."[713]

b. The Events of June 9, 2016

i. Arrangements for the Meeting

Veselnitskaya was in New York on June 9, 2016, for appellate proceedings in the *Prevezon* civil forfeiture liti ation.[714] That da Veselnitskaya called Rinat Akhmetshin, a Soviet-born U.S. lobbyist and when she learned that he was in New York, invited him to lunch. Akhmetshin told the O fice that he had worked on issues relating to the Magnitsky Act and had worked on the *Prevezon* litigation.[716] Kaveladze and Anatoli Samochornov, aRussian-born translator who had assisted Veselnitska *Prevezon* case also attended the lunch.[717]

Meeting asked Akhmetshin what she should tell him. According to several participants in the lunch, Veselnitskaya showed Akhmetshin a document alleging financial misconduct by Bill Browder and the Ziff brothers (Americans with business in Russia and those individuals subse uentl makin olitical donations to the DNC.[719]

The group then went to Trump Tower for the meeting.P'

ii. *Conduct of the Meeting*

Trump Jr., Manafort, and Kushner participated on the Trump side, while Kaveladze, Samochomov, Akhmetshin, and Goldstone attended with Veselnitskaya.F' The Office spoke to every participant except Veselnitska a and Trum Jr. the latter of whom declined to be voluntaril interviewed b the Office The meeting lasted approximately 20 minutes.[723] Grand Jury

████ eal hat Trump Jr. invited Veselnitskaya to begin but did not say anything about the subject of the meeting.'?" Participants agreed that Veselnitskaya stated that the Ziff brothers had? According to Akhmetshin, Trump Jr. aske ollow-up questions about how the alleged payments could be tied specifically to the Clinton Campaign, but Veselnitskaya indicated that she could not trace the money once it entered the United States.[729] Kaveladze similarly recalled that Trump Jr. asked what they have on Clinton, and Kushner became aggravated and asked "[w]hat are we doing here?"[730]

Akhmetshin then spoke about U.S. sanctions imposed under the Magnitsky Act and Russia's response prohibiting U.S. adoption of Russian children.[731] Several participants recalled that Trump Jr. commented that Trump is a private citizen, and there was nothing they could do at that time.[732] Trump Jr. also said that they could revisit the issue if and when they were in government.[733] Notes that Manafort took on his phone reflect the general flow of the conversation, although not all of its details.[734]

At some point in the meeting, Kushner sent an iMessage to Manafort stating "waste of time," followed immediately by two separate emails to assistants at Kushner Companies with requests that they call him to give him an excuse to leave.[735] Samochornov recalled that Kushner departed the meeting before it concluded; Veselnitskaya recalled the same when interviewed by the press in July 2017.[736]

Veselnitskaya's press interviews and written statements to Congress differ materially from other accounts. In a July 2017 press interview, Veselnitskaya claimed that she has no connection to the Russian government and had not referred to any derogatory information concerning the Clinton Campaign when she met with Trump Campaign officials.[737] Veselnitskaya's November 2017 written submission to the Senate Judiciary Committee stated that the purpose of the June 9 meeting was not to connect with "the Trump Campaign" but rather to have "a private meeting with Donald Trump Jr.—a friend of my good acquaintance's son on the matter of assisting me or my colleagues in informing the Congress members as to the criminal nature of manipulation and interference with the legislative activities of the US Congress."[738] In other words, Veselnitskaya claimed her focus was on Congress and not the Campaign. No witness, however, recalled any reference to Congress during the meeting. Veselnitskaya also maintained that she "attended the meeting as a lawyer of Denis Katsyv," the previously mentioned owner of Prevezon Holdings, but she did not "introduce [her]self in this capacity."[739]

In a July 2017 television interview, Trump Jr. stated that while he had no way to gauge the reliability, credibility, or accuracy of what Goldstone had stated was the purpose of the meeting, if "someone has information on our opponent . . . maybe this is something. I should hear them out."[740] Trump Jr. further stated in September 2017 congressional testimony that he thought he should "listen to what Rob and his colleagues had to say."[741] Depending on what, if any, information was provided, Trump Jr. stated he could then "consult with counsel to make an informed decision as to whether to give it any further consideration."[742]

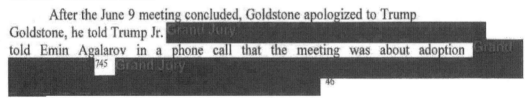

After the June 9 meeting concluded, Goldstone apologized to Trump Goldstone, he told Trump Jr. ████████ told Emin Agalarov in a phone call that the meeting was about adoption ████ [745] ████████ 46

Aras Agalarov asked Kaveladze to report in after the meeting, but before Kaveladze could call, Aras Agalarov called him.[747] With Veselnitskaya next to him, Kaveladze reported that the meeting had gone well, but he later told Aras Agalarov that the meeting about the Magnitsky Act had been a waste of time because it was not with lawyers and they were "preaching to the wrong crowd."[748]

c. *Post-June 9 Events*

Veselnitskaya and Aras Agalarov made at least two unsuccessful attempts after the election to meet with Trump representatives to convey similar information about Browder and the Magnitsky Act.[749] On November 23, 2016, Kaveladze emailed Goldstone about setting up another meeting "with T people" and sent a document bearing allegations similar to those conveyed on June 9.[750] Kaveladze followed up with Goldstone, stating that "Mr. A," which Goldstone understood to mean Aras Agalarov, called to ask about the meeting.[751] Goldstone emailed the document to Rhona Graff, saying that "Aras Agalarov has asked me to pass on this document in the hope it can be passed on to the appropriate team. If needed, a lawyer representing the case is in New York currently and happy to meet with any member of his transition team."[752] According to Goldstone, around January 2017, Kaveladze contacted him again to set up another meeting, but Goldstone did not make the request.[753] The investigation did not identify evidence of the transition team following up.

Participants in the June 9, 2016 meeting began receiving inquiries from attorneys representing the Trump Organization starting in approximately June 2017.[754] On approximately June 2, 2017, Goldstone spoke with Alan Garten, general counsel of the Trump Organization, about his participation in the June 9 meeting.[755] The same day, Goldstone emailed Veselnitskaya's name to Garten, identifying her as the "woman who was the attorney who spoke at the meeting from Moscow."[756] Later in June 2017, Goldstone participated in a lengthier call with Garten and Alan Futerfas, outside counsel for the Trump Organization (and, subsequently, personal counsel for Trump Jr.).[757] On June 27, 2017, Goldstone emailed Emin Agalarov with the subject "Trump attorneys" and stated that he was "interviewed by attorneys" about the June 9 meeting who were "concerned because it links Don Jr. to officials from Russia—which he has always denied meeting."[758] Goldstone stressed that he "did say at the time this was an awful idea and a terrible meeting."[759] Emin Agalarov sent a screenshot of the message to Kaveladze."?

The June 9 meeting became public in July 2017. In a July 9, 2017 text message to Emin Agalarov, Goldstone wrote "I made sure I kept you and your father out of [t]his story,"[761] and "[i]f contacted I can do a dance and keep you out of it."[762] Goldstone added, "FBI now investigating," and "I hope this favor was worth for your dad—it could blow up."[763] On July 12, 2017 Emin Agalarov complained to Kaveladze that his father, Aras, "never listens" to him and that their relationship with "mr T has been thrown down the drain."[764] The next month, Goldstone commented to Emin Agalarov about the volume of publicity the June 9 meeting had generated, stating that his "reputation [was] basically destroyed by this dumb meeting which your father insisted on even though Ike and Me told him would be bad news and not to do."[765] Goldstone added, "I am not able to respond out of courtesy to you and your father. So am painted as some mysterious link to Putin."[766]

After public reporting on the June 9 meeting began, representatives from the Trump Organization again reached out to participants. On July 10, 2017, Futerfas sent Goldstone an email with a proposed statement for Goldstone to issue, which read:

> As the person who arranged the meeting, I can definitively state that the statements I have read by Donald Trump Jr. are 100% accurate. The meeting was a complete waste of time and Don was never told Ms. Veselnitskaya's name prior to the meeting. Ms. Veselnitskaya mostly talked about the Magnitsky Act and Russian adoption laws and the meeting lasted
> 20 to 30 minutes at most. There was never any follow up and nothing ever came of the meeting.[7]

[67]

Grand Jury ～～～～ ment drafted by Trump Organization
Grand Jury ～～～～ was
[768] He proposed a different statement, asserting that he had been asked "by [his] client in Moscow – Emin Agalarov – to facilitate a meeting between a Russian attorney (Natalia Veselnitzkaya [sic])

and Donald Trump Jr. The lawyer had apparently stated that she had some information regarding funding to the DNC from Russia, which she believed Mr. Trump Jr. might find interesting."[769] Goldstone never released either statement."?

On the Russian end, there were also communications about what participants should say about the June 9 meeting. Specifically, the organization that hired Samochornov—an anti• Magnitsky Act group controlled by Veselnitskaya and the owner of Prevezon—offered to pay $90,000 of Samochornov's legal fees.[771] At Veselnitskaya's request, the organization sent Samochornov a transcript of a Veselnitskaya press interview, and Samochornov understood that the organization would pay his legal fees only if he made statements consistent with Veselnitskaya's.T? Samochornov declined, telling the Office that he did not want to perjure himself.T?

The individual who conveyed Veselnitskaya's request to Samochornov stated that he did not expressly condition payment on following Veselnitskaya's answers but, in hindsight, recognized that by sending the transcript, Samochornov could have interpreted the offer of assistance to be conditioned on his not contradicting Veselnitskaya's account.[774]

Volume II, Section ILG, *infra,* discusses interactions between President Trump, Trump Jr., and others in June and July 2017 regarding the June 9 meeting.

6. Events at the Republican National Convention

Trump Campaign officials met with Russian Ambassador Sergey Kislyak during the week of the Republican National Convention. The evidence indicates that those interactions were brief and non-substantive. During platform committee meetings immediately before the Convention, J.D. Gordon, a senior Campaign advisor on policy and national security, diluted   a proposed amendment to the Republican Party platform expressing support   for providing "lethal" assistance to   Ukraine   in response to Russian aggression.   Gordon requested that platform committee personnel   revise   the proposed amendment to state that only "appropriate" assistance be provided to Ukraine.   The original   sponsor of the "lethal"   assistance amendment stated that Gordon told her (the sponsor) that he was on the phone with candidate Trump in connection with his request to dilute the language.   Gordon denied making that statement to the   sponsor, although   he acknowledged it was possible he mentioned having previously spoken to the candidate   about the subject matter.   The investigation did not establish that Gordon   spoke to or was directed   by the candidate to make that proposal.   Gordon   said that he sought the change   because   he believed   the proposed language was inconsistent with Trump's position on Ukraine.

a. *Ambassador Kislyak's Encounters with Senator Sessions and J.D. Gordon the Week of the RNC*

In July 2016, Senator   Sessions and Gordon   spoke   at the Global Partners   in Diplomacy event, a conference co-sponsored by the   State Department and the Heritage Foundation held in Cleveland,   Ohio   the same   week   as   the   Republican National Convention (RNC   or "Convention'tj.T" Approximately 80 foreign ambassadors to the United States, including Kislyak, were invited to the conference.?"

On July 20, 2016, Gordon and Sessions delivered their speeches at the conference.F? In his speech, Gordon stated in pertinent part that the United States should have better relations with Russia.?" During Sessions's speech, he took questions from the audience, one of which may have been asked by Kislyak.F? When the speeches concluded, several ambassadors lined up to greet the speakers.P? Gordon shook hands with Kislyak and reiterated that he had meant what he said in the speech about improving U.S.-Russia relations.[781] Sessions separately spoke with between six and 12 ambassadors, including Kislyak.[782] Although Sessions stated during interviews with the Office that he had no specific recollection of what he discussed with Kislyak, he believed that the two spoke for only a few minutes and that they would have exchanged pleasantries and said some things about U.S.-Russia relations.[783]

Later that evening, Gordon attended a reception as part of the conference.[784] Gordon ran into Kislyak as the two prepared plates of food, and they decided to sit at the same table to eat.[785]

They were joined at that table by the ambassadors from Azerbaijan and Kazakhstan, and by Trump Campaign advisor Carter Page.[786] As they ate, Gordon and Kislyak talked for what Gordon estimated to have been three to five minutes, during which Gordon again mentioned that he meant what he said in his speech about improving U.S.-Russia relations.[787]

b. Change to Republican Party Platform

In preparation for the 2016 Convention, foreign policy advisors to the Trump Campaign, working with the Republican National Committee, reviewed the 2012 Convention's foreign policy platform to identify divergence between the earlier platform and candidate Trump's positions.[788] The Campaign team discussed toning down language from the 2012 platform that identified Russia as the country's number one threat, given the candidate's belief that there needed to be better U.S. relations with Russia.[789] The RNC Platform Committee sent the 2016 draft platform to the National Security and Defense Platform Subcommittee on July 10, 2016, the evening before its first meeting to propose amendments.

Although only delegates could participate in formal discussions and vote on the platform, the Trump Campaign could request changes, and members of the Trump Campaign attended committee meetings.[791] John Mashburn, the Campaign's policy director, helped oversee the Campaign's involvement in the platform committee meetings.[792] He told the Office that he directed Campaign staff at the Convention, including J.D. Gordon, to take a hands-off approach and only to challenge platform planks if they directly contradicted Trump's wishes.[793]

On July 11, 2016, delegate Diana Denman submitted a proposed platform amendment that included provision of armed support for Ukraine.[794] The amendment described Russia's "ongoing military aggression" in Ukraine and announced "support" for "maintaining (and, if warranted, increasing) sanctions against Russia until Ukraine's sovereignty and territorial integrity are fully restored" and for "providing lethal defensive weapons to Ukraine's armed forces and greater coordination with NATO on defense planning."[795] Gordon reviewed the proposed platform changes, including Denman's.[796] Gordon stated that he flagged this amendment because of Trump's stated position on Ukraine, which Gordon personally heard the candidate say at the March 31 foreign policy meeting—namely, that the Europeans should take primary responsibility for any assistance to Ukraine, that there should be improved U.S.-Russia relations, and that be did not want to start World War III over that region.[797] Gordon told the Office that Trump's statements on the campaign trail following the March meeting underscored those positions to the point where Gordon felt obliged to object to the proposed platform change and seek its dilution.[798]

On July 11, 2016, at a meeting of the National Security and Defense Platform Subcommittee, Denman offered her amendment.[799] Gordon and another Campaign staffer, Matt Miller, approached a committee co-chair and asked him to table the amendment to permit further discussion.f? Gordon's concern with the amendment was the language about providing "lethal defensive weapons to Ukraine."[801] Miller did not have any independent basis to believe that this language contradicted Trump's views and relied on Gordon's recollection of the candidate's views.[802]

According to Denman, she spoke with Gordon and Matt Miller, and they told her that they had to clear the language and that Gordon was "talking to New York."[803] Denman told others that she was asked by the two Trump Campaign staffers to strike "lethal defense weapons" from the proposal but that she refused.[804] Denman recalled Gordon saying that he was on the phone with candidate Trump, but she was skeptical whether that was true.[805] Gordon denied having told Denman that he was on the phone with Trump, although he acknowledged it was possible that he mentioned having previously spoken to the candidate about the subject matter.[806] Gordon's phone records reveal a call to Sessions's office in Washington that afternoon, but do not include calls directly to a number associated with Trump.[807] And according to the President's written answers to the Office's questions, he does not recall being involved in the change in language of the platform amendment.[808]

Gordon stated that he tried to reach Rick Dearborn, a senior foreign policy advisor, and Mashburn, the Campaign policy director. Gordon stated that he connected with both of them (he could not recall if by phone or in person) and apprised them of the language he took issue with in the proposed amendment. Gordon recalled no objection by either Dearborn or Mashburn and that all three Campaign advisors supported the alternative formulation ("appropriate assistance").[809]

Dearborn recalled Gordon warning them about the amendment, but not weighing in because Gordon was more familiar with the Campaign's foreign policy stance.!!"[810] Mashburn stated that Gordon reached him, and he told Gordon that Trump had not taken a stance on the issue and that the Campaign should not intervene.[811]

When the amendment came up again in the committee's proceedings, the subcommittee changed the amendment by striking the "lethal defense weapons" language and replacing it with"appropriate assistance."[812] Gordon stated that he and the subcommittee co-chair ultimately agreed to replace the language about armed assistance with "appropriate assistance."[813] The subcommittee accordingly approved Denman's amendment but with the term "appropriate assistance."[814] Gordon stated that, to his recollection, this was the only change sought by the Campaign.[815] Sam Clovis, the Campaign's national co-chair and chief policy advisor, stated he was surprised by the change and did not believe it was in line with Trump's stance.[816] Mashburn stated that when he saw the word "appropriate assistance," he believed that Gordon had violated Mashburn's directive not to intervene.[817]

7. Post-Convention Contacts with Kislyak

Ambassador Kislyak continued his efforts to interact with Campaign officials with responsibility for the foreign-policy portfolio—among them Sessions and Gordon—in the weeks after the Convention. The Office did not identify evidence in those interactions of coordination between the Campaign and the Russian government.

a. Ambassador Kislyak Invites J.D. Gordon to Breakfast at the Ambassador's Residence

On August 3, 2016, an official from the Embassy of the Russian Federation in the United States wrote to Gordon "[o]n behalf of" Ambassador Kislyak inviting Gordon "to have breakfast/tea with the Ambassador at his residence" in Washington, D.C. the following week.[818]

Gordon responded five days later to decline the invitation. He wrote, "[t]hese days are not optimal for us, as we are busily knocking down a constant stream of false media stories while also preparing for the first debate with HRC. Hope to take a raincheck for another time when things quiet down a bit. Please pass along my regards to the Ambassador."[819] The investigation did not identify evidence that Gordon made any other arrangements to meet (or met) with Kislyak after this email.

b. Senator Sessions's September 2016 Meeting with Ambassador Kislyak

Also in August 2016, a representative of the Russian Embassy contacted Sessions's Senate office about setting up a meeting with Kislyak.P? At the time, Sessions was a member of the Senate Foreign Relations Committee and would meet with foreign officials in that capacity.[821] But Sessions's staff reported, and Sessions himself acknowledged, that meeting requests from ambassadors increased substantially in 2016, as Sessions assumed a prominent role in the Trump Campaign and his name was mentioned for potential cabinet-level positions in a future Trump Administration.[822]

On September 8, 2016, Sessions met with Kislyak in his Senate office.[823] Sessions said that he believed he was doing the Campaign a service by meeting with foreign ambassadors, including Kislyak.[824] He was accompanied in the meeting by at least two of his Senate staff: Sandra Luff, his legislative director; and Pete Landrum, who handled military affairs.[825] The meeting lasted less than 30 minutes.[826] Sessions voiced concerns about Russia's sale of a missile• defense system to Iran, Russian planes buzzing U.S. military assets in the Middle East, and Russian aggression in emerging democracies such as Ukraine and Moldova.[827] Kislyak offered explanations on these issues and complained about NATO land forces in former Soviet-bloc countries that border Russia.[828] Landrum recalled that Kislyak referred to the presidential campaign as "an interesting campaign,"[829] and Sessions also recalled Kislyak saying that the Russian government was receptive to the overtures Trump had laid out during his campaign.P" None of the attendees, though, remembered any discussion of Russian election interference or any request that Sessions convey information from the Russian government to the Trump Campaign.[831]

During the meeting, Kislyak invited Sessions to further discuss U.S.-Russia relations with him over a meal at the ambassador's residence.[832] Sessions was non-committal when Kislyak extended the invitation. After the meeting ended, Luff advised Sessions against accepting the one• on-one meeting with Kislyak, whom she assessed to be an "old school KGB guy."[833] Neither Luff nor Landrum recalled that Sessions followed up on the invitation or made any further effort to dine or meet with Kislyak before the November 2016 election.[834] Sessions and Landrum recalled that, after the election, some efforts were made to arrange a meeting between Sessions and Kislyak.[835]

According to Sessions, the request came through CNI and would have involved a meeting between Sessions and Kislyak, two other ambassadors, and the Governor of Alabama.[836] Sessions, however, was in New York on the day of the anticipated meeting and was unable to attend.[837] The investigation did not identify evidence that the two men met at any point after their September 8

.

8. Paul Manafort

Paul Manafort served on the Trump Campaign, including a period as campaign chairman, from March to August 2016.[838] Manafort had connections to Russia through his prior work for Russian oligarch Oleg Deripaska and later through his work for a pro-Russian regime in Ukraine. Manafort stayed in touch with these contacts during the campaign period through Konstantin Kilimnik, a longtime Manafort employee who previously ran Manafort's office in Kiev and who the FBI assesses to have ties to Russian intelligence.

Manafort instructed Rick Gates, his deputy on the Campaign and a longtime employee,[839] to provide Kilimnik with updates on the Trump Campaign—including internal polling data, although Manafort claims not to recall that specific instruction. Manafort expected Kilimnik to share that information with others in Ukraine and with Deripaska. Gates periodically sent such polling data to Kilimnik during the campaign.

Manafort also twice met Kilimnik in the United States during the campaign period and conveyed campaign information. The second meeting took place on August 2, 2016, in New York City. Kilimnik requested the meeting to deliver in person a message from former Ukrainian President Viktor Yanukovych, who was then living in Russia. The message was about a peace plan for Ukraine that Manafort has since acknowledged was a "backdoor" means for Russia to control eastern Ukraine. Several months later, after the presidential election, Kilimnik wrote an email to Manafort expressing the view—which Manafort later said he shared—that the plan's success would require U.S. support to succeed: "all that is required to start the process is a very minor 'wink' (or slight push) from [Donald Trump]."[840] The email also stated that if Manafort were designated as the U.S. representative and started the process, Yanukovych would ensure his reception in Russia "at the very top level."

Manafort communicated with Kilimnik about peace plans for Ukraine on at least four occasions after their first discussion of the topic on August 2: December 2016 (the Kilimnik email described above); January 2017; February 2017; and again in the spring of 2018. The Office reviewed numerous Manafort email and text communications, and asked President Trump about the plan in written questions.[841] The investigation did not uncover evidence of Manafort's passing along information about Ukrainian peace plans to the candidate or anyone else in the Campaign or the Administration. The Office was not, however, able to gain access to all of Manafort's electronic communications (in some instances, messages were sent using encryption applications). And while Manafort denied that he spoke to members of the Trump Campaign or the new Administration about the peace plan, he lied to the Office and the grand jury about the peace plan and his meetings with Kilimnik, and his unreliability on this subject was among the reasons that the district judge found that he breached his cooperation agreement.[842]

The Office could not reliably determine Manafort's urose in sharin internal oiling data with Kilimnik during the campaign period. Manafort did not see a downside to sharing campaign information, and told Gates that his role in the Campaign would be "good for business" and potentially a way to be made whole for work he previously completed in the Ukraine. As to Deripaska, Manafort claimed that by sharing campaign information with him, Deripaska might see value in their relationship and resolve a "disagreement"—a reference to one or more outstanding lawsuits. Because of questions about Manafort's credibility and our limited ability to gather evidence on what happened to the polling data after it was sent to Kilimnik, the Office could not assess what Kilimnik (or others he may have given it to) did with it. The Office did not identify evidence of a connection between Manafort's sharing polling data and Russia's interference in the election, which had already been reported by U.S. media outlets at the time of the August 2 meeting. The investigation did not establish that Manafort otherwise coordinated with the Russian government on its election-interference efforts.

a. Paul Manafort's Ties to Russia and Ukraine

Manafort's Russian contacts during the campaign and transition periods stem from his consulting work for Deripaska from approximately 2005 to 2009 and his separate political consulting work in Ukraine from 2005 to 2015, including through his company DMP International LLC (DM1). Kilimnik worked for Manafort in Kiev during this entire period and continued to communicate with Manafort through at least June 2018. Kilimnik, who speaks and writes Ukrainian and Russian, facilitated many of Manafort's communications with Deripaska and Ukrainian oligarchs.

i. *Oleg Deripaska Consulting Work*

In approximately 2005, Manafort began working for Deripaska, a Russian oligarch who has a global empire involving aluminum and power companies and who is closely aligned with Vladimir Putin.[843] A memorandum describing work that Manafort performed for Deripaska in 2005 regarding the post-Soviet republics referenced the need to brief the Kremlin and the benefits that the work could confer on "the Putin Government."[844] Gates described the work Manafort did for Deripaska as "political risk insurance," and explained that Deripaska used Manafort to install friendly political officials in countries where Deripaska had business interests.[845]

Manafort's company earned tens of millions of dollars from its work for Deripaska and was loaned millions of dollars by Deripaska as well.[846]

In 2007, Deripaska invested through another entity in Pericles Emerging Market Partners L.P. ("Pericles"), an investment fund created by Manafort and former Manafort business partner Richard Davis. The Pericles fund was established to pursue investments in Eastern Europe.[847] Deripaska was the sole investor.[848] Gates stated in interviews with the Office that the venture led to a deterioration of the relationship between Manafort and Deripaska.[849] In particular, when the fund failed, litigation between Manafort and Deripaska ensued. Gates stated that, by 2009, Manafort's business relationship with Deripaska had "dried up."[850] According to Gates, various interactions with Deripaska and his intermediaries over the past few years have involved trying to resolve the legal dispute.[851] As described below, in 2016, Manafort, Gates, Kilimnik, and others engaged in efforts to revive the Deripaska relationship and resolve the litigation.

ii. Political Consulting Work

Through Deripaska, Manafort was introduced to Rinat Akhmetov, a Ukrainian oligarch who hired Manafort as a political consultant.[852] In 2005, Akhmetov hired Manafort to engage in political work supporting the Party of Regions,[853] a political party in Ukraine that was generally understood to align with Russia. Manafort assisted the Party of Regions in regaining power, and its candidate, Viktor Yanukovych, won the presidency in 2010. Manafort became a close and trusted political advisor to Yanukovych during his time as President of Ukraine. Yanukovych served in that role until 2014, when he fled to Russia amidst popular protests.[854]

iii.　Konstantin Kilimnik

Kilimnik is a Russian national who has lived in both Russia and Ukraine and was a longtime Manafort employee.[855]　Kilimnik had direct and close access to Yanukovych and his senior entourage, and he facilitated communications between Manafort and his clients, including Yanukovych and multiple Ukrainian oligarchs.[856] Kilimnik also maintained a relationship with Deripaska's deputy, Yiktor Boyarkin,[857] a Russian national who previously served in the defense attache office of the Russian Embassy to the United States.[858]

Manafort told the Office that he did not believe Kilimnik was working as a Russian "spy."[859]　The FBI, however, assesses that Kilimnik has ties to Russian intelligence.P?　Several pieces of the Office's evidence--including witness interviews and emails obtained through court· authorized search warrants—support that assessment:

- Kilimnik was born on April 27, 1970, in Dnipropetrovsk Oblast, then of the Soviet Union, and attended the Military Institute of the Ministry of Defense from 1987 until 1992.[861]　Sam Patten, a business partner to Kilimnik,[862] stated that Kilimnik told him that he was a translator in the Russian army for seven years and that he later worked in the Russian armament industry selling arms and military equipment.[863]

- U.S. government visa records reveal that Kilimnik obtained a visa to travel to the United States with a Russian diplomatic passport in 1997.[864]

- Kilimnik worked for the International Republican Institute's (IRI) Moscow office, where he did translation work and general office management from 1998 to 2005.[865]　While another official recalled the incident differently,[866] one former associate of Kilimnik's at IRI told the FBI that Kilimnik was fired from his post because his links to Russian intelligence were too strong. The same individual stated that it was well known at IRI that Kilimnik had links to the Russian government.[867]

• Jonathan Hawker, a British national who was a public relations consultant at FTI Consulting, worked with DMI on a public relations campaign for Yanukovych. After Hawker's work for DMI ended, Kilimnik contacted Hawker about working for a Russian government entity on a public-relations project that would promote, in Western and Ukrainian media, Russia's position on its 2014 invasion of Crimea.[868]

• Gates suspected that Kilimnik was a "spy," a view that he shared with Manafort, Hawker, and Alexander van der Zwaan,[869] an attorney who had worked with DMI on a report for the Ukrainian Ministry of Foreign Affairs.F

b. Contacts during Paul Manafort's Time with the Trump Campaign

i. Paul Manafort Join the Campaign

Manafort served on the Trump Campaign from late March to August 19, 2016. On March 29, 2016, the Campaign announced that Manafort would serve as the Campaign's "Convention Manager."[871] On May 19, 2016, Manafort was promoted to campaign chairman and chief strategist, and Gates, who had been assisting Manafort on the Campaign, was appointed deputy campaign chairman.[872]

Thomas Barrack and Roger Stone both recommended Manafort to candidate Trump.[873] In early 2016, at Manafort's request, Barrack suggested to Trump that Manafort join the Campaign to manage the Republican Convention.[874] Stone had worked with Manafort from approximately 1980 until the mid-1990s through various consulting and lobbying firms. Manafort met Trump in 1982 when Trump hired the Black, Manafort, Stone and Kelly lobbying firm.[875] Over the years, Manafort saw Trump at political and social events in New York City and at

Stone's wedding, and Trump requested VIP status at the 1988 and 1996 Republican conventions worked by Manafort.876

According to Gates, in March 2016, Manafort traveled to Trump's Mar-a-Lago estate in Florida to meet with Trump. Trump hired him at that time.877 Manafort agreed to work on the Campaign without pay. Manafort had no meaningful income at this point in time, but resuscitating his domestic political campaign career could be financially beneficial in the future. Gates reported that Manafort intended, if Trump won the Presidency, to remain outside the Administration and monetize his relationship with the Administration.878

ii. *Paul Manafort's Campaign-Period Contacts*

Immediately upon joining the Campaign, Manafort directed Gates to prepare for his review separate memoranda addressed to Deripaska, Akhmetov, Serhiy Lyovochkin, and Boris Kolesnikov,879 the last three being Ukrainian oligarchs who were senior Opposition Bloc officials.P? The memoranda described Manafort's appointment to the Trump Campaign and indicated his willingness to consult on Ukrainian politics in the future. On March 30, 2016, Gates emailed the memoranda and a press release announcing Manafort's appointment to Kilimnik for translation and dissemination.881 Manafort later followed up with Kilimnik to ensure his messages had been delivered, emailing on April 11, 2016 to ask whether Kilimnik had shown "our friends" the media coverage of his new role.882 Kilimnik replied, "Absolutely. Every article." Manafort further asked: "How do we use to get whole. Has Ovd [Oleg Vladimirovich Deripaska] operation seen?" Kilimnik wrote back the same day, "Yes, I have been sending everything to Victor [Boyarkin, Deripaska's deputy], who has been forwarding the coverage directly to OVD."883

Gates reported that Manafort said that being hired on the Campaign would be "good for business" and increase the likelihood that Manafort would be paid the approximately $2 million he was owed for previous political consulting work in Ukraine.[884]   Gates also explained to the Office that Manafort thought his role on the Campaign could help "confirm" that Deripaska had dropped the Pericles lawsuit, and that Gates believed Manafort sent polling data to Deripaska (as discussed further below) so that Deripaska would not move forward with his lawsuit against Manafort.[885]   Gates further stated that Deripaska wanted a visa to the United States, that Oeripaska could believe that having Manafort in a position inside the Campaign or Administration might be helpful to Deripaska, and that Manafort's relationship with Trump could help Deripaska in other ways as well.[886] Gates stated, however, that Manafort never told him anything specific about what, if anything, Manafort might be offering Deripaska.[887]

Gates also reported that Manafort instructed him in April 2016 or early May 2016 to send Kilimnik Campaign internal polling data and other updates so that Kilimnik, in turn, could share it with Ukrainian oli archs.[888]   Gates understood that the information would also be shared withDeripaska[889]
Gates reported to the Office that he did not know why Manafort wanted him to send polling information, but Gates thought it was a way to showcase Manafort's work, and Manafort wanted to open doors to jobs after the Trump Campaign ended.[890]   Gates said that Manafort's instruction included sending internal polling data prepared for the Trump Campaign by pollster Tony Fabrizio.[891]   Fabrizio had worked with Manafort for years and was brought into the Campaign by Manafort. Gates stated that, in accordance with Manafort's instruction, he periodically sent Kilimnik polling data via WhatsApp; Gates then deleted the communications on a daily basis.[892]   Gates further told the Office that, after Manafort left the Campaign in mid-August, Gates sent Kilimnik polling data less frequently and that the data he sent was more publicly available information and less internal data.[893]

The Office also obtained contemporaneous emails that shed light on the purpose of the communications with Deripaska and that are consistent with Oates's account. For example, in response to a July 7, 2016, email from a Ukrainian reporter about Manafort's failed Deripaska• backed investment, Manafort asked Kilimnik whether there had been any movement on "this issue with our friend."[897] Gates stated that "our friend" likely referred to Deripaska,[898] and Manafort told the Office that the "issue" (and "our biggest interest," as stated below) was a solution to the Deripaska-Pericles issue.[899] Kilimnik replied:

> I am carefully optimistic on the question of our biggest interest.
>
> Our friend [Boyarkin] said there is lately significantly more attention to the campaign in his boss' [Deripaska's] mind, and he will be most likely looking for ways to reach out to you pretty soon, understanding all the time sensitivity. I am more than sure that it will be resolved and we will get back to the original relationship with V.'s boss [Deripaska].[900]

Eight minutes later, Manafort replied that Kilimnik should tell Boyarkin's "boss," a reference to Deripaska, "that if he needs private briefings we can accommodate.t'Y' Manafort has alleged to the Office that he was willing to brief Deripaska only on public campaign matters and gave an example: why Trump selected Mike Pence as the Vice-Presidential running mate.[902] Manafort said he never gave Deripaska a briefing.[903] Manafort noted that if Trump won, Deripaska would want to use Manafort to advance whatever interests Deripaska had in the United States and elsewhere.P''

iii. Paul Manafort's Two Campaign-Period Meetings with Konstantin Kilimnik in the United States

Manafort twice met with Kilimnik in person during the campaign period-once in May and again in August 2016. The first meeting took place on May 7, 2016, in New York City.[905] In the days leading to the meeting, Kilimnik had been working to gather information about the political situation in Ukraine. That included information gleaned from a trip that former Party of Regions official Yuriy Boyko had recently taken to Moscow—a trip that likely included meetings between Boyko and high-ranking Russian officials.P'' Kilimnik then traveled to Washington, D.C. on or about May 5, 2016; while in Washington, Kilimnik had pre-arranged meetings with State Department employees.P'"

Late on the evening of May 6, Gates arranged for Kilimnik to take a 3:00 a.m. train to meet Manafort in New York for breakfast on May 7. 908 According to Manafort, during the meeting, he and Kilimnik talked about events in Ukraine, and Manafort briefed Kilimnik on the Trump Campaign, expecting Kilimnik to pass the information back to individuals in Ukraine and elsewhere.P" Manafort stated that Opposition Bloc members recognized Manafort's position on the Campaign was an opportunity, but Kilimnik did not ask for anything.910 Kilimnik spoke about a plan of Boyko to boost election participation in the eastern zone of Ukraine, which was the base for the Opposition Bloc.911 Kilimnik returned to Washington, D.C. right after the meeting with Manafort.

Manafort met with Kilimnik a second time at the Grand Havana Club in New York City on the evening of August 2, 2016. The events leading to the meeting are as follows. On July 28, 2016, Kilimnik flew from Kiev to Moscow.[912] The next day, Kilimnik wrote to Manafort requesting that they meet, using coded language about a conversation he had that day.[913] In an email with a subject line "Black Caviar," Kilimnik wrote:

I met today with the guy who gave you your biggest black caviar jar several years ago. We spent about 5 hours talking about his story, and I have several important messages from him to you. He asked me to go and brief you on our conversation. I said I have to run it by you first, but in principle I am prepared to do it. ... It has to do about the future of his Manafort identified "the guy who gave you your biggest black caviar jar" as Yanukovych. He explained that, in 2010, he and Yanukovych had lunch to celebrate the recent presidential election. Yanukovych gave Manafort a large jar of black caviar that was worth approximately $30,000 to $40,000.[915] Manafort's identification of Yanukovych as "the guy who gave you your biggest black caviar jar" is consistent with Kilimnik being in Moscow — where Yanukovych resided — when Kilimnik wrote "I met today with a December 2016 email in which Kilimnik referred to Yanukovych as "BG," —— [916] Manafort replied to Kilimnik's July 29 email, "Tuesday [August 2] is best ... Tues or weds in NYC."[917]

Three days later, on July 31, 2016, Kilimnik flew back to Kiev from Moscow, and on that same day, wrote to Manafort that he needed "about 2 hours" for their meeting "because it is a long caviar story to tell."[918] Kilimnik wrote that he would arrive at JFK on August 2 at 7:30 p.m., and he and Manafort agreed to a late dinner that night.[919] Documentary evidence — including flight, phone, and hotel records, and the timing of text messages exchanged[920] – confirms the dinner took place as planned on August 2.[921]

As to the contents of the meeting itself, the accounts of Manafort and Gates — who arrived late to the dinner--differ in certain respects. But their versions of events, when assessed alongside available documentary evidence and what Kilimnik told business associate Sam Patten, indicate that at least three principal topics were discussed.

First, Manafort and Kilimnik discussed a plan to resolve the ongoing political problems in Ukraine by creating an autonomous republic in its more industrialized eastern region of Donbas,[922] and having Yanukovych, the Ukrainian President ousted in 2014, elected to head that republic.[923]

That plan, Manafort later acknowledged, constituted a "backdoor" means for Russia to control eastern Ukraine.P' Manafort initially said that, if he had not cut off the discussion, Kilimnik would have asked Manafort in the August 2 meeting to convince Trump to come out in favor of the peace plan, and Yanukovych would have expected Manafort to use his connections in Europe and Ukraine to support the plan.[925] Manafort also initially told the Office that ████████████████

to Kilimnik that the plan was crazy, that the discussion ended, and that he did not recall Kilimnik askin Manafort to reconsider the lan after their Au ust 2 meetin.[926] Manafort said that he reacted negatively to Yanukovych sending—years later—an "urgent" request when Yanukovych needed him.[927] When confronted with an email written by Kilimnik on or about December 8, 2016, however, Manafort acknowledged Kilimnik raised the peace plan again in that email.[928] Manafort ultimately acknowleded Kilimnik also raised the eace lan in

ary 2017 meetings with Manafort ████████████

Second, Manafort briefed Kilimnik on the state of the Trump Campaign and Manafort's plan to win the election.P? That briefing encompassed the Campaign's messaging and its internal polling data. According to Gates, it also included discussion of "battleground" states, which ████████████████ Manafort identi ████████████████████████████ Manafort did no ████████████████ refer ex licit! to battle round states in his tellin of the August 2 discussion

Third, according to Gates and what Kilimnik told Patten, Manafort and Kilimnik discussed two sets of financial disputes related to Manafort's previous work in the region. Those consisted of the unresolved Deripaska lawsuit and the funds that the Opposition Bloc owed to Manafort for his political consulting work and how Manafort might be able to obtain payment.[933]

After the meeting, Gates and Manafort both stated that they left separately from Kilimnik because they knew the media was tracking Manafort and wanted to avoid media reporting on his connections to Kilimnik.[934]

c. Post-Resignation Activities

Manafort resigned from the Trump Campaign in mid-August 2016, approximately two weeks after his second meeting with Kilimnik, amidst negative media reporting about his political consulting work for the pro-Russian Party of Regions in Ukraine. Despite his resignation, Manafort continued to offer advice to various Campaign officials through the November election. Manafort told Gates that he still spoke with Kushner, Bannon, and candidate Trump,[935] and some of those post-resignation contacts are documented in emails. For example, on October 21, 2016, Manafort sent Kushner an email and attached a strategy memorandum proposing that the Campaign make the case against Clinton "as the failed and corrupt champion of the establishment" and that "Wikileaks provides the Trump campaign the ability to make the case in a very credible way – by using the words of Clinton, its campaign officials and DNC members."[936] Later, in a November 5, 2016 email to Kushner entitled "Securing the Victory," Manafort stated that he was "really feeling good about our prospects on Tuesday and focusing on preserving the victory," and that he was concerned the Clinton Campaign would respond to a loss by "mov[ing] immediately to discredit the [Trump] victory and claim voter fraud and cyber-fraud, including the claim that the Russians have hacked into the voting machines and tampered with the results."[937]

Trump was elected President on November 8, 2016. Manafort told the Office that, in the wake of Trump's victory, he was not interested in an Administration job. Manafort instead preferred to stay on the "outside," and monetize his campaign position to generate business given his familiarity and relationship with Trump and the incoming Administration.[938] Manafort appeared to follow that plan, as he traveled to the Middle East, Cuba, South Korea, Japan, and China and was paid to explain what a Trump presidency would entail.[939]

Manafort's activities in early 2017 included meetings relating to Ukraine and Russia. The first meeting, which took place in Madrid, Spain in January 2017, was with Georgiy Oganov. Oganov, who had previously worked at the Russian Embassy in the United States, was a senior executive at a Deripaska company and was believed to report directly to Deripaska.[P']? Manafort initially denied attending the meeting. When he later acknowledged it, he claimed that the meeting had been arranged by his lawyers and concerned only the Pericles lawsuit.[941] Other evidence, however, provides reason to doubt Manafort's statement that the sole topic of the meeting was the Pericles lawsuit. In particular, text messages to Manafort from a number associated with Kilimnik suggest that Kilimnik and Boyarkin — not Manafort's counsel — had arranged the meeting between Manafort and Oganov.[942] Kilimnik's message states that the meeting was supposed to be "not about money or Pericles" but instead "about recreating [the] old friendship" — ostensibly between Manafort and Deripaska — "and talking about global politics."[943] Manafort also replied by text that he "need[s] this finished before Jan. 20,"[944] which appears to be a reference to resolving Pericles before the inauguration.

On January 15, 2017, three days after his return from Madrid, Manafort emailed K.T. McFarland, who was at that time designated to be Deputy National Security Advisor and was formally appointed to that position on January 20, 2017.[945] Manafort's January 15 email to McFarland stated: "I have some important information I want to share that I picked up on my travels over the last month."[946] Manafort told the Office that the email referred to an issue regarding Cuba, not Russia or Ukraine, and Manafort had traveled to Cuba in the past month.[947] Either way, McFarland — who was advised by Flynn not to respond to the Manafort inquiry ━ appears not to have responded to Manafort.[948]

Manafort told the Office that around the time of the Presidential Inauguration in January, he met with Kilimnik and Ukrainian oligarch Serhiy Lyovochkin at the Westin Hotel in Alexandria, Virginia.[949] During this meeting, Kilimnik again discussed the Yanukovych peace plan that he had broached at the August 2 meeting and in a detailed December 8, 2016 message found in Kilirnnik's DMP email account."? In that December 8 email, which Manafort acknowledged having read,[951] Kilimnik wrote, "[a]ll that is required to start the process is a very minor 'wink' (or slight push) from DT"—an apparent reference to President-elect Trump—"and a decision to authorize you to be a 'special representative' and manage this process." Kilimnik assured Manafort, with that authority, he "could start the process and within 10 days visit Russia [Yanukovych] guarantees your reception at the very top level," and that "DT could have peace in Ukraine basically within a few months after inauguration."[952]

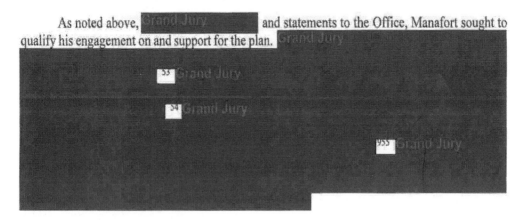

On February 26, 2017, Manafort met Kilimnik in Madrid, where Kilimnik had flown from Moscow.[956] In his first two interviews with the Office, Manafort denied meeting with Kilimnik on his Madrid trip and then—after being confronted with documentary evidence that Kilimnik was in Madrid at the same time as him—recognized that he met him in Madrid. Manafort said that Kilimnik had updated him on a criminal investigation into so-called "black ledger" payments to Manafort that was bein conducted b Ukraine's National Anti-Corru tion Bureau.[957]

Manafort remained in contact with Kilimnik throughout 2017 and into the spring of 2018.

Those contacts included matters pertaining to the criminal charges brought by the Office,[959] and the Ukraine peace plan. In early 2018, Manafort retained his longtime polling firm to craft a draft poll in Ukraine, sent the pollsters a three-page primer on the plan sent by Kilimnik, and worked with Kilimnik to formulate the polling questions.t'" The primer sent to the pollsters specifically called for the United States and President Trump to support the Autonomous Republic of Donbas with Yanukovych as Prime Minister.l"! and a series of questions in the draft poll asked for opinions on Yanukovych's role in resolving the conflict in Donbas.[962] (The poll was not solely about Donbas; it also sought participants' views on leaders apart from Yanukovych as they pertained to the 2019 Ukraine presidential election.)

The Office has not uncovered evidence that Manafort brought the Ukraine peace plan to the attention of the Trump Campaign or the Trump Administration. Kilimnik continued his efforts to promote the peace plan to the Executive Branch (e.g., U.S. Department of State) into the summer of 2018.[963]

B. Post-Election and Transition-Period Contacts

Trump was elected President on November 8, 2016. Beginning immediately after the election, individuals connected to the Russian government started contacting officials on the Trump Campaign and Transition Team through multiple channels—sometimes through Russian Ambassador Kislyak and at other times through individuals who sought reliable contacts through U.S. persons not formally tied to the Campaign or Transition Team. The most senior levels of the Russian government encouraged these efforts. The investigation did not establish that these efforts reflected or constituted coordination between the Trump Campaign and Russia in its election• interference activities.

1. Immediate Post-Election Activity

As soon as news broke that Trump had been elected President, Russian government officials and prominent Russian businessmen began trying to make inroads into the new Administration. They appeared not to have preexisting contacts and struggled to connect with senior officials around the President-Elect. As explained below, those efforts entailed both official contact through the Russian Embassy in the United States and outreaches—sanctioned at high levels of the Russian government—through business rather than political contacts.

a. Outreach from the Russian Government

At approximately 3 a.m. on election night, Trump Campaign press secretary Hope Hicks received a telephone call on her personal cell phone from a person who sounded foreign but was calling from a number with a DC area code.[964] Although Hicks had a hard time understanding the person, she could make out the words "Putin call."[965] Hicks told the caller to send her an email.[966]

The following morning, on November 9, 2016, Sergey Kuznetsov, an official at the Russian Embassy to the United States, emailed Hicks from his Gmail address with the subject line, "Message from Putin."[967] Attached to the email was a message from Putin, in both English and Russian, which Kuznetsov asked Hicks to convey to the President-Elect.[968] In the message, Putin offered his congratulations to Trump for his electoral victory, stating he "look[ed] forward to working with [Trump] on leading Russian-American relations out of crisis."[969]

Hicks forwarded the email to Kushner, asking, "Can you look into this? Don't want to get duped but don't want to blow off Putin!"[970] Kushner stated in Congressional testimony that he believed that it would be possible to verify the authenticity of the forwarded email through the

Russian Ambassador, whom Kushner had previously met in April 2016.[971] Unable to recall the Russian Ambassador's name, Kushner emailed Dimitri Simes of CNI, whom he had consulted previously about Russia, see Volume I, Section IV.A.4, supra, and asked, "What is the name of Russian ambassador?"[972] Kushner forwarded Simes's response— which identified Kislyak by name—to Hicks.[973] After checking with Kushner to see what he had learned, Hicks conveyed Putin's letter to transition officials.[974] Five days later, on November 14, 2016, Trump and Putin spoke by phone in the presence of Transition Team members, including incoming National Security Advisor Michael Flynn.[975]

b. High-Level Encouragement of contacts through Alternative Channels

As Russian officials in the United States reached out to the President-Elect and his team, a number of Russian individuals working in the private sector began their own efforts to make contact. Petr Aven, a Russian national who heads Alfa-Bank, Russia's largest commercial bank, described to the Office interactions with Putin during this time period that might account for the flurry of Russian activity.[976]

Aven told the Office that he is one of approximately 50 wealthy Russian businessmen who regularly meet with Putin in the Kremlin; these 50 men are often referred to as "oligarchs."?" Aven told the Office that he met on a quarterly basis with Putin, including in the fourth quarter (Q4) of 2016, shortly after the U.S. presidential election.[978] Aven said that he took these meetings seriously and understood that any suggestions or critiques that Putin made during these meetings were implicit directives, and that there would be consequences for Aven if he did not follow through.[979] As was typical, the 2016 Q4 meeting with Putin was preceded by a preparatory meeting with Putin's chief of staff, Anton Vaino.[980]

According to Aven, at his Q4 2016 one-on-one meeting with Putin,[981] Putin raised the prospect that the United States would impose additional sanctions on Russian interests, including sanctions against Aven and/or Alfa-Bank.[982] Putin suggested that Aven needed to take steps to protect himself and Alfa-Bank.[983] Aven also testified that Putin spoke of the difficulty faced by the Russian government in getting in touch with the incoming Trump Administration.[984] According to Aven, Putin indicated that he did not know with whom formally to speak and generally did not know the people around the President-Elect.[985]

Aven told Putin he would take steps to protect himself and the Alfa-Bank shareholders from potential sanctions, and one of those steps would be to try to reach out to the incoming Administration to establish a line of communication.[986] Aven described Putin responding with skepticism about Aven's prospect for success.[987] According to Aven, although Putin did not expressly direct him to reach out to the Trump Transition Team, Aven understood that Putin expected him to try to respond to the concerns he had raised.[988] Aven's efforts are described in Volume I, Section IV.B.5, *infra.*

2. Kirill Dmitriev's Transition-Era Outreach to the Incoming Administration

Aven's description of his interactions with Putin is consistent with the behavior of Kiri ll Dmitriev, a Russian national who heads Russia's sovereign wealth fund and is closely connected to Putin. Dmitriev undertook efforts to meet members of the incoming Trump Administration in the months after the election. Dmitriev asked a close business associate who worked for the United Arab Emirates (UAE) royal court, George Nader, to introduce him to Trump transition officials, and Nader eventually arranged a meeting in the Seychelles between Dmitriev and Erik Prince, a 'frump Campaign supporter and an associate of Steve Bannon.[989] In addition, the UAE national security advisor introduced Dmitriev to a hedge fund manager and friend of Jared Kushner, Rick Gerson, in late November 2016. In December 2016 and January 2017, Dmitriev and Gerson worked on a proposal for reconciliation between the United States and Russia, which Dmitriev implied he cleared through Putin. Gerson provided that proposal to Kushner before the inauguration, and Kushner later gave copies to Bannon and Secretary of State Rex Tillerson.

a. Background

Dmitriev is a Russian national who was appointed CEO of Russia's sovereign wealth fund, the Russian Direct Investment Fund (RDIF), when it was founded in 2011.[990] Dmitriev reported directly to Putin and frequently referred to Putin as his "boss."[991]

RDIF has co-invested in various projects with UAE sovereign wealth funds.[992] Dmitriev regularly interacted with Nader, a senior advisor to UAE Crown Prince Mohammed bin Zayed(Crown Prince Mohammed), in connection with RDIF's dealings with the UAE.[993] Putin wanted Dmitriev to be in charge of both the financial and the political relationship between Russia and the Gulfstates, in part because Dmitriev had been educated in the West and spoke English fluently.[994]
Nader considered Dmitriev to be Putin's interlocutor in the Gulf region, and would relay Dmitriev's views directly to Crown Prince Mohammed.[995]

Nader developed contacts with both U.S. presidential campaigns during the 2016 election, and kept Dmitriev abreast of his efforts to do so.[996] According to Nader, Dmitriev said that his and the government of Russia's preference was for candidate Trum to win and asked Nader to assist him in meetin members of the Trum Cam ai n.[997]   Na
der did not introduce Dmitriev to anyone associated with the Trump Campaign before t e election.[999]

Erik Prince is a businessman who had relationships with various individuals associated with the Trump Campaign, including Steve Bannon, Donald Trump Jr., and Roger Stone.[1005] Prince did not have a formal role in the Campaign, although he offered to host a fundraiser for Trump and sent unsolicited policy papers on issues such as foreign policy, trade, and Russian election interference to Bannon.[1006]

After the election, Prince frequently visited transition offices at Trump Tower, primarily to meet with Bannon but on occasion to meet Michael Flynn and others.[1007] Prince and Bannon would discuss, *inter alia,* foreign policy issues and Prince's recommendations regarding who should be appointed to fill key natiositions.[1008] Although ===== affiliated with the transition, Nader —— received assurances ➤ that the incoming Administration considered Prince a trusted associate.'?

b. Kirill Dmitriev's Post-Election Contacts With the Incoming Administration

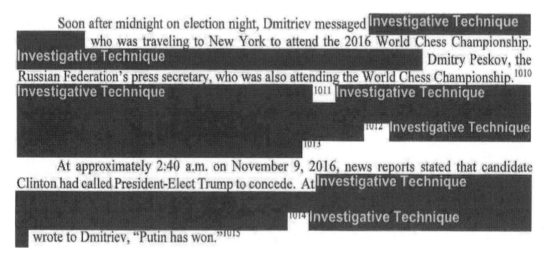

Soon after midnight on election night, Dmitriev messaged Investigative Technique who was traveling to New York to attend the 2016 World Chess Championship. Investigative Technique Dmitry Peskov, the Russian Federation's press secretary, who was also attending the World Chess Championship.[1010] Investigative Technique [1011] Investigative Technique

[1012] Investigative Technique

[1013]

At approximately 2:40 a.m. on November 9, 2016, news reports stated that candidate Clinton had called President-Elect Trump to concede. At Investigative Technique

[1014] Investigative Technique

wrote to Dmitriev, "Putin has won."[1015]

Later that morning, Dmitriev contacted Nader, who was in New York, to request a meeting with the "key people" in the incoming Administration as soon as possible in light of the "[g]reat results."[1016] He asked Nader to convey to the incoming Administration that "we want to start rebuilding the relationship in whatever is a comfortable pace for them. We understand all of the sensitivities and are not in a rush."[1017] Dmitriev and Nader had previously discussed Nader introducing him to the contacts Nader had made within the Trump Campaign.[1018] Dmitriev also told Nader that he would ask Putin for permission to travel to the United States, where he would be able to speak to media outlets about the positive impact of Trump's election and the need for reconciliation between the United States and Russia.[1019]

Later that day, Dmitriev flew to New York, where Peskov was separately traveling to attend the chess tournament.[1020] Dmitriev invited Nader to the opening of the tournament and noted that, if there was "a chance to see anyone key from Trump camp," he "would love to start building for the future."[1021] Dmitriev also asked Nader to invite Kushner to the event so that he (Dmitriev) could meet him.[1022] Nader did not pass along Dmitriev's invitation to anyone connected with the incoming Administration.[1'F'] Although one World Chess Federation official recalled hearing from an attendee that President-Elect Trump had stopped by the tournament, the investigation did not establish that Trump or any Campaign or Transition Team official attended the event.[1024] And the President's written answers denied that he had.[1025]

Nader stated that Dmitriev continued to press him to set up a meeting with transition officials, and was particularly focused on Kushner and Trump Jr.[1026] Dmitriev told Nader that [1028] Grand Jury [029] According to Nader, Dmitriev was very anxious to connect with the incoming Administration and told Nader that he would try other routes to do so besides Nader himself.[1030] Nader did not ultimately introduce Dmitriev to anyone associated with the incoming Administration during Dmitriev's post-election trip to New York.[1031]

In early December 2016, Dmitriev again broached the topic of meeting incoming Administration officials with Nader in January or February.[P"] Dmitriev sent Nader a list of publicly available quotes of Dmitriev speaking positively about Donald Trump "in case they [were] helpful."[1033]

c. Erik Prince and Kirill Dmitriev Meet in the Seychelles

i. George Nader and Erik Prince Arrange Seychelles Meeting with Dmitriev

Nader traveled to New York in early January 2017 and had lunchtime and dinner meetings with Erik Prince on January 3, 2017.[1034] Nader and Prince discussed Dmitriev.[1035] Nader informed Prince that the Russians were looking to build a link introduce him to someone from the incoming incoming Trump Administration.Y" with the someone from the incoming he told Prince that Dmitriev had been ushin Nader relationship with Transition Team officials. that Pr to

After his dinner with Prince, Nader sent Prince a link to a Wikipedia entry about Dmitriev, and sent Dmitriev a message stating that he had just met "with some key people within the family and inner circle" — a reference to Prince — and that he had spoken at length and positively about Drnitriev.P'? Nader told Dmitriev that the people he met had asked for Dmitriev's bio, and Dmitriev replied that he would update and send it.[1041] Nader later received from Dmitriev two files concerning Dmitriev: one was a two-page biography, and the other was a list of Dmitriev's positive quotes about Donald Trump.[1042]

The next morning, Nader forwarded the message and attachments Dmitriev had sent him to Prince.[1043] Nader wrote to Prince that these documents were the versions "to be used with some additional details for them" (with "them" referring to members of the incoming Adrninistrationj.P" Prince opened the attachments at Trump Tower within an hour of receiving them.[1045] Prince stated that, while he was at Trump Tower that day, he spoke with Kellyanne Conway, Wilbur Ross, Steve Mnuchin, and others while waiting to see Bannon.P" Cell-site location data for Prince's mobile phone indicates that Prince remained at Trump Tower for approximately three hours.P'? Prince said that he could not recall whether durin those three hours he met with Bannon and discussed Dmitriev with him.[1048] [049]

Prince booked a ticket to the Seychelles on January 7, 2017.[1050] The following day, Nader wrote to Dmitriev that he had a "pleasant surprise" for him, namely that he had arranged for Dmitriev to meet "a Special Guest" from "the New Team," referring to Prince.[P] Nader asked Dmitriev if he could come to the Seychelles for the meeting on January 12, 2017, and Dmitriev agreed.[1052]

The following day, surance from Nader that the Seychelles meeting would be worthwhile.[P] —— Dmitriev was not enthusiastic about the idea of meeting with Prince, and that Nader assured him that Prince wielded influence with the incoming Administration.[P] Nader wrote to Dmitriev, "This guy [Prince] is designated by Steve [Bannon] to meet you! I know him and he is very very well connected and trusted by the New Team. His sister is now a Minister of Education."[1055] According to Nader, Prince had led him to believe that Bannon was aware of Prince's upcoming meeting with Dmitriev, and Prince acknowledged that it was fair for Nader to think that Prince would pass information on to the Transition Team.[1056] Bannon, however, told the Office that Prince did not tell him in advance about his meeting with Dmitriev.[P]?

iii. The Seychelles Meetings

Dmitriev arrived with his wife in the Seychelles on January 11, 2017, and checked into the Four Seasons Resort where Crown Prince Mohammed and Nader were staying.[1058] Prince arrived that same day.[1059] Prince and Dmitriev met for the first time that afternoon in Nader's villa, with Nader present.[1060] The initial meeting lasted approximately 30-45 minutes.[P]

[062]

Prince described the eight years o the Obama Administration in negative terms, and stated that he was looking forward to a new era of cooperation and conflict resolution.[P]! According to Prince, he told Dmitriev that Bannon was effective if not conventional, and that Prince provided policy papers to Bannon.[P]

[1066] [067] [1068] The

175

Afterwards, Prince returned to his room, where he learned that a Russian aircraft carrier had sailed to Libya, which led him to call Nader and ask him to set up another meeting with Dmitriev.[1073] According to Nader, Prince called and said he had checked with his associates back home and needed to convey to Dmitriev that Libya was "off the table."[1074] Nader wrote to Dmitriev that Prince had "received an urgent message that he needs to convey to you immediately," and arranged for himself, Dmitriev, and Prince to meet at a restaurant on the Four Seasons property.[1015]

After the brief second meeting concluded, Nader and Dmitriev discussed what had transpircd.[F"] Dmitriev told Nader that he was disappointed in his meetings with Prince for two reasons: first, he believed the Russians needed to be communicating with someone who had more authority within the incoming Administration than Prince had.[1079] Second, he had hoped to have a discussion of greater substance, such as outlinin a strate ic roadmap for both countries to follow.[1080]

Hours after the second meeting, Prince sent two text messages to Bannon from the Seychelles.[l'P] As described further below, investigators were unable to obtain the content of these or other messages between Prince and Bannon, and the investigation also did not identify evidence of any further communication between Prince and Dmitriev after their meetings in the Seychelles.

iii. Erik Prince's Meeting with Steve Bannon after the Seychelles trip

After the Seychelles meetings, Prince told Nader that he would inform Bannon about his discussion with Dmitriev and would convey that someone within the Russian power structure was interested in seeking better relations with the incoming Administration.[l'P!] On January 12, 2017, Prince contacted Bannon's personal assistant to set up a meeting for the following week.[1084] Several days later, Prince messaged her again asking about Bannon's schedule.[P"]

Prince said that he met Bannon at Bannon's home after returning to the United States in mid-January and briefed him about several topics, including his meeting with Dmitriev.[1086] Prince told the Office that he explained to Bannon that Dmitriev was the head of a Russian sovereign wealth fund and was interested in improving relations between the United States and Russia.P'" Prince had on his cellphone a screenshot of Dmitriev's Wikipedia page dated January 16, 2017, and Prince told the Office that he likely showed that image to Bannon.[1088] Prince also believed he provided Bannon with Dmitriev's contact information.l'"? According to Prince, Bannon instructed Prince not to follow up with Dmitriev, and Prince had the impression that the issue was not a priority for Bannon.P'" Prince related that Bannon did not appear angry, just relatively uninterested.l?"

> Bannon, by contrast, told the Office that he never discussed with Prince anything regarding Dmitriev, RDIF, or any meetings with Russian individuals or people associated with Putin.[1092] Bannon also stated that had Prince mentioned such a meeting, Bannon would have remembered it, and Bannon would have objected to such a meeting having taken place.[1093]

The conflicting accounts provided by Bannon and Prince could not be independently clarified by reviewing their communications, because neither one was able to produce any of the messages they exchanged in the time period surrounding the Seychelles meeting. Prince's phone contained no text messages prior to March 2017, though provider records indicate that he and Bannon exchanged dozens of messages.F'" Prince denied deleting any messages but claimed he did not know why there were no messages on his device before March 2017.[1095] Bannon's devices similarly contained no messages in the relevant time period, and Bannon also stated he did not know why messages did not appear on his device.[1096] Bannon told the Office that, during both the months before and after the Seychelles meeting, he regularly used his personal Blackberry and personal email for work-related communications (including those with Prince), and he took no steps to preserve these work communications.P?

d. *Kirill Dmitriev's Post-Election Contact with Rick Gerson Regarding U.S.• Russia Relations*

Dmitriev's contacts during the transition period were not limited to those facilitated by Nader. In approximately late November 2016, the UAE national security advisor introduced Dmitriev to Rick Gerson, a friend of Jared Kushner who runs a hedge fund in New York.[1098] Gerson stated he had no formal role in the transition and had no involvement in the Trump Campaign other than occasional casual discussions about the Campaign with Kushner.F" After the election, Gerson assisted the transition by arranging meetings for transition officials with former UK prime minister Tony Blair and a UAE delegation led by Crown Prince Mohammed.U'"

When Dmitriev and Gerson met, they principally discussed potential joint ventures between Gerson's hedge fund and RDIF.[1101] Dmitriev was interested in improved economic cooperation between the United States and Russia and asked Gerson who he should meet with in the incoming Administration who would be helpful towards this goal.[1102] Gerson replied that he would try to figure out the best way to arrange appropriate introductions, but noted that confidentiality would be required because of the sensitivity of holding such meetings before the new Administration took power, and before Cabinet nominees had been confirmed by the Senate.l'F' Gerson said he would ask Kushner and Michael Flynn who the "key person or people" were on the topics of reconciliation with Russia, joint security concerns, and economic matters.l'""

Dmitriev told Gerson that he had been tasked by Putin to develop and execute a reconciliation plan between the United States and Russia. He noted in a text message to Gerson that if Russia was "approached with respect and willingness to understand our position, we can have Major Breakthroughs quickly."[1105] Gerson and Dmitriev exchanged ideas in December 2016 about what such a reconciliation plan would include.U'" Gerson told the Office that the Transition Team had not asked him to engage in these discussions with Dmitriev, and that he did so on his own initiative and as a private citizen.U'"

On January 9, 2017, the same day he asked Nader whether meeting Prince would be worthwhile, Dmitriev sent his biography to Gerson and asked him if he could "share it with Jared (or somebody else very senior in the team) – so that they know that we are focused from our side on improving the relationship and my boss asked me to play a key role in that."[1108] Dmitriev alsoasked Gerson if he knew Prince, and if Prince was somebody important or worth spending time with.[1109] After his trip to the Seychelles, Dmitriev told Gerson that Bannon had asked Prince to meet with Dmitriev and that the two had had a positive meeting.[1110]

On January 16, 2017, Dmitriev consolidated the ideas for U.S.-Russia reconciliation that he and Gerson had been discussing into a two-page document that listed five main points: (I) jointly fighting terrorism; (2) jointly engaging in anti-weapons of mass destruction efforts; (3) developing "win-win" economic and investment initiatives; (4) maintaining an honest, open, and continual dialogue regarding issues of disagreement; and (5) ensuring proper communication and trust by "key people" from each country.[1111] On January 18, 2017, Gerson gave a copy of the document to Kushner.[1112] Kushner had not heard of Dmitriev at that time.[1113] Gerson explained that Dmitriev was the head of RDIF, and Gerson may have alluded to Dmitriev's being well connected.[1114] Kushner placed the document in a file and said he would get it to the right people.[1115] Kushner ultimately gave one copy of the document to Bannon and another to Rex Tillerson; according to Kushner, neither of them followed up with Kushner about it.[1116] On January 19, 2017, Dmitriev sent Nader a copy of the two-page document, telling him that this was "a view from our side that I discussed in my meeting on the islands and with you and with our friends. Please share with them—we believe this is a good foundation to start from.?"[1117]

Gerson informed Dmitriev that he had given the document to Kushner soon after delivering it.[1118] On January 26, 2017, Dmitriev wrote to Gerson that his "boss"—an apparent reference to Putin—was asking if there had been any feedback on the proposal.[1119] Dmitriev said, "[w]e do not want to rush things and move at a comfortable speed. At the same time, my boss asked me to try to have the key US meetings in the next two weeks if possible."[1120] He informed Gerson that Putin and President Trump would speak by phone that Saturday, and noted that that information was "very confidential."[1121]

The same day, Dmitriev wrote to Nader that he had seen his "boss" again yesterday who had "emphasized that this is a great priority for us and that we need to build this communication channel to avoid bureaucracy."[1122] On January 28, 2017, Dmitriev texted Nader that he wanted "to see ifI can confirm to my boss that your friends may use some of the ideas from the 2 pager I sent you in the telephone call that will happen at 12 EST,"[1123] an apparent reference to the call scheduled between President Trump and Putin. Nader replied, "Definitely paper was so submitted to Team by Rick and me. They took it seriously!"[1124] After the call between President Trump and Putin occurred, Dmitriev wrote to Nader that "the call went very well. My boss wants me to continue making some public statements that us [sic] Russia cooperation is good and important."[1125] Gerson also wrote to Dmitriev to say that the call had gone well, and Dmitriev replied that the document they had drafted together "played an important role."[1126]

Gerson and Dmitriev appeared to stop communicating with one another in approximately March 2017, when the investment deal they had been working on together showed no signs of progressing.[1127]

3. Ambassador Kislyak's Meeting with Jared Kushner and Michael Flynn in Trump Tower Following the Election

On November 16, 2016, Catherine Vargas, an executive assistant to Kushner, received a request for a meeting with Russian Ambassador Sergey Kislyak.[1128] That same day, Vargas sent Kushner an email with the subject, "MISSED CALL: Russian Ambassador to the US, Sergey Ivanovich Kislyak . . . ."[1129] The text of the email read, "RE: setting up a time to meet w/you on 12/1. LMK how to proceed." Kushner responded in relevant part, "I think I do this one -- confirm with Dimitri [Simes of CNI] that this is the right guy."[1130] After reaching out to a colleague of Simes at CNI, Vargas reported back to Kushner that Kislyak was "the best go-to guy for routine matters in the US," while Yuri Ushakov, a Russian foreign policy advisor, was the contact for "more direct/substantial matters."[1131]

Bob Foresman, the UBS investment bank executive who had previously tried to transmit to candidate Trump an invitation to speak at an economic forum in Russia, *see* Volume I, Section IV.A.I .d.ii, *supra,* may have provided similar information to the Transition Team. According toForesman, at the end ofan early December 2016 meeting with incoming National Security Advisor Michael Flynn and his designated deputy (K.T. McFarland) in New York, Flynn asked Foresman for his thoughts on Kislyak. Foresman had not met Kislyak but told Flynn that, while Kislyak was an important person, Kislyak did not have a direct line to Putin.[1132] Foresman subsequently traveled to Moscow, inquired of a source he believed to be close to Putin, and heard back from that source that Ushakov would be the official channel for the incoming U.S. national security advisor.[1133] Foresman acknowledged that Flynn had not asked him to undertake that inquiry in Russia but told the Office that he nonetheless felt obligated to report the information back to Flynn, and that he worked to get a face-to-face meeting with Flynn in January 2017 so that he could do so.[1134] Email correspondence suggests that the meeting ultimately went forward,[1133] but Flynn has no recollection of it or of the earlier December meeting.[1136] (The investigation did not identify evidence of Flynn or Kushner meeting with Ushakov after being given his name.[1137]

In the meantime, although he had already formed the impression that Kislyak was not necessarily the right point of contact,[1138] Kushner went forward with the meeting that Kislyak had requested on November 16. It took place at Trump Tower on November 30, 2016.[1139] At Kushner's invitation, Flynn also attended; Bannon was invited but did not attend.[1140] During the meeting, which lasted approximately 30 minutes, Kushner expressed a desire on the part of the incoming Administration to start afresh with U.S.-Russian relations.[1141] Kushner also asked Kislyak to identify the best person (whether Kislyak or someone else) with whom to direct future discussions—someone who had contact with Putin and the ability to speak for him.[1142]

The three men also discussed U.S. policy toward Syria, and Kislyak floated the idea of having Russian generals brief the Transition Team on the topic using a secure communications line.[1143] After Flynn explained that there was no secure line in the Transition Team offices Kushner asked Kislyak if they could communicate using secure facilities at the Russian Embassy.[1144] Kislyak quickly rejected that idea.[1145]

4. Jared Kushner's Meeting with Sergey Gorkov

On December 6, 2016, the Russian Embassy reached out to Kushner's assistant to set up a second meeting between Kislyak and Kushner.[1146] Kushner declined several proposed meeting dates, but Kushner's assistant indicated that Kislyak was very insistent about securing a second meeting.[1147] Kushner told the Office that he did not want to take another meeting because he had already decided Kislyak was not the right channel for him to communicate with Russia, so he arranged to have one of his assistants, Avi Berkowitz, meet with Kislyak in his stead.[1148] Although embassy official Sergey Kuznetsov wrote to Berkowitz that Kislyak thought it "important" to "continue the conversation with Mr. Kushner in person,"[1149] Kislyak nonetheless agreed to meet instead with Berkowitz once it became apparent that Kushner was unlikely to take a meeting.

Berkowitz met with Kislyak on December 12, 2016, at Trump Tower.[1150] The meeting lasted only a few minutes, during which Kislyak indicated that he wanted Kushner to meet someone who had a direct line to Putin: Sergey Gorkov, the head of the Russian-government• owned bank Vnesheconombank (VEB).

Kushner agreed to meet with Gorkov.[1151] The one-on-one meeting took place the next day, December 13, 2016, at the Colony Capital building in Manhattan, where Kushner had previously scheduled meetings.[1152] VEB was (and is) the subject of Department of Treasury economic sanctions imposed in response to Russia's annexation of Crimea.[1153] Kushner did not, however, recall any discussion during his meeting with Gorkov about the sanctions against VEB or sanctions more generally.[1154] Kushner stated in an interview that he did not engage in any preparation for the meeting and that no one on the Transition Team even did a Google search for Gorkov's name.[1155]

At the start of the meeting, Gorkov presented Kushner with two gifts: a painting and a bag of soil from the town in Belarus where Kushner's family originated.[1156]

The accounts from Kushner and Gorkov differ as to whether the meeting was diplomatic or business in nature. Kushner told the Office that the meeting was diplomatic, with Gorkov expressing disappointment with U.S.-Russia relations under President Obama and hopes for improved relations with the incoming Administration.[1157] According to Kushner, although Gorkov told Kushner a little bit about his bank and made some statements about the Russian economy, the two did not discuss Kushner's companies or private business dealings of any kind.[1158] (At the time of the meeting, Kushner Companies had a debt obligation coming due on the building it owned at 666 Fifth Avenue, and there had been public reporting both about efforts to secure lending on the property and possible conflicts of interest for Kushner arising out of his company's borrowing from foreign lenders.[1159]

In contrast, in a 2017 public statement, VEB suggested Gorkov met with Kushner in Kushner's capacity as CEO of Kushner Companies for the purpose of discussing business, rather than as part of a diplomatic effort. In particular, VEB characterized Gorkov's meeting with Kushner as part of a series of "roadshow meetings" with "representatives of major US banks and business circles," which included "negotiations" and discussion of the "most promising business lines and sectors."[1160]

Foresman, the investment bank executive mentioned in Volume I, Sections IV.A.I and IV.B.3, *supra,* told the Office that he met with Gorkov and VEB deputy chairman Nikolay Tsekhomsky in Moscow just before Gorkov left for New York to meet Kushner.[1161] According to Foresman, Gorkov and Tsekhomsky told him that they were traveling to New York to discuss post• election issues with U.S. financial institutions, that their trip was sanctioned by Putin, and that they would be reporting back to Putin upon their return.[1162]

The investigation did not resolve the apparent conflict in the accounts of Kushner and Gorkov or determine whether the meeting was diplomatic in nature (as Kushner stated), focused on business (as VEB's public statement indicated), or whether it involved some combination of those matters or other matters. Regardless, the investigation did not identify evidence that Kushner and Gorkov engaged in any substantive follow-up after the meeting.

Rather, a few days after the meeting, Gorkov's assistant texted Kushner's assistant, "Hi, please inform your side that the information about the meeting had a very positive response!"[1163] Over the following weeks, the two assistants exchanged a handful of additional cordial texts.[1164] On February 8, 2017, Gorkov's assistant texted Kushner's assistant (Berkowitz) to try to set up another meeting, and followed up by text at least twice in the days that followed.[1165] According to Berkowitz, he did not respond to the meeting request in light of the press coverage regarding the Russia investigation, and did not tell Kushner about the meeting request.[1166]

5. Petr Aven's Outreach Efforts to the Transition Team

In December 2016, weeks after the one-on-one meeting with Putin described in Volume I, Section IV.B.1.b, *supra*, Petr Aven attended what he described as a separate "all-hands" oligarch meeting between Putin and Russia's most prominent businessmen.[1167] As in Aven's one-on-one meeting, a main topic of discussion at the oligarch meeting in December 2016 was the prospect of forthcoming U.S. economic sanctions.[1168]

After the December 2016 all-hands meeting, Aven tried to establish a connection to the Trump team. Aven instructed Richard Burt to make contact with the incoming Trump Administration. Burt was on the board of directors for LetterOne (LI), another company headed by Aven, and had done work for Alfa-Bank.[1169] Burt had previously served as U.S. ambassador to Germany and Assistant Secretary of State for European and Canadian Affairs, and one of his primary roles with Alfa-Bank and L1 was to facilitate introductions to business contacts in the United States and other Western countries.1'""

While at a L1 board meeting held in Luxembourg in late December 2016, Aven pulled Burt aside and told him that he had spoken to someone high in the Russian government who expressed interest in establishing a communications channel between the Kremlin and the Trump Transition Team.[1171] Aven asked for Burt's help in contacting members of the Transition Team.[1172] Although Burt had been responsible for helping Aven build connections in the past, Burt viewed Aven's request as unusual and outside the normal realm of his dealings with Aven.[1173]

Burt, who is a member of the board of CNI (discussed at Volume I, Section IV.A.4, *supra)[1174]*, decided to approach CNI president Dimitri Simes for help facilitating Aven's request, recalling that Simes had some relationship with Kushner.[1175] At the time, Simes was lobbying the Trump Transition Team, on Burt's behalf, to appoint Burt U.S. ambassador to Russia.[1176]

Burt contacted Simes by telephone and asked if he could arrange a meeting with Kushner to discuss setting up a high-level communications channel between Putin and the incoming Administration.[1177] Simes told the Office that he declined and stated to Burt that setting up such a channel was not a good idea in light of the media attention surrounding Russian influence in the U.S. presidential election.[1178] According to Simes, he understood that Burt was seeking a secret channel, and Simes did not want CNI to be seen as an intermediary between the Russian government and the incoming Administration.[1179] Based on what Simes had read in the media, he stated that he already had concerns that Trump's business connections could be exploited by Russia, and Simes said that he did not want CNI to have any involvement or apparent involvement in facilitating any connection.U'"

If this is unclear or you would like to discuss, don't hesitate to call.[1181]
According to Burt, the "very influential person" referenced in his email was Simes, and the reference to a "trusted third party" was a fabrication, as no such third

party existed. "Project A" was a term that Burt created for Aven's effort to help establish a communications channel between Russia and the Trump team, which he used in light of the sensitivities surrounding what Aven was requesting, especially in light of the recent attention to Russia's influence in the U.S. presidential election.[1182] According to Burt, his report that there was "interest" in a communications channel reflected Simes's views, not necessarily those of the Transition Team, and in any event, Burt acknowledged that he added some "hype" to that sentence to make it sound like there was more interest from the Transition Team than may have actually existed.[1183]

Aven replied to Burt's email on the same day, saying "Thank you. All clear."[1184] According to Aven, this statement indicated that he did not want the outreach to continue.[1185] Burt spoke to Aven some time thereafter about his attempt to make contact with the Trum team that the current environment made it impossible,

Burt did not recall discussing Aven's request with Simes again, nor did he recall speaking to anyone else about the request.[1186][1187]

In the first quarter of 2017, Aven met again with Putin and other Russian officials.[1188] At that meeting, Putin asked about Aven's attem t to build relations with the Trum Administration and Aven recounted his lack of success.[1189]

— [1190] Putin continued to inquire about Aven's efforts to connect to the Trump Administration in several subsequent quarterly meetings.[1191]

Aven also told Putin's chief of staff that he had been subpoenaed by the FBI.[1192] As part of that conversation, he reported that he had been asked by the FBI about whether he had worked to create a back channel between the Russian government and the Trump Administration.[1193]

According to Aven, the official showed no emotion in response to this report and did not appear to care.[1194]

6. Carter Page Contact with Deputy Prime Minister Arkady Dvorkovich

In December 2016, more than two months after he was removed from the Trump Campaign, former Campaign foreign policy advisor Carter Pa e a ain visited ████████████ ███████████████████ b█████████████████████.[1196]

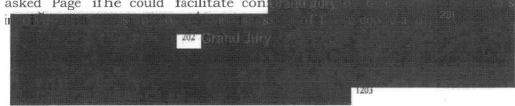

According to Konstantin Kilimnik, Paul Manafort's associate, Page also gave some individuals in Russia the impression that he had maintained his connections to President-Elect Trump. In a December 8, 2016 email intended for Manafort, Kilimnik wrote, "Carter Page is in Moscow today, sending messages he is authorized to talk to Russia on behalf of DT on a range of issues of mutual interest, including Ukraine."[1197]

On December 9, 2016, Page went to dinner with NES employees Shlomo Weber and Andrej Krickovic.[1198] Weber had contacted Dvorkovich to let him know that Page was in town and to invite him to stop by the dinner if he wished to do so, and Dvorkovich came to the restaurant for a few minutes to meet with Page.[1199] Dvorkovich congratulated Page on Trump's election and expressed interest in starting a dialogue between the United States and Russia.[1200] Dvorkovich asked Page if he could facilitate con██████████████████████████ i█████████████████████████████████[1201]███████████ [202] Grand Jury ██[1203]

7. Contacts With and Through Michael T. Flynn

Incoming National Security Advisor Michael Flynn was the Transition Team's primary conduit for communications with the Russian Ambassador and dealt with Russia on two sensitive matters during the transition period: a United Nations Security Council vote and the Russian government's reaction to the United States's imposition of sanctions for Russian interference in the 2016 election.[1207] Despite Kushner's conclusion that Kislyak did not wield influence inside the Russian government, the Transition Team turned to Flynn's relationship with Kislyak on both issues. As to the sanctions, Flynn spoke by phone to K.T. McFarland, his incoming deputy, to prepare for his call to Kislyak; McFarland was with the President-Elect and other senior members of the Transition Team at Mar-a-Lago at the time. Although transition officials at Mar• a-Lago had some concern about possible Russian reactions to the sanctions, the investigation did not identify evidence that the President-Elect asked Flynn to make any request to Kislyak. Flynn asked Kislyak not to escalate the situation in response to U.S. sanctions imposed on December 29, 2016, and Kislyak later reported to Flynn that Russia acceded to that request.

a. *United Nations Vote on Israeli Settlements*

On December 21, 2016, Egypt submitted a resolution to the United Nations Security Council calling on Israel to cease settlement activities in Palestinian territory.F''' The Security Council, which includes Russia, was scheduled to vote on the resolution the following day.[1209]

According to Flynn, the Transition Team regarded the vote as a significant issue and wanted to support Israel by opposing the resolution.[1211] On December 22, 2016, multiple members of the Transition Team, as well as President-Elect Trump, communicated with foreign government officials to determine their views on the resolution and to rally support to delay the vote or defeat the resolution.[1212] Kushner led the effort for the Transition Team; Flynn was responsible for the Russian government.[1213] Minutes after an early morning phone call with Kushner on December 22, Flynn called Kislyak.[1214] According to Flynn, he informed Kislyak about the vote and the Transition Team's opposition to the resolution, and requested that Russia vote against or delay the resolution.[1215] Later that day, President-Elect Trump spoke with Egyptian President Abdel Fattah al-Sisi about the vote.[1216] Ultimately, Egypt postponed the vote.[1217]

On December 23, 2016, Malaysia, New Zealand, Senegal, and Venezuela resubmitted the resolution.[1218] Throughout the day, members of the Transition Team continued to talk with foreign leaders about the resolution, with Flynn continuing to lead the outreach with the Russian government through Kislyak.[1219] When Flynn again spoke with Kislyak, Kislyak informed Flynn that if the resolution came to a vote, Russia would not vote against it.[1220] The resolution later passed 14-0, with the United States abstaining.[1221] There was speculation in the media that the Obama Administration would not oppose the resolution.P'?

b. U.S. Sanctions Against Russia

Flynn was also the Transition Team member who spoke with the Russian government when the Obama Administration imposed sanctions and other measures against Russia in response to Russia's interference in the 2016 presidential election. On December 28, 2016, then-President Obama signed Executive Order 13757, which took effect at 12:01 a.m. the following day and imposed sanctions on nine Russian individuals and entities.[1222] On December 29, 2016, the Obama Administration also expelled 35 Russian government officials and closed two Russian government-owned compounds in the United States.[1223]

During the rollout of the sanctions, President-Elect Trump and multiple Transition Team senior officials, including McFarland, Steve Bannon, and Reince Priebus, were staying at the Mar• a-Lago club in Palm Beach, Florida. Flynn was on vacation in the Dominican Republic,[1224] but was in daily contact with McFarland.[1223]

The Transition Team and President-Elect Trump were concerned that these sanctions would harm the United States's relationship with Russia.[1226] Although the details and timing of sanctions were unknown on December 28, 2016, the media began reporting that retaliatory measures from the Obama Administration against Russia were forthcoming.[1227] When asked about imposing sanctions on Russia for its alleged interference in the 2016 presidential election, President-Elect Trump told the media, "I think we ought to get on with our lives."[1228]

Russia initiated the outreach to the Transition Team. On the evening of December 28, 2016, Kislyak texted Flynn, "can you kindly call me back at your convenience."[1229] Flynn did not respond to the text message that evening. Someone from the Russian Embassy also called Flynn the next morning, at 10:38 a.m., but they did not talk.[1230]

The sanctions were announced publicly on December 29, 2016.[1231] At 1:53 p.m. that day, McFarland began exchanging emails with multiple Transition Team members and advisors about the impact the sanctions would have on the incoming Administration.[1232] At 2:07 p.m., a Transition Team member texted Flynn a link to a New York Times article about the sanctions[1233] At 2:29 p.m., McFarland called Flynn, but they did not talk.[1234] Shortly thereafter, McFarland and Bannon discussed the sanctions[1235]. According to McFarland, Bannon remarked that the sanctions would hurt their ability to have good relations with Russia, and that Russian escalation would make things more difficult.[1236] McFarland believed she told Bannon that Flynn was scheduled to talk to Kislyak later that night.[1237] McFarland also believed she may have discussed the sanctions with Priebus, and likewise told him that Flynn was scheduled to talk to Kislyak that night.[1238] A 3:14 p.m., Flynn texted a Transition Team member who was assisting McFarland, "Time for a call???"[1239]

The Transition Team member responded that McFarland was on the phone with Tom Bossert, a Transition Team senior official, to which Flynn responded, "Tit for tat w Russia not good. Russian AMBO reaching out to me today."[1240]

Flynn recalled that he chose not to communicate with Kislyak about the sanctions until he had heard from the team at Mar-a-Lago.[1241] He first spoke with Michael Ledeen,[1242] a Transition Team member who advised on foreign policy and national security matters, for 20 minutes.[1243]

Flynn then spoke with McFarland for almost 20 minutes to discuss what, if anything, to communicate to Kislyak about the sanctions.[1244] On that call, McFarland and Flynn discussed the sanctions, including their potential impact on the incoming Trump Administration's foreign policy goals.[1245] McFarland and Flynn also discussed that Transition Team members in Mar-a-Lago did not want Russia to escalate the situation.[1246] They both understood that Flynn would relay a message to Kislyak in hopes of making sure the situation would not get out of hand.[1247]

Immediately after speaking with McFarland, Flynn called and spoke with Kislyak.[1248]

Flynn discussed multiple topics with Kislyak, including the sanctions, scheduling a video teleconference between President-Elect Trump and Putin, an upcoming terrorism conference, and Russia's views about the Middle East.[1249] With respect to the sanctions, Flynn requested that Russia not escalate the situation, not get into a "tit for tat," and only respond to the sanctions in a reciprocal manner.[1250]

Multiple Transition Team members were aware that Flynn was speaking with Kislyak that day. In addition to her conversations with Bannon and Reince Priebus, at 4:43 p.m., McFarland sent an email to Transition Team members about the sanctions, informing the group that "Gen [F]lynn is talking to russian ambassador this evening."[1251] Less than an hour later, McFarland briefed President-Elect Trump. Bannon, Priebus, Sean Spicer, and other Transition Team members were present.[1252] During the briefing, President-Elect Trump asked McFarland if the Russians did "it," meaning the intrusions intended to influence the presidential election.[1253] McFarland said yes, and President-Elect Trump expressed doubt that it was the Russians.[1254] McFarland also discussed potential Russian responses to the sanctions, and said Russia's response would be an indicator of what the Russians wanted going forward.[1255] President-Elect Trump opined that the sanctions provided him with leverage to use with the Russians.[1256] McFarland recalled that at the end of the meeting, someone may have mentioned to President-Elect Trump that Flynn was speaking to the Russian ambassador that evening.[1257]

After the briefing, Flynn and McFarland spoke over the phone.[1258] Flynn reported on the substance of his call with Kislyak, including their discussion of the sanctions.[1259] According to McFarland, Flynn mentioned that the Russian response to the sanctions was not going to be escalatory because they wanted a good relationship with the incoming Administration.[1260]

McFarland also gave Flynn a summary of her recent briefing with President-Elect Trump.[1261]

The next day, December 30, 2016, Russian Foreign Minister Sergey Lavrov remarked that Russia would respond in kind to the sanctions.[1262] Putin superseded that comment two hours later, releasing a statement that Russia would not take retaliatory measures in response to the sanctions at that time.[1263] Hours later President-Elect Trump tweeted, "Great move on delay (by V. Putin)."[1264] Shortly thereafter, Flynn sent a text message to McFarland summarizing his call with Kislyak from the day before, which she emailed to Kushner, Bannon, Priebus, and other Transition Team members.[1265] The text message and email did not include sanctions as one of the topics discussed with Kislyak.[1266] Flynn told the Office that he did not document his discussion of sanctions because it could be perceived as getting in the way of the Obama Administration's foreign policy.[1267]

On December 31, 2016, Kislyak called Flynn and told him the request had been received at the highest levels and that Russia had chosen not to retaliate to the sanctions in response to the request.[1268] Two hours later, Flynn spoke with McFarland and relayed his conversation with Russia. He believed his phone call had made a difference.[1271] McFarland recalled congratulating Flynn in response.F'? Flynn spoke with other Transition Team members that day, but does not recall whether they discussed the sanctions.[1273] Flynn recalled discussing the sanctions with Bannon the next day and that Bannon appeared to know about Flynn's conversation with Kislyak.[1274] Bannon, for his part, recalled meeting with Flynn that day, but said that he did not remember discussing sanctions with him.[1275]

Additional information about Flynn's sanctions-related discussions with Kislyak, and the handling of those discussions by the Transition Team and the Trump Administration, is provided in Volume II of this report.

In sum, the investigation established multiple links between Trump Campaign officials and individuals tied to the Russian government. Those links included Russian offers of assistance to the Campaign. In some instances, the Campaign was receptive to the offer, while in other instances the Campaign officials shied away. Ultimately, the investigation did not establish that the Campaign coordinated or conspired with the Russian government in its election-interference activities.

****

288 For example, on August 18, 2015, on behalf of the editor-in-chief of the internet newspaper Vzglyad, Georgi Asatryan emailed campaign press secretary Hope Hicks asking for a phone or in-person candidate interview. 8/18/15 Email, Asatryan to Hicks. One day earlier, the publication's founder (and former Russian parliamentarian) Konstantin Rykov had registered two Russian websites-Trump2016.ru and DonaldTrump2016.ru. No interview took place.

289 See, e.g., Interview of Donald J. Trump, Jr, Senate Judiciary Committee, 1 15th Cong. 151-52 (Sept. 7, 2017) (discussing licensing deals of specific projects).

290 As noted in Volume I, Section 111.D.l, supra, in November 2018, Cohen pleaded guilty to making false statements to Congress concerning, among other things, the duration of the Trump Tower

Moscow project. See Information ,r 7(a), United States v. Michael Cohen, 1 :18-cr-850 (S.D.N.Y. Nov. 29,

2018), Doc. 2 ("Cohen Information").

291 See Interview of Donald J. Trump, Jr, Senate Judiciary Committee, 115th Cong. 13 (Sept. 7,

2017) ("Following the pageant the Trump Organization and Mr. Agalarov's company, Crocus Group, began preliminarily discussion [sic] potential real estate projects in Moscow."). As has been widely reported, the Miss Universe pageant-which Trump co-owned at the time-was held at the Agalarov-owned Crocus City Hall in Moscow in November 2013. Both groups were involved in organizing the pageant, and Aras Agalarov's son Emin was a musical performer at the event, which Trump attended.

292 Kaveladze 11/16/17 302, at 2, 4-6; OSC- KAV_00385 (12/6/13 Email, Trump Jr. to Kaveladze & E. Agalarov).

294

295 OSC-KAV_00452 (12/23/13 Email, Trump Jr. to Kaveladze & E. Agalarov).

296 See, e.g., OSC-KAV_01158 (Letter agreement signed by Trump Jr. & E. Agalarov); OSC· KAV_01147 (1/20/14 Email, Kaveladze to Trump Jr. et al.).

297 See, e.g., OSC-KAV_00972 (10/14/14 Email, McGee to Khoo et al.) (email from Crocus Group contractor about specifications); OSC-KAV_00540 (1/24/14 Email, McGee to Trump Jr. et al.).

298 See OSC-KAV 00631 (2/5/14 Email E. A%alarov to Ivanka Trump Jr. & Kaveladze); Goldstone Facebook post, 2/4/14 (8:01 a.m.)ji,t_fifh.,;\ftjj(DPilMU·-

299 See, e.g., OSC-KAV_00791 (6/3/14 Email, Kaveladze to Trump Jr. et al.; OSC-KAV_00799 (6/10/14 Email, Trump Jr. to Kaveladze et al.); OSC-KAV_00817 (6/16/14 Email, Trump Jr. to Kaveladze et al.).

300 OSC-KAV 00870 (7/17/14 Email, Khoo to McGee et al.).

301 OSC-KAV_00855 (8/4/14 Email, Khoo to McGee et al.).

302 OSC-KAV_00903 (9/29/14 Email, Tropea to McGee & Kaveladze (noting last response was on August 26, 2014)); OSC-KAV_00906 (9/29/14 Email, Kaveladze to Tropea & McGee (suggesting silence "proves my fear that those guys are bailing out of the project")); OSC-KAV_00972 (10/14/14 Email, McGee to Khoo et al.) (email from Crocus Group contractor about development specifications)).

303 OSC-KAV_01140 (11/24/14 Email, Khoo to McGee et al.).

307 Sater 9/19/17 302, at 3.

308 Rozov 1/25/18 302, at 1.

309 Rozov 1/25/18 302, at 1; see also 11 /2/15 Email, Cohen to Rozov et al. (sending letter ofintent).

31° Cohen 9/12/18 302, at 1-2, 4-6.

311 Cohen 9/12/18 302, at 5.

312 Cohen 9/12/18 302, at 4-5.

314 Cohen 9/12/18 302, at 12; see also Rtskhiladze 5/10/18 302, at I. ars 9/22/15 Email, Rtskhiladze to Nizharadz

316 9/24/15 Email, Rtskhiladze to Cohen.

317 9/24/15 Email, Rtskhiladze to Cohen.

318 9/27/15 Email, Rtskhiladze to Cohen.

319 Cohen 9/12/18 302, at 12

320 11/2/1 5 Email, Cohen to Rozov et al. (attachment) (hereinafter "LOI"); see also 1 0/13/15 Email, Sater to Cohen & Davis (attaching proposed letter of intent).

321 LO[, p. 2.

322 The LOI called for the Trump Organization to receive 5% of all gross sales up to $100 million;

4% of all gross sales from $100 million to $250 million; 3% of all gross sales from $250 million to $500 million; 2% of all gross sales from $500 million to $1 billion; and 1 % of all gross sales over $1 billion. LOI, Schedule 2.

323 LOI, Schedule 2.

324 LOI, Schedule 1.

325 LOI, Schedule 2.

326 Cohen 9/12/18 302, at 3.

327 11/3/15 Email, Sater to Cohen (12:14 p.m.).

328 11/3/15 Email, Sater to Cohen (12:40 p.m.).

329 Cohen 9/12/18 302, at 3-4; Cohen 8/7/18 302, at 15.

330   Sater 12/15/17 302, at 2.

331 Sater 12/15/17 302, at 3-4.

332 1 0/12/15 Email, Sater to Cohen (8:07 a.m.).

333

334 Ivanka Trump received an email from a woman who identified herself as "Lana E. Alexander," which said in part, "If you ask anyone who knows Russian to google my husband Dmitry Klokov, you'll see who he is close to and that he has done Putin's political campaigns." 11/16/15 Email, Erchova to l. Trump

335 11/16/15 Email, I. Trump to Cohen.

336 Cohen 8/7/18 302, at 17. During his interviews with the Office, Cohen still appeared to believe that the Klokov he spoke with was that Olympian. The investigation, however, established that the email address used to communicate with Cohen belongs to a different Dmitry Klokov, as described above.

337 11/18/15 Email, Klokov to Cohen (6:51 a.m.).

338 In July 2018, the Office received an unsolicited email purporting to be from Erchova, in which she wrote that "[a]t the end of2015 and beginning of2016 I was asked by my ex-husband to contact Ivanka Trump ... and offer cooperation to Trump's team on behalf of the Russian officials." 7/27/18 Email, Erchova to Special Counsel's Office. The email claimed that the officials wanted to offer candidate Trump "land in Crimea among other things and unofficial meeting with Putin." Id. In order to vet the email's claims, the Office responded requesting more details. The Office did not receive any reply.

339 11/18/15 Email, Cohen to Klokov (7: 15 a.m.).

340 11/18/15 Email, Klokov to Cohen (6:51 a.m.).

341   11/18/15 Email, Klokov to Cohen (6:51 a.m.) ("I would suggest separating your negotiations and our proposal to meet. I assure you, after the meeting level of projects and their capacity can be completely different, having the most important support.").

342 11/19/15 Email, Klokov to Cohen (7:40 a.m.).

343 11/19/15 Email, Cohen to Klokov (12:56 p.m.).

344 Cohen 9/18/18 302, at 12.

345 FS00004 (12/30/15 Text Message, Cohen to Sater (6:17 p.m.)).

346 1/11/16 Email, Cohen to pr_peskova@prpress.gof.ru (9:12 a.m.).

347 1/14/16 Email, Cohen to info@prpress.gov.ru (9:21 a.m.).

348 1/16/16 Email, Cohen to pr_peskova@prpress.gov.ru (10:28 a.m.).

349 Cohen Information ,i,i 4, 7. Cohen's interactions with President Trump and the President's lawyers when preparing his congressional testimony are discussed further in Volume II. See Vol. II, Section ll.K.3, infra.

350 1/20/16 Email, Poliakova to Cohen (5:57 a.m.) ("Mr. Cohen[,] I can't get through to both your phones. Pis, call me.").

351 Telephone records show a 20-minute call on January 20 2016 between Cohen and the number Poliakova provided in her email. Call Records of Michael Cohen After the call, Cohen saved Poliakova's contact information in his Trump Organization Outlook contact list. 1/20/16 Cohen Microsoft Outlook Entry (6:22 a.m.).

352 Cohen 9/12/18 302, at 2-3.

353 FSOOOI 1 (1/21/16 Text Messages, Sater to Cohen).

354 The invitation purported to be from Genbank, a Russian bank that was, according to Sater, working at the behest of a larger bank, VTB, and would consider providing financing. FS00008 (12/31/15

Text Messages, Sater & Cohen). Additional information about Genbank can be found infra.

355 FSOOOll (1/21/16 Text Message, Sater to Cohen (7:44 p.m.)); 1/21/16 Email, Sater to Cohen(6:49 p.m.).

356 1/25/16 Email, Sater to Cohen (12:01 p.m.) (attachment).

357 Cohen 9/12/18 302, at 6-7.

358 See, e.g., 12/1/15 Email, Sater to Cohen (12:41 p.m.) ("Please scan and send me a copy ofyour passport for the Russian Ministry of Foreign Affairs.").

359 Toll records show that Sater was speaking to Evgeny Dvoskin. Call Records of Felix Sater Dvoskin is an executive of Genbank, a large bank with lending focused in Crimea, Ukraine. At the time that Sater provided this financing letter to Cohen, Genbank was subject to U.S. government sanctions, see Russia/Ukraine-related Sanctions and Identifications, Office of Foreign Assets Control (Dec. 22, 2015), available at https://www.treasury.gov/resource-center/sanctions/OFAC• Enforcement/Pages/20151222.aspx. Dvoskin, who had been deported from the United States in 2000 for criminal activity, was under indictment in the United States for stock fraud under the aliases Eugene Slusker and Gene Shustar. See United States v. Rizzo, et al., 2:03-cr-63 (E.D.N.Y. Feb. 6, 2003).

360 12/19/15 Email, Sater to Cohen (10:50 a.m.); FS00002 (12/19/15 Text Messages, Sater to
Cohen, (10:53 a.m.).

361 FS00004 (12/19/15 Text Message, Cohen to Sater); ERT_0198-256 (12/19/15 Text Messages, Cohen & Sater).

362 Cohen 9/12/18 302, at 5.

363 On December 21, 2015, Sater sent Cohen a text message that read, "They need a copy of DJT passport," to which Cohen responded, "After I return from Moscow with you with a date for him." FS00004 (12/21 /15 Text Messages, Cohen & Sater).

364 FS00014 (4/20/16 Text Message, Sater to Cohen (9:06 p.m.)).

365 FS00015 (5/4/16 Text Message, Sater to Cohen (7:38 p.m.)).

366 FS00015 (5/4/16 Text Message, Cohen to Sater (8:03 p.m.)).

367 Sater 12/15/17 302, at 4.

368 FSOOO 16 (5/5/16 Text Messages, Sater to Cohen (6:26 & 6:27 a.m.)).

369 FS00016 (5/6/16 Text Messages, Cohen & Sater).

37° FSOOO 18 (6/9/16 Text Messages, Sater & Cohen).

371 6/13/16 Email, Sater to Cohen (2:10 p.m.).

372 FS00018 (6/13/16 Text Message, Sater to Cohen (2:20 p.m.)); 6/13/16 Email, Sater to Cohen.

373 Cohen 9/12/18 302, at 6-8.

374 FS00019 (6/14/16 Text Messages, Cohen & Sater (12:06 and 2:50 p.m.)).

375 Cohen 9/12/18 302, at 2.

376 Cohen 9/12/18 302, at 7.

377 12/21/15 Email, Mira to Ivanka Trump (6:57 a.m.) (attachments); TRUMPORG_l6_000057 (1/7/16 Email, I. Trump to Graff (9:18 a.m.)).

378 1/14/16 Email, Graff to Mira.

379 1/15/16 Email, Mira to Graff.

380 As explained in Volume II and Appendix C, on September 17, 2018, the Office sent written questions to the President's counsel. On November 20, 2018, the President provided written answers to those questions through counsel.

381 Written Responses of Donald J. Trump (Nov. 20, 2018), at 17 (Response to Question IV, Part (e)) ("[D]ocuments show that Ms. Graff prepared for my signature a brief response declining the invitation.").

382 Written Responses of Donald J. Trump (Nov. 20, 2018), at 17 (Response to Question IV, Part

(e)); see also TRUMPORG_16_000134 (unsigned letter dated March 31, 2016).

383 TRUMPORG_l6_000134 (unsigned letter).

384 TRUMPORG 16 000133 (3/31/16 Email, Graff to Macchia).

385 Foresman 10/17/18 302, at 3-4.

386 See TRUMPORG_l6_00136 (3/31/16 Email, Foresman to Graff); see also Foresman 10/17/18

302, at 3-4.

387 See TRUMPORG_l6_00136 (4/4/16 Email, Graff to Macchia).

388 See TRUMPORG_l6_00137 (4/26/16 Email, Foresman to Graft); TRUMPORG_l6_00141 (4/30/16 Email, Foresman to Graff).

389 See TRUMPORG_l6_00139 (4/27/16 Email, Graff to Foresman); TRUMPORG_16_00137 (4/27/16 Email, Graff to Lewandowski).

390 TRUMPORG_l6_00142 (5/2/16 Email, Graff to S. Miller); see also TRUMPORG_l6_00143 (5/2/16 Email, Graff to S. Miller) (forwarding March 2016 email from Foresman).

391 Foresman's contacts during the transition period are discussed further in Volume I, Section

IV.B.3, infra.

392 Foresman 10/17/18 302, at 4.

393 Foresman 10/17/18 302, at 8-9.

395 A Transcript of Donald Trump's Meeting with the Washington Post Editorial Board,

Washington Post (Mar. 21, 2016).

396 7/15/15 Linkedin Message, Papadopoulos to Lewandowski (6:57 a.m.); 9/30/15 Email, Glassner to Papadopoulos (7:42:21 a.m.).

397 Papadopoulos 8/10/17 302, at 2.

398 Papadopoulos 8/10/17 302, at 2; 2/4/16 Email, Papadopoulos to Idris.

399 London Centre of International Law Practice, at https://www.lcilp.org/ (via web.archive.org).

400 2/4/16 Email, Papadopoulos to Idris.

401 2/5/16 Email, Idris to Papadopoulos (6: 11 :25 p.m.); 2/6/16 Email, Idris to Papadopoulos(5:34:15 p.m.).

402 2/4/16 LinkedIn Message, Papadopoulos to Lewandowski (1 :28 p.m.); 2/4/16 Email, Papadopoulos to Glassner (2: 10:36 p.m.).

403 3/2/16 Email, Papadopoulos to Glassner (11: 17:23 a.m.).

404 3/2/16 Email, Lutes to Papadopoulos (10:08:15 p.m.).

405 Clovis 10/3/17 302 (1 of2), at 4.

406 Clovis 10/3/17 302 (1 of2), at 4.

407 ; 3/3/16 Email, Lutes to Clovis & Papadopoulos(6:05:47 p.m.).

408 3/6/16 Email, Papadopoulos to Clovis (4:24:21 p.m.).

409 Statement of Offense 1 4, United States v. George Papadopoulos, 1: 1 7-cr-182 (D.D.C. Oct. 5,

2017), Doc. 19 ("Papadopoulos Statement of Offense").

410 Papadopoulos 8/10/17 302, at 2.

411 Papadopoulos 8/10/17 302, at 2-3; Papadopoulos Statement of Offense ,r 5.

412 Papadopoulos 8/10/17 302, at 2-3; Stephanie Kirchgaessner et al., Joseph Mifsud: more questions than answers about mystery professor linked to Russia, The Guardian (Oct. 31, 2017) ("Link Campus University ... is headed by a former Italian interior minister named Vincenzo Scotti.").

413 Papadopoulos Statement of Offense ,r 5.

414 Papadopoulos 8/10/17 302, at 3

416 Papadopoulos Statement of Offense ,r 5.

417 Papadopoulos Statement of Offense ,r 5.

418 Papadopoulos 8/10/17 302, at 3; Papadopoulos 8/11/17 302, at 2.

419 Papadopoulos Statement of Offense ,r 5.

420 Papadopoulos 8/10/17 302, at 2.

421 Phillip Rucker & Robert Costa, Trump Questions Needfor NATO, Outlines Noninterventionist

Foreign Policy, Washington Post (Mar. 21, 2016).

422 Papadopoulos 8/10/17 302, at 3; 3/24/16 Text Messages, Mifsud & Papadopoulos.

423 Papadopoulos 8/10/17 302, at 3.

424 Papadopoulos 8/10/17 302, at 3; Papadopoulos 2/10/17 302, at 2-3; Papadopoulos Internet Search History (3/24/16) (revealing late-morning and early-afternoon searches on March 24, 2016 for "putin's niece," "olga putin," and "russian president niece olga," among other terms). m Papadopoulos 8/10/17 302, at 3.

426 Papadopoulos Statement of Offense ,i 8 n. l.

427 3/24/16 Email, Papadopoulos to Page et al. (8:48:21 a.m.).

428 Papadopoulos's statements to the Campaign were false. As noted above, the woman he met was not Putin's niece, he had not met the Russian Ambassador in London, and the Ambassador did not also serve as Russia's Deputy Foreign Minister.

429 3/24/16 Email, Papadopoulos to Page et al. (8:48:21 a.m.).

431 3/24/16 Email, Clovis to Papadopoulos et al. (8:55:04 a.m.).

432 Papadopoulos 8/10/17 302, at 4; Papadopoulos 8/11 /17 302, at 3.

433 Sessions 1/17/18 302, at 16-17.

434 Papadopoulos 8/10/17 302, at 4.

435 Papadopoulos 8/10/17 302, at 4.

436 Papadopoulos 8/10/17 302, at 4.

437 Papadopoulos Statement of Offense ,r 9; see Gordon 8/29/17 302, at 14; Carafano 9/12/17 302, at 2; Hoskins 9/14/17 302, at 1.

438 Papadopoulos 8/10/17 302, at 4-5; Gordon 9/7/17 302, at 4-5.

439 Papadopoulos 8/10/17 302, at 5; Papadopoulos 8/11/17 302, at 3.

440 Sessions 1/17/18 302, at 17; Gordon 9/7/17 302, at 5; Hoskins 9/14/17 302, at 1; Carafano 9/12/17 302, at 2.

441 Papadopoulos 8/10/17 302, at 4-5; Papadopoulos 8/11/17 302, at 3; Papadopoulos 9/20/17 302,

442 Papadopoulos Statement of Offense j 10.

443 Papadopoulos Statement of Offense n 10-15.

444 3/29/16 Emails, Mifsud to Polonskaya (3:39 a.rn. and 5:36 a.m.).

445 4/10/16 Email, Papadopoulos to Polonskaya (2:45:59 p.m.).

446 4/11/16 Email, Polonskaya to Papadopoulos (3: 11 :24 a.m.).

447 4/11/16 Email, Papadopoulos to Polonskaya (9:21 :56 a.m.).

448 4/11/16 Email, Mifsud to Papadopoulos (11:43:53).

449 Papadopoulos Statement of Offense j lO(c).

450 Anton Troianovski, Putin Ally Warns ofArms Race as Russia Considers Response to US. Nuclear Stance, Washington Post (Feb. 10, 2018).

451 4/11/16 Email, Papadopoulos to Mifsud (11 :51 :53 a.m.).

452 4/12/16 Email, Polonskaya to Papadopoulos (4:47:06 a.m.).

453 Papadopoulos 9/19/17 302, at 7.

454 4/12/16 Email, Mifsud to Papadopoulos (5:44:39 a.m.) (forwarding Libya-related document); 4/12/16 Email, Mifsud to Papadopoulos & Obaid (10:28:20 a.m.); Papadopoulos Internet Search History (Apr. 11, 2016 10:56:49 p.m.) (search for "andaz hotel liverpool street"); 4/12/16 Text Messages, Mifsud & Papadopoulos.

455 See, e.g., 4/18/16 Email, Mifsud to Papadopoulos (8:04:54 a.m.).

456 Papadopoulos 8/10/17 302, at 5.

457 Papadopoulos Statement of Offense ,r 11.

458 During the campaign period, Papadopoulos connected over LinkedIn with several MFA• affiliated individuals in addition to Timofeev.   On April 25, 2016, he connected with Dmitry Andreyko, publicly identified as a First

Secretary at the Russian Embassy in Ireland. In July 2016, he connected with Yuriy Melnik, the spokesperson for the Russian Embassy in Washington and with Alexey Krasilnikov,

publicly identified as a counselor with the MFA. And on September 16, 2016, he con

Nalobin also identified as an MFA official. See Papadopoulos Linked In Connections 1111111111111111

459 Papadopoulos Statement of Offense ,r 11.

460 Papadopoulos 8/10/17 302, at 5; Papadopoulos 9/19/17 302, at 10.

461 4/25/16 Email, Timofeev to Papadopoulos (8:16:35 a.m.).

462 4/22/16 Email, Mifsud to Papadopoulos (12:41:01 a.m.).

463 Papadopoulos Statement ofOffense 14; 4/25/16 Text Messages, Mifsud & Papadopoulos.

464 Papadopoulos Statement of Offense   14.

46s This information is contained in the FBI case-opening document and related materials.   :i:he iAf.erm!lticA is !av+' eAf.ereemeAt seAsitive (LES) BAS must be tfeatee aeeereiAgly iA BAY eifterAal eisseffliAatieA. The foreign government conveyed this information to the U.S. government on July 26, 2016, a few days after WikiLeaks's release of Clinton-related emails. The FBI opened its investigation of potential coordination between Russia and the Trump Campaign a few days later based on the information.

466 4/25/16 Email, Papadopoulos to S. Miller (8:12:44 p.m.).

467 4/27/16 Email, Papadopoulos to S. Miller (6:55:58 p.m.).

468 4/27/16 Email, Papadopoulos to Lewandowski (7:15:14 p.m.).

469 5/4/16 Email, Papadopoulos to Lewandowski (8:14:49 a.m.).

470 5/5/16 Email, Papadopoulos to Clovis (7:15:21 p.m.).

471 5/21/16 Email, Papadopoulos to Manafort (2:30: 14 p.m.).

472 Papadopoulos Statement ofOffense 19 n.2.

473 6/1/16 Email, Papadopoulos to Lewandowski (3 :08: 18 p.m.).

474 6/1/16 Email, Lewandowski to Papadopoulos (3:20:03 p.m.); 6/1/16 Email, Papadopoulos toClovis (3:29:14 p.m.).

 475 6/1/16 Email, Papadopoulos to Clovis (3:29:14 p.m.). Papadopoulos's email coincided in time with another message to Clovis suggesting a Trump-Putin meeting. First, on May 15, 2016, David Klein• a distant relative of then-Trump Organization lawyer Jason Greenblatt-emailed Clovis about a potential Campaign meeting with Berel Lazar, the Chief Rabbi of Russia. The email stated that Klein had contacted Lazar in February about a possible Trump-Putin meeting and that Lazar was "a very close confidante of Putin." DJTFPOOOl 1547 (5/15/16 Email, Klein to Clovis (5:45:24 p.m.)). The investigation did not find evidence that Clovis responded to Klein's email or that any further contacts of significance came out of Klein's subsequent meeting with Greenblatt and Rabbi Lazar at Trump Tower. Klein 8/30/18 302, at 2.

476 Papadopoulos Statement of Offense, 2 l(a).

477

478 6/19/16 Email, Papadopoulos to Lewandowski (I: 11: 11 p.m.).

479 6/19/16 Email, Papadopoulos to Lewandowski (1: 11: 11 p.m.).

480 Papadopoulos Statement of Offense, 21; 7/14/16 Email, Papadopoulos to Timofeev (11 :57:24 p.m.); 7/15/16 Email, Papadopoulos to Mifsud; 7/27/16 Email, Papadopoulos to Mifsud (2:14:18 p.m.).

481 Papadopoulos 9/19/17 302, at 16-17; 9th TAG Summit in Washington DC, Transatlantic

Parliament Group on Counter Terrorism.

482 9th TAG Summit in Washington DC, Transatlantic Parliament Group on Counter Terrorism.

483

484 Papadopoulos 9/19/17 302, at 16-17.

485 7/11/16 Email, Phares to Papadopoulos.

486 7/12/16 Email, Phares to Papadopoulos (14:52:29).

487 7/27/16 Email, Papadopoulos to Mifsud (14:14:18).

488 Papadopoulos 9/20/17 302, at 3.

489 Papadopoulos declined to assist in deciphering his notes, telling investigators that he could not read his own handwriting from the journal. Papadopoulos 9/19/17 302, at 21. The notes, however, appear to read as listed in the column to the left ofthe image above.

490 8/15/16 Email, Papadopoulos to Clovis (11 :59:07 a.m.).

491 8/15/16 Email, Clovis to Papadopoulos (12:01 :45 p.m.).

492 George Papadopoulos: Sanctions Have Done Little More Than to Turn Russia Towards China,

Interfax (Sept. 30, 2016).

493 Papadopoulos 9/19/17 302, at 14-15; Def. Sent. Mem., United States v. George Papadopoulos, l:17-cr-182 (D.D.C. Aug. 31, 2018), Doc. 45.

494 See footnote 465 of Volume I, Section IV.A.2.d, supra.

495 Papadopoulos 8/10/17 302, at 5; Papadopoulos 8/11/17 302, at 5; Papadopoulos 9/20/17 302,

at 2.

496 S. Miller 12/14/17 302, at 10.

499

500 7/15/16 Linkedln Message, Millian to Papadopoulos.

501 7/15/16 Linkedln Message, Millian to Papadopoulos.

502 7/22/16 Facebook Message, Papadopoulos to Timofeev (7:40:23 p.m.); 7/26/16 Facebook

Message, Papadopoulos to Timofeev (3:08:57 p.m.).

503 7/23/16 Facebook Message, Timofeev to Papadopoulos (4:31:37 a.m.); 7/26/16 Facebook

Message, Timofeev to Papadopoulos (3:37: 16 p.m.).

504 7/16/16 Text Messages, Papadopoulos & Millian (7:55:43 p.m.).

505 7/30/16 Text Messages, Papadopoulos & Millian (5:38 & 6:05 p.m.); 7/31/16 Text Messages, Millian & Papadopoulos (3:48 & 4:18 p.m.); 8/1/16 Text Message, Millian to Papadopoulos (8:19 p.m.).

506 8/2/16 Text Messages, Millian & Papadopoulos (3 :04 & 3 :05 p.m.); 8/3/16 Facebook Messages, Papadopoulos & Millian (4:07:37 a.m. & 1:11:58 p.m.).

507 7/31/16 Email, Papadopoulos to Denysyk (12:29:59 p.m.).

508 7/31/16 Email, Denysyk to Papadopoulos (21 :54:52).

509 8/23/16 Facebook Message, Millian to Papadopoulos (2:55:36 a.m.).

510 Papadopoulos 9/20/17 302, at 2.

511 11/10/16 Facebook Message, Millian to Papadopoulos (9:35:05 p.m.).

512 11/14/16 Facebook Message, Millian to Papadopoulos (1:32:11 a.m.).

513 Papadopoulos 9/19/17 302, at 19.

514 E.g., 11/29/16 Facebook Messages, Papadopoulos & Millian (5:09 - 5:11 p.m.); 12/7/16 Facebook Message, Millian to Papadopoulos (5:10:54 p.m.).

515 1/20/17 Facebook Messages, Papadopoulos & Millian (4:37-4:39 a.m.).

516 Page was interviewed b Counsel's appointment.

517 Testimony of Carter Page, Hearing Before the US. House of Representatives, Permanent Select Committee on Intelligence, 115th Cong. 40 (Nov. 2, 2017) (exhibit).

518 Page 3/30/17 302, at 10.

519

520

521

523

524

525

Complaint j'[22, 24, 32, United States v. Buryakov, 1: 15-mj-215 (S.D.N.Y. Jan. 23, 2015), Doc. 1 ("Buryakov Complaint").

526 Buryakov Complaint 1 34.

527 Buryakov Complaint 1 34.

528 Buryakov Complaint'[32

529 Buryakov Complaint.

530 Buryakov Complaint.

531 Buryakov Complaint.

532 See Buryakov Com Jaint· see also Indictment United States v. Buryakov, 1: 15-cr-73 (S.D.N. Y. Feb. 9, 2015), Doc. 10;

534

536 Page 3/16/17 302, at 4;

537 Page 3/30/17 302, at 6; Page 3/31/17 302, at 1.

538 Page 3/31/17 302, at I.

539 Page 3/16/17 302, at 1;

540 Page 3/10/17 302, at 2.

541 See, e.g., 1/30/16 Email, Page to Glassner et al.; 3/17/16 Email, Page to Clovis (attaching a "President's Daily Brief' prepared by Page that discussed the "severe de radation of U.S.-Russia relations following Washington's meddling" in Ukraine);

542 1/30/16 Email, Page to Glassner et al.

543 1/30/16 Email, Page to Glassner et al.

544   1/30/16 Email, Page to Glassner et al.

545

546 A Transcript of DonaldWashington Post (Mar. 21, 2016);

549 See, e.g., 3/28/16 Email, Clovis to Lewandowski et al. (forwarding notesprepared by Page and stating, "I wanted to let you know the type of work some of our advisors are capable of."). sso Page 3/16/17 302, at 2-3; Page 3/10/17 302, at 3.

551 S. Weber 7/28/17 302, at 3.

552 Y. Weber 6/1/17 302, at 4-5; S. Weber 7/28/17 302, at 3.

553 See Y. Weber 6/1/17 302, at 4; S. Weber 7/28/17 302, at 3.m De. Klimentov 6/9/17 302, at 2.

555 S. Weber 7/28/17 302, at 3.

556 See 5/16/16 Email, Page to Phares et al. (referring to submission of a "campaign advisor request

557 ; 5/16/16 Email, Page to Phares et al.

558 6/19/16 Email, Page to Gordon et al.

559 6/19/16 Email, Lewandowski to Page et al.

s63 7/5/16 Email, Klimentov to Zakharova (translated).

s64 Dm. Klimentov 11/27/18 302, at 1-2.

sss 7/6/16 Email, Peskov to Klimentov (translated).

s66 Page 3/10/17 3 02, at 3.

s67   See Carter W. Page, The Lecture of Trump's Advisor Carter Page in Moscow, YouTube Channel Katehon Think Tank, Posted July 7, 2016, available at https://www.youtube.com/watch? time_continue=28&v=lCYF29saA9w. Page also provided the FBI with a copy of his speech and slides from the speech. See Carter Page, "The Evolution of the World Economy: Trends and Potential," Speech at National Economic Speech (July 7, 2016).

s68 Page 3/10/17 302, at 3.

s69 Page 3/16/17 302, at 3.

S?o S. Weber 7/28/17 302, at 4.

571 m Page 3/10/17 302, at 3; Page 3/30/17 302, at 3; Page 3/31/17 302, at 2. m Page 3/30/17 302, at 3.

576 Page 3/10/17 302, at 3; Page 3/30/17 302, at 7; Page 3/31/17 302, at 2.

577

578

579

580

581

582 7/8/16 Email, Page to Dahl & Gordon.

583 Page 3/10/17 302, at 4; Page 3/16/17 302, at 3.

584 Page 3/10/17 302, at 4; Page 3/16/17 302, at 3. SSS   Page to Gordon & Schmitz.

; 7/23/16 Email, Page to Clovis; 7/25/16 Email,

586

587   See, e.g., Steven Mufson & Tom Hamburger, Trump Advisor's Public Comments, Ties to Moscow Stir Unease in Both Parties, Washington Post (Aug. 5, 2016).

588 Michael Isikoff, U.S. Intel Officials Probe Ties Between Trump Adviser and Kremlin, Yahoo! News (Sept. 23, 2016).

589 Michael Isikoff, U.S. Intel Officials Probe Ties Between Trump Adviser and Kremlin, Yahoo! News (Sept. 23, 2016); see also 9/25/16 Email, Hicks to Conway & Bannon (instructing that inquiries about Page should be answered with "[h]e was announced as an informal adviser in March.   Since then he has had no role or official contact with the campaign. We have no knowledge of activities past or present and he now officially has been removed from all lists etc.").

590 Page 3/16/17 302, at 2; see, e.g., 9/23/16 Email, J. Miller to Bannon & S. Miller (discussing plans to remove Page from the campaign). "Transition Online Form," 11/14/16

593 Simes 3/8/18 302, at 1-2.

594 About the Center, CNI, available at https://cftni.org/about/.

595   Advisory Counsel, CNI, available at https://web.archive.org/web/20161030025331/ http://cftni.org/about/advisory-council/; Simes 3/8/18 302, at 3-4; Saunders 2/15/18 302, at 4; Sessions 1/17/18 302, at 16.

596 Simes 3/8/18 302, at 2

. 597 Simes 3/8/18 302, at 1-2; Simes 3/27/18 302, at 19.

598 Simes 3/27/18 302, at 10-15.

599 COOOl 1656 (Rethinking U.S.-Russia Relations, CNI (Apr. 18, 2015)).

600 Simes 3/8/18 302, at 5; Saunders 2/15/18 302, at 29-30; Zakheim 1/25/18 302, at 3.

601 Simes 3/8/18 302, at 6; C00006784 (3/11/16 Email, Gilbride to Saunders (3:43:12 p.m.); cf Zakheim 1/25/18 302, at I (Kissinger was CNI's "Honorary Chairman of the Board"); Boyd 1/24/18 302, at 2; P. Sanders 2/15/18 302, at 5.

602 Simes 3/8/18 302, at 5-6; Simes 3/27/18 302, at 2.

603 Simes 3/8/18 302, at 6; Kushner 4/11 /18 302 at 2.

604 Kushner 4/11/18 302, at 2.

605 Simes 3/8/18 302, at 6-7

606   see Volume I, Section IV.A.2, supra.

607 Simes 3/8/18 302, at 7-9.

608 Simes 3/8/18 302, at 7-8.

609 Simes 3/8/18 302, at 8; see also Boyd 1/24/18 302, at 2.

61° C00008187 (6/17/16 Email, Simes to Gordon (3:35:45 p.m.)).

611 Simes 3/8/18 302, at 7.

612 Simes 3/8/18 302, at 8-11; C00008923 (4/6/16 Email, Simes to Burt (2:22:28 p.m.)); Burt 2/9/18 302, at 7.

613 C00008551 (4/17/16 Email, Kushner to Simes (2:44:25 p.m.)); C00006759 (4/14/16 Email Kushner to Simes & S. Miller (12:30 p.m.)).

614 Burt 2/9/18 302, at 7; Saunders 2/15/18 302, at 7-8.

615 Simes 3/8/18 302, at 13; Saunders 2/15/18 302, at 7-8.

616 Simes 3/8/18 302, at 13; Saunders 2/15/18 302, at7-8.

617 Saunders 2/15/18 302, at 8; Simes 3/8/18 302, at 12; C00003834-43 (4/22/16 Email, Simes to Boyd et al. (8:47 a.m.)).

618 Simes 3/8/18 302, at 12, 18; Saunders 2/15/18 302, at 11.

619 Saunders 2/15/18 302, at 11-12; C00006651-57 (Mayflower Group Sales Agreement).

620 Saunders 2/15/18 302, at 12-13.

621 Saunders 2/15/18 302, at 12.

622 C00002575 (Attendee List); C00008536 (4/25/16 Email, Simes to Kushner (4:53:45 p.m.)).

623 Simes 3/8/18 302, at 19-20.

624 Simes 3/8/18 302, at 21.

625 Simes 3/8/18 302, at 21.

626 Simes 3/8/18 302, at 21.

627 Simes 3/8/18 302, at 21.

628 Kushner 4/11/18 302, at 4.

629 See, e.g., Ken Dilanian, Did Trump, Kushner, Sessions Have an Undisclosed Meeting With Russian?, NBC News (June 1, 2016); Julia Ioffe, Why Did Jef!Sessions Really Meet With Sergey Kislyak, The Atlantic (June 13, 2017).

630 Sessions 1/17/18 302, at 22.

631 Simes 3/8/18 302, at 21; Saunders 2/15/18 302, at 14, 21; Boyd 1/24/18 302, at 3-4; Heilbrunn 2/1/18 302, at 6; Statement Regarding President Trump's April 27, 2016 Foreign Policy Speech at the Center/or the National Interest, CNI (Mar. 8, 2017).

632 Simes 3/8/18 302, at 22; Heilbrunn 2/1/18 302, at 7.

633 Luff 1/30/18 302, at 4.

634 Saunders 2/15/18 302, at 15.

635 Sessions 1/17/18 302, at 22; Saunders 2/15/18 302, at 17.

636 Saunders 2/15/18 302, at 17; C00004779-80 (5/23/16 Email, Cantelmo to Saunders & Hagberg (9:30: 12 a.m.); C00004362 (5/23/16 Email, Bauman to Cantelmo et al. (2:02:32 a.m.).

637 C00004362 (5/23/16 Email Bauman to Cantelmo et al. (2:02:32 a.m.).

638 Sessions l/17/18 302, at 22.

639 Boyd 1/24/18 302, at 4.

640 Simes 3/8/18 302, at 23; Saunders 2/15/18 302, at 18; Heilbrunn 2/1/18 302, at 7.

641 Simes 3/8/18 302, at 31; Saunders 2/15/18 302, at 19; Burt 2/9/18 302, at 9-10; Khalilzad 1/9/1302, at 5.

642 Butt 2/9/18 302, at 9-1 O; Khalilzad 1/9/18 302, at 1-2, 5.

643 Khalilzad 1/9/18 302, at 5-6.

644 Simes 3/8/18 302, at 31; Burt 2/9/18 302, at 9-1 O; Khalilzad 1/9/18 302, at 5.

645 Saunders 2/15/18 302, at 20.

646 Khalilzad 1/9/18 302, at 6.

647 Saunders 2/15/18 302, at 19-20.

648 Simes 3/8/18 302, at 27.

649 Simes 3/8/18 302, at 27.

650 Simes 3/8/18 302, at 27.

651 Simes 3/8/18 302, at 27. During this period of time, the Campaign received a request for a high• level Campaign official to meet with an officer at a Russian state-owned bank "to discuss an offer [that officer] claims to be carrying from President Putin to meet with" candidate Trump. NOSC00005653 (5/17/16 Email, Dearborn to Kushner (8: 12 a.m.j). Copying Manafort and Gates, Kushner responded, "Pass on this. A lot of people come claiming to carry messages. Very few are able to verify. For now I think we decline such meetings. Most likely these people go back home and claim they have special access to gain importance for themselves. Be careful." NOSC00005653 (5/17/16 Email, Kushner to Dearborn).

652 Kushner 4/11 /18 302, at 11-13.

655 C00007981 (8/9/16 Email, Simes to Kushner (6:09:21 p.m.)).

656 DJTFP00023459 (8/10/16 Email, Kushner to S. Miller et al. (11 :30: 13 a.m.)).

657 DJTFP00023484 (8/11/16 Email, Hagan to Manafort (5:57:15 p.m.)).

658 Simes 3/8/18 302, at 29-30; Simes 3/27/18 302, at 6; Kushner 4/11/18 302, at 12.

659 Simes 3/8/18 302, at 30; Simes 3/27/18 302, at 6.

660 Simes 3/8/18 302, at 30.

661 Simes 3/8/18 302, at 30; Simes 3/27/18 302, at 6.

662 Kushner 4/11/18 302, at 12

670 Goldstone 2/8/18 302, at 1-2; Beniaminov 1/6/18 302,

671 Goldstone 2/8/18 302, at 1-5; DJTJR00008 (2/29/19 Email, Goldstone to Trump Jr.); Beniaminov 1/6/18 302, at 3; Shugart 9/25/17 302, at 2; TRUMPORG_18_001325 (6/21/13 Email, Goldstone to Graft); TRUMPORG_18_001013 (6/24/13 Email, Goldstone to Graff); TRUMPORG_18_001014 (6/24/13 Email, Graff to Shugart); TRUMPORG_18_001018 (6/26/13 Email, Graff to Goldstone); TRUMPORG_18_001022 (6/27/13 Email, Graff to L. Kelly); TRUMPORG_18_001333 (9/12/13 Email, Goldstone to Graff, Shugart); MU000004289 (7/27/13 Email, Goldstone to Graff, Shugart).

672

673

674see Goldstone 2/,8/18 302, at 6-7.

675

676 In December 2018, a grand jury in the Southern District of New York returned an indictment charging Veselnitskaya with obstructing thePrevezon litigation discussed in the text above. See Indictment, United States v. Natalia Vladimirovna Veselnitskaya, No. 18-cr-904 (S.D.N.Y.). The indictment alleges, among other things, that

Veselnitskaya lied to the district court about her relationship to the Russian Prosecutor General's Office and her involvement in responding to a U.S. document request sent to the Russian government.

677 Veselnitska a 11/20/17 Statement to the Senate Committee on the Judiciary, at 2;-

678 Testimony of Natalia Veselnitskaya Before the Senate Committee on Judiciary (Nov. 20, 2017) at 33; Keir Simmons & Rachel Elbaum, Russian Lawyer Veselnitskaya Says She Didn't Give Trump Jr. Info on Clinton, NBC News (July 11, 2017); Maria Tsvetkova & Jack Stubbs, Moscow Lawyer Who Met Trump Jr. Had Russian Spy Agency As Client, Reuters (July 21, 2017); Andrew E. Kramer & Sharon Lafraniere, Lawyer Who Was Said to Have Dirt on Clinton Had Closer Ties to Kremlin than She Let On, New York Times (Apr. 27, 2018).

679 See Pub. L. No. 112-208 §§ 402, 404(a)(l), 126 Stat. 1502, 1502-1506. Sergei Magnitsky was a Russian tax specialist who worked for William Browder, a former investment fund manager in Russia. Browder hired Magnitsky to investigate tax fraud by Russian officials, and Magnitsky was charged with helping Browder embezzle money. After Magnitsky died in a Russian prison, Browder lobbied Congress to pass the Magnitsky Act. See, e.g., Andrew E. Kramer, Turning Tables in Magnitsky Case, Russia Accuses Nemesis of Murder, New York Times (Oct. 22, 2017); Testimony of Natalia Veselnitskaya Before the Senate Committee on Judiciary (Nov. 20, 2017), Exhibits at 1-4; Rosie Gray, Bill Browder's Testimony to the Senate Judiciary Committee, The Atlantic (July 25, 2017).

680 Ellen Barry, Russia Bars 18 Americans After Sanctions by US, New York Times (Apr. 13, 2013); Tom Porter, Supporters of the Magni/sky Act Claim They've Been Targets of Russian Assassination and Kidnapping Bids, Newsweek (July 16, 2017).

681 Testimony of Natalia Veselnitskaya Before the Senate Committee on Judiciary (Nov. 20, 2017), at 21.

682 See Veselnitskaya Deel., United States v. Prevezon Holdings, Ltd., No. 13-cv-6326 (S.D.N.Y.); see Prevezon Holdings, Second Amended Complaint; Prevezon Holdings, Mem. and Order; Prevezon Holdings, Deposition of Oleg Lurie.

683 See Gribbin 8/31/17 302, at 1-2 & lA (undated one-page document given to congressional delegation). The Russian Prosecutor General is an official with broad national responsibilities in the Russian legal system. See Federal Law on the Prosecutor's Office of the Russian Federation (1992, amended 2004).

684 RG000006l (6/3/16 Email, Goldstone to Trump Jr.); DJTJR00446 (6/3/16 Email, Goldstone to Donald Trump Jr.); @DonaldJTrumpJr 07/11/17 (11 :00) Tweet.

685 DJTJR00446 (6/3/16 Email, Trump Jr. to Goldstone); @DonaldJTrumpJr 07/11/17 (11 :00) Tweet; RG000061 (6/3/16 Email, Trump Jr. to Goldstone).

686 RG000062 (6/3/16 Email, Goldstone & Trump Jr.).

687 RG000063 (6/6/16 Email, A. Agalarov to Goldstone); RG000064 (6/6/16 Email, Goldstone to A. Agalarov).

688 RG000065 (6/6/16 Email, Goldstone to Trump Jr.); DJTJR00446 (6/6/16 Email, Goldstone to Trump Jr.).

689 DJTJR00445 (6/6/16 Email, Goldstone and Trump Jr.); RG000065-67 (6/6/16 Email, Goldstone and Trump Jr.); [Grand Jury]

690 DJTJR00499 (Call Records of Donald Trump Jr. [Grand Jury] of Donald Trump Jr. [Grand Jury].

691 Kaveladze 11/16/17 302, at 6; [Grand Jury]

692 Kaveladze 11/16/17 302, at 1-2; [Grand Jury] Beniaminov 1/6/18 302, at 2-3; [Grand Jury]

693 Kaveladze 11/16/17 302, at 6.

699 NOSC0000007-08 (6/8/18 Email, Kushner to Vargas).

700 NOSC00000039-42 (6/8/16 Email, Trwnp Jr. to Kushner & Manafort); DJTJR00485 (6/8/16 Email, Trump Jr. to Kushner & Manafort).

701 NOSC0000004 (6/8/16 Email, Kushner to Vargas).

702 6/8/16 Email, Manafort to Trump Jr.

703 Gates l/30/18 302, at 7; Gates 3/1/18 302, at 3-4. Although the March 1 302 refers to "June 19," that is likely a typographical error; external emails indicate that a meeting with those participants occurred on June 6. See NOSC00023603 (6/6/16 Email, Gates to Trump Jr. et al.).

704 Gates 1/30/18 302, at 7. Aras Agalarov is originally from Azerbaijan, and public reporting indicates that his company, the Crocus Group, has done substantial work in Kyrgyzstan. See Neil MacFarquhar, A Russian Developer Helps Out the Kremlin on Occasion. Was He a Conduit to Trump?, New York Times (July 16, 2017).

7os Gates 3/1/18 302, at 3-4.

706 Hicks 12/7/17 302, at 6.

707 Kushner 4/11/18 302, at 8.

708 Cohen 8/7/18 302, at 4-6.

709 Cohen 8/7/18 302, at 4-5.

71° Cohen 9/12/18 302, at 15-16.

711 Interview of Donald J. Trump, Jr., Senate Judiciary Committee, 11 Sth Cong. 28-29, 84, 94-95 (Sept. 7, 2017). The Senate Judiciary Committee interview was not under oath, but Trump Jr. was advised that it is a violation of 18 U.S.C. § 1001 to make materially false statements in a congressional investigation. Id. at 10-11.

712 Manafort 9/11/18 302, at 3-4; Kushner 4/11/18 302, at 10.

713 Written Responses of Donald J. Trump (Nov. 20, 2018), at 8 (Response to Question I, Parts (a)• (c)). We considered whether one sequence of events suggested that candidate Trump had contemporaneous knowledge of the June 9 meeting. On June 7, 2016 Trump announced his intention to give "a major speech" "probably Monday of next week"-which would have been June 13-about "all of the things that have taken place with the Clintons." See, e.g., Phillip Bump, What we know about the Trump Tower meeting, Washington Post (Aug. 7, 2018). Following the June 9 meeting, Trump changed the subject of his planned speech to national security. But the Office did not find evidence that the original idea for the speech was connected to the anticipated June 9 meeting or that the change of topic was attributable to the failure of that meeting to produce concrete evidence about Clinton. Other events, such as the Pulse nightclub shooting on June 12, could well have caused the change. The President's written answers to our questions state that the speech's focus was altered "[i]n light of' the Pulse nightclub shooting. See Written Responses, supra. As for the original topic of the June 13 speech, Trump has said that "he expected to give a speech referencing the publicly available, negative information about the Clintons," and that the draft of the speech prepared by Campaign staff "was based on publicly available material, including, in particular, information from the book Clinton Cash by Peter Schweizer." Written Responses, supra. In a later June 22 speech, Trump did speak extensively about allegations that Clinton was corrupt, drawing from the

Clinton Cash book. See Full Transcript: Donald Trump NYC Speech on Stakes of the Election, politico.com (June 22, 2016).

714 Testimony of Natalia Veselnitskaya Before the Senate Committee on Judiciary (Nov. 20, 2017) at 41, 42; Alison Frankel, How Did Russian Lawyer Veselnitskaya Get into US.for Trump Tower Meeting? Reuters, (Nov. 6, 2017); Michael Kranish et al., Russian Lawyer who Met with Trump Jr. Has Long History Fighting Sanctions, Washington Post (July 1 l, 2017); see OSC-KAVOOl 13 (6/8/16 Email, Goldstone to Kaveladze); RG000073 (6/8/16 Email, Goldstone to Trump Jr.); Lieberman 12/13/17 302, at 5; see also Prevezon Holdings Order (Oct. 17, 2016).

733 Akhmetshin 11/14/17 302, at 12-13; Samochornov 7/13/17 302, at 3. Trump Jr. confirmed this in a statement he made in July 2017 after news of the June 2016 meeting broke. Interview of Donald J Trump, Jr., Senate Judiciary Committee US. Senate Washington DC, 1 15th Cong. 57 (Sept. 7, 2017).

734 Manafort's notes state: Bill browder Offshore – Cyprus 133m shares Companies Not invest - loan

Value in Cyprus as inter Illici Active sponsors of RNC Browder hired Joanna Glover Tied into Cheney Russian adoption by American families

735 NOSC00003992 (6/9/16 Text Message, Kushner to Manafort); Kushner 4/11/18 302, at 9; Vargas 4/4/18 302, at 7; NOSC00000044 (6/9/16 Email, Kushner to Vargas); NOSC00000045 (6/9/16

Email, Kushner to Cain).

736 Samochornov 7/12/17 302, at 4; Kushner 4/11/18 302, at 9-1 O; see also Interview of Donald J. Trump, Jr., Senate Judiciary Committee, 1 15th Cong. 48-49 (Sept. 7, 2017).

737 Russian Lawyer Veselnitskaya Says She Didn't Give Trump Jr. Info on Clinton, NBC News

(July 11, 2017).

738 Testimony of Natalia Vese/nitskaya before the UnitedStates Senate Committee on the Judiciary,

1 15th Cong. 1 0. (Nov 20, 2017).

739 Testimony of Natalia Vese/nitskaya before the United States Senate Committee on the Judiciary,

1 1 51 Cong. 21 (Nov. 20, 20 1 7).

740 Sean Hannity, Transcript-Donald Trump Jr, Fox News (July 11, 2017).

741 Interview of DonaldJ. Trump, Jr, Senate Judiciary Committee, 1 15th Cong. 16 (Sept. 7, 2017).

742 Interview of Donald J. Trump, Jr, Senate Judiciary Committee, 1 15th Cong. 16-17 (Sept. 7, 2017).

746

747 Kaveladze 11/16/17 302, at 8; Call Records of Ike Kaveladze

748 Kaveladze 11/16/17 302, at 8; Call Records of Ike Kaveladze On June 14, 2016 Kaveladze's teenage daughter emailed asking how the June 9 meeting had gone, and Kaveladze responded, "meeting was boring. The Russians did not have an bad info on Hilar " OSC•KAV_00257 (6/14/16 Email, I. Kaveladze to A. Kaveladze;

749 Goldstone 2/8/18 302, at 11;

750 OSC-KAV 00138 11/23/16 Email Goldstone to Kaveladze);

751 RG000196 (11/26-29/16 Text Messages, Goldstone & Kaveladze

764 OSC-KAV 01197 (7/11-12/17 Text Messages, Kaveladze & E. Agalarov);

765 Investigative Technique

766 Investigative Technique

767 7/10/17 Email, Goldstone to Futerfas & Garten.

768

769 7/10/17 Email, Goldstone to Futerfas & Garten.

773 Samochornov 7/13/17 302, at l.

774

775 Gordon 8/29/17 302, at 9; Sessions 1/17/18 302, at 22; Allan Smith, We Now Know More About whyJeffSessions and a Russian Ambassador CrossedPaths at the Republican Convention, Business Insider (Mar. 2, 2017).

776 Gordon 8/29/17 302, at 9; Laura DeMarco, Global Cleveland and Sen. Bob Corker Welcome International Republican National Convention Guests, Cleveland Plain Dealer (July 20, 2016).

777 Gordon 8/29/17 3 02, at 9; Sessions 1 /17I 18 3 02, at 22.

778 Gordon 8/29/17 302, at 9.

779 Sessions 1/17/18 302, at 22; Luff 1/30/18 302, at 3.

780 Gordon 8/29/17 302, at 9; Luff 1/30/18 302, at 3.

781 Gordon 8/29/17 302, at 9.

782 Sessions 1/17/18 302, at 22; Luff 1/30/18 302, at 3; see also Volume I, Section IV.A.4.b, supra (explaining that Sessions and Kislyak may have met three months before this encounter during a reception held on April 26, 2016, at the Mayflower Hotel).

783 Sessions 1/17/18 302, at 22.

784 Gordon 8/29/17 302, at 9-10. rss Gordon 8/29/17 302, at 9-10.

786 Gordon 8/29/17 302, at 10; see also Volume I, Section IV.A.3.d, supra (explaining that Page acknowledged meeting Kislyak at this event).

787 Gordon 8/29/17 302, at 10.

788 Gordon 8/29/17 302, at 10.

789 Gordon 8/29/17 302, at 10.

790 Gordon 8/29/17 302, at 1 O; Hoff 5/26/17 302, at 1-2.

791 Hoff5/26/17 302, at 1; Gordon 9/7/17 302, at 10.

792 Mashburn 6/25/18 302, at 4; Manafort 9/20/18 302, at 7-8.

793 Mashburn 6/25/ 18 302, at 4; Gordon 8/29/17 302, at l 0.

794 DENMAN 000001-02, DENMAN 000012, DENMAN 000021-22; Denman 12/4/17 302, at l; Denman 6/7/17 302, at 2.

795 DENMAN 000001-02, DENMAN 000012, DENMAN 000021-22.

796 Gordon 8/29/17 302, at I 0-11.

797 Gordon 8/29/17 302, at 11; Gordon 9/7/17 302, at I l; Gordon 2/14/19 302, at 1-2, 5-6.

798 Gordon 2/14/19 302, at 5-6.

799 Denman 6/7/17 302, at 2; see DENMAN 000014.

800 Denman 6/7/17 302, at 2; Denman 12/4/17 302, at 2; Gordon 9/7/17 302, at 11-12; see Hoff 5/26/17 302, at 2.

801 Denman 6/7/17 302, at 3.

802 M. Miller 10/25/17 302 at 3.

803 Denman 12/4/17 302, at 2; Denman 6/7/17 302, at 2.

804 Hoff 5/26/17 302, at 2.

805 Denman 6/7/17 302, at 2-3, 3-4; Denman 12/4/17 302, at 2.

806 Gordon 2/l4/19 302, at 7.

807 Call Records of J.D. Gordon   . Gordon stated to the Office that his calls with Sessions were unrelated to the platform c ange. Gordon 2 14/19 302, at 7.

808 Written Responses of Donald J. Trump (Nov. 20, 2018), at 17 (Response to Question IV, Part (f)).

809 Gordon 2/14/19 302, at 6-7; Gordon 9/7/17 302, at 11-12; see Gordon 8/29/17 302, at 11.

810 Dearborn 11/28/l 7 302, at 7-8.

811 Mashburn 6/25/18 302, at 4.

812 Hoff 5/26/17 302, at 2-3; see Denman 12/4/17 302, at 2-3; Gordon 8/29/17 302, at 11.

813 Gordon 8/29/17 302, at 11; Gordon 9/7/17 302, at 12.

814 Hoff 5/26/17 302, at 2-3.

81 5 Gordon 2/14/19 302, at 6.

816 Clovis 10/3/17 302, at 10-11.

817 Mashburn 6/25/18 302, at 4.

818 DJTFP00004828 (8/3/16 Email, Pchelyakov [embassy@russianembassy.org] to Gordon).

819 DJTFP00004953 (8/8/16 Email, Gordon to embassy@russianembassy.org).

820 Luff 1/30/18 302, at 5.

821 Sessions 1/17/18 302, at 23-24; Luff 1/30/18 302, at 5.

822 Sessions 1/17/18 302, at 23-24; Luff l/30/18 302, at 5; Landrum 2/27/18 302, at 3-5.

823 Sessions 1/17/18 302, at 23.

824 Sessions 1/17/l 8 302, at 23.

825 Sessions 1/17/18 302, at 23; Luff 1/30/18 302, at 5-6; Landrum 2/27/18 302, at 4-5 (stating he could not remember if election was discussed).

826 Luff 1/30/18 302, at 6; Landrum 2/27/18 302, at 5.

827 Luff 1/30/18 302, at 6; Landrum 2/27/18 302, at 4-5.

828 Luff 1/30/18 302, at 6; Landrum 2/27/18 302 at 4-5.

829 Landrum 2/27/18 302, at 5.

830 Sessions 1/17/18 302, at 23. Sessions also noted that ambassadors came to him for information about Trump and

hoped he would pass along information to Trump. Sessions 1/17/18 302, at 23-24.

831 Sessions 1/17/18 302, at 23; Luff 1/30/18 302, at 6; Landrum 2/27/18 302, at 5.

832 Luff 1/30/18 302, at 5; Landrum 2/27/18 302, at 4.

833 Luff 1/30/18 302, at 5.

834 Luff 1/30/18 302, at 6; Landrum 2/27/18 302, at 4-5.

835 Sessions 1/17/18 3 02, at 23.

836 Sessions 1/17/18 302, at 23.

837 Sessions 1 /17/18 302, at 23.

838 On August 21, 2018, Manafort was convicted in the Eastern District of Virginia on eight tax, Foreign Bank Account Registration (FBAR), and bank fraud charges. On September 14, 2018, Manafort pleaded guilty in the District of Columbia to (1) conspiracy to defraud the United States and conspiracy to commit offenses against the United States (money laundering, tax fraud, FBAR, Foreign Agents Registration Act (FARA), and FARA false statements), and (2) conspiracy to obstruct justice (witness tampering). Manafort also admitted criminal conduct with which he had been charged in the Eastern District of Virginia, but as to which the jury hung. The conduct at issue in both cases involved Manafort's work in Ukraine and the money he earned for that work, as well as crimes after the Ukraine work ended. On March 7, 2019, Manafort was sentenced to 47 months of imprisonment in the Virginia prosecution. On March 13, the district court in D.C. sentenced Manafort to a total term of 73 months: 60 months on the Count 1 conspiracy (with 30 of those months to run concurrent to the Virginia sentence), and 13 months on the Count 1 conspiracy, to be served consecutive to the other two sentences. The two sentences resulted in a total term of 90 months.

839 As noted in Volume I, Section III.D. l.b, supra, Gates pleaded guilty to two criminal charges in the District of Columbia, including making a false statement to the FBI, pursuant to a plea agreement. He has provided information and in-court testimony that the Office has deemed to be reliable. See also Transcript at 16, United States v. Paul J Manafort, Jr., 1 :17-cr-201 (D.D.C. Feb. 13, 2019), Doc. 514 ("Manafort 2/13/19 Transcript") (court's explanation of reasons to credit Gates's statements in one instance).

841 According to the President's written answers, he does not remember Manafort communicating to him any particular positions that Ukraine or Russia would want the United States to support. Written Responses of Donald J. Trump (Nov. 20, 2018), at 16-17 (Response to Question IV, Part (d)).

842 Manafort made several false statements during debriefings. Based on that conduct, the Office determined that Manafort had breached his plea agreement and could not be a cooperating witness. The judge presiding in Manafort's D.C. criminal case found by a preponderance of the evidence that Manafort intentionally made multiple false statements to the FBI, the Office, and the grand jury concerning his interactions and communications with Kilimnik (and concerning two other issues). Although the report refers at times to Manafort's statements, it does so only when those statements are sufficiently corroborated to be trustworthy, to identify issues on which Manafort's untruthful responses may themselves be of evidentiary value, or to provide Manafort's explanations for certain events, even when we were unable to determine whether that explanation was credible.

843 Pinchuk et al., Russian Tycoon Deripaska in Putin Delegation to China, Reuters (June 8, 2018).

844 6/23/05 Memo, Manafort & Davis to Deripaska & Rothchild.

845 Gates 2/2/18 302, at 7.

846 Manafort 9/20/18 302, at 2-5; Manafort Income by Year, 2005 - 2015; Manafort Loans from Wire Transfers, 2005 - 2015.

847 Gates 3/12/18 302, at 5.

848 Manafort 12/16/15 Dep., at 157:8-11.

849 Gates 2/2/18 302, at 9.

850 Gates 2/2/18 302, at 6.

851 Gates 2/2/18 302, at 9-10.

852 Manafort 7/30/14 302, at 1; Manafort 9/20/18 302, at 2.

853 Manafort 9/11/18 302, at 5-6.

854 Gates 3/16/18 302, at 1; Davis 2/8/18 302, at 9; Devine 7/6/18 302, at 2-3.

855 Patten 5/22/18 302, at 5; Gates 1/29/18 302, at 18-19; 10/28/97 Kilimnik Visa Record, U.S. Department of State.

856 Gates 1/29/18 302, at 18-19; Patten 5/22/18 302, at 8; Gates 1/31/18 302, at 4-5; Oates 1/30/18

302, at 2; Gates 2/2/18 302, at 11.m Gates 1/29/18 302, at 18; Patten 5/22/18 302, at 8.

858 Boyarkin Visa Record, U.S. Department of State.

859 Manafort 9/11/18 302, at 5.

860 The Office has noted Kilimnik's assessed ties to Russian intelligence in public court filings.

E.g., Gov't Opp. to Mot. to Modify, United States v, Paul J Manafort, Jr., 1 :17-cr-201 (D.D.C. Dec. 4,

2017), Doc. 73, at 2 ("Manafort (D.D.C.) Gov't Opp. to Mot. to Modify").

861 12/17/16 Kilimnik Visa Record, U.S. Department of State.

862 In August 2018, Patten pleaded guilty pursuant to a plea agreement to violating the Foreign Agents Registration Act, and admitted in his Statement of Offense that he also misled and withheld documents from the Senate Select Committee on Intelligence in the course of its investigation of Russian election interference. Plea Agreement, United States v. W Samuel Patten, 1 :18-cr-260 (D.D.C. Aug. 31,

20 I 8), Doc. 6; Statement of Offense, United States v, W Samuel Patten, 1: I 8-cr-260 (D.D.C. Aug. 31,

2018), Doc. 7.

863 Patten 5/22/18 302, at 5-6.

864 10/28/97 Kilimnik Visa Record, U.S. Department of State.

865 Nix 3/30/18 302, at 1-2.

866 Nix 3/30/18 302, at 2.

867 Lenzi 1 /30/18 302, at 2.

868 Hawker 1/9/18 302, at 13; 3/18/14 Email, Hawker & Tulukbaev.

869 van der Zwaan pleaded guilty in the U.S. District Court for the District of Columbia to making false statements to the Special Counsel's Office. Plea Agreement, United States v. Alex van der Zwaan, l: 18-cr-3 1 (D.D.C. Feb. 20, 2018), Doc. 8.

870 Hawker 6/9/18 302, at 4; van der Zwaan 11/3/17 302, at 22. Manafort said in an interview that Gates had joked with Kilimnik about Kilimnik's going to meet with his KGB handler. Manafort 10/16/18 302, at 7.

871 Press Release - DonaldJ Trump Announces Campaign Convention Manager Paul J Manafort, The American Presidency Project- U.C. Santa Barbara (Mar. 29, 2016).

872 Gates 1/29/18 302, at 8; Meghan Keneally, Timeline ofManafort 's role in the Trump Campaign, ABC News (Oct. 20, 2017).

873 Gates 1/29/18 302, at 7-8; Manafort 9/11/18 302, at 1-2; Barrack 12/12/17 302, at 3.

874 Barrack 12/12/17 302, at 3; Gates 1/29/18 302, at 7-8.

875 Manafort 10/16/18 302, at 6.

876 Manafort l 0/16/18 302, at 6.

877 Gates 2/2/18 302, at 10.

878 Gates 1/30/18 302, at 4.

879 Gates 2/2/18 302, at 11.

880 See Sharon LaFraniere, Manafort's Trial Isn't About Russia, but It Will Be in the Air, New York Times (July 30, 2018); Tierney Sneed, Prosecutors Believe Manafort Made $60 Million Consulting in Ukraine, Talking Points Memo (July 30, 2018); Mykola Vorobiov, How Pro-Russian Forces. Will Take Revenge on Ukraine, Atlantic Council (Sept. 23, 2018); Sergii Leshchenko, Ukraine's Oligarchs Are Still Calling the Shots, Foreign Policy (Aug. 14, 2014); Interfax-Ukraine, Kolesnikov: Inevitability of PunishmentNeededfor Real Fight Against Smuggling in Ukraine, Kyiv Post (June 23, 2018); Igor Kossov, Kyiv Hotel Industry Makes Room for New Entrants, Kyiv Post (Mar. 7, 2019); Markian Kuzmowycz, How the Kremlin Can Win Ukraine's Elections, Atlantic Council (Nov. 19, 2018). The Opposition Bloc is a Ukraine political party that largely reconstituted the Party ofRegions.

881 3/30/16 Email, Gates to Kilimnik.

882 4/11/16 Email, Manafort & Kilimnik.

883 4/11/16 Email, Manafort & Kilimnik.

884 Gates 2/2/18 302, at 10.

885 Gates 2/2/18 302, at 11; Gates 9/27/18 302 (serial 740), at 2.

886 Gates 2/2/18 302, at 12.

887 Gates 2/2/18 302, at 12.

888 Gates 1/31/18 302, at 17; Gates 9/27/18 302 (serial 740), at 2. In a later interview with the Office, Gates stated that Manafort directed him to send polling data to Kilimnik after a May 7, 2016 meeting between Manafort and Kilimnik in New York, discussed in Volume I, Section IY.A.8.b.iii, infra. Gates11/7/18 302, at 3.

889 Gates 9/27/l 8 302, Part II, at 2;

890 'Gates 2/12/18 302, at IO; Gates 1/31/18 302, at 17.

891 Gates 9/27/18 302 (serial 740), at 2; Gates 2/7/18 302, at 15.

892 Gates 1/31/18 302, at 17.

893 Gates 2/12/18 302, at 11-12. According to Gates, his access to internal polling data was more limited because Fabrizio was himself distanced from the Campaign at that point.

894

89s 8/18/16 Email, Kilimnik to Dirkse; 8/18/16 Email, Kilimnik to Schultz; 8/18/16 Email, Kilimnik to Marson; 7/27/16 Email, Kilimnik to Ash; 8/18/16 Email, Kilimnik to Ash; 8/18/16 Email, Kilimnik to Jackson; 8/18/16 Email, Kilimnik to Mendoza-Wilson; 8/19/16 Email, Kilimnik to Patten.

896

897 7/7/16 Email, Manafort to Kilimnik.

898 Gates 2/2/18 302, at 13.

899 Manafort 9/11/18 302, at 6.

900 7/8/16 Email, Kilimnik to Manafort.

901 7/8/16 Email, Kilimnik to Manafort; Gates 2/2/18 302, at 13.

902 Manafort 9/11/18 302, at 6.

903 Manafort 9/11 /18 3 02, at 6.

904 Manafort 9/11/18 302, at 6

90S Investigative Technique

906 4/26/16 Email, Kilimnik to Purcell, at 2; Gates 2/2/18 302, at 12; Patten 5/22/18 302, at 6-7;
Gates 11/7/18 302, at 3.

907 5/7/16 Email, Kilimnik to Charap & Kimmage; 5/7/16 Email, Kasanof to Kilimnik.

908 5/6/16 Email, Manafort to Gates; 5/6/16 Email, Gates to Kilimnik.

909 Manafort 10/11/18 302, at I.

910 Manafort 10/11/18 302, at I.

911 Manafort 10/11/18 302, at 1.

912 7/25/16 Email, Kilimnik to katrin@yana.kiev.ua (2: 17:34 a.m.).

913 7/29/16 Email, Kilimnik to Manafort (10:51 a.m.).

914 7/29/16 Email, Kilimnik to Manafort (10:51 a.m.).

915 Manafort 9/12/18 302, at 3.Investigative Technique

917 7/29/16 Email, Manafort to Kilimnik.

918 7/31/16 Email, Manafort to Kilimnik.

919 7/31/16 Email, Manafort to Kilimnik.

920 Kilimnik 8/2/16 CBP Record·   Call Records of Konstantin Kilimnik   Call Records of Rick Gates
; 8/2-3/16, Kilimnik Park Lane Hotel Receipt.

921 Deripaska's private plane also flew to Teterboro Airport in New Jersey on the evening of August

2, 2016.   According to Customs and Border Protection records, the only passengers on the plane were

Deripaska's wife, daughter, mother, and father-in-law, and separate records obtained by our Office confirm that Kilimnik
flew on a commercial flight to New York.

922   The Luhansk and Donetsk People's Republics, which are located in the Donbas region of Ukraine, declared
themselves independent in response to the popular unrest in 2014 that removed President Yanukovych from power.   Pro-
Russian Ukrainian militia forces, with backing from the Russian military, have occupied the region since 2014.   Under
the   Yanukovych-backed plan,   Russia would assist in withdrawing the military, and Donbas would become an
autonomous region within Ukraine with its own

925 Manafort 9/11/18 302, at 4.

926 Manafort 9/12/18 302, at 4.

927 Manafort 9/11/18 302, at 5; Manafort 9/12/18

302, at 4.

928 Manafort 9/12/18 302, at 4; Investigative Techniqu

V.

PROSECUTION AND DECLINATION DECISIONS

The Appointment Order authorized the Special Counsel's Office "to prosecute federal crimes arising from [its] investigation" of the matters assigned to it. In deciding whether to exercise this prosecutorial authority, the Office has been guided by the Principles of Federal Prosecution set forth in the Justice (formerly U.S. Attorney's) Manual. In particular, the Office has evaluated whether the conduct of the individuals considered for prosecution constituted a federal offense and whether admissible evidence would probably be sufficient to obtain and sustain a conviction for such an offense. Justice Manual § 9-27.220 (2018). Where the answer to those questions was yes, the Office further considered whether the prosecution would serve a substantial federal interest, the individuals were subject to effective prosecution in another jurisdiction, and there existed an adequate non-criminal alternative to prosecution. *Id.*

As explained below, those considerations led the Office to seek charges against two sets of Russian nationals for their roles in 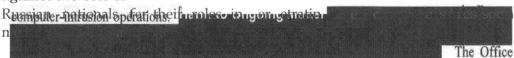 computer-intrusion operations. The Office similarly determined that the contacts between Campaign officials and Russia-linked individuals either did not involve the commission of a federal crime or, in the case of campaign-finance offenses, that our evidence was not sufficient to obtain and sustain a criminal conviction. At the same time, the Office concluded that the Principles of Federal Prosecution supported charging certain individuals connected to the Campaign with making false statements or otherwise obstructing this investigation or parallel congressional investigations.

A. Russian "Active Measures" Social Media Campaign

On February 16, 2018, a federal grand jury in the District of Columbia returned an indictment charging 13 Russian nationals and three Russian entities—including the Internet Research Agency (IRA) and Concord Management and Consulting LLC (Concord)—with violating U.S. criminal laws in order to interfere with U.S. elections and political processes.[1276]
The indictment charges all of the defendants with conspiracy to defraud the United States (Count One), three defendants with conspiracy to commit wire fraud and bank fraud (Count Two), and five defendants with aggravated identity theft (Counts Three through Eight). *Internet Research Agency* Indictment. Concord, which is one of the entities charged in the Count One conspiracy, entered an appearance through U.S. counsel and moved to dismiss the charge on multiple grounds. In orders and memorandum opinions issued on August 13 and November 15, 2018, the district court denied Concord's motions to dismiss. *United States v. Concord Management & Consulting LLC*, 347 F. Supp. 3d 38 (D.D.C. 2018). *United States v. Concord Management & Consulting LLC*, 317 F. Supp. 3d 598 (D.D.C. 2018). As of this writing, the prosecution of Concord remains ongoing before the U.S. District Court for the District of Columbia. The other defendants remain at large.

Although members of the IRA had contact with individuals affiliated with the Trump Campaign, the indictment does not charge any Trump Campaign official or any other U.S. person with participating in the conspiracy. That is because the investigation did not identify evidence that any U.S. person who coordinated or communicated with the IRA knew that he or she was speaking with Russian nationals engaged in the criminal conspiracy. The Office therefore determined that such persons did not have the knowledge or criminal purpose required to charge them in the conspiracy to defraud the United States (Count One) or in the separate count alleging a wire- and bank-fraud conspiracy involving the IRA and two individual Russian nationals (Count Two).

The Office did, however, charge one U.S. national for his role in supplying false or stolen bank account numbers that allowed the IRA conspirators to access U.S. online payment systems by circumventing those systems' security features. On February 12, 2018, Richard Pinedo pleaded guilty, pursuant to a single-count information, to identity fraud, in violation of 18 U.S.C. § 1028(a)(7) and (b)(I)(O). Plea Agreement, *United States v. Richard Pinedo*, No. 1: 1 8-cr-24(D.D.C. Feb. 12, 2018), Doc. 10. The investigation did not establish that Pinedo was aware of the identity of the IRA members who purchased bank account numbers from him. Pinedo's sales of account numbers enabled the IRA members to anonymously access a financial network through which they transacted with U.S. persons and companies. *See* Gov't Sent. Mem. at 3, *United States v. Richard Pinedo*, No. 1: 18-cr-24 (O.O.C. Sept. 26, 2018), Doc. 24. On October 10, 2018, Pinedo was sentenced to six months of imprisonment, to be followed by six months of home confinement, and was ordered to complete 100 hours of community service

B. Russian Hacking and Dumping Operations

1. Section 1030 Computer-Intrusion Conspiracy

a. *Background*

On July 13, 2018, a federal grand jury in the District of Columbia returned an indictment charging Russian military intelligence officers from the GRU with conspiring to hack into various U.S. computers used by the Clinton Campaign, DNC, DCCC, and other U.S. persons, in violation of 18 U.S.C. §§ 1030 and 371 (Count One); committing identity theft and conspiring to commit money laundering in furtherance of that hacking conspiracy, in violation of 18 U.S.C. §§ 1028A and 1 956(h) (Counts Two through Ten); and a separate conspiracy to hack into the computers of U.S. persons and entities responsible for the administration of the 2016 U.S. election, in violation of 18 U.S.C. §§ 1030 and 371 (Count Eleven). *Netyksho* Indictment.F" As of this writing, all 12 defendants remain at large.

The *Netyksho* indictment alleges that the defendants conspired with one another and with others to hack into the computers of U.S. persons and entities involved in the 2016 U.S. presidential election, steal documents from those computers, and stage releases of the stolen documents to interfere in the election. *Netyksho* Indictment 12. The indictment also describes how, in staging the releases, the defendants used the Guccifer 2.0 persona to disseminate documents through WikiLeaks. On July 22, 2016, WikiLeaks released over 20,000 emails and other documents that the hacking conspirators had stolen from the DNC. *Netyksho* Indictment ,r 48. In addition, on October 7, 2016, WikiLeaks began releasing emails that some conspirators had stolen from Clinton Campaign chairman John Podesta after a successful spearphishing operation. *Netyksho* Indictment ,r 49.

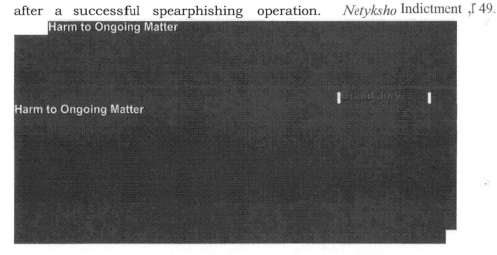

b. *Charging Decision As to*

2. Potential Section 1030 Violation B y

See United States v. Willis, 476 F.3d 1121, 1125 n.1 (10th Cir. 2007) (explaining that the 1986 amendments to Section
1030 reflect Congress's desire to reach "'intentional acts of unauthorized access—rather than mistaken, inadvertent, or careless ones'") (quoting S. Rep. 99-432, at 5 (1986)). In addition, the likely qualifies as a "protected" one under the statute, which computer reaches "effectively all computers with Internet access." United States v. Nosal 676 F.3d 854 859 (9th Cir. 2012) (en banc).

C. Russian Government Outreach and Contacts

As explained in Section IV above, the Office's investigation uncovered evidence of numerous links (i.e., contacts) between Trump Campaign officials and individuals having or claiming to have ties to the Russian government. The Office evaluated the contacts under several sets of federal laws, including conspiracy laws and statutes governing foreign agents who operate in the United States. After considering the available evidence, the Office did not pursue charges under these statutes against any of the individuals discussed in Section IV above—with the exception of FARA charges against Paul Manafort and Richard Gates based on their activities on behalf of Ukraine.

One of the interactions between the Trump Campaign and Russian-affiliated individuals ⬤ the June 9, 2016 meeting between high-ranking campaign officials and Russians promising derogatory information on Hillary Clinton—implicates an additional body of Jaw: campaign• finance statutes. Schemes involving the solicitation or receipt of assistance from foreign sources raise difficult statutory and constitutional questions. As ex lained below the Office evaluated those questions in connection with the June 9 **meeting**

The Office ultimately concluded that, even if the principal legal questions were resolved favorably to the government, a prosecution would encounter difficulties proving that Campaign officials or individuals connected to the Campaign willfully violated the law.

Finally, although the evidence of contacts between Campaign officials and Russia• affiliated individuals may not have been sufficient to establish or sustain criminal charges, several U.S. persons connected to the Campaign made false statements about those contacts and took other steps to obstruct the Office's investigation and those of Congress. This Office has therefore charged some of those individuals with making false statements and obstructing justice.

1. Potential Coordination: Conspiracy and Collusion

As an initial matter, this Office evaluated potentially criminal conduct that involved the collective action of multiple individuals not under the rubric of "collusion," but through the lens of conspiracy law. In so doing, the Office recognized that the word "collud[e]" appears in the Acting Attorney General's August 2, 2017 memorandum; it has frequently been invoked in public reporting; and it is sometimes referenced in antitrust law, *see, e.g., Brooke Group v. Brown & Williamson Tobacco Corp.,* 509 U.S. 209, 227 (1993). But collusion is not a specific offense or theory of liability found in the U.S. Code; nor is it a term of art in federal criminal law.

To the contrary, even as defined in legal dictionaries, collusion is largely synonymous with conspiracy as that crime is set forth in the general federal conspiracy statute, 18 U.S.C. § 371. *See Black's Law Dictionary* 321 (10th ed. 2014) (collusion is "[a]n agreement to defraud another or to do or obtain something forbidden by law"); 1 Alexander Burrill, *A Law Dictionary and Glossary* 311 (1871) ("An agreement between two or more persons to defraud another by the forms of law, or to employ such forms as means of accomplishing some unlawful object."); 1 *Bouvier's Law Dictionary* 352(1897) ("An agreement between two or more persons to defraud a person of his rights by the forms of law, or to obtain an object forbidden by law.").

For that reason, this Office's focus in resolving the question of joint criminal liability was on conspiracy as defined in federal law, not the commonly discussed term "collusion." The Office considered in particular whether contacts between Trump Campaign officials and Russia-linked individuals could trigger liability for the crime of conspiracy—either under statutes that have their own conspiracy language *(e.g,* 18 U.S.C. §§ 1349, 1951(a)), or under the general conspiracy statute (18 U.S.C. § 371). The investigation did not establish that the contacts described in Volume I, Section IV, *supra,* amounted to an agreement to commit any substantive violation of federal criminal law—including foreign-influence and campaign-finance laws, both of which are discussed further below. The Office therefore did not charge any individual associated with the Trump Campaign with conspiracy to commit a federal offense arising from Russia contacts, either under a specific statute or under Section 371's offenses clause.

The Office also did not charge any campaign official or associate with a conspiracy under Section 371 's defraud clause. That clause criminalizes participating in an agreement to obstruct a lawful function of the U.S. government or its agencies through deceitful or dishonest means. *See Dennis v. United States,* 384 U.S. 855, 861 (1966); *Hammerschmidt v. United States,* 265 U.S. 182, 188 (1924); *see also United States v. Concord Mgmt. & Consulting LLC,* 347 F. Supp. 3d 38, 46 (D.D.C. 2018). The investigation did not establish any agreement among Campaign officials — or between such officials and Russia-linked individuals — to interfere with or obstruct a lawful function of a government agency during the campaign or transition period. And, as discussed in Volume I, Section V.A, *supra,* the investigation did not identify evidence that any Campaign official or associate knowingly and intentionally participated in the conspiracy to defraud that the Office charged, namely, the active-measures conspiracy described in Volume I, Section II, *supra.* Accordingly, the Office did not charge any Campaign associate or other U.S. person with conspiracy to defraud the United States based on the Russia-related contacts described in Section IV above.

2. **Potential Coordination: Foreign Agent Statutes** (FARA and 18 U .S.C. § 951)

The Office next assessed the potential liability of Campaign-affiliated individuals under federal statutes regulating actions on behalf of, or work done for, a foreign government.

a. Governing Law

Under 18 U.S.C. § 951, it is generally illegal to act in the United States as an agent of a foreign government without providing notice to the Attorney General. Although the defendant must act on behalf of a foreign government (as opposed to other kinds of foreign entities), the acts need not involve espionage; rather, acts of any type suffice for liability. See United States v. Duran, 596 F.3d 1283, 1293-94 (11th Cir. 2010); UnitedStates v. Latchin, 554 F.3d 709, 715 (7th Cir. 2009); United States v. Dumeisi, 424 F.3d 566, 581 (7th Cir. 2005). An "agent of a foreign government" is an "individual" who "agrees to operate" in the United States "subject to the direction or control of a foreign government or official." 18 U.S.C. § 951 (d).

The crime defined by Section 951 is complete upon knowingly acting in the United States as an unregistered foreign-government agent. 18 U.S.C. § 95 l(a). The statute does not require willfulness, and knowledge of the notification requirement is not an element of the offense. *United States v. Campa,* 529 F.3d 980, 998-99 (11th Cir. 2008); *Duran,* 596 F.3d at 1291-94; *Dumeisi,* 424 F.3d at 581.

The Foreign Agents Registration Act (FARA) generally makes it illegal to act as an agent of a foreign principal by engaging in certain (largely political) activities in the United States without registering with the Attorney General. 22 U.S.C. §§ 611-621. The triggering agency relationship must be with a foreign principal or "a person any of whose activities are directly or indirectly supervised, directed, controlled, financed, or subsidized in whole or in major part by a foreign principal." 22 U.S.C. § 61 l(c)(1). That includes a foreign government or political party and various foreign individuals and entities. 22 U.S.C. § 61 l(b). A covered relationship exists if a person "acts as an agent, representative, employee, or servant" or "in any other capacity at the order, request, or under the [foreign principal's] direction or control." 22 U.S.C. § 61 l(c)(1). It is sufficient if the person "agrees, consents, assumes or purports to act as, or who is or holds himself out to be, whether or not pursuant to contractual relationship, an agent of a foreign principal." 22 U.S.C. § 61 l(c)(2).

The triggering activity is that the agent "directly or through any other person" in the United States (1) engages in "political activities for or in the interests of [the] foreign principal," which includes attempts to influence federal officials or the public; (2) acts as "public relations counsel, publicity agent, information-service employee or political consultant for or in the interests of such foreign principal"; (3) "solicits, collects, disburses, or dispenses contributions, loans, money, or other things of value for or in the interest of such foreign principal"; or (4) "represents the interests of such foreign principal" before any federal agency or official. 22 U.S.C. § 611 (c)(1).

It is a crime to engage in a "[w]illful violation of any provision of the Act or any regulation thereunder." 22 U.S.C. § 618(a)(l). It is also a crime willfully to make false statements or omissions of material facts in FARA registration statements or supplements. 22 U.S.C. § 618(a)(2). Most violations have a maximum penalty of five years of imprisonment and a $10,000 fine. 22 U.S.C. § 618.

b. *Application*

The investigation uncovered extensive evidence that Paul Manafort's and Richard Oates's pre-campaign work for the government of Ukraine violated FARA. Manafort and Gates were charged for that conduct and admitted to it when they pleaded guilty to superseding criminal informations in the District of Columbia prosecution.F'" The evidence underlying those charges is not addressed in this report because it was discussed in public court documents and in a separate prosecution memorandum submitted to the Acting Attorney General before the original indictment in that case.

In addition, the investigation produced evidence of FARA violations involving Michael Flynn. Those potential violations, however, concerned a country other than Russia *(i.e.,* Turkey) and were resolved when Flynn admitted to the underlying facts in the Statement of Offense that accompanied his guilty plea to a false-statements charge. Statement of Offense, *United States v. Michael T. Flynn,* No. 1 :1 7-cr-232 (D.D.C. Dec. 1, 2017), Doc. 4 *("Flynn* Statement of Offense").[1281]

The investigation did not, however, yield evidence sufficient to sustain any charge that any individual affiliated with the Trump Campaign acted as an agent of a foreign principal within the meaning of FARA or, in terms of Section 951, subject to the direction or control of the government of Russia, or any official thereof. In particular, the Office did not find evidence likely to prove beyond a reasonable doubt that Campaign officials such as Paul Manafort, George Papadopoulos, and Carter Page acted as agents of the Russian overnment—or at *its* direction, control, or re uest—durin the relevant time eriod.[1282]

As a result, the O ice did not charge   any other Trump Campaign official with violating FARA or Section 951, or attempting or conspiring to do so, based on contacts with the Russian government or a Russian principal.

Finally, the Office investigated whether one of the above campaign advisors — George Papadopoulos — acted as an agent of, or at the direction and control of, the government of Israel. While the investigation revealed significant ties between Papadopoulos and Israel (and search warrants were obtained in part on that basis), the Office ultimately determined that the evidence was not sufficient to obtain and sustain a conviction under FARA or Section 951.

3. Campaign Finance

Several areas of the Office's investigation involved efforts or offers by foreign nationals to provide negative information about candidate Clinton to the Trump Campaign or to distribute that information to the public, to the anticipated benefit of the Campaign. As explained below, the Office considered whether two of those efforts in particular Matter —the June 9, 2016 meeting at Trump   The Office d

a. *Overiew of Governing Law*

"[T]he United States has a compelling interest ... in limiting the participation of foreign citizens in activities of democratic self-government, and in thereby preventing foreign influence over the U.S. political process." *Bluman v. FEC*, 800 F. Supp. 2d 281, 288 (D.D.C. 2011) (Kavanaugh, J., for three-judge court), *aff'd,* 565 U.S. 1104 (2012). To that end, federal campaign• finance law broadly prohibits foreign nationals from making contributions, donations, expenditures, or other disbursements in connection with federal, state, or local candidate elections, and prohibits anyone from soliciting, accepting, or receiving such contributions or donations. As relevant here, foreign nationals may not make — and no one may "solicit,' accept, or receive" from them — "a contribution or donation of money or other thing of value" or "an express or implied promise to make a contribution or donation, in connection with a Federal, State, or local election."52 U.S.C. § 30121(a)(1)(A), (a)(2).[1283] The term "contribution," which is used throughout the campaign-finance law, "includes" "any gift, subscription, loan, advance, or deposit of money or anything of value made by any person for the purpose of influencing any election for Federal office." 52 U.S.C. § 30101(8)(A)(i). It excludes, among other things, "the value of [volunteer] services." 52 U.S.C. § 30101(8)(B)(i).

Foreign nationals are also barred from making "an expenditure, independent expenditure, or disbursement for an electioneering communication." 52 U.S.C. § 30121(a)(1)(C). The term "expenditure" "includes" "any purchase, payment, distribution, loan, advance, deposit, or gift of money or anything of value, made by any person for the purpose of influencing any election for Federal office." 52 U.S.C. §,30101(9)(A)(i). It excludes, among other things, news stories and non-partisan get-out-the-vote activities. 52 U.S.C. § 30101(9)(B)(i)-(ii). An "independent expenditure" is an expenditure "expressly advocating the election or defeat of a clearly identified candidate" and made independently of the campaign. 52 U.S.C. § 30101(17). An "electioneering communication" is a broadcast communication that "refers to a clearly identified candidate for Federal office" and is made within specified time periods and targeted at the relevant electorate. 52 u.s.c. § 30104(f)(3).

The statute defines "foreign national" by reference to FARA and the Immigration and Nationality Act, with minor modification. 52 U.S.C. § 30121(b) (cross-referencing 22 U.S.C.§ 61 1(b)(1)-(3) and 8 U.S.C. § 1 101(a)(20), (22)). That definition yields five, sometimes• overlapping categories of foreign nationals, which include all of the individuals and entities relevant for present purposes—namely, foreign governments and political parties, individuals outside of the U.S. who are not legal permanent residents, and certain non-U.S. entities located outside of the U.S.

A "knowing[']" and willful[]" violation involving an aggregate of $25,000 or more in a calendar year is a felony. 52 U.S.C. § 30109(d)(1)(A)(i); *see Bluman,* 800 F. Supp. 2d at 292 (noting that a willful violation will require some "proof of the defendant's knowledge of the law"); *United States v. Danielczyk,* 917 F. Supp. 2d 573, 577 (E.D. Va. 2013) (applying willfulness standard drawn from *Bryan v. United States,* 524 U.S. 184, 191–92 (1998)); *see also Wagner v. FEC,* 793 F.3d 1, 19 n.23 (D.C. Cir. 2015) (en banc) (same). A "knowing[j] and willful[]" violation involving an aggregate of $2,000 or more in a calendar year, but less than $25,000, is a misdemeanor. 52 U.S.C. § 30109(d)(1)(A)(ii).

b. Application to June 9 Trump Tower Meeting

The Office considered whether to charge Trump Campaign officials with crimes in connection with the June 9 meeting described in Volume I, Section IV.A.5, *supra.* The Office concluded that, in light of the government's substantial burden of proof on issues of intent ("knowing" and "willful"), and the difficulty of establishing the value of the offered information, criminal charges would not meet the Justice Manual standard that "the admissible evidence will probably be sufficient to obtain and sustain a conviction." Justice Manual § 9-27.220.

In brief, the key facts are that, on June 3, 2016, Robert Goldstone emailed Donald Trump Jr., to pass along from Emin and Aras Agalarov an "offer" from Russia's "Crown prosecutor" to "the Trump campaign" of "official documents and information that would incriminate Hillary and her dealings with Russia and would be very useful to [Trump Jr.'s] father." The email described this as "very high level and sensitive information" that is "part of Russia and its government's support to Mr. Trump-helped along by Aras and Emin." Trump Jr. responded: "if it's what you say I love it especially later in the summer." Trump Jr. and Emin Agalarov had follow-up conversations and, within days, scheduled a meeting with Russian representatives that was attended by Trump Jr., Manafort, and Kushner. The communications setting up the meeting and the attendance by high-level Campaign representatives support an inference that the Campaign anticipated receiving derogatory documents and information from official Russian sources that could assist candidate Trump's electoral prospects.

This series of events could implicate the federal election-law ban on contributions and donations by foreign nationals, 52 U.S.C. § 30121 (a)(l)(A). Specifically, Goldstone passed along an offer purportedly from a Russian government official to provide "official documents and information" to the Trump Campaign for the purposes of influencing the presidential election. Trump Jr. appears to have accepted that offer and to have arranged a meeting to receive those materials. Documentary evidence in the form of email chains supports the inference that Kushner and Manafort were aware of that purpose and attended the June 9 meeting anticipating the receipt of helpful information to the Campaign from Russian sources.

The Office considered whether this evidence would establish a conspiracy to violate the foreign contributions ban, in violation of 18 U.S.C. § 371; the solicitation of an illegal foreign• source contribution; or the acceptance or receipt of "an express or implied promise to make a[foreign-source] contribution," both in violation of 52 U .S.C. § 30121 (a)(I)(A), (a)(2). There are reasonable arguments that the offered information would constitute a "thing of value" within the meaning of these provisions, but the Office determined that the government would not be likely to obtain and sustain a conviction for two other reasons: first, the Office did not obtain admissible evidence likely to meet the government's burden to prove beyond a reasonable doubt that these individuals acted "willfully," i.e., with general knowledge of the illegality of their conduct; and, second, the government would likely encounter difficulty in proving beyond a reasonable doubt that the value of the promised information exceeded the threshold for a criminal violation, see 52U.S.C. § 30109(d)(l)(A)(i).

i. *Thing-of-Value Element*

A threshold legal question is whether providing to a campaign "documents and information" of the type involved here would constitute a prohibited campaign contribution. The foreign contribution ban is not limited to contributions of money. It expressly prohibits "a contribution or donation of money or *other thing of value.*" 52 U.S.C. § 30121(a)(1)(A), (a)(2) (emphasis added). And the term "contribution" is defined throughout the campaign-finance laws to "includej]" "any gift, subscription, loan, advance, or deposit of money or *anything of value.*" 52 U.S.C. § 30101(8)(A)(i) (emphasis added).

The phrases "thing of value" and "anything of value" are broad and inclusive enough to encompass at least some forms of valuable information. Throughout the United States Code, these phrases serve as "term[s] of art" that are construed "broad[ly]." *United States v. Nilsen,* 967 F.2d 539, 542 (11th Cir. 1992) (per curiam) ("thing ofvalue" includes "both tangibles and intangibles"); *see also, e.g,* 18 U.S.C. §§ 201(b)(1), 666(a)(2) (bribery statutes); *idS* 641 (theft of government property). For example, the term "thing of value" encompasses law enforcement reports that would reveal the identity of informants, *United States v. Girard,* 601 F.2d 69, 71 (2d Cir. 1979); classified materials, *United States v. Fowler,* 932 F.2d 306, 310 (4th Cir. 1991); confidential information about a competitive bid, *United States v. Matzkin,* 14 F.3d 1014, 1020 (4th Cir. 1994); secret grand jury information, *United States v. Jeter,* 775 F.2d 670, 680 (6th Cir. 1985); and information about a witness's whereabouts, *United States v. Sheker,* 618 F.2d 607, 609 (9th Cir.1980) (per curiam). And in the public corruption context, "'thing of value' is defined broadly to include the value which the defendant subjectively attaches to the items received." *United States v. Renzi,* 769 F.3d 731, 744 (9th Cir. 2014) (internal quotation marks omitted).

Federal Election Commission (FEC) regulations recognize the value to a campaign of at least some forms of information, stating that the term "anything of value" includes "the provision of any goods or services without charge," such as "membership lists" and "mailing lists." 11 C.F.R. § 100.52(d)(l). The FEC has concluded that the phrase includes a state-by-state list of activists. See Citizens for Responsibility and Ethics in Washington v. FEC, 475 F.3d 337, 338 (D.C. Cir. 2007) (describing the FEC's findings). Likewise, polling data provided to a campaign constitutes a "contribution." FEC Advisory Opinion 1990-12 (Strub), 1990 WL 153454 (citing 11C.F.R. § 106.4(b)). And in the specific context of the foreign-contributions ban, the FEC has concluded that "election materials used in previous Canadian campaigns," including "flyers, advertisements, door hangers, tri-folds, signs, and other printed material," constitute "anything of value," even though "the value of these materials may be nominal or difficult to ascertain." FEC Advisory Opinion 2007-22 (Hurysz), 2007 WL 5172375, at *5.

These authorities would support the view that candidate-related opposition research given to a campaign for the purpose of influencing an election could constitute a contribution to which the foreign-source ban could apply. A campaign can be assisted not only by the provision of funds, but also by the provision of derogatory information about an opponent. Political campaigns frequently conduct and pay for opposition research. A foreign entity that engaged in such research and provided resulting information to a campaign could exert a greater effect on an election, and a greater tendency to ingratiate the donor to the candidate, than a gift of money or tangible things of value. At the same time, no judicial decision has treated the voluntary provision of uncompensated opposition research or similar information as a thing of value that could amount to a contribution under campaign-finance law. Such an interpretation could have implications beyond the foreign-source ban, see 52 U.S.C. § 30116(a) (imposing monetary limits on campaign contributions), and raise First Amendment questions. Those questions could be especially difficult where the information consisted simply of the recounting of historically accurate facts. It is uncertain how courts would resolve those issues.

ii. *Willfuness*

Even assuming that the promised "documents and information that would incriminate Hillary" constitute a "thing of value" under campaign-finance law, the government would encounter other challenges in seeking to obtain and sustain a conviction. Most significantly, the government has not obtained admissible evidence that is likely to establish the scienter requirement beyond a reasonable doubt. To prove that a defendant acted "knowingly and willfully," the government would have to show that the defendant had general knowledge that his conduct was unlawful. U.S. Department of Justice, *Federal Prosecution of Election Offenses* 123 (8th ed. Dec.2017) *("Election Offenses"); see Bluman,* 800 F. Supp. 2d at 292 (noting that a willful violation requires "proof of the defendant's knowledge of the law"); *Danielczyk,* 917 F. Supp. 2d at 577 ("knowledge of general unlawfulness"). "This standard creates an elevated scienter element requiring, at the very least, that application of the law to the facts in question be fairly clear. When there is substantial doubt concerning whether the law applies to the facts of a particular matter, the offender is more likely to have an intent defense." *Election Offenses* 123.

On the facts here, the government would unlikely be able to prove beyond a reasonable doubt that the June 9 meeting participants had general knowledge that their conduct was unlawful. The investigation has not developed evidence that the participants in the meeting were familiar with the foreign-contribution ban or the application of federal law to the relevant factual context. The government does not have strong evidence of surreptitious behavior or efforts at concealment at the time of the June 9 meeting. While the government has evidence of later efforts to prevent disclosure of the nature of the June 9 meeting that could circumstantially provide support for a showing of scienter, *see* Volume II, Section II.G, *infra,* that concealment occurred more than a year later, involved individuals who did not attend the June 9 meeting, and may reflect an intention to avoid political consequences rather than any prior knowledge of illegality. Additionally, in light of the unresolved legal questions about whether giving "documents and information" of the sort offered here constitutes a campaign contribution, Trump Jr. could mount a factual defense that he did not believe his response to the offer and the June 9 meeting itself violated the law. Given his less direct involvement in arranging the June 9 meeting, Kushner could likely mount a similar defense. And, while Manafort is experienced with political campaigns, the Office has not developed evidence showing that he had relevant knowledge of these legal issues.

iii. Difficulties in Valuing Promised Information

The Office would also encounter difficulty proving beyond a reasonable doubt that the value of the promised documents and information exceeds the $2,000 threshold for a criminal violation, as well as the $25,000 threshold for felony punishment. See 52 U.S.C. § 30109(d)(l). The type of evidence commonly used to establish the value of non-monetary contributions-such as pricing the contribution on a commercial market or determining the upstream acquisition cost or the cost of distribution-would likely be unavailable or ineffective in this factual setting.

Although damaging opposition research is surely valuable to a campaign, it appears that the information ultimately delivered in the meeting was not valuable. And while value in a conspiracy may well be measured by what the participants expected to receive at the time of the agreement, see, e.g., United States v. Tombrello, 666 F.2d 485, 489 (11th Cir. 1982), Goldstone's description of the offered material here was quite general. His suggestion of the information's value-i.e., that it would "incriminate Hillary" and "would be very useful to [Trump Jr.'s] father"-was non• specific and may have been understood as being of uncertain worth or reliability, given Goldstone's lack of direct access to the original source. The uncertainty over what would be delivered could be reflected in Trump Jr.'s response ("if it's what you say I love it") (emphasis added).

Accordingly, taking into account the high burden to establish a culpable mental state in a campaign-finance prosecution and the difficulty in establishing the required valuation, the Office decided not to pursue criminal campaign-finance charges against Trump Jr. or other campaign officials for the events culminating in the June 9 meeting.

ii. Willfuness

As discussed, to establish a criminal campaign-finance violation, the government must prove that the defendant acted "knowingly and willfully." 52 U.S.C. § 30109(d)(1)(A)(i). That standard requires proof that the defendant knew generally that his conduct was unlawful. *Election Offenses* 123. Given the uncertainties noted above, the "willfulness" requirement would pose a substantial barrier to prosecution.

4. False Statements and Obstruction of the Investigation

The Office determined that certain individuals associated with the Campaign lied to investigators about Campaign contacts with Russia and have taken other actions to interfere with the investigation. As explained below, the Office therefore charged some U.S. persons connected to the Campaign with false statements and obstruction offenses.

a. Overvie of Governing Law

False Statements. The principal federal statute criminalizing false statements to government investigators is 18 U.S.C. § 1001. As relevant here, under Section 1001 (a)(2), it is a crime to knowingly and willfully "make[] any materially false, fictitious, or fraudulent statement or representation" "in any matter within the jurisdiction of the executive . . . branch of the Government." An FBI investigation is a matter within the Executive Branch's jurisdiction. *United States v. Rodgers,* 466 U.S. 475, 479 (1984). The statute also applies to a subset of legislative branch actions — viz., administrative matters and "investigation[s] or review[s]" conducted by a congressional committee or subcommittee. 18 U.S.C. § t00t(c)(1) and (2); *see United States v. Pickett,* 353 F.3d 62, 66 (D.C. Cir. 2004).

Whether the statement was made to law enforcement or congressional investigators, the government must prove beyond a reasonable doubt the same basic non-jurisdictional elements: the statement was false, fictitious, or fraudulent; the defendant knew both that it was false and that it was unlawful to make a false statement; and the false statement was material. See, e.g., United States v. Smith, 831 F.3d 1207, 1222 n.27 (9th Cir. 2017) (listing elements); see also Ninth Circuit Pattern Instruction 8.73 & cmt. (explaining that the Section 1001 jury instruction was modified in light ofthe Department ofJustice's position that the phrase "knowingly and willfully" in the statute requires the defendant's knowledge that his or her conduct was unlawful).

In the D.C. Circuit, the government must prove that the statement was actually false; a statement that is misleading but "literally true" does not satisfy Section 1001(a)(2). See United States v. Milton, 8 F.3d 39, 45(D.C. Cir. 1993); United States v. Dale, 991 F.2d 819, 832-33 & n.22 (D.C. Cir. 1993). For that false statement to qualify as "material," it must have a natural tendency to influence, or be capable of influencing, a discrete decision or any other function of the agency to which it is addressed. See United States v. Gaudin, 515 U.S. 506, 509 (1995); United States v. Moore, 612 F.3d 698, 701 (D.C. Cir. 2010).

Perjury. Under the federal perjury statutes, it is a crime for a witness testifying under oath before a grand jury to knowingly make any false material declaration. *See* 18 U.S.C. § 1623. The government must prove four elements beyond a reasonable doubt to obtain a conviction under Section 1623(a): the defendant testified under oath before a federal grand jury; the defendant's testimony was false in one or more respects; the false testimony concerned matters that were material to the grand jury investigation; and the false testimony was knowingly given. *United States v. Bridges,* 717 F.2d 1444, 1449 n.30 (D.C. Cir. 1983). The general perjury statute, 18U.S.C. § 1621, also applies to grand jury testimony and has similar elements, except that it requires that the witness have acted willfully and that the government satisfy "strict common-law requirements for establishing falsity." *See Dunn v. United States,* 442 U.S. 100, 106 & n.6 (1979) (explaining "the two-witness rule" and the corroboration that it demands).

Obstruction of Justice. Three basic elements are common to the obstruction statutes pertinent to this Office's charging decisions: an obstructive act; some form of nexus between the obstructive act and an official proceeding; and criminal *(i.e.,* corrupt) intent. A detailed discussion of those elements, and the law governing obstruction of justice more generally, is included in Volume II of the report.

c. *Application to Certain Individuals*

i. *George Papadopoulos*

Investigators approached Papadopoulos for an interview based on his role as a foreign policy advisor to the Trump Campaign and his suggestion to a foreign government representative that Russia had indicated that it could assist the Campaign through the anonymous release of information damaging to candidate Clinton. On January 27, 2017, Papadopoulos agreed to be interviewed by FBI agents, who informed him that the interview was part of the investigation into potential Russian government interference in the 2016 presidential election.

During the interview, Papadopoulos lied about the timing, extent, and nature of his communications with Joseph Mifsud, Olga Polonskaya, and Ivan Timofeev. With respect to timing, Papadopoulos acknowledged that he had met Mifsud and that Mifsud told him the Russians had "dirt" on Clinton in the form of "thousands of emails." But Papadopoulos stated multiple times that those communications occurred before he joined the Trump Campaign and that it was a "very strange coincidence" to be told of the "dirt" before he started working for the Campaign. This account was false. Papadopoulos met Mifsud for the first time on approximately March 14, 2016, after Papadopoulos had already learned he would be a foreign policy advisor for the Campaign. Mifsud showed interest in Papadopoulos only after learning of his role on the Campaign. And Mifsud told Papadopoulos about the Russians possessing "dirt" on candidate Clinton in late April 2016, more than a month after Papadopoulos had joined the Campaign and been publicly announced by candidate Trump. Statement of Offense ,r,r 25-26, United States v. George Papadopoulos, No. 1: 17-cr-182 (D.D.C. Oct. 5, 2017), Doc. 19 ("Papadopoulos Statement of Offense").

Papadopoulos also made false statements in an effort to mmirruze the extent and importance of his communications with Mifsud. For example, Papadopoulos stated that "[Mifsud]'s a nothing," that he thought Mifsud was "just a guy talk[ing] up connections or something," and that he believed Mifsud was "BS'ing to be completely honest with you." In fact, however, Papadopoulos understood Mifsud to have substantial connections to high-level Russian government officials and that Mifsud spoke with some of those officials in Moscow before telling Papadopoulos about the "dirt." Papadopoulos also engaged in extensive communications over a period of months with Mifsud about foreign policy issues for the Campaign, including efforts to arrange a "history making" meeting between the Campaign and Russian government officials. In addition, Papadopoulos failed to inform investigators that Mifsud had introduced him to Timofeev, the Russian national who Papadopoulos understood to be connected to the Russian Ministry of Foreign Affairs, despite being asked if he had met with Russian nationals or "[a]nyone with a Russian accent" during the campaign. *Papadopoulos* Statement of Offense ¶¶ 27-29.

Papadopoulos also falsely claimed that he met Polonskaya before he joined the Campaign, and falsely told the FBI that he had "no" relationship at all with her. He stated that the extent of their communications was her sending emails — "Just, 'Hi, how are you?' That's it." In truth, however, Papadopoulos met Polonskaya on March 24, 2016, after he had joined the Campaign; he believed that she had connections to high-level Russian government officials and could help him arrange a potential foreign policy trip to Russia. During the campaign he emailed and spoke with her over Skype on numerous occasions about the potential foreign policy trip to Russia. *Papadopoulos* Statement of Offense ¶¶ 30-31.

Papadopoulos's false statements in January 2017 impeded the FBI's investigation into Russian interference in the 2016 presidential election. Most immediately, those statements hindered investigators' ability to effectively question Mifsud when he was interviewed in the lobby of a Washington, D.C. hotel on February 10, 2017. *See* Gov't Sent. Mem. at 6, *United States v. George Papadopoulos*, No. 1:17-cr-182 (D.D.C. Aug. 18, 2017),

Doc. 44. During that interview, Mifsud admitted to knowing Papadopoulos and to having introduced him to Polonskaya and Timofeev. But Mifsud denied that he had advance knowledge that Russia was in possession of emails damaging to candidate Clinton, stating that he and Papadopoulos had discussed cybersecurity and hacking as a larger issue and that Papadopoulos must have misunderstood their conversation. Mifsud also falsely stated that he had not seen Papadopoulos since the meeting at which Mifsud introduced him to Polonskaya, even though emails, text messages, and other information show that Mifsud met with Papadopoulos on at least two other occasions—April 12 and April 26, 2016. In addition, Mifsud omitted that he had drafted (or edited) the follow-up message that Polonskaya sent to Papadopoulos following the initial meeting and that, as reflected in the language of that email chain ("Baby, thank you!"), Mifsud may have been involved in a personal relationship with Polonskaya at the time. The false information and omissions in Papadopoulos's January 2017 interview undermined investigators' ability to challenge Mifsud when he made these inaccurate statements.

Given the seriousness of the lies and omissions and their effect on the FBI's investigation, the Office charged Papadopoulos with making false statements to the FBI, in violation of 18 U.S.C. § 1001. Information, *United States v. George Papadopoulos*, No. 1:17-cr-182 (D.D.C. Oct. 3, 2017), Doc. 8. On October 7, 2017, Papadopoulos pleaded guilty to that charge pursuant to a plea agreement. On September 7, 2018, he was sentenced to 14 days of imprisonment, a $9,500 fine, and 200 hours of community service.

iii. Michael Flynn

Michael Flynn agreed to be interviewed by the FBI on January 24, 2017, four days after he had officially assumed his duties as National Security Advisor to the President. During the interview, Flynn made several false statements pertaining to his communications with the Russian ambassador.

First, Flynn made two false statements about his conversations with Russian Ambassador Kislyak in late December 2016, at a time when the United States had imposed sanctions on Russia for interfering with the 2016 presidential election and Russia was considering its response. See Flynn

Statement of Offense. Flynn told the agents that he did not ask Kislyak to refrain from escalating the situation in response to the United States's imposition of sanctions. That statement was false. On December 29, 2016, Flynn called Kislyak to request Russian restraint. Flynn made the call immediately after speaking to a senior Transition Team official (K.T. McFarland) about what to communicate to Kislyak. Flynn then spoke with McFarland again after the Kislyak call to report on the substance of that conversation. Flynn also falsely told the FBI that he did not remember a follow-up conversation in which Kislyak stated that Russia had chosen to moderate its response to the U.S. sanctions as a result of Flynn's request. On December 31, 2016, Flynn in fact had such a conversation with Kislyak, and he again spoke with McFarland within hours of the call to relay the substance of his conversation with Kislyak. See Flynn Statement of Offense 13.

Second, Flynn made false statements about calls he had previously made to representatives of Russia and other countries regarding a resolution submitted by Egypt to the United Nations Security Council on December 21, 2016. Specifically, Flynn stated that he only asked the countries' positions on how they would vote on the resolution and that he did not request that any of the countries take any particular action on the resolution. That statement was false. On December 22, 2016, Flynn called Kislyak, informed him of the incoming Trump Administration's opposition to the resolution, and requested that Russia vote against or delay the resolution. Flynn also falsely stated that Kislyak never described Russia's response to his December 22 request regarding the resolution. Kislyak in fact told Flynn in a conversation on December 23, 2016, that Russia would not vote against the resolution if it came to a vote. *See Flynn Statement of Offense* 4.

Flynn made these false statements to the FBI at a time when he was serving as National Security Advisor and when the FBI had an open investigation into Russian interference in the 2016 presidential election, including the nature of any links between the Trump Campaign and Russia. Flynn's false statements and omissions impeded and otherwise had a material impact on that ongoing investigation. *Flynn* Statement of Offense ¶¶ 1-2. They also came shortly before Flynn made separate submissions to the Department of Justice, pursuant to FARA, that also contained materially false statements and omissions. *Id* ,r 5. Based on the totality of that conduct, the Office decided to charge Flynn with making false statements to the FBI, in violation of 18 U.S.C.§ 1001(a). On December 1, 2017, and pursuant to a plea agreement, Flynn pleaded guilty to that charge and also admitted his false statements to the Department in his FARA filing. *See id.;* Plea Agreement, *United States v. Michael T Flynn,* No. 1:17-cr-232 (D.D.C. Dec. 1, 2017), Doc. 3. Flynn is awaiting sentencing.

iv. Michael Cohen

Michael Cohen was the executive vice president and special counsel to the Trump Organization when Trump was president of the Trump Organization. Information ,r 1, *United States v. Cohen,* No. 1 :18-cr-850 (S.D.N.Y. Nov. 29, 2018), Doc. 2 *("Cohen* Information"). From the fall of 2015 through approximately June 2016, Cohen was involved in a project to build a Trump-branded tower and adjoining development in Moscow. The project was known as Trump Tower Moscow.

In 2017, Cohen was called to testify before the House Permanent Select Committee on Intelligence (HPSCI) and the Senate Select Committee on Intelligence (SSCI), both of which were investigating Russian interference in the 2016 presidential election and possible links between Russia and the presidential campaigns. In late August 2017, in advance of his testimony, Cohen caused a two-page statement to be sent to SSCI and HPSCI addressing Trump Tower Moscow. Cohen Information ,r,r 2-3. The letter contained three representations relevant here. First, Cohen stated that the Trump Moscow project had ended in January 2016 and that he had briefed candidate Trump on the project only three times before making the unilateral decision to terminate it. Second, Cohen represented that he never agreed to travel to Russia in connection with the project and never considered asking Trump to travel for the project. Third, Cohen stated that he did not recall any Russian government contact about the project, including any response to an email that he had sent to a Russian government email account. Cohen Information f 4. Cohen later asked that his two-page statement be incorporated into his testimony's transcript before SSCI, and he ultimately gave testimony to SSCI that was consistent with that statement. Cohen Inforrnation f 5.

Each of the foregoing representations in Cohen's two-page statement was false and misleading. Consideration of the project had extended through approximately June 2016 and included more than three progress reports from Cohen to Trump. Cohen had discussed with Felix Sater his own travel to Russia as part of the project, and he had inquired about the possibility of Trump traveling there-both with the candidate himself and with senior campaign official Corey Lewandowski. Cohen did recall that he had received a response to the email that he sent to Russian government spokesman Dmitry Peskov-in particular, that he received an email reply and had a follow-up phone conversation with an English-speaking assistant to Peskov in mid-January 2016. Cohen Information 7. Cohen knew the statements in the letter to be false at the time, and admitted that he made them in an effort (1) to minimize the links between the project and Trump (who by this time was President), and (2) to give the false impression that the project had ended before the first vote in the Republican Party primary process, in the hopes of limiting the ongoing Russia investigations. Id.

Given the nature of the false statements and the fact that he repeated them during his initial interview with the Office, we charged Cohen with violating Section 1001. On November 29, 2018, Cohen pleaded guilty pursuant to a plea agreement to a single-count information charging him with making false statements in a matter within the jurisdiction of the legislative branch, in violation of 18 U.S.C. § 1001(a)(2) and (c). *Cohen Information.* The case was transferred to the district judge presiding over the separate prosecution of Cohen pursued by the Southern District of New York (after a referral from our Office). On December 7, 2018, this Office submitted a letter to that judge recommending that Cohen's cooperation with our investigation be taken into account in sentencing Cohen on both the false-statements charge and the offenses in the Southern District prosecution. On December 12, 2018, the judge sentenced Cohen to two months of imprisonment on the false-statements count, to run concurrently with a 36-month sentence imposed on the other counts.

vi. Jeff Sessions

As set forth in Volume I, Section IV.A.6, supra, the investigation established that, while a U.S. Senator and a Trump Campaign advisor, former Attorney General Jeff Sessions interacted with Russian Ambassador Kislyak during the week of the Republican National Convention in July 2016 and again at a meeting in Sessions's Senate office in September 2016. The investigation also established that Sessions and Kislyak both attended a reception held before candidate Trump's foreign policy speech at the Mayflower Hotel in Washington, D.C., in April 2016, and that it is possible that they met briefly at that reception.

The Office considered whether, in light of these interactions, Sessions committed perjury before, or made false statements to, Congress in connection with his confirmation as Attorney General. In January 2017 testimony during his confirmation hearing, Sessions stated in response to a question about Trump Campaign communications with the Russian government that he had "been called a surrogate at a time or two in that campaign and I didn't have - did not have communications with the Russians." In written responses submitted on January 17, 2017, Sessions answered "[n]o" to a question asking whether he had "been in contact with anyone connected to any part of the Russian government about the 2016 election, either before or after election day." And, in a March 2017 supplement to his testimony, Sessions identified two of the campaign-period contacts with Ambassador Kislyak noted above, which had been reported in the media following the January 2017 confirmation hearing. Sessions stated in the supplemental response that he did "not recall any discussions with the Russian Ambassador, or any other representatives of the Russian government, regarding the political campaign on these occasions or any other occasion."

Although the investigation established that Sessions interacted with Kislyak on the occasions described above and that Kislyak mentioned the presidential campaign on at least one occasion, the evidence is not sufficient to prove that Sessions gave knowingly false answers to Russia-related questions in light of the wording and context of those questions. With respect to Sessions's statements that he did "not recall any discussions with the Russian Ambassador ... regarding the political campaign" and he had not been in contact with any Russian official "about the 2016 election," the evidence concerning the nature of Sessions's interactions with Kislyak makes it plausible that Sessions did not recall discussing the campaign with Kislyak at the time of his statements. Similarly, while Sessions stated in his January 2017 oral testimony that he "did not have communications with Russians," he did so in response to a question that had linked such communications to an alleged "continuing exchange of information" between the Trump Campaign and Russian government intermediaries. Sessions later explained to the Senate and to the Office that he understood the question as narrowly calling for disclosure of interactions with Russians that involved the exchange of campaign information, as distinguished from more routine contacts with Russian nationals. Given the context in which the question was asked, that understanding is plausible

. Accordingly, the Office concluded that the evidence was insufficient to prove that Sessions was willfully untruthful in his answers and thus insufficient to obtain or sustain a conviction for perjury or false statements. Consistent with the Principles of Federal Prosecution, the Office therefore determined not to pursue charges against Sessions and informed his counsel of that decision in March 2018

vii.   Others Interviewed During the Investigation

The Office considered whether, during the course of the investigation, other individuals interviewed either omitted material information or provided information determined to be false. Applying the Principles of Federal Prosecution, the Office did not seek criminal charges against any individuals other than those listed above.   In some instances, that decision was due to evidentiary hurdles to proving falsity. In others, the Office determined that the witness ultimately provided truthful information and that considerations of culpability, deterrence, and resource- reservation wei hed a ainst   rosecution. *See* Justice Manual   9-27.220 9-27.230

VOLUME II OF II

INTRODUCTION TO VOLUME II

This report is submitted to the Attorney General pursuant to 28 C.F.R. § 600.8(c), which states that, "[a]t the conclusion of the Special Counsel's work, he ... shall provide the Attorney General a confidential report explaining the prosecution or declination decisions [the Special Counsel] reached."

Beginning in 2017, the President of the United States took a variety of actions towards the ongoing FBI investigation into Russia's interference in the 2016 presidential election and related matters that raised questions about whether he had obstructed justice. The Order appointing the Special Counsel gave this Office jurisdiction to investigate matters that arose directly from the FBT's Russia investigation, including whether the President had obstructed justice in connection with Russia-related investigations. The Special Counsel's jurisdiction also covered potentially obstructive acts related to the Special Counsel's investigation itself. This Volume of our report summarizes our obstruction-of-justice investigation of the President.

We first describe the considerations that guided our obstruction of justice investigation, and then provide an overview of this Volume:

> **First,** a traditional prosecution or declination decision entails a binary determination to initiate or decline a prosecution, but we determined not to make a traditional prosecutorial judgment. The Office of Legal Counsel (OLC) has issued an opinion finding that "the indictment or criminal prosecution of a sitting President would impermissibly undermine the capacity of the executive branch to perform its constitutionally assigned functions" in violation of "the constitutional separation of powers."! Given the role of the Special Counsel as an attorney in the Department of Justice and the framework of the Special Counsel regulations, *see* 28 U.S.C. § 515; 28 C.F.R. §

600.7(a), this Office accepted OLC's legal conclusion for the purpose of exercisingprosecutorialjurisdiction. And apart from OLC's constitutional view, we recognized that a federal criminal accusation against a sitting President would place burdens on the President's capacity to govern and potentially preempt constitutional processes for addressing presidential misconduct.[2]

Second, while the OLC opinion concludes that a sitting President may not be prosecuted, it recognizes that a criminal investigation during the President's term is permissible.[3] The OLC opinion also recognizes that a President does not have immunity after he leaves office.[4] And if individuals other than the President committed an obstruction offense, they may be prosecuted at this time. Given those considerations, the facts known to us, and the strong public interest in safeguarding the integrity of the criminal justice system, we conducted a thorough factual investigation in order to preserve the evidence when memories were fresh and documentary materials were available.

Third, we considered whether to evaluate the conduct we investigated under the Justice Manual standards governing prosecution and declination decisions, but we determined not to apply an approach that could potentially result in a judgment that the President committed crimes. The threshold step under the Justice Manual standards is to assess whether a person's conduct "constitutes a federal offense." U.S. Dep't of Justice, Justice Manual § 9-27.220 (2018) (Justice Manual). Fairness concerns counseled against potentially reaching thatjudgment when no charges can be brought. The ordinary means for an individual to respond to an accusation is through a speedy and public trial, with all the procedural protections that surround a criminal case. An individual who believes he was wrongly accused can use that process to seek to clear his name. In contrast, a prosecutor's judgment that crimes were committed, but that no charges will be brought, affords no such adversarial opportunity for public name-clearing before an impartial adjudicator.[5]

The concerns about the fairness of such a determination would be heightened in the case of a sitting President, where a federal prosecutor's accusation of a crime, even in an internal report, could carry consequences that extend beyond the realm of criminal justice. OLC noted similar concerns about sealed indictments. Even if an indictment were sealed during the President's term, OLC reasoned, "it would be very difficult to preserve [an indictment's] secrecy," and if an indictment became public, "[t]he stigma and opprobrium" could imperil the President's ability to govern."[6] Although a prosecutor's internal report would not represent a formal public accusation akin to an indictment, the possibility of the report's public disclosure and the absence of a neutral adjudicatory forum to review its findings counseled against potentially determining "that the person's conduct constitutes a federal offense." Justice Manual § 9-27.220.

Fourth, if we had confidence after a thorough investigation of the facts that the President clearly did not commit obstruction of justice, we would so state. Based on the facts and the applicable legal standards, however, we are unable to reach that judgment. The evidence we obtained about the President's actions and intent presents difficult issues that prevent us from conclusively determining that no criminal conduct occurred. Accordingly, while this report does not conclude that the President committed a crime, it also does not exonerate him.

This report on our investigation consists of four parts. Section I provides an overview of obstruction of justice principles and summarizes certain investigatory and evidentiary considerations. Section II sets forth the factual results of our obstruction investigation and analyzes the evidence. Section III addresses statutory and constitutional defenses. Section IV states our conclusion.

*****

1 A Sitting President's Amenability to Indictment and Criminal Prosecution, 24 Op. O.L.C. 222, 222, 260 (2000) (OLC Op.).

2 See U.S. CONST. Art. I § 2, cl. 5; § 3, cl. 6; cf OLC Op. at 257-258 (discussing relationship between impeachment and criminal prosecution of a sitting President).

3 OLC Op. at 257 n.36 ("A grand jury could continue to gather evidence throughout the period of immunity").

4 OLC Op. at 255 ("Recognizing an immunity from prosecution for a sitting President would not preclude such prosecution once the President's term is over or he is otherwise removed from office by resignation or impeachment").

5 For that reason, criticisms have been lodged against the practice of naming unindicted co-conspirators in an indictment. See United States v. Briggs, 514 F.2d 794, 802 (5th Cir. 1975) ("The courts have struck down with strong language efforts by grand juries to accuse persons of crime while affording them no forum in which to vindicate themselves."); see also Justice Manual § 9-11.130.

6 OLC Op. at 259 & n.38 (citation omitted).

EXECUTIVE SUMMARY TO VOLUME II

Our obstruction-of-justice inquiry focused on a series of actions by the President that related to the Russian-interference investigations, including the President's conduct towards the law enforcement officials overseeing the investigations and the witnesses to relevant events.

FACTUAL RESULTS OF THE OBSTRUCTION INVESTIGATION

The key issues and events we examined include the following:

The Campaign's response to reports about Russian support for Trump. During the 2016 presidential campaign, questions arose about the Russian government's apparent support for candidate Trump. After WikiLeaks released politically damaging Democratic Party emails that were reported to have been hacked by Russia, Trump publicly expressed skepticism that Russia was responsible for the hacks at the same time that he and other Campaign officials privately sought information about any further planned WikiLeaks releases. Trump also denied having any business in or connections to Russia, even though as late as June 2016 the Trump Organization had been pursuing a licensing deal for a skyscraper to be built in Russia called Trump Tower Moscow. After the election, the President expressed concerns to advisors that reports of Russia's election interference might lead the public to question the legitimacy of his election.

Conduct involving FBI Director Comey and Michael Flynn. In mid-January 2017, incoming National Security Advisor Michael Flynn falsely denied to the Vice President, other administration officials, and FBI agents that he had talked to Russian Ambassador Sergey Kislyak about Russia's response to U.S. sanctions on Russia for its election interference. On January 27, the day after the President was told that Flynn had lied to the Vice President and had made similar statements to the FBI, the President invited FBI Director Corney to a private dinner at the White House and told Corney that he needed loyalty. On February 14, the day after the President requested Flynn's resignation, the President told an outside advisor, "Now that we fired Flynn, the Russia thing is over." The advisor disagreed and said the investigations would continue.

Later that afternoon, the President cleared the Oval Office to have a one-on-one meeting with Corney. Referring to the FBI's investigation of Flynn, the President said, "I hope you can see your way clear to letting this go, to letting Flynn go. He is a good guy. I hope you can let this go." Shortly after requesting Flynn's resignation and speaking privately to Corney, the President sought to have Deputy National Security Advisor K.T. McFarland draft an internal letter stating that the President had not directed Flynn to discuss sanctions with Kislyak. McFarland declined because she did not know whether that was true, and a White House Counsel's Office attorney thought that the request would look like a quid pro quo for an ambassadorship she had been offered.

The President's reaction to the continuing Russia investigation. In February 2017, Attorney General Jeff Sessions began to assess whether he had to recuse himself from campaign•related investigations because of his role in the Trump Campaign. In early March, the President told White House Counsel Donald McGahn to stop Sessions from recusing. And after Sessions announced his recusal on March 2, the President expressed anger at the decision and told advisors that he should have an Attorney General who would protect him. That weekend, the President took Sessions aside at an event and urged him to "unrecuse." Later in March, Corney publicly disclosed at a congressional hearing that the FBI was investigating "the Russian government's efforts to interfere in the 2016 presidential election," including any links or coordination between the Russian government and the Trump Campaign. In the following days, the President reached out to the Director of National Intelligence and the leaders of the Central Intelligence Agency (CIA) and the National Security Agency (NSA) to ask them what they could do to publicly dispel the suggestion that the President had any connection to the Russian election-interference effort. The President also twice called Corney directly, notwithstanding guidance from McGahn to avoid direct contacts with the Department of Justice. Corney had previously assured the President that the FBI was not investigating him personally, and the President asked Corney to "lift the cloud" of the Russia investigation by saying that publicly.

The President's termination of Comey. On May 3, 2017, Comey testiftied in a congressional hearing, but declined to answer questions about whether the President was personally under investigation. Within days, the President decided to terminate Comey. The President insisted that the termination letter, which was written for public release, state that Comey had informed the President that he was not under investigation. The day of the firing, the White House maintained that Comey's termination resulted from independent recommendations from the Attorney General and Deputy Attorney General that Comey should be discharged for mishandling the Hillary Clinton email investigation. But the President had decided to fire Comey before hearing from the Department of Justice. The day after firing Comey, the President told Russian officials that he had "faced great pressure because of Russia," which had been "taken off" by Comey's firing. The next day, the President acknowledged in a television interview that he was going to fire Comey regardless of the Department of Justice's recommendation and that when he "decided to just do it," he was thinking that "this thing with Trump and Russia is a made-up story." In response to a question about whether he was angry with Comey about the Russia investigation, the President said, "As far as I'm concerned, I want that thing to be absolutely done properly," adding that firing Comey "might even lengthen out the investigation."

The appointment of a Special Counsel and efforts to remove him. On May 17, 2017, the Acting Attorney General for the Russia investigation appointed a Special Counsel to conduct the investigation and related matters. The President reacted to news that a Special Counsel had been appointed by telling advisors that it was "the end of his presidency" and demanding that Sessions resign. Sessions submitted his resignation, but the President ultimately did not accept it. The President told aides that the Special Counsel had conflicts ofinterest and suggested that the Special Counsel therefore could not serve. The President's advisors told him the asserted conflicts were meritless and had already been considered by the Department of Justice.

On June 14, 2017, the media reported that the Special Counsel's Office was investigating whether the President had obstructed justice. Press reports called this "a major turning point" in the investigation: while Comey had told the President he was not under investigation, following Comey's firing, the President now was under investigation. The President reacted to this news with a series of tweets criticizing the Department of Justice and the Special Counsel's investigation. On June 17, 2017, the President called McGahn at home and directed him to call the Acting Attorney General and say that the Special Counsel had conflicts of interest and must be removed. McGahn did not carry out the direction, however, deciding that he would resign rather than trigger what he regarded as a potential Saturday Night Massacre.

Efforts to curtail the Special Counsel's investigation. Two days after directing McGahn to have the Special Counsel removed, the President made another attempt to affect the course of the Russia investigation. On June 19, 2017, the President met one-on-one in the Oval Office with his former campaign manager Corey Lewandowski, a trusted advisor outside the government, and dictated a message for Lewandowski to deliver to Sessions. The message said that Sessions should publicly announce that, notwithstanding his recusal from the Russia investigation, the investigation was "very unfair" to the President, the President had done nothing wrong, and Sessions planned to meet with the Special Counsel and "let [him] move forward with investigating election meddling for future elections." Lewandowski said he understood what the President wanted Sessions to do.

One month later, in another private meeting with Lewandowski on July 19, 20 I 7, the President asked about the status of his message for Sessions to limit the Special Counsel investigation to future election interference. Lewandowski told the President that the message would be delivered soon. Hours after that meeting, the President publicly criticized Sessions in an interview with the New York Times, and then issued a series of tweets making it clear that Sessions's job was in jeopardy.

Lewandowski did not want to deliver the President's message personally, so he asked senior White House official Rick Dearborn to deliver it to Sessions. Dearborn was uncomfortable with the task and did not follow through.

Efforts to prevent public disclosure of evidence. Tn the summer of 2017, the President learned that media outlets were asking questions about the June 9, 2016 meeting at Trump Tower between senior campaign officials, including Donald Trump Jr., and a Russian lawyer who was said to be offering damaging information about Hillary Clinton as "part of Russia and its government's support for Mr. Trump." On several occasions, the President directed aides not to publicly disclose the emails setting up the June 9 meeting, suggesting that the emails would not leak and that the number of lawyers with access to them should be limited. Before the emails became public, the President edited a press statement for Trump Jr. by deleting a line that acknowledged that the meeting was with "an individual who [Trump Jr.] was told might have information helpful to the campaign" and instead said only that the meeting was about adoptions of Russian children. When the press asked questions about the President's involvement in Trump Jr. 's statement, the President's personal lawyer repeatedly denied the President had played any role.

Further efforts to have the Attorney General take control of the investigation. In early summer 2017, the President called Sessions at home and again asked him to reverse his recusal from the Russia investigation. Sessions did not reverse his recusal. In October 20 I 7, the President met privately with Sessions in the Oval Office and asked him to "take [a] look" at investigating Clinton. in December 2017, shortly after Flynn pleaded guilty pursuant to a cooperation agreement, the President met with Sessions in the Oval Office and suggested, according to notes taken by a senior advisor, that if Sessions unrecused and took back supervision of the Russia investigation, he would be a "hero." The President told Sessions, "I'm not going to do anything or direct you to do anything. I just want to be treated fairly." In response, Sessions volunteered that he had never seen anything "improper" on the campaign and told the President there was a "whole new leadership team" in place. He did not unrecuse.

Efforts to have McGahn deny that the President had ordered him to have the Special Counsel removed. in early 2018, the press reported that the President had directed McGahn to have the Special Counsel removed in June 2017 and that McGahn had threatened to resign rather than carry out the order. The President reacted to the news stories by directing White House officials to tell McGahn to dispute the story and create a record stating he had not been ordered to have the Special Counsel removed. McGahn told those officials that the media reports were accurate in stating that the President had directed McGahn to have the Special Counsel removed. The President then met with McGahn in the Oval Office and again pressured him to deny the reports. In the same meeting, the President also asked McGahn why he had told the Special Counsel about the President's effort to remove the Special Counsel and why McGahn took notes of his conversations with the President. McGahn refused to back away from what he remembered happening and perceived the President to be testing his mettle.

Conduct towards Flynn, Manafort, ... After Flynn withdrew from a joint defense agreement with the President and began cooperating with the government, the President's personal counsel left a message for Flynn's attorneys reminding them of the President's warm feelings towards Flynn, which he said "still remains," and asking for a "heads up" if Flynn knew "information that implicates the President." When Flynn's counsel reiterated that Flynn could no longer share information pursuant to a joint defense agreement, the President's personal counsel said he would make sure that the President knew that Flynn's actions reflected "hostility" towards the President. During Manafort's prosecution and when the jury in his criminal. trial was deliberating, the President praised Manafort in public, said that Manafort was being treated unfairly, and declined to rule out a pardon.

Conduct involving Michael Cohen. The President's conduct towards Michael Cohen, a former Trump Organization executive, changed from praise for Cohen when he falsely minimized the President's involvement in the Trump Tower Moscow project, to castigation of Cohen when he became a cooperating witness. From September 2015 to June 2016, Cohen had pursued the Trump Tower Moscow project on behalf of the Trump Organization and had briefed candidate Trump on the project numerous times, including discussing whether Trump should travel to Russia to advance the deal. In 2017, Cohen provided false testimony to Congress about the project, including stating that he had only briefed Trump on the project three times and never discussed travel to Russia with him, in an effort to adhere to a "party line" that Cohen said was developed to minimize the President's connections to Russia.

While preparing for his congressional testimony, Cohen had extensive discussions with the President's personal counsel, who, according to Cohen, said that Cohen should "stay on message" and not contradict the President. After the FBI searched Cohen's home and office in April 2018, the President publicly asserted that Cohen would not "flip," contacted him directly to tell him to "stay strong," and privately passed messages of support to him. Cohen also discussed pardons with the President's personal counsel and believed that if he stayed on message he would be taken care of. But after Cohen began cooperating with the government in the summer of 2018, the President publicly criticized him, called him a "rat," and suggested that his family members had committed crimes.

Overarching factual issues. We did not make a traditional prosecution decision about these facts, but the evidence we obtained supports several general statements about the President's conduct. Several features of the conduct we investigated distinguish it from typical obstruction-of justice cases. First, the investigation concerned the President, and some of his actions, such as firing the FBI director, involved facially lawful acts within his Article IT authority, which raises constitutional issues discussed below.

At the same time, the President's position as the head of the Executive Branch provided him with unique and powerful means of influencing official proceedings, subordinate officers, and potential witnesses-all of which is relevant to a potential obstruction-of-justice analysis. Second, unlike cases in which a subject engages in obstruction of justice to cover up a crime, the evidence we obtained did not establish that the President was involved in an underlying crime related to Russian election interference. Although the obstruction statutes do not require proof of such a crime, the absence of that evidence affects the analysis of the President's intent and requires consideration ofother possible motives for his conduct. Third, many of the President's acts directed at witnesses, including discouragement of cooperation with the government and suggestions of possible future pardons, took place in public view. That circumstance is unusual, but no principle of law excludes public acts from the reach of the obstruction laws. Ifthe likely effect ofpublic acts is to influence witnesses or alter their testimony, the harm to the justice system's integrity is the same.

Although the series of events we investigated involved discrete acts, the overall pattern of the President's conduct towards the investigations can shed light on the nature of the President's acts and the inferences that can be drawn about his intent. In particular, the actions we investigated can be divided into two phases, reflecting a possible shift in the President's motives. The first phase covered the period from the President's first interactions with Comey through the President's firing of Comey. During that time, the President had been repeatedly told he was not personally under investigation. Soon after the firing of Comey and the appointment of the Special Counsel, however, the President became aware that his own conduct was being investigated in an obstruction-of-justice inquiry. At that point, the President engaged in a second phase of conduct, involving public attacks on the investigation, non-public efforts to control it, and efforts in both public and private to encourage witnesses not to cooperate with the investigation. Judgments about the nature of the President's motives during each phase would be informed by the totality of the evidence.

STATUTORY AND CONSTITUTIONAL DEFENSES

The President's counsel raised statutory and constitutional defenses to a possible obstruction-of-justice analysis of the conduct we investigated. We concluded that none of those legal defenses provided a basis for declining to investigate the facts.

Statutory defenses. Consistent with precedent and the Department of Justice's general approach to interpreting obstruction statutes, we concluded that several statutes could apply here. See 18 U.S.C. §§ 1503, 1505, 1512(b)(3), 1512(c)(2). Section 1512(c)(2) is an omnibus obstruction-of-justice provision that covers a range of obstructive acts directed at pending or contemplated official proceedings. No principle of statutory construction justifies narrowing the provision to cover only conduct that impairs the integrity or availability of evidence. Sections 1503 and 1505 also offer broad protection against obstructive acts directed at pending grand jury, judicial, administrative, and congressional proceedings, and they are supplemented by a provision in Section I 5 I 2(b) aimed specifically at conduct intended to prevent or hinder the communication to law enforcement of information related to a federal crime.

Constitutional defenses. As for constitutional defenses arising from the President's status as the head of the Executive Branch, we recognized that the Department of Justice and the courts have not. definitively resolved these issues. We therefore examined those issues through the framework established by Supreme Court precedent governing separation-of-powers issues. The Department of Justice and the President's personal counsel have recognized that the President is subject to statutes that prohibit obstruction ofjustice by bribing a witness or suborning perjury because that conduct does not implicate his constitutional authority. With respect to whether the President can be found to have obstructed justice by exercising his powers under Article II of the Constitution, we concluded that Congress has authority to prohibit a President's corrupt use of his authority in order to protect the integrity of the administration ofjustice

Under applicable Supreme Court precedent, the Constitution does not categorically and permanently immunize a President for obstructing justice through the use of his Article II powers. The separation-of-powers doctrine authorizes Congress to protect official proceedings, including those of courts and grand juries, from corrupt, obstructive acts regardless of their source. We also concluded that any inroad on presidential authority that would occur from prohibiting corrupt acts does not undermine the President's ability to fulfill his constitutional mission. The term "corruptly" sets a demanding standard. It requires a concrete showing that a person acted with an intent to obtain an improper advantage for himself or someone else, inconsistent with official duty and the rights of others.

 A preclusion of "corrupt" official action does not diminish the President's ability to exercise Article II powers. For example, the proper supervision of criminal law does not demand freedom for the President to act with a corrupt intention of shielding himself from criminal punishment, avoiding financial liability, or preventing personal embarrassment. To the contrary, a statute that prohibits official action undertaken for such corrupt purposes furthers, rather than hinders, the impartial and evenhanded administration of the law.

It also aligns with the President's constitutional duty to faithfully execute the laws. Finally, we concluded that in the rare case in which a criminal investigation of the President's conduct is justified, inquiries to determine whether the President acted for a corrupt motive should not impermissibly chill his performance of his constitutionally assigned duties. The conclusion that Congress may apply the obstruction laws to the President's corrupt exercise of the powers of office accords with our constitutional system of checks and balances and the principle that no person is above the law.

CONCLUSION

Because we determined not to make a traditional prosecutorial judgment, we did not draw ultimate conclusions about the President's conduct. The evidence we obtained about the President's actions and intent presents difficult issues that would need to be resolved if we were making a traditional prosecutorial judgment. At the same time, if we had confidence after a thorough investigation of the facts that the President clearly did not commit obstruction ofjustice, we would so state. Based on the facts and the applicable legal standards, we are unable to reach that judgment. Accordingly, while this report does not conclude that the President committed a crime, it also does not exonerate him.

I. BACKGROUND LEGAL AND EVIDENTIARY PRINCIPLES

A. Legal Framework of Obstruction of Justice

The May 17, 2017 Appointment Order and the Special Counsel regulations provide this Office with jurisdiction to investigate "federal crimes committed in the course of, and with intent to interfere with, the Special Counsel's investigation, such as perjury, obstruction of justice, destruction of evidence, and intimidation of witnesses." 28 C.F.R. § 600.4(a). Because of that description ofourjurisdiction, we sought evidence for our obstruction-of-justice investigation with the elements of obstruction offenses in mind. Our evidentiary analysis is similarly focused on the elements of such offenses, although we do not draw conclusions on the ultimate questions that govern a prosecutorial decision under the Principles of Federal Prosecution. See Justice Manual § 9-27.000 et seq. (2018).

Here, we summarize the law interpreting the elements of potentially relevant obstruction statutes in an ordinary case. This discussion does not address the unique constitutional issues that arise in an inquiry into official acts by the President. Those issues are discussed in a later section of this report addressing constitutional defenses that the President's counsel have raised. See Volume II, Section 111.B, infra.

Three basic elements are ommon to most of the relevant obstruction statutes: (1) an obstructive act; (2) a nexus between the obstructive act and an official proceeding; and (3) a corrupt intent. See, e.g., 18 U.S.C. §§ 1503, 1505, I 512(c)(2). We describe those elements as they have been interpreted by the courts. We then discuss a more specific statute aimed at witness tampering, see 18 U.S.C. § 1 5 1 2(b), and describe the requirements for attempted offenses and endeavors to obstructjustice, see 18 U.S.C. §§ 1503, 1512(c)(2).

Obstructive act. Obstruction-of-justice law "reaches all corrupt conduct capable of producing an effect that prevents justice from being duly administered, regardless of the means employed." United States v. Silverman, 745 F.2d 1386, 1393 (11th Cir. 1984) (interpreting 18 U.S.C. § 1503).
An "effort to influence" a proceeding can qualify as an endeavor to obstruct justice even if the effort was "subtle or circuitous" and "however cleverly or with whatever cloaking of purpose" it was made. United States v. Roe, 529 F.2d 629, 632 (4th Cir. 1975); see also UnitedStates v. Quattrone, 441 F.3d 153, 173 (2d Cir. 2006). The verbs "'obstruct or impede' are broad" and "can refer to anything that blocks, makes difficult, or hinders." Marinello v. United States, 138 S. Ct. 1101, 1106 (2018) (internal brackets and quotation marks omitted).An improper motive can render an actor's conduct criminal even when the conduct would otherwise be lawful and within the actor's authority. See United States v. Cueto, 151 F.3d 620,631 (7th Cir. 1998) (affirming obstruction conviction of a criminal defense attorney for "litigation• related conduct"); United States v. Cintolo, 818 F.2d 980, 992 (1st Cir. 1987) ("any act by any party-whether lawful or unlawful on its face-may abridge § 1503 if performed with a corrupt motive").

Nexus to a pending or contemplated official proceeding. Obstruction of justice law generally requires a nexus, or connection, to an official proceeding. In Section 1503, the nexus must be to pending "judicial or grand jury proceedings." United States v. Aguilar, 515 U.S. 593, 599 (1995). In Section 1505, the nexus can include a connection to a "pending" federal agency proceeding or a congressional inquiry or investigation. Under both statutes, the government must demonstrate "a relationship in time, causation, or logic" between the obstructive act and the proceeding or inquiry to be obstructed. Id. at 599; see also Arthur Andersen LLP v. UnitedStates,544 U.S. 696, 707-708 (2005). Section I 5 I 2(c) prohibits obstructive efforts aimed at official proceedings including judicial or grand jury proceedings. 18 U.S.C. § 151 S(a)(I)(A). "For purposes of Section 1512, "an official proceeding need not be pending or about to be instituted at the time ofthe offense." 18 U.S.C. § I 5 I 2(f)(I). Although a proceeding need not already be in progress to trigger liability under Section I 512(c), a nexus to a contemplated proceeding still must be shown. United States v. Young, 916 F.3d 368, 386 (4th Cir. 2019); United States v. Petruk, 781F.3d 438, 445 (8th Cir. 2015); United States v. Phillips, 583 F.3d 1261, 1264 (10th Cir. 2009); United States v. Reich, 479 F.3d 179, 186 (2d Cir. 2007). The nexus requirement narrows the scope of obstruction statutes to ensure that individuals have "fair warning" of what the law proscribes. Aguilar, 515 U.S. at 600 (internal quotation marks omitted).

The nexus showing has subjective and objective components. As an objective matter, a defendant must act "in a manner that is likely to obstruct justice," such that the statute "excludes defendants who have an evil purpose but use means that would only unnaturally and improbably be successful." Aguilar, 515 U.S. at 601-602 (emphasis added; internal quotation marks omitted). "[T[he endeavor must have the natural and probable effect of interfering with the due administration of justice." Id. at 599 (citation and internal quotation marks omitted).   As a subjective matter, the actor must have "contemplated a particular, foreseeable proceeding." Petruk, 781 F .3d at 445-446.   A defendant need not directly impede the proceeding.   Rather, a nexus exists if "discretionary actions of a third person would be required to obstruct the judicial proceeding if it was foreseeable to the defendant that the third party would act on the [defendant's] communication in such a way as to obstruct the judicial proceeding." United States v. Martinez, 862 F.3d 223, 238 (2d Cir.2017) (brackets, ellipses, and internal quotation marks omitted).

Corruptly. The word "corruptly" provides the intent element for obstruction ofjustice and means acting "knowingly and dishonestly" or "with an improper motive."   United States v. Richardson, 676 F.3d 491, 508 (5th Cir. 2012); United States v. Gordon, 710 F.3d I 124, 1151 (I 0th Cir. 2013) (to act corruptly means to "actj] with an improper purpose and to engage in conduct knowingly and dishonestly with the specific intent to subvert, impede or obstruct" the relevant proceeding) (some quotation marks omitted); see 18 U.S.C. § 15 I 5(b) ("As used in section 1505, the term 'corruptly' means acting with an improper purpose, personally or by influencing another."); see also Arthur Andersen, 544 U.S. at 705-706 (interpreting "corruptly" to mean "wrongful, immoral, depraved, or evil" and holding that acting "knowingly ... corruptly" in 18U.S.C. § I 5 I 2(b) requires "consciousness of wrongdoing").

The requisite showing is made when a person acted with an intent to obtain an "improper advantage for [him]self or someone else, inconsistent with official duty and the rights of others." BALLENTTNE'S LAW DICTIONARY 276 (3d ed. 1969); see United States v. Pasha, 797 F .3d 1122, 1132 (D.C. Cir. 2015); Aguilar, 515 U.S. at616 (Scalia, J., concurring in part and dissenting in part) (characterizing this definition as the"longstanding and well-accepted meaning" of "corruptly").

Witness tampering. A more specific provision in Section 1512 prohibits tampering with a witness. See 18 U.S.C. § I 512(b)(I), (3) (making it a crime to "knowingly use[] intimidation ... or corruptly persuade[] another person," or "engage[] in misleading conduct towards another person," with the intent to "influence, delay, or prevent the testimony of any person in an official proceeding" or to "hinder, delay, or prevent the communication to a law enforcement officer ... of information relating to the commission or possible commission of a Federal offense").

To establish corrupt persuasion, it is sufficient that the defendant asked a potential witness to lie to investigators in contemplation of a likely federal investigation into his conduct. United States v. Ed/ind, 887 F.3d 166, 174 (4th Cir. 2018); United States v. Sparks, 791 F.3d 1188, 1191-1192 (10th Cir. 2015); United States v. Byrne, 435 F.3d 16, 23-26 (!st Cir. 2006); United States v. LaShay, 417 F.3d 715, 718-719 (7th Cir. 2005); United States v. Burns, 298 F.3d 523, 539-540 (6th Cir. 2002); United States v. Pennington, 168 F.3d 1060, 1066 (8th Cir. 1999).

The "persuasion" need not be coercive, intimidating, or explicit; it is sufficient to "urge," "induce," "askO," "argu[e]," "giv[e] reasons," Sparks, 791 F.3d at 1192, or "coach[] or remind[] witnesses by planting misleading facts," Ed/ind, 887 F.3d at 174. Corrupt persuasion is shown "where a defendant tells a potential witness a false story as if the story were true, intending that the witness believe the story and testify to it." United States v. Rodolitz, 786 F.2d 77, 82 (2d Cir. 1986); see United States v. Gabriel, 125 F .3d 89, I 02 (2d Cir. 1997). It also covers urging a witness to recall a fact that the witness did not know, even if the fact was actually true. See LaShay, 417 F.3d at 719. Corrupt persuasion also can be shown in certain circumstances when a person, with an improper motive, urges a witness not to cooperate with law enforcement. See United States v. Shotts, 145 F.3d 1289, 1301 (l Ith Cr. 1998) (telling Secretary "not to [say] anything [to the FBI] and [she] would not be bothered").

When the charge is acting with the intent to hinder, delay, or prevent the communication of information to law enforcement under Section I 5 I 2(b)(3), the "nexus" to a proceeding inquiry articulated in Aguilar-that an individual have "knowledge that his actions are likely to affect the judicial proceeding," 515 U.S. at 599-does not apply because the obstructive act is aimed at the communication of information to investigators, not at impeding an official proceeding.

Acting "knowingly ... corruptly" requires proof that the individual was "conscious of wrongdoing." Arthur Andersen, 544 U.S. at 705-706 (declining to explore "[t]he outer limits of this element" but indicating that an instruction was infirm where it permitted conviction even if the defendant "honestly and sincerely believed that [the] conduct was lawful"). It is an affirmative defense that "the conduct consisted solely oftawful conduct and that the defendant's sole intention was to encourage, induce, or cause the other person to testify truthfully." 18 U.S.C. § I 512(e).

Attempts and endeavors. Section 1512(c)(2) covers both substantive obstruction offenses and attempts to obstruct justice. Under general principles of attempt law, a person is guilty of an attempt when he has the intent to commit a substantive offense and takes an overt act that constitutes a substantial step towards that goal. See United States v. Resendiz-Ponce, 549 U.S. I 02, I 06-107 (2007). "[T]he act [must be] substantial, in that it was strongly corroborative of the defendant's criminal purpose." United States v. Pratt, 351 F.3d 131, 135 (4th Cir. 2003). While "mere abstract talk" does not suffice, any "concrete and specific" acts that corroborate the defendant's intent can constitute a "substantial step." UnitedStates v. Irving, 665 F.3d 1184, 1198-1205 (10th Cir. 2011). Thus, "soliciting an innocent agent to engage in conduct constituting an element ofthe crime" may qualify as a substantial step. Model Penal Code§ 5.01 (2)(g); see United States v. Lucas, 499 F.3d 769, 781 (8th Cir. 2007).

The omnibus clause of 18 U.S.C. § 1503 prohibits an "endeavor" to obstructjustice, which sweeps more broadly than Section 1 5 I 2's attempt provision. See United States v. Sampson, 898 F.3d 287, 302 (2d Cir. 2018); United States v. Leisure, 844 F.2d 1347, 1366-1367 (8th Cir. 1988) (collecting cases). "It is well established that a[n] [obstruction-of-justice] offense is complete when one corruptly endeavors to obstruct or impede the due administration of justice; the prosecution need not prove that the due administration of justice was actually obstructed or impeded." United States v. Davis, 854 F.3d 1276, 1292 (11th Cir. 2017) (internal quotation marks omitted).

B.   Investigative and Evidentiary Considerations

After the appointment of the Special Counsel, this Office obtained evidence about the following events relating to potential issues ofobstruction ofjustice involving the President:

(a) The President's January 27, 2017 dinner with former FBI Director James Comey in which the President reportedly asked for Comey's loyalty, one day after the White House had been briefed by the Department of Justice on contacts between former National Security Advisor Michael Flynn and the Russian Ambassador;

(b) The President's February 14, 2017 meeting with Comey in which the President reportedly asked Comey not to pursue an investigation of Flynn;

(c) The President's private requests to Comey to make public the fact that the President was not the subject of an FBI investigation and to lift what the President regarded as a cloud;

(d) The President's outreach to the Director of National Intelligence and the Directors of the National Security Agency and the Central Intelligence Agency about the FBI's Russia investigation;

(e) The President's stated rationales for terminating Comey on May 9, 2017, including statements that could reasonably be understood as acknowledging that the FBI's Russia investigation was a factor in Comey's termination; and

(f) The President's reported involvement in issuing a statement about the June 9, 2016 Trump Tower meeting between Russians and senior Trump Campaign officials that said the meeting was about adoption and omitted that the Russians had offered to provide the Trump Campaign with derogatory information about Hillary Clinton.

Taking into account that information and our analysis of applicable statutory and constitutional principles (discussed below in Volume II, Section III, infra), we determined that there was a sufficient factual and legal basis to further investigate potential obstruction-of-justice issues involving the President.

Many of the core issues in an obstruction-of-justice investigation turn on an individual's actions and intent. We therefore requested that the White House provide us with documentary evidence in its possession on the relevant events. We also sought and obtained the White House's concurrence in our conducting interviews of White House personnel who had relevant information. And we interviewed other witnesses who had pertinent knowledge, obtained documents on a voluntary basis when possible, and used legal process where appropriate. These investigative steps allowed us to gather a substantial amount of evidence.

We also sought a voluntary interview with the President. After more than discussion the President declined to be interviewed.

During the course of our discussions, the President did agree to answer written questions on certain Russia-related topics, and he provided us with answers. He did not similarly agree to provide written answers to questions on obstruction topics or questions on events during the transition. Ultimately, while we believed that we had the authority and legal justification to issue a grand jury subpoena to obtain the President's testimony, we chose not to do so. We made that decision in view of the substantial delay that such an investigative step would likely produce at a late stage in our investigation. We also assessed that based on the significant body of evidence we had already obtained of the President's actions and his public and private statements describing or explaining those actions, we had sufficient evidence to understand relevant events and to make certain assessments without the President's testimony. The Office's decision-making process on this issue is described in more detail in Appendix C, infra, in a note that precedes the President's written responses.

In assessing the evidence we obtained, we relied on common principles that apply in any investigation. The issue of criminal intent is often inferred from circumstantial evidence. See, e.g., United States v. Croteau, 819 F.3d 1293, 1305 (I Ith Cir. 2016) ("[G]uilty knowledge can rarely be established by direct evidence.... Therefore, mens rea elements such as knowledge or intent may be proved by circumstantial evidence.") (internal quotation marks omitted); United States v. Robinson, 702 F.3d 22, 36 (2d Cir. 2012) ("The government's case rested on circumstantial evidence, but the mens rea elements of knowledge and intent can often be proved through circumstantial evidence and the reasonable inferences drawn therefrom.") (internal quotation marks omitted). The principle that intent can be inferred from circumstantial evidence is a necessity in criminal cases, given the right ofa subject to assert his privilege against compelled self-incrimination under the Fifth Amendment and therefore decline to testify. Accordingly, determinations on intent are frequently reached without the opportunity to interview an investigatory subject.

Obstruction of justice cases are consistent with this rule. See, e.g., Ed/ind, 887 F.3d at 174, 176 (relying on "significant circumstantial evidence that [the defendant] was conscious ofher wrongdoing" in an obstruction case; "[b]ecause evidence of intent will almost always be circumstantial, a defendant may be found culpable where the reasonable and foreseeable consequences of her acts are the obstruction ofjustice") (internal quotation marks, ellipses, and punctuation omitted); Quattrone, 441 F.3d at 173-174. Circumstantial evidence that illuminates intent may include a pattern of potentially obstructive acts. Fed. R. Evid. 404(b) ("Evidence of a crime, wrong, or other act ... may be admissible ... [to] prov[e] motive, opportunity, intent, preparation, plan, knowledge, identity, absence ofmistake, or lack of accident."); see, e.g., United States v. Frankhauser, 80 F.3d 641, 648-650 (1st Cir. 1996); United States v. Arnold, 773 F.2d 823, 832-834 (7th Cir. 1985); Cintolo, 818 F.2d at 1000.

Credibility judgments may also be made based on objective facts and circumstantial evidence. Standard jury instructions highlight a variety of factors that are often relevant in assessing credibility. These include whether a witness had a reason not to tell the truth; whether the witness had a good memory; whether the witness had the opportunity to observe the events about which he testified; whether the witness's testimony was corroborated by other witnesses; and whether anything the witness said or wrote previously contradicts his testimony. See, e.g., First Circuit Pattern Jury Instructions § 1.06 (2018); Fifth Circuit Pattern Jury Instructions (Criminal Cases)§ 1.08 (2012); Seventh Circuit Pattern Jury Instruction§ 3.01 (2012).

In addition to those general factors, we took into account more specific factors in assessing the credibility of conflicting accounts of the facts. For example, contemporaneous written notes can provide strong corroborating evidence. See United States v. Nobles, 422 U.S. 225, 232 (1975) (the fact that a "statement appeared in the contemporaneously recorded report ... would tend strongly to corroborate the investigator's version of the interview"). Similarly, a witness's recitation of his account before he had any motive to fabricate also supports the witness's credibility. See Tome v. United States, 513 U.S. 150, 158 (1995) ("A consistent statement that predates the motive is a square rebuttal of the charge that the testimony was contrived as a consequence of that motive.").

Finally, a witness's false description of an encounter can imply consciousness of wrongdoing. See Al-Adahi v. Obama, 613 F .3d 1102, 1107 (D.C. Cir. 20 I 0) (noting the "well-settled principle that false exculpatory statements are evidence-often strong evidence-of guilt"). We applied those settled legal principles in evaluating the factual results of our investigation.

II. FACTUAL RESULTS OF THE OBSTRUCTION INVESTIGATION

This section of the report details the evidence we obtained. We first provide an overview of how Russia became an issue in the 2016 presidential campaign, and how candidate Trump responded. We then turn to the key events that we investigated: the President's conduct concerning the FBI investigation of Michael Flynn; the President's reaction to public confirmation of the FBI's Russia investigation; events leading up to and surrounding the termination of FBI Director Comey; efforts to terminate the Special Counsel; efforts to curtail the scope of the Special Counsel's investigation; efforts to prevent disclosure of information about the June 9, 2016 Trump Tower meeting between Russians and senior campaign officials; efforts to have the Attorney General unrecuse; and conduct towards McGahn, Cohen, and other witnesses.

We summarize the evidence we found and then analyze it by reference to the three statutory obstruction-of-justice elements: obstructive act, nexus to a proceeding, and intent. We focus on elements because, by regulation, the Special Counsel has "jurisdiction ... to investigate ... federal crimes committed in the course of, and with intent to interfere with, the Special Counsel's investigation, such as perjury, obstruction of justice, destruction of evidence, and intimidation of witnesses." 28 C.F.R. § 600.4(a). Consistent with our jurisdiction to investigate federal obstruction crimes, we gathered evidence that is relevant to the elements of those crimes and analyzed them within an elements framework-while refraining from reaching ultimate conclusions about whether crimes were committed, for the reasons explained above. This section also does not address legal and constitutional defenses raised by counsel for the President; those defenses are analyzed in Volume II, Section III, infra.

The Campaign's Response to Reports About Russian Support for Trump

During the 2016 campaign, the media raised questions about a possible connection between the Trump Campaign and Russia.[7]   The questions intensified after WikiLeaks released politically damaging Democratic Party emails that were reported to have been hacked by Russia. Trump responded to questions about possible connections to Russia by denying any business involvement in Russia—even though the Trump Organization had pursued a business project in Russia as late as June 2016. Trump also expressed skepticism that Russia had hacked the emails at the same time as he and other Campaign advisors privately sought information about any further planned WikiLeaks releases. After the election, when questions persisted about possible links between Russia and the Trump Campaign, the President-Elect continued to deny any connections to Russia and privately expressed concerns that reports of Russian election interference might lead the public to question the legitimacy of his election.[8]

Press Reports Allege Links Between the Trump Campaign and Russia

On June 16, 2015, Donald J. Trump declared his intent to seek nomination as the Republican candidate for President.[9]   By early 2016, he distinguished himself among Republican candidates by speaking of closer ties with Russia,[10] saying he would get along well with Russian President Vladimir Putin,[11]   questioning whether the NATO alliance was obsolete,[12] and praising Putin as a "strong leader."[13]   The press reported that Russian political analysts and commentators perceived Trump as favorable to Russia.[14]

Beginning in February 2016 and continuing through the summer, the media reported that several Trump campaign advisors appeared to have ties to Russia. For example, the press reported that campaign advisor Michael Flynn was seated next to Vladimir Putin at an RT gala in Moscow in December 2015 and that Flynn had appeared regularly on RT as an analyst.[15] The press also reported that foreign polic advisor Carter Page had ties to a Russian state-run gas company,[16] and that campaign chairman Paul Manafort had done work for the "Russian-backed former Ukrainian president Viktor Yanukovych."[17] In addition, the press raised questions during the Republican National Convention about the Trump Campaign's involvement in changing the Republican platform's stance on giving "weapons to Ukraine to fight Russian and rebel forces.?"

2. The Trump Campaign Reacts to WikiLeaks's Release of Hacked Emails

On June 14, 2016, a cybersecurity firm that had conducted in-house analysis for the Democratic National Committee (DNC) posted an announcement that Russian government hackers had infiltrated the DNC's computer and obtained access to documents.[19]

On July 22, 2016, the day before the Democratic National Convention, WikiLeaks posted thousands of hacked DNC documents revealing sensitive internal deliberations. Soon thereafter, Hillary Clinton's campaign manager publicly contended that Russia had hacked the DNC emails and arranged their release in order to help candidate Trump.[21] On July 26, 2016, the New York Times reported that U.S. "intelligence agencies ha[d] told the White House they now have 'high confidence' that the Russian government was behind the theft of emails and documents from the Democratic National Committee."[22]

3. The Trump Campaign Reacts to Allegations That Russia was Seeking to Aid Candidate Trump

In the days that followed WikiLeaks's July 22, 2016 release of hacked DNC emails, the Trump Campaign publicly rejected suggestions that Russia was seeking to aid candidate Trump. On July 26, 2016, Trump tweeted that it was "[c]razy" to suggest that Russia was "dealing with Trump"[32] and that "[f]or the record," he had "ZERO investments in Russia."[33]

In a press conference the next day, July 27, 2016, Trump characterized "this whole thing with Russia" as "a total deflection" and stated that it was "farfetched" and "ridiculous."?' Trump said that the assertion that Russia had hacked the emails was unproven, but stated that it would give him "no pause" if Russia had Clinton's emails.[35] Trump added, "Russia, if you're listening, I hope you're able to find the 30,000 emails that are missing. I think you will probably be rewarded mightily by our press."[36] Trump also said that "there's nothing that I can think of that I'd rather do than have Russia friendly as opposed to the way they are right now," and in response to a question about whether he would recognize Crimea as Russian territory and consider lifting sanctions, Trump replied, "We'll be looking at that. Yeah, we'll be looking."[37]

During the press conference, Trump repeated "I have nothing to do with Russia" five times.[38] He stated that "the closest [he] came to Russia" was that Russians may have purchased a home or condos from him.[39] He said that after he held the Miss Universe pageant in Moscow in 2013 he had been interested in working with Russian companies that "wanted to put a lot of money into developments in Russia" but "it never worked out.?" He explained, "[f]rankly, I didn't want to do it for a couple of different reasons. But we had a major developer ... that wanted to develop property in Moscow and other places. But we decided not to do it."[41] The Trump Organization, however, had been pursuing a building project in Moscow—the Trump Tower Moscow project — from approximately September 2015 through June 2016, and the candidate was regularly updated on developments, including possible trips by Michael Cohen to Moscow to promote the deal and by Trump himself to finalize it.[42]

Cohen recalled speaking with Trump after the press conference about Trump's denial of any business dealings in Russia, which Cohen regarded as untrue.[43] Trump told Cohen that Trump Tower Moscow was not a deal yet and said, "Why mention it if it is not a deal?"[44] According to Cohen, at around this time, in response to Trump's disavowal of connections to Russia, campaign advisors had developed a "party line" that Trump had no business with Russia and no connections to Russia.[45]

In addition to denying any connections with Russia, the Trump Campaign reacted to reports of Russian election interference in aid of the Campaign by seeking to distance itself from Russian contacts. For example, in August 2016, foreign policy advisor J.D. Gordon declined an invitation to Russian Ambassador Sergey Kislyak's residence because the timing was "not optimal" in view of media reports about Russian interference.[46] On August 19, 2016, Manafort was asked to resign amid media coverage scrutinizing his ties to a pro-Russian political party in Ukraine and links to Russian business.[47] And when the media published stories about Page's connections to Russia in September 2016, Trump Campaign officials terminated Page's association with the Campaign and told the press that he had played "no role" in the Campaign.[48]

On October 7, 2016, WikiLeaks released the first set of emails stolen by a Russian intelligence agency from Clinton Campaign chairman John Podesta.[49] The same day, the federal government announced that "the Russian Government directed the recent compromises of e-mails from US persons and institutions, including from US political organizations.'P" The government statement directly linked Russian hacking to the releases on WikiLeaks, with the goal of interfering with the presidential election, and concluded "that only Russia's senior-most officials could have authorized these activities" based on their "scope and sensitivity.?"

On October 11, 2016, Podesta stated publicly that the FBI was investigating Russia's hacking and said that candidate Trump might have known in advance that the hacked emails were going to be released.[52] Vice Presidential Candidate Mike Pence was asked whether the TrumpCampaign was "in cahoots" with WikiLeaks in releasing damaging Clinton-related information and responded, "Nothing could be further from the truth."[53]

4. After the Election, Trump Continues to Deny Any Contacts or Connections with Russia or That Russia Aided his Election

On November 8, 2016, Trump was elected President. Two days later, Russian officials told the press that the Russian government had maintained contacts with Trump's "immediate entourage" during the campaign.[54] In response, Hope Hicks, who had been the Trump Campaign spokesperson, said, "We are not aware of any campaign representatives that were in touch with any foreign entities before yesterday, when Mr. Trump spoke with many world leaders."[55] Hicks gave an additional statement denying any contacts between the Campaign and Russia: "It never happened. There was no communication between the campaign and any foreign entity during the campaign."[56]

On December 10,2016, the press reported that U.S. intelligence agencies had "concluded that Russia interfered in last month's presidential election to boost Donald Trump's bid for the White House."[57] Reacting to the story the next day, President-Elect Trump stated, "I think it's ridiculous. I think it's just another excuse."[58] He continued that no one really knew who was responsible for the hacking, suggesting that the intelligence community had "no idea if it's Russia or China or somebody. It could be somebody sitting in a bed some place."[59] The President-Elect also said that Democrats were "putting out" the story of Russian interference "because they suffered one of the greatest defeats in the history of polttics.?"

On December 18, 2016, Podesta told the press that the election was "distorted by the Russian intervention" and questioned whether Trump Campaign officials had been "in touch with the Russians."[61] The same day, incoming Chief of Staff Reince Priebus appeared on Fox News Sunday and declined to say whether the President-Elect accepted the intelligence community's determination that Russia intervened in the election.[62] When asked about any contact or coordination between the Campaign and Russia, Priebus said, "Even this question is insane. Of course we didn't interface with the Russians."[63] Priebus added that "this whole thing is a spin job" and said, "the real question is, why the Democrats ... are doing everything they can to delegitimize the outcome of the election?"[64]

On December 29, 2016, the Obama Administration announced that in response to Russian cyber operations aimed at the U.S. election, it was imposing sanctions and other measures on several Russian individuals and entities.[65] When first asked about the sanctions, President-Elect Trump said, "I think we ought to get on with our lives."[66] He then put out a statement that said "It's time for our country to move on to bigger and better things," but indicated that he would meet with intelligence community leaders the following week for a briefing on Russian interference.[67]

The briefing occurred on January 6, 2017.[68] Following the briefing, the intelligence community released the public version of its assessment, which concluded with high confidence that Russia had intervened in the election through a variety of means with the goal of harming Clinton's electability.[69] The assessment further concluded with high confidence that Putin and the Russian government had developed a clear preference for Trump.l?

Several days later, BuzzFeed published unverified allegations compiled by former British intelligence officer Christopher Steele during the campaign about candidate Trump's Russia connections under the headline "These Reports Allege Trump Has Deep Ties To Russia."?' In a press conference the next day, the President-Elect called the release "an absolute disgrace" and said, "I have no dealings with Russia. I have no deals that could happen in Russia, because we've stayed away.... So I have no deals, I have no loans and I have no dealings. We could make deals in Russia very easily if we wanted to, I just don't want to because I think that would be a conflict."[72]

Several advisors recalled that the President-Elect viewed stories about his Russian connections, the Russia investigations, and the intelligence community assessment of Russian interference as a threat to the legitimacy of his electoral victory.[73] Hicks, for example, said that the President-Elect viewed the intelligence community assessment as his "Achilles heel" because, even if Russia had no impact on the election, people would think Russia helped him win, taking away from what he had accomplished.[74] Sean Spicer, the first White House communications director, recalled that the President thought the Russia story was developed to undermine the legitimacy of his election.[75] Gates said the President viewed the Russia investigation as an attack on the legitimacy of his win.[76] And Priebus recalled that when the intelligence assessment came out, the President-Elect was concerned people would question the legitimacy of his win."

*****

7 This section summarizes and cites various news stories not for the truth of the information contained in the stories, but rather to place candidate Trump's response to those stories in context. Volume I of this report analyzes the underlying facts of several relevant events that were reported on by the media during the campaign.

8 As discussed in Volume I, while the investigation identified numerous links between individuals with ties to the Russian government and individuals associated with the Trump Campaign, the evidence was not sufficient to charge that any member of the Trump Campaign conspired or coordinated with representatives of the Russian government to interfere in the 2016 election.

9 @realDonaldTrump 6/16/15 (11 :57 a.m. ET) Tweet.

10 See, e.g., Meet the Press Interview with Donald J. Trump, NBC (Dec. 20, 2015) (Trump: "! think it would be a positive thing if Russia and the United States actually got along"); Presidential Candidate Donald Trump News Conference, Hanahan, South Carolina, C-SPAN (Feb. 15, 2016) ("You want to make a good deal for the country, you want to deal with Russia.").

11 See, e.g., Anderson Cooper 360 Degrees, CNN (July 8, 2015) ("! think I get along with [Putin] fine."); Andrew Rafferty, Trump Says He Would "Get Along Very Well" With Putin, NBC (July 30, 2015) (quoting Trump as saying, "I think T would get along very well with Vladimir Putin.").

12 See, e.g., @realDonaldTrump Tweet 3/24/16 (7:47 a.m. ET);@realDonaldTrump Tweet 3/24/16 (7:59 a.m. ET).

13 See, e.g., Meet the Press Interview with Donald J. Trump, NBC (Dec. 20, 2015) ("[Putin] is a strong leader. What am I gonna say, he's a weak leader? He's making mincemeat out of our President."); Donald Trump Campaign Rally in Vandalia, Ohio, C-SPAN (Mar. 12, 2016) ("I said [Putin] was a strong leader, which he is. I mean, he might be bad, he might be good. But he's a strong leader."). 14 See, e.g., Andrew Osborn, From Russia with love: why the Kremlin backs Trump, Reuters (Mar. 24, 2016); Robert Zubrin, Trump: The Kremlin's Candidate, National Review (Apr. 4, 2016).

15 See, e.g., Mark Hosenball & Steve Holland, Trump being advised by ex-US. Lieutenant General whofavors closer Russia ties, Reuters (Feb. 26, 2016); Tom Hamburger et al., Inside Trump'sfinancial ties to Russia and his unusual flattery of Vladimir Putin, Washington Post (June 17, 2016). Certain matters pertaining to Flynn are described in Volume I, Section IV.B.7, supra.

16 See, e.g., Zachary Mider, Trump's New Russia Advisor Has Deep Ties to Kremlin's Gazprom, Bloomberg (Mar. 30, 2016); Julia Jofee, Who is Carter Page?, Politico (Sep. 23, 2016). Certain matters pertaining to Page are described in Volume I, Section IV.A.3, supra.

17 Tracy Wilkinson, In a shift, Republican platform doesn't cal/for arming Ukraine against Russia, spurring outrage, Los Angeles Times (July 21, 2016); Josh Ragin, Trump campaign guts GOP 's anti• Russia stance on Ukraine, Washington Post (July 18, 2016).

18 Josh Rogin, Trump campaign guts GOP 's anti-Russia stance on Ukraine, Washington Post, Opinions (July 18, 2016). The Republican Platform events are described in Volume I, Section IV.A.6, supra.

19 Bears in the Midst: Intrusion into the Democratic National Committee, CrowdStrike (June 15,2016) (post originally appearing on June 14, 2016, according to records of the timing provided by CrowdStrike); Ellen Nakashima, Russian government hackers penetrated DNC, stole opposition research on Trump, Washington Post (June 14, 2016).

20 Tom Hamburger and Karen Tumulty, Wikil.eaks releases thousands ofdocuments about Clinton and internal deliberations, Washington Post (July 22, 2016).

21 Amber Phillips, Clinton campaign manager: Russians leaked Democrats' emails to help Donald Trump, Washington Post (July 24, 2016).

22 David E. Sanger and Eric Schmitt, Spy Agency Consensus Grows That Russia Hacked D.NC., New York Times (July 26, 2016).

23 Gates 4/10/18 302, at 5; Newman 8/23/18 302, at I.

24 Gates 4/11/18 302, at 2-3 (SM-2180998); Gates I 0/25/18 302, at 2; see also Volume I, Section III.D. l, supra.

25 Cohen 8/7/18 302, at 8; see also Volume I, Section III.D. I, supra. According to Cohen, after WikiLeaktolen DNC emails on July 22, 2016, Trump said to Cohen words to the effect of, Cohen 9/18/18 302, at 10. Cohen's role in the candidate's and later

26 Cohen 8/7/18 302, at 8.

27 . As explained in footnote 197 of Volume I, Section III.D. l .b, supra, this Office has included Manafort's account of these events because it aligns with those of other witnesses and is corroborated to that extent.

28 Gates 10/25/18 302, at 4.

29 Gates I 0/25/ 18 302, at 4.

30 Bannon 1/18/19 302, at 3.

31 Gates 4/11/18 302, at 1-2 (SM-2180998); Gates I 0/25/18 302, at 2 (messa formed in June/Jul timeframe based on claims b Assan e on June 12, 2016, ...   ).

32@realDonaldTrump 7/26/16 (6:47 p.m, ET) Tweet.

33 @rea!DonaldTrump 7/26/16 (6:50 p.m. ET) Tweet.

34 Donald Trump News Conference, Doral, Florida, C-SPAN (July 27, 2016).

35 Donald Trump News Conference, Doral, Florida, C-SPAN (July 27, 2016).

36 Donald Trump News Conference, Doral, Florida, C-SPAN (July 27, 2016). Within five hours of Trump's remark, a Russian intelligence service began targeting email accounts associated with Hillary Clinton for possible hacks. See Volume I, Section HI, supra. In written answers submitted in this investigation, the President stated that he made the "Russia, if you're listening" statement "in jest and sarcastically, as was apparent to any objective observer." Written Responses of Donald J. Trump (Nov. 20, 2018), at 13 (Response to Question II, Part (d)).

37 Donald Trump News Conference, Doral, Florida, C-SPAN (July 27, 2016). In his written answers submitted in this investigation, the President said that his statement that "we'll be looking" at Crimea and sanctions "did not communicate any position." Written Responses of Donald J. Trump (Nov. 20, 2018), at 17 (Response to Question IV, Part (g)).

38 Donald Trump News Conference, Doral, Florida, C-SPAN (July 27, 2016).

39 Donald Trump News Conference, Doral, Florida, C-SPAN (July 27, 2016).

40 Donald Trump News Conference, Doral, Florida, C-SPAN (July 27, 2016).

41 Donald Trump News Conference, Doral, Florida, C-SPAN (July 27, 2016).

42   The Trump Tower Moscow project and Trump's involvement in it is discussed in detail in Volume I, Section IV.A. I, supra, and Volume II, Section ILK, infra.

43 Cohen 9/18/18 302, at 4.

44 Cohen 9/18/18 302, at 4-5.

45   Cohen 11/20/18 302, at I; Cohen 9/18/18 302, at 3-5.   The formation of the "party line" is described in greater detail in Volume TI, Section 11.K, infra.

46 DJTFP00004953 (8/8/16 Email, Gordon to Pchelyakov) (stating that "[t]hese days are not optimal for us, as we are busily knocking down a stream of false media stories").   The invitation and Gordon's response are discussed in Volume I, Section IV.A.7.a, supra.

47 See, e.g., Amber Phillips, Paul Manafort's complicated ties to Ukraine, explained, Washington Post (Aug. 19, 2016) ("There were also a wave of fresh headlines dealing with investigations into [Manafort's] ties to a pro-Russian political party in Ukraine."); Tom Winter & Ken Dilanian, Donald Trump Aide Paul Manafort Scrutinized for Russian Business Ties, NBC (Aug. 18, 2016).   Relevant events involving Manafort are discussed in Volume 1, Section IV.A.8, supra.

48 Michael lsikoff, U.S. intel officials probe ties between Trump adviser and Kremlin, Yahoo News (Sep. 23, 2016); see, e.g., 9/25/16 Email, Hicks to Conway & Bannon; 9/23/16 Email, J. Miller to Bannon & S. Miller; Page 3/ 16/17 302, at 2.

49 @WikiLeaks 10/7/16 (4:32 p.m. ET) Tweet.

50 Joint Statement from the Department Of Homeland Security and Office of the Director of National Intelligence on Election Security, OHS (Oct. 7, 2016).

51 Joint Statement from the Department Of Homeland Security and Office of the Director of National Intelligence on Election Security, OHS (Oct. 7, 2016).

52 John Wagner & Anne Gearan, Clinton campaign chairman ties email hack to Russians, suggests Trump had early warning, Washington Post (Oct. 11, 2016).

53 Louis Nelson, Pence denies Trump camp in cahoots with Wikil.eaks, Politico (Oct. 14, 2016).

54 Ivan Nechepurenko, Russian Officials Were in Contact With Trump Allies, Diplomat Says, New York Times (Nov. I 0, 2016) (quoting Russian Deputy Foreign Minister Sergey Ryabkov saying, "[t]here were contacts" and "I cannot say that all, but a number of them maintained contacts with Russian representatives"); Jim Heintz & Matthew Lee, Russia eyes better ties with Trump; says contacts underway, Associated Press (Nov. 11, 2016) (quoting Ryabkov saying, "I don't say that all of them, but a whole array of them supported contacts with Russian representatives").

55 Ivan Nechepurenko, Russian Officials Were in Contact With Trump Allies, Diplomat Says, NewYork Times (Nov. 11, 2016) (quoting Hicks).

56   Jim Heintz & Matthew Lee, Russia eyes better ties with Trump; says contacts underway, Associated Press (Nov. I 0, 2016) (quoting Hicks).   Hicks recalled that after she made that statement, she spoke with Campaign advisors Kellyanne Conway, Stephen Miller, Jason Miller, and probably Kushner and Bannon to ensure it was accurate, and there was no hesitation or pushback from any of them. Hicks 12/8/17 302, at 4.

57   Damien Gayle, CIA concludes Russia interfered to help Trump win election, say reports,Guardian (Dec. 10, 2016).

58   Chris Wallace Hosts "Fox News Sunday," Interview with President-Elect Donald Trump, CQ Newsmaker Transcripts (Dec. 11, 2016).6° Chris Wallace Hosts "Fox News Sunday," Interview with President-Elect Donald Trump, CQ Newsmaker Transcripts (Dec. 11, 2016).

61   David Morgan, Clinton campaign: It's an 'open question' ifTrump team colluded with Russia, Reuters Business Insider (Dec. 18, 2016).

62 Chris Wallace Hosts "Fox News Sunday," Interview with Incoming While House ChiefofStaff Reince Priebus, Fox News (Dec. 18, 2016).

63 Chris Wallace Hosts "Fox News Sunday," Interview with Incoming While House ChiefofStaff Reince Priebus, Fox News (Dec. 18, 2016).

64 Chris Wallace Hosts "Fox News Sunday, "Interview with Incoming White House ChiefofStaff Reince Priebus, Fox News (Dec. 18, 2016).

65 Statement by the President on Actions in Response to Russian Malicious Cyber Activity and Harassment, White House (Dec. 29, 2016); see also Missy Ryan et al., Obama administration announces measures to punish Russiafor 2016 election interference, Washington Post (Dec. 29, 2016).

66 John Wagner, Trump on alleged election interference by Russia: 'Get on with our lives,' Washington Post (Dec. 29, 2016).

67 Missy Ryan et al., Obama administration announces measures to punish Russiafor 2016 election interference, Washington Post (Dec. 29, 2016).68 Corney 11/15/17 302, at 3.

69 Office of the Director ofNational Intelligence, Russia's Influence Campaign Targeting the 2016 US Presidential Election, at I (Jan. 6, 2017).

70 Office ofthe Director ofNational Intelligence, Russia's Influence Campaign Targeting the 2016 US Presidential Election, at I (Jan. 6, 2017).

71 Ken Bensinger et al., These Reports Allege Trump Has Deep Ties To Russia, BuzzFeed (Jan. I 0, 2017).

72 Donald Trump's News Conference: Full Transcript and Video, New York Times (Jan. 11, 2017), available at https://www.nytimes.com/2017/0 I /11 /us/politics/trump-press-conference•transcript.html.

73 Priebus I 0/13/17 302, at 7; Hicks 3/13/18 302, at 18; Spicer 10/16/17 302, at 6; Bannon 2/14/18 302, at 2; Gates 4/ 18/18 302, at 3; see Pompeo 6/28/17 302, at 2 (the President believed that the purpose of the Russia investigation was to delegitimize his presidency).

74 Hicks 3/13/18 302, at 18.

75 Spicer 10/17/17 302, at 6.

76 Gates 4/18/18 302, at 3.

77 Priebus I 0/ 13/ 17 302, at 7.

B. The President's Conduct Concerning the Investigation of Michael Flynn

Overview

During the presidential transition, incoming National Security Advisor Michael Flynn had two phone calls with the Russian Ambassador to the United States about the Russian response to U.S. sanctions imposed because of Russia's election interference. After the press reported on Flynn's contacts with the Russian Ambassador, Flynn lied to incoming Administration officials by saying he had not discussed sanctions on the calls. The officials publicly repeated those lies in press interviews. The FBI, which previously was investigating Flynn for other matters, interviewed him about the calls in the first week after the inauguration, and Flynn told similar lies to the FBI. On January 26, 2017, Department of Justice (DOJ) officials notified the White House that Flynn and the Russian Ambassador had discussed sanctions and that Flynn had been interviewed by the FBI. The next night, the President had a private dinner with FBI Director James Comey in which he asked for Comey's loyalty. On February 13, 2017, the President asked Flynn to resign. The following day, the President had a one-on-one conversation with Comey in which he said, "I hope you can see your way clear to letting this go, to letting Flynn go."

Evidence

1. Incoming National Security Advisor Flynn Discusses Sanctions on Russia with Russian Ambassador Sergey Kislyak

Shortly after the election, President-Elect Trump announced he would appoint Michael Flynn as his National Security Advisor.[78] For the next two months, Flynn played an active role on the Presidential Transition Team (PTT) coordinating policy positions and communicating with foreign government officials, including Russian Ambassador to the United States Sergey Kislyak.[79]

On December 29, 2016, as noted in Volume II, Section II.A.4, *supra,* the Obama Administration announced that it was imposing sanctions and other measures on several Russian individuals and entities." That day, multiple members of the PTT exchanged emails about the sanctions and the impact they would have on the incoming Administration, and Flynn informed members of the PTT that he would be speaking to the Russian Ambassador later in the day.[81]

Flynn, who was in the Dominican Republic at the time, and K.T. McFarland, who was slated to become the Deputy National Security Advisor and was at the Mar-a-Lago resort in Florida with the President-Elect and other senior staff, talked by phone about what, if anything, Flynn should communicate to Kislyak about the sanctions.[82] McFarland had spoken with incoming Administration officials about the sanctions and Russia's possible responses and thought she had mentioned in those conversations that Flynn was scheduled to speak with Kislyak.[83] Based on those conversations, McFarland informed Flynn that incoming Administration officials at Mar-a• Lago did not want Russia to escalate the situation.[84] At 4:43 p.m. that afternoon, McFarland sent an email to several officials about the sanctions and informed the group that "Gen [F]lynn is talking to russian ambassador this evening."[85]

Approximately one hour later, McFarland met with the President-Elect and senior officials and briefed them on the sanctions and Russia's possible responses.[86] Incoming Chief of Staff Reince Priebus recalled that McFarland may have mentioned at the meeting that the sanctions situation could be "cooled down" and not escalated.[87] McFarland recalled that at the end of the meeting, someone may have mentioned to the President-Elect that Flynn was speaking to the Russian Ambassador that evening.[88] McFarland did not recall any response by the President• Elect.89 Priebus recalled that the President-Elect viewed the sanctions as an attempt by the Obama Administration to embarrass him by delegitimizing his election.?"

Immediately after discussing the sanctions with McFarland on December 29, 2016, Flynn called Kislyak and requested that Russia respond to the sanctions only in a reciprocal manner, without escalating the situation.[91] After the call, Flynn briefed McFarland on its substance.l"

Flynn told McFarland that the Russian response to the sanctions was not going to be escalatory because Russia wanted a good relationship with the Trump Administration.[93] On December 30, 2016, Russian President Vladimir Putin announced that Russia would not take retaliatory measures in response to the sanctions at that time and would instead "plan ... further steps to restore Russian• US relations based on the policies of the Trump Administration."[94] Following that announcement, the President-Elect tweeted, "Great move on delay (by V. Putin) - I always knew he was very smart!"[95]

On December 31, 2016, Kislyak called Flynn and told him that Flynn's request had been received at the highest levels and Russia had chosen not to retaliate in response to the request." Later that day, Flynn told McFarland about this follow-up conversation with Kislyak and Russia's decision not to escalate the sanctions situation based on Flynn's request.[97] McFarland recalled that Flynn thought his phone call had made a difference.[98] Flynn spoke with other incoming Administration officials that day, but does not recall whether they discussed the sanctions.[99]

Flynn recalled discussing the sanctions issue with incoming Administration official Stephen Bannon the next day.[100] Flynn said that Bannon appeared to know about Flynn's conversations with Kislyak, and he and Bannon agreed that they had "stopped the train on Russia's response" to the sanctions.'?' On January 3, 2017, Flynn saw the President-Elect in person and thought they discussed the Russian reaction to the sanctions, but Flynn did not have a specific recollection of telling the President-Elect about the substance of his calls with Kislyak.l'?

Members of the intelligence community were surprised by Russia's decision not to retaliate in response to the sanctions.I''' When analyzing Russia's response, they became aware of Flynn's discussion of sanctions with Kislyak.l''' Previously, the FBI had opened an investigation of Flynn based on his relationship with the Russian government.l'" Flynn's contacts with Kislyak became a key component of that investigation.'?"

2. President-Elect Trump is Briefed on the Intelligence Community's Assessment of Russian Interference in the Election and Congress Opens Election• Interference Investigations

On January 6, 2017, as noted in Volume II, Section 11.A.4, *supra,* intelligence officials briefed President-Elect Trump and the incoming Administration on the intelligence community's assessment that Russia had interfered in the 2016 presidential election.I'" When the briefing concluded, Corney spoke with the President-Elect privately to brief him on unverified, personally sensitive allegations compiled by Steele.'" According to a memorandum Corney drafted immediately after their private discussion, the President-Elect began the meeting by telling Corney he had conducted himself honorably over the prior year and had a great reputation.'

The President-Elect stated that he thought highly of Corney, looked forward to working with him, and hoped that he planned to stay on as FBI director.!"? Corney responded that he intended to continue serving in that role.[111]   Corney then briefed the President-Elect on the sensitive material in th Steele reporting.[112] Corney recalled that the President-Elect seemed defensive, so Corney decided Michael Cohen received a text from Russian businessman Giorgi Rtskhiladze that said, "Stopped flow of tapes from Russia but not sure if there's anything else. Just so you know ...." 10/30/16 Text Message, Rtskhiladze to Cohen. Rtskhiladze said "tapes" referred to compromising tapes of Trump rumored to be held by persons associated with the Russian real estate conglomerate Crocus Group, which had helped host to assure him that the FBI was not investigating him personally.[113]   Corney recalled he did not want the President-Elect to think of the conversation as a "J. Edgar Hoover move."!"

On January 1 0, 2017, the media reported that Corney had briefed the President-Elect on the Steele reporting,[115] and BuzzFeed News published information compiled by Steele online, stating that the information included "specific, unverified, and potentially unverifiable allegations of contact between Trump aides and Russian operatives."[116]   The next day, the President-Elect expressed concern to intelligence community leaders about the fact that the information had leaked and asked whether they could make public statements refuting the allegations in the Steele reports.[117]

In the following weeks, three Congressional committees opened investigations to examine Russia's interference in the election and whether the Trump Campaign had colluded with Russia.[118]   On January 13, 2017, the Senate Select Committee on Intelligence (SSCT) announced that it would conduct a bipartisan inquiry into Russian interference in the election, including any "links between Russia and individuals associated with political campaigns."!"?   On January 25, 2017, the House Permanent Select Committee on Intelligence (HPSCI) announced that it had been conducting an investigation into Russian election interference and possible coordination with the political campaigns.P?   And on February 2, 2017, the Senate Judiciary Committee announced that it too would investigate Russian efforts to intervene in the election.[121]

3. Flynn Makes False Statements About his Communications with Kislyak to Incoming Administration Officials, the Media, and the FBI

On January 12, 2017, a Washington Post columnist reported that Flynn and Kislyak communicated on the day the Obama Administration announced the Russia sanctions.[122] The column questioned whether Flynn had said something to "undercut the U.S. sanctions" and whether Flynn's communications had violated the letter or spirit of the Logan Act.[123]

President-Elect Trump called Priebus after the story was published and expressed anger about it.[124] Priebus recalled that the President-Elect asked, "What the hell is this all about?"[125] Priebus called Flynn and told him that the President-Elect was angry about the reporting on Flynn's conversations with Kislyak.[126] Flynn recalled that he felt a lot of pressure because Priebus had spoken to the "boss" and said Flynn needed to "kill the story."[127] Flynn directed McFarland to call the Washington Post columnist and inform him that no discussion of sanctions had occurred.[128] McFarland recalled that Flynn said words to the effect of, "I want to kill the story."[129] McFarland made the call as Flynn had requested although she knew she was providing false information, and the Washington Post updated the column to reflect that a "Trump official" had denied that Flynn and Kislyak discussed sanctions.[130]

When Priebus and other incoming Administration officials questioned Flynn internally about the Washington Post column, Flynn maintained that he had not discussed sanctions with Kislyak.[131] Flynn repeated that claim to Vice President-Elect Michael Pence and to incoming press secretary Sean Spicer.[132] In subsequent media interviews in mid-January, Pence, Priebus, and Spicer denied that Flynn and Kislyak had discussed sanctions, basing those denials on their conversations with Flynn.[133]

The public statements of incoming Administration officials denying that Flynn and Kislyak had discussed sanctions alarmed senior DOJ officials, who were aware that the statements were not true.[134] Those officials were concerned that Flynn had lied to his colleagues—who in turn had unwittingly misled the American public—creating a compromise situation for Flynn because the Department of Justice assessed that the Russian government could prove Flynn lied.[135] The FBI investigative team also believed that Flynn's calls with Kislyak and subsequent denials about discussing sanctions raised potential Logan Act issues and were relevant to the FBI's broader Russia investigation."

On January 20, 2017, President Trump was inaugurated and Flynn was sworn in as National Security Advisor. On January 23, 2017, Spicer delivered his first press briefing and stated that he had spoken with Flynn the night before, who confirmed that the calls with Kislyak were about topics unrelated to sanctions.[137] Spicer's statements added to the Department of Justice's concerns that Russia had leverage over Flynn based on his lies and could use that derogatory information to compromise him.[138]

On January 24, 2017, Flynn agreed to be interviewed by agents from the FBI.[139] During the interview, which took place at the White House, Flynn falsely stated that he did not ask Kislyak to refrain from escalating the situation in response to the sanctions on Russia imposed by the Obama Administration.[140] Flynn also falsely stated that he did not remember a follow-up conversation in which Kislyak stated that Russia had chosen to moderate its response to those sanctions as a result of Flynn's request.[141]

4. Officials Notify the White House of Their Concerns About Flynn

On January 26, 2017, Acting Attorney General Sally Yates contacted White House Counsel Donald McGahn and informed him that she needed to discuss a sensitive matter with him in person.[142] Later that day, Yates and Mary McCord, a senior national security official at the Department of Justice, met at the White House with McGahn and White House Counsel's Office attorney James Burnham.[143] Yates said that the public statements made by the Vice President denying that Flynn and Kislyak discussed sanctions were not true and put Flynn in a potentially compromised position because the Russians would know he had lied.[144] Yates disclosed that Flynn had been interviewed by the FBI.[145] She declined to answer a specific question about how Flynn had performed during that interview,[146] but she indicated that Flynn's statements to the FBI were similar to the statements he had made to Pence and Spicer denying that he had discussed sanctions.[147] McGahn came away from the meeting with the impression that the FBI had not pinned Flynn down in lies,[148] but he asked John Eisenberg, who served as legal advisor to the National Security Council, to examine potential legal issues raised by Flynn's FBI interview and his contacts with Kislyak.[149]

That afternoon, McGahn notified the President that Yates had come to the White House to discuss concerns about Flynn.[P"] McGahn described what Yates had told him, and the President asked him to repeat it, so he did.[151] McGahn recalled that when he described the FBI interview of Flynn, he said that Flynn did not disclose having discussed sanctions with Kislyak, but that there may not have been a clear violation of 18 U.S.C. § 1001.[152] The President asked about Section 1001, and McGahn explained the law to him, and also explained the Logan Act.[153] The President instructed McGahn to work with Priebus and Bannon to look into the matter further and directed that they not discuss it with any other officials.[154] Priebus recalled that the President was angry with Flynn in light of what Yates had told the White House and said, "not again, this guy, this stuff."[155]

That evening, the President dined with several senior advisors and asked the group what they thought about FBI Director Comey.[156] According to Director of National Intelligence Dan Coats, who was at the dinner, no one openly advocated terminating Comey but the consensus on him was not positive.[157] Coats told the group that he thought Comey was a good director.[158] Coats encouraged the President to meet Comey face-to-face and spend time with him before making a decision about whether to retain him.[159]

5. McGahn has a Follow-Up Meeting About Flynn with Yates; President Trump has Dinner with FBI Director Comey

The next day, January 27, 2017, McGahn and Eisenberg discussed the results of Eisenberg's initial legal research into Flynn's conduct, and specifically whether Flynn may have violated the Espionage Act, the Logan Act, or 18 U.S.C. § 1001.[160] Based on his preliminary research, Eisenberg informed McGahn that there was a possibility that Flynn had violated 18 U.S.C. § 1001 and the Logan Act.[161] Eisenberg noted that the United States had never successfully prosecuted an individual under the Logan Act and that Flynn could have possible defenses, and told McGahn that he believed it was unlikely that a prosecutor would pursue a Logan Act charge under the circumstances.[162]

That same morning, McGahn asked Yates to return to the White House to discuss Flynn again.[163] In that second meeting, McGahn expressed doubts that the Department of Justice would bring a Logan Act prosecution against Flynn, but stated that the White House did not want to take action that would interfere with an ongoing FBI investigation of Flynn.[164] Yates responded that Department of Justice had notified the White House so that it could take action in response to the information provided.[165] McGahn ended the meeting by asking Yates for access to the underlying information the Department of Justice possessed pertaining to Flynn's discussions with Kislyak.[166]

Also on January 27, the President called FBI Director Comey and invited him to dinner that evening.[167] Priebus recalled that before the dinner, he told the President something like, "don't talk about Russia, whatever you do," and the President promised he would not talk about Russia at the dinner.[168] McGahn had previously advised the President that he should not communicate directly with the Department of Justice to avoid the perception or reality of political interference in law enforcement.[169] When Bannon learned about the President's planned dinner with Comey, he suggested that he or Priebus also attend, but the President stated that he wanted to dine with Comey alone.[170] Comey said that when he arrived for the dinner that evening, he was surprised and concerned to see that no one else had been invited.[171]

Comey provided an account of the dinner in a contemporaneous memo, an interview with this Office, and congressional testimony. According to Corney's account of the dinner, the President repeatedly brought up Corney's future, asking whether he wanted to stay on as FBI director.[172] Because the President had previously said he wanted Comey to stay on as FBI director, Comey interpreted the President's comments as an effort to create a patronage relationship by having Comey ask for his job.[173] The President also brought up the Steele reporting that

Corney had raised in the January 6, 2017 briefing and stated that he was thinking about ordering the FBI to investigate the allegations to prove they were false.[174] Comey responded that the President should think carefully about issuing such an order because it could create a narrative that the FBI was investigating him personally, which was incorrect.[175] Later in the dinner, the President brought up Flynn and said, "the guy has serious judgment issues."[177] Comey did not comment on Flynn and the President did not acknowledge any FBI interest in or contact with Flynn.[177]

According to Comey's account, at one point during the dinner the President stated, "I need loyalty, I expect loyalty."[178] Comey did not respond and the conversation moved on to other topics, but the President returned to the subject of Corney's job at the end of the dinner and repeated, "I need loyalty."[179] Comey responded, "You will always get honesty from me."[180] The President said, "That's what I want, honest loyalty."[181] Corney said, "You will get that from me."[182]

After Corney's account of the dinner became public, the President and his advisors disputed that he had asked for Corney's loyalty.[183] The President also indicated that he had not invited Corney to dinner, telling a reporter that he thought Corney had "asked for the dinner" because "he wanted to stay on."[184] But substantial evidence corroborates Corney's account of the dinner invitation and the request for loyalty. The President's Daily Diary confirms that the President "extend[ed] a dinner invitation" to Corney on January 27.[185] With respect to the substance of the dinner conversation, Corney documented the President's request for loyalty in a memorandum he began drafting the night of the dinner;[186] senior FBT officials recall that Corney told them about the loyalty request shortly after the dinner occurred;[187] and Corney described the request while under oath in congressional proceedings and in a subsequent interview with investigators subject to penalties for lying under 18 U.S.C. § 1001. Corney's memory of the details of the dinner, including that the President requested loyalty, has remained consistent throughout.[188]

6. Flynn's Resignation

On February 2, 2017, Eisenberg reviewed the underlying information relating to Flynn's calls with Kislyak.[189] Eisenberg recalled that he prepared a memorandum about criminal statutes that could apply to Flynn's conduct, but he did not believe the White House had enough information to make a definitive recommendation to the President.'?" Eisenberg and McGahn discussed that Eisenberg's review of the underlying information confirmed his preliminary conclusion that Flynn was unlikely to be prosecuted for violating the Logan Act.[191] Because White House officials were uncertain what Flynn had told the FBI, however, they could not assess his exposure to prosecution for violating 18 U.S.C. § 1001.[192]

The week of February 6, Flynn had a one-on-one conversation with the President in the Oval Office about the negative media coverage of his contacts with Kislyak.[193] Flynn recalled that the President was upset and asked him for information on the conversations.[194] Flynn listed the specific dates on which he remembered speaking with Kislyak, but the President corrected one of the dates he listed.[195] The President asked Flynn what he and Kislyak discussed and Flynn responded that he might have talked abou sanctions.[196]

On February 9, 2017, the Washington Post reported that Flynn discussed sanctions with Kislyak the month before the President took office.[197] After the publication of that story, Vice President Pence learned of the Department of Justice's notification to the White House about the content of Flynn's calls.[198]

He and other advisors then sought access to and reviewed the underlying information about Flynn's contacts with Kislyak.[199]   FBI Deputy Director Andrew McCabe, who provided the White House officials access to the information and was present when they reviewed it, recalled the officials asking him whether Flynn's conduct violated the Logan Act.[200] McCabe responded that he did not know, but the FBI was investigating the matter because it was a possibility.'?'   Based on the evidence of Flynn's contacts with Kislyak, McGahn and Priebus concluded that Flynn could not have forgotten the details of the discussions of sanctions and had instead been lying about what he discussed with Kislyak.i'''   Flynn had also told White House officials that the FBI had told him that the FBI was closing out its investigation of him,[203] but Eisenberg did not believe him.[204]   After reviewing the materials and speaking with Flynn, McGahn and Priebus concluded that Flynn should be terminated and recommended that course of action to the President.i'''

That weekend, Flynn accompanied the President to Mar-a-Lago.P'' Flynn recalled that on February 12, 2017, on the return flight to D.C. on Air Force One, the President asked him whether he had lied to the Vice President.F' Flynn responded that he may have forgotten details of his calls, but he did not think he lied.[208] The President responded, "Okay. That's fine. T got it."[209]

On February 13, 2017, Priebus told Flynn he had to resign.[210] Flynn said he wanted to say goodbye to the President, so Priebus brought him to the Oval Office.[211] Priebus recalled that the President hugged Flynn, shook his hand, and said, "We'll give you a good recommendation. You're a good guy. We'll take care of you."[212]

Talking points on the resignation prepared by the White House Counsel's Office and distributed to the White House communications team stated that McGahn had advised the President that Flynn was unlikely to be prosecuted, and the President had determined that the issue with Flynn was one of trust.[213] Spicer told the press the next day that Flynn was forced to resign "not based on a legal issue, but based on a trust issue, [where] a level of trust between the President and General Flynn had eroded to the point where [the President] felt he had to make a change."[214]

7. The President Discusses Flynn with FBI Director Corney

On February 14, 2017, the day after Flynn's resignation, the President had lunch at the White House with New Jersey Governor Chris Christie.[215] According to Christie, at one point during the lunch the President said, "Now that we fired Flynn, the Russia thing is over."[216] Christie laughed and responded, "No way."[217] He said, "this Russia thing is far from over" and "[w]e'll be here on Valentine's Day 2018 talking about this."[218] The President said, "[w]hat do you mean? Flynn met with the Russians. That was the problem. I fired Flynn. It's over."[219] Christie recalled responding that based on his experience both as a prosecutor and as someone who had been investigated, firing Flynn would not end the investigation.[220] Christie said there was no way to make an investigation shorter, but a lot of ways to make it longer.[221] The President asked Christie what he meant, and Christie told the President not to talk about the investigation even if he was frustrated at times.[222] Christie also told the President that he would never be able to get rid of Flynn, "like gum on the bottom of your shoe."[223]

Towards the end of the lunch, the President brought up Comey and asked if Christie was still friendly with him.[224] Christie said he was.[225] The President told Christie to call Comey and tell him that the President "really like[s] him. Tell him he's part of the team."[226] At the end of the lunch, the President repeated his request that Christie reach out to Comey.[227] Christie had no intention of complying with the President's request that he contact Comey.[228] He thought the President's request was "nonsensical" and Christie did not want to put Comey in the position of having to receive such a phone call.[229] Christie thought it would have been uncomfortable to pass on that message.?

At 4 p.m. that afternoon, the President met with Comey, Sessions, and other officials for a homeland security briefing.[231] At the end of the briefing, the President dismissed the other attendees and stated that he wanted to speak to Comey alone.[232] Sessions and senior advisor to the President Jared Kushner remained in the Oval Office as other participants left, but the President excused them, repeating that he wanted to speak only with Comey.[233] At some point after others had left the Oval Office, Priebus opened the door, but the President sent him away.[234]

According to Corney's account of the meeting, once they were alone, the President began the conversation by saying, "I want to talk about Mike Flynn."[235] The President stated that Flynn had not done anything wrong in speaking with the Russians, but had to be terminated because he had misled the Vice President.[236] The conversation turned to the topic of leaks of classified information, but the President returned to Flynn, saying "he is a good guy and has been through a lot."[237] The President stated, "I hope you can see your way clear to letting this go, to letting Flynn go. He is a good guy. I hope you can let this go."[238] Corney agreed that Flynn "is a good guy," but did not commit to ending the investigation of Flynn.[239] Corney testified under oath that he took the President's statement "as a direction" because of the President's position and the circumstances of the one-on-one meeting.[240]

Shortly after meeting with the President, Corney began drafting a memorandum documenting their conversation.[241] Corney also met with his senior leadership team to discuss the President's request, and they agreed not to inform FBI officials working on the Flynn case of the President's statements so the officials would not be influenced by the request.[242] Corney also asked for a meeting with Sessions and requested that Sessions not leave Corney alone with the President again.[243]

8. The Media Raises Questions About the President's Delay in Terminating Flynn

After Flynn was forced to resign, the press raised questions about why the President waited more than two weeks after the DOJ notification to remove Flynn and whether the President had known about Flynn's contacts with Kislyak before the DOJ notification.[244] The press also continued to raise questions about connections between Russia and the President's campaign.[245]

On February 15, 2017, the President told reporters, "General Flynn is a wonderful man. I think he's been treated very, very unfairly by the media."[246] On February 16, 2017, the President held a press conference and said that he removed Flynn because Flynn "didn't tell the Vice President of the United States the facts, and then he didn't remember. And that just wasn't acceptable to me."[247] The President said he did not direct Flynn to discuss sanctions with Kislyak, but "it certainly would have been okay with me if he did. T would have directed him to do it if I thought he wasn't doing it. I didn't direct him, but T would have directed him because that's his job."[248] In listing the reasons for terminating Flynn, the President did not say that Flynn had lied to him.[249]

The President also denied having any connection to Russia, stating, "I have nothing to do with Russia. I told you, T have no deals there. T have no anything."[250] The President also said he "had nothing to do with" WikiLeaks's publication of information hacked from the Clinton campaign.[251]

9. The President Attempts to Have K.T. McFarland Create a Witness Statement Denying that he Directed Flynn's Discussions with Kislyak

On February 22, 2017, Priebus and Bannon told McFarland that the President wanted her to resign as Deputy National Security Advisor, but they suggested to her that the Administration could make her the ambassador to Singapore.[252] The next day, the President asked Priebus to have McFarland draft an internal email that would confirm that the President did not direct Flynn to call the Russian Ambassador about sanctions.[253] Priebus said he told the President he would only direct McFarland to write such a letter if she were comfortable with it.[254] Priebus called McFarland into his office to convey the President's request that she memorialize in writing that the President did not direct Flynn to talk to Kislyak.[255] McFarland told Priebus she did not know whether the President had directed Flynn to talk to Kislyak about sanctions, and she declined to say yes or no to the request.[256] Priebus understood that McFarland was not comfortable with the President's request, and he recommended that she talk to attorneys in the White House Counsel's Office.[257]

McFarland then reached out to Eisenberg.[258] McFarland told him that she had been fired from her job as Deputy National Security Advisor and offered the ambassadorship in Singapore but that the President and Priebus wanted a letter from her denying that the President directed Flynn to discuss sanctions with Kislyak.[259]

Eisenberg advised McFarland not to write the requested letter[260]. As documented by McFarland in a contemporaneous "Memorandum for the Record" that she wrote because she was concerned by the President's request: "Eisenberg ... thought the requested email and letter would be a bad idea— from my side because the email would be awkward. Why would I be emailing Priebus to make a statement for the record? But it would also be a bad idea for the President because it looked as if my ambassadorial appointment was in some way a quid pro quo."[261] Later that evening, Priebus stopped by McFarland's office and told her not to write the email and to forget he even mentioned it.[262]

Around the same time, the President asked Priebus to reach out to Flynn and let him know that the President still cared about him.[263] Priebus called Flynn and said that he was checking in and that Flynn was an American hero.[264] Priebus thought the President did not want Flynn saying bad things about him.[265]

On March 31, 2017, following news that Flynn had offered to testify before the FBI and congressional investigators in exchange for immunity, the President tweeted, "Mike Flynn should ask for immunity in that this is a witch hunt (excuse for big election loss), by media & Dems, of historic proportion!"[266] In late March or early April, the President asked McFarland to pass a message to Flynn telling him the President felt bad for him and that he should stay strong.[267]

Analysis

In analyzing the President's conduct related to the Flynn investigation, the following evidence is relevant to the elements of obstruction of justice:

a.   Obstructive act. According to Comey's account of his February 14, 2017 meeting in the Oval Office, the President told him, "I hope you can see your way clear to letting this go, to letting Flynn go.... I hope you can let this go." In analyzing whether these statements constitute an obstructive act, a threshold question is whether Comey's account of the interaction is accurate, and, if so, whether the President's statements had the tendency to impede the administration of justice by shutting down an inquiry that could result in a grand jury investigation and a criminal charge.

After Comey's account of the President's request to "let[] Flynn go" became public, the President publicly disputed several aspects of the story. The President told the New York Times that he did not "shoo other people out of the room" when he talked to Comey and that he did not remember having a one-on-one conversation with Comey.[268] The President also publicly denied that he had asked Comey to "let[] Flynn go" or otherwise communicated that Comey should drop the investigation of Flynn.[269] In private, the President denied aspects of Corney's account to White House advisors, but acknowledged to Priebus that he brought Flynn up in the meeting with Comey and stated that Flynn was a good guy.[270] Despite those denials, substantial evidence corroborates Comey's account.

First, Comey wrote a detailed memorandum of his encounter with the President on the same day it occurred. Comey also told senior FBI officials about the meeting with the President that day, and their recollections of what Corney told them at the time are consistent with Corney's account.[271]

Second, Comey provided testimony about the President's request that he "letO Flynn go" under oath in congressional proceedings and in interviews with federal investigators subject to penalties for lying under 18 U.S.C. § 1001. Corney's recollections of the encounter have remained consistent over time.

Third, the objective, corroborated circumstances of how the one-on-one meeting came to occur support Corney's description of the event. Comey recalled that the President cleared the room to speak with Comey alone after a homeland security briefing in the Oval Office, that Kushner and Sessions lingered and had to be shooed out by the President, and that Priebus briefly opened the door during the meeting, prompting the President to wave him away. While the President has publicly denied those details, other Administration officials who were present have confirmed Corney's account of how he ended up in a one-on-one meeting with the President.' And the President acknowledged to Priebus and McGahn that he in fact spoke to Comey about Flynn in their one-on-one meeting.

Fourth, the President's decision to clear the room and, in particular, to exclude the Attorney General from the meeting signals that the President wanted to be alone with Comey, which is consistent with the delivery of a message of the type that Comey recalls, rather than a more innocuous conversation that could have occurred in the presence of the Attorney General.

Finally, Comey's reaction to the President's statements is consistent with the President having asked him to "let[] Flynn go." Comey met with the FBI leadership team, which agreed to keep the President's statements closely held and not to inform the team working on the Flynn investigation so that they would not be influenced by the President's request. Comey also promptly met with the Attorney General to ask him not to be left alone with the President again, an account verified by Sessions, FBT Chief of Staff James Rybicki, and Jody Hunt, who was then the Attorney General's chief of staff.

A second question is whether the President's statements, which were not phrased as a direct order to Comey, could impede or interfere with the FBI's investigation of Flynn. While the President said he "hope[d]" Comey could "letO Flynn go," rather than affirmatively directing him to do so, the circumstances of the conversation show that the President was asking Comey to close the FBI's investigation into Flynn. First, the President arranged the meeting with Corney so that they would be alone and purposely excluded the Attorney General, which suggests that the President meant to make a request to Comey that he did not want anyone else to hear. Second, because the President is the head of the Executive Branch, when he says that he "hopes" a subordinate will do something, it is reasonable to expect that the subordinate will do what the President wants. Indeed, the President repeated a version of "let this go" three times, and Corney testified that he understood the President's statements as a directive, which is corroborated by the way Comey reacted at the time.

b.   Nexus to a proceeding. To establish a nexus to a proceeding, it would be necessary to show that the President could reasonably foresee and actually contemplated that the investigation of Flynn was likely to lead to a grand jury investigation or prosecution.

At the time of the President's one-on-one meeting with Corney, no grand jury subpoenas had been issued as part of the FBI's investi ation into Fl nn. But Fl nn's lies to the FBI violated federal criminal law, , and resulted in Flynn's prosecution for violating 18 U.S.C. § 1001. By the time the President spoke to Corney about Flynn, DOJ officials had informed McGahn, who informed the President, that Flynn's statements to senior White House officials about his contacts with Kislyak were not true and that Flynn had told the same version of events to the FBI. McGahn also informed the President that Flynn's conduct could violate 18 U.S.C. § 1001. After the Vice President and senior White House officials reviewed the underlying information about Flynn's calls on February 10, 2017, they believed that Flynn could not have forgotten his conversations with Kislyak and concluded that he had been lying. In addition, the President's instruction to the FBI Director to "let[] Flynn go" suggests his awareness that Flynn could face criminal exposure for his conduct and was at risk of prosecution.

c.   Intent. As part of our investigation, we examined whether the President had a personal stake in the outcome of an investigation into Flynn—for example, whether the President was aware of Flynn's communications with Kislyak close in time to when they occurred, such that the President knew that Flynn had lied to senior White House officials and that those lies had been passed on to the public. Some evidence suggests that the President knew about the existence and content of Flynn's calls when they occurred, but the evidence is inconclusive and could not be relied upon to establish the President's knowledge. In advance of Flynn's initial call with Kislyak, the President attended a meeting where the sanctions were discussed and an advisor may have mentioned that Flynn was scheduled to talk to Kislyak. Flynn told McFarland about the substance of his calls with Kislyak and said they may have made a difference in Russia's response, and Flynn recalled talking to Bannon in early January 2017 about how they had successfully "stopped the train on Russia's response" to the sanctions. It would have been reasonable for Flynn to have wanted the President to know of his communications with Kislyak because Kislyak told Flynn his request had been received at the highest levels in Russia and that Russia had chosen not to retaliate in response to the request, and the President was pleased by the Russian response, calling it a "[g]reat move." And the President never said publicly or internally that Flynn had lied to him about the calls with Kislyak.

But McFarland did not recall providing the President-Elect with Flynn's read-out of his calls with Kislyak, and Flynn does not have a specific recollection of telling the President-Elect directly about the calls. Bannon also said he did not recall hearing about the calls from Flynn. And in February 2017, the President asked Flynn what was discussed on the calls and whether he had lied to the Vice President, suggesting that he did not already know. Our investigation accordingly did not produce evidence that established that the President knew about Flynn's discussions of sanctions before the Department of Justice notified the White House of those discussions in late January 2017. The evidence also does not establish that Flynn otherwise possessed information damaging to the President that would give the President a personal incentive to end the FBI's inquiry into Flynn's conduct.

Evidence does establish that the President connected the Flynn investigation to the FBI's broader Russia investigation and that he believed, as he told Christie, that terminating Flynn would end "the whole Russia thing." Flynn's firing occurred at a time when the media and Congress were raising questions about Russia's interference in the election and whether members of the President's campaign had colluded with Russia. Multiple witnesses recalled that the President viewed the Russia investigations as a challenge to the legitimacy of his election. The President paid careful attention to negative coverage of Flynn and reacted with annoyance and anger when the story broke disclosing that Flynn had discussed sanctions with Kislyak. Just hours before meeting one-on-one with Comey, the President told Christie that firing Flynn would put an end to the Russia inquiries. And after Christie pushed back, telling the President that firing Flynn would not end the Russia investigation, the President asked Christie to reach out to Comey and convey that the President liked him and he was part of "the team." That afternoon, the President cleared the room and asked Comey to "let[] Flynn go."

We also sought evidence relevant to assessing whether the President's direction to Corney was motivated by sympathy towards Flynn. In public statements the President repeatedly described Flynn as a good person who had been harmed by the Russia investigation, and the President directed advisors to reach out to Flynn to tell him the President "care[d]" about him and felt bad for him. At the same time, multiple senior advisors, including Bannon, Priebus, and Hicks, said that the President had become unhappy with Flynn well before Flynn was forced to resign and that the President was frequently irritated with Flynn. Priebus said he believed the President's initial reluctance to fire Flynn stemmed not from personal regard, but from concern about the negative press that would be generated by firing the National Security Advisor so early in the Administration. And Priebus indicated that the President's post-firing expressions of support for Flynn were motivated by the President's desire to keep Flynn from saying negative things about him.

The way in which the President communicated the request to Comey also is relevant to understanding the President's intent. When the President first learned about the FBI investigation into Flynn, he told McGahn, Bannon, and Priebus not to discuss the matter with anyone else in the White House. The next day, the President invited Comey for a one-on-one dinner against the advice of an aide who recommended that other White House officials also attend. At the dinner, the President asked Comey for "loyalty" and, at a different point in the conversation, mentioned that Flynn had judgment issues. When the President met with Comey the day after Flynn's termination—shortly after being told by Christie that firing Flynn would not end the Russia investigation—the President cleared the room, even excluding the Attorney General, so that he could again speak to Corney alone. The President's decision to meet one-on-one with Corney contravened the advice of the White House Counsel that the President should not communicate directly with the Department of Justice to avoid any appearance of interfering in law enforcement activities. And the President later denied that he cleared the room and asked Corney to "let[] Flynn go"—a denial that would have been unnecessary if he believed his request was a proper exercise of prosecutorial discretion.

Finally, the President's effort to have McFarland write an internal email denying that the President had directed Flynn to discuss sanctions with Kislyak highlights the President's concern about being associated with Flynn's conduct. The evidence does not establish that the President was trying to have McFarland lie. The President's request, however, was sufficiently irregular that

McFarland—who did not know the full extent of Flynn's communications with the President and thus could not make the representation the President wanted—felt the need to draft an internal memorandum documenting the President's request, and Eisenberg was concerned that the request would look like a quid pro quo in exchange for an ambassadorship.

*****

78 Flynn 11/16/17 302, at 7; President-Elect Donald.! Trump Selects U.S. Senator JeffSessionsfor Attorney General, Lt. Gen. Michael Flynn as Assistant to the Presidentfor National Security Affairs and U.S. Rep. Mike Pompeo as Director ofthe Central Intelligence Agency, President-Elect Donald J. Trump Press Release (Nov. 18, 2016); see also, e.g., Bryan Bender, Trump names Mike Flynn national security adviser, Politico, (Nov. 17, 2016).

79 Flynn 11/16/17 302, at 8-14; Priebus I 0/13/17 302, at 3-5.

80 Statement by the President on Actions in Response to Russian Malicious Cyber Activity and Harassment, The White House, Office of the Press Secretary (Dec. 29, 2016).

81 12/29/16 Email, O'Brien to McFarland et al.; 12/29/16 Email, Bossert to Flynn et al.; 12/29/16 Email, McFarland to Flynn et al.; SFOOOOOI (12/29/16 Text Message, Flynn to Flaherty) ("Tit for tat w Russia not good. Russian AMBO reaching out to me today."); Flynn 1/19/18 302, at 2.

82 Statement of Offense at 2-3, United States v. Michael T. Flynn, I: 1 7-cr-232 (0.0.C. Dec. I, 2017), Doc. 4 (Flynn Statement of Offense); Flynn 11/17/17 302, at 3-4; Flynn 11/20/17 302, at 3; McFarland 12/22/17 302, at 6-7.

83 McFarland 12/22/17 302, at 4-7 (recalling discussions about this issue with Bannon and Priebus). M Flynn Statement of Offense, at 3; Flynn 11/17/17 302, at3-4; McFarland 12/22/17 302, at 6-7.

85 12/29/16 Email, McFarland to Flynn et al.

86 McFarland 12/22/17 302, at 7.

87 Priebus 1 /18/18 302, at 3

88 McFarland 12/22/17 302, at 7. Priebus thought it was possible that McFarland had mentioned Flynn's scheduled call with Kislyak at this meeting, although he was not certain. Priebus 1/18/18 302, at

89 McFarland 12/22/17 302, at 7.

90 Priebus 1/18/18 302, at 3.

91 Flynn Statement of Offense, at 3; Flynn 11/17/17 302, at 3-4.

92 Flynn Statement of Offense, at 3; McFarland 12/22/17 302, at 7-8; Flynn 11/17/17 302, at 4.

93 McFarland 12/22/17 302, at 8.

94 Statement by the President ofRussia, President of Russia (Dec. 30, 2016) 12/30/16.

95 @realDonaldTrump 12/30/ 16 (2:41 p.m. ET) Tweet.% Flynn 1/19/18 302, at 3; Flynn Statement of Offense, at 3.

97 Flynn 1/19/18 302, at 3; Flynn 11/17/17 302, at 6; McFarland 12/22/17 302, at 10; Flynn Statement ofOffe

98 McFarland 12/22/17 302, at IO; see Flynn I I 1 9/ 18 302, at 4.

99 Flynn 11/17/17 302, at 5-6.

10° Flynn 1/19/18 302, at 4-5. Bannon recalled meeting with Flynn that day, but said he did not remember discussing sanctions with him. Bannon 2/12/18 302, at 9.

101 Flynn 11/21/17 302, at I; Flynn I /19/18 302, at 5.

102 Flynn 1/19/18 302, at 6; Flynn 11/17/17 302, at 6.

103 McCord 7/17/17 302, at 2.

104 McCord 7/17/17 302, at 2.

105 McCord 7/17/17 302, at 2-3; Corney 11/15/17 302, at 5.

106 McCord 7/17/17 302, at 2-3.

107 Hearing on Russian Election Interference Before the Senate Select Intelligence Committee, I 15th Cong. (June 8, 2017) (Statement for the Record of James B. Corney, former Director of the FBI, at1-2).

108 Corney I I /15/ 17 302, at 3; Hearing on Russian Election Interference Before the Senate Select Intelligence Committee, I 15th Cong. (June 8, 2017) (Statement for the Record of James B. Corney, former Director of the FBI, at 1-2).

109 Corney 1/7/17 Memorandum, at I. Corney began drafting the memorandum summarizing the meeting immediately after it occurred. Corney 11/15/17 302, at 4. He finished the memorandum that evening and finalized it the following morning. Corney 11/15/17 302, at 4.

11° Corney 1/7/17 Memorandum, at I; Corney 11/15/17 302, at 3. Corney identified several other occasions in January 2017 when the President reiterated that he hoped Corney would stay on as FBI director. On January 11, President-Elect Trump called Corney to discuss the Steele reports and stated that he thought Corney was doing great and the President-Elect hoped he would remain in his position as FBI director. Corney 11 /15/17 302, at 4; Hearing on Russian Election Interference Before the Senate Select Intelligence Committee, I 15th Cong. (June 8, 2017) (testimony of James B. Corney, former Director of the FBI), CQ Cong. Transcripts, at 90. ("[D]uring that call, he asked me again, 'Hope you're going to stay, you're doing a great job.' And I told him that I intended to."). On January 22, at a White House reception honoring law enforcement, the President greeted Corney and said he looked forward to working with him. Hearing on Russian Election Interference Before the Senate Select Intelligence Committee, I 15th Cong. (June 8, 2017) (testimony ofJames B. Corney, former Director of the FBI), CQ Cong. Transcripts, at 22. And as discussed in greater detail in Volume II, Section 11.D, infra, on January 27, the President invited Corney to dinner at the White House and said he was glad Corney wanted to stay on as FBI Director.

111 Corney 1/7/17 Memorandum, at I; Corney 11/15/17 302, at 3.

112 Corney 1/7/17 Memorandum, at 1-2; Corney 11/15/17 302, at 3. Corney's briefing included the Steele reporting's unverified allegation that the Russians had compromising tapes ofthe President involving conduct when he was a private citizen during a 2013 trip to Moscow for the Miss Universe Pageant. During the 2016 presidential campaign, a similar claim may have reached candidate Trump. On October 30, 2016,

113 Corney 11 /15/17 302, at 3-4; Hearing on Russian Election Interference Before the Senate Select Intelligence Committee, I 15th Cong. (June 8, 2017) (Statement for the Record of James 8. Corney, former Director of the FBI, at 2).

114 Corney 11/15/17 302, at 3.

115 See, e.g., Evan Perez et al., Intel chiefs presented Trump with claims of Russian efforts to compromise him, CNN (Jan. 1 0, 2017; updated Jan. 12, 2017).

116 Ken Bensinger et al., These Reports Allege Trump Has Deep Ties To Russia, BuzzFeed News (Jan. 1 0, 2017).

117 See 1/11/17 Email, Clapper to Corney ("He asked ifl could put out a statement. He would prefer of course that I say the documents are bogus, which, of course, I can't do."); I /12/17 Email, Corney to Clapper ("He called me at 5 yesterday and we had a very similar conversation."); Corney 11/15/17 302, at4-5.

118 See 2016 Presidential Election Investigation Fast Facts, CNN (first published Oct. 12, 2017; updated Mar. I, 2019) (summarizing starting dates of Russia-related investigations).

119 Joint Statement on Commillee Inquiry into Russian Intelligence Activities, SSC[(Jan. 13, 2017).

120 Joint Statement on Progress ofBipartisan HPSCJ Inquiry into Russian Active Measures, HPSCI (Jan. 25, 2017).

121 Joint Statementfrom Senators Graham and Whitehouse on Investigation into Russian Influence on Democratic Nations' Elections (Feb. 2, 2017).

122 David Ignatius, Why did Obama dawdle on Russia's hacking?, Washington Post (Jan. 12, 2017).

123 David Ignatius, Why did Obama dawdle on Russia's hacking?, Washington Post (Jan. 12, 2017). The Logan Act makes it a crime for "[a]ny citizen of the United States, wherever he may be" to "without authority of the United States, directly or indirectly commence[] or carr[y] on any correspondence or intercourse with any foreign government or any officer or agent thereof, in relation to any disputes or controversies with the United States, or to defeat the measures of the United States." 18 U.S.C. § 953.

124 Priebus 1/18/18 302, at 6.

125 Priebus 1/18/18 302, at 6.

126 Priebus 1/18/18 302, at 6.

127 Flynn 11/21/17 302, at 1; Flynn 11/20/17 302, at 6.

128 McFarland 12/22/17 302, at 12-13.

129 McFarland 12/22/ 17 302, at 12.

130 McFarland 12/22/ 17 302, at 12-13; McFarland 8/29/17 302, at 8; see David Ignatius, Why did Obama dawdle on Russia's hacking?, Washington Post (Jan. 12, 2017).

131 Flynn 11/17/17 302, at I, 8; Flynn 1/19/18 302, at 7; Priebus 10/13/17 302, at 7-8; S. Miller 8/3 I /17 3 02, at 8-1 I .

132 Flynn 11/17/17 302, at I, 8; Flynn 1/19/18 302, at 7; S. Miller 8/31 I 17 302, at I 0-11

133 Face the Nation Interview with Vice President-Elect Pence, CBS (Jan. 15, 2017); Julie Hirschfield Davis et al., Trump National Security Advisor Called Russian Envoy Day Before Sanctions Were Imposed, Washington Post (Jan. 13, 2017); Meet the Press Interview with Reince Priebus, NBC (Jan.15,2017).

134 Yates 8/15/17 302, at 2-3; McCord 7/17/17 302, at 3-4; McCabe 8/17/17 302, at 5 (DOJ officials were "really freaked out about it").

135 Yates 8/15/17 302, at 3; McCord 7/17/17 302, at 4.

136 McCord 7/17/17 302, at 4; McCabe 8/17/17 302, at 5-6.

137 Sean Spicer, White House Daily Briefing, C-SPAN (Jan. 23, 2017).

138 Yates 8/15/17 302, at 4; Axelrod 7/20/17 302, at 5.

139 Flynn Statement of Offense, at 2.

14° Flynn Statement of Offense, at 2

141 Flynn Statement of Offense, at 2. On December I, 2017, Flynn admitted to making these false statements and pleaded guilty to violating 18 U.S.C. § I 00 I, which makes it a crime to knowingly and willfully "make[] any materially false, fictitious, or fraudulent statement or representation" to federal law enforcement officials. See Volume I, Section fV.A.7, supra

142 Yates 8/15/17 302, at 6.

143 Yates 8/15/17 302, at 6; McCord 7/17/17 302, at 6; SCR015_000198 (2/15/17 Draft Memorandum to file from the Office of the Counsel to the President).

144 Yates 8/15/17 302, at 6-8; McCord 7/17/17 302, at 6-7; Burnham 11/3/17 302, at 4; SCRO t 5_000198 (2/ 15/17 Draft Memorandum to file from the Office of the Counsel to the President).

145 McGahn 11/30/17 302, at 5; Yates 8/15/17 302, at 7; McCord 7/17/17 302, at 7; Burnham 11/3/17 302, at

146 Yates 8/15/17 302, at 7; McCord 7/17/17 302, at 7.

147 SCR015_000198 (2/15/17 Draft Memorandum to file from the Office of the Counsel to the President); Burnham 11 /3/ 17 302, at 4.

148 McGahn 11/30/17 302, at 5.

149 SCRO 15 000198 (2/15/17 Draft Memorandum to file from the Office of the Counsel to the President); McGahn 11 /30/17 302, at 6, 8.

150 McGahn 11/30/17 302, at 6; SCR015_000278 (White House Counsel's Office Memorandum re: "Flynn Tick Tock") (on January 26, "McGahn IMMEDIATELY advises POTUS"); SCR015_000198 (2/15/17 Draft Memorandum to file from the Office of the Counsel to the President).

151 McGahn 11/30/17 302, at 6.

152 McGahn 11/30/17 302, at 7.

153 McGahn 11/30/17 302, at 7.

154 McGahn 11/30/17 302, at 7; SCRO 15 000198-99 (2/15/17 Draft Memorandum to file from the Office of the Counsel to the President).

155 Priebus I 0/13/17 302, at 8. Several witnesses said that the President was unhappy with Flynn for other reasons at this time. Bannon said that Flynn's standing with the President was not good by December 2016. Bannon 2/12/18 302, at 12. The President-Elect had concerns because President Obama had warned him about Flynn shortly after the election. Bannon 2/ 12/ 18 302, at 4-5; Hicks 12/8/17 302, at 7 (President Obama's comment sat with President-Elect Trump more than Hicks expected). Priebus said that the President had become unhappy with Flynn even before the story of his calls with Kislyak broke and had become so upset with Flynn that he would not look at him during intelligence briefings. Priebus I I 18/ 18 302, at 8. Hicks said that the President thought Flynn had bad judgment and was angered by tweets sent by Flynn and his son, and she described Flynn as "being on thin ice" by early February 2017. Hicks 12/8/17302,at7, 10.

156 Coats 6/14/17 302, at 2.

157 Coats 6/14/ 17 302, at 2.

158 Coats 6/14/17 302, at 2.

159 Coats 6/14/17 302, at 2.

160 SCR015 000199 (2/15/17 Draft Memorandum to file from the Office of the Counsel to the President); McGahn 11/30/17 302, at 8.

161   SCR015_000199 (2/15/17 Draft Memorandum to file from the Office of the Counsel to the President); Eisenberg 11/29/17 302, at 9.

162   SCR015_000199 (2/15/17 Draft Memorandum to file from the Office of the Counsel to thePresident); Eisenberg 11 /29/17 302, at 9.

163   SCR015_000199 (2/15/17 Draft Memorandum to file from the Office of the Counsel to the President); McGahn 11/30/17 302, at 8; Yates 8/15/17 302, at 8.

164   Yates 8/15/17 302, at 9; McGahn 11/30/17 302, at 8.

165   Yates 8/15/17 302, at 9; Burnham 11/3/17 302, at 5; see SCR015_00199 (2/15/17 Draft Memorandum to file from the Office of the Counsel to the President) ("Yates was unwilling to confirm or deny that there was an ongoing investigation but did indicate that the Department of Justice would not object to the White House taking action against Flynn.").

166   Yates 9/15/17 302, at 9; Burnham 11/3/17 302, at 5. In accordance with McGahn's request, the Department of Justice made the underlying information available and Eisenberg viewed the information in early February. Eisenberg 11/29/17 302, at 5; FBI 2/7/17 Electronic Communication, at I (documenting
2/2/17 meeting with Eisenberg).

167   Corney 11/15/17 302, at 6; SCROl2b_OOOOOI (President's Daily Diary, 1/27/17); Hearing on Russian Election Interference Before the Senate Select Intelligence Committee, I 15th Cong. (June 8, 2017) (Statement for the Record of James B. Corney, former Director of the FBI, at 2-3).

168   Priebus I 0/13/17 302, at 17.

169   See McGahn 11/30/17 302, at 9; Dhillon 11/21/17 302, at 2; Bannon 2/12/18 302, at 17.

170   Bannon 2/12/18 302, at 17.

171   Hearing on Russian Election Interference Before the Senate Select Intelligence Committee, I 15th Cong. (June 8, 2017) (Statement for the Record of James B. Corney, former Director of the FBI, at
3); see Corney 11/15/17 302, at 6.

172   Corney 11/15/17 302, at 7; Corney 1/28/17 Memorandum, at I, 3; Hearing on Russian Election Interference Before the Senate Select Intelligence Committee, I 15th Cong. (June 8, 2017) (Statement for the Record of James B Corney, former Director of the FBI, at 3).

173   Corney 11/15/17 302, at 7; Hearing on Russian Election Interference Before the Senate Select Intelligence Committee, I 15th Cong. (June 8, 2017) (Statement for the Record of James B. Corney, former Director ofthe FBI, at 3).

174   Corney 1/28/17 Memorandum, at 3; Hearing on Russian Election Interference Before the Senate Select Intelligence Committee, I 15th Cong. (June 8, 2017) (Statement for the Record of James B. Corney, former Director of the FBI, at

175   Corney 1/28/17 Memorandum, at 3; Hearing on Russian Election Interference Before the Senate Select Intelligence Committee, I 15th Cong. (June 8, 2017) (Statement for the Record of James B. Corney, former Director of the FBI, at 4).

176   Corney 1/28/17 Memorandum, at 4; Corney 11/15/17 302, at 7.

177   Corney 1/28/17 Memorandum, at 4; Corney 11/15/17 302, at 7.

178 Corney 1/28/18 Memorandum, at 2; Corney 11/15/17 302, at 7; Hearing on Russian Election Interference Before the Senate Select Intelligence Committee, I 15th Cong. (June 8, 2017) (Statement for the Record of James B. Corney, former Director of the FBI, at 3).

179 Corney 1/28/17 Memorandum, at 3; Corney 11/15/17 302, at 7; Hearing on Russian Election Interference Before the Senate Select Intelligence Committee, I 15th Cong. (June 8, 2017) (Statement for the Record of James B. Corney, former Director of the FBI, at 3-4).

18° Corney 1/28/17 Memorandum, at 3; Corney 11/15/17 302, at 7; Hearing on Russian Election Interference Before the Senate Select Intelligence Committee, I 15th Cong. (June 8, 2017) (Statement for the Record of James B. Corney, former Director of the FBI, at 4).

181 Corney 1/28/17 Memorandum, at 3; Corney 11/15/17 302, at 7; Hearing on Russian Election Interference Before the Senate Select Intelligence Committee, I 15th Cong. (June 8, 2017) (Statement for the Record ofJames B. Corney, former Director of the FBI, at 4).

182 Corney 1/28/17 Memorandum, at 3; Corney 11/15/17 302, at 7; Hearing on Russian Election Interference Before the Senate Select Intelligence Committee, I 15th Cong. (June 8, 2017) (Statement for the Record ofJames 8. Corney, former Director of the FBI, at 4).

183 See, e.g., Michael S. Schmidt, In a Private Dinner, Trump Demanded Loyalty. Corney Demurred., New York Times (May 11, 2017) (quoting Sarah Sanders as saying, "[The President] would never even suggest the expectation of personal loyalty"); Ali Vitali, Trump Never Asked for Corney's Loyalty, President's Personal Lawyer Says, NBC (June 8, 2017) (quoting the President's personal counsel as saying, "The president also never told Mr. Corney, 'I need loyalty, T expect loyalty,' in form or substance."); Remarks by President Trump in Press Conference, White House (June 9, 2017) ("T hardly know the man. I'm not going to say 'T want you to pledge allegiance.' Who would do that? Who would ask a man to pledge allegiance under oath?"). In a private conversation with Spicer, the President stated that he had never asked for Corney's loyalty, but added that if he had asked for loyalty, "Who cares?" Spicer I 0/16/17 302, at 4. The President also told McGahn that he never said what Corney said he had. McGahn 12/12/17 302, at 17.

184 Interview ofDonald J Trump, NBC (May 11, 2017).

185 SCRO I 2b_OOOOOI (President's Daily Diary, 1/27/17) (reflecting that the President called Corney in the morning on January 27 and "[t]he purpose ofthe call was to extend a dinner invitation"). In addition, two witnesses corroborate Corney's account that the President reached out to schedule the dinner, without Corney having asked for it. Priebus I 0/13/17 302, at 17 (the President asked to schedule the January 27 dinner because he did not know much about Corney and intended to ask him whether he wanted to stay on as FBI Director); Rybicki 11/21/18 302, at 3 (recalling that Corney told him about the President's dinner invitation on the day of the dinner).

186 Corney 11/15/17 302, at 8; Hearing on Russian Election Interference Before the Senate Select Intelligence Committee, I 15th Cong. (June 8, 2017) (Statement for the Record of James B. Corney, former Director of the FBT, at 4).

187 McCabe 8/17/17 302, at 9-10; Rybicki 11/21/18 302, at 3. After leaving the White House, Corney called Deputy Director of the FBI Andrew McCabe, summarized what he and the President had discussed, including the President's request for loyalty, and expressed shock over the President's request. McCabe 8/17/17 302, at 9. Corney also convened a meeting with his senior leadership team to discuss what the President had asked of him during the dinner and whether he had handled the request for loyalty properly. McCabe 8/17/17 302, at 10; Rybicki 11/21/18 302, at 3. In addition, Corney distributed his

188 There also is evidence that corroborates other aspects of the memoranda Corney wrote documenting his interactions with the President. For example, Corney recalled, and his memoranda reflect, that he told the President in his January 6, 2017 meeting, and on phone calls on March 30 and April 11, 2017, that the FBI was not investigating the President personally. On May 8, 2017, during White House discussions about firing Corney, the President told Rosenstein and others that Corney had told him three times that he was not under investigation, including once in person and twice on the phone. Gauhar-000058 (Gauhar 5/16/17 Notes).

189 Eisenberg 11/29/17 302, at 5; FBI 2/7/17 Electronic Communication, at I (documenting 2/2/17 meeting with Eisenberg).

190 Eisenberg 11/29/17 302, at 6.

191 Eisenberg 11/29/17 302, at 9; SCROl5_000200 (2/15/17 Draft Memorandum to file from the Office of the Counsel to the President).

192 Eisenberg 11/29/17 302, at 9.

193 Flynn 11/21/ 17 302, at 2.

194 Flynn 11/21/17 302, at 2.

195 Flynn 11/21/17 302, at 2.

196 Flynn 11/21/17 302, at 2-3.

197 Greg Miller et al., National security adviser Flynn discussed sanctions with Russian ambassador, despite denials, officials say, Washington Post (Feb. 9, 2017).

198 SCR015_000202 (2/15/17 Draft Memorandum to file from the Office of the Counsel to the President); McGahn 11 /30/17 302, at 12.

199 SCR015_000202 (2/15/17 Draft Memorandum to file from the Office of the Counsel to the President); McCabe 8/17/17 302, at 11-13; Priebus 10/13/17 302, at 10; McGahn 11/30/17 302, at 12.

200 McCabe 8/17/17 302, at 13.

201 McCabe 8/17/17 302, at 13.

202 McGahn 11130/17 302, at 12; Priebus 1/18/18 302, at 8; Priebus 10/13/17 302, at 10; SCRO 15_000202 (2/15/17 Draft Memorandum to file from the Office of the Counsel to the President).

203 McGahn 11/30/17 302, at 11; Eisenberg 11/29/17 302, at 9; Priebus 10/13/17 302, at 11.

204 Eisenberg 11/29/17 302, at 9.

205 SCRO 15 000202 (2/ 15/17 Draft Memorandum to file from the Office of the Counsel to the President); Priebus I 0/13/17 302, at IO; McGahn 11130/17 302, at 12.

206 Flynn 11/17/17 302, at 8.

207 Flynn I I 19118 302, at 9; Flynn 11 /17/17 302, at 8.

208 Flynn 11/17/17 302, at 8; Flynn 1/19/18 302, at 9.

209 Flynn 1/19/18 302, at 9.

210 Priebus l/18/18 302, at 9.

211 Priebus l/18/18302,at9;Flynn 11/17/17302,at 10.

212 Priebus 1/18/18 302, at 9; Flynn 11/17(17 302, at I 0.

213 SCR004_00600 (2/ 16/ 17 Email, Burnham to Donaldson).

214 Sean Spicer, White House Daily Briefing, C-SPAN (Feb. 14, 2017). After Flynn pleaded guilty to violating 18 U.S.C. § 100 I in December 2017, the President tweeted, "I had to fire General Flynn because he lied to the Vice President and the FBI." @realDonaldTrump 12/2/17 (12: 14 p.m. ET) Tweet. The next day, the President's personal counsel told the press that he had drafted the tweet. Maegan Vazquez et al., Trump's lawyer says he was behind President's tweet about firing Flynn, CNN (Dec. 3, 2017).

215 Christie 2/13/19 302, at 2-3; SCROl2b_000022 (President's Daily Diary, 2/14/17).

216 Christie 2/13/19 302, at 3.

217 Christie 2/13/19 302, at 3.

218 Christie 2/13/19 302, at 3. Christie said he thought when the President said "the Russia thing" he was referring to not just the investigations but also press coverage about Russia. Christie thought the more important thing was that there was an investigation. Christie 2/13/19 302, at 4.

219 Christie 2/13/19 302, at 3.

22° Christie 2/13/ 19 302, at 3.

221 Christie 2/ 13/19 302, at 3.

222 Christie 2/13/19 302, at 3-4.

223 Christie 2/13/19 302, at 3. Christie also recalled that during the lunch, Flynn called Kushner, who was at the lunch, and complained about what Spicer had said about Flynn in his press briefing that day. Kushner told Flynn words to the effect of, "You know the President respects you. The President cares about you. I'll get the President to send out a positive tweet about you later." Kushner looked at the President when he mentioned the tweet, and the President nodded his assent. Christie 2/13/19 302, at 3. Flynn recalled getting upset at Spicer's comments in the press conference and calling Kushner to say he did not appreciate the comments. Flynn 1/19/18 302, at 9.

224 Christie 2/ 13/19 302, at 4.

225 Christie 2/13/19 302, at 4

226 Christie 2/ 13/I 9 302, at 4-5.

227 Christie 2/13/19 302, at 5.

228 Christie 2/13/19 302, at 5.

229 Christie 2/13/19 302, at 5.no Christie 2/13/19 302, at 5.

231 SCRO I 2b_000022 (President's Daily Diary, 2/14/17); Corney 11/15/17 302, at 9.

232 Corney I 1/15/17 302, at IO; 2/14/17 Corney Memorandum, at I; Hearing on Russian Election Interference Before the Senate Select Intelligence Committee, I 15th Cong. (June 8, 2017) (Statement for the Record of James B. Corney, former Director of the FBI, at 4); Priebus I 0/13/17 302, at 18 (confirming that everyone was shooed out "like Corney said" in his June testimony).

233 Comey 11/15/17 302, at 10; Corney 2/14/17 Memorandum, at 1; Hearing on Russian Election Interference Before the Senate Select Intelligence Committee, I 15th Cong. (June 8, 2017) (Statement for the Record of James 8. Corney, former Director of the FBI, at 4). Sessions recalled that the President asked to speak to Corney alone and that Sessions was one of the last to leave the room; he described Corney's testimony about the events leading up to the private meeting with the President as "pretty accurate." Sessions 1/17/18 302, at 6. Kushner had no recollection of whether the President asked Corney to stay behind. Kushner 4/11/18 302, at 24.

234 Corney 2/14/17 Memorandum, at 2; Priebus I 0/13/17 302, at 18.

235 Comey 11/15/17 302, at IO; Comey 2/14/17 Memorandum, at I; Hearing on Russian Election Interference Before the Senate Select Intelligence Committee, I 15th Cong. (June 8, 2017) (Statement for the Record of James B. Comey, former Director of the FBI, at 4).

236 Comey 2/14/ 17 Memorandum, at I; Hearing on Russian Election Interference Before the Senate Select Intelligence Committee, I 15th Cong. (June 8, 2017) (Statement for the Record of James 8. Comey, former Director of the FBI, at 5).

237 Comey 11/15/17 302, at IO; Comey 2/14/17 Memorandum, at 2; Hearing on Russian Election Interference Before the Senate Select Intelligence Committee, I 15th Cong. (June 8, 2017) (Statement for the Record of James B. Comey, former Director of the FBI, at 5).

238 Hearing on Russian Election Interference Before the Senate Select Intelligence Committee,
I 15th Cong. (June 8, 2017) (Statement for the Record of James B. Comey, former Director of the FBI, at
5); Comey 2/14/17 Memorandum, at 2. Comey said he was highly confident that the words in quotations in his Memorandum documenting this meeting were the exact words used by the President. He said he knew from the outset of the meeting that he was about to have a conversation of consequence, and he remembered the words used by the President and wrote them down soon after the meeting. Comey 11/15/17
302, at 10-11.

239 Comey 11/15/17 302, at IO; Comey 2/14/17 Memorandum, at 2.

240 Hearing on Russian Election Interference Before the Senate Select Intelligence Committee,
I 15th Cong. (June 8, 2017) (CQ Cong. Transcripts, at 31) (testimony of James B. Comey, former Director of the FBI). Comey further stated, "I mean, this is the president of the United States, with me alone, saying,
'I hope' this. I took it as, this is what he wants me to do." Id.; see also Comey I I I 15/ 17 302, at IO (Comey took the statement as an order to shut down the Flynn investigation).

241 Comey 11/15/17 302, at 11; Hearing on Russian Election Interference Before the Senate Select Intelligence Committee, 115th Cong. (June 8, 2017) (Statement for the record of James B. Comey, former Director of the FBI, at 5).

242 Comey 11/15/17 302, at 11; Rybicki 6/9/17 302, at 4; Rybicki 6/22/17 302, at I; Hearing on Russian Election Interference Before the Senate Select Intelligence Committee, 115th Cong. (June 8, 2017) (Statement for the record of James B. Comey, former Director of the FBI, at 5-6).

243 Comey 11/15/17 302, at 11; Rybicki 6/9/17 302, at 4-5; Rybicki 6/22/17 302, at 1-2; Sessions
1/17/18 302, at 6 (confirming that later in the week following Comey's one-on-one meeting with the President in the Oval Office, Comey told the Attorney General that he did not want to be alone with the President); Hunt 2/1 /18 302, at 6 (within days of the February 14 Oval Office meeting, Comey told Sessions he did not think it was appropriate for the FBI Director to meet alone with the President); Rybicki 11/21/18
302, at 4 (Rybicki helped to schedule the meeting with Sessions because Comey wanted to talk about his concerns about meeting with the President alone); Hearing on Russian Election Interference Before the Senate Select Intelligence Committee, 115th Cong. (June 8, 2017) (Statement for the record of James 8. Comey, former Director of the FBI, at 6).

244 See, e.g., Sean Spicer, White House Daily Briefing, C-SPAN (Feb. 14, 2017) (questions from the press included, "if [the President] was notified 17 days ago that Flynn had misled the Vice President, other officials here, and that he was a potential threat to blackmail by the Russians, why would he be kept on for almost three weeks?" and "Did the President instruct [Flynn] to talk about sanctions with the [Russian ambassador]?"). Priebus recalled that the President initially equivocated on whether to fire Flynn because it would generate negative press to lose his National Security Advisor so early in his term. Priebus 1/18/18 302, at 8.

245 E.g., Sean Sullivan et al., Senatorsfrom both parties pledge to deepen probe ofRussia and the 2016 election, Washington Post (Feb. 14, 2017); Aaron Blake, 5 times Donald Trump's team denied contact with Russia, Washington Post (Feb. 15, 2017); Oren Dorell, Donald Trump's ties to Russia go back 30 years, USA Today (Feb. 15, 2017); Pamela Brown et al., Trump aides were in constant touch with senior Russian officials during campaign, CNN (Feb. 15, 2017); Austin Wright, Camey briefs senators amidfuror over Trump-Russia ties, Politico (Feb. 17, 2017); Megan Twohey & Scott Shane, A Back-Channel Planfor Ukraine and Russia, Courtesy ofTrump Associates, New York Times (Feb. 19, 2017).

246 Remarks by President Trump and Prime Minister Netanyahu oflsrael in Joint Press Conference, White House (Feb. IS, 2017).

247 Remarks by President Trump in Press Conference, White House (Feb. 16, 2017).

248 Remarks by President Trump in Press Conference, White House (Feb. 16, 2017). The President also said that Flynn's conduct "wasn't wrong - what he did in terms of the information he saw." The President said that Flynn was just "doing the job," and "if anything, he did something right."

249 Remarks by President Trump in Press Conference, White House (Feb. 16, 2017); Priebus 1/18/18 302, at 9.

250 Remarks by President Trump in Press Conference, White House (Feb. 16, 2017).

251 Remarks by President Trump in Press Conference, White House (Feb. 16, 2017).

252 KTMF_00000047 (McFarland 2/26/17 Memorandum for the Record); McFarland 12/22/17 302, at 16-17.

253 See Priebus 1/18/18 302, at 11; see also KTMF_00000048 (McFarland 2/26/17 Memorandum for the Record); McFarland 12/22/17 302, at 17.

254 Priebus I /18/18 302, at 1 I.

255 KTMF_00000048 (McFarland 2/26/17 Memorandum for the Record); McFarland 12/22/17 302, at 17.

256 KTMF_00000047 (McFarland 2/26/17 Memorandum for the Record) ("I said l did not know whether he did or didn't, but was in Maralago the week between Christmas and New Year's (while Flynn was on vacation in Carribean) and I was not aware of any Flynn-Trump, or Trump-Russian phone calls"); McFarland 12/22/17 302, at 17.

257 Priebus 1/18/18 302, at 11.

258 McFarland 12/22/17 302, at 17.

259 McFarland 12/22/17 302, at 17.

260 KTMF_00000048 (McFarland 2/26/17 Memorandum for the Record); McFarland 12/22/17 302, at 17.

261 KTMF_00000048 (McFarland 2/26/17 Memorandum for the Record); see McFarland 12/22/17

302, at 17.

262 McFarland 12/22/ 17 302, at 17; KTMF_00000048 (McFarland 2/26/ 17 Memorandum for the Record).

263 Priebus 1/18/18 302, at 9.

264 Priebus 1/18/18 302, at 9; Flynn 1/19/18 302, at 9.

265 Priebus 1/18/18 302, at 9-10.

266 @realDonaldTrump 3/31 /17 (7:04 a.m. ET) Tweet; see Shane Harris at al., Mike Flynn Offers to Testify in Exchangefor Immunity, Wall Street Journal (Mar. 30, 2017).

267 McFarland 12/22/17 302, at 18.

268 Excerpts From The Times's Interview With Trump, New York Times (July 19, 2017). Hicks recalled that the President told her he had never asked Corney to stay behind in his office. Hicks 12/8/17 302, at 12.

269 In a statement on May 16, 2017, the White House said: "While the President has repeatedly expressed his view that General Flynn is a decent man who served and protected our country, the President has never asked Mr. Corney or anyone else to end any investigation, including any investigation involving General Flynn. . . . This is not a truthful or accurate portrayal of the conversation between the President and Mr. Corney." See Michael S. Schmidt, Corney Memorandum Says Trump Asked Him to End Flynn Investigation, New York Times (May 16, 2017) (quoting White House statement); @realDonaldTrump
12/3/17 (6: 15 a.m. ET) Tweet ("I never asked Corney to stop investigating Flynn. Just more Fake News covering another Corney lie!").

270 Priebus recalled that the President acknowledged telling Corney that Flynn was a good guy and he hoped "everything worked out for him." Priebus 10/13/17 302, at 19. McGahn recalled that the President denied saying to Corney that he hoped Corney would let Flynn go, but added that he was "allowed to hope." The President told McGahn he did not think he had crossed any lines. McGahn 12/14/17 302, at
8. 271 Rybicki 11/21/18 302, at4; McCabe 8/17/17 302, at 13-14.

272 See Priebus 1 0/13/17 302, at 18; Sessions I I 17/18 302, at 6.

C. The President's Reaction to Public Confirmation of the FBI's Russia Investigation

Overview

In early March 2017, the President learned that Sessions was considering recusing from the Russia investigation and tried to prevent the recusal. After Sessions announced his recusal on March 2, the President expressed anger at Sessions for the decision and then privately asked Sessions to "unrecuse." On March 20, 2017, Comey publicly disclosed the existence of the FBI's Russia investigation. In the days that followed, the President contacted Comey and other intelligence agency leaders and asked them to push back publicly on the suggestion that the President had any connection to the Russian election-interference effort in order to "lift the cloud" of the ongoing investigation.

Evidence

Attorney General Sessions Recuses From the Russia Investigation

In late February 20 1 7, the Department of Justice began an internal analysis of whether Sessions should recuse from the Russia investigation based on his role in the 2016 Trump Campaign.[273] On March 1, 2017, the press reported that, in his January confirmation hearing to become Attorney General, Senator Sessions had not disclosed two meetings he had with Russian Ambassador Kislyak before the presidential election, leading to congressional calls for Sessions to recuse or for a special counsel to investigate Russia's interference in the presidential election.[274]

Also on March 1, the President called Comey and said he wanted to check in and see how Comey was doing.[275] According to an email Corney sent to his chief of staff after the call, the President "talked about Sessions a bit," said that he had heard Comey was "doing great," and said that he hoped Comey would come by to say hello when he was at the White House.[276] Corney interpreted the call as an effort by the President to "pull [him] in," but he did not perceive the call as an attempt by the President to find out what Corney was doing with the Flynn investigation."

The next morning, the President called McGahn and urged him to contact Sessions to tell him not to recuse himself from the Russia investigation.[278] McGahn understood the President to be concerned that a recusal would make Sessions look guilty for omitting details in his confirmation hearing; leave the President unprotected from an investigation that could hobble the presidency and derail his policy objectives; and detract from favorable press coverage of a Presidential Address to Congress the President had delivered earlier in the week.[279] McGahn reached out to Sessions and reported that the President was not happy about the possibility of recusal.[280] Sessions replied that he intended to follow the rules on recusal.[281] McGahn reported back to the President about the call with Sessions, and the President reiterated that he did not want Sessions to recuse.[282] Throughout the day, McGahn continued trying on behalf of the President to avert Sessions's recusal by speaking to Sessions's personal counsel, Sessions's chief of staff, and Senate Majority Leader Mitch McConnell, and by contacting Sessions himself two more times.[283]
Sessions recalled that other White House advisors also called him that day to argue against his recusal.[284]

That afternoon, Sessions announced his decision to recuse "from any existing or future investigations of any matters related in any way to the campaigns for President of the United States."[285] Sessions believed the decision to recuse was not a close call, given the applicable language in the Code of Federal Regulations (CFR), which Sessions considered to be clear and decisive.[286] Sessions thought that any argument that the CFR did not apply to him was "very thin."[287] Sessions got the impression, based on calls he received from White House officials, that the President was very upset with him and did not think he had done his duty as Attorney General.[288]

Shortly after Sessions announced his recusal, the White House Counsel's Office directed that Sessions should not be contacted about the matter.[289] Internal White House Counsel's Office notes from March 2, 2017, state "No contact w/Sessions" and "No comms / Serious concerns about obstruction."[290]

On March 3, the day after Sessions's recusal, McGahn was called into the Oval Office.[291] Other advisors were there, including Priebus and Bannon.[292] The President opened the conversation by saying, "I don't have a lawyer."[293] The President expressed anger at McGahn about the recusal and brought up Roy Cohn, stating that he wished Cohn was his attorney.[294]

McGahn interpreted this comment as directed at him, suggesting that Cohn would fight for the President whereas McGahn would not.[295] The President wanted McGahn to talk to Sessions about the recusal, but McGahn told the President that DOJ ethics officials had weighed in on Sessions's decision to recuse.[296] The President then brought up former Attorneys General Robert Kennedy and Eric Holder and said that they had protected their presidents.[297] The President also pushed back on the DOJ contacts policy, and said words to the effect of, "You're telling me that Bobby and Jack didn't talk about investigations? Or Obama didn't tell Eric Holder who to investigate?"[298]

Bannon recalled that the President was as mad as Bannon had ever seen him and that he screamed at McGahn about how weak Sessions was.[299] Bannon recalled telling the President that Sessions's recusal was not a surprise and that before the inauguration they had discussed that Sessions would have to recuse from campaign-related investigations because of his work on the Trump Campaign.[300]

That weekend, Sessions and McGahn flew to Mar-a-Lago to meet with the President.[301] Sessions recalled that the President pulled him aside to speak to him alone and suggested that Sessions should "unrecuse" from the Russia investigation.[302] The President contrasted Sessions with Attorneys General Holder and Kennedy, who had developed a strategy to help their presidents where Sessions had not.[303] Sessions said he had the impression that the President feared that the investigation could spin out of control and disrupt his ability to govern, which Sessions could have helped avert if he were still overseeing it.[304]

On March 5, 2017, the White House Counsel's Office was informed that the FBI was asking for transition-period records relating to Flynn—indicating that the FBI was still actively investigating him.[305] On March 6, the President told advisors he wanted to call the Acting Attorney General to find out whether the White House or the President was being investigated, although it is not clear whether the President knew at that time of the FBI's recent request concerning Flynn.[306]

2. FBI Director Comey Publicly Confirms the Existence of the   Russia Investigation in Testimony Before HPSC

On March 9, 2017, Comey briefed the "Gang of Eight" congressional leaders about the FBI's investigation of Russian interference, including an identification of the principal U.S. subjects of the investigation.[P?] Although it is unclear whether the President knew of that briefing at the time, notes taken by Annie Donaldson, then McGahn's chief of staff, on March 12, 2017, state, "POTUS in panic/chaos ... Need binders to put in front of POTUS. (1) All things related to Russia."[308] The week after Comey's briefing, the White House Counsel's Office was in contact with SSCI Chairman Senator Richard Burr about the Russia investigations and appears to have received information about the status of the FBI investtgatlon.[P?]

On March 20, 2017, Comey was scheduled to testify before HPSCI.[310] In advance of Comey's testimony, congressional officials made clear that they wanted Comey to provide information about the ongoing FBI investigation.[311] Dana Boente, who at that time was the Acting Attorney General for the Russia investigation, authorized Comey to confirm the existence of the Russia investigation and agreed that Comey should decline to comment on whether any particular individuals, including the President, were being investigated.[312]

In his opening remarks at the HPSCI hearing, which were drafted in consultation with the Department of Justice, Comey stated that he had "been authorized by the Department of Justice to confirm that the FBI, as part of [its] counterintelligence mission, is investigating the Russian government's efforts to interfere in the 2016 presidential election and that includes investigating the nature of any links between individuals associated with the Trump campaign and the Russian government and whether there was any coordination between the campaign and Russia's efforts. As with any counterintelligence investigation, this will also include an assessment of whether any crimes were committed."[313] Comey added that he would not comment further on what the FBI was "doing and whose conduct [it] [was] examining" because the investigation was ongoing and classified—but he observed that he had "taken the extraordinary step in consultation with the Department of Justice of briefing this Congress's leaders ... in a classified setting in detail about the investigation."[314] Comey was specifically asked whether President Trump was "under investigation during the campaign" or "under investigation now."[315] Comey declined to answer, stating, "Please don't over interpret what I've said as—as the chair and ranking know, we have briefed him in great detail on the subjects of the investigation and what we're doing, but I'm not gonna answer about anybody in this forum."[316] Comey was also asked whether the FBI was investigating the information contained in the Steele reporting, and he declined to answer.[317]

According to McGahn and Donaldson, the President had expressed frustration with Comey before his March 20 testimony, and the testimony made matters worse.[318] The President had previously criticized Comey for too frequently making headlines and for not attending intelligence briefings at the White House, and the President suspected Comey of leaking certain information to the media.[319] McGahn said the President thought Comey was acting like "his own branch of government."[320]

Press reports following Comey's March 20 testimony suggested that the FBI was investigating the President, contrary to what Comey had told the President at the end of the January 6, 2017 intelligence assessment briefing.[321] McGahn, Donaldson, and senior advisor Stephen Miller recalled that the President was upset with Comey's testimony and the press coverage that followed because of the suggestion that the President was under investigation.[322] Notes from the White House Counsel's Office dated March 21, 2017, indicate that the President was "beside himself" over Corney's testimony.[323] The President called McGahn repeatedly that day to ask him to intervene with the Department of Justice, and, according to the notes, the President was "getting hotter and hotter, get rid?"[324] Officials in the White House Counsel's Office became so concerned that the President would fire Comey that they began drafting a memorandum that examined whether the President needed cause to terminate the FBI director.[325]

At the President's urging, McGahn contacted Boente several times on March 21, 2017, to seek Boente's assistance in having Comey or the Department of Justice correct the misperception that the President was under investigation.[326] Boente did not specifically recall the conversations, although he did remember one conversation with McGahn around this time where McGahn asked if there was a way to speed up or end the Russia investigation as quickly as possible.[327] Boente said McGahn told him the President was under a cloud and it made it hard for him to govern.[328] Boente recalled telling McGahn that there was no good way to shorten the investigation and attempting to do so could erode confidence in the investigation's conclusions.[329] Boente said McGahn agreed and dropped the issue.[330] The President also sought to speak with Boente directly, but McGahn told the President that Boente did not want to talk to the President about the request to intervene with Comey.[331] McGahn recalled Boente telling him in calls that day that he did not think it was sustainable for Comey to stay on as FBI director for the next four years, which McGahn said he conveyed to the President.[332] Boente did not recall discussing with McGahn or anyone else the idea that Comey should not continue as FBI director.[333]

3. The President Asks Intelligence Community Leaders to Make Public Statements that he had No Connection to Russia

In the weeks following Comey's March 20, 2017 testimony, the President repeatedly asked intelligence community officials to push back publicly on any suggestion that the President had a connection to the Russian election-interference effort.

On March 22, 2017, the President asked Director of National Intelligence Daniel Coats and CIA Director Michael Pompeo to stay behind in the Oval Office after a Presidential Daily Briefing.[334] According to Coats, the President asked them whether they could say publicly that no link existed between him and Russia.[335] Coats responded that the Office of the Director of National Intelligence (ODNI) has nothing to do with investigations and it was not his role to make a public statement on the Russia investigation.[336] Pompeo had no recollection of being asked to stay behind after the March 22 briefing, but he recalled that the President regularly urged officials to get the word out that he had not done anything wrong related to Russia.[337]

Coats told this Office that the President never asked him to speak to Comey about the FBI investigation.[338] Some ODNI staffers, however, had a different recollection of how Coats described the meeting immediately after it occurred. According to senior ODNI official Michael Dempsey, Coats said after the meeting that the President had brought up the Russia investigation and asked him to contact Comey to see if there was a way to get past the investigation, get it over with, end it, or words to that effect.[339] Dempsey said that Coats described the President's comments as falling "somewhere between musing about hating the investigation" and wanting Coats to "do something to stop it."[340] Dempsey said Coats made it clear that he would not get involved with an ongoing FBI investigation.[341] Edward Gistaro, another ODNI official, recalled that right after Coats's meeting with the President, on the walk from the Oval Office back to the Eisenhower Executive Office Building, Coats said that the President had kept him behind to ask him what he could do to "help with the investigation."[342] Another ODNI staffer who had been waiting for Coats outside the Oval Office talked to Gistaro a few minutes later and recalled Gistaro reporting that Coats was upset because the President had asked him to contact Comey to convince him there was nothing to the Russia investigation.[343]

On Saturday, March 25, 2017, three days after the meeting in the Oval Office, the President called Coats and again complained about the Russia investigations, saying words to the effect of ,"I can't do anything with Russia, there's things I'd like to do with Russia, with trade, with ISIS, they're all over me with this."[344] Coats told the President that the investigations were going to go on and the best thing to do was to let them run their course.[345] Coats later testified in a congressional hearing that he had "never felt pressure to intervene or interfere in any way and shape—with shaping intelligence in a political way, or in relationship . _ _ to an ongoing investigation."[346]

On March 26, 2017, the day after the President called Coats, the President called NSA Director Admiral Michael Rogers.[347] The President expressed frustration with the Russia investigation, saying that it made relations with the Russians difficult.[348] The President told Rogers "the thing with the Russians [wa]s messing up" his ability to get things done with Russia.[349]

The President also said that the news stories linking him with Russia were not true and asked Rogers if he could do anything to refute the stories.P? Deputy Director of the NSA Richard Ledgett, who was present for the call, said it was the most unusual thing he had experienced in 40 years of government service.[351] After the call concluded, Ledgett prepared a memorandum that he and Rogers both signed documenting the content of the conversation and the President's request, and they placed the memorandum in a safe.[352] But Rogers did not perceive the President's request to be an order, and the President did not ask Rogers to push back on the Russia investigation itself.[353] Rogers later testified in a congressional hearing that as NSA Director he had "never been directed to do anything [he] believe[d] to be illegal, immoral, unethical or inappropriate" and did "not recall ever feeling pressured to do so."[354]

In addition to the specific comments made to Coats, Pompeo, and Rogers, the President spoke on other occasions in the presence of intelligence community officials about the Russia investigation and stated that it interfered with his ability to conduct foreign relations.[355] On at least two occasions, the President began Presidential Daily Briefings by stating that there was no collusion with Russia and he hoped a press statement to that effect could be issued.[356] Pompeo recalled that the President vented about the investigation on multiple occasions, complaining that there was no evidence against him and that nobody would publicly defend him.[357] Rogers recalled a private conversation with the President in which he "vent[ed]" about the investigation, said he had done nothing wrong, and said something like the "Russia thing has got to go away."[358] Coats recalled the President bringing up the Russia investigation several times, and Coats said he finally told the President that Coats's job was to provide intelligence and not get involved in investigations.[359]

4. The President Asks Comey to "Lift the Cloud" Created by the Russia Investigation

On the morning of March 30, 2017, the President reached out to Comey directly about the Russia investigation"? According to Corney's contemporaneous record of the conversation, the President said "he was trying to run the country and the cloud of this Russia business was making that difficult."[361] The President asked Corney what could be done to "lift the cloud."[362] Corney explained "that we were running it down as quickly as possible and that there would be great benefit, if we didn't find anything, to our Good Housekeeping seal of approval, but we had to do our work."[363] Corney also told the President that congressional leaders were aware that the FBI was not investigating the President personally.P"

The President said several times, "We need to get that fact out."[365] The President commented that if there was "some satellite" (which Corney took to mean an associate of the President's or the campaign) that did something, "it would be good to find that out" but that he himself had not done anything wrong and he hoped Corney "would find a way to get out that we weren't investigating him."[366] After the call ended, Corney called Boente and told him about the conversation, asked for guidance on how to respond, and said he was uncomfortable with direct contact from the President about the investigation.[367] On the morning of April 11, 2017, the President called Corney again.[368]

According to Corney's contemporaneous record of the conversation, the President said he was "following up to see if [Corney] did what [the President] had asked last time—getting out that he personally is not under investigation."[369] Corney responded that he had passed the request to Boente but not heard back, and he informed the President that the traditional channel for such a request would be to have the White House Counsel contact DOJ leadership.F?

The President said he would take that step.[371] The President then added, "Because I have been very loyal to you, very loyal, we had that thing, you know."[372] In a televised interview that was taped early that afternoon, the President was asked if it was too late for him to ask Corney to step down; the President responded, "No, it's not too late, but you know, I have confidence in him. We'll see what happens. You know, it's going to be interesting."[373] After the interview, Hicks told the President she thought the President's comment about Corney should be removed from the broadcast of the interview, but the President wanted to keep it in, which Hicks thought was unusual.[374]

Later that day, the President told senior advisors, including McGahn and Priebus, that he had reached out to Corney twice in recent weeks.[375] The President acknowledged that McGahn would not approve of the outreach to Corney because McGahn had previously cautioned the President that he should not talk to Corney directly to prevent any perception that the White House was interfering with investigations.[376] The President told McGahn that Corney had indicated the FBI could make a public statement that the President was not under investigation if the Department of Justice approved that action."?

After speaking with the President, McGahn followed up with Boente to relay the President's understanding that the FBI could make a public announcement if the Department of Justice cleared it.[378] McGahn recalled that Boente said Corney had told him there was nothing obstructive about the calls from the President, but they made Corney uncomfortable.[379] According to McGahn, Boente responded that he did not want to issue a statement about the President not being under investigation because of the potential political ramifications and did not want to order Corney to do it because that action could prompt the appointment of a Special Counsel.? Boente did not recall that aspect of his conversation with McGahn, but did recall telling McGahn that the direct outreaches from the President to Corney were a problem.[381] Boente recalled that McGahn agreed and said he would do what he could to address that issue.[382]

Analysis

In analyzing the President's reaction to Sessions's recusal and the requests he made to Coats, Pompeo, Rogers, and Comey, the following evidence is relevant to the elements of obstruction of justice:

a.   Obstructive act. The evidence shows that, after Corney's March 20, 2017 testimony, the President repeatedly reached out to intelligence agency leaders to discuss the FBT's investigation. But witnesses had different recollections of the precise content of those outreaches. Some ODNT officials recalled that Coats told them immediately after the March 22 Oval Office meeting that the President asked Coats to intervene with Comey and "stop" the investigation. But the first-hand witnesses to the encounter remember the conversation differently. Pompeo had no memory of the specific meeting, but generally recalled the President urging officials to get the word out that the President had not done anything wrong related to Russia. Coats recalled that the President asked that Coats state publicly that no link existed between the President and Russia, but did not ask him to speak with Comey or to help end the investigation. The other outreaches by the President during this period were similar in nature. The President asked Rogers if he could do anything to refute the stories linking the President to Russia, and the President asked Comey to make a public statement that would "lift the cloud" of the ongoing investigation by making clear that the President was not personally under investigation. These requests, while significant enough that Rogers thought it important to document the encounter in a written memorandum, were not interpreted by the officials who received them as directives to improperly interfere with the investigation.

b.   Nexus to a proceeding. At the time of the President's outreaches to leaders of the intelligence agencies in late March and early April 2017, the FBT's Russia investigation did not yet involve grand jury proceedings. The outreaches, however, came after and were in response to Corney's March 20, 2017 announcement that the FBT, as a part of its counterintelligence mission, was conducting an investigation into Russian interference in the 2016 presidential election. Comey testified that the investigation included any links or coordination with Trump campaign officials and would "include an assessment of whether any crimes were committed."

c.   Intent. As described above, the evidence does not establish that the President asked or directed intelligence agency leaders to stop or interfere with the FBI's Russia investigation ▬ and the President affirmatively told Comey that if "some satellite" was involved in Russian election interference "it would be good to find that out."   But the President's intent in trying to prevent Sessions's recusal, and in reaching out to Coats, Pompeo, Rogers, and Comey following Corney's public announcement of the FBJ's Russia investigation, is nevertheless relevant to understanding what motivated the President's other actions towards the investigation.

The evidence shows that the President was focused on the Russia investigation's implications for his presidency—and, specifically, on dispelling any suggestion that he was under investigation or had links to Russia. In early March, the President attempted to prevent Sessions's recusal, even after being told that Sessions was following DOJ conflict of interest rules. After Sessions recused, the White House Counsel's Office tried to cut off further contact with Sessions about the matter, although it is not clear whether that direction was conveyed to the President.   The President continued to raise the issue of Sessions's recusal and, when he had the opportunity, he pulled Sessions aside and urged him to unrecuse.   The President also told advisors that he wanted an Attorney General who would protect him, the way he perceived Robert Kennedy and Eric Holder to have protected their presidents.   The President made statements about being able to direct the course of criminal investigations, saying words to the effect of, "You're telling me that Bobby and Jack didn't talk about investigations?   Or Obama didn't tell Eric Holder who to investigate?"

After Comey publicly confirmed the existence of the FBI's Russia investigation on March 20, 2017, the President was "beside himself" and expressed anger that Comey did not issue a statement correcting any misperception that the President himself was under investigation.   The President sought to speak with Acting Attorney General Boente directly and told McGahn to contact Boente to request that Comey make a clarifying statement.   The President then asked other intelligence community leaders to make public statements to refute the suggestion that the President had links to Russia, but the leaders told him they could not publicly comment on the investigation.   On March 30 and April 11, against the advice of

White House advisors who had informed him that any direct contact with the FBI could be perceived as improper interference in an ongoing investigation, the President made personal outreaches to Comey asking him to "lift the cloud" of the Russia investigation by making public the fact that the President was not personally under investigation.

Evidence indicates that the President was angered by both the existence of the Russia investigation and the public reporting that he was under investigation, which he knew was not true based on Comey's representations. The President complained to advisors that if people thought Russia helped him with the election, it would detract from what he had accomplished.

Other evidence indicates that the President was concerned about the impact of the Russia investigation on his ability to govern. The President complained that the perception that he was under investigation was hurting his ability to conduct foreign relations, particularly with Russia. The President told Coats he "can't do anything with Russia," he told Rogers that "the thing with the Russians" was interfering with his ability to conduct foreign affairs, and he told Comey that "he was trying to run the country and the cloud of this Russia business was making that difficult."

*****

273 Sessions 1/17/18 302, at I; Hunt 2/11 18 302, at 3.

274 E.g., Adam Entous et al., Sessions met with Russian envoy twice last year, encounters he later did not disclose, Washington Post (Mar. I, 2017).

275 3/1/17 Email, Corney to Rybicki; SCRO 12b_000030 (President's Daily Diary, 3/1/17, reflecting call with Corney at 11:55 am.)

276 3/1/17 Email, Corney to Rybicki; see Hearing on Russian Election Interference Before the Senate Select Intelligence Committee, I 15th Cong. (June 8, 2017) (CQ Cong. Transcripts, at 86) (testimony

277 Corney 11/15/17 302, at 17-18.

278 McGahn 11/30/17 302, at 16.

279 McGahn 11/30/17 302, at 16-17; see SC_AD_00123 (Donaldson 3/2/17 Notes) ("Just in the middle of another Russia Fiasco.").

280 Sessions 1/17/18 302, at 3.

281 McGahn 11/30/17 302, at 17.

282 McGahn 11/30/17 302, at 17.

283 McGahn 11/30/17 302, at 18-19; Sessions 1/17/18 302, at 3; Hunt 2/1/18 302, at 4; Donaldson 11/6/17 302, at 8-1 O; see Hunt-000017; SC AD 00121 (Donaldson 3/2/17 Notes).

284 Sessions 1/17/18 302, at 3.

285 Attorney General Sessions Statement on Recusal, Department ofJustice Press Release (Mar. 2, 2017) ("During the course of the last several weeks, I have met with the relevant senior career Department officials to discuss whether I should recuse myself from any matters arising from the campaigns for President of the United States. Having concluded those meetings today, I have decided to recuse myself from any existing or future investigations of any matters related in any way to the campaigns for President of the United States."). At the time of Sessions's recusal, Dana Boente, then the Acting Deputy Attorney General and U.S. Attorney for the Eastern District of Virginia, became the Acting Attorney General for campaign-related matters pursuant to an executive order specifying the order of succession at the Department of Justice. Id. ("Consistent with the succession order for the Department of Justice, ... Dana

286 Sessions 1/17/18 302, at 1-2. 28 C.F.R. § 45.2 provides that "no employee shall participate in a criminal investigation or prosecution if he has a personal or political relationship with ... [a]ny person or organization substantially involved in the conduct that is the subject of the investigation or prosecution," and defines "political relationship" as "a close identification with an elected official, a candidate (whether or not successful) for elective, public office, a political party, or a campaign organization, arising from service as a principal adviser thereto or a principal official thereof."

287 Sessions 1/17/18 302, at 2.

288 Sessions 1/17/18 302, at 3.

289 Donaldson 11/6/17 302, at 11; SC_AD_00123 (Donaldson 3/2/17 Notes). It is not clear whether the President was aware of the White House Counsel's Office direction not to contact Sessions about his recusal.

290 SC_AD_OOl23 (Donaldson 3/2/17 Notes). McGahn said he believed the note "No comms I Serious concerns about obstruction" may have referred to concerns McGahn had about the press team saying "crazy things" and trying to spin Sessions's recusal in a way that would raise concerns about obstruction. McGahn I 1/30/17 302, at 19. Donaldson recalled that "No comms" referred to the order that no one should contact Sessions. Donaldson I 1/6/17 302, at I I.

291 McGahn I 2/12/17 302, at 2.

292 McGahn 12/ 12/ 17 302, at 2.

293 McGahn 12/ 12/ 17 302, at 2.

294 McGahn 12/12/17 302, at 2. Cohn had previously served as a lawyer for the President during his career as a private businessman. Priebus recalled that when the President talked about Cohn, he said Cohn would win cases for him that had no chance, and that Cohn had done incredible things for him. Priebus 4/3/ 18 302, at 5. Bannon recalled the President describing Cohn as a winner and a fixer, someone who got things done. Bannon 2/14/ 18 302, at 6.

295 McGahn 12/12/17 302, at 2.

296 McGahn 12/12/17 302, at 2.

297 McGahn 12/12/17 302, at 3. Bannon said the President saw Robert Kennedy and Eric Holder as Attorneys General who protected the presidents they served. The President thought Holder always stood up for President Obama and even took a contempt charge for him, and Robert Kennedy always had his brother's back. Bannon 2/14/18 302, at 5. Priebus recalled that the President said he had been told his entire life he needed to have a great lawyer, a "bulldog," and added that Holder had been willing to take a contempt-of-Congress charge for President Obama. Priebus 4/3/18 302, at 5.

298 McGahn 12/12/17 302, at 3.

299 Bannon 2/14/18 302, at 5.

300 Bannon 2/14/18 302, at 5.

301 Sessions 1/17/18 302, at 3; Hunt 2/1/18 302, at 5; McGahn 12/12/17 302, at 3.

302 Sessions 1/17/18 302, at 3-4.

303 Sessions 1/17/18 302, at 3-4

304 Sessions 1/17/18 302, at 3-4. Hicks recalled that after Sessions recused, the President was angry and scolded Sessions in her presence, but she could not remember exactly when that conversation occurred. Hicks 12/8/17 302, at 13. 305 SC

306 Donaldson 11/6/17 302, at 14; see SC_AD_000168 (Donaldson 3/6/17 Notes) ("POTUS wants to call Dana [then the Acting Attorney General for campaign-related investigations] I Is investigation I No I We know something on Flynn I GSA got contacted by FBI I There's something hot").

307 Corney 11/15/17 302, at 13-14; SNS-Classified-0000140-44 (3/8/17 Email, Gauhar to Page et al.).

308 SC_AD_00188 (Donaldson 3/12/18 Notes). Donaldson said she was not part of the conversation that led to these notes, and must have been told about it from others. Donaldson 11/6/17 302, at 13.

309 Donaldson 11/6/17 302, at 14-15. On March 16, 2017, the White House Counsel's Office was briefed by Senator Burr on the existence of "4-5 targets." Donaldson 11/6/17 302, at 15. The "targets" were identified in notes taken by Donaldson as "Flynn (FBI was in-wra in u -+DOJ looking for phone records"; "Corney-s-Manafort (Ukr + Russia, not campaign)"; "Carter Page ($ game)"; and "Greek Guy" (potentially referring to George Papadopoulos, ater charged with violating 18 U.S.C. § I 001 for lying to the FBI). SC_AD_OOl98 (Donaldson 3/16/17 Notes). Donaldson and McGahn both said they believed these were targets of SSCI. Donaldson 11/6/17 302, at 15; McGahn 12/12/17 302, at 4. But SSCI does not formally investigate individuals as "targets"; the notes on their face reference the FBI, the Department of Justice, and Corney; and the notes track the background materials prepared by the FBI for Corney's briefing to the Gang of 8 on March 9. See SNS-Classitied-0000140-44 (3/8/17 Email, Gauhar to Page et al.); see also Donaldson 11/6/17 302, at 15 (Donaldson could not rule out that Burr had told McGahn those individuals were the FBI's targets).

313 Hearing on Russian Election Tampering Before the House Permanent Select Intelligence Committee, I 15th Cong. (Mar. 20, 2017) (CQ Cong. Transcripts, at 11) (testimony by FBI Director James 8. Corney); Corney 11/15/17 302, at 17; Boente 1/31/18 302, at 5 (confirming that the Department of Justice authorized Corney's remarks).

314 Hearing on Russian Election Tampering Before the House Permanent Select Intelligence Committee, I 15th Cong. (Mar. 20, 2017) (CQ Cong. Transcripts, at 11) (testimony by FBI Director James B. Corney).

315 Hearing on Russian Election Tampering Before the House Permanent Select Intelligence Committee, I 15th Cong. (Mar. 20, 2017) (CQ Cong. Transcripts, at 130) (question by Rep. Swalwell).

316 Hearing on Russian Election Tampering Before the House Permanent Select Intelligence Committee, I 15th Cong. (Mar. 20, 2017) (CQ Cong. Transcripts, at 130) (testimony by FBI Director James B. Corney).

317 Hearing on Russian Election Tampering Before the House Permanent Select intelligence Committee, I 15th Cong. (Mar. 20, 2017) (CQ Cong. Transcripts, at 143) (testimony by FBI Director James B. Corney).

318 Donaldson 11/6/17 302, at 21; McGahn 12/12/17 302, at 7.

319 Donaldson 11/6/17 302, at 21; McGahn 12/12/17 302, at 6-9.

320 McGahn 12/12/17 302, at 7.

321 E.g., Matt Apuzzo et al., F.B.l Is Investigating Trump's Russia Ties, Corney Confirms, New York Times (Mar. 20, 2017); Andy Greenberg. The FBI Has Been Investigating Trump's Russia Ties Since July, Wired (Mar. 20, 2017); Julie Borger & Spencer Ackerman, Trump-Russia collusion is being investigated by FBI, Corney confirms, Guardian (Mar. 20, 2017); see Corney 1 /6/17 Memorandum, at 2.

322 Donaldson 11/6/17 302, at 16-17; S. Miller 10/31/17 302, at4; McGahn 12/12/17 302, at 5-7.

323 SC AD 00213 (Donaldson 3/21/17 Notes). The notes from that day also indicate that the President referred to the "Corney bombshell" which "made [him] look like a fool." SC_AD_00206 (Donaldson 3/21/17 Notes).

324 SC AD 00210 (Donaldson 3/21 I 1 7 Notes).

325 SCR016_000002-05 (White House Counsel's Office Memorandum). White House Counsel's Office attorney Uttam Dhillon did not recall a triggering event causing the White House Counsel's Office to begin this research. Dhillon 11 /21 /17 302, at 5. Metadata from the document, which was provided by the White House, establishes that it was created on March 21, 2017.

326 Donaldson 11 /6/ 17 302, at 16-21; McGahn 12/12/17 302, at 5-7.

327 Boente I /31/18 302, at 5.

328 Boente 1/31/18 302, at 5.

329 Boente I /31/18 302, at 5.

330 Boente 1/31/18 302, at 5.

331 SC_AD_00210 (Donaldson 3/21/17 Notes); McGahn 12/12/17 302, at 7; Donaldson 11/6/17 302, at 19.

332 McGahn 12/12/17 302, at 7; Burnham 11/03/17 302, at 11.

333 Boente 1/31/18 302, at 3.

334 Coats 6/14/17 302, at 3; Culver 6/14/17 302, at 2.

335 Coats 6/14/ 17 302, at 3.

336 Coats 6/14/17 3 02, at 3.

337 Pompeo 6/28/17 302, at 1-3.

338 Coats 6/14/17 302, at 3.

339 Dempsey 6/14/17 302, at 2.

340 Dempsey 6/14/17 302, at 2-3.

341 Dempsey 6/14/ 17 302, at 3.

342 Gistaro 6/14/17 302, at 2.

343 Culver 6/14/17 302, at 2-3.

344 Coats 6/14/17 302, at 4.

345 Coats 6/14/17 302, at 4; Dempsey 6/14/17 302, at 3 (Coats relayed that the President had asked several times what Coats could do to help "get [the investigation] done," and Coats had repeatedly told the President that fastest way to "get it done" was to let it run its course).

346 Hearing on Foreign Intelligence Surveillance Act Before the Senate Select Intelligence Committee, I 15th Cong. (June 7, 2017) (CQ Cong. Transcripts, at 25) (testimony by Daniel Coats, Director ofNational Intelligence).

347 Rogers 6/12/17 302, at 3-4.

348 Rogers 6/12/17 302, at 4.

349 Ledgett 6/13/ 17 302, at 1-2; see Rogers 6/12/ 17 302, at 4.

350 Rogers 6/12/17 302, at 4-5; Ledgett 6/13/17 302, at 2.

351 Ledgett 6/13/17 302, at 2.

352 Ledgett 6/13/17 302, at 2-3; Rogers 6/12/17 302, at 4.

353 Rogers 6/12/17 302, at 5; Ledgett 6/ 13/17 302, at 2.

354 Hearing on Foreign Intelligence Surveillance Act Before the Senate Select Intelligence Committee, I 15th Cong. (June 7, 2017) (CQ Cong. Transcripts, at 20) (testimony by Admiral Michael Rogers, Director of the National Security Agency).

355 Gistaro 6/14/17 302, at I, 3; Pompeo 6/28/17 302, at 2-3.

356 Gistaro 6/14/17 302, at I.

357 Pompeo 6/28/17 302, at 2.

358 Rogers 6/ I 2/17 302, at 6.

359 Coats 6/ 14/17 302, at 3-4.

360 SCRO I 2b_000044 (President's Daily Diary, 3/30/17, reflecting call to Corney from 8: I 4 - 8:24 a.m.); Corney 3/30/17 Memorandum, at 1 ("The President called me on my CMS phone at 8: 13 am today .. . . The call lasted 1 1 minutes (about IO minutes when he was connected)."; Hearing on Russian Election

361 Corney 3/30/17 Memorandum, at 1. Corney subsequently testified before Congress about this conversation and described it to our Office; his recollections were consistent with his memorandum. Hearing on Russian Election Interference Before the Senate Select Intelligence Committee, 115th Cong. (June 8, 2017) (Statement for the Record of James B. Corney, former Director of the FBI, at 6); Corney 11/15/17 302, at 18.

362 Corney 3/30/ 17 Memorandum, at I; Corney I I I I 5/ 17 302, at 18.

363 Corney 3/30/17 Memorandum, at I; Corney 11/15/17 302, at 18.

364 Corney 3/30/17 Memorandum, at I; Hearing on Russian Election Interference Before the Senate Select Intelligence Committee, 1 ISth Cong. (June 8, 2017) (Statement for the Record of James B. Corney, former Director of the FBI, at 6).

365 Corney 3/30/17 Memorandum, at 1; Hearing on Russian Election Interference Before the Senate Select Intelligence Committee, 115th Cong. (June 8, 2017) (Statement for the Record of James B. Corney, former Director of the FBT, at 6). ·

366 Corney 3/30/17 Memorandum, at I; Hearing on Russian Election Interference Before the Senate Select Intelligence Committee, 115th Cong. (June 8, 2017) (Statement for the Record of James B. Corney, former Director of the FBI, at 6-7).

367 Corney 3/30/17 Memorandum, at 2; Boente I /31 I 18 302, at 6-7; Hearing on Russian Election Interference Before the Senate Select Intelligence Committee, I I 5th Cong. (June 8, 2017) (Statement for the Record of James B. Corney, former Director of the FBI, at 7).

368 SCROl2b_OOOOS3 (President's Daily Diary, 4/11/17, reflecting call to Corney from 8:27 - 8:3 l a.m.); Corney 4/11/17 Memorandum, at I ("I returned the president's call this morning at 8:26 am EDT. We spoke for about four minutes.").

37° Corney 4/11 /17 Memorandum, at I.

371 Corney 4/11/17 Memorandum, at I.

372 Corney 4/11/17 Memorandum, at I. In a footnote to this statement in his memorandum, Corney wrote, "His use of these words did not fit with the flow of the call, which at that point had moved away from any request of me, but I have recorded it here as it happened."

373 Maria Bartiromo, Interview with President Trump, Fox Business Network (Apr. 12, 2017); SCR012b_000054 (President's Daily Diary, 4/11/17, reflecting Bartiromo interview from 12:30 - 12:55 p.m.).

374 Hicks 12/8/17 302, at 13.

375 Priebus I Of13/17 302, at 23; McGahn 12/ 12/ 17 302, at 9.

376 Priebus I 0/13/17 302, at 23; McGahn 12/12/ 17 302, at 9; see McGahn I J/30/17 302, at 9; Dhillon 11/21/17 302, at 2 (stating that White House Counsel attorneys had advised the President not to contact the FBI Director directly because it could create a perception he was interfering with investigations). Later in April, the President told other attorneys in the White House Counsel's Office that he had called Corney even though he knew they had advised against direct contact. Dhillon 11/21/17 302, at 2 (recalling that the President said, "I know you told me not to, but I called Corney anyway.").

377 McGahn 12/12/17 302, at 9.

378 McGahn 12/12/17 302, at 9.

379 McGahn 12/12/17 302, at 9; see Boente 1/31/18 302, at 6 (recalling that Corney told him after the March 30, 2017 call that it was not obstructive).

380 McGahn 12/J 2/17 302, at 9-10.

381 Boente 1/31/18 302, at 7; McGahn 12/12/17 302, at 9.

382 Boente 1/31/18 302, at 7

D.   Events Leading Up To and Surrounding the Termination of FBI Director Comey

Overview

Comey was scheduled to testify before Congress on May 3, 2017. Leading up to that testimony, the President continued to tell advisors that he wanted Comey to make public that the President was not under investigation. At the hearing, Comey declined to answer questions about the scope or subjects of the Russia investigation and did not state publicly that the President was not under investigation. Two days later, on May 5, 2017, the President told close aides he was going to fire Comey, and on May 9, he did so, using his official termination letter to make public that Comey had on three occasions informed the President that he was not under investigation. The President decided to fire Comey before receiving advice or a recommendation from the Department of Justice,. but he approved an initial public account of the termination that attributed it to a recommendation from the Department ofJustice based on Comey's handling of the Clinton email investigation. After Deputy Attorney General Rod Rosenstein resisted attributing the firing to his recommendation, the President acknowledged that he intended to fire Comey regardless of the DOJ recommendation and was thinking ofthe Russia investigation when he made the decision. The President also told the Russian Foreign Minister, "I just fired the head of the F.B.I. He was crazy, a real nut job. I faced great pressure because of Russia. That's taken off. . . I'm not under investigation."

Evidence

I. Comey Testifies Before the Senate Judiciary Committee and Declines to Answer Questions About Whether the President is Under Investigation

On May 3, 2017, Comey was scheduled to testify at an FBI oversight hearing before the Senate Judiciary Committee.[383] McGahn recalled that in the week leading up to the hearing, the President said that it would be the last straw if Comey did not take the opportunity to set the record straight by publicly announcing that the President was not under investigation.

The President had previously told McGahn that the perception that the President was under investigation was hurting his ability to carry out his presidential duties and deal with foreign leaders.[385] At the hearing, Comey declined to answer questions about the status of the Russia investigation, stating "[t]he Department of Justice ha(d] authorized (him] to confirm that (the Russia investigation] exists," but that he was "not going to say another word about it" until the investigation was completed.[386] Comey also declined to answer questions about whether investigators had "ruled out anyone in the Trump campaign as potentially a target of th[e] criminal investigation," including whether the FBI had "ruled out the president of the United States."[387]

Corney was also asked at the hearing about his decision to announce 11 days before the presidential election that the FBI was reopening the Clinton email investigation.[388] Corney stated that it made him "mildly nauseous to think that we might have had some impact on the election," but added that "even in hindsight" he "would make the same decision."[389] He later repeated that he had no regrets about how he had handled the email investigation and believed he had "done the right thing at each turn."[390]

In the afternoon following Comey's testimony, the President met with McGahn, Sessions, and Sessions's Chief of Staff Jody Hunt.[391] At that meeting, the President asked McGahn how Comey. had done in his testimony and McGahn relayed that Comey had declined to answer questions about whether the President was under investigation.[392] The President became very upset and directed his anger at Sessions.[393] According to notes written by Hunt, the President said, "This is terrible Jeff It's all because you recused. AG is supposed to be most important appointment. Kennedy appointed his brother. Obama appointed Holder. I appointed you and you recused yourself. You left me on an island. I can't do anything."[394] The President said that the recusal was unfair and that it was interfering with his ability to govern and undermining his authority with foreign leaders.[395] Sessions responded that he had had no choice but to recuse, and it was a mandatory rather than discretionary decision.[396] Hunt recalled that Sessions also stated at some point during the conversation that a new start at the FBI would be appropriate and the President should consider replacing Comey as FBI director.[397] According to Sessions, when the meeting concluded, it was clear that the President was unhappy with Comey, but Sessions did not think the President had made the decision to terminate Comey.[398]

Bannon recalled that the President brought Comey up with him at least eight times on May3 and May 4, 2017.[399] According to Bannon, the President said the same thing each time: "He told me three times I'm not under investigation. He's a showboater. He's a grandstander. I don't know any Russians. There was no collusion.t"?" Bannon told the President that he could not fire Comey because "that ship had sailed."?" Bannon also told the President that firing Comey was not going to stop the investigation, cautioning him that he could fire the FBI director but could not fire the FBI.[40]

2. The President Makes the Decision to Terminate Comey

The weekend following Corney's May 3, 2017 testimony, the President traveled to his resort in Bedminster, New Jersey.t'" At a dinner on Friday, May 5, attended by the President and various advisors and family members, including Jared Kushner and senior advisor Stephen Miller, the President stated that he wanted to remove Comey and had ideas for a letter that would be used to make the announcement/?'

The President dictated arguments and specific language for the letter, and Miller took notes.[405] As reflected in the notes, the President told Miller that the letter should start, "While I greatly appreciate you informing me that I am not under investigation concerning what I have often stated is a fabricated story on a Trump-Russia relationship – pertaining to the 2016 presidential election, please be informed that I, and I believe the American public – including Ds and Rs – have lost faith in you as Director of the FBT."[406]   Following the dinner, Miller prepared a termination letter based on those notes and research he conducted to support the President's arguments." Over the weekend, the President provided several rounds of edits on the draft letter.[408]   Miller said the President was adamant that he not tell anyone at the White House what they were preparing because the President was worried about leaks.[409]

In his discussions with Miller, the President made clear that he wanted the letter to open with a reference to him not being under investigatlon."?   Miller said he believed that fact was important to the President to show that Comey was not being terminated based on any such investigation.[411] According to Miller, the President wanted to establish as a factual matter that Comey had been under a "review period" and did not have assurance from the President that he would be permitted to keep his job.[412]

The final version of the termination letter prepared by Miller and the President began in a way that closely tracked what the President had dictated to Miller at the May 5 dinner: "Dear Director Comey, While I greatly appreciate your informing me, on three separate occasions, that I am not under investigation concerning the fabricated and politically-motivated allegations of a Trump-Russia relationship with respect to the 2016 Presidential Election, please be informed that I, along with members of both political parties and, most importantly, the American Public, have lost faith in you as the Director of the FBI and you are hereby terminated."[413] The four-page letter went on to critique Corney's judgment and conduct, including his May 3 testimony before the Senate Judiciary Committee, his handling of the Clinton email investigation, and his failure to hold leakers accountable.[414] The letter stated that Comey had "asked [the President] at dinner shortly after inauguration to let [Comey] stay on in the Director's role, and [the President] said that [he] would consider it," but the President had "concluded that [he] had no alternative but to find new leadership for the Bureau – a leader that restores confidence and trust."[415]

In the morning of Monday, May 8, 2017, the President met in the Oval Office with senior advisors, including McGahn, Priebus, and Miller, and informed them he had decided to terminate Comey.[416] The President read aloud the first paragraphs of the termination letter he wrote with Miller and conveyed that the decision had been made and was not up for discussion.[417] The President told the group that Miller had researched the issue and determined the President had the authority to terminate Corney without cause.[418] In an effort to slow down the decision-making process, McGahn told the President that DOJ leadership was currently discussing Corney's status and suggested that White House Counsel's Office attorneys should talk with Sessions and Rod Rosenstein, who had recently been confirmed as the Deputy Attorney General.[419] McGahn said that previously scheduled meetings with Sessions and Rosenstein that day would be an opportunity to find out what they thought about firing Comey."

At noon, Sessions, Rosenstein, and Hunt met with McGahn and White House Counsel's Office attorney Uttam Dhillon at the White House.[421] McGahn said that the President had decided to fire Corney and asked for Sessions's and Rosenstein's views.[422] Sessions and Rosenstein criticized Corney and did not raise concerns about replacing him.[423] McGahn and Dhillon said the fact that neither Sessions nor Rosenstein objected to replacing Corney gave them peace of mind that the President's decision to fire Corney was not an attempt to obstruct justice.[424] An Oval Office meeting was scheduled later that day so that Sessions and Rosenstein could discuss the issue with the President.[425]

At around 5 p.m., the President and several White House officials met with Sessions and Rosenstein to discuss Comey.[426] The President told the group that he had watched Corney's May3 testimony over the weekend and thought that something was "not right" with Comey.[427] The President said that Corney should be removed and asked Sessions and Rosenstein for their views.[428] Hunt, who was in the room, recalled that Sessions responded that he had previously recommended that Corney be replaced.[429] McGahn and Dhillon said Rosenstein described his concerns about Corney's handling of the Clinton email investigation.P?

The President then distributed copies of the termination letter he had drafted with Miller, and the discussion turned to the mechanics of how to fire Corney and whether the President's letter should be used.[431] McGahn and Dhillon urged the President to permit Corney to resign, but the President was adamant that he be fired.[432] The group discussed the possibility that Rosenstein and Sessions could provide a recommendation in writing that Corney should be removed.[433] The President agreed and told Rosenstein to draft a memorandum, but said he wanted to receive it first thing the next morning.[434] Hunt's notes reflect that the President told Rosenstein to include in his recommendation the fact that Corney had refused to confirm that the President was not personally under investigation.[435] According to notes taken by a senior DOJ official of Rosenstein's description of his meeting with the President, the President said, "Put the Russia stuff in the memo."[436] Rosenstein responded that the Russia investigation was not the basis of his recommendation, so he did not think Russia should be mentioned.[437] The President told Rosenstein he would appreciate it if Rosenstein put it in his letter anyway.[438] When Rosenstein left the meeting, he knew that Corney would be terminated, and he told DOJ colleagues that his own reasons for replacing Corney were "not [the President's] reasons."[439]

On May 9, Hunt delivered to the White House a letter from Sessions recommending Corney's removal and a memorandum from Rosenstein, addressed to the Attorney General, titled "Restoring Public Confidence in the FBJ."[440] McGahn recalled that the President liked the DOJ letters and agreed that they should provide the foundation for a new cover letter from the President accepting the recommendation to terminate Comey.[441]

Notes taken by Donaldson on May 9 reflected the view of the White House Counsel's Office that the President's original termination letter should "not [see the] light of day" and that it would be better to offer "[n]o other rationales" for the firing than what was in Rosenstein's and Sessions's memoranda.[442] The President asked Miller to draft a new termination letter and directed Miller to say in the letter that Corney had informed the President three times that he was not under investigation.[443] McGahn, Priebus, and Dhillon objected to including that language, but the President insisted that it be included.[444] McGahn, Priebus, and others perceived that language to be the most important part of the letter to the President.[445] Dhillon made a final pitch to the President that Corney should be permitted to resign, but the President refused.[446]

Around the time the President's letter was finalized, Priebus summoned Spicer and the press team to the Oval Office, where they were told that Corney had been terminated for the reasons stated in the letters by Rosenstein and Sessions.[447] To announce Corney's termination, the White House released a statement, which Priebus thought had been dictated by the President.[448] In full, the statement read: "Today, President Donald J. Trump informed FBI Director James Corney that he has been terminated and removed from office. President Trump acted based on the clear recommendations of both Deputy Attorney General Rod Rosenstein and Attorney General Jeff Sessions."[449]

That evening, FBI Deputy Director Andrew McCabe was summoned to meet with the President at the White House.[450] The President told McCabe that he had fired Corney because of the decisions Corney had made in the Clinton email investigation and for many other reasons.[451]

The President asked McCabe if he was aware that Corney had told the President three times that he was not under investigation.[452] The President also asked McCabe whether many people in the FBI disliked Corney and whether McCabe was part of the "resistance" that had disagreed with Corney's decisions in the Clinton investigation.[453] McCabe told the President that he knew Corney had told the President he was not under investigation, that most people in the FBI felt positively about Corney, and that McCabe worked "very closely" with Corney and was part of all the decisions that had been made in the Clinton investigation.[454]

Later that evening, the President told his communications team he was unhappy with the press coverage of Corney's termination and ordered them to go out and defend him.[455] The President also called Chris Christie and, according to Christie, said he was getting "killed" in the press over Corney's termination.[456] The President asked what he should do.[457] Christie asked, "Did you fire [Corney] because of what Rod wrote in the memo?", and the President responded, "Yes."[458] Christie said that the President should "get Rod out there" and have him defend the decision.[459] The President told Christie that this was a "good idea" and said he was going to call Rosenstein right away."?

That night, the White House Press Office called the Department of Justice and said the White House wanted to put out a statement saying that it was Rosenstein's idea to fire Comey.[461]Rosenstein told other DOJ officials that he would not participate in putting out a "false story."[462]

The President then called Rosenstein directly and said he was watching Fox News, that the coverage had been great, and that he wanted Rosenstein to do a press conference.[463] Rosenstein responded that this was not a good idea because if the press asked him, he would tell the truth that Corney's firing was not his idea.[464] Sessions also informed the White House Counsel's Office that evening that Rosenstein was upset that his memorandum was being portrayed as the reason for Corney's termination.[465]

In an unplanned press conference late in the evening of May 9, 2017, Spicer told reporters, "It was all [Rosenstein]. No one from the White House. It was a DOJ decision."[466] That evening and the next morning, White House officials and spokespeople continued to maintain that the President's decision to terminate Corney was driven by the recommendations the President received from Rosenstein and Sessions.[467]

In the morning on May 10, 2017, President Trump met with Russian Foreign Minister Sergey Lavrov and Russian Ambassador Sergey Kislyak in the Oval Office.[468] The media subsequently reported that during the May 10 meeting the President brought up his decision the prior day to terminate Corney, telling Lavrov and Kislyak: "I just fired the head of the F.B.I. He was crazy, a real nut job. I faced great pressure because of Russia. That's taken off ... I'm not under investigation."[469] The President never denied making those statements, and the White House did not dispute the account, instead issuing a statement that said: "By grandstanding and politicizing the investigation into Russia's actions, James Corney created unnecessary pressure on our ability to engage and negotiate with Russia. The investigation would have always continued, and obviously, the termination of Corney would not have ended it. Once again, the real story is that our national security has been undermined by the leaking of private and highly classified information.v'?? Hicks said that when she told the President about the reports on his meeting with Lavrov, he did not look concerned and said of Corney, "he *is* crazy."[471] When McGahn asked the President about his comments to Lavrov, the President said it was good that Corney was fired because that took the pressure off by making it clear that he was not under investigation so he could get more work done.[472]

That same morning, on May 10, 2017, the President called McCabe.[473] According to a memorandum McCabe wrote following the call, the President asked McCabe to come over to the White House to discuss whether the President should visit FBI headquarters and make a speech to employees.[474] The President said he had received "hundreds" of messages from FBI employees indicating their support for terminating Comey.[475]

The President also told McCabe that Comey should not have been permitted to travel back to Washington, D.C. on the FBI's airplane after he had been terminated and that he did not want Comey "in the building again," even to collect his belongings.[476] When McCabe met with the President that afternoon, the President, without prompting, told McCabe that people in the FBI loved the President, estimated that at least 80% of the FBI had voted for him, and asked McCabe who he had voted for in the 2016 presidential election."?

In the afternoon of May 10, 2017, deputy press secretary Sarah Sanders spoke to the President about his decision to fire Comey and then spoke to reporters in a televised press conference.[478] Sanders told reporters that the President, the Department of Justice, and bipartisan members of Congress had lost confidence in Comey, "[a]nd most importantly, the rank and file of the FBI had lost confidence in their director. Accordingly, the President accepted the recommendation of his Deputy Attorney General to remove James Comey from his position."?" Jn response to questions from reporters, Sanders said that Rosenstein decided "on his own" to review Comey's performance and that Rosenstein decided "on his own" to come to the President on Monday, May 8 to express his concerns about Comey. When a reporter indicated that the "vast majority" of FBI agents supported Comey, Sanders said, "Look, we've heard from countless members of the FBI that say very different things.'[480] Following the press conference, Sanders spoke to the President, who told her she did a good job and did not point out any inaccuracies in her comments.[481] Sanders told this Office that her reference to hearing from "countless members of the FBI" was a "slip of the tongue."[482] She also recalled that her statement in a separate press interview that rank-and-file FBI agents had lost confidence in Comey was a comment she made "in the heat of the moment" that was not founded on anything.[483]

Also on May 10, 2017, Sessions and Rosenstein each spoke to McGahn and expressed concern that the White House was creating a narrative that Rosenstein had initiated the decision to fire Comey.[484] The White House Counsel's Office agreed that it was factually wrong to say that the Department of Justice had initiated Comey's termination,[485] and McGahn asked attorneys in the White House Counsel's Office to work with the press office to correct the narrative.[486]

The next day, on May 11, 2017, the President participated in an interview with Lester Holt. The President told White House Counsel's Office attorneys in advance of the interview that the communications team could not get the story right, so he was going on Lester Holt to say what really happened.[487] During the interview, the President stated that he had made the decision to fire Comey before the President met with Rosenstein and Sessions. The President told Holt, "I was going to fire regardless of recommendation . . . . [Rosenstein] made a recommendation. But regardless of recommendation, I was going to fire Comey knowing there was no good time to do it."[488] The President continued, "And in fact, when I decided to just do it, I said to myself—I said, you know, this Russia thing with Trump and Russia is a made-up story. It's an excuse by the Democrats for having lost an election that they should've won."[489]

In response to a question about whether he was angry with Comey about the Russia investigation, the President said, "As far as I'm concerned, I want that thing to be absolutely done properly."[490] The President added that he realized his termination of Comey "probably maybe will confuse people" with the result that it "might even lengthen out the investigation," but he "had to do the right thing for the American people" and Comey was "the wrong man for that position."[491] The President described Comey as "a showboat" and "a grandstander," said that "[t]he FBI has been in turmoil," and said he wanted "to have a really competent, capable director."[492] The President affirmed that he expected the new FBI director to continue the Russia investigation.[493]

On the evening of May 11, 2017, following the Lester Holt interview, the President tweeted, "Russia must be laughing up their sleeves watching as the U.S. tears itself apart over a Democrat EXCUSE for losing the election."[494] The same day, the media reported that the President had demanded that Comey pledge his loyalty to the President in a private dinner shortly after being sworn in.[495] Late in the morning of May 12, 2017, the President tweeted, "Again, the story that there was collusion between the Russians & Trump campaign was fabricated by Dems as an excuse for losing the election."[496] The President also tweeted, "James Comey better hope that there are no 'tapes' of our conversations before he starts leaking to the press!" and "When James Clapper himself, and virtually everyone else with knowledge of the witch hunt, says there is no collusion, when does it end?"[497]

Analysis

In analyzing the President's decision to fire Comey, the following evidence is relevant to the elements of obstruction of justice:

a.   Obstructive act. The act of firing Corney removed the individual overseeing the FBI's Russia investigation. The President knew that Comey was personally involved in the investigation based on Corney's briefing of the Gang of Eight, Corney's March 20, 2017 public testimony about the investigation, and the President's one-on-one conversations with Corney.

Firing Comey would qualify as an obstructive act if it had the natural and probable effect of interfering with or impeding the investigation—for example, if the termination would have the effect of delaying or disrupting the investigation or providing the President with the opportunity to appoint a director who would take a different approach to the investigation that the President perceived as more protective of his personal interests. Relevant circumstances bearing on that issue include whether the President's actions had the potential to discourage a successor director or other law enforcement officials in their conduct of the Russia investigation. The President fired Comey abruptly without offering him an opportunity to resign, banned him from the FBI building, and criticized him publicly, calling him a "showboat" and claiming that the FBI was "in turmoil" under his leadership. And the President followed the termination with public statements that were highly critical of the investigation; for example, three days after firing Comey, the President referred to the investigation as a "witch hunt" and asked, "when does it end?" Those actions had the potential to affect a successor director's conduct of the investigation.

The anticipated effect of removing the FBI director, however, would not necessarily be to prevent or impede the FBI from continuing its investigation. As a general matter, FBI investigations run under the operational direction of FBI personnel levels below the FBI director. Bannon made a similar point when he told the President that he could fire the FBI director, but could not fire the FBI. The

White House issued a press statement the day after Comey was fired that said, "The investigation would have always continued, and obviously, the termination of Comey would not have ended it." In addition, in his May 11 interview with Lester Holt, the President stated that he understood when he made the decision to fire Corney that the action might prolong the investigation. And the President chose McCabe to serve as interim director, eventhough McCabe told the President he had worked "very closely" with Comey and was part of all the decisions made in the Clinton investigation.

   b.   Nexus to a proceeding. The nexus element would be satisfied by evidence showing that a grand jury proceeding or criminal prosecution arising from an FBI investigation was objectively foreseeable and actually contemplated by the President when he tertninated Corney.

Several facts would be relevant to such a showing. At the time the President fired Corney, a grand jury had not begun to hear evidence related to the Russia investigation and no grand jury subpoenas had been issued. On March 20, 2017, however, Comey had announced that the FBI was investigating Russia's interference in the election, including "an assessment of whether any crimes were committed." It was widely known that the FBI, as part of the Russia investigation, was investigating the hacking of the DNC's computers—a clear criminal offense.

In addition, at the time the President fired Comey, evidence indicates the President knew that Flynn was still under criminal investigation and could potentially be prosecuted, despite the President's February 14, 2017 request that Comey "letl] Flynn go." On March 5, 2017, the White House Counsel's Office was informed that the FBI was asking for transition-period records relating to Flynn—indicating that the FBI was still actively investigating him. The same day, the President told advisors he wanted to call Dana Boente, then the Acting Attorney General for the Russia investigation, to find out whether the White House or the President was being investigated. On March 31, 2017, the President signaled his awareness that Flynn remained in legal jeopardy by tweeting that "Mike Flynn should ask for immunity" before he agreed to provide testimony to the FBI or Congress. And in late March or early April, the President asked McFarland to pass a message to Flynn telling him that the President felt bad for him and that he should stay strong, further demonstrating the President's awareness of Flynn's criminal exposure.

c.   Intent.   Substantial evidence indicates that the catalyst for the President's decision to fire Comey was Corney's unwillingness to publicly state that the President was not personally under investigation, despite the President's repeated requests that Corney make such an announcement. In the week leading up to Corney's May 3, 2017 Senate Judiciary Committee testimony, the President told McGahn that it would be the last straw if Comey did not set the record straight and publicly announce that the President was not under investigation. But during his May 3 testimony, Comey refused to answer questions about whether the President was being investigated. Comey's refusal angered the President, who criticized Sessions for leaving him isolated and exposed, saying "You left me on an island."

Two days later, the President told advisors he had decided to fire Comey and dictated a letter to Stephen Miller that began with a reference to the fact that the

President was not being investigated: "While I greatly appreciate you informing me that I am not under investigation concerning what I have often stated is a fabricated story on a Trump-Russia relationship ...." The President later asked Rosenstein to include "Russia" in his memorandum and to say that Comey had told the President that he was not under investigation. And the President's final termination letter included a sentence, at the President's insistence and against McGahn's advice, stating that Comey had told the President on three separate occasions that he was not under investigation.

The President's other stated rationales for why he fired Comey are not similarly supported by the evidence. The termination letter the President and Stephen Miller prepared in Bedminster cited Comey's handling of the Clinton email investigation, and the President told McCabe he fired Comey for that reason. But the facts surrounding Comey's handling of the Clinton email investigation were well known to the President at the time he assumed office, and the President had made it clear to both Comey and the President's senior staff in early 2017 that he wanted Comey to stay on as director. And Rosenstein articulated his criticism of Comey's handling of the Clinton investigation after the President had already decided to fire Comey. The President's draft termination letter also stated that morale in the FBJ was at an all-time low and Sanders told the press after Comey's termination that the White House had heard from "countless" FBI agents who had lost confidence in Comey. But the evidence does not support those claims. The President told Comey at their January 27 dinner that "the people of the FBI really like [him]," no evidence suggests that the President heard otherwise before deciding to terminate Comey, and Sanders acknowledged to investigators that her comments were not founded on anything.

We also considered why it was important to the President that Comey announce publicly that he was not under investigation. Some evidence indicates that the President believed that the erroneous perception he was under investigation harmed his ability to manage domestic and foreign affairs, particularly in dealings with Russia. The President told Comey that the "cloud" of "this Russia business" was making it difficult to run the country. The President told Sessions and McGahn that foreign leaders had expressed sympathy to him for being under investigation and that the perception he was under investigation was hurting his ability to address foreign relations issues. The President complained to Rogers that "the thing with the Russians [was] messing up" his ability to get things done with Russia, and told Coats, "I can't do anything with Russia, there's things I'd like to do with Russia, with trade, with ISIS, they're all over me with this." The President also may have viewed Comey as insubordinate for his failure to make clear in the May 3 testimony that the President was not under investigation.

Other evidence, however, indicates that the President wanted to protect himself from an investigation into his campaign. The day after learning about the FBI's interview of Flynn, the President had a one-on-one dinner with Comey, against the advice of senior aides, and told Comey he needed Comey's "loyalty." When the President later asked Comey for a second time to make public that he was not under investigation, he brought up loyalty again, saying "Because I have been very loyal to you, very loyal, we had that thing, you know." After the President learned of Sessions's recusal from the Russia investigation, the President was furious and said he wanted an Attorney General who would protect him the way he perceived Robert Kennedy and Eric Holder to have protected their presidents. The President also said he wanted to be able to tell his Attorney General "who to investigate."

In addition, the President had a motive to put the FBT's Russia investigation behind him. The evidence does not establish that the termination of Comey was designed to cover up a conspiracy between the Trump Campaign and Russia: As described in Volume I, the evidence uncovered in the investigation did not establish that the President or those close to him were involved in the charged Russian computer-hacking or active-measure conspiracies, or that the President otherwise had an unlawful relationship with any Russian official. But the evidence does indicate that a thorough FBI investigation would uncover facts about the campaign and the President personally that the President could have understood to be crimes or that would give rise to personal and political concerns. Although the President publicly stated during and after the election that he had no connection to Russia, the Trump Organization, through Michael Cohenwas pursuing the proposed Trump Tower Moscow project through June 2016 and candidate Trump was repeatedly briefed on the ro ress of those efforts.498 In addition, some witnesses said that

.   .

. - at a time when public reports stated that Russian intelligence officials were behind the hacks, and that Trump privately sought information about future WikiLeaks releases.499 More broadly, multiple witnesses described the President's preoccupation with press coverage of the Russia investigation and his persistent concern that it raised questions about the legitimacy of his election.P"

Finally, the President and White House aides initially advanced a pretextual reason to the press and the public for Corney's termination. In the immediate aftermath of the firing, the President dictated a press statement suggesting that he had acted based on the DOJ recommendations, and White House press officials repeated that story. But the President had decided to fire Comey before the White House solicited those recommendations. Although the President ultimately acknowledged that he was going to fire Corney regardless of the Department ofJustice's recommendations, he did so only after DOJ officials made clear to him that they would resist the White House's suggestion that they had prompted the process that led to Comey's termination. The initial reliance on a pretextual justification could support an inference that the President had concerns about providing the real reason for the firing, although the evidence does not resolve whether those concerns were personal, political, or both.

******

383 Hearing on Oversight ofthe FBI before the Senate Judiciary Committee, I 15th Cong. (May 3,
384 McGahn 12/12/17 302, at I 0-11.
385 McGahn 12/12/17 302, at 7, 10-11 (McGahn believed that two foreign leaders had expressed sympathy to the President for being under investigation); SC_AD_00265 (Donaldson 4/11/17 Notes) ("P Called Corney - Day we told him not to? 'You are not under investigation' NK/China/Sapping Credibility").
387 Hearing on FBI Oversight Before the Senate Judiciary Committee, I 15th Cong. (May 3, 2017) (CQ Cong. Transcripts, at 87-88) (questions by Sen. Blumenthal and testimony by FBI Director James B. Corney).
388 Hearing on FBI Oversight Before the Senate Judiciary Committee, I 15th Cong. (May 3, 2017) (CQ Cong. Transcripts, at 15) (question by Sen. Feinstein).
389 Hearing on FBI Oversight Before the Senate Judiciary Committee, I 15th Cong. (May 3, 2017) (CQ Cong. Transcripts,at 17) (testimony by FBI Director James 8. Corney).
390 Hearing on FBI Oversight Before the Senate Judiciary Committee, I 15th Cong. (May 3, 2017) (CQ Cong. Transcripts, at 92) (testimony by FBI Director James B. Corney).

391 Sessions 1/17/18 302, at 8; Hunt 2/1/18 302, at 8.

392 Sessions 1/17/18 302, at 8; Hunt-000021 (Hunt 5/3/17 Notes); McGahn 3/8/18 302, at 6.

393 Sessions 1/17/18 302, at 8-9.

394 Hunt-000021 (Hunt 5/3/17 Notes). Hunt said that he wrote down notes describing this meeting and others with the President after the events occurred. Hunt 2/1 /17 302, at 2.

395 Hunt-000021-22 (Hunt 5/3/17 Notes) ("I have foreign leaders saying they are sorry I am being investigated."); Sessions 1/17/18 302, at 8 (Sessions recalled that a Chinese leader had said to the President that he was sorry the President was under investigation, which the President interpreted as undermining his authority); Hunt 2/1/18 302, at 8.

396 Sessions 1/17/18 302, at 8; Hunt-000022 (Hunt 5/3/17 Notes).

397 Hunt-000022 (Hunt 5/3/17 Notes).

398 Sessions 1/17/18 302, at 9.

399 Bannon 2/ 12/18 302, at 20.

400 Bannon 2/12/18 302, at 20.

401 Bannon 2/12/18 302, at 20.

402 Bannon 2/12/18 302, at 20-21; see Priebus I 0/13/17 302, at 28.

403 S. Miller I 0/31/17 302, at 4-5; SCR025_000019 (President's Daily Diary, 5/4/17).

404 S. Miller 10/31/17 302, at 5.

405 S. Miller 10/31/17 302, at5-6.

406 S. Miller 5/5/17 Notes, at I; see S. Miller I 0/31/17 302, at 8.

407 S. Miller 10/31 /17 302, at 6.

408 S. Miller 10/31/17 302, at 6-8.

409 S. Miller I 0/31 /17 302, at 7. Miller said he did not want Priebus to be blindsided, so on Sunday night he called Priebus to tell him that the President had been thinking about the "Corney situation" and there would be an important discussion on Monday. S. Miller I 0/31/17 302, at 7.

410 S. Miller 10/31/17 302, at 8.

411 S. Miller I 0/31/17 302, at 8.

412 S. Miller 10/31/17 302, at I 0.

413 SCROl3c_000003-06 (Draft Termination Letter to FBI Director Corney).

414 SCROl3c_000003-06 (Draft Termination Letter to FBI Director Comey). Kushner said that the termination letter reflected the reasons the President wanted to fire Corney and was the truest representation of what the President had said during the May 5 dinner. Kushner 4/11 /18 302, at 25.

415 SCRO I 3c_000003 (Draft Termination Letter to FBI Director Corney).

416 McGahn 12/12/17 302, at 11; Priebus 10/13/17 302, at 24; S. Miller 10/31/17 302, at 11; Dhillon 11/21/17 302, at 6; Eisenberg 11/29/17 302, at 13.

417 S. Miller I 0/31/17 302, at 11 (observing that the President started the meeting by saying, "I'm going to read you a letter. Don't talk me out of this. I've made my decision."); Dhillon 11/21/17 302, at 6 (the President announced in an irreversible way that he was firing Corney); Eisenberg I 1/29/17 302, at 13 (the President did not leave whether or not to fire Corney up for discussion); Priebus 10/13/17 302, at 25; McGahn 12/12/17 302, at 11-12.

418 Dhillon 302 11/21/17, at 6; Eisenberg 11/29/17 302, at 13; McGahn 12/12/_ 17 302, at 11.

419 McGahn 12/12/17 302, at 12, 13; S. Miller 10/31/17 302, at 11; Dhillon 11/21/17 302, at 7. Because of the Attorney General's recusal, Rosenstein became the Acting Attorney General for the Russia investigation upon his confirmation as Deputy Attorney General. See 28 U.S.C. § 508(a) ("In case of a vacancy in the office of Attorney General, or of his absence or disability, the Deputy Attorney General may exercise all the duties of that office").

420 McGahn 12/12/17 302, at 12.

421 Dhillon 11/21/17 302, at 7; McGahn 12/12/17 302, at 13; Gauhar-000056 (Gauhar 5/16/17 Notes); see Gauhar-000056-72 (2/11/19 Memorandum to File attaching Gauhar handwritten notes) ("Ms. Gauhar determined that she likely recorded all these notes during one or more meetings on Tuesday, May 16, 2017.").

422 McGahn 12/12/17 302, at 13; see Gauhar-000056 (Gauhar 5/16/17 Notes).

423 Dhillon 11/21/17 302, at 7-9; Sessions 11/17/18 302, at 9; McGahn 12/12/17 302, at 13.

424 McGahn 12/12/17 302, at 13; Dhillon 11/21/17 302, at 9.

425 Hunt-000026 (Hunt 5/8/17 Notes); see Gauhar-000057 (Gauhar 5/16/17 Notes).

426 Rosenstein 5/23/17 302, at 2; McGahn 12/12/17 302, at 14; see Gauhar-000057 (Gauhar 5/16/17 Notes).

427 Hunt-000026-27 (Hunt 5/8/17 Notes).

428 Sessions 1/17/18 302, at IO; see Gauhar-000058 (Gauhar 5/16/17 Notes) ("POTUS to AG: What is your rec?").

429 Hunt-000027 (Hunt 5/8/17 Notes).

430 McGahn 12/12/17 302, at 14; Dhillon 11/21/17 302, at 7.

431 Hunt-000028 (Hunt 5/8/17 Notes).

432 McGahn 12/12/17 302, at 13.

433 Hunt-000028-29 (Hunt 5/8/17 Notes).

434 McCabe 9/26/17 302, at 13; Rosenstein 5/23/17 302, at 2; see Gauhar-000059 (Gauhar 5/16/17 Notes) ("POTUS tells DAG to write a memo").

435 Hunt-000028-29 (Hunt 5/8/17 Notes) ("POTUS asked if Rod's recommendation would include the fact that although Corney talks about the investigation he refuses to say that the President is not under investigation.... So it would be good if your recommendation would make mention of the fact that Corney refuses to say public[ly] what he said privately 3 times.").

436 Gauhar-000059 (Gauhar 5/16/17 Notes).

437 Sessions 1/17/18 302 at IO; McCabe 9/26/17 302, at 13; see Gauhar-000059 (Gauhar 5/16/17 Notes).

438 Gauhar-000059 (Gauhar 5/16/17 Notes); McCabe 5/16/17 Memorandum I; McCabe 9/26/17 302, at 13.

439 Rosenstein 5/23/17 302, at 2; Gauhar-000059 (Gauhar 5/16/17 Notes) ("DAG reasons not their reasons [POTUS]"); Gauhar-000060 (Gauhar 5/16/17 Notes)(" I 51 draft had a recommendation. Took it out b/c knew decision had already been made.").

440 Rosenstein 5/23/17 302, at 4; McGahn 12/12/17 302, at 15; 5/9/17 Letter, Sessions to President Trump ("Based on my evaluation, and for the reasons expressed by the Deputy Attorney General in the attached memorandum, I have concluded that a fresh start is needed at the leadership of the FBI."); 5/9/17

Memorandum, Rosenstein to Sessions (concluding with, "The way the Director handled the conclusion of the email investigation was wrong. As a result, the FBI is unlikely to regain public and congressional trust until it has a Director who understands the gravity ofthe mistakes and pledges never to repeat them. Having refused to admit his errors, the Director cannot be expected to implement the necessary corrective actions.").

441 S. Miller I 0/31/17 302, at 12; McGahn 12/12/17 302, at I 5; Hunt-000031 (Hunt 5/9/17 Notes).

442 SC_AD_00342 (Donaldson 5/9/17 Notes). Donaldson also wrote "[i]s this the beginning of the end?" because she was worried that the decision to terminate Corney and the manner in which it was carried out would be the end of the presidency. Donaldson 1 l/6/17 302, at 25.

443 S. Miller 10/31/17 302, at 12; McGahn 12/12/17 302, at 15; Hunt-000032 (Hunt 5/9/17 Notes).

444 McGahn 12/12/17 302, at 15; S. Miller 10/31/17 302, at 12; Dhillon I 1/21/17 302, at 8, 10; Priebus 10/13/17 302, at 27; Hunt 2/1/18 302, at 14- I 5; Hunt-000032 (Hunt 5/9/17 Notes).

445 Dhillon 11/21/ 17 302, at IO; Eisenberg 11/29/17 302, at 15 (providing the view that the President's desire to include the language about not being under investigation was the "driving animus of the whole thing"); Burnham 1 l/3/17 302, at 16 (Burnham knew the only line the President cared about was the line that said Corney advised the President on three separate occasions that the President was not under investigation). According to Hunt's notes, the reference to Corney's statement would indicate that "notwithstanding" Corney's having informed the President that he was not under investigation, the President was terminating Corney. Hunt-000032 (Hunt 5/9/17 Notes). McGahn said he believed the President wanted the language included so that people would not think that the President had terminated Corney because the President was under investigation. McGahn 12/12/17 302, at 15.

446 McGahn 12/12/17 302, at 15; Donaldson 11/6/17 302, at 25; see SC_AD_00342 (Donaldson5/9/17 Notes) ("Resign vs. Removal. - POTUS/removal.").

447 Spicer 10/16/17 302, at9; McGahn 12/12/17 302, at 16.

448 Priebus 10/13/17 302, at 28.

449 Statement ofthe Press Secretary, The White House, Office ofthe Press Secretary (May 9, 2017).

450 McCabe 9/26/17 302, at 4; SCR025_000044 (President's Daily Diary, 5/9/17); McCabe 5/ I 0/17 Memorandum, at I.

451 McCabe 9/26/17 302, at 5; McCabe 5/10/17 Memorandum, at I.

452 McCabe 9/26/17 302, at 5; McCabe 5/10/17 Memorandum, at 1-2.

453 McCabe 9/26/17 302, at 5; McCabe 5/10/17 Memorandum, at 1-2.

454 McCabe 9/26/17 302, at 5; McCabe 5/I0/17 Memorandum, at 1-2.

455 Spicer I 0/16/17 302, at 11; Hicks 12/8/17, at 18; Sanders 7/3/18 302, at 2.

456 Christie 2/13/19 302, at 6.

451 Christie 2/13/19 302, at 6.

458 Christie 2/13/19 302, at 6.

459 Christie 2/13/19 302, at 6.

46° Christie 2/13/19 302, at 6.

461 Gauhar-000071 (Gauhar 5/16/17 Notes); Page Memorandum, at 3 (recording events of 5/16/17); McCabe 9/26/17 302, at 14.

462 Rosenstein 5/23/17 302, at 4-5; Gauhar-000059 (Gauhar 5/16/17 Notes).

463 Rosenstein 5/23/17 302, at 4-5; Gauhar-000071 (Gauhar 5/16/17 Notes).

464 Gauhar-000071 (Gauhar 5/16/17 Notes). DOJ notes from the week of Corney's firing indicate that Priebus was "screaming" at the DOJ public affairs office trying to get Rosenstein to do a press conference, and the DOJ public affairs office told Priebus that Rosenstein had told the President he was not doing it. Gauhar-000071-72 (Gauhar 5/16/17 Notes).

465 McGahn 12/12117 302, at 16-17; Donaldson 11/6/17 302, at 26-27; Dhillon 11/21/17 302, at 11.

466 Jenna Johnson, After Trump fired Corney, While House staff scrambled to explain why, Washington Post (May 10, 2017) (quoting Spicer).

467 See, e.g., Sarah Sanders, White House Daily Briefing, C-SPAN (May 10, 2017); SCR013_001088 (5/10/17 Email, Hemming to Cheung et al.) (internal White House email describing comments on the Corney termination by Vice President Pence).

468 SCR08_000353 (5/9/17 White House Document, "Working Visit with Foreign Minister Sergey Lavrov of Russia"); SCR08_001274 (5/10/17 Email, Ciaramella to Kelly et al.). The meeting had been planned on May 2, 2017, during a telephone call between the President and Russian President Vladimir Putin, and the meeting date was confirmed on May 5, 2017, the same day the President dictated ideas for the Corney termination letter to Stephen Miller. SCR08_001274 (5/10/17 Email, Ciaramella to Kelly et al.).

469 Matt Apuzzo et al., Trump Told Russians That Firing "Nut Job" Corney Eased Pressure From Investigation, New York Times (May 19, 2017).

470 SCR08_002 I I 7 (5/19/17 Email, Walters to Farhi (CBS News)); see Spicer I Oil 6/17 302, at 13 (noting he would have been told to "clean it up" if the reporting on the meeting with the Russian Foreign Minister was inaccurate, but he was never told to correct the reporting); Hicks 12/8/17 302, at 19 (recalling that the President never denied making the statements attributed to him in the Lavrov meeting and that the President had said similar things about Corney in an off-the-record meeting with reporters on May 18, 2017, calling Corney a "nutjob" and "crazy").

471 Hicks 12/8/17 302, at 19.

472 McGahn 12/12/17 302, at 18.

473 SCR025_000046 (President's Daily Diary, 5/10/17); McCabe 5/10/17 Memorandum, at

474 McCabe 5/10/17 Memorandum, at 1.

475 McCabe 5/10/17 Memorandum, at I.

476 McCabe 5/ I 0/17 Memorandum, at 1; Rybicki 6/13/ 17 302, at 2. Corney had been visiting the FBI's Los Angeles office when he found out he had been terminated. Corney I 1/15/17 302, at 22.

477 McCabe 5/10/17 Memorandum, at 1-2. McCabe's memorandum documenting his meeting with the President is consistent with notes taken by the White House Counsel's Office. See SC_AD_00347 (Donaldson 5/10/17 Notes).

478 Sanders 7/3/18 302, at 4; Sarah Sanders, While House Daily Briefing, C-SPAN (May I 0, 20 I 7).

479 Sarah Sanders, White House Daily Briefing, C-SPAN (May I 0, 2017); Sanders 7/3/ I 8 302, at 4.

480 Sarah Sanders, White House Daily Briefing, C-SPAN (May I 0, 2017).

481 Sanders 7/3/18 302, at 4.

482 Sanders 7/3/18 302, at 4.

483 Sanders 7/3/18 302, at 3.

484 McGahn 12/12/17 302, at 16-17; Donaldson 11/6/17 302, at 26; see Dhillon 11/21/17 302, at

485 Donaldson 11 /6/ 17 302, at 27.

486 McGahn 12/12/17 302, at 17.

487Dhillon 11/21/17302,at 11.

488 Interview with President Donald Trump, NBC (May 11, 2017) Transcript, at 2.

489 Interview with President Donald Trump, NBC (May 11, 2017) Transcript, at 2.

495 Michael S. Schmidt, In a Private Dinner, Trump Demanded Loyalty. Corney Demurred., New York Times (May 11, 2017).

496 @realDonaldTrump 5/12/17 (7:51 a.m. ET) Tweet.

497 @realDonaldTrump 5/12/17 (8:26 a.m. ET) Tweet; @realDonaldTrump 5/12/17 (8:54 a.m. ET)

498 See Volume II, Section 11.K.1, infra.

499 See Volume l, Section III.D. l, supra.

500 Tn addition to whether the President had a motive related to Russia-related matters that an FBI investigation could uncover, we considered whether the President's intent in firing Corney was connected to other conduct that could come to light as a result of the FBI's Russian-interference investigation. In particular, Michael Cohen was a potential subject of investigation because of his pursuit of the Trump Tower Moscow project and involvement in other activities. And facts uncovered in the Russia investigation, which our Office referred to the U.S. Attorney's Office for the Southern District of New York, ultimately led to the conviction of Cohen in the Southern District ofNew York for campaign-finance offenses related to payments he said he made at the direction of the President. See Volume II, Section

11.K.5, infra. The investigation, however, did not establish that when the President fired Corney, he was

considering the possibility that the FBI's investigation would uncover these payments or that the President's intent in firing Corney was otherwise connected to a concern about these matters coming to light.

E. The President's Efforts to Remove the Special Counsel

Overview

The Acting Attorney General appointed a Special Counsel on May 17, 2017, prompting the President to state that it was the end of his presidency and that Attorney General Sessions had failed to protect him and should resign. Sessions submitted his resignation, which the President ultimately did not accept. The President told senior advisors that the Special Counsel had conflicts of interest, but they responded that those claims were "ridiculous" and posed no obstacle to the Special Counsel's service. Department of Justice ethics officials similarly cleared the Special Counsel's service. On June 14, 2017, the press reported that the President was being personally investigated for obstruction of justice and the President responded with a series of tweets.

Evidence

I. The Appointment of the Special Counsel and the President's Reaction

On May 17, 2017, Acting Attorney General Rosenstein appointed Robert S. Mueller, ITT as Special Counsel and authorized him to conduct the Russia investigation and matters that arose from the investigation.t" The President learned of the Special Counsel's appointment from Sessions, who was with the President, Hunt, and McGahn conducting interviews for a new FBI Director.[502] Sessions stepped out of the Oval Office to take a call from Rosenstein, who told him about the Special Counsel appointment, and Sessions then returned to inform the President of the news.[503]

According to notes written by Hunt, when Sessions told the President that a Special Counsel had been appointed, the President slumped back in his chair and said, "Oh my God. This is terrible. This is the end of my Presidency. I'm fucked."[504] The President became angry and lambasted the Attorney General for his decision to recuse from the investigation, stating, "How could you let this happen, Jeff?"[505] The President said the position of Attorney General was his most important appointment and that Sessions had "let [him] down," contrasting him to Eric Holder and Robert Kennedy.[506] Sessions recalled that the President said to him, "you were supposed to protect me," or words to that effect.[507] The President returned to the consequences of the appointment and said, "Everyone tells me if you get one of these independent counsels it ruins your presidency. It takes years and years and I won't be able to do anything. This is the worst thing that ever happened to me."[508]

The President then told Sessions he should resign as Attorney General.[509] Sessions agreed to submit his resignation and left the Oval Office.[510] Hicks saw the President shortly after Sessions departed and described the President as being extremely upset by the Special Counsel's appointment.[511] Hicks said that she had only seen the President like that one other time, when the Access Hollywood tape came out during the campaign.[512]

The next day, May 18, 2017, FBI agents delivered to McGahn a preservation notice that discussed an investigation related to Comey's termination and directed the White House to preserve all relevant documents.[513] When he received the letter, McGahn issued a document hold to White House staff and instructed them not to send out any burn bags over the weekend while he sorted things out.[514]

Also on May 18, Sessions finalized a resignation letter that stated, "Pursuant to our conversation of yesterday, and at your request, I hereby offer my resignation."[515] Sessions, accompanied by Hunt, brought the letter to the White House and handed it to the President.[516] The President put the resignation letter in his pocket and asked Sessions several times whether he wanted to continue serving as Attorney General.[517] Sessions ultimately told the President he wanted to stay, but it was up to the President.[518] The President said he wanted Sessions to stay.[519]

At the conclusion of the meeting, the President shook Sessions's hand but did not return the resignation letter.[520]

When Priebus and Bannon learned that the President was holding onto Sessions's resignation letter, they became concerned that it could be used to influence the Department of Justice.[521] Priebus told Sessions it was not good for the President to have the letter because it would function as a kind of "shock collar" that the President could use any time he wanted; Priebus said the President had "DOJ by the throat."[522] Priebus and Bannon told Sessions they would attempt to get the letter back from the President with a notation that he was not accepting Sessions's resignation.[523]

On May 19, 2017, the President left for a trip to the Middle East.[524] Hicks recalled that on the President's flight from Saudi Arabia to Tel Aviv, the President pulled Sessions's resignation letter from his pocket, showed it to a group of senior advisors, and asked them what he should do about it.[525] During the trip, Priebus asked about the resignation letter so he could return it to Sessions, but the President told him that the letter was back at the White House, somewhere in the residence.[526] It was not until May 30, three days after the President returned from the trip, that the President returned the letter to Sessions with a notation saying, "Not accepted."[527]

3. The President Asserts that the Special Counsel has Conflicts of nterest

In the days following the Special Counsel's appointment, the President repeatedly told advisors, including Priebus, Bannon, and McGahn, that Special Counsel Mueller had conflicts of interest.[528] The President cited as conflicts that Mueller had interviewed for the FBI Director position shortly before being appointed as Special Counsel, that he had worked for a law firm that represented people affiliated with the President, and that Mueller had disputed certain fees relating to his membership in a Trump golf course in Northern Virginia.[529]

The President's advisors pushed back on his assertion of conflicts, telling the President they did not count as true contlicts.P" Bannon recalled telling the President that the purported conflicts were "ridiculous" and that none of them was real or could come close to justifying precluding Mueller from serving as Special Counsel.[531] As for Mueller's interview for FBI Director, Bannon recalled that the White House had invited Mueller to speak to the President to offer a perspective on the institution of the FBJ.[532]

Bannon said that, although the White House thought about beseeching Mueller to become Director again, he did not come in looking for the job.[533] Bannon also told the President that the law firm position did not amount to a conflict in the legal community.[534] And Bannon told the President that the golf course dispute did not rise to the level of a conflict and claiming one was "ridiculous and petty."[535] The President did not respond when Bannon pushed back on the stated conflicts of interest.[536]

On May 23, 2017, the Department of Justice announced that ethics officials had determined that the Special Counsel's prior law firm position did not bar his service, generating media reports that Mueller had been cleared to serve.[537] McGahn recalled that around the same time, the President complained about the asserted conflicts and prodded McGahn to reach out to Rosenstein about the issue.[538] McGahn said he responded that he could not make such a call and that the President should instead consult his personal lawyer because it was not a White House issue.[539] Contemporaneous notes of a May 23, 2017 conversation between McGahn and the President reflect that McGahn told the President that he would not call Rosenstein and that he would suggest that the President not make such a call either.[540] McGahn advised that the President could discuss the issue with his personal attorney but it would "look like still trying to meddle in [the] investigation" and "knocking out Mueller" would be "[a]nother fact used to claim obst[ruction] of just[ice]."[541] McGahn told the President that his "biggest exposure" was not his act of firing Corney but his "other contacts" and "calls," and his "ask re: Flynn."[542] By the time McGahn provided this advice to the President, there had been widespread reporting on the President's request for Corney's loyalty, which the President publicly denied; his request that Corney "[let] Flynn go," which the President also denied; and the President's statement to the Russian Foreign Minister that the termination of Corney had relieved "great pressure" related to Russia, which the President did not deny.[543]

On June 8, 2017, Corney testified before Congress about his interactions with the President before his termination, including the request for loyalty, the request that Corney "let[] Flynn go," and the request that Corney "lift the cloud" over the presidency caused by the ongoing investigation.[544] Corney's testimony led to a series of news reports about whether the President had obstructed justice.[545] On June 9, 2017, the Special Counsel's Office informed the White House Counsel's Office that investigators intended to interview intelligence community officials who had allegedly been asked by the President to push back against the Russia investigation.[546]

On Monday, June 12, 2017, Christopher Ruddy, the chief executive of Newsmax Media and a longtime friend of the President's, met at the White House with Priebus and Bannon.[547] Ruddy recalled that they told him the President was strongly considering firing the Special Counsel and that he would do so precipitously, without vetting the decision through Administration officials.[548] Ruddy asked Priebus if Ruddy could talk publicly about the discussion they had about the Special Counsel, and Priebus said he could.[549] Priebus told Ruddy he hoped another blow up like the one that followed the termination of Corney did not happen.P? Later that day, Ruddy stated in a televised interview that the President was "considering perhaps terminating the Special Counsel" based on purported conflicts of interest.[551] Ruddy later told another news outlet that "Trump is definitely considering" terminating the Special Counsel and "it's not something that's being dismissed."[552] Ruddy's comments led to extensive coverage in the media that the President was considering firing the Special Counsel.[553]

White House officials were unhappy with that press coverage and Ruddy heard from friends that the President was upset with him.[554] On June 13, 2017, Sanders asked the President for guidance on how to respond to press inquiries about the possible firing of the Special Counsel.[555] The President dictated an answer, which Sanders delivered, saying that "[w]hile the president has every right to" fire the Special Counsel, "he has no intention to do so."[556]

Also on June 13, 2017, the President's personal counsel contacted the Special Counsel's Office and raised concerns about possible conflicts.[557] The President's counsel cited Mueller's previous partnership in his law firm, his interview for the FBI Director position, and an asserted personal relationship he had with Comey.[558] That same day, Rosenstein had testified publicly before Congress and said he saw no evidence of good cause to terminate the Special' Counsel, including for conflicts of interest.[559] Two days later, on June 15, 2017, the Special Counsel's Office informed the Acting Attorney General's office about the areas of concern raised by the President's counsel and told the President's counsel that their concerns had been communicated to Rosenstein so that the Department of Justice could take any appropriate action.[560]

3. The Press Reports that the President is Being Investigated for Obstruction of Justice and the President Directs the White House Counsel to Have the Special Counsel Removed

On the evening of June 14, 2017, the Washington Post published an article stating that the Special Counsel was investigating whether the President had attempted to obstruct justice.[561] This was the first public report that the President himself was under investigation by the Special Counsel's Office, and cable news networks quickly picked up on the report.[562]

The Post story stated that the Special Counsel was interviewing intelligence community leaders, including Coats and Rogers, about what the President had asked them to do in response to Corney's March 20, 2017 testimony; that the inquiry into obstruction marked "a major turning point" in the investigation; and that while "Trump had received private assurances from then-FBI Director James B. Corney starting in January that he was not personally under investigation," "[o]fficials say that changed shortly after Corney's firing."[563] That evening, at approximately 10:31 p.m., the President called McGahn on McGahn's personal cell phone and they spoke for about 15 minutes.[564] McGahn did not have a clear memory of the call but thought they might have discussed the stories reporting that the President was under investigation.[565]

Beginning early the next day, June 15, 2017, the President issued a series of tweets acknowledging the existence of the obstruction investigation and criticizing it. He wrote: "They made up a phony collusion with the Russians story, found zero proof, so now they go for obstruction of justice on the phony story. Nice";[566] "You are witnessing the single greatest WITCH HUNT in American political history—led by some very bad and conflicted people!";[567] and "Crooked H destroyed phones w/ hammer, 'bleached' emails, & had husband meet w/AG days before she was cleared—& they talk about obstruction?"[568] The next day, June 16, 2017, the President wrote additional tweets criticizing the investigation: "After 7 months of investigations & committee hearings about my 'collusion with the Russians,' nobody has been able to show any proof. Sad!";[569] and "Jam being investigated for firing the FBI Director by the man who told me to fire the FBI Director! Witch Hunt."[570]

On Saturday, June 17, 2017, the President called McGahn and directed him to have the Special Counsel removed.[571] McGahn was at home and the President was at Camp David.[572] Jn interviews with this Office, McGahn recalled that the President called him at home twice and on both 'occasions directed him to call Rosenstein and say that Mueller had conflicts that precluded him from serving as Special Counsel.[573]

On the first call, McGahn recalled that the President said something like, "You gotta do this. You gotta call Rod."[574] McGahn said he told the President that he would see what he could do.[575] McGahn was perturbed by the call and did not intend to act on the request.[576] He and other advisors believed the asserted conflicts were "silly" and "not real," and they had previously communicated that view to the President." McGahn also had made clear to the President that the White House Counsel's Office should not be involved in any effort to press the issue of conflicts.[578] McGahn was concerned about having any role in asking the Acting Attorney General to fire the Special Counsel because he had grown up in the Reagan era and wanted to be more like Judge Robert Bork and not "Saturday Night Massacre Bork."[579] McGahn considered the President's request to be an inflection point and he wanted to hit the brakes.[580]

When the President called McGahn a second time to follow up on the order to call the Department of Justice, McGahn recalled that the President was more direct, saying something like, "Call Rod, tell Rod that Mueller has conflicts and can't be the Special Counsel."[581] McGahn recalled the President telling him "Mueller has to go" and "Call me back when you do it."[582] McGahn understood the President to be saying that the Special Counsel had to be removed by Rosenstein.[583] To end the conversation with the President, McGahn left the

President with the impression that McGahn would call Rosenstein.[584] McGahn recalled that he had already said no to the President's request and he was worn down, so he just wanted to get off the phone.[585]

McGahn recalled feeling trapped because he did not plan to follow the President's directive but did not know what he would say the next time the President called.[586] McGahn decided he had to resign.[587] He called his personal lawyer and then called his chief of staff, Annie Donaldson, to inform her of his decision.[588] He then drove to the office to pack his belongings and submit his resignation letter.[589] Donaldson recalled that McGahn told her the President had called and demanded he contact the Department of Justice and that the President wanted him to do something that McGahn did not want to do.[590] McGahn told Donaldson that the President had called at least twice and in one of the calls asked "have you done it?"[591] McGahn did not tell Donaldson the specifics of the President's request because he was consciously trying not to involve her in the investigation, but Donaldson inferred that the President's directive was related to the Russia investigation.[592] Donaldson prepared to resign along with McGahn.[593]

That evening, McGahn called both Priebus and Bannon and told them that he intended to resign.[594] McGahn recalled that, after speaking with his attorney and given the nature of the President's request, he decided not to share details of the President's request with other White House staff.[595] Priebus recalled that McGahn said that the President had asked him to "do crazy shit," but he thought McGahn did not tell him the specifics of the President's request because McGahn was trying to protect Priebus from what he did not need to know.[596] Priebus and Bannon both urged McGahn not to quit, and McGahn ultimately returned to work that Monday and remained in his position.[597] He had not told the President directly that he planned to resign, and when they next saw each other the President did not ask McGahn whether he had followed through with calling Rosenstein.[598]

Around the same time, Chris Christie recalled a telephone call with the President in which the President asked what Christie thought about the President firing the Special Counsel.[599] Christie advised against doing so because there was no substantive basis for the President to fire the Special Counsel, and because the President would lose support from Republicans in Congress if he did so.[600]

Analysis

In analyzing the President's direction to McGahn to have the Special Counsel removed, the following evidence is relevant to the elements of obstruction of justice:

a.   Obstructive act. As with the President's firing of Corney, the attempt to remove the Special Counsel would qualify as an obstructive act if it would naturally obstruct the investigation and any grand jury proceedings that might flow from the inquiry. Even if the removal of the lead prosecutor would not prevent the investigation from continuing under a new appointee, a factfinder would need to consider whether the act had the potential to delay further action in the investigation, chill the actions of any replacement Special Counsel, or otherwise impede the investigation.

A threshold question is whether the President in fact directed McGahn to have the Special Counsel removed. After news organizations reported that in June 2017 the President had ordered McGahn to have the Special Counsel removed, the President publicly disputed these accounts, and privately told McGahn that he had simply wanted McGahn to bring conflicts of interest to the Department of Justice's attention. See Volume H, Section II.I, infra. Some of the President's specific language that McGahn recalled from the calls is consistent with that explanation. Substantial evidence, however, supports the conclusion that the President went further and in fact directed McGahn to call Rosenstein to have the Special Counsel removed.

First, McGahn's clear recollection was that the President directed him to tell Rosenstein not only that conflicts existed but also that "Mueller has to go." McGahn is a credible witness with no motive to lie or exaggerate given the position he held in the White House.P''' McGahn spoke with the President twice and understood the directive the same way both times, making it unlikely that he misheard or misinterpreted the President's request. In response to that request, McGahn decided to quit because he did not want to participate in events that he described as akin to the Saturday Night Massacre. He called his lawyer, drove to the White House, packed up his office, prepared to submit a resignation letter with his chief of staff, told Priebus that the President had asked him to "do crazy shit," and informed Priebus and Bannon that he was leaving. Those acts would be a highly unusual reaction to a request to convey information to the Department of Justice.

Second, in the days before the calls to McGahn, the President, through his counsel, had already brought the asserted conflicts to the attention of the Department of Justice. Accordingly, the President had no reason to have McGahn call Rosenstein that weekend to raise conflicts issues that already had been raised.

Third, the President's sense of urgency and repeated requests to McGahn to take immediate action on a weekend-"You gotta do this. You gotta call Rod."-support McGahn's recollection that the President wanted the Department of Justice to take action to remove the Special Counsel. Had the President instead sought only to have the Department of Justice re-examine asserted conflicts to evaluate whether they posed an ethical bar, it would have been unnecessary to set the process in motion on a Saturday and to make repeated calls to McGahn.

Finally, the President had discussed "knocking out Mueller" and raised conflicts of interest in a May 23, 2017 call with McGahn, reflecting that the President connected the conflicts to a plan to remove the Special Counsel. And in the days leading up to June 17, 2017, the President made clear to Priebus and Bannon, who then told Ruddy, that the President was considering terminating the Special Counsel. Also during this time period, the President reached out to Christie to get his thoughts on firing the Special Counsel. This evidence shows that the President was not just seeking an examination of whether conflicts existed but instead was looking to use asserted conflicts as a way to terminate the Special Counsel.

b.   Nexus to an official proceeding.   To satisfy the proceeding requirement, it would be necessary to establish a nexus between the President's act of seeking to terminate the Special Counsel and a pending or foreseeable grand jury proceeding.

Substantial evidence indicates that by June I 7, 2017, the President knew his conduct was under investigation by a federal prosecutor who could present any evidence of federal crimes to a grand jury. On May 23, 2017, McGahn explicitly warned the President that his "biggest exposure" was not his act of firing Corney but his "other contacts" and "calls," and his "ask re: Flynn." By early June, it was widely reported in the media that federal prosecutors had issued grand jury subpoenas in the Flynn inquiry and that the Special Counsel had taken over the Flynn investigation.s'" On June 9, 2017, the Special Counsel's Office informed the White House that investigators would be interviewing inteltigence agency officials who allegedly had been asked by the President to push back against the Russia investigation. On June 14, 2017, news outlets began reporting that the President was himself being investigated for obstruction of justice.   Based on widespread reporting, the President knew that such an investigation could include his request for Corney's loyalty; his request that Corney "let[] Flynn go"; his outreach to Coats and Rogers; and his termination of Corney and statement to the Russian Foreign Minister that the termination had relieved "great pressure" related to Russia.   And on June 16, 2017, the day before he directed McGahn to have the Special Counsel removed, the President publicly acknowledged that his conduct was under investigation by a federal prosecutor, tweeting, "I am being investigated for firing the FBI Director by the man who told me to fire the FBI Director!"

c.   Intent. Substantial evidence indicates that the President's attempts to remove the Special Counsel were linked to the Special Counsel's oversight of investigations that involved the President's conduct-and, most immediately, to reports that the President was being investigated for potential obstruction of justice.

Before the President terminated Corney, the President considered it critically important that he was not under investigation and that the public not erroneously think he was being investigated. As described in Volume II, Section II.D, supra, advisors perceived the President, while he was drafting the Corney termination letter, to be concerned more than anything else about getting out that he was not personally under investigation. When the President learned of the appointment of the Special Counsel on May 17, 2017, he expressed further concern about the investigation, saying "[t]his is the end of my Presidency." The President also faulted Sessions for recusing, saying "you were supposed to protect me."

On June 14, 2017, when the Washington Post reported that the Special Counsel was investigating the President for obstruction of justice, the President was facing what he had wanted to avoid: a criminal investigation into his own conduct that was the subject of widespread media attention. The evidence indicates that news of the obstruction investigation prompted the President to call McGahn and seek to have the Special Counsel removed. By mid-June, the Department of Justice had already cleared the Special Counsel's service and the President's advisors had told him that the claimed conflicts of interest were "silly" and did not provide a basis to remove the Special Counsel. On June 13, 2017, the Acting Attorney General testified before Congress that no good cause for removing the Special Counsel existed, and the President dictated a press statement to Sanders saying he had no intention of firing the Special Counsel. But the next day, the media reported that the President was under investigation for obstruction of justice and the Special Counsel was interviewing witnesses about events related to possible obstruction-spurring the President to write critical tweets about the Special Counsel's investigation. The President called McGahn at home that night and then called him on Saturday from Camp David. The evidence accordingly indicates that news that an obstruction investigation had been opened is what led the President to call McGahn to have the Special Counsel terminated.

There also is evidence that the President knew that he should not have made those calls to McGahn. The President made the calls to McGahn after McGahn had specifically told the President that the White House Counsel's Office-and McGahn himself-could not be involved in pressing conflicts claims and that the President should consult with his personal counsel if he wished to raise conflicts. Instead ofrelying on his personal counsel to submit the conflicts claims, the President sought to use his official powers to remove the Special Counsel. And after the media reported on the President's actions, he denied that he ever ordered McGahn to have the Special Counsel terminated and made repeated efforts to have McGahn deny the story, as discussed in Volume II, Section II.I, infra. Those denials are contrary to the evidence and suggest the President's awareness that the direction to McGahn could be seen as improper.

******

501 Office of the Deputy Attorney General, Order No. 3915-2017, Appointment ofSpecial Counsel to Investigate Russian Interference with the 2016 Presidential Election and Related Matters (May 17,2017).

502 Sessions 1/17/18 302, at 13; Hunt.2/1/18 302, at 18; McGahn 12/14/17 302, at 4; Hunt-000039 (Hunt 5/17/17 Notes).

503 Sessions 1/17/18 302, at 13; Hunt 2/1/18 302, at 18; McGahn 12/14/17 302, at 4; Hunt-000039 (Hunt 5/17/17 Notes).

504 Hunt-000039 (Hunt 5/17/17 Notes).

505 Hunt-000039 (Hunt 5/17/17 Notes); Sessions 1/17/18 302, at 13-14.

506 Hunt-000040; see Sessions 1/17/18 302, at 14.

507 Sessions 1/17/18 302, at 14.

508 Hunt-000040 (Hunt 5/17/17 Notes); see Sessions 1 /17/18 302, at 14. Early the next morning, the President tweeted, "This is the single greatest witch hunt of a politician in American history!" @realDonaldTrump 5/18/17 (7:52 a.m. ET) Tweet

509Hunt-000041 (Hunt5/17/17Notes);Sessions 1/17/18302,at 14.

510 Hunt-000041 (Hunt 5/17/17 Notes); Sessions 1/17/18 302, at 14.

511 Hicks 12/8/17 302, at 21.

512 Hicks 12/8/17 302, at 21. The Access Hollywood tape was released on October 7, 2016, as discussed in Volume I, Section 111.D.1, supra.

513 McGahn 12/14/17 302, at 9; SCR015_000175-82 (Undated Draft Memoranda to White House Staff).

514 McGahn 12/14/17 302, at 9; SCR015_000175-82 (Undated Draft Memoranda to White House
Staff). The White House Counsel's Office had previously issued a document hold on February 27, 2017. SCR015_000171
(2/17/17 Memorandum from McGahn to Executive Office of the President Staff).

515 Hunt-000047 (Hunt 5/18/17 Notes); 5/18/17 Letter, Sessions to President Trump (resigning as Attorney General).

516 Hunt-000047-49 (Hunt 5/18/17 Notes); Sessions 1/17/18 302, at 14. m Hunt-000047-49 (Hunt 5/18/17 Notes); Sessions
1/17/18 302, at 14

518 Hunt-000048-49 (Hunt 5/18/17 Notes); Sessions 1/17/18 302, at 14.

519 Sessions 1/17/18 302, at 14.

520 Hunt-000049 (Hunt 5/18/17 Notes).

521 Hunt-000050-51 (Hunt 5/18/17 Notes).

522 Hunt-000050 (Hunt 5/18/17 Notes); Priebus I 0/ 13/17 302, at 21; Hunt 2/1 /18 302, at 21.

523 Hunt-000051 (Hunt 5/18/17 Notes).

524 SCR026_000110 (President's Daily Diary, 5/19/17).

525 Hicks 12/8/17 302, at 22.

526 Priebus I 0/ 13/17 302, at 21. Hunt's notes state that when Priebus returned from the trip, Priebus told Hunt that the
President was supposed to have given him the letter, but when he asked for it, the President "slapped the desk" and said
he had forgotten it back at the hotel. Hunt-000052 (Hunt Notes, undated).

527 Hunt-000052-53 (Hunt 5/30/17 Notes); 5/18/17 Letter, Sessions to President Trump (resignation letter).   Robert Porter,
who was the White House Staff Secretary at the time, said that in the days after the President returned from the Middle East
trip, the President took Sessions's letter out ofa drawer in the Oval Office and showed it to Porter. Porter 4/13/18 302 at 8.

528 Priebus 1/18/18 302, at 12; Bannon 2/14/18 302, at 10; McGahn 3/8/18 302, at I; McGahn 12/14/17 302, at 10;
Bannon 10/26/18 302, at 12.

529 Priebus 1/18/18 302, at 12; Bannon 2/14/18 302, at 10. In October 2011, Mueller resigned his family's membership
from Trump National Golf Club in Sterling, Virginia, in a letter that noted that "we live in the District and find that we are
unable to make full use of the Club" and that inquired "whether we would be entitled to a refund of a portion ofour initial
membership fee," which was paid in 1994. I 0/12/11
Letter, Muellers to Trump National GolfClub. About two weeks later, the controller of the club responded that the Muellers'
resignation would be effective October 31, 2011, and that they would be "placed on a waitlist to be refunded on a first
resigned I first refunded basis" in accordance with the club's legal documents.   10/27/11 Letter, Muellers to Trump
National Golf Club. The Muellers have not had further contact with the club.

530 Priebus 4/3/18 302, at 3; Bannon 10/26/18 302, at 13 (confirming that he, Priebus, and McGahn pushed back on the
asserted conflicts).

531 Bannon I 0/26/18 302, at 12-13.

532 Bannon 10/26/18 302, at 12.

533 Bannon 10/26/18 302, at 12.

534 Bannon 10/26/ I 8 302, at 12.

535 Bannon 10/26/18 302, at 13.

536 Bannon 10/26/18 302, at 12.

537 Matt Zapotosky & Matea Gold, Justice Department ethics experts clear Mueller to lead Russia probe, Washington Post
(May 23, 2017).

538 McGahn 3/8/18 302, at l; McGahn 12/14/17 302, at 10; Priebus 1/18/18 302, at 12.

539 McGahn 3/8/18 302, at I. McGahn and Donaldson said that after the appointment of the Special Counsel, they considered themselves potential fact witnesses and accordingly told the

541 SC_AD_00361 (Donaldson 5/31/17 Notes).

542 SC AD 00361 (Donaldson 5/31/17 Notes).

543 See, e.g., Michael S. Schmidt, In a Private Dinner, Trump Demanded Loyalty. Comey Demurred., New York Times (May 11, 2017); Michael S. Schmidt, Comey Memorandum Says Trump Asked Him to End Flynn Investigation, New York Times (May 16, 2017); Matt Apuzzo et al., Trump Told Russians That Firing 'Nut Job' Comey Eased Pressure From Investigation, New York Times (May 19, 2017).

544 Hearing on Russian Election Interference Before the Senate Select Intelligence Committee, I 15th Cong. (June 8, 2017) (Statement for the Record of James B. Corney, former Director of the FBI, at 5-6). Corney testified that he deliberately caused his memorandum documenting the February 14, 2017 meeting to be leaked to the New York Times in response to a tweet from the President, sent on May 12, 2017, that stated "James Corney better hope that there are no 'tapes' of our conversations before he starts leaking to the press!," and because he thought sharing the memorandum with a reporter "might prompt the appointment of a special counsel." Hearing on Russian Election Interference Before the Senate Select Intelligence Committee, I 15th Cong. (June 8, 2017) (CQ Cong. Transcripts, at 55) (testimony by James B. Corney, former Director of the FBT).

545 See, e.g., Matt Zapotosky, Camey lays out the case that Trump obstructed justice, Washington Post (June 8, 2017) ("Legal analysts said Corney's testimony clarified and bolstered the case that the president obstructed justice.").

546 6/9/17 Email, Special Counsel's Office to the White House Counsel's Office. This Office made the notification to give the White House an opportunity to invoke executive privilege in advance of the interviews. On June 12, 2017, the Special Counsel's Office interviewed Admiral Rogers in the presence of agency counsel. Rogers 6/12/17 302, at I. On June 13, the Special Counsel's Office interviewed Ledgett. Ledget 6/13/17 302, at I. On June 14, the Office interviewed Coats and other personnel from his office. Coats 6/14/17 302, at I; Gistaro 6/14/17 302, at I; Culver 6/ 14/17 302, at I.

547 Ruddy 6/6/ 18 302, at 5.

548 Ruddy 6/6/18 302, at 5-6.

549 Ruddy 6/6/18 302, at 6.

sso Ruddy 6/6/18 302, at 6.

551 Trump Confidant Christopher Ruddy says Mueller has "real conflicts" as special counsel, PBS (June 12, 2017); Michael D. Shear & Maggie Haberman, Friend Says Trump Is Considering Firing Mueller as Special Counsel, New York Times (June 12, 2017).

552 Katherine Faulders & Veronica Stracqualursi, Trump friend Chris Ruddy says Spicer 's 'bizarre' statement doesn't deny claim Trump seeking Mueller firing, ABC (June 13, 2017).

553 See, e.g., Michael D. Shear & Maggie Haberman, Friend Says Trump Is Considering Firing Mueller as Special Counsel, New York Times (June 12, 2017).

554 Ruddy 6/6/18 302, at 6-7.

555 Sanders 7/3/18 302, at 6-7.

556 Glenn Thrush et al., Trump Stews, Sta.f!Steps In, and Mueller Is Safe/or Now, New York Times (June 13, 2017); see Sanders 7/3/18 302, at 6 (Sanders spoke with the President directly before speaking to the press on Air Force One and the answer she gave is the answer the President told her to give).

557 Special Counsel's Office Attorney 6/13/17 Notes.

558 Special Counsel's Office Attorney 6/13/17 Notes.

560 Special Counsel's Office Attorney 6/ 15/17 Notes.

561 Devlin Barrett et al., Special counsel is investigating Trump for possible obstruction of justice, officials say, Washington Post (June 14, 2017).

562 CNN, for example, began running a chyron at 6:55 p.m. that stated: "WASH POST: MUELLER INVESTIGATING TRUMP FOR OBSTRUCTION OF JUSTICE." CNN, (June 14, 2017, published online at 7: 15 p.m. ET).

563 Devlin Barrett et al., Special counsel is investigating Trump for possible obstruction of justice, officials say, Washington Post (June I 4, 2017).

564 SCR026_000183 (President's Daily Diary, 6/14/17) (reflecting call from the President to McGahn on 6/14/17 with start time 10:31 p.m. and end time 10:46 p.m.); Call Records of Don McGahn.

565 McGahn 2/28/19 302, at 1-2. McGahn thought he and the President also probably talked about the investiture ceremony for Supreme Court Justice Neil Gorsuch, which was scheduled for the following day. McGahn 2/28/18 302, at 2.

566 @realDonaldTrump 6/15/17 (6:55 a.m. ET) Tweet.

567 @realDonaldTrump 6/15/17 (7:57 a.m. ET) Tweet

568 @realDonaldTrump 6/15/17 (3:56 p.m. ET) Tweet.

569 @realDonaldTrump 6/16/17 (7:53 a.m. ET) Tweet.

570 @realDonaldTrump 6/16/17 (9:07 a.m. ET) Tweet.

571 McGahn 3/8/18 302, at 1-2; McGahn 12/14/17 302, at 10.

572 McGahn 3/8/18 302, at I, 3; SCR026_000196 (President's Daily Diary, 6/17/17) (records showing President departed the White House at 11 :07 a.m. on June 17, 2017, and arrived at Camp David at 11 :37 a.m.).

573 McGahn 3/8/18 302, at 1-2; McGahn 12/14/17 302, at I 0. Phone records show that the President called McGahn in the afternoon on June 17, 2017, and they spoke for approximately 23 minutes. SCR026_000196 (President's Daily Diary, 6/17/17) (reflecting call from the President to McGahn on

6/17/17 with start time 2:23 p.m. and end time 2:46 p.m.); (Call Records of Don McGahn). Phone records do not show another call between McGahn and the President that day. Although McGahn recalled receiving multiple calls from the President on the same day, in light of the phone records he thought it was possible that the first call instead occurred on June 14, 2017, shortly after the press reported that the President was under investigation for obstruction of justice. McGahn 2/28/19 302, at 1-3. While McGahn was not certain of the specific dates of the calls, McGahn was confident that he had at least two phone conversations with the President in which the President directed him to call the Acting Attorney General to have the Special Counsel removed. McGahn 2/28/19 302, at 1-3.

574 McGahn 3/8/ 18 302, at I.

575 McGahn 3/8/18 302, at I.

576 McGahn 3/8/18 302, at I.

577 McGahn 3/8/ 18 302, at 1-2.

578 McGahn 3/8/18 302, at 1-2.

579 McGahn 3/8/18 302, at 2.

580 McGahn 3/8/18 302, at 2.

581 McGahn 3/8/18 302, at 5.

582 McGahn 3/8/18 302, at 2, 5; McGahn 2/28/19 302, at 3.

583 McGahn 3/8/18 302, at 1-2, 5.

584 McGahn 3/8/18 302, at 2.

585 McGahn 2/28/19 302, at 3; McGahn 3/8/18 302, at 2.

586 McGahn 3/8/18 302, at 2.

587 McGahn 3/8/18 302, at 2.

588 McGahn 3/8/18 302, at 2-3; McGahn 2/28/19 302, at 3; Donaldson 4/2/18 302, at 4; Call Records of Don McGahn.

589 McGahn 3/8/18 302, at 2; Donaldson 4/2/18 302, at 4.

590 Donaldson 4/2/18 302, at 4.

591 Donaldson 4/2/18 302, at 4.

592 McGahn 2/28/19 302, at 3-4; Donaldson 4/2/18 302, at 4-5. Donaldson said she believed McGahn consciously did not share details with her because he did not want to drag her into the investigation. Donaldson 4/2/18 302, at 5; see McGahn 2/28/19 302, at 3.

593 Donaldson 4/2/18 302, at 5.

594 McGahn 12/14/17 302, at 1 O; Call Records of Don McGahn; McGahn 2/28/19 302, at 3-4; Priebus 4/3/1 8 302, at 6-7.

595 McGahn 2/28/19 302, at 4. Priebus and Bannon confirmed that McGahn did not tell them the specific details of the President's request. Priebus 4/3/18 302, at 7; Bannon 2/14/18 302, at JO.

596 Priebus 4/3/18 302, at 7.

597 McGahn 3/8/18 302, at 3; McGahn 2/28/19 302, at 3-4.

598 McGahn 3/8/18 302, at 3.

599 Christie 2/13/19 302, at 7. Christie did not recall the precise date of this call, but believed it was after Christopher Wray was announced as the nominee to be the new FBI director, which was on June 7,

2017. Christie 2/13/19 302, at 7. Telephone records show that the President called Christie twice after that time period, on July 4, 2017, and July 14, 2017. Call Records of Chris Christie.

60° Christie 2/13/19 302, at 7.

601 When this Office first interviewed McGahn about this topic, he was reluctant to share detailed information about what had occurred and only did so after continued questioning. See McGahn 12/14/17

302 (agent notes).

602 See, e.g., Evan Perez et al., CNN exclusive·: Grand jury subpoenas issued in FB/'s Russia investigation, CNN (May 9, 2017); Matt Ford, Why Mueller Is Taking Over the Michael Flynn Grand Jury, The Atlantic (June 2, 2017).

F.   The President's Efforts to Curtail the Special Counsel Investigation

Overview

Two days after the President directed McGahn to have the Special Counsel removed, the President made another attempt to affect the course of the Russia investigation. On June 19, 2017, the President met one-on-one with Corey Lewandowski in the Oval Office and dictated a message to be delivered to Attorney General Sessions that would have had the effect of limiting the Russia investigation to future election interference only. One month later, the President met again with Lewandowski and followed up on the request to have Sessions limit the scope of the Russia investigation. Lewandowski told the President the message would be delivered soon. Hours later, the President publicly criticized Sessions in an unplanned press interview, raising questions about Sessions's job security.

1. The President Asks Corey Lewandowski to Deliver a Message to Sessions to Curtail the Special Counsel Investigation

On June 19, 2017, two days after the President directed McGahn to have the Special

Counsel removed, the President met one-on-one in the Oval Office with his former campaign manager Corey Lewandowski.f?' Senior White House advisors described Lewandowski as a "devotee" of the President and said the relationship between the President and Lewandowski was "close."[604]

During the June 19 meeting, Lewandowski recalled that, after some small talk, the President brought up Sessions and criticized his recusal from the Russia investigation.f" The President told Lewandowski that Sessions was weak and that if the President had known about the likelihood of recusal in advance, he would not have appointed Sessions.f" The President then asked Lewandowski to deliver a message to Sessions and said "write this down."[607] This was the first time the President had asked Lewandowski to take dictation, and Lewandowski wrote as fast as possible to make sure he captured the content correctly.r'"

> The President directed that Sessions should give a speech publicly announcing:
>
> I know that I recused myself from certain things having to do with specific areas. But our POTUS ... is being treated very unfairly. He shouldn't have a Special Prosecutor/Counsel b/c he hasn't done anything wrong. I was on the campaign w/ him for nine months, there were no Russians involved with him. I know it for a fact b/c I was there. He didn't do anything wrong except he ran the greatest campaign in American history.[609]

The dictated message went on to state that Sessions would meet with the Special Counsel to limit his jurisdiction to future election interference:

> Now a group of people want to subvert the Constitution of the United States. I am going to meet with the Special Prosecutor to explain this is very unfair and let the Special Prosecutor move forward with investigating election meddling for future elections so that nothing can happen in future elections."?

The President said that if Sessions delivered that statement he would be the "most popular guy in the country."[611] Lewandowski told the President he understood what the President wanted Sessions to do.[612]

Lewandowski wanted to pass the message to Sessions in person rather than over the phone.[613] He did not want to meet at the Department of Justice because he did not want a public log of his visit and did not want Sessions to have an advantage over him by meeting on what Lewandowski described as Sessions's turf.[614] Lewandowski called Sessions and arranged a meeting for the following evening at Lewandowski's office, but Sessions had to cancel due to a last minute conflict.[615]   Shortly thereafter, Lewandowski left Washington, D.C., without having had an opportunity to meet with Sessions to convey the President's message.[616]   Lewandowski stored the notes in a safe at his home, which he stated was his standard procedure with sensitive items.[617]

2. The President Follows Up with Lewandowski

Following his June meeting with the President, Lewandowski contacted Rick Dearborn, then a senior White House official, and asked if Dearborn could pass a message to Sessions.[618] Dearborn agreed without knowing what the message was, and Lewandowski later confirmed that Dearborn would meet with Sessions for dinner in late July and could deliver the message then.[619] Lewandowski recalled thinking that the President had asked him to pass the message because the President knew Lewandowski could be trusted, but Lewandowski believed Dearborn would be a better messenger because he had a longstanding relationship with Sessions and because Dearborn was in the government while Lewandowski was not.[620]

On July 19, 2017, the President again met with Lewandowski alone in the Oval Office.[621] In the preceding days, as described in Volume TT, Section ILG, *infra,* emails and other information about the June 9, 2016 meeting between several Russians and Donald Trump Jr., Jared Kushner, and Paul Manafort had been publicly disclosed. In the July 19 meeting with Lewandowski, the President raised his previous request and asked if Lewandowski had talked to Sessions.[622] Lewandowski told the President that the message would be delivered soon.[623] Lewandowski recalled that the President told him that if Sessions did not meet with him, Lewandowski should tell Sessions he was fired.[624]

Immediately following the meeting with the President, Lewandowski saw Dearborn in the anteroom outside the Oval Office and gave him a typewritten version of the message the President had dictated to be delivered to Sessions.[625] Lewandowski told Dearborn that the notes were the message they had discussed, but Dearborn did not recall whether Lewandowski said the message was from the President.[626] The message "definitely raised an eyebrow" for Dearborn, and he recalled not wanting to ask where it came from or think further about doing anything with it.[627]

Dearborn also said that being asked to serve as a messenger to Sessions made him uncomfortable.[628] He recalled later telling Lewandowski that he had handled the situation, but he did not actually follow through with delivering the message to Sessions, and he did not keep a copy of the typewritten notes Lewandowski had given him.[629]

3. The President Publicly Criticizes Sessions in a New York Times Interview

Within hours of the President's meeting with Lewandowski on July 19, 2017, the President gave an unplanned interview to the New York Times in which he criticized Sessions's decision to recuse from the Russia investigation. The President said that "Sessions should have never recused himself and if he was going to recuse himself, he should have told me before he took the job, and I would have picked somebody else."[631] Sessions's recusal, the President said, was "very unfair to the president. How do you take a job and then recuse yourself? If he would have recused himself before the job, I would have said, 'Thanks, Jeff, but I can't, you know, I'm not going to take you.' It's extremely unfair, and that's a mild word, to the president."[632] Hicks, who was present for the interview, recalled trying to "throw [herself] between the reporters and [the President]" to stop parts of the interview, but the President "loved the interview."[633]

Later that day, Lewandowski met with Hicks and they discussed the President's New York Times interview.[634] Lewandowski recalled telling Hicks about the President's request that he meet with Sessions and joking with her about the idea of firing Sessions as a private citizen if Sessions would not meet with him.[635]   As Hicks remembered the conversation, Lewandowski told her the President had recently asked him to meet with Sessions and deliver a message that he needed to do the "right thing" and resign.[636]   While Hicks and Lewandowski were together, the President called Hicks and told her he was happy with how coverage of his New York Times interview criticizing Sessions was playing out.[637]

4. The President Orders Priebus to Demand Sessions's Resignation

Three days later, on July 21, 2017, the Washington Post reported that U.S. intelligence intercepts showed that Sessions had discussed campaign-related matters with the Russian ambassador, contrary to what Sessions had said publicly.[638]   That evening, Priebus called Hunt to talk about whether Sessions might be fired or might resign.[639]   Priebus had previously talked to Hunt when the media had reported on tensions between Sessions and the President, and, after speaking to Sessions, Hunt had told Priebus that the President would have to fire Sessions if he wanted to remove Sessions because Sessions was not going to quit.[640]   According to Hunt, who took contemporaneous notes of the July 21 call, Hunt told Priebus that, as they had previously discussed, Sessions had no intention of resigning.[641]   Hunt asked Priebus what the President would accomplish by firing Sessions, pointing out there was an investigation before and there would be an investigation after.[642]

Early the following morning, July 22, 2017, the President tweeted, "A new INTELLIGENCE LEAK from the Amazon Washington Post, this time against A.G. Jeff Sessions. These illegal leaks, like Corney's, must stop!"[643]   Approximately one hour later, the President tweeted, "So many people are asking why isn't the A.G. or Special Council looking at the many Hillary Clinton or Corney crimes. 33,000 e-mails deleted?',6[44]   Later that morning, while aboard Marine One on the way to Norfolk, Virginia, the President told Priebus that he had to get Sessions to resign immediately.[645]   The President said that the country had lost confidence in Sessions and the negative publicity was not tolerable.[646] According to contemporaneous notes taken by Priebus, the President told Priebus to say that he "need[ed] a letter of resignation on [his] desk immediately" and that Sessions had "no choice" but "must immediately resign."[647] Priebus replied that if they fired Sessions, they would never get a new Attorney General confirmed and that the Department of Justice and Congress would turn their backs on the President, but the President suggested he could make a recess appointment to replace Sessions.[648]

Priebus believed that the President's request was a problem, so he called McGahn and asked for advice, explaining that he did not want to pull the trigger on something that was "all wrong."[649] Although the President tied his desire for Sessions to resign to Sessions's negative press and poor performance in congressional testimony, Priebus believed that the President's desire to replace Sessions was driven by the President's hatred of Sessions's recusal from the Russia investigation.v" McGahn told Priebus not to follow the President's order and said they should consult their personal counsel, with whom they had attorney-client privilege.[651] McGahn and Priebus discussed the possibility that they would both have to resign rather than carry out the President's order to fire Sessions.[652]

That afternoon, the President followed up with Priebus about demanding Sessions's resignation, using words to the effect of, "Did you get it? Are you working on it?"[653] Priebus said that he believed that his job depended on whether he followed the order to remove Sessions, although the President did not directly say so.[654] Even though Priebus did not intend to carry out the President's directive, he told the President he would get Sessions to resign.[655] Later in the day, Priebus called the President and explained that it would be a calamity if Sessions resigned because Priebus expected that Rosenstein and Associate Attorney General Rachel Brand would also resign and the President would be unable to get anyone else confirmed.[656] The President agreed to hold off on demanding Sessions's resignation until after the Sunday shows the next day, to prevent the shows from focusing on the firing.[657]

By the end of that weekend, Priebus recalled that the President relented and agreed not to ask Sessions to resign.[658] Over the next several days, the President tweeted about Sessions. On the morning of Monday, July 24, 2017, the President criticized Sessions for neglecting to investigate Clinton and called him "beleaguered."[659] On July 25, the President tweeted, "Attorney General Jeff Sessions has taken a VERY weak position on Hillary Clinton crimes (where are E• mails & DNC server) & Intel leakers!"[660] The following day, July 26, the President tweeted, "Why didn't A.G. Sessions replace Acting FBI Director Andrew McCabe, a Corney friend who was in charge of Clinton investigation."[661] According to Hunt, in light of the President's frequent public attacks, Sessions prepared another resignation letter and for the rest of the year carried it with him in his pocket every time he went to the White House.[662]

Analysis

In analyzing the President's efforts to have Lewandowski deliver a message directing Sessions to publicly announce that the Special Counsel investigation would be confined to future election interference, the following evidence is relevant to the elements of obstruction of justice:

a.   Obstructive act. The President's effort to send Sessions a message through Lewandowski would qualify as an obstructive act if it would naturally obstruct the investigation and any grand jury proceedings that might flow from the inquiry.

The President sought to have Sessions announce that the President "shouldn't have a Special Prosecutor/Counsel" and that Sessions was going to "meet with the Special Prosecutor to explain this is very unfair and let the Special Prosecutor move forward with investigating election meddling for future elections so that nothing can happen in future elections." The President wanted Sessions to disregard his recusal from the investigation, which had followed from a formal DOJ ethics review, and have Sessions declare that he knew "for a fact" that "there were no Russians involved with the campaign" because he "was there." The President further directed that Sessions should explain that the President should not be subject to an investigation "because he hasn't done anything wrong." Taken together, the President's directives indicate that Sessions was being instructed to tell the Special Counsel to end the existing investigation into the President and his campaign, with the Special Counsel being permitted to "move forward with investigating election meddling for future elections."

b.   Nexus to an official proceeding. As described above, by the time of the President's initial one-on-one meeting with Lewandowski on June 19, 2017, the existence of a grand jury investigation supervised by the Special Counsel was ublic knowled e. B the time of the President's follow-u meetin with Lewandowski

See Volume II, Section 11.G, infra. To satisfy the nexus requirement, it would be necessary to show that limiting the Special Counsel's investigation would have the natural and probable effect of impeding that grand jury proceeding.

c.   Intent. Substantial evidence indicates that the President's effort to have Sessions limit the scope of the Special Counsel's investigation to future election interference was intended to prevent further investigative scrutiny of the President's and his campaign's conduct.

As previously described, see Volume II, Section II.B, supra, the President knew that the Russia investigation was focused in part on his campaign, and he perceived allegations of Russian interference to cast doubt on the legitimacy of his election. The President further knew that the investigation had broadened to include his own conduct and whether he had obstructed justice. Those investigations would not proceed ifthe Special Counsel's jurisdiction were limited to future election interference only.

The timing and circumstances of the President's actions support the conclusion that he sought that result. The President's initial direction that Sessions should limit the Special Counsel's investigation came just two days after the President had ordered McGahn to have the Special Counsel removed, which itself followed public reports that the President was personally under investigation for obstruction of justice. The sequence of those events raises an inference that after seeking to terminate the Special Counsel, the President sought to exclude his and his campaign's conduct from the investigation's scope. The President raised the matter with Lewandowski again on July 19, 2017, just days after emails and information about the June 9, 2016 meeting between Russians and senior campaign officials had been publicly disclosed, generating substantial media coverage and investigative interest.

The manner in which the President acted provides additional evidence of his intent. Rather than rely on official channels, the President met with Lewandowski alone in the Oval Office. The President selected a loyal "devotee" outside the White House to deliver the message, supporting an inference that he was working outside White House channels, including McGahn, who had previously resisted contacting the Department of Justice about the Special Counsel. The President also did not contact the Acting Attorney General, who had just testified publicly that there was no cause to remove the Special Counsel. Instead, the President tried to use Sessions to restrict and redirect the Special Counsel's investigation when Sessions was recused and could not properly take any action on it.

The July 19, 2017 events provide further evidence of the President's intent. The President followed up with Lewandowski in a separate one-on-one meeting one month after he first dictated the message for Sessions, demonstrating he still sought to pursue the request. And just hours after Lewandowski assured the President that the message would soon be delivered to Sessions, the President gave an unplanned interview to the New York Times in which he publicly attacked Sessions and raised questions about his job security. Four days later, on July 22, 2017, the President directed Priebus to obtain Sessions's resignation. That evidence could raise an inference that the President wanted Sessions to realize that his job might be on the line as he evaluated whether to comply with the President's direction that Sessions publicly announce that, notwithstanding his recusal, he was going to confine the Special Counsel's investigation to future election interference.

****

604 Kelly 8/2/18 302, at 7; Dearborn 6/20/18 302, at 1   (describing Lewandowski as a "comfort to the President" whose loyalty was appreciated). Kelly said that when he was ChiefofStaffand the President had meetings with friends   like Lewandowski,   Kelly tried   not to be there and to push the meetings to the residence to create distance from the West Wing. Kelly 8/2/18 302, at 7.

605 Lewandowski 4/6/18 302, at 2.

606 Lewandowski 4/6/18 302, at 2.

607 Lewandowski 4/6/18 302, at 2.

608 Lewandowski 4/6/ 18 302, at 3.

609 Lewandowski 4/6/18 302, at 2-3; Lewandowski 6/19/17 Notes, at 1-2.

610 Lewandowski 4/6/18 302, at 3; Lewandowski 6/19/17 Notes, at 3.

611 Lewandowski 4/6/18 302, at 3; Lewandowski 6/19/17 Notes, at 4.

612 Lewandowski 4/6/18 302, at 3.

613 Lewandowski 4/6/ I 8 302, at 3-4.

614 Lewandowski 4/6/18 302, at 4.

615 Lewandowski 4/6/18 302, at 4.

616 Lewandowski 4/6/18 302, at 4.

617 Lewandowski 4/6/18 302, at 4.

618 Lewandowski 4/6/18 302, at 4; see Dearborn 6/20/18 302, at 3

619 Lewandowski 4/6/18 302, at 4-5.

620 Lewandowski 4/6/18 302, at 4, 6.

621   Lewandowski 4/6/18 302, at 5; SCR029b 000002-03 (6/5/18 Additional Response to Special Counsel Request for Certain Visitor Log Information).

622 Lewandowski 4/6/ 1 8 3 02, at 5.

623 Lewandowski 4/6/18 302, at 5.

624 Lewandowski 4/6/18 302, at 6. Priebus vaguely recalled Lewandowski telling him that in approximately May or June 2017 the President had asked Lewandowski to get Sessions's resignation. Priebus recalled that Lewandowski described his reaction as something like, "What can I do? I'm not an employee of the administration. I'm a nobody." Priebus 4/3/18 302, at 6.

62s Lewandowski 4/6/18 302, at 5. Lewandowski said he asked Hope Hicks to type the notes when he went in to the Oval Office, and he then retrieved the notes from her partway through his meeting with the President. Lewandowski 4/6/18 302, at 5.

626 Lewandowski 4/6/18 302, at 5; Dearborn 6/20/18 302, at 3.

627 Dearborn 6/20/ 18 302, at 3.

628 Dearborn 6/20/ 1 8 302, at 3.

629 Dearborn 6/20/18 302, at 3-4.

630 Peter Baker et al., Excerpts From The Times 's Interview With Trump, New York Times (July19, 2017).

631 Peter Baker et al., Excerpts From The Times 's Interview With Trump, New York Times (July19,2017).

632 Peter Baker et al., Excerpts From The Times 's Interview With Trump, New York Times (July19, 2017).

633 Hicks 12/8/17 302, at 23.

634 Hicks 3/13/18 302, at IO; Lewandowski 4/6/18 302, at 6.

635 Lewandowski 4/6/18 302, at 6.

636 Hicks 3/13/18 302, at I 0. Hicks thought that the President might be able to make a recess appointment of a new Attorney General because the Senate was about to go on recess. Hicks 3/ 13/ 18 302, at I 0. Lewandowski recalled that in the afternoon of July 19, 2017, following his meeting with the President, he conducted research on recess appointments but did not share his research with the President. Lewandowski 4/6/18 302, at 7.

637 Lewandowski 4/6/18 302, at 6.

638   Adam Entous et al., Sessions discussed Trump campaign-related matters with Russian ambassador, US. intelligence intercepts show, Washington Post (July 21, 2017).   The underlying events concerning the Sessions-Kislyak contacts are discussed in Volume I, Section IV.A.4.c, supra.

639 Hunt 2/1/18 302, at 23.

640 Hunt 2/1/18 302, at 23.

641 Hunt 2/1/18 302, at 23-24; Hunt 7/21/17 Notes, at I.

642 Hunt 2/1/18 302, at 23-24; Hunt 7/21/17 Notes, at 1-2.

643 @realDonaldTrump 7/22/17 (6:33 a.m. ET) Tweet.

644 @realDonaldTrmp 7/22/17 (7:44 a.m. ET) Tweet. Three minutes later, the President tweeted, "What about all of the Clinton ties to Russia, including Podesta Company, Uranium deal, Russian Reset, big dollar speeches etc." @realDonaldTrump 7/22/17 (7:47 a.m. ET) Tweet.

645 Priebus I /18/18 302, at 13-14.

646 Priebus 1/18/18 302, at 14; Priebus 4/3/18 302, at 4-5; see RP 000073 (Priebus 7/22/17 Notes).

647 RP_000073 (Priebus 7/22/17 Notes).

648 Priebus 4/3/18 302, at 5.

649 Priebus 1/18/18 302, at 14; Priebus 4/3/18 302, at 4-5.

650 Priebus 4/3/18 302, at 5.

651 RP 000074 (Priebus 7/22/17 Notes); McGahn 12/14/17 302, at 11; Priebus 1/18/18 302, at 14. Priebus followed McGahn's advice and called his personal attorney to discuss the President's request because he thought it was the type of thing about which one would need to consult an attorney.   Priebus1/18/18 302, at 14.

652 McGahn 12/14/17 302, at 11; RP_000074 (Priebus 7/22/17 Notes) ("discuss resigning together").

653 Priebus 1/18/18 302, at 14; Priebus 4/3/18 302, at 4.

654 Priebus 4/3/18 302, at 4.

655 Priebus 1/18/18 302, at 15.

656 Priebus 1/18/18 302, at 15.

657 Priebus 1/18/18 302, at 15.

658 Priebus 1 /18/18 302, at 15.

659 @realDonaldTrump 7/24/17 (8:49 a.m. ET) Tweet ("So why aren't the Committees and investigators, and of course our beleaguered A.G., looking into Crooked Hillarys crimes & Russia relations?").

660 @realDonaldTrump 7/25/17 (6: 12 a.m. ET) Tweet. The President sent another tweet shortly before this one asking "where is the investigation A.G." @realDonaldTrump 7/25/17 (6:03 a.m. ET) Tweet

661 @realDonaldTrump 7/26/17 (9:48 a.m. ET) Tweet.

662 Hunt 2/1/18 302, at 24-25.

G. The President's Efforts to Prevent Disclosure of Emails About the June 9, 2016 Meeting Between Russians and Senior Campaign Officials

Overview

By June 2017, the President became aware of emails setting up the June 9, 2016 meeting between senior campaign officials and Russians who offered derogatory information on Hillary Clinton as "part of Russia and its government's support for Mr. Trump." On multiple occasions in late June and early July 2017, the President directed aides not to publicly disclose the emails, and he then dictated a statement about the meeting to be issued by Donald Trump Jr. describing the meeting as about adoption.

Evidence

I. The President Learns About the Existence of Emails Concerning the June 9, 2016 Trump Tower Meeting

Tn mid-June 2017-the same week that the President first asked Lewandowski to pass a message to Sessions-senior Administration officials became aware of emails exchanged during the campaign arranging a meeting between Donald Trump Jr., Paul Manafort, Jared Kushner, and a Russian attorney.[663]

As described in Volume I, Section TV.A.5, *supra,* the emails stated that the "Crown [P]rosecutor of Russia" had offered "to provide the Trump campaign with some official documents and information that would incriminate Hillary and her dealings with Russia" as part of "Russia and its government's support for Mr. Trump."[664] Trump Jr. responded, "[I]f it's what you say I love it,"[665] and he, Kushner, and Manafort met with the Russian attorney and several other Russian individuals at Trump Tower on June 9, 2016.[666] At the meeting, the Russian attorney claimed that funds derived from illegal activities in Russia were provided to Hillary Clinton and other Democrats, and the Russian attorney then spoke about the Magnitsky Act, a 2012 U.S. statute that imposed financial and travel sanctions on Russian officials and that had resulted in a retaliatory ban in Russia on U.S. adoptions of Russian children.[667]

According to written answers submitted by the President in response to questions from this Office, the President had no recollection of learning of the meeting or the emails setting it up at the time the meeting occurred or at any other time before the election.[668]

The Trump Campaign had previously received a document request from SSCI that called for the production of various information, including, "[a] list and a description of all meetings" between any "individual affiliated with the Trump campaign" and "any individual formally or informally affiliated with the Russian government or Russian business interests which took place between June 16, 2015, and 12 pm on January 20, 2017," and associated records.[669] Trump Organization attorneys became aware of the June 9 meeting no later than the first week of June

2017, when they began interviewing the meeting participants, and the Trump Organization attorneys provided the emails setting up the meeting to the President's personal counsel. Mark Corallo, who had been hired as a spokesman for the President's personal legal team, recalled that he learned about the June 9 meeting around June 21 or 22, 2017.[671] Priebus recalled learning about the June 9 meeting from Fox News host Sean Hannity in late June 2017.[672] Priebus notified one of the President's personal attorneys, who told Priebus he was already working on it.[673] By late June, several advisors recalled receiving media inquiries that could relate to the June 9 meeting.[674]

2. The President Directs Communications Staff Not to Publicly Disclose Information About the June 9 Meeting

Communications advisors Hope Hicks and Josh Raffel recalled discussing with Jared Kushner and Ivanka Trump that the emails were damaging and would inevitably be leaked.[675] Hicks and Raffel advised that the best strategy was to proactively release the emails to the press.[676] On or about June 22, 2017, Hicks attended a meeting in the White House residence with the President, Kushner, and Ivanka Trump.[677] According to Hicks, Kushner said that he wanted to fill the President in on something that had been discovered in the documents he was to provide to the congressional committees involving a meeting with him, Manafort, and Trump Jr.[678] Kushner brought a folder of documents to the meeting and tried to show them to the President, but the President stopped Kushner and said he did not want to know about it, shutting the conversation down.[679]

On June 28, 2017, Hicks viewed the emails at Kushner's attorney's office.[680] She recalled being shocked by the emails because they looked "really bad."[681] The next day, Hicks spoke privately with the President to mention her concern about the emails, which she understood were soon going to be shared with Congress.[682] The President seemed upset because too many people knew about the emails and he told Hicks that just one lawyer should deal with the matter.[683] The

President indicated that he did not think the emails would leak, but said they would leak if everyone had access to them.[684]

Later that day, Hicks, Kushner, and Ivanka Trump went together to talk to the President.[685]

Hicks recalled that Kushner told the President the June 9 meeting was not a big deal and was about Russian adoption, but that emails existed setting up the meeting.[686] Hicks said she wanted to get in front of the story and have Trump Jr. release the emails as part of an interview with "softball questions."[687] The President said he did not want to know about it and they should not go to the press.[688] Hicks warned the President that the emails were "really bad" and the story would be "massive" when it broke, but the President was insistent that he did not want to talk about it and said he did not want details.[689] Hicks recalled that the President asked Kushner when his document production was due.[690] Kushner responded that it would be a couple of weeks and the President said, "then leave it alone."[691] Hicks also recalled that the President said Kushner's attorney should give the emails to whomever he needed to give them to, but the President did not think they would be leaked to the press.[692] Raffel later heard from Hicks that the President had directed the group not to be proactive in disclosing the emails because the President believed they would not leak.[693]

3. The President Directs Trump Jr.'s Response to Press Inquiries About the June 9 Meeting

The following week, the President departed on an overseas trip for the G20 summit in Hamburg, Germany, accompanied by Hicks, Raffel, Kushner, and Ivanka Trump, among others.[694] On July 7, 2017, while the President was overseas, Hicks and Raffel learned that the New York Times was working on a story about the June 9 meeting.[695] The next day, Hicks told the President about the story and he directed her not to comment.[696] Hicks thought the President's reaction was odd because he usually considered not responding to the press to be the ultimate sin.[697] Later that day, Hicks and the President again spoke about the story.[698] Hicks recalled that the President asked her what the meeting had been about, and she said that she had been told the meeting was about Russian adoption.[699] The President responded, "then just say that."[700]

On the flight home from the G20 on July 8, 2017, Hicks obtained a draft statement about the meeting to be released by Trump Jr. and brought it to the President."?' The draft statement began with a reference to the information that was offered by the Russians in setting up the meeting: "I was asked to have a meeting by an acquaintance I knew from the 2013 Miss Universe pageant with an individual who I was told might have information helpful to the campaign."[702]

Hicks again wanted to disclose the entire story, but the President directed that the statement not be issued because it said too much.[703] The President told Hicks to say only that Trump Jr. took a brief meeting and it was about Russian adoption.'" After speaking with the President, Hicks texted Trump Jr. a revised statement on the June 9 meeting that read:

> It was a short meeting. I asked Jared and Paul to stop by. We discussed a program about the adoption of Russian children that was active and popular with American families years ago and was since ended by the Russian government, but it was not a campaign issue at that time and there was no follow up.[705]

Hicks's text concluded, "Are you ok with this? Attributed to you."[706] Trump Jr. responded by text message that he wanted to add the word "primarily" before "discussed" so that the statement would read, "We primarily discussed a program about the adoption of Russian children."[707] Trump Jr. texted that he wanted the change because "[t]hey started with some Hillary thing which was bs and some other nonsense which we shot down fast."[708] Hicks texted back, "I think that's right too but boss man worried it invites a lot of questions[.] [U]ltimately [d]efer to you and [your attorney] on that word Be I know it's important and I think the mention of a campaign issue adds something to it in case we have to go further."[709] Trump Jr. responded, "If I don't have it in there it appears as though I'm lying later when they inevitably leak something.v'!" Trump Jr.'s statement—adding the word "primarily" and making other minor additions—was then provided to the New York Times.[711] The full statement provided to the *Times* stated:

It was a short introductory meeting. I asked Jared and Paul to stop by. We primarily discussed a program about the adoption of Russian children that was active and popular with American families years ago and was since ended by the Russian government, but it was not a campaign issue at the time and there was no follow up. I was asked to attend the meeting by an acquaintance, but was not told the name of the person I would be meeting with beforehand.[712]

The statement did not mention the offer of derogatory information about Clinton or any discussion of the Magnitsky Act or U.S. sanctions, which were the principal subjects of the meeting, as described in Volume I, Section IV.A.5, *supra*.

A short while later, while still on Air Force One, Hicks learned that Priebus knew about the emails, which further convinced her that additional information about the June 9 meeting would leak and the White House should be proactive and get in front of the story.[713] Hicks recalled again going to the President to urge him that they should be fully transparent about the June 9 meeting, but he again said no, telling Hicks, "You've given a statement. We're done."[714]

Later on the flight home, Hicks went to the President's cabin, where the President was on the phone with one of his personal attorneys.[715] At one point the President handed the phone to Hicks, and the attorney told Hicks that he had been working with Circa News on a separate story, and that she should not talk to the New York Times.[716]

4. The Media Reports on the June 9, 2016 Meeting

Before the President's flight home from the G20 landed, the New York Times published its story about the June 9, 2016 meeting.[717] In addition to the statement from Trump Jr., the Times story also quoted a statement from Corallo on behalf of the President's legal team suggesting that the meeting might have been a setup by individuals working with the firm that produced the Steele reporting.[718] Corallo also worked with Circa News on a story published an hour later that questioned whether Democratic operatives had arranged the June 9 meeting to create the appearance of improper connections between Russia and Trump family members.[719] Hicks was upset about Corallo's public statement and called him that evening to say the President had not approved the statement.[?"]

The next day, July 9, 2017, Hicks and the President called Corallo together and the President criticized Corallo for the statement he had released.P' Corallo told the President the statement had been authorized and further observed that Trump Jr. 's statement was inaccurate and that a document existed that would contradict it.[722] Corallo said that he purposely used the term "document" to refer to the emails setting up the June 9 meeting because he did not know what the President knew about the emails.[723] Corallo recalled that when he referred to the "document" on the call with the President, Hicks responded that only a few people had access to it and said "it will never get out."[724] Corallo took contemporaneous notes of the call that say: "Also mention existence of doc. Hope says 'only a few people have it. It will never get out.'"[725] Hicks later told investigators that she had no memory of making that comment and had always believed the emails would eventually be leaked, but she might have been channeling the President on the phone call because it was clear to her throughout her conversations with the President that he did not think the emails would leak.[726]

On July 11, 2017, Trump Jr. posted redacted images of the emails setting up the June 9 meeting on Twitter; the New York Times reported that he did so "[a]fter being told that The Times was about to publish the content of the emails."? Later that day, the media reported that the President had been personally involved in preparing Trump Jr.'s initial statement to the New York Times that had claimed the meeting "primarily" concerned "a program about the adoption of Russian children."? Over the next several days, the President's personal counsel repeatedly and inaccurately denied that the President played any role in drafting Trump Jr.'s statement.P" After consulting with the President on the issue, White House Press Secretary Sarah Sanders told the media that the President "certainly didn't dictate" the statement, but that "he weighed in, offered suggestions like any father would do."[730] Several months later, the President's personal counsel stated in a private communication to the Special Counsel's Office that "the President dictated a short but accurate response to the New York Times article on behalf of his son, Donald Trump, Jr."[731] The President later told the press that it was "irrelevant" whether he dictated the statement and said, "It's a statement to the New York Times.... That's not a statement to a high tribunal of judges."[732]

On July 19, 2017, the President had his follow-up meeting with Lewandowski and then met with reporters for the New York Times. In addition to criticizing Sessions in his Times interview, the President addressed the June 9, 2016 meeting and said he "didn't know anything about the meeting" at the time.[734] The President added, "As I've said—most other people, you know, when they call up and say, 'By the way, we have information on your opponent,' I think most politicians — I was just with a lot of people, they said ... , 'Who wouldn't have taken a meeting like that?'"[735]

Analysis

In analyzing the President's actions regarding the disclosure of information about the June 9 meeting, the following evidence is relevant to the elements of obstruction of justice:

a.   Obstructive act. On at least three occasions between June 29, 2017, and July 9, 2017, the President directed Hicks and others not to publicly disclose information about the June9, 2016 meeting between senior campaign officials and a Russian attorney. On June 29, Hicks warned the President that the emails setting up the June 9 meeting were "really bad" and the story would be "massive" when it broke, but the President told her and Kushner to "leave it alone." Early on July 8, after Hicks told the President the New York Times was working on a story about the June 9 meeting, the President directed her not to comment, even though Hicks said that the President usually considered not responding to the press to be the ultimate sin. Later that day, the President rejected Trump Jr.'s draft statement that would have acknowledged that the meeting was with "an individual who I was told might have information helpful to the campaign." The President then dictated a statement to Hicks that said the meeting was about Russian adoption (which the President had twice been told was discussed at the meeting). The statement dictated by the President did not mention the offer of derogatory information about Clinton.

Each of these efforts by the President involved his communications team and was directed at the press. They would amount to obstructive acts only if the President, by taking these actions, sought to withhold information from or mislead congressional investigators or the Special Counsel. On May 17, 2017, the President's campaign received a document request from SSCI that clearly covered the June 9 meeting and underlying emails, and those documents also plainly would have been relevant to the Special Counsel's investigation.

But the evidence does not establish that the President took steps to prevent the emails or other information about the June 9 meeting from being provided to Congress or the Special Counsel. The series of discussions in which the President sought to limit access to the emails and prevent their public release occurred in the context of developing a press strategy. The only evidence we have of the President discussing the production of documents to Congress or the Special Counsel is the conversation on June 29, 2017, when Hicks recalled the President acknowledging that Kushner's attorney should provide emails related to the June 9 meeting to whomever he needed to give them to. We do not have evidence of what the President discussed with his own lawyers at that time.

b.   Nexus to an official proceeding. As described above, by the time of the President's attempts to prevent the public release of the emails regarding the June 9 meeting, the existence of a grand jury investigation supervised by the Special Counsel was public knowledge, and the President had been told that the emails were responsive to congressional inquiries. To satisfy the nexus requirement, however, it would be necessary to show that preventing the release of the emails to the public would have the natural and probable effect of impeding the grand jury proceeding or congressional inquiries. As noted above, the evidence does not establish that the President sought to prevent disclosure of the emails in those official proceedings.

c.   Intent. The evidence establishes the President's substantial involvement in the communications strategy related to information about his campaign's connections to Russia and his desire to minimize public disclosures about those connections. The President became aware of the emails no later than June 29, 2017, when he discussed them with Hicks and Kushner, and he could have been aware of them as early as June 2, 2017, when lawyers for the Trump Organization began interviewing witnesses who participated in the June 9 meeting. The President thereafter repeatedly rejected the advice of Hicks and other staffers to publicly release information about the June 9 meeting. The President expressed concern that multiple people had access to the emails and instructed Hicks that only one lawyer should deal with the matter. And the President dictated a statement to be released by Trump Jr. in response to the first press accounts of the June 9 meeting that said the meeting was about adoption.

But as described above, the evidence does not establish that the President intended to prevent the Special Counsel's Office or Congress from obtaining the emails setting up the June 9 meeting or other information about that meeting. The statement recorded by Corallo-that the emails "will never get out"-can be explained as reflecting a belief that the emails would not be made public if the President's press strategy were followed, even if the emails were provided to Congress and the Special Counsel.

*****

663 Hicks 3/13/18 302, at I; Raffel 2/8/18 302, at 2.
664 RG000061 (6/3/16 Email, Goldstone to Trump Jr.); @DonaldJTrumpJR 7/11/17 (11:01 a.m. ET) Tweet.
665 RG000061 (6/3/16 Email, Trump Jr. to Goldstone); @DonaldJTrumpJR 7/11/17 (11:01 a.m. ET) Tweet.
666 Samochornov 7/12/17 302, at 4.
667 See Volume I, Section TV.A.5, supra (describing meeting in detail).
668 Written Responses of Donald J. Trump (Nov. 20, 2018), at 8 (Response to Question I, Parts (a) through (c)). The President declined to answer questions about his knowledge of the June 9 meeting or other events after the election.
669 DJTFP_SCO_PDF_00000001-02 (5/17/17 Letter, SSCT to Donald J. Trump for President, Inc.).

670 Goldstone 2/8/18 302, at 12; 6/2/17 and 6/5/17 Emails, Goldstone & Garten; Raffel 2/8/18 302, at 3; Hicks 3/13/18 302, at 2.

671 Corallo 2/15/18 302, at 3.

672 Priebus 4/3/18 302, at 7.

673 Priebus 4/3/18 302, at 7.

674 Corallo 2/15/ 18 302, at 3; Hicks 12/7/ 17 302, at 8; Raffel 2/8/18 302, at 3.

675 Raffel 2/8/18 302, at 2-3; Hicks 3/13/18 302, at 2.

676 Raffel 2/8/18 302, at 2-3, 5; Hicks 3/13/18 302, at 2; Hicks 12/7/17 302, at 8.

677 Hicks 12/7/17 302, at 6-7; Hicks 3/13/18 302, at I.

678 Hicks 12/7/ 17 302, at 7; Hicks 3/13/18 302, at I.

679 Hicks 12/7/17 302, at 7; Hicks 3/13/18 302, at 1. Counsel for Ivanka Trump provided an attorney proffer that is consistent with Hicks's account and with the other events involving Ivanka Trump set forth in this section of the report. Kushner said that he did not recall talking to the President at this time about the June 9 meeting or the underlying emails. Kushner 4/11/18 302, at 30.

680 Hicks 3/13/18 302, at 1-2.

681   Hicks 3/13/18 302, at 2.

682 Hicks 12/7/17 302, at 8.

683 Hicks 3/13/18 302, at 2-3; Hicks 12/7/17 302, at 8.

685 Hicks 12/7I 17 302, at 8; Hicks 3/13/ 18 302, at 2.

686 Hicks 3/13/18 302, at 2; Hicks 12/7/17 302, at 9.

687 Hicks 3/13/18 302, at 2-3.

688 Hicks 3/13/18 302, at 2-3; Hicks 12/7/17 302, at 9.

689 Hicks 3/13/18 302, at 3; Hicks 12/7/17 302, at 9.

690 Hicks 3/13/18 302, at 3.

691   Hicks 3/13/18 302, at 3.

692 Hicks 12/7/17 302, at 9.

693 Raffel 2/8/18 302, at 5.

694   Raffel 2/8/18 302, at 6.

695   Raffel 2/8/18 302, at 6-7; Hicks 3/13/18 302, at 3.

696 Hicks 12/7/17 302, at 10; Hicks 3/13/18 302, at 3.

697 Hicks 12/7/17302,at 10.

699   Hicks 3/13/18 302, at 3; Hicks 12/7/17 302, at 10.

700   Hicks 3/ 13/18 302, at 3; see Hicks 12/7I17 302, at I 0.

701   Hicks 3/13/18 302, at 4.

702   Hicks 7/8/17 Notes.

703 Hicks 3/13/18 302, at 4-5; Hicks 12/7/17 302, at 11.

704   Hicks 12/7/17 302, at 11.

705 SCRO! la 000004 (7/8/17 Text Message, Hicks to Trump Jr.).

706 SCROJ Ja_000004 (7/8/17 Text Message, Hicks to Trump Jr.).

707 SCROl la_000005 (7/8/17 Text Message, Trump Jr. to Hicks).

708 SCRO l la_000005 (7/8/17 Text Message, Trump Jr. to Hicks).

709 SCRO 11 a_000005 (7/8/17 Text Message, Hicks to Trump Jr.).

710 SCRO 11 a_000006 (7/8/17 Text Message, Trump Jr. to Hicks).

711 Hicks 3/13/18 302, at 6; see Jo Becker et al., Trump Team Met With Lawyer Linked to Kremlin During Campaign, New York Times (July 8, 2017).

712 See Jo Becker et al., Trump Team Met With Lawyer Linked to Kremlin During Campaign, New York Times (July 8, 2017).

713 Hicks 3/13/18 302, at 6; Raffo! 2/8/18 302, at 9-10.

714 Hicks 12/7/17 302, at 12; Raffel 2/8/18 302, at 10.

715 Hicks 3/13/18 302, at 7.

716 Hicks 3/13/18 302, at 7.

717 See Jo Becker et al., Trump Team Met With Lawyer Linked to Kremlin During Campaign, New York Times (July 8, 2017); Raffel 2/8/18 302, at 10.

718 See Jo Becker et al., Trump Team Met With Lawyer Linked to Kremlin During Campaign, New York Times (July 8, 2017).

719 See Donald Trump Jr. gathered members ofcampaignfor meeting with Russian lawyer before election, Circa News (July 8, 2017).

720 Hicks 3/13/18 302, at 8; Corallo 2/15/18 302, at 6-7.

721 Corallo 2/15/18 302, at 7.

722 Corallo 2/15/18 302, at 7.

723 Corallo 2/15/18 302, at 7-9.

724 Corallo 2/15/18 302, at 8.

725 Corallo 2/15/18 302, at 8; Corallo 7/9/17 Notes ("Sunday 9lh - Hope calls w/ POTUS on line"). Corallo said he is" I 00% confident" that Hicks said "It will never get out" on the call. Corallo 2/15/18 302, at 9.

726 Hicks 3/13/18 302, at 9.

727 @DonaldJTrumpJR 7/11/17 (11:01 a.m. ET) Tweet; Jo Becker et al., Russian Dirt on Clinton? 'I Love It, 'Donald Trump Jr. Said, New York Times (July 11, 2017).

728 See, e.g., Peter Baker & Maggie Haberman, Rancor at White House as Russia Story Refuses to let the Page Turn, New York Times (July 11, 2017) (reporting that the President "signed off" on Trump Jr. 's statement

729 See, e.g., David Wright, Trump lawyer: President was aware of t'nothing", CNN (July 12, 2017) (quoting the President's personal attorney as saying, "I wasn't involved in the statement drafting at all nor was the President."); see also Good Morning America, ABC (July 12, 2017) ("The President didn't sign off on anything.... The President wasn't involved in that."); Meet the Press, NBC (July 16, 2017) ("I do want to be clear-the President was not involved in the drafting of the statement.").

730 Sarah Sanders, White House Daily Briefing, C-SPAN (Aug. I, 2017); Sanders 7/3/ 18 302, at 9 (the President told Sanders he "weighed in, as any father would" and knew she intended to tell the press what he said),

731 1/29/18 Letter, President's Personal Counsel to Special Counsel's Office, at 18.

732 Remarks by President Trump in Press Gaggle (June 15, 2018).

733

734 Peter Baker et al., Excerpts From The Times's Interview With Trump, New York Times (July19,2017).

735 Peter Baker et al., Excerpts From The Times 's Interview With Trump, New York Times (July19, 2017).

H. The President's Further Efforts to Have the Attorney General Take Over the Investigation

Overview

From summer 2017 through 2018, the President attempted to have Attorney General Sessions reverse his recusal, take control of the Special Counsel's investigation, and order an investigation of Hillary Clinton.

Evidence

I. The President Again Seeks to Have Sessions Reverse his Recusal

After returning Sessions's resignation letter at the end of May 2017, but before the President's July 19, 2017 New York Times interview in which he publicly criticized Sessions for recusing from the Russia investigation, the President took additional steps to have Sessions reverse his recusal.

In particular, at some point after the May 17, 2017 appointment of the Special Counsel, Sessions recalled, the President called him at home and asked if Sessions would "unrecuse" himself[736] According to Sessions, the President asked him to reverse his recusal so that Sessions could direct the Department of Justice to investigate and prosecute Hillary Clinton, and the "gist" of the conversation was that the President wanted Sessions to unrecuse from "all of it," including the Special Counsel's Russia investigation.[737] Sessions listened but did not respond, and he did not reverse his recusal or order an investigation of Clinton.[738]

In early July 2017, the President asked Staff Secretary Rob Porter what he thought of Associate Attorney General Rachel Brand.[739] Porter recalled that the President asked him if Brand was good, tough, and "on the team."[740] The President also asked if Porter thought Brand was interested in being responsible for the Special

Counsel's investigation and whether she would want to be Attorney General one day.[741] Because Porter knew Brand, the President asked him to sound her out about taking responsibility for the investigation and being Attorney General.[742] Contemporaneous notes taken by Porter show that the President told Porter to "Keep in touch with your friend," in reference to Brand.[743] Later, the President asked Porter a few times in passing whether he had spoken to Brand, but Porter did not reach out to her because he was uncomfortable with the task.[744] In asking him to reach out to Brand, Porter understood the President to want to find someone to end the Russia investigation or fire the Special Counsel, although the President never said so explicitly.[745] Porter did not contact Brand because he was sensitive to the implications of that action and did not want to be involved in a chain of events associated with an effort to end the investigation or fire the Special Counsel.[746]

McGahn recalled that during the summer of 2017, he and the President discussed the fact that if Sessions were no longer in his position the Special Counsel would report directly to a non-recused Attorney General.[747] McGahn told the President that things might not change much under a new Attorney General.[748] McGahn also recalled that in or around July 2017, the President frequently brought up his displeasure with Sessions.[749] Hicks recalled that the President viewed Sessions's recusal from the Russia investigation as an act of disloyalty.[750] In addition to criticizing Sessions's recusal, the President raised other concerns about Sessions and his job performance with McGahn and Hicks.[751]

2. Additional Efforts to Have Sessions Unrecuse or Direct Investigations Covered by his Recusal

Later in 2017, the President continued to urge Sessions to reverse his recusal from campaign-related investigations and considered replacing Sessions with an Attorney General who would not be recused.

On October 16, 2017, the President met privately with Sessions and said that the Department of Justice was not investigating individuals and events that the President thought the Department should be investigating.[752]   According to contemporaneous notes taken by Porter, who was at the meeting, the President mentioned Clinton's emails and said, "Don't have to tell us, just take [a] look."[753] Sessions did not offer any assurances or promises to the President that the Department of Justice would comply with that request.[754] Two days later, on October 18, 2017, the President tweeted, "Wow, FBI confirms report that James Corney drafted letter exonerating Crooked Hillary Clinton long before investigation was complete. Many people not interviewed, including Clinton herself. Corney stated under oath that he didn't do this-obviously a fix? Where is Justice Dept?"[755]   On October 29, 2017, the President tweeted that there was "ANGER & UNITY" over a "lack of investigation" of Clinton and "the Corney fix," and concluded: "DO SOMETHING!"[756]

On December 6, 2017, five days after Flynn pleaded guilty to lying about his contacts with the Russian government, the President asked to speak with Sessions in the Oval Office at the end of a cabinet meeting.[757]   During that Oval Office meeting, which Porter attended, the President again suggested that Sessions could "unrecuse," which Porter linked to taking back supervision of the Russia investigation and directing an investigation of Hillary Clinton.[758]   According to contemporaneous notes taken by Porter, the President said, "I don't know if you could un-recuse yourself. You'd be a hero. Not telling you to do anything. Dershowitz says POTUS can get involved. Can order AG to investigate. I don't want to get involved. I'm not going to get involved. I'm not going to do anything or direct you to do anything. I just want to be treated fairly."[759] According to Porter's notes, Sessions responded, "We are taking steps; whole new leadership team. Professionals; will operate according to the law."[760] Sessions also said, "I never saw anything that was improper," which Porter thought was noteworthy because it did not fit with the previous discussion about Clinton.[761]

Porter understood Sessions to be reassuring the President that he was on the President's team.[762]

At the end of December, the President told the New York Times it was "too bad" that Sessions had recused himself from the Russia investigation.[763] When asked whether Holder had been a more loyal Attorney General to President Obama than Sessions was to him, the President said, "I don't want to get into loyalty, but I will tell you that, I will say this: Holder protected President Obama. Totally protected him. When you look at the things that they did, and Holder protected the president. And I have great respect for that, I'll be honest."[764]

Later in January, the President brought up the idea of replacing Sessions and told Porter that he wanted to "clean house" at the Department of Justice.[765] In a meeting in the White House residence that Porter attended on January 27, 2018, Porter recalled that the President talked about the great attorneys he had in the past with successful win records, such as Roy Cohn and Jay Goldberg, and said that one of his biggest failings as President was that he had not surrounded himself with good attorneys, citing Sessions as an example.[766] The President raised Sessions's recusal and brought up and criticized the Special Counsel's investigation.[767]

Over the next several months, the President continued to criticize Sessions in tweets and media interviews and on several occasions appeared to publicly encourage him to take action in the Russia investigation despite his recusal.[768] On June 5, 2018, for example, the President tweeted, "The Russian Witch Hunt Hoax continues, all because Jeff Sessions didn't tell me he was going to recuse himself ... I would have quickly picked someone else. So much time and money wasted, so many lives ruined ... and Sessions knew better than most that there was No Collusion!"[769] On August 1, 2018, the President tweeted that "Attorney General Jeff Sessions should stop this Rigged Witch Hunt right now."[770] On August 23, 2018, the President publicly criticized Sessions in a press interview and suggested that prosecutions at the Department of Justice were politically motivated because Paul Manafort had been prosecuted but Democrats had not.[771] The President said, "I put in an Attorney General that never took control of the Justice Department, Jeff Sessions. That day, Sessions issued a press statement that said, "I took control of the Department of Justice the day I was sworn in .... While I am Attorney General, the actions of the Department of Justice will not be improperly influenced by political considerations.

The next day, the President tweeted a response: "'Department of Justice will not be improperly influenced by political considerations.' Jeff, this is GREAT, what everyone wants, so look into all of the corruption on the 'other side' including deleted Emails, Corney lies & leaks, Mueller conflicts, McCabe, Strzok, Page, Ohr, FISA abuse, Christopher Steele & his phony and corrupt Dossier, the Clinton Foundation, illegal surveillance of Trump campaign, Russian collusion by Dems – and so much more. Open up the papers & documents without redaction? Come on Jeff, you can do it, the country is waiting!"[774]

On November 7, 2018, the day after the midterm elections, the President replaced Sessions with Sessions's chief of staff as Acting Attorney General.[775]

Analysis

In analyzing the President's efforts to have Sessions unrecuse himself and regain control of the Russia investigation, the following considerations and evidence are relevant to the elements of obstruction of justice:

a.   Obstructive act.   To determine if the President's efforts to have the Attorney General unrecuse could qualify as an obstructive act, it would be necessary to assess evidence on whether those actions would naturally impede the Russia investigation. That inquiry would take into account the supervisory role that the Attorney General, if unrecused, would play in the Russia investigation. It also would have to take into account that the Attorney General's recusal covered other campaign-related matters. The inquiry would not turn on what Attorney General Sessions would actually do if unrecused, but on whether the efforts to reverse his recusal would naturally have had the effect of impeding the Russia investigation.

On multiple occasions in 2017, the President spoke with Sessions about reversing his recusal so that he could take over the Russia investigation and begin an investigation and prosecution of Hillary Clinton. For example, in early summer 2017, Sessions recalled the President asking him to unrecuse, but Sessions did not take it as a directive. When the President raised the issue again in December 2017, the President said, as recorded by Porter, "Not telling you to do anything.... I'm not going to get involved. I'm not going to do anything or direct you to do anything. I just want to be treated fairly." The duration of the President's efforts-which spanned from March 2017 to August 2018-and the fact that the President repeatedly criticized Sessions in public and in private for failing to tell the President that he would have to recuse is relevant to assessing whether the President's efforts to have Sessions unrecuse could qualify as obstructive acts.

b. Nexus to an official proceeding. As described above, by mid-June 2017, the existence of a grand jury investigation supervised by the Special Counsel was public knowledge. In addition, in July 2017, a different grand jury supervised by the Special Counsel was empaneled in the District of Columbia, and the press reported on the existence of this grand jury in early August 2017.776 Whether the conduct towards the Attorney General would have a foreseeable impact on those proceedings turns on much of the same evidence discussed above with respect to the obstructive-act element.

c. **Intent.** There is evidence that at least one purpose of the President's conduct toward Sessions was to have Sessions assume control over the Russia investigation and supervise it in a way that would restrict its scope. By the summer of 2017, the President was aware that the Special Counsel was investigating him personally for obstruction of justice. And in the wake of the disclosures of emails about the June 9 meeting between Russians and senior members of the campaign, see Volume IT, Section ILG, supra, it was evident that the investigation into the campaign now included the President's son, son-in-law, and former campaign manager. The President had previously and unsuccessfully sought to have Sessions publicly announce that the Special Counsel investigation would be confined to future election interference. Yet Sessions remained recused. In December 2017, shortly after Flynn pleaded guilty, the President spoke to Sessions in the Oval Office with only Porter present and told Sessions that he would be a hero if he unrecused. Porter linked that request to the President's desire that Sessions take back supervision of the Russia investigation and direct an investigation of Hillary Clinton. The President said in that meeting that he "just want[ed) to be treated fairly," which could reflect his perception that it was unfair that he was being investigated while Hillary Clinton was not. But a principal effect of that act would be to restore supervision of the Russia investigation to the Attorney General-a position that the President frequently suggested should be occupied by someone like Eric Holder and Bobby Kennedy, who the President described as protecting their presidents. A reasonable inference from those statements and the President's actions is that the President believed that an unrecused Attorney General would play a protective role and could shield the President from the ongoing Russia investigation.

******

736 Sessions 1/17/18 302, at 15. That was the second time that the President asked Sessions to reverse his recusal from campaign-related investigations. See Volume H, Section Tl.C.1, supra (describing President's March 2017 request at Mar-a-Lago for Sessions to unrecuse).

737 Sessions 1/17/18 302, at 15.

738 Sessions 1/17/18 302, at 15.

739 Porter 4/13/18 302, at I 1; Porter 5/8/18 302, at 6.

740 Porter 4/ I 3/I 8 302, at 11; Porter 5/8/ 18 302, at 6.

741 Porter 4/13/18 302, at 11; Porter 5/8/18 302, at 6. Because of Sessions's recusal, if Rosenstein were no longer in his position, Brand would, by default, become the DOJ official in charge of supervising the Special Counsel's investigation, and if both Sessions and Rosenstein were removed, Brand would be next in line to become Acting Attorney General for all DOJ matters. See 28 U.S.C. § 508.

742 Porter 4/ 13/ 18 302, at I 1; Porter 5/8/ 18 302, at 6.

743 SC RRP000020 (Poiter 7/10/17 Notes).

744 Porter 4/ 13/18 302, at I 1-12.

745 Porter 4/ 13/18 302, at 11-12.

746 Porter 4/13/18 302, at 11-12. Brand confirmed that no one ever raised with her the prospect of taking over the Russia investigation or becoming Attorney General. Brand 1/29/19 302, at 2.

747 McGahn 12/14/17 302, at 11.

748 McGahn 12/14/17 302, at 11.

749 McGahn 12/14/17 302, at 9.150 Hicks 3/13/18 302, at 10.

751 McGahn 12/14/17 302, at 9; Hicks 3/13/18 302, at I 0

752 Porter 5/8/18 302, at 10.

753 SC_RRP000024 (Porter I 0/16/17 Notes); see Porter 5/8/18 302, at I 0.

754 Porter 5/8/18 302, at 10.

755 @realDonaldTrump I 0/18/17 (6:21 a.m. ET) Tweet; @realDonaldTrump I 0/18/17 (6:27 a.m. ET) Tweet.

756@rea!DonaldTrump 10/29/17 (9:53 a.m. ET) Tweet; @realDonaldTrump 10/29/17 (10:02 a.m. ET) Tweet; @realDonaldTrump I 0/29/17 (I 0: 17 a.m. ET) Tweet.

757 Porter 4/13/18 302, at 5-6; see SC_RRP00003 1 (Porter 12/6/17 Notes) C' l 2:45pm With the President, Gen. Kelly, and Sessions (who I pulled in after the Cabinet meeting)"); SC_RRP000033 (Porter

12/6/17 Notes) ("Post-cabinet meeting - POTUS asked me to get AG Sessions. Asked me to stay. Also COS Kelly.").

758 Porter 5/8/18 302, at 12; Porter 4/ 13/18 302, at 5-6.

759 SC_RRP000033 (Porter 12/6/17 Notes); see Porter 4/13/18 302, at 6; Porter 5/8/18 302, at 12.

760 SC_RRP000033 (Porter 12/6/17 Notes); see Porter 4/13/18 302, at 6.

761 SC_RRP000033 (Porter 12/6/17 Notes); Porter 4/13/18 302, at 6.

762 Porter 4/ 13/18 302, at 6-7.

763 Michael S. Schmidt & Michael D. Shear, Trump Says Russia Inquiry Makes U.S. "Look Very Bad", New York Times (Dec. 28, 2017).

764 Michael S. Schmidt & Michael D. Shear, Trump Says Russia Inquiry Makes U.S. "Look Very Bad", New York Times (Dec. 28, 2017).

765 Porter 4/13/18 302, at 14.

766 Porter 5/8/ 18 302, at 15. Contemporaneous notes Porter took of the conversation state, "Roy Cohn (14-0) I Jay Goldberg (12-0)." SC_RRP000047 (Potter I /27/18 Notes).

767 Porter 5/8/18 302, at 15-16.

768 See, e.g.,@realDonaldTrurnp 2/28/18 (9:34 a.rn. ET) Tweet ("Why is A.G. Jeff Sessions asking the Inspector General to investigate potentially massive FISA abuse. Will take forever, has no prosecutorial power and already late with reports on Corney etc.   Isn't the I.G. an Obama guy?   Why not use Justice Department lawyers? DISGRACEFUL!");@realDonaldTrump 4/7/J 8 (4:52 p.m. ET) Tweet ("Lawmakers of the House Judiciary Committee are angrily accusing the Department of Justice of missing the Thursday Deadline for turning over UNREDACTED Documents relating to FISA abuse, FBI, Corney, Lynch, McCabe, Clinton Emails and much more. Slow walking- what is going on? BAD!"); @realDonaldTrump
4/22/18 (8:22 a.m. ET) Tweet ("'GOP Lawmakers asking Sessions to Investigate Corney and Hillary
Clinton.' @FoxNews Good luck with that request!"); @realDonaldTrump 12/16/18 (3:37 p.m. ET) Tweet
769 @realDonaldTrump 6/5/18 (7:31 a.m. ET) Tweet.

770 @realDonaldTrump 8/1/18 (9:24 a.m. ET) Tweet.
771 Fox & Friends Interview ofPresident Trump, Fox News (Aug. 23, 2018).
772 Fox & Friends Interview of President Trump, Fox News (Aug. 23, 2018).
773 Sessions 8/23/18 Press Statement.
774 @realDonaldTrump 8/24/18 (6: 17 a.m. ET) Tweet;@ realDonaldTrump 8/24/18 (6:28 a.m. ET) Tweet.
775 @realDonaldTrump 11/7/18 (2:44 p.m. ET) Tweet.
776 E.g., Del Quentin Wilbur & Byron Tau, Special Counsel Robert Mueller Impanels Washington Grand Jury in Russia Probe, Wall Street Journal (Aug. 3, 2017); Carol D. Leonnig et al., Special Counsel Mueller using grandjury in federal court in Washington as part ofRussia investigation, Washington Post (Aug. 3, 2017).

I. The President Orders McGahn to Deny that the President Tried to Fire the Special Counsel

Overview

In late January 2018, the media reported that in June 2017 the President had ordered McGahn to have the Special Counsel fired based on purported conflicts of interest but McGahn had refused, saying he would quit instead. After the story broke, the President, through his personal counsel and two aides, sought to have McGahn deny that he had been directed to remove the Special Counsel. Each time he was approached, McGahn responded that he would not refute the press accounts because they were accurate in reporting on the President's effort to have the Special Counsel removed. The President later personally met with McGahn in the Oval Office with only the Chief of Staff present and tried to get McGahn to say that the President never ordered him to fire the Special Counsel. McGahn refused and insisted his memory of the President's direction to remove the Special Counsel was accurate. In that same meeting, the President challenged McGahn for taking notes of his discussions with the President and asked why he had told Special Counsel investigators that he had been directed to have the Special Counsel removed.

Evidence

I. The Press Reports that the President Tried to Fire the Special Counsel

On January 25, 2018, the New York Times reported that in June 2017, the President had ordered McGahn to have the Department of Justice fire the Special Counsel."? According to the article, "[a]mid the first wave of news media reports that Mr. Mueller was examining a possible obstruction case, the president began to argue that Mr. Mueller had three conflicts of interest that disqualified him from overseeing the investigation."[778] The article further reported that "[a]fter receiving the president's order to fire Mr. Mueller, the White House counsel ... refused to ask the Justice Department to dismiss the special counsel, saying he would quit instead."[779]

The article stated that the president "ultimately backed down after the White House counsel threatened to resign rather than carry out the directive."[780] After the article was published, the President dismissed the story when asked about it by reporters, saying, "Fake news, folks. Fake news. A typical New York Times fake story."[781]

The next day, the Washington Post reported on the same event but added that McGahn had not told the President directly that he intended to resign rather than carry out the directive to have the Special Counsel terminated.[782] In that respect, the Post story clarified the Times story, which could be read to suggest that McGahn had told the President of his intention to quit, causing the President to back down from the order to have the Special Counsel fired.[783]

2. The President Seeks to Have McGahn Dispute the Press Reports

On January 26, 2018, the President's personal counsel called McGahn's attorney and said that the President wanted McGahn to put out a statement denying that he had been asked to tire the Special Counsel and that he had threatened to quit in protest.P" McGahn's attorney spoke with McGahn about that request and then called the President's personal counsel to relay that McGahn would not make a statement.I'" McGahn's attorney informed the President's personal counsel that the Times story was accurate in reporting that the President wanted the Special Counsel removed.[786] Accordingly, McGahn's attorney said, although the article was inaccurate in some other respects, McGahn could not comply with the President's request to dispute the story.[787] Hicks recalled relaying to the President that one of his attorneys had spoken to McGahn's attorney about the issue.[788]

Also on January 26, 2017, Hicks recalled that the President asked Sanders to contact McGahn about the story.[789] McGahn told Sanders there was no need to respond and indicated that some of the article was accurate.P? Consistent with that position, McGahn did not correct the *Times* story.

On February 4, 2018, Priebus appeared on Meet the Press and said he had not heard the President say that he wanted the Special Counsel fired.[791] After Priebus's appearance, the President called Priebus and said he did a great job on Meet the Press.[792] The President also told Priebus that the President had "never said any of those things about" the Special Counsel.[793]

The next day, on February 5, 2018, the President complained about the *Times* article to Porter.[794] The President told Porter that the article was "bullshit" and he had not sought to terminate the Special Counsel.[795] The President said that McGahn leaked to the media to make himself look good.[796] The President then directed Porter to tell McGahn to create a record to make clear that the President never directed McGahn to fire the Special Counsel."? Porter thought the matter should be handled by the White House communications office, but the President said he wanted McGahn to write a letter to the file "for our records" and wanted something beyond a press statement to demonstrate that the reporting was inaccurate.[798] The President referred to McGahn as a "lying bastard" and said that he wanted a record from him.[799] Porter recalled the President saying something to the effect of, "If he doesn't write a letter, then maybe I'll have to get rid of him."[800]

Later that day, Porter spoke to McGahn to deliver the President's message.[""] Porter told McGahn that he had to write a letter to dispute that he was ever ordered to terminate the Special Counsel. McGahn shrugged off the request, explaining that the media reports were true.[803]
McGahn told Porter that the President had been insistent on firing the Special Counsel and that McGahn had planned to resign rather than carry out the order, although he had not personally told the President he intended to quit.[804] Porter told McGahn that the President suggested that McGahn would be fired if he did not write the letter.[805] McGahn dismissed the threat, saying that the optics would be terrible if the President followed through with firing him on that basis.[806] McGahn said he would not write the letter the President had requested.[P"] Porter said that to his knowledge the issue of McGahn's letter never came up with the President again, but Porter did recall telling Kelly about his conversation with McGahn.[808]

The next day, on February 6, 2018, Kelly scheduled time for McGahn to meet with him and the President in the Oval Office to discuss the Times article.[809] The morning of the meeting, the President's personal counsel called McGahn's attorney and said that the President was going to be speaking with McGahn and McGahn could not resign no matter what happened in the meeting.

The President began the Oval Office meeting by telling McGahn that the New York Times story did not "look good" and McGahn needed to correct it.[811] McGahn recalled the President said, "I never said to fire Mueller. I never said 'fire.' This story doesn't look good. You need to correct this. You're the White House counsel."[812]

In response, McGahn acknowledged that he had not told the President directly that he planned to resign, but said that the story was otherwise accurate.[813] The President asked McGahn, "Did I say the word 'fire'?"[814] McGahn responded, "What you said is, 'Call Rod [Rosenstein], tell Rod that Mueller has conflicts and can't be the Special Counsel.'"[815] The President responded, "I never said that."[816] The President said he merely wanted McGahn to raise the conflicts issue with Rosenstein and leave it to him to decide what to do.[817] McGahn told the President he did not understand the conversation that way and instead had heard, "Call Rod. There are conflicts. Mueller has to go."[818] The President asked McGahn whether he would "do a correction," and McGahn said no.[819] McGahn thought the President was testing his mettle to see how committed McGahn was to what happened.[820] Kelly described the meeting as "a little tense."[821]

The President also asked McGahn in the meeting why he had told Special Counsel's Office investigators that the President had told him to have the Special Counsel removed.[822] McGahn responded that he had to and that his conversations with the President were not protected by attorney-client privilege.[823] The President then asked, "What about these notes? Why do you take notes? Lawyers don't take notes. I never had a lawyer who took notes."[824] McGahn responded that he keeps notes because he is a "real lawyer" and explained that notes create a record and are not a bad thing.[825] The President said, "I've had a lot of great lawyers, like Roy Cohn. He did not take notes."[826]

After the Oval Office meeting concluded, Kelly recalled McGahn telling him that McGahn and the President "did have that conversation" about removing the Special Counsel.[827] McGahn recalled that Kelly said that he had pointed out to the President after the Oval Office that McGahn had not backed down and would not budge.[828] Following the Oval Office meeting, the President's personal counsel called McGahn's counsel and relayed that the President was "fine" with McGahn.[829]

Analysis

In analyzing the President's efforts to have McGahn deny that he had been ordered to have the Special Counsel removed, the following evidence is relevant to the elements of obstruction of justice:

a.   Obstructive act. The President's repeated efforts to get McGahn to create a record denying that the President had directed him to remove the Special Counsel would qualify as an obstructive act if it had the natural tendency to constrain McGahn from testifying truthfully or to undermine his credibility as a potential witness if he testified consistently with his memory, rather than with what the record said.

There is some evidence that at the time the New York Times and Washington Post stories were published in late January 2018, the President believed the stories were wrong and that he had never told McGahn to have Rosenstein remove the Special Counsel. The President correctly understood that McGahn had not told the President directly that he planned to resign. Tn addition, the President told Priebus and Porter that he had not sought to terminate the Special Counsel, and in the Oval Office meeting with McGahn, the President said, "I never said to fire Mueller. I never said 'fire.'" That evidence could indicate that the President was not attempting to persuade McGahn to change his story but was instead offering his own-but different-recollection of the substance of his June 2017 conversations with McGahn and McGahn's reaction to them.

Other evidence cuts against that understanding of the President's conduct. As previously described, see Volume II, Section ILE, supra, substantial evidence supports

McGahn's account that the President had directed him to have the Special Counsel removed, including the timing and context of the President's directive; the manner in which McGahn reacted; and the fact that the President had been told the conflicts were insubstantial, were being considered by the Department of Justice, and should be raised with the President's personal counsel rather than brought to McGahn. In addition, the President's subsequent denials that he had told McGahn to have the Special Counsel removed were carefully worded. When first asked about the New York Times story, the President said, "Fake news, folks. Fake news. A typical New York Times fake story." And when the President spoke with McGahn in the Oval Office, he focused on whether he had used the word "fire," saying, "I never said to fire Mueller. I never said 'fire'" and "Did I say the word 'fire'?" The President's assertion in the Oval Office meeting that he had never directed McGahn to have the Special Counsel removed thus runs counter to the evidence.

In addition, even if the President sincerely disagreed with McGahn's memory of the June 17, 2017 events, the evidence indicates that the President knew by the time of the Oval Office meeting that McGahn's account differed and that McGahn was firm in his views. Shortly after the story broke, the President's counsel told McGahn's counsel that the President wanted McGahn to make a statement denying he had been asked to fire the Special Counsel, but McGahn responded through his counsel that that aspect of the story was accurate and he therefore could not comply with the President's request. The President then directed Sanders to tell McGahn to correct the story, but McGahn told her he would not do so because the story was accurate in reporting on the President's order. Consistent with that position, McGahn never issued a correction. More than a week later, the President brought up the issue again with Porter, made comments indicating the President thought McGahn had leaked the story, and directed Porter to have McGahn create a record denying that the President had tried to fire the Special Counsel. At that point, the President said he might "have to get rid of" McGahn if McGahn did not comply. McGahn again refused and told Porter, as he had told Sanders and as his counsel had told the President's counsel, that the President had in fact ordered him to have Rosenstein remove the Special Counsel. That evidence indicates that by the time of the Oval Office meeting the President was aware that McGahn did not think the story was false and did not want to issue a statement or create a written record denying facts that McGahn believed to be true. The President nevertheless persisted and asked McGahn to repudiate facts that McGahn had repeatedly said were accurate.

      b.   Nexus to an official proceeding. By January 2018, the Special Counsel's use of a grand jury had been further confirmed by the return of several indictments. The President also was aware that the Special Counsel was investigating obstruction-related events because, among other reasons, on January 8, 2018, the Special Counsel's Office provided his counsel with a detailed list of topics for a possible interview with the President.P? The President knew that McGahn had personal knowledge of many of the events the Special Counsel was investigating and that McGahn had already been interviewed by Special Counsel investigators. And in the Oval Office meeting, the President indicated he knew that McGahn had told the Special Counsel's Office about the President's effort to remove the Special Counsel. The President challenged McGahn for disclosing that information and for taking notes that he viewed as creating unnecessary legal exposure. That evidence indicates the President's awareness that the June 17, 2017 events were relevant to the Special Counsel's investigation and any grand jury investigation that might grow out of it.

      To establish a nexus, it would be necessary to show that the President's actions would have the natural tendency to affect such a proceeding or that they would hinder, delay, or prevent the communication of information to investigators. Because McGahn had spoken to Special Counsel investigators before January 2018, the President could not have been seeking to influence his prior statements in those interviews. But because McGahn had repeatedly spoken to investigators and the obstruction inquiry was not complete, it was foreseeable that he would be interviewed again on obstruction-related topics. If the President were focused solely on a press strategy in seeking to have McGahn refute the New York Times article, a nexus to a proceeding or to further investigative interviews would not be shown. But the President's efforts to have McGahn write a letter "for our records" approximately ten days after the stories had come out-well past the typical time to issue a correction for a news story-indicates the President was not focused solely on a press strategy, but instead likely contemplated the ongoing investigation and any proceedings arising from it.

c.   Intent. Substantial evidence indicates that in repeatedly urging McGahn to dispute that he was ordered to have the Special Counsel terminated, the President acted for the purpose of influencing McGahn's account in order to deflect or prevent further scrutiny of the President's conduct towards the investigation.

Several facts support that conclusion. The President made repeated attempts to get McGahn to change his story. As described above, by the time of the last attempt, the evidence suggests that the President had been told on multiple occasions that McGahn believed the President had ordered him to have the Special Counsel terminated. McGahn interpreted his encounter with the President in the Oval Office as an attempt to test his mettle and see how committed he was to his memory of what had occurred. The President had already laid the groundwork for pressing McGahn to alter his account by telling Porter that it might be necessary to fire McGahn if he did not deny the story, and Porter relayed that statement to McGahn. Additional evidence of the President's intent may be gleaned from the fact that his counsel was sufficiently alarmed by the prospect of the President's meeting with McGahn that he called McGahn's counsel and said that McGahn could not resign no matter what happened in the Oval Office that day. The President's counsel was well aware of McGahn's resolve not to issue what he believed to be a false account of events despite the President's request. Finally, as noted above, the President brought up the Special Counsel investigation in his Oval Office meeting with McGahn and criticized him for telling this Office about the June 17, 2017 events. The President's statements reflect his understanding-and his displeasure-that those events would be part of an obstruction-of-justice inquiry.

******

777 Michael S. Schmidt & Maggie Haberman, Trump Ordered Mueller Fired, but Backed Off When White House Counsel Threatened to Quit, New York Times (Jan. 25. 2018).

778 Michael S. Schmidt & Maggie Haberman, Trump OrderedMueller Fired, but Backed Off When White House Counsel Threatened to Quit, New York Times (Jan. 25. 2018).

779 Michael S. Schmidt & Maggie Haberman, Trump OrderedMueller Fired, but Backed Off When White House Counsel Threatened to Quit, New York Times (Jan. 25. 2018).

780 Michael S. Schmidt & Maggie Haberman, Trump OrderedMueller Fired, but Backed Off When White House Counsel Threatened to Quit, New York Times (Jan. 25. 2018).

781 Sophie Tatum & Kara Scannell, Trump denies he calledfor Mueller's firing, CNN (Jan. 26, 2018); Michael S. Schmidt & Maggie Haberman, Trump Ordered Mueller Fired, but Backed Off WhenWhite House Counsel Threatened to Quit, New York Times (Jan. 25, 2018).

782 The Post article stated, "Despite internal objections, Trump decided to assert that Mueller had unacceptable conflicts of interest and moved to remove him from his position. . . . In response, McGahn said he would not remain at the White House if Trump went through with the move.... McGahn did not deliver his resignation threat directly to Trump but was serious about his threat to leave." Rosalind S. Helderman & Josh Dawsey, Trump moved to fire Mueller in June, bringing White House counsel to the brink ofleaving, Washington Post (Jan. 26, 2018).

783 Rosalind S. Helderman & Josh Dawsey, Trump moved to fire Mueller in June, bringing White House counsel to the brink ofleaving, Washington Post (Jan. 26, 2018); see McGahn 3/8/17 302, at 3-4.

784 McGahn 3/8/18 302, at 3 (agent note).

785 McGahn 3/8/18 302, at 3 (agent note).

786 McGahn 3/8/18 302, at 3-4 (agent note).

787 McGahn 3/8/18 302, at 4 (agent note).

788 Hicks 3/13/18 302, at 11. Hicks also recalled that the President spoke on the phone that day with Chief of Staff John Kelly and that the President said Kelly told him that McGahn had totally refuted the story and was going to put out a statement. Hicks 3/13/18 302, at 11. But Kelly said that he did not speak to McGahn when the article came out and did not tell anyone he had done so. Kelly 8/2/18 302, at1-2.

789 Hicks 3/13/18 302, at 11. Sanders did not recall whether the President asked her to speak to McGahn or if she did it on her own. Sanders 7/23/18 302, at 2.

790 Sanders 7/23/18 302, at 1-2.

791 Meet the Press Interview with Reince Priebus, NBC (Feb. 4, 2018).

792 Priebus 4/3/18 302, at 10.

793 Priebus 4/3/18 302, at 10.

794 Porter 4/13/18 302, at 16-17. Porter did not recall the timing of this discussion with the President. Porter 4/13/18 302, at 17. Evidence indicates it was February 5, 2018. On the back of a pocket card dated February 5, 2018, Porter took notes that are consistent with his description of the discussion: "COS: (1) Letter from OM - Never threatened to quit- DJT never told him to fire M." SC_RRP000053 (Porter Undated Notes). Porter said it was possible he took the notes on a day other than February 5. Porter 4/13/18 302, at 17. But Porter also said that "COS" referred to matters he wanted to

discuss with Chief of Staff Kelly, Porter 4/13/18 302, at 17, and Kelly took notes dated February 5, 2018, that state "POTUS - Don McGahn letter - Mueller+ resigning." WHOOOOl 7684 (Kelly 2/5/18 Notes). Kelly said he did not recall what the notes meant, but thought the President may have "mused" abo.ut having McGahn write a letter. Kelly 8/2/18 302, at 3. McGahn recalled that Porter spoke with him about the President's request about two weeks after the New York Times story was published, which is consistent with the discussion taking place on or about February 5. McGahn 3/8/18 302, at 4.

795 Porter 4/13/18 302, at 17.
796 Porter 4/13/18 302, at 17.
797 Porter 4/13/18 302, at 17.
798 Porter4/13/18 302, at 17; Porter 5/8/18 302, at 18.
799 Porter 4/13/18 302, at 17; Porter 5/8/18 302, at 18.
800 Porter 4/13/18 302, at 17.
801 Porter 4/13/18 302, at 17; McGahn 3/8/18 302, at 4.
802 Porter 4/13/18 302, at 17; McGahn 3/8/18 302, at 4.
803 Porter 4/13/18 302, at 17; McGahn 3/8/18 302, at 4.
804 Porter 4/13/18 302, at 17; McGahn 3/8/18 302, at 4.
805 Porter 4/13/18 302, at 17; McGahn 3/8/18 302, at 4.
806 Porter 4/13/18 302, at 17-18; McGahn 3/8/18 302, at 4.
807 McGahn 3/8/18 302, at 4.
808 Potter 4/ 13/18 302, at 18.
809 McGahn 3/8/ 18 302, at 4; WHOOO 17685 (Kelly 2/6/ 18 Notes). McGahn recalled that, before the Oval Office meeting, he told Kelly that he was not inclined to fix the article. McGahn 3/8/ 18 302, at 4.
810 McGahn 3/8/18 302, at 5 (agent note); 2/26/19 Email, Counsel for Don McGahn to Special Counsel's Office (confirming February 6, 2018 date of call from the President's personal counsel).

811 McGahn 3/8/18 302, at 4; Kelly 8/2/18 302, at 2.
812 McGahn 3/8/18 302, at 4; Kelly 8/2/18 302, at 2.
813 McGahn 3/8/18 302, at 4.
814 McGahn 3/8/18 302, at 4; Kelly 8/2/18 302, at 2.
815 McGahn 3/8/18 302, at 5.
816 McGahn 3/8/18 302, at 5.
817 McGahn 3/8/18 302, at 5.
818 McGahn 3/8/18 302, at 5.
819 McGahn 3/8/18 302, at 5; Kelly 8/2/18 302, at 2.
820 McGahn 3/8/18 302, at 5.
821 Kelly 8/2/18 302, at 2.
822 McGahn 3/8/18 302, at 5.
823 McGahn 3/8/18 302, at 5.
824 McGahn 3/8/18 302, at 5. McGahn said the President was referring to Donaldson's notes, which the President thought of as McGahn's notes. McGahn 3/8/18 302, at 5.
825 McGahn 3/8/18 302, at 5.

826 McGahn 3/8/18 302, at 5.

827 Kelly 8/2/ 18 302, at 2

828 McGahn 3/8/18 302, at 5.   Kelly did not recall discussing the Oval Office meeting with the President after the fact. Kelly 8/2/18 302, at 2.   Handwritten notes taken by Kelly state, "Don[:] Mueller discussion in June. - Bannon Priebus - came out okay." WHOOOO 17685 (Kelly 2/6/18 Notes).

829 McGahn 3/8/18 302, at 5 (agent note).

830 1/29/18 Letter, President's Personal Counsel to Special Counsel's Office, at 1-2 ("In our conversation of January 8, your office identified the following topics as areas you desired to address with the President in order to complete your investigation on the subjects of alleged collusion and obstruction of justice"; listing 16 topics).

J.   The President's Conduct Towards Flynn, Manafort, mllll

Overview

In addition to the interactions with McGahn described above, the President has taken other actions directed at possible witnesses in the Special Counsel's investigation, including Flynn, Manafort, mand as described in the next section, Cohen. When Flynn withdrew from a joint defense agreement with the President, the President's personal counsel stated that Flynn's actions would be viewed as reflecting "hostility" towards the President. During Manafort's prosecution and while the jury was deliberating, the President repeatedly stated that Manafolt was bein treated unfair! and made it known that Manafort could receive a ardon.

Evidence

Conduct Directed at Michael Flynn

As previously noted, see Volume II, Section II.B, supra, the President asked for Flynn's resignation on February 13, 2017. Following Flynn's resignation, the President made positive public comments about Flynn, describing him as a "wonderful man," "a fine person," and a "very good person."[831] The President also privately asked advisors to pass messages to Flynn conveying that the President still cared about him and encouraging him to stay strong.[832]

In late November 2017, Flynn began to cooperate with this Office. On November 22, 2017, Flynn withdrew from a joint defense agreement he had with the President.[833] Flynn's counsel told the President's personal counsel and counsel for the White House that Flynn could no longer have confidential communications with the White House or the President.[834]   Later that night, the President's personal counsel left a voicemail for Flynn's counsel that said:

> I understand your situation, but let me see if I can't state it in starker terms. . . .   (T]t wouldn't surprise me if you've gone on to make a deal with ... the government. ... If_ _   there's information that implicates the President, then we've got a national security issue, . . . so, you know, . . . we need some kind of heads up. Um, just for the sake of protecting all our interests if we can. . . . [R]emember what we've always said about the President and his feelings toward Flynn and, that still remains .... [835]

On November 23, 2017, Flynn's attorneys returned the call from the President's personal counsel to acknowledge receipt of the voicemail.[836]   Flynn's attorneys reiterated that they were no longer in a position to share information under any sort of privilege.[837]   According to Flynn's attorneys, the President's personal counsel was indignant and vocal in his disagreement.[838]   The President's personal counsel said that he interpreted what they said to him as a reflection of Flynn's hostility towards the President and that he planned to inform his client of that interpretation.[839]

Flynn's attorneys understood that statement to be an attempt to make them reconsider their position because the President's personal counsel believed that Flynn would be disturbed to know that such a message would be conveyed to the President.F'?

On December 1, 2017, Flynn pleaded guilty to making false statements pursuant to a cooperation agreement.[841]   The next day, the President told the press that he was not concerned about what Flynn might tell the Special Counsel.[842]   In response to a question about whether the President still stood behind Flynn, the President responded, "We' ll see what happens."[843]   Over the next several days, the President made public statements expressing sympathy for

Flynn and indicating he had not been treated fairly.[844] On December 15, 2017, the President responded to a press inquiry about whether he was considering a pardon for Flynn by saying, "I don't want to talk about pardons for Michael Flynn yet. We'll see what happens. Let's see. I can say this: When you look at what's gone on with the FBI and with the Justice Department, people are very, very angry."s4s

2. Conduct Directed at Paul Manafort

On October 27, 2017, a grand jury in the District of Columbia indicted Manafort and former deputy campaign manager Richard Gates on multiple felony counts, and on February 22, 2018, a grand jury in the Eastern District of Virginia indicted Manafort and Gates on additional felony counts.[846] The charges in both cases alleged criminal conduct by Manafort that began as early as 2005 and continued through 2018.[847]

In January 2018, Manafort told Gates that he had talked to the President's personal counsel and they were "going to take care of us."[848] Manafort told Gates it was stupid to plead, saying that he had been in touch with the President's personal counsel and repeating that they should "sit tight" and "we'll be taken care of."[849] Gates asked Manafort outright if anyone mentioned pardons and Manafort said no one used that word.[850]

As the proceedings against Manafort progressed in court, the President told Porter that he never liked Manafort and that Manafort did not know what he was doing on the campaign.[851] The President discussed with aides whether and in what way Manafort might be cooperating with the Special Counsel's investigation, and whether Manafort knew any information that would be harmful to the President.[852]

In public, the President made statements criticizing the prosecution and suggesting that Manafort was being treated unfairly. On June 15, 2018, before a scheduled court hearing that day on whether Manafort's bail should be revoked based on new charges that Manafort had tampered with witnesses while out on bail, the President told the press, "I feel badly about a lot of them because I think a lot of it is very unfair. I mean, I look at some of them where they go back 12 years. Like Manafort has nothing to do with our campaign. But I feel so–I tell you, I feel a little badly about it. They went back 12 years to get things that he did 12 years ago? ... I feel badly for some people, because they've gone back 12 years to find things about somebody, and I don't think it's right."[853] In response to a question about whether he was considering a pardon for Manafort or other individuals involved in the Special Counsel's investigation, the President said, "I don't want to talk about that. No, I don't want to talk about that. ... But look, I do want to see people treated fairly. That's what it's all about."[854] Hours later, Manafort's bail was revoked and the President tweeted, "Wow, what a tough sentence for Paul Manafort, who has represented Ronald Reagan, Bob Dole and many other top political people and campaigns. Didn't know Manafort was the head of the Mob. What about Comey and Crooked Hillary and all the others? Very unfair!"[855]

Immediately following the revocation of Manafort's bail, the President's personal lawyer, Rudolph Giuliani, gave a series of interviews in which he raised the possibility of a pardon for Manafort. Giuliani told the New York Daily News that "[w]hen the whole thing is over, things might get cleaned up with some presidential pardons."[856]

Giuliani also said in an interview that, although the President should not pardon anyone while the Special Counsel's investigation was ongoing, "when the investigation is concluded, he's kind of on his own, right?"[857] In a CNN interview two days later, Giuliani said, "I guess I should clarify this once and for all. . . . The president has issued no pardons in this investigation. The president is not going to issue pardons in this investigation.... When it's over, hey, he's the president of the United States.

He retains his pardon power. Nobody is taking that away from him."[858] Giuliani rejected the suggestion that his and the President's comments could signal to defendants that they should not cooperate in a criminal prosecution because a pardon might follow, saying the comments were "certainly not intended that way."[859] Giuliani said the comments only acknowledged that an individual involved in the investigation would not be "excluded from [a pardon],i f in fact the president and his advisors ... come to the conclusion that you have been treated unfairly."[860] Giuliani observed that pardons were not unusual in political investigations but said, "That doesn't mean they're going to happen here. Doesn't mean that anybody should rely on it. ... Big signal is, nobody has been pardoned yet.[H86)]

On July 31, 2018, Manafort's criminal trial began in the Eastern District of Virginia, generating substantial news coverage.[862] The next day, the President tweeted, "This is a terrible situation and Attorney General Jeff Sessions should stop this Rigged Witch Hunt right now, before it continues to stain our country any further. Bob Mueller is totally conflicted, and his 17 Angry Democrats that are doing his dirty work are a disgrace to USA!"[863] Minutes later, the President tweeted, "Paul Manafort worked for Ronald Reagan, Bob Dole and many other highly prominent and respected political leaders. He worked for me for a very short time. Why didn't government tell me that he was under investigation. These old charges have nothing to do with Collusion—a Hoax!"[864] Later in the day, the President tweeted, "Looking back on history, who was treated worse, Alfonse Capone, legendary mob boss, killer and ' Public Enemy Number One,' or Paul Manafort, political operative & Reagan/Dole darling, now serving solitary confinement—although convicted of nothing? Where is the Russian Collusion?"[865] The President's tweets about the Manafort trial were widely covered by the press.[866] When asked about the President's tweets, Sanders told the press, "Certainly, the President's been clear. He thinks Paul Manafort's been treated unfairly."[867]

On August 16, 2018, the Manafort case was submitted to the jury and deliberations began. At that time, Giuliani had recently suggested to reporters that the Special Counsel investigation needed to be "done in the next two or three weeks,"[868] and media stories reported that a Manafort acquittal would add to criticism that the Special Counsel investigation was not worth the time and expense, whereas a conviction could show that ending the investigation would be premature.[869]

On August 17, 2018, as jury deliberations continued, the President commented on the trial from the South Lawn of the White House. In an impromptu exchange with reporters that lasted approximately five minutes, the President twice called the Special Counsel's investigation a "rigged witch hunt."[870] When asked whether he would pardon Manafort if he was convicted, the President said, "I don't talk about that now. I don't talk about that."[871] The President then added, without being asked a further question, "I think the whole Manafort trial is very sad when you look at what's going on there. I think it's a very sad day for our country. He worked for me for a very short period of time. But you know what, he happens to be a very good person. And I think it's very sad what they've done to Paul Manafort The President did not take further questions.[873] In response to the President's statements, Manafort's attorney said, "Mr. Manafort really appreciates the support of President Trump."[874]

On August 21, 2018, the jury found Manafort guilty on eight felony counts. Also on August 21, Michael Cohen pleaded guilty to eight offenses, including a campaign-finance violation that he said had occurred "in coordination with, and at the direction of, a candidate for federal office."[875] The President reacted to Manafort's convictions that day by telling reporters, "Paul Manafort's a good man" and "it's a very sad thing that happened."[876] The President described the Special Counsel's investigation as "a witch hunt that ends in disgrace."[877] The next day, the President tweeted, "I feel very badly for Paul Manafort and his wonderful family. 'Justice' took a 12 year old tax case, among other things, applied tremendous pressure on him and, unlike Michael Cohen, he refused to 'break'—make up stories in order to get a 'deal.' Such respect for a brave man! "[878]

In a Fox News interview on August 22, 2018, the President said: "[Cohen] makes a better deal when he uses me, like everybody else. And one of the reasons I respect Paul Manafort so much is he went through that trial—you know they make up stories. People make up stories. This whole thing about flipping, they call it, I know all about flipping."[879] The President said that flipping was "not fair" and "almost ought to be outlawed."[880] In response to a question about whether he was considering a pardon for Manafort, the President said, "I have great respect for what he's done, in terms of what he's gone through.... He worked for many, many people many, many years, and I would say what he did, some of the charges they threw against him, every consultant, every lobbyist in Washington probably does."[881] Giuliani told journalists that the President "really thinks Manafort has been horribly treated" and that he and the President had discussed the political fallout if the President pardoned Manafort.[882] The next day, Giuliani told the Washington Post that the President had asked his lawyers for advice on the possibility of a pardon for Manafort and other aides, and had been counseled against considering a pardon until the investigation concluded.[883]

On September 14, 2018, Manafort pleaded guilty to charges in the District of Columbia and signed a plea agreement that required him to cooperate with investigators.[884] Giuliani was reported to have publicly said that Manafort remained in a joint defense agreement with the President following Manafort's guilty plea and agreement to cooperate, and that Manafort's attorneys regularly briefed the President's lawyers on the topics discussed and the information Manafort had provided in interviews with the Special Counsel's Office.[885] On November 26, 2018, the Special Counsel's Office disclosed in a public court filing that Manafort had breached his plea agreement by lying about multiple subjects.[886] The next day, Giuliani said that the President had been "upset for weeks" about what he considered to be "the un-American, horrible treatment of Manafort."[887] In an interview on November 28, 2018, the President suggested that it was "very brave" that Manafort did not "flip":

> If you told the truth, you go to jail. You know this flipping stuff is terrible. You flip and you lie and you get—the prosecutors will tell you 99 percent of the time they can get people to flip. It's rare that they can't. But T had three people: Manafort, Corsi—I don't know Corsi, but he refuses to say what they demanded.[888] Manafort, Corsi It's actually very brave.[889]

In response to a question about a potential pardon for Manafort, the President said, "It was never discussed, but I wouldn't take it off the table. Why would T take it off the table?"[890]

Analysis

In analyzing the President's conduct towards Flynn, Manafort, lil:illll, the following evidence is relevant to the elements of obstruction of justice:

a.   Obstructive act. The President's actions towards witnesses in the Special Counsel's investigation would qualify as obstructive if they had the natural tendency to prevent particular witnesses from testifying truthfully, or otherwise would have the probable effect of influencing, delaying, or preventing their testimony to law enforcement.

With regard to Flynn, the President sent private and public messages to Flynn encouraging him to stay strong and conveying that the President still cared about him before he began to cooperate with the government. When Flynn's attorneys withdrew him from a joint defense agreement with the President, signaling that Flynn was potentially cooperating with the government, the President's personal counsel initially reminded Flynn's counsel of the President's warm feelings towards Flynn and said "that still remains." But when Flynn's counsel reiterated that Flynn could no longer share information under a joint defense agreement, the President's personal counsel stated that the decision would be interpreted as reflecting Flynn's hostility towards the President. That sequence of events could have had the potential to affect Flynn's decision to cooperate, as well as the extent of that cooperation. Because of privilege issues, however, we could not determine whether the President was personally involved in or knew about the specific message his counsel delivered to Flynn's counsel.

With respect to Manafort, there is evidence that the President's actions had the potential to influence Manafort's decision whether to cooperate with the government. The President and his personal counsel made repeated statements suggesting that a pardon was a possibility for Manafort, while also making it clear that the President did not want Manafort to "flip" and cooperate with the government. On June 15, 2018, the day the judge presiding over Manafort's D.C. case was considering whether to revoke his bail, the President said that he "felt badly" for Manafort and stated, "I think a lot of it is very

unfair." And when asked about a pardon for Manafort, the President said, "I do want to see people treated fairly. That's what it's all about." Later that day, after Manafort's bail was revoked, the President called it a "tough sentence" that was "Very unfair!" Two days later, the President's personal counsel stated that individuals involved in the Special Counsel's investigation could receive a pardon "if in fact the [P]resident and his advisors
... come to the conclusion that you have been treated unfairly"-using language that paralleled how the President had already described the treatment of Manafort. Those statements, combined with the President's commendation of Manafort for being a "brave man" who "refused to 'break'," suggested that a pardon was a more likely possibility if Manafort continued not to cooperate with the government. And while Manafort eventually pleaded guilty pursuant to a cooperation agreement, he was found to have violated the agreement by lying to investigators.

The President's public statements during the Manafort trial, including during jury deliberations, also had the potential to influence the trial jury. On the second day of trial, for example, the President called the prosecution a "terrible situation" and a "hoax" that "continues to stain our country" and referred to Manafort as a "Reagan/Dole darling" who was "serving solitary confinement" even though he was "convicted of nothing." Those statements were widely picked up by the press. While jurors were instructed not to watch or read news stories about the case and are presumed to follow those instructions, the President's statements during the trial generated substantial media coverage that could have reached jurors if they happened to see the statements or learned about them from others. And the President's statements during jury deliberations that Manafort "happens to be a very good person" and that "it's very sad what they've done to Paul Manafort" had the potential to influence jurors who learned of the statements, which the President made just as jurors were considering whether to convict or acquit Manafort.

b.   Nexus to an official proceeding. The President's actions towards Flynn, Manafort, appear to have been connected to pending or official proceedings involving each individual. The President's conduct towards Flynn principally occurred when both were under criminal investigation by the Special Counsel's Office and press reports speculated about whether they would cooperate with the Special Counsel's investigation. And the

President's conduct towards Manafort was directly connected to the official proceedings involving him. The President made statements about Manafort and the charges against him during Manafort's criminal trial. And the President's comments about the prospect of Manafort "flipping" occurred when it was clear the Special Counsel continued to oversee grand jury proceedings.

c. Intent. Evidence concerning the President's intent related to Flynn as a potential witness is inconclusive. As previously noted, because of privilege issues we do not have evidence establishing whether the President knew about or was involved in his counsel's communications with Flynn's counsel stating that Flynn's decision to withdraw from the joint defense agreement and cooperate with the government would be viewed as reflecting "hostility" towards the President. And regardless of what the President's personal counsel communicated, the President continued to express sympathy for Flynn after he pleaded guilty pursuant to a cooperation agreement, stating that Flynn had "led a very strong life" and the President "fe(lt) very badly" about what had happened to him.

Evidence concerning the President's conduct towards Manafort indicates that the President intended to encourage Manafort to not cooperate with the government. Before Manafort was convicted, the President repeatedly stated that Manafort had been treated unfairly. One day after Manafort was convicted on eight felony charges and potentially faced a lengthy prison term, the President said that Manafort was "a brave man" for refusing to "break" and that "flipping" "almost ought to be outlawed." At the same time, although the President had privately told aides he did not like Manafort, he publicly called Manafort "a good man" and said he had a "wonderful family." And when the President was asked whether he was considering a pardon for Manafort, the President did not respond directly and instead said he had "great respect for what [Manafort]'s done, in terms of what he's gone through." The President added that "some of the charges they threw against him, every consultant, every lobbyist in Washington probably does." In light of the President's counsel's previous statements that the investigations "might get cleaned up with some presidential pardons" and that a pardon would be possible if the President "come[s] to the conclusion that you have been treated unfairly," the evidence supports the inference that the President intended Manafort to believe that he could receive a pardon, which would make cooperation with the government as a means of obtaining a lesser sentence unnecessary.

We also examined the evidence of the President's intent in making public statements about Manafort at the beginning of his trial and when the jury was deliberating. Some evidence supports a conclusion that the President intended, at least in part, to influence the jury. The trial generated widespread publicity, and as the jury began to deliberate, commentators suggested that an acquittal would add to pressure to end the Special Counsel's investigation. By publicly stating on the second day of deliberations that Manafort "happens to be a very good person" and that "it's very sad what they've done to Paul Manafort" right after calling the Special Counsel's investigation a "rigged witch hunt," the President's statements could, if they reached jurors, have the natural tendency to engender sympathy for Manafort among jurors, and a factfinder could infer that the President intended that result. But there are alternative explanations for the President's comments, including that he genuinely felt sorry for Manafort or that his goal was not to influence the jury but to influence public opinion. The President's comments also could have been intended to continue sending a message to Manafort that a pardon was possible. As described above, the President made his comments about Manafort being "a very good person" immediately after declining to answer a question about whether he would pardon Manafort.

******

831 See, e.g., Remarks by President Trump in Press Conference, White House (Feb. 16, 2018) (stating that "Flynn is a fine person" and "I don't think [Flynn] did anything wrong. If anything, he did something right ... You know, he was just doing his job"); Interview of Donald J. Trump, NBC (May 11, 2017) (stating that Flynn is a "very good person").

832 See Priebus 1/18/17 302, at 9-10 (the President asked Priebus to contact Flynn the week he was terminated to convey that the President still cared about him and felt bad about what happened to him; Priebus thought the President did not want Flynn to have a problem with him); McFarland 12/22/17 302, at 18 (about a month or two after Flynn was terminated, the President asked McFarland to get in touch with Flynn and tell him that he was a good guy, he should stay strong, and the President felt bad for him); Flynn 1/19/18 302, at 9 (recalling the call from Priebus and an additional call from Hicks who

said she wanted to relay on behalf of the President that the President hoped Flynn was okay); Christie 2/13/19 302, at 3 (describing a phone conversation between Kushner and Flynn the day after Flynn was fired where Kushner said, "You know the President respects you. The President cares about you. I'll get the President to send out a positive tweet about you later," and the President nodded his assent to Kushner's comment promising a tweet).
833 Counsel for Flynn 3/1/18 302, at I.

834 Counsel for Flynn 3/1/18 302, at I.
835 11/22/17 Voicemail Transcript, President's Personal Counsel to Counsel for Michael Flynn.
836 Counsel for Flynn 3/1/18 302, at 1.
837 Counsel for Flynn 3/1I18 302, at I.
838 Counsel for Flynn 3/1/18 302, at I.
839 Counsel for Flynn 3/1/18 302, at 2. Because of attorney-client privilege issues, we did not seek to interview the President's personal counsel about the extent to which he discussed his statements to Flynn's attorneys with the President.
84° Counsel for Flynn 3/1/18 302, at 2.
841 Information, United States v. Michael T Flynn, 1: 17-cr-232 (D.D.C. Dec. I, 2017), Doc. I; Plea Agreement, United States v. Michael T Flynn, I: 17-cr-232 (D.D.C. Dec. I, 2017), Doc. 3.
842 President Trump Remarks on Tax Reform and Michael Flynn's Guilty Plea, C-SPAN (Dec. 2, 2017).
843 President Trump Remarks on Tax Reform and Michael Flynn's Guilty Plea, C-SPAN (Dec. 2,
844 See @realDonaldTrump 12/2/17 (9:06 p.m. ET) Tweet ("So General Flynn lies to the FBI and his life is destroyed, while Crooked Hillary Clinton, on that now famous FBI holiday 'interrogation' with no swearing in and no recording, lies many times ... and nothing happens to her? Rigged system, orjust a double standard?"); President Trump Departure Remarks, C-SPAN (Dec. 4, 2017) ("Well, I feel badly for General Flynn. I feel very badly. He's led a very strong life. And I feel very badly.").
845 President Trump White House Departure, C-SPAN (Dec. 15, 2017).

846 Indictment, United States v. Paul J Manofort, Jr. andRichard W. Gates III, I: I 7-cr-20 I (D.D.C. Oct, 27, 2017), Doc. 13 ("Manafort and Gates D.D.C. Indictment"); Indictment, United States v. Paul J Manafort, Jr. and Richard W. Gates III, I: I 8-cr-83 (E.D. Va. Feb. 22, 2018), Doc. 9 ("Manafort and Gates E.D. Va. Indictment")
847 Manafort and Gates D.D.C. Indictment; Manafort and Gates E.D. Va. Indictment.

848 Gates 4/18/18 302, at 4. In February 2018, Gates pleaded guilty, pursuant to a cooperation plea agreement, to a superseding criminal information charging him with conspiring to defraud and commit multiple offenses (i.e., tax fraud, failure to report foreign bank accounts, and acting as an unregistered agent of a foreign principal) against the United States, as well as making false statements to our Office. Superseding Criminal Information, United States v. Richard W. Gates ff!, I: I 7-cr-201 (D.D.C. Feb. 23, 2018), Doc. 195; Plea Agreement, United States v. Richard W. Gates III, I: 17-cr-20 I (D.D.C. Feb. 23,2018), Doc. 205. Gates has provided information and in-court testimony that the Office has deemed to be reliable.
849 Gates 4/18/18 302, at 4.
850 Gates 4/18/18 302, at 4. Manafort told this Office that he never told Gates that he had talked to the President's personal counsel or suggested that they would be taken care of. Manafort also said he hoped for a pardon but never discussed one with the President, although he noticed the President's public comments about pardons. Manafort I 0/1/18 302, at 11.

As explained in Volume I, Section IV.A.8, supra, Manafort entered into a plea agreement with our Office. The U.S. District Court for the District of Columbia determined that he breached the agreement by being untruthful in proffer sessions and before the grand jury. Order, United States v. Manafort, I: 17-cr-201 (D.D.C. Feb. 13, 2019), Doc. 503.

851 Porter 5/8/18 302, at 11. Priebus recalled that the President never really liked Manafort. See Priebus 4/3/18 302, at 11. Hicks said that candidate Trump trusted Manafort's judgment while he worked on the Campaign, but she also once heard Trump tell Gates to keep an eye on Manafort. Hicks 3/13/18 302, at 16.

852 Porter 5/8/18 302, at 11; McGahn 12/14/17 302, at 14.

853 Remarks by President Trump in Press Gaggle, White House (June 15, 2018).

854 Remarks by President Trump in Press Gaggle, White House (June 15, 2018).

855 @realDonaldTrump 6/15/18 (I :41 p.m. ET) Tweet.

856 Chris Sommerfeldt, Rudy Giuliani says Mueller probe 'might get cleaned up' with 'presidential pardons' in light ofPaul Manafort going to jail, New York Daily News (June 15, 2018).

857 Sharon LaFraniere, Judge Orders Paul Manafort Jailed Before Trial, Citing New Obstruction Charges, New York Times (June 15, 2018) (quoting Giuliani).

858 State ofthe Union with Jake Tapper Transcript, CNN (June 17, 2018); see Karoun Demirjian, Giuliani suggests Trump may pardon Manafort after Mueller's probe, Washington Post (June 17, 2018).

859 State ofthe Union with Jake Tapper Transcript, CNN (June 17, 2018).

860 State ofthe Union with Jake Tapper Transcript, CNN (June 17, 2018).

861 State ofthe Union with Jake Tapper Transcript, CNN (June 17, 2018).

862 See, e.g., Katelyn Polantz, Takeaways from day one ofthe Paul Mana/or/ trial, CNN (July 31, 2018); Frank Bruni, Paul Manafort 's Trial Is Donald Trump's, Too, New York Times Opinion (July 31, 2018); Rachel Weiner et al., PaulManafort trial Day 2: Witnesses describe extravagant clothingpurchases, home remodels, lavish cars paid with wire transfers, Washington Post (Aug. I, 2018).

863 @realDonaldTrump 8/1/18 (9:24 a.m. ET) Tweet. Later that day, when Sanders was asked about the President's tweet, she told reporters, "It's not an order. It's the President's opinion." Sarah Sanders, White House Daily Briefing, C-SPAN (Aug. I, 2018).

864 @realDonaldTrump 8/1/18 (9:34 a.m. ET) Tweet.

865 @realDonaldTrump 8/1/18 (11 :35 a.m. ET) Tweet.

866 See, e.g., Carol D. Leonnig et al., Trump calls Manafort prosecution "a hoax," says Sessions should stop Mueller investigation "right now", Washington Post (Aug. I, 2018); Louis Nelson, Trump claims Manafort case has "nothing to do with collusion", Politico (Aug. 1. 2018).

867 Sarah Sanders, White House Daily Briefing, C-SPAN (Aug. 1, 2018).

868 Chris Strohm & Shannon Pettypiece, Mueller Probe Doesn't Need to Shut Down Before Midterms, Officials Say, Bloomberg (Aug. 15, 2018).

869 See, e.g., Katelyn Polantz et al., Manafortjury endsfirst day ofdeliberations without a verdict, CNN (Aug. 16, 2018); David Voreacos, What Mueller's Manafort Case Means for the Trump Baille to Come, Bloomberg (Aug. 2, 2018); Gabby Morrongiello, What a guilty verdict for Manafort would mean for Trump andMueller, Washington Examiner (Aug. 18, 2018).

870 President Trump Remarks on John Brennan and Mueller Probe, C-SPAN (Aug. 17, 2018).

871 President Trump Remarks on John Brennan and Mueller Probe, C-SPAN (Aug. 17, 2018).

872 President Trump Remarks on John Brennan and Mueller Probe, C-SPAN (Aug. 17, 2018).

873 President Trump Remarks on John Brennan and Mueller Probe, C-SPAN (Aug. 17, 2018).

874 Trump calls Manafort "verygoodperson," All In with Chris Hayes (Aug. 17, 2018) (transcript); Mana/art lawyer: We appreciate Trump's support, CNN (Aug. 17, 20 I 8) (https://www.cnn.com/videos/politics/2018/08/17/paul-manafort-attorney-trump-jury-deliberations- schneider-lead-vpx.cnn).

875 Transcript at 23, United States v. Michael Cohen, 1: 18-cr-602 (S.D.N.Y. Aug. 21, 2018), Doc. 7 (Cohen 8/21/18 Transcript).

876 President Trump Remarks on Mana/art Trial, C-SPAN (Aug. 21, 2018).

877 President Trump Remarks on Manafort Trial, C-SPAN (Aug._ 21, 2018).

878 @realDonaldTrump 8/22/18 (9:21 a.m. ET) Tweet.

879 Fox & Friends Exclusive Interview with President Trump, Fox News (Aug. 23, 2018) (recorded the previous day).

88° Fox & Friends Exclusive Interview with President Trump, Fox News (Aug. 23, 2018) (recorded the previous day).

881 Fox & Friends Exclusive Interview with President Trump, Fox News (Aug. 23, 2018) (recorded the previous day).

882 Maggie Haberman & Katie Rogers, "How Did We End Up Here?" Trump Wonders as the White House Soldiers On, New York Times (Aug. 22, 2018).

883 Carol D. Leonnig & Josh Dawsey, Trump recently sought his lawyers' advice on possibility of pardoning Manafort, Giuliani says, Washington Post (Aug. 23, 2018).

884 Plea Agreement, United States v. Paul J. Manafort, Jr., I: I 7-cr-20 I (D.D.C. Sept. 14, 2018), Doc. 422.

885 Karen Freifeld & Nathan Layne, Trump lawyer: Manafort said nothing damaging in Mueller interviews, Reuters (Oct. 22, 2018); Michael S. Schmidt et al., Manafort 's Lawyer Said to Brief Trump Attorneys on What He Told Mueller, New York Times (Nov. 27, 2018); Dana Bash, Manafort team briefed Giuliani on Mueller meetings, CNN, Posted 11/28/18, available at https ://www.cnn.com/videos/pol itics/2018/11 /28/manafort-lawyers-keeping-trump-lawyers-gi ul iani- updated-muel ler-probe-bash-sot-nr-vpx.cnn; see Sean Hannity, Interview with Rudy Giuliani, Fox News (Sept. 14, 2018) (Giuliani: "[T]here was a quote put out by a source close to Manafort that the plea agreement has, and cooperation agreement has, nothing to do with the Trump campaign.... Now, I know that because I've been privy to a lot of facts I can't repeat.").

886 Joint Status Report, United States v. Paul J. Manafort, Jr., (D.D.C Nov. 26, 2018), Doc. 455.

887 Stephen Collinson, Trump appears consumed by Mueller investigation as details emerge, CNN (Nov. 29, 2018).

888 "Corsi" is a reference to Jerome Corsi, !Il.!.li!i::mll who was involved in efforts to coordinate with WikiLeaks and Assange, and wme that he had refused a plea offer fro's Office because he was "not going to sign a lie." Sara Murray & Eli Watkins, says he won't agree to plea deal, CNN (Nov. 26, 2018).

889 Marisa Schultz & Nikki Schwab, Oval Office Interview with President Trump: Trump says pardon/or Paul Manaforl still apossibility, New York Post (Nov. 28, 2018). That same day, the President tweeted: "While the disgusting Fake News is doing everything within their power not to report it that way, at least 3 major players are intimating that the Angry Mueller Gang of Dems is viciously telling witnesses to lie about facts & they will get relief. This is our Joseph McCarthy Era!" @realDonaldTrump 11/28/18 (8:39 a.m. ET) Tweet.

890 Marisa Schultz & Nikki Schwab, New York Post Oval Office Interview with President Trump: Trump says pardonfor Paul Manaforl still a possibility, New York Post (Nov. 28, 2018).

K.   The President's Conduct Involving Michael Cohen

Overview

The President's conduct involving Michael Cohen spans the full period of our investigation. During the campaign, Cohen pursued the Trump Tower Moscow project on behalf of the Trump Organization. Cohen briefed candidate Trump on the project numerous times, including discussing whether Trump should travel to Russia to advance the deal. After the media began questioning Trump's connections to Russia, Cohen promoted a "party line" that publicly distanced Trump from Russia and asserted he had no business there. Cohen continued to adhere to that party line in 2017, when Congress asked him to provide documents and testimony in its Russia investigation. In an attempt to minimize the President's connections to Russia, Cohen submitted a letter to Congress falsely stating that he only briefed Trump on the Trump Tower Moscow project three times, that he did not consider asking Trump to travel to Russia, that Cohen had not received a response to an outreach he made to the Russian government, and that the project ended in January 2016, before the first Republican caucus or primary. While working on the congressional statement, Cohen had extensive discussions with the President's personal counsel, who, according to Cohen, said that Cohen should not contradict the President and should keep the statement short and "tight." After the FBI searched Cohen's home and office in April 2018, the President publicly asserted that Cohen would not "flip" and privately passed messages of support to him. Cohen also discussed pardons with the President's personal counsel and believed that if he stayed on message, he would get a pardon or the President would do "something else" to make the investigation end. But after Cohen began cooperating with the government in July 2018, the President publicly criticized him, called him a "rat," and suggested his family members had committed crimes.

Evidence

1. Candidate Trump's Awareness of and Involvement m the Trump Tower Moscow Project

The President's interactions with Cohen as a witness took place against the background of the President's involvement in the Trump Tower Moscow project. As described in detail in Volume I, Section IV.A. I, *supra,* from September 2015 until at least June 2016, the Trump Organization pursued a Trump Tower Moscow project in Russia, with negotiations conducted by Cohen, then-executive vice president of the Trump Organization and special counsel to Donald J. Trump.[909] The Trump Organization had previously and But after Cohen pleaded guilty to offenses in the Southern District of New York on August 21, 2018, he met with investigators again and corrected the record. The Office found Cohen's testimony in these subsequent proffer sessions to be consistent with and corroborated by other information obtained in the course of the Office's investigation. The Office's sentencing submission in Cohen's criminal case stated: "Starting with his second meeting with the [Special Counsel's Office] in September 2018, the defendant has accepted responsibility not only for unsuccessfully pursued a building project in Moscow.t'" According to Cohen, in approximately September 2015 he obtained internal approval from Trump to negotiate on behalf of the Trump Organization to have a Russian corporation build a tower in Moscow that licensed the Trump name and brand.[911] Cohen thereafter had numerous brief conversations with Trump about the project.[912]

Cohen recalled that Trump wanted to be updated on any developments with Trump Tower Moscow and on several occasions brought the project up with Cohen to ask what was happening on it.[913] Cohen also discussed the project on multiple occasions with Donald Trump Jr. and Ivanka

In the fall of 2015, Trump signed a Letter of Intent for the project that specified highly lucrative terms for the Trump Organization.[915] In December 2015, Felix Sater, who was handling negotiations between Cohen and the Russian corporation, asked Cohen for a copy of his and Trump's passports to facilitate travel to Russia to meet with government officials and possible financing partners.[916] Cohen recalled discussing the trip with Trump and requesting a copy of Trump's passport from Trump's personal secretary, Rhona Graff.[917]

By January 2016, Cohen had become frustrated that Sater had not set up a meeting with Russian government officials, so Cohen reached out directly by email to the office of Dmitry Peskov, who was Putin's deputy chief of staff and press secretary.[918] On January 20, 2016, Cohen received an email response from Elena Poliakova, Peskov's personal assistant, and phone records confirm that they then spoke for approximately twenty minutes, during which Cohen described the Trump Tower Moscow project and requested assistance in moving the project forward.[919] Cohen recalled briefing candidate Trump about the call soon afterwards.F" Cohen told Trump he spoke with a woman he identified as "someone from the Kremlin," and Cohen reported that she was very professional and asked detailed questions about the project.[921] Cohen recalled telling Trump he wished the Trump Organization had assistants who were as competent as the woman from the Kremlin.[922]

Cohen thought his phone call renewed interest in the project.[923] The day after Cohen's call with Poliakova, Sater texted Cohen, asking him to "[c]all me when you have a few minutes to chat... It's about Putin they called today."[924] Sater told Cohen that the Russian government liked the project and on January 25, 2016, sent an invitation for Cohen to visit Moscow "for a working visit."[925] After the outreach from Sater, Cohen recalled telling Trump that he was waiting to hear back on moving the project forward.

After January 2016, Cohen continued to have conversations with Sater about Trump Tower Moscow and continued to keep candidate Trump updated about those discussions and the status of the project.[927] Cohen recalled that he and Trump wanted Trump Tower Moscow to succeed and that Trump never discouraged him from working on the project because of the campaign.F" In March or April 2016, Trump asked Cohen if anything was happening in Russia.[929] Cohen also recalled briefing Donald Trump Jr. in the spring—a conversation that Cohen said was not "idle chit chat" because Trump Tower Moscow was potentially a $1 billion deal.[930]

Cohen recalled that around May 2016, he again raised with candidate Trump the possibility of a trip to Russia to advance the Trump Tower Moscow project.[931] At that time, Cohen had received several texts from Sater seeking to arrange dates for such a trip.[932] On May 4, 2016, Sater wrote to Cohen, "I had a chat with Moscow.

ASSUMING the trip does happen the question is before or after the convention . . . . .
Obviously the premeeting trip (you only) can happen anytime you want but the 2 big
guys [is] the question. I said I would confirm and revert."[933] Cohen responded,
"My trip before Cleveland. Trump once he becomes the nominee after the
convention."[934] On May 5, 2016, Sater followed up with a text that Cohen thought
he probably read to Trump:

> Peskov would like to invite you as his guest to the St. Petersburg
> Forum which is Russia's Davos it's June 16-19. He wants to meet
> there with you and possibly introduce you to either Putin or
> Medvedev. . . . This is perfect. The entire business class of Russia will
> be there as well. He said anything you want to discuss including dates
> and subjects are on the table to discuss.[935]

Cohen recalled discussing the invitation to the St. Petersburg Economic
Forum with candidate Trump and saying that Putin or Russian Prime Minister Dmitry
Medvedev might be there.[936] Cohen remembered that Trump said that he would be
willing to travel to Russia if Cohen could "lock and load" on the deal.[937] In June
2016, Cohen decided not to attend the St. Petersburg Economic Forum because Sater
had not obtained a formal invitation for Cohen from Peskov.[938]
Cohen said he had a quick conversation with Trump at that time but did not tell him that
the project was over because he did not want Trump to complain that the deal was
on-again-off-again if it were revived.[939]

During the summer of 2016, Cohen recalled that candidate Trump publicly claimed that
he had nothing to do with Russia and then shortly afterwards privately checked with
Cohen about the status of the Trump Tower Moscow project, which Cohen found
"interesting."[940] At some point that summer, Cohen recalled having a brief
conversation with Trump in which Cohen said the Trump Tower Moscow project
was going nowhere because the Russian development company had not secured a
piece of property for the project.[941] Trump said that was "too bad," and Cohen did not
recall talking with Trump about the project after that.[942] Cohen said that at no time
during the campaign did Trump tell him not to pursue the project or that the
project should be abandoned.[943]

2. Cohen Determines to Adhere to a "Party Line" Distancing Candidate Trump From Russia

As previously discussed, *see* Volume II, Section II.A, *supra,* when questions about possible Russian support for candidate Trump emerged during the 2016 presidential campaign, Trump denied having any personal, financial, or business connection to Russia, which Cohen described as the "party line" or "message" to follow for Trump and his senior advisors.[944]

After the election, the Trump Organization sought to formally close out certain deals in advance of the inauguration.[945] Cohen recalled that Trump Tower Moscow was on the list of deals to be closed out.[946] In approximately January 2017, Cohen began receiving inquiries from the media about Trump Tower Moscow, and he recalled speaking to the President-Elect when those inquiries came in.[947] Cohen was concerned that truthful answers about the Trump Tower Moscow project might not be consistent with the "message" that the President-Elect had no relationship with Russia.[948]

In an effort to "stay on message," Cohen told a New York Times reporter that the Trump Tower Moscow deal was not feasible and had ended in January 2016.[949] Cohen recalled that this was part of a "script" or talking points he had developed with President-Elect Trump and others to

[941] Cohen 3/19/19 302, at 2. Cohen could not recall the precise timing of this conversation, but said he thought it occurred in June or July 2016. Cohen recalled that the conversation happened at some point after candidate Trump was publicly stating that he had nothing to do with Russia. Cohen 3/19/19 302, at dismiss the idea of a substantial connection between Trump and Russia.[950] Cohen said that he discussed the talking points with Trump but that he did not explicitly tell Trump he thought they were untrue because Trump already knew they were untrue.[951] Cohen thought it was important to say the deal was done in January 2016, rather than acknowledge that talks continued in May and June 2016, because it limited the period when candidate Trump could be alleged to have a relationship with Russia to an early point in the campaign, before Trump had become the party's presumptive nominee.[952]

3. Cohen Submits False Statements to Congress Minimizing the Trump Tower Moscow Project in Accordance with the Party Line

In early May 2017, Cohen received requests from Congress to provide testimony and documents in connection with congressional investigations of Russian interference in the 2016 election.[953] At that time, Cohen understood Congress's interest in him to be focused on the allegations in the Steele reporting concerning a meeting Cohen allegedly had with Russian officials in Prague during the campaign.[954] Cohen had never traveled to Prague and was not concerned about those allegations, which he believed were provably false.[955] On May 18, 2017, Cohen met with the President to discuss the request from Congress, and the President instructed Cohen that he should cooperate because there was nothing there.[956]

Cohen eventually entered into a joint defense agreement (JDA) with the President and other individuals who were part of the Russia investigation.[957] In the months leading up to his congressional testimony, Cohen frequently spoke with the President's personal counsel.[958] Cohen matters, we asked the President's personal counsel if he wished to provide information to us about his conversations with Cohen related to Cohen's congressional testimony about said that in those conversations the President's personal counsel would sometimes say that he had just been with the President.[959] Cohen recalled that the President's personal counsel told him the JOA was working well together and assured him that there was nothing there and if they stayed on message the investigations would come to an end soon.[960] At that time, Cohen's legal bills were being paid by the Trump Organization.P" and Cohen was told not to worry because the investigations would be over by summer or fall of 2017.[962] Cohen said that the President's personal counsel also conveyed that, as part of the JOA, Cohen was protected, which he would not be if he "went rogue."[963] Cohen recalled that the President's personal counsel reminded him that "the President loves you" and told him that if he stayed on message, the President had his back.[964]

In August 2017, Cohen began drafting a statement about Trump Tower Moscow to submit to Congress along with his document production.[965] The final version of the statement contained several false statements about the project.[966] First, although the Trump Organization continued to pursue the project until at least June 2016, the statement said, "The proposal was under consideration at the Trump Organization from September 2015 until the end of January 2016. By the end of January 2016, I determined that the proposal was not feasible for a variety of business reasons and should not be pursued further. Based on my business determinations, the Trump Organization abandoned the proposal."[967] Second, although Cohen and candidate Trump had discussed possible travel to Russia by Trump to pursue the venture, the statement said, "Despite overtures by Mr. Sater, I never considered asking Mr. Trump to travel to Russia in connection with this proposal. I told Mr. Sater that Mr. Trump would not travel to Russia unless there was a definitive agreement in place."[968] Third, although Cohen had regularly briefed Trump on the status of the project and had numerous conversations about it, the statement said, "Mr. Trump was never in contact with anyone about this proposal other than me on three occasions, including signing a non-binding letter of intent in 2015."[969]

Fourth, although Cohen's outreach to Peskov in January 2016 had resulted in a lengthy phone call with a representative from the Kremlin, the statement said that Cohen did "not recall any response to my email [to Peskov], nor any other contacts by me with Mr. Peskov or other Russian government officials about the proposal."?"

> Cohen's statement was circulated in advance to, and edited by, members of the JDA.[971]

Before the statement was finalized, early drafts contained a sentence stating, "The building project led me to make limited contacts with Russian government officials."[972] In the final version of the statement, that line was deleted.[973] Cohen thought he was told that it was a decision of the JOA to take out that sentence, and he did not push back on the deletion.[974] Cohen recalled that he told the President's personal counsel that he would not contest a decision of the JOA.[975]

Cohen also recalled that in drafting his statement for Congress, he spoke with the President's personal counsel about a different issue that connected candidate Trump to Russia: Cohen's efforts to set up a meeting between Trump and Putin in New York during the 2015 United Nations General Assembly.[976] In September 2015, Cohen had suggested the meeting to Trump, who told Cohen to reach out to Putin's office about it.[977] Cohen spoke and emailed with a Russian official about a possible meeting, and recalled that Trump asked him multiple times for updates on the proposed meeting with Putin.[978] When Cohen called the Russian official a second time, she told him it would not follow proper protocol for Putin to meet with Trump, and Cohen relayed that message to Trump.[979] Cohen anticipated he might be asked questions about the proposed Trump•Putin meeting when he testified before Congress because he had talked about the potential meeting on Sean Hannity's radio show.[980] Cohen recalled explaining to the President's personal counsel the "whole story" of the attempt to set up a meeting between Trump and Putin and Trump's role in it.[981] Cohen recalled that he and the President's personal counsel talked about keeping Trump out of the narrative, and the President's personal counsel told Cohen the story was not relevant and should not be included in his statement to Congress.[982]

Cohen said that his "agenda" in submitting the statement to Congress with false representations about the Trump Tower Moscow project was to minimize links between the project and the President, give the false impression that the project had ended before the first presidential primaries, and shut down further inquiry into Trump Tower Moscow, with the aim of limiting the ongoing Russia investigations.[983] Cohen said he wanted to protect the President and be loyal to him by not contradicting anything the President had said.[984] Cohen recalled he was concerned that if he told the truth about getting a response from the Kremlin or speaking to candidate Trump about travel to Russia to pursue the project, he would contradict the message that no connection existed between Trump and Russia, and he rationalized his decision to provide false testimony because the deal never happened.[985] He was not concerned that the story would be contradicted by individuals who knew it was false because he was sticking to the party line adhered to by the whole group.[986] Cohen wanted the support of the President and the White House, and he believed that following the party line would help put an end to the Special Counsel and congressional investigations.[987]

Between August 18, 2017, when the statement was in an initial draft stage, and August 28, 2017, when the statement was submitted to Congress, phone records reflect that Cohen spoke with the President's personal counsel almost daily.[988] On August 27, 2017, the day before Cohen submitted the statement to Congress, Cohen and the President's personal counsel had numerous contacts by phone, including calls lasting three, four, six, eleven, and eighteen minutes.[989] Cohen recalled telling the President's personal counsel, who did not have first-hand knowledge of the project, that there was more detail on Trump Tower Moscow that was not in the statement, including that there were more communications with Russia and more communications with candidate Trump than the statement reflected.[990] Cohen stated that the President's personal counsel responded that it was not necessary to elaborate or include those details because the project did not progress and that Cohen should keep his statement short and "tight" and the matter would soon come to an end.[991] Cohen recalled that the President's personal counsel said "his client" appreciated Cohen, that Cohen should stay on message and not contradict the President, that there was no need to muddy the water, and that it was time to move on.[992] Cohen said he agreed because it was what he was expected to do.[993] After Cohen later pleaded guilty to making false statements to Congress about the Trump Tower Moscow project, this Office sought to speak with the President's personal counsel about these conversations with Cohen, but counsel declined, citing potential privilege concerns.[994]

At the same time that Cohen finalized his written submission to Congress, he served as a source for a Washington Post story published on August 27, 2017, that reported in depth for the first time that the Trump Organization was "pursuing a plan to develop a massive Trump Tower in Moscow" at the same time as candidate Trump was "running for president in late 2015 and early 2016."[995] The article reported that "the project was abandoned at the end of January 2016, just

445

before the presidential primaries began, several people familiar with the proposal said."[996] Cohen recalled that in speaking to the Post, he held to the false story that negotiations for the deal ceased in January 2016.[997]

On August 28, 2017, Cohen submitted his statement about the Trump Tower Moscow project to Congress.[998] Cohen did not recall talking to the President about the specifics of what the statement said or what Cohen would later testify to about Trump Tower Moscow.[999] He recalled speaking to the President more generally about how he planned to stay on message in his testimony.[1000] On September 19, 2017, in anticipation of his impending testimony, Cohen orchestrated the public release of his opening remarks to Congress, which criticized the allegations in the Steele material and claimed that the Trump Tower Moscow project "was terminated in January of 2016; which occurred before the Iowa caucus and months before the very first primalyl."[1001] Cohen said the release of his opening remarks was intended to shape the narrativeand let other people who might be witnesses know what Cohen was saying so they could follow the same message.[1002] Cohen said his decision was meant to mirror Jared Kushner's decision to release a statement in advance of Kushner's congressional testimony, which the President's personal counsel had told Cohen the President liked.[1003] Cohen recalled that on September 20, 2017, after Cohen's opening remarks had been printed by the media, the President's personal counsel told him that the President was pleased with the Trump Tower Moscow statement that had gone out.[1004]

On October 24 and 25, 2017, Cohen testi tied before Congress and repeated the false statements he had included in his written statement about Trump Tower Moscow.[1005] Phone records show that Cohen spoke with the President's personal counsel immediately after his testimony on both days.[1006]

4. The President Sends Messages of Support to Cohen

In January 2018, the media reported that Cohen had arranged a $130,000 payment during the campaign to prevent a woman from publicly discussing an alleged sexual encounter she had with the President before he ran for office.[1""]? This Office did not investigate Cohen's campaign· period payments to women.[P"] However, those events, as described here, are potentially relevant to the President's and his personal counsel's interactions with Cohen as a witness who later began to cooperate with the government.

On February 13, 2018, Cohen released a statement to news organizations that stated, "In a private transaction in 2016, I used my own personal funds to facilitate a payment of $130,000 to [the woman]. Neither the Trump Organization nor the Trump campaign was a party to the transaction with [the woman], and neither reimbursed me for the payment, either directly or indirectly.?'?" In congressional testimony on February 27, 2019, Cohen testified that he had discussed what to say about the payment with the President and that the President had directed Cohen to say that the President "was not knowledgeable ... of[Cohen's] actions" in making the payment[P'"] On February 19, 2018, the day after the New York Times wrote a detailed story attributing the payment to Cohen and describing Cohen as the President's "fixer," Cohen received a text message from the President's personal counsel that stated, "Client says thanks for what you do."[1011]

On April 9, 2018, FBI agents working with the U.S. Attorney's Office for the Southern District of New York executed search warrants on Cohen's home, hotel room, and office.[P'?] That day, the President spoke to reporters and said that he had "just heard that they broke into the office of one of my personal attorneys—a good man."[1013] The President called the searches "a real disgrace" and said, "It's an attack on our country, in a true sense. It's an attack on what we all stand for."[1014] Cohen said that after the searches he was concerned that he was "an open book," that he did not want issues arising from the payments to women to "come out," and that his false statements to Congress were "a big concern."[1015]

A few days after the searches, the President called Cohen.[1016] According to Cohen, the President said he wanted to "check in" and asked if Cohen was okay, and the President encouraged Cohen to "hang in there" and "stay strong."?"' Cohen also recalled that following the searches he heard from individuals who were in touch with the President and relayed to Cohen the President's support for him.[1018] Cohen recalled that   , a friend of the President's, reached out to say that he was with "the Boss" in M - -   e President had said "he loves you" and not to worry.1'"? Cohen recalled that   for the Trump Organization, told him, "the boss loves   , a friend of the President's, told him, "everyone knows the boss has your back."

On or about April 17, 2018, Cohen began speaking with an attorney, Robert Costello, who had a close relationship with Rudolph Giuliani, one of the President's personal lawyers.P? Costello told Cohen that he had a "back channel of communication" to Giuliani, and that Giuliani had said the "channel" was "crucial" and "must be maintained."[1023] On April 20, 2018, the New York Times published an article about the President's relationship with and treatment of Cohen.[1024] The President responded with a series of tweets predicting that Cohen would not "flip":

> The New York Times and a third rate reporter ... are going out of their way to destroy Michael Cohen and his relationship with me in the hope that he will 'flip.' They use non• existent 'sources' and a drunk/drugged up loser who hates Michael, a fine person with a wonderful family. Michael is a businessman for his own account/lawyer who I have always liked & respected. Most people will flip if the Government lets them out of trouble, even if it means lying or making up stories. Sorry, I don't see Michael doing that despite the horrible Witch Hunt and the dishonest media![1025]

In an email that day to Cohen, Costello wrote that he had spoken with Giuliani.[1026] Costello told Cohen the conversation was "Very Very Positive[.] You are 'loved' ... they are in our comer.... Sleep well tonight[], you have friends in high places."[1027]

Cohen said that following these messages he believed he had the support of the White House if he continued to toe the party line, and he determined to stay on message and be part of the team.[1028] At the time, Cohen's understood that his legal fees were still being paid by the Trump Organization, which he said was important to him.[1029] Cohen believed he needed the power of the President to take care of him, so he needed to defend the President and stay on message.l'P?

Cohen also recalled speaking with the President's personal counsel about pardons after the searches of his home and office had occurred, at a time when the media had reported that pardon discussions were occurring at the White House.[1031] Cohen told the President's personal counsel he had been a loyal lawyer and servant, and he said that after the searches he was in an uncomfortable position and wanted to know what was in it for him.[1032] According to Cohen, the President's personal counsel responded that Cohen should stay on message, that the investigation was a witch hunt, and that everything would be fine.[1033] Cohen understood based on this conversation and previous conversations about pardons with the President's personal counsel that as long as he stayed on message, he would be taken care of by the President, either through a pardon or through the investigation being shut down.[1034]

On April 24, 2018, the President responded to a reporter's inquiry whether he would consider a pardon for Cohen with, "Stupid question."[1035] On June 8, 2018, the President said he "hadn't even thought about" pardons for Manafort or Cohen, and continued, "It's far too early to be thinking about that. They haven't been convicted of anything. There's nothing to pardon."[1036] And on June 15, 2018, the President expressed sympathy for Cohen, Manafort, and Flynn in a press interview and said, "I feel badly about a lot of them, because I think a lot of it is very unfair."[1037]

5. The President's Conduct After Cohen Began Cooperating with the Government

On July 2, 2018, ABC News reported based on an "exclusive" interview with Cohen that Cohen "strongly signaled his willingness to cooperate with special counsel Robert Mueller and federal prosecutors in the Southern District of New York--even if that puts President Trump in jeopardy.v'P" That week, the media reported that Cohen had added an attorney to his legal team who previously had worked as a legal advisor to President Bill Clinton.[1039]

Beginning on July 20, 2018, the media reported on the existence of a recording Cohen had made of a conversation he had with candidate Trump about a payment made to a second woman who said she had had an affair with Trump.[1040] On July 21, 2018, the President responded: "Inconceivable that the government would break into a lawyer's office (early in the moming}-• almost unheard of. Even more inconceivable that a lawyer would tape a client—totally unheard of & perhaps illegal. The good news is that your favorite President did nothing wrongl'"?" On July 27, 2018, after the media reported that Cohen was willing to inform investigators that Donald Trump Jr. told his father about the June 9, 2016 meeting to get "dirt" on Hillary Clinton,[1042] the President tweeted: "[S]o the Fake News doesn't waste my time with dumb questions, NO, I did NOT know of the meeting with my son, Don jr. Sounds to me like someone is trying to make up stories in order to get himself out of an unrelated jam (Taxi cabs maybe?). He even retained Bill and Crooked Hillary's lawyer. Gee, I wonder if they helped him make the choicel'"?"

On August 21, 2018, Cohen pleaded guilty in the Southern District of New York to eight felony charges, including two counts of campaign-finance violations based on the payments he had made during the final weeks of the campaign to women who said they had affairs with the President.'?" During the plea hearing, Cohen stated that he had worked "at the direction of" the candidate in making those payments.'?" The next day, the President contrasted Cohen's cooperation with Manafort's refusal to cooperate, tweeting, "I feel very badly for Paul Manafort and his wonderful family. 'Justice' took a 12 year old tax case, among other things, applied tremendous pressure on him and, unlike Michael Cohen, he refused to 'break'—make up stories in order to get a 'deal.' Such respect for a brave man!"[1046]

On September 17, 2018, this Office submitted written questions to the President that included questions about the Trump Tower Moscow project and attached Cohen's written statement to Congress and the Letter of Intent signed by the President. Among other issues, the questions asked the President to describe the timing and substance of discussions he had with Cohen about the project, whether they discussed a potential trip to Russia, and whether the President "at any time direct[ed] or suggest[ed] that discussions about the Trump Moscow project should cease," or whether the President was "informed at any time that the project had been abandoned."?"

On November 20, 2018, the President submitted written responses that did not answer those questions about Trump Tower Moscow directly and did not provide any information about the timing of the candidate's discussions with Cohen about the project or whether he participated in any discussions about the project being abandoned or no longer pursued.P'? Instead, the President's answers stated in relevant part:

I had few conversations with Mr. Cohen on this subject. As I recall, they were brief, and they were not memorable. I was not enthused about the proposal, and I do not recall any discussion of travel to Russia in connection with it. I do not remember discussing it with anyone else at the Trump Organization, although it is possible. I do not recall being aware at the time of any communications between Mr. Cohen and Felix Sater and any Russian government official regarding the Letter of Intent.[1050]

On November 29, 2018, Cohen pleaded guilty to making false statements to Congress based on his statements about the Trump Tower Moscow project.[1051] In a plea agreement with this Office, Cohen agreed to "provide truthful information regarding any and all matters as to which this Office deems relevant."[1052] Later on November 29, after Cohen's guilty plea had become public, the President spoke to reporters about the Trump Tower Moscow project, saying:

> I decided not to do the project. . . . I decided ultimately not to do it. There would have been nothing wrong if I did do it. If I did do it, there would have been nothing wrong. That was my business. . . . It was an option that I decided not to do. . . . I decided not to do it. The primary reason . . . I was focused on running for President. . . . I was running my business while I was campaigning. There was a good chance that I wouldn't have won, in which case I would've gone back into the business. And why should I lose lots of opportunities

The President also said that Cohen was "a weak person. And by being weak, unlike other people that you watch—he is a weak person. And what he's trying to do is get a reduced sentence. So he's lying about a project that everybody knew about."[1054] The President also brought up Cohen's written submission to Congress regarding the Trump Tower Moscow project: "So here's the story: Go back and look at the paper that Michael Cohen wrote before he testified in the House and/or Senate. It talked about his position."[1055] The President added, "Even if [Cohen] was right, it doesn't matter because I was allowed to do whatever I wanted during the campaign."[1056]

In light of the President's public statements following Cohen's guilty plea that he "decided not to do the project," this Office again sought information from the President about whether he participated in any discussions about the project being abandoned or no longer pursued, including when he "decided not to do the project," who he spoke to about that decision, and what motivated the decision.'?" The Office also again asked for the timing of the President's discussions with Cohen about Trump Tower Moscow and asked him to specify "what period of the campaign" he was involved in discussions concerning the project.[1058] In response, the President's personal counsel declined to provide additional information from the President and stated that "the President has fully answered the questions at issue."[1059]

In the weeks following Cohen's plea and agreement to provide assistance to this Office, the President repeatedly implied that Cohen's family members were guilty of crimes. On December 3, 2018, after Cohen had filed his sentencing memorandum, the President tweeted,

"'Michael Cohen asks judge for no Prison Time.' You mean he can do all of the TERRIBLE, unrelated to Trump, things having to do with fraud, big loans, Taxis, etc., and not serve a long prison term? He makes up stories to get a GREAT & ALREADY reduced deal for himself, and get his wife and father-in-law (who has the money?) off Scott Free. He lied for this outcome and should in m o inion serve a full and com lete sentence.t"P'"

On December 12, 2018, Cohen was sentenced to three years of imprisonment.[1P?] The next day, the President sent a series of tweets that said:

I never directed Michael Cohen to break the law.... Those charges were just agreed to by him in order to embarrass the president and get a much reduced prison sentence, which he did—including the fact that *his family was temporarily let off the hook*. As a lawyer, Michael has great liability to me![1063]

On December 16, 2018, the President tweeted, "Remember, Michael Cohen only became a 'Rat' after the FBI did something which was absolutely unthinkable & unheard of until the Witch Hunt was illegally started. They BROKE INTO AN

AITORNEY'S OFFICE! Why didn't they break into the DNC to get the Server, or Crooked's office?"[1064]

Jn January 2019, after the media reported that Cohen would provide public testimony in a congressional hearing, the President made additional public comments suggesting that Cohen's family members had committed crimes. In an interview on Fox on January 12, 2019, the President was asked whether he was worried about Cohen's testimony and responded:

> [I]n order to get his sentence reduced, [Cohen] says "I have an idea, I'll ah, tell—I'll give you some information on the president." Well, there is no information. But *he should give information maybe on his father-in-law because that's the one that people want to look at because where does that money–that's the money in the Family And I guess he didn't want to talk about his father-in-law,* he's trying to get his sentence reduced. So it's ah, pretty sad. You know, it's weak and it's very sad to watch a thing like that.[1065]

On January 18, 2019, the President tweeted, "Kevin Corke, @FoxNews 'Don't forget, Michael Cohen has already been convicted of perjury and fraud, and as recently as this week, the Wall Street Journal has suggested that he may have stolen tens of thousands of dollars....' Lying to reduce his jail time! *Watch father-in-law!*"

On January 23, 2019, Cohen postponed his congressional testimony, citing threats against his family.[1067] The next day, the President tweeted, "So interesting that bad lawyer Michael Cohen, who sadly will not be testifying before Congress, is using the lawyer of Crooked Hillary Clinton to represent him–, how did that happen?"[1068]

Also in January 2019, Giuliani gave press interviews that appeared to confirm Cohen's account that the Trump Organization pursued the Trump Tower Moscow project well past January 2016. Giuliani stated that "it's our understanding that [discussions about the Trump Moscow project] went on throughout 2016. Weren't a lot of them, but there were conversations. Can't be sure of the exact date. But the president can remember having conversations with him about it. . . . The president also remembers—yeah, probably could be up to as far as October, November."[1069] In an interview with the New York Times, Giuliani quoted the President as saying that the discussions regarding the Trump Moscow project were "going on from the day I announced to the day I won."[1070] On January 21, 2019,

Giuliani issued a statement that said: "My recent statements about discussions during the 2016 campaign between Michael Cohen and candidate Donald Trump about a potential Trump Moscow 'project' were hypothetical and not based on conversations I had with the president.t"?"

Analysis

In analyzing the President's conduct related to Cohen, the following evidence is relevant to the elements of obstruction of justice.

a.   Obstructive act. We gathered evidence of the President's conduct related to Cohen on two issues: (i) whether the President or others aided or participated in Cohen's false statements to Congress, and (ii) whether the President took actions that would have the natural tendency to prevent Cohen from providing truthful information to the government.

i.   First, with regard to Cohen's false statements to Congress, while there is evidence, described below, that the President knew Cohen provided false testimony to Congress about the Trump Tower Moscow project, the evidence available to us does not establish that the President directed or aided Cohen's false testimony.

Cohen said that his statements to Congress followed a "party line" that developed within the campaign to align with the President's public statements distancing the President from Russia. Cohen also recalled that, in speaking with the President in advance of testifying, he made it clear that he would stay on message-which Cohen believed they both understood would require false testimony. But Cohen said that he and the President did not explicitly discuss whether Cohen's testimony about

455

the Trump Tower Moscow project would be or was false, and the President did not direct him to provide false testimony. Cohen also said he did not tell the President about the specifics of his planned testimony. During the time when his statement to Congress was being drafted and circulated to members of the JOA, Cohen did not speak directly to the President about the statement, but rather communicated with the President's personal counsel-as corroborated by phone records showing extensive communications between Cohen and the President's personal counsel before Cohen submitted his statement and when he testified before Congress.

Cohen recalled that in his discussions with the President's personal counsel on August 27, 2017-the day before Cohen's statement was submitted to Congress-Cohen said that there were more communications with Russia and more communications with candidate Trump than the statement reflected. Cohen recalled expressing some concern at that time. According to Cohen, the President's personal counsel-who did not have first-hand knowledge of the project• responded by saying that there was no need to muddy the water, that it was unnecessary to include those details because the project did not take place, and that Cohen should keep his statement short and tight, not elaborate, stay on message, and not contradict the President. Cohen's recollection of the content of those conversations is consistent with direction about the substance of Cohen's draft statement that appeared to come from members of the IDA. For example, Cohen omitted any reference to his outreach to Russian government officials to set up a meeting between Trump and Putin during the United Nations General Assembly, and Cohen believed it was a decision of the JDA to delete the sentence, "The building project led me to make limited contacts with Russian government officials."

The President's personal counsel declined to provide us with his account of his conversations with Cohen, and there is no evidence available to us that indicates that the President was aware of the information Cohen provided to the President's personal counsel. The President's conversations with his personal counsel were presumptively protected by attorney-client privilege, and we did not seek to obtain the contents of any such communications. The absence of evidence about the President and his counsel's conversations about the drafting of Cohen's statement precludes us from assessing what, if any, role the President played.

ii.   Second, we considered whether the President took actions that would have the natural tendency to prevent Cohen from providing truthful information to criminal investigators or to Congress.

Before Cohen began to cooperate with the government, the President publicly and privately urged Cohen to stay on message and not "flip." Cohen recalled the President's personal counsel telling him that he would be protected so long as he did not go "rogue." In the days and weeks that followed the April 2018 searches of Cohen's home and office, the President told reporters that Cohen was a "good man" and said he was "a fine person with a wonderful family ... who I have always liked & respected." Privately, the President told Cohen to "hang in there" and "stay strong." People who were close to both Cohen and the President passed messages to Cohen that "the President loves you," "the boss loves you," and "everyone knows the boss has your back." Through the President's personal counsel, the President also had previously told Cohen "thanks for what you do" after Cohen provided information to the media about payments to women that, according to Cohen, both Cohen and the President knew was false. At that time, the Trump Organization continued to pay Cohen's legal fees, which was important to Cohen. Cohen also recalled discussing the possibility of a pardon with the President's personal counsel, who told him to stay on message and everything would be fine. The President indicated in his public statements that a pardon had not been ruled out, and also stated publicly that "[m]ost people will flip if the Government lets them out of trouble" but that he "d[idn't] see Michael doing that."

After it was reported that Cohen intended to cooperate with the government, however, the President accused Cohen of "mak[ing] up stories in order to get himself out of an unrelated jam (Taxi cabs maybe?)," called Cohen a "rat," and on multiple occasions publicly suggested that Cohen's family members had committed crimes. The evidence concerning this sequence of events could support an inference that the President used inducements in the form of positive messages in an effort to get Cohen not to cooperate, and then turned to attacks and intimidation to deter the provision of information or undermine Cohen's credibility once Cohen began cooperating.

b.   Nexus to an official proceeding. The President's relevant conduct towards Cohen occurred when the President knew the Special Counsel's Office, Congress, and the U.S. Attorney's Office for the Southern District ofNew York were investigating Cohen's conduct. The President acknowledged through his public statements and tweets that Cohen potentially could cooperate with the government investigations c.   Intent. In analyzing the President's intent in his actions towards Cohen as a potential witness, there is evidence that could support the inference that the President intended to discourage Cohen from cooperating with the government because Cohen's information would shed adverse light on the President's campaign-period conduct and statements.

i.   Cohen's false congressional testimony about the Trump Tower Moscow project was designed to minimize connections between the President and Russia and to help limit the congressional and DOJ Russia investigations-a goal that was in the President's interest, as reflected by the President's own statements. During and after the campaign, the President made repeated statements that he had "no business" in Russia and said that there were "no deals that could happen in Russia, because we've stayed away." As Cohen knew, and as he recalled communicating to the President during the campaign, Cohen's pursuit of the Trump Tower Moscow project cast doubt on the accuracy or completeness of these statements.

In connection with his guilty plea, Cohen admitted that he had multiple conversations with candidate Trump to give him status updates about the Trump Tower Moscow project, that the conversations continued through at least June 2016, and that he discussed with Trump possible travel to Russia to pursue the project. The conversations were not off-hand, according to Cohen, because the project had the potential to be so lucrative. In addition, text messages to and from Cohen and other records further establish that Cohen's efforts to advance the project did not end in January 2016 and that in May and June 2016, Cohen was considering the timing for possible trips to Russia by him and Trump in connection with the project.

The evidence could support an inference that the President was aware of these facts at the time of Cohen's false statements to Congress. Cohen discussed the project with the President in early 2017 following media inquiries. Cohen recalled that on September 20, 2017, the day after he released to the public his opening remarks to Congress-which said the project "was terminated in January of 2016"-the President's personal counsel told him the President was pleased with what Cohen had said about Trump Tower Moscow. And after Cohen's guilty plea, the President told reporters that he had ultimately decided not to do the project, which supports the inference that he remained aware of his own involvement in the project and the period during the Campaign in which the project was· being pursued.

ii.   The President's public remarks following Cohen's guilty plea also suggest that the President may have been concerned about what Cohen told investigators about the Trump Tower Moscow project. At the time the President submitted written answers to questions from this Office about the project and other subjects, the media had reported that Cohen was cooperating with the government but Cohen had not yet pleaded guilty to making false statements to Congress. Accordingly, it was not publicly known what information about the project Cohen had provided to the government. In his written answers, the President did not provide details about the timing and substance of his discussions with Cohen about the project and gave no indication that he had decided to no longer pursue the project. Yet after Cohen pleaded guilty, the President publicly stated that he had personally made the decision to abandon the project. The President then declined to clarify the seeming discrepancy to our Office or answer additional questions. The content and timing of the President's provision of information about his knowledge and actions regarding the Trump Tower Moscow project is evidence that the President may have been concerned about the information that Cohen could provide as a witness.

111.   The President's concern about Cohen cooperating may have been directed at the Southern District of New York investigation into other aspects of the President's dealings with Cohen rather than an investigation of Trump Tower Moscow. There also is some evidence that the President's concern about Cohen cooperating was based on the President's stated belief that Cohen would provide

false testimony against the President in an attempt to obtain a lesser sentence for his unrelated criminal conduct. The President tweeted that Manafort, unlike Cohen, refused to "break" and "make up stories in order to get a 'deal.'" And after Cohen pleaded guilty to making false statements to Congress, the President said, "what (CohenJ's trying to do is get a reduced sentence. So he's lying about a project that everybody knew about." But the President also appeared to defend the underlying conduct, saying, "Even if [Cohen] was right, it doesn't matter because I was allowed to do whatever I wanted during the campaign." As described above, there is evidence that the President knew that Cohen had made false statements about the Trump Tower Moscow project and that Cohen did so to protect the President and minimize the President's connections to Russia during the campaign.

iv.   Finally, the President's statements insinuating that members of Cohen's family committed crimes after Cohen began cooperating with the government could be viewed as an effort to retaliate against Cohen and chill further testimony adverse to the President by Cohen or others. It is possible that the President believes, as reflected in his tweets, that Cohen "ma[d]e[] up stories" in order to get a deal for himself and "get his wife and father-in-law ... off Scott Free." It also is possible that the President's mention of Cohen's wife and father-in-law were not intended to affect Cohen as a witness but rather were part of a public-relations strategy aimed at discrediting Cohen and deflecting attention away from the President on Cohen-related matters. But the President's suggestion that Cohen's family members committed crimes happened more than once, including just before Cohen was sentenced (at the same time as the President stated that Cohen "should, in my opinion, serve a full and complete sentence") and again just before Cohen

was scheduled to testify before Congress. The timing of the statements supports an inference that they were intended at least in part to discourage Cohen from further cooperation.

****

909 In August 2018 and November 2018, Cohen pleaded guilty to multiple crimes of deception, including making false statements to Congress about the Trump Tower Moscow project, as described later in this section.

When Cohen first met with investigators from this Office, he repeated the same lies he told Congress about the Trump Tower Moscow project. Cohen 8/7/18 302, at 12-17. his false statements concerning the [Trump Tower] Moscow Project, but also his broader efforts through public statements and testimony before Congress to minimize his role in, and what he knew about, contacts between the [Trump Organization] and Russian interests during the course of the campaign. . . . The information provided by Cohen about the [Trump Tower] Moscow Project in these proffer sessions is consistent with and corroborated by other information obtained in the course of the [Special Counsel's Office's] investigation. . . . The defendant, without prompting by the [Special Counsel's Office], also corrected other false and misleading statements that he had made concerning his outreach to and contacts with Russian officials during the course ofthe campaign." Gov't Sentencing Submission at 4, UnitedStates v, Michael Cohen, I: 18-cr-850 (S.D.N. Y. Dec. 7, 2018), Doc. 14. At Cohen's sentencing, our Office further explained that Cohen had "provided valuable information ... while taking care and being careful to note what he knows and what he doesn't know." Transcript at 19, United States v. Michael Cohen, 1: I 8-cr-850 (S.D.N.Y. Dec. 12, 2018), Doc. 17 (Cohen 12/12/18 Transcript).

910 See Volume I, Section IV .A. I, supra (noting that starting in at least 2013, several employees of the Trump Organization, including then-president of the organization Donald J. Trump, pursued a Trump Tower Moscow deal with several Russian counterparties).

911 Cohen 9/12/18 302, at 1-4; Cohen 8/7/18 302, at 15.

912 Cohen 9/12/18 302, at 2, 4.

913 Cohen 9/12/18 302, at 4.

918 See FS00004 (12/30/15 Text Message, Cohen to Sater); TRUMPORG MC 000233 (1/11/16 Email, Cohen to pr_peskova@prpress.gof.ru); MDC-H-000690 (1/14/16- Eail, Cohen to info@prpress.gov.ru); TRUMPORG_MC_000235 (l/16/16 Email, Cohen to pr_peskova@prpress.gov.ru).

919 1/20/16 Email, Poliakova to Cohen; Call Records ofMichael Cohen. (Showing a 22-minute call on January 20, 2016, between Cohen and the number Poliakova provided in her email); Cohen 9/12/18 302, at 2-3. After the call, Cohen saved Poliakova's contact information in his Trump Organization Outlook contact list. I /20/16 Cohen Microsoft Outlook Entry (6:22 a.m.).

92° Cohen l 1/20/18 302, at 5.

921 Cohen 11 /20/18 302, at 5-6; Cohen I J"/12/18 302, at 4.

922 Cohen 11/20/18 302, at 5.

923 Cohen 9/12/18 302, at 5.

924 FSOOOI J (1/21/16 Text Messages, Sater & Cohen).

925 Cohen 9/12/l 8 302, at 5; 1/25/16 Email, Sater to Cohen (attachment).

926 Cohen 11/20/18 302, at 5.

927 Cohen 9/12/18 302, at 6. In later congressional testimony, Cohen stated that he briefed Trump on the project approximately six times after January 2016. Hearing on Issues Related to Trump Organization Before the House Oversight and Reform Cammi/lee, I 16th Cong. (Feb. 27, 2019) (CQ Cong. Transcripts, at 24) (testimony of Michael Cohen).

928 Cohen 9/12/18 302, at 6.

929 Cohen 9/18/18 302, at 4.

914 Cohen 9/12/18 302, at 4, 10.

915 MDC-H-000618-25 (1 0/28/15 Letter ofIntent, signed by Donald J. Trump, Trump Acquisition, LLC and Andrey Rozov, I.C. Expert Investment Company); Cohen 9/12/18 302, at 3; Written Responses of Donald J. Trump (Nov.20,2018), at 15 (Response to Question III, Parts (a) through (g)).

916 MDC-H-000600 (12/19/15 Email, Sater to Cohen).

917 Cohen 9/12/18 302, at 5.

93° Cohen 9/12/18 302, at I 0.

931 Cohen 9/12/18 302, at 7.

932 Cohen 9/12/18 302, at 7.

933 FSOOO 15 (5/4/16 Text Message, Sater to Cohen).

934 FSOOO 15 (5/4/16 Text Message, Cohen to Sater).

935 FSOOO 16-17 (5/5/16 Text Messages, Sater & Cohen).

936 Cohen 9/12/ 18 302, at 7.

937 Cohen 9/12/18 302, at 7.

938 Cohen 9/12/18 302, at 7-8.

939 Cohen 9/12/18 302, at 8.

94° Cohen 3/19/19 302, at 2.

941   Cohen 3/19/19 302, at 2. Cohen could not recall the precise timing of this conversation, but said he thought it occurred in June or July 2016. Cohen recalled that the conversation happened at some point after candidate Trump was publicly stating that he had nothing to do with Russia. Cohen 3/19/19 302, at2.

942 Cohen 3/19/19 302, at 2.

943 Cohen 3/19/19 302, at 2.

944 Cohen 11/20/18 302, at I; Cohen 9/18/18 302, at 3, 5; Cohen 9/12/ 18 302, at 9.

945 Cohen 9/18/18 302, at 1-2; see also Rtskhiladze 4/4/18 302, at 8-9.

946 Cohen 9/ 18/18 3 02, at 1-2.

947 Cohen 9/ 18/18 302, at 3.

948 Cohen 11/20/18 302, at 4.

949 Cohen 9/18/18 302, at 5. The article was published on February 19, 2017, and reported that Sater and Cohen had been working on plan for a Trump Tower Moscow "as recently as the fall of 2015" but had come to a halt because of the presidential campaign. Consistent with Cohen's intended patty line message, the article stated, "Cohen said the Trump Organization had received a letter of intent for a project in Moscow from a Russian real estate developer at that time but determined that the project was not feasible." Megan Twohey & Scott Shane,A Back-Channel Planfor Ukraine and Russia, Courtesy a/Trump Associates, New York Times (Feb. 19, 2017).

95° Cohen 9/18/18 302, at 5-6.

951 hen 9/18/18 302, at 6.

952 Cohen 9/12/18 302, at I 0.

953 P-SC0-000000328 (5/9/17 Letter, HPSCI to Cohen); P-SC0-000000331 (5/12/17 Letter, SSC!to Cohen).

954 Cohen 1 1 /20/1 8 302, at 2-3.

955 Cohen 11/20/18 302, at 2-3.

956 Cohen I 1/12/1 8 302, at 2; Cohen I 1/20/19 302, at 3.

957 Cohen 11/12/18 302, at 2.

958   Cohen   11/12/18 302, at 2-3; Cohen   11/20/18, at 2-6. Cohen told investigators about his conversations with the President's personal counsel after waiving any privilege of his own and after this Office

advised his counsel not to provide any communications that would be covered by any other privilege, including communications protected by a joint defense or common interest privilege. As a result, most of what Cohen told us about his conversations with the President's personal counsel concerned what Cohen had communicated to the President's personal counsel, and not what was said in response. Cohen described certain statements made by the President's personal counsel, however, that are set forth in this section. Cohen and his counsel were better positioned than this Office to evaluate whether any privilege protected those statements because they had knowledge of the scope of their joint defense agreement and access to privileged communications that may have provided context for evaluating the statements they shared. After interviewing Cohen about these Trump Tower Moscow. The President's personal counsel declined and, through his own counsel, indicated that he could not disaggregate information he had obtained from Cohen from information he had obtained from other parties in the IDA. Tn view of the admonition this Office gave to Cohen's counsel to withhold communications that could be covered by privilege, the President's personal counsel's uncertainty about the provenance of his own knowledge, the burden on a privilege holder to establish the elements to support a claim of privilege, and the substance of the statements themselves, we have included relevant statements Cohen provided in this report. Tf the statements were to be used in a context beyond this report, further analysis could be warranted.

959 Cohen 11 /20/18 302, at 6.

96° Cohen 11 /20/18 3 02, at 2, 4.

961 Cohen 11/20/18 302, at 4.

962 Cohen 9/18/18 302, at 8; Cohen 11 /20/ 18 302, at 3-4.

963 Cohen 11 /20/18 302, at 4.

964 Cohen 9/18/18 302, at 11; Cohen 11/20/18 302, at 2.

965 P-SC0-000003680 and P-SC0-0000003687 (8/ 16/ 17 Email and Attachment, Michael Cohen's Counsel to Cohen). Cohen said it was not his idea to write a letter to Congress about Trump Tower Moscow. Cohen 9/18/18 302, at 7.

966 P-SC0-00009478 (Statement of Michael D. Cohen, Esq. (Aug. 28, 2017)).

967 P-SC0-00009478 (Statement of Michael D. Cohen, Esq. (Aug. 28, 2017)).

968 P-SC0-00009478 (Statement of Michael D. Cohen, Esq. (Aug. 28, 2017)).

969 P-SC0-00009478 (Statement of Michael D. Cohen, Esq. (Aug. 28, 2017)).

970 P-SC0-00009478 (Statement of Michael D. Cohen, Esq. (Aug. 28, 2017)).

971 Cohen 9/12/18 302, at 8-9. Cohen also testified in Congress that the President's counsel reviewed and edited the statement. Hearing on Issues Related to Trump Organization Before the House Oversight and Reform Committee, I 16th Cong. (Feb. 27, 2019) (CQ Cong. Transcripts, at 24-25) (testimony by Michael Cohen). Because ofconcerns about the common interest privilege, we did not obtain or review all drafts of Cohen's statement. Based on the drafts that were released through this Office's filter process, it appears that the substance of the four principal false statements described above were contained in an early draft prepared by Cohen and his counsel. P-SC0-0000003680 and P-SC0-0000003687 (8/16/17Email and Attachment, Cohen's counsel to Cohen).

972 P-SC0-0000003687 (8/16/17 Draft Statement of Michael Cohen); Cohen 11/20/18 302, at 4.

973 Cohen 11/20/18 302, at 4. A different line stating that Cohen did "not recall any response to my email [to Peskov in January 2016], nor any other contacts by me with Mr. Peskov or other Russian government

officials about the proposal" remained in the draft. See P-SC0-0000009478 (Statement of Michael D. Cohen, Esq. (Aug. 28, 2017)).

974 Cohen 11/20/18 3 02, at 4.

975 Cohen 11/20/18 302, at 5.

976 Cohen 9/18/18 302, at 10-11.

977 Cohen 9/18/18 302, at 11; Cohen 11/12/18 302, at 4.

978 Cohen 9/18/18 302, at 11; Cohen 11/12/18 302, at 5.

979 Cohen 11/12/18 302, at 5.

98° Cohen 9/18/18 302, at 11.

981 Cohen 3/19/19 302, at 2.

982 Cohen 3/19/19 302, at 2; see Cohen 9/18/18 302, at 11 (recalling that he was told that if he stayed on message and kept the President out of the narrative, the President would have his back).

983 Cohen 9/12/18 302, at 8; Information at 4-5, United States v. Michael Cohen, 1:18-cr-850 (S.D.N.Y. Nov. 29, 2018), Doc. 2 (Cohen Information).

984 Cohen 11/20/18 302, at 4.

985 Cohen 11/20/18 302, at 4; Cohen 11/12/18 302, at 2-3, 4, 6.

986 Cohen 9/12/18 302, at 9.

987 Cohen 9/12/18 302, at 8-9.

988 Cohen 11/12/18 302, at 2-3; Cohen 11/20/18 302, at 5; Call Records of Michael Cohen (Reflecting three contacts on August 18, 2017 (24 seconds; 5 minutes 25 seconds; and 10 minutes 58 seconds); two contacts on August 19 (23 seconds and 24 minutes 26 seconds); three contacts on August 23 (8 seconds; 20 minutes 33 seconds; and 5 minutes 8 seconds); one contact on August 24 (11 minutes 59 seconds); 14 contacts on August 27 (28 seconds; 4 minutes 37 seconds; 1 minute 16 seconds; 1 minutes 35seconds; 6 minutes 16 seconds; 1 minutes 10 seconds; 3 minutes 5 seconds; 18 minutes 55 seconds; 4 minutes 56 seconds; 11 minutes 6 seconds; 8 seconds; 3 seconds; 2 seconds; 2 seconds).

989 Cohen 11/20/18 302, at 5; Call Records of Michael Cohen. (Reflecting 14 contacts on August 27, 2017 (28 seconds; 4 minutes 37 seconds; 1 minute 16 seconds; 1 minutes 35 seconds; 6 minutes 16 seconds; 1 minutes 10 seconds; 3 minutes 5 seconds; 18 minutes 55 seconds; 4 minutes 56 seconds; 11 minutes 6 seconds; 8 seconds; 3 seconds; 2 seconds; 2 seconds)).

990 Cohen 11/20/18 302, at 5.

991 Cohen 11/20/18 302, at 5. Cohen also vaguely recalled telling the President's personal counsel that he spoke with a woman from the Kremlin and that the President's personal counsel responded to the effect of "so what?" because the deal never happened. Cohen 11/20/18 302, at 5.

992 Cohen 11/20/18 3 02, at 5.

993 Cohen 11/20/18 302, at 5.

994 2/8/19 email, Counsel for personal counsel to the President to Special Counsel's Office

995 Cohen 9/18/18 302, at 7; Carol D. Leonnig et al., Trump's business sought deal on a Trump Tower in Moscow while he ran/or president, Washington Post (Aug. 27, 2017).

996 Carol D. Leonnig et al., Trump's business sought deal on a Trump Tower in Moscow while he ran/or president, Washington Post (Aug. 27, 2017).

997 Cohen 9/18/18 302, at 7.

998 P-SC0-000009477 - 9478 (8/28/17 Letter and Attachment, Cohen to SSCI).

999 Cohen 11/12/18 302, at 2; Cohen 9/12/18 302, at 9. 100° Cohen 9/12/18 302, at 9.

1001   Cohen 9/18/18 302, at 7; see, e.g., READ: Michael Cohen's statement to the Senate intelligence committee, CNN (Sept. 19, 2017).

1002   Cohen 9/18/18 302, at 7.

1003   Cohen 9/18/18 302, at 7; Cohen 11/20/18 302, at 6.

1004   Cohen 11/20/18 302, at 6. Phone records show that the President's personal counsel called Cohen on the morning of September 20, 2017, and they spoke for approximately 11 minutes, and that they had two more contacts that day, one of which lasted approximately 18 minutes. Call Records of Michael Cohen. (Reflecting three contacts on September 20, 2017, with calls lasting for 11 minutes 3 seconds; 2 seconds; and 18 minutes 38 seconds).

1005   Cohen Information, at 4; Executive Session, Permanent Select Committee on Intelligence, U.S. House of Representatives, Interview of Michael Cohen (Oct. 24, 2017), at I 0-11, 117-119.

1006   Call Records of Michael Cohen. (Reflecting two contacts on October 24, 2017 (12 minutes 8 seconds and 8 minutes 27 seconds) and three contacts on October 25, 2017 (I second; 4 minutes 6 seconds; and 6 minutes 6 seconds)).

1007   See, e.g., Michael Rothfeld & Joe Palazzolo, Trump Lawyer Arranged $130, 000 Paymentfor Adult-Film Star's Silence, Wall Street Journal (Jan. 12, 2018).

1008   The Office was authorized to investigate Cohen's establishment and use of Essential Consultants LLC, which Cohen created to facilitate the $130,000 payment during the campaign, based on evidence that the entity received funds from Russian-backed entities. Cohen's use of Essential Consultants to facilitate the $130,000 payment to the woman during the campaign was part of the Office's referral of certain Cohen-related matters to the U.S. Attorney's Office for the Southern District ofNew York.

1009   See, e.g., Mark Berman, Longtime Trump attorney says he made $130, 000 payment to Stormy Daniels with his money, Washington Post (Feb. 14, 2018).

1010   Hearing on Issues Related to Trump Organization Before the House Oversight and Reform Committee, I 16th Cong. (Feb. 27, 2019) (CQ Cong. Transcripts, at 147-148) (testimony ofMichael Cohen). Toll records show that Cohen was connected to a White House phone number for approximately five minutes on January 19, 2018, and for approximately seven minutes on January 30, 2018, and that Cohen called Melania Trump's cell phone several times between January 26, 2018, and January 30, 2018. Call Records of Michael Cohen.

1011   2/19/18 Text Message, President's personal counsel to Cohen; see Jim Rutenberg et al., Tools ofTrump's Fixer: Payouts, Intimidation and the Tabloids, New York Times (Feb. 18, 2018).

1012   Gov't Opp. to Def. Mot. for Temp. Restraining Order, In the Matter of Search Warrants Executed on April 9, 2018, 18-mj-3161 (S.D.N.Y. Apr. 13, 2018), Doc. I ("On April 9, 2018, agents from the New York field office of the Federal Bureau of Investigation ... executed search warrants for Michael Cohen's residence, hotel room, office, safety deposit box, and electronic devices.").

1013   Remarks by President Trump Before Meeting with Senior Military Leadership, White House (Apr. 9, 2018).

1014   Remarks by President Trump Before Meeting with Senior Military Leadership, White House (Apr. 9, 2018).

1015   Cohen, I 0/17/18 302, at I I.

1016   Cohen 3/19/19 302, at 4.

1017 Cohen 3/19/19 302, at 4.

1018 Cohen 9/12/18 302, at I I.

1019 Cohen 9/12/18 302, at I I.

102° Cohen 9/12/18 302, at 11.

1021 Cohen 9/12/18 302, at I I.

1022 4/17/18 Email, Citron to Cohen; 4/19/18 Email, Costello to Cohen; MC-SC0-001 (7/7/18 redacted billing statement from Davidoff, Hutcher & Citron to Cohen).

1023 4/21/18 Email, Costello to Cohen.

1024 See Maggie Haberman et al., Michael Cohen Has Said He Would Take a Bullet for Trump. Maybe Not Anymore., New York Times (Apr. 20, 2018).

1025 @realDonaldTrump 4/21/18 (9: 10 a.m. ET) Tweets.

1026 4/21/18 Email, Costello to Cohen.

1028 Cohen 9/12/18 302, at I I.

1029 Cohen 9/12/18 302, at 10.

103° Cohen 9/12/18 302, at 10.

1031 Cohen 11/20/18 302, at 7. At a White House press briefing on April 23, 2018, in response to a question about whether the White House had "close[d] the door one way or the other on the President pardoning Michael Cohen," Sanders said, "It's hard to close the door on something that hasn't taken place. I don't like to discuss or comment on hypothetical situations that may or may not ever happen. I would refer you to personal attorneys to comment on anything specific regarding that case, but we don't have anything at this point." Sarah Sanders, White House Daily Briefing, C-SPAN (Apr. 23, 2018).

1032 Cohen 11/20/18 302, at 7; Cohen 3/19/19 302, at 3.

1033 Cohen 3/19/19 302, at 3.

1034 Cohen 3/19/19 302, at 3-4.

1035 Remarks by President Trump and President Macron of France Before Restricted Bilateral Meeting, The White House (Apr. 24, 2018).

1036 President Donald Trump Holds Media Availability Before Departingfor the G-7 Summit, CQ Newsmaker Transcripts (June 8, 2018).

1037 Remarks by President Trump in Press Gaggle, The White House (June 15, 2018).

1038 EXCLUSIVE: Michael Cohen says family and country, not President Trump, is his 'first loyalty', ABC (July 2, 2018). Cohen said in the interview, "To be crystal 'clear, my wife, my daughter and my son, and this country have my first loyalty."

1039 See e.g., Darren Samuelsohn, Michael Cohen hires Clinton scandal veteran Lanny Davis, Politico (July 5, 2018).

1040 See, e.g., Matt Apuzzo et al., Michael Cohen Secretly Taped Trump Discussing Payment to Playboy Model, New York Times (July 20, 2018).

1041 @ralDonaldTrump 7/21/18 (8: IO a.m. ET) Tweet.

1042 See, e.g., Jim Sciutto, Cuomo Prime Time Transcript, CNN (July 26, 2018).

1043@realDonaldTrump 7/27/18 (7:26 a.m. ET) Tweet;@realDonaldTrump 7/27/18 (7:38 a.m. ET) Tweet; @realDonaldTrump 7/27/18 (7:56 a.m. ET) Tweet. At the time of these tweets, the press had reported that Cohen's financial interests in taxi cab medallions were being scrutinized by investigators. See, e.g., Matt

Apuzzo et al., Michael Cohen Secretly Taped Trump Discussing Payment to Playboy Model, New York Times (July 20, 2018).

1044 Cohen Information.

1045 Cohen 8/21/18 Transcript, at 23.

1046 @rea!DonaldTrump 8/22/18 (9:21 a.m. ET) Tweet.

1047 9/17/18 Letter, Special Counsel's Office to President's Personal Counsel (attaching written questions for the President, with attachments).

1048 9/17/18 Letter, Special Counsel's Office to President's Personal Counsel (attaching written questions for the President), Question III, Parts (a) through (g).

1049 Written Responses of Donald J. Trump (Nov. 20, 2018).

1050 Written Responses of Donald J. Trump (Nov. 20, 2018), at 15 (Response to Question III, Parts (a) through (g)).

1051 Cohen Information; Cohen 8/21/ I 8 Transcript.

1052 Plea Agreement at 4, United States v. Michael Cohen, I: 18-cr-850 (S.D.N.Y. Nov. 29, 2018).

1053 President Trump Departure Remarks, C-SPAN (Nov. 29, 2018). In contrast to the President's remarks following Cohen's guilty plea, Cohen's August 28, 2017 statement to Congress stated that Cohen, not the President, "decided to abandon the proposal" in late January 2016; that Cohen "did not ask or brief Mr. Trump ... before I made the decision to terminate further work on the proposal"; and that the decision

·   to abandon the proposal was "unrelated" to the Campaign. P-SC0-000009477 (Statement of Michael D. Cohen, Esq. (Aug. 28, 2017)).

1054 President Trump Departure Remarks, C-SPAN (Nov. 29, 2018).

1055 President Trump Departure Remarks, C-SPAN (Nov. 29, 2018).

1057 1/23/19 Letter, Special Counsel's Office to President's Personal Counsel.

1058 I /23/19 Letter, Special Counsel's Office to President's Personal Counsel.

1059 2/6/19 Letter, President's Personal Counsel to Special Counsel's Office.

1060 @rea1DonaldTrump 12/3/18 (10:24 a.m. ET and 10:29 a.m. ET) Tweets (emphasis added).

1061 @realDonaldTrump 12/3/18 (I 0:48 a.m. ET) Tweet.

1062 Cohen 12/12/18 Transcript.

1063 @rea1DonaldTrump 12/13/18 (8: 17 a.m. ET, 8:25 a.m. ET, and 8:39 a.m. ET) Tweets (emphasis

1064 @realDonaldTrump 12/16/18 (9:39 a.m. ET) Tweet

1065 Jeanine Pirro Interview with President Trump, Fox News (Jan. 12, 2019) (emphasis added).

1066 @realDonaldTrump 1 /18/19 (I 0:02 a.m. ET) Tweet (emphasis added).

1067 Statement by Lanny Davis, Cohen's personal counsel (Jan. 23, 2019).

1068 @realDonaldTrump 1/24/19 (7:48 a.m. ET) Tweet.

1069 Meet the Press Interview with Rudy Giuliani, NBC (Jan. 20, 2019).

1070 Mark Mazzetti et al., Moscow Skyscraper Talks Continued Through "the Day I Won," Trump Is Said to Acknowledge, New York Times (Jan. 20, 2019).

1071 Maggie Haberman, Giuliani Says His Moscow Trump Tower Comments Were "Hypothetical", New York Times (Jan. 21, 2019). In a letter to this Office, the President's counsel stated that Giuliani's public comments "were not intended to suggest nor did they reflect knowledge of the existence or timing

L.   Overarching Factual Issues

Although this report does not contain a traditional prosecution decision or declination decision, the evidence supports several general conclusions relevant to analysis of the facts concerning the President's course of conduct.

1.   Three features of this case render it atypical compared to the heartland obstruction of justice prosecutions brought by the Department of Justice.

First, the conduct involved actions by the President. Some of the conduct did not implicate the President's constitutional authority and raises garden-variety obstruction-of-justice issues. Other events we investigated, however, drew upon the President's Article II authority, which raised constitutional issues that we address in Volume II, Section IU.B, infra. A factual analysis of that conduct would have to take into account both that the President's acts were facially lawful and that his position as head of the Executive Branch provides him with unique and powerful means of influencing official proceedings, subordinate officers, and potential witnesses

Second, many obstruction cases involve the attempted or actual cover-up of an underlying crime. Personal criminal conduct can furnish strong evidence that the individual had an improper obstructive purpose, see, e.g., United States v. Willoughby, 860 F.2d 15, 24 (2d Cir. 1988), or that he contemplated an effect on an official proceeding, see, e.g., United States v. Binday, 804 F.3d 558, 591 (2d Cir. 2015). But proof of such a crime is not an element of an obstruction offense. See United States v. Greer, 872 F.3d 790, 798 (6th Cir. 2017) (stating, in applying the obstruction sentencing guideline, that "obstruction of a criminal investigation is punishable even if the prosecution is ultimately unsuccessful or even if the investigation ultimately reveals no underlying crime"). Obstruction of justice can be motivated by a desire to protect non-criminal personal interests, to protect against investigations where underlying criminal liability falls into a gray area, or to avoid personal embarrassment. The injury to the integrity of the justice system is the same regardless of whether a person committed an underlying wrong.

In this investigation, the evidence does not establish that the President was involved in an underlying crime related to Russian election interference. But the evidence does point to a range of other possible personal motives animating the President's conduct. These include concerns that continued investigation would call into question the legitimacy of his election and potential uncertainty about whether certain events-such as advance notice of WikiLeaks's release of hacked information or the June 9, 2016 meeting between senior campaign officials and Russians• could be seen as criminal activity by the President, his campaign, or his family.

Third, many of the President's acts directed at witnesses, including discouragement of cooperation with the government and suggestions of possible future pardons, occurred in public view. While it may be more difficult to establish that public-facing acts were motivated by a corrupt intent, the President's power to influence actions, persons, and events is enhanced by his unique ability to attract attention through use of mass communications. And no principle of law excludes public acts from the scope of obstruction statutes. If the likely effect of the acts is to intimidate witnesses or alter their testimony, the justice system's integrity is equally threatened.

2.   Although the events we investigated involved discrete acts-e.g., the President's statement to Comey about the Flynn investigation, his termination of Comey, and his efforts to remove the Special Counsel-it is important to view the President's pattern of conduct as a whole. That pattern sheds light on the nature of the President's acts and the inferences that can be drawn about his intent.

a.   Our investigation found multiple acts by the President that were capable of exerting undue influence over law enforcement investigations, including the Russian-interference and obstruction investigations. The incidents were often carried out through one-on-one meetings in which the President sought to use his official power outside of usual channels. These actions ranged from efforts to remove the Special Counsel and to reverse the effect of the Attorney General's recusal; to the attempted use of official power to limit the scope of the investigation; to direct and indirect contacts with witnesses with the potential to influence their testimony. Viewing the acts collectively can help to illuminate their significance. For example, the President's direction to McGahn to have the Special Counsel removed was followed almost immediately by his direction to Lewandowski to tell the Attorney General to limit the scope of the Russia investigation to prospective election-interference only-a temporal connection that suggests that both acts were taken with a related purpose with respect to the investigationThe President's efforts to influence the investigation were mostly unsuccessful, but that is largely because the persons who surrounded the President declined to carry out orders or accede to his requests. Comey did not end the investigation ofFlynn, which ultimately resulted in Flynn's prosecution and conviction for lying to the FBI. McGahn did not tell the Acting Attorney General that the Special Counsel must be removed, but was instead prepared to resign over the President's order.   Lewandowski and Dearborn did not deliver the President's message to Sessions that he should confine the Russia investigation to future election meddling only. And McGahn refused to recede from his recollections about events surrounding the President's direction to have the Special Counsel removed, despite the President's multiple demands that he do so. Consistent with that pattern, the evidence we obtained would not support potential obstruction charges against the President's aides and associates beyond those already filed.

b.   In considering the full scope of the conduct we investigated, the President's actions can be divided into two distinct phases reflecting a possible shift in the President's motives. In the first phase, before the President fired Comey, the President had been assured that the FBI had not opened an investigation of him personally. The President deemed it critically important to make public that he was not under investigation, and he included that information in his termination letter to Comey after other efforts to have that information disclosed were unsuccessful.

Soon after he fired Comey, however, the President became aware that investigators were conducting an obstruction-of-justice inquiry into his own conduct. That awareness marked a significant change in the President's conduct and the start of a second phase of action. The President launched public attacks on the investigation and individuals involved in it who could possess evidence adverse to the President, while in private, the President engaged in a series of targeted efforts to control the investigation. For instance, the President attempted to remove the Special Counsel; he sought to have Attorney General Sessions unrecuse himself and limit the investigation; he sought to prevent public disclosure of information about the June 9, 2016 meeting between Russians and campaign officials; and he used public forums to attack potential witnesses who might offer adverse information and to praise witnesses who declined to cooperate with the government. Judgments about the nature of the President's motives during each phase would be informed by the totality of the evidence.

Made in the USA
Lexington, KY
07 May 2019

Contents

S0-BYE-693

 **Ideas** The best writing begins with a strong idea.

A. Read this brainstorming web for a school newspaper article. Think about the purpose and audience. Cross out the topics that don't fit the purpose or audience.

Purpose: <u>to provide news and information about things going on at school</u>

Audience: <u>students, teachers, and parents</u>

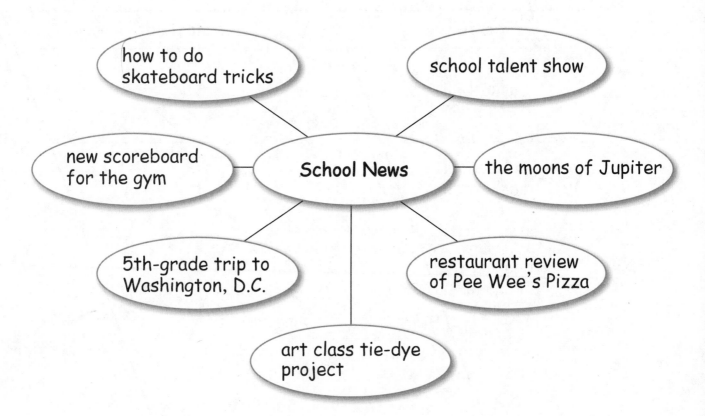

B. What would you write about if you were writing an article for your school newspaper? List three ideas below.

1. _____

2. _____

3. _____

 **Ideas** Make your ideas stronger by narrowing your focus.

A. A narrowing triangle can help you choose an idea that is specific enough to write about. Read Triangle 1 as an example. Then use Triangle 2 to think of a specific idea of your own. Complete the triangle.

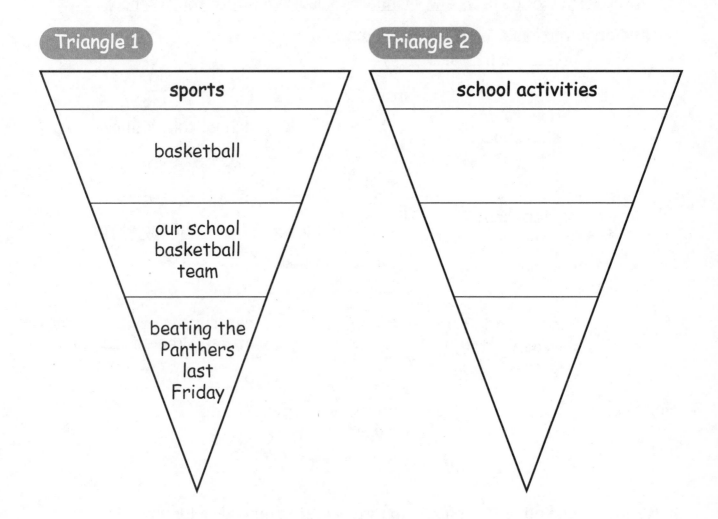

Triangle 1

sports

basketball

our school basketball team

beating the Panthers last Friday

Triangle 2

school activities

B. Find the proper nouns in Triangle 1. Write them below.

1. Team name: _____

2. Day of the week: _____

 **Ideas** To choose a strong idea, think about your audience and purpose for writing.

A. Read the list of purposes for writing. For each audience given, choose a purpose from the list and think of a specific idea to fit that purpose.

Purposes for Writing	
to explain how to do something	to tell a funny story
to report facts or information	to describe what something is like
to express your feelings	to persuade someone to take action

1. **Audience:** a young child

   Purpose: _____

   Idea: _____

2. **Audience:** the people of your community

   Purpose: _____

   Idea: _____

3. **Audience:** your teacher and classmates

   Purpose: _____

   Idea: _____

4. **Audience:** a pen pal in another country

   Purpose: _____

   Idea: _____

B. Write the names of two people who have recently read something you wrote. Be sure to capitalize their names and titles.

_____   _____

Think of many ideas, but choose the strongest one. A strong idea is specific and fits your purpose and audience.

A. Look back at the ideas you wrote on Day 3. Choose one of them to develop into a stronger, more specific idea. Fill in the audience and purpose. Then use the narrowing triangle below to help you choose a strong idea.

Audience: _____

Purpose: _____

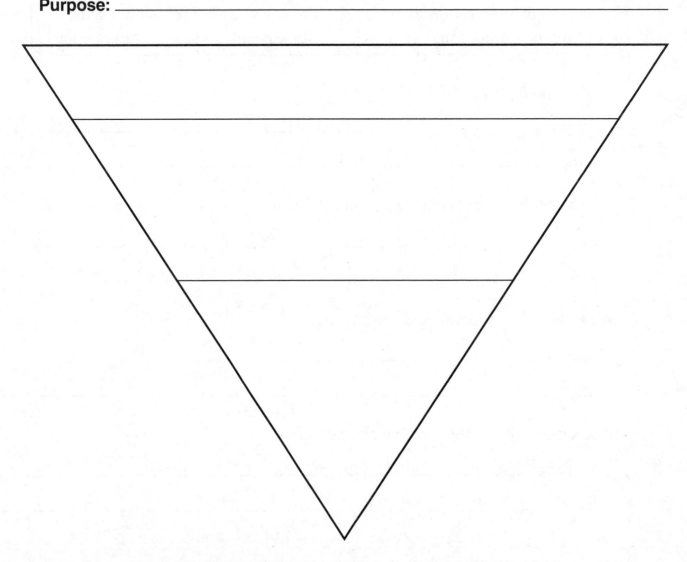

B. Write the names of three people who could be in your audience. Remember to capitalize their names and titles.

_____ _____ _____

Ideas

Use the idea you chose on Day 4 to develop into a paragraph or story. Make sure that your writing fits the purpose and audience.

Be sure to capitalize proper nouns.

 **Ideas** | A topic sentence clearly states the main idea of a paragraph.

A. Read each paragraph and pair of topic sentences beneath it. Choose the best topic sentence for the paragraph and write it where you think it should go in the paragraph.

Paragraph 1

Hurricanes blow through with very high winds. The winds often lift roofs from buildings and send cars sailing through the air. Flooding is very common during hurricanes. The large amounts of rain they bring can make the water level of lakes, oceans, and other bodies of water rise quickly and flood streets, homes, and businesses.

Topic Sentences: Hurricanes are dangerous storms.
Hurricanes cause flooding.

Paragraph 2

Thousands of years ago, during the Ice Age, glaciers crawled across North America. These sheets of ice were so heavy that they carved out giant valleys. Then the glaciers melted, leaving behind rocks and gravel. These changes in the land created the Great Lakes: Huron, Ontario, Michigan, Erie, and Superior. These are some of the largest lakes in the world! Without them, the land would look a lot different.

Topic Sentences: Glaciers are slow-moving masses of ice.
The Great Lakes are proof of the power of glaciers.

B. Read each sentence. Which one uses verbs correctly? Write an X next to it.

1. ___ The lakes is full of fresh water.

   ___ The lakes are full of fresh water.

2. ___ A hurricane sometimes has 100-mile-per-hour winds.

   ___ A hurricane sometimes have 100-mile-per-hour winds.

 **Ideas**

Clearly state the main idea in the topic sentence.
Give strong details to support the main idea.

A. Read this paragraph. Circle its topic sentence. Underline three details that support its main idea.

When you were younger, did you ever read the books **The Very Hungry Caterpillar** or **Brown Bear, Brown Bear, What Do You See?** If so, then you have seen the art of Eric Carle. Eric Carle is a successful artist whose style is known all over the world. To make his illustrations, he paints papers. Then he cuts the papers and makes them into a collage. Since the 1950s, he has illustrated more than 70 books. Now, 75 million copies of his books exist all over the world. That's a lot of books! Carle has inspired children everywhere to make collages of their own. Sometimes they send him pictures of their art.

B. This paragraph is missing a topic sentence. Figure out the main idea of the paragraph, and write a topic sentence for it. Then fix any verbs that do not agree with their subjects.

First, form a ball of clay. Then press your thumb halfway into the ball. Use your other hand to pinch the clay around your thumb. Keep pinching as you turn the ball of clay. Soon, you will have a clay bowl! After your bowl dry, you can paint it any color you wish.

Topic Sentence:

_____

_____

Ideas Every detail in a paragraph must support the main idea, or it doesn't belong in the paragraph.

A. Read each how-to paragraph. Check the one that needs improvement. Then cross out the details in that paragraph that are not important.

Paragraph 1

☐ It's easy to cut off part of a pothos vine and plant it somewhere else. First, cut off part of the vine, but keep the leaves attached. Then, put the vine in a cup of water. Leave the cup near a window so it gets plenty of sunlight. In a week or two, small roots will start growing on the vine. When the roots are a few inches long, plant the pothos in a pot of soil. Finally, place the pot near a window and water the plant regularly.

Paragraph 2

☐ Baseball is a fun sport that's easy to set up. First, choose two teams of at least seven people. Mauricio and I always play on the same team. Then, make a diamond by setting up four bases. It's very different from football. Have a team member from one team stand at each base. The other team members stand outside the diamond. These are called outfielders. Did you ever see Angels in the Outfield? It's a good movie.

B. Read the topic sentence. Write four detail sentences that support it.

Topic Sentence: This is how I get to school every morning.

1. _____

2. _____

3. _____

4. _____

C. Reread each sentence you wrote in Activity B. Underline each verb. Make sure that it agrees with its subject.

 **Ideas** Write an interesting topic sentence to state your main idea. Support it with clear details that stick to the topic.

Think of an activity you could write a how-to paragraph about. Write a topic sentence about the activity in the center of the web. Use the following questions to think of details that support the topic sentence:

- What is the activity?

- What are the steps in the activity? Why is each step important?

- What equipment, materials, or ingredients do you need? Where can you get them?

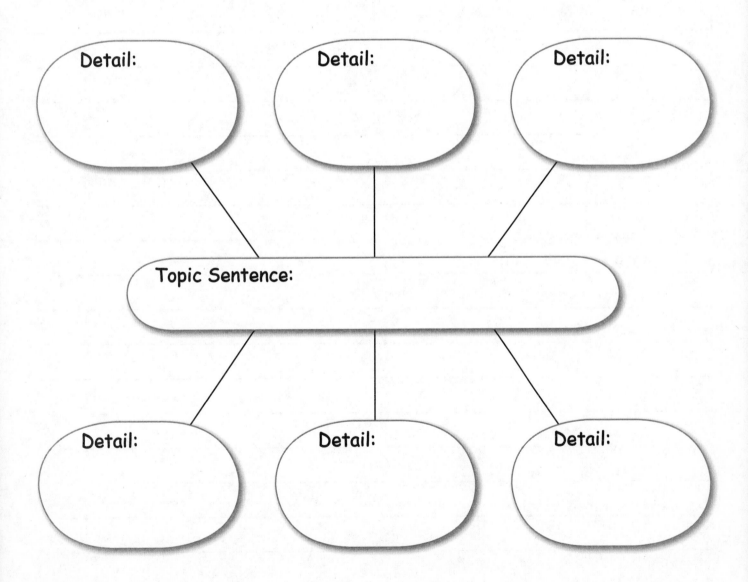

Detail:

Detail:

Detail:

Topic Sentence:

Detail:

Detail:

Detail:

Ideas

Use the web you completed on Day 4 to write a how-to paragraph with a clear topic sentence and supporting details.

Be sure that your subjects and verbs agree.

_____

_____

_____

_____

_____

_____

_____

_____

_____

_____

_____

_____

_____

_____

_____

_____

_____

_____

_____

_____

 **Ideas** : Use interesting details to make your characters come to life.

A. Read the story. Then use your imagination to answer the questions about the character. Try to think of details that would make George more interesting.

> George sat on the steps of his apartment building. The steaming sun beat down on his shoulders, and the street was almost deserted. George heard the old grandfather clock inside the apartment chime noon. He thought about his sister's request. She wanted him to enter a local talent contest. Before the accident, he would've done it in a heartbeat. But now he'd do just about anything to get out of it.

1. What is George's full name? How old is he?

   _____

2. What does George look like?

   _____

3. What are George's goals?

   _____

4. What are George's strengths?

   _____

5. What are George's weaknesses?

   _____

B. Reread the story. Find the two contractions and write them below.
   Then write the two words that form each contraction.

   1. _____ = _____ + _____

   2. _____ = _____ + _____

 **Ideas** Use vivid details to make your setting interesting.

A. Read the story. Then use your imagination to answer the questions about the setting.

> Greta looked around with dread. She couldn't believe her eyes! She let out a long sigh. This wouldn't be the first time her science experiments had gotten her into trouble. She could've gone to summer camp, but instead she'd spent her entire vacation trying to earn enough money to pay for the damage her last experiment caused. And now, she had made an even bigger mess! When her parents got home, they'd ground her for life!

1. At what time of day does the story take place?

   _____

2. Where does the story take place? Be specific.

   _____

3. What does the place look like? Describe it.

   _____

   _____

4. What can you hear in the setting? Smell? Feel? Touch?

   _____

B. Reread the story. Find the contractions formed from *have, had,* or *would* and write them below. Then write the two words that form each contraction.

1. _____ = _____ + _____

2. _____ = _____ + _____

3. _____ = _____ + _____

 **Ideas**   Develop a good plot by planning an exciting sequence of events.

A. Read the basic plot. Fill in the plot diagram to show the sequence of events.

> **Basic plot:** Two boys are walking in the woods. They hear a strange sound. They see a bear and her cubs! They get scared and hide. The bears go away. The boys run back and tell all of the other campers about it.

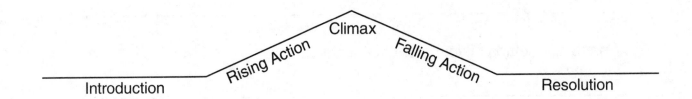

Climax

Rising Action   Falling Action

Introduction   Resolution

B. The plot above is clear, but it needs to be developed. Answer the questions to give more details about each event.

1. How does the story begin?

_____

2. What happens next?

_____

_____

3. What is the climax of the story?

_____

_____

4. How does the story end?

_____

_____

 **Ideas**

Develop your characters, setting, and plot to make your story interesting and detailed.

Answer the questions and fill in the plot diagram to plan your own short story about someone who wakes up on another planet.

1. Who is the main character of your story? Describe him or her.

   _____

   _____

2. What is the setting of your story? Describe it.

   _____

   _____

3. How does your story begin?

   _____

   _____

4. What is the climax of the story?

   _____

   _____

5. What happens at the end?

   _____

   _____

Climax

Rising Action

Falling Action

Introduction

Resolution

Write a short story about someone who wakes up on another planet. Include the plot, character, and setting ideas you developed on Day 4.

Use at least one contraction with *have, had,* or *would* in your story.

_____

_____

_____

_____

_____

_____

_____

_____

_____

_____

_____

_____

_____

_____

_____

_____

_____

_____

_____

_____

_____

_____

 **Ideas** Good writers elaborate on ideas and details to paint a meaningful picture for the reader.

A. Two students wrote letters to their principal. Read the letters and answer the question.

> Dear Ms. Wong,
>
>   We want the Writer's Club to come back. We used to have fun. Now we don't have anyplace to meet, and it's hard to find times to get together. Some teachers said they could help. We need to meet sometime at school.
>
> Sincerely,
Pat Johnston

> Dear Ms. Wong,
>
>   We don't want the Writer's Club to end. The other club members and I used to have fun after school, thinking of plots and characters. Now there's nowhere for us to meet. We want to talk about our stories and read each other's work, but we live miles from each other. There's no way to get together after school except for the Writer's Club. Mr. Gonzales and Ms. Zane have both said we can use their rooms.
>
> Sincerely,
Rula Paz

Which writer did a better job of elaborating? Give at least two examples of specific details to support your answer.

_____

_____

B. Use proofreading marks to correct the double negatives in these sentences.

1. The students don't live nowhere near each other.

2. We're not never going to have a place to meet.

 **Ideas** Look for ways to elaborate on your ideas by making your details and examples more specific.

A. Read this short essay. The words in bold are not very specific. How could the writer have elaborated more on her ideas? Use the chart below to write more specific examples the writer might have included instead.

> Photographs are a good way to help remember **things**. **Important events** in my life are shown through photos. Photos help me remember the **fun times** with my friends.

Too General	More Specific
things	
important events	
fun times	

B. Rewrite each sentence to fix the double negative.

1. I couldn't never give up my camera.

   _____

2. Stacey doesn't want nobody to take her picture.

   _____

3. There's not nothing better than taking pictures.

   _____

 **Ideas**

Elaborate on your ideas to be persuasive. Use specific details and examples that support your argument.

A. Read Joey's first draft of a letter to a newspaper. Use proofreading marks to fix any sentences that have double negatives. Then underline vague words and phrases that Joey could improve to provide details that support his argument.

> Dear Editor:
>
> I heard that the city wants to close the Bevington Library because it doesn't have no more money to pay the staff or buy no more books. We need to keep the library open. My family uses the library a lot. We check out lots of things. We go there a lot in the summer. Whenever I write a report, people help me find information there. If the library closes, where will kids go?

B. Read Joey's revision. Underline the specific details and examples he added to support his argument.

> I heard that the city wants to close the Bevington Library because it doesn't have anymore money to pay the staff or buy anymore books. We need to keep the library open so students like me can use it. My family goes to the library every Saturday. My dad checks out books to read, and my brothers rent CDs and DVDs that they can't afford to buy. In the summer, my sister and I always join the reading program and earn prizes for reading books. And, whenever I need to write a report, Mr. Jue helps me find tons of information about my topic. If the library closes, where will kids go to get help like that?

C. Imagine that a library in your area has to close. Write two reasons why you think it shouldn't.

_____

_____

 **Ideas** When you want to be persuasive, choose meaningful details that support your reasons.

Think of a change you would like to see in your community or school and prepare to write a letter to the editor of your local newspaper about it. Use the questions below to plan your ideas.

1. What change or action would you like to see taken?

   _____

   _____

2. Why is this change or action necessary?

   _____

   _____

   _____

3. How could the change or action take place? Who would be involved?

   _____

   _____

   _____

   _____

4. Who might be against the idea? What would you say to them?

   _____

   _____

   _____

   _____

 **Ideas**

Use your ideas from Day 4 to write a letter to the editor about an important issue. Include specific details, examples, and reasons that elaborate on your ideas. Be sure to fix any double negatives in your letter.

_____
date

_____
greeting

_____

_____

_____

_____

_____

_____

_____

_____

_____

_____

_____

_____

_____

_____
closing

_____
signature

 **Ideas** Keep the focus on your topic as you write.

A. Read each descriptive paragraph. Then:
   - Check the paragraph that does not keep its focus.
   - Cross out the unnecessary details in that paragraph.

Paragraph 1

☐ Bright, fragrant flowers and plants filled the shop. The scent of blooming petunias drew me toward the back of the store. I thought about the library books I needed to return. The musty odor of nearby potting soil was strong. Another strong odor is the coffee my mom makes every morning. The flowers were lined up and stacked on shelves near the potting soil. I grabbed a couple of boxes to use for carrying flowers. I chose daisies and pansies. I hoped I'd remember to buy my mom's birthday cake!

Paragraph 2

☐ Bright, fragrant flowers and plants filled the shop. Wind chimes near the deep purple petunias rang out a tune. The sweet smell of honeysuckle vines drew me toward the back of the shop. There, near an open window, I saw tall elephant plants with huge leaves waving in the breeze. Customers filled the tiny shop. They pulled flowers and plants from the shelves and put them in their carts. Cheerful yellow marigolds filled tiny pots near the cash register. I put a couple of them in my cart before I checked out.

B. Circle the plural nouns in Paragraph 1. Then write the singular form of each noun below.

_____   _____

_____   _____

_____   _____

_____   _____

 **Ideas** Keep the focus on your topic as you write.

A. Read this article for a school newspaper. Then:
- Cross out the sentences that do not focus on the topic.
- Use proofreading marks to insert the sentences from the box that focus on the topic.

From the first day, the fifth-grade class trip to New York City was an amazing experience. Some students had asked to go to Washington, D.C., instead. The students saw hundreds of people jamming the streets in Times Square. Lighted ads blinked as far as the eye could see. One student was thinking about the new glasses he'd be getting after the trip. Restaurants also lined the streets. They offered many kinds of food. When they left Times Square, the students traveled to the Statue of Liberty. The story about the statue was printed on stands all around it. A few of the students had sore feet. Close to the statue was Ellis Island. This is where immigrants from other countries used to enter the United States.

Sentences

Some students bought sandwiches, and others bought pizza.

It seemed as if there was a souvenir shop under each ad.

Some students found the names of their ancestors on its lists of immigrants!

B. Write the plural form of each noun.

1. glass _____   3. journey _____

2. ceremony _____   4. torch _____

Keep the focus on your topic as your write.
Include only details that are important to the topic.

Alonzo completed this web so he could write a description of his first day on his uncle's farm. Cross out the details that don't stick to Alonzo's topic. Then write a paragraph about Alonzo's day. Be sure to correct any misspelled plural nouns.

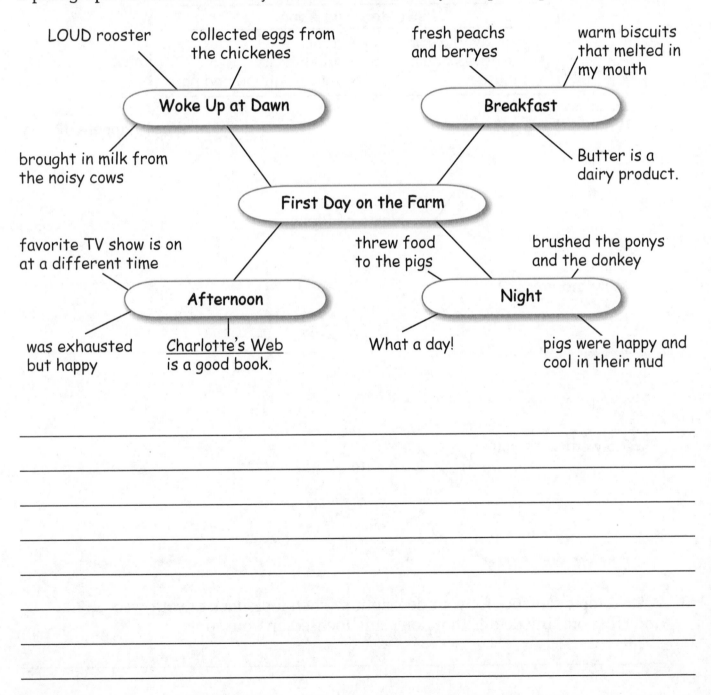

_____

_____

_____

_____

_____

_____

_____

Ideas

Keep your focus as you write. Write a topic sentence and provide details that support it.

A. Think about a trip you have taken to one of the places listed in the box. How would you describe your visit? Fill in the web to help you think of details.

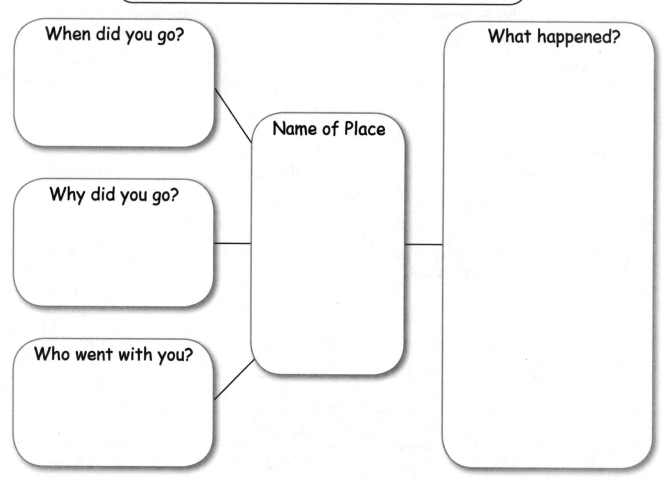

Places to Write About

- your favorite store
- a relative's home
- a museum
- a zoo
- another city
- your neighborhood park

When did you go?

Why did you go?

Who went with you?

Name of Place

What happened?

B. Write a topic sentence for your description. Then look back at your web and cross out any details that don't stay focused on your topic.

_____

_____

Use the details you wrote on Day 4 to write a descriptive paragraph about a place you have been. Remember to stay focused on your topic.

Be sure to spell plural nouns correctly.

_____

_____

_____

_____

_____

_____

_____

_____

_____

_____

_____

_____

_____

_____

_____

_____

_____

_____

_____

_____

_____

When you write about steps in a process, be sure to put the steps in sequential order.

A. In the recipe below, the steps for making a burrito are out of order. Reorder the steps by writing the number that each step should be. Then correct the misspellings of *to, too,* and *two.*

How two Make a Burrito

____ Sprinkle cheese on top of the beans.

____ Eat and enjoy your burrito.

____ Place a soft tortilla flat on a plate.

____ Spoon salsa onto the flat tortilla. Don't use to much!

____ Roll up the tortilla with all of the fillings inside.

____ Place too spoonfuls of beans on top of the salsa.

B. Using the numbered steps in Activity A and the transition words and phrases in the box below, write a paragraph explaining how to make a burrito. Be sure to spell *to, too,* and *two* correctly.

Transition Words				
next	then	after that	finally	first

How to Make a Burrito

_____

_____

_____

_____

_____

_____

_____

Organization

In an autobiography, the events of someone's life should be in the order in which they happened.

The timeline below shows events in Adrienne's life. Read her autobiography. Then use proofreading marks to insert the missing events, based on her timeline. Find and correct the misspelled words in the paragraph.

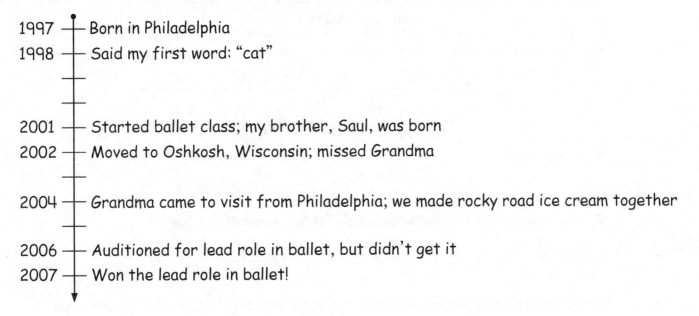

1997 — Born in Philadelphia
1998 — Said my first word: "cat"

2001 — Started ballet class; my brother, Saul, was born
2002 — Moved to Oshkosh, Wisconsin; missed Grandma

2004 — Grandma came to visit from Philadelphia; we made rocky road ice cream together

2006 — Auditioned for lead role in ballet, but didn't get it
2007 — Won the lead role in ballet!

I came into this world on August 5, 1997, in Philadelphia. My parents said I loved animals from the time I was born. When I was four, to important things happened: I started ballet class, and my little brother, Saul, was born. I had always wanted a little brother. Now I had someone to call me "Big Sis" for the rest of my life. We had fun when Grandma Merrill came too visit from Philadelphia in 2004. In 2006, I auditioned for the lead role in a ballet, but I didn't get it. However, I auditioned for the role again in 2007, and finally I got it! I had achieved my dreams threw hard work.

 **Organization**

When you write in chronological order, use transition words to guide your reader.

Use this timeline of George Washington's life to write a short biography of him. Be sure to keep the events in chronological order and use transition words to connect the events.

Transition Words				
however	then	before	next	throughout
after that	later	eventually	finally	

The Life of George Washington

1732	Born in Virginia
1749	Starts his own business
1753–1758	Serves in British army; helps defend frontier against France
1759–1775	Marries Martha Dandridge Curtis; lives and farms at Mt. Vernon
1775	Revolutionary War begins; elected commander in chief of the Continental army
1789	Elected as the first president of the United States
1792	Elected for a second term as president
1799	Dies at Mt. Vernon

_____

_____

_____

_____

_____

_____

_____

 Daily 6-Trait Writing • EMC 6795 • © Evan-Moor Corp.

 **Organization** When you write a biography, put the events of your subject's life in chronological order.

A. Use these questions to interview a classmate about his or her life.

   1. When were you born? Where?

    _____

    _____

   2. What important events have happened in your life? When did they happen?

    _____

    _____

   3. What special memories do you have? When did they happen?

    _____

    _____

B. Make a timeline of events of your classmate's life. On one side, write his or her age or the year. On the other side, write what happened.

Organization

Use the timeline you created on Day 4 to write a short biography of your classmate. Remember to use chronological order.

Be sure to spell *to, too, two, threw,* and *through* correctly.

_____

_____

_____

_____

_____

_____

_____

_____

_____

_____

_____

_____

_____

_____

_____

_____

_____

_____

Organization — Use logical organization so your writing makes sense. Group similar ideas and details together.

A. Read this friendly letter from Marilyn to Stefan. Find and circle the sentence fragment. Then:
   - Use a <u>straight line</u> to underline the details about Marilyn's school.
   - Use a <u>wavy line</u> to underline the details about her neighborhood.

Dear Stefan,

We have finally finished moving! Last week was my first week at my new school. I now go to Jane Addams School. My new teacher is Mr. Yi. He's nice and likes to tell jokes. I love Fridays because he lets us play soccer in the afternoon! I like my neighborhood, too. There is an ice-cream store called Mariana's. Lots of flavors. We also have a park with a playground and a baseball diamond. I miss you, but I do like my new school and neighborhood. Good luck with your soccer team this year!

Your friend,
Marilyn

B. The details in this short paragraph are not in logical order. Rewrite it so that the details about each soccer position are grouped together.

Two positions in soccer are the goalie and the sweeper. A sweeper tries to steal the ball from the other team. A goalie can touch the ball with his or her hands. A goalie blocks the other team's goal. Sweepers must be very fast.

_____

_____

_____

_____

_____

Organization When you write a description of how something looks, you can organize your details by where things are in relation to each other.

A. Look at the floor plan of Neil's room and read the description. Then:
- Use proofreading marks to fix the sentence fragments.
- Draw a line on the floor plan to show the order in which the items were presented in the description.

Neil shares a bunk bed. With his brother Wade. On Neil's desk is his microscope. It's for looking at the bugs he finds outside. The closets. Are a big mess. Sometimes when Neil and Wade clean, they just throw everything. In their closets. Through the window, they can see the backyard. There's a <u>Star Wars</u> rug on the floor. They have two dressers.

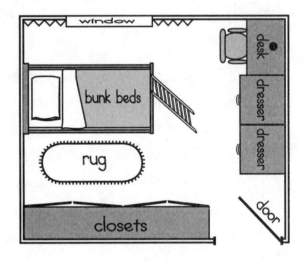

B. Look back at the line you drew. Draw another line to show a more logical order that you could follow to describe the room. Then rewrite the description. Use position words and phrases to create transitions from one detail to the next.

Position Words and Phrases				
behind	top	in front of	inside	near
on the other side	between	to the left	to the right	beside

_____

_____

_____

_____

_____

_____

 **Organization** When you write an explanation, you can organize your details by cause and effect—how or why one thing makes another thing happen.

A. Read this cause-and-effect paragraph. Use proofreading marks to correct any sentence fragments.

> There are many ways to prevent catching a cold. Eat a lot of vegetables so your body will get more vitamins. Get plenty of sleep so your body has the energy. To fight cold viruses. The most important thing you can do is to wash your hands. Often. By washing your hands, you wash away viruses!

B. Read the cause-and-effect diagram. Then complete a cause-and-effect paragraph about the rhinovirus, a germ that often causes colds. Use the transition words and phrases in the box.

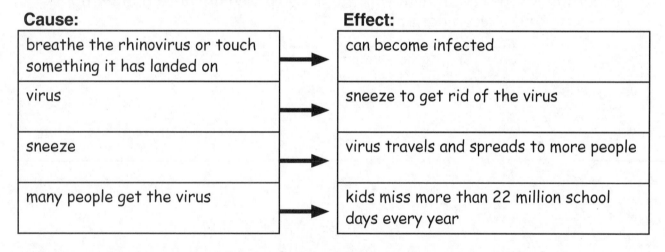

Cause:

| breathe the rhinovirus or touch something it has landed on |
| virus |
| sneeze |
| many people get the virus |

Effect:

| can become infected |
| sneeze to get rid of the virus |
| virus travels and spreads to more people |
| kids miss more than 22 million school days every year |

Transition Words and Phrases

as a result   because   if   then   when   consequently   therefore

> The rhinovirus is not a large animal that lives in Africa. The rhinovirus is a virus that can make you catch a bad cold! _____
>
> _____
>
> _____

Organization

Choose the form of organization that works best for your writing.

A. Read the writing assignments below. Mark the one you would like to complete.

☐ **Assignment 1:** Write a description of your favorite room in your home.

☐ **Assignment 2:** Write a paragraph that tells what you liked and disliked about the last movie you saw.

☐ **Assignment 3:** Write a paragraph that tells how to do well in school. Explain the effects of good behavior and study habits.

B. Draw and complete the graphic organizer that will best help you plan your paragraph for the assignment you chose. Use a web or chart, a drawing, or a cause-and-effect diagram.

Organization

Write a paragraph in response to the assignment you chose on Day 4. Use the graphic organizer you completed.

Have a partner check your writing for sentence fragments. Correct any that are found.

_____

_____

_____

_____

_____

_____

_____

_____

_____

_____

_____

_____

_____

_____

_____

_____

_____

_____

_____

_____

_____

_____

 **Organization** When you write to compare and contrast, you can use point-by-point order to organize your details.

Read the compare-and-contrast paragraph. Then:
- Complete the outline by filling in the missing details from the paragraph.
- Insert the missing commas.

Have you ever been to Portland? "Well, which one?" you may ask. That is a good question, because in the United States, more than ten states have cities or towns named Portland. The two largest are in Oregon and Maine. Portland, Oregon, is the largest Portland, with around 500,000 residents. Portland Maine, has only 63,000 residents. Portland, Oregon is known as The Rose City, because roses grow very well in the city's rainy weather. Portland, Maine, however, is known for its Italian sandwiches. They are made with soft bread, sour pickles, and oil. Portland Maine is on the Atlantic Coast and became a city in 1786. It was named for its large shipping port. Portland, Oregon on the other hand, is on the Pacific Coast. It became a city in 1851 and was named after—you guessed it!—the city of Portland Maine!

I. Population

  A. Portland, Oregon: 500,000

  B. _____

II. What the City Is Known For

  A. _____

  B. Portland, Maine: Italian sandwiches

III. Location

  A. _____

  B. Portland, Maine: Atlantic Coast

IV. When It Became a City

  A. _____

  B. Portland, Maine: 1786

 **Organization** Use signal words to tell how things are similar or different.

A. Read the paragraphs. Then:
- Circle the signal words that indicate that the cities are alike.
- Underline the signal words that indicate that the cities are different.
- Insert any missing commas.

You've probably heard of Paris, France, but did you know there is a Paris, Tennessee? These two cities are very different at first glance. For one thing, Paris, France is in Europe, while Paris, Tennessee is in the U.S. There are also a lot more people in Paris, France. It has a population of about 2.2 million, as opposed to only 10,000 in Paris Tennessee. This may be partly because Paris France has been around for more than 2,000 years! Paris, Tennessee on the other hand, is only about 200 years old.

However, the two cities are similar in some ways. For example, both cities are near rivers. Paris, France lies on the Seine River, and Paris, Tennessee, lies near the West Sandy River. They even both have Eiffel Towers! The Eiffel Tower in France was built in 1889 and stands 1,063 feet tall. The one in Tennessee is a lot smaller. It's only 60 feet tall and is a copy of the original. Nonetheless, its citizens love their tower just like the French love theirs.

B. Look back at the paragraphs. List two ways in which the cities are different and two ways in which they are the same. Use commas correctly in the place names.

Different: 1. _____

2. _____

Same: 1. _____

2. _____

Organization

A Venn diagram can help you see how two things are similar or different so you can plan and organize your writing.

Use the Venn diagram below to write a short compare-and-contrast paragraph. You do not have to include all of the information that is in the diagram. Remember to use signal words.

Rocky Mountains   **Both**   **Appalachian Mountains**

- were home to Apache, Cheyenne, Crow, and Sioux

- highest peak is Mount Elbert at 14,440 feet

- stretch 3,000 miles from British Columbia, Canada, to New Mexico, USA

- endangered species: whooping crane

- lie west of the Mississippi

- stretch from Canada to the U.S.

- were home to Native American tribes

- have bears and wolves

- open for hiking, camping, fishing, skiing

- have endangered species

- were home to Iroquois, Creek, and Cherokee

- highest peak is Mount Mitchell at 6,684 feet

- stretch 1,500 miles from Newfoundland, Canada, to Alabama, USA

- endangered species: red wolf, eastern cougar

- lie east of the Mississippi

_____

_____

_____

_____

_____

_____

_____

_____

_____

_____

 **Organization** Use a Venn diagram to plan your writing about how two things are similar and different.

Think about two cities or towns in your state or region. How are they similar and different? Answer the questions to help you think of details to compare and contrast. Then fill in the Venn diagram.

Comparing _____ to _____

1. How many people live in each place?

   _____

2. What landforms or bodies of water are nearby?

   _____

3. What are some fun things to do or places to go?

   _____

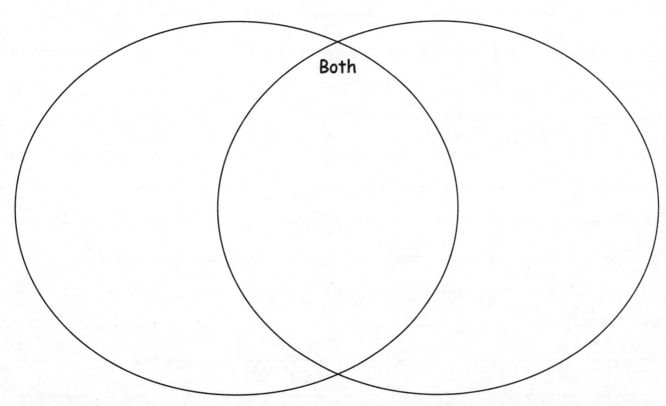

Organization

Use your Venn diagram from Day 4 to write a compare-and-contrast paragraph about two cities or towns. Be sure to use commas correctly between the names of the cities and states.

_____

_____

_____

_____

_____

_____

_____

_____

_____

_____

_____

_____

_____

_____

_____

_____

_____

_____

_____

_____

_____

 **Organization** When you want to be persuasive, organize your ideas to build your argument. State your opinion, and then give reasons with supporting examples.

Read Cody's persuasive speech. Then fill in the opinion diagram to show how Cody organized his opinion, reasons, and supporting examples.

You should vote for me, Cody Walker. I'm running for class president! Most of you have seen me running before—running through the halls, in the library, and around the lunch tables! Well, I'll use my energy to improve our school. For example, I would hold a playground cleanup day. That way, we could go outside for an hour to work off some energy. Also, I spend a lot of time in the principal's office. Hey! It's a great way to stay on top of what's going on around school. Plus, I know the principal personally from chatting with her so much. Oh, you may not think I'm serious enough to be class president. But I am serious about having fun! If you want more parties, talent shows, and extra-dessert days, I'm your guy!

Cody's Opinion Statement:

Reason 1:

Examples:

Reason 2:

Examples:

Possible Objection:

Response to Objection:

 **Organization**

An opinion statement tells how you feel about your topic. It should be clear and specific.

A. Read these opinion statements. Mark the stronger one in each pair.

1. ☐ It would be nice to have soft drinks at school sometimes.

   ☐ Students at Old Mill Elementary should be able to choose whatever they want to drink at lunch, including soft drinks.

2. ☐ Starkey Elementary should allow fourth-grade students with musical experience to join the fifth-grade band.

   ☐ If you're in fourth grade at Starkey Elementary, I think it's OK if you play in the fifth-grade band.

3. ☐ I wish I could take my cellphone to school.

   ☐ It's important for students to be able to take their cellphones to school.

B. This movie review is missing an opinion statement. Read the review and write a strong opinion statement for it. Then fix the interjections that need correct capitalization and punctuation.

Cooking Up Fun with the Film <u>Ratatouille</u>

The main character is Remy, a special rat who wants to be a chef. The plot of the movie is funny because Remy helps his human friend, Linguini, cook in a fancy French restaurant. But he has to hide inside Linguini's hat! He tells Linguini what to do by pulling his hair. Ouch The best part of <u>Ratatouille</u> is the end, when Remy saves Linguini's restaurant. hooray. Some people might not want to see a movie about rats because they think rats are gross. But these rats aren't gross—they're adorable and funny! Rent <u>Ratatouille</u> tonight!

Opinion Statement: _____

_____

 **Organization**

Use transition words and phrases to connect your opinion, reasons, and details.

Read the opinion diagram. Then use the ideas in it to write an editorial for your school newspaper about a way to help people in need. Be sure to include transition words and phrases to connect your ideas.

Opinion Statement: On our birthdays, we should tell people to donate to a charity instead of buying us presents.

Reason 1: There are other people who need the money more than we do.

Examples: Some people have lost their homes due to natural disasters or wars. Other people don't have enough food or clothing.

Reason 2: We don't need more stuff.

Examples: Your closet is probably already full.

Possible Objection: Some kids might not want to give up their presents.

Response to Objection: You can live without new toys or games more easily than people can live without food, clothing, and shelter.

Transition Words and Phrases

also	as a result	first of all	for example	in addition	most importantly

_____

_____

_____

_____

_____

_____

Organization

Use an opinion diagram to plan how to persuade others about your ideas.

Plan a short editorial to persuade others to do volunteer work in your community. Fill in the opinion diagram to organize your ideas.

Opinion Statement:

Reason 1:

Examples:

Reason 2:

Examples:

Reason 3:

Examples:

Possible Objection:

Response to Objection:

Organization

Write a short editorial persuading others to do volunteer work in your community. Use the ideas from the diagram you completed on Day 4.

Be sure to capitalize and punctuate interjections correctly.

Organization The best way to organize your writing depends on your topic and purpose.

Decide which type of organization each paragraph uses. Write the correct letter on the line. Then fill in the missing parts of the organizers.

Paragraph

1. _____ Taylor Elementary should have a science fair. First of all, we could have fun while learning about science. We could make and display creative projects. The science fair at my former school was great. Over 100 students participated. Although it would take up a lot of time, a science fair will get more students interested in science.

2. _____ Acid rain has become a serious problem. The gases that cause acid rain come from power plants, factories, and cars that burn fossil fuels. Acid rain harms the environment in many ways. It pollutes the soil, which poisons plants. When it falls on lakes and streams, it kills fish and other aquatic life.

3. _____ Video games and board games are alike in some ways and different in others. Both can be enjoyed by more than one player. However, video games require a computer or television, unlike a board game. You can play a board game any place you want to. You can even play a board game when the power goes out.

How It Is Organized

a. Cause and Effect:

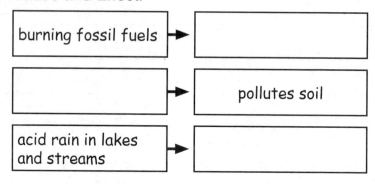

b. Compare and Contrast:

Video Games: require a computer or television

Both

Board Games: play anywhere

c. Persuasive:

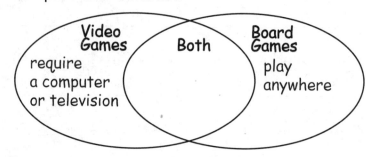

Opinion Statement:

Reason 1:
Example: make and display creative projects

Reason 2: science fair at former school was great
Example:

Possible Objection:
Answer: will get more students interested in science

 **Organization**

When you are given a writing assignment, decide which type of organization best fits the assignment.

A. Read each writing assignment. Which type of organization would you use to write the paragraph? Write it on the line. Then circle the words that provide clues to the organization.

Types of Organization		
Persuasive	Cause and Effect	Compare and Contrast
Position Order	Chronological Order	

Assignment 1: Write a paragraph that compares the Amazon River to the Nile River. Describe the ways in which they are similar and different.

_____

Assignment 2: Write a paragraph that explains the reasons you think your school should add a new item to the lunch menu.

_____

Assignment 3: Write a paragraph that describes how fossils can be formed by water and minerals.

_____

Assignment 4: Write a paragraph that tells about the life of someone you admire.

_____

B. Read each run-on sentence. Rewrite it as one correct sentence or two separate sentences.

1. The Amazon is in South America, the Nile is in Africa.

_____

2. We like burritos please add them to our cafeteria choices.

_____

Organization

Choose a graphic organizer that matches your purpose and form of organization.

A. Read the writing assignment. Then look at each graphic organizer. Circle the organizer that you would use to organize your paragraph.

Assignment: Write a paragraph that explains how popcorn pops when it is heated. Tell what the heat does to the inside of the kernels.

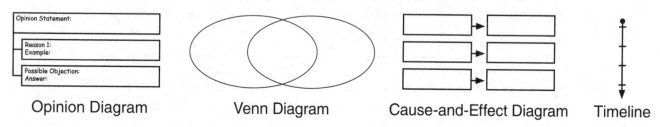

Opinion Diagram   Venn Diagram   Cause-and-Effect Diagram   Timeline

B. Read the sentences. Find and correct the run-on sentences. Then draw the graphic organizer you circled in Activity A. Write each sentence's number where it belongs on the organizer.

1. A microwave oven heats the kernels.

2. The heat causes moisture inside the kernels to expand.

3. The expansion puts pressure on the kernels' outer shells.

4. The kernels' shells explode.

5. Starch inside the kernels becomes inflated, the starch bursts.

6. The kernels turn inside out they make a popping sound.

 **Organization**

Choose the best way to organize your writing. Make your method of organization clear to the reader.

A. Choose one of the writing prompts below, and think about how you would respond to it. Draw and complete a graphic organizer to help you organize your ideas.

☐ Explain the difference between a skateboard and a surfboard.

☐ Describe something that makes you mad, and what happens as a result.

☐ Write a summary of your school year so far.

B. Write a topic sentence for your paragraph. Be sure it's not a run-on sentence.

_____

_____

Write a paragraph responding to the prompt you chose on Day 4. Use the diagram you completed to organize your paragraph.

Trade papers with a partner to check for run-on sentences. Correct any that are found.

_____

_____

_____

_____

_____

_____

_____

_____

_____

_____

_____

_____

_____

_____

_____

_____

Word Choice — Choose strong, specific verbs to show exactly what is happening. Avoid tired, overused verbs.

A. Read each paragraph. Then answer the questions.

Paragraph A

> A cold wind went through the forest, blowing the leaves of the trees. A deer ran by as owls sat on branches and called in the dark. Rain fell. Mice ran under piles of leaves to stay dry. Far in the distance, a train went by.

Paragraph B

> A cold wind whistled through the forest, rustling the leaves of the trees. A deer dashed by as owls perched on branches and hooted to each other in the dark. Rain pelted the ground. Mice scurried under piles of leaves to take shelter from the rain. Far in the distance, a train roared by.

1. What are three examples of verbs that changed from Paragraph A to Paragraph B? Write them below.

Paragraph A	**Paragraph B**
_____	_____
_____	_____
_____	_____

2. Circle all of the specific verbs in Paragraph B that replaced the tired verbs in Paragraph A.

B. Read the paragraph. Use proofreading marks to fix the verbs that are in the wrong tense.

> Horns blared. Cars blocked the crosswalk where Talia wanted to cross the street. Suddenly, Talia caught a glimpse of a hot dog cart. She quickly swings to her left and bolts down the crowded city street. Her stomach screamed in hunger! Luckily, she finds a few dollars in her wallet. "I'll take a jumbo dog with everything on it!" Talia called.

Word Choice

Choose just the right verb to convey your meaning.

A. Read the paragraph. Choose the better action verb to complete each sentence. Write the word on the line.

Byron _____ out of the bushes and _____ onto
        (darted / crawled)   (climbed / jumped)

his bike. He _____ home, trying to _____ as fast
             (raced / rode)   (go / pedal)

as he could. He _____ through the door, _____ up
                (burst / entered)   (climbed / flew)

the stairs, and turned on the bathtub faucet. Hearing the commotion, his

mother slowly _____ into the bathroom. As soon as she saw
               (stepped / crept)

Byron's legs, she _____, "Byron, you've got poison ivy all
                   (cried out / said)

over you!"

"I know," Byron _____. "I'm doomed!"
                 (moaned / whined)

B. Read the paragraph. Circle the verbs that are in the wrong tense.
    Then rewrite those sentences, changing the verbs to the correct tense.

Last weekend, Lorena visits the YMCA with her parents. She

participated in a gymnastics class. The teacher comments that Lorena

does well. Lorena's parents signed her up for a regular class.

_____

_____

_____

_____

 **Word Choice**

Look for tired verbs in your writing. Change them to strong, specific action verbs.

Read Lucy's personal narrative. Then rewrite it, changing weak verbs to strong ones. Also, fix any verbs that are not in the right tense.

Felix and I walked slowly through the parking lot. I'm cold. When we were inside, I put on skates for the first time. I was sure that this would be easy. I walk over to the rink and step onto the ice. All of a sudden, I started to fall. I looked for Felix. He wasn't there!

I went over to the wall. I hold onto the railing and slowly move along the ice. Meanwhile, small children were quickly passing me. I realized that I needed to do this more!

_____

_____

_____

_____

_____

_____

_____

_____

_____

_____

_____

Word Choice Use strong, specific verbs in your writing.

A. Think of a time when you visited a new place, such as an amusement park, a neighborhood, a mall, or a beach. Then complete the web with the name of the place and what you did or saw there.

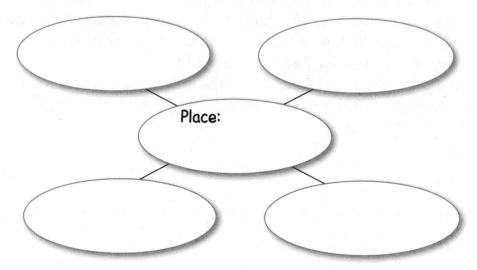

Place:

B. Copy each verb you wrote in your web in the top boxes. Then write stronger, more specific verbs that mean the same thing.

Verb:

Specific Verbs:

Verb:

Specific Verbs:

Verb:

Specific Verbs:

Verb:

Specific Verbs:

Word Choice

Write a personal narrative about your first visit to a new place. Use the strong action verbs you wrote on Day 4. Trade papers with a partner to make sure that all of your verbs are in the past tense.

Word Choice

Use specific nouns and precise, descriptive language to paint a clear picture for your reader.

A. Read each paragraph. Circle the words and phrases in Paragraph 2 that replaced the bold words in Paragraph 1. Then answer the question.

Paragraph 1

Our field trip to Museum Park was **fun**. First, we ate **lunch** on the **lawn**. I decided to lie on my back and watch the **clouds in the sky**. Suddenly, I heard a dog barking **loudly**. I was worried that it might be a **mean** dog, but I looked up to see **the dog** barking at a **pretty** kite that had crashed to the ground. After cleaning up from lunch, we went inside the art museum and **looked at** the **interesting** paintings and sculptures on display.

Paragraph 2

Our trip to Museum Park was full of excitement. First, we ate gigantic submarine sandwiches on the cool, green, freshly mowed grass. I decided to lie on my back and watch the fluffy white clouds drifting through the sky. Suddenly, I heard a dog barking urgently. I was worried that it might be an aggressive dog, but I looked up to see a French poodle barking at a rainbow-colored kite that had crashed to the ground. After cleaning up from lunch, we went inside the art museum and examined the expressive paintings and carefully crafted sculptures on display.

Which paragraph does a better job of describing? Give an example to support your answer.

_____

_____

B. Read each sentence. Write an X next to the one that uses the underlined word correctly.

_____ 1. The dog <u>lays</u> down on the grass.

_____ 2. The dog <u>lies</u> down on the grass.

_____ 3. The girl <u>lays</u> her books on the table.

_____ 4. The girl <u>lies</u> her books on the table.

Word Choice

Use vivid adjectives to make your descriptions clear and precise.

A. Use each given word or phrase to write a strong descriptive sentence. Be as creative as possible. Remember to use *a* and *an* correctly.

Example: The audience cringed when the singer hit an **eardrum-shattering** note.

1. **eardrum-shattering:** _____

_____

2. **peppery:** _____

_____

3. **brightly spotted:** _____

_____

4. **pungent:** _____

_____

5. **towering:** _____

_____

6. **100-year-old:** _____

_____

B. Read the paragraph. Use *lay* or *lie* and *a* or *an* to complete each sentence.

Please _____ your sleeping bag in _____ tent. But don't

_____ down and take _____ nap! Help me _____ the

tablecloth on _____ unclaimed picnic table.

 **Word Choice**

Replace overused words with specific nouns and vivid adjectives to make your descriptions clear and precise.

A. Read the description of a painting. Then:

- Use proofreading marks to replace each word in bold with a better descriptive word or phrase. Remember to change the article before it to *a* or *an,* if necessary.

- Use proofreading marks to fix any incorrect uses of *lay* or *lie.*

My brother's friend Ismael painted an **interesting** painting in his art class. The painting shows an **old** cabin in the woods, with **old, broken** doors and windows. You can see some **tall** trees in the background. Their **colorful** autumn leaves lie scattered on the ground. A rusted rake lays against one wall of the cabin, and in front of the door, a peacock stands with its **colorful** feathers spread wide open. Facing the peacock is a **little** boy on an **old** tricycle. The boy is leaning over the handlebars and staring **hard** at the peacock. The peacock is looking back with a **weird** look. Ismael titled this painting "Standoff." He entered it in the county fair, where it competed against many paintings and won first place!

B. Rewrite each sentence correctly.

1. There was a ugly brown snake laying across the trail.

   _____

2. I saw a squirrel scurry off with an nut and lie it in a hole.

   _____

Word Choice

Use precise nouns and adjectives to write a strong description.

A. If you were going to write a description of the picture below, what could you say? Write eight strong descriptive phrases to describe the truck, the kids, or other things in the picture.

_____   _____

_____   _____

_____   _____

_____   _____

B. Write one sentence you could use in your description. Remember to use _a_ and _an_ correctly.

_____

_____

Word Choice

Use precise, descriptive language to write a description of the picture on Day 4.

Be sure to use the articles *a* and *an* correctly, as well as the verbs *lie* and *lay*.

_____

_____

_____

_____

_____

_____

_____

_____

_____

_____

_____

_____

_____

_____

_____

_____

_____

_____

Word Choice

Using similes and metaphors makes your writing richer. A simile compares two things using *like* or *as*. A metaphor does not use *like* or *as*.

A. Read the free-verse poem. Underline each simile, and circle each metaphor.

Autumn Night

Golden leaves crunch under my feet like cornflakes at breakfast.

My cheeks are red roses in bloom.

Cotton balls of smoke puff out of chimneys, and

Jen and Grandma Josie are cozy cats in their blankets.

I'm as warm as a mug of cocoa,

Falling like leaves, falling asleep.

B. Pretend you are writing about a baseball game. For each subject below, read the simile or the metaphor that has been written about it. Then write your own simile or metaphor.

1. **Subject:** baseball diamond before a game

    Simile: The empty diamond is like a kite lying on the ground, waiting for the wind.

    Metaphor: _____

2. **Subject:** the pitcher throwing a fastball

    Simile: _____

    Metaphor: The pitcher shoots a white bullet into the catcher's glove.

3. **Subject:** the umpire making a call

    Simile: The umpire watches the ball like an eagle eyeing its prey.

    Metaphor: _____

4. **Subject:** runner stealing a base

    Simile: _____

    Metaphor: The runner is on fire, burning toward second base.

Word Choice

Using personification, or giving nonliving things human form or characteristics, brings your writing to life.

A. Read the description of the moon. Underline the words or phrases that make the moon seem human. Then use proofreading marks to correct any errors in subject-verb agreement.

> The moon is fickle. She's always changing her mind. Some nights you
>
> sees her, some nights you don't. Sometimes she smile down on you with her
>
> moonbeams. Other nights she hides in the dark. Dogs howls at the moon.
>
> Maybe they want her to slow down so they can catch her. But she keep
>
> strolling across the sky, never stopping in one place for too long.

B. Pretend you're writing about a street scene. Describe each subject below by writing a sentence that includes personification.

Example:

   Subject: stop sign

   Description: <u>The stop sign stands there sternly, waiting to command "Stop!"</u>

1. **Subject:** traffic light

   Description: _____

   _____

2. **Subject:** bus shelter

   Description: _____

   _____

3. **Subject:** mailbox

   Description: _____

   _____

 **Word Choice**

Use similes, metaphors, and personification to make your descriptions memorable.

Read Jack's description of his first roller coaster ride. Then:
- Help him finish some of the similes, metaphors, and personification by filling in the blanks.
- Use proofreading marks to correct any errors in subject-verb agreement.

"Who's up for the Mountain of Mayhem?" asked Sam. That were the LAST ride I wanted to go on, but I couldn't show my fear in front of my friends. So I put on a brave face, like a pirate walking the plank.

This coaster was **as high as a** _____. Every time I looked at it, my stomach became a pancake flipping in a frying pan. As we moved closer to the front of the line, I began trembling **like** a _____.

When it were our turn, I listened carefully to the safety instructions. I pulled the harness as tight as it would go and clung to the safety bar **like** _____.

Suddenly, the train was a _____, shooting away from the platform. The track tossed us around **as if it** _____. Then we roared into a tunnel. The darkness gobbled me up, and the car slowly started to climb up, and up, and up.

Finally, we was at the top. The car hung suspended for a moment, like the calm before a storm. Then I was _____, hanging in midair as I rose out of my seat. All I remember is screaming **like a** _____.

As we exited the ride, my legs was _____.

"Want to go again?" Sam asked.

"Maybe later," I whispered, running for the bathroom.

Word Choice

Use similes, metaphors, and personification to develop your ideas for a description.

A. Think of the first time you did something. Plan a description of that event. Answer the questions to help you.

The First Time I _____

1. How did you feel before the event?

    _____

2. Write a simile that describes how you felt.

    _____

3. How did you feel during the event?

    _____

4. Write a metaphor that describes how you felt.

    _____

5. What verbs could describe the event or how you felt?

    _____

6. What adjectives could you use to describe the event?

    _____

7. Write an example of personification that describes the event or how you felt.

    _____

B. Have a partner check your answers for errors in subject-verb agreement. Fix any that are found.

Word Choice

Write a description about the first time you did something exciting or scary. Include similes, metaphors, and personification. You may use the ones you wrote on Day 4.

Be sure that subjects and verbs agree with each other.

_____

_____

_____

_____

_____

_____

_____

_____

_____

_____

_____

_____

_____

_____

_____

_____

_____

_____

_____

_____

_____

_____

Word Choice

When you write to someone you know well, it's OK to use informal language. Use formal language for anyone else.

A. Read each letter. Underline the words in the formal letter that replaced the bolded words in the informal letter.

Informal

Hey Luiz,

    I'd love to get the **guy** who just won the **bike** race, Mr. Armstrong, to come **talk** to our bike club. We could **set up a time that would work for him** to come out here. I bet he'd have some tips he could give us for our next **few** races. **What do you think?** How cool would that be? I think that our members would be **totally psyched** to have someone like him **give us an edge** over the other bike clubs in the upcoming races.

Formal

Dear Sir:

I am writing to request that the man who won the recent bicycle race, Mr. Armstrong, come give a presentation to our bicycle club. We would schedule the meeting at a convenient time for Mr. Armstrong. He could discuss skills that would help us in our future races. Do you think this would be possible? Our club would be honored to have someone like Mr. Armstrong advise us on how to win races.

B. Complete each sentence with the word *who's* or *whose*.

1. _____ going on the bicycle ride tomorrow?

2. _____ bicycle was left in front of the door?

3. Do you know _____ helmet this is?

 **Word Choice**

Choose words that fit your audience. When you write informally or for younger children, use simpler words.

A. Read the journal entry. Choose the word or phrase below each line that sounds more informal. Write it on the line.

November 7

Today, we had a _____ _____ about
              (long / lengthy)   (talk / presentation)

school safety in the _____. All students had to
              (gymnasium / gym)

_____. One of my _____ asked some
(attend / go)   (BFFs / friends)

_____ questions!
(amusing / funny)

After everyone spoke, we _____ to the cafeteria to
           (went / proceeded)

_____. We _____ what the speakers had said.
(stuff our faces / dine) (discussed / talked about)

B. Read this paragraph about a school's safety plan. Use proofreading marks to correct any incorrect usage of *its* or *it's*. Then rewrite the paragraph in simpler language so a first-grade student could understand it.

> When the alarm activates, there's no need to be frightened. Simply line up behind your teacher in an orderly fashion. You may then leave the classroom and proceed to the rear door of the school. Its critical that you maintain a calm, quiet composure. Remain outside until the emergency personnel can ensure the safety of the building and it's classrooms.

_____

_____

_____

_____

_____

Word Choice

When your audience is someone important or someone you don't know well, use formal language. Choose serious-sounding words.

Susan wrote a letter to a judge, but she did not use formal enough language. She also made mistakes with *whose* and *its*. Rewrite her letter, correcting the mistakes and using formal language. Use the words in the box to give you ideas.

Hey Judge Lee,

In our class, we've been learning all about trials, lawyers, judges, and other legal things. We've learned about who does what, and we even had a pretend trial. Also, some old judge came to our classroom. He told us about the law and it's history, but now we wanna meet a judge whose still in court. We also want to check out your courtroom. We could see your robe and your gavel, and everything. And some of us want to be lawyers when we grow up, so you could tell us what to do and stuff. That would be totally cool! Thanks!

TTYL,
Susan Zack

| Dear | understanding | features | consider | system | request |
| experience | appreciate | thank you | Sincerely | explain | process |

_____

_____

_____

_____

_____

_____

_____

_____

_____

Word Choice

Choose words that fit your audience. Think about whom you're writing to. Ask yourself what type of writing he or she would best respond to.

A. Think about someone whom you would like to visit your classroom. Write a letter in which you ask that person to visit. Complete the chart to plan your ideas.

Whom would you like to visit?	
What would you like this person to do, show you, or tell you about?	
Why do you want this person to visit?	
When would you like this person to visit?	
How would you convince this person to visit?	

B. Fill in the blanks to complete each sentence with the correct word. Use *whose, who's, it's,* or *its.*

1. I want to meet somebody _____ job is to protect wild animals.

2. Donnie wants to talk with someone _____ involved with computers.

3. Malik thinks _____ fun to talk about our future careers.

4. Wendy wants to go to State University and be on _____ basketball team.

Word Choice

Use your ideas from Day 4 to write a letter inviting someone to visit your classroom. Use the type of language most appropriate for the person receiving the letter.

Be sure to spell *whose, who's, it's,* and *its* correctly.

_____
date

_____
greeting

_____

_____

_____

_____

_____

_____

_____

_____

_____

_____

_____

_____

_____
closing

_____
signature

Word Choice

To write a strong opening and get your reader's attention, use powerful, precise language.

A. Read each opening for a persuasive essay. Circle the precise word or phrase in Opening 2 that replaces each boldface word in Opening 1.

Opening 1

Money is often **taken** from **musicians**. It happens because musicians own their music, just as store owners own their **stuff**. When people **copy** music for free, they're **taking** the money from musicians.

Opening 2

Millions of dollars are stolen from musicians' pockets every day! How does it happen? Just as a store owner owns the items on his or her shelves, musical artists own their music. When people download music without paying for it, they are stealing. And every dollar adds up!

B. Read this opening paragraph for a story. Complete the sentences by writing the words or phrases that are more likely to grab the reader's attention.

The fact that Dan's science fair entry was _____
(broken / trampled)

by his darling _____ would certainly have
(German shepherd / dog)

_____ any other boy into _____.
(put / thrown)   (hysterics / a mood)

However, Dan was different from all the other boys. He had

_____—his mom! She just happened to be an expert
(a secret weapon / help)

_____, who could put his clay volcano model back
(artist / sculptor)

together _____.
(lickety-split / quickly)

Word Choice

Review and revise your opening to make it stronger. Use words and phrases that will get your reader's attention.

A. Read each pair of opening sentences. Write an *X* next to the opening that gets your attention more. Then use proofreading marks to fix any misspelled words ending in *or, er,* or *ar.*

1. ___ You've got the whole day ahead of you. Where do you go to pass the time? You hit the road and head to beautiful Lake Romana.

   ___ If you are looking for a nice place to spend the day, you might considor going to Lake Romana.

2. ___ Helen Tarrosa is a great doctor who is known around town for helping others.

   ___ Everyone in town is familier with Dr. Helen Tarrosa, who has helped hundreds of people in need.

3. ___ The T-shirt Factory sells any T-shirt you could ever want! In fact, it sells shirts in more than 60 different colers and styles.

   ___ The T-shirt Factory sells many kinds of T-shirts.

4. ___ Imagine waking up on a farm, surrounded by quiet cows, cheerful chickens, cozy cats, and one very happy hound.

   ___ At Old Farm Inn, you can wandor all around a real farm.

B. Read this opening for a restaurant ad. Then rewrite it, using more powerful, precise language.

Think about having dinner at Pete's Pizza. His interesting flavors will probably surprise you.

_____

_____

_____

_____

Word Choice

Use powerful, precise language to make your reader want to keep reading.

A. Read this interview. Use a dictionary to check the spellings of words ending in *or, er,* or *ar,* and use proofreading marks to fix any that are misspelled.

Reportor:	What happened?
Mayor Ruiz:	There was a small fire in Public Square on Tuesday night.
Reporter:	How did it start?
Mayar Ruiz:	A small tremer caused a huge, tall light to fall over. It landed on a movie camera and knocked it to the ground. There were sparks, which started a small fire.
Reporter:	Who was involved at the fire?
Mayar Ruiz:	The acters, directar, and film crew, who were in town to make a movie.
Reporter:	How did they react?
Mayor Ruiz:	The most populor actor ran from the scene. A crew member knocked over the food table. Some of the food fell into the fire, and it smelled like a skunk!
Reporter:	How was the fire put out?
Mayor Ruiz:	Firefightors arrived and put out the fire. Thankfully, no one was hurt.

B. Use the interview above to write a short article describing what happened in Public Square. Be sure to write a beginning that grabs the reader's attention.

_____

_____

_____

_____

_____

_____

Word Choice

Use powerful, precise language to write a strong opening that makes your reader want to read more.

Imagine that you're a reporter on the scene of one of the events listed in the box below. Complete the chart with information about the event. Use words that will grab your reader's attention.

> • A bear is found wandering through a shopping mall.
> • School bus drivers compete in a bus race.
> • Famous actors come to town for the premier of a new movie.

Event:

Who was there?	
What happened?	
Where did it happen?	
When did it happen?	
Why did it happen?	
How did it happen?	

Word Choice

Use your chart from Day 4 to write a newspaper article about the event you chose. Get your reader's attention by using powerful, precise language.

Be sure to spell words ending in *or, er,* or *ar* correctly.

_____

_____

_____

_____

_____

_____

_____

_____

_____

_____

_____

_____

_____

_____

_____

_____

_____

_____

_____

_____

_____

_____

_____

_____

_____

Sentence Fluency

Make your writing flow by combining short, choppy sentences into compound sentences. Use conjunctions (*and, but, or,* and *so*) to make compound sentences.

A. Read this description. Underline each compound sentence, and circle its conjunction.

> Have you ever been to the Bug Museum? This museum is dedicated to helping kids know more about the many roles that bugs play on Earth. You may not love bugs, but this museum will help you understand why they're so important! You can discover how bees communicate, and you can learn how ladybugs help farmers. You can touch some live beetles, and you can crawl around in a giant ant farm. The museum offers tours, or you can explore on your own. There is even a place to have lunch. Just remember that the museum is crowded on weekends, so it's better to go during the week.

B. Read this description. Underline the short, choppy sentences that could be combined. Then combine them to write three compound sentences, using a comma and a conjunction.

> The Museum of Communication has collected telephones for the past century. They have old phones. They have new ones. Many phones are antiques. Some still work. My favorite phone is the one with an earpiece that you hold to your ear while talking into a box on the wall. It reminds me of old movies. I tried using an old phone. It was hard to hear. I had to talk loudly. My friend and I pretended to be living when people used those phones. People had less privacy then. You couldn't move or carry around the phone. The closest thing to text messaging was the telegraph machine.

1. _____

2. _____

3. _____

Sentence Fluency

When you combine sentences to make your writing flow, be careful not to form rambling sentences.

A. Underline the rambling sentences in this paragraph. Then rewrite the paragraph, changing the rambling sentences to compound or simple sentences.

Most creatures have some sort of way to protect themselves from predators, but there are some creatures that have very unusual defense mechanisms, and some animals use toxic chemicals to protect themselves. For example, the poison dart frog has many poison glands all over its body, and the fire salamander squirts poison at its enemies from glands on its back, but other animals use camouflage to hide from their enemies. For instance, the chameleon changes its color to match its surroundings, and so do some octopuses, but one type of octopus, the mimic octopus, even changes its shape to look like other animals, so it just goes to show that animals will do anything to keep from being eaten!

_____

_____

_____

_____

_____

_____

_____

_____

_____

B. Look back at the paragraph you wrote. Check to make sure you used commas correctly. Circle the commas, and add them if necessary.

Sentence Fluency

When you revise your writing, look for ways to make it flow better with compound sentences.

A. Read Dean's journal entry. Then rewrite the entry, combining the shorter sentences into compound sentences and breaking up the rambling sentence.

March 18, 2009

   Today was the first day of volunteering at the science museum. I had fun. It was hard work. First, I carried boxes for a new exhibit, and then I unloaded them all, and then a group of first-grade students came for a tour, and I showed them around. They were cute. Some of them were hard to control. They climbed on the exhibits. They ran away from the group! After lunch, I assisted with a demonstration. I was nervous. Luckily, all I had to do was pass around some fossils. At the end, everyone thanked me. I guess I did a good job!

_____

_____

_____

_____

_____

_____

_____

_____

_____

_____

_____

B. Trade papers with a partner. Check each other's paragraphs to make sure commas and conjunctions are used correctly in each compound sentence.

Sentence Fluency

Use compound sentences to make your writing flow.

A. Imagine that you work at a museum. Choose from the list of museums below, or think of your own. Then use the web to plan an exhibit for that museum.

- Museum of Pirate History
- Museum of Games
- Museum of Pizza
- Museum of Socks

Name of Museum: _____

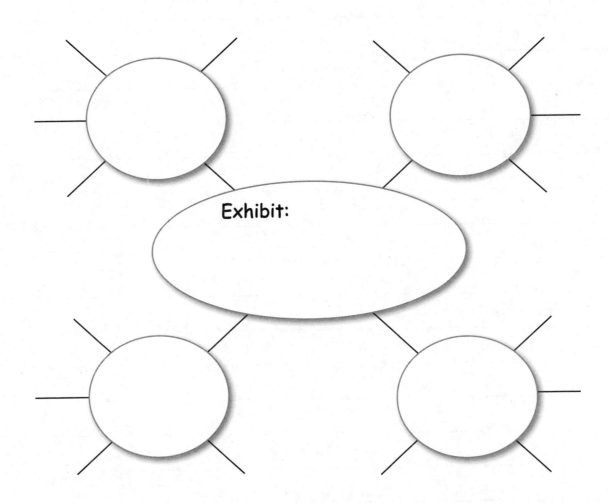

B. Write one compound sentence you could use in your description.

_____

_____

Sentence Fluency

Use your web from Day 4 to write a description of a museum exhibit you would design.

Be sure to use commas in compound sentences correctly, and avoid writing rambling sentences.

_____

_____

_____

_____

_____

_____

_____

_____

_____

_____

_____

_____

_____

_____

_____

_____

_____

_____

_____

_____

Sentence Fluency

Complex sentences help your writing flow. A complex sentence is an independent clause and a dependent clause joined by a subordinating conjunction.

A. Underline the complex sentences in this paragraph. Then, for each sentence you underlined:

- Circle the subordinating conjunction.
- Draw a second line under the independent clause.

Subordinating Conjunctions				
after	because	when	while	until

On Saturday, I helped my mom get ready to open her new bookstore. My job was to straighten all the bookshelves while Mom prepared the cash register. We were expecting a lot of customers because Mom had put a big ad in the paper. Finally, Mom was ready to open the store, but there was a problem. When she tried to open the door from the inside, it was stuck! She had to call a locksmith. He said he couldn't get there until he finished another job. Mom was frantic! While we waited nervously, customers started gathering outside. After twenty minutes, the locksmith finally arrived. He fixed the door and let everyone in. We all cheered, especially Mom!

B. Combine each pair of sentences to write a complex sentence, using the conjunction in parentheses. Remember, the conjunction can come at the beginning or in the middle of the sentence.

1. Rafael writes the story. Jessie will draw the pictures. *(if)*

_____

2. Please help me think of plot ideas. I have to start writing. *(before)*

_____

3. I revised my story. Yuki liked it better. *(after)*

_____

Sentence Fluency

When you write a complex sentence, you can start with either the dependent clause or the independent clause. Choose the way that sounds the most natural.

A. Read the clauses. Match each dependent clause to an independent clause to write six complex sentences. Be sure to think about which way the sentence makes more sense—with the dependent clause or the independent clause first.

Dependent Clause	Independent Clause
once he has finished his homework	he writes in his reading journal
when Eli has time	Eli's mom built him a bookcase
while he reads	Eli is also interested in historical fiction
before his little sister goes to bed	he reads her a story
although he likes fantasy novels	Eli will read his book
because he has so many books	Eli always makes a snack to eat

1. _____

2. _____

3. _____

4. _____

5. _____

6. _____

B. Exchange papers with a partner. Check to make sure commas are used correctly in the sentences that begin with a dependent clause. Circle the commas, or add them if necessary.

Sentence Fluency : Use complex sentences to help your writing flow smoothly.

A. Rewrite this book review to make it flow more smoothly. Combine some sentences into complex sentences, using any of the conjunctions in the box.

A Wrinkle in Time

   I don't normally enjoy reading fantasy books. I really liked the fantasy A Wrinkle in Time by Madeleine L'Engle. The story is about a brother and sister. They have to work hard to save their father. He is trapped on another planet. They journey through time and space to reach him. They find out more about themselves. They realize that the power of love is stronger than evil. They return home—with their father. This book had me hooked. I couldn't stop reading. I finally got to the end. You will love this book. You'll finish reading it. You'll want to read it again!

Subordinating Conjunctions				
after	because	if	unless	when
although	before	once	until	while

_____

_____

_____

_____

_____

_____

_____

B. Exchange papers with another student. Underline each complex sentence in the rewritten review. Check to make sure commas have been used correctly.

 **Sentence Fluency** Use complex sentences to help your writing flow smoothly.

Think of a book you have read that you could write a review about. Then complete the items.

1. What is the name of the book? Remember to underline the title.

_____

2. Who is the author?

_____

3. What happens in the book? Write a few sentences to summarize the plot. Use subordinating conjunctions such as *before, after,* or *while* in your answer.

_____

_____

_____

_____

4. Did you like or dislike the book? Why? Use the word *because* in your answer. Write at least one complex sentence.

_____

_____

_____

5. Who would like or dislike this book? Answer the question using a complex sentence.

_____

_____

Sentence Fluency

Use your ideas from Day 4 to write a book review. Explain what you thought of the book and who would or would not like it. Include complex sentences to help your writing flow smoothly.

Be sure to use commas correctly.

Sentence Fluency

Use parallel structure in your writing.
Keep lists of words or phrases in the same form.

A. Read each pair of sentence fragments. In each pair:

- Make a check next to the fragment in which all three words or phrases are parallel.

- Write an *X* next to the fragment whose words or phrases are not parallel. Circle the word or phrase that does not match.

1. _____ to walk, to climb, and hiking

   _____ to walk, to climb, and to hike

2. _____ my sneakers, my baseball bat, and my mitt

   _____ my sneakers, baseball bat, and my mitt

3. _____ two flies, a beetle, a grasshopper, and an ant

   _____ two flies, a beetle, grasshopper, and an ant

4. _____ sweep the floor, do the laundry, and the dishes

   _____ sweep the floor, do the laundry, and wash the dishes

B. Write the correct pronoun to complete each sentence.

1. My sister Dara and _____ are taking karate lessons this year.
   (I / me)

2. _____ are learning how to kick, how to block, and how to punch.
   (We / Us)

3. Dad takes _____ to the gym on Tuesdays, Thursdays, and Saturdays.
   (her and me / she and I)

4. A lot of my friends want to take karate now. _____ have heard how fun it is!
   (Them / They)

5. They always ask _____ to demonstrate kicks.
   (I / me)

Sentence Fluency

When you write a series of words or phrases in a sentence, be sure to use parallel structure.

A. Complete each sentence with the word or phrase that keeps the sentence parallel.

1. Kira needs to perform twenty sit-ups, _____, and run a mile.

   a. ten push-ups   b. do ten push-ups

2. To make a fruit shake, you need some milk, several strawberries,

   a banana, and _____.

   a. blender   b. a blender

3. Mr. Milos likes running in races, swimming laps, and _____.

   a. playing basketball   b. basketball

B. Write a complete sentence with parallel structure to answer each question.

1. What are three things you will do this weekend?

   _____

2. What are three things you need to make your favorite sandwich?

   _____

C. Use proofreading marks to fix the incorrect pronouns in this paragraph.

   Jay is my best friend. Him and me go everywhere together. Our

   parents are friends, too. Them go to football games together. Jay's dad

   taught us how to play football. Next year, me and Jay will try out for

   the team.

Sentence Fluency

When you revise your writing, check to make sure you have used parallel structure in each sentence.

Read this compare-and-contrast paragraph. Then:

- Circle the incorrect pronouns.
- Underline the sentences that do not have parallel structure.
- Rewrite the paragraph correctly.

   Two of the hardest athletic events are marathons and triathlons. These competitions aren't for regular people like you and I. They are only for really good athletes. A marathon is a running race. A triathlon is a race with three parts. First, you run, then you swim, and riding a bike. For a marathon, athletes need a running outfit and comfortable shoes. For a triathlon, them also need a swimsuit, a bicycle, and they need a helmet. In a marathon, an athlete runs 26 miles. Him or her might take a few hours to finish. In a triathlon, an athlete swims 2 miles, bikes 4 miles, and runs 26. This can take ten hours or more to complete! So you can see why both marathons and triathlons require special training, incredible endurance, and you have to work hard.

_____

_____

_____

_____

_____

_____

_____

_____

Sentence Fluency

Use parallel structure in your writing.
Keep series of words or phrases in the same form.

Think of two sports you like to watch or play. Complete the chart below to plan a compare-and-contrast paragraph. Remember to use parallel structure in your answers.

Sport 1:	Sport 2:
Name three actions you do while playing it.	Name three actions you do while playing it.
Name three things you need to play it.	Name three things you need to play it.
Name three things you need to do well in order to win.	Name three things you need to do well in order to win.

Sentence Fluency

Write a compare-and-contrast paragraph about two sports. Use the lists you created on Day 4 to write sentences that have parallel structure.

Be sure to use pronouns correctly.

_____

_____

_____

_____

_____

_____

_____

_____

_____

_____

_____

_____

_____

_____

_____

_____

_____

_____

_____

 **Sentence Fluency**

If you begin your sentences in different ways, your writing will sound more interesting.

A. Read each personal narrative. Circle the first word in each sentence. Draw a star next to the narrative that has more variety in the way the sentences begin.

Narrative 1

I looked for Aunt Linda as I stepped off the train. I wondered where she was. I saw her standing outside the station. I was so happy! I raced over to her, and we hugged.

Aunt Linda exclaimed, "You're growing like a weed!" We walked to the parking lot and climbed into her car. We talked about all sorts of things as we drove. I looked out the window at all the tall buildings.

We pulled up in front of my aunt's apartment building. I carefully climbed the stairs to her apartment. I didn't want to fall. I was so tired! I knew I needed a nap.

Narrative 2

As I stepped off the train, I looked for Aunt Linda. Where was she? Finally, I saw her standing outside the station. It was so good to see her! We raced toward each other and hugged.

"You're growing like a weed!" Aunt Linda exclaimed. Then we walked to the parking lot and climbed into her car. We talked about all sorts of things. I asked her about the tall buildings we were passing, and she told me their names.

Soon, my aunt pulled the car up in front of her building. Carefully, I climbed the stairs to her apartment. The last thing I needed was to fall! Boy, was I tired. A nap was certainly in store for me.

B. Make a check next to the sentences that are punctuated correctly.

☐ Rita cried, "Oh no, the elevator is broken! We'll have to take the stairs!"

☐ "How many floors does this building have?", Jeffrey asked nervously.

☐ "There are ten floors!" exclaimed Rita.

☐ Jeffrey said "Well, I guess we'd better start climbing!"

☐ "How long do you think it will take us?" wondered Rita.

 **Sentence Fluency** Begin sentences in different ways. Use different types of words and phrases to add variety to your writing.

A. Read each pair of sentences. Rewrite the underlined sentence so it begins in a different way.

Example: I left the playground. <u>I followed the muddy tracks that headed into the forest.</u>

<u>Following the muddy tracks, I headed into the forest.</u>

1. <u>I heard strange high-pitched noises coming from the bushes.</u> I trembled in my boots!

   _____

2. I saw a tiny raccoon suddenly rocket past me. <u>I felt silly for being scared.</u>

   _____

3. <u>I returned to my house and immediately called my best friend.</u> I told her what had happened.

   _____

B. Read each sentence. Use proofreading marks to add punctuation to the dialogue.

1. What's up? Tiana asked.

2. Arthur replied I just saw a raccoon in the forest!

3. I see raccoons all the time Tiana said.

4. That high-pitched noise is weird! Arthur exclaimed.

5. It's just the raccoon complaining that you're too close explained Tiana.

Sentence Fluency

Look for sentences that begin the same way. Revise them so they begin differently.

Read this personal narrative. Then:

- Correct the punctuation errors in the dialogue.
- Underline at least five sentences that could be revised to begin differently.
- Rewrite the narrative, changing the sentences you underlined.

We had all gathered at Auntie Giselle's house by 6 o'clock for Grandpa's surprise party. She had invited him to dinner at 6:15. We had parked around the corner so Grandpa wouldn't see our cars. Then Auntie Giselle got a phone call while we were waiting for Grandpa to arrive. He was calling to say he wasn't coming! He wanted to stay home and watch the ballgame. She convinced him that they could watch it together at her house. She saved the party!

Grandpa finally rang the doorbell at 6:30. We darted behind the furniture. Auntie Giselle threw open the door. We yelled "Surprise!"

Grandpa gasped. "I was not expecting this he said, in a daze.

_____

_____

_____

_____

_____

_____

_____

_____

 **Sentence Fluency**   Begin your sentences in different ways to keep your reader interested.

A. Think about a time when something surprising or unexpected happened to you. Then complete the chart to plan a personal narrative about that event.

Event:	
What I saw:	
What I heard:	
What I smelled:	
What I felt:	
What I tasted:	

B. Write a sentence that describes something that happened during the event. Then rewrite the sentence, using a different beginning.

1. _____

_____

2. _____

_____

C. Write something you said or heard someone else say. Use correct punctuation.

_____

Sentence Fluency

Use your completed chart from Day 4 to write a personal narrative of a time when something unexpected happened to you. Be sure to begin your sentences in different ways and include dialogue in your narrative. Be sure to punctuate the dialogue correctly.

_____

_____

_____

_____

_____

_____

_____

_____

_____

_____

_____

_____

_____

_____

_____

_____

_____

_____

_____

_____

_____

_____

_____

_____

Sentence Fluency

To write a smooth paragraph, vary the types of sentences you use. Include simple, compound, and complex sentences.

A. Read each student's autobiography. Then:

- Use a <u>straight line</u> to underline each compound sentence.
- Use a <u>wavy line</u> to underline each complex sentence.

Larry Alvarez

On December 1, 1997, I was born in Las Vegas. I already had a brother, but my sister wasn't born yet. She didn't arrive until I was two years old. When I was three, we adopted a puppy. We named him Racer, and he sure lived up to his name! We also moved from an apartment to a house that year. This was important because Racer really needed a yard to run in. When I was eight, I joined City League Sports and Recreation. Unfortunately, I could only pick one team to be on. I could play soccer, or I could swim. I chose soccer, and the rest is history!

Renee Narcizo

I was born on January 27, 1998. I was born in Chicago. I don't remember much about it. In 2002, we moved to Alabama. We moved to Florida two years later. My dad is in the military, so we have moved a lot. I don't mind. I have made some great friends. We have visited friends and family in a lot of places! I have a baby brother. I have a baby sister. Their names are Damon and Valeria. They are twins. They were born when I was seven. They are fun to watch.

B. Choose two pairs of short sentences in Renee's autobiography. Combine them to write compound or complex sentences.

1. _____

2. _____

Sentence Fluency

Use transition words and phrases to improve the flow of your sentences.

A. Read the paragraph. Use the words and phrases in the box to fill in the blanks.

Transition Words and Phrases		
as a result	in fact	furthermore
for example	of course	

Accidents happen all the time, so all kids should have a basic knowledge of first aid. _____, do you know what to do if your friend falls and cuts his arm? _____, you should seek an adult's help. But what if there are no adults around and your friend needs immediate attention? You may not have time to wait for help. _____, you wouldn't want to just stand there doing nothing while your friend is in pain. So ask your parents to sign you up for a first-aid class. There is a free one, _____, being offered at the community center next week. You'll learn some simple things that even kids can do if someone is bleeding, choking, or injured. _____, you will know what to do in an emergency.

B. Underline the sentence fragments in this short paragraph. Then rewrite the paragraph, using complete sentences.

We've lived next door to Mr. Green for a long time. Like forever. He's very nice. When we ride our bikes. Lets us cut through his yard. To thank him, we take him cookies. Chocolate chip! His favorite.

_____

_____

_____

_____

 **Sentence Fluency** Include different kinds of sentences for a smooth-sounding paragraph.

Read this persuasive letter. Look for sentences that can be revised or improved. Then rewrite the body of the letter by:

- Correcting any sentence fragments.
- Combining simple sentences into compound or complex sentences.
- Beginning sentences in different ways.
- Using parallel structure.
- Adding transition words and phrases.

Dear Mayor,

Tia Shin deserves an award. The Best Neighbor Award. She is kind, friendly, and she cares. She treats us like family. Although she is just a neighbor. Once we were sick. She took care of us. My mom had to go to work. Nobody else could take us to the doctor. Tia did.

She watches out for all the kids on our street. She will flag a driver down. If she sees a car speeding down our street. She will tell the driver to slow down. Children play around here. Best neighbor in the city.

Sincerely,
Zane Childers

_____

_____

_____

_____

_____

_____

_____

_____

 **Sentence Fluency**

Include different kinds of sentences for a smooth-sounding paragraph.

Think of an adult you know. Is there an award you think he or she should win, such as Best Coach or Greatest Custodian? What would you tell someone about the person you chose? Use the questionnaire below to plan a letter recommending this person for the award.

1. Whom will you write about?

   _____

2. What kind of award should this person win?

   _____

3. What does your favorite person do that is so great? Write your answer as a **compound sentence**.

   _____

   _____

4. Give a specific example of a time when your favorite person helped others. Write your answer as a **complex sentence**.

   _____

   _____

5. Write a sentence that tells three things about what your favorite person looks like. Use **parallel structure** in your sentence.

   _____

   _____

6. What else would you want to say about this person?

   _____

   _____

Sentence Fluency

Write a persuasive letter recommending an adult you know for an award. Use the sentences you wrote on Day 4 to make your letter flow smoothly. Exchange papers with a partner to check for sentence fragments. Correct any that are found.

_____
date

_____
greeting

_____

_____

_____

_____

_____

_____

_____

_____

_____

_____

_____

_____

_____

_____
closing

_____
signature

 **Voice** Your voice can come through your writing in a variety of ways. For example, you can write with a mysterious voice.

A. Read Ms. West's narrative about a strange event that happened in her classroom. Fill in the words and phrases that help make it mysterious.

startled	flew through the window	no one
theories	thoroughly mystified	we still don't know
screamed	phantom offender	erupted into confusion

A Real "Whodunit"

This morning, as I was about to give my students a math test,

something odd happened. Just as I was giving directions, a soccer

ball _____ and bounced off my desk!

Naturally, this _____ everyone. A few students

_____ . The class _____ .

A student ran to the window, but there was _____

in sight. We were all _____ . The students came

up with various _____ about who might have been the

_____ . Some thought it was a student in another

class. Other kids wondered if it was the gym teacher, the custodian, or

someone from the house across the street. The true scary part is that

_____ who did it—or why!

B. Commas are used to separate words in a series. Underline the sentence in Ms. West's story that contains a series. Circle the commas.

C. Imagine you are a student in Ms. West's class. How would you have told the story? Rewrite the beginning, using your own mysterious voice.

_____

_____

 **Voice** Some writers use a playful voice that makes their writing fun to read.

A. Read Sam's funny narrative. Underline the sentences that contain a series. Add commas where they are needed.

Fascinating Fifth-Grade Flying Soccer Ball Mystery

You won't believe what happened in math class today! We were getting ready to take a test when a soccer ball zoomed through the window! It just missed bopping Ms. West on the head and bounced off her desk instead. Then it whacked the wall the whiteboard and the wastebasket. I jumped to my feet and hotfooted it to the window. I looked left right up and down, but there was no one to be seen. I did hear one teeny-tiny thing, however. The back door to Mr. Ventura's classroom clicked shut. Was he playing a joke on us? You're probably wondering why in the world I'd suspect a teacher! Well, guess who once turned all the maps upside down when we were studying the fifty states. Guess who once filled the closet with crumpled newspaper. I concluded that the phantom soccer player was the marvelous, mischievous Mr. Ventura!

B. How did Sam make his writing fun to read? Write two examples of each way listed below.

1. Alliteration: _____

_____

2. Amusing Words and Phrases: _____

_____

3. Informal Language: _____

_____

 **Voice** Sometimes it's important to write with a formal, serious-sounding voice.

A. Read this letter of apology. The writer used formal language to match her purpose, and she used facts to explain what happened. Underline the facts and circle examples of formal language.

> Dear Ms. West and Class,
>
> My sincere apologies to you for disturbing your class yesterday. I am a college student who hopes to be a professional soccer player one day. So, I was using the grassy area in front of your school to practice my dribbling. However, I got carried away imagining that I was a soccer star and tried a banana kick. Unfortunately, the ball curved in a different direction than I planned. When I realized that it was flying through your window, I panicked and ran. I am terribly embarrassed by my carelessness, rudeness, and improper behavior. Please accept my apology.
>
> Yours sincerely,
> Becky Beckham

B. Pretend you are Ms. West. Write three sentences to Becky, accepting her apology and offering the ball back. Use a formal style.

_____

_____

_____

_____

C. Insert commas where they belong in these sentences.

1. To be a good soccer player, you must know how to dribble pass and kick.

2. The goalie fullback halfback and forward are four different positions in soccer.

 **Voice** When you plan your writing, think about the voice you will use. For instance, it can be mysterious, playful, or serious.

A. Plan a story about something that mysteriously disappears from your school. Fill in the events in this flowchart. Then choose which voice you want to use for your story.

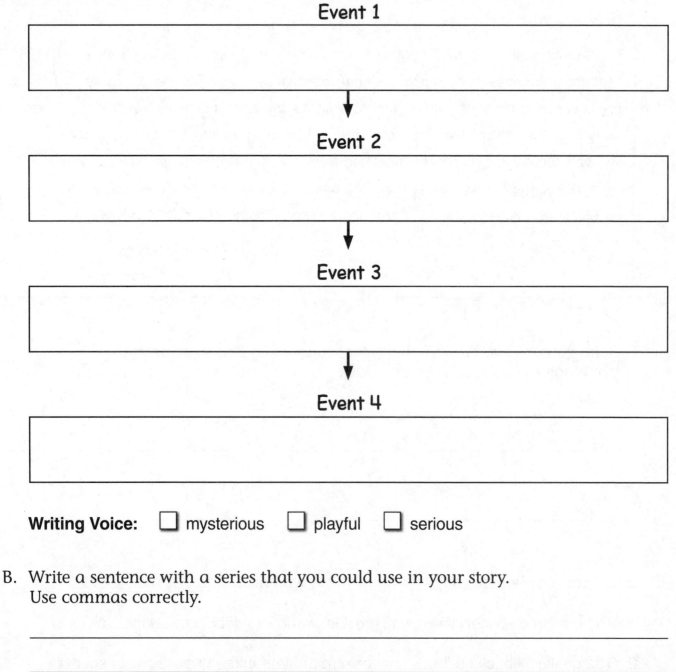

Event 1

Event 2

Event 3

Event 4

Writing Voice: ☐ mysterious ☐ playful ☐ serious

B. Write a sentence with a series that you could use in your story. Use commas correctly.

_____

_____

Write a story about something that mysteriously disappears from school. Use your ideas from Day 4, and write in a mysterious, serious, or playful voice.

Be sure to use commas in a series correctly.

_____

_____

_____

_____

_____

_____

_____

_____

_____

_____

_____

_____

_____

_____

_____

_____

_____

_____

_____

_____

_____

_____

 **Voice**

The voice you use depends on your purpose. For example, you can use your voice to persuade.

A. Read the e-mail Dani wrote to persuade her cousin to visit. Then:

- Underline three activities that Dani listed to persuade Ellie.
- List six emotional words that Dani used to persuade Ellie.

Dear Ellie,

Are you looking forward to summer vacation? I am! I'm writing with some amazing news. Are you ready for this? Pete and the Pugs will be performing at this year's county fair—our absolute favorite band! Don't you just love the band's new song, "Chili Dog"? So I begged and begged my parents, and guess what! They said they'd get us tickets! So you must come and visit me in July. We'll have other awesome things to do while you're here, too. You can borrow my sister's tennis racket, and we can play every day at the high school. Also, our town's new water park, Wild Waters, just opened. We would have a blast there! So try to e-mail me back sometime, because I think the concert tickets probably go on sale kind of soon.

Hugs from your cousin,

Dani

_____ _____ _____

_____ _____ _____

B. The last sentence of the e-mail isn't very persuasive. Rewrite it in a stronger voice to persuade Ellie to write back to Dani right away.

_____

_____

C. Circle the possessive nouns in Dani's e-mail. Write them next to their meanings below.

(of this year) _____   (of my sister) _____

(of the band) _____   (of our town) _____

 **Voice**   You can use your voice to be entertaining.

A. Ethan wanted to write a funny paragraph about eating hot dogs. His purpose was to entertain, but some of the language he used sounds more formal than funny. Use proofreading marks to replace the words in bold with more entertaining words and phrases from the box.

Entertaining Words and Phrases

tickle the taste buds	splattered	head straight for	mouthwatering
a huge, sloppy mess	if you ask me	slaps on heaps	

Hot Dogs

For the most **flavorful** hot dogs in town, **I recommend** Charley's Burger Place. Most customers' favorite meal there is the Charley Burger. However, **in my opinion,** the best thing on the menu is Charley's chili dogs. They really **are quite delicious.** First, Charley **applies generous amounts** of mustard and ketchup. Next, he adds a special chili sauce. I always have to ask for extra napkins because the hot dogs can be **difficult to eat.** One time, I even **managed to drip** chili on my shoes! It was worth every bite, though.

B. Write the plural possessive form of each word in parentheses to complete the sentences.

1. The _____ trays were loaded with plates of steaming food.
   (server)

2. The customers inhaled the _____ spicy aroma.
   (hot dog)

3. After dinner, the _____ bellies were full.
   (boy)

4. Their _____ wallets were empty!
   (parent)

 **Voice** Be sure your voice matches your purpose.

A. Kim's assignment was to write an exciting description. However, she didn't use a very exciting voice. Read what Kim wrote. Rewrite the paragraph in a more exciting voice. Use the words in the box to help you.

Exciting Words						
amazing	colossal	dare	dark	deep	hottest	longest
plunge	roaring	soar	splash	thrilling	wild	zoom

A Day at the Water Park

A trip to Wild Waters on a hot day is a lot of fun. You will like the park's Turbo Slide. The slide has twists and turns through a tunnel. At the tunnel's end is a pool that you land in. You can do some bodysurfing in another pool called the Boogie Blast. It has waves for surfing. You can also ride in an inner tube on the Master Blaster. The ride's track is like a roller coaster of water that moves you up and down. You climb as high as a two-story building. Then you drop into the water.

_____

_____

_____

_____

_____

B. Use proofreading marks to fix the possessive noun in each sentence.

1. My two best friends favorite ride at Wild Waters is the Turbo Slide.

2. Jeremy and Ahmed love swooshing through the slides tunnel.

3. During the summer, the parks hours are from 10:00 a.m. to 8:00 p.m.

 **Voice** Be sure your voice matches your purpose.

Where would you like to go on a class trip? Complete the chart to plan a paragraph persuading your teacher to take you there. List three things that would be exciting to see or do there. Then write descriptive words and strong verbs about each of those things.

Name of Place: _____

Things to Do or See	Descriptive Words	Strong Verbs
1		
2		
3		

 **Voice**

Use your chart from Day 4 to write a paragraph persuading your teacher to take your class on a trip. Use an exciting voice to show your enthusiasm.

Be sure to spell possessive nouns correctly.

_____

_____

_____

_____

_____

_____

_____

_____

_____

_____

_____

_____

_____

_____

_____

_____

_____

_____

 **Voice** Images are pictures that a writer creates with words to describe something. Images can add voice to a poem.

A. Read the poem. Then answer the questions.

Little Things by Ebenezer Brewer

Little drops of water,
  Little grains of sand,
Make the mighty ocean,
  And the pleasant land.

Thus the little minutes,
  Humble though they be,
Make the mighty ages
  Of eternity.

1. In the first stanza, what are two small things that Brewer writes about? What are the two big things that they make up?

Small things: _____   _____

Big things: _____   _____

2. In the second stanza, what small thing does Brewer write about? What is the big thing?

Small thing: _____

Big thing: _____

3. How would you describe the voice of this poem? Circle the words.

funny   simple   exciting   serious

thoughtful   mysterious   quiet

B. "Little Things" uses images to describe something invisible—time. For each invisible thing below, write an image that could describe it.

Something Invisible	Image
1. time	
2. friendship	
3. summer	

 **Voice**

Certain kinds of poems have a specific number of syllables. This gives the poems a rhythmic voice.

A. Read each poem. Then:

- Use proofreading marks to make the use of capital letters the same at the beginning of each line.
- Write the syllables in each line of the poem.
- Circle the words that describe the voice of the poem.

Haiku

	Syllables
loud, icy pebbles	_____
Marbles falling from the sky	_____
hail plonks on the roof	_____

Voice: funny   informal   serious   quiet   lighthearted

Cinquain

	Syllables
Garbage	_____
smelly, stinky,	_____
Throwing, crushing, piling,	_____
Filled with things we no longer want	_____
the dump	_____

Voice: formal   sad   enthusiastic   informal   funny

B. Read each word. Think of a word that has a similar or more specific meaning but a different number of syllables. Write the word.

1. scary _____   3. red _____

2. tree _____   4. run _____

 **Voice**

You can bring your own voice and ideas to a common poetry form, such as haiku.

Write a line to complete each haiku. Be sure that the line has the correct number of syllables (in parentheses) and matches the use of capitalization in other lines. Then draw a picture to illustrate your haiku.

1. **Subject:** the sun

   (5)   Yellow like pencils

   (7)   Always sketching a new day

   (5)   _____

2. **Subject:** a cat

   (5)   _____

   (7)   it stretches from front to back

   (5)   tail up in the air

3. **Subject:** winter

   (5)   bundled up in coats

   (7)   _____

   (5)   the year's coldest time

 **Voice**   Use your own images and voice to write a haiku.

Haikus are usually about nature. Think of two things in nature that you would like to write a haiku about, such as animals, flowers, weather events, or bodies of water. Then use the chart to plan your poems.

	Haiku 1	**Haiku 2**
Subject:		
Words related to the subject:		
Images that come to mind:		

Daily 6-Trait Writing • EMC 6795 • © Evan-Moor Corp.

Voice Choose one of the subjects you wrote about on Day 4 to write a haiku. Be sure that the first and third lines have five syllables, and the second line has seven. Use consistent capitalization at the beginning of each line.

 **Voice** — Everyone has a unique point of view and a unique voice.

A. Read each version of this story about a girl, her dad, and their dog. From whose point of view is each version told? Circle the name. Then write an adjective to describe the voice.

1. **Point of View:** Aubrey   Dad   Bowser   **Voice:** _____

   We were in the living room watching TV, waiting for our lasagna to cool. Well, we should have known better than to leave it on the table, because the next thing you know, my dog Bowser walked in with lasagna all over his snout! I could have cried. I had worked so hard to make that lasagna after school, and I was so hungry! Now everything was totally ruined.

2. **Point of View:** Aubrey   Dad   Bowser   **Voice:** _____

   After a very long day, I finally got to sit down for a few minutes and watch TV. The lasagna smelled delicious, and we were only minutes away from enjoying it. Suddenly, I heard the rattle of Bowser's collar in the kitchen. I could have gotten up and checked on him, but I was too comfortable to move. So that's how Bowser ended up having lasagna for dinner, and we ended up having takeout pizza!

3. **Point of View:** Aubrey   Dad   Bowser   **Voice:** _____

   Oh boy, it's dinnertime! Where's my bowl? I am STARVING! Ooooh, what's that yummy smell? Whatever it is, it's right on the edge of the table, so that must mean it's mine. YUMMMM! That's delicious! I would have behaved better today if I'd known I was going to get a reward like this! I'll go show the family how much I love them. They're the best!

B. Circle the phrases *should have, could have,* and *would have* in the story versions above. Write them as contractions.

_____   _____   _____

When you write a story, think about what kind of voice your character would have. Use that voice to write from his or her point of view.

A. Read what each character says about losing a softball game. Then write what else he or she might say. Use the same voice and point of view.

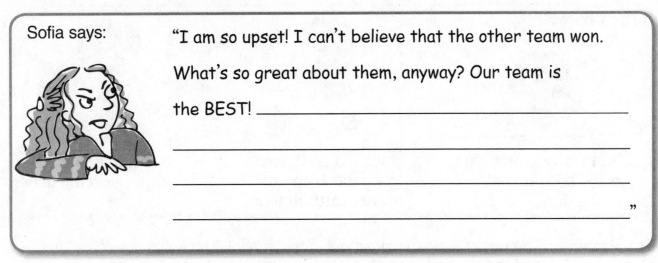

Sofia says:

"I am so upset! I can't believe that the other team won. What's so great about them, anyway? Our team is the BEST! _____ _____ _____ _____ "

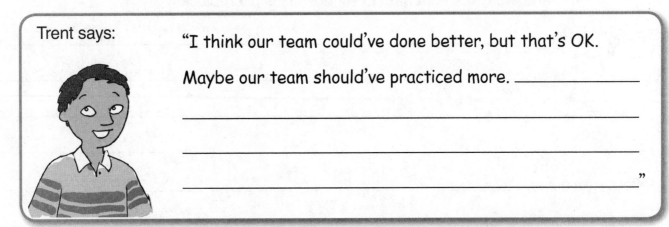

Trent says:

"I think our team could've done better, but that's OK. Maybe our team should've practiced more. _____ _____ _____ _____ "

B. Use proofreading marks to fix the incorrect forms of *could have, should have,* and *would have.*

1. "You should of seen the home run I hit yesterday," boasted Emily.

2. "I woulda made it to the game on time if my sister hadn't gotten sick," explained Rudy.

3. "We could'uv scored a lot more runs, but our best hitter had a sore arm," said Louis.

 **Voice**

When you write a story, give each of your characters a unique voice. Imagine how each character would react in a given situation.

Read each character description. Then read the problem. Imagine what each character would say about it.

The Characters:

Berto, a nervous, shy boy who is afraid of the dark

Kiara, a confident girl who is captain of her softball team

Mr. Savio, a calm, experienced teacher

The Problem: The power suddenly goes out in the school. The lights are off, and the classroom has no windows. It's pitch-black!

Berto would say: _____

_____

_____

_____

Kiara would say: _____

_____

_____

_____

Mr. Savio would say: _____

_____

_____

_____

 **Voice**

When you develop different characters, think about their different points of view. Give each character a unique voice.

Read about Gio's problem. Then fill in the chart to create two characters who have two different opinions about what Gio should have done.

The Problem: Gio received money for his birthday. He could have saved it for a skateboard, but he bought a lot of candy instead. Then he ate all of the candy at once and got sick!

	Character 1	**Character 2**
Character's Name:		
Two words to describe personality:		
Reaction to Gio's problem:		
What character would say to Gio:		
Two words to describe voice:		

Voice

Use your ideas from the chart on Day 4 to write a dialogue between the characters you created. Have them discuss what Gio did with his birthday money, expressing their particular points of view.

Be sure to use *should have, could have,* and *would have* correctly.

_____

_____

_____

_____

_____

_____

_____

_____

_____

_____

_____

_____

_____

_____

_____

_____

_____

_____

_____

_____

_____

_____

_____

 **Voice** When you write persuasively, think about the emotions you want your reader to feel.

A. Read each editorial. Then answer the questions.

Editorial 1

Earth Day is coming up on April 22. There is a lot of trash around. You can see soda cans, plastic bags, and other litter everywhere along Dodge River. It's good to pick up trash so that everything looks clean. Also, it helps birds and other animals, who often mistake litter for food. They can get sick from it, so come pick up trash on Earth Day.

Editorial 2

What will you be doing this April 22? If you're smart, you'll be having fun and helping out on Earth Day. Here's a simple way to participate: join the Dodge River Cleanup. We have gloves, bags, and hats for everyone. There will be a big party afterward, too, so bring your friends! April 22 doesn't have to be just another day. You could spend it hanging out with your friends, cleaning up your environment, and saving the wildlife. It's your choice. Which will you do?

1. Which editorial makes the event sound more fun? _____
   Underline three phrases that the writer used to do this.

2. Which editorial makes the cleanup job sound easier? _____
   Circle one word and one sentence that the writer used to do this.

3. Why do you think the writer of the second editorial used the phrase "If you're smart"?

   _____

   _____

B. Use proofreading marks to fix the use of commas.

1. Celia, Marcus, Julio and, Cassandra planted a garden on Earth Day.

2. They pulled weeds dug up rocks and planted vegetables.

 **Voice** : Use a strong, confident voice when you write persuasively.

A. Read each topic for a persuasive paragraph. What would your topic sentence be? Write it as a strong, confident opinion statement.

Example: **Topic:** avoiding the worst restaurant in town
   Opinion statement: <u>If you want to enjoy your food, don't go to Angie's Pizza.</u>

1. **Topic:** joining a specific club or team
   Opinion statement: _____

2. **Topic:** making the school day longer
   Opinion statement: _____

B. Write an *X* next to the movie review that does not have a confident voice. Then rewrite it to make it sound more confident.

☐ <u>The Flying Finkelsteins</u> is a pretty good movie. Mr. and Mrs. Finkelstein are superheroes trying to teach their kids how to fly. I enjoyed the scene where they all jump off the roof of their house together. If you have time this weekend, you might go see <u>The Flying Finkelsteins.</u>

☐ <u>Little Bo Beep</u> is the funniest movie ever! It's about a robot who thinks he's a sheepdog. Bo Beep tries to protect his flock of sheep from mutant coyotes—with hilarious results! If you want to laugh your head off, go see <u>Little Bo Beep</u> today!

_____

_____

_____

_____

C. Use proofreading marks to insert the missing commas.

1. If you have any books that you don't want please donate them to the library.

2. Although plastic bags are convenient they can also be harmful.

 **Voice**

When writing persuasively, use a strong, confident voice to appeal to your reader's emotions.

A. Read this persuasive paragraph. Then rewrite the paragraph so it has a stronger persuasive voice. Be sure to:

- Appeal to your reader's emotions.
- Be confident in your writing.

> Marshall Elementary School is collecting pennies, nickels, and dimes for The Children of the World Fund. This organization builds schools all over the world. It helps some children get an education. Pennies may not seem like they're worth very much, but they can add up to a lot of money. Most people have some spare change hiding around the house. If every family in town gave twenty-five or fifty cents, it might make a difference.

_____

_____

_____

_____

_____

_____

_____

_____

B. Use proofreading marks to insert the missing commas.

1. Please remember to bring in canned vegetables meat and soup for the food drive.

2. If you want to help distribute food you should be at the Community Center at 5:00.

3. Not everyone can afford to give money so they donate their time instead.

Voice

When you plan your persuasive writing, think about the reasons and voice you will use to convince your reader.

Use the opinion diagram below to plan a paragraph persuading people to contribute their time or money to an important cause at your school. Use one of the ideas below, or think of your own.

- Volunteer to be a homework tutor.
- Help start and run a new after-school club.
- Donate computers or art supplies to the school.
- Help raise money to pay for a class field trip.

Opinion Statement:

Reason 1:

Examples:

Reason 2:

Examples:

Reason 3:

Examples:

Possible Objection:

Response to Objection:

Write a persuasive paragraph urging your readers to contribute their time or money to an important cause at your school. Use your ideas from Day 4 to help you.

Be sure to use commas correctly.

_____

_____

_____

_____

_____

_____

_____

_____

_____

_____

_____

_____

_____

_____

_____

_____

_____

_____

_____

_____

_____

_____

Proofreading Marks

Mark	Meaning	Example
℘	Take this out (delete).	I love ℘ to read.
⊙	Add a period.	It was late⊙
≡	Make this a capital letter.	First prize went to maria.
/	Make this a lowercase letter.	We saw a ₿lack ₵at.
‾‾‾	Fix the spelling.	This is our house. ~~hause~~.
∧	Add a comma.	Goodnight∧Mom.
∨	Add an apostrophe.	That∨s Lil∨s bike.
! ? ∧ ∧	Add an exclamation point or a question mark.	Help!∧Can you help me?∧
∧	Add a word or a letter.	The red∧pen is mine.
# ∧	Add a space between words.	I like#∧pizza.
‾‾‾	Underline the words.	We read <u>Old Yeller</u>.
" " ∨ ∨	Add quotation marks.	∨Come in,∨he said.

Daily 6-Trait Writing • EMC 6795 • © Evan-Moor Corp.

A Land of Aching Hearts

LEILA TARAZI FAWAZ

A Land of Aching Hearts

The Middle East in the Great War

▐▐▐ Harvard University Press Cambridge, Massachusetts, and London, England
2014

First printing

Library of Congress Cataloging-in-Publication Data

Fawaz, Leila Tarazi
  A land of aching hearts : the Middle East in the Great War / Leila Tarazi Fawaz.
    pages   cm
Includes bibliographical references and index.
ISBN 978-0-674-73549-1
1. World War, 1914–1918—Social aspects—Middle East. 2. World War,
1914–1918—Social aspects—Syria. 3. Middle East—History—1914–1923.
4. Civilians in war—Middle East—History—20th century. 5. Soldiers—
Middle East—History—20th century. 6. Middle East—History, Military—
20th century. 7. Syria—History, Military—20th century. 8. Middle
East—Social conditions—20th century. 9. Syria—Social conditions—20th
century. I. Title.
D524.7.M53F39 2014
940.3'56—dc23
2014012879

To Karim Fawaz

Contents

Illustrations follow Chapter 4

Preface

WORLD WAR I is very much alive in the memory of what was once "Greater Syria," the focus of this book, but it also holds resonance throughout the entire Middle East. Indeed, the war transformed the political choices of the entire region and exposed its populations to social and economic duress on a scale never before known. In Lebanon, before the civil war that enveloped the country broke out in 1975, it was the Great War that people talked about most. I owe my own interest in the topic to my father, who used to talk about how the war had marked our family and others in Lebanon. Later, my own research into war and society from a historical perspective touched on World War I, in particular as I studied another great conflict—the conflict that broke out in Mount Lebanon and Syria in 1860.

The Great War marked the end of one historical era and the beginning of another. When I took up this project, I relished turning my attention from my previous focus on the prewar Middle East to that rupturing event itself. In the twentieth century, the region experienced perennial conflict—of which Lebanon endured its unhappy share—but it is the outsized importance of World War I that has held particular interest for me. I was fortunate that excellent scholars had pioneered research into the war and the decades immediately preceding it, for I was able to profit from their careful analysis and findings. This book will try to follow in their footsteps and build on their work to bring to life the social history of those who endured the Great War.

In this book, as in my other work, "Syria," "Syrian region," "Mount Lebanon," and "Lebanon" are not used in their modern sense but as they were used until the end of World War I. At the time "Greater Syria," "Syria," and "Syrian region" referred to the territory stretching from the Taurus Mountains in the north to the Sinai peninsula in the south, and from the Mediterranean in the west to the Syrian desert in the east. "Syria" and the "Syrian provinces" will therefore be used to refer to both the areas that comprise the modern states of Lebanon, Syria, Jordan, Israel, and Palestine and those areas of northern "Greater Syria" and southern modern Turkey that were ceded to Turkey in the 1920s, as well as to western Iraq. This area had been under Ottoman rule from 1516 to the end of World War I.

"Lebanon," "Mount Lebanon," and "the Mountain" will refer to the old territory of Mount Lebanon rather than the present-day republic. Between the late eighteenth century and the close of World War I, the Mountain included both the northern and southern districts of the Lebanon range. Northern Mount Lebanon extended into the areas around the renowned Cedars of Lebanon to the limits of Jabal Akkar and south across Kisrawan; it included the districts of Bisharri, Kura, Batrun, Jubayl, Munaytra, and Kisrawan (which, before the late eighteenth century, made up the original Mount Lebanon). The southern region covered the area south of Kisrawan and was separated from it by the Beirut-Damascus road. It included the districts known at that time as "Jabal al-Duruz" (Druze Mountain) of Gharb (upper and lower), Jurd, Urqub, and Shuf, and the districts of the Matn, Biqa', Jazzin, al-Tuffah, al-Kharrub, and Jabal al-Rayhan.

I would like to mention two other terms that occasionally are used by secondary sources and experts and merit special explanation. "Levant" and "Levantine" refer to the coastal areas that border the eastern Mediterranean from Anatolia to Egypt, including today's Lebanon, Syria, Jordan, Israel, Palestine, Cyprus, and parts of southern Turkey (Iraq and the Sinai peninsula are also sometimes included). The term has been used by French travelers and scholars of centuries past, but it is now mostly associated with colonial rule, particularly the French Mandate over Syria and Lebanon in the interwar period. It has acquired a slightly negative cultural meaning not only for its colonial antecedents but also because a "Levantine" is understood to be someone who supplemented cosmopolitan business acumen with something like a wheeler-dealer approach. However, the term has its uses for historians of the Ottoman period in that it is associated with the key centers of exchange with Europe, such as the great port cities of the eastern Mediterranean. This population of middlemen connected the interior with the West as trade expanded along the coast. The term thus captures a unique geography and the set of actors who peopled those areas. It is worth noting the sophistication and worldliness of these Levantines, their openness to outside cultures and influences, their tolerance of difference, and how they adjusted during rapidly changing times.

I would also like to caution the reader about the use of the word "Turk." In this book, the term "Turk" is used to designate ethnic Turks except in direct quotations, which cannot be changed. In mostly Western but also Arabic sources, the term "Turk" is used to refer not only to ethnic Turks but also to Arabs, Kurds, and others serving in Ottoman military or political functions. The Ottoman Empire was multiethnic, multilinguistic, multireligious, and multinational, but to traditional Western and other observers, including some local minorities from the region, such nuances were not always noted. Therefore, this book uses the term "Ottoman" as appropriate when designating a larger set of persons or actors. It is important to remember how diverse the population of the empire was, even when our sources simplify its composition.

Note on Transliteration

I HAVE CHOSEN to simplify the transliteration of Arabic by omitting most diacritics; in addition, initial ayns or hamzas are usually dropped in the text proper but they are retained in bibliographical references, which will facilitate tracing them in databases. For other Arabic words or names, I transliterate place names in accordance with the anglicized spelling commonly found in Western literature (for example, Beirut for Bayrut); if not a very everyday place name, I use modern standard Arabic as opposed to a colloquial spelling. Names of people appear in the form most commonly used by the individuals or families themselves (such as Baroody for Barudi); and the definite article *al-* is written only upon first mention, omitted subsequently.

Note on Exchange Rates

BECAUSE OF THE several different types of currency in circulation in the late nineteenth and early twentieth centuries and the continuously changing nature of relative prices due to debasement and depreciation, it is difficult to determine exact exchange rates. In addition, not all sources use the same rates of exchange. Therefore, the rates of exchange have been approximated for the purposes of this study. The silver coin introduced around 1688, the Ottoman kuruş (*qirsh* in Arabic), was known to Europeans as the piaster. During the period 1860–1888, 125 piasters were exchanged for a pound sterling. The pound sterling came to 25 French francs, which meant that 5 piasters equaled a French franc. The *kis, kise,* or purse was introduced in the seventeenth century as a unit of account; 500 piasters equaled one purse.

The Balkan Wars of 1912–1913 and World War I led to enormous fluctuations in the currency, and prices increased about twentyfold until the end of 1918. The three major gold units, known as liras, were the Ottoman, the English, and the French. In Syria, the gold dinar was made up of 100 Syrian piasters and a silver Syrian riyal was issued and was valued at 25 piasters.

Paper money began to circulate in 1915. By 1917 a banknote of 1 lira was exchanged for 35 piasters in Istanbul, for 25 in Aleppo, and for 10 in Mosul. By August 1917, 1 gold lira exchanged for 430 piasters of paper currency in Istanbul, 450 piasters in Bursa and Izmir, 540 in Aleppo, 555 in Beirut, and 766 in Mosul.

The Middle East at the outbreak of World War I.

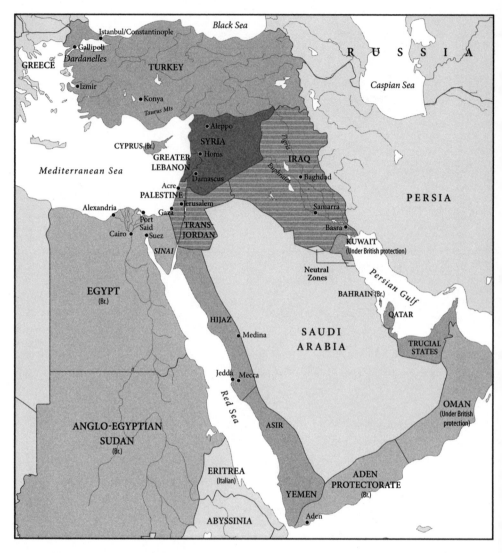

The Middle East at the end of World War I.

Theaters of war in the Middle East.

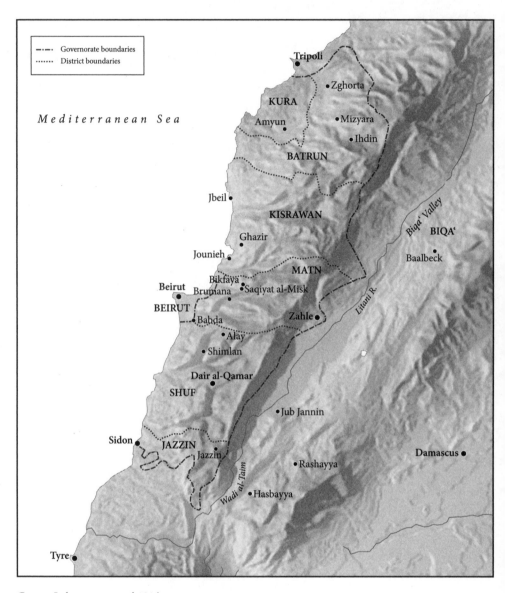

Greater Lebanon, around 1914.

A Land of Aching Hearts

Introduction

Everyday Heroes

IN HER MEMOIR, the pioneering Arab educator Wadad Makdisi Cortas (al-Maqdisi Qurtas) recalls the fishermen of Beirut plying their trade in the waters of coastal Lebanon. "Day after day," she reminisces, "we would watch the fishermen in their small white boats casting their nets in the thunderous waves, and we would wait for them to come back with their bounty. Mustafa the fisherman . . . would cast his rod from the rocks repeating, 'Fortune is by the grace of God.' He would wait for hours to catch one or two fish before the day ended but he would not complain, only constantly repeat, 'God is good and will ultimately make it better.' "[1]

In 1914, those small white boats were suddenly overshadowed by steel hulks lurking on the horizon of the Mediterranean. The first battleships steamed into the eastern Mediterranean, interrupting the rhythm of daily life and bringing with them the war that would sap the local economy and contribute to four years of devastation. When her memoir begins in 1917, eight-year-old Wadad is building castles on the warm sands of the shore, but no longer would she be unbothered by the broader world.

Through it all, Mustafa the fisherman resolutely carried on, committed to carrying out his daily task. "I still remember how he used to stand on that beautiful coast while the warships were cruising and spelling danger, but [Mustafa] would always stand on his scarlet rock full of determination, repeating: 'only what is meant to happen will happen and God will provide to his faithful servants.'"[2]

Such small acts of personal resistance were no match for the military shockwaves that shook the Middle East during World War I. For four years, the tremors of the Great War rocked the region. So vast was the resulting devastation that the social architecture of the region is still in the process of being rebuilt. Published on the centennial of the war, this book delves beneath the steel skyscrapers, eye-catching monuments, and political changes of today's Middle East to excavate the foundational experience of the modern Middle East: the Great War of 1914–1918. It does so by telling the story of men like Mustafa the fisherman, women like Wadad Cortas, and the millions of others who lived through the trauma of World War I. This book stands, in many ways, as a tribute to the everyday heroes who faced adversity as best they could. To them, and in this book, World War I was not only a global event, but also a personal story that varied across the broad Middle Eastern landscape.

Geographically, this book encompasses the broader Middle East, but specifically focuses on the eastern Mediterranean, or what was then known as Greater Syria. It will also touch on happenings beyond this area that nonetheless affected it; we accompany the soldiers of India as they stream into the unknown terrain of Mesopotamia, the men of Australia and New Zealand as they assault the Gallipoli peninsula, and the officers of Great Britain as they charge across the Sinai Desert into Palestine. These foreign soldiers were themselves often changed by war; their perspectives offer insights into the challenge of adjusting to a new world while coping with the trauma of combat.

Within the region, the presence of these foreigners in such unprecedented numbers affected local identities and reshaped regional politics for decades after the war. However secluded in their small villages or removed from the battlefield, local populations interacted with a larger and less familiar mix of people than ever before. The war brought people together from all over the world. On occasion, this led to the growth of prejudice, with some developing stereotypes about the "other" and, in general, a deeper anchoring in traditional ways. But there was also a concurrent openness to the new, the modern, and even the avant-garde. For these reasons, and due to the political settlement that followed, World War I stands as the defining moment that shaped the direction of the Middle East for the next hundred years.

This book chronicles the course of Greater Syrians in the Middle East during four years of conflict. But its primary purpose is to elucidate the experiences of the civilians and soldiers who lived the war in all its variety and diversity. It documents how they adapted to and endured the challenges war poses, particularly as they lived the Great War in the form of many small wars. The people of the Middle East did not suffer passively through the war. Although circumstances beyond their control made them victims in a variety of ways, they persistently fought back with every means at their disposal. Most often this meant small efforts to make life as routine and as normal as possible, but it also included emigration to distant lands or draft evasion when confronted with military conscription. Overwhelmingly, however, it meant seizing the best deals available in everyday life. From the money exchanges to the long lines at the bakeries (which often kept people queued up for hours), to the rummaging through street garbage for a morsel of food, people fought to make the best of their desperate lot.

While those in more modest social circles avoided drawing the attention of officials, relying for survival on their own wit, resourcefulness, and networks of family and friends, others played the system and sought out ways to profit from the war. For social elites, currying favor with public officials and collaborating with those in power could mean access to exclusive markets that eased the burdens of war. By hosting governors in their homes, some well-connected people gained access to luxury items and an escape from military conscription. Many actively profited from the war. For these economic entrepreneurs, cast by some as wartime opportunists, their ventures constituted a means of striving in the midst of hardship.

To accomplish their goals, profiteers were prepared to engage in a variety of endeavors. They tried new, overlooked lines of work, seized openings to turn small profits into larger successes, worked both for and against their governments for monetary gain, and alternately solicited assistance from others or stepped on other people's rights, as needed.

To survive during the war, individuals had to find any escape hatch available for themselves and their loved ones. This book highlights the resilience and initiative of military deserters and civilian émigrés, loyal Arab units and wartime entrepreneurs, and their varied reactions to crisis. But no matter which rung one occupied on the social ladder, the right mix of ingenuity and practicality often meant the difference between success and failure, life and death.

The dichotomy of rich and poor, exacerbated by the exigencies of war, reinforced class consciousness and privilege, but the conflict also highlighted other social identities. As members of families, clans, villages, city quarters, regions, sects, and ethnicities, individuals prioritized their identities in different ways depending on the context, which invariably transcended any notion of traditional primordialism. Out of the crucible of multiple identities emerged a sense of national consciousness.

How nationalist people became and precisely when they moved from the immediate to the larger forms of political identities are matters of debate. Several reputable historians have argued that before World War I, Arabs were largely content with belonging to a multireligious, multiethnic, and multilingual Ottoman Empire. Others have identified an incipient, even assertive, Arab nationalism in some prewar political agendas of federalism and in the programs of a few secret societies among writers or other politically conscious groups. These individuals and collectivities were already cognizant and supportive of some forms of distinctive national and supralocal identities. In reality and on balance, a variety of conflicting views and political beliefs ebbed and flowed in the coffee shops and other public meeting places of Beirut, Damascus, and Aleppo.

There is no reason to reduce the complexity of these competing political positions and options, or to assume that people had to choose between clear-cut denials or acceptances of integration or separatism. All sorts of political sentiments coexisted among different groups and sometimes within the same groups. On occasion, the upper social strata would claim an Ottoman identity to preserve their privileges; at other times, they would distance themselves from Istanbul in favor of European protection. Such protean politics existed alongside loyalists who tacitly accepted the centuries-old Ottoman political framework, as well as others who became uncomfortable with some of the decisions made by Ottoman leaders during the war and who increasingly thought in terms of a separate political identity. Such thinking was particularly common among minorities susceptible to the political and economic enticements of Europeans at war with the Ottoman government.

In Egypt, political sentiment was as varied as it was elsewhere, but also adapted to its unique circumstances. Since 1882, Egypt had been under the British, who ruled the Nile Delta in the name of the Ottoman Empire until the outbreak of World War I. British control over Egypt was so complete that Britain declared Egypt a protectorate in December 1914. For most Egyptians, therefore, the Ottomans were a distant, almost abstract power. It was the British who elicited varying degrees of loyalty and enmity. On the other hand, many of the Syrians in Egypt sympathized not with the Ottoman Empire and its allies but with the Entente powers, and did so freely from British-controlled Egypt.

In addition to nationalism, and often in a complex relationship with it, religious identity also took on a new salience in the aftermath of World War I. For decades before the war, the weakness of the Ottoman Empire and the growth of European influence in the Middle East accelerated the pace of change in daily life. European players took a more active role in local rivalries and conflicts, and the Great War aggravated the resulting tensions. In the aftermath of the war, the victorious European powers assumed a more direct colonial role, took sides in local conflicts more frequently and openly than they had done previously, and increased their support of minorities. During the Mandate period, the French institutionalized confessional politics in the *Grand Liban,* while European powers reinforced preferential arrangements with religious minorities and local proxies willing and able to assist in ruling over the broader population. This was particularly true in the case of Christians in Lebanon and Jews in Palestine. Nothing would be the same after the Great War for the peoples of the region; it is the war that everyone in the region remembers, far more than World War II. But even if the European powers had not charted such an interventionist course, a reversion to the political state before the war would have been impossible; the Great War not only opened partially isolated geographies but also closed off the option of a multinational empire.

The Great War earned its name in large part due to the immense suffering it wrought. As a result, the legacy of suffering and the memory of hardship play leading parts in the story that follows, partly because they set the stage for the political developments that ensued in the Mandate period. The considerable misery caused by World War I shaped people's views of governments for decades to come. People saw at close quarters what manipulative governments were capable of in order to achieve their ends. In the midst of hunger, disease, injury, and death, the region suffered under rulers who imposed their will and maintained their power.

But the war era also featured great military and political actors. Yusuf al-Azma, Minister of Defense in King Faysal ibn Husayn's Arab Kingdom, who died heroically at Maysalun in 1920 fighting the French, is still remembered each year in Syria and his statue stands at the entrance to the Salihiyye quarter in Damascus. Faysal ibn Husayn himself, whom some later considered to have bowed too quickly to colonial pressure, advocated tolerance as tensions flared. This son of the sharif of Mecca traveled to Aleppo in June 1919 to proclaim, famously, that Arabs preceded Moses, Muhammad, Jesus, and Abraham, and that only death could separate Arabs, meaning that each is buried according to his or her own creed.[3] In Egypt, Sa'd Zaghlul altered the course of Egyptian politics when he established the Wafd Party in response to the British barring him from leading a delegation to the Paris Peace Conference at Versailles. In Turkey, Mustafa Kemal irrevocably altered the course of twentieth-century Middle Eastern history through his establishment of the state of Turkey in 1923. This very small sample of important actors on the stage of World War I could be supplemented by many others, but that is not the aim of this book. For this project, the connection between leaders and the masses is only relevant insofar as many in the region grew disillusioned after the Great War, when postwar political promises went mostly unfulfilled both at home and on the international scene.[4]

As a result, for some cynicism became a defining feature of twentieth-century politics, leading citizens either to withdraw to "cultivate their gardens" or to join in the opportunities exemplified and afforded by those in power. Some notable exceptions notwithstanding, there were few truly great political leaders to admire and military heroes to emulate in the successor states of the Ottoman Syrian and Iraqi provinces. Generally, power was something to be seized by using populist slogans and appeals.

Yet if a lofty political vision became an exception rather than the rule, the experiences of World War I had something to do with this eventuality. During the four years between 1914 and 1918, some starved while others feasted, some fought while others fled, and some died while others survived. As disillusionment with the state spread, many turned to money and connections to protect their interests. This initiation into twentieth-century politics was a precursor for Egyptians, Syrians, and Iraqis who were to be subjected to the harsh politics of the future.

In time, what happened to trust in politics is a bit like what happens in poorly functioning municipalities. In many such cities, inhabitants keep their homes impeccably clean while they ignore the increasingly filthy streets. In short, people focus on that which they can control, and ignore that which they cannot. On a larger scale, a similar phenomenon occurred in Middle Eastern politics after the war. Some tended to their immediate families but surrendered active citizenship and public service, because the latter constituted mostly futile pursuits. In a region of politicized armies and militarized parties, there were citizens who tacitly allowed authoritarian government whether foreign or local to last, and they did so with little struggle, turning their energies inward toward that which they could control. There were many others who tried to resist, participated in political protests and coups, and believed in shared and democratic governance. However, once they attained power, they typically did not open up the political process, even if they accomplished a measure of success in modernizing their societies from above.

This book focuses on the social history of Greater Syria because it helps us understand the attitudes toward politics in the decades to follow and because the story of the Great War features not only heroes who figure in textbooks but also everyday heroes who faced tragedy and survived as best they could. This matters because it restores faith not in leaders but in civil society during times of great duress. Many variations of this theme played out in the Middle East after the war, with civil, regional, and international conflicts becoming widespread in the eastern Mediterranean and beyond. The principal heroes of these conflicts, as in World War I, are the regular folks who face the worst and make the best of it. Their courage is not sufficiently recorded or acknowledged. This book aims to restore them to their rightful place in history.

CHAPTER ONE

A Changing Middle East

AS THE SUN rose on the imperial capital city of Vienna on Saturday, May 20, 1882, a fresh day beckoned the laborers, merchants, and officials slumbering in their beds on the right bank of the majestic Danube. Unbeknownst to them—and secret even to the diplomatic milieu of late nineteenth-century Europe—the Austro-Hungarian foreign minister and the German and Italian representatives to Vienna were busy finalizing an agreement that would reshape the European security architecture. For as the sun set that day on that epicenter of European intrigue, espionage, and diplomacy, the three diplomats committed their governments to a newly created Triple Alliance. The savvy first chancellor of the German Reich, Otto von Bismarck, exulted at the agreement, "No one will dare to measure himself with the Teuton fury which is manifested in case of an attack."[1]

Even so, the signing of the Triple Alliance may have distracted Berlin, Vienna, and Rome from a perhaps even more important geopolitical event occurring that very day 2,200 kilometers to the south. For on May 20, 1882, British and French warships arrived off the coast of Alexandria in the warm waters of the eastern Mediterranean, ostensibly to protect the Egyptian khedive, Tawfiq Pasha, from the revolt of Colonel Ahmad Urabi, in rebellion in part over pay and other disparities between Europeans and Egyptians.[2] Seven weeks later, after rioters in Alexandria killed dozens of Europeans, the fleet moved into action, unleashing a massive reprisal on the city. Amid the destruction, Her Majesty Queen Victoria's forces rushed ashore, and with their superior technology, destroyed Urabi's fledgling forces at the battle of Tall al-Kabir, restored the khedive, and garrisoned the country. Thus the great crown jewel of the Arab world, Egypt and the Suez, was added to Queen Victoria's already studded imperial diadem, an arrangement formalized in December 1914 after the outbreak of World War I.

That historic spring day combined great-power politics and political colonialism across multiple continents, two dynamics that fed decades of tensions from which the Arab world is still reeling. But occasionally overlooked is that the British action that day both served and depended upon technological superiority made possible by economic dominance. Although the Middle East of 1882 was part and parcel of a rapidly accelerating and globalizing world, European economic dominance and political expansion collided regularly with Middle Eastern development to yield an imbalanced relationship in favor of the great European powers.

European political colonialism nipped hard at the heels of the rapid economic changes that characterized the nineteenth-century Middle East. While to the rioters in Alexandria the world was still closer to what it had been for centuries than to what it would become, the pace of change in their lifetimes was unlike any other period preceding it. The Industrial Revolution drove that change, as Middle Easterners experienced the West in a decidedly new capacity.

Rulers and ruled, sultans and subjects, empire and province, millets and guilds, these were still the familiar dichotomies that defined life in the late nineteenth century, as they had for centuries before it. It was a world in which family, clan, village, or city quarter dominated one's worldview rather than larger social or political affiliations, and where a limited and predictable circle of relatives, friends, business partners, and acquaintances took precedence over distant events in distant lands.[3] And yet the integration of the Middle East into the world economy, and the social, cultural, and political disruption it caused, loosened expectations that had been moored to centuries of tradition. Again, at the heart of that process stood the Industrial Revolution.

The European industrial breakthrough powered the Middle East toward modernity as nothing else could have done so comprehensively. The arrival of steam navigation on the eastern Mediterranean coast, the consequent re-orientation of markets so that trade with different parts of Asia and Africa became less central than trade with Europe, the integration of the region into a Western-dominated economy in the course of the century, the attraction of rural and other populations to the new centers of exchange and productivity, the growth of a merchant community eager and able to participate in the new opportunities at hand, all led to a reshuffling of business and traditional life. The Western-dominated economic system overwhelmed many processes of traditional exchange. It lessened the isolation of different parts of the region, but it also altered the balance between areas drawn into the new economy and others where crops did not matter to the export trade or where artisanal handicrafts became redundant in the face of new manufactured imports from Europe.

These changes in economic patterns invariably reshaped the constellation of economic power in the Arab provinces. Some previously remote regions shed their isolation and were assimilated into the burgeoning global economy, while others writhed and chafed under the economic revolution. By the twentieth century, the Middle East was exporting a variety of raw materials, led by cotton, while importing finished manufactured goods, especially cotton textiles. The diversity in exports reflected the rich Ottoman mosaic—raw silk constituted almost one quarter of Greater Syria's exports, while cotton blanketed the ports of Egypt and Turkestan.[4] Sugar, coffee, tea, and grain complemented those dominant twin commodities of Middle Eastern trade bound for Liverpool, Marseilles, Trieste, and the other great ports of Europe.

Even more directly, Middle Eastern rulers allowed European public and private investors into vast cross-sections of the economy. After decades of fiscal challenges, they surrendered an elaborate system of exclusive economic concessions for road, telegraph, port, and railway development to Europe. Although intended to revitalize a woeful economic base and reinvigorate the struggling Ottoman economy, these monopolistic arrangements invited European "financiers, merchants, physicians, skilled workers, and the adventurers of all sorts who joined a gold rush."[5]

Europeans held controlling stakes in enterprises ranging from public utilities (gas, electricity, and water) to public transport (riverboats and streetcars), mining, and manufacturing. With the exception of Egypt, the Sudan, and an extension into the Arabian desert, Europeans owned and operated every major railway connecting the interior to the coast. But European dominance did not end at the coastal railhead; port and shipping facilities were similarly controlled by European interests, as were the banking sectors financing the trading cycle. And in the early twentieth century, in perhaps their most enduring legacy, Europeans began drilling for petroleum in Iran while Egyptian wells had entered into production by the outbreak of World War I. Indeed, from acquisition to sale, the complete life cycle of virtually every major economic activity in the broader Middle East was dominated and financed by Europe.[6]

Of course, as four years of war would make clear, Europe was not a monolithic political entity. The great powers managing the delicate post-Napoleonic balance in Europe acted with foresight in establishing spheres of influence in Asia and Africa. In varying degrees, the Germans, French, and British struggled for power in the Ottoman capital at Istanbul;[7] the Belgians, French, and British controlled Egypt; the Russians and British eyed Iran; and the French pressured the Levant. Most directly, the French occupied Algeria in 1830, established a Tunisian protectorate in 1881, and a Moroccan one in 1912. A joint British, French, Italian, and Russian condominium established control over Crete in 1898, followed by an Italian invasion of Libya in 1911 that was completed the following year. By the eve of World War I, the Mediterranean Sea had been reduced to a European lake.

This European political and economic penetration jolted territories controlled by essentially the same Ottoman dynasty for centuries. For four hundred years, from the early sixteenth to the early twentieth centuries, much of the Arab world was ruled from Istanbul as part of the Ottoman Empire. Spanning thirty-six sultans, the empire had humble origins, stemming from a Turkish principality that had been converted to Sunni Islam. These early Ottomans swept across the Eurasian steppes and into the Anatolian heartland, sensing weakness in the aging Byzantine Empire. Over the centuries, this incipient Ottoman Empire transformed into a full-fledged intercontinental force, conquering territories from southeastern Europe to southwestern Asia. In the process, its capital moved from Bursa in northwestern Anatolia in 1326 to Edirne in eastern Thrace in 1366 to Constantinople in 1453. The sacking of Constantinople, modern-day Istanbul, on Tuesday, May 29, 1453, completed the collapse of the Byzantine Empire, and with it, the last vestige of the Roman Empire. At its peak in the second half of the sixteenth century, the Ottoman Empire extended from Algeria to Azerbaijan and from central Europe to central Africa. Twice, in 1529 and in 1683, Ottoman armies besieged Vienna.

Rebuffed at Vienna after centuries of expansion but still straddling three continents, the Ottoman Empire turned to internal consolidation in the face of regional rebellions. Even so, as late as the nineteenth century the Ottoman Empire still weighed heavily on the European balance of power through its Balkan presence. To maintain the empire's heavyweight status alongside a rapidly modernizing Europe, the Ottomans decided to implement a massive reorganization, known as the Tanzimat reforms. Although launched earlier by reforming Sultans, this Western-style modernization was officially proclaimed in November 1839; it sought to counter centrifugal forces, including European meddling, with centripetal reforms. In practice, this meant permanent Ottoman vigilance in Ottoman Europe, where secessionist sentiment had already seized Serbia and the Peloponnese (via the 1821–1832 Greek War of Independence), and in the Ottoman Middle East, which generally remained more tolerant of Istanbul's rule.

Accompanying this political centralization were economic investments in public security and infrastructure, most visibly the five-year-long construction of a railway connecting Damascus and Medina, completed in 1908. Long-distance transport before the nineteenth century often required laborious treks by animal carriage across kilometers of desert. Traders may have enjoyed the luxury of the navigable Nile, Euphrates, and Tigris in Egypt and Mesopotamia, and in Greater Syria merchants could hug the Mediterranean coastline, but most interior geographies dependent on the caravan trade could not be connected to the Mediterranean before the nineteenth century's sudden advancements in transportation infrastructure.

The steamboat charged into Middle Eastern ports in the 1830s, changing the pace, pattern, and potential of international trade, and in the second half of the century railways created new links between distant cities—one could now travel from Alexandria to Cairo via Suez, from Konya to Basra via Baghdad, from Scutari to Ankara across the Bosporus, from Izmir to the Anatolian hinterland, and from Damascus to the Hijaz. Although the motorcar remained relatively rare—roadways were generally neglected—a major road facilitating expansion in trade by linking the Syrian rural interior to the Mediterranean trading coast was completed in 1863.[8]

As European demand increased, camel caravans crisscrossed the Syrian and Saharan deserts, railways rolled through rural regions, and ships steamed the Suez in larger numbers and with greater frequency. This voluminous growth in trade directly affected peasants. For while merchants and financiers directed trade from metropolitan hubs, that commerce directly determined the scope and scale of cultivation in the interior. Between 1860 and 1914, the allure of profit steadily encroached on nomadism. In Egypt, the insatiable European demand for raw cotton led businessmen to double the amount of land apportioned to cotton cultivation. In Syria and Mesopotamia, similar market forces incentivized the mass production of grain, olives, oil, and sesame seeds; in Mount Lebanon, the commodity of choice was raw silk.

These dual pillars of Ottoman modernization and European globalization quickly spilled from the economic and political to the social and cultural spheres. In particular, they reshaped the social composition of the countryside and cities. Advances in public health, including in battling contagious diseases, resulted in rapid population expansion throughout the century, most notably in the cities.[9] Istanbul and Cairo, the glittering capital of the Empire and the largest Arab city, respectively, benefited disproportionally from these improvements.

The port cities prospered most in this era of seaborne trade, rail navigation, and improving public health. At the top was Alexandria, dominating the Egyptian cotton trade and long the second largest city in the Arab world. A confident Beirut also grew steadily, until it dominated the Syrian coast as its main port. Izmir, the principal pivot of the Aegean region and a major Mediterranean outlet, expanded its port in the last quarter of the nineteenth century; not long thereafter, in 1901, Istanbul and Salonika undertook similar port renovations and expansions. From Casablanca to Algiers and Tunis, booming North African ports rapidly expanded their commercial activities. Basra, situated along the Shatt al Arab waterway in Mesopotamia, linked the Gulf to the Arabian Sea and the Indian Ocean. Ships rounding the Arabian peninsula into the Red Sea and through the Suez Canal, past the teeming ports of Aden, Jedda, Suez, and Port Said, were gliding through one seamless maritime trading corridor from the Arabian to the Mediterranean Seas.

These ports became the dominant centers of finance and trade, import and export, and politics and authority in the Ottoman Empire. Throughout the Middle East, infrastructure upgrades were prioritized to accommodate the mercantilist export of raw materials and the importation of finished products. The dredging and expansion of ports facilitated the docking of ever larger vessels, while the somewhat erratic expansion of road networks connected the coast to the interior. Alongside these transportation networks, telegraph and postal services linked communications between subregions and regions as never before.[10] As cities strained under the weight of new populations, municipalities were established to administer affairs, leading to the planning and construction of sewage systems in Alexandria and Cairo in the first decade of the new century.[11]

The magnetic allure of opportunity easily outshone the dangers of growing crime, leading to expanding urbanization. Since land transport was relatively undeveloped, the cities of the interior struggled to keep pace with their coastal cousins. By the twentieth century, the port cities of the eastern and southern Mediterranean served as the beating heart of Middle Eastern life, sustained by transfusions of people and materials through newly established transportation arteries. Alexandria, in particular, exemplified the myriad political, cultural, economic, and social dimensions of modern trade.[12]

This ancient city, situated in the western Nile Delta on the Mediterranean coast, equaled the greatness of its conquering founder. As the central hub of nineteenth-century southern Mediterranean trade with Europe, it burst with entrepreneurs, activity, and importance. Second only to Cairo in the Arab world, Alexandria was essential to the all-important cotton trade.

In the 1840s, Alexandria was quintessentially Egyptian. Local Christians and Jews, comprising fully one quarter of the population, mingled with local Muslims in the beehive of shops that inhabited the ancient bazaar. By the second half of the nineteenth century, however, waves of economic migrants dreaming of fame and fortune painted the city in the rich hues of diversity. Armenians were among the migrants to Egypt in the course of the nineteenth century, starting with traders and money changers from Izmir, Istanbul, and Aleppo, and followed by peasants and others. The migrant "Greeks"—an all-encompassing label applied not only to the Greek subjects of the Ottoman Empire but also to other non-Greeks who may have been independent of it—reveled in the cities' cafés, casinos, and coastlines. At night these foreigners retired to their homogeneous city quarters, whether North African, Jewish, Italian, or Greek.[13] By the time its stock exchange was opened in 1883, Alexandria resembled more a European than an Egyptian or Ottoman city.

By 1907 Alexandria's population was estimated at over 400,000, with large communities of Greeks, Italians, English, and French, in descending order of size; Greek Orthodox and Jews freely attended their religious services and performed their rituals. Even Coptic Christians, descendants of the dominant pre-Islamic Egyptian Christians but by then reduced to only 2 percent of the population, thrived in Alexandria's urbane cosmopolitanism. This transformation and rapid growth—spanning prostitutes and profiteers—resembled a "Klondike on the Nile."[14]

Six hundred kilometers to Alexandria's northeast sits Beirut, the dominant port city of the nineteenth-century eastern Mediterranean coast. Beirut's commercial enterprises and political activities secured it a position second only to Alexandria. Like Alexandria, Beirut was also dependent on a single commodity—raw silk in its case, not cotton. Beginning in the 1820s it performed an added function in housing the European consulates-general on the Syrian coast. In 1888 Istanbul added to Beirut's prestige by appointing it the administrative capital of a newly created Ottoman province overseeing sections of the Palestinian coast. Over the next quarter century, as the city experienced pronounced urban growth, this fledgling administrative apparatus grew into a major municipal authority charged with large-scale development.[15]

Nine hundred kilometers northwest of Beirut, tucked away in the Gulf of Izmir in the Aegean Sea, lies the port of Izmir, once the ancient city of Smyrna. Restored in classical antiquity, largely by Alexander of Macedonia, Smyrna could point to a proud history even before it entered the Hellenistic and Roman periods. Today, anthropologists and archeologists flock to Izmir to unlock its historical treasures, but in the 1830s the city was focused on an intense period of economic modernization. As the western Anatolian hinge in the Ottoman trading network, Izmir bridged Asiatic Anatolia with the European Balkans, allowing it to join Alexandria and Beirut as a major trading post in the empire. One of the most cosmopolitan Anatolian cities, Izmir hosted diverse ethnic and religious groups that thrived alongside foreign diplomats, traders, and sailors. Its municipal council, established in 1868, embodied that diversity, at one point listing among its membership six Muslims, five Greeks, three Armenians, one Jew, and nine foreigners.[16]

In time Izmir's vivid diversity created a unique anthropology, interweaving Greek and Turkish peasants, non-Muslim and Muslim merchants, and marauding bands of Greek and Muslim bandits who alternately targeted and sponsored wealthy notables. When apprehended, these criminals often appealed to Mediterranean power brokers to ease the grip of justice, no matter their sectarian affiliation. Indeed, as the employment of Muslims in the Public Debt Administration and in foreign banks suggests, religion and ethnicity were not politically, economically, or even socially decisive.[17] All three cities—Alexandria, Beirut, and Izmir—were open and welcoming ports thriving during a century of change.

In these great cities of the Ottoman Empire, an upper echelon of society steadily separated from the masses. Enjoying preferential status and profiting from the new economy, merchant traders, government administrators, and landed notables flourished in close association with one another.[18] By the second decade of the twentieth century, these upper classes could be clearly distinguished from the majority struggling to cope with change, at least in part because the privileged elite increasingly adopted Western ways.[19]

Continuing a process begun in Istanbul in the first decades of the nineteenth century, non-Muslims and elite Muslims often embraced cultural changes. These subjects of the sultan dressed in the most fashionable Parisian styles and imitated European representatives in their choice of home decorations. Traditional flat roofs gave way to pitched red tiling, complementing the fashionable stone decorations and wrought-iron facades below.[20] These nouveaux riches promenaded through the streets or traveled by horse-drawn carriage to newly opened cinemas, the public theater (in Izmir), or the opera house (in Cairo). In several major cities, trams signaled the arrival of modernity and represented the height of fashion. In 1903, the first motorcar careened through the streets of Cairo; in 1908, an Englishman successfully drove from Aleppo to Baghdad; and in 1909, just as the Anglo-Persian Oil Company—the future British Petroleum—formed for operations in the Gulf, the first motorcar crossed from Alexandretta to Aleppo.[21]

Paradoxically, while urban centers increasingly absorbed rural migrants, the pace of social change also slowed at times to accommodate the traditional customs and sectarian identities that villagers carried with them. Tens of thousands—in some cases hundreds of thousands—of peasants moved into cities, reshaping those metropolitan centers as much as the cities transformed them. Individuals with rural backgrounds grappled with their newfound urban existence, until continued urban growth overwhelmed, subsumed, or co-opted many of their traditions.[22]

The unnerving pace of change led some to repudiate reform and instead retrench in a familiar circle of family and friends. Some businessmen reactivated traditional networks, trading on interpersonal trust rather than on perceived excess. Others, such as some esteemed notables of old money, were able to straddle traditional culture and modern economics. In this way, many respected families grew wealthy while preserving their domestic traditions. Buffeted by the winds of change, this balance was often difficult to sustain, but many did so successfully.

For many, the new world meant extraordinary opportunity, empowering some to petition consulates general and local authorities to air grievances, suggest reforms, or sideline rivals. This era of privilege spawned a new set of social actors some foreign observers labeled as "Levantine." These nouveaux riches were derided as profiteers whose ostentation underscored their spoiled and spendthrift ways.[23]

More positively, on the opposite end of the spectrum, attitudes toward the marginalized shifted somewhat for the better. The taboo of mental illness slowly lifted as missionaries reached out to the mentally challenged, until then consigned to an underworld of shame and neglect. In the 1890s a Swiss couple established an asylum in the village of Asfuriyya near Beirut, growing from a modest fourteen patients in 1900 to over one hundred within the decade. The mere existence of such an institution—and the willingness of families to commit their loved ones to it—lifted a veil of shame after centuries of neglect. Successive Ottoman governors subsidized treatment for patients unable to afford it, tacitly acknowledging the imperial system's role in providing medical care.[24]

On a much larger scale, the nineteenth century constituted a turning point in education. Although most of the population remained illiterate well into the twentieth century, literacy spread among the upwardly mobile classes during the nineteenth century. These educational advances, fueled by the proliferation of printing, publications, and pedagogy, can be traced in part to the presence of American missionaries, whose drive gave the initial impetus to change. Roberts College (renamed Boğaziçi University in 1971) was founded in Istanbul in 1863 as one of the first American colleges outside the United States, and in 1866 the Syrian Protestant College in Beirut (renamed the American University of Beirut in 1920) welcomed its first class of sixteen students under the direction of President Daniel Bliss. With the establishment of the American University of Cairo by the United Presbyterian Church of North America just after the war in 1919, eventually as many as 23,000 students from throughout the Middle East, but especially from the mountains of Lebanon, were enrolled in American missionary schools.[25]

European missionaries had been journeying to the Middle East for centuries, but with the backing of powerful European patrons, they intensified and deepened their reach in the nineteenth century, occasionally in association with local groups. In Egypt, Syria, and Mount Lebanon, Maronites established schools consistent with their traditional emphasis on education.[26] Under French protection, Catholic religious orders with a deep commitment to education founded schools in Mount Lebanon, culminating in the Jesuit Université Saint-Joseph in 1875, which was expanded to include a French Faculty of Medicine in 1883. As a result, Turkish and Arab notables adopted French as the lingua franca of their professional and private lives.[27] At the same time, and consistent with the heavy Islamic emphasis on charity, Muslims established charitable associations, including the Sunni al-Maqasid in Beirut in 1878, which educated poor children before broadening its mission to include a host of benevolent social services.[28]

The Ottomans complemented these private efforts with their own public initiatives. At the start of the nineteenth century, professional schools had already begun training civilian officials and military officers, along with medical doctors and engineers; but always keen on improving the quality of its armed forces and its civilian bureaucracy, and intent on expanding its educational system in an age of competitive imperialism, Istanbul prioritized the spread of secondary and higher education as "a major state enterprise" expanding beyond limited vocational training.[29]

During the course of the nineteenth century, a system of primary, secondary, and collegiate education was therefore created that included technical training and teacher instruction. Moreover, increased mobility allowed educated young men to leave their provinces and complete their education in the prestigious institutions of Istanbul, after which they were recruited into the imperial service. This Ottoman commitment to expanded public education never diminished, even during the trauma of war. As late as the war years, the military governor of Greater Syria sponsored schools in Jerusalem, Aleppo, and the Syrian interior.[30]

The increase in literacy both enabled and benefited from the rise of mass publication. In the eighteenth century, Turkish and Arabic books were rare, and printed materials were largely irrelevant,[31] but with the spread of literacy in administrative centers such as Beirut and Cairo, the reading public yearned for printed materials. In Beirut alone, sixty newspapers were founded between 1908 and 1914, while thirty-five additional newspapers were founded in Syria in the twelve months after the 1908 revolution.[32] In Cairo, Beirut, and Istanbul, publishing houses strained to print enough newspapers, serialized novels, and textbooks. The government sponsored the first newspapers in Istanbul, Cairo, and Tunis, but it was not long before private newspapers under the management of Lebanese Christians and Cairo-based journalists published independent views as well. With people long starved of written information, even an encyclopedia was compiled and published for Arab consumption. Indeed, in the late nineteenth century, the public debated a cornucopia of topics, ranging from politics to culture to science.[33]

Invariably, this spread in print publications enabled political dissent. In cultural and literary productions, which subtly explored questions of political consciousness, writers considered the tensions between moral justice and power and between individuals and the state. Depending on the decade, nineteenth-century intellectuals tackled issues ranging from the compatibility of Islam with modernity to the role of Europe within the empire. Inevitably, issues pertaining to the multiethnic, multinational, and multireligious character of the Ottoman Empire spilled from print into public discussion, spawning questions of federalism, autonomy, and devolution. These discussions included elections, the formation of parliament, and the writing of a constitution as potential checks on Ottoman power and European colonialism. But in the pre–World War I era, these debates were conducted timidly and within the construct of the established order.

From behind the Sublime Porte, which marked the governing complex of Istanbul, officials carefully monitored the Arab transition from eighteenth-century primordialism to twentieth-century nationalism. By the second half of the nineteenth century, the Porte had seen—and read—enough; it began reeling in Arab (and Turkish) reformers through an extensive program of political centralization. After 1876, this trend accelerated under the reign of Sultan Abdulhamid II.

At the time of his coronation, Abdulhamid eyed the maelstrom of change enveloping his empire with extreme circumspection. For over thirty years he had watched his predecessors champion Western-style reforms. And yet Ottoman decline and humiliation had continued apace. Worse, his two

immediate predecessors had both been deposed. From Abdulhamid's perspective, the Tanzimat only encouraged European political, cultural, and
territorial encroachments at the expense of the Porte. Moreover, by the early
1870s the Ottoman economy was in atrophy and its political functions in
disrepair. Abdulhamid therefore moved to reassert central control and snuff
out political liberalism. In 1878 the sultan suspended the newly elected
General Assembly, which had convened only once, and cast aside the Constitution of 1876, which would remain inoperative for thirty years. While
Abdulhamid continued to pilot the Ottoman Empire toward economic modernity, he veered toward political repression.

In his Arab territories, the sultan co-opted notables into his palace administration and imperial bureaucracy. His carrot-and-stick policy kept Arabs off
balance and deterred them from coalescing into a unified opposition.[34] Even
in Greater Syria, where internal instability and regional tensions occasionally
simmered under the surface, popularly based political movements could not
gain momentum.[35] Most of all, however, Abdulhamid profited from the
latent loyalty of the silent majority to his dynasty. For Arabs he was the ruler
in a long lineage of sultans, and therefore was generally accepted as sultan of
the Ottoman Empire, caliph of Islam, and "custodian of the two holy mosques
[of Mecca and Medina]" (*khadim al-haramayn*). Moreover, the Ottoman territories witnessed continued expansion and improvement in professional and
other schools, public services, building operations on public lands and along
waterways, communications, roads, railroads, telegraphs, postal services, port
works, and in the management of government personnel, public administrators, and jurists.[36]

While interpretations of the Tanzimat as an era of reform and the reign
of Abdulhamid as a period of despotism have generally been discredited,
the economic modernization that occurred in the last quarter of the nineteenth century was nonetheless accompanied by deepening autocracy.[37]
Abdulhamid embraced censorship of the media, suspicion of some minority groups, and crackdowns on political liberals. As with other rulers, he
utilized an extensive network of secret police and spies.

Recognizing its importance to his legitimacy, Abdulhamid also reinvigorated his status as caliph of Islam. In doing so, he subtly reminded Europe
not only of the Islamic solidarity that strengthened his empire but also of
Islam's universal threat to European colonial legitimacy from North Africa
to South Asia. To French and British colonialists with large Muslim popu-

lations under their rule, the prospect of pan-Islamic rebellion under the banner of the caliph was a perennial concern.

Despite these political maneuvers on the regional and international levels, Abdulhamid could not reverse the steady slide of the Ottoman great power.[38] In 1908, a group of junior army officers and bureaucrats joined forces, and with the support of key army groups demanded the reinstitution of the constitution and the reopening of the parliament. As these winds of political challenge intensified, Abdulhamid's thirty-year balancing act finally came to an end. A group styling themselves the Young Turks seized control of the government, leading to the end of Abdulhamid's reign after a last gasp in 1909. Four years later, as the empire suffered defeats in the two Balkan wars that lasted from October 1912 until July 1913, a Young Turk faction known as the Committee of Union and Progress (CUP) upturned Istanbul yet again by taking power in a coup. The CUP was mostly "conservative in outlook, with little or no interest in promoting social change," but it effectively exploited public frustration with military defeats and perceived Ottoman weakness to take the helm.[39] It was the CUP that would ultimately shepherd the empire through World War I.

Upon taking power the Young Turks did revise the constitution to strengthen parliament at the expense of the Sultan and the palace bureaucracy, but they essentially practiced "the old formula of Ottomanism, centralization, a strong, modern army and administration and a modernized, secularized educational and legal system."[40] Ottomanism was adjusted and updated to reflect the military defeats in the Balkans, which ejected the empire from all but a thin European hinterland stretching from Edirne to Istanbul.[41] With its empire suddenly heavily Arab, Istanbul championed pan-Islamism and a form of nationalism alongside this reworked Ottomanism. As the historian Feroz Ahmad contends, after the two Balkan defeats in 1912 and 1913, the ideological "change was one of emphasis. . . . The three ingredients—Ottomanism, Islam, and nationalism, all undefined—continued to constitute the recipe for the ideological cake; only the proportions had changed."[42]

In the Arab provinces, public opinion of the Young Turks ranged from a marked skepticism to a palpable antagonism and all points in between. But despite this public Arab weariness, the Young Turks should not be understood as synonymous with Turkish nationalism, a popular belief that the historians of the Young Turks reject. In fact, the Young Turk umbrella sheltered many non-Turks, non-Muslims, and Arabs. Indeed, the leadership remained steadfastly committed to an ideologically multinational empire.

In fact, Arabs sent their sons to schools in Istanbul, and shared similar outlooks with their Turkish counterparts in a world where privilege and connections put them on top of the social order. Some prospered as leading notables and interacted regularly and closely with their local government representatives. Others became representatives of Arab cities and districts, and aired Arab views in favor of federalism and local representation in parliament. Sometimes, locals deployed such arguments in order to consolidate their advantageous position. Syria's Sunnis in earlier periods

> had stood outside government and measured their status in competition for religious offices. The progress of centralization had made government employment much more important than in the past, both for income and the possibilities of patronage. . . . The leading Damascus families were now those who were most successful in the pursuit of government jobs. The competition for jobs led to disputes among themselves and between them and the Ottoman authorities. In previous times these disputes might have been expressed in religious terms or even in the vocabulary of Arab politics. Exposure to European ideas had presented the Damascus notables with a new range of ideas, which, in a modernizing world, could serve as a more suitable vehicle of their ambitions.[43]

The arduous prospect of building a separate ethnic geography was not the preference of most Arabs, even after Istanbul increased its focus on its Arab provinces and introduced Arabic into official administration.[44] Indeed, for the great majority of Arab notables, the advantages of elitism complemented a form of Islamic Ottomanism, limiting the growth and attraction of nascent nationalism.

And yet, by the beginning of the twentieth century politically aware Arabs agitated with increasing ardor for autonomy, an issue still unresolved at the outbreak of the "Great War," as it became known. In the increasingly interconnected Arab world, concepts pertaining to federalism, self-determination, and representation circulated further and quicker than ever before. Periodically, campaigns and elections stoked these simmering embers of self-rule, especially when clumsy policies surfaced. In Beirut in 1912, the Ottoman authorities enlisted local muscle and thuggish bosses to steal an election.

While such heavy-handed tactics, supported by campaign propaganda, were useful arrows in the government's quiver, they also may have punctured the central authority's legitimacy, thus reviving the very truculence the Ottomans were working to avoid in the first place.[45]

Although Europeans often grafted their own ideas of nationalism onto their observations of the region, incipient nationalism did make some headway in the Arab provinces. Before 1914, this took the form of Arab opposition to centralization rather than an articulated, aggressive nationalism, but it is clearly detectable in the Greater Syrian disenchantment with Young Turk policies.[46] Across the Syrian desert in Mesopotamia, Arab notables clamoring for local elections and autonomy projected the same form of incipient nationalism.[47] In 1912, for example, Arab notables in Iraq expressed unhappiness and dismay at government changes to local elections.[48]

Istanbul was aware of this criticism; in 1911 one high-ranking Ottoman official commented to the British ambassador that the government was "already being accused of being too Ottoman and too much inclined to neglect the interests of the other races of the Empire, especially the Arabs."[49] As a countervailing force, European threats against the Ottoman Empire, such as the Italian takeover of Libya, triggered Arab and other Muslims' popular sympathy and support for their rulers.[50] So the trend was not uniform, nor was it the equivalent of twentieth-century Arabism. Rather, it was the manifestation of Arabs feeling their way in a rapidly changing world that facilitated introspection and reassessment.

At times, that introspection did explode into public violence. In Greater Syria and on the Arabian peninsula, uprisings occurred in 1910 and 1911, respectively. But here, too, while ostensibly the manifestation of a new national awareness, rebellion was more the outgrowth of demands for power and autonomy. In the Syrian interior, Druze and Bedouin tribes briefly chose rebellion, but they quickly retreated in the face of an Ottoman crackdown, as they had in centuries past. On the Najd plateau of Arabia and in Yemen, tribal revolts continued, but these uprisings were more a function of long-standing defiance than a turn toward an Arab identity. When Ottoman forces did trek across the desert to crush these rebellions, they sometimes did so in collaboration with rival tribal leaders. Power and interests, it seems, prevailed.[51]

The First Balkan War from October 1912 to May 1913 only burdened the brittle politics of the region further. Rumors of the possibility of imperial collapse ricocheted through the winding bazaars and into the cafés. Residents shared the latest news, expressing their fear of tax increases and the draining of local coffers. Political societies in Istanbul, Beirut, and elsewhere debated what to do next. As Istanbul commenced peace negotiations at the end of 1912, Arab notables were authorized by Istanbul to form mixed-religious reform committees in Beirut and Damascus. However, in January 1913 the CUP military takeover signaled reversal and confrontation, as did the promulgation of a spring provincial law, opposed by Arab reformists in Beirut.[52] At the same time, the strains of military mobilization and requisitioning, especially in Aleppo, uncorked spiraling inflation on staple goods, including bread and meat. This led to mass demonstrations—which included women—in February 1913 that escalated into rioting in Damascus and Aleppo.[53] In response, the government closed down several newspapers in Beirut and suppressed the reform societies, causing yet more political agitation across the spectrum. Leading Sunnis withdrew from government in protest while notables penned articles in the remaining independent newspapers decrying the clampdown.[54] Public and secret societies arose, some with their own programs for the future of the empire.[55]

At the apogee of the crisis, the second war in the Balkans rocked the empire. Although it lasted only one month in the summer of 1913, Istanbul recognized that it could no longer afford unrest in its Arab rear and thus shifted perceptibly from confrontation to conciliation. The use of Arabic was expanded in official matters and the language was taught with greater frequency in schools.[56] Most of all Istanbul tacitly acknowledged that Arab grievances existed by dispatching a delegation to the first Arab Congress, convened in the great rooms of the Geographical Society in Saint-Germain, Paris, in June 1913.[57]

Strolling along the Seine that summer, Syrian delegates to the congress mingled with representatives from Cairo and elsewhere to vent their frustrations at Ottoman handling of nascent nationalists, non-Muslims, and liberals. But even while the congress highlighted a common yearning for greater freedom, the delegates differed in their outlook. Coastal Syrians who had more experience with Europe were on the whole more intent on a pluralistic decentralization than those who represented the remote interior. Similarly, delegates representing the sizeable urban Christian and Muslim populations of Beirut and Aleppo were more inclined to trust French and Western motives than were their rural counterparts, who still preferred the Sublime

Porte to Europe.[58] To summarize the proceedings, "in a general Ottoman reform there should be autonomy for the Arab provinces, with Arabic as an official language there and in the Ottoman Parliament, and local military service. There was, however, no wish to leave the Ottoman Empire and there were specific requests for more jobs for Arabs in Istanbul and more Ottoman government financial assistance for the mutasarrifate [governorate] of Lebanon."[59]

In Egypt, the political evolution toward nationalism took place in a different context than in Syria or Iraq. Although nominally still subjects of the Porte, Egyptians occupied a separate rung in the Ottoman Empire. At the height of Queen Victoria's imperial power, the British occupation actually accelerated Egyptian identity formation; Egyptian opposition leaders rallied their followers around the clear political objective of uniting in opposition to British colonialism and expelling a European colonial power. The British gradually allowed political parties and debate in the early twentieth century, but the Egyptian opposition remained steadfast in its demand for self-government and later for independence.

The general consensus among Arabs subject to Istanbul's rule was that the Young Turk era was a grim period. Yet a unified opposition to Istanbul did not exist and would not materialize before the Great War. Even for an empire that "was a general refuge for every sort of foreign dissenter," the relationship between the Porte and the periphery was accepted by Muslims and acquiesced to by Christians.[60]

In the years preceding the war, the Europeans also established their own relationships with local networks. Sectarian groups were selected and advantaged by European wedge policies, contributing to socioeconomic imbalance and a spiraling cycle of tensions. Up in Mount Lebanon and below on the Syrian coast, the British protected the Druze and also the Jews while the French protected the Maronites. Local leaders rushed to ingratiate themselves with key Westerners, but also hedged by maintaining close contacts with the local Ottoman representatives.[61] In weaving such political webs, European and Ottoman officials contributed to a rise in distrust, but also inadvertently prepared the local population for the complex politics surrounding national sovereignty during the post–World War I era.

The example of Beirut is telling. In that port city decades of immigration, education, and exposure to modernity had united people of various socioeconomic and religious backgrounds in their calls for reform and decentralization. But Beirut's citizens allowed outsiders to weaken their resolve and unity. The government set policies to position one group against the other, triggering dissent among them. By turning to Ottoman or European outsiders to intervene on their behalf, notables from different communities exacerbated these differences. These divisions foreshadowed a difficult postwar future.

Invariably the political, economic, and social penetration brought on by the nineteenth-century forerunner to modern globalization electrified a reservoir of antipathy toward new norms. In 1908 the ringleader of a reactionary crowd in Istanbul petitioned the sultan to shutter saloons, prohibit photography, and reverse Muslim women's right to walk out on their own. Other protesters agitated in the mosque and in the theater, while sporadic violent attacks occurred against Muslim women deemed improperly veiled in public.[62] But even then such outbursts of violence were relatively rare and confined to certain segments of the population.

The structural cracks in the social foundation of the nineteenth-century Middle East widened in the years leading up to the Great War.[63] In the cities, the optimism of modernization began to fracture, in part due to the expanding fault lines of inequality. For the most part, the opportunities of the early twentieth century were confined to the privileged stratum of society. For others in urban Syria and Iraq, life was still lived in the economic shadows without bright prospects in education or employment.

In Egypt at the turn of the century, the working class lived in poverty while a select group reveled in wealth.[64] In Cairo and Alexandria, urban explosion and high inflation spawned a housing crisis. From the deterioration of some old quarters, rendering them practically uninhabitable, to the complete overhaul of other quarters, pricing them out of the reach of the lower classes, the housing shortage precipitated social unrest. The historian Robert Ilbert has characterized "the period of 1890–1910 . . . as the first of the modern housing crisis in Egypt."[65] These juxtapositions between the haves and the have-nots were most pronounced in cities that experienced the greatest population increases.

Some peasants struggled to overcome the vicissitudes of global markets, as entire classes of craftspeople—men and women—were challenged by manufactured goods. In Mount Lebanon, some traditional artisans toiled in futility to keep pace with mass-production factories that flooded the marketplace with inexpensive silk and other fabrics.[66] Others grew frustrated by working conditions in the industrializing economy. Beginning in the 1890s workers began collectively organizing with increasing frequency. Textile journeymen struck over wages among other grievances in Damascus, while in Mount Lebanon female workers in the silk-reeling factories protested.[67] In Alexandria, the urban crisis affected workers who were both Ottomans (Egyptians but also Turks, Syrians, Armenians, local Jews, and others) and Europeans, as urban growth included several thousand Italians, Greeks, and others. In 1899 Egyptian cigarette workers went on strike for the first time, followed by another work stoppage in 1903.[68] In 1902, ten strikes were documented in Alexandria alone, including one mass march staged through the city by over one thousand typographers, hair dressers, and employees in cigarette factories.[69] In 1908, approximately half the urban wage laborers in the empire went on strike.[70] From Istanbul to Cairo, Alexandria, Beirut, Izmir, and Tunis, labor unrest occurred frequently, even if many strikes were short-lived.[71]

Other forms of protest were also on the rise, but it is not always discernible whether economic discontent, political dissatisfaction, social frustration, or a combination of the three motivated public mobilization. In 1907 crowds in Fez, Morocco, angry at high inflation and interest rates, burned a government post at the town's entrance and attacked the shops of merchants under European mentorship along with the local offices of the French telegraph company.[72] One year later, in 1908, officials in Istanbul, Izmir, and Salonika beat back strikers demanding more pay and upset at the system of foreign concessions. Similarly, in Beirut a boycott of Austrian goods signaled the unpopularity of foreign concessions, and of local groups enjoying foreign protection.[73]

A series of escalated, violent peasant uprisings constituted the most radical form of confrontation. On the whole, peasants are apt to put up with harsh economic conditions and much more before they revolt; not until the nineteenth century did they revolt so frequently.[74] Tied to all the unrest was the rise in migration, sometimes made possible by improvements in transportation. Throughout its industrial development, the Ottoman Empire witnessed migration in search of opportunity and security. For those emigrating due to political crisis or civil conflict, resentment at past wrongs could be defining, and occasionally spill into violence in response to grievances in the new setting. As memories of past disputes in native lands were passed from one generation to another, narratives of persecution and moral justice aggravated differences. As a result, migrants reinforced their estrangement from rival groups that migrated alongside them, or from new groups that shared ethnic or religious commonalities with their rivals back home. This social tension and the socioeconomic divide could sometimes spawn violence.

During the Egyptian campaign to occupy Syria in the 1830s, Palestinian peasants rebelled against forced labor, conscription, and a new levy, and they kept the memory of those rebellions alive in 1852 and 1854 with similar uprisings. Financial pressures caused uprisings against local lords, who in turn channeled the protests against the central government.[75] Uprisings troubled Greater Syria between the 1820s and 1850s in Mount Lebanon, between the 1870s and 1890s in Hawran, and in the 1850s in Alawi areas.[76] In Egypt, land reforms meant to improve the cotton crop had the ancillary effect of enriching the large estates at the expense of the peasantry, who often lost their land and were forced to migrate. Although the countryside simmered, the historian Ilham Khuri-Makdisi has painted a nuanced picture of this period, writing that Egypt was "neither a straightforward tale of dispossession . . . nor a tale of perpetual confrontation between new owners and old land users."[77]

As the historian Jens Hanssen notes, "By and large . . . late Ottoman cosmopolitanism . . . was confined to elite spaces. It was also overwhelmingly male-dominated, though women slowly entered 'respectable' public positions through education and health work from the 1870s and 1880s onwards."[78] Perhaps too much was happening too quickly by the standards of slower times, but from national debt to military occupation and from upheaval in the Balkan periphery to instability at the Porte, the Ottoman Empire became more unsettled, uncertain, and uneasy. Moreover, the political censorship of liberals, the growth in economic inequality, the popular dislike of conscription, and "the sense of living in a stagnant society while other parts of the world were fast progressing"[79] propelled intercontinental emigration to new levels.

Improvements in education and transportation accompanied those social and economic changes, crucially enabling migration. Between 1860 and 1914, total emigration from Greater Syria approached 330,000, of which 15,000 emigrated annually between 1900 and 1914. Thousands of Syrian émigrés moved to the United States, especially after the civil war that ravaged Mount Lebanon and Damascus in 1860. So significant was the Syrian presence in America that émigré remittances constituted over 40 percent of the total income of Mount Lebanon.[80] A contemporary observer noted that about one-quarter of the mostly Christian population of Mount Lebanon had emigrated, although many Muslims left as well.[81] In fact, so many young men left Mount Lebanon that single Christian women reportedly emigrated just to find husbands.[82] By the early twentieth century in Egypt, tens of thousands of Syrians lived and worked along the Nile and among the pyramids.

To those Syrians who undertook the arduous journey across the Atlantic, America represented a higher rung on the economic and political ladder of stability. But behind them, Turkoman, Circassian, and trans-Caucasian peasants dreamed of immigrating to Syria to escape their own, even more wretched conditions. As Syrians departed, tens of thousands of central Asians, Armenians, and Jews swept into Syria and Iraq to escape their conditions and start anew. The social disruption this sometimes caused in areas already fraught with tensions often correlated with the size and suddenness of the migration.

As the birthplace of the world's three great monotheistic religions, the Middle East featured practically every variety of sect and subsect of these faiths.[83] From the seventh century—when the message of Islam, rising from the Arabian desert, ultimately spread through the Middle East—Sunni ("orthodox") Muslims headed the dynasties and dominated in numbers, with few exceptions. Believing in the sanctity of the Qur'an, God's word transmitted to the Prophet Muhammad, and relying on accounts of the Prophet's behavior as a revealed guide to a moral life, Muslims captured far-flung domains, spreading Islam from India to North Africa and beyond. With their focus on love and union with God, Sufi mystical orders gained in popularity and were instrumental, as well, in converting other religionists to Islam.

The Sunnis recognized the first four successors (caliphs) who followed the Prophet Muhammad as "rightly guided" and temporal, but early in the first Islamic century, a group—known as shi'at Ali, or partisans of Ali—broke off following a dispute over the lines of succession to the Prophet, asserting that it ran through his family, starting with his cousin and son-in-law, Ali. As their split from the Sunnis grew, the Shi'is rejected the two dynasties of caliphs that followed the rightly guided caliphs—the Umayyads in Damascus and the Abbasids in Baghdad—and instead followed the descendants of Ali (Imams), whom they consider the legitimate leaders of the Muslim community and the infallible interpreters of Islamic law and dogma. In time, a majority of Shi'is, known as Twelvers or Imamis, believed that the succession of Imams ended with the twelfth Imam, who disappeared in the ninth century and has since remained hidden, to reappear one day as the divinely guided Mahdi to rule the world. Other Shi'is, known as the Seveners or Isma'ilis, believe the eldest son of the sixth Imam to be the hidden Imam; and a third group, the Zaydis, broke off even earlier to follow a son of the fourth Imam, Zayd ibn Ali (d. 740).

One offshoot of Shi'ism is the Druze. Sevener Shi'is believe that one of the followers of Isma'il founded an Egyptian dynasty, the Fatimids, of which two followers founded the Druze sect. The Druze do not proselytize, and believe with the Seveners in the transmigration of souls, in supernatural hierarchies, and in emanations of God. Not uncommon in Shi'ism because of their persecuted past, Druze conceal their beliefs in order to protect against outside pressure, and they maintain a secret leadership class of initiates who guide their noninitiate followers. An additional offshoot from Shi'ism is made up of the Nusayris or Alawis, ensconced in the Latakia Mountains of Syria. Although their rituals originate from Christianity and they believe in a divine triad, reincarnation, and the transmigration of souls, they also venerate Imam Ali and possess a secret set of beliefs known only to the initiates.

Christian and Jewish minorities continued to reside in the Middle East following the arrival of Islam, albeit in declining numbers. After centuries of disputes and divisions, practically every Christian denomination was present somewhere in the broader Middle East. The Eastern Orthodox constituted the largest such Christian community; it followed the Orthodox Byzantine teaching on the dual nature of Jesus Christ—as both human and divine—that was adopted at the Council of Chalcedon in 451. Six hundred years later, in 1054, Rome and Constantinople ceased ecclesiastic relations after the Great Schism, leading the Eastern Orthodox to deny the authority of the Roman pope and instead rally behind the four Eastern patriarchs of Antioch, Alexandria, Jerusalem, and (most importantly) Constantinople.

In the late seventeenth and early eighteenth centuries, some Eastern Orthodox factions recognized the Roman papacy and became known as one of the Uniate churches accepting papal supremacy while maintaining their own customs and Byzantine rites. These Uniates include Greek Catholics; non-Uniates are known as Greek Orthodox. Other Uniates include Syrian Catholics, Armenian Catholics, Chaldean Catholics, and Roman Catholics of the Latin rite.

Other Middle Eastern Christians accepted the belief that Jesus was one composite, divine nature or a synthesis of divine and human, rejecting the idea of his dual nature. These Monophysites were condemned at the Council of Chalcedon and pronounced heterodox by both Constantinople and Rome. Among the Monophysites are Egyptian Copts, Armenian Orthodox or Gregorians, and Syriac-speaking Syrian Orthodox or Jacobites, after the sixth-century bishop Jacob Baradeus who propagated their beliefs.

In the seventh century, in an attempt at compromise between the Monophysites and Orthodox positions, Monothelites established the Monothelete doctrine that Christ possessed both a divine and human nature, but only one divine will. The Council of Constantinople rejected this doctrine as heresy in 680, but the doctrine survived among a Christian community in Syria known as the Maronites, named after their fifth-century patron saint Mar Marun. These Maronites originally inhabited the valley of the Orontes River (which runs through Lebanon, Syria, and southern Turkey before draining into the Mediterranean Sea) and parts of northern Syria, but by the end of the eleventh century they were concentrated almost exclusively in Mount Lebanon.

Still other communities rejected the Council of Chalcedon's duality from the opposite end of the spectrum, arguing for a more pronounced distinction between the human and divine natures of Christ. To them, the full humanity of Christ and the Word of God lived in the man Jesus from his formation. These Nestorians, named after the fifth-century Patriarch of Constantinople, are found among the Assyrians of Syria and Iraq, a Semitic people who speak and write distinct dialects of Eastern Aramaic.

Catholic missionaries were active in the Middle East before Ottoman rule and their numbers grew during Istanbul's reign. Franciscan friars served as custodians of the holy shrines in the Holy Land in the fifteenth century, followed by Jesuits, Carmelites, Dominicans, and others. Missionary priests departed for Roman colleges, returning to spread Latin, Italian, and Arabic and contributing to an important cultural revival of increased theological study and scholarly inquiry.[84] The pope established a number of colleges in the Middle East to train priests from the late sixteenth century onward, including Maronite and Greek schools. As the number of missions—and missionary priests—increased, so did the number of eastern churches that again accepted the pope, without surrendering their own liturgies, customs, and laws. In the eighteenth century, the Maronites reaffirmed their original

commitment to the papacy. In the nineteenth century, Protestants also began preaching in the Holy Land. Initially focused on evangelizing non-
Christians, they proved more successful at converting Christians of other
denominations, mostly the alienated and the Greek Orthodox.

Although smaller in number, Jewish communities made a significant impact as well. Small communities of Jewish traders and craftsmen dotted the
Middle East and North Africa from Morocco to Yemen, congregating primarily in the coastal towns but also extending into the Syrian and Iraqi interior. These communities fluctuated in size and location, often in response
to external events. Jews sought refuge in the Ottoman Empire after the Re-
conquista of Andalusia in the fifteenth century, bringing Sephardic traditions to Istanbul and the other great imperial cities, including the Kabbala
mystical interpretation associated with the sixteenth-century Rabbi Isaac
Luria, one of the greatest mystics of all time.

Religious groups tended to aggregate in homogeneous groupings. Centuries of limited transportation and communication meant that at times
they worshiped and lived in relative isolation from one another, and religious
space was often compartmentalized from social venues, limiting the spread
of interreligious empathy. This communal autonomy, however, did not entirely preclude cooperation. For much of Middle Eastern history, different
religious communities not only lived in relative peace with one another but
even thrived in pluralistic settings. In the guild documents of the Damascene law-court registers the historian Abdul-Karim Rafeq discovered that
members of different communities could live side-by-side, and did business
together.[85] Indeed, these groups represented sects embedded within a larger
community.

The correspondence of leading families shows that merchants knew one
another by name and exchanged inquiries about the families of those they
did business with, irrespective of their affiliation. It appears that a working
trust, accrued over years of partnership, supplanted religious affiliation in the
structuring of business practices. Although city quarters were for the most
part ethnically and religiously differentiated, in the social melting-pot of the
central marketplace workers and vendors often mixed, while different communities cooperated in the caravan trade. All of this suggests that interreligious links existed across professions and classes.

However, when the effects of the Industrial Revolution began disrupting
the established political, economic, and social balance on a large scale, the

resulting tensions could find sectarian expression. Uneven economic opportunities, greater mobility, better communications, regional or local instability, the manipulation of local groups, and just about any disruption of
the status quo caused people to find strength in their traditional loyalties.
Many migrants gravitated toward those bonds and identities that withstood
the transition to the new milieu and setting. Often, the strongest loyalty
was to sectarian identity. Migrants identified with others of similar ethnic,
racial, religious, or cultural background even beyond the initial period of
adjustment.

This rise in religious tension varied by region, depending on the pace of
change, the composition of the province, the scope and nature of Ottoman
governance and European activity, and the depth of European favoritism
toward religious minorities. This tension more often reflected economic
grievance than confessional politics.

Communal rioting broke out in Aleppo in 1850 when Muslims in the
eastern quarters of the city, fearful of conscription and angered by direct
taxation, attacked the city's prosperous Christian minority. Violence also
broke out in Iraq in mid-century, in Nablus and Gaza in 1856, in Jaffa the
following year, and in Jedda the year after that. In Nablus a variety of factors combined to trigger violence. Christians hoisted French and British
flags over their houses at news of the Russian defeat in the Crimean War,
while an Ottoman edict privileged religious minorities, creating tensions
between the state and locality. A new bell was mounted over a Protestant
missionary school, and a European missionary shot a Muslim beggar for
allegedly attempting to steal his coat. Mobs gathered at the British mission
and tore down the Union Jack before proceeding to the governor's house
to demand justice. The outbreak ended with the ransacking and burning of
some Christian houses and the killing of a number of foreigners.[86]

By far the most important sectarian outbreak in the Syrian provinces occurred in Mount Lebanon and Damascus in 1860. In the 1820s, and between the 1840s and 1860, a crescendo of disquiet in Mount Lebanon led
up to clashes in 1860 between Druze and mostly Maronite Christians, spilling into the Syrian interior when Muslims of a populous quarter of Damascus attacked Christians of a more affluent quarter. The solution to this violence was the creation of a special administration for Lebanon whereby the
distribution of offices was set by sect on the basis of quotas.[87] In this case,
institutional development reinforced sectarian separation by encouraging

the maintenance of a sectarian identity that conveyed a special place in the political landscape. Thus, in addition to inherited religious affiliations and growing economic imbalances, the development of confessional politics was a contributing factor to the persistence of sectarian identities. In time it became difficult to distinguish political and sectarian rivalries since they often merged and overlapped, but the main factor was less religious difference than political and monetary ambition.

North Africa was not spared the nineteenth-century social disharmony. In Tunisia in 1864, violence erupted against foreign merchants and affluent local groups; in 1882, the riot that precipitated the British occupation killed some fifty foreigners in Alexandria; and in 1899, interethnic clashes erupted in the low-income quarters of Alexandria.[88] It is hard at times to untangle tensions and clashes, especially since a major source of unrest was the novelty of political participation, however limited it may have been. Overall, though, these trends reflected the new social disharmonies of the century.

After centuries without the experience of governance, it was inevitable that new political opportunities and structures would create problems of corruption and management. In the case of Egypt, where so much was at stake with the cultivation and trade of cotton, corruption was pervasive, involving European financiers, top government officials, and businessmen. In the Syrian and Iraqi provinces, areas with more compartmentalized geographies and societies, politics was more local. And in Mount Lebanon, residents regularly complained of political favoritism and patronage. The result was pervasive distrust, bordering on cynicism toward government, but this also signaled that people were intensely involved with their local administration and politics.[89]

Indeed, tensions mixed and matched with broader questions of governance to shape the political consciousness. A short-lived project in 1909 to merge an Ottoman navigation company with a British outfit led Arab deputies in the Ottoman parliament to protest in Baghdad. While it is likely true that some protesters simply favored rival German ambitions and wanted to check British expansion in Iraq whenever possible, other politically aware Arab deputies simply preferred the Ottomans over the British, a possible foreshadowing of the development of Arab identity or of Arab assertions in the face of British economic penetration.[90]

In sum, at the turn of the twentieth century tensions were on the rise among mixed areas and in the key cities of trade and administration. Despite Beirut's earned reputation for religious tolerance and plurality from the seventeenth to the nineteenth century, the city began to feel the after-shocks of communal tensions from Mount Lebanon and from the Syrian interior. As Beirut entered the twentieth century on a note of prosperity, observers started to report sectarian clashes between Muslims and Christians as regular occurrences. Amid this rising tide of tension, wealthy merchants sought to keep afloat their intercommunal business associations, political advocacy, and social gatherings.[91]

Such was the state of the key Ottoman regions as the calendar turned to 1914. In retrospect, given what we now know was looming, it is ironic that the year 1914 began as more stable than the preceding six years. There seemed to be less unrest in the Arab provinces than in the years since the Young Turk revolution of 1908. By 1914, the Ottoman government had shifted from re-capturing its former European domains to focusing more on its Arab lands. As a result, it accommodated some Arab concerns, cultivated key notables and members of the Arab press, allowed larger Arab representation in elections, and generally supported reform initiatives. Arab criticism of the government did not disappear—in fact, two secret societies with anti-Ottoman separatist platforms, al-Fatat (the Youth) and al-Ahd (the Covenant), had come into existence in 1909 and 1913—but on the whole, the government had tighter control over its Syrian and Iraqi provinces than in the immediate past, and the majority of the population accepted Ottomanism. In British-controlled Egypt, the population generally would have traded British for Ottoman rule, but that choice was an abstraction in the days when the sun never seemed to set on a British Empire at the height of its global power.[92]

At the periphery of the Arab Ottoman lands and left to its own devices for much of its history, Arabia remained primarily an arena of traditional tribal politics. Because this area did not experience the convulsions of rapid change, it remained relatively isolated. But this Arabia was bursting with life when it came to local and regional politics of a more traditional type—the politics of notables and tribal rivalries. Among those rivalries, and as a sign of things to come, relations deteriorated in 1914 between the sharif of Mecca, Husayn bin Ali, and the Ottoman governor in the Hijaz. Ironically, in this very traditional place, the dreams of an Arab nation would find an outlet in Sharif Husayn's 1916 Arab Revolt. The story could not have been more unexpected; the Arab provinces that were politically active before the war ended up playing a minor role in the national movement during the war, while the traditional Arabian peninsula, engrossed in tribal politics, led the way in marshaling the first Arab Revolt.

The Great War itself was triggered by events beyond the Middle East. Rivalry between Russia and Austria and the assassination of Archduke Franz Ferdinand, heir to the Austro-Hungarian throne, and of his wife, Sophie, the Duchess of Hohenberg, in Sarajevo on June 28, 1914, unleashed a war in August that continued on many fronts for the next four years. The Great War involved groups of nations that fought on opposite sides: the Entente powers were on one side, including Britain, France, and Russia, later joined by Italy, Greece, Portugal, Serbia, Romania, the United States, and others; the Central Powers opposed them, dominated by Germany and Austria-Hungary, and later joined by the Ottoman Empire and Bulgaria.

How the war was fought and how it was won determined how it was re-membered by the peoples of the region. The Great War had a lasting effect not only on relations between the peoples of the Middle East and all those who took part in the war from outside the region, but also on relations be-tween various national groups within the Middle East. But before we turn to that story, and the war itself, let us sail back in time to 1882 and rejoin Admiral Frederick Beauchamp Seymour, commanding the British fleet at Alexandria aboard HMS *Alexandra*.

When Seymour arrived off the Egyptian coastline in 1882, Victorian Britain commanded the seas unlike any force in history. The ships that he ordered into action reduced the defenses at Alexandria to rubble, making short work of the Egyptian fortresses guarding the harbor. Yet both the *Alexandra* and HMS *Invincible,* to which Seymour transferred his flag during the bombardment, appear upon closer inspection as if stuck between eras. These British ships featured both engines and sails. The presence of those sails unfurls recollections of the great voyages of discovery, while the use of engine propulsion foreshadows the dreadnought battleships that would dominate the early twentieth century. Indeed, in the spring of 1882 maritime steam engines were still somewhat new to the scene, and the British navy was still adjusting.

The British focus on naval modernization and its fleet's conversion to coal-fired and even petroleum propulsion systems can be explained by the island power's dependency on sea travel to maintain its vast empire. In the years before World War I, however, a complementary explanation for British modernization loomed, returning us to the imperial court at Vienna and the alliance it enjoyed with Berlin.

By the early twentieth century, the unified German Reich was a rising power, increasingly dominating continental Europe. Ready to claim his place at the top of the European order, Kaiser Wilhelm II charged ahead with an armaments program and naval buildup that disrupted the delicate post-Napoleonic Concert of Europe. With the outbreak of the First Balkan War in 1912, the German Imperial Navy dispatched one battle cruiser and one light cruiser from Kiel for the Mediterranean. As they cut into the North Sea and passed the British Isles and steamed purposefully toward the Strait of Gibraltar, these powerful ships announced a new era of sea power.

Within days, the two German ships began a series of port calls in the Mediterranean, where they would remain for almost two years. The Middle East would forever be changed by the arrival of the 22,000-ton Moltke-class battle cruiser SMS *Goeben* and its companion, the 4,500-ton Magdeburg-class light cruiser SMS *Breslau.*

CHAPTER TWO

The Empire at War

AT 5:00 IN the late afternoon of Monday, August 10, 1914, the battle cruiser SMS *Goeben* steamed into the entrance of the Dardanelles.[1] Accompanied by the light cruiser SMS *Breslau,* SMS *Goeben* embodied the pride of the German Imperial Navy and was one of the most formidable ships in the Mediterranean Sea. For the past eight days, under the command of Rear Admiral Wilhelm Souchon, commander of the Reich's Mediterranean fleet, the two cruisers had roared across the sea, the *Goeben*'s boilers scalding its sailors at a scorching 24 knots, in an attempt to evade their British and French pursuers.[2] Their derring-do voyage, which included the bombardment of French North Africa and a frenetic breakout into the eastern Mediterranean after coaling at Messina, Sicily, constituted the first naval action in the Mediterranean of World War I.[3] But as *The Ship That Changed the World* demonstrates, the Germans' arrival in the Dardanelles, welcome at Istanbul, and subsequent passage into the Black Sea signaled more than the permanent bottling of Russia's southern naval outlet. Indeed, as Admiral Souchon later put it to his men: "Do your utmost: the future of Turkey is at stake."[4]

In retrospect, the actions of the two German cruisers and their arrival on that late summer afternoon at the crossing between Europe and Asia decisively shaped not only the future of Turkey, but also the future of the entire Ottoman Empire—and with it, the world. For upon arriving in Ottoman waters, and with the consent of the German government, SMS *Goeben* and SMS *Breslau* were reflagged and their crew transferred to the sultan's Ottoman navy, along with Admiral Souchon. Eleven weeks later, near the end of October, the newly outfitted flagship of the Ottoman navy, *Yavuz Sultan Selim* (formerly *Goeben*), ever loyally accompanied by *Midilli* (formerly *Breslau*), set out under secret instructions from the pro-German Ottoman Minister of War to "gain command of the Black Sea."[5] Days later, *Yavuz* led four squadrons in a dawn raid on the Russian bases of Sevastopol, Feodosia, Yalta, Odessa, and Novorossiysk.[6] Overrun by events, the Tsarist government declared war on the Ottoman Empire on November 2.[7] Thus, thanks to *Yavuz*'s foray along the north shore of the Black Sea and the maneuvers of the Young Turks in Istanbul, a proud, centuries-old empire set course for four years of agony and suffering, ending in its defeat and destruction with the signing of the armistice in the port of Mudros in 1918.[8]

Look past the smoke of *Yavuz*'s 11-inch guns, however, and a broader rationale for the Ottoman entry into the war comes into focus. The historian Mustafa Aksakal's recent study has shown that it was the Ottomans who had made the request for the German ships to sail to the Ottoman capital.[9] Indeed, beneath the surface of the Ottoman naval action lurked several strategic imperatives that pressed the Ottoman leadership into forging a continental alliance, ultimately choosing Germany as its ally. In the summer of 1914, as the Hofburg planned to dispatch its promising heir to the Austro-Hungarian throne, Archduke Franz Ferdinand, to Sarajevo for a routine troop inspection, the Ottoman Empire suffered from mounting economic imbalances, a collapsing position in the Balkans, and a series of military defeats that left its public "aggrieved"; moreover, Europe's indifference to the disintegration of Ottoman Europe in the aftermath of the Balkan Wars had shocked the Ottoman Turks.[10] As the historian Feroz Ahmad summarized, "The treasury was empty, the army demoralized, and the Turks diplomatically isolated."[11]

The Ottoman leadership had sought to arrest its decline, protect against partition, shore up its finances, and reactivate its Balkan presence through a new power constellation centered on Turkey, Bulgaria, and Romania.[12] Achieving such a system would effectively isolate Greece and advance Ottoman irredentist claims on Chios and Mytilene in the Aegean Sea.[13] Accomplishing these ambitions, however, would require great-power patronage. Thus, after seizing power in January 1913, some members of the Young Turks had pushed for an Anglo-Ottoman alliance. London proved uninterested, however, as did Russia and France, which rejected alliance overtures in May and July 1914, respectively.[14] Rebuffed by the Triple Entente, Istanbul turned to the single strongest power on the European continent, Germany.

The alliance with Germany, nonetheless, was not arrived at by a simple process of elimination: an agreement with Berlin had its own compelling strategic rationale and supporters. Of the European powers only Germany represented the "combination of military strength on the continent with its weakness in Asia Minor."[15] Germany "was one European power that had no, or at least limited, territorial ambitions in the Ottoman Empire."[16] In contrast to Britain and France, Germany's peacetime interests in the Ottoman Empire—embodied in Deutsche Bank's 1903 financing of a railway from Berlin to Baghdad—appeared mostly commercial and its negotiations with Istanbul remained unfettered by Russian desiderata.[17] Thus, the Ottomans forwarded an alliance proposal to Berlin based on defensive deterrence that would eventually nudge Sofia and Bucharest toward Istanbul and isolate Greece.[18]

As the delicate diplomatic dance of the post-Napoleonic Concert of Europe neared its last stanza early in the twentieth century, Europe viewed "co-operation with Turkey . . . as desirable, but its pursuit . . . second to the management" of the European alliance system.[19] With the activation of the interlocking alliance system following Archduke Ferdinand's assassination in Sarajevo, however, Berlin's perspective changed. Germany now perceived a value in an Ottoman southern flank to relieve pressure on the Austro-Hungarian eastern front and to threaten the colonial possessions of the Triple Entente. People in German official circles but also in church groups and the universities were attracted to the idea that acquiring Ottoman territories would enhance Germany's status in the Middle East and beyond.[20] Berlin's response to Istanbul's offer of alliance, therefore, was to urge the Ottomans to enter the war.

The CUP leadership thus faced a conundrum. As Feroz Ahmad writes, "There was a general consensus among Turks in favour of the German alliance, for it ended Turkey's isolation—a factor of great psychological significance in 1914. But Unionists differed as to whether or when Turkey should become a belligerent. After all the disasters the Empire had suffered in the recent past, most Unionists would have preferred to stay out of the war, maintaining a benevolent neutrality in favor of Germany."[21] Still, an opportunity seemingly existed. Surveying the geopolitical setting from Istanbul in the summer of 1914, the Young Turks viewed Germany as a guarantor of potential postwar Ottoman gains in Europe in the event of a swift Serbian defeat.[22] Moreover, it was thought that if the Austro-Serbian Balkan crisis escalated into a wider European conflagration, the geostrategic significance of the Bosporus would perhaps vitiate Ottoman neutrality as a viable option anyway.[23] Thus, hard-pressed for financing, recognizing the difficulty of neutrality, and inclined toward Germany, the Ottoman leadership felt compelled to act.[24] On August 2 it chose to ally itself with Germany, while attempting to navigate the tightrope of nonbelligerence.[25]

In the meantime, the British government repossessed what were to be the first modern Ottoman battleships, *Sultan Osman* and *Reschadieh* (*Reşadiye*) still moored in their British shipyards but ready for delivery. Istanbul awaited these ships with "an eager pride that was all the more general because the purchase-money had been raised by collections among the people."[26] Therefore, one week later, when *Goeben* and *Breslau* steamed through the Greek archipelago and set their course for history, "popular outcry was at its height."[27]

Before burning out, the Great War ignited conflict from the Egyptian desert to the Anatolian mountains, and beyond. As the scholar Orhan Koloğlu wrote, "The major impact of World War I stems from the fact that this was the first large scale war ever fought within the territory of the Ottoman Empire. Previously during the war in Libya or even the Balkan Wars, only some part of the empire was fighting against the enemy while the rest of the empire was living in peace."[28] The brief introduction that follows therefore recapitulates the military action across five different fronts of the Middle East: Anatolia, Gallipoli, Persia, Mesopotamia, and Egypt and the Levant. It begins in eastern Anatolia.

EASTERN ANATOLIA

Over 1,100 kilometers east of the steep bluffs of the Bosporus, nestled along a bend in the Aras River in the rugged eastern Anatolian topography south of the Cakir Baba mountains, sits the outpost of Koprukoy. Today it is a sleepy hamlet of 1,500, but in late 1914 it constituted the bustling forward headquarters of the Ottoman Third Army, charged with protecting the Anatolian heartland to its rear from the Russian Caucasian corps looming in the mountain approaches ahead.

On December 10, 1914, the Ottoman Minister of War, Enver Pasha, arrived in Koprukoy and was promptly briefed by his field commander, General Hassan Izzet.[29] Stressing the disorganized state of his army—the Tenth Corps of the Third Army alone was short seventeen thousand overcoats and boots—Izzet counseled patience and prudence as the front stabilized following a brief Russian incursion.[30] The ambitious Enver Pasha had a different idea, however: an attack deep into the mountains, in the dead of winter. The powerful war minister had long sensed weakness in Russia's southern underbelly, which tracked neatly with his desire to break through into the Caucasus.[31] He therefore proceeded to dismiss Izzet, assume personal command of the Third Army, and plot a complex, multipronged flank offensive that would divide his ill-equipped forces. Such an attack would have to contend not only with the Russians, but also with the subfreezing conditions of an eastern Anatolian winter: "roads are impassable, and wise peasants bring their animals and themselves indoors and remain there for months."[32] Nevertheless, Enver's mind was made up: the Third Army, consisting of three corps, would attack.

Enver's flanking attack called for the Ninth Corps to follow a path known as *top yol* ("cannon way") along the Cakir Baba mountain ridge until descending on the exposed Russian right flank near Sarikamish.[33] The path followed the crest of the ridge, which, lacking ravines, sat exposed to recurring winds and therefore would be blown clear of heavy winter snow. Of course, the same winds that guaranteed a swept path brought with them an unbearable frost. Since the pass was too high for trees, soldiers could not warm themselves with fire;[34] to compound their suffering, many marched without greatcoats and knapsacks in order to facilitate rapid movement.[35] In fact, they possessed "few winter uniforms or warm coats, no winter boots."[36] As the Ninth Corps marched its grueling mountain path, the

Tenth Corps would attempt an even deeper encirclement of the Russian right in order to protect and reinforce the Ninth Corps attack.[37] It too faced the hardship of bitter cold and waist-level snow as it pushed to capture the Russian-held Oltu. Meanwhile, the Eleventh Corps had the task of occupying two Russian corps while the Ninth and Tenth Corps completed their flanking attack.[38]

The surprise offensive began on December 22, and until Christmas Eve developed promisingly enough. The advance columns of the Tenth Corps took Oltu on December 23 and the leading division of the Ninth Corps entered the pivot of Bardiz on the road to Sarikamish the next day.[39] At the high point of the offensive, the confident thirty-year-old commander of the Tenth Corps, Hafiz Hakki, spoke of needing only " 'a few hours' to destroy the Russians."[40]

Somewhat confused, the Russian commander, General Aleksandr Myshlayevsky, reacted to the Ottoman movements by ordering a general retreat through Sarikamish, but not before one of his own corps launched a counterattack.[41] Fortuitously for Myshlayevsky and his men, the Russians thereby sustained interior lines of operations, dislodged the Ottomans from key road systems, and reinforced their men by the time the Ottoman attack on Sarikamish took place on December 27.[42]

The Ottomans entered the battle badly depleted and exhausted; an entire division of the Ottoman Ninth Corps, scheduled to lead the assault, had already lost half its strength on Christmas night to frostbite while Hakki's Tenth Corps was delayed after marching through blizzard conditions.[43] The reinforced Russian garrison was therefore able to withstand waves of Ottomans as they hurled themselves against the Russian trenches.[44] By New Year's Eve the threat to Sarikamish had passed and a Russian counterattack commenced, devastating the two flanking Turkish corps (Ninth and Tenth). In the attack's aftermath, the Russians "found 30,000 frozen bodies around Sarikamish alone" and by the end of January the entire Third Army's strength was estimated at less than 12,500 men.[45] Indeed, the Ottoman dream of a breakthrough into the Russian Caucasus, assisted by nationalist rebellions, died along with the Third Army in the snows of Sarikamish.[46]

The Battle of Sarikamish was a major operational defeat with strategic consequences for the Ottoman Empire; the Caucasus would remain in the tenuous grip of Moscow for the duration of the war. Complex and foolhardy, the attack at Sarikamish inaugurated a slow but steady Russian advance westward. It also took place parallel to what some scholars describe as "the beginning of a civil war" with Armenians, whom the Ottomans accused of collaborating with the Russians.[47] This interpretation has been contested by others who argue that the Ottomans attacked Armenian communities unprovoked, and on the scale of genocide.[48] Even so, 1915 was the key year in which the "relocation and massacre of the Greek and Armenian communities in Anatolia began."[49]

There would be other major confrontations, but the decisive battle for the Caucasus front did not occur until 1917, and then in the distant streets of Saint Petersburg. Two communist revolutionaries, Leon Trotsky and Vladimir Lenin, stoked the Russian Revolution that ultimately would lead to the March 3, 1918, Treaty of Brest-Litovsk, terminating Russian participation in World War I. The conflict in the Caucasus smoldered on in the ethnic mélange of the Caspian Sea basin even after Brest-Litovsk, but the Russian threat to the Anatolian heartland was extinguished.

GALLIPOLI

On Christmas Day 1914, the Russian High Command headquarters, Stavka, received several pressing, panicked situation reports from Myshlayevsky in the Caucasus, detailing his eroding position in the face of Enver Pasha's offensive. Fearing Myshlayevsky's imminent collapse, Grand Duke Nicholas Nikolaevich, commander in chief of all Russian forces, requested a British diversionary attack to support his enfeebled commander.[50] Although the danger to Myshlayevsky quickly dissipated, the Russians did not withdraw their request for action.[51]

In London, the message was taken up urgently. Upon receipt, the First Lord of the Admiralty, the forty-year-old liberal politician Winston Churchill, conferred with the already legendary British Secretary for War, Lord Herbert Kitchener, and suggested an attack on the peninsula of Gallipoli that guards the Dardanelles strait.[52] In Churchill's opinion, such an operation would not only relieve the Russians but potentially bring Greece and Bulgaria into alliance with the Entente and divert Ottoman attention from the vital Suez Canal.[53] Ultimately, whoever controlled the Dardanelles controlled the Sea of Marmara and thus threatened Istanbul. After a wide-ranging session on

January 13, 1915, the War Council adopted Churchill's proposal, resolving that "the Admiralty should prepare a naval expedition 'to invade and take the Gallipoli Peninsula with Constantinople as its objective,' commencing February 1915."[54] By the end of January, the decision to execute such a proposal was finalized.[55]

The Dardanelles strait runs northeast for seventy kilometers to the Sea of Marmara, splitting the peninsula of Gallipoli from the Anatolian mainland; at its narrowest point only 1,400 meters separate the shores.[56] Beginning on February 19 and continuing for the next month the British and French navies, led ultimately by the super-dreadnought HMS *Queen Elizabeth,* steamed cautiously into the strait, their superior guns trained on Ottoman shore installations in the heights above while converted North Sea fishing trawlers swept for enemy mines.[57] The Ottomans eyed the approaching British with an "air of expectancy"[58] until suddenly "the whole coast burst forth in vicious, splitting bursts of flame."[59] As one officer, Captain Sarkis Torossian, noted, "The strait had become a bedlam, an inferno, a crazy picture in a mad world, a confusion of ships and gunfire and tons of boiling mud hurled high in the air by exploding shells; shells seemed to fly in every direction without reason, without sense. The very earth shook under the barrage and the thunderous din."[60]

Even so, the main naval attack into the Dardanelles did not commence March 18, when the *Queen Elizabeth,* supported by British and French battleships, trained its 15-inch guns on the concentration of Ottoman batteries and forts that constituted the main obstacles to passage.[61] By most accounts, the combined Anglo-French fleet had exhausted most of the Ottoman ammunition and defense that day; however, when breaking contact in the early afternoon HMS *Irresistible,* HMS *Ocean,* and the French battleship *Bouvet* struck an overlooked minefield in the shallows and sank.[62] The Ottoman defenses protecting Istanbul had held, but just barely. So narrow was the Ottoman victory that in precaution "all the archives, stores of money, etc., had already been removed" from Istanbul.[63]

Checked in the strait, the Admiral of the Fleet, John de Robeck, concluded that a naval forcing should be reassessed: "To attack Narrows now with Fleet would be a mistake."[64] Instead, as he notified London, a full-scale amphibious operation on the peninsula of Gallipoli, the largest attempted in modern warfare, would be "essential" to forcing passage.[65] Thus the stage was set for a landing on Gallipoli.

On March 26, 1915, the newly appointed commander of the Ottoman Fifth Army, Prussian General Otto Liman von Sanders, established his headquarters in the harbor town of Gallipoli, located on the eastern shore of the peninsula jutting southwest from the Thracian European mainland.[66] From that vantage point Liman von Sanders could observe the primary features of the peninsula, its small beaches and series of hills that loom over the landscape.[67] As identified by Liman von Sanders and the Ottoman defenders in the early months of World War I, the three major high points of Gallipoli that would prove critical were the Anafarta Ridge near Suvla Bay, over halfway down the peninsula on its west coast; the Sari Bair Range just northeast of Ari Burnu, itself several kilometers to the south of Suvla Bay on the peninsula's west coast; and the central Achi Baba heights, ten kilometers north of Cape Helles, at the southernmost tip of the peninsula.[68]

Upon inspection the Ottoman commanders found the Fifth Army spread out like the "frontier detachments of the good old days" along Gallipoli's entire coastline.[69] These thin formations were positioned to meet an attack against any part of the island, but would be susceptible to subsequent breakthrough and encirclement. The Ottomans therefore instituted a centralized reserve system with only a light detachment of troops to screen along the coast and temporarily slow any British landing.[70] Such a strategy, premised on rapid maneuver and flexible mobility, required a drastic upgrading of Gallipoli's infrastructure. Liman von Sanders ordered "supply dumps laid and field bakeries built," while Ottoman labor battalions hurriedly transformed narrow donkey trails into passable paths.[71] Fortunately for the Ottomans, the long delay between the Dardanelles naval action and the Gallipoli amphibious assault provided the time necessary to prepare for the enemy landing.

The Scotsman, Ian Hamilton, commanded the enemy in question, the Mediterranean Expeditionary Force (MEF). Hamilton planned a two-pronged attack, consisting of an assault by the Australian and New Zealand Army Corps (ANZAC) south of Ari Burnu, followed by the British Twenty-Ninth Division attacking along the Cape Helles peninsular tip.[72] ANZAC was to capture the Sari Bair heights and then cross the peninsula almost six kilometers toward Maidos.[73] In Hamilton's thinking, from that vantage point the main fort of Kilid Bahr—standing since Sultan Mehmed II ordered it built to guard his newly acquired prize of Istanbul in 1453— could be taken from the rear and Ottoman communications severed.[74] In the southern theater, the British Twenty-Ninth Division was expected to capture five small beaches and quickly push north to envelope Achi Baba Ridge near the town of Krithia.[75] Once in control of these heights, Hamilton planned on landing reinforcements, pushing north, linking up with ANZAC, and taking the entire peninsula. He recognized that success in such an endeavor would imperil Istanbul's participation in the war.

But Hamilton could not have reckoned with the tenacity of the Ottoman fighting force. When his attack came in the early morning of April 25, the ANZAC covering force faced little opposition at their Ari Burnu landing cove; it then proceeded to capture several key ridges quickly while advancing inland, from where it could even "see the waters of the Narrows only 3 miles away."[76] Quite suddenly, however, its advance was checked by a ferocious Ottoman counterattack.

Based near Maidos, the Ottoman Nineteenth Division constituted the primary inland defense hub tasked with rushing to check the enemy's amphibious landing.[77] Commanding the Nineteenth Division was a thirty-three-year-old lieutenant colonel, Mustafa Kemal, whose performance over the ensuing months would change the outcome of the campaign and catapult him to glory.

Born into the cosmopolitan port city of Salonica in the winter of 1880 or 1881, Mustafa Kemal was an ambitious, proud young man with the talents to match.[78] In Salonica, which "had undergone a major transformation during the reform era and had begun to look like a Western European city," the young Kemal attended both primary and (military) preparatory school.[79] Kemal enrolled in the War College in Istanbul and reveled in his era's secular scientism, a paradigm reinforced by one leisurely posting in Sofia.[80] Like many of his soldiering contemporaries, Kemal believed himself destined for greatness long before the Great War.[81] He saw himself as Turkey's savior, and thus undertook a program of politicking that at one point it almost landed him in prison for being away from his post.[82] For Kemal, nothing short of rebuilding the fundamental basis of Turkish politics on enlightened secularism would suffice. As the Turkish Cypriot sociologist Niyazi Berkes argues, "Mustafa Kemal's extraordinary personality was such a part of all the secularizing developments that almost nothing of them can be understood properly without taking it into account. It was his leadership that developed nationalism, populism, and secularism as a response to the challenges of

imperialism, communism, and theocracy."[83] Kemal's aptitude for soldiering, his exacting precision, and his bias for action ultimately proved the
means to that end decades later. Ironically, he initially opposed Ottoman
entry into the war that would launch him from relative obscurity as a lieutenant colonel to national fame, as the Father of the Turks and founder of
the modern state of Turkey. But once he was involved, Kemal's confidence
and military acumen would prove critical, especially on that first day on
Gallipoli. His heroism as a soldier generated a wellspring from which Atatürk
the politician would profit for years.

Upon hearing reports of a small enemy force advancing up the western
slope of Chunuk Bair, a 260-meter peak of the Sari Bair ridge, Kemal
quickly grasped the enemy battle plan and—on his own initiative—ordered
an entire regiment into action, committing Liman von Sanders's inland reserve on the basis of piecemeal evidence and strong intuition.[84]

Had Kemal been wrong, and the attack on Chunuk Bair a ruse or feint,
the Ottomans would have been wrong-footed and the consequences potentially disastrous. But as one of his more admiring biographers recounts,
Kemal "knew he was right" and therefore personally led his Fifty-Seventh
Regiment across the peninsula, with map and compass in hand.[85] Upon
arrival, he ordered his men into action with legendary bravado: "I don't order you to attack, I order you to die. In the time it takes us to die, other
troops and commanders can come and take our places."[86] Facing a furnace
of fire, virtually the entire Fifty-Seventh Regiment did just that, obeying
Kemal's order as a final soldiering act to blunt the charges of the ANZAC
forces. Through its efforts, the regiment held the top of the strategically vital Chunuk Bair until Kemal's primarily Arab Seventy-Second and Seventy-
Seventh Regiments arrived to reinforce the line.[87] These troops hailed from
modern-day Lebanon, Jordan, Syria, and Palestine and acted a central part
in one of the most defining victories of Turkish history.[88]

The race to bring up reserves, allowing the Ottomans to erase their numerical disadvantage, was critical to the Ottoman defensive concept. As the
sun set over the eastern Mediterranean, it appeared as though the Ottomans had won that contest. They had met the initial ANZAC attack with
courage, pinned the landing force against the surrounding heights, and arrested the advance when it threatened breakthrough. But Kemal knew that
the bitter fight had only just begun, later issuing inspirational orders to his

men that infused them with pride and purpose: "Every soldier who fights here with me must realise that he is in honour bound not to retreat one step. Let me remind you all that if you want to rest there may be no rest for our whole nation throughout eternity."[89]

Forty minutes after the first ANZAC landings, the First King's Own Scottish Borderers swept into two narrow gullies, twenty-three kilometers to the south, that split the 150-foot cliffs guarding the northwestern flank of the Cape Helles peninsula.[90] Luckily for the Borderers the cliffs constituted their only obstacle and they quickly reached the top.[91] Yet despite having landed unopposed, the Scots failed to press the initiative, "achieved nothing of any military importance," and settled on the cliffs after a brief sojourn toward the unopposed town of Krithia.[92] By the time the attackers sought to link up, "a portion of the Turkish Infantry Regiment 26, which was literally everywhere, threw itself between the two English battalions which were striving to reach each other. The way lay only over their dead bodies."[93]

Thanks to the decisive action of the Ninth Division commander Colonel Sami Bey, who immediately ordered the forced march of Lieutenant Colonel Nail Bey's Twenty-Fifth Regiment, the Ottomans counterattacked and left the Scots teetering on the cliff's edge at bayonet point.[94] Compounding the mistake of delay, confusion at the landing zone the next morning led to the evacuation of a detachment of Scottish Borderers seeking ammunition; that withdrawal quickly steamrolled into a full-fledged clearing of nearly the entire British force.[95]

The real linchpins of Hamilton's amphibious assault at Cape Helles, however, were the early morning landings at Tekke Bay and Ertugral Bay, which constitute the far southern tips of Cape Helles. Tekke Bay features a beach from which a direct advance toward Achi Baba was possible, to be commenced by the First Battalion Lancashire Fusiliers. Ertugral Bay formed a similar landing area for the British vanguard, led by the First Royal Dublin Fusiliers.[96] These landing zones were not unknown to the Ottomans, who had belts of barbed wire placed in the shallows and on the beaches to accompany a series of mines.[97] These defenses complemented other features, as one German colonel observed: "Here the country is extremely difficult, scarcely welcoming for a landing-party apart from the flat but narrow beach, because starting close to the massive old walls of the ancient Beach fort a high cliff rises in a half circle from Cape Helles entirely shutting in the landing-place. Like the seats in an amphitheatre the cliffs rise to a height of 40 metres."[98]

When the Lancashire Fusiliers approached Tekke Bay, the Ottoman riflemen defending the beachhead waited for the attackers to pour out of their vessels and struggle in the barbed wire before opening fire.[99] By dusk the British had made progress, but not without real cost: Tekke Bay's sandy beach was stained dark red by the blood of some 600 casualties out of the 957 who made the landing.[100] Six Victoria Crosses—the most distinguished British military decoration—were famously won "before breakfast."[101] The Ottomans fought with similar heroism. In one letter home, an Ottoman soldier named Ismail detailed the courage of his comrades: "[T]he earth trembled from the thunder of our rifles, and our holy Hodja, who had previously prayed with us, sprang from the trenches like a youngster although his hair was white, and he certainly was more than one hundred years old, and we stormed forwards behind him swinging our rifle butts and what showed itself before us was killed without mercy."[102]

When the First Royal Dublin Fusiliers approached Ertugral Bay in the early morning of April 25, "It was a lovely spring day, the sea glassy, the sun a blood-red orb over the Asian coast."[103] But when they came ashore, supported by troops in the refitted collier *River Clyde,* they were devastated by Ottoman rifle fire. So impassioned was the defense that one Turkish sergeant named Mehmet even charged a British sailor with a rock after his weapon jammed.[104] Patrolling over the battle, Royal Navy Air Commodore Charles Samson reported that "the sea for a distance of about 50 yards from the beach was absolutely red with blood."[105] An Ottoman major of the Ninth Division described the action: "The fire changed the colour of the sea with the blood from the bodies of the enemy—a sea whose colour had remained the same for years. Shells and machine gun bullets fell ceaselessly at the points where rifle fire was observed but, in spite of this, heavy fire was opened from all our trenches. . . . The shore became full of enemy corpses, like a shoal of fish."[106]

Eventually, despite their fierce determination, the outnumbered Ottomans broke during the afternoon of April 26, fighting a tough retiring action that slowed the British advance northward.[107] These Ottoman troops gave the British pause as they streamed out into the "olive groves on the lower slopes of Achi Baba."[108] By the time the British launched a full-scale attack on April 28, the primary objective of Hamilton's Cape Helles campaign, Achi Baba Ridge, had been transformed into an invincible Ottoman fortress.[109]

With the initial seaborne assault checked by the Ottoman troops, Gallipoli assumed the familiar, predictable rhythm of trench warfare that defined the European theater, replete with scrambles over the parapet, futile charges through no-man's-land, and hand-to-hand fighting near the enemy's trench. Hoping to smash through and sweep away their enemies, and fueled by the prospect of near victory, each side ordered ever-larger charges, battering the other with waves of rifle fodder. It was "a caricature of all that was tactically wrong with World War I. . . . Great bravery led to incredible carnage."[110] In the Mediterranean summer heat it was not long before rotting corpses announced the front from a great distance. Amplifying the stench was the narrow distance between the trenches, purposefully dug close by the Ottomans to escape British naval bombardments. So ubiquitous were the corpses that one New Zealand officer was able to calculate the distance between the two front-line trenches by adding up the corpses lying head to foot between them.[111]

In the midst of this killing, or perhaps because of it, the best of the human spirit often shone through. A British corporal, Charles Livingstone, described an armistice called in late May 1915 in order to clear the corpses. As with the Christmas Day truce of 1914 on the Western front, during which German and English troops serenaded one another with Christmas carols and even struck up a soccer match before resuming combat, the armistice between the Ottomans and the English that May was observed with preternatural politeness. "We stood together some 12 feet apart, quite friendly, exchanging coins and other articles," reports Livingstone. "A Turk gave me a beautiful Sultan's guard's belt buckle made of brass with a silver star and crescent embossed with the Sultan's scroll in Arabic. . . . Our troops carried the dead Turkish bodies over the dividing line and the Turkish troops did the same for our dead."[112] A similar sentiment is encountered in the reflections of Captain Aubrey Herbert, who himself spoke Turkish and had been instrumental in bringing about the truce. "About a dozen Turks came out. I chaffed them, and said they would shoot me [*sic*] next day. They said, in horrified chorus: 'God forbid!' . . . Then the Australians began coming up, and said: 'Goodbye, old chap; good luck!' And the Turks said: 'Smiling may you go and smiling come again.' "[113]

That camaraderie extended beyond the truce itself. On Kereves Dere in Cape Helles, near the Dardanelles, sits a monument to Lieutenant Colonel Hasan Bey, killed by a wounded Frenchman. His final words: "Don't kill the Frenchman—he did his duty."[114]

The action on the peninsula was punctuated by several major, escalating battles, in which more and more troops were committed. In all of these attacks, and in several that were to follow, both sides failed to appreciate the defense dominance brought on by a shift in firepower—specifically, machine guns and improved rifles—and in method, including barbed-wire protection for well-dug trenches. Interconnecting fields of fire made assaults difficult, as Lieutenant Colonel Mehmet Sefk bemoaned after one fruitless frontal assault in mid-May: "The line which they held was a bent line with indentations and salients which defended each other by flanking fire. . . . It was a perfect defensive position with ammunition and bomb dumps; arms, especially machine guns; perfect and completely adequate manpower; with naval aid immediately to the rear."[115] The British calculated the futility of conventional charges on Cape Helles: on June 4, the British conquered up to 500 yards in return for 6,500 casualties; on June 21, 200 yards was paid for by 2,500 casualties; on June 28, 1,000 yards required 3,800 casualties; and on July 12, 400 yards meant 6,000 casualties.[116]

Even so, Liman von Sanders identified British hesitancy in following up their attacks as a key factor in the outcome of the campaign: "It was fortunate for us that the British attacks never lasted more than one day, and were punctuated by pauses of several days. Otherwise it would have been impossible to replenish our artillery ammunition."[117] A similar conclusion was reached by Churchill, who was forced to resign as First Lord of the Admiralty with the collapse of the Liberal government in May 1915: "Time was the dominating factor. The extraordinary mobility and unexpectedness of amphibious power can, as has been shown, only be exerted in strict relation to limited periods of time. . . . A week lost was about the same as a division. Three divisions in February could have occupied the Gallipoli Peninsula with little fighting. . . . Eleven might have sufficed at the beginning of July. Fourteen were to prove insufficient on August 7."[118]

As Churchill's comments reveal, General Hamilton's final gambit came in August. He proposed an assault on the Sari Bair range, including the peak of Chunuk Bair inland from Ari Burnu, where ANZAC had identified weaknesses in the Ottoman lines.[119] Concomitantly, reinforced with fresh divisions, Hamilton planned an attack on the large amphitheater of Suvla Plain, north of Ari Burnu, which was thought lightly defended.[120] This two-pronged attack included one hundred thousand men at three fronts.[121]

Liman von Sanders anticipated an attack—Berlin had warned him as much on July 22—but he did not know its location.[122] The one Ottoman officer who did was the newly promoted Colonel Mustafa Kemal.[123] Recognizing the Sari Bair range as central to the entire island, he argued vehemently that an advance from the northeast at Suvla Plain, with little opposition, could outflank his entire division and take Chunuk Bair.[124]

Hamilton attacked during the night of August 6.[125] It was the flanking maneuver Mustafa Kemal had feared and predicted. As the Ottoman troops marched on the evening of August 7, he famously telephoned with headquarters: "There is one moment left," he instructed. "If we lose that moment, we are faced with a general catastrophe."[126] Asked what he was proposing, he replied, "A unified command. The only remedy is to put all the available troops under my command."[127] When Liman von Sanders's chief of staff asked, "Won't that be too many?" Kemal replied, "It will be too few."[128] Given command, Kemal raced his men to a summit called Tekke Tepe, and to Anafarta Ridge near Suvla Bay, arriving a half hour before the enemy. He then ordered a massive counterattack.[129] The fighting was fierce, and most of his men were exhausted. Kemal's chief of staff, Major Izzetin, described the scene as "critical. . . . The divisional adjutant sustained a grave wound as he went to find out what was happening. His assistant Hakki has been taken to hospital at Lapseki suffering from dysentery. . . . There is no one left and work has stopped in the headquarters."[130] At one point in the fighting for Anafarta Ridge, Kemal ordered a cavalry commander into action, who assented but then hesitated for a moment.[131] Kemal called him back, heatedly demanding, "Did you understand what I said?" The officer responded, "Yes, Sir. . . . You ordered us to die."[132]

Many did die, but in the process the Ottomans broke the enemy line at Tekke Tepe, killing virtually every enemy officer and overrunning the enemy battalion and brigade headquarters.[133] As Kemal later reflected: "All men, all creatures suffer from tiredness. But men have a mental force which allows them to go on without resting."[134] By going beyond exhaustion, the

Battle of Suvla Bay had been won, yet Kemal chose to dig in and halt his advance, for looming in the distance lay another existential danger: the attackers' advance at Sari Bair.[135]

At Sari Bair Kemal planned a major frontal assault from Chunuk Bair itself. Stepping forward, he raised his riding whip to signal his troops, who poured over their trenches and stormed as little as twenty to thirty yards into Hamilton's front lines, breaking the enemy front.[136] Both sides fought valiantly at Chunuk Bair, enveloped in the smoke of British naval support. Kemal himself remained in the line of fire giving orders when shrapnel suddenly exploded near his chest. As if by fate, it shattered his pocket watch and left him unwounded.[137] Others were not so lucky; asked by Kemal where his men were, one officer replied, "Here are my troops. . . . Those who lie dead."[138] Another Ottoman officer who marveled at the courage of his men later reminisced about the "solemn wonderment" with which he watched men charge the British lines on Gallipoli: "If you have gone through battle and known the havoc that shell fire causes among men and things, you cannot but stand in awe at the folly and courage of line after line of marching men, starting bravely down a hill-side as the first faint streaks of dawn break through the lingering darkness."[139]

By August 10 the battle for Chunuk Bair was decided, and with it the Gallipoli campaign.[140] Having shot their bolt, the British-led force would withdraw under cover of darkness in January 1916. Remaining behind for the remainder of the war would be almost 58,000 of Hamilton's men and 66,000 Ottoman troops.[141] "Casualties at Gallipoli were, in proportion, similar to those in the great battles in France: approximately 210,000 Allied and 120,000 Ottoman casualties. In the end, the strategic position was exactly as it had been."[142] Death had the victory.[143]

The Gallipoli campaign had inspired real fear in Istanbul. The German news correspondent for the *Kölnische Zeitung* in Istanbul, Harry Stürmer, would later confide that "money and archives were hurried off from Constantinople to Asia, and a German officer in Constantinople gave me the entertaining information that he had really seriously thought of hiring a window in the Grande Rue de Péra so that he and his family might watch the triumphal entry of the Entente troops."[144] Instead, it was the CUP that organized celebrations to take place in the Istanbul streets as Ottoman morale surged at the news of "great victory."[145]

PERSIA

Eight decades before Hamilton's last stand at Gallipoli, a young intelligence officer of the British East India Company's Sixth Bengal Native Light Cavalry, Captain Arthur Conolly, described the great-power rivalry unfolding between London and Saint Petersburg across Central and Southwest Asia as "the great game."[146] Conolly was soon thereafter beheaded by the emir of Bukhara, in modern-day Uzbekistan, for volunteering to rescue a fellow officer who had attempted to solicit the emir's assistance against the Russians.[147] But Conolly's description of the developing great-power competition outlived him and became his permanent legacy. Indeed, ever since he coined the phrase, "the great game"—or "tournament of shadows," as it is described in Russia—has been known to encompass the vast nineteenth-century strategic rivalry between the British and Russian Crowns, culminating in the Anglo-Russian Convention of 1907, in which Russia and Great Britain divided Persia into exclusive spheres of influence: Russia in the north and Britain in the southeast. Eight years later, in March 1915, Tsar Nicholas II secretly updated the Constantinople Agreement by ceding the remaining Persian zones to Britain as a quid pro quo for British postwar assurances in the Sea of Marmara, on the western shore of the Bosporus, and over Istanbul.[148] With the exchange of a few clandestine diplomatic communiqués—crafted without consulting those most affected in Persia—the fate of an entire people was sealed.

Even without these maneuvers, however, it can be posited that Persia could not have withstood the international aftershocks of Sarajevo. Persia's geopolitical footprint, standing sentry over the Gulf and stretching from the Ottoman and Russian borders in the northwest to colonial British India in the southeast, made it as a central player in southwest Asia. If Persia went the way of Istanbul, crucial Triple Entente war supplies from Ukrainian grain to Mesopotamian oil would be imperiled.[149] Persia's attempt at neutrality—officially announced on November 1, 1914—was therefore immediately subsumed by the cold reality of power politics; that very day, British landing parties were in action steaming toward southern Persia.[150] Their eagerness is explained largely by the presence of that great commodity of the twentieth century, crude oil.

At the turn of the twentieth century, the Englishman William Knox D'Arcy wrestled some five hundred thousand square miles in drilling concessions from the Persian government and then struck oil near Shushtar, in southern Persia.[151] With the conversion of the British Navy from coal to oil, then–First Lord of the Admiralty Churchill acquired a controlling stake in the Anglo-Persian Oil Company (today's BP) for the British government. With the British Isles' most powerful force dependent on southern Persia, the strategic imperative of maintaining British dominance in the Gulf littoral was fixed.

On the eve of war, as Vienna's ultimatum expired in Belgrade, Persia's public finances were still in bad shape—key economic concessions to Britain and Russia had created a natural parallel to the economic plight of Istanbul. On the security front, the Swedish and Persian gendarmes of Ahmad Shah, the last Qajar ruler of Persia, were slowly extending their control across Iran.[152] These checked the influence of Russian Cossacks in the north and preempted any British temptations in the south, but at the time of *Goeben*'s foray into the Black Sea Tehran was still struggling to extend its writ across the Persian countryside.[153]

Despite Persian insistence on neutrality, British forces moved with alacrity at the outbreak of the war to occupy the south Persian province of Khuzistan, which constitutes the critical northern boundary of the Gulf. In doing so, and by occupying the southern Mesopotamian city of Basra, the British guaranteed their dominance over Khuzistan's abundant oil fields and safeguarded the Anglo-Persian Oil Company's lengthy pipeline extending from the wells near the city of Shushtar to the refineries on the island of Abadan. By the summer of 1915, the British had installed themselves throughout Khuzistan and augmented their garrison at Bushahr, the critical port city on the eastern bank of the Gulf.[154]

With the British methodically taking over southern Persia, the Russians descended from the Caucasus to claim their agreed-upon share. The British may have disembarked their men in Khuzistan, but the Russians consolidated their troops in Persian Azerbaijan while redeploying some forces to the Caucasus to check Enver Pasha's strike at Sarikamish. The upshot of these two moves, straddling Ottoman Anatolia while drawing off men and thinning the consolidated force, was to invite an Ottoman attack on Persian Azerbaijan. When that Ottoman attack did come, however, it was overshadowed by the central battle raging in the Caucasus.[155] After successfully defending Sarikamish and even threatening Erzurum, the Russians were free to counterattack, recapturing Tabriz just east of Lake Urmia in late January 1915.[156]

In May 1915 Russian Cossacks disembarked at the Caspian Sea port of Enzeli and marched to Qazvin, 140 kilometers west of Tehran, causing alarm in the defenseless capital.[157] Russian activity in the north directly affected Tehran throughout the war, owing to its proximity. As in Istanbul during the tensest moments of the Gallipoli campaign, Russian action in the northwest reverberated like an earthquake, strengthening and weakening political factions in the capital. When the Cossacks left Qazvin and steered a westerly course toward Tehran to signal Saint Petersburg's disapproval of Persian policies, the government debated its future prospects while shopkeepers assessed the fate of the Persian empire.[158]

In fact, the landing of a newly formed Russian Expeditionary Corps unleashed such alarm that the young Ahmad Shah felt compelled to install pro-Russian ministers, confiscate Ottoman material and men, and accept the patronage of Russian and British officials, while pro-Allied officials fled to Qom and onward to Kermanshah.[159] This military-political interplay is a central thread weaving together the Persian canvas, and it greatly explains the instability of successive Persian governments during the war years. Less than one year into the Great War, then, the "great game" had been partially revised and updated: the Russians controlled Azerbaijan and the north, the British lorded over Khuzistan and the south, and an Anglo-Russian condominium cordoned off eastern Persia.

Although Ottoman hopes for Persian Azerbaijan foundered in the snows of Sarikamish, the German and Ottoman powers did hold one powerful trump card in wartime Persia: Persian sympathy for the Triple Alliance, which yielded a variety of outcomes, from subtle pro-German and pro-Ottoman governmental policies to the granting of unencumbered Ottoman passage through Persian territory.[160] This was unsurprising given that in 1915 Kaiser Wilhelm had no large-scale forces in Asia and had carefully cultivated his public image in the Middle East.[161] In fact, German agents had miraculously discovered "an astonishing new family tree" for the Hohenzollerns, descending from the Prophet Muhammad's sister, and earnestly spread the news of the Kaiser's conversion to Islam after a holy trip to Mecca. The Kaiser's supposed conversion fit neatly with the Triple Alliance propaganda of an Anglo-Russian crusade against Islam.[162] The seeds of rebellion were therefore already sown early in the war; since British and Russian actions did nothing to discourage this Persian perspective, under German-Ottoman care it blossomed into an outright uprising.

With Ottoman reversals in the Caucasus extinguishing all hope for a breakthrough in Persian Azerbaijan, Berlin and Istanbul turned to the world of unconventional warfare. Utilizing the political cover provided by sympathetic political parties and playing on the narrative of imperialism, local German and Ottoman officers won the assistance of many key players, including members among the gendarmerie force, their pro-German Swedish officers, and several rural tribal authorities.[163] The most legendary of the German agents was Wilhelm Wassmuss, known to the world today as "Wassmuss of Persia" and the "German Lawrence." Wassmuss's energy and enthusiasm for Persian and Iraqi culture reflected an overall romanticism for the Islamic world, which was equaled only by his knowledge of the tribal landscape dotting the deserts and mountains from Kut to Kabul. Through his efforts—and those of others—agitation against Allied personnel grew from a petty nuisance into a regular menace. By the fall of 1915 German agents had arranged for an assassination attempt on T. G. Graham, the British consul in Isfahan, prompting the British and Russian representatives to quit the city altogether, and by late autumn, the German representative at Shiraz had succeeded in arresting the British consulate's chief officer, Major W. F. T. O'Connor, before expelling the British from the city.[164]

As rebellions spread across a string of cities, Wassmuss moved "among the south Persian tribes like a native, playing particularly on the anti-British resentments of the large south-Persian tribe, the Tangistani."[165] These attempts to spark resistance throughout the Persian countryside aimed to embolden tribal actors, most importantly the anti-British Qashqais, which one German official hoped might ignite native rebellions "from the Caucasus to Calcutta."[166] Antagonisms over policy between Ottomans and Germans sometimes handicapped these efforts, however, and German agents often misinterpreted the indigenous complexities of local tribal society. Moreover, the Shah's unwillingness to leave Tehran in the face of advancing Russian columns to join the resistance greatly weakened the potential for, and the legitimacy of, an uprising.

Despite the Anglo-Russian thrust eastward to cordon off the Persian heartland and ostensibly shield Afghanistan and India from any threat, major pockets of unrest existed in Persia, requiring the Russians and British to apply pressure in Tehran. By late 1915, spurred on by rumors of an uprising in Tehran and the threat of irregular troops, a Russian Expeditionary Force was dispatched under the command of General Nikolai Baratoff to crush the Persian irregulars.[167] By spring 1916 the Russians had swept through several tribes and put an end to German interference.[168] Indeed, it was the investment of Russian boots on the ground that outmuscled the German irregular campaign.

Having lost influence in Tehran, and with its irregular forces subdued, it was now Berlin's turn to fret about a formal Iranian war entry alongside the Anglo-Russian alliance. In no uncertain terms, Berlin communicated to Persia that if it entered the war as a hostile power, its fate would mirror that of Serbia, once Germany's victory in Europe freed it to turn its wrath on India and Persia.[169] Hemmed in by tens of thousands of Russian troops in the north, a major British action in neighboring Mesopotamia, unruly tribes in its hinterlands, and German diplomatic threats, Ahmad Shah maintained his tenuous neutrality while bowing to military realities with a pro-Russian cabinet and the dismissal of pro-German Swedish gendarme officers.[170]

In the south, the British commander General Percy Sykes organized the South Persia Rifles as a local force to mask his numerical deficiencies, since the majority of British soldiers were tied up in neighboring Mesopotamia.[171] The South Persia Rifles was in places deeply unpopular, but it did free Anglo-Indian forces for the Mesopotamian campaign. In April 1916, however, a British disaster in Mesopotamia—the surrender of a thirteen-thousand-strong Anglo-Indian garrison at Kut—buoyed an Ottoman offensive into western Persia.[172] In the political seesaw of Tehran, news of the Ottoman advance unleashed concern once more, this time among British and Russian sympathizers.[173] Russia responded by pressing an attack into Azerbaijan, thus threatening Ottoman communication lines and forcing a decisive confrontation near Urmia, which Russia won.[174] With the Ottoman sword dulled, Baratoff then forced the Ottomans westward. By March 1917, as Baghdad surrendered to the British, the Ottomans were busily evacuating Persia, a process they completed entirely by the end of April.[175]

The operational themes of irregular warfare and insurgency burst onto the Persian political scene because of the great variety of Persian society spread across an expansive geography. The diversity of Persia's political culture was a natural outgrowth of its tribal configuration. Tribes resented foreign interference—be it Ottoman or British—and therefore seized opportune moments for open confrontation, as they did during the apparently successful 1918 German offensive on the western front. In the reminiscences of British soldiers, the shifting sands of tribal cooperation—often tied to developments on the battlefield—are a regular theme and perpetual worry. Late in the war the British responded to tribal rebellions with a pacification campaign that targeted essentially any tribe within their broader sphere of influence, a sphere that gravitated steadily north in the aftermath of the Russian Revolution.[176]

On March 15, 1917, Tsar Nicholas II renounced his throne, but it was not until December 3, after the October Revolution, that Russia truly shifted its stance on Persia, formally rejecting Tsarist Russia's policies toward Iran as imperialist and interventionist. Moreover, the new Russian government published the secret March 1915 Anglo-Russian Constantinople Agreement, to the great embarrassment of London. Having deployed tens of thousands of men to conquer Persia, Russia now withdrew its Russian Expeditionary Corps; of the seventy-five-thousand-man force, only two thousand remained in Persia by the end of 1917.[177] For Britain the resulting vacuum was irresistible, and in late 1917 it launched an invasion of western Persia from Mesopotamia and occupied eastern Persia up to the Russian border. Powerless against the British airplane and the armored car, former Russian strongholds transferred easily to British control.[178] By the summer of 1918, a fifty-five-thousand-strong Anglo-Indian occupation force, supplemented by local allies and commanded by General Lionel Dunsterville, was master of Iran.

The British conquest of northern Persia transformed the Persian empire into a British "semi-colony."[179] The indignity of that de facto colonial status came in the wake of mass death and famine, which continued into the immediate postwar period. At the mercy of military events, its politics conducted at gunpoint, Tehran was doomed to a series of short-lived governments while squeezed from both sides by the Great Powers. The Persian agricultural cycle was destroyed by conflict and ground to a halt, leading to mass starvation. "Invading armies had ruined farmland and irrigation works, crops and livestock were stolen or destroyed, and peasants had been taken from their fields and forced to serve as laborers in the various armies.

Famine killed as many as two million Iranians out of a population of little more than ten million while an influenza pandemic killed additional tens of thousands."[180] In a sad irony, the Persian Empire that had chosen neutrality at the outset of war suffered millions of casualties.

MESOPOTAMIA

The large British presence in Persia highlighted what was simultaneously one of Britain's greatest strengths and greatest vulnerabilities: its global communications system. Gliding through the Mediterranean and Suez before rounding the Indian subcontinent, passing through the Straits of Malacca, and turning north after reaching Singapore on the tip of the Malay peninsula, the Royal Navy was permanently attuned to any threats arising between the British Isles and Hong Kong, along the Chinese mainland.

The German-Ottoman interest in Muslim-majority Persia, Arabia, and Afghanistan therefore alarmed Britain.[181] Most crucially, although Britain reigned supreme on the high seas, Ottoman control of Mesopotamia threatened to open a hostile land corridor to India.[182] Indeed, "Civil and military planners in India considered the Gulf to be a vital flank on the sea route to India."[183] In retrospect, the prospect of a widespread regional rebellion opening such a corridor was highly unlikely, but at the time the specter of revolt unleashed genuine concern among Britain's 125,000-man contingent—of whom only three-fifths were soldiers—deployed among millions of Muslim Indians.[184] Moreover, the petroleum wells that cursed southern Persia in 1914 also doomed Mesopotamia to great-power competition. With the outbreak of World War I, an already heated geopolitical rivalry between Berlin and London, carried on by regional proxies and evident in commercial competition, intensified in Mesopotamia.

Mesopotamia is one level plain of sandy desert, divided by the snaking Tigris River, the winding Euphrates River, and their resulting alluvium.[185] From their origins in the mountains of northeastern Turkey, these rivers descend into the Mesopotamian plateau, breathing life into their surroundings before draining into the marshes of southern Iraq.[186] Predictably, each spring the melting snows of the Taurus and Zagros Mountains spawned river torrents that flooded vast stretches of desert, transforming the landscape into a "quagmire of greasy mud."[187] Some ten thousand square miles could be underwater by late spring. Not until summer would the water begin to recede, usually reaching its nadir around October. However, while both the Tigris and Euphrates act as dual arteries animating the Mesopotamian desert, only the Tigris could sustain river transport. In high-water flood season, vessels with a draught of five feet could traverse its length, but even then only with a skilled navigator who knew its sandbanks and meandering channels. During low-water season vessels of no more than a draught of three feet dared attempt the journey.[188]

This dichotomy of the riverine Iraqi provinces matches their climactic extremes.[189] From May through October unbearable heat blankets the area, which can transition quickly into a shivering cold from December through March.[190] Moreover, the arid desert contrasts sharply with the swampy humidity of the marshy south, where the geographic key to the Gulf, Basra, lies—five hundred miles downstream from the ancient Mesopotamian capital of Baghdad. Basra was known in the Western imagination and referenced in British soldiering accounts as Ali Baba's fabled city, but for all its literary eminence it was in reality a weakly outfitted port city ill-suited for any significant military expedition at the start of the war.[191]

Major J. D. Crowdy, who served Great Britain in the Mesopotamia campaign, arrived in Basra in January 1916. It was raining the day of his arrival, and although he wore nailed boots, "the mud was so slippery that I could hardly get along, while my companions could do little more than slide."[192] Even at that late date Crowdy bemoaned the lack of "even a vestige of metalled or corrugated track. There is insufficient labour and barge accommodation to unload all the steamers anchored here; at one time, and that is not so long ago either, there were no ramps available for disembarking animals!"[193] Major Roger Evans similarly relays that Basra's harbor works, troop facilities, and quays were virtually nonexistent.[194]

Yet despite its dilapidated state and the unhealthy nearby marshes, seizing Basra was vital for Britain, since Basra stood astride the confluence of the Tigris and Euphrates, known as the Shatt al-Arab, and guarded the Anglo-Persian Oil Company pipeline. The British envisioned occupying southern Mesopotamia as a defensive phalanx around Persian Ahvaz and Mesopotamian Abadan.[195] Anything beyond that was "liable to be severely hindered—in the winter by rain and mud, in the spring by floods, in the summer by heat and sickness, in the autumn by exhaustion following upon the summer, at all times by the extreme difficulty of maintaining an Army in a country which has neither communications nor local resources."[196]

On November 5, 1914, the Sixth Indian Division "steamed across the bar of the Shatt al-Arab into Turkish waters," occupied the old Ottoman fort at Fao, and advanced on Basra.[197] For Istanbul, preoccupied by an offensive at the Suez Canal and warily eyeing Russia in the Caucasus, the Gulf constituted a secondary theater.[198] At the sight of the approaching British, the local commander, Colonel Subhi Bey, ordered a general retreat.[199] From Basra, the Sixth Poona Division set off in December to consolidate control of the surrounding region. In doing so, as A. J. Barker relates, the force met stiff resistance, including from guns concealed in the "thick belt of date palms fringing the river" Tigris.[200] These ambushes were intended to protect the strategic town of al-Qurna, which occupied the fork of the Euphrates and Tigris. Eventually, the British Indian Division overwhelmed the Ottoman position, awaited the arrival of another Indian division, and consolidated their forces into the newly formed Indian Second Army Corps.[201]

To the great benefit of the Anglo-Indian force, but to the deep consternation of the Ottomans, the Second Corps formed just in time to meet a massive Ottoman counterattack from Nasiriyya, commanded by Lieutenant Colonel Suleiman Askeri. In April 1915 Askeri attacked for over three days in an attempt to turn and roll up the British left flank in the Euphrates River Valley and push on to Basra, but his efforts shattered in the face of the reinforced Indian defenses.[202] During retreat, tribesmen turned on the Ottomans, recasting an Ottoman defeat into disaster. Despondent, Suleiman committed suicide.

Having swallowed Basra and retained it in the face of Ottoman counterattack, the British appetite might have been satiated. Instead, fanciful aspirations of sacking the minarets of Baghdad, glittering some five hundred miles upstream, appeared as enticing as a Mesopotamian desert mirage. This meant supplying a large-scale expeditionary force operating in hostile desert territory and reliant on rickety infrastructure. At regional command in India, the allure of taking Baghdad as a means of augmenting British prestige in the Muslim world overwhelmed any on-the-spot military reservations. In operational terms, the British commander in theater, General John Nixon, voiced such ambitions by arguing for a forward perimeter to protect Qurna. The issue was decided: Britain would advance into the Mesopotamian heartland.

In the short run, the dangers of attack were disguised by the thrill of victory. At the end of May 1915, the commander of the Sixth Division, General Charles Townshend, attacked up the Tigris. Relieved of their misery at Qurna, where the conditions were truly awful, Townshend's men charged with anticipation into the surrounding marshes, plodding through thick weeds and high water toward the enemy force, commanded by Halim Bey.[203] While flooding had slowed the British maneuver, it also had inhibited the construction of Ottoman defensive works, leaving the Ottomans exposed to strafing biplanes and gunboats. As described in virtually every account of the action, small units of men, subsequently known as "Townshend's Regatta," climbed aboard local boats, called bellums, to carry the battle through weeds and marshes and force an Ottoman retreat. Aboard HMS *Espiegle,* and after grounding her, HMS *Comet,* Townshend and a small detachment of no more than one hundred sailors and soldiers offered relentless pursuit of the Ottoman retreat, bluffing their way up the Tigris to Amara.[204] In the process Townshend overtook elements of the Ottoman retreat, which disintegrated as the gunboats approached. As the British saw it, by June 1915 they successfully had fought their way from Basra, the "Venice of the East" and home port of Sinbad the Sailor, past Qurna and the biblical Garden of Eden to conquer Amara, the purported Garden of Tears.

Brimming with confidence, General Nixon shifted his campaign plan from defensive consolidation into offensive warfare.[205] This fit neatly with the outlook of the British political officers who worked the India portfolio. For them, maintaining the strategic initiative and elevating British prestige in the Muslim world were like two blazing suns that never set on British strategy. The British riverine adventure was on.

In what should have been a warning, the British apparatus struggled to supply Amara, which had compelled Townshend to slow his pursuit in the first place. Despite its sleek elegance, Amara turned into a cockpit of deprivation and disease much like the British strongholds downriver. With heat reaching 120°F (48°C), and British garrisons poorly supported once they settled, the town became a living hell.[206] Soldiers on sentry duty were known to faint from heat stroke, while patients recovered in inadequate medical facilities overwhelmed by cases of dysentery, paratyphoid, and fever.[207] With his memory still fresh, an officer in the Royal Army Medical Corps wrote, "I do not know of any other malady so dramatic, or so painful to witness, as heat-stroke, with the exception, perhaps, of acute cholera."[208] During the campaign British officers recorded cases of "men going mad from the heat, stripping off their clothes and dancing about in No Man's Land until they were shot by the enemy."[209]

Nevertheless, by August 1915, the Union Jack flew over Basra, Amara, Qurna, and Nasiriyya, stoking Nixon's confidence to seek his next objective, Kut al-Amara.[210] Upriver ninety miles from the British at Amara, Kut sits at the intersection of the Tigris and the Shatt al-Hayy, which connects the Tigris to the Euphrates near Nasiriyya. As such, Kut represented a worthy prize in the riverine web of Mesopotamia, which is why waiting at Kut was the Ottoman commander, Colonel Nureddin Bey. Relying on ramshackle, improvised supply lines and with thirteen thousand men, Townshend left Amara in late September 1915. By the end of the month he had managed to outflank Nureddin's Ottoman defenses at Kut cleverly, but the Ottomans rallied to prepared positions in Salman Pak at Ctesiphon, eighty miles above Kut.[211] In a replay of his exploits at Qurna, Townshend launched a pursuit, but his attempts ground down in the shallows of the Tigris with his men exhausted, and his administration buckled.[212] Recognizing these deficiencies, Townshend pulled up while Nureddin installed his men into defenses and received reinforcements.

Tempted by victory, the British eventually pressed forward to Salman Pak, the ancient Parthian and Sassanid capital of Ctesiphon. For the British to succeed 463 miles from Basra, nothing less than a decisive victory at Salman Pak would suffice. Nixon even counted on taking Baghdad, thirty-five miles behind the Ottoman lines, to resupply and provision his men.[213] As the civil engineer General George Buchanan wrote, so confident was Nixon that he "even anticipated evacuating his wounded to Baghdad."[214] Bedazzled by Baghdad, and ascribing superhuman qualities to their men, Nixon and Townshend planned for victory and nothing else. As Major Evans observed: "If strategically the situation contained possibilities of perils, administratively it had all the elements of disaster."[215]

Between the British and Baghdad waited thousands of entrenched and motivated Ottomans under the shadow of the great Arch of Ctesiphon. For generations before the Islamic conquest, the great arch had epitomized Sassanid splendor and stood sentry as Sassanid soldiers ventured forth to defend their Persian empire.[216] To Colonel Nureddin's men, and those of his newly arrived deputy, Colonel Khalil Bey, Ctesiphon was known as Salman Pak, the final resting place of Salman the Persian, a follower of the Prophet known as the first Persian convert to Islam. As such, Salman Pak imbued the city with religious significance and recalled past glories. When Townshend ordered his attack on November 22, the sacred legacy of Salman Pak combined with the martial valor of Ctesiphon to yield an impregnable fortress.[217] By that evening, the British had sustained 4,500 casualties, forcing Townshend to consolidate his remaining forces and guard against a potential counterattack.[218]

What followed was one of the more difficult scenes of the campaign. The British wounded were hauled away on iron mule carts[219]—"iron frameworks suspended between two iron-tired wheels, drawn by mules and driven by an Indian driver" with "no springs in their make-up."[220] Rather than endure such transport across the rough desert, despite their broken limbs some men flung themselves off the carts and crawled across the desert floor, pocketed with irrigation channels, toward ships where they were "stuffed . . . closer than hounds are packed into a hound-van . . . to endure the voyage to Basra."[221] Many of the men did not have their dressings examined until they reached Basra, up to thirteen days later.[222] So unsanitary were the conditions that one officer in Basra recalled seeing one ship arrive looking "as if she was festooned with ropes. The stench when she was close was quite definite, and I found that what I mistook for ropes were dried stalactites of human faeces."[223] In Basra, Major Crowdy reported in early 1916 that "the hospitals are in tents and mat huts . . . situated in veritable seas of mud, while the mat huts leak."[224]

Colonel Nureddin, too, had suffered tremendous casualties but his supply lines had been shortened considerably by his earlier retreat up the Tigris. At Salman Pak he insisted on standing his ground, forcing General Townshend to turn away first.[225] It was now Nureddin's turn to pursue the retreating British. For days he pressed Townshend as he returned to Kut, screened by cavalry while protecting his flotilla.[226] After a brief halt at Aziziyeh to recover, the British march resumed until the Sixth Division finally collapsed into Kut on December 3, 1915. Townshend's decision to hold at Kut was meant to salvage British prestige, rescue his supplies, hold the strategic confluence of the Tigris and Hayy rivers, and refit his exhausted men.[227] On the assumption that he could be quickly resupplied, thus justifying his position hundreds of miles from Basra, Townshend considered the retreat to Kut a brief interlude before a renewed offensive could be mounted on Baghdad. His forces simply needed to reorganize and await their resupply.

In truth, with his Anglo-Indian force stretched from Basra to Kut and tottering on a flimsy supply base, Townshend would find himself hard pressed to sustain his defensive position, let alone plan a new offensive. In pursuit, Nureddin recognized his opportunity and moved downstream past Kut on December 7, 1915.[228] The blockade of the thirteen-thousand-man British force had begun.

To rescue the stranded force, General Nixon turned to "a distinguished Sapper officer, Lieutenant General Sir Fenton Aylmer."[229] The recipient of the Victoria Cross as a captain in 1891, Aylmer was asked to do the extraordinary once more in leading a hastily cobbled-together force without adequate river transport against an entrenched enemy of superior numbers. Aylmer advanced up the Tigris without his divisions assembled, a proper corps staff in place, medical arrangements completed, or adequate river transport prepared—that is, he was asked to bend the logistical laws of modern warfare and dislodge a heavily entrenched and emboldened enemy while his reinforcements scrambled in echelon to join the fight.[230] Starting off on his mission, virtually the only thing Aylmer did have to satisfaction was his orders.

Aylmer's Relief Force, as it became known, comprised twenty thousand men, including the Seventh Meerut (Indian) Division.[231] This relief force faced a rapidly strengthening Ottoman defense arrayed along the Tigris under the command of the Prussian strategist, General Colmar von der Goltz, who appointed Khalil Bey as his field commander after sacking Nureddin for fighting an earlier delaying action of which he disapproved.[232] As Aylmer's men flung themselves toward Kut with increasing desperation, the clatter of gunfire piercing the air, the Ottomans stood their ground resolutely; despite repeated artillery barrages and bayonet charges, the Ottomans refused to bend. By January 22, after yet another futile British charge, a truce called to collect the wounded confirmed the British failure. In poor health, Nixon had been relieved of command, and after one last battle, so too was Aylmer.[233]

In Crowdy's account, the British wounded "had to lie in the rain where they had been put, covered by a waterproof sheet only, in this icy wind.

Mind you, we passed barge loads of wounded on our way up, laid out just like this, exposed to the wind and rain."[234] As described by the medical officer writing under the pseudonym Martin Swayne, "The appearance of the sick and wounded defies description. Like the Gallipoli lot, only worse, they were lean, gaunt, haggard skeletons, hollow-eyed, with rivulets of perspiration furrowing the dirt of their faces."[235] Even so, as on the other fronts, a soldiering camaraderie deriving from the common travails of the Mesopotamia campaign managed to dull the pain and suffering somewhat. For example, infantrymen cooperated to mitigate the risk of drawing water from the river: "Whoever wanted water stood on his parapet and waved; if one of his opponents got up and answered the wave, all was well and the man went down and got his water. On the other hand, if there was no response, the man got under cover again recognizing that there was nothing doing at that time, probably owing to the inconvenient presence of an officer."[236]

After an interlude during which the Anglo-Indian forces were consolidated at around thirty thousand men and the wounded were cleared from the battlefront, General George Gorringe inherited Aylmer's impossible predicament, made more difficult as Ottoman reinforcements reached the trenches.[237] In early April, Gorringe's final assault failed to close the gap separating his men from Townshend. The fate of Kut was sealed.

From January to April 1916 the Ottomans suffered ten thousand battlefield casualties. By comparison, the British lost well over double that in their relief efforts, and all for naught, since Townshend's thirteen-thousand-strong force remained locked in Kut.[238] In the Kut cauldron, conditions were just as bad, if not worse than they had been. Townshend's "waterlogged, hungry, shelled, bombed, flea-ridden, thin, ailing and constantly sniped at" men were reduced to eating grass and rotten oats while slaughtering their horses for protein.[239] Opium pills were issued to dull the pangs of hunger.[240] As nights grew colder, "wooden crosses began to disappear from the cemetery, to be used as fire-wood, and a billion lice, appearing from nowhere, snuggled into the seams of any garment covering warm flesh."[241] Shelling was a constant terror.

With his division disintegrating, Townshend spiked his guns, destroyed his equipment, ordered the consumption of the final rations, lowered the Union Jack, and hoisted the white flag of surrender.[242] His men had staved off bullets and bombs, only to surrender to misery and hunger. On April

29, 1916, after 144 days of blockade, Townshend surrendered his sword and pistol to Khalil Bey (who declined them) and went into captivity.[243] As Townshend traveled upriver in a launch, his men marched along the riverbanks, cheering and saluting their defeated general.[244] Such support contrasted with the mood in the House of Commons, where Townshend's final transmission was read to members of Parliament listening in stunned silence. It was the greatest military debacle for the British Army since General Charles Cornwallis surrendered to the Americans at Yorktown in 1781.

For the next several months, British policy retrenched into defensive warfare intent on protecting British oil wells from any Ottoman advance southward.[245] At the same time the British command busied itself with dredging the port of Basra and refitting its installations, thus allowing for a steady stream of military transport. Defeated at Kut, and now baking in their trenches—their ranks fighting off swarms of diseased sandflies and mosquitoes—the British were content to immobilize the Ottomans and keep them out of southern Persia.[246]

Considering his deep defenses and secure flanks, coupled with the defensive British posture, Khalil Bey felt confident enough to launch just such an attack, dispatching two divisions into Persia against the Russians.[247] This suddenly tilted the balance of forces back in favor of the new British commander, General Stanley Maude.[248] Upon taking command, Maude had intensified the British administrative offensive capacities and had built an outfit on the backs of his laborers capable of resourcing a military expedition. By 1917 these improvements were undeniable, leading one observer to conclude that "Basra looks as if she really were doing her best for those of us whose work lies up river";[249] meanwhile, medical facilities had "electric light and fans in each ward, not to mention beds and sheets."[250] Sensing opportunity in December 1916 Maude ordered an attack with a force superiority of at least three-to-one, overcoming the twenty-five-mile-long Ottoman trenches.[251]

It took the British months of bitter fighting through multiple positions to clear Kut and its surroundings. But on February 24, 1917, the Ottomans retreated toward Baghdad. Authorized to exploit his successes, and more importantly organized to do so, Maude pursued the Ottomans until he forced a decisive victory at the Diyala River.[252] At sunset on March 10, the now-promoted Khalil Pasha surrendered Baghdad.[253] British soldiers "white with dust, thirsty, hungry and bone-weary . . . gazed on the Sacred City through bloodshot eyes."[254] Maude was rewarded for his months of tedious, meticulous administrative planning by steaming into Baghdad as "the Man of Mesopotamia."[255] Fighting would continue north of Baghdad for the remainder of the war, but with the fall of the city of the Abbasid caliphs, the Ottoman Empire had breathed its last in Mesopotamia. All that remained was its final defeat in the eastern Mediterranean.

EGYPT AND THE LEVANT

The Suez Canal flows for approximately one hundred miles from Suez on the Red Sea in the south to Port Said on the Mediterranean Sea in the north. For the British, the Suez was of critical geostrategic significance as a gateway from Europe to its Persian oilfields and Indian colonies. Life on the Suez itself depended on another canal, the Sweet Water Canal, winding from the Nile at Cairo to Ismailia on the Suez, just north of the Great Bitter Lake. From there, the Sweet Water Canal branched north and south to sustain life all along the waterway. As Colonel A. P. Wavell concludes in his study of the Palestine campaigns, if the attacking Ottomans gained "control of the gates and sluices at Ismailia," which regulated the fresh water flow to the Canal area, the British-led defenders on the northern and southern flanks of the Suez Canal would be cut off from their water supply and wither away in dehydration.[256]

The key to the Suez defense system, therefore, was the fork of the Sweet Water Canal at Ismailia, even if the length of the Suez Canal had to be protected against sabotage.[257] This was also the analysis of the Ottoman military governor of Syria, Jamal Pasha. Jamal commanded the sixty-five-thousand-man Ottoman Fourth Army, which he organized into two corps. In mid-January 1915, at Jamal's direction, the highly respected Bavarian Chief of Staff of the Eighth Corps, Colonel Kress von Kressenstein, assembled a task force at Beersheba in Palestine. Even the most optimistic Ottoman planners recognized that this small force could not possibly charge across the Sinai desert and break through across Egypt. But Jamal Pasha believed that the presence of an Ottoman force advancing into the Sinai would spark an Egyptian rebellion, thereby easing the military task of retaking the Nile Delta. Already in late 1914 Syrian Bedouin irregulars, with Ottoman encouragement, occupied al-Arish and had overrun much of the Sinai.[258] As Jamal wrote in his memoir, "I had staked everything upon surprising the English and being able to hold the stretch of the Canal. . . . During this time I hoped that the Egyptian patriots, encouraged by the capture of Ismaila [*sic*] by the Turkish army, would rise *en masse,* and Egypt would be freed in an unexpectedly short time by the employment of quite a small force and insignificant technical resources."[259]

The Pasha ordered his men to advance from Beersheba at night along a central route across the Sinai.[260] Although watering in the central Sinai was more difficult than along the coast, this desert route outranged British naval guns.[261] Moreover, as Liman von Sanders wrote: "They never thought that such a small force would dare to advance against Egypt. The scouting officers of the expeditionary corps saw British officers calmly playing football when the leading Turkish troops were within twenty-five kilometers of the canal."[262] In the early hours of February 3, 1915, the Pasha launched a bevy of pontoons and rafts across the Suez Canal near Ismailia. The British-Indian garrison spotted the rafts gliding across the canal, however, and unleashed a sheet of fire. Another attempt was made at daylight, but the element of surprise was lost. Before long, the Ottoman forces were dragging their heavy equipment back across the desert toward Beersheba.[263]

With their attack sunk in the sands of the Sinai, the Ottomans looked beyond the Nile Delta to a tribal Sufi order roaming the Libyan desert. For years, the Sanusi tribes of Libya had resented European territorial encroachments in North Africa. They sympathized with the Ottomans and their desire to retake Egypt, and eyed nearby Egyptian grains.[264] Operating from the major oases that dot eastern Libya, the Sanusiyya repeatedly launched attacks on British forces in Egypt, but they were outmatched by superior British technology.[265] By the end of 1915 all Ottoman efforts at uprising, invasion, and insurgency had ended in failure. Moreover, "the British, fearful of the possible success of other attacks, began to divert men and war materials to Egypt, marshaling their forces."[266]

If the new year brought new Ottoman hopes of taking Egypt, they were quickly dashed—planning for another Ottoman campaign against Egypt was disrupted in February 1916 by news from the Caucasus. The Russians had sacked the eastern Anatolian city of Erzurum in a wide-reaching offensive, distracting Istanbul from Egypt and the Levant. In the resulting interlude, the British strengthened, expanded, and deepened their defenses. Most importantly, they constructed miles of railway and piping deep into the desert.[267] Interlocking trenches were synchronized with artillery on the east bank of the Suez, silencing those critics who asked whether the Suez was guarding the British or the British the Suez.

But the Egypt campaign was too important to the Ottomans to be abandoned, even if it was delayed. In April 1916 Jamal launched his second foray into Egypt. Colonel von Kressenstein led several thousand men toward the Mediterranean coast, where the British were busy extending their railhead.[268] Achieving complete surprise, Kressenstein recorded a quick victory before withdrawing to await German technical reinforcements. In July, he would attack again in an attempt to entrench his guns within range of the canal.[269] The main attack struggled in the sand dunes, however, and the force was saved only by the searing heat that accompanied the British counterattack.[270] Due to the rigorous marching of the Ottoman infantry, and the tenacious efforts of their rearguard, the Ottomans escaped envelopment and returned to Palestine. They would never threaten Egypt or the Suez again.

On June 5, 1916, military preparations on both sides were interrupted yet again. This time news came from the Arabian peninsula, and for the Ottomans it would prove even more discouraging than the events of February. In March 1916 Sharif Husayn and Henry MacMahon, the British High Commissioner for Egypt, had reached an agreement after months of protracted negotiations that suggested Husayn would receive a pan-Arabian empire in return for open revolt against the Ottomans.[271] As the historian William Cleveland wrote in his superior survey, this was the "famous Husayn-MacMahon correspondence (July 1915–March 1916), an exchange of ten letters that lie at the root of an immense controversy over whether Britain pledged to support an independent Arab state and then reneged on that pledge."[272] While the precise contours of the wartime agreements remain contentious to this day, in June 1916 Sharif Husayn revolted against the Ottomans and overwhelmed the port of Jedda before overcoming the light garrison at Mecca.[273] Medina would be different, however. For the duration of the war, and even for a time thereafter, the reinforced Medina garrison, led by the veteran Ottoman officer Fakhr al-Din Pasha, refused to yield the sacred city to Sharif Husayn. So tenacious was his defense that the Ottomans even attempted to retake Mecca. Meanwhile, Sharif Husayn's third son and field commander, Faysal, was so bereft of supplies and money that he employed the ruse of filing a chest with stones, and "had it locked and corded carefully, guarded on each daily march by his own slaves, and introduced meticulously into his tent each night."[274] With the Arab Revolt seemingly stalling, Istanbul appeared on the brink of reasserting itself over the peninsula. As Faysal deliberated over his next move near Medina, an enterprising British Arab specialist briefly joined his camp before vanishing and rejoining him for operations throughout the Hijaz. This was T. E. Lawrence, famously known in the West as Lawrence of Arabia.

Born in North Wales in 1888, Thomas Edward Lawrence was a precocious adolescent who ignored social convention in favor of a life of rugged individualism. At Oxford his fascination with topics as varied as the Hittites, Crusaders, Fortresses, European military strategy, ancient archeology, and cartography defied the conventional categorization of university life. Lawrence pursued his interests as he wished and wherever they led, including into the Middle East, which he crisscrossed by foot and rail during lengthy expeditions. His vagabond lifestyle led to an appreciation of local cultures and peoples. This proved invaluable during the war, just as his obsessive study of military strategy and leadership helped him shape the Arab Revolt.

Since the war, however, this image of the adventuring mastermind has been challenged by some of Lawrence's soldiering contemporaries and academic historians. One member of the Arab Revolt claimed that "Lawrence to my knowledge did nothing to foment the Arab revolution, nor did he play any part in the Arab military tactics. When first I heard of him he was a paymaster, nothing more. And so he was to Prince Emir Abdulah, brother of King Feisal, whom I knew."[275] In his extensive criticism of Lawrence, Suleiman Mousa argues that "for the whole of his life, Lawrence embellished his stories."[276] For Mousa, his "exaggerated fondness for the exotic and romantic, combined with the imaginative efforts of Western writers with their heads full of *The Arabian Nights,* gradually built up a legend round Lawrence, depicting him as one of the Emirs or Sharifs of Mecca—a far cry from the truth."[277] George Antonius similarly argued that "so much limelight has been projected on Lawrence that his colleagues have remained in comparative obscurity."[278]

Lawrence was enthralled by Faysal's enterprising personality and urged him to undertake an irregular, mobile style of warfare to threaten Ottoman supply lines and spread the revolt northward toward Damascus (thus avoiding a costly direct attack on Medina).[279] He proposed a program of propaganda and raiding that would confine the Ottoman garrison to Medina and force Istanbul to redeploy its troops along the Hijaz Railway.[280] Mousa argues that this initiative was mostly at the urging of Sharif Husayn and his sons, who he claims developed the operational outlines of the Arab Revolt together. To Mousa, Lawrence played mostly a tangential role as a British adviser.[281] Critiquing the myth surrounding Lawrence as "between fact and fancy," Mousa laments that "foreign sources have habitually attributed any Arab military success to the British or French officers on the scene."[282] Irrespective of the contours of that debate, it is indisputable that Lawrence and Faysal soon began harassing the Ottomans in the desert while avoiding pitched battles. In his memoir, Ja'far al-Askari describes one raid, typical of Faysal's operations: "I . . . led a small Bedouin detachment under the leadership of Sharif Ali bin Hussain Al-Harithi and some Egyptian soldiers . . . on a reconnaissance mission to the railway, our intention being also to destroy stretches of track where possible. We scouted the area . . . and decided to dynamite the tracks. . . . We crept up to the tracks at the dead of a very dark night, and when the dynamite went off in a series of terrifying explosions I could see the silhouettes of a horde of Turkish soldiers coming towards us."[283]

The men of the Arab Revolt consisted of a disparate crew of irregulars. Ja'far al-Askari relates one anecdote concerning a certain Captain Hasan Ma'ruf. His men "failed to obey his orders on parade not because they were insubordinate, but because they were completely unable to understand his Baghdadi dialect, which is very different from their own Hijazi."[284] Perplexed by his Arabic, the platoon even protested that Captain Ma'ruf "always addresses us in Turkish!"[285]

In January 1917 Faysal and his men bypassed Medina and trekked over two hundred miles north to al-Wajh on the Red Sea, directly threatening the Hijaz Railway. Faysal's stroke threatened to choke the Ottoman garrison holding Medina and eliminated the threat to Mecca by forcing Istanbul to disperse its troops along the railway. Buoyed by his success, Faysal ordered his men overland to Aqaba, at the head of the Gulf of Aqaba, where he sacked the Ottoman fortifications. By July 1917, these masterstrokes combined with sabotage operations to threaten the entire Ottoman southern flank in Palestine—where the war in the Middle East would be decided.

Indeed, while the Arab Revolt was under way, both sides had made intensive preparations for the battles that lay ahead in Egypt and Palestine. The Egyptian Labour Corps extended the British railway all along the Sinai coastline and laid piping for the transporting of water from the Sweet Water Canal.[286] "It is estimated that upward of half a million men served in" the Egyptian Labour Corps and Camel Transport Corps between 1915 and 1919, "though Egyptian historians dispute this and claim that the real figure is more than one million."[287] The two units "formed the backbone of the logistical system, without which the advance into Palestine would not have been possible."[288]

Thousands of camels of the Camel Transport Corps trekked toward Palestine and eventually seized Raffa (Rafah) after a difficult battle in January 1917. As sand gave way to soil, both sides focused their attention on the ancient gateway sitting astride the traditional invasion route to Palestine: the fortress of Gaza. Two dozen miles to the south, Beersheba complements Gaza as the other major city of southern Palestine. It is also the last watering outpost before the mountains that bracket it to the south and east.[289] The Ottomans held this Beersheba-Gaza line.[290]

The first battle for Gaza began on March 26, 1917, with a large British mounted and infantry attack across the gardens and fields of the city outskirts. But the British, despite their best efforts, could not overcome the cactus hedges, dense fog, and enfilading fire of the Ottoman defense. As dusk signaled the end to a daylong battle, the British retreated. The Ottomans reoccupied by daylight the all-important al-Muntar ridge of Gaza, commanding the city and outfitted with strong trenches. Reinvigorated and apprised of British intentions, the Ottomans reinforced their lines while the British extended their railhead to less than ten miles from Gaza.[291] Another British attack in mid-April, this time utilizing poison gas and armored tanks, ended in Ottoman victory once more.[292]

From the British perspective, however, the Ottoman Empire represented the vulnerable chink in the German armor. A breakthrough in Palestine would imperil Istanbul's Arab provinces and thereby strike a serious blow against Germany. As Wavell summarizes: "Early in 1917 Turkey was in evil plight. During the latter half of 1916 her best remaining troops had been taken to fight Germany's battles against Russia and Rumania. Meanwhile her starved and ragged armies on the Caucasus front wasted away in the rigours of a bitter winter; her forces in Iraq suffered a decisive defeat; those on the Palestine front were falling back in the face of the British advance; and the expedition to recover Mecca and to quench the Arab Revolt had been dramatically checked by Feisal's flank move to Wejh."[293]

Twice stymied, London determined to force the issue a third time, dispatching General Edmund Allenby to take command of the Egyptian Expeditionary Force (EEF) and "to demand 'such reinforcements and supplies as he found necessary to Jerusalem by Christmas.'"[294] As for Istanbul, activity in Palestine was viewed with similar anxiety. Mecca and Baghdad had fallen, Medina was under threat, and the British were eyeing Jerusalem. The Young Turks therefore assembled the Ottoman Seventh Army at Aleppo for the purpose of retaking Baghdad or defending Palestine. In London these troop movements only reinforced the need to press on into Palestine. Rather than resupply General Maude, an arduous task in the best of conditions, Allenby was ordered to advance.[295]

Allenby's strategy was to capture Beersheba rapidly and then unleash his mounted and infantry divisions around the Ottoman left flank, rolling up the defenses at Gaza.[296] The key to the plan was an elaborate scheme to deceive the Ottomans that the initial attack would occur at Gaza. So successful was the military ruse that on October 31, 1917, when Allenby's attack did come, only a few thousand Ottomans manned the single-line Beersheba trenches. But it was also prepared by the heaviest non-European artillery bombardment of the entire war, "with a gun concentration equivalent to that of 1 July 1916 on the Somme."[297] At bayonet point, the Desert Mounted Corps galloped through the Ottoman defense and into Beersheba.

The man in overall Ottoman command, the former chief of the German General Staff Eric von Falkenhayn, now faced a major threat to his forces. Twice the Ottomans had beaten back assaults on Gaza, but they had not anticipated an attack on Beersheba. Compounding their difficulties, many of the scattered Ottoman troops, already inferior in numbers to the British, were ill.[298] And the Ottoman Seventh Army—rushing from Syria to meet the British offensive—had not yet arrived.[299] Thus, after sacking Beersheba, Allenby successfully turned the Ottoman flank at Gaza in the early hours of November 2.[300] Several days of tough fighting later, just after midnight on November 6, 1917, the British breached a series of defensive works and seized Muntar.[301]

Allenby was not to be contented with his Gaza prize and ordered the immediate exploitation of his success, driving his mounted men north along the coast as the Ottomans fought a tenacious rearguard action. Eventually, however, the front stabilized as the Ottoman Eighth Army withdrew behind the Auja River, surrendering Jaffa, while the Ottoman Seventh Army retreated into the central highlands of Palestine.[302] In just over two weeks, Allenby had split the Ottoman armies, inflicted thousands of casualties, and charged up the coast to Jaffa. Allenby's next objective was fixed: Jerusalem.

Jerusalem's western approaches are framed by steep and craggy outcrops that have protected the city from invasion since antiquity. The terrain is ideal for ambush warfare. Nevertheless, on November 19, Allenby ordered his men to attack into the Palestinian highlands to pressure the separated and disorganized Ottoman armies. Over the next five days, the British struggled through valleys and hills, buffeted by fog, rain, and enfilading fire from seemingly invisible men lurking behind rocks and ridges. On November 24 Allenby was forced to order a general retreat.

On December 8, 1917, Allenby plunged once more into the Jerusalem hills, this time dislodging the Ottoman Seventh Army.[303] One Armenian soldier recorded the unease in Jerusalem at the approach of the British: "The city of Jerusalem was in great turmoil, all the Turkish soldiers were in a hurry to withdraw."[304] Shortly thereafter, on December 11, Allenby passed on foot through the Jaffa Gate into the city, where "the victors met with a genuine, if subdued, welcome from a population shrunken to half its size by hunger, exile and deportation."[305] For Istanbul, the loss of Jerusalem represented a catastrophe: Baghdad, Mecca, and now Jerusalem were all firmly under enemy control, and while Medina was still garrisoned by an Ottoman force, the city increasingly constituted an isolated Ottoman outpost. With the capture of Jerusalem, Allenby slowed to synchronize his supply situation and railways with the demands of his next target: Greater Syria.

By February 1918 he felt sufficiently secure to descend the eastern edge of the central Palestinian highlands into the Jordan River valley.[306] At this point Allenby linked his operations to those of Faysal.[307] After capturing Aqaba, Prince Faysal had enlisted the tribes south of the Dead Sea in a series of rapid-fire raids against the Ottoman cornbelt between the Dead Sea and the Hijaz Railway.[308] Faysal worked to protect Allenby's southern flank as Allenby twice launched spring offensives across the Jordan River valley in the direction of Amman. Both times, however, bad weather, steep terrain, and obdurate defense stymied the attacks, forcing Allenby's cavalry to decamp in the choking dust and summer heat of the valley.

As the last-gasp German offensive collapsed in Europe, the Ottomans consolidated their Palestinian front into three sectors: the Ottoman Seventh Army operated west of the Jordan River, the Ottoman Eighth Army protected the coastal plain, and the Ottoman Fourth Army headquartered at Amman east of the Jordan River.[309] The key to their supply was Dar'a Junction, the railway node between Damascus and Amman. From Dar'a, the railway cut west to Haifa on the Mediterranean to supply the Seventh and Eighth Armies. Along the way, at al-Afula, a branch extended south to Nablus on the Jordan River's West Bank, where the Ottoman Seventh Army was headquartered.

Allenby sought to destroy the Ottoman Seventh and Eighth Armies through an infantry breakthrough that would facilitate a mounted ride up the coastal plain and around enemy lines, converging on al-Afula.[310] In the east, Allenby charged Faysal with cutting Ottoman communications around Dar'a, while his regular forces in the Jordan River valley feinted toward Amman in the hopes of convincing the Ottomans that the main attack would occur inland instead of along the coast. On September 19, 1918, after a massive preparatory infantry assault surprised the Ottomans, Allenby's mounted men swept up the coast. The Ottomans retreated inland toward their railway junctions. At dawn the next day, September 20, British cavalry reached Nazareth—Liman von Sanders's headquarters—and occupied al-Afula before falling on Jenin from the rear. By nighttime, the natural lines of retreat for the Ottoman Seventh and Eighth Armies were eliminated.[311] The advancing infantry pushed both armies toward the enveloping charge of the British cavalry. Pressed on three sides, the Ottomans' only escape route was eastward toward the Jordan River.

The tangled web of the central highlands of Palestine, so advantageous in defense, proved deadly in open retreat. British airmen and troops unleashed terror on frantic columns trapped in the narrow valleys that stretched to the Jordan River. As the army disintegrated, troops faded into the surrounding hills. All that remained was the Ottoman Fourth Army, east of the Jordan

River. Observing the disaster from Amman, that force could do nothing but beat a hasty retreat toward Damascus. On September 22, they began their treacherous, thirst-ridden march toward Dar'a (Faysal had destroyed the railway).[312] Along the way, the countryside rose in revolt, slowing progress and frustrating the retreat. Harried by Faysal's fighters on their flank and marching through hostile territory, the Ottoman Fourth Army could not check the advancing British southwest of Damascus.

When the first riders reached the main square of Damascus, they "beheld the Arab flag flying. Four hundred years of Ottoman domination had passed into history."[313] At dawn on October 1, they entered Damascus, encountering "a frenzy of joy" while taking thousands of prisoners.[314] The French fleet took Beirut a few days later and Aleppo fell thereafter, leading to "similar scenes of rejoicing as had greeted the liberators in Damascus."[315] On October 31, 1918, the Armistice of Mudros formalized what had already been established on the battlefield.[316] "With the occupation of Damascus and the rest of Syria by the Anglo-Arab forces in October 1918 and the Ottoman surrender at the Mudros cease-fire at the end of the month, it became clear that the Istanbul government had lost its hold on the Arab provinces."[317]

From a military perspective, the great lesson of Allenby's sweep through the Levant, coupled with the success of the Arab Revolt, was the value of mobile warfare and indirect attack. In contrast to the bludgeoning direct warfare of western Europe, Allenby built an administrative apparatus and insisted on executing a mobile military campaign. A second striking development was the transformation of the colonial British political economy.[318] Especially in Mesopotamia and Palestine, "the demands of war imposed novel logistical and administrative requirements" that meant far greater coercion and extraction.[319]

In January 1918, months before the fall of Damascus, two old friends, *Yavuz* and *Midilli*, had attempted to steam to the rescue and relieve the pressure building on the Ottomans in Palestine. Under the command of Vice Admiral Hubert von Rebeur-Paschwitz, the successor to Admiral Souchon, the pair passed through the Dardanelles. On their first foray through the narrow straits since Souchon's desperate dash almost three and a half years earlier, the ships sought to break into the Aegean Sea and support the embattled Ottomans in Palestine. The mission began promisingly enough, for after exiting the Dardanelles the two ships sank a pair of British monitors.

As they steamed near the island of Imbros, however, both repeatedly struck mines. *Midilli* sank mere miles from the port of Mudros. *Yavuz,* however, was spared such a fate. Three and a half years after steaming into the Dardanelles as SMS *Goeben,* the ship returned, limping at a mere fourteen knots, a shell of its former glory. Embodying the exhaustion of the empire it had served, *Yavuz* bypassed one final minefield before collapsing onto the Asiatic shores of the Dardanelles, struggling to fend off its British pursuers.[320] The ship would survive the war, but much like the Ottoman Empire, it would never be the same again.

CHAPTER THREE

Living the Great War

IN HER NOVEL *Shirwal Barhum: Ayyam min safarbarlik,* the Damascene Nadiya al-Ghazzi tells the story of a humble Syrian peasant, Maryam, who travels to the historic Azm Palace in the heart of Damascus. In Maryam's possession is an elaborately embroidered pair of colorful pants, known as a *shirwal,* which she presents upon arrival to the manager of the palace, Mr. Shafik al-Imam. "I was a young bride when they took away my husband of one month to the military," Maryam explains, now worn with age. "I was hoping that when he came back and people and friends would come to greet him, he would be wearing a nice *shirwal,* so I bought fabric . . . and I used to go to the fountain (*shadharwan*) where I would sit and look at the colors of flowers . . . and embroider them on the *shirwal.*"[1]

Yet Maryam's labor of love went unrequited, ending in tragic heartbreak: "The war ended . . . and I waited . . . and I waited . . . and my husband did not come back . . . so I put this *shirwal* in a trunk and every time I longed for my husband, I would open the trunk, take out the *shirwal* then put it back where it was . . . this went on for forty years."[2] Maryam offered this final object of value, her sentimental *shirwal,* to Mr. Imam in return for one gold coin to pay for her medicines.

From her sadness at his conscription to her growing anxiety over his fate and her ultimate resignation at his death, Maryam turned to the *shirwal* to ease the burden of losing her husband and the dreams he represented. Her grief was shared by millions of women, devastated by the loss of husbands, sons, uncles, and cousins. The Turkish feminist writer Halidé Edib captured the heightened anxiety of such women, still hopeful of a happy reunion, during one memorable expedition across Syria in 1916. Two years into the war, Edib traveled by rail from Anatolia to Homs, where she encountered an unforgettable scene: "The women whose husbands and sons were in the army had come to the station because a military train was passing and there was a chance of meeting their men. They were wringing their hands and calling in inexpressible excitement to the soldiers in the cars."[3] As the train idled at the Homs station, her travel companion had to turn away would-be passengers as bundles, water jugs, and fruit baskets were hurled into their carriage. Men and women squeezed in through the window and the train strained to capacity while Edib watched women running "up and down the platform, wringing their hands."[4]

Earlier on that same trip, Edib stopped in a small village before Konya, Anatolia. Although the village contained twenty-five houses or so, "there was hardly a man to be seen." She elaborated:

Old women sat at the door of their huts, and little children played about, while a group of young women returned from the fields, with their scythes on their shoulders. The heat, the dust, and the sadness of the lonely women were beyond description; the younger ones squatted in the dust and asked us when the war would end and told us the names of their husbands. We were in the second year of the war, and already they looked as if they were at the end of their strength. The end of the war was their concern more than any one's. They not only had their beloved at the front, but they also had to supply Turkey and her army with the means of living.[5]

The despair of families is a continual reality of war that extends long after the last shots echo through the air: "Behind the fronts women who once had listened to the words of men whom they had loved, now had but memories to thrill them. Instead of men to embrace, they had dreams."[6] As Edib wrote, "I have seen, I have gone through, a land full of aching hearts and torturing remembrances."[7]

In the imagined peasant world of *Shirwal Barhum,* the years leading up to the Great War are described as idyllic; contented villagers passed their time planting all sorts of fruits and vegetables, and waited for the seasons to deliver their bounty while lying in fields among cucumbers, tomatoes, lettuce, and corn. In June they picked apricots and made jam, which the tale's heroine stored in big jars on the white roof of her home. July was spent chatting amiably on straw mats with neighbors to pass the time. Communications from the outside world were slow, information was rare, and the first bulletins of war did not always immediately penetrate the far reaches of the Ottoman Empire. In fact, as news of the possibility of war reached the cities and countryside of the Arab provinces in the summer of 1914, some took it in stride, leisurely processing the news as if it were some distant event or remote abstraction irrelevant to their daily lives.

Yet the heartbreak of war was anticipated by many subjects of the sultan from the very start. As news of Ottoman participation in the war began to spread in November 1914, unease blew throughout Greater Syria like a cannon shot, foreshadowing foreboding and fear. Jirjis Makdisi, who himself experienced the war and later became chair of the Arabic Department at the Syrian Protestant College, has even argued that widespread apprehension at news of the war triggered a migratory wave, with Muslims congregating in the interior while Christians sheltered along the coast. For some coastal Muslims and rural Christians, escaping to their safe havens offered peace of mind as the turbulence of war approached.[8]

The story of the Beiruti George Korkor demonstrates this flight to safety. A man of moderate means, Korkor struggled on occasion to make ends meet. In his unpublished handwritten memoir, he confides that his business suffered greatly at the outbreak of World War I. Even so, he moved his family to the Mediterranean seaport of Jounieh, fifteen kilometers northeast of Beirut in the Kisrawan district of Mount Lebanon. Life was not easy: "We went to Jounieh with the family and stayed there for twelve terrible months."[9] He added that his family crammed into two bedrooms and a kitchen lacking all conveniences while he traveled back and forth from Beirut, which entailed additional expenses. Eventually the entire family moved back from Jounieh.

Like the Korkors, Ja'far ibn Muhsin al-Amin's family responded to the exigencies of war by moving from the city to the countryside. In his posthumously published autobiography, Ja'far recalled that his father, a Shi'i scholar and imam, Muhsin al-Amin, reacted to the food shortages in the cities by transporting his entire family from Damascus to his native village of Shaqra in the mountainous region of Jabal Amil in southern Lebanon. He outfitted camels for the women and children and packed two fabric-covered wooden baskets on each side to haul the family possessions.[10]

What people feared most of all was military conscription. Before 1908, the Ottoman imperial narrative had focused on obedience to the sultan; after the revolution, this was redirected toward the Ottoman fatherland (*vatan*). Through this subtle yet meaningful shift, the Ottoman authorities sought to transform society from one of traditional subjects (the *kulluk* system) into one of modern citizenship (*vatandaşlık*). Reforming the conscription system was considered part and parcel of this social endeavor. Thus in 1909 the Ottoman parliament (*Meclis-i mebusan*) abolished preferential religious treatment throughout the empire and ordered the conscription of Christians and Jews into the army with the intent of uniting the people around an Ottoman identity.

Already during the Balkan Wars of 1912 and 1913, this military reorganization raised alarm in the Arab provinces.[11] By 1914, even before the empire abandoned neutrality, Istanbul was forced to issue multiple (and more pressing) decrees announcing general mobilization.[12] On the scene, one British officer interpreted this "as indication of the unpopularity of the war, and unwillingness to serve of a large part of the population."[13] Indeed, from the start to the end of the war, the call to general mobilization met with considerable opposition in many localities, such as Hawran, Kurdistan, Arabia, and Mount Lebanon.[14]

Apprehension regarding conscription was exacerbated by its inconsistent implementation. Some escaped service through bribery, which was welcomed by some officials as Ottoman finances deteriorated, or by appealing to powerful intermediaries:

> It was a common sight to see the police chasing those who were called to the military, looking for them on the streets, in the fields, in the corners of their houses, and if they caught someone who had a family with some money, the family would intercede in his favor to the notable of the town who in turn would talk to the police to convince them to let him escape, and share with them the money given by the family. . . . Others who were caught would have a nice sister or a mother still looking young or in some cases a

wife who would go to the notable and plead for their freedom. Then the soldiers would look the other way if only to please the notable who could not resist temptation.[15]

Ja'far ibn Muhsin al-Amin hints at the unpopularity of conscription while bemoaning the fate of certain soldiers:

As for those who had not been granted money or a pretty sister by God, or who did not have legs like the legs of a deer to escape, or a way to disappear like the fox, they would be taken away. Not always did they reach the front and if they did they did not come back because of hunger and disease and hardship, and if they managed to flee they fell prey to bandits who were killing for a coat or a few coins or just to kill, especially if they found out that the man had blue bones and from the Abu Dhanab people ["those with a tail," in other words, adds the author, Shi'i].[16]

The Damascene notable Khalid al-Azm similarly offered that by "the order of Military Headquarters, Syrian soldiers were taken away to faraway fronts such as Sinai, Gallipoli or the Caucasus. Many of these young men lost their lives, were wounded or sent to captivity. *The number of those who went into hiding to avoid service outnumbered those who joined the military service.*"[17] This tendency toward draft evasion and desertion is confirmed by the historian Abdallah Hanna, who interviewed 303 peasants of more than seventy-five years of age between July and September 1984. These peasants hailed from 245 villages in various parts of Syria, providing a sample of the perspectives of commoners during the Great War. Hanna's findings confirm that thousands of young men fled various theaters of war during their deployments.[18]

To avoid conscription and hardship, many even chose to emigrate beyond the Ottoman Empire, including to the distant shores of the Americas. In 1916 the army recruited ten thousand young Christians and put them to hard labor on the railway between Damascus and Palestine.[19] News of this draft accelerated international migration, which had been gathering steam in the Ottoman seaports for decades. As Hanna points out, in popular memory the wars in Yemen and the Balkans in 1912 and 1913 mixed with World War I to spur emigration. After the 1890s many Syrians set sail for South America to avoid conscription; more broadly, during the two periods 1890–1914 and 1920–1939, people migrated to the Americas.[20]

In 1919 Paul Huvelin, a legal historian from the University of Lyon, led a French mission to Syria and Cilicia at the behest of the Lyon and Marseilles chambers of commerce. In his detailed report, Huvelin documented the "petty annoyances" and political causes that contributed to these migrations. Among them were motivations well beyond an aversion to military service. As Huvelin established, the migrants were not peasants but artisans, small merchants, employees, and sometimes small-business owners. It was a self-selected exodus by those with the professional skills to match. They migrated to nearby Egypt and to distant America not to work the land or till the soil, but to sell their olives, cigars, carpets, and merchandise in new markets, and to practice other professions.[21] This entrepreneurial emigration, which included women,[22] only intensified before the war. By 1922, one French report noted that many Lebanese had grown accustomed to trading in Europe, the Americas, and even parts of Africa.[23]

Many of the half-million Syrians whom Huvelin estimates to have migrated abroad traveled by ship, often stopping in Alexandria.[24] It was aboard these ships, and in the train stations, where the scope and scale of the Great War could be observed. The sheer volume of movement, from military deployments to civilian migrations, manifested itself in the emotional hustle and bustle of people bidding goodbye and saying hello. From one end of the Ottoman Empire to the other, railway stations exuded anxiety, excitement, and fear, all at once. This charged atmosphere extended to foreigners as well. The American ambassador in Istanbul between 1913 and 1916, Henry Morgenthau, whose memoir is critical of the Ottoman government in general and its treatment of the Armenians in particular, described one scene in Istanbul around the onset of hostilities. Morgenthau had come to the train station to arrange for the departure of foreigners:

> As soon as I arrived at the railroad station, the day following the break, I saw that my task was to be a difficult one. I had arranged with the Turkish authorities for two trains; one for the English and French residents, which was to leave at seven o'clock, and one for the diplomats and their staff, which was to go at nine. But the arrangement was not working according to schedule. The station was a surging mass of excited and frightened people; the police were there in full force, pushing the crowds back; the scene was an indescribable mixture of soldiers, gendarmes, diplomats, baggage, and Turkish functionaries.[25]

In the process of making arrangements, Ambassador Morgenthau noticed Bedri Bey, a member of the Committee of Union and Progress who served as a police prefect and who Morgenthau thought exuded "a hatred of foreigners": "Bedri would let no one get on the diplomatic train until I had personally identified them. So I had to stand at a little gate, and pass upon each applicant. Everyone, whether he belonged to the diplomatic corps or not, attempted to force himself through this narrow passageway, and we had an old-fashioned Brooklyn Bridge crush on a small scale. People were running in all directions, checking baggage, purchasing tickets, arguing with officials, consoling distracted women and frightened children, while Bedri, calm and collected, watched the whole pandemonium with an unsympathetic smile."[26]

At times, the scene was almost comical but for an all-pervading fear: "Hats were knocked off, clothing was torn. . . . One lady dropped her baby in my arms, later another handed me a small boy, and still later, when I was standing at the gate, identifying Turkey's departing guests, one of the British secretaries made me the custodian of his dog. . . . As the train left the station I caught my final glimpse of the British Ambassador, sitting in a private car, almost buried in a mass of trunks, satchels, boxes, and diplomatic pouches, surrounded by his embassy staff, and sympathetically watched by the secretary's dog."[27]

As wartime conditions deteriorated, such scenes from the train stations turned even more dreary. In 1916, far from fashionable Istanbul, in the heartland of traditional Asia Minor, a sad scene captured the attention of Halidé Edib, who was traveling in the relative comfort that was typical of the wealthy: "In Konia the station greeted us with a scene of misery. A large number of Eastern Anatolians, mostly refugees and Kurds, were crowded with their families and few belongings in the station. They were the remainder of the Armenian victims, running from the Armenian massacres. Under the glare of the station lights, huddled together in their bright-colored but tattered costumes, their faces hopeless and entirely expressionless, as refugee faces usually are, they waited for the train. There was that smell of misery peculiar to a human crowd, unwashed, and in physical as well as moral suffering."[28]

From her Bebek village on the Bosporus, Edib regularly traveled both by train and by boat. While she once dismissed "the lower classes . . . expressing themselves in their dumb but very forcible way," Edib nonetheless noted that the "scenes on the trams and the boats enlightened me every day."[29] In her memoir, she records tensions that spilled over into ethnic disputes. "Blows between Turkish women and Christian women were frequent"; one time, traveling by boat, a Greek woman with a second-class ticket insisted on sitting in first class. She pushed the other women and insulted them as prostitutes, and would not relent, despite the intervention and protestations of the controller and inspector. Edib resolved henceforth to sit only in second class. It is in Edib's move to second class that the story earns its keep. Her reaction to second class testifies to the vast chasm separating the wartime notables from the disadvantaged masses, for her disapproval at the quarrel in first class faded once she witnessed "the poorer women, dressed in loose *charshafs* [cloaks], their face always unveiled" who made a place for her to sit among them. She empathized with these "neither articulate nor demonstrative" passengers, and interpreted their emotional states as profoundly affected and sad.

For some, the sea did represent a waterway leading to a better future in Europe or the Americas. But for most it represented a source of human suffering. It was from the sea that foreign armies descended on Ottoman shores; it was at sea where British and French warships floated, their cannons bombarding Ottoman defenses; and it was across the sea that the population gazed in disappointment when promised food supplies failed to materialize. For the civilians of the Ottoman territories, it was this last threat—starvation—that combined with disease to form the most likely source of death.

The great famine of World War I had many origins. The sea blockade by the British in collusion with the French combined with Ottoman maladministration, hoarding, speculation, and the inevitable vicissitudes of war to devastate the eastern Mediterranean and beyond. From the Aegean to the Arabian seas, Ottomans blamed their government for the shortages. Some Greeks, for example, criticized the Ottomans after refugees from Izmir reported that Greeks "were being atrociously treated in the interior by the Turks, who stop their water supply, so that the people are dying of thirst."[30] Meanwhile, in the Arabian peninsula, rumors of food boycotts contributed to Arab disenchantment. As one British officer reported to the High Commissioner for Egypt, "There are rumours that Arabs are preparing to attack Jeddah in consequence of Turks having prohibited removal of food-stuffs from Jeddah."[31]

For the Ottoman authorities, blame for the famine was floating offshore, in the form of the Entente warships. Great Britain implemented a naval blockade all along the Ottoman coastline, not just in the Mediterranean. British correspondence in May 1916 makes explicit reference to "the blockade of the Yemen Coasts and prevention of the exportation of grain and other necessaries to Jeddah in particular and all other Hijaz ports in general."[32] In October 1916 one British officer reported from Egypt that camel convoys appeared to be circumventing the blockade and delivering supplies into the interior: "I have already successfully taken action with armoured cars and camel corps, against several of these convoys, which have been rounded up and captured while approaching the Egyptian Oases [sic] from Italian territory," he proudly reports, "but I would point out that *my work of maintaining the blockade in Egypt* is very seriously interfered with by this continual traffic, which the local Italian authorities have, up to now, not been successful in preventing."[33]

The Ottoman authorities did sequester foodstuffs and other products in order to feed and equip their army.[34] In March 1915 Jamal Pasha reportedly ordered the relocation of foodstuffs (including produce), pack animals, transport carriages, and all other means of transportation from the Syrian coast to the interior. Moreover, fearful of an enemy landing along the coast, which never did come to pass, Jamal ordered the burning of whatever grain remained in storage. In warning of such an invasion, Jamal's order had great effect; their goods subject to the arbitrary whims of the authorities, and with military action apparently imminent, scores of coastal townsmen and farmers fled with their cattle and belongings in tow.[35]

In 1915 Jamal Pasha appropriated Greater Syrian foodstuffs in what he interpreted as a strategic necessity. As the Entente powers closed Istanbul's last surviving seaborne supply routes to its provinces, the Pasha authorized the transfer of up to ten carloads of food from Damascus to Medina in an effort to maintain Sharif Husayn's loyalty.[36] Damascus was already experiencing food shortages, but he defended his decision as a necessary evil. In his memoir, he also emphasized the cost of supplying his force in Medina after the outbreak of the Arab Revolt, which he succeeded in doing regularly until December 1917: "The sacrifices necessarily involved in feeding the garrison in Medina and supplying the troops echelonned [sic] between Medina and Maan with food and ammunition compelled us to halve the supplies provided for Palestine and Sinai and prevented us from reinforcing our Sinai front when and how we liked."[37]

Jamal Pasha's seizure of vast amounts of grain alongside a steadily tightening blockade contributed to hyperinflation in basic commodities, including vegetables and meats.[38] Prices increased fourteenfold in Istanbul, compared to a fourfold increase in Paris; some items rose as much as 1,350 percent, while in London and Paris they increased 200 and 300 percent.[39] Sa'id Jawmar from the Syrian town of Dayr Atiya survived deployments to Palestine, the Suez Canal, and the Dardanelles before returning home in 1918. He wrote a poem about his experiences, in which he highlighted what a terrible strain the requisitioning of "half of the wheat, oats, maize, raisins, and all other crops" had put on the population, as tax collectors "practically rob the houses" of all those with back taxes. Jawmar added, "The men have fled, all work and the management of property is on the shoulders of women."[40]

Jamal Pasha also appropriated iron, wood, cement, cloth, and a variety of other materials, for which his officers tendered payment only sporadically, and then at arbitrary prices.[41] In part, as in the case of the Medina garrison, he did so in order to satiate the appetite of the thousands of soldiers exerting themselves in marches to the front and in battle against the enemy. The plight of these soldiers is covered elsewhere in this book, but their nourishment is so closely interwoven with the civilian famine that it deserves special mention here. Lacking transport, these soldiers often embarked on barefoot marches while undernourished and badly clothed. Indeed, it was "not unusual for Turkish troops to fight—and march— barefoot. As a matter of fact, the war is still known as the 'barefoot war' in Syria today."[42]

Those in charge of the military worried constantly about food. At the very beginning of the war, troops could sometimes be provisioned, in large part because the Ottoman system prioritized military well-being over civilian comfort. In Palestine, "compulsory work gangs"—euphemistically labeled "volunteer labor battalions"—helped "build roads, railroad tracks, army encampments, and military installations."[43] These men suffered enormous deprivations and often lost their lives in unknown lands among unknown people for an unknown cause. But while they labored, they grew accustomed to meat, biscuits, jam, and the luxury of three meals per day.[44] For many in the military, particular items, such as dates, seem to have been readily obtainable early in the war.[45] One Arab fisherman, interviewed on August 16, 1915, stated that food at al-Muwaylih on the Arabian peninsula was sufficient; the British had not yet tightened their stranglehold over the overland route from Syria and cut the seaborne trade at Jedda.[46]

In principle, then, the army should have been adequately fed; in reality, the situation fluctuated enormously, and never approached an overall satisfactory condition.[47] The purchase of military wheat and barley was dependent on the chief administrator of each army, whose success at provisioning his men often depended on an overburdened transportation network. As a result, "the food situation of the different armies varied enormously, depending on whether they were close to, or far away from, grain-producing areas."[48]

With the onset of the conflict, food production plummeted, declining by 40 percent. Even so, Anatolia possessed a surplus of wheat, while Greater Syria maintained sufficient supplies (disregarding the locust plague of 1915). In Egypt, the return of the Mediterranean Expeditionary Force from Gallipoli in 1916 overwhelmed existing supplies and triggered a food crisis arrested only by the mass importation of bread and hay from India. Similar military consumption spikes caused shortfalls in the last two years of the war.[49] As the war unraveled on the Syrian front, soldiers "had often not only to live on half rations, but they were given the same flour soup for months and months and at last became incapable of touching a spoonful of it."[50] Already in 1915 British military intelligence reported discontented Ottoman officers, poorly clothed rank-and-file troops, and the malnourished state of the enemy.[51] Many of the troops "were ill-paid or not paid at all, worn out marching, undernourished and badly clothed."[52]

On both sides, the inadequate soldiering diet eventually led to outbreaks of scurvy, "a serious problem, with teeth falling out and large sores forming in their mouths or even through their cheeks. According to one report, 20 percent of the army was affected by scurvy";[53] due to their poor diet, it particularly ravaged Indian troops.[54] In April 1916, as the siege of Kut al-Amara reached its apogee, an Indian soldier wrote about his fellow men, trapped and reduced to consuming their own pack animals: "The 7th Brigade is surrounded in Mesopotamia. Attempts have been made to rescue them, but without success. There was a fight on 6th March and heavy losses to us in the attempt to relieve them. Some men of ours are in the besieged force, twenty in number. They have eaten their horses and mules. They have a quarter of a pound of flour each per diem."[55] The soldier ended that section of his letter with a remarkable claim given the ferocity of the fighting conditions: "We are hopeful of being sent to join the relieving force."

Jamal Pasha cast similar challenges in a more positive light in his postwar memoir. Revisiting the Suez expedition, he praised the determination and unity of the men from "Arab and Turkish stock" who charged across the Sinai in 1915, while conceding that "the supply of food for officers and men right through the desert to the Canal was impossible," requiring the imposition of a new system of desert rations: "It was based on a list of comestibles, the weight of which was not to exceed one kilogram per man, and comprised biscuits, dates, and olives. As regards water, no man must carry more than contents of a gourd."[56] Jamal Pasha claimed that such provisioning restrictions applied to the commanders as much as to the rank-and-file and suggested that shortages were mitigated by the troops' enthusiasm: "It may well be believed that this army, in which no one from the Commander-in-Chief down to the humblest private was allowed more than 650 grammes of biscuit and a few dates and olives, and every man had to keep his consumption of water down to bare necessity, was borne along by glowing hopes as it approached its goal."[57]

Since food was mostly inadequate during the war, soldiers often lived off the land and looted villages and towns to satiate their hunger. Leaving their barracks, they attacked the markets to pilfer whatever they could from food stores: "Every time a battalion passed in the streets we would see the street vendors running away with their trays and their carts that carried food and sweets for fear that the hungry soldiers would snatch them from their hands."[58] In this way, the shortage of food supplies resulted in a negative interplay between soldiers and civilians.

Much of this activity was born of desperation. In late 1917 Ottoman forces stationed in Mesopotamia requested food of the Syrian army, only to be told that the "food situation in the Fourth Army [in Syria] is so dreadful that only 250 grams of flour can be given to men and 2.5 kilograms of forage to animals. If communications are not improved it is doubtful we can go on."[59] The situation in Palestine was described similarly:

> The Turkish soldiers concentrated at that time in Palestine had not enough
> bread to maintain their strength. They received almost no meat, no butter,
> no sugar, no vegetables, no fruits. Only a thin tent gave a semblance of pro-

tection from the hot sun by day, and from the cold of the night. They were wretchedly clothed. They had no boots at all, or what they had were so bad that they meant injury to the feet of many who wore them. Soldiers had been without word from home for years and years. Owing to the bad communications no leave was ever given. There was no amusement of any sort, no tobacco, no coffee. And men so placed could not but see that their German comrades on the same front were well fed, and enjoyed every sort of comfort and amusement.[60]

Detained Ottoman soldiers confirmed the destitute, famished state of the force. In the Hijaz, after the destruction of miles of telegram lines, one British officer reported the capture of some thirty enemy soldiers, adding: "The captives were all very hungry and state that they get only a water-bottle of water and one small loaf per day."[61] The effect of famine conditions on military health is confirmed in other contemporary reports.[62] The German commander Liman von Sanders estimated that the Ottoman army in Syria lost some seventeen thousand men to starvation in the winter and early spring of 1918 alone.[63] The hunger and misery of the soldiers was such that military desertion, already as high as three hundred thousand by December 1917, reached nearly five hundred thousand by the end of the war.[64] German observers note that pay was regularly in arrears, at best, and that desertion among soldiers was extremely difficult to slow, let alone stop.[65]

In addition to the burdens the sea blockade placed on an already patchwork transportation network and the hardships distribution decisions caused for the civilian population, overall agricultural production suffered in at least two other respects. First, many peasant farmers fighting on the front could not also till their fields, plant their seeds, and harvest their crops. Second, the deportation of the Armenians on the eastern front and the deportation of the Greeks from the coastal plains on the western front created what Zürcher describes as an agricultural "wasteland."[66] Of course, not all agricultural downturns were attributable to the war. In Palestine, three years of drought, beginning in 1914, parched production at precisely the time when heavy conscription robbed the land of local peasants and animals.[67] Most vivid of all, however, was the devastating locust attack of 1915.

In *Year of the Locust* the historian Salim Tamari discusses the memoirs of three soldiers in the Ottoman army, a rare luxury considering few of the diaries from that era are from soldiers of the region—in this case two from Jerusalem and one from Mersin.[68] One of the Jerusalem men, Private Ihsan Turjman (1893–1917), wrote a diary between March 28, 1915, and August 8, 1916, which Tamari edited and published. In an early entry Private Turjman laments the scourge of locusts: "Locusts are attacking all over the country. The locust invasion started seven days ago and covered the sky. Today it took the locust clouds two hours to pass over the city. God protect us from the three plagues: war, locusts, and disease, for they are spreading through the country. Pity the poor."[69]

Locust invasions were not unprecedented in the region. In his memoir, George Korkor described the abundance of food available in Homs, where prices were the lowest in the empire: large watermelons, fish, and good fruit were plentiful in the market. But in 1908, he noted, the locusts ravaged crops and created serious shortages.[70] According to oral history, in Lebanon (and presumably throughout the locust-infested areas of the region) people would send children into the fields to rattle tin cans in the hopes of scaring away the locusts.[71]

During the Great War, the effects of these swarming grasshoppers were felt everywhere, compounding the inherent misery that accompanies war.[72] In April 1915 the populations of al-Alamayn and Tabi'a al-Shaykh in Egypt tried to corral an outbreak of locusts, with some success.[73] In May 1915 locusts appeared in Alexandria, destroying significant cultivation in the area.[74] And in July 1915, as the Egyptian Ministry of Agriculture prematurely announced the departure of locusts from all Egyptian provinces,[75] they swarmed throughout Sudan. "The damage left is indescribable," noted the Cairo-based daily *al-Muqattam,* which added that the summer harvest and many palm trees were shorn clean. Descending from the Bayuda desert, located north of modern-day Khartoum, they razed the land like an impenetrable sandstorm to which all resistance seemed futile.[76]

In 1915 locusts also ravaged Haifa before passing over Jordan and heading to Hawran, destroying green fields as they went.[77] The website of the American Colony in Jerusalem describes the "biblical proportions" of these attacks in Palestine, lasting from March to October and stripping "areas in and around Palestine of almost all vegetation."[78] With the food supply already depleted, this disastrous development severely burdened Jerusalemites.[79] The density of the locust cloud over Beirut and Lebanon was so extreme in April 1916 that it even eclipsed the sun.[80] In order to clean the water cisterns of these pestilent pollutants, the Beirut water authority interrupted the water supply for two days (on the heels of three consecutive days of interrupted food distribution). When locusts attacked their next target—the fertile Biqa' valley—they were described as covering the ground to the depth of an arm's length.[81] An Arab publication in Argentina, *al-Shams,* reported that in the town of Damur, south of Beirut, "prices are inflating. Locusts, the lack of rain, and war impoverished the population."[82] In 1916 one Lebanese émigré in America received a letter revealing that four of his neighbors had succumbed to hunger in the wake of the locust attack. "This incident is considered to be a first in the East," reported *al-Ahram,* which added that not only had the locusts ravaged all the green fields of the country, but that the agricultural stock from the preceding year had been entirely depleted. In turn, Syrians living in the United States launched philanthropic endeavors to assist their countrymen.[83]

Jean Touma, a young man from Dayr al-Qamar in the Shuf district of Mount Lebanon, kept a diary before his early death, which occurred sometime during the last two years of the war (his family is uncertain of the exact date). His unpublished diary is written in French and English, as Touma was an educated young man who taught in the village of Barja, also located in the Shuf district. It conveys a carefree attitude as well as a great interest in music, since Touma was a mandolin player. Yet Touma's youthfulness—he turned twenty-one in 1915—was dampened by the Great War, which imposed all sorts of restrictions on the population. In April 1915 he wrote that for several years he had not seen such a quantity of locusts and that "the sun is almost veiled."[84]

According to Touma, the government did attempt to combat the locust plague. At one point authorities ordered each household to capture or kill two to four *oqqa* (over five kilograms) of locusts. Before dawn, drums and bugles woke the population, and Touma dutifully proceeded to chase locusts with the housemaid. After filling a bag of almost four *oqqa* and sending it to the military barracks, Touma noted, "many are still visible in the sky but much less than yesterday."[85] The program was not entirely successful; eleven months later, Touma again remarked upon locusts flying through the skies in search of crops.[86] On his way to Mosul from Tell-Halif, another man reported battling "a storm of locusts . . . continuously for two days. Millions upon millions of white wings filled the air like opaque snow and hid the sun."[87]

Postwar novels picked up on the epic destruction of the locusts, illustrating their resonance in the collective memory of the region. Born in 1911, Tawfiq Yusuf Awwad wrote a novel at the outbreak of World War II concerning the Great War. The novel—*al-Raghif* (The Loaf of Bread)—is set primarily in his mother's village, Saqiyat al-Misk, in the Matn district of Mount Lebanon and highlights villagers who fought against the Ottomans while collaborating with them for economic gain. His descriptions of dust-blown fields underscore the lack of flower and plant growth, both casualties of the locusts, and contrasts with the normally picturesque setting of the eastern Mediterranean.[88] Similarly, in words echoing Linda Schatkowski Schilcher's description of the poor subsisting on orange and lemon peels, sugarcane, weeds, and other greens in 1916 Cairo,[89] the novel *Shirwal Barhum* ties famine to locusts: "Have you forgotten the locust attack in 1915 when they spread over Syria . . . have you forgotten how they destroyed all the vegetation . . . have you forgotten how people started fighting over the peel of lemons and oranges and sugar cane that had been sucked on in northern Lebanon?"[90]

As refugees moved into and throughout the empire, the Arab provinces experienced an increased competition for food, straining an already tenuous situation. In addition to floods (in 1914 major floods destroyed more than 2,500 homes) and a cholera epidemic, by 1917 Baghdad had experienced an influx of refugees from other regions of Mesopotamia.[91] These population dislocations added to the pressures of feeding the population at a time when serious shortages already existed. Conditions were only exacerbated by retributive sanctions imposed by Jamal Pasha to punish alleged nationalists for collaborating with the French. So focused was Jamal on this threat that at one point he exiled more than two hundred families from Beirut and Damascus to Anatolia. In other cases, residents were displaced because they had been deemed troublemakers or classified as deserters. The historian Elizabeth Thompson uncovered one such case of exile: "Ahmad al-Jundi tells of how his father, a court employee in northern Syria, was banished to a small town of Anatolia in late 1916. The entire family made the trip by cart, carriage, and train in winter weather."[92]

Jamal Pasha paints a different picture. In his memoir, he argued that it was only out of precaution that he "invited" a few Maronite and Druze Lebanese to settle in Jerusalem, where they remained "free to reside exactly where they liked" for the duration of his Egyptian campaign, and to do so at his expense. Jamal justified this wartime measure on the grounds that many of these men were not only friendly with the French and English, but strongly suspected of inciting unrest.[93] For Ambassador Morgenthau, distrustful of the Pasha, such arguments rang false. But to others he came across as sympathetic. Edib wrote of his protection of Armenians exiled in Syria and of his charitable children's organizations, both Armenian and Arab.[94]

The image of hunger, disease, and lawlessness swirling around the gates of the Porte became a dominant postwar memory in the memoirs and secondary sources that survived the strict Ottoman wartime censorship. Despite considerable effort, the misery of war could seem almost impossible to evade. Although Ja'far ibn Muhsin al-Amin's family had moved from Damascus to the countryside, it was not long before the situation deteriorated there too, with supplies diminished and cholera spreading. "Death was everywhere and whoever could escape to the countryside did so and lived in tents fearful of contamination. . . . We were the only ones left from this family in Shaqra and had my father not been lucky to find a few men who were ready to help evacuate the dead bodies many would have remained without a tomb because healthy people refused to get close to sick people for fear of contagion."[95] So all the Amin family packed their camels and moved once again, this time to the Siddiqin area in the south and to Niha in the Biqa' valley where there were fewer people.

In the capital Istanbul, where the population numbered almost one million, some basic necessities became rare, while others disappeared altogether.[96] One visitor in 1916 observed that the "lines in front of the baker shops awaiting their daily ration of bread were of people obviously undernourished, their faces thin, pale and drawn."[97] Reflecting this scarcity, the price of bread spiked while its quality tumbled. In the provinces, even before the war, food shortages had sparked bread riots, which de-escalated only after government intervention.[98] During the war, in the cities and countryside alike, bakery lines stretched for hours as people waited for a single loaf.[99] In Palestine, "women and children (most young men were already conscripted) formed long queues in front of bakeries and fought for meager amounts of bread."[100] As bread supplies cratered, substitute goods entered the Ottoman economy. Authentic white bread was replaced by a mix of flour and cut-up wheat straw.[101] In the spring of 1916, shortages resulting from slackening grain deliveries from the Hawran even caused fights to break out in front of bakeries.[102] In June, for example, Beirut was without bread for three days.[103]

The accompanying discontent caused some people to take risks. Bechara Baroody (Bishara al-Barudi), a resident of the town of Rayaq in the Biqaʻ valley, recounts a scene of protest in which women registered their dissatisfaction with the quality of bread: "And I still remember the coming of Jamal Pasha . . . as he passed in front of the pharmacy in a red car and the day was rainy and the road muddy. . . . He had a thick beard and fiery eyes and wore a black kalpak and the women threw black bread at him to show him what the people were eating. He became angry and had the women arrested and ordered to have them flogged."[104]

Basic necessities such as fat for cooking, cracked wheat, and coffee became rare luxuries, but the rarest commodity of all was sugar. Sugar was already entirely imported at the start of the war; the blockade ensured that it was virtually impossible for the average person to procure.[105] In less than a year, by October 1915, the price of a pound of sugar had inflated to 60 piasters in the Arab provinces, reflecting widespread shortages.[106] The creation of a central food provisions office in 1916 could not slow its meteoric rise, unmatched by any other staple food during the war.[107] From memoirs and war accounts it is possible to glean anecdotal insight into just how precious sugar was to daily life. In his memoir, Baroody vividly illustrates how fiercely sugar was protected and how indelibly it was bound up in the memory of war. In this scene Baroody is describing his family's home in Rayak in the Biqaʻ valley, in the midst of the explosions of war:

> In this house we witnessed the battle between the British and the Germans and the explosions in Rayaq and what happened is that it was in the afternoon and my mother was making figs with molasses because there was no sugar in those days and it is worth mentioning that we had a "sugar loaf" and I used to look at it with delight but it was forbidden to touch it because it was kept for the moment of deep need. We were hovering around my mother and smelling the aroma of figs and we heard four planes flying high in the sky toward Rayaq. Suddenly we heard the rumble of the DCA and the bombs were exploding around the planes. The planes in turn, were bombarding the ammunition warehouses with bombs and we understood later that one of the planes had been downed. . . . An hour after the planes had left, explosions started rocking the air and the fires erupted in all the German warehouses in Rayaq. The fires raged for three days. And the people went

looting so that you could see people walking on the railroad track toward Rayaq as if they were groups of ants. The house we were in was requisitioned by the Germans and we had to move to another house.[108]

Irrespective of their causes, such hardships were very hard on a civilian population largely bereft of its men. Virtually every part of the empire was affected in some form, even if the famine spread with varying intensity across the Ottoman provinces, towns, and cities. For one author, the Ottoman territories suffered differently from the scarcity of food, but harsh famines appeared specifically in four regions—Kut, Khanikin, Mosul, and Lebanon. In the first three areas, the famine was limited in time and scope. Yet starting in the spring of 1916, widespread famine in Lebanon engulfed some areas bordering Syria that overlooked Lebanon, and lasted for more than two years. People suffered tremendously.[109]

From the spring of 1916 on, the misery was particularly acute, as *L'Asie française* noted in a postwar article that blamed the abandonment of towns, the dilapidated state of housing, and the grave social conditions for the outbreak of famine.[110] Mount Lebanon and the Syrian coast, including Tripoli, Jounieh, and Beirut, were devastated early on, as were the towns of Haifa and Acre.[111] Initially in the war, the population of south Lebanon, the Syrian interior, and the Biqaʿ valley emerged relatively unscathed, mostly because of their proximity to the grain-producing areas.[112] But despite Syria's usual water abundance and the agricultural self-sufficiency of Mount Lebanon and other areas, the harvest of 1915 was disappointing, and unable to meet the needs even of the troops stationed in the area. Harry Stürmer, the German correspondent in Istanbul for the *Kölnische Zeitung* from 1915 to 1916, recalled that "reliable reports of a still worse state of affairs" emerged from the Syrian interior.[113]

To portray the misery in Syria, in April 1915 one correspondent of the London *Times* in Cairo cited a Syrian refugee who had escaped from Beirut overland to Basra. This refugee's narrative dovetailed with detailed reporting in *al-Muqattam,* which covered the eyewitness accounts of Syrian refugees. The condition of the country is "worse than in 1860," wrote the *Times* correspondent, referring to the devastating civil war that had shaken Mount Lebanon and Damascus five decades before, adding that "locusts have much ravaged the country, famine reigns, and people are dying on the roadside by the hundreds."[114] Again, this was in large part attributed to myriad miscues in transportation, which made scarce foods virtually inaccessible: "Grain is obtainable in isolated parts but it is impossible to move it to the more needy districts owing to lack of transport. Fodder is scarce, and there are no horses or mules, while the sole train facilities are a weekly service between Beirut and Damascus."[115]

As Schilcher comments, "At least during 1917 and 1918, the interior joined the coastal towns in suffering. By that time the streets of all cities and towns of greater Syria were filled with their own starving poor."[116] By then, too, refugees had flooded Syria, adding to the number of deprived. In the third year of the war, "conditions in Aleppo had deteriorated badly; hardly any food or medical supplies were left," and not even a gold coin could buy bread because not a loaf could be found in any marketplace.[117] Before long it became widely known that hundreds of thousands in Syria were dying of hunger and scarcity. "By the end of 1918 mortality in the coastal towns of Lebanon may have reached 500,000."[118] Baroody later recalled that in World War II "we lived like emperors," but in World War I "Lebanon was hell."[119]

Among those who suffered extraordinary hardship and loss during the Great War were the Armenians. In 1915 British and other reports circulated from every direction with increasing frequency concerning the genocide of the Armenians. One report dated September 1, 1915, mentioned an ongoing extermination and the mass expulsion of Armenian men from Istanbul, of whom almost ten thousand died in the mountains.[120] Other reports echoed and reinforced such assessments, referring to Armenians dying by famine and disease or at the hands of Turks and Kurds.[121] Intelligence reports poured in concerning systematic deportations and deaths, including in Diyarbakir, Urfa, Erzurum, and Sivas, as well as in other areas of eastern Anatolia.[122] The reports added that the German and Austrian ambassadors sheltered many Armenians in Istanbul from their Ottoman allies.[123]

British officials expressed worry to their superiors about the dislocations in 1917, [124] and as late as 1918 T. E. Lawrence reported on "a swarm of destitute . . . Armenians" arriving in Tafila in southern Jordan.[125] While the men often died quickly in their enfeebled state, many Armenian women were distributed among harems as far away as Persia. Armenian children were also exploited sexually, or turned into slaves.[126] In the ensuing decades, countless firsthand accounts spread from the Middle East to Europe, the

Americas, and beyond. Wherever they settled, Armenians rebuilt their lives and became important scions of local societies. In Syria and Lebanon, in particular, they became major contributors to the economic boom of the middle of the twentieth century, but they never forgot what they went through or what it taught them.[127] Of such sensitive topics, there are always multiple interpretations. Yet even the official Ottoman view that Armenians were a fifth column helping the Russian enemy does not explain why the innocent and guilty were punished equally, en masse, and why no judicial process was established to distinguish between the combatant and the civilian.[128] What happened to the Armenian population will remain one of the great tragedies of World War I in the Middle East.

The suffering of wartime populations is brought home by the emotional renderings of eyewitnesses, whose grim encounters produced detailed memories that would haunt them for many years. Ja'far Muhsin al-Amin recalled watching weak and sickly children walk through the streets on rooster-thin legs supporting bloated stomachs.[129] The Lebanese writer Anis Freiha (Furayha), a native of Ra's al-Matn in Mount Lebanon, has written extensively about Lebanese traditional life. He experienced the Great War as a secure youth, sheltered and surrounded by family and village traditions that imbued his formative years with stability and joy: "As for us, youngsters, we did not care much about the war and the news. We were happy during that summer of 1914 because we were back to our playgrounds. . . . We left the news of the war to the adults."[130] But even he could not long escape the human catastrophe unfolding all around him. Freiha described the famine, the locusts, and the discovery of an abandoned, malnourished baby that looked like a skeleton: "I remember an evening where I was coming back home and saw something that scared me terribly: the skeleton of a baby wrapped in a blanket. The head was shaved. I really got scared: who was this child? He was a child found on the street dying."[131] The rescued child was taken to Brumana, in the Matn district of Mount Lebanon, some ten kilometers east of Beirut. There the orphan was entrusted to Mr. Oliver, the headmaster of Brumana High School, a prestigious secondary school established in 1873 by Quakers and where Freiha had been enrolled: "He [the baby] had been taken to Mr. Oliver who sent [returned] him to us until he could prepare a room for him at the seraglio. And he told my mother not to feed him anything except for water and milk because his intestines were not working. This child was the first orphan who entered the seraglio. I remember that he was from Arsun. . . . And that's why Jamal Pasha had given a large sum of money."[132]

The Nablus-born author, historian, and politician Muhammad Izzat Darwaza also recounts the mounting social crises among the poor families of the mountains and their effect on children. These families migrated to Beirut to escape famine, but in fact "they escaped from hunger to hunger."[133] The children of these families appeared ghostlike in worn-out clothes that slumped over their skeletal bodies. Many of them, and their parents, died of hunger on the railway tracks or among the garbage while scavenging for food. The correspondent Stürmer relayed similar scenes from the capital, where "some dozen human beings literally died of hunger daily in Constantinople alone. With my own eyes I have repeatedly seen women collapsing from exhaustion in the streets."[134]

In pity Darwaza began cutting two loaves of bread into small pieces every day and distributing them to hungry children in his neighborhood. At news of this deliverance, a crowd of children began gathering in front of his house to compete over bread crumbs as if they were manna from heaven.[135] 'Anbara Salam al-Khalidi, a member of the Sunni elite, recalls that the weak and hungry lay in the street, imploring "[I am] hungry! [I am] hungry!" Like Darwaza, she—and presumably other members of her family—would rush to the windows and verandas of her family home and beckon those who could walk to come near and catch the food she would toss them. She would watch children rummaging through garbage searching for leftovers, quarreling with dogs for whatever prized scraps they discovered. She also recalled her mother regularly leaving the house armed with bread or dried food that she would distribute to the poor.[136] At one point, she and her family bought bananas, which attracted tens of children who hungrily eyed the peels. Bishara al-Buwari, whose memoir details his wartime service to the French, confirms how the war transformed discarded fruit peels into luxury items. After returning to his native Beirut in 1918, he called on one store owner who had assisted him: "I felt like eating some grapes, a kind that I had not eaten all through the war. So he brought me a grape that weighed no less than half a kilogram and I started sucking the grains and throwing the skin on the pavement which was all muddy from the rain. In less than a second, about ten children came towards me and started fighting over the peel. My eyes welled up with tears and I gave them the grape and some coins and left."[137]

The historian Khairia Kasmieh similarly writes that "nobody had the luxury of peeling an orange in the street, as it would have caused a starving crowd to gather, to fight over it."[138] The sociologist Ali al-Wardi cites the Turkish eyewitness Falih Rifki Bey, then a journalist who also served as secretary to Jamal Pasha, and who visited Beirut in the midst of the famine.[139] Falih Rifki Bey's memoir is haunted with "terrible sights, naked kids with distended abdomens fighting over orange peels, devouring it to calm their hunger, and skeletal women covered in faded rags lying on the streets asking for a piece of bread."[140]

Thompson described "the horror that befell those who stayed behind" in 1915 Beirut as "immeasurable." In February 1916, Mary Bliss Dale, Daniel Bliss's daughter, mentioned in her unpublished journal that an eyewitness reported "adults and children lying by the side of the road beyond Beyrout river bridge—actually dying."[141] At the medical gate of the college, a woman who had had nothing to eat but grass for two days was found exhausted by hunger.[142] In May of the same year, Mary Bliss Dale wrote that one woman had attempted to give up her baby boy in order to save him from starvation while adults and children were "lying around the streets weak and starving."[143] Thompson refers to the American consul, who found the streets of Beirut in July 1916 "filled with starving women and children" and "people lying dead in the gutter."[144] In response, the American consulate asked American ladies living in Beirut, with the support of locals, to distribute money among the needy in order to help them fend off starvation. These women then offered apprenticeships in printing and devised jobs such as street sweeping and guarding the Syrian Protestant College. They also taught local women in handicrafts, which helped stave off hunger and the general misery for a while.[145] Similarly, Mariam Cortas, along with two of her sisters, responded to shortages by fundraising for mothers who were still nursing their infants. Cortas established a distribution system for these young women: "The mothers went every day at noon to the backyard of the Cortas's home to receive their ration."[146] She also launched a soup kitchen with her husband, Tanios,[147] although Western sources credit an English doctor for its existence.[148] In truth, the doctor had found it difficult to distribute raw food to the hungry because local thugs would steal it and then resell it. So the Cortases suggested that a kitchen be built in a neighboring house that belonged to a certain Umm Bishara. The Cortases were responsible for storing the food in their cellar and in the doctor's house.

They were supported by a large number of women and children from Brumana, Roumieh, Joura, and Qinnabeh, who helped run the kitchen with
Mariam's younger sisters and other women and young boys from the village. Of course, such charitable acts could alleviate only a small percentage
of the suffering that had spread throughout the region. Wardi cites Jirjis
al-Khuri Makdisi: "Those who did not flee to inner Syria looking for food
became part of the beggars who saw their numbers increase steadily in
Beirut; among the beggars there were those who had some energy to roam
the streets and go from door to door or step over the piles of trash looking
for dead animal carcasses and those who could not, would lie down in
the streets begging the passersby for help with their hands outstretched and
weak voices. Some people, and there were kids among them, would talk
with their eyes. . . . When 1918 came, the lower strata of the society had
virtually disappeared and were replaced by the middle class."[149]

Usually, it was the most vulnerable, predominantly women and children,
who suffered the most. One eyewitness reported that "crowds of starving
men, women and children, many of whom die on the roadside" could be seen
on the road between Beirut and the mountains.[150] In the summer of 1916
Halidé Edib was asked by Jamal Pasha to increase the number of schools
in Lebanon, Damascus, and Beirut. As a result, she visited an orphanage in
Antura located in the Matn district of Mount Lebanon, a small valley that
faced the Mediterranean Sea and was otherwise shut in by mountains. She
was taken aback by the filth and misery those children suffered: "Each
child, each bed, and each piece of furniture was covered with vermin, and
most of the children had mouth disease. The children themselves looked
like little wild beasts and acted as such. There seemed to be no human de-
cency or cleanliness left among them. The smell, the dirt, the din, and the
sickly sight quite overcame the new staff. They had not imagined such a
state possible." The "complete degradation of the children" frightened the
new director, Loutfi Bey.[151]

In 1918 a German medical officer also noted the sad, haggard state of so
many children: "every morning, one could see the bodies of starved children in the streets."[152] Such reports are substantiated by the gruesome photos that have survived the ensuing century. The haggard, gaunt expressions
of the starving women and children of World War I are interchangeable
with the worst refugee and concentration camp images of later decades.
Their suffering, if they somehow managed to survive the conflict, did not

necessarily end with the war. As late as the spring and fall of 1920, bread riots were reported in Hama while many Aleppine families went without evening meals.[153]

Throughout Mount Lebanon, whole families lived on nuts, fruit peels, and the rare, luxurious slice of bread. As Jean Touma commented, "No one talks about war anymore . . . everyone is in search of bread, which can be found only with difficulty. In the Lebanon the famine is even more terrible; it would take volumes to write all that is related to it."[154] Muhammad Darwaza relays rumors that "people in Beirut and in areas in the mountain ate cats and dogs and dead cadavers; and it was also said that mothers ate the cadavers of their children."[155] For visitors, the contrast in Lebanon was particularly haunting. Wardi's eyewitness, Falih Rifki Bey, wrote that

> as soon as we crossed that road situated on one of the hills of the city and reached neighboring areas I felt a sadness that forced me to stop, for I started hearing voices around me expressing the pain of hunger and begging the passersby for a piece of bread. Then I started seeing skeletal shapes lying around incapable of moving. And I saw a carriage with hands extended from the back so I looked closer and found out that these were the corpses of women and children who had succumbed to the famine. The city of Beirut had assigned these carriages for the living to roam around and pick up the dead people who had succumbed in the streets to dispose of them. These carriages were ferrying dozens of these wretched people every night and sometimes they would take people who had fainted from hunger with no one to take care of them. On waking up these people would find themselves among the dead and the fear and hunger would overcome them and they would die. One of the carriage drivers told me that he had often seen that happening and no one was available to help.[156]

No wonder, then, that in his book on Lebanon during the Great War, the writer Antun Yammin characterizes the Lebanese famine and those "black days" as singular in scope and size.[157] In Ras Beirut (west Beirut), near the Sanayi' school, he witnessed children picking up sesame grains from garbage piles, while others gathered around dead animal bones to suck out the marrow. In Harat Hurayk (Hreik), a suburb south of Beirut, men, women, and children competed over ant hives, because grain could be collected from the ants' mouths. The destitute even searched for grains in the excrement of horses and donkeys near wheat mills. In the Biqa' valley, dogs and humans competed over the flesh and bones of camel corpses, whether or not the camels had succumbed to disease.[158] In other instances, people ate their own domesticated animals. Such desperate measures were dangerous and risky. One source who used to work with Germans in Rayak informed Yammin that the Germans had once discarded a diseased horse. The foxes and wolves of the region refused to consume the carcass, but some forty people "ate the horse from head to toe" and subsequently died of disease.[159]

Hunger and misery were not confined to wartime Lebanon, even if it was the hardest-hit region. In Damascus life was difficult for all but the wealthy—especially so for the historian Nicola Ziadeh. In his account, personal tragedy combined with public hardship to paint an unsettling picture of conditions in the city. Ziadeh's family struggled to locate even molasses, while sugar and imported rice from Egypt disappeared completely.[160] After his father's conscription into the Ottoman army, his impoverished family turned destitute altogether. Originally from Nazareth, Ziadeh's father was educated in the German Syrian orphanage in Jerusalem, and thereafter found work as a foreman helping construct the Hijaz Railway. Eventually he was transferred to the Damascus headquarters of the German railway company. "This is why I was accidentally born in Damascus on 2 December 1907," Ziadeh explains, before recalling "the scarcity of so many commodities in the markets. We could not get sugar, coffee, rice, or tea."[161] Ziadeh eventually joined his maternal grandfather in Nazareth during the war: "What was scarce in Damascus was even worse in Nazareth and other parts of the region. At least in Damascus there was quite a lot of molasses made of grapes. Grapes in the Nazareth area were not good for molasses. They were not even good for *araq* [the alcoholic drink], as they are in Lebanon."[162] Ziadeh's situation deteriorated at the news of his father. Like so many other conscripts, his father had never deployed to the Suez front for which he had mobilized, but instead had been herded from one Damascene mosque or home to another, eventually growing infirm and dying. Ziadeh's family anxiously searched for him in the local hospitals. Ziadeh later recalled that his "experience of those days, which lasted for more than three weeks—seeing all those people sick, neglected, abandoned, and the smell—made a lasting impression upon me. The rooms were dirty. The treatment was bad. Most of the nurses had never received proper training."[163] Perhaps most searing of all, however, was that one hospital official directed the eight-year-old to a set of corpses lying "on the pavement" awaiting identification. Thus, as a young boy Ziadeh experienced the scene of an exposed, outdoor morgue, preserved only by the rush of cold water spilling over the unshielded dead bodies. One old man, searching through the same corpses for his son, compared the grotesque scene to vegetable squash (*kusa*) sitting in salt water to ensure proper stuffing. Ziadeh later summarized it as "the things the terrified city experienced."[164] For a young boy, it must have been painful.

In his diary, a founder of several Jerusalem private schools vividly recounts the desolation of Damascus during the war. Brought to the city in 1917 as an Ottoman prisoner of war, Khalil Sakakini escaped the following year to join the Arab rebellion in Hawran,[165] but while still in Damascus he encountered the pleas of desperate women, their sad eyes and gaunt hands entreating passersby to save their emaciated children from starvation. In his remembrances, Sakakini reproached those passersby who ignored such pleas "as if their hearts had turned to stone."[166] As the renowned Lebanese dancer Badi'a Masabni discovered firsthand, however, some people were so deprived of food that well-intentioned but ill-timed generosity could prove fatal.

Although born in Beirut, Masabni moved to Cairo where she opened the Casino Opera nightclub in 1926. Ali Wardi describes her as a beautiful artist and singer with "a skin soft like no other" and a charming personality.[167] To the broader world she is known for her contribution to modern belly dancing. After her death in Beirut in the 1970s, a Cairo bridge was even named in her honor.[168] Yet before she attained fame and celebrity, Masabni was courted by an Ottoman officer, Salah al-Din, whose influence ensured her a steady supply of grain during the war. Wardi relays one anecdote from Masabni's memoir in which her good intentions backfire:

One morning, while I was standing on the balcony of our house, I saw a child looking for food in the garbage on the street, so I called my sister Nazla and asked her to bring the hungry child. As soon as the little girl saw all the food that Nazla prepared for her to eat, she threw herself on the food and started eating like a little animal. I let her eat all she wanted without thinking that overeating could harm her and she quickly started showing the signs of bloating; she died a week later. She did not die from hunger but died from too much food! What an irony! . . . and the same thing happened again with a poor mother who, with her child, was looking for something to eat so we sheltered her and gave her food for her and her frail child. The woman was not hurt and was able to overcome the hunger and the bloating but her child did not last long and suffered the same fate as the other child.[169]

Invariably, such scenes proved impossible to erase from the collective memory, leaving a prominent mark on identity formation. The specific form of that memory varied—from Ziadeh's macabre morgue to Masabni's famished girl—but thousands of such experiences rippled throughout the region. One Arab novelist, Hanna Mina, stands out for his portrayal of hardship in Syria in the first decades of the century, and how it maintained its resonance decades later. Born in Latakia in 1924, Mina "moved with his family to the port of Al-Suwaydiya, in the Iskenderon province—which shortly thereafter was captured by the French and annexed to Turkey. . . . He started school at the age of eight and completed his primary education in 1936." His *Fragments of Memory* captures the period afterward, when "extreme poverty forced him into employment as a dock worker, a hairdresser, and a journalist."[170]

In this novel, published six decades after the war, Mina portrays Syrian society in the 1930s and 1940s through the struggle of an impoverished family—one that is neither rural nor urban—that moves from the city to the countryside and back to the city in a constant search for human security. The poet, critic, translator, and anthologist Salma Khadra Jayyusi described Mina's novel as "unique among his multi-faceted work in that, while it characteristically excels in the depiction of the malaise of a life lived under great stress, the experience it presents has two further qualities: first, it is mostly the experience of the author himself during his sadly deprived childhood, and second, it is an experience directly tied to a mode of life prevalent in the early decades of the century that is no longer in existence."[171] This characterization of Mina's "sadly deprived childhood" and a life "no longer in existence" demonstrate how much the Middle East changed with the war, and what an impact it had on the memory of those whom it challenged. In *Fragments of Memory* Mina narrates the life of a family encountering death and remembering war. He writes of their survival in an abandoned shack and of the father harvesting licorice roots "along with the rest of the poor."[172] In the midst of this struggle, the mother would gather her three daughters and son around an old mattress and pass the evenings telling stories. The mother was an orphan raised by relatives on the coast near Antioch. Her only brother, the middle child Rizkallah, was conscripted into the Ottoman army early in the Great War, and thereafter called for his two sisters to come to him at Mersin. The sisters set out in a sailing ship along with other women, and the ship was buffeted by such fierce winds that it nearly sank, but after two weeks at sea it sailed into Mersin and the sisters set about working as housemaids. Their brother died of pneumonia, and the mother's sister was lost in the *safarbarlik*,[173] a comprehensive term referring to the wartime tragedy of mobilization, forced displacement, and migration.[174] As disease and locusts swarmed the countryside, the mother was surrounded by mass starvation. Rendered too weak to steal or fight over discarded fruit peels, children with the sunken eyes of desperation would lie down in the streets to beg. Later, from the old mattress, the mother would intone of those days:[175] "Your uncle, son, was a man amongst men: as lively, generous, and brave as any hero in a story. Everyone loved him, even death. Death loved him and took him. I was still young. After he and your aunt were gone, I was a piece broken off a rock: alone, a stranger in a land where people were lost fleeing from the war. I wasn't the only one who lost their folks through death but I was the only one, in this exile, who had no relative left. Our village was far away and the *Safar Barr* terrible. Columns of refugees filled the roads. I worked as a servant for a station manager in a town called Baleemadak."[176]

Even from a distance, the horrors of the war are similarly clear in Ghazzi's *Shirwal Barhum,* discussed at the opening of this chapter. At the start of the war, as news of the Suez expedition arrived in Lebanon, and more and more young men donned their military uniforms, Maryam prepares for her wedding to Barhum: "My cheeks became rosy and I had a healthy glow on my face . . . and I was not that interested anymore in sitting in the evening with the guests who would come to tell their stories. I could not care less about the war now. Peace was all around me! I had become like a selfish kitten who cared only about its food and drink and shelter and I cared only about my dear life companion Barhum!"[177]

The year 1915 began full of promise for Maryam. She dismisses the possibility that misfortune could afflict them: "We . . . consider ourselves lucky because we are hiding in a deep spacious valley where we can, thanks to the work of our peasants, plant all sorts of crops . . . we can raise lamb and chicken away from the prying eyes of soldiers and robbers . . . and we can dream of the future because our isolation allows us a unique chance for tranquility."[178]

One evening, Barhum's anxiety, visible as Maryam's father offers him tea, is revealed as a neighbor curses the *safarbarlik*. Maryam hears people talking about hunger, suffering on the front in Suez, hardship in the Caucasus, and, ultimately, death by starvation and combat. Even her bountiful and protected valley is eventually confronted with the threat of hunger.[179] In imagery that would undoubtedly resonate, Maryam is told of brides so hungry, young, and brittle that they were carried off like dolls by bridegrooms.[180] As she learns of abject suffering, military losses, and the resulting death by hunger and disease, her outlook shifts:

> The pangs of hunger had reached everyone . . . by then, we had had to share the bread and share the wheat and help the many who came from both capitals . . . and some who came to the neighboring towns. Then we started getting really hungry . . . and the grandmothers started a very effective rationing . . . for, from what I remember from back then, we were still able to get wheat . . . but we could not have bread as much as we wanted to . . . and the olives that we had stored became our food . . . and in the early morning . . . my grandmother would milk the cow that we had hidden from the eyes of the soldiers and the guards, then she would boil the milk and turn it into yogurt and we would dip in it the bread that had become stale then hardened . . . and we would often eat it even after the mold had started to show on it . . . and we would remove the moldy parts to give to the chickens which would hurry to pick the bits of bread instead of taking their time before pecking like they used to do in the old days. And we would say: Thanks be to God . . . our house is still hidden among the hills . . . and our field still has many furrows and overlooks the railway road . . . and Barhum is still waiting for me to become his wife . . . because as a matter of course the wedding has been delayed by a year . . . because of the situation . . . which has become hard on everybody . . . for neither were we capable of buying clothes, dresses and carpets . . . nor was Barhum capable of selling the plants from his small greenhouse because the city ladies had stopped indulging in this practice after the spread of the war and were content to use the plants they had.[181]

As malnutrition turned to famine and starvation, disease spread among the people of the Middle East. Tuberculosis became the leading epidemic in

Istanbul and Anatolia during and after the war, and it was closely associated with poor living standards.[182] In 1915 *al-Muqattam* reported that fever
had spread in Cairo and that the number of deaths was increasing to the
point at which the Department of Health issued weekly statistics of total
people infected and killed. The paper added that the number of typhoid
dead had surpassed the number killed by the plague.[183]

Even so, the plague was a perpetual concern. In April 1915 bubonic
plague was discovered in two villages approximately one hundred kilometers southwest of Cairo, resulting in the death of twelve and the infection of
a further nine people.[184] Although at the start of May the newspaper announced that the number of fever infections had been halved,[185] by the end
of the month it compared the number of deaths in 1915 to 1914 and revealed that the infection total had apparently increased by over half.[186]
Then in July 1915 *al-Muqattam* reported that typhoid fever had decreased
in Cairo with no more than twenty persons infected daily, yet no reduction
in the mortality rate from the previous year was observed.[187] While the paper recognized that the Department of Health had insufficient staff to clean
all the houses, "this should not stop it from guiding the people in newspapers and posters reminding them of the right ways to protect themselves
from epidemics."[188] Moreover, *al-Muqattam* counseled, the Department of
Health "should also provide the poor with the necessary disinfectants for
free. Doctors should also publish articles to explain to people how to prevent these diseases."[189]

The paper again pushed for action one month later, noting that there
were many proven ways to prevent typhoid and typhus in Egypt. The Department of Health's staff, argued *al-Muqattam,* was large enough to treat
persons in each infected region; the country should utilize the tens of hospitals, staffed with hundreds of medical doctors and nurses, spread across
the regions.[190] Yet the next year typhus stubbornly reappeared in Cairo and
spread to the point where residents and officials alike feared an epidemic
outbreak.[191]

In his two-volume study of Alexandria, the French historian Robert Ilbert mentions that relatively few people paid to properly filter water and
prevent cholera.[192] In 1915 *al-Muqattam* expounded on some commercial
side effects of the spread of fever: an increased demand for mineral and
spring water imported from Europe caused many factories to imitate those
bottles by labeling their own products with identical seals. Of course, while

the labels suggested purified water, the bottles were in fact often filled with ordinary water.[193] As the war wore on, sanitary conditions worsened, leading to a steady decline in birthrates to go along with the general poor health of the population. By 1920, two years after the war, plague, typhoid, and especially tuberculosis had found a home in Alexandria.[194]

Not only Alexandria but the farthest reaches of the Ottoman Empire were wracked by disease. In the first year of the war, the plague claimed more than forty lives per week in the Iraqi provinces. If one survived the clutches of the plague or of deadly tuberculosis, a range of other diseases threatened, from smallpox to cholera and jaundice. All of these maladies were dangerous, since nearly all medicines were sent to the front and pharmacists were scarce.[195]

In the spring of 1916 newspapers reported on the spread of typhoid in Syria, Armenia, and Iraq; four American doctors succumbed to the disease. As a consequence, the American Red Cross sent a medical delegation of doctors and nurses to assist in treatment.[196] In his report on Syria Huvelin wrote that typhus and famine had hit the working classes particularly hard.[197] By 1916, the people of Syria's interior cities were dying by the thousands, and famine and disease, particularly typhus and malaria, "reached far beyond worst-hit Lebanon and far beyond the 1918 armistice."[198] Nicola Ziadeh, whose childhood in Damascus was darkened by his family's poverty and the search for his father's body, noted that in 1916 his mother contracted typhus in the contaminated hospitals during the search for her husband.[199]

Hanna Mina humanized the impact of disease on loved ones, recounting what his mother told them about her brother:

One day when he was in the city, he was arrested and conscripted. The men said, "This time he'll definitely eat the *qarwana*."[200] But he didn't eat it. He fled across the mountains through the snow. He reached us on his last legs. He was coughing and had a burning fever. He threw himself upon the bed from which he did not rise. "My oil has run out, brothers," he said to those who came to visit him, "and this little one," pointing to me, "is entrusted to your care!" The older men answered, "Don't talk like that, Rizk, our beloved friend. Tomorrow you'll get up as strong as a lion." He smiled at them, turned away . . . and asked for water. . . . He was burning up inside and the fire was coming out of his forehead. . . . I didn't know anything about death and it never occurred to me that he would die. It was difficult for me to believe that in that room he could so quickly leave me alone in the world.[201]

Disease spread among soldiers at a rapid pace. Ambassador Morgenthau criticized the Ottomans for their "most inadequate medical and sanitary service." He noted that typhus and dysentery had spread in all the camps and had caused the death of some hundred thousand men, and that rumors circulated widely about the suffering of the soldiers.[202] Animals were also prone to infection, compounding problems. Fever suspected to have come from Sudan spread among animals in Egypt and villagers were advised to boil milk before drinking it. A newspaper article sought to reassure readers that while fever occasionally spread in Egypt, causing infected cattle and sheep to become emaciated, they could be cured after a short treatment period. The article added that two veterinarians were assigned to the western province, while another was assigned elsewhere. The best way to prevent the spread of disease, the article concluded, was to alert these veterinarians.[203]

The historian François Georgeon has offered insight into just how difficult life was in the Middle East, setting aside the usual issues of hunger and disease. Even in the imperial capital of Istanbul clothes and shoes were rare among middle-income groups, the scarcity of wood and coal made winters unbearable, and entire city quarters existed cut off from water. With the war reducing public transport, people could either ride on overcrowded trams or walk for long stretches with ragged shoes on streets infested with rats. The humorist journal *Karagöz* commented in jest that rats had their uses, as following them would lead inhabitants directly to where the profiteers hoarded supplies of coffee and sugar.[204] The Armenian Sarkis Torossian, on leave from the front, described the scene in Istanbul in early 1916:

> As I strolled idly along, I began to notice the great change that had taken place. . . . No longer women and children paraded in fashionable finery; their clothing was seedy and even their postures seemed shabby and worn out. Hardships and scarcity were beginning to take their toll. I was witnessing a people on the verge of ruin. . . . Every second doorway seemed draped in mourning. Stamboul, that beautiful spot of the Marmora, had the appearance of a woman who, through sickness, grief, and old age, had lost her beauty and charm. German officers crowded the few markets which remained open,

buying up all available provisions for their families in the fatherland. Exor-bitant prices were demanded for the poorest foodstuffs, and in the markets household treasures daily were bartered for the merest necessities. If such was the condition of the middle classes, I dreaded to think of the predica-ment of the poor which by far was the more numerous of the two. In one market, through which I loitered, I heard people talking of thousands of children dying of undernourishment and disease. I heard tell of bands of desperate women sallying forth at night to sack foodshops or attack an un-suspecting traveler. Beggars lined the streets.[205]

T. E. Lawrence summarized in one report that even the "Turks are no bet-ter off than we are" in the Arab territories.[206]

Paradoxically, among those affected most severely by the war in Istanbul were government employees whose wages lost their purchasing power due to the enormous inflation that racked the city for the entirety of the war and beyond.[207] A telegraph operator with a large family, who received the equivalent of $24 per month, submitted a letter to the editor in which he wrote: "We are literally starving. Members of our families are suffering from diseases directly caused by hunger. . . . I have had to sell everything we had, merely to keep my family and myself alive."[208] This official was proud to have resisted the temptation to trade in illicit items, but he added that the temptation was growing steadily.[209]

What was the outgrowth of such hardship and to what exactly did that government official, and millions of impoverished like him, turn in trying times? For some the hardship was unbearable. As early as August 1915 Syr-ian immigrants to Egypt reported that suicide had spread like an epidemic, with men despairing because they had been unable to support their families or had lost all their belongings.[210]

There were also reports of cannibalism. However unbelievable, these sto-ries are telling in that they convey how people felt. Horror tales circulated of mothers eating their own children in desperation, although such charges were based more in prejudice against women than in fact.[211] According to Yammin, one woman from the Matn district of Lebanon ate the corpse of her nephew.[212] Yammin also heard from the commissary of customs in Bei-rut, Philip Effendi Faris, about an incident in Tripoli that quickly became known throughout the country. As the story goes, four women from the village of Hardin near Batrun in north Lebanon traveled to the nearby port of Tripoli where they slaughtered and ate four children before discarding their bones in wells. The incident was investigated by one of the commissioners in the Tripoli police force, the women were arrested, and within a week they died in their prison cells.[213]

Various other sources repeated or added to the tales of women who ate their children to satiate their hunger. Ali Wardi writes about a woman in the town of al-Qalamun near Tripoli who confronted her neighbor whom she had found eating her child, which she had cooked in a pot. The woman replied: "My child died of hunger so I am eating him so that I don't die in turn. Another child died before and I ate him as well."[214] According to the narrator, the children had not died a natural death but instead had been knifed. The authorities arrested her and she too eventually died in jail.[215] Linda Schatkowski Schilcher has recorded that "a German Vice-Consul personally investigated and reported on the case of two impoverished Maronite women, living in the port area of the Lebanese town of Tripoli, who had abducted, murdered, dismembered and eaten at least five children."[216] George Antonius quotes several sources about the famine, of which one, an American woman, wrote in the London *Times* on September 15, 1916, that "everywhere women could be seen seeking eatable weeds among the grass along the roads."[217] Commented Wardi: "We don't know how true all these stories are and it must have been the kind of exaggerations that the people had gotten used to tell in such situations. However we know that in terrible famines people can be driven to eat human flesh."[218]

Of course, reports of such extremes were very rare, and it is difficult to believe that they happened at all. Most gritted their teeth and endured by other means; one British naval commander noted in April 1916 that "there seems [*sic*] to be very few provisions in the block-house."[219] In Kut, for example, surplus grain was stored behind fake walls and in hidden compartments.[220] As the flour shortage intensified, beginning in 1915, the fear of starvation set people against one another, even for those residing in the tough, weathered deserts, accustomed to hardship.[221]

In 1918, while observing events in Tafila, T. E. Lawrence observed a pervasive distrust and division among the population (and between the population and the British) that manifested itself in nightly shootouts in the streets. According to Lawrence, the British took steps to police and secure the area with over five hundred men, but the insecurity persisted. Flour and barley were costly and difficult to find in Tafila, contributing to an escalating and reinforcing cycle of anxiety. Even in the west-central Jordanian town of Karak, where foods were generally cheaper, the expectation of imminent fighting drove supplies out of the open and into the underworld markets.[222]

At Edib's orphanage in Antura, among those too young to be conscripted, bullies prospered: "There were a few big healthy-looking children who seemed to dominate the whole place. Loutfi Bey told me that they took the bread of the smaller children and sold it in the village, gambled in all sorts of ways, and did other things which could not be told."[223] Similar bullying occurred in the dining halls of the schools, especially as some students grew weak and "looked as if they would be much better in a sanatorium." Two soldiers stood at the entrance to the hall with two large sacks of bread, rationing it to children as they arrived, while the matron and a few other teachers attempted to pour soup rations: "Before all the children had got into the hall, a tremendous uproar and fighting began. It was a scene for students of anthropology to see, for it illustrated the terrific struggle for existence among the lowest kinds of animals. The stronger boys were snatching the bread from the weaker ones, and the weaker ones were struggling to keep from giving up their bread. It was a wild fight, with all the children wrestling and tearing each other, crying and screaming."[224]

Begging became a regular means of survival. In Jerusalem, the poor relied on soup kitchens and traditional food distribution methods during peacetime. During the war, however, many of these programs collapsed, in large part due to food shortages but also because of the breakdown in traditional loyalties.[225] As a result, in one book on Australians in Egypt during the war, the photo caption reads: "Arabs scrambling for coins and food."[226]

A steady growth in crime to cope with deprivation was also observable. In 1916 the *Times* reported that "Lebanon, which is usually the most exemplary district, is now the most criminal."[227] Crime often constitutes the only means of survival in war; during the Great War, much of it took the form of petty theft. Some of the famished, especially the young and fleet of foot, stole food from people's hands and disappeared before the act could even register.[228] Wardi cites one eyewitness, Munir al-Rayyis, who was deeply saddened by the sight of children stealing food in Damascus: "The sight of the hungry youth and children roaming the streets and the souks trying to steal from the grocers and get anything they could from the hands of the people was painful: one would dip his hands in the yogurt bucket, another would be watching, barefoot, standing behind the person carrying the bucket, waiting for the chance to get some yogurt for himself and running away, his hands and mouth dripping."[229] Khalil Sakakini similarly empathized with the plight of children stealing in Damascus: "The harsh living and the skyrocketing prices left children with no other choice but to plunder the bakeries and restaurants. I personally would have participated if I had been a child facing these conditions."[230] Khairia Kasmieh also laments "the bitter poverty" registered by Badr al-Din al-Shallah, whom she describes as a member of a famous trading family: "No one would have dared to carry a loaf of bread in public, as it would have provoked the hungry to lunge upon it."[231]

The government sought to stem the rising tide of criminality by imposing stiff penalties. But considering the reason for the growth in crime—the battle for daily existence—such threats were largely ineffectual. In one case uncovered in Istanbul in November 1917, several women from destitute families formed together to steal hundreds of items valued at around $80,000: "Some of the members of the band sold the stolen goods in distant towns, bought food supplies with the proceeds, and sold such food to advantage in the streets of Constantinople."[232] That same year in the imperial capital, the authorities apprehended three other similarly organized bands consisting of both men and women.[233]

Already before the war, lax public morality offended Jamal Pasha's moral sensibilities: "There were many people in Constantinople who indulged in the vicious habit of making amorous remarks to Mohammedan ladies as they passed them out walking, on the boats and bridges, or in the streets and bazaars. Among them were even old women, who made indecent suggestions and even laid hands on elegant and well dressed women."[234] One can therefore only imagine Jamal's displeasure at the growth of another war industry in Istanbul—prostitution. An increase in open prostitution occurred alongside the growth of secret prostitution;[235] as a result, newspapers bemoaned the rise in immorality while the government established courts charged with protecting public morality.[236] But even these measures were largely ineffective. As Ahmed Emin Yalman discovered, the burdens of war—including rampant poverty among soldiers' families—were the main causes of this "general wave of prostitution."[237] This trend toward criminality was not confined to Istanbul.[238] In Jerusalem "begging, theft, and prostitution became daily features in the streets."[239] The soldier Turjman lamented that the war forced many honorable women and young girls of varying religions to turn to prostitution in order to provide for their families.[240] In Beirut prostitutes were already common in the late nineteenth century, but their numbers increased during the war.[241] Wardi noted that women first sold their jewelry, then their clothes, and ultimately themselves in honorable and dishonorable ways. Indeed, those hard days witnessed the growth of an industry of house servants and prostitutes.[242]

One of the main characters in the novel *al-Raghif* is the young Lebanese woman Zayna. Her stepmother, a café owner and woman of questionable morality, pressures Zayna repeatedly to submit to the desires of her older suitors in order to generate income for the family. In this postwar novel, the stepmother is angry that Zayna would not trade her good looks for food, and perhaps some niceties, too.[243] The pressure of prostitution as a means to survival is a recurring theme in the literature about Lebanon in the Great War, but it was immortalized in Bishara al-Khuri's poem, *The Poor*. In the poem, brought to us by Khuri's friend, Yammin, a young woman is forced into prostitution in order to provide for her daughter, since her husband is serving at the front. She is paid with a counterfeit coin, and so eventually ends up in prison while her daughter is forced onto the street.[244]

Egypt similarly abounded with tales of women forced into prostitution and its unhappy repercussions. In the land of the Nile, just as in Lebanon, poverty was the primary motivator. Unlike in Lebanon, however, prostitution in Egypt also serviced the large numbers of foreigners present during the war. It was a well-organized system, abetted by high-ranking officials intent on ensuring the comfort of important foreign guests, officials, and officers.[245] Above all, prostitution thrived in the bustling port cities such as Alexandria.

The presence of troops in Egypt accounted for an upsurge in prostitution.[246] Large numbers of British troops were stationed at a mass camp at the foot of the Pyramids, some ten miles from Cairo. One soldier wrote his mother that some considered Cairo to be "one of the world's most sinful cities, full of brothels and gambling dens where those intent on pleasure can enjoy everything from narcotics to naked dancers."[247] He also discovered that soldiers took the local train to Cairo: "The train is usually packed with soldiers searching for recreation and there are frequently passengers even on the roofs of the carriages. In the evenings the streets of the great city are full of Australian, New Zealand, British and Indian soldiers."[248] With such a large presence of British forces (including Australians) and other soldiers,[249] who on the whole had the reputation of being lawless and undisciplined, Cairo's brothels descended into even greater disrepute.[250] Another soldier stationed in the camp just outside Cairo wrote his mother on April 16, 1915, about riots in Cairo's red-light district that had occurred, of all days, on Good Friday two weeks prior. Primarily Australians and New Zealanders had "started running amok," "smashed up bars and brothels, hurled the fittings out into the street and set fire to them." When the military police arrived to intervene, they were bombarded with bottles, provoking the police to open fire in return. The result was four wounded soldiers and a battered image for the foreign Australian and New Zealand troops in the city.[251]

Although not all of the soldiers reinforced this negative reputation—one enlisted Australian soldier was known to prefer sophisticated settings and elegant female company—"for most, the fleshpots were more alluring, and enticed many to nocturnal, drunken debauchery in 'disgusting' back alleys."[252] Many of those alleys were probably in Cairo's Wazir quarter, where the red light area was frequented by Australians. One Australian estimated the number of prostitutes at thirty-five thousand.[253] He had little basis for such a figure, but such an extraordinary estimate suggests prostitution was rampant. Where prostitution existed, so did venereal diseases and theft, which Australians training in Egypt referred to as the "red plague."[254] While "some men 'got off scot free' after paying a prostitute five piasters (one shilling) in the notorious Wazir district," some "found themselves in the worst possible trouble for one hundred or two hundred piasters."[255]

A serial killing case in 1920 that captured headlines illustrates the deadly dangers prostitutes faced. The saga began in Alexandria when a prostitute named Sakina contracted a sexually transmitted disease, for which she was treated in a hospital where she met her eventual husband.[256] Sakina and another prostitute, Raya, their husbands, and two other men allegedly then went on to kill seventeen other prostitutes in Labban, a poor and unsafe neighborhood of the city abutting the western harbor.[257] They were convicted and hanged the following year. Other such crimes were reported near the end of the war in *al-Ahram* from the town of Tanta, when the pressures of the preceding years contributed to the breakup of social norms, and thus, to the social upheaval of the immediate postwar period.[258]

In the opinion of some observers of the 1975–1990 civil war, the mental trauma of that conflict sometimes outpaced its physical destruction. Waiting for the worst could sometimes be more agonizing than living with the physical wounds of war. While this rings particularly true for modern warfare, it also applies to conflict in the early twentieth century, with its own form of anguish. For long stretches civilians were in the dark about the well-being of their loved ones, and their separation often lasted years. On the home front, the physical ordeals and mental challenges of the war turned those four years into a living hell. Rather than give up, those who could fought to make ends meet.

CHAPTER FOUR

Entrepreneurs and Profiteers

"ONE OF THE characteristics of famine is that it is sensitive to social classes, poor people are those who suffer the most from it but rich people are hardly affected by it," commented Ali Wardi, adding about the rich: "They see their fortunes grow and the scope of their pleasures expand."[1]

The chasm between rich and poor predated World War I, but it was evident to contemporaries that the rich not only weathered the war but also profited from it, while the poor suffered immensely. A daily paper in Istanbul wrote in September 1918 that the hardships of the past four years had been distributed unevenly and that "for some sections of the population it had been an extraordinary occasion for profit and for enjoyment."[2] Like other conflicts of great duration and magnitude, the Great War provided new opportunities to those already favored with status and wealth. At the very top of society, privileged political, administrative, and military leaders lived lavishly. The journalist Ahmed Emin Yalman noted: "Whenever a minister had to travel on government business, his table had to be supplied with luxuries, unusual even in times of peace."[3] Meanwhile, government ministers played "their daily game of poker or billiards in the fashionable club, in the days of anxiety in 1915."[4] In contrast, peasants' earnings were raided for the profit of powerful officials and tradesmen—the Ottoman establishment requisitioned the peasant crop of Hawran, especially wheat, at cheap prices, and the Committee of Union and Progress indulged in sugar and maintained monopolies in most basic necessities.[5] Of the provisions collected in the name of military necessity, most benefited the upper ranks and failed to reach the average soldier: "Food supplies . . . were consumed behind the front, and never reached the fighting units."[6] All the while, the less privileged strata of the population suffered.

We have details of how this worked from the private papers of the Syrian politician Faris al-Khuri, published by his granddaughter Colette al-Khuri, herself a Syrian novelist. Born in the 1870s in Hasbayya into a Greek Orthodox family that later converted to Presbyterianism, Faris al-Khuri rose to political prominence in Syria in the 1940s. Already during the Great War, however, he had interacted with a range of important officials. One such contact was Michel Ibrahim Sursock (Sursuq), a Beiruti delegate elected in 1914 to the Ottoman parliament and member of the prominent Greek Orthodox Sursock family.[7] The Sursocks described themselves as Ottomans, and in his papers, Khuri noted the friendship that Jamal Pasha had with Michel Sursock, a friendship which some family members believed extended to Sursock's wife and cousin, Linda Sursock.[8]

Sursock visited Khuri in mid-May 1916, just after the public hangings in Greater Syria that year. Sursock confided in him that he had come on a sensitive mission—to requisition grain from the Hawran. At Jamal Pasha's direction, Hawran's farmers and villagers were to sell all their grain to Sursock for cash at low prices, keeping only enough for their own families. Khuri agreed to be of assistance.[9] In such ways, the war provided middlemen such as Khuri with the opportunity to turn a profit, even if the authorities would later exercise personal discretion over the disbursement of the collected grain, part of it going to the army.

During the war, Sursock also profited from the concession for wheat, which he controlled. To generate more income, he reputedly manipulated supply by closing granaries and, along with another family, the Asfars, engaging in price speculation.[10] Critics also accused him of hoarding grain during the war, which—considering his monopoly—may have deepened the famine. One source reported that in the summer of 1918, Sursock "refused to sell grain bought at 40 piasters the measure for less than 250 piasters even to save at least a portion of the children fed by the American relief organization."[11]

A young man at the time of his death, Sursock may have died of typhus, although some allege that he was murdered. Either way, his body was never found.[12] But while alive, Sursock and those like him with great wealth enjoyed advantages that proved decisive. These farmers, businessmen, or merchants bought provisions in bulk and at discounted prices. As Jirjis Maqdisi summarized, "Whoever has is given even more."[13]

Those with influence used their positions to land exclusive arrangements for rare commodities. Often, they needed Ottoman officials to get land and other projects started.[14] The governor's partners in the monopolization of sugar and petrol were wealthy Muslim and Christian Beirutis, respectively. The importation of flour and wheat from Aleppo was structured to reinforce monopolies.[15] Those who controlled such rare commodities guarded their concessions because these could be used as leverage to strengthen loyalties with members of their constituencies. This often raised the ire of other notables, who could not similarly strengthen their ties with their own followers. Control over entire economic sectors allowed some to consolidate control among their constituents, while their counterparts in other communities came up short. In September 1918, the press reported that Beiruti merchants had sent a telegram to the Ministry of Justice demanding that the wealthy businessman Salim Ali Salam be brought to justice for siphoning forty thousand kilograms of sugar from the General Food Directorate for distribution among his constituency.[16]

In wartime, Beirut notables entertained top Ottoman officials in their homes in extravagant style, hoping to curry favor and perhaps land such exclusive arrangements. When Jamal Pasha arrived in Syria, "one of the wealthy Beiruti people gave a dancing party in his opulent palace for Jamal Pasha at the same time when the streets of Beirut were filled with starving people and dead people because of the famine that we have described. . . . The dinner tables were laden with all sorts of delicious dishes and vintage wine and arak from Zahle, the guests who were attending were beautifully dressed, and the women were wearing precious jewelry. And there were smiles and signs of happiness on the faces around."[17] We can assume that during the war, the upper middle class mingled with the wealthy at such parties. Moreover, dignitaries and officers of similar ranks and opposing sides may have met at the same social gatherings before facing one another in battle.

Jamal Pasha was greeted with such smiles in Syria that Father Antun Yammin recounts high-society Syrians throwing themselves at the feet of the Ottoman "oppressors," showering them with gifts and invitations.[18] Christians and Muslims, such as the Sursock, Trad, Asfar, Bayhum, Ghandour, and Mkhaysh families, catered to Ottoman officials, as did "all the wealthy from one end to the other in Beirut and the Mountain."[19] In Damascus, the practice was no different: Muhammad Fawzi al-Azm, then Minister of Religious Endowments (*awqaf*), held a major banquet attended by leading public officials and local notables in honor of Jamal Pasha at his request in the summer of 1916.[20]

Nevertheless, upper-income families also turned their attention to the poor, and deployed their resources in service of the needy. The Sursocks are one family who took an active interest in the plight of the needy, chartering a school for girls in the 1880s, upgrading infrastructure around Beirut during the Great War, and building the Beirut hippodrome, an equestrian arena initiated during the war which some family members believe helped employ the poor.[21] Most directly, during the war they and other wealthy families distributed food to the needy.[22] At the age of just twenty, the future Lebanese man-of-letters, automobile tycoon, and philanthropist Charles Corm set off on a relief journey across Mount Lebanon. He traveled through many mountain villages, coming up with ingenious ways of providing food to the hungry. For instance, having noted the influx of starving countrymen to Beirut, Corm had the idea of making a sweet paste from dried grapes ("raisinée") in abandoned vineyards. He produced several tons, which he personally distributed to the needy. In fact, the initiative was such a success that it caught the attention of the French authorities just at the end of the war and they asked Corm to head the food supplies of Beirut in 1918–1919.[23]

By the middle decades of the nineteenth century, the Sursocks were already renowned as a leading Beiruti family. Their origins trace to Mersin, a town near Adana in southern Anatolia, much of which was built on Sursock land. From Mersin, the family business empire spread into Anatolia, Egypt, Lebanon, Palestine, and beyond. By the outbreak of World War I, the Sursocks lived in palatial homes, including several on Rue Sursock in the Ashrafieh district of Beirut, and moved in aristocratic circles from Istanbul to Paris. In the nineteenth and early twentieth centuries, one rhyme (in colloquial Arabic) was "I would love to be a horse in the Sursock household so that I am fed pistachios and nuts."[24]

Many families inherited or acquired wealth from traditional real estate investments, commerce with Asia and Africa, or through the expanded trade with Europe that characterized the nineteenth-century economic boom. One of them, the Sunni Salam family, was already firmly established at the beginning of the twentieth century. The scion of the family, Ali Salam, prospered as a merchant trading in staple goods with important connections in Aleppo, Damascus, Jaffa, and Alexandria. He married well, dressed in European fashion, and became so successful that he bought a home in the Musaytiba quarter of Beirut, which he remodeled into a stately mansion, and soon "was recognized as a leading citizen of the locality."[25]

Ali Salam's eldest son was Salim, who ran the family business from an office in the port area of Beirut after his father's death. The historian Kamal Salibi left us a lively description of Salim, acknowledging how families accrued connections and wealth over generations, but also appreciating the importance of Salim's savoir faire. As Salibi wrote, "Families like the Bayhums may have been richer; others, like the Barbīrs and Agharrs, may have claimed more distinguished ancestries; but among the Muslim notables of Beirut at the turn of the century few communicated with their fellow men as easily and readily as Salīm ʿAli Salām."[26]

Salim's charm likely proved helpful to his philanthropic endeavors, which extended to his involvement with the charitable Islamic society of the Maqasid, and with education. He and others from the society established two schools for girls and two schools for boys, which proved successful and enjoyed increasing enrollment. By 1912, in part thanks to Salim, the society was in strong enough shape to weather a government takeover during the war years.[27] In such ways, powerful families could make a real difference for the broader population. Salibi described Salim's entrepreneurial personality, his energetic approach to life, and the manifold activities of some of the well-to-do:

Leading citizen of the populous quarter of al-Musaytiba, at the southwestern end of the city, Abu ʿAli (as he was commonly called) was a successful merchant and an active public figure. Well-built and handsome, despite a paralysis of the right eye which was reportedly the result of a childhood accident, and smartly dressed in the latest European fashion topped by an Ottoman tarboosh, he was, with his modish moustache and carefully trimmed goatee, an elegant man about town. From his office in the port area, Abu Ali conducted a profitable business, mainly in staples; yet he did not lack the leisure to indulge in other activities. At different times he was a member and vice-president of the commercial court, a member and president of the municipal council, a member of the administrative council of the *vilayet* of Beirut, and a deputy for the *sanjak* of Beirut in the Ottoman parliament; he was also a leading member, and at one time the president, of the Moslem Society of Benevolent Intentions . . . which sought to promote modern education among the Moslems of Beirut.[28]

At times of acute crisis, the opulence of wealth contrasted sharply with the painful deprivation of poverty. In a short unpublished play he wrote in 1914, Charles Corm chastised the rich for playing tennis and for being so carefree at the Lebanese mountain resort of Sofar, when those less fortunate suffered so much.[29] Even the powerful could see the wretchedness of wartime Beirut, and they sought to obscure its most miserable features. Jirjis Makdisi wrote that before Enver Pasha's inaugural visit to Beirut in 1916—accompanied by several German generals—the governor (*wali*) of Beirut, Azmi Bey, ordered public decorations affixed around the city to mask the sight of the hungry and poor, herding them into the khans of Beirut, away from the visiting dignitaries.[30] Perhaps equal attention should have been paid to other jarring displays of wealth. Some German observers, themselves no strangers to luxurious treatment, were struck by the contrast they observed in Beirut. Despite the stagnating economy and the harbor at standstill, they found that an easy, shockingly privileged life prevailed among certain sections of the population.[31]

Halidé Edib shared a similar recollection from the same city in 1916: "The poorer population looked haggard and underfed. But women of the richer classes, gorgeously dressed and elaborately painted, drove about the town in luxurious carriages. The famine had not reached its climax, but one felt it coming, and the prosperity of the rich hurt one's eyes."[32] A similarly unperturbed existence permeated the upper classes of Damascus, where Edib traveled next. She attended one party where "the ladies gave a musical evening in the Arab fashion. There was no end of sweets and delicious fruit and of Arab women dancing and singing."[33] These singers and dancers wore

European clothes, much like Istanbul's Armenian dancing girls, and performed alongside Bedouin dancers clad in traditional draperies. The undisputed highlight of the evening was the arrival of Hedie, a Christian Arab singer who arrived unveiled and in European clothing. "The ladies sat around her and served her with fruit, delicious apricots and grapes, such as one gets only in Damascus," as she enraptured her audience with a famous desert song: "Although I am a great chief of the desert, I am thy humblest slave."[34]

At times, this upper social circle seemed disconnected from their times: "People who witnessed the famine in Lebanon say that some rich people managed to increase their wealth by way of monopoly or usury and the purchase of properties and expensive things at very low prices and they used to eat in their homes in the same way that they always did and some of them would have feasts with delicious food and they would laugh and enjoy themselves without caring for all the terrible suffering that was happening nearby."[35] Amplifying this point was a planned casino in Beirut, which thrived and was "much to the amazement of certain German observers, crowded even during the famine."[36] People enjoyed "all aspects of pleasure—organising elaborate trips, private parties and dances, and special games."[37] Khalid al-Azm, who spent summers in Lebanon in the village of Suq al-Gharb, located a few kilometers from the mountain city of Alay, derided the profligacy of one wedding banquet held in 1917.[38] Meanwhile, Muhammad Sa'id al-Jaza'iri observed in his memoir that some starving Beirutis were "reduced to eating Lupine" (lupini beans, or *turmus*), a practice that they ordinarily would have avoided.[39] To these observers, and others, the wealthy just carried on, deaf to the trumpets of war and the pleas of the masses.

Ottoman officials were blamed for reveling in luxury while all around them the masses suffered. For the Syrian journalist Muhammad Kurd Ali, Enver Pasha in particular deserved criticism. Belying his religiosity, purity, and commitment, he had diverted four thousand men to his farm near the end of the war, while the government stood in desperate need of fighters.[40] Kurd Ali's criticism extended to several of the Pasha's senior colleagues within the CUP, who pocketed tens of millions of liras through the sugar trade at a time when that commodity was virtually unobtainable in the markets.[41] Unabashed, Kurd Ali fingered an entire set of officials who profited from the war, including the Ottoman ambassador to Vienna, Husayn

Hilmi Pasha, who made thousands of liras from the sugar trade.[42] He even relayed an informant's unsubstantiated observation of four military men loading ten very heavy suitcases onto Jamal Pasha's wife's train one morning, which he suspected were filled with gold.[43] Irrespective of the claim's veracity, the anecdote underscores the perception of widespread profiteering by the Ottoman elite and the frustration it engendered.

In June 1915 al-Muqattam reported that while the Ottoman government authorized 200 Ottoman liras for the governor of Beirut to fight locusts that were annihilating every green plant in their path, "no one knows what happened to that money."[44] Moreover, al-Muqattam continued, the Beirut municipality monopolized flour, selling only two hundred grams to every family of less than five per month, while larger families could purchase one bag. In Lebanon, the poor regularly ground chickpeas and ate flour since wheat was generally unavailable. Al-Muqattam criticized this monopolization of flour, sugar, and petrol, linking the public's excessive hardship to such policies.

As the veteran politician Adib Pasha has argued, public works constituted another thinly veiled form of self-enrichment. Roads suitable for coach travel and funded by special taxes were prioritized over agricultural, industrial, and trading sectors that lacked powerful patrons. No effort, for example, was made to regulate deforestation.[45] In Beirut, one governor constructed the aforementioned casino in the hopes of creating a "sort of 'Oriental Nice' after the war."[46] For Yammin, such profiteering, aided by the Ottomans, represented the true calamity of the Lebanese people. The resulting ostentatious displays of wealth manifested themselves in well-dressed, perfumed, and bejeweled public appearances by the wealthy, which grated on the general public.[47] In the following anecdote that Yammin relates about Anis—"Mr. Khawaja" (master of the house)—and Sara—a simple waif—power even devolves into other forms of exploitation.

In January 1917, Sara's father, Sharbil, passed away, her mother following him one month later. The orphaned children—Sara, her brother Nassif, and sister Zayna—were left with nothing but a bed and a cotton cover. Since their father had sold his vineyard for a miserly thirty Turkish paper pounds before his death, they also had no access to food. Hunger soon engulfed them. The hamlet where the three siblings lived was mortgaged by a wealthy man named Anis. In him, the frail Sara placed her and her siblings' hopes for salvation. On a cold winter night, she trudged to his home, where the wealthy man received her, taking her to his private rooms and closing the door.

Sara told Anis about the death of her parents and the children's subsequent plight. He agreed to bring her siblings to his house in the morning. As it was already late, Anis instructed his maid to heat water and bring Sara new clothes. She spent the night in the comfort of his big house, and the next morning he retrieved her siblings. As promised, Anis fed them and supplied them with clothes, and for the next two weeks, he generously provided for the three of them. When Nassif grew stronger, Anis even bought five goats and a cow and sent him to shepherd his lands. For her part, Zayna worked in the house while Sara became the house caretaker. After all their suffering, life had turned for the better.

Sara's recovery, however, became her own undoing. As she regained her health and her beauty, Anis began to visit Sara in her lodgings. Despite his persistent advances, she refused his sexual approaches. The frustrated Anis dismissed Sara's brother and sister in the hopes that she would ensure the lives of her siblings "with the blood of her virginity." But she steadfastly refused, and ultimately all three siblings left Anis's protection; Sara told him that they would rather live in poverty with honor than in wealth with shame. The price Anis asked was one she could not pay: "You asked that I deliver you myself, so understand that I do not want to die covered with shame. How sweet is death for the sake of virtue." Sara, Zayna, and Nassif were reduced to eating grass and leaves, until finally, they tasted the sweetness of virtue in death.[48]

In recounting this story, Yammin lamented that if only the rich had spent a dirham on charity, if only "their hard hearts had become softer at the sight of tragedies that bloodied the hearts and cut the livers," he might have suppressed his criticisms.[49] Instead, he indicted the cruelty of the rich: "Sorry, you rich who are wicked, we said that we are not afraid and we will not be afraid as long as we strive for what is right and what is right transcends and is not transcended."[50]

In moments of crisis, personal networks proved indispensable. Poor Sara and her siblings had nowhere to turn; others with stronger connections or prestigious positions could escape the worst of the suffering, even if they remained aware of it. Wadad Makdisi Cortas wrote in her memoir that World War I was painful for the people of Lebanon as they endured tremendous hunger, disease, and general misery, but in her own circle life was

much better since her father was professor and chair of the Arabic department at the Syrian Protestant College.[51] He enjoyed special privilege and
respect across Beirut, including access to goods others found impossible to
procure.

In the Ottoman capital of Istanbul, a thriving black market blossomed
after 1915, giving rise to scores of speculators and public embezzlers. The
sea blockade cut off trade and created scarcity; from the resulting disruption profiteers emerged who made vast profits meeting the basic needs of
the million-strong inhabitants of Istanbul.[52] The rapidly growing nouveaux
riches flaunted their wealth, in stark contrast to the discreet lifestyles of the
old wealthy.[53] Turkish novelists interpreted this materialistic consumerism
as symptomatic of a general moral decay.[54] Ahmed Emin Yalman argued
that the uneven distribution of burdens and the contrast between fortune
and famine contributed to a general breakdown in public morality.[55] The
wealthy patronized the pastry shops of Beyoğlu, then a relatively new and
elegant district in European Istanbul, while luxurious boutiques featuring
the most fashionable items enticed the diplomats and merchants who
strolled along Pera Street (since renamed İstiklal Caddesi). As the historian
François Georgeon put it, "The rest, that is the immense majority of Istanbul's population could only salivate (*lèche-vitrine*) outside Lebon, the best
candy store (*confiserie*) on Pera Street."[56]

The war did stir a growth in class consciousness. The contrast between
the enjoyment of wealth and the reality of poverty made people more conscious of social inequalities and of class differences than before. The historian James Gelvin highlighted the growing income gap between rich and
poor in his discussion of the rise of speculators and smugglers. Gelvin
quotes Kurd Ali, who chastised merchants and bureaucrats for transforming Lebanon into "a nation of ease and opulence."[57] As Georgeon argues,
one of the by-products of the rise of the nouveaux riches was a collapse in
the illusion of equality, which had long prevailed in the Ottoman Empire,
especially in Istanbul. In the past, even the wealthy could fall prey to government whims, thereby blunting class differences—the rich could join the
ranks of the dispossessed at any time. During the Great War, however, some
nouveaux riches loosened their dependence on government, and therefore gained some autonomy in ways that the traditional upper classes tied
to the government for their opportunities had not.[58] The inequality Georgeon observed in Istanbul applied to the Arab provinces as well, leading to

the growth of class consciousness. In T. E. Lawrence's opinion, in Beirut, "which itself produced nothing," the Christian merchants were "fat men living by exchange" while "the next strongest component was the class of returned emigrants."[59]

For those neither traditionally nor newly wealthy, the deterioration in political conditions, linked to military exigency in the first decades of the century, exacerbated the business environment. George Korkor, a Beiruti of moderate means, embodied the struggles of small traders who enjoyed the highs and endured the lows of business in insecure times. In his handwritten journal that covers the years 1892 to 1915, Korkor brings to life the vicissitudes of life in the early twentieth century, challenges that were made more difficult by the war.

Korkor was a bon viveur who enjoyed a good laugh, delving into poetry at weddings, and dabbling in palm readings at European fairs. Although never quite financially secure, he unmistakably relished the pleasures of everyday life, even finding entertainment in observing the hangings in the public square.[60] Korkor was never destitute, but he lived on the modern equivalent of one paycheck to the next. That did not stop him from buying a home, which he paid for by working in Germany, even if it left him short on cash. In 1902, he traveled to Egypt, Paris, Vienna, and Düsseldorf, attended European fairs, and also did business in Damascus. Korkor attempted to deal in fur, but finding that trade unprofitable he switched to importing hats from Paris to Beirut and Damascus with the help of his nephew. He then sought to round up investors to buy a women's and men's apparel store, but the project failed on account of insufficient funds. It is astonishing how many trades he contemplated, and even attempted, and how difficult it was for someone even as entrepreneurial as Korkor to turn a profit. His situation deteriorated to the point where he sold all but his most indispensable possessions, including two gold chains inherited from his mother and a piano: "I started to sell anything that came my way and that I did not need."[61]

Short on cash, Korkor switched to buyer-seller arbitrage opportunities. To protect his capital base, he even began buying smaller amounts of stamps for 200 piasters at a time, instead of his usual bulk purchases for 2,000 or 3,000 piasters, but the stamp seller informed Korkor that the administration did not sell stamps to any one person more than twice a month, meaning that he did not want small payments. Complicating his situation, Korkor's cousin Mitri asked him to loan his wife some money, with assurances that he would repay the loan later. Korkor felt obliged to meet this request even though he was short on money, so he collected whatever cash was at his disposal and gave it to her.

Then his own sister began asking for money, and he again felt that he could not refuse: "I started borrowing from someone, repaid him from someone else, and so on and so forth until I had spent 300 piasters." At that point, he wrote to Mitri asking for repayment of his loan. His cousin grew upset that Korkor apparently did not trust him to repay his debt. Too embarrassed to reveal the actual reason—his own financial challenges—Korkor replied that it was all a misunderstanding and quickly dropped the subject. Indeed, it was not easy to survive when the needs of one's extended family added to existing economic burdens.

Short on cash, Korkor quickly learned the quality of his so-called friends, because some were unwilling to lend him even a cent: "I thought that human nature was amazing and may no one ever need someone else and that is how I spent some time in dire need." He decided that his best option was to spend the summer at his sister's Damascus home, and to the north between Damascus and Saydnaya in the mountains.[62] His financial problems bedeviled him in Damascus, too, where he discovered that his Damascene relatives also needed loans, which he could not afford. His uncle's daughter desperately needed food, even though she once "had known days of plenty and glory." The same applied across his uncle's household, where the women worked alone without the advice and benefit of their men, who were off at war during this period of regular conflict. So he provided as much as he could in the one currency at his disposal—advice, counsel, and expertise. As he explored ways to earn money, he discovered that the easiest way was lending. Since he had no capital base from which to lend, he returned to Beirut to once again try his hand in the fur business. That too failed, as business in the winter was bad "as usual."

In 1902, Korkor set off for the fairs of Europe. After enjoying himself in Germany and Paris, he returned so impressed with Europe and the German medical system that he chronicled his trip in a letter to the Beiruti daily *Lisan al-Hal.* As he confided in his journal, however, the trip had not been easy, and he had had difficulty finding work and renting booths at the great fairs: "I met the man . . . and told him what I wanted. . . . He said that the fortune teller place had been taken by an Englishwoman who wanted a store to sell cigarettes. I asked for a perfume store, he said it was not possible. I asked for a store between 2000 and 8000 marks that he had advertised and I looked at one in the 6000 to 8000 range but he did not accept and made fun of me, saying 'this gentleman has talk but no money.' At that moment I was really upset at this and I left the market and went to sleep because I was so angry and because nothing was working."

Korkor redoubled his efforts to find a booth, presumably at the Düsseldorf fair (his memoir is not clear), but his frustrations underscore just how difficult life was without access to credit. The space he initially wanted at the fair was instead allocated to a cigarette store. He offered its holder a payment of 50 English pounds, but was rejected; he then tried to purchase some merchandise from a nearby man. After initially accepting, the man changed his mind. Unbowed, Korkor decided that he would do "whatever it took." He approached the fortune teller and offered his services as an assistant or translator, in the hopes that she would employ him once she saw the number of clients he could attract. She too refused. Korkor grew desperate and concluded that the trip had been doomed from the start.

Nevertheless, he refused to let these hardships get the best of him. "Suddenly one day as I was looking around at the fair, God opened a door to me by helping me find a place that was flying hot air balloons, whose name was 'The Garden of Happiness.' I asked its manager if he had any empty space and he said they had space at the end of the park, if not the end of the fairgrounds. I accepted the space and asked for a lower price, and when the man saw how desperate I was, he offered to give me an answer the next day on lowering the price. But I refused to wait and asked him to commit himself on his word of honor. After thinking a bit he said he was giving me his word and so I left happy."[63]

Eventually, after he was cleared of some accusation by the courts, Korkor made a profit, rejoicing in his memoir: "Thank God, this was a good year because I had never had as much money as I had this year." In 1902, after contracting the flu but recovering with some money in his pocket, he decided to settle down. After marrying and starting a family, he began to relax. Thanks to his import business, his financial situation stabilized until World War I. Korkor was the first to import children's sandals into Syria, building an exclusive brand with a factory stamp of his name on each pair of shoes. Even in that period of relative financial ease, his expenses mushroomed. The start of the war drove him to Jounieh for a year, with little cash remaining and his family crowded into two rooms. Eventually, Korkor returned to Beirut. The war is not mentioned again in his journal, which ends in 1915 with an entry about a wedding.

George Korkor's story describes the challenges of pre–World War I middle-class merchants and middlemen, fighting to make ends meet in the midst of competition. His story also speaks to the slow and steady Middle Eastern integration into the world economy, and the resourcefulness that enabled some to break through when given an opportunity. In an era when credit and financing were still relatively undeveloped, people leaned on family members for loans and business ventures. Moreover, in Korkor's time, specialization through comparative advantage had not yet imposed its will, and people moved frequently between professions. Judging by his journal, and his family memories, Korkor's propensity for a good laugh and for social company never diminished, despite his challenges.

In Korkor's case, the Great War hurt his business just as his family was growing (he had four surviving daughters). Therefore, the widening income gap during the war was not simply a function of the exponential growth in wealth, but also a reflection of the struggles of the upper-middle class, and just as much, the strivings of the poor. Overall, the high cost of living and diminishing production led to a decline in the standard of living during World War I.[64] It took an optimistic spirit like Korkor's to remain positive during those trying years.

These dynamics also applied to rural areas, where economic disruptions, limited access to raw materials, and lack of manufactured goods cut people off from regional and external markets. Profits tied to French, British, and Italian trade disappeared. As agricultural production diminished, including sericulture and the silk factory industry in Syria, incomes declined and unemployment spiked. This all had a ripple effect on many other aspects of the local economy. Commerce stagnated, hard hit by the British blockade,[65] and in turn, the brokers, merchants, and middlemen who depended on trading, commissions, and services related to the movement of goods by land or sea were left stranded as merchant ships steamed off onto the horizon.

Remittances from abroad slowed from a steady stream into a minor trickle. For the many families relying on remittances not merely as a supplement but as a primary source of income, the collapse was devastating. Tourism, a relatively new and limited form of income, also came to an end. It has been estimated that in the *vilayet* of Beirut, income declined at least 80 percent, while the collapse of the silk industry created a loss of at least 90 percent.[66] These losses were huge elsewhere, as well.[67]

When war erupted in 1914, business transactions froze as people rushed to creditors, tradesmen, and banks to withdraw their deposits.[68] With credit tightening and a run on the banks under way, the government froze all debt obligations that threatened the viability of debtors and creditors.[69] The greedy undermined the order by fabricating outlandish excuses to circumvent it,[70] and some borrowers refused to repay their debts, even if it was within their means to do so. As a consequence, some lenders and merchants who had worked long and hard to amass a capital base fell on hard times,[71] while those who had borrowed freely spent as they pleased.[72] Still others leveraged their capital base by charging extremely high interest rates.

In 1915, the Ottoman government introduced paper currency reforms and imposed currency controls, particularly on gold. Intended to build confidence in paper money, the decision partially backfired. The issuance of paper currency added to economic uncertainty as money fluctuated and devalued, contributing to a decline in living standards.[73] It also led to the hoarding of metallic currency as people spirited away whatever gold and silver they could find.[74] The prohibition on the transport of gold made it almost irresistible to smuggle, as the public discovered when university professors were caught smuggling gold from Germany and Austria.[75] This was considered such a breach of academic ethics that the Faculty of Arts at the University of Constantinople passed a motion in December 1917 against its participation in commercial enterprises.[76] Halidé Edib wrote about emergency currency measures during the Great War and the smuggling they spawned: "A strict examination of gold was made of every passenger during the war. The Turkish population somehow never feels real confidence in paper money, and there was enough secret dealing in gold to justify the application of strict measures. There were a great many Anatolian women who traveled over the country for trading purposes, and they managed to smuggle all sorts of things, the discovery of which would have baffled any government."[77]

Everywhere, and in the provinces in particular, people distrusted paper money, trading paper money for gold and silver at lightning speeds. First-hand accounts of people who lived through the war in Mount Lebanon and

in the *vilayet* of Beirut during World War I open a window into this difficult period. Among them was the Brumana native Ra'if Abi l-Lama', who
spent the war with his family in Beirut. In 1916, Ra'if concluded his medical studies and was drafted into the Ottoman army. In the course of his
travels, he dined in an Aleppo restaurant, but after Ra'if paid his bill in
paper currency, the owner of the restaurant refused to give him change,
because he had only the much more valuable gold coins in his possession.
Rather than part with his precious metals, the owner decided that the meal
was on the house![78] Ra'if also recounted the story of a shepherd tending to
his sheep in the Hawran. Ottoman soldiers approached him and attempted
to buy a sheep from him with paper money. Although he initially resisted,
they forced him to accept the payment. After the soldiers departed, the
sheep in tow, he tore up the money and resignedly decided that he would
view his sheep loss as if it had been eaten by a wolf.[79] Another confirmation
of the collapse of paper money is given by Mary Dale Dorman, who was
the granddaughter of Daniel Bliss, the founder of the Syrian Protestant
College. In an entry dated March 22, 1916, from her journal, Dorman
noted that she had gone into downtown Beirut but was unable to change
her paper money anywhere, and thus was unable to pay for goods.[80]

As a result, everyday objects transformed into treasures. Father Sarloute
was the director of a school in the Lebanese town of Antura, which sits on
a sloping hill overlooking the Mediterranean Sea. In June 1916 he traveled
to French-controlled Arwad Island just off the Syrian coast to serve as chap-
lain of the troops. He had a friendly disposition and succeeded in easing
tensions and disputes on the island. Every ten days, a boat arrived from Port
Said with provisions and goods from all over the world—except Germany
and its allies—to be distributed to the needy. The priest's house filled with
boxes of clothes, sweets, blankets, raingear, beer, soda, woolen underwear,
and other goods that he gave to the soldiers and the poor. He once received
one hundred men's suits, of which twenty-five were given to a Lebanese intelligence man, Bechara Buwari (Bishara al-Buwari). Buwari gave one suit
to his servant, who returned the next day holding a small watch in his
hand, saying that he had found it in the small pocket of the vest. After examination, it turned out that all of Buwari's suits contained something extra of value, such as a pin, a tie, socks, or two or five francs.[81]

In such ambiguous credit markets, profiteers and entrepreneurs could
make their mark, with money changers pocketing the difference between

paper and metal money, especially in the provincial towns. Many people were also forced to change their gold coins into smaller coins, in the process losing more than one-tenth of their value.[82] Some debtors who had borrowed money on the basis of gold before the war rushed to repay their debts in less valuable paper money, thereby hurting creditors. Moreover, the difficulties of moving between areas during the war meant that exchange rates could not be shopped across the provinces but had to be accepted as offered locally.[83]

Thus, smuggling during the war became all the more difficult and all the more profitable. For powerful officials and connected profiteers, this was an ideal combination, since monopolies could be established. It was more difficult for unconnected, middle-income individuals to turn profits, but they, too, found a variety of ways to make money. Some merchants found novel ways of trading commodities, the rarer the better: "Goods changed hands not from merchant to consumer, but from one merchant to another without ever reaching the consumer. . . . It was possible for one and the same commodity to double or triple in price in a single day."[84] Corruption eventually became so blatant and pervasive that, by 1917, the government took measures against these profiteers.[85]

The collapse in industry meant that virtually the only way to import goods for private use was to conceal them as war supplies and procure them from people with influence. The scarcity in these markets caused prices and profits to skyrocket for a whole range of imported goods, from sugar and paper (both in high demand) to services such as the issuance of transportation permits, which became a very lucrative business.[86] Even upper-middle-class individuals unconnected to the rich or the well-placed found ways to make profits on all sorts of commodities.

War conditions created a field day for crafty smugglers who prospered during the war. In his memoir of the period around World War I, the Lebanese Bechara Baroody mentions that one advantage of the town of Zahle was that it straddled the governorate of Mount Lebanon and the province of Syria, so that smugglers could be safe from pursuit the instant they changed districts. The town's pharmacy was on the Lebanese side of the dividing line, and in front of it was a covered canal for running water. Crossing the covered canal (only a meter wide) meant crossing into the province of Syria. Near the pharmacy, still in Lebanon, was a store that sold tobacco. Whoever was caught carrying this Lebanese tobacco in Syria was fined because

Syria had the monopoly on tobacco: "How many times did we see groups of men running toward the pharmacy carrying smuggled cigarettes and when they enter the pharmacy the police of the tobacco company would stop at the door and not move further?"[87]

The war also provided opportunities for those who launched businesses, despite the odds of doing so in difficult times. That task could be made easier by government involvement. In December 1915, for example, the governor of Beirut asked locals to form a company for the production of carpets, leading to the formation of "The Beirut Carpet Company," which took up operations in the building of the nuns of 'Azariyya in Ras Beirut.[88] Usually, however, average citizens started businesses through sheer hard work and individual initiative, importing goods that had not been available on the market before. In 1912 the Baroody family started a company—Baroody Bros and Co.—primarily active in the import-export business. We know about this enterprise principally through the unpublished memoir of one member of the family, Bechara Baroody, and through interviews with his family descendants. The business was located first at Suq al-Tawila in Beirut, which was the first and at that time the most prominent market district, and then moved to Avenue des Français. The business was started by Bechara's uncle Benjamin Baroody, who married Sumaya Makdisi, sister of Wadad Makdisi Cortas who also left a memoir. Bechara's father was Shukri Baroody, Benjamin's brother-in-law.

On Shukri's shoulders fell the responsibility of feeding, clothing, sheltering, and answering the needs of everyone in the household, which included some members of his extended family, a practice typical for much of the region. Shukri was a pharmacist in charge of vaccination in Zahle and the surrounding area. He was also an official representative of the Ottoman government whose duties were to search the Damascus and Beirut trains and make sure that none of the passengers had contracted a contagious disease. He visited the houses of the sick to check for smallpox, cholera, or typhus and twice a week went to the army hospital in Zahle to prepare medications for the soldiers (at that time medications were compounded by the pharmacist).[89]

Benjamin Baroody, educated at the Syrian Protestant College in Beirut, imported goods from the United States and England that did not exist on the local market and for which there was demand, such as clothes, socks, electrical appliances, and other goods. The business kept growing during the war and flourished despite the difficulties he faced. At one point, the Ottoman authorities even took Benjamin away for questioning—all the way to Anatolia, his family believed, although that is unlikely—presumably because they wanted to know the nature of his contacts with Europeans (and probably with Westerners in general), a development that caused deep anxiety among his family members. Benjamin explained to the authorities that his relationships were for business reasons and he was released, but the incident underscores the challenges of conducting business at the time.[90]

One of the most important enterprises for carpentry and furniture making was in place already before World War I. It was owned by Ilyas Jirji Sioufi in the Ashrafieh hill in the eastern part of Beirut alongside the shore, which Muhammad Kurd Ali visited in 1912.[91] The Sioufi factories were so modern that he wrote:

> When one visits them one would think himself in one of the big factories of the West and what catches your eye as you enter are the two clocks, one on the right and one on the left. Near them are two boxes hanging and divided in small partitions, and in each there is a card on which the name of a worker is written and typed on it are the times of entry, lunch, and departure so that when the employee comes after dawn and before sunrise in winter for example, he inserts his card in the slot and the hour and minute of his arrival is automatically inscribed in Arabic numerals. At the end of the day or week the manager refers to these cards and computes the times and what is owed to the employee according to a special system like the one in Switzerland, Belgium, Austria and Germany.[92]

It would seem that the Sioufi stayed in business during the war and even prospered for a while thereafter.[93] The Lebanese writer Elias Khoury was born in Beirut in 1948. In his youth, he would walk in Ashrafieh with a certain Abu George, whom he described as a friend since his earliest days of leisurely walking around the hill. Abu George regaled Khoury with stories of a bygone era—the interwar period after World War I, the coming of the French, and World War II. Abu George likely embellished where memory failed him, but his tales serve as a window into how the interwar period was remembered. In Abu George's telling, the Sioufi factories used to be a huge property owned by Yusuf al-Saghir, which is why the hill on which Ashrafieh was located was called "little mountain," since *Saghir* means "small." George told Khoury that the Sioufi brothers, Ilyas and Nicolas, bought Sioufi "dirt cheap" and built a furniture factory after World War I (Abu George's chronology may be wrong, as Kurd Ali wrote that he visited the factory in 1912; moreover, according to Abu George, the factory was owned by the two brothers, whereas Kurd Ali wrote that it belonged to Ilyas Jirji Sioufi). Regardless, Abu George said that Ilyas died, the business soured, and Nicolas sold the property, after which it was split into small holdings.[94]

One long-term effect of the war that may have contributed to the Sioufi business losses was the spread of thievery. On his walks with Khoury, Abu George lamented that the days of old-fashioned robbery—of simply taking from the rich and giving to the poor—had been replaced by organized robbery, as exemplified in one incident at the Sioufi factory when thieves took advantage of shifting norms.

After burglarizing the factory, the thieves distracted workers by throwing coins on the floor. The ploy worked, as workers forgot about the thieves and scrambled for the coins. In times past the workers might have caught the thieves, but now the lure of money ended the chase: "They were lenient with the thieves and took the factory's money. That is when the decline set it [in]. And the story has it the factory started going bankrupt then." Of course, more systemic causes are mentioned as well, but Khoury's anecdote highlights the onset of a new era.[95]

Alongside the Sioufi and Baroody families, other entrepreneurs made fortunes, including refugees who rose from nothing to build business empires. The historian Keith Watenpaugh describes the dynamic, growing commercial middle class in Aleppo and other cities of the eastern Mediterranean in the first decades of the twentieth century.[96] As Watenpaugh shows, this middle class was dominated by religious minorities, including Greek Catholics, Jews, and Armenians. Armenians had already been in the Middle East for centuries.[97] But in the second half of the nineteenth and early twentieth centuries, Cairo and Alexandria attracted Armenians, contributing to those cities' remarkable social, economic, and cultural growth.

Armenians controlled the tobacco and shoe industries of Egypt, and played a significant part in international trade. During World War I, far more Armenian refugees moved to Greater Syria than Egypt (numbers in Egypt never exceeded forty thousand), partly because they could cross into the Arab provinces of southwest Asia by land, while the distances and difficulties of traveling to Egypt were logistically more complex.[98]

In Lebanon, the Armenian community was relatively established, with people mostly involved in commerce and the crafts, but it remained relatively small until World War I. At that point, a massive migration occurred. By 1925, it is estimated that well over two hundred thousand Armenian refugees had settled in the Arab lands.[99] These migrations in the interwar period and after occurred in clusters, such as in the early 1920s and in the 1930s.

During the Great War, Armenians escaped from genocide to Syria and elsewhere in large numbers.[100] These refugees settled in various areas, but principally in Aleppo, because it sat at the intersection of long-distance trade routes that had attracted "merchants from all around the Mediterranean, northern Europe, and south and Central Asia" for centuries.[101] Aleppo's refugee camps, where many died of disease, malnutrition, and general neglect, became the main resettlement centers for hundreds of thousands of Armenians, mostly women and children.[102] "During the deportations of 1915–16, some of the [Armenian] victims managed to slip into the narrow-laned Christian quarters of old Aleppo as their caravans of death passed near the city *en route* to the desert."[103] Local sources reported scenes of rape and suicide among those fleeing into Syria.[104]

Armenians also settled in large numbers in Beirut; one of their biggest concentrations was in Bourj Hammoud of the Matn district of Mount Lebanon, not far from Beirut. But they also settled in other areas of the Matn, from Antaliyas to Bikfaya. Armenians also moved into areas of the Biqa' valley, such as the town of Zahle. During the Mandate period, after the French ceded the sanjak of Iskenderun to the Turks,[105] the Armenians were settled at Anjar ('Anjar) in the Biqa'—built for them and by them—mostly from an agricultural Armenian population.[106] The number of Armenians who settled in Lebanon during the early twentieth century remains unclear. The local press reported as many as one hundred thousand, a number Armenians consider exaggerated.[107] A few thousand Armenian refugees also settled in the areas of Palestine and Transjordan after World War I.[108]

The two-part memoir of one Armenian pharmacist, Hagop Arsenian—translated into English by his granddaughter, the scholar Arda Arsenian Ekmekji—sheds light on their plight. In his first set of remembrances, compiled in 1919, Arsenian discusses the period 1880 to 1916 (from his birth year to his family's settlement in Jerusalem); in the second part he describes life in interwar Palestine. Arsenian spent his early life in the Izmit region of northwestern Anatolia. In July 1915 he, his wife, and their two sons were deported by rail to the railway station at Meskin (Meskene) in northeastern Syria, a destination for many Armenian refugees. His march through Anatolia and across the Syrian desert toward Aleppo was filled with trepidation and suffering, but after several detours, he and his family eventually arrived in Jerusalem.[109]

Arsenian's memoir describes how, after months of suffering in Meskin, he was allowed to leave for Aleppo. On July 13, 1916, entrusting his wife and sons to his father-in-law in Meskin, Arsenian set out with three friends on a difficult journey to Aleppo. Along the way he experienced "terror and fear," especially when Anza ('Anaza) tribesmen chased their horse cart (presumably with the intention of robbing them). The cart driver never slowed his pace, and by evening the travelers had reached a khan resting point on the way to Aleppo. Exhausted, one of their horses collapsed and died on the spot. After procuring a new horse the next morning, they set out and reached Aleppo, where "the policemen and the guards" pursued undocumented refugees with the zeal of Anza tribesmen. Unfortunately for Hagop, he was detained and sent to Dayr al-Zur, some 450 kilometers northeast of Damascus on the Euphrates River. Despondent, Hagop managed to turn his trade, pharmacy, into a means of escape, with the help of his friends. After navigating bureaucratic hurdles, he attained a position as a military pharmacist at the former French hospital in Jerusalem, for which he departed on July 25, 1916.

From Jerusalem he requested the transfer of his family, a prospect over which he agonized, considering the erratic nature of wartime bureaucracy. The Ottomans granted Hagop fifteen days' leave to collect his family, now in Aleppo, and they all arrived back in Jerusalem on September 25, 1916. Although Hagop feared the draft and service at the front—in September 1918 he was taken prisoner of war—he survived the war and lived to the age of eighty-three.[110] That moment of reunion with his family remained seared in Hagop's memory:

> After fourteen months of deadly and torturous exile, arriving in Jerusalem and settling as a family in one of the quarters of the Armenian Convent was of the utmost bliss and happiness. Gone were the fearful swords and bayonets of the *gendarmes,* gone were the *gachken, khekhen, chekhen* shouts which struck us like lightning and filled us with terror and fear. Gone were the insecure days and the deadly Damoclean sword which had haunted us for weeks.

Also gone were our marching days like the errant Jew—walk, walk, always walk. Now my mind was preoccupied with all the family members and friends we had left behind, and who still did not have the good fortune of escaping that destructive, painful fate.[111]

The suffering that these Armenians endured should not overshadow their myriad social, political, and economic contributions to the growth and vitality of the region. Many Armenians were less victims of war than drivers of social change in a process that began decades earlier and continued for decades hence. For while the war irrevocably altered the political trajectory of the region, populations like the Armenians contributed to a parallel social transformation in the region. Of all the communities that settled in Greater Syria, Armenians were admired most for their entrepreneurial drive and perseverance in the face of adversity. One common saying in Lebanon during the second half of the twentieth century was that one could never find an Armenian beggar, because they invariably outworked their dire circumstances.

In 1920 the American secretary of the Beirut chapter of the Red Cross, Margaret McGilvary, published *The Dawn of a New Era in Syria,* a firsthand account of the relief operation in Syria during the war. The book describes the American Red Cross, the American Mission, and the philanthropic efforts of other countries. In the course of describing visits to three hospitals— one for men, one for women, and one for eye cases—where student doctors and nurses from the Syrian Protestant College provided medical treatment to those who relied on the soup kitchens of Mount Lebanon, she mentions the Armenian doctor Dikran Utidjian. McGilvary praised Dr. Utidjian, who at the time was the resident physician, for his management of the medical department, describing his work and that of the other Syrian assistants to the chief physician, Dr. Arthur Dray, as tireless.[112]

In 1908, the Armenian Sarkis Bakalian founded a mill in Adana; his family speculates that the government spared his life in return for his flour. Between 1915 and 1920, Sarkis sought refuge from the authorities in Beirut after a stint in Marseilles (a city that he did not enjoy). There he started small, buying a mill in the center of town before expanding his business so that it produced twenty-five tons of flour per day by the 1930s. Still today, his fourth-generation descendants churn out freshly milled flour from the family business.[113]

Others thrived in the arts, including photography and the new field of postcards that took hold in the late nineteenth century. The first illustrated postcards to appear in France date back to the 1890s; Beirut received its first lot of postcards, with general views of Beirut and Baalbek, from Germany and Austria in 1897. One year later, new methods in printing allowed for the production of panoramic postcards snapped by the first (mostly) French photographers, such as Bonfils, Dumas, and Bézier. Within the region, photographers such as Sabounji, Sarrafian, and Tarazi soon began producing the first local postcards.[114] Yet Armenians too played a critical role in the further expansion and growth of Middle Eastern photography, beginning in Jerusalem and Beirut.[115]

The three Sarrafian brothers—Abraham, Boghos, and Samuel—illustrate how some Armenians prospered over decades despite the interruptions and setbacks of war. The family hailed from a small town east of Diyarbakir in southeastern Anatolia. Their father worked as a banker, carpet merchant, antiquarian, and numismatist, reflecting the roving, nonspecialized ways of the late nineteenth century. After completing primary and secondary school and traveling, Abraham and Boghos opened a photo laboratory. Thereafter, however, a government crackdown on Armenians forced the Sarrafian brothers to flee to Beirut, where they settled with their families with the help of Lebanese and Protestant missionaries. Back home, Abraham had married a local woman from the Garabedian family, which also became well known in Beirut. These brothers became extremely successful in photography. Their photographs of people, monuments, and even archeological sites catapulted them to fame in Beirut and beyond. Before the turn of the century, they had opened a studio in the Bab Idriss section of downtown Beirut, which prospered until the beginning of the Lebanese civil war in 1975.[116] The brothers' talent was the foundation for their postcard and photography empire, enabling them to open branches as far away as Syria and Palestine. As their reputation spread, they became the official photographers of the Syrian Protestant College and established themselves as the main publishers of postcards in the Middle East. In 1925 Abraham Sarrafian won first prize in photography in Dhour Shweir in the Matn region of Lebanon; his brother, Samuel, sold the art and postcards.[117]

Far from the fine arts looms the mysterious world of espionage and conspiracy, which also constituted a form of entrepreneurship during the Great

War. For those close to the sea or living along the Syrian coast, intelligence became a means of survival.

The British were the first to put a naval blockade of the coast in place, and perhaps the first to initiate an intelligence operation to collect information on the Ottomans, although their operations sometimes suffered from problems in communications between their war office in London and their government in India. The British coordinated their efforts with the French to develop a relatively widespread system of spies.[118] After the war, a British captain by the name of Lewen Weldon published a book of diaries he kept between 1914 and 1919. On January 16, 1916, Weldon arrived at Port Said to take up a new assignment: "I was to be a kind of mixture of Liaison, Intelligence and Commanding Officer rolled into one, and that the seaplanes with which I was to work were French, but it soon appeared that this was not all. Someone was wanted to distribute spies, or more politely 'agents,' behind Turkish lines, and this little job also fell to my lot."[119]

Working with the British, the French dropped agents behind enemy lines and collected their information using French seaplanes. Intelligence operations continued throughout the war as the Entente controlled the Syrian coast and monitored it continually with steamers and other ships capable of carrying airplanes and seaplanes. The system worked relatively well, and on the whole these operations ran smoothly. However, the weather made a big difference to the success of operations, and many a time "our old enemy, a heavy sea," prevented ships from landing. It was easier to call regularly at set stations along the coast during the summer than during the winter, when landing was impossible half the time.[120]

All methods at the disposal of the military were used for intelligence, even pigeons. They transported messages, but they could also create danger. One night, their cooing frightened Weldon: "That night on the beach I realized how loudly pigeons can coo. It seemed to me that the little brutes made enough noise to bring half the Turkish army down on me."[121] Most of the time, however, intelligence depended on local collaborators who spoke the languages of the areas under observation and could melt into the population. In this way, people from Anatolia and Syria were recruited to serve in intelligence and to man the intelligence ships. Their work consisted mostly in gathering information on the enemy's position and in gauging how the local population felt and coped. In the last year of the war, some agents were also used for sabotage.[122] On the whole, they remained safe;

Weldon wrote that he did not think that more than seven were captured, six of whom were hanged, and one who had his head cut off.[123]

Local people were very eager to be recruited for intelligence work, perhaps out of conviction for the Allied cause, but perhaps even more out of pecuniary need. The head of intelligence for the Fourth Army in Syria during the war, Aziz Bek, published a book in the 1930s about intelligence gathering during the war. He wrote that spying played an important role in Lebanon and that its non-Muslim population was the enemy of the state. Indeed, Aziz protested that the population of Lebanon was "in its entirety against us" (the Ottoman side) because they considered the Ottomans their enemy and the French their friends and protectors.[124]

More generally, the eagerness of local people in Syria, Egypt, and probably elsewhere to work in intelligence did not impress outside observers. "The indigenous contacts used by the Allies for collecting and reporting information were, almost without exception, untrained and generally ill-equipped for performing such tasks. The information they provided at times was really nothing spectacular but just common knowledge or that culled from the local rumor mills."[125] Weldon also did not seem to have a high opinion of the locals and did not mince words: "On shore I had to interview any number of likely 'agents,' or rather people who thought they were likely. As a matter of fact good agents were very few and far between, and my experience taught me that while most of them were very brave in Port Said, it was only one in a hundred who was worth a damn when once at sea."[126]

One of the problems of these local collaborators, as Ajay points out, was that many of them allowed their sentiments to color their findings: "Their strong feelings about the Turks [Ottomans] undoubtedly influenced their judgment when reporting on the plight of the local populace. Being inclined to accept the worst about anything connected with the Turks [Ottomans], they would report in a highly exaggerated or dramatic manner without really substantiating it. As to the ultimate value of the information supplied the Allies on the Turks' [Ottomans'] position in Syria during the war, none of the sources consulted revealed just how good or worthwhile was the whole intelligence operation."[127]

The agents seem to have been paid well, although on occasion their requests for additional funds were turned down. One local agent told Weldon that a British officer was being held prisoner not very far away and that he could arrange his escape if he could have three hundred guineas with which to cover "what we might call 'traveling expenses,' which meant bribes for the guards, and of these guineas no doubt a fair, or probably unfair, proportion would stick to his palm." The request was turned down, although Weldon reassures his readers that the British prisoner ended up alive and safe.[128] Most of the time, however, money was available to agents. Those who worked with the British were paid in gold sovereigns that were never dated later than 1914, as the possession of money of a later year could have been awkward for "friends" of the Entente and arouse the enemy's suspicions.[129] The French also paid their agents with their currency.

The Ottomans and their allies did the same. During the war they paid between one hundred and fifty to four hundred Turkish gold pounds per month to their spies, of whom there were eighteen in Beirut, three in Sidon, three in Nablus, two in Tyre, and five each in Acre, Latakia, and Tripoli. In Mount Lebanon, the Ottomans paid five hundred Turkish gold pounds to twenty-two spies and sometimes asked them to spy on one another. The Ottomans also had twenty-eight spies inside religious organizations, especially inside the Maronite patriarchate; sixty-two in Damascus; eighteen in Aleppo; and twenty-two in Jerusalem.[130] Port Said was believed to be filled with Ottoman and German spies, which drove the French navy to move their own supporters cautiously by back routes so as to protect their identities from the enemy.[131]

The Ottoman network of spies was not restricted to the coast and the cities, but extended to the desert where Jamal Pasha utilized Bedouins. Secret funds were spent on tribes that aided the government and on which Jamal Pasha depended to back his personal politics. One of the desert people by the name of Ahmad ibn Walid al-Jasem became a double agent for the Ottomans and the British. He was not discovered until 1916 but could not be arrested because he escaped to the British.[132] A few Muslim clerics were Ottoman collaborators. Jamal Pasha depended on them to assist him and he had a secret fund from which he could draw money and supplies for their living expenses. The amount spent on them was more than one thousand gold liras per month. The Mufti of Beirut, Mustafa Naja (d. 1931), refused the money, but the Ottomans found enough people willing to work for them in return for handsome payments.[133]

Aziz Bek complained to Jamal Pasha that the government spies were ineffective, that the stipend paid to spies was too low, and that more money was needed to form a counterespionage organization. When Jamal Pasha questioned Aziz about his suggestion, he replied: "Who will volunteer for such a job without money?" Aziz did not believe that the inhabitants of Greater Syria would serve the government just because it was their government. As he put it, the Muslims were not that loyal and the Christians were known to be enemies of the government.[134]

At the forefront of Aziz's worries was Bechara al-Buwari, who despite a bounty and death sentence (in absentia) was never captured.[135] Aziz disdained him, perhaps because of his success, or because he thought Buwari was motivated by greed. In fact, Aziz divided the French enemy spies into two groups: those that spied to earn the protection of the French or who considered it their duty to defend the independence of their regions against Ottoman encroachments, and those who spied purely for financial gain. Aziz placed Buwari and his friends in the latter group, and thought of them as mercenaries: "Had the Ottoman government given that second group money, they would not have hesitated to spy for the government against the French."[136]

Other sources confirm that many local people worked for the French and the British. Yammin mentions someone named Michel Dahruj from Zahle as an important spy in the English military intelligence network in Syria. Buwari was Dahruj's counterpart with the French, but he did not trust him. Such caution was necessary for Buwari in the treacherous underworld that was wartime espionage.[137] Another agent, who spied for the French out of Egypt (although he did not like to use the word "spy" but instead insisted he was "serving" the Maronite leadership), was Q. B. Khuwayri. Recruited from Egypt in 1916, Khuwayri traveled to Syria to collect intelligence on subjects ranging from the spread of locusts to the trial of seamen caught with incriminating intelligence. At each turn, he relied on his wit and intuition to evade capture and survive.[138]

In his memoir of the four years of the Great War, the Lebanese businessman and French protégé Bechara Buwari from Jounieh described his wartime service to the French, both on land and aboard the naval ships that patrolled the Mediterranean.[139] Resourceful from the start, as soon as he heard news of the war, Buwari looked for ways to control his life and shape his future. Every day he would visit George Picot, then French consul-general in Beirut, to learn the latest telegraphed news from the battlefield. When the Ottoman Empire formally entered the war in November 1914,

Picot left the country; an official of France, he had become a war enemy to the Ottomans. Buwari lost no time preparing to leave as well. At first, he attempted to board a small boat at nearby Sidon bound for Cyprus, but was unsuccessful. On January 15, 1915, he boarded the Italian *Syracusa*, reaching Alexandria on February 3.

Business opportunities presented themselves immediately to Buwari. With war declared, the British seized all Ottoman ships that were in the seaports of Cyprus and Egypt. Among them were two ships loaded with wheat belonging to two Lebanese, Khalil al-Bustani and Tannus al-Qadi, who gave Buwari powers of attorney so that he could help them liberate their ships. Buwari worked on this while in Alexandria, meeting several times with Picot, who presumably had moved from Syria to Egypt. Buwari obtained the permissions he needed to secure the boats, noting that shortly after his arrival the two ships were allowed to travel between Cyprus and Egypt along with other Lebanese boats. In record time, then, he had procured the powerful foreign backing he needed, becoming something along the lines of an intermediary between the French and other Lebanese.

After arriving in Alexandria, Buwari became a reference point for the former French consul in Tripoli concerning the situation in the Syrian provinces, including Lebanon. To increase his effectiveness, the French secured special authorization from the British authorities to expedite Buwari's access to boats traveling from Syria to Egypt. The French general consul in Alexandria, Monsieur de Rivet, even introduced Buwari to the French Captain Libran. In turn, Captain Libran introduced Buwari to Superintendent Langlais at the Central Command Bureau. Armed with these connections and a permit affording him free movement, Buwari prepared to translate and offer cultural advice aboard one of the French warships.

On April 15, 1915, the same day warships departed Alexandria for the Dardanelles, Buwari was offered the position of translator and guide for one of the warships, which he accepted gratefully. The next morning, he boarded the train for Port Said, where he was met by a priest, Father Ni'matullah Salama, who escorted him to the French consulate. In the company of the consulate secretary, Monsieur Bellevie, Buwari was taken aboard a French warship under the command of Rear Admiral Dario. After introductions, the terms of Buwari's service were discussed, and he adamantly declined any payment. In doing so, he solidified his ties with his interlocutors and raised his status in their eyes:

When I entered, the Chief of the General Staff asked about my age and my country, and then asked about how much money I wanted to compensate me for my services. I answered, "Nothing—because I want to serve France out of love only." He insisted, however, and I told him that it would be a shame for me or for any Lebanese to be compensated for what was a duty toward France, especially in these circumstances, but he insisted again, saying that he could not accept me if I did not get a salary. I answered that in that case it would be better for me to go back to where I came from rather than accept any salary, so he thanked me profusely and talked to the admiral. He then told me that I would have a private room and that my assignment would be on the cruiser *D'Estrées* stationed in Alexandretta. Half an hour later we were sailing to an unknown destination.[140]

So impressed were his newfound allies that the French chief of war staff at Port Said outfitted him with a letter of introduction that instructed the commander of the *D'Estrées* to seat him at the officers' table, and treat him accordingly: "I ask for your special attention to Mr. Bechara Buwari, the carrier of this letter, whose task will be to serve as your guide and translator. He was introduced to us by the French consul and the French attaché in Cairo."[141] The letter continued, "It is imperative that Mr. Buwari has his meals at the officers' table and that you prepare for him a fitting place, as circumstances allow."[142]

In effect, through his intensity, focus, and personal skills, Buwari gained the confidence of the French. He navigated between cultures and knew when and how to adjust his style to meet his objectives. For example, knowing French preferences, when famine and war made life unbearable in Lebanon, he advised his local contacts to ask the French for loans that could be repaid after the war rather than the usual donations.[143]

By April 1915, weeks after his arrival in Egypt, he was finally aboard the destroyer *D'Estrées,* and by December 1915 he moved to naval intelligence, where he would remain until the end of the war. Buwari would help organize intelligence operations on Arwad Island, just off the coast of Syria.[144] For his service, he was recognized with the French Medal of War.[145]

Buwari's work for the French was essentially that of a spy, but on another level it can be seen as an example of local entrepreneurship. Some may have worked in intelligence out of loyalty to the Entente and opposition to the Central Powers, or because they believed in higher causes such as patriotism or nationalism which they could serve best by joining the Entente.

It is likely, however, that others worked in intelligence out of pragmatism—as an avenue to survival that bypassed the roadblocks of war. Buwari admired the French government and disliked the Ottomans, but by siding with the French he also ensured his livelihood. However hard and perilous life was for a wartime collaborator, it helped him acquire a larger network of useful connections than he otherwise would have had in the relatively contained Mount Lebanon, and it presented him with a number of potentially profitable opportunities. This bypasses Aziz Bek's frustrated interpretation of someone he never arrested or knew, and assesses collaboration as a porthole into a new world of opportunity.

After months of working for the French, Buwari eventually accepted regular payments.[146] By December 1915 his role was clarified. Albert Trabaud, governor at Arwad Island, issued him written instructions spelling out Buwari's mission as a translator and government employee on Arwad who would answer directly to him.[147] Part of Buwari's time was spent enlisting Lebanese sailors to the French service; he tells us that he recruited about one hundred people during the four years he spent with the French navy.[148]

Arwad Island sits three kilometers from the Syrian coastal town of Tartus, south of the principal port city of Syria, Latakia. Arwad was occupied at the end of August 1915 in order to support France's Maronite protégés, but it also served as a launching point for the takeover of Damascus in 1918. After capturing the island, the French appointed a governor by the name of Albert Trabaud. He worked with a French and Lebanese intelligence staff to gather information on Syria, but he also collaborated with British and French naval authorities operating out of Port Said, so that for the duration of the war the island served as the principal center for intelligence operations off the coast, while Egypt remained the center for recruitment and other administrative and logistical operations.[149]

Buwari is an example of entrepreneurship enhanced by close contact with European representatives. He seized every opportunity to solidify his relationship with the French, and was valued for his resolve and hard work. By rejecting compensation at the start, he earned their esteem. Life was not easy for this entrepreneur, however, and his survival required perseverance. Personal skills were everything. After two months on Arwad Island, isolated in that remote area, he went into a deep dejection. He wrote of his despair and disillusionment after several cold months of sailing between the island

and the coast of Lebanon. He found it particularly difficult to get ashore with only three men in small boats while buffeted by heavy winds. He naturally missed his homeland, such a short yet unobtainable distance away. In April 1916, Buwari accepted an invitation to dinner by the Lebanese leader Yusuf Karam, "if only to remember later on that I had had a meal on the soil of Lebanon during the war."[150]

The food restrictions added to his misery. There were no vegetables, yogurt, or milk; meat was offered only occasionally (and then, only goat meat); even water was limited to well water and that which ships sometimes brought from Port Said or Cyprus. There also was no one to prepare or serve the food to Buwari because, as he put it, all the inhabitants were Muslim and their women veiled "even if the age of one of them was 100 years or more."[151] So he resigned himself to cooking—despite his ignorance in the matter—or pickled foods.

Buwari was also discouraged by what he describes as the governor's bad temper, his militant ways, and his insistence that Buwari execute his orders no matter their implication, with no consideration for his inexperience in military matters or his Lebanese background.[152] Later, Buwari regretted criticizing the governor to the French admiral in Alexandria after discovering that he had not only praised him, but actually recommended him for promotion.[153] There was no doubt, however, that he loathed his time on the island; once during the winter of 1916, hearing from the governor that the *D'Estrées* was coming at midnight to ferry him from Arwad to Port Said, he packed all of his belongings and secretly resolved never to return.[154] With time, he seems to have more or less come to terms with his stay on the island—he got to know people and to help and be helped by them as the occasion demanded. But he never liked the island. His reaction when he was informed in 1917 that he had been assigned to assist someone in Cyprus was unequivocal: "I was elated by the good news because it meant the end of the difficult life at Arwad and because Cyprus would be a much better place for me."[155] Although he was summoned back to the island at the end of August 1918, it was only for a short stay, and then the island basked in the illuminating glow of victory. On December 30, Buwari sailed with his wife, son, and maid to Beirut, where he spent the night before reaching Jounieh the next morning: "My absence from my country had lasted a total of four years."[156]

Buwari could grow irritable when his challenges were not appreciated. In 1917, the Lebanese Michel Jabre, who lived in Marseilles, wrote to him asking for Buwari's help in getting Jabre's wife, Julia, and daughter Mary out of Jounieh to Arwad and then onward to Alexandria where he would meet them. Jabre implied that such a task would be easy since Jounieh and Arwad Island were only a few miles apart.

He inquired about the cost of having a boat with six seamen and their captain navigate the trip, and wondered if it would be possible once the boat reached Jounieh to moor it near the house of Jabre's uncle, Faris. Apparently Jabre also wrote to Picot about the same matter. Jabre frustrated Buwari, who wrote in his memoir: "Reading these two letters showed me that Mr. Jabre thought that the matter was an easy one, amounting to a walk in the park, and that is why he wanted to be assured of its success before paying, as if I were the owner of a travel agency. What made me laugh even more was the fact that he wanted me to tie the boat by the house of [his] uncle Faris because he did not want the lady to be bothered to walk to the mooring place!"[157]

The stress and the tension of espionage operations never abated. Buwari was most familiar with the inhabitants of Lebanon, the Maronites in particular, and his memoir makes clear that several worked with the French and with him, and did so while frightened of the Ottoman authorities. Traveling between the coast and Arwad was among these missions, attempted even by priests.

In the dark of night, small boats would cast into the Mediterranean to rendezvous with their targets, but sometimes the sailors grew too scared to draw close enough to shore and missed their targets. In 1916, one man signaled a boat by lighting matchsticks, coming aboard trembling: "I took his hand to bring him onto the boat and asked him why he was trembling now that he was saved. He said that he was not trembling from fear but from happiness for having escaped from the tricky situation he was in while in Lebanon."[158] Another time in 1916, Buwari traveled by boat to the town of Byblos or Jbeil northeast of Beirut in the Jbeil district of Mount Lebanon, and found twelve men waiting for him. They started calling one another loudly "as if they did not know how critical the situation was in case a soldier from the locality came by suddenly and found us." One priest by the name of Elias sat next to Buwari in the boat and started calling out in a loud voice, asking for his suitcase from one friend and for his shoes from another. Buwari begged him to lower his voice, to no avail. "Finally, I could not control myself and directed my gun at his head and threatened him and everyone else." The priest fell silent.[159]

Buwari also seized other opportunities to turn a profit when they came his way. Although he was keen on demonstrating his loyalty to the French and declined a salary at first, he was certainly aware of the unique commercial and financial opportunities that his position with the French generated. Buwari pounced on these with the same creativity and eagerness as he had demonstrated in building his relationship with the French. Serving the French navy might have helped Buwari become a well-compensated middleman between the French and the local population. He was a bit of a wheeler-dealer; his experiences embody some of the creative ways in which locals lived the war, caught between warring powers while attempting to make a profit.

Profit might also have been in the back of his mind when he worried about the fate of confiscated provisions and tried to help locals recover their boats—perhaps in the hope of a reward, although that is not spelled out in his memoir. The Entente frequently impounded provisions, raising the conundrum of what to do with seized goods. Buwari deplored the discarding of seized provisions during such times of deprivation and need and argued that releasing them could buy goodwill, or even some loyalty, among the local population.

In 1915 Buwari traveled aboard a French ship to Mount Carmel. Those onboard saw several boats speeding toward Jaffa.[160] They seized two boats, one owned by Jirji Zakka from the 'Ukayba area near Damascus[161] and the other by Sijan Kazzi from Jounieh in the Kisrawan district of Mount Lebanon. The two boats carried flour and other provisions, apparently destined for the Ottoman army stationed around Gaza and al-Arish. The French then seized another two boats, one full of oranges and captained by a man from Jaffa. The commander ordered these four boats scuttled; upon learning the news, Zakka and Kazzi turned despondent. Buwari grew weary of their "crying and lamenting" and ended up "paying no attention to them." However, he did convince the French to spare their boats and cargo. He transferred four sailors to each of the two boats, keeping the owners and their crew onboard his own, since he worried that they would go over to the

Ottomans if released. The next day, the remaining two boats were scuttled and Buwari and his French allies steamed onward to Port Said.

On land he met up again with the owners of the two surviving boats, who told him that the French admiral had summoned them, offered them financial help, arranged that they be paid fifty pounds [presumably French pounds] and provided them with a document authorizing them to hoist the French flag and travel between Cyprus and Egypt. The boat owners then asked Buwari to appeal for still more money from the French, a request which he refused: "Zakka got angry at me and cursed me all through the war forgetting that he owed me his freedom and the safe return of his boat."[162]

When he could, Buwari used his influence to maneuver the French into outcomes he desired. Earlier, in the summer of 1915, the French navy sunk two ships carrying flour. Buwari could not but feel regretful that the ships and their loads were sunk, "given the high price of goods these days." Therefore, "I went to the commander and told him that we had used twenty five mortars of 100mm that cost two hundred and fifty French pounds to sink two ships and their loads that probably cost over two thousand five hundred French pounds. If we had Lebanese sailors it would have been possible for us to take these two ships to Port Said or Cyprus and save the Treasury the price of the bombs and make money instead. So he promised me to talk to the admiral about it and get permission and when we reached Port Said, he got permission."[163]

In 1917, he displayed similar savvy in the case of Yusuf al-Hani. Hani wrote to him from Paris asking him for help in arranging for the escape of his mother and brothers from Syria. Hani asked Buwari to assist in the matter and promised to show his gratitude by paying twenty-five thousand francs to the crew.[164]

Buwari's intercession not only profited him; he also helped launch the business careers of others. One such example is the entrepreneur Tawfiq Hadid from Tyre (Sur), the ancient Phoenician port on the Mediterranean, now part of Lebanon and located south of Sidon and Beirut. Hadid lived in Jounieh in the north and owned a boat in which Faris Buwari, Bechara's cousin, owned a stake. After the French seized his boat and imprisoned him, Hadid approached Buwari and asked him to vouch for him. Buwari was a cautious man, however, and it was typical of him to be suspicious of those he did not know during those troubled war years: "I told him that I was not going to vouch for anyone I did not know, especially in days like this."[165] His reluctance was overcome only when he reached Port Said and several Lebanese assured him that Hadid was indeed trustworthy. Buwari agreed to vouch for him, leading the French to free Hadid and give him back his boat. Ironically, though, he may have regretted helping Hadid. As he later wrote in his memoir, Hadid began working (we do not know at what) between Cyprus and Egypt, amassing "a fortune he would never have dreamed of."[166] When he returned to Tyre at the end of the war he denied the widow of Faris Buwari and her small children their fair share of the boat. The stone-hearted could make money during the war, sometimes at the expense of the vulnerable.[167]

Ships, however small, became a means to making profit. With the outbreak of war, the movement of Ottoman sailboats ceased and the Ottomans scuttled the remaining sailboats moored in the Syrian ports for fear of enemy capture. At Arwad, the boats remained unharmed and stayed in port until after the French invasion of the island. As the war progressed and the number of German submarines increased, the British stopped ferrying their merchandise in big ships, relying instead on the smaller sailboats. These boats ferried merchandise between Egypt and Cyprus, making huge amounts of money for their owners.

The case of the dilapidated sailboat of Buwari's cousin, Yusuf, illustrates just how local entrepreneurs profited from changing circumstances. About thirty-five years before Buwari committed his story to paper, Yusuf had owned a sailboat with a capacity of approximately sixty tons. Yusuf sold it and left for Australia with his brother, one of many émigrés in those days. Buwari did not hear about the boat thereafter, nor did he expect to; he thought that Syrian boats did not last more than twenty years because of their rickety build. Yet one day, as he sat in a café on Arwad Island, two friends drew his attention to a very old boat moored in the port and told him that it was his cousin Yusuf's boat.

At first, Buwari was incredulous, but after looking into the matter, he found out that it was in fact true. He learned that someone named Abdul Jalil Sabra had bought the boat from his cousin for five hundred piasters, intending to use it for firewood, but when he realized just how much money could be made in shipping, he tarred the boat and sent it to Cyprus. For transporting carob from Cyprus to Port Said he was paid seven hundred

British pounds, of which three hundred went to various expenses and four hundred he kept himself. He then sent the boat on another trip to Port Said and Alexandria under the same terms. When he sailed from Alexandria to Cyprus he shipped kerosene, sugar, and rice to traders.[168]

Alongside shipping, sailors also made money by collecting insurance. Some owners apparently even instructed their men to scuttle their boats, in the hope of collecting insurance fees. Abdul Jalil Sabra once attempted to collect 1,500 British pounds, claiming a submarine had sunk his boat after his men returned on rafts. In fact, he had instructed them to purposely sink the boat. During an investigation, their ruse was uncovered and they spent the rest of the war in an Egyptian jail. The scheme was realistic, however; submarines sank a number of small boats during the war, and many sailors survived only by transferring onto small rafts. Their owners would collect an insurance payout.[169]

Survival was not only about making money, but also about exercising caution. Buwari repeatedly warned the French and others to avoid disclosing valuable information, such as the names of spies, to curious outsiders that were unvetted. Locals in the service of the French devised simple yet effective communications schemes to avoid Ottoman notice. For example, informants on shore hung special objects, such as carpets, on their balconies to convey messages to those on ship.[170] In this way, as one French boat reached Jounieh in north Lebanon in January 1916, Buwari saw his brother Hanna "walking in front of his house hanging a red sign, which meant that there was a submarine in the port of Beirut. We became very worried and our men started getting ready to pursue the submarine if we could get a glimpse of it, but soon after we saw a white sign near the red one, which meant that he was requesting a meeting."[171]

The conspirators worked on codes. At least once they arranged for the same Hanna to travel aboard a French ship to Arwad for twenty-four hours to establish communication methods, such as how and where to leave written messages and signals from the window of his house. However, as they approached the island, Arwad's governor instructed them to make only basic arrangements and turn around so that the Ottoman spies on the island would not learn of Hanna's involvement with the French.[172] The governor's instructions proved prescient, as Hanna was eventually jailed and beaten on suspicion of espionage before escaping (and surrendering again).[173]

Spies worked on both sides of the conflict, and one of those in the service
of the Ottomans was named Hasan Hammud. He operated on Arwad
Island, from the heart of the French intelligence effort, and signed his reports with the fictitious name of Ma'ruf al-Kirji. Hasan sent his handlers
messages through bottles that were carried across the sea by the current,
washing ashore near the port of Tartus. In the spring of 1916, Buwari sought
to ferret out this enemy spy. He made a list of the inhabitants of Arwad
who could read and write and asked them to submit a writing sample under
the guise of building an education plan for the island. He then compared
the writing of each with the seized missives and before long discovered that the
spy was in fact Hasan Hammud. Hammud was tried and condemned to
death, but the governor commuted his sentence to ten years in jail. Exiled to
Europe, Hammud died before he could complete his sentence,[174] but Buwari
ensured that his methods lived on, suggesting to the governor that they
mimic his bottle messages as part of a deception campaign. Each week,
bottles were dropped near the shore or thrown into the sea from the port,
but the information they contained was fabricated.[175]

World War I in the Middle East also had its share of double agents. Two
such spies were Khayr al-Din Abd al-Wahhab from Tripoli and his brother
Adil. Khayr al-Din knew everything there was to know about the docks of
Tripoli. Well respected by the sailors, he was recruited by the Ottomans to
spy on French activities along the Syrian coast and at Arwad Island. Instead, Khayr al-Din informed the Arwad governor of his mission, and expressed an interest in working for the French, to whom he pledged fealty.
He carried a Masonic card, which at least one French priest disapproved of
(he kept accusing Buwari of freemasonry as well, a charge Buwari denied).

If some doubted the value of local agents, Khayr al-Din proved an exception. On at least one occasion, he alerted the French of an Ottoman plan to
bombard Arwad, enabling them to take precautions against the attack.
Like many others who risked their lives in espionage, Khayr al-Din seemed
to have courage in the face of danger. On one occasion in January 1917, he
was sent by the Ottomans to visit Arwad. He used the opportunity to sur-
reptitiously bring along one brother and five or six other young men from
the prominent families of Tripoli, to free them from military service. They
started their journey at night from Tripoli, launching by sailboat into the
Mediterranean. At daybreak, they faced a fierce storm before taking shelter
on a big abandoned rock some miles south of the island. They secured the

sailboat and waited for the storm to abate. Instead the storm doubled in fury, causing the boat to be stuck on the rock and dashing their hopes of escape.[176]

Things only got worse. In the afternoon, the stranded sailors discussed whether it might not be better to risk swimming back to shore rather than remain on the rock. They all opted to go back, removed their clothes, leaving them on the rock, and plunged into the stormy seas. All drowned except for Khayr al-Din, who reached the shore around sunset, totally exhausted. A local patrol found him and took him on foot to Tartus, from where a cable was sent to Tripoli requesting instructions on how to proceed. The commanding officer at Tripoli ordered Khayr al-Din sent back home with all the comforts and honors due him.[177] It appears that Khayr al-Din remained in good standing with the Ottoman military authorities in Tripoli despite this misadventure.[178]

Toward the end of June 1917, the authorities asked 'Adil, Khayr al-Din's brother, to ship a load of soap to Beirut. He sailed by night and on the evening of the next day he reached an area west of the port of Jounieh, where a French ship caught him by surprise. He was brought back to Arwad Island, arrested, and imprisoned in the citadel. The French vice governor wanted him released without his connection to the French revealed. Buwari assisted the vice governor in concocting a scheme in which the island's notables supposedly paid for Adil's release. Before long, Adil returned to Tartus boasting that he had escaped from the French by swimming from the island. The Ottoman authorities talked of awarding him a medal, while the French naval officer who had arrested him, unaware of his collaboration with the French, was upset that his prisoner had been released. One man was skeptical of Adil's escape and saw it for the bluff that it really was, so Buwari threatened him with exile if he repeated his views. Such were the adventures of two modestly valuable double agents operating in precarious waters.[179]

Across the social spectrum and also across industries, the presence of large foreign armies combined with the vicissitudes of war to close some doors and open others. As some basic goods spiked in value, the powerful wartime authorities monopolized and controlled the flow of goods and money. Below the surface, however, profiteers and entrepreneurs charted their own path to survival. On board their sailboats, or in the marketplace, people identified money-making opportunities. In the aftermath of the war, the rich and the poor alike carried memories that changed over the decades. These myths surrounding the wartime experience transformed into a powerful variable, shaping the social and political relations of the Middle East in the century that followed.

Alongside those civilians was another group that shaped the postwar region. These were the soldiers, whose experiences on the front and in the labor battalions revealed to them new worlds of foreign fighters and local soldiers, city dwellers, and rural peasants.

Café in a public garden, Beirut, 1909. *(Library of Congress.)*

Fig tree after devastation by locusts, Palestine, 1915. *(Library of Congress.)*

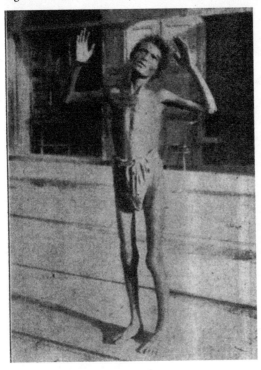

Wartime measures, as well
as natural disasters, caused a
devastating famine in parts
of the region. *(L'Asie française,
February 1922.)*

Famine killed large numbers of civilians, including these victims being removed for burial. (L'Asie française, *February 1922.*)

Local militia in Antioch. *(Courtesy of Nadim Shehadi.)*

Opening of the Beersheba railway station. *(Middle East Centre Archive, St. Antony's College, Oxford, Saunders Collection, 5/1/14.)*

A hanging at Damascus Gate, Jerusalem, 1915. *(Courtesy of the Library of the Institute for Palestine Studies.)*

Armenian woman kneeling beside dead child near Aleppo. *(Library of Congress.)*

Railroad station in Beirut with Armenian refugees. *(Courtesy of Nadim Shehadi.)*

Ottoman soldiers returning from military review in Damascus. Postcard. *(Courtesy of Nadim Shehadi.)*

Jamal Pasha and members of the Ottoman Parliament, 1916. *(Library of Congress)*

Indian cavalry on the Tigris. *(Library of Congress.)*

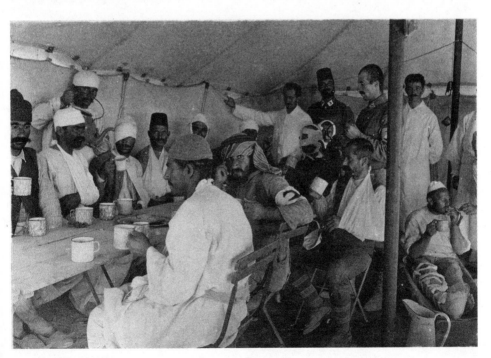

A dining tent at a Red Crescent hospital, Hafir, 1916. *(Library of Congress.)*

The first British regiment entering Jerusalem's Old City by the Jaffa Gate. *(Courtesy of Nadim Shehadi.)*

Gaza in ruins, 1917. *(Library of Congress.)*

An Australian officer at the head of troops in Damascus. *(Courtesy of Nadim Shehadi.)*

Turkish prisoners marching through Nablus. *(Middle East Centre Archive, St. Antony's College, Oxford, PA 1-995-023.)*

Relief committee for Beirut, 1919. *(Courtesy of Carole Corm.)*

CHAPTER FIVE

The Soldiering Experience

OVER ONE HUNDRED miles west of the Turkish capital of Ankara sits the central Anatolian province of Eskişehir, framed by the subtle arch of its surrounding mountains. On Wednesday, April 2, 2008, amid the red-tiled roofs that dot the central Anatolian landscape, an old man drew his last breath while comforted by his closest family members.[1] The simple passing of Yakup Satar—matched only by his own gentle, unassuming nature—seems at first a commonplace event. Yet the death of this old man with the sparse gray beard soon made international headlines. For, at 110 years, Yakup Satar was the sultan's last living Turkish soldier of the Great War.[2] With his death, the final living historical entry point to the Turkish trenches of 1914–1918 was barricaded shut, never to be breached again.

Over the decades, that barrier to information has been reinforced by the reliance on a steady stream of mobilized, convalescent, and discharged Ottoman soldiers to relay news orally between front lines and hometowns.[3] Ottoman soldiers—approximately 80 percent of whom were rural, with only 11 percent of these literate—did not leave behind a trail of diaries and letters detailing the war.[4] However, many of these troops were able to carry messages home orally, and some letters have survived. Hans Kannengiesser, operating alongside Ottoman forces, explained the modus operandi in his memoir: "The connection of the soldier with his home was not, as is usually the case, by exchange of letters through the post, but more often one of the older men decided to visit the troops in the field. He travelled around in his neighbourhood to collect messages from the parents or other relatives. Then he sought the troops in the field. After many months he found them and was able to exchange letters and news with the soldiers from his neighbourhood. Finally, after further months he arrived back home, eagerly awaited by everybody."[5] In the ensuing decades, most of these letters have been lost.

Even so, the World War I historian must soldier on, making use of whatever source material—memoirs, diaries, memoranda, newspapers—can be uncovered to gain an imperfect glimpse into the four years of devastation wrought by the Great War. The resulting image of the Ottoman soldiering experience, long past and lacking living witnesses, is as diverse as the empire itself. There is no unitary experience, no singular narrative, that defines the Ottoman soldier.

Counting less than 19 million subjects in its core provinces, burgeoning to perhaps 25 million with its outlying regions counted, the early twentieth-century Ottoman Empire faced a decisive manpower disadvantage relative to the conscripted mass armies of Europe.[6] Doubly debilitating, when Ottoman leaders transitioned to a Prussian-inspired mass mobilization campaign prior to World War I, those efforts were buffeted by two structural deficiencies: the legacy of nineteenth-century Ottoman warfare and the weakness of the Ottoman industrial base. Even before World War I, the attraction of military service in faraway lands was tarnished by irregular campaigns, decade-long tours, and sporadic pay, which the Ottoman soldier could expect to be regularly in arrears.[7]

Moreover, lacking the industrial infrastructure necessary to supply a mobile force properly, the Ottoman soldier of the late nineteenth and early twentieth centuries deployed in disparate environments—from the Hijaz desert to the Albanian mountains—with inadequate uniforms and insufficient food. Dependent on an erratic single-track railway, Istanbul was unable to sustain supply depots as close as thirty miles away, forcing its troops to live off the land.[8]

Given these challenges, more Ottoman troops perished from starvation and disease than from battle wounds in major confrontations with Russia

(1877–1878) and the Balkans (1912–1913).[9] As war clouds rumbled over the Balkans in the summer of 1914, the Ottomans had just suffered through two wars in the Balkans. Because so many experienced and entrepreneurial Ottoman officers died in those campaigns, Istanbul entered World War I without many of its most battle-hardened, savvy officers.[10] In sum, the hardship of military service was all too familiar to the sultan's subjects.

That hardship was not shared equally, however. In the decades before the Great War, Ottoman conscription was handicapped by a system of detailed exemptions in which authorities issued periodic regulations redefining the pool of eligible military men. Most notably, Ottoman Christians and Jews were regularly absent from frontline military service despite constituting 20 to 30 percent of the population.[11] Specific geographical areas, including the imperial capital of Istanbul and the holy cities of Mecca and Medina, also enjoyed exemption from service, along with entire professional classes, religious students, mullahs, and women.[12] For practical purposes *muinsiz*, or irreplaceable breadwinners, and nomads, who were eligible in theory but overlooked in practice, were also given a pass by the authorities. These exemption categories were closely monitored by the general population; tellingly, the number of young pilgrims to Mecca spiked during recruitment.[13] For the less pious, two popular options for circumventing military service remained—substitution (sending a personal replacement) and payment.[14]

Thus, by this process of elimination, we return to the Anatolian countryside, to provinces like Eskişehir, and to men like Yakup Satar. Indeed, throughout World War I, the backbone of the sultan's army was the Anatolian infantryman.[15] As one distinguished scholar of the early twentieth-century Ottoman military observed: "The Ottoman army was . . . an army of sedentary Muslim men, and, as over 80 percent of the population was rural even at the dawn of the twentieth century, primarily one of sedentary Muslim peasants."[16] Nonetheless, in an attempt to remedy its manpower shortage and build imperial cohesion across confessional lines in the years preceding World War I, the Ottoman leadership significantly expanded the pool of eligible troops by jettisoning several previous exemption categories, such as for Christians.[17]

In response, a majority of Christians chose to change nationalities, flee abroad, or pay the individual exemption fee.[18] In this last respect, the authorities were somewhat complicit. Although the CUP decreed the payment as applicable only in peacetime, "it seems doubtful that the Ottoman government, always hungry for money, actually suspended the practice during World War I."[19] For poor Greeks or Armenians who could not afford either to pay or flee abroad, the manual labor battalions beckoned. On the eve of war, therefore, the CUP's mobilization efforts were still in transition, cajoling a mostly reluctant population into military service. As a result, the Ottoman army remained to the very end a largely Anatolian peasant force.[20]

Once ordered, mobilization was proclaimed publicly and prominently. In exploring the social dimensions of conscription, the historian Najwa al-Qattan has described the notification process: "Announcements calling for mobilization were posted in public areas in Ottoman towns and distributed to local leaders, and the word *seferberlik* was prominently printed on top. Following such announcements, conscription would begin. The names of 'eligible' young men were sent to city councils, drummers and criers announced the draft in city quarters, and Ottoman officials collected the men and promptly dispatched them to the front."[21] In a memorandum addressed to "His Britannic Majesty's Ambassador at Constantinople," the British consul in Baghdad reported on the "bright colored placards" adorning Baghdad's walls announcing general mobilization of the army following the outbreak of hostilities in Europe.[22] A scan of contemporary newspapers reinforces the impression that conscription was a dominant topic of discussion in the summer and fall of 1914.

Despite this notification system, the Ottoman effort was slowed by incomplete population census data. For the central administrators setting recruitment quotas and for the local officers administering the conscription, faulty census data created a maze of inefficiencies.[23] Brigadier General Ziya Yergök, stationed in eastern Anatolia, assisted in military recruitment after the declaration of general mobilization on August 2, 1914. In his memoir, he recalls the confusion resulting from erroneous population data: "Men who were called up for the army rushed to the recruiting offices in order not to become a criminal. However, records of recruiting offices were not accurate and their personnel were limited in number to manage the recruitment process. As a result, front doors of the offices were filled by reserved soldiers. Many of them had to stay on the streets or in the gardens of mosques for days and nights. Complaints among them increased and some of them had to go back to their home."[24] Yergök added that mobilization was ordered in the summer during Ramadan, creating additional complications, despite an order prohibiting soldiers from fasting.[25]

The confusion and challenge inherent in mobilizing a culturally diverse force with incomplete population data are uniquely captured in the experiences of one Syrian conscript:

> I had finished my military service [but] the Ottomans were recruiting young men to serve in their army. I decided to visit the barracks the next day. They informed me that the Ottomans were trying to recruit around 300 men but that only 10 of different confessions showed up. . . . We didn't have the time to settle our business or to say goodbye to our families. We were imprisoned in the barracks and an officer told us that we will be moved to another region in 18 days. He told us that we will not receive any military training, ignoring the fact that none of us knew how to handle a rifle. My father offered to pay the 50 liras military allowance to exempt me from joining the army. The officer refused. . . . So my father suggested to pay 50 liras anyway to allow me to sleep at my house during those 18 days. . . . The officer agreed. So I left to close my shop and spend some time with my family before leaving.[26]

At the end of his eighteen-day leave, this young man was sent to Damascus with a diverse group of conscripts:

> I joined the rest of the recruited on the 19th day and we took the train to Damascus. . . . We were all originally from Aleppo and its surrounding villages: around 100 Christians, 3 Jewish and the rest were Muslims. The barracks were stuffed with soldiers and ammunitions. We couldn't find a place to sleep so we decided to cover the floor with some blankets and sleep despite the cold weather. We were moved the next morning to Daraa, a small village next to the road of the Hejaz railway. We stayed there for 5 days, sleeping next to each other in the tents in an attempt to warm one another. We were separated the next day. . . . We were suffering from the cold so we asked our commanding officer to allow us to leave Daraa. He did and we left with no food or water and walked around 9 hours before we reached the village of Salkhat near Jabal al-Druze. We came across an Ottoman troop and stayed with them for the night. A doctor checked us the next day and judged that we were ready to military service. We were then given military clothes and some food and joined the military exercises. We got really scared every time an Ottoman officer insulted us. He ignored the fact that we didn't understand the language. He would even beat us. My friend couldn't take it anymore, so he escaped and never returned back.[27]

Indeed, the push for rapid mobilization in anticipation of war, within the context of limited administrative capacity, combined with cultural obstacles to create a jolting process. As the historian Salim Tamari suggests, many soldiers "were uprooted from their traditional communities, and traveled throughout the empire for the first time [coming] in contact with 'ethnic others' in the imperial army: Turks, Kurds, Syrians, Albanians, and Bulgarians, as well as Austrian and German officers from the European Allies."[28] One transition memo for an incoming German commander, Major General Hans von Seeckt, describes the resulting mix of culture shock and an acute desire to escape: "When sent to the railroad station, the men for the most part did not know each other or their superiors. They only knew that they were being sent to some bad place. Hence they ran away whenever they could, and risked being shot while running. They jumped from the cars in motion, from the marching column in covered terrain, or from the bivouac, or from their billets."[29]

Throughout the war, Ottoman administrators grappled with the general popular aversion to the newly instituted system of mass conscription. In July 1914 in British-controlled Egypt al-Ahram reported on popular reaction— "all Arabs strongly opposed the new law"[30]—while al-Muqattam wrote that the religious leadership and civic notables of Beirut had even telegraphed Istanbul to register their opposition: "The application of this new military law will ruin the population. Thus, we completely reject it as we seek to protect our interests as well as those of the Porte."[31] Another telegram intoned, "We know that all the social norms compel the governments to abide by its peoples wishes and the people refuse this law."[32] As the British Intelligence Department reported from Cairo, "the enforcement of the recruiting measures has met with considerable opposition in localities such as Kurdistan, the Hauran, and Arabia, so that for the moment the full member of recruits are by no means secured."[33]

Whatever initial enthusiasm may have existed for service was further dampened by widespread property confiscations. Even before the outbreak of war, the British consul in Baghdad reported that "the military authorities since the mobilization began, have been requisitioning mules, horses, cloth, sugar, flour, shoes, cooking pots, sewing machines, etc."[34] In Aleppo, Ottoman military detachments roamed markets and warehouses as early as the summer of 1914, registering goods and ordering some merchants to inventory rather than sell their items. From the cool climes of Mount Lebanon's resorts, wealthy Egyptian and Syrian families followed such unprecedented measures with great apprehension. With the assassination of Archduke Ferdinand, many rushed "to crowd the boats or carriages that carried them home" to attend to their affairs.[35] Not surprisingly, "their hasty departure was a confirmation of the worst fears of less mobile onlookers."[36]

Nonetheless, the advent of modern warfare and the humiliation of decisive military defeats reinforced the Ottoman leadership's conviction that a modern conscription system was an essential political and military unifier. The threshold for attaining official exemption from military service therefore proved quite high. In her study of Jerusalem during the Great War, Abigail Jacobson explains that attempts "to escape from military service are described (by locals) as extremely difficult. In his diary, [the Palestinian Christian] Khalil al-Sakakini describes at length his attempts to change his conscription order in order to perform his military service in Jerusalem. He describes his failed attempts, as well as those of Mayor Hussein Selim al-Husayni, to negotiate this issue with Commander Rusen Bey."[37] Thus, as modern conscription crept forward and the Ottoman leadership pressed on, the practice of draft evasion picked up in both sophistication and frequency. To corral the most brazen evaders, military policemen hunted through "attics, basements, synagogues, mosques, and churches."[38] In Jerusalem, as elsewhere, neighborhood representatives and village leaders (*mukhtars*) accepted bribes to divert policemen from hiding places.[39] As Abdallah Hanna discovered in his study of Syrian commoners in the war: "The slogan 'We will not capitulate!' [to the army] circulated among the young men, who hid in villages, in prepared hiding places in the houses, in the fields, in caves, with Bedouin families or in other out-of-the-way places."[40]

By degrees, evading conscription in rural areas proved easier than in the cities; indeed, "leaving for the mountains" was an established exercise in evasion throughout the Balkans and in Anatolia.[41] Even then, one could not be assured of success. In *Fragments of Memory* the Syrian novelist Hanna Mina recounts the fate of one boy's uncle who grew ill and ultimately died after fleeing across the mountains to avoid military service.[42] When apprehended, suspected draft evaders were usually convicted by military court— usually without trial—and often sentenced to flogging.[43] Since the ultimate consequence of capture was often military service, applying effective deterrent measures was nearly impossible.[44] As a result, the Ottomans adopted a "system of material and personal sureties, whereby those who had no property were required to have a male family member (father, brother or uncle) vouch for them."[45] In the summer of 1914, *al-Muqattam* captured the anguish unleashed by conscription, quoting one father imploring authorities, "Have pity for my seven children! I am their only financial supporter" as he was hauled away to service.[46] The article proceeded to question the compatibility and adaptability of an imported military conscription system. In Germany, wives could take on the responsibilities of their conscripted husbands, but "is it possible for Muslim women to do the same?"[47]

Set aside *al-Muqattam*'s agenda, however, and it remains difficult today to imagine the extreme pressure such a system of total mobilization placed on Ottoman society. In an empire devoted to victory and pressed repeatedly by its allies to increase its contribution, the exhaustive scale of mobilization remains a lasting legacy of the Great War. This found expression in the newly emerging term *safarbarlik*, which announced general mobilization by headlining placards and conscription lists. In her study of Greater Syria during World War I, Najwa al-Qattan compellingly argues that "in its most focused form, *safarbarlik* is also the sultan's war, a war that (as described in a contemporary play) 'has nothing to do with us . . . our young men prefer to mutilate themselves rather than serve.' [In Syrian postwar writings] the Great War, as the *safarbarlik*, was first and foremost a very local civilian catastrophe, a war at home."[48] Yet it also invoked "bounty hunters (rather than agents of a bureaucratized state) who roamed city streets hoping to 'catch' young men. They carried ropes with them to encircle, tie up, and carry off boys and men on the run."[49]

The heartbreak of war is personalized through a young woman, Maryam, the protagonist in a novel by Nadiya al-Ghazzi, whom we met earlier. At war's outbreak, the young Maryam is engaged to Barhum, who is destined for death on the battlefield. Maryam's story traumatizes and humanizes "the wedding that never was, of a war that reduced young women to spinsterhood or loveless marriage, of a dream that was cut down by history and war."[50] As Abdallah Hanna explains, in Syria "*Safar Barlik* or *al-tajammu'* . . . 'the collection' in Arabic, refers to the collection or 'rounding up' of recruits before their departure. The Ottoman term *Safar Barlik* referred to mobilization in Turkish; the Persian *seferber* means 'being ready for war.' In its Arabic usage, *safar barlik* is understood as 'the journey over land.' Since the end of the 19th century (the Yemen war) and the Balkan Wars . . . this term became a popular synonym for the march of the recruits . . . to the Ottoman theatres of war."[51] Indeed, conscription served as such a traumatic departure point for the Great War that it grew to be synonymous with the horror of war itself.

For many living in Greater Syria, the image of the "bounty hunter" was inextricably bound up with the person of Jamal Pasha.[52] Nicknamed "the murderer" and "the butcher" by some Syrians, Jamal Pasha was depicted in popular narratives as terrorizing "Damascenes through rigged courts martial and the scaffolds."[53] In the late summer of 1915, when Jamal Pasha arrived in Nazareth, British military intelligence reported that "old men, very often physical wrecks, are being sent for military service; the young men are hiding."[54] As the war intensified, this capricious system of mobilization steadily intensified as Enver Pasha's strike into eastern Anatolia squandered thousands of lives. Other soldiers were lost to unbearable conditions and rampant disease; before long, a steady stream of deserters fled the army.[55] In combination, these factors meant perpetual mobilization campaigns throughout the war as the authorities sought to replenish the ill, dead, or deserted of their force.

In this context, reports of Istanbul accepting, and at times even preferring, payment over service as early as the fall of 1914 attest to the delicate state of Ottoman finances.[56] As early as one month after mobilization, non-Muslims were invited to return to Beirut to pay an exemption fee as part of an Ottoman amnesty initiative. While the drive raised funds, the upshot of such policies may have been to deepen socioeconomic divisions between those who could afford exemption and those who faced service.[57] The poor could neither afford exemption nor scramble aboard the last Italian ships steaming out of Lebanese ports.[58] Eventually, the yawning gap between the powerful and the powerless spawned a drama genre in which self-mutilation symbolized defection from a war few understood and defiance of a CUP increasingly disrespected. In one play, a man turned mad by the prospect of conscription amputates his own leg, while another mutilates his own arm as the police close in on him.[59] The fact that these plays required little explanation or context suggests popular cynicism toward—and historical memory of—Ottoman conscription policies.[60]

As the war took shape, and Jamal Pasha contemplated his gamble across the Sinai desert against Suez, Jerusalem registered a spike in popular resistance to military service.[61] In response, in April 1915 the authorities issued regulations that eliminated still more exemption categories and substantially increased the exemption payment.[62] In particular, Muslim foreigners living in the Ottoman Empire were made eligible under the pretext of jihad, which one could nonetheless avoid for a more earthly forty-five liras.[63] By August, official pronouncements mixed disappointment with retribution: "Men of the 1310 Class (1894) were called up nearly a month ago; we regret to say that the non-Moslems particularly have not displayed great eagerness to respond to the summons. Young men of the 1310 Class, either Moslems or non-Moslems, who do not report themselves the day after this notice, deserve more than men of other classes, the penalty of death, which is the legal penalty; they will be immediately tried by court-martial."[64] The failure of these efforts was confirmed through reports, published in the ensuing months, of conscription of boys as young as sixteen and men as old as fifty-five.[65] Al-Muqattam published one Syrian's complaint that only "women, children, and old men are left living in the villages."[66]

The mass conscription of Ottoman soldiers strained an already-overwhelmed support system. The shortage of medical personnel in particular proved troubling for an army dispersed geographically and expanding exponentially. In Syria, physicians were mass enrolled; by January 1915 medical students were enlisted to alleviate the shortage in deployed doctors.[67] The journalist Ahmed Emin Yalman estimated the number of physicians for the entire health service at 2,555, serving alongside 1,202 active surgeons and 1,353 reserve surgeons. These doctors were predictably overwhelmed by the almost three million men who were enrolled during the war.[68] In light of their rarity, for doctors who ignored conscription orders, as one physician from the Kisrawan district of Lebanon dared, property seizures could follow.[69]

The physician in Kisrawan may be forgiven for ignoring his summons since Mount Lebanon always represented a unique geography. As the British Intelligence Department noted, most residents of Mount Lebanon served in the "Lebanon militia: This militia force is not liable for service outside its own district, where its duties are chiefly those of police. . . . Turkish officers are said to have been put in command of them."[70] In December 1915 al-Muqattam reported that "Lebanese working in Beirut have been exempted from military service, under the condition that their houses must be located outside Beirut. The Ottoman government still respects Lebanon's autonomy for reasons Jamal Pasha only knows."[71]

In a related manner, Christian labor battalions only rarely participated in battle at the front, and were almost universally unarmed. Nonetheless, they proved indispensable to the war effort by constructing transportation systems, repairing dilapidated infrastructure, and carrying essential supplies to the front lines.[72] One Ottoman officer recalled encountering "gangs of working men constructing a railway line under German supervision. . . . They toiled like slaves, their backs blistering in the sun."[73] These bustling workers, laying piping and repairing infrastructure, transformed Greater Syria "into one major construction site."[74] The British Intelligence Department recognized this contribution, reporting that although the "introduction of the law applying conscription to the Christians was at first the occasion of much controversy and recrimination, and the Christians themselves showed little enthusiasm to serve in the army," in 1914 and 1915 "the great majority of Christians and Jews enrolled were drafted into unarmed labor battalions, used for road making, etc."[75] Salim Tamari has written that "the misery of these conscripts, often sent to die in the distant expanses of Anatolia or in Gallipoli or the Sinai desert, was tempered by a salutary side: they were offered free food, lodging."[76] Although ineligible to rise above the rank of lieutenant—except for doctors who were conscripted as captains—Ottoman Christian work battalions performed indispensable work in exceptionally harsh conditions throughout the war.[77] That contribution came at a social price, however. A primary duty of these battalions was the removal of wounded and corpses, and these soldiers "became immune to death, and the mass carnage of war," forever disrupting their prewar notions of life and death.[78]

In sum, the ever-tightening noose of Ottoman conscription choked Ottoman society. As Thompson observed, at least by the latter part of 1916, "The Ottomans were conscripting men aged 17 to 55, both Muslims and Christians (except those in Mount Lebanon), in an army that recruited 2.85 million troops. About three-fourths of all adult men were mobilized. Casualties neared one million. Figures on battlefield deaths vary between 325,000 and 600,000 men."[79] In addition, hundreds of thousands of soldiers died of disease while "250,000 others were listed as missing or as enemy prisoners by war's end."[80] Sensing the extreme cost of war and the alienation it was causing, in July 1915 al-Muqattam attacked the governors of Syria as having "gone mad. They decided to recruit Syrian men to military service and took them to die in Sinai, Caucasus, Iraq and the Dardanelles.

The governors also confiscated all the goods, crops, livestock and animals."[81] These measures, along with the possibility of death, loomed large for the Ottoman soldier, and therefore spawned mass desertion.

As with draft evaders, Ottoman deserters captured the attention of decision makers throughout the conflict. In fact, the head of the German military mission in Istanbul identified desertion as a major vulnerability: "The British very skillfully used all imaginable means to influence the disposition of the Turkish soldier. They used gold freely. . . . Propaganda was also made openly. Among many other kinds of papers the British airplanes dropped wagon loads of the most beautifully illustrated pamphlets showing the physical comforts the Turkish soldier enjoyed in British captivity. The effect of such means on men that never got enough to eat and in many ways received no care of any kind should not be underestimated."[82] One Ottoman officer recalled that on Gallipoli, the British dropped "leaflets telling us to have nothing to do with the Germans, that they would establish friendly relations with us."[83]

Daring British agents often went beyond dropping leaflets; operating behind enemy lines in Ottoman uniforms, they distributed "handbills" persuading units to desert, including an entire battalion "at the station of Affuleh, in which the Turkish situation is described as hopeless."[84] The Russians organized similar information campaigns. During the Arab Revolt in August 1916, "two Arab officers, Shukri al-Shurbaji [. . .] and Ahmad Shaykha, deserted to the Russian lines in Kermanshah. They said that they had made up their minds to desert after reading propaganda leaflets dropped by Russian planes, and in which the outbreak of the Arab revolt was reported."[85]

Desertion occurred on every Ottoman military front: "The deserters who joined the revolt army came from the various battle fronts, from Gallipoli, Iraq, Palestine, and even from the besieged Medina. Arab deserters from Medina slipped through to the Arab rebel lines from the beginning of the revolt until the end of the war."[86] Most especially, however, "recruits fled while en route to the front, or from the army on the march, especially when they passed close to their home town or village. They roamed the countryside, living off the land and turning into robber bands. Further troops had to be detached in ever greater numbers to deal with the insecurity these bands created behind the front lines. The population often sympathised with the deserters and hid them in their homes."[87] Such bands

informally parceled out the countryside among each other, living off villagers or attacking railways in order to survive.[88]

To escape the war, others even defected to the French navy patrolling the
Mediterranean shore. Buwari recounts several such scenes. On the afternoon of September 7, 1915, as his French ship passed the coastal town of
Shikka, located just south of Tripoli, a man and woman were observed running toward the sea. As the two reached the water, the man took off his
clothes and threw himself into the water, swimming toward the French,
while the woman took his discarded clothes and slipped back into town.
The French commander of the ship dispatched a small boat to retrieve the
man, who turned out to be a construction worker named Constantine,
from Tripoli. Constantine ended up enlisting in the French navy and deployed to the French-controlled island of Arwad.[89] It is unclear whether
Constantine defected from a life of civilian hardship or military duty, but
he did go on to serve with the French until the end of the war.

Buwari witnessed a similar rescue scene ten months later, in July 1916,
off the coast of Tabarja, north of Beirut in the Kisrawan district of Lebanon. This time, however, the captain of the French vessel refused Buwari's
request to pick up the young man swimming toward them, arguing that
doing so might endanger the crew. So Buwari turned to a sailor whom he
had met in Cyprus and recruited to join the French navy, and instructed
him and two others to pull the young man from the water. The Ottomans
responded with a bombardment, the very threat the French captain had
feared, but the young man was brought safely on board while the crew lay
low on deck.[90]

Armenians from around the world also voluntarily enlisted with the
Triple Entente, helping to form a foreign legion within the French army.
This *Légion d'Orient* included disparate members of the Ottoman Empire
who fought with Allenby against the Ottomans in Syria.[91] Captain Sarkis
Torossian was wounded in Gallipoli and fought in Palestine before joining
the Arab Revolt. Torossian's shock at the condition of his fellow Armenians,
trekking across the Syrian desert in refugee columns, was made all the more
painful by his own sister's hardship and eventual death. Having already lost
his family and friends to the Great War, and his commitment to the Ottoman cause sullied, he chose to defect. Even then, however, he remained powerless to stem the tide of suffering that washed over his life. In one moving
passage of his memoir, Torossian recalls the death by disease of his fiancée

at Gaza: "I raised Jemileh in my arms, the pain and terror in her eyes melted until they were bright as stars again, stars in an oriental night, the lids drooped slowly and so she died, as a dream passing."[92]

To forestall men like Torossian from deserting, Syrian and Lebanese soldiers were transferred to distant battlefronts, ranging from Galicia to Gallipoli and from Suez to Samarra.[93] In his seminal study *The Arab Awakening*, George Antonius describes the political scene that Faysal encountered during a return trip to Damascus during the war. Faysal "found conditions changed beyond recognition. He had come with the settled purpose of fomenting a revolt of the Arab divisions in the Turkish army and a mass rising of the population on a signal from his father. . . . The last remaining Arab divisions had been transferred . . . and their place taken by battalions manned by Turks."[94]

As battlefield conditions deteriorated and the number of military deserters ballooned, "the government released a pamphlet warning every family whose members fled that they'd be sent to Anatolia or somewhere far away in the Ottoman Empire."[95] In fact, Jamal Pasha's new policy mixed inducements with punishments: "(1) The family of the defector will be deported from its country to a far province. (2) Those who come back before the end of the grace period will be acquitted from the tribute. The rest will be arrested and gravely punished. (3) The responsible division and the nearest local government should be informed about the defections."[96]

At the front, military measures were implemented, but as one German lieutenant wrote, the "Turks were tired of war and unwilling to fight, as evidenced by the mass desertions of the Turkish soldiers. These deserters took with them not only their rifles and hand grenades, but also machine guns. The headquarters of the Eighth Army took energetic steps by guarding the country in rear, but trucks with armed infantry had to be sent after these deserters, with whom sometimes regular actions took place."[97] The historian Erik Zürcher observed that "troops, especially those consisting of Arab recruits, were mistrusted so much that they were sometimes brought to the front unarmed, and under armed escort of Turkish guards. In Palestine and Syria, Beduins were offered a reward of five Ottoman pounds for every deserter they captured and returned."[98] During the steady retreat into Palestine in 1917, one account recalled times "when we had to turn our machine-guns upon our own Arab troops in order to prevent them from deserting."[99]

Indeed, during the occasional disorganized Ottoman retreat, a hazardous journey through tribal realms threatened.[100]

One Venezuelan adventurer, Rafael de Nogales Méndez, left a memoir in which he recounts that "desertions from the Army, daily became more frequent, especially from the Arab troops. . . . Hard-pressed by hunger or overcome by homesickness for their native hills, the detachments of our Arab line and labor battalions kept disintegrating in such fashion as finally to alarm Djemal Pasha."[101] As Nogales Méndez saw it, especially during his time in Palestine, Jamal Pasha utilized the "most severe measures": "There was never a morning . . . which did not show two or three corpses of Arab deserters dangling from some beam or telegraph pole. Since the desertions nevertheless increased, Djemal Pasha decreed an ostentatious execution by shooting for the next offender, to see if this means might check the disorder. . . . The victim chanced to be no less a personage than an Arab priest."[102]

Nonetheless, "when deserters were caught, they generally were punished only lightly and returned to their units as soon as possible in order not to deplete the strength of the army any further."[103] Indeed, large numbers of deserters—hundreds could be arrested in one action—crowded public jails and peopled labor projects.[104] The *Times* of London may have characterized Ottoman policies as producing a "reign of terror" in which "courts-martial are sentencing suspects wholesale to death," but "only rarely do we find reports of deserters being executed."[105]

British officers similarly encouraged the speedy processing of deserters. One Regimental Order, dated June 1915, instructed: "The trials of men accused of desertion should take place at once, and only those whom it is necessary to execute as a public example will be executed. Others to be put to hard labour. Information has been received that there are very large numbers of such persons detained in many different places, and it is most undesirable that they should be kept for a long time awaiting trial. Steps should therefore be taken to try them and report results."[106] As in the Ottoman territories, restorative justice could take precedence over retributive punishment. Therefore, in the case of a certain "Osman Chaous," a deserting sergeant, he was "to be punished . . . and if he does it again, he will be very severely punished. This is to be communicated to the men."[107]

For the British in Egypt, the Great War meant balancing the exigencies of war with the maintenance of popular support. Cairo bustled with foreign troops, which ebbed and flowed depending on military developments. In his memoir, Colonel Alfred Parker describes Cairo in the aftermath of the Gallipoli debacle as "a bewildering place. . . . Thousands of Australians and New Zealanders [joined] the British and Indian troops who thronged the streets and bazaars, and made every day a festival for the belly-dancers and bar and brothel owners. Wide-brimmed hats, open-tunics and unfamiliar accents vied with spit-and-polish and . . . parade-ground chants of the grammar-school officers. A British intelligence officer likened Staff HQ at the Savoy to an oriental railway station."[108] The threat of Egyptian social upheaval forced the British to tread lightly, but as the war ground on the demand for labor steadily increased.[109] The Egyptian Labour Corps began in 1915 with a modest five hundred workers from southern Egypt sent to Mudros.[110] The workers so impressed the British that the Corps was quickly expanded even while recruiting proved difficult.[111]

By the summer of 1917 "it was plain that a crisis was approaching," for all factions were struggling to meet the seemingly insatiable appetite of the British war machine.[112] General Archibald Murray, commander of the Egyptian Expeditionary Force, argued as much in a memorandum: "There can be no doubt that Egypt is not feeling the strain of war, and it may be that I shall have to ask you for power to conscript native labour as the work and anxiety of keeping a voluntary Labour Corps, of which the members only serve for 3 months at a time, are very great."[113] In theory enlistment was voluntary, but in practice recruitment into the indigenous Egyptian Labour Corps and its offspring the Camel Transport Corps evolved into forced conscription.[114] For the peasantry (*fellahin*) who enabled the vast logistical undertaking of crossing the Sinai, "pay was low, the discipline often harsh, and the clothing simple."[115] As the historian David Woodward writes, "The best workers came from the southern provinces of Egypt, but many of them refused to sign a contract for more than three months. Nor would they agree to return to work until their savings had been depleted."[116] Lieutenant Colonel G. E. Badcock, who had firsthand experience, knew whereof he wrote: "The first recruits were volunteers which is to say that of every three, one came to avoid the Police, one was sent by the Police, and one was a respectable wage-earner."[117]

British officers were persuaded by call-and-response singing among the laborers that morale was good, when, in fact, the words bemoaned the seemingly endless years of drudgery: "A work party began this chant by

asking . . . how much longer would they have to work before returning to
their homes. . . . A soloist would respond with a prediction, perhaps one
hundred years, which would be greeted with much wailing and wringing of
hands. The group would then repeat the question, and the soloist with each
response reduced the number of years. . . . His final response would be 'one
day, one night,' and his fellow workers would clap their hands with pleasure. And the song was over."[118] British newspapers merrily reported on "the
happy, singing Egyptians" and made no effort to correct the misconception
that laborers were offering voluntary rather than compulsory service.[119]
While building railways and laying pipe in the searing desert, these men
endured the punishment of enemy artillery and the scars of the overseer's
lash. Many gave their lives laboring under an abusive master for a cause
they did not understand.

From Egypt, the British demanded "labour, food, and animals."[120] As
Allenby advanced deep into Palestine, the British demanded more resources
transported across even longer supply lines. As Lieutenant Colonel Elgood
wrote, Egypt had "yielded to the Army her labour, her food, and her money.
She had no more to give but cotton, and on the 18th June 1918 His Majesty's
Government announced by military proclamation their intention of purchasing and distributing the next crop."[121]

In the Ottoman provinces, the rationale for desertion was bound up in
the ragged nature of the soldiering existence. On one particularly devastating day, Liman von Sanders observed that "the number of Turkish deserters
is higher today than that of the men under arms. A guaranty for the subsistence of the troops can never be given by the Turks. The promises are made
and broken. The clothing of my army is so bad that many officers are wearing ragged uniforms and even battalion commanders have to wear tschariks
in lieu of boots."[122] The young Fawzi al-Qawuqji—who himself deserted to
join the Arab Revolt and later commanded troops during the 1948 war—
pinned the high rate of desertion on the woeful supply situation. He commented that there was hunger at the war front and a lack of clothes, supplies, and ammunition, which led to high numbers of soldiers deserting the
army.[123] Zürcher summarized the situation: "Both the vulnerability of the
troops to disease and their tendency to desert were increased immeasurably
by the lack of basic care for their welfare: the troops were ill-paid or not paid
at all, worn out marching, undernourished and badly clothed—all factors
which made them susceptible to disease and desertion. Time and again lack

of pay and lack of food are mentioned as reasons to desert in the British reports."[124]

The Ottoman force was so plagued by desertion that the authorities were forced to issue a general amnesty in July 1918 in an attempt to lure deserters back into the fight. The proclamations asked "by whom is our internal safety endangered in war-time? By soldiers, corporals, and sergeants who have been summoned to arms to defend the honor and rights of their country. In many cases they have become the tools of sedition and have left their companies to retire to the mountains. Such men endanger the public safety by their revolt against the laws and regulations of the country. Yet the Government has chosen to forgive and not punish. All offenders will surely profit by such good will, and return to their formations. It will strengthen the country's power to produce, and at the same time fill the army's ranks once more."[125] Days later, another proclamation shamed the deserters: "Deserters! You were asked to take the road that leads to God. If you had encountered on this road not military service, but even hell itself you should not have thought of deserting. You ought to have been patient and remained at the front, even if you were being deliberately cut to pieces. Privation and pain should not have influenced your actions. But you thought only of your good pleasure and put butter on our enemies' bread."[126] By September 1918, to avoid further desertion, the Ottoman Fourth Army issued an order "banning the stationing of soldiers in their own townships."[127]

In 1918, the burdens of full-scale warfare—exacerbated by military adventure and repeated defeat—trounced the Ottoman war machine, unleashing a tidal wave of deserters. After the fall of Damascus, reports surfaced of soldiers fleeing for home en masse. Although during four years of warfare almost five hundred thousand men deserted, some two hundred thousand did so in 1918 alone.[128] Eager to relieve their families' uncertainty and insecurity, relatively few soldiers joined the British forces or the Arab Revolt.[129]

On October 10, 1918, the Ottoman assembly convened to debate proposing a separate peace with London and Paris. Six days later, General Nuri Bey reported that "out of the million-and-a-half soldiers only seventy-two thousand had rifles, a number hardly sufficient to defend the country. He thought that Aleppo, Adana, and Mosul would be occupied within a few days, and the Straits, Izmir, and Istanbul could come under attack."[130] With that pronouncement, the assembly's deliberations were exposed as irrelevant, for without an army, the fate of the empire was sealed.

Early in World War I, as he deployed to the Ottoman front, Captain T. H. Chamberlain of the Berkshire Yeomanry observed that his men "had heard of the Turks but few had ever seen one—some had vague memories of a picture in a school book showing a large dark man, bare chested, large muscles and an enormous sword."[131] Four years later, for those lucky British servicemen who survived the Ottoman cauldron, a newfound appreciation for the Ottoman serviceman emerged. Back in Britain after the war, British veterans infused their encomiums to the Ottoman martial spirit with all variations of reverence and respect. The *Australian Official History* even admiringly cast the "Turk as a fighter . . . unlike any other soldier in the world. Even when he is wretchedly fed and miserably equipped . . . he will continue month after month and year after year a dangerous foe to troops of a higher civilization fighting under the happiest conditions. No set of circumstances, however depressing, appears able to diminish his dogged resistance, while if the opportunity is propitious he can always be stirred to the offensive."[132]

Western stereotypes of the Ottoman Empire proved ubiquitous in postwar remembrances. Considering the brittle state of the Ottoman Empire in 1914, the conjured image of a tenacious, formidable Ottoman opponent is particularly impressive. The German colonel Kress von Kressenstein reminds us that when "judging Turkey's performance during the World War, both in the larger operational and in the individual troop sense, one cannot forget that Turkey had experienced three defeats and a revolution. Despite sincere efforts, Turkey had not yet recuperated from the heavy losses in officers, troops, and materials incurred therein. At the outbreak of the war, the Ottoman treasury was empty, its troops poorly uniformed and equipped with antiquated weapons."[133] Recast in this light, the endurance, accomplishment, and valor of individual Ottoman soldiers was nothing short of extraordinary. With a touch of hyperbole, New Zealand private Digger Craven vividly recounts one battle on Gallipoli. His respect for the enemy is evident:

> They descended upon us in a dense, black, screaming mass, so thickly ranked that they could advance shoulder to shoulder, and six to eight deep. They came and we sprayed them with machine-gun bullets, threw bombs in the packed mass, tore gaps into them with volley after volley of rifle-fire. From our miserable holes and bits of breast-works we annihilated their advance line. Then we rose to meet the second with bayonets, knives, entrenching

tools, cut and battered them to bits . . . the din of battle was deafening. . . .
They came on us in storming waves. The third line broke us, forced us back
on our pitiful apology for trenches, leapt into our holes and hacked right
and left in a confused jumble of destruction and death. The remnants fell
back to the second line of trenches, rallied, stiffened. . . . But we could not
hold them. . . . It is no mere expression to say we caught one another by the
throat. We rolled about the dirt locked in death grips. We used stones, knives,
bayonets, clubs, even fists, hurled ourselves upon one another in a fiendish
bestiality such as the battlefield rarely sees.[134]

Most of all, however, the Ottomans earned a reputation for dogged defense and proficient marching, covering vast distances while under duress.
A. P. Wavell, the famed World War II Field Marshal and eventual Viceroy
of India, recalled the Ottoman soldier as "a fine marcher [who] could dis-
pense with many of the impedimenta necessary to European armies. On
the defensive, his eye for ground, his skill in planning and entrenching a
position, and his stubbornness in holding it made him really a formidable
adversary to engage."[135] Wavell praised the "finest qualities" of the Ottoman soldier after one particular battle, reminiscing how he "struggled
gamely when checked in his assault, outmarched the British infantry when
he withdrew, and held off the pursuing horsemen in his retreat."[136] Woodward has summarized it thus: "The British soldier, as reflected in his letters,
diaries, and memoirs, developed considerable respect for the fighting ability
of the enemy, especially the Anatolian Turk. The Turkish peasant proved
tenacious in defense and courageous in attack. Although often poorly supplied, his power of endurance proved extraordinary, as did his ability to
cover ground on foot."[137]

Similarly, the German and Austrian soldiers deployed in the Middle
East praised their Ottoman comrades as exceptionally tough. Germans remarked "again and again on the barefoot, hungry soldiers who fought so
well."[138] Tensions did develop, however, between the German and Ottoman high command. Some of this is likely explained by rudimentary cultural differences: "There were so many opportunities for misunderstanding,
quite apart from the translation errors of the interpreters. Take, for instance,
the particularly important matter of time: six o'clock in the morning is, *à la
franca,* six o'clock in the morning, that is, six hours after midnight whether
it is dark or light, but six o'clock in the morning, *à la turca,* is six hours after
the continually changing sunrise."[139]

Anecdotal evidence also suggests that Jamal Pasha dispatched spies, posing as staff officers, among German commanders. In his memoir, Liman von Sanders wrote that as chief of the military mission, "I had several unpleasant conflicts with Enver [Pasha]."[140] The natural tensions arising in warfare and the cultural differences between Germans and Ottomans were exacerbated by Ottoman frustration at supposed German domineering and German frustration with perceived Ottoman inefficiency.

Liman von Sanders charged that Enver Pasha "fully recognized the value of the German work, but later was unable to recognize the salutary limitation that should have been imposed on it in his army where a different religion, language and interior organism required special considerations."[141] He also turned the spotlight on the German command, however, recognizing that there were too many officers "who would not accommodate themselves to the peculiarities of the country and of the Turkish administration, and thought all that was necessary was to apply German standards and German methods to Turkish conditions."[142] This led the British to judge that cultural tensions caused "mutual recrimination" and resulted in the Germans putting "almost as much grit as oil into the military machine."[143]

In contrast to the military elite, a more typical and unique camaraderie developed among the common soldiers on the front, where in the midst of the Great War's madness a mutual respect borne out of common hardship developed between the warring sides. Lieutenant Robert Goodsall of the Royal Field Artillery recalled that at one point along the Gaza-Beersheba lines "the heat produced what the men called a 'mirage,' and a rifle fire under such conditions was apt to be erratic. . . . By a sort of natural agreement, both sides shut down the war until the hours of dusk and darkness."[144] From Mesopotamia, Major Crowdy reported on one incident in which an "enemy drabi . . . was quietly driving a water cart along the road to Tikrit about 200 yards in front of our advancing firing line. Our firing line continued advancing and the Turk went on driving his cart, neither of them taking the slightest notice of the other."[145] The "exasperated" local British commander "sent up a message to his firing line asking them to at least to have a drink, even though they did not appear to want the cart. However, in the meanwhile, our men had stopped while the Turkish drabi had gone on out of sight."[146] At times, the Ottomans showed similar restraint, as the historian Edward Woodfin details in his study of the Palestine front: "When a party of foolhardy Scottish officers chased a jackal, foxhunt style, into no-man's land, the Turks did not open fire, though they had registered the entire sector for their guns and thus could have destroyed the Scots with ease and great accuracy."[147]

This camaraderie played out within the troops as well. Writing his father and mother from Gallipoli, one Ottoman soldier, Ismail, described the feeling as "we lay in our tents at night we saw the flash of the enemy's guns who had many great ships lying out at sea, and whether by day or night we heard continuously the thunder of the cannons and the rattle of small arms and our hearts were very sad."[148] As the fighting raged in the distance, another soldier leapt to his feet and shouted, "Truly my Mother did not bear me that I should die here in this tent while my comrades outside take part in the greatest blessing of Allah."[149] Several men marched to gain permission from headquarters for voluntary action on the front, which was granted.

Few issues animated soldiering camaraderie or inspired more hostility and enmity than prisoners of war (POWs). Kermit Roosevelt, the son of US President Theodore Roosevelt and an honorary captain in the British army, wrote that he and his men "always felt that the Turk was a clean fighter. Our officers he treated well as long as he had anything to give or share with them."[150] From Switzerland, the anti-Ottoman correspondent Stürmer conceded that "the Turk, when he does take prisoners, treats them kindly and chivalrously; but he takes few prisoners. . . . The primitive Turk is all too sadly lacking in the comforts of life himself to be able to provide them for his prisoners."[151]

In a typical dispatch, after capturing thirty Ottomans in the Hijaz, British intelligence commented that "the captives were all very hungry and state that they get only a water-bottle of water and one small loaf per day."[152] Ottoman detainees, Roosevelt maintained, "would thrive on what was starvation issue to our men. The attitude of many of the Turkish officers was amusing, if exasperating. They seemed to take it for granted that they would be greeted with every consideration due an honored guest. They would complain bitterly about not being supplied with coffee."[153] *Al-Muqattam* and *al-Ahram*, both published in British-controlled Egypt, did much to highlight the humane British treatment of Ottoman soldiers, reporting that prisoners were provided three meals a day and given their own plate, fork, and cup for water. To convey religious sensibilities—an important priority for British officers commanding Indian Muslims from their headquarters in Muslim Egypt—the military government built a small mosque for prisoners and offered daily religious courses.[154]

While the two Cairo newspapers circulated their reports, a censored cablegram arrived from London on September 4, 1915, complaining that "no theatre of war is so fruitful of mendacities in Germany as Dardanelles. Latest report from Constantinople published in German Press speaks of printing matter thrown among Turkish troops by Allied aviators, containing glowing descriptions of how Turkish prisoners treated b [sic] Allies. To counter-act effect of these circulars, Turkish Headquarters distributed papers stating treatment meted out to Turkish prisoners in Egypt was disgraceful, men being badly housed, badly fed, and subjected to every indignity. Wounded officers had to walk entire way to Ismailia and men were bound all night to trees."[155] Indeed, on both sides governments tried to paint a particular image of how the enemy treated soldiers held in captivity.[156]

Beyond the physical reality of internment and the dueling propaganda campaigns it spawned, lengthy imprisonment also shifted traditional social and political alignments. Wrenched from their units and marched into foreign confinement, internment constituted a bewildering experience that undoubtedly affected the prisoner's self-identity.[157] Salim Tamari has explored the effect of Siberian internment on Ottoman prisoners of war.[158] In the camps, "prisoners were separated along ethnic categories. . . . Since the Russians employed most of the rank and file POWs to work in mines, railroads and digging canals, they assumed that prisoners work better in an environment of 'common culture.' "[159] Citing the excellent findings of the Turkish historian Yücel Yanikdağ, Tamari argues that "initially there was little tension between Ottoman prisoners along ethnic lines, and Islam seems to have been a bonding element among prisoners. . . . Possibly because of their religious identity in a hostile environment, Ottoman prisoners experienced less friction on the basis of class identity and social standing than was commonly observed among Austro-Hungarian and German prisoners."[160] Eventually, however, "two factors began to produce Turkish-Arab tensions within the prison camps. One was Russian favoritism towards Arab soldiers and officers over Turkish soldiers, and secondly, the news of Arab rebellion in Hijaz and Syria (June 1916)."[161]

It does appear that the Shaykh al-Islam's fatwa declaring jihad upon the outbreak of the war gained traction in the traditional quarters of cities like

Aleppo and Baghdad, and Islam long constituted a powerful bonding force among soldiers.[162] "In order to secure allegiance to the state, the government continued to resort to religious propaganda on the one hand and time-honored tactics of enticement and alliances on the other," concludes the historian Hasan Kayali.[163] But in the prisons, special camp newspapers eroded Islamic solidarity by accentuating the delineation between Turkish and Arab political identities.[164] Through this emphasis on ethnic differences, Islam at times melted into the background. As evidence, Salim Tamari points to the Siberian imprisonment of Lieutenant Arif Shahada, an Arab officer in the Ottoman Fifth Army, whose self-conception hardened into a durable Arabism during confinement.[165]

Arif Shahada would go on (as Arif al-Arif) to enjoy an illustrious postwar career as a journalist and politician, including as mayor of east Jerusalem during the Mandate. Prior to his imprisonment, however, he was a firm believer in the Ottoman Empire; speaking Turkish, he worked as a translator in the Ministry of Foreign Affairs, advocated decentralization within the Ottoman umbrella (rather than a break from Istanbul), and enlisted in the Ottoman Fifth Army rather than pay an exemption fee.[166] But during his imprisonment in Krasnoyarsk in Siberia, Arif's views shifted. By the time he and several fellow prisoners took advantage of the collapsing Tsarist administration to flee captivity, they carried in their hearts "the love of the great Arab nation, that makes no difference between religions."[167]

This trend was facilitated by three factors: "The camp segregated dwellings for Ottoman prisoners by ethnicity (and the implicit favoritism extended by the Russians towards Arab officers); the spread of clandestine publications . . . providing a separatist platform for Arab soldiers and officers; and (most importantly) news of the Hijazi Arab rebellion and the subsequent collapse of the Ottoman fronts at Suez, Gaza, and southern Iraq (Kut al Amara). What was experienced as a potential for emancipation of the Arab provinces from autocratic rule among Arab soldiers, was seen as Arab betrayal by the Turkish soldiers."[168]

Ja'far al-Askari—the future prime minister of Iraq—tells a similar tale of conversion while locked up in an Egyptian prison. In March 1916, after meeting General Maxwell at his Egyptian Expeditionary Force headquarters in the Savoy Hotel, Askari settled into a life of sequestered boredom as an imprisoned Ottoman officer.[169] One day, however, he obtained a copy of the Syrian newspaper *Public Opinion:* "It carried an apologia by Jamal Pasha for his infamous actions against the Arab leaders and the hangings that had taken place, including that of the late Salim Bey Al-Jazairi. I was deeply grieved by this news and wept bitter tears for one of my oldest and dearest friends."[170] After learning of "various Arab secret societies" Askari discovered that "many members of these societies had been arrested, savagely humiliated and subjected to the most inhumane and outrageous torture. I made up my mind there and then to seek revenge, and to make every effort to join the Sharif of Makkah at the earliest possible opportunity."[171]

Askari recruited "Arab prisoners, officers and enlisted men alike, being held at detention centres in Maadi, Heliopolis and Sidi Bishr in Alexandria. . . . They assembled the prisoners for us on a spacious parade ground [at Heliopolis]. There I delivered an impassioned speech, urging them to volunteer for the Sharifian Army so that they could play their part in ridding their countries of foreign domination, and so that they could become citizens of independent sovereign countries under the flag of King Hussain. My words had an electrifying effect on the men. Many of them clamoured to enlist at once and be transported to the Hijaz without further ado."[172] In other recruiting sessions, such as at Maadi camp, Askari was less successful, since in those camps "a considerable number of Turks intermingled with the Arabs" and the prisoners "were fearful for their futures and anxious about what might befall their families at the hands of the Turks."[173] Even so, the "largest potential reservoir of skilled manpower for the army of the Arab revolt, that is, officers and men, was in the prisoner-of-war camps in India and Egypt."[174] Of course, some men also deserted to the Arab Revolt, but "the number of deserters who joined the revolt was smaller even than the number of prisoners who had agreed to volunteer."[175]

Because units were regularly recruited from the same geographic area, the Ottoman army was "ethnically uniform up to the level of regiments or even divisions."[176] Ethnically mixed units did not exist until quite late in the war, when degraded units were disbanded and merged with others.[177] Initially Arab troops were envisioned for garrison and communication duties, but as the war progressed, they increasingly fought on the front lines. By 1915 anywhere from one hundred thousand to perhaps three hundred thousand Arab soldiers served in the Ottoman force.[178] By late 1918 four out of ten divisions defending Palestine from Allenby were Arab.[179] Nomadic tribes, especially Kurds, also fought in the war, but mostly as an irregular cavalry auxiliary that was loosely affiliated with the regular army and did not regularly coordinate its actions with Ottoman commanders.[180]

The ethnic uniformity of military units may have prejudiced postbattle accounts. In most postwar histories, Gallipoli has been presented as a signature Turkish military victory achieved under the command of Lieutenant Colonel Mustafa Kemal. That it was, but the Arab contribution was real; Syrians comprised the critical regiments of Kemal's nineteenth division, which absorbed the shock of the initial ANZAC amphibious assault and checked the British expeditionary force altogether.[181] Turkish officers sometimes distrusted these Arab units, at least so it seems from the British reports. In prisoner exchange negotiations Ottoman commanders demanded " 'real Turkish troops, not Arabs' in exchange for British troops and offered only Indian troops in exchange for Arabs."[182] At Kut, the Ottoman commander Colonel Halil Pasha initially offered Englishmen for Turks and Indians for Arabs, since "he said he had a poor opinion of both the latter." However, he quickly reversed his position as "one in ten of his Turkish troops had proved to be a coward but only one Arab in a hundred was brave. He continued: 'You can send them back to me if you like but I have already condemned them to death. I should like to have them to hang.' "[183]

In part, wherever such denunciations existed, they often reflected the legacy of past confrontations. One lieutenant colonel suggested as much, writing "The Arab tribes of Mesopotamia . . . were armed with the old pattern Mauser. . . . These arms and ammunition had been captured from the Turkish troops which had been sent from time to time to try and restore order amongst the Arabs."[184]

Tribal distrust of external authority disrupted Ottoman cooperation. Some tribal elements moved regularly at night into camps to steal ammunition stocks and rifles, which they sold to the enemy.[185] In Mesopotamia, "it was never safe to have the hospital barges tie up to the banks for the night on their way down the river."[186] And in the Jordan River valley, one sheikh, suspected by the British of being a local smuggler, was described by one source as "a friend only because friendship profited him."[187] This tells us as much about the source, who struggled to appreciate local perspectives, as it does about military cooperation within the Ottoman ranks. But tensions did exist.

For the tribesmen, the conflict was local. The number of fighters vacillated widely.[188] Intent on preserving their local sovereignty, tribes cooperated with Istanbul when their interests aligned, and did not when those interests diverged.[189] The fierce defense of local suzerainty also shines through in Murphy's assessment of tribal loyalty in Mesopotamia, where he says locals "were genuinely pleased to see the Turks being ejected, but they did not want us or anyone else to take their places."[190]

In the rough-and-tumble settings of the Sinai, Hijaz, and Mesopotamian deserts, and in the midst of conflict, tribesmen sought out advantage whenever possible. The Arab Revolt undermined the already tense relationship between Ottoman Turkish and non-Turkish soldiers, causing Liman von Sanders to exclaim in exasperation that no one "can long ward off attacks from the enemy in front, and assaults from the rear."[191] The frustration some felt toward opportunistic locals produced several incidents. Kermit Roosevelt recalls being "told, and I believe it to be true, that during the fighting at Sunnaiyat, the Turks sent over to know if we would agree to a three days' truce, during which time we should join forces against the Arabs, who were watching on the flank to pick off stragglers or ration convoys."[192] Regardless of the anecdote's veracity, Roosevelt's readiness to accept it underscores Western officers' attitudes. Reportedly, an artillery exchange in the summer of 1918 was interrupted by a group of locals gathering on a distant ridge to observe the spectacle. "To everyone's astonishment, the Turkish and Austrian gunners shifted their fire off the New Zealand trenches and began shelling the civilian onlookers."[193]

From the local perspective, enduring a foreign war with modern technologies must have been a novel experience. New technology appeared in rural tribal territories, inspiring both wonder and fear. At one point several sheikhs traveled near Samarra by motorcar for the first time. When the car stopped for a moment, one sheikh "fairly flew out of the car. It didn't seem possible that a man able to ride ninety miles at a stretch on a camel, could be made ill by the motion of an automobile."[194] In another instance a Kurdish chief, who attempted to expedite his journey from Istanbul to Baghdad by driving, reported several harrowing experiences "for the villagers had never before seen an automobile and regarded it as a devil; often stones were thrown . . . only escaped by driving full speed through the crowd."[195] The sudden appearance of modern weaponry, in particular warships and airplanes, made quite an impression on the soldiers of the region as well. Sa'id Jawmar, a young man from Dayr Atiya, a town north of Damascus on the road to Homs, served on the Palestine front and wrote in amazement that the British "have produced something that is like a bird. It is an aeroplane which has wings like a bird. It makes its rounds in the sky and can discern anything that is happening on the earth. As its sign, frigates from the sea shoot at the Ottoman soldiers, and hit them! And the divers make enemy ships explode."[196]

For the most part, however, tribes sought shelter and security. For all his categorical rhetoric, Liman von Sanders understood that "by far the greater part of the people longed for orderly conditions regulated by law."[197] Indeed, in one frontline village near the river Diyala, sporadic British and Ottoman patrols intermixed with Kurdish raiders to create an atmosphere of perpetual distrust and insecurity. In this geography of conflict, as the front line ebbed, flowed, and rotated, one old sheikh wondered why one side "couldn't make an advance and put his village safely behind our lines, so that the children could grow fat and the herds graze unharmed."[198]

The local townspeople conscripted into regular service varied in their interpretations of the war. One Damascene, Fakhri al-Barudi, fought the British in Beersheba. In his poetry he focused primarily on the challenging desert conditions before being captured and joining the Arab Revolt.[199] Another Damascene, Nabih al-Azma, interpreted the attacks and looting in the wake of the Turkish retreat as an expression of tribal aspirations for freedom.[200] Some soldiers reveled in the presence of Arab flags fluttering in Damascus after the Ottomans' retreat, while others, such as Fawzi al-Qawuqji, remained proud, loyal fighters at the disposal of their Ottoman commanders.[201] In his memoir, Jamal Pasha interpreted the loyalty of Arab soldiers as irreproachable, with an obvious exception for Sharif Husayn's treachery. In the force that made the first Suez Canal expedition, Jamal says "a fine feeling of brotherly affection prevailed, and not a man hesitated to sacrifice himself for his comrades . . . a brilliant revelation of the fact that the majority of the Arabs stood by the Khalifate with heart and soul."[202]

In his diary Ihsan Turjman, the earlier-mentioned cleric in the Ottoman civil service and translator in the Islamic court who served as a soldier in the Notre Dame compound of Jerusalem, takes a different course.[203] In August 1915 he asked himself: "Will I go to protect my country? . . . I am not an Ottoman, only in name, but a citizen of the world. . . . Had the state treated me as part of it, it would have been worthwhile for me to give my life to it. However, since the country does not treat me in such way, it is not worthwhile for me to give my blood to the Turkish state."[204] Stationed as he was in Jerusalem, Turjman's perspective bridges the civilian and military worlds of wartime urban Syria. He reserves considerable blame for the local authorities, chiding the government for failing "to store flour so that it would be able to sell it during these difficult days to the poor. . . . The government should wake up before the people revolt."[205]

Turjman also complained of excessive revelry and prostitution during the festivals of wartime Jerusalem. He disapprovingly notes that the "men are telling the secrets of the state to these women without noticing, because they are drunk."[206] In Jerusalem, as well as in cities like Jaffa, Beirut, Aleppo, and Damascus, alcohol- and hashish-fueled festivals created a licentious environment, bolstering the prostitution trade.[207]

Almost certainly, these excesses frayed Turjman's affiliation with the Ottoman state; following the hanging of activists in Beirut, he "disengages himself completely from the empire."[208] In July 1916 Turjman unloads his frustration into his diary: "The Ottomans killed our sons, offended our honor—why would we like to remain under it [the empire]? . . . Every Arab is zealous for his race. It is enough for us! . . . The Arabs will harass the Ottoman government until it gets out of the Arab countries . . . humiliated as it got out of any other place. . . . God bless you, Sharif Hussein, and hurt those who try to hurt you. You Arabs proved to the world that you are men who refuse to be humiliated and proved to God that you are the sons of Arab ancestors. You proved that you protect your Arab nation in your life for ending up . . . the barbaric Ottoman nation."[209] For some, then, it was the Ottoman leadership that made the situation unbearable.[210] Instead of focusing on criticisms of the tribes, officers could interpret those riverine tribes as heroic. In his memoir Qawuqji praises the generosity of nomads along the Tigris, singing "songs and Bedouin poems that aroused our enthusiasm as we heard our common language being spoken in its different dialects."[211]

The Ottoman high command took practical logistical measures to prevent revolt. By 1916, for example, several divisions suspected of plotting against the Porte were redeployed from Greater Syria,[212] which in turn triggered other acts of defiance. As Eliezer Tauber reports, one officer "stood in the streets of Aleppo and spoke before Arab soldiers about the need to desert and to stop fighting for the Turks, the oppressors of the Arabs. According to one estimate 300 Syrian soldiers deserted as a result of this. Jamal Pasha issued an order to take the officer dead or alive, but he escaped to the Syrian desert and from there continued on to the British in southern Iraq."[213]

In January 1915 Liman von Sanders left Istanbul for the coast of Asia Minor to conduct a brief inspection.[214] Despite his stature as the top German officer in the Ottoman Empire, the general struggled over one river by using "high buffalo carts"—the bridge had been washed away—before being "overtaken by a blizzard and we crossed the mountains . . . with considerable difficulty. For many hours we marched on foot through deep snow" before reaching a railroad that "had been rendered impassable by landslides."[215] If such conditions characterized travel for the top Ottoman officer "in the best parts of Turkey,"[216] the difficulty of travel for the common soldier must be imagined as exponentially worse. Indeed, the physician Abdülkadir Noyan, in his own trip from Istanbul to Baghdad in December 1915, observed such transport difficulties firsthand. "He first took the train from Istanbul to Pozanti. He then traveled from Pozanti to Mosul on horseback and from there to Baghdad on *keleks* (a kind of raft mounted on animal skins filled with air). All Ottoman troops deployed to the Iraqi front could reach that region only after a two-month walk, which naturally had a very adverse effect on their health condition."[217]

The heavy marching required in World War I had a detrimental impact on soldiers' health, and was a direct reflection of the underdeveloped Ottoman rail infrastructure. In total, the Ottoman Empire possessed just "5,700 kilometers of railway—one kilometer per 304 square kilometers of territory"—compared to one kilometer per ten square kilometers in France.[218] Moreover, these 5,700 kilometers were single track and periodically changed gauge, thus requiring the repeated unloading and reloading of cargo.[219] The single track, steep grades, and sharp curves of the railway that connected the German and Ottoman Empires constrained the flow of heavy equipment and supplies.[220] Moreover, in light of the Triple Entente's command of the seas, nearly the entire volume of cargo from Europe fed through the narrow Istanbul corridor, creating a natural supply bottleneck.

From Istanbul, the railroad snaked into the Arab interior. Until the fall of 1918, however, cargo had to be unloaded onto wagons, camels, and autos for transport across the Taurus and Nur mountains, and by the time the tunnel passage was completed in the fall of 1918 it was too late.[221] Until October 1918 no train could travel uninterrupted from Istanbul to Aleppo, and the lines from Aleppo into the Syrian heartland and the Hijaz were never sufficient.[222] As for the railway extending from Istanbul into the Anatolian heartland, soldiers could enjoy rail travel for no more than sixty kilometers before disembarking for a thirty-day march from the railhead to Erzurum.[223]

The German artillery officer Waldemar Frey eloquently details the challenges posed by the Taurus and Nur mountain crossings in his book *Kut El-Amara*. Alongside references to historical conquests and military adventures, Frey describes ascending the torturously steep mountain passes before descending into ethnically mixed frontier lands.[224] Lacking a railway, soldiers traveled over winding, often-unkempt passages while guiding pack horses along steep mountain cliffs.[225] Frey resumed his rail travel at Islahiye in southeastern Anatolia, alongside soldiers who were packed into freight cars.[226]

Throughout the war, the Ottomans faced an emergency shortage in locomotives, despite acquiring them from Europe, and in the coal or wood necessary to fuel their engines. Instead of European-style deforestation, "large sections of the olive groves in Syria were cut down. . . . Because wood is bulkier than coal, the locomotives had to stop frequently to refill their bunker, and they had to reduce speed in order to save fuel."[227] Thus, short on rolling stock and fuel, and traveling on incomplete, single-track rails that periodically changed in gauge, rail transport was exceedingly cumbersome. For much of the war, travel from Istanbul to Palestine and Mesopotamia took up to six and seven weeks, respectively.[228]

Before long, freight space turned into a traded good from which politically connected officers profited by exploiting arbitrage opportunities.[229] Since transport within the Ottoman Empire was sporadic at best, market prices for basic commodities differed widely in different parts of the empire. For those controlling access to the freight cars, easy money was made by those who could exploit price differentials by buying goods in a low-priced area for shipment to market in a high-priced area.[230] Similarly, commanding officers received money as a lump sum, with total discretionary authority over expenditures. As a result, officers succumbed to the temptations such arrangements presented, using their monetary allotments to purchase supplies that they then resold, pocketing the proceeds.[231]

Bureaucratic oversight and control of this type of profiteering was lax, as most administrative sections struggled with the immediate exigencies of war. Liman von Sanders complained that in most personnel sections "there existed an incredible confusion. Sometimes it required months to ascertain with what organizations Turkish officers sought were serving. It happened that officers killed long ago were ordered transferred."[232] Fakhr al-Din Pasha, the commander of the encircled garrison at Medina, "repeatedly telegraphed to the Army Group that he and his men were condemned to starvation," but that was interpreted only as "the customary exaggeration" by administrators coping with nonstop emergencies.[233]

Where the bureaucracy failed to successfully process basic inquiries, the tried and trusted intrigue of the bazaar often filled the gap. Roosevelt explains how the "bazaar rumors always told of our advances long before they were officially given out. Once in Baghdad I heard of an attack we had launched. On going around to G.H.Q. I mentioned the rumor, and found that it was not yet known there, but shortly after was confirmed."[234] Similarly, currency fluctuations tracked the latest tug and pull of the front lines. From small towns to metropolitan Baghdad, the money market value of the Indian rupee fluctuated to reflect the military fortunes of the British.[235] In fact, during the surrender negotiations at Kut, an Ottoman escort inquired "if the British officers ever had difficulty changing paper money in Mesopotamia. They did not know what to make of this until the questioner continued that he always had difficulty changing Turkish scrip until recently. 'Now the Arabs accept it quite readily. Tell me gentlemen, to what do you attribute this change of heart?' he asked."[236] From the dry desert to the bustling bazaar, it was difficult to maintain military secrets.

Barring modern rail transport, many Ottomans instead reverted to more traditional, reliable methods of shipment. The historian C. A. Bayly describes the Ottoman army floating supplies down the Tigris "on huge rafts made from thousands of stitched skins brought from Kurdistan. Ashurbanipal and Alexander the Great had done the same."[237] Roosevelt admired these goatskins while in Tikrit: "Their rafts have been made in the same manner since before the days of Xerxes and Darius. Inflated goatskins are used as a basis for a platform of poles, cut in the up-stream forests. On these, starting from Diarbekr or Mosul, they float down all their goods. When they reach Tekrit they leave the poles there, and start up-stream on foot, carrying their deflated goatskins. The Turks used this method a great deal bringing down their supplies."[238] Reporting from Samarra, one British officer observed that Mesopotamian tribes were constantly passing our camp, drifting downstream on their inflated skins and guiding their rafts. This seems to be the normal mode of travel in these parts. When a member of the local aristocracy wishes to go to town or to visit a friend of his, whose estate is downstream, he twists his shirt round his neck—they wear nothing else hereabouts—blows up his [raft] and floats off. They go down in parties of half a dozen like this, shouting at each other and singing all the while. A couple of them created some excitement the other night by coming down the river on their skins after dark. They were picked up by the searchlight and the anti-mine machine guns opened a heavy fire on them. However . . . these two continued on their way . . . and—alas for the efficiency of our anti-mine defences!—unharmed.[239]

Most of all, however, the Ottomans depended on pack animals as the "legs and arms of the army."[240] As Izzet Pasha put it, this "poor nation has just gone out of the Balkan Wars. These animals are acquired with greatest difficulties. We have to fight this war with these animals because there are no others to replace them. Without them, we can carry neither food nor weapon. Then, defeat would be inevitable. We have to take better care of these animals . . . than the soldiers."[241] For the most part, the Ottomans relied on oxen and mules as draught animals, and loaded camels for carrying.[242] Of these pack animals, the Ottomans "had between five and ten thousand (the estimates vary) . . . in service behind the Palestinian front alone. But they were reared by the Arab Beduin and these had to be paid in gold. Paper money was impopular [sic] everywhere and in the settled areas those who refused it faced heavy penalties, but the Beduin could not be coerced in this way."[243] In fact, tribal rivalries also complicated transactions immensely, and after the Arab Revolt in 1916, led to the importation of Anatolian camels via the already overburdened railway.[244]

Moreover, sporadic transport made it difficult to rotate troops away from the front lines for rest and recuperation. After the Second Battle of Gaza in April 1917, the Ottoman front lines were manned by the same men continuously for almost seven months.[245] Although adequately armed—using rifles captured from Belgium to Russia—these soldiers endured harsh living conditions thanks to the poor industrial infrastructure of the Ottoman Empire.[246] The "British official history's description of the forces opposing Allenby is striking: 'hungry, ragged, verminous, comfortless, hopeless, out-numbered'" while Liman von Sanders described his men as "ragged," "wretched," and "infested."[247]

From the Anatolian winter, where temperatures could drop to a mind-numbing −20°C (−4°F) at night, to the summer in the Jordan River valley, where temperatures could spike to an unbearable 55°C (131°F) during the day, the Ottoman troops rarely possessed the protective insulation of modern uniforms.[248] On every front "the enormous need for tents, greatcoats, clothes, shoes, and the like could hardly be met."[249] On Gallipoli, officers took particular care to guard sandbags intended for trenching, for "there was danger of their being used by the troop leaders for patching the ragged uniforms of their men."[250] Moreover, due to administrative error, soldiers equipped for desert campaigns were on occasion transferred to the Caucasus in the depths of winter.[251]

In that "Turkish Siberia," as the Russians referred to the Caucasus, troops feared death by frost as much as they feared combat: "whichever direction one turned one's gaze, there was nothing to be seen but snow, ice, and a gray sky which seemed to press down over that accursed land like a vault of lead."[252] As fatalities increased, packs of dogs "passed entire days . . . in the snow among the trenches of the dead, and did not leave off until the bodies were completely devoured."[253] One officer on inspection described a cavalry division as having only "underclothes on, and instead of military greatcoats were wearing *mashlahs* (long, open-fronted cloak). They were sleeping on the ground, on earth in the narrow and dirty rooms of the miserable village, and they did not have any blankets to cover their bodies while sleeping. At a temperature of 5 degrees below 0 Celsius . . . the whole division was on horses for inspection in the early morning, I saw their naked feet twisted on the iron stirrups because of the cold."[254] To this report, General Izzet Pasha, who later signed the Armistice of Mudros formalizing Ottoman surrender, replied: "In the Balkan War, our Army was well clothed and equipped, yet we were defeated. This time, let's fight without equipment."[255]

Troops often marched barefoot or in rags. The Ottoman soldier Mehmet Arif Ölçen recorded twenty-one months of captivity, spent mostly in Varnavino, three hundred miles northeast of Moscow, in a diary that offers rich detail on life in that provincial town and hints at shifts in his own identity.[256] Equally striking, however, is what the historian Azade-Ayse Rorlich interprets as his "sense of betrayal" in comparing the "warmly dressed and well-fed Russians with the plight of the Ottoman soldiers."[257] On the Palestine front, as a last resort, "the troops in the front line were given yellow Beduin slippers, which were bound to the feet with throngs. Those on garrison duty had to make do with shoes made of straw, with wooden soles."[258] One colonel reported that owing to the sporadic resupply situation, soldiers self-equipped to whatever extent was possible: "The soldiers could carry their rations in the bags they brought from their villages; however they have no means to carry their ammunition. Furthermore, the shoes of many of the soldiers are in a very bad condition. It is obvious that the tired and weakened soldiers cannot walk as desired with those shoes."[259] In eastern Anatolia a division commander described "great losses" due to the "lack of subsistence and lack of warm clothing."[260] For shoes, his men wrapped their feet in rags "from which the toes protrude," while many soldiers "dressed in thin summer garments, have no overcoats."[261] The report was made in November 1916, before the onset of the most merciless months of the eastern Anatolian winter. Another officer wrote that "the covering for the feet differed widely, often only a piece of cloth tied round with a string. String was often used to replace leather in the equipment. Later I saw a good deal of English equipment and clothing used."[262]

Indeed, Ottoman soldiers eyed the far superior British- and Russian-issued uniforms as a major prize. Zürcher writes that "in at least one instance, an Ottoman regiment after a successful attack on a British trench, returned unrecognisable, because the soldiers had exchanged their own rags with British uniforms, taken from the dead."[263] Liman von Sanders added that Ottoman soldiers "regarded with jealous eyes the felt soles of the boots of British dead and prisoners, which were nailed on to deaden the sound of marching on rocky ground. Their own feet were often wrapped in rags, or at best they wore tschariks, i.e., animal skins tied with strings. Many officers had no other foot gear."[264] So difficult was the Ottoman situation that even in the two most decisive Ottoman victories of the war, the troops plundered until exhaustion. At Kut a surrendered British medical officer discovered "three hefty, ragged Turks trying on his uniforms and bashing open his boxes with rifle butts" while in the hospital Ottoman soldiers "were robbing the patients of blankets, boots, and valuables."[265] After Gallipoli, "What the ragged and insufficiently nourished Turkish soldiers took away, cannot be estimated."[266] The commanding general "tried to stop plundering by a dense line of sentinels but the endeavor was in vain. During the ensuing time we saw the Turkish soldiers on the peninsula in the most incredible garments which they had made up from every kind of uniform. They even carried British gas masks for fun."[267] He concluded that such behavior "is not to be looked upon as intentional cruelty. It appeared to the Turkish soldiers as the only means of procuring clothing, linen or boots. All orders against the spoliation of the dead were in vain. European drill at such times does not hold the men, the loosely donned garment of culture is quickly thrown aside by the Turkish soldier."[268] Since the Russians marched in leather boots, wore sturdy underclothes, and wrapped themselves with full-body greatcoats while enjoying "haversacks full of daily food rations, including even tea and sugar," Russian prisoners and casualties could similarly expect their possessions confiscated.[269] After stripping prisoners, soldiers would often hand the prisoners their own rags in return.[270] By the end of the war Ottoman soldiers even began foraging among the enemy dead for tins of meat.[271]

Nevertheless, the Ottoman Empire had within it the means for self-sufficiency had it not traded its butter for guns. In a mass barter arrangement the Ottomans exported wheat to its allies in return for weapons and ammunition.[272] Each year during the war administrators confiscated 10 percent of the wheat and barley harvest as tithe, which it supplemented by purchasing an additional 30 to 40 percent at market rates.[273] From this it bartered with its allies and fed its force. In theory soldiers could expect "900 grams of bread, 600 grams of biscuit, 250 grams of meat, 150 grams of bulgur (broken wheat), 20 grams of butter, 20 grams of salt," but in practice the Ottoman soldier subsisted on much less.[274] Often the daily ration depended on the soldiers' geographic deployment; since transport was unreliable, food was adequate near agricultural breadbaskets and virtually nonexistent elsewhere.[275] Even so, the system was arranged to give priority to the front lines, followed by garrisons, and lastly, the civilian population.

Al-Muqattam reported on Ottoman provisioning early in the war, writing in October 1914 that soldiers ate lentil soup or grit for lunch and eggplant or beans for dinner. Every soldier, it claimed, was allowed three loaves of bread per day. "These soldiers are complaining of lack of food because the food given to four persons is not actually enough for two persons."[276] Moreover, *al-Muqattam* wanted its readership to know, the soldiers stationed in Beirut, Damascus, and Tripoli often bought their own food as an alternative to the "terrible" army variety.[277] When that "terrible" staple, wheat, was scarce, bread was baked with barley or ground beans. In addition, troops received two warm meals per day, consisting of flour soup or bulgur, with an occasional (perhaps weekly) stew or meat provided as supplement. In fact when "there was meat, it had to be shared out among a lot of people: according to one report the daily supply was one ox or four sheep for 450 men. Most often, though, the meat was camel meat, as dead camels were not in short supply."[278] Hans Kannengiesser observed that for Ottomans "rice and flesh is a feast. . . . Their iron rations, as and when available, consisted of a piece of bread and some olives, the latter generally wrapped in the corner of a more than doubtful-looking handkerchief. In the morning a soup, towards evening a soup again, sometimes with meat in it and always prepared with oil. The main diet was bulgur, particularly when the rations were short owing to the English having seized several supply ships in the Sea of Marmora. Bulgur is rolled barley generally cooked in rancid oil and served cold."[279] The rations were carried to the troops by "small donkeys with a pannikin or old petrol tin right and left of their saddles, each tin covered with an old cloth to prevent spilling." Kannengiesser added that passing "such a donkey column a European could easily be sick from the smell of old cart grease."[280]

Ibrahim Tali, the chief doctor of the Ottoman Third Army, was taken aback by his army's meat ration, reporting after inspection that "meat given to them had a gelatinous appearance and seemed to have lost all its nutritive value."[281] For bread to be baked, and for meat to be cooked, wood was necessary. Without the luxury of European forests, and competing with the demands of the locomotive, the daily Ottoman wood ration dwindled as well.[282] As for vegetables and fruits, soldiers scavenged for dates and olives whenever possible, but consumed them so rarely that scurvy spread. Before long, reports surfaced of "soldiers' teeth falling out and large sores forming in their mouths or even through their cheeks."[283] Some soldiers, in a desperate search for nutrients, consumed poisonous leaves.[284]

By the end of 1917, therefore, the Ottoman Fourth Army responded to a request for food from Mesopotamia by outlining its own grim condition: "The food situation in the Fourth Army is so dreadful that only 350 grams of flour can be given to men and 2.5 kilograms of forage to animals. If communications are not improved it is doubtful whether we can go on."[285] In late 1917, on the eve of the Third Battle of Gaza, Major General Hüseyin Hüsnü minced few words in his report: the soldiers "concentrated at that time in Palestine had not enough bread to maintain their strength. They received almost no meat, no butter, no sugar, no vegetables, no fruits. Only a thin tent gave a semblance of protection from the hot sun by day, and from the cold of the night. They were wretchedly clothed. They had no boots at all, or what they had were so bad that they meant injury to the feet of many who wore them. Soldiers had been without word from home for years and years. Owing to the bad communications no leave was ever given."[286] Indeed, the Ottoman soldier, "often with no other nourishment than a crust of bread or a handful of olives, kept on bleeding and dying of starvation among the snows of the Caucasus and the sands of the desert without ever letting a complaint or a whisper of dismay cross his livid, fever-paled lips."[287]

Yet despite these pitiful conditions, no significant mutinies occurred among the regular troops (although many fled the front). Even during meals a certain soldiering camaraderie existed. "It was quite a pleasure to see them at meals," Hans Kannengiesser wrote. "Eight men sat round a tin tray having a common meal *à la turca*. Each threw a piece of bread into the soup and calmly and dignified, each without haste, recovered it with his spoon. I have never seen a battle for food, no matter how great the hunger."[288] Captain Torossian observed a slightly different mealtime routine:

> Their daily rations were one-quarter of a pound of meat, six ounces of rice and two and a quarter pounds of bread per man with the consequence that they were always famished. When the dinner trumpet blew, there was a scramble for a place on the floor of the barracks. Each company of eight sat in a circle holding wooden spoons raised in the air as though awaiting a charge. Ten-quart pails of thin soup with a small portion of boiled meat in it were placed in the center of each group by the corporals who then proceeded to cut the meat up into nine small pieces. Then the signal to proceed was given and each one thrust his spoon ravenously into the pail and tried to swallow as much of the liquid as possible. Dinner over—greasy fingers, spoons wiped in the folds of uniforms, and Allah praised.[289]

Brigadier General Yergök claimed that during combat the soldiers were full of joy and thought of little else but defeating the enemy. For days they silenced their hunger without warm meals, subsisting in the best of circumstances on bread and dried meat.[290] Perhaps this resilience is attributable to troops receiving stimulants before entering battle. As Qawuqji reported, "I ordered the soldiers to lessen their luggage and carry only the ammunition and grenades. When it was the time to move, they were awakened and given tea mixed with rum."[291]

Beyond such episodes, however, there "was no amusement of any sort, no tobacco, no coffee. And men so placed could not but see that their German comrades on the same front were well fed, and enjoyed every sort of comfort and amusement."[292] Since the soldiers' monthly salary barely satisfied their monthly tobacco habit, tobacco became a metaphor for scarcity.[293] Hans Kannengiesser wrote that the Ottoman "chief desire" was " 'Tütün' (tobacco)": "It gave me particular pleasure, when in the trenches, to say to each man I found actively employed at his loop-hole, 'Hold your left hand out behind you.' I always put two cigarettes in his hand and I seldom received even a very soft 'teschekürderim' (I thank you), but I felt how grateful they were, these brave Askers [Turkish troops]."[294]

When an opportunity for entertainment did present itself, the soldiers seized it. During the Ottoman pursuit of the British to Kut, for example, "the patrols, instead of following in pursuit as ordered, decided that enough had been done for one day. This conclusion was no doubt arrived at after the discovery of a considerable quantity of abandoned stores, including some alcoholic refreshment. The party, in which it appears the entire Turkish cavalry took part, was soon in full swing. According to the Turkish account, as soon as these troops reached Aziziya they went off duty and 'there passed the night in drunkenness among this priceless display of plunder.' "[295]

Another episode from the Kut cauldron demonstrates how morale-boosting news was speedily passed to the front lines. On the morning of January 9, 1916, scouts "on the Kut roofs noticed that the steamers at Shumran bend were decked with bunting. Cheering, bugling and volleys of rifle fire came from the Turkish trenches. The British troops were somewhat mystified by this cheerful demonstration until the answer was supplied by the Arab coffee shops. It was bad news indeed. The British troops were being evacuated from Gallipoli after suffering heavy losses."[296]

Another perspective into the morale of the fighting men comes from war songs sung to pass the time in the trenches.[297] These Ottoman ditties predominantly borrowed from the bloody experiences of nineteenth-century warfare. In a nod to Yemen, the "prevailing sentiment in the lyrics of the songs is . . . nearly always that those who went on campaign had no chance of returning and that they would die in some far off desert."[298] As Zürcher explains, there was "no heroism here, and no patriotism. Nor do the songs express the kind of dogged determination of contemporary Western front hits. . . . More than anything they express a feeling of homesickness, hopelessness and doom, of being sacrificed."[299]

For so many soldiers, it seems, the call to soldiering amounted to a death sentence. As one letter from a Turkish soldier killed during the retreat from Jerusalem put it forlornly: "God has so far granted me health and strength and brought me through, but where can it all end? We are tormented by the English; no rest do we receive, and very little food, and our men are dying in hundreds of disease."[300]

Establishing precise figures of Ottoman war casualties is quite difficult. Although wartime Ottoman officers kept meticulous records, "much of the widespread deaths from diseases took place in regions, or at times, where and when nobody was available or in a position to count the human toll. In other cases, nobody cared to count the death toll at a time when the country was overwhelmed by the contingencies of the war."[301] In fact, since the Ottomans did not publish "postwar statistics, most estimates of their casualties are based on supposition and flawed perceptions of Turkish losses."[302] For those killed in combat, the total of 325,000 military dead has long been the most commonly used figure.[303] Added to this total, however, must be the 60,000 soldiers, out of a total of 400,000 permanently disabled veterans, who ultimately succumbed to their wounds.[304] Another 400,000 died of disease, while 250,000 more were considered prisoners or missing (this does not account for the estimated 500,000 deserters).[305] In his deconstruction of casualty data, Edward Erickson argues that most likely "the Ottoman Empire suffered a death rate of 10.6 percent (as a percentage of men mobilized) of men who were either killed or missing in action, or who died of combat wounds. . . . However, when the horrific numbers of men who died of disease are considered, the death rate skyrockets to [an] astounding 26.9 percent of men mobilized. When the wounded who suffered permanent injury are considered, every third man mobilized died or became crippled."[306]

In his study of death and disease in the Ottoman force, historian Hikmet Özdemir argues that "the number of soldiers dying from infectious diseases in the Ottoman Army was far greater than that of combat-related fatalities."[307] Malaria was the most widely known of those diseases, but typhus and dysentery were similarly deadly. Studies suggest typhus killed almost half of those it infected who did not receive treatment.[308] In winter the established routes to and from the fronts served as cockpits of disease, as lice-infested troops—unable to bathe or change en route—carried or contracted typhus during their marches.[309] In the summer many of these same areas were ravaged by malarial mosquitoes lurking in contaminated drinking water, which in turn yielded to cholera in the fall.[310] As a result "the casualty rate among local men sent to serve on remote fronts (as a disciplinary measure and to forestall desertion) was so high that the term 'army' became synonymous with 'cholera.'"[311] As the Ottoman army retreated, the wounded and diseased surged back through these towns, adding to the risk of epidemic.

Disease spared no one and spread even into the highest officer ranks. In fact, Marshall Goltz and General Maude succumbed in Baghdad to typhus and cholera, respectively.[312] In Mesopotamia soap was often unavailable, even if men could bathe in the public baths.[313] Lice therefore became a pernicious carrier of typhus. Similarly, in the wasteland of eastern Anatolia, almost half the Ottoman Third Army in 1915 contracted a disease, including one of its senior commanders, Hafiz Hakki, who died of typhus.[314]

The chronically malnourished state of the force only increased its susceptibility to disease.[315] The winter of 1916–1917 proved especially brutal in eastern Anatolia. A German surgeon observed "how little power of resistance these debilitated men have even for slight operations. If we do not operate on them, they die; if we do operate they die also."[316] From the Black Sea coastal city of Trebizond, the German consul reported that "typhus is raging in all the hospitals of the city. The extent of the epidemic is approaching a catastrophe," echoing the horror of two Red Cross surgeons who characterized the "lack of sanitary arrangements and sufficient medical help" as decimating "the ranks of the Turkish soldiers in a manner unthinkable under German conditions."[317] As Liman von Sanders ultimately concluded, "Mass dying in the Second Army had begun."[318]

During his service on the eastern Anatolian front, Yergök described the quintessential conditions for disease. After one march, soldiers began to eat any animal they could find—devouring it from its maw to its intestine—without so much as chewing. Others drank boiled wheat like horses eating barley soaked in water.[319]

In the immediate aftermath of combat, conditions were generally even more gruesome. After the bayonet battles of Gallipoli, the wounded lay exposed in the blazing sun while "great ugly flies were feasting" on nearby corpses.[320] One witness recalled the collective moans of the wounded who were "trying to clean their wounds of maggots by washing them with seawater, or even by putting lime on those wounds."[321] Before long, "viruses carried by those flies transformed into a mosquito-borne infectious disease called 'dengue.'"[322]

Movement in the Hijaz was more sporadic and often tethered to the railway, but in the desert sunstroke, scurvy, and even malaria especially limited military effectiveness.[323] Askari recounts after crossing the Hijaz how "one of our mules in desperation leapt into the 60-foot-deep well we were drinking from, but so overcome were we all by thirst that we paid no heed at all to the beast's filth, and voraciously carried on gulping down the contaminated water. Never in my life have I experienced a thirst as intense as the one on this journey."[324] At another point he felt "as if one were being incinerated in the flames of an infernal valley."[325] The Mesopotamian desert was similarly unforgiving. The German officer Frey zigzagged across the desert from Ra's al-Ayn in Syria to Mosul in northern Mesopotamia, leading his camels from one watering source to the next. Arriving in Baghdad Frey saw "many disgusting sicknesses, nasty boils . . . typhus, this plague spread through lice, floats around us constantly like a ghost."[326]

On the Palestinian front soldiers were ravaged by typhoid, cholera, malaria, and dysentery, all of which exacted a particularly heavy price in the summer of 1918.[327] In fact, British officers ordered prisoners to be submerged in barrels of corrosive sublimate to avoid the spread of typhus.[328] For the soldiers in the cities, especially Istanbul and Beirut, syphilis and gonorrhea were also a constant threat.[329] One German officer recalled a large placard outside Aleppo warning travelers: "The city is contaminated!"[330]

Furthermore, the Ottoman authorities were unable to address the extreme scourge of war with timely medical interventions. The resources and capacities of the Ottoman medical system were simply no match for the scope and scale of the suffering. The Triple Entente's blockade, the weak transportation links, and the tug and pull of resourcing multiple fronts all combined to make such a prospect impossible. Alcohol, iodine, and quinine were all in short supply. Medical evacuation sometimes meant walking from the front to the rear, even if badly wounded.[331] During the collapse of the Palestinian front in late 1917, one witness spoke of a "'heart-rending scene' of wounded Ottoman soldiers transported on horses with nothing to cover them from the harsh winter weather."[332] Another account, from Anatolia, paints an even grimmer scene: "I watched the ill to be left here: all of them were scrawny, and their cheeks were sunken. Some of them were throwing up, while some others were defecating in one corner. Some of them were bathing in a large puddle in front of the village. I shouted at them: 'is it a good time to do that?' One of the soldiers replied to me: 'Sir, it is cholera. They are afraid of dying without ablution.' It was a tragic scene: There was no hospital, nor anybody to look after them. We left by saying, 'May God protect you.'"[333] As a German officer dryly summarized, "Great difficulties were encountered in the transfer of the patients to the areas in the interior. No railroads or automobiles were available for that purpose."[334]

So dire were the circumstances that many serious surgeries near the end of the war were undertaken without the aid of anesthesia.[335] The "alarming" conditions of hospitals, where "dirt and every imaginable bad odor made the overcrowded rooms unsanitary and almost intolerable abodes," sapped the spirit and strength of many men.[336] In her memoir, the Turkish writer Halidé Edib describes the "newly arrived and gravely wounded soldiers" in the hospital: "One heard their low moan, and their eyes held the far and strange vision of the dying."[337] In the haphazardly ventilated and makeshift hospital setting, where the "sick lay confusedly mixed," the attending medical personnel often contracted their patients' diseases.[338]

As the British advanced through Palestine and into Syria with increasing speed, they began to overrun the major metropolitan centers of the empire. In Damascus they encountered thousands of abandoned wounded surviving in "indescribably hideous and inhuman" conditions.[339] At one facility, more than six hundred wounded were discovered on their own, "starved for three days, and suffocated by the stench of their own offal and the unburied dead."[340] The most crowded of such facilities included 900 wounded and sick soldiers attended to "by seven Syrian doctors who worked continuously without any help. There was neither food nor medical stores."[341]

To sum up, the Ottoman Turk "fought for ten years, from 1912 to 1922 (the first Balkan War through to the Turkish War of Independence), often without basic supplies or clothing. To modern readers, stories of soldiers marching over mountains with rags wound around their feet rather than shoes appear melodramatic and unlikely. In the Ottoman wars, the stories were true."[342] As troops struggled to survive, the political alignments that anchored the region shifted as well, eventually yielding the tremors and full-blown earthquakes of the postwar years. Some Syrian officers adopted self-determination—as evidenced by the heavy flying of Arab flags in Damascus during the Ottoman withdrawal—while others preferred other identities or a blend of identities to shape their ideological orientation. To what degree the challenging conditions of war affected these orientations is difficult to know, but they inevitably did influence the population.

The size and shape of society were changed by the war, too, as larger collective identities challenged the previously dominant provincialism.[343] Salim Tamari argues that "the war created a new sense of time (discreteness) and geography (decentralizing of Palestine within the imperial domain); increased people's mobility through the advent of the railroad and the automobile, introduced greater discipline in military work, and conquered the night (through electrification and the positioning of guards on the streets outside the city walls)."[344] In the vanguard of all of these developments were Ottoman soldiers, whose mobility, interactions, and experiences constituted an accelerated and alien departure from their traditional existence.[345]

That departure proved so transformative in large part because World War I brought the world to the Middle East on a scale never seen before. Europeans who had never dreamed of traveling there marched on its lands and sailed its seas, but it also drew the peoples of South Asia into the Middle East on an unrivaled scale and at an unmatched level of intensity.

CHAPTER SIX

South Asians in the War

NEARLY THIRTY KILOMETERS southwest of Basra, just off the open road to Nasiriyya, stands a sun-bleached stone monument to a forgotten era. In contrast to the grandeur of some of Iraq's more modern monuments, the Basra War Memorial blends modestly and unobtrusively into the surrounding sandy desert. Its windswept and dilapidated stone edifice commemorates the 40,500 members of the British Empire's operations in Mesopotamia whose final resting places are unknown. Among those names chiseled into immortality in the lengthy stone walkway framing a central pillar are the sons of India. An engraved sentence "as sad as any I've read in war" caught the eye of BBC reporter Fergal Keane while he accompanied coalition troops during the 2003 Iraq war. "It says simply: For Subhadar Mahanga and 1,770 other Indian soldiers."[1]

Such unassuming memorials as in that empty stretch of desert near Basra pay tribute to the extraordinary sacrifice of Indian soldiers, among others, who deployed to fight in the Great War. As the historian Sugata Bose states, "Indian soldiers formed an important population of South Asians who followed the British imperial flag across the globe and around the Indian Ocean rim."[2]

Yet despite these soldiers' journey across the seas and into the heartland of the Ottoman Empire, the Indian contribution to World War I in the Middle East is considerably less acknowledged outside the British Isles and the Indian subcontinent. In truth, the links between the Middle East and South Asia go back centuries; the Great War served to bring the two populations even closer and in larger numbers than ever before. It was Indians, Egyptians, Australians, and other colonial subjects who manned the trenches and peopled the platoons that fought and won the war in the Middle East for the British. The presence of such large numbers of foreigners in the heart of the Middle East represented an opening that built on centuries-old contacts between South Asia and the Middle East.[3]

As 1914 dawned major combat operations seemed a distant prospect to the soldiers of the Indian army. At the start of monsoon season that summer, the Indian army comprised a mere 155,000 men organized into nine divisions and eight cavalry brigades, of which seven divisions and five cavalry brigades were equipped, trained, and organized for combat in the North West Frontier Province (NWFP).[4] Despite the presence of a seventy-five-thousand-strong British garrison, complemented by the Imperial Service Troops of India's princes, "none of the units were equipped for fighting a modern war."[5] Instead they were narrowly focused on combating internal threats to colonial rule, patrolling the NWFP, and maintaining a field force for potential war in Afghanistan.[6]

To the Indian soldier of early 1914 it would have been unimaginable that by the time the Armistice was signed in the forest of Compiègne four years later, India would have "provided over 1.27 million men, including 827,000 combatants, contributing roughly one man in ten to the war effort of the British Empire."[7] The Indian army had more than tripled in size to a wartime high of "573,000 combatants, with a maximum of 273,000 men serving outside the Indian Subcontinent at any one time (mostly in Mesopotamia)."[8] Moreover, that impressive Indian mobilization was scaled rapidly to meet imperial demand: by the time of the British surrender at Kut in April 1916, over 210,000 Indians had already been deployed to fight in Egypt, East Africa, France, and Mesopotamia.[9] Altogether, nearly sixty thousand Indians died "on the battlefields of Mesopotamia and France during World War 1."[10]

It was in Mesopotamia, in particular, where the Indian soldier experienced the trials, tribulations, and triumphs of war. Along the Tigris and at Kut rash decisions triggered the envelopment of an entire Indian army quickly beset by hunger. Its predicament tightened London's oversight of the theater; its eventual surrender revamped Great Britain's approach to the entire Middle East. During the year after Kut, Indians fought impressively up the Tigris before marching into Baghdad to claim that ancient capital for the empire. Financing that advance to Baghdad (and beyond) strained Delhi's finances: "The cost in terms of Indian revenue was not insignificant . . . although the British Exchequer bore the larger part of the cost of the Indian expeditionary forces, the Indian government's military expenditure rose from £20 million in 1913–1914 to £140 million in 1918–1919."[11]

Early in the conflict, the British insisted on conscripting only particular types of Indians. In 1857, the great Indian rebellion involving soldiers and civilians alike swept across a broad belt of central and northern India, shocking Britain and spelling the end of the British East India Company, the commercial outfit through which London long ruled India. In fact, "The Indian Army of 1914 was the product of recruitment and retention strategies developed in response to the 1857 Mutiny."[12] After 1857, the British pushed their recruitment efforts into what were considered more reliable parts of the north. Bypassing the educated masses of urban India, the sedentary Indians of the Indo-Gangetic plain, and the populations of the vast Deccan, British officers trained their recruitment on the illiterate teenage peasants from the north and northwest whom they judged as infused with a warrior ethos.[13] This trend, which accelerated from the 1880s onward, meant that by the summer of 1914 an overwhelming percentage of the Indian army was composed of soldiers from Punjab, the NWFP, and the independent kingdom of Nepal.[14]

In organizing their Indian forces, the British reinforced such martial class demarcations by "assigning recruits from specific ethnic, religious, and linguistic groups such as Gurkhas, Sikhs, and Rajputs to homogenous companies and even regiments."[15] Emphasizing such group distinctions mitigated the potential for uprising, as the distinctive "religious practices, dietary restrictions and religious ceremonies" of homogeneously constructed regiments fostered separate and cohesive identities.[16] The limits of such tight recruiting parameters, however, were exposed early in the war at the battle of Neuve Chapelle, which initiated many colonial troops to the mass killing of the European theater.[17] After General Townshend's defeat at Kut in the spring of 1916, the policy of limited recruitment became even more unsustainable as London ordered British divisions from secondary theaters transferred to the Western front.[18] Moreover, ample evidence of heroism by groups outside the martial classes dealt a powerful blow to the theory of martial recruitment.

On a practical level the chaos of warfare had repeatedly broken down the strict segregation of units, as "Punjabi Muslims, Sikhs, and Rajputs mingled on the front, in the hospitals, or as prisoners. . . . The letters left behind by soldiers stationed in the Suez Canal also indicate that religious and class mixing was a regular feature of army life in spite of the reluctance of some men."[19] The Labor Corps in Mesopotamia, reported the wartime correspondent Edmund Candler, "introduced the nearest thing to Babel since the original confusion of tongues. Coolies and artisans came in from China and Egypt, and from the East and West Indies, the aboriginal Santals and Paharias from Bengal, Moplahs, Thyas, and Nayars from the West Coast, Nepalise quarrymen, Indians of all races and creeds, as well as the Arabs and Chaldeans of the country."[20] In July 1917, Major J. D. Crowdy reported:

> Labourers seem to have been collected from all parts of the world. Most of the carpenters are Chinese or Japanese, & all the members of the Labour Corps are recognized from all classes in India. There are Egyptian & Arab Porter Corps and . . . one from Mauritius, the members of which speak French & English & are as black as negroes! There is also a battalion of the West Indian Regt . . . of Jamaica. When to these are added Persian & Kurdish Labour Corps, you can form a faint conception of the appearance of this cosmopolitan crowd.[21]

The largest contribution of Indian combat soldiers, however, still came from the Punjab; "out of a total of 683,149 combat troops recruited in India between August 1914 and November 1918, 349,688—about 60 percent—came from the Punjab."[22] Alongside them served Sikhs, Rajputs, Gurkhas, Jats, Dogras, Pathans, Hindustani Muslims and Ahirs—and almost seventy other population groups—who accompanied Punjabis across the Indian Ocean and into foreign territories to do battle on behalf of the Crown.[23]

How did Indian soldiers interpret their recruitment? There is ripe speculation among historians as to "the extent to which Indians were coaxed, cajoled, or coerced into fighting for Britain."[24] Many Indians were perhaps skeptical of the British narrative of war, and few likely rode the wave of emotional patriotism that swept the British home isles. The historian David Omissi's careful combing of Indian soldiers' war letters shows that "people never mentioned in the letters read like a political Who's Who of World War I: Woodrow Wilson, Lloyd George, Herbert Asquith, Lenin, Trotsky, and Gandhi."[25] More than anything, it seems that the focus, instead, on "family, clan, and caste" helped inspire the Indian soldiers as warfare intensified from frontier patrols to frontal charges.[26] A sense of solidarity also sprang from the prestige of regimental duty in the selective, relatively small prewar Indian military. The structure of these units reinforced the potency of that camaraderie: organized and initially deployed as socially cohesive units walled off from other communal groups, Indian regiments demonstrated intense pride born of accomplishment. The 47th Sikhs official war record, for example, opens with the boast that it "was raised as a Class Regiment of Jat Sikhs in 1901. . . . Above all things esprit de corps amongst all ranks was undoubtedly excellent. . . . It never lost a yard of trench in any theatre of War. . . . On no occasion was it ever withdrawn for reconstruction."[27]

An illustration of this solidarity comes from the trenches near al-Shaykh Sa'ad on the banks of the Tigris in January 1916. Four Indian companies— Sikh, Punjabi Muslim, Dogra, and Pathan—that were engaged in relief operations went on the offensive,[28] but a brave initial charge by the Sikh and Punjabi companies was cut down by enemy fire, despite their utmost exertion. With their fate in clear view, Dogra and Pathan men charged in a second wave, but apparently somewhat tentatively, resulting in severe losses. Six days later, during another attack, the Dogras led the charge, rushing through hundreds of yards of enemy fire. As one Sikh commander later recalled: "Seventy yards short of the Wadi was a ditch. The Turkish bank of the Wadi was much higher, giving them a wonderful field of fire to the ditch. I saw men in that deadly seventy yards get up singly and make a dash forward until killed. Not one here and there but man after man. . . . I have never seen such heroism. They did it to redeem the name of their clan which they thought had been besmirched."[29]

In 1914 80 percent of India's 57 million Muslims lived in the broad arc of upper India stretching from Punjab to Bengal, with the populations in each of these bookend provinces half-Muslim.[30] Even before the Ottoman war entry, therefore, Britain's Crown Raj (which replaced Company Raj in 1858) heavily censored the press and prepared the monarch's subjects for the possibility of war: "Great Britain, the greatest Muhammadan Power in the world, and the faithful and consistent friend of Turkey, whom she has steadfastly helped to maintain her position in Europe and to recover her stability, which was shaken in the Balkan wars, would see with the greatest regret that Turkey had been decoyed into ranging herself on the side of England's enemies."[31] As soon as the appearance of *Goeben* announced Ottoman intentions in the Black Sea, the government in India issued an additional proclamation meant to assuage the concerns of Muslim Indians:

> In view of the outbreak of war between Great Britain and Turkey, which, to the regret of Great Britain, has been brought about by the ill-advised, unprovoked and deliberate action of the Ottoman Government, his Excellence the Viceroy is authorized by His Majesty's Government to make the following public announcement in regard to the Holy Places of Arabia, including the Holy Shrines of Mesopotamia and the port of Jeddah, in order that there may be no misunderstanding on the part of His Majesty's most loyal Moslem subjects as to the attitude of His Majesty's Government in this war, in which no question of a religious character is involved. These Holy Places and Jeddah will be immune from attack or molestation by the British naval and military forces so long as there is no interference with pilgrims from India to the Holy Places and shrines in question. At the request of his Majesty's Government the Governments of France and Russia have given similar assurances.[32]

Sympathetic newspapers, such as Bombay's *Jame-e-Jamshad,* propagandized: "This is the time when India should feel it to be her duty to show to the world . . . how ready and willing she is to make any sacrifice she can in men and treasure, for the defence . . . and assertion of her honour and dignity."[33]

The Ottomans were well aware of the Indian Muslim presence in the British lines and they moved promptly to exploit their status as coreligionists. Because almost one-third of the Egyptian Expeditionary Force's new infantry was Muslim,[34] frontline patrols were "accompanied by the regimental *imam,* who would sing holy greeting and prayers at the British lines" in the hopes of luring defectors: "these men [the sepoys] being Moslems, will not fight against us; therefore it is advisable to choose from each Battalion and from each Company, men with good voices to accompany patrols at night."[35] In response, British staff officers ordered intensified vigilance when Indian soldiers "were on leave, or [at] training courses in Egypt, or when employed as guards over Turkish prisoners of war."[36] Intelligence officers at Suez, Ismailia, and al-Qantara kept watch for Ottoman propaganda, while military police "toured front live divisions providing [soldiers] with photographs showing the appalling conditions Indian prisoners of war were kept in by the Turks."[37] If possible, "leave parties were . . . organized to Jerusalem to allow the sepoys to see the religious sites. In addition, after the end of hostilities small groups were taken from regiments to participate in the pilgrimage to Mecca."[38] After capturing Nablus during his push north in the fall of 1918, General Edmund Allenby placed a guard at the Grand Mosque, a signal to his men that he took religious sensibilities seriously.[39] Across the desert in Mesopotamia similar precautions were taken as men fought their way past holy sites.[40]

In retrospect, the Ottoman effort was mostly ineffective at sparking Indian military defections: "There were relatively few instances of unrest in the Indian Army during the First World War. . . . The EEF was fortunate to only suffer a total of 30 Indian desertions in 1918."[41] When religion proved ineffective, the Ottomans attempted other propaganda strategies. One Indian battalion in Mesopotamia was greeted by a shower of Hindi pamphlets warning them that "England was starving and would soon be unable to feed and clothe them."[42] Highlighting their loyalty, the Indian officers wrote a reply and requested it be dropped on the Ottomans. It included the lines, "We have never been fed and clothed so well but prisoners taken from you are in rags. . . . We will never cease to fight for the King Emperor Jarj Panjam [George V] until the evil Kaiser is utterly trodden into the mud, as was the ten-headed demon Rawan by Ramchandarji."[43] One Punjabi Muslim stationed in Persia wrote to a comrade deployed in France that he "must have heard that the Indian forces of our King of Kings, George V, have achieved a splendid victory and taken Baghdad the Holy. It is a matter of the greatest joy to us Muslims that this sacred place has escaped out of the hands of the evil Germans, and has come into the possession of our just King."[44] Such a tone was sure to pass censorship.

The Ottoman effort failed in part because so many Indian Muslims separated political duty from religious fealty, thereby easing their anxieties over the war. "War has nothing to do with religion," *al-Ahram* intoned in British-controlled Cairo. "Thus, the Indian pilgrims can travel to Mecca or anywhere else they wish to."[45] Although she offers her statement in the context of anticolonialist nationalism, the historian Ayesha Jalal hints at the possibility of layered identities when writing, "An emotional affinity toward the *Ummah* had never kept Muslims from identifying with patriotic sentiments in their own homelands."[46] This may be why one soldier found it possible to argue in a letter to his brother that he could not find a "better occasion . . . to prove the loyalty of my family to the British government. Turkey, it is true, is a Muslim power, but what has it to do with us? Turkey is nothing at all to us."[47] Another soldier in Punjab addressed a comrade: "Remember this, that you must always do the Sirkar's work faithfully. It is very difficult to get such a King. The Turks are not our paternal uncle's children! I firmly rely on you, that you remain the well-wisher of the Sirkar. Still, it is proper that I should advise you. The Turks made war against our Sirkar without any cause. Our Sirkar repeatedly told the Turks before the war to remain neutral, and that their security would be arranged for in every way. But the Turks would not be advised, and now they are giving away their country with their own hands."[48]

That loyalty also strained to hurdle cultural obstacles. Sikhs, for example, refused to wear steel shrapnel helmets, citing religious prohibitions against the wearing of such hats, and instead "decided that they should be carried as trench stores."[49] Meanwhile, the war diary of a Punjabi regiment describes the challenges the British faced during one cholera inoculation campaign in Mesopotamia in the spring of 1916: "The Khattacks except the Indian officers and NCOs refused to be done as they still believed the stories they had heard in Egypt about all inoculation rendering men impotent. Even when told in turn that this inoculation was not voluntary but by order they still refused and had to be marched back to camp under arrest. Subedar Major Mir Akbar found out who was at the bottom of this refusal and persuaded them to agree to be inoculated the following day."[50]

In targeting the home front, Enver Pasha launched efforts to "stir up" holy war by creating regional commands and dispatching espionage missions.[51] Ottoman efforts at pan-Islamic revolution across multiple continents were encouraged by Germany, even if frictions existed between the two allies. In the instructions of German Chancellor Theobald von Bethmann-Hollweg to his Foreign Office, "England appears determined to wage war to the bitter end. . . . Thus one of our main tasks is gradually to wear England down through unrest in India and Egypt."[52] In 1913–1914, prominent Ottoman emissaries, including Tevfik Bey of the paper *Sebilürreşad,* Adnan Bey and Kemal Omer Bey, both of the Red Crescent Society, and military envoys Sami Bey and Muhammed Sadik Bey, traveled to India to appeal to lingering pro-Ottoman sentiment, push for closer collaboration, and build an alliance network within India.[53] After arriving in the spring of 1913, Tevfik Bey took to the pages of the Urdu newspaper *al-Hilal* and urged an expanded outreach to influential Muslim leaders, while Adnan Bey and Kemal Omer Bey, the (ostensible) Red Crescent representatives, carefully appealed to pan-Islamist solidarity in the event of war.[54] Similarly, another prominent episode that has received historical attention is the so-called silk letter conspiracy—an attempt to support Indian Muslim demands for independence—but it was mostly an indigenous affair that was quickly unraveled.[55] At least one American consular report from Baghdad in the summer of 1915 did raise the possibility of a volunteer corps of Indians revolting, adding "many British Indian subjects have become spies for the Ottoman Government here and they are constantly seeking information at this consulate."[56] Many Indian Muslim intellectuals, including Maulana Abul Kalam Azad, preached the virtues of an anticolonial jihad and a string of small uprisings from the Middle East to Southeast Asia did take place in February 1915.[57] Yet after 1915, Ottoman efforts at pan-Islamic political coordination in India slackened; most Indian Muslim soldiers' loyalties proved relatively robust.[58] Even such destitute populations as Indians captured during the siege of Kut remained supportive of the British.[59]

Indian Muslims did react to the news of war with serious apprehension: "The principal mosque in Dhaka was thronged by persons anxious to hear whether the Sultan, as Caliph of Islam, would be mentioned as usual in the opening prayer, because there was a rumor that the British Government had forbidden this. They were much relieved to find that no change had been made in the form of prayer."[60] As with troops in the field, on the Indian subcontinent "an attempt was made to make out [sic] a distinction between the political and religious aspects of the situation. It was pointed out that the war that Turkey was fighting was political and that while the Indian Muslims had some religious ties with the Sultan Caliph, they were by no means bound to treat their political interest as identical with that of

Turkey."[61] The pan-Islamist Mazharul Haq argued for contextualizing Islam within the political state, while members of the Delhi ulema instructed: "We and the Turk . . . have a spiritual relation with each other. The religious duties that are binding on us are binding on them, but their material responsibilities and ours are quite different. They have their own political needs just as we have ours. At the same time it should be borne in mind that our material responsibilities, which relate to India and the British Government, are not only material, but moral and to a certain extent religious."[62]

Despite the best efforts of the British, public opinion in colonial India included a noticeable sympathy for the Ottomans. "The revocation of the partition of Bengal in 1912 had encouraged" Indian Muslims predisposed to extraneous cultural influences and sensitive to their Muslim status to reflect on their loyalties.[63] These potentially pro-Ottoman predispositions were given voice in newspapers such as *Comrade, Hamdard, Al-Hilal,* and *Zamindar,*[64] which expressed regret at the Ottoman entry into the war but emphasized pan-Islamic solidarity, the sacredness of the Islamic holy sites, the British annexation of Egypt, and Ottoman victories in places such as Gallipoli.[65]

At the beginning of the war, Sultan Mehmed V issued a fatwa for jihad in order to address the question of loyalty: "The Moslem subjects of Russia, of France, of England and of all the countries that side with them in their land and sea attacks dealt against the Caliphate for the purpose of annihilating Islam, must these subjects, too, take part in the Holy War against the respective governments from which they depend? Yes."[66] Although Indians may have interpreted the fatwa as a ploy for wartime cooperation, one Council of India member related that "the anguish with which they (Indian Muslims) see England attacking Turkey is the most terrible trial that they have experienced since the beginning of British rule in India."[67] The British fear of uprising was real during the war but after 1915 "this threat was never more than potential."[68] Ultimately, proof of Indian sympathy for the Ottoman caliphate emerged after the war in the form of the Khilafat movement of 1919 to 1924, organized by Muslims in India in support of the Ottoman Empire. None other than Mahatma Gandhi lent strong support to the cause of the Khilafat during the mass noncooperation movement against the British in the aftermath of the Great War.

For Indians, tales told by the returning wounded constituted a central source of news and information. The impressions created were of a brutal, grim conflict, sowing doubts among prospective Indian soldiers who weighed the promised rewards for enlistment against the dangers of combat.[69] Tellingly "certain Punjabi folk songs from this period also seem to indicate equidistance from all war parties and an understanding that the war meant suffering for the poor."[70] The British counted on military convention and soldiering camaraderie—along with an extensive censorship program—to overcome such doubts. For the troops, in addition to the fear of the consequences of quitting the force, loyalty was sustained by British attention to the "traditional beliefs and practices, including religious ceremonies and dietary requirements" of Indians.[71] When Shi'i soldiers "expressed concern about fighting near holy cities and sites in Mesopotamia, such as Karbala and Salman Pak," the British "secured statements of support from Indian Muslim leaders such as the Nizam of Hyderabad," thereby assuaging most Muslim soldiers' concerns.[72]

Although Indian soldiers knew their missives faced the probing eyes of British censors, and therefore likely shaped their letters to pass muster, some felt a genuine connection to the war. One soldier wrote that this was "the time to show one's loyalty to the Sirkar, to earn a name for oneself. To die on the battlefield is glory. For a thousand years one's name will be remembered."[73] Moreover, bonds forged in the crucible of trench combat reinforced morale. Echoing a refrain heard across military history, one soldier confided, "I cannot describe to you how great fascination there is in fighting at the front. One experiences a feeling of exhilaration."[74] These concomitant feelings of loyalty and exhilaration were doubly tested at the outset of Sharif Husayn's Arab Revolt in June 1916. It was a jolting event for Indian Muslims, whose incredulity hardened into criticism at the revolt for risking the sanctity of Islam's holy sites.[75] Throughout India, "anti-Arab feeling was apparent. The Sharif was considered to have been ungrateful to the Porte."[76] The All-India Muslim League in Lucknow embodied the reaction of political actors across Muslim India: "The Arab rebels headed by the Sharif of Mecca, whose outrageous conduct may place in jeopardy the safety and sanctity of the holy places of Islam in the Hejaz and Mesopotamia."[77]

Nonetheless, in the letters that Omissi curates, ideological discussions or broader political dynamics generally rank behind concerns of the familial strains caused by war. One Punjabi soldier argued that while "those who do not put their hearts into the work of fighting the King's enemies are clearly worthy of the greatest blame," it is incumbent on the king to ameliorate the burdens of extended deployment. He continued, "[The Caliph] Hazrat Umar . . . had a law passed that in future every married soldier should be allowed to return to his home on leave once every six months. I have been astonished to think that when we have such a King, renowned through-out the world for his kindness and justice, he has never considered this problem. . . . Unless a law like that of Hazrat Umar is passed I believe that the wives and families will never believe that the men are alive at all."[78] Although primarily concerned with soldiers active on the western front, Omissi's study confirms that "many relatives wrote letters lamenting the long separation, imploring soldiers to return on leave or for marriage."[79] One anonymous, candid letter stated "your family is in misery" before tak-ing the rare step of advocating desertion: "What you ought to do is raise your fellow caste-men against the English and join the army of Islam. If you die in its service it would be better than living as you are doing now."[80] While such an appeal was exceptional, it underscores the strain of families coping with lengthy deployments. Alarming reports of drought and disease began to reach the front in 1915, compounding such anxieties among sol-diers.[81] Sugata Bose describes Indian soldiers writing of "unprecedented death and destruction."[82] As the war ground on, an increasing number sought to escape the front through self-inflicted wounds, often to their left hands and feet,[83] while night blindness in one unit—the Third Brahmans—was discovered to be mostly "self-induced disease by croton seeds."[84]

Indian soldiers faced a mixture of socioeconomic hardship and ideologi-cal pressure. Three units—the 130th Baluchis at Rangoon, the Fifth Light Infantry at Singapore, and the Fifteenth Lancers at Basra—mutinied rather than face their brethren on the battlefield, while some Pathans even fired on their own sentries before deserting their ranks.[85] According to official figures, after four years of war almost half of the Punjabi deserters remained at large, "suggesting considerable local support for those who decided to evade military service."[86]

Yet with the exception of Pathans, "although sometimes praising the bravery of the Turkish Army, most Muslim Indian sepoys decided, after some debate, to fight the Turks if need be."[87] The reaction of Indian soldiers to the Fifteenth Lancers who refused to advance from Basra was generally to bemoan the decision. One soldier wrote that when he "read about the behavior of the regiment I was overwhelmed with grief. It was indeed a great pity that they should have acted thus at such a time. . . . Our duty is loyalty and bravery. I again say I am deeply grieved and hurt by the behavior of our people." He concludes that "this is the time to show loyalty and give help to the government and not to be false to one's salt."[88] Still another asserted "this was a great mistake to behave to our King in this way."[89]

Other soldiers worried over the condition of their Indian comrades who were imprisoned after mutinying. "It is a thousand pities that I, poor creature as I am, can do nothing in the matter," wrote one;[90] another voiced his displeasure at what he perceived as an excessively vindictive punishment, excusing the Fifteenth Lancers who "declined to take up arms against their brother Muslims and asked to be sent to some other theater of war. . . . It is very sad that fate should have dealt thus cruelly with this regiment in the end, after they had done such good service and gained so much renown elsewhere. . . . My idea is that the Government have acted in this way simply to vindicate their authority, and that after the war all these unfortunates will be released."[91]

In the wake of the 1857 revolt, the British offered an avenue for Indian advancement in the form of the Viceroy's Commissioned Officer (VCO).[92] Limited to Indian troops, VCOs commanded most of the platoons and companies in Indian regiments, and were selected after years of loyal service.[93] Their power of command, however, did not extend to holders of the King's Commission (KCO), which included all British and colonial officers, nor to enlisted men in British regiments.[94] At the war's outset, each Indian battalion featured seventeen VCOs and thirteen British KCOs.[95] The hierarchy of Indian society, transplanted to the battlefield, shaped the interactions of, and colored the relationships within, Indian units. As losses undermined homogeneity and replacement officers dwindled in quality and numbers, Indian units suffered along with their British counterparts.[96] On the flip side, however, the dynamics of Indian society may also have triggered great acts of courage. Countless examples of heroism and valor emerge in the story of Indian soldiers in the Great War, to their credit and to the benefit of their British officers.[97] The history of the Maratha Light Infantry tracks one example of Indian heroism in Mesopotamia in January 1917:

> The morning was very misty and the lines, soon after they moved out, almost disappeared from view. The first line of Turkish trenches was just in front of them. . . . The leading companies, though slightly mixed up in the

mist, dashed forward and reached their objectives. Captain Wilson who was leading C Company was wounded . . . and the command devolved on Subedar Chimaji Garud. He was held up by a Turkish machine-gun. Determined to knock out this hurdle, he, with two other sepoys, sprang forward to attack the gun-position. The Subedar's two comrades were killed before they could grapple with the Turkish machine-gunners but the Subedar rushed ahead alone and with his revolver shot the gunners.[98]

After this action, a colonel reported that the "name of the Regiment rings from Basra to Kut. In the words of the Corps Commander the men fought like tigers. Some Gorkhas led by their Colonel turned out to cheer them and the Corps Commander congratulated a British Regiment on being brigaded with us."[99] Another British officer later gushed to the regiment, "You belong to the type of men whom nothing in the world can stop."[100] During the charge on Baghdad, "wild Indians" "emerging out of dust and smoke" shook the enemy, attacking "amidst a din of 'Har har Mahadev' going fully 100 yards a minute."[101] In the midst of such violent combat, the Maratha soldiers apparently went about their duties in good cheer: "No one had anything but praise for the Maratha, of whom there were five battalions in Mesopotamia."[102] Newly joined subaltern Cyril Hancock remarked on the unit: "Whatever was said to them and wherever they found themselves they were always happy and smiling. Never did I see a sullen Mahratta."[103] In the case of the Ninth Bhopal Infantry, known colloquially as the Bo-Peeps, such a happy disposition yielded a generosity of spirit befitting the close officer-soldier relationship. As one of the propagandists of empire relates of the relief operations of Kut, "During an attack on a Turkish entrenched position, the commanding officer, Colonel Thomas, was hit and fell within 200 yards of the Turkish lines. There was no cover. Sepoy Chatta Singh went forward to Thomas's help, bandaged him and covered him with his own body while digging cover for them both. Thomas's leg was shattered and he was in great pain; Chatta Singh stayed with him till night when he brought him in. He was awarded the Victoria Cross."[104] A British major described another Indian soldier's unflinching performance during an attack in January 1917: "We advanced in quick time, no rushing, over 3000 yards of flat ground with no cover. . . . We went through three belts of it [machine guns]. Whole platoons dropped. . . . Only two British officers left and three Indian, instead of eight and fifteen. For the third time in a year we have lost half the regiment in one swoop. . . . My greatcoat changed hands four times. My orderly was carrying it first. He was hit and threw it to another man and so on. My Mahomedans made it a point of honour that my greatcoat must get in."[105]

Invariably, from Egypt *al-Ahram* reported expansively on the "physical strength" of the Indians and their "bravery and courage on the battlefield."[106] One Saturday in March 1915, the newspaper headlined "An Indian Champion," whose "flock was all killed, so the commander asked him to withdraw but he refused to. He kept firing on the enemies until he forced them to retreat."[107] As anecdotes of Indian valor spread, the Australian George MacKay remarked on the Indians' ferocity: "The famous Gurkha Regiment . . . are short and nuggety of build, Nepalese men and most wonderful fighters and as fearless as the lion. Each man carries a knife known as a kugri, a curved knife broadening towards the point which they throw at the enemy. I have watched them practice and came to the conclusion that I would rather be on their side than against them."[108]

Indian activity on the front also led to unlikely interconfessional camaraderie forged through battle. Despite British attempts at regimental compartmentalization, on the battlefield such arrangements were often superseded by acts of selflessness and valor:

On September 11, 1917 . . . thirty men of the 2nd Battalion, commanded by Lieutenant O'Shea, met an enemy party about a hundred strong. O'Shea was hit early in the action but would not give up command. He fought till he judged it necessary to order a retreat. The senior N.C.O., Naik Fazal Ahmad, who saw that O'Shea was much more severely wounded than he knew, refused to obey the order. . . . With the help of Lance-Naik Sher Mohammad he got O'Shea under cover and continued the fight. O'Shea died of his wound; Fazal Ahmad was hit and died; Sher Mohammad was hit and the enemy overran the position where the bodies of O'Shea and Fazal Ahmad lay. But Lance-Naik Prabhu Singh took charge, rallied the men, led a spirited counterattack and recovered the two bodies. They were Irish, Muslim, Sikh—but between them was an overriding loyalty to each other.[109]

Since the British takeover of Egypt in 1882, maintaining control over the Suez Canal became the sine qua non of London's regional strategy. For Great Britain, Egypt also acted as an equidistant geopolitical hub between the Middle East and Europe for deployments ranging from Basra to Marseilles. As a result, Indian forces shared Egypt with troops from around the British Empire. *Al-Ahram* anticipated the arrival of Indian troops, and the logistical strain it would place on the country, reporting in 1914 that "40,000 Indians and English soldiers are expected to arrive."[110] In fact, for "legions of the Indian army" a reception was "being prepared in Alexandria."[111] By January 1915 the British had increased the Suez defense to 70,000 soldiers drawn from across the empire: Australian and New Zealand Army Corps, "the 10th Indian Division, 11th Indian Division, and the Bikanir Camel Corps" all defended Suez.[112] Although the government controlled any reporting on troop movements, the disembarkation of thousands of Indians at railway stations inevitably sparked curiosity. "The streets of Egypt were packed with English and Indian soldiers staying at Heliopolis and Zeytun," *al-Ahram* reported. "The crowds gathered to watch them and some thought that the Indians looked exactly like the Japanese."[113] In four years of war India sent 95,000 combatants and 135,000 noncombatants to the Egyptian and Palestine front.[114] Just as interested Egyptians observed the novelty of a mass of marching Indians, so too these Indian soldiers experienced real culture shock at being deployed so far from home. In August 1916, one soldier in Cairo wrote a friend concerning the "very strange" celebration of the holy festival of 'Id (Eid):

> Roundabouts were erected everywhere on which "nightingales" and "cuckoos" [women] of Egypt, each with an admirer, sang songs to allure the listening foreigners. . . . Each man encountered was more or less the worse for drink, and, having at least one "nightingale" sitting beside him in his carriage, indulged in all kinds of lewd and obscure songs. It was all very wrong. . . . On one side a "nightingale" in the possession of an Arab sang loudly. On the other, a "nightingale" embraced an Egyptian, while some poor Hindustani looked on and wondered when his turn would come. . . . Shame! Shame! The very ground cried out for protection, and praying to God, said "for a day like this make a new earth, because I am no longer able to endure the suggestive gait, and the thrust of the pointed heels of these creatures."[115]

The same soldier went on to contrast his own customs with the sinful Egyptian variety, lamenting that "there was no trace of the Hindustani customs of friends meeting and partaking of the Id banquets. Each one went about 'empty-handed' after his own pleasure. . . . Nothing that we have seen in Hindustan, even during the Holi festivals of the Hindus, approaches the things we have seen here during the Id. Thank God, for this Our Country!"[116] In Egypt, separate military cantonments did limit somewhat the interaction between Indians and Egyptians,[117] and British apprehension at the prospect of thousands of Indian men stationed in Egypt caused them to declare Port Said—a noted prostitution center—as entirely "out of bounds."[118] Some, however, readily resigned themselves to their new milieu, even taking to their new setting enthusiastically. One Hindu soldier volunteered that "not only I but numbers of other Hindus . . . have eaten from the hands of sweepers. . . . We used to go openly to hotels [cafes, restaurants and refreshment rooms in Suez]. Of course, this was not known in India. . . . Now everyone knows it and I am not alone in having transgressed. I have no compunction."[119]

Ultimately, however, these Indians deployed to Egypt for war, and one of their first major tasks was to defend the Suez Canal. Thirty-four feet deep, 100 miles long, and 190 feet wide at minimum, the canal constituted a formidable waterway.[120] Luckily for the British, "more than one-third was protected by lakes and inundations."[121] The rest, however, would need to be protected by troops. In the predawn hours of early February 1915, Indian sentries spied the silhouetted mass of an Ottoman attacking force silently pushing off the east bank of the canal and making its way toward their defensive works.[122] In the ensuing battle Punjabis trained heavy fire on pontoons and other amphibious assault craft, sinking them in rapid succession, with Rajputs, Egyptians, and Sikhs participating in the operation.[123] As one of the first Egyptian-Indian actions of the war against the Ottomans, the first Suez offensive set the tone for the ensuing battle over Palestine.[124] Several Indian divisions, such as the Third Lahore and Seventh Meerut, saw action on disparate fronts, from the lush countryside of France to the barren desert of Mesopotamia. Then, following the surrender of Baghdad, these troops joined newly arrived Indian cavalry—redeployed from Europe—to help form the Egyptian Expeditionary Corps.[125] Although they would win him brilliant victories, culminating in the Battle of Megiddo in northern Palestine in September 1918, Allenby invoked some of the same stereotypes as his contemporaries in discussing his colonial men. In the aftermath of one Pathan outpost deserting to the Ottomans, Allenby was piqued. "If I could be reinforced by 3 or 4 good divisions . . . I could, I think, really get a move on my Turks."[126] So it must have been disheartening to Allenby when in late 1917 London accelerated the "Indianization" of his force. Increasing the number of Indians in the Egyptian Expeditionary Corps was Britain's effort to build up Allenby's troops "without having to make recourse to fresh drafts from Britain, which was facing accumulating manpower problems."[127] British planners also hoped to draw on the organizational skills and combat experiences of Indian units acclimated to three years of war in the Middle East.[128] The perceived downside to such a move was the risk of stationing in Palestine large numbers of Indian Muslims in direct opposition and in proximity to their coreligionists, the Ottomans.[129]

By late 1917, the gears of the Indian recruiting system were rotating at full speed, enabling such a policy shift. On December 11, 1917, Allenby dismounted and walked into Jerusalem, prompting Prime Minister Lloyd George to advocate a major offensive to break out into Greater Syria, thereby refocusing "a Eurocentric effort he regarded as counterproductive."[130] In response, Allenby submitted his resourcing requirements for further action. Allenby's plans, however, were soon interrupted by a massive, last-ditch German offensive launched in March 1918 in Flanders and France, an attack that ripped large holes in two British armies.[131] Allenby's hopes for British reinforcements died along with entire British divisions in the fields of Flanders and France. As the War Office rapidly recalled troops to Europe to stem the rising German tide, the pace of "Indianization" in Palestine quickened. Indeed, the "instrument of victory was being reformed with raw material from an unexpected quarter: Britain's Indian Army."[132] In fact, while Allenby's deceptions eventually outmaneuvered the Germans and Ottomans, the war itself was fought and won largely by an Indian and Egyptian force.[133]

Integral to that victory was "the last great cavalry campaign in history."[134] Although Indian infantry prepared, assaulted, and broke through the Ottoman lines during Allenby's fall offensive, it was the Desert Mounted Corps, including the Fourth and Fifth Indian Cavalry divisions, that pushed through the Ottoman gaps and prohibited an orderly Ottoman retreat.[135] This sweeping cavalry ride accomplished what European troops had been unable to do in the stalemate of Europe, raising the stature of the Imperial Service Troops.[136] The *New York Times* correspondent, W. T. Massey, reported on "great feats by the cavalry" and described Indian charges as "brilliantly . . . perfectly timed . . . masterly success . . . performed a feat almost without parallel in this war." Lavishing compliments on the rest of the force, Massey described that "bold use of cavalry" as accompanied by the "superb skill and endurance" of the Indian infantry.[137]

As in past conflicts, the cavalry also served as raiding parties and intelligence gatherers. Charles Trench, an Indian army officer in the 1930s who became known for his popular historical works, relates one such raid during the "dash up the coast" and toward Damascus.[138] "Just short of Damascus a squadron of the Poona Horse charged in error a body of Arabs who proved too elusive for them. They did, however, bag a large motor-car containing a European splendidly Arab-garbed. Suspecting a German spy, Risaldar Major Hamir Singh demanded his surrender, and there ensued a heated altercation, neither understanding one word the other said. It transpired that this individual's name was Lawrence, and that he had something to do with the Sharif of Mecca's forces."[139]

As Trench suggests, this incident may in part account for T. E. Lawrence's general bias toward the Indian army, even if a "machine-gun section of Hodson's Horse, Pathans commanded by Risaldar Hassan Shah, took part in many of Lawrence's raids."[140] The incident notwithstanding, Allenby's attack up the coastal plain, through the central Palestinian highlands, and across the Jordan River valley inspired pride among Indian troops. Their official histories and diaries record Ottoman surrenders, swift-moving victories, and valorous performances in battle. Testifying to their momentum, in all of 1918 the Egyptian Expeditionary Force suffered only a few dozen desertions.[141]

That is not to say, however, that Allenby's thrust through Palestine was simple. Although it is often portrayed as swift and active in comparison to the static European front, conditions in Palestine were far from ideal and cost Allenby almost ten thousand Indian and native troops (9,980).[142] While British captains often fixed bayonets and ordered charges, it was mostly Indian units who executed those orders.[143] Their suffering is exemplified in the Indian experience at Kut, while their determination was rewarded with the eventual capture of Baghdad. Indeed, it was in Mesopotamia where the pain of defeat and the exhilaration of victory merged into one.

It began in November 1914 when the Indian Sixth Division was dispatched to capture Basra and secure the Anglo-Persian oil installations.[144]

Facing them in Mesopotamia were "17,000 infantry, 380 cavalry, 44 field guns, and three machine guns."[145] By the time of the Armistice, over six hundred thousand men of India, in one form or another, had experienced the great convulsion of Mesopotamian warfare.[146] In the beginning, such a large-scale war along the Tigris seemed unlikely. However, after a series of initial victories, British decision makers in the "cool climes of the resort towns of Simla" were tempted by the ease of their early advances and cast strategic prudence aside.[147] As one writer put it, "the temptation theme is played fortissimo. [The British prime minister] Mr. Asquith was eager for a resounding success; everyone had heard of Baghdad, the city of the Arabian Nights, and the news that it had fallen would reassure a British public who knew that Gallipoli had been a failure."[148] Echoing that sentiment, Lord Hardinge, the British viceroy, argued in November 1915 that "our success hitherto in Mesopotamia has been the main factor which has kept Persia, Afghanistan, and India itself quiet."[149] Ultimately, however, the blame for one of the greatest catastrophes in British military history—the defeat at Kut—rests on the commanders on the spot, in particular General John Nixon.[150] Nixon's preference for an ethos of inspirational leadership came at the expense of logistical preparation. The Tigris expedition faced one logistical hurdle after another; unfortunately, Nixon's confidence in the fighting spirit of his men came at the expense of such indispensable administrative work as the development of the port of Basra.[151] In fact, in the staff college instruction of the time, maintaining lines of communications took a backseat to an operational emphasis on freedom of maneuver.[152] This approach would prove doubly costly during the attack at Ctesiphon and throughout the operations to relieve Kut. Martial valor proved no substitute for careful preparation.

Unaware of the foreign conditions of Mesopotamia, British officers in India also misjudged the logistical requirements that a major undertaking toward Baghdad would demand. As late as October 1915, Lord Hardinge wrote, "I still hope to be the Pasha of Baghdad before I leave India," a departure scheduled for April 1916.[153] Instead, impending defeat at Kut caused the chief of the Imperial General Staff to assert control over Delhi in early 1916, thereby aligning London's "world-wide priorities and the needs of India's semi-independent campaign in Mesopotamia."[154] From that point on, it would be little more than a year before Punjabi and Gurkha regiments marched at the head of General Stanley Maude's columns into Baghdad.[155] Maude had reversed the errors of his predecessors by emphasizing the painstaking work of logistical preparation, altering the command structure to emphasize flexibility, and adapting infantry-artillery coordination to utilize the latest advances in modern warfare.[156] The pivotal point in the campaign, however, was the defeat at Kut.

From the beginning, life inside besieged Kut was emotionally and physically torturous. As the historian Nikolas Gardner has detailed, the Ottomans bombarded Kut with "leaflets printed in various Indian languages calling on sepoys to murder their British officers and join the Turks."[157] As elsewhere, this Ottoman initiative had little effect, but it reminded Townshend of the dilemma Indian soldiers faced fighting in a foreign land against coreligionists while subsisting on inadequate provisions and receiving insufficient medical care.[158] As the siege dragged on, conditions only worsened.

On January 20, 1916, as the prospect of immediate relief was dwindling and vegetables and other food grew scarce inside Kut, Townshend ordered his men to halve their rations.[159] The garrison's tinned meat supplies—the disdained "bully beef"—gave way to an even less appetizing reality: the consumption of pack animals.[160] Although famished, many Indians refused to incorporate horse and mule into their daily diet, as they considered themselves prohibited by religious rules from doing so.[161] Gardner explains, "By 1916, the original ranks of many battalions had been depleted by casualties and diluted by reinforcements, but many men from the same community or region still served together in the same unit. Sepoys were therefore concerned that if they broke dietary taboos at the front without the complicity of their comrades, news of their conduct would reach their home communities and they would be ostracized upon their return."[162] Townshend sought to overcome his soldiers' hesitations by soliciting statements from Indian religious leaders, posted throughout Kut, "sanctioning the consumption of horseflesh."[163] Townshend stated that "only by drastic measures have I been able to accomplish this even after they had received permission by telegram from their religious leaders in India to eat horse flesh!"[164]

Moreover, the soldiers' reliance on diminishing and already inadequate rations of flour and unprocessed grain led to outbreaks of pneumonia, jaundice, and dysentery at alarmingly high levels.[165] On March 7 the daily ration was set at "ten ounces of barley flour and four ounces of parched barley grain";[166] by the end of the month, rations were further reduced to six ounces of barley flour and four ounces of unground barley.[167] Throughout March the physical toll that the siege exerted threatened the basic readiness of the force; soldiers fainted while digging trenches and sentries simply sat listlessly on duty. The weakest soldiers succumbed to starvation, while over ten others died of disease per day.[168]

Even so, it was not until mid-April, when rations were reduced to four ounces of flour, that ten thousand Sikhs, Hindus, and Muslims relented and began consuming horsemeat, although for some it was too late.[169] One author documented malnutrition among British and Indian troops; in consuming less than half the calories necessary to maintain their strength, British soldiers lost an average of 12.5 pounds while Indians lost approximately 17 pounds during the siege.[170]

One soldier's memoir aptly summarized the effect of Kut: "We are a sick army, a skeleton army rocking with cholera and disease."[171] A small percentage of the force despaired; 147 Indians deserted, while others committed suicide.[172] Yet by and large the fighting spirit of the Indian soldiers remained unbowed by the adversity of Kut. This is notably exemplified by the story of Subedar Akbar Khan, who was shot in the knee during early action, later wounded in his other leg, and finally knocked down by an airplane bomb. Each time, he rejoined the action after brief medical care, the last time "permanently deaf in one ear."[173] Of the lucky few who survived until surrender, an even much smaller number of Indians lived to tell of their lengthy, brutal march into captivity. While Townshend was prized as a celebrity captive, 30 percent of his Indian force would not survive their Ottoman internment.[174] In an appendix to *The Campaign in Mesopotamia,* based on official documents and released in 1924, British Captain A. J. Shakeshaft's diary describes the conditions faced by men left behind after Townshend's surrender:

We met a number of unfortunate British and Indian soldiers who were standing at the door of a miserable yard, where they were herded together. They looked ghastly. They were sick[,] left behind by one of the columns. . . . They were in a miserable plight, many suffering from dysentery. Others were fairly fit, but had no boots for marching. There were about 80 British and Indian. They received only a ration of wheat. The Arabs used to bring milk and eggs to sell and asked exorbitant prices; consequently they would soon have no money and would die of starvation and neglect. There were no guards over them and they were completely abandoned. Sometimes, when a sick man would crawl out of the hovel they lived in, Arabs would throw stones and chase him back into the yard. I will spare the reader any description of the dark, filthy hovel where they slept.[175]

The British-Indian force charged with rescuing the garrison at Kut operated in barely better conditions. Riverine resupplies of medicines, along with cases of whisky and cigarettes and other parcels, often did not reach the front lines because troops pilfered them along the way.[176] Moreover, the dearth of cold storage facilities in Mesopotamia meant that shipments of onions and potatoes often spoiled below deck, disproportionally affecting Indians because they received smaller rations than the British.[177] In a letter to his wife written while participating in the relief operation, one British officer, J. D. Crowdy, reported, "Rations are short, & at times we have been reduced to bully, biscuits & tea only—no sugar, potatoes, or anything else. Being a scratch mess, we are very short of stores, but have managed to pick up odd tins of milk at intervals, & occasional cones of white sugar, for which we pay fabulous prices. The Indian troops are getting no sugar or gur, & as there is no fresh meat available, they are having a very rough time of it. They suffer very much from the cold, but bear their hardships extraordinarily well."[178]

British authorities did attempt to buttress Indian soldiers' daily intake by providing an allowance that could be used to purchase food matching their "custom, caste, and religion."[179] Although well intentioned, far too few goods were available for purchase in what one Indian soldier described as "desolate" and "uninhabited" Mesopotamia.[180] The policy struggled to meet the emergency of the moment.

The British engineer George Buchanan, whose expertise Nixon ignored during the relief operations of Kut, described the consequences of the rickety British logistics network: "At lunch on Sunday, Major Cook Young, Indian Medical Service, arrived, straight from the front. . . . He had come down, the only doctor in charge of over 500 wounded, all packed on to an iron barge, in bitter cold weather and without even the bare necessities of life. Major Young said he was ashamed of himself as a man, ashamed of himself as a doctor, and ashamed to look the miserable dying men in the face. I have never heard a more dreadful tale of preventable suffering."[181]

Another soldier described life in Basra, the supply headquarters for the British effort in Mesopotamia, by relaying the sentiments of his deployed brother, who lamented that "the heat is unbearable and that the country [Mesopotamia] is the very opposite of France . . . except for dates and the heat, nothing is to be found."[182] If such was the state of Basra, one can only imagine conditions at the front. Several soldiers tried to paint a vivid picture of the action there, and also chose as their contrast the comforts of France. From one regimental history: "The country we were now in was in every way a complete contrast to our late theater of War [France]. The climate was tropical, excessively hot in summer, and during that season the flat country became scorched and bare. In the short winter the climate was usually bright and cold. . . . The monotony of the hot weather was very great. The flat desert country had little of interest, and we often sighed for the comfortable billets behind the line in France."[183]

Unlike the temperate European climate, near Kut "the air felt like a blast from a furnace" while stormy winds brought "sudden darkness, a rustle and a deep shadow, and [a] wall of dust . . . across the desert and through the bivouac, blowing down shelters."[184] By the time the black smoke of Kut signaled its surrender, swarms of flies had made conditions even more unbearable. In fact, "Everything and everywhere was black with [flies]. To eat without swallowing flies was impossible and many preferred to forego food during the day, eating only in the early morning or after sundown when the plague abated somewhat."[185]

Conditions did not change quickly after the fall of Kut. One major summarized the state of conditions while entrenched with Punjabis in simple, unexaggerated staccato: "Heat is appalling and only just beginning. Flies bite hard and are in thousands. Cholera has started. . . . We lie and gasp all day. . . . Food now is disgusting; we exist on bully beef—fly-blown—and stale bread. . . . Meals are practically an impossibility on account of the flies."[186] In a sad literary twist, he later describes a march in which "men fell like flies" as more than "1,000 collapsed from heat and lack of water. . . . Men simply crumpled up."[187] These conditions were endured by a particularly large number of Indian soldiers, since more than twice as many fought in Mesopotamia as in France (or Palestine).[188] The influence of these theaters could not have been equal; Mesopotamia, more than Palestine or France, shaped the Indian soldier.

Lest we forget about Indian contributions outside Palestine and Meso-potamia, however, it should be noted that Indians fought all around the world, and showed a basic awareness of the battles ongoing in the various theaters of the Great War. In August 1915, one Punjabi wrote admiringly about the Ottoman victory on Gallipoli to a comrade in France, "There is a country belonging to the Turks too which they call Dadarnes [the Darda-nelles]. There has been fighting there with the Turks, about which I cannot tell you. There France, Italy, England, and another four Kings had their armies. The Turk smashed and bashed the whole lot, and the losses were heavy. The Turks are the bravest of all. We are ever praying that the victory may be granted to our King, the King of peace."[189]

What that soldier may not have known is that a small number of Indians were at the center of the amphibious assault against the Ottoman positions on Gallipoli. Sikhs, Gurkhas, and Punjabis held the left flank of the Cape Helles line "where the smell of corpses was so awful that men stuffed their noses with 'four-by-two,' the flannelette patches used to clean rifles,"[190] and it was the Indian Twenty-Ninth Infantry Brigade that landed with the AN-ZACs on the west coast of Gallipoli. They would be the only unit to "gaze down on the waters of the Dardanelles" after fighting their way inland atop an elevated position.[191]

By most accounts Indians and Australians got along on Gallipoli, de-spite difficulties of communication and translation.[192] One amusing anec-dote underscores Indian resourcefulness: "Water was short, and a water-expert told [an Australian] that he must water his mules only once a day. [The Australian] replied that they would then be unable to hump stores every night for the Australians, and was told to dig his own well. This he did, in a spot chosen by the Havildar Major who had done this in the Pun-jab. It watered 200 mules twice a day, and the expert was understandably cross."[193]

More seriously indicative of Australian-Indian solidarity were the per-formances of Indian field ambulances. Australians suffering from diarrhea and dysentery on Gallipoli often preferred Indian over Australian medical care: "From their doctors all they got was bully-beef, biscuits and Number 9 which the heaving stomach rejected, but the Indians gave them dhal and chupattis, which was fair dinkum, and dried them up."[194] As on the other fronts, the Indians' resourcefulness was matched by their courage in combat.

Commanding a group of Sikhs, one British officer boasted of his men withstanding an Ottoman charge that left ANZACs in panic: "My Sikhs . . . stood firm and edged into the side of the ravine."[195]

Unbeknownst to many, Indians even served in sub-Saharan Africa. Trench uncovered an illuminating anecdote from early 1916 in which Indians served alongside South Africans under the South African General Jan Smuts, and joined "the main attacking force . . . the South African Mounted Brigade, rough and tough, mainly Boers, equally scornful of the 'Kaffirs' against whom they would be fighting and the 'Coolies' who were on their side."[196] Struggling through the East African brush in February 1916, the Boers raided a deadly German machine-gun nest under the command of General Paul von Lettow. In the ensuing battle, "shrieking blacks . . . charged down on [the Boers] leaving six hundred dead and wounded. On [the South Africans'] flanks the 2nd Rhodesians and the 129th Baluchis stood firm. . . . The next day the Rhodesians and Baluchis exchanged compliments. To the South Africans the Baluchis returned the machine guns they had lost, together with a request 'that you do not refer to our sepoys as coolies.'"[197]

This demand was not confined to the jungles of East Africa. The historian Mario Ruiz highlights the diary of the commissioned Indian army officer Amar Singh, who noted, "I hear that in Egypt Tommies [ordinary British soldiers] have to salute Egyptian officers. Why not in India? These fellows have got a commission after all but unfortunately this right is not given to them."[198]

As the war ground to a close, Indian troops arrived in the heart of the Ottoman Arab territories. The London *Times* reported in October 1918 that the "infantry of the 7th Indian Division, which during the war has fought from far Tekrit to Tripoli, marched through the town [Tripoli]. The people were amazed at the condition and equipment of the splendid Seaforth Highlanders, and some of the Leicesters and Indians, artillery and sappers, were magnificent samples of Imperial troops."[199] Arab newspapers also covered the arrival of Indians and reported on their courage, with *al-Ahram* even musing that the "Germans are disappointed after the defeat they suffered at the hands of Indian soldiers and they fear confronting them because of their physical strength."[200] In Tikrit, "The bazaar was doing a great trade in cigarettes and was full of soldiers—British and Indian—buying tobacco and anything else they could get, which was very little."[201]

Many locals accepted, even preferred, Indian currency: "He [the "Arab"] seems to be accepting our presence with equanimity, if without enthusiasm, and it says a great deal for our reputation that Indian paper money is positively sought after."[202]

As the historian Dina Rizk Khoury shows, it is also possible to trace the formative experience of Iraqi Arabs interned as Indian POWs. Some Arab prisoners were successfully recruited from Sumerpur camp—between Delhi and Bombay—to join the Arab revolt, ultimately facilitating Faysal's transition into Iraq. Turkish POWs, by contrast, were separately interned in Thayetmoyo in Upper Burma, where they languished: "By early March of 1917, the International Committee of the Red Cross found 3,369 Ottoman prisoners of war in Sumerpur, 2,734 of them from Iraq. The number of Ottoman prisoners of war in Thayetmoyo was 3,591, although there is no indication of how many were from Iraq. After 1917, some of the Ottoman prisoners of war were interned in Egypt, while the camps in India took in 2,300 more prisoners after the fall of Baghdad in March of 1917."[203]

Dina Khoury traces the long arc of imprisonment of Mahmud al-Shaykhli. "Taken prisoner in Kut al-Zayn on the 17th of November 1914, only 10 days after the British landed in Fao [until] April 1919."[204] Al-Shaykhli kept a detailed diary as he passed from prison camp to prison camp: "[H]is journey into India . . . was a harbinger of the new world order and al-Shaykhli's, as well as Iraq's, place in it. From the beginning of his imprisonment, al-Shaykhli came across what he perceived as a contradiction: colonized dark-skinned people fighting the colonizers' war."[205] While al-Shaykhli was impressed by Britain's modern administration of India, "he remained acutely aware of the division between European colonizer and the colonized. For example, he commented on the divisions in the British army between officers, primarily white, and ordinary Indian soldiers."[206] Such experiences affected identity formation among Indian and Arab soldiers.

In the Great War, South Asians were critical to Triple Entente victories around the Gulf, in Palestine, and throughout Greater Syria. This fact alone justifies paying increased attention to the Indians who fought in the Middle East, especially when compared to the enormous scholarship devoted to their European counterparts. Set aside their military contributions, however, and an additional rationale for studying these South Asians emerges. By traveling across the Indian Ocean and into the Middle East, these men experienced new worlds and new people. In Palestine they fought with the

Arab Revolt; in Mesopotamia they suffered among riverine tribes; on Gallipoli they charged Ottoman Turks; and in Cairo they experienced cosmopolitan urbanites. A diverse array of Indians encountered an equally diverse group of Middle Easterners for four intensive years, deepening and broadening a long-standing connection between the two regions. Thus, as the Middle East transitioned into its postwar era, its interactions and experiences with South Asia became an important part of its historical memory.

CHAPTER SEVEN

Cooperation and Disaffection

IN HER NOVEL *Shirwal Barhum,* Nadiya al-Ghazzi tells us about a seventeen-year-old conscript, Muhyiddin Talib, who was taken from Damascus to the front with other youth in 1917, never to be heard from again. Long after the war had ended, after his parents had lost all hope of seeing him again, a man arrived barefoot on camel in their village in 1940, and threw himself on the ground. His father, who was still alive, did not recognize him at first, especially since Muhyiddin now spoke with a Yemeni accent and had to gesture to be fully understood. After Muhyiddin's dramatic return, "He settled in his town and never left."[1]

Home was the point of reference, especially for those experiencing dislocation, resettlement, or disruption in the aftermath of the war. The yearning for the familiar was so strong during the war that many other soldiers insisted on returning home, even if only to die. We saw how Hanna Mina, in his novel *Fragments of Memory,* described his uncle, a conscript in the Ottoman army, fleeing across mountains through snow on his last legs, coughing and burning with fever, only to reach his family: "He threw himself upon the bed from which he did not rise."[2]

Home was also important because, for many, World War I was not one Great War but a series of local or regional wars. Whatever local issues dominated mattered most, and caring about home was part of this broader focus on all things local. In that sense, "Great War" is a bit of a misnomer: the war was experienced more as a series of local and regional engagements than as one epic conflagration. In the provinces, and on the front lines, local dynamics and news from home mattered. Even in the larger geopolitical context, the Great War was not considered a single event. Rather, it was viewed as the historical bookend to decades of warfare. This impression of multiple wars was due in part to the fact that people centered on their own region, subregion, area, family, clan, village, town, and other affiliations that they identified with and cared about. This perception was also reinforced by the fact that the Great War followed decades of war beginning with the nineteenth-century conflicts with Russia, spanning the campaigns against rebels and tribes in the Arabian peninsula, and concluding with the Balkan Wars immediately preceding World War I. In the eleven years between September 1911 and September 1922 alone, Ottoman soldiers fought in five wars that included only twenty-two months of peace.[3] No wonder that "for the Ottomans [World War I] did not stand on its own. It was the second phase in a period of almost continuous warfare."[4]

Moreover, émigrés tended to identify with their places of origin—not necessarily with the broader region or empire. Being away sometimes caused them to sentimentalize their homeland and become even more attached to it. They sent remittances, exchanged letters with their loved ones, identified with news and poetry about their homeland, and once they had secured themselves financially, often returned to their places of origin to build large houses and claim a notable local identity. No measure of success was perhaps more satisfying than to be acknowledged as having finally succeeded in one's own original circles.

People expressed their attachment to places of origin in many ways, including in literature and fiction. Some of the best-known poetry of the war was composed by those living abroad, including the renowned poet Gibran Khalil Gibran, who in a celebrated poem entitled "Dead Are My People," wrote:

My people died from hunger, and he who
Did not perish from starvation was

Butchered with the sword; and I am
Here in this distant land, roaming
Amongst a joyful people . . . who sleep
Upon soft beds, and smile at the days
While the days smile upon them.[5]

The renowned and more critically acclaimed poet Mikhail Naima—a close associate of Gibran's in the United States–based group of *Mahjar* (Arab diaspora) poets in the early 1900s—also called on an imaginary "comrade" or brother to:

Kneel silently with me awhile
And let your heart be bowed in woe
And bleed,
As we lament our dead.

Comrade, the soldier from the wars
Comes to his fatherland again
To find him healing for his scars,
And friends to ease him of his pain.
Look not to find, if you shall come
Homeward, old comrades waiting here;
Hunger has left us none at home
To welcome us with loving cheer
Beside
The ghosts of those who died.[6]

More generally, the Great War occasioned what historian Christoph Schumann refers to as a "collective memory," mostly made up of Arab auto-biographies, which refer to shared experiences, myths, and recollections of the past and the way in which people placed their own individual experiences, however small, within that context.[7] Often people wrote memoirs for their families, transmitting the knowledge of their experiences down the generations. Although their audience was mostly a familial one, they often also appreciated their place in the larger picture of the times they lived in. For example, Schumann relays the reminiscences of the Islamic scholar Sa'id Abu l-Husn, who recalled black donkeys roaming in the courtyard of his family's home in Jabal al-Druze. Abu l-Husn remembers being told as a four-year-old toddler that these donkeys belonged to relatives fleeing the great famine in Lebanon. Seemingly trivial, the anecdote reveals the strength of kinship bonds and Druze solidarity under duress.[8]

Many of those who left recollections of the Great War were immersed in the immediacies of their lives and did not dwell on the larger regional world. In fact, as Schumann notes, some memoirs evince only a vague idea about what was going on in the world of politics. This category includes Anis Freiha's memoir, *Qabla an ansa* (Before I Forget), valuable for its depiction of a bygone world of village life in Lebanon, and the unpublished memoir of George Korkor, who opens a window into the lower-to-middle-class world of Beirut in the early 1900s. In contrast, some autobiographers were politically astute—for example, Salim Ali Salam, the influential Sunni notable and Beiruti member of the Ottoman parliament who participated in the Paris Conference of 1913. As Schumann points out, Salim Ali Salam wrote about Jamal Pasha and the Ottoman oppression of his social class during World War I, rather than about the suffering of the general population. In between these extremes are the recollections of Wadad Makdisi Cortas, who grew up in a politically informed urban middle-class milieu exposed to both Arab and Western influences. She was acutely aware of the world beyond her family, loved her country "from the bottom of my heart," was very sensitive to the sufferings of her people across social classes, and felt deeply rooted in her familial world and that of her Beirut neighborhood.[9]

In some ways, the war strengthened tradition rather than weakening it. In particular, people's sense of a communal identity—emerging from shared circumstances as much as from shared beliefs or traditions—was reinforced by the dislocations of war and later by the institutions imposed by the new Mandatory powers. Even before the victorious powers took control of the region after the war, communal identity was an important resource for surviving the war. Cooperation with other communities existed, and perhaps increased, as common catastrophes—locusts, famine, foreign troops—created closer bonds that tended to run along socioeconomic class lines. Yet paradoxically all eyewitness accounts reveal a strong sense of familial and sectarian belonging during the war and after. This is not surprising; in the great shakeups of war, people naturally look for something to hold on to.

In fact, a sense of what one might call primordial identity can be reinforced by the traumas of war. The anthropologist Fuad Khuri has shown that in modern Lebanon, primordial ties of family, clan, village, and sect are deeply affected by forced dislocations. Refugees who have to give up elements of identity tied to their places of origin cling even more to the mobile aspects of their identities—for example, religious identity.[10] In this way, sectarianism is sometimes strengthened by war. Often refugees from the Great War found support from coreligionists in the areas they fled to, which reinforced mobile identities. This is illustrated in the case of the Armenians who, after leaving their homes under traumatic conditions during World War I, received support from local and international Christian groups. Their religious identification remained undiminished during their exile. National identification also was reinforced with time for the Armenians and other war refugees, which helped them to survive and eventually rebuild their lives in the face of adversity, relocation, and reconstruction. The sheer will to survive was strengthened by a sense of belonging to a community.

The colonial troops of the British Empire, like others from other nations, were transferred from front to front and from battlefield to battlefield, suffered through unbearable temperatures and standoffs, but were also exposed to new understandings, distant worlds, and unfamiliar traditions. In their service, they developed a transnational soldiering camaraderie with other subjects of the vast British Empire. But they also became aware of their separate identities. Safely home, veterans showed pride for their countrymen in action from Gallipoli to Gaza. For many, the diversity of their experiences crystalized the distinctive signature that defined them. By the time these soldiers returned to their homelands, they possessed a heightened self-awareness that would affect the postwar political constellations. All over the Arab world, the dislocations of war reshuffled the decks of identity.

In an age of growing national consciousness, people subjected to foreign rule developed an increasingly well-defined sense of their identity. At times, they preferred any outside occupiers to their rulers. Thus, to many the Ottoman caliphate was preferable to European rule.[11] To Muslims of Algeria and of Russia, the Ottoman Empire was an ally against their French or Russian colonizers. As far away as Indonesia, some Muslims hoped the Ottoman power would be a counterbalance to Dutch colonialism.[12] To many Muslim Indians in the subcontinent, it was shameful that Muslim Arabs would oppose the Ottoman power and side with the colonizing British.

Egyptian notables were acutely aware of the power of the British even before the war, because although Egypt was under Ottoman rule officially, in reality it had been under British occupation since 1882. The treatment of Egyptians by the British in the Great War caused lasting damage in their relations. The Egyptian Labour Corps, made up of about 1.5 million conscripted Egyptians, included instances of terrible treatment, which outraged some contemporary observers. For example, one wrote: "The treatment of these Egyptians is a scandal. They talk about modern civilization and abolishing slavery yet these men have task masters paid by the British government to whip them like dogs with long leather whips. Even the British and Australians kick and bully them unmercifully."[13] Another contemporary writer conveyed similar humiliations:

> More than one Australian said that he would clear the lot out if he had his way. They treated the natives with cruelty and contempt. In the canteen in which I worked, a very good native servant was kicked and knocked about simply because he did not understand an order given him by a soldier. An educated native in the town was struck in the mouth, and had his inlaid walking stick snatched from him by a soldier who wanted it. . . . I spoke with great severity frequently to the soldiers, telling them that by their conduct they were proving themselves the enemies of England; that the Germans maltreated the enemy, but that they were attacking their own side and would make enemies. This surprised them very much. They were absolutely ignorant of the situation.[14]

In contrast to the Egyptians, the people in the lands of the eastern Mediterranean had not yet experienced direct European rule, and their immediate problem was not distant Europe but the very present Ottoman government. Under Ottoman rule, the people of Greater Syria became increasingly aware of their distinctiveness and found wartime imperial rule high handed. Alienation from the Ottoman government took place during the war at one point or another for many groups in the Arab provinces, and took many forms. The more politicized segments of the population became increasingly aware of issues larger than themselves—for example, imperial policy or shifting identities. For most, however, the wear and tear of daily life was simply exacerbated by war measures—conscription and food rationing among other things—and a heavy-handed government. These ordinary citizens simply wanted to control their day-to-day lives and have the freedom to pursue economic and other opportunities.[15] Although the majority of the population still accepted Ottoman rule, many started to question government regulations and war policies, to blame the government for the suffering they endured, and to associate their plight with Ottoman mismanagement or actual antagonism. War measures and deprivations irrevocably widened the gap between those who took orders and those who gave them.

In Iraq, continuous fighting during World War I alienated the population from both the Ottomans and the British. Minority communities suffered as the Ottomans deported Christians and Jews suspected of supporting the British. Nor were wealthy and respected Sunni and Shi'i Iraqis spared; they were also subjected to humiliation and various indignities.[16] These Iraqis, some imprisoned or exiled, lamented the British and Ottoman oppression. Many had been conscripted into the Ottoman army, fought on the Ottoman side, perhaps witnessed Ottoman mistakes in the conduct of war, deserted, or joined the enemy camp. They ended up in prison camps in Iraq, Anatolia, Egypt, India, or Burma. Some of these veterans perceived these experiences as personal traumas, but others viewed their individual suffering through the wider prism of the costs to pay for an Arab cause.[17]

Nazik Ali Jawdat, the daughter of a Circassian father and an Aleppine mother, was born in 1903 in a Circassian village in the province of Aleppo.[18] She grew up in Aleppo and in 1919 married Ali Jawdat al-Ayubi who after the independence of Iraq had a decorated political career as military governor of Aleppo, ambassador, and prime minister. Jawdat tells us that "leading up to and during the First World War, the fervor of Turkish nationalism reached Aleppo in the form of new reforms."[19] It is particularly interesting to study her account, not only because accounts of the war by women are relatively rare but also because she sympathized with the Ottoman Empire and came to believe in the "Turkification" policies that Jamal Pasha and some of her contemporaries denied[20]—and which some scholars think were applied less widely than the general myth about these policies leads us to think.[21]

Nazik Ali Jawdat recalled that in her youth the Turkish language was imposed on students. The teacher's training college for girls where she studied was created on Turkish orders, and

teaching was entirely in Turkish and we were forbidden to speak Arabic—
even during the breaks. . . . The change from Ottoman patriotism to strong
Turkish nationalism gave rise to an opposite reaction in my case; instead of
reinforcing my "Turkishness," it awakened a consciousness of my Circassian
identity which had been dormant for years. The Great Jemal Pasha, as he
was known, while visiting our art class, stopped to look at my drawing. After complimenting me, he said, "You're Turkish, aren't you, young lady?"
"No, Sir, I'm Circassian," I answered. "Well, Circassian means Turkish," he
replied.[22]

As the war continued, rumors circulated of Ottoman defeats and
treacherous Arabs who had deserted the Ottoman army to join the Arab
rebellion in the Hijaz. Nazik Ali Jawdat's sympathy was not with the rebels
("We were all frightened of these barbarous men who were said to regard
women as their inferiors"[23]) but neither did she feel as supportive of the Ottomans as she had once been, before their emphasis on Turkish identity.
She added, "I had been brought up as an Ottoman patriot, and I was one,
but now things had changed; the Ottomans were divided and killing
each other. The war had forced us—Turks, Arabs, Kurds, Circassians—to
question our identity. On which side did I belong and what was I expected
to do?"[24]

If one person can be singled out for creating this widespread alienation it
is Jamal Pasha. Most contemporary Arab accounts and others, such as that
of T. E. Lawrence,[25] are critical of Jamal Pasha and blame him for hardships that probably were caused either by Ottoman central decisions or by
the Entente powers bent on defeating the Ottomans and making them
unpopular with their subjects. The historian Mas'ud Dahir points out that
during the war Jamal Pasha's actions led all the people of Syria to call for
the end of Ottoman rule and for total independence, regardless of their differences in other facets of political life.[26] Youssef Mouawad, a Lebanese legal scholar, observes that Jamal Pasha was the most despised dignitary in
the history of Lebanon, condemned by all in the formal version of Lebanese
history. Such unanimity about him, added Mouawad, was all the more astonishing in the case of Lebanon because the country is so factionalized;
typically, it is enough for one community to side with someone for others to
take the opposite viewpoint.[27] Another author, Aziz Bek, who during the
war had been head of intelligence for the Fourth Army in Syria, began a

chapter in his history of Syria and Lebanon during World War I with a list
of vivid epithets used for the pasha:

Jamal al-Saffah! (The Blood Shedder!)
Jamal al-Zalim! (The Oppressor!)
Jamal al-Taghiya! (The Tyrant!)
Jamal Mujawiʻ al-bilad! (Who Starved the People!)
Jamal Hatik al-aʻrad! (The Violator of Women's Honor!)
Jamal! Jamal! Jamal![28]

Another anecdote from Mount Lebanon conveys the enduring negativ-
ity surrounding Jamal Pasha, even decades later. In 1957, a professor at the
American University of Beirut and his family rented a house in the village
of Brumana for a year. The professor's family discovered that the villagers
were surprised that they had rented that house, known in the village as *bayt
al-muna* ("the house of provisions"), for the villagers considered it haunted
by their ancestors who had built the house in World War I. The house belonged to the widow of Doctor Arthur Dray, an Englishman who was head
of the dental department and a member of the faculty at the Syrian Protestant College of Beirut, which in 1910 opened a school of dentistry that operated for thirty years. When the war broke out in December 1914, he and
two other British doctors on the faculty were deported from Syria with
their fellow countrymen, but were later allowed to return to Beirut so that
the medical school could continue to function and produce doctors who,
upon graduation, could be drafted into the Ottoman army. In the summer
of 1915, one midnight, Turkish police came with orders from Jamal Pasha
for Doctor Dray to proceed immediately to Jerusalem, where he was asked
to help an influential Turkish guest of the pasha who had received serious
facial wounds from a bullet fired into their carriage—probably meant for
the pasha—and was in very serious condition.[29] The operation was successful and the pasha received Dr. Dray's assurance that he would keep the attack confidential. The pasha was delighted, sent him back to Beirut with a
letter with the highest recommendation to its governor, and "thenceforth
he could not do too much for Dr. Dray, and there were even times when the
Doctor was forced to remind his 'grateful patient' that he was himself a
British patriot, and therefore an enemy of the Turk. Even this defiance,
however, only seemed to increase the Pasha's respect, and as long as he was

in power he manifested consistent friendliness to the Doctor, and through him to the College."[30]

The closeness of Dr. Dray to Jamal Pasha was what the villagers of Brumana remembered. Western sources describe the apparently benevolent work that Dr. Dray was able to accomplish due to this relationship, which began in the summer of 1916 and continued "until the American Red Cross arrived in November 1918, a month after the British occupation, to take over all the relief work in Syria."[31] Because of his relationship with Jamal Pasha, Dr. Dray was given the title to a new house (located today on the promenade that goes behind the Park Hotel from the Brumana High School to the Belvedere Hotel), as well as enough supplies of flour to pay villagers for their labor in kind. However, according to village oral tradition, people never forgave Dr. Dray or the pasha for making starving villagers work—at the height of the famine—not for money, but for a basic staple like flour that only Dr. Dray could get his hands on. Whether the famine was caused by Allied blockade or not, the inhabitants of Mount Lebanon felt particularly deprived by Jamal Pasha and also hated him for what were perceived as his other punitive policies in Syria.[32]

Immersed in the effort to survive, most people in Syria were not aware of the nuances of politics in distant Istanbul. They had no idea where Jamal Pasha stood in the eyes of his peers or how much support he had in the capital. All they knew was that Jamal Pasha was frightening and that he had been sent to the Syrian provinces with great powers in the name of the Ottoman government. Jamal Pasha was so disliked that people even criticized his personal appearance. Anis Freiha recalled that as a youth he once saw the pasha:

> I remember seeing him from a distance of two or three meters. The municipality of Hamana had prepared a feast for him in the cafe by the waterfall in Hamana. The news spread to the neighboring towns and the young people decided to go . . . to see the man whose name scared people. We reached the waterfall of Hamana towards noon and after a short while the convoy of the Pasha made its appearance. He was riding a horse and was surrounded by a number of officers who were carrying swords that dragged on the ground. He was short, with a black beard and wearing a black hat (kalpak). He looked unimpressive among his companions who were young tall men. And we heard our leader say: Let's go back lads! We thought the Pasha was a Pasha, it turns out that the Pasha is [only] a man albeit half a man![33]

Jamal Pasha spent three years in Syria, between December 1914 and December 1917,[34] which became the basis for the Ottoman campaigns against the British at the Suez Canal in 1915 and 1916 and the campaigns into western Arabia and Yemen.[35] Upon his arrival in Syria he sought to cultivate good relations with the population as he planned his Suez expedition. But as his beaten army came back across the Suez and into Palestine, and as the Arab Revolt threatened his flank on the peninsula, he toughened his Syrian policy. He replaced governors with ones he could trust and he instituted what historians have labeled a "policy of terror" against the population. Members of Arab committees who had called for autonomy for Arabs before the war and who turned to European powers and tribal leaders in Syria for support once the war started were hunted down. Some activists escaped to Egypt; others to the Druze Mountains.[36] For the general population left behind, daily life became very difficult: "The situation in Syria and Mount Lebanon rapidly deteriorated. A tax of 50 per cent was levied on personal property and one of 25 per cent on lands, sheep, cattle, camels, crops and oil. All the trees of the country were cut down and used to fuel trains. Wagons and beasts of burden were confiscated to tow artillery. The army took over many houses and quartered soldiers in them."[37]

By 1916 a Damascene informant wrote that discontent in Syria was "general and shared by all classes and creeds," and that the exactions of the Ottoman government had alienated essentially all classes.[38] The depth of the unhappiness of the population toward the Ottoman government in general and toward Jamal Pasha in particular was the result of numerous unpopular policies, including the deportation of many Palestinian families involved with the Arab nationalism movement, the exile of a great number of people to Anatolia and to Jerusalem, the establishment of courts-martial in Syria that tried and condemned many Arab leaders,[39] and the public hangings in Beirut and Damascus in 1915 and 1916.[40] The hangings took place in Beirut downtown, at "Cannons Square" or the "Burj," subsequently also known as Martyrs' Square, and in Damascus they took place at Marja Square, which also became known as Martyrs' Square.

A large number of people had been arrested over the past months. They were brought before a military tribunal that had first been set up in Beirut and then moved, in mid-December 1914, to the town of Alay in Mount Lebanon, located alongside other popular summer resorts about seventeen kilometers uphill southeast of Beirut—the first major railway stop between

Beirut and Damascus. All those accused of being involved in political associations were kept separate from other prisoners at a location at or near
the railway station. These prisoners were forbidden to smoke, to look out
from or even go near the windows, or to get in touch with anyone. Most of
them were whipped at night. One Ottoman official by the name of Uth-
man was reportedly relieved of his duties and then imprisoned because he
once allowed the prisoners to sleep on a clean bed.[41]

Cases were tried before the Alay tribunal in late 1915 and lasted until
the spring of 1916. "Thirteen of those [arrested] were sentenced to death;
forty-five others who were abroad or had escaped, to the same sentence in
absence, and a number to varying terms of imprisonment and deportation—
all of them men of standing." The first executions took place on August 20,
1915, "of the thirteen who were present to hear their death-sentence, two
were reprieved and the rest executed at dawn on the 21st of August 1915."
The eleven notables numbered ten Muslims and one Christian, and they
were taken from Alay to Beirut on August 20 and hanged by dawn of the
next day. "They came from different parts of Syria—Bairut, Baalbek,
Hama, Damascus, Jenin; and most of them were young and died well."[42]
Among the first nationalists to be arrested in 1915 were Shi'is from Jabal
'Amil.[43]

More arrests, deportations, and executions followed in late 1915; more
executions took place on May 6, 1916, when twenty-one more notables
(seventeen Muslims and four Christians) were hanged, fourteen in Beirut
and seven in Damascus. Sentences were not announced ahead of time: a
prison guard at Alay would enter the hall of the prison, read out the names
of the accused, and command them to get dressed and follow him. Those
destined for Damascus were taken by train to the city and then made to
walk to the main square. Those to be executed in Beirut were driven to the
city in carriages and taken to the main square. "A shudder shook the country," writes George Antonius in his vivid style.[44]

Trials continued, with some indicted and sometimes executed, in both
Beirut and Damascus; no fewer than seventy-one notables were condemned
to death in absentia. In addition, many families were deported and their
property confiscated. Among those who died were two brothers of the Lebanese Christian Khazin family, who were tried at Alay and hanged along
with Muslims in Beirut on June 6, 1916.[45] Those put to death in Beirut and
Damascus included dozens of prominent local figures, including several

former members of the Ottoman parliament, newspaper editors, army offi-cers, and other public figures. The numbers of those imprisoned and exiled varies; families exiled to Anatolia without trial are estimated at three hundred; the number of deportees during the war is estimated at fifty thousand.[46]

Blame for these persons' fate partly fell on the seizure of incriminating files left behind in Beirut by George Picot, then French consul-general, who left Beirut on short notice at the start of the war but expected to return soon thereafter. He had been advised by Stanley Hollis, the American consul-general in Beirut, to destroy incriminating files, but instead chose to hide them behind a false wall in the consulate, a location revealed to Jamal Pasha by scared translators at the consulate.[47] Shortly after the executions of May 6, 1916, in the name of the commander of the Fourth Army, Jamal Pasha, the government made its case by publishing several of the French documents it had seized in French, Arabic, and Turkish.[48] Lists of others who were given lengthy prison sentences were also circulated in the press.

Hanging was an established punishment long before the Great War, and it left its mark by the crudeness of its design. From the unpublished memoir of George Korkor, we have a description of one such hanging: "A criminal was hanged but I did not go to see that and no one from this area did and when the constitution was established . . . [he] was to be hanged after fif-teen years in jail and that was on Sunday morning June 6th 1909 and for that they brought a big ladder to which a rope was attached and they brought the criminal from the seraglio. The soldiers made a circle around him some on horses and some on foot and representatives from the court came and they asked for his pardon from the family of the victim who did not answer. They hung the criminal and removed the chair from under his feet and he suffocated."[49]

But the hangings of 1915 and 1916 had a special effect on the people of Syria because they saw them as a collective punishment. Nicholas Ajay gives us a detailed picture of what it felt like to be at the hanging of the eleven prisoners court-martialed in Alay and executed in Beirut. On Friday, August 20, 1915, under tight security throughout Beirut's roads and city quarters, the prisoners were first taken to the central police station to make their last testaments and then walked over to their scaffolds at Cannons Square. They were given an opportunity to speak from the platform before being hanged in front of local officials and members of the military tribunal, and some used the opportunity to proclaim their innocence in statements that are part of the legend surrounding the executions. These final statements include the last words of Muhammad Mahmasani, a graduate of the school of law in Paris and one of the founders of the secret society *al-Fatat,* who protested his innocence until the very last moment and proclaimed that he had committed no crime by loving freedom and giving his life for his Arab nation.[50] He and others among the executed are remembered for their passionate denials of guilt and assertions of patriotism on the gallows.[51]

Bodies were left suspended for some hours after the hangings. A student who happened to be walking to class found himself at the Burj, in the middle of a crowd of people who had just witnessed the hangings. He recollected decades later: "I looked up and saw them [the "martyrs"] hanging there. I almost fainted. The people were silent and depressed. I saw hatred and fear on their faces. There was no trouble but only silent protest. The Turks had filled the city with troops and would have squashed any protest instantly."[52]

In Damascus, the hanging of seven men took place at Marja Square. The square was lit up, with the gallows in its center. Unlike Beirut, the townspeople were allowed to witness the executions, which they watched in silence.[53]

The emotions created by the hangings are vividly expressed by a young Muslim resident of Jerusalem in his unpublished diary: "The government killed eleven people, but they were worth more than 11,000 people. They were killed because they demanded reforms, they were killed in Beirut . . . but no one said a word—people were afraid for their lives. The government killed the best of our young men. . . . The death of these people will be repaid. The government claimed that you are traitors, but you are not. You are loyal to your nation, country, and family."[54]

Such a reaction is confirmed by other sources, including a secret British military intelligence report from Cairo dated September 8, 1915, where the fear and anger of the local populations are described as palpable: "An American, who arrived in BEIRUT about 20th of August from DAMASCUS found the town deserted and the shops shut; when he inquired what had happened he was informed that the Government had that day hanged eleven Syrian Nationalists in the public square. The report was that eight had been hanged in ALAI, and fifteen in DAMASCUS as well. BEIRUT was very frightened, and DAMASCUS was very angry. All the hanged were civilians. Two ulema were forgiven for their extreme age, and banished to IRAK."[55]

The martyrs of May 6, 1916, have been immortalized in history textbooks,[56] and the events of the Great War and their retelling have shaped Lebanese history and provided a precious, if humanly tragic, opportunity for a communally shared history. Both Christians and Muslims suffered for a higher patriotic cause, as Ottomans were pitted against Syrians, Palestinians, and Lebanese nationals. How important that memory is varies with the time period and the interpreter, but it cannot be ignored. Nicholas Ajay is among those who consider it of the utmost importance. For his meticulous and original dissertation from 1973 on Lebanon during World War I, Ajay interviewed many who had witnessed the hangings and been affected by them. This was before the outbreak of the civil war of 1975–1990, which shook Lebanon to its core and made all previous suffering seem relatively insignificant. Writing before that cataclysm of 1975, Ajay went so far as to compare the consequence of the 1915 and 1916 hangings for the Lebanese to that of Pearl Harbor for Americans; he also equated Ottomans and modern-day Turks in ways that many historians have distanced themselves from. Although more nuance has entered the discussions, even an admission that Ajay might have overstated his point, one cannot deny the "martyr's squares" in both Beirut and Damascus and the persistent memories of the hangings of World War I.

Despite the vastly different contexts, Ajay does portray how relevant the memory of the hangings is for local history and folklore: "It is difficult to describe the profound effect the Turks' suppressive acts, and the hangings in particular, have had upon the people of Lebanon. To them, 6 May 1916 is what 7 December 1941 is to Americans. The martyrs have become not only part of the country's recorded history but also part of its oral history. Eye-witness accounts are passed on from one generation to another, with time and patriotic fervor taking their toll of accuracy. This situation has prevailed down to today and has a great influence upon the feelings of the Lebanese toward the Turks, something akin to that of the feelings of Armenians or Greeks toward the Turks. It seems every nation must have a national epic, and for Lebanon, the martyrs are an important chapter in its development."[57]

The historian Zeine Zeine was no admirer of nationalism, but even he recognized that "whatever the motives were, the consequences of Djemal

Pasha's anti-Arab policy were to widen still further the gulf between Arabs and Turks and thus to intensify the Arab struggle to obtain their independence. Indeed, it may not be an exaggeration to say that Djemal Pasha's rule in Syria was one of the determining factors which helped most of the Muslim Arab leaders to make up their minds once for all to break away completely from the Turkish Empire. After the executions of May 6, 1916, Arab nationalism gathered momentum and strength. Arab political independence and Arab national sovereignty became a tangible reality and an absolute necessity for sheer survival if for no other reason."[58]

Tarif Khalidi succinctly sums it up in an article that relies on a rich variety of autobiographical sources: "Perhaps no single political event of the war could compare with the impact of the public hangings of prominent nationalists in 1915–16, in Beirut and Damascus. The shock waves were felt throughout Greater Syria all the way to Baghdad and Arabia. Anger, horror, sullen resentment, were directed at Jamal Pasha, Commander of the Fourth Ottoman Army and Ottoman supremo in Greater Syria. Many of the 'martyrs' were personally known to our autobiographers. But these widespread feeling of grief were soon to transmute into the glum realisation that the days of the Empire were numbered. It may be that our sources reproduce in this respect a judgment formed after the events, a sort of retrojected wisdom, but these sources do nevertheless reflect a sense of nationalist rupture between Turks and Arabs, of an empire that could no longer stand firmly on all its ethnic pillars."[59]

It was Jamal Pasha whom people held responsible for their suffering, not the Ottomans in general. As Hasan Kayali has pointed out, the wartime devastation and suffering in Syria formed a centerpiece in the narratives of the successor states to Ottoman Syria, particularly Lebanon and Syria, and much of it has been blamed on Jamal Pasha.[60] In the opinion of one researcher, Jamal Pasha's policies in Syria led to a "point of no return" in relations between Arabs and Turks in that period.[61] "For many of those who had not decided to revolt [against the Ottomans]," Rashid Khalidi sums up, "Cemal Pasa made the decision for them. By hanging the best and brightest among an entire generation of Arab leaders in Syria, Lebanon and Palestine in 1915 and 1916, he gave the revolt both a number of martyrs and an impetus it would not otherwise have had."[62]

Opposite points of view do exist, of course. It is common to have different, even revisionist, interpretations of historical events and figures and this applies to Jamal Pasha as well. The fact that he arrived at the start of the war, following a period of exceptional openness that war conditions could not allow, acted against him. There was a "feverish" journalistic outburst in Greater Syria in the post-1908 period, with some thirty-five new papers established in the twelve months after the revolution and some sixty published in Beirut between 1908 and 1914, which served to accentuate Jamal Pasha's oppression of free speech when he settled in Syria. Stagnation and active suppression of the press during the war occurred elsewhere as well, and it cannot be blamed on Jamal Pasha alone. However, his arrival in Syria was also accompanied by a close monitoring of those suspected of disloyalty to the state. A large number of journalists were among those Jamal Pasha singled out for punishment as dissenters, and only a few newspapers continued to be distributed in Syria.[63]

There are historians who have recognized many of the achievements of Jamal Pasha while also noting that his policies toward Syrian notables and his execution of Arab leaders led to estrangement and alienation and radicalized officers in the Ottoman army.[64] Jamal Pasha himself defended his actions in his memoir and elsewhere. In "The Truth about the Syrian Question," he went out of his way to justify the trial and sentencing of Syrians whom he considered traitors and spoke of evidence proving the treachery of the criminals condemned and executed in Syria.[65] When he first came to Syria, he cultivated relationships with some newspaper owners and editors, and invited well-known writers to spend time with him.[66] He also tried to win over Arab reformists (whom he also referred to as Arab revolutionaries). He included them in a literary festival held in Damascus soon after his arrival, delivered a speech in which he expressed his commitment to the Arabic language and the common religion that Turks and Arabs shared, and told the leaders of the Arab reformers in the group that "Turkish and Arab ideals do not conflict." His goal in Syria was to pursue a policy of "clemency and tolerance" and to leave "no stone unturned to create unity of views and sentiments in all the Arab countries." To achieve this, he included the reformers in whatever he did and wherever he went, thus displaying "great confidence in the 'Reform' Party." He also ordered that nothing in Syria and Palestine be taken as requisition from the population—be it food, equipment, or clothing—but that everything must be paid for, a policy that was not practiced in other parts of the empire where food and other articles were simply requisitioned. He also recommended to the government that the same policy be put in place throughout the Ottoman Empire.[67]

Arab reformers had a very different interpretation of how he welcomed them. One member of the *al-Fatat* secret society, Fa'iz al-Ghusayn, left a memoir in which he describes meeting with the pasha in Damascus at the Damascus Hotel. His version is that Jamal Pasha told him right away that all of Syria had come out to welcome him, showing enthusiasm for the empire and expressing obedience and loyalty to the sultan-caliph, except for Ghusayn's group of political activists. He then ordered Ghusayn to return with another activist by the name of Sheikh Sa'adeddin. Fa'iz al-Ghusayn came back alone to meet with Jamal Pasha, and was made to wait for hours. When he explained that his colleague could not make the meeting due to illness, the pasha objected that no, the absent fellow was not sick, he was a donkey (a grave insult). The pasha left incensed, adding that he had sent for the sheikh knowing that he would not come, and with a final comment that you, young Arabs, do not blame me if I erect hanging poles and execute you. Fa'iz al-Ghusayn and his group knew that the pasha would use every opportunity to punish them, so he appealed to the governor in Damascus, who advised him to leave town. Ghusayn ended up in prison on several occasions, including at Alay, before being exiled to the town of Diyarbakır in southeastern Anatolia from which he escaped on foot. He eventually reached Iraq, went on to India, and then joined the Arab Revolt in the Hijaz.[68]

Among those who defended Jamal Pasha was Halidé Edib, who was impressed with much of what the pasha had accomplished in Syria during the war: "He restored order, which had never been so complete in Syria since he began his constructive policy of building roads, fighting disease, and opening schools. His energies were always most valuable when used for constructive purposes. Wherever he sojourned as governor the people still enjoy good roads and good public buildings and have the memory of a period of great security and public order."[69]

Another defender was Aziz Bek, who, after listing some of the pejorative titles given by the population to Jamal Pasha, wrote that he did not hang the innocent, only punished the guilty, and simply followed orders in the execution of his mission.[70] Other contemporaries were cautious in their assessment of the pasha, either out of fear or because they came to appreciate some of his accomplishments in Syria. Among them was Muhammad Kurd

Ali, the editor of the journal *al-Muqtabas* and man of letters. During the war years he became close to the establishment, and revised his originally very negative views of the Ottomans. Although he did not believe in the guilt of those arrested and executed by the government, he believed that Jamal Pasha had a positive side and was preferable to British outsiders.[71]

Foreign observers, especially Germans, also noted Jamal Pasha's merits, admiring his achievements in Greater Syria, appreciating his public works in the major Syrian cities,[72] and deeming the situation in the Syrian provinces "infinitely better" than in the Iraqi ones. One archeologist noted that what made such improvements possible was that, instead of being subjected to committees that prevented efficiency, in Syria there was "one will, one order, one work."[73] For some German contemporary observers perhaps influenced by the Ottoman-German war alliance, the hanging of Arab notables was completely warranted.[74] Contemporary analysts also point to circumstances in 1915, when the government was fiercely determined to suppress any dissent—the first Suez campaign had failed, the Gallipoli campaign had started, and the numbers of Ottoman troops stationed in Syria, Lebanon, and Palestine were inadequate because so many had been sent to various fronts.[75]

Generally, however, historians have begun to revise the negative image of the Young Turks and their era. As C. A. Bayly pointed out, Reşat Kasaba's work on communal conflict in Izmir revises stereotypes and suggests that it was international conflict and not local ethnic hatreds that divided the population.[76] As Bayly also points out, Feroz Ahmad, Hasan Kayali, and Engin Akarli are among those whose works demonstrate that the Young Turks were "essentially Ottoman patriots."[77] Whether the Young Turks tried to impose Turkish nationalism on others in their multinational empire is a subject of debate. Research by Ahmad, Kayali, Akarli, and others suggests that the Young Turks did not impose Turkification on the populations and did not have a language policy that was substantially different from that of the period of Abdulhamid II, but used centralization for purposes of integration as a safeguard against secessionist trends and planned for an Ottoman multinational imperial entity that, after 1914, they conceived of as more focused on Islam.[78] Jamal Pasha in particular expected the Ottomans to win the war and built institutions in Greater Syria premised on the idea that Ottomans would remain in control of their Arab lands in the long run. With that expectation in mind, the pasha worked

with Ottoman and German experts on a broad program of urban development and a wide range of public works—all with an eye to posterity.[79]
Some of these historians also point to the dangers of an Arab nationalist
historiography, which reduced late Ottoman policies in the Arab provinces
to a Turkish-centered agenda and ignored the ambivalence of a majority of
Arabs who felt loyal to the Ottoman Muslim state, thus essentially project-
ing onto the last two decades of the Ottoman period an unambiguously
nationalist drive more distinctive of the postwar period.[80] Clearly, the picture is not black and white, but must be shaded with nuances when one is
evaluating particular governments and individuals.

New generations of Arab historians appreciate much in the Ottoman
Empire and give the Ottomans more credit than some of their predecessors
did. The predominant view, however, remains one of weariness about the
last two decades of Ottoman history and, particularly, about the CUP's
intentions and vision. Arab historians appreciate that the challenges facing
Ottoman governments at the beginning of the twentieth century were enormous with regard to both foreign and internal threats. They acknowledge
that only some Syrians joined the opposition to the Ottomans during the
war and that their turn toward nationalism came in 1919. They also recognize that the vast majority of Arab notables and of the populace were loyal
to the Ottomans until the end of the empire, and that most of the politically conscious supporters of Arabist ideas cooperated with the Ottoman
government once it joined the war and for its duration. On the whole, however, the dominant view remains that the Young Turks' emphasis on centralization and unity for the empire was tantamount to a tendency in the
direction of Turkish nationalism, and that the CUP was simply not committed to an Ottoman vision in which Arabs and other non-Turks would be
their equal.[81]

Other historians make similar points. Scholars of Turkey and the central
Ottoman lands such as François Georgeon do mention that the Young
Turks had a policy of centralization and Turkification that alienated the
middle classes and the intellectuals in the Arab world, even though it would
be an exaggeration to conclude that the Arab provinces had turned away
completely from the empire before the war.[82] Albert Hourani mentions "the
growing division between Turks and Arabs after the Young Turk revolution
of 1908"[83] and, as he put it in his typically tactful way, "since by the time
the empire had become largely a Turco-Arab state, any attempt to empha-

size the paramountcy of the Turkish element was bound to upset the balance between them and the Arabs, and by reaction Arab nationalism gradually became explicit."[84]

World War I exacerbated the chasm between Ottoman Turks and non-Turks, especially after the start of the Arab Revolt, though the war did not create it. Reportedly Ottoman urbanites and high-level functionaries had little regard for Arab peasants, and Ottoman Turkish bureaucrats looked down upon Arab townsmen and nomads. Their reservations about Arabs were moderated by their shared religion, by respect for the role Arabs played in Islamic history, and by centuries of coexistence on many levels,[85] but some government officials and others viewed themselves as bringing civilization to what they saw as a tribal society unequal to theirs. In the assessment of the Turkish historian Şükrü Hanioğlu, "Although Arabs were of the same religion as the Turks, the Young Turks viewed them as the most inferior ethnic group of the empire."[86]

Such negative opinions of Arabs expressed by Young Turks need additional substantiation by further research, but to the degree that they existed among some high-level functionaries and others, these opinions must have been developed and spread after the Great War began, and after Arab soldiers and some Arab leaders such as Sharif Husayn deserted or joined the enemy. Arabs and others under Ottoman rule, on their end, tended to blame Ottoman Turks for shortcomings in local and regional government that they could have contributed to, and they also blamed them for past deficiencies as well as present ones.

The CUP period was a turning point. Although opposition to the CUP was not coherent, and although many Arabs believed that the Ottoman Empire was here to stay and that their differences with the government had more to do with rivalries of elites than any new ideology such as nationalism, the centralizing policies of the government weighed heavily on the Arab provinces, particularly the towns and cities, already before the Great War. Whatever reason lay behind the use of Turkish in court proceedings, in government offices, and in school curricula, the implementation of the policy of using Turkish was unpopular. Arab officers felt diminished in the Ottoman army; local officials were removed from positions of relative influence and were replaced by new ones who were not familiar with Arabic or with local customs and traditions.[87] The memoir of one Arab infantry officer in the Ottoman army in the war, Muhammad Sharif al-Faruqi, reveals his disappointment with the CUP. Born in Mosul, he went to military school in Baghdad, then to the military academy in Istanbul, and became a supporter of the CUP. After serving in the Balkan Wars and returning to Mosul in 1913, "his Arab identity was rekindled when he discovered that the CUP was anti-Arab in its orientations."[88] He joined the *al-Ahd* secret society, defected to the British side in 1915 (although he later grew disappointed with them), served as Sharif Husayn's representative in Egypt in 1916, and was dismissed a year later. He was killed in Iraq during the 1920 revolt against the British.[89]

Fear of government centralization and suspicion of its motivation for imposing new census registration, taxation, and other burdens provoked local chiefs to lead a number of mutinies in parts of the Arab provinces, particularly in Syria and Arabia in 1910 and 1911. The Druze revolted, having done so before in the Hawran area; they were again defeated, but not before lending support to uprisings by Bedouin of the Transjordan area, who, as part of their own rebellion in east Jordan, destroyed a station on the new Hijaz Railway, widely seen as emblematic of the new policies of Ottoman centralization. There were also rebellions in the region of Asir ('Asir) and in Yemen, which were provoked by traditional leaders fighting Ottoman centralization and the threat it presented to their privileges. Some Western observers have understood these rebellions to be expressions of a nationalist sentiment.[90]

It was mostly in the urban areas that educated and politicized Arab elites became concerned over government policies. In Beirut, Damascus, Tripoli, Jerusalem, Haifa, and possibly elsewhere, "there was much intellectual ferment and appreciable cultural activity reflected, immediately, in the appearance and wide circulation of dailies and magazines as well as in the many individual works on a variety of literary, theological and scientific subjects."[91] A politically aware intelligentsia enjoyed this "sustained intellectual activity,"[92] joined clubs and societies, and was "well in advance of Syrian public opinion."[93] Some belonged to Arab societies, public or secret, and called for reform and decentralization; others were public figures or writers who were concerned about what they observed. Outside the urban areas, such as in Mount Lebanon, as well as among the Lebanese emigrant communities in Egypt and elsewhere, elites called for more autonomy for the Arab provinces.[94]

Although the majority of the notables connected with Ottoman government and much of the population did not question the government, the literate Syrian population tended to be critical of it and had sympathy for Arabism, "a tendency that was reflected in public opinion."[95] As Rashid Khalidi notes, there were "a large number of Syrian, Palestinian, Cairo, and Istanbul newspapers that consistently opposed the CUP and expressed Arab nationalist sentiments."[96] By his count, there were at least twenty major newspapers in the period after 1910 that expressed such Arab nationalist sentiments. He also points out that by the time Syrian deputies who had been elected to the Ottoman parliament in 1908 ran for reelection in 1912 and again in 1914, they were in opposition to the CUP, in support of decentralization and reform, and in favor of a focus on Arabic language, culture, and history. As these notables were campaigning and "presumably had the exquisite concern for their own self-interest that politicians have in all places and all times," they must have understood that their upper-class electors shared their views.[97]

Muhammad Kurd Ali, who had his differences with the CUP, received a pardon when after 1914 the CUP adopted a lenient attitude toward its former Arab critics and toward the Arab provincial press: he then wrote more positively about the Ottomans, including Jamal Pasha's rule, and was critical of the leaders of the Arab nationalist movement. Before that, however, he had belittled Turkish culture and language and blamed the Ottomans for Arab decline.[98] Another intellectual who became critical of Ottoman supporters and enthusiastic about the Arab Revolt was Khalil al-Sakakini. Yet another was Nabih al-Azma, despite his family's ties to the Ottoman government. Azma came from a notable Damascene family and he served the government well in a department that provided the army with supplies and provisions. He supported Ottoman policies and believed that the religious link shared by Arabs and Turks was important, but eventually he concluded that the Ottoman state could not be saved.[99]

Even some with more supportive views of the Ottomans came to question the CUP—for example, Shukri al-Asali, an Arab deputy to the Ottoman parliament who in 1909 had been an ardent supporter of the CUP and a believer in a new era of Arab-Turkish cooperation. Within two years, however, he became skeptical of what could be achieved and called for Arab rights and for instruction in the Arabic language. He returned to Syria in

1911 and although he never called for Arab independence after that, he became more openly hostile to the CUP. Although in 1914 he accepted a post as a civil inspector in the province of Syria—at least in part because he needed the salary—in the end his opposition to the CUP cost him his life, when he was hanged in 1916 by Jamal Pasha. Despite his opposition to the power of the CUP and its hegemony, he never called for a revolutionary change and the end of the Ottoman Empire, but only for an affirmation of Arab identity.[100] However, few walked as thin a line between cooperating with the government and criticizing it as Shakib Arslan, a prominent Druze from the village of Shuwayfat in the mountains southeast of Beirut. He was an Ottoman loyalist before and during the war, serving in the Ottoman parliament and acting as an informal intermediary between his local peers and Jamal Pasha. He made a lot of enemies in Mount Lebanon and elsewhere for his early enthusiasm and closeness to Jamal Pasha, and was accused of being a collaborator with the pasha in the executions of Syrian activists. In his memoir and other publications, Arslan tried to defend himself and argued that he had been deeply shocked by the executions and had tried to intercede with the CUP, to no avail.[101]

Others were ambivalent in different ways. Some understood that the Ottoman state had its shortcomings, but they preferred it to the alternatives. Khalid al-Azm's father preferred a Muslim Ottoman state to the French and the British and remained loyal to the Ottomans, but he was torn between his allegiance to the Ottoman sultan and his Arab national sentiment.

Specific government policies helped a consciousness of Arab identity trickle down from politicized elites to larger segments of Arab society. The issue of language was such a policy; justifiably or not, it inflamed Arab popular opinion against the government. Although historians have established that the Young Turks did not have a particularly consistent and novel language policy or pursue deliberate language or cultural indoctrination, "opposition to the government came to be expressed in an anti-Turkish idiom by different sectors of the Arab population."[102] In particular, the Young Turks were accused of demanding that Turkish be used as the sole official language of the government and were blamed for it. In Beirut, "a furor" developed in 1910 over this matter when students, probably instigated by city residents, protested the appointment of a Turk as professor in Arabic at the state preparatory school. Likewise, Damascenes were angry that a

Turkish official was appointed as examining magistrate despite his ignorance or limited knowledge of Arabic, which he needed to discharge his
responsibilities.[103]

Also unpopular was the creation of an intelligence bureau to find out
about subjects in touch with the Entente powers or active in Arab societies;
it kept files on suspects, who were then harshly interrogated: "The suspects
under interrogation were chained and beaten until their clothing stuck to
their bodies from the dried and clotted blood. The interrogators would
pierce them with needles and cane the soles of their feet held in the falqa
[*falaqa*].[104] Hot boiled eggs would be put in their armpits. A special instrument would press the temples of those being tortured until they felt their
brains were bursting through their eye sockets. They would be given bread
and water once every two days, and they were kept awake for three successive nights. After the interrogation stage they would be put on trial."[105]

Thanks to interviews conducted by Nicholas Ajay and Antun Yammin's
two-volume study of the war, *Lubnan fi l-harb,* it is possible to know how
arrests and punishments of individuals and family members resonated in
the small societies of the cities of Syria in those days. The vivid details of the
indignities that Nakhla Pasha al-Mutran—a prominent notable from the
town of Baalbek in the Biqaʿ valley of Lebanon—had to bear tell us about
the way history is remembered.

Mutran seems to have been among the first victims of the Ottoman
clampdown on dissidents.[106] He was arrested in Damascus on November
20, on the basis of what Jamal Pasha describes as "important documents,"
which, Jamal Pasha implied, implicated Mutran in treason.[107] Yammin describes the arrest giving details that, however imprecise, convey how some
bystanders recalled it. He tells us that on the morning of January 6, 1915,
Mutran was brought to the government building in Damascus where the
governor read him the summary of his sentence and condemned him to
"penal servitude for life" for treason, especially for attempting to make
Baalbek part of Lebanon and under French protection. Mutran's sentence
was written on a piece of cloth that he was made to wear on his chest. He
was also made to wear his jacket in reverse, his hands were shackled, and a
hat made of hair was put on his head. The governor spit on him before
handing him over to an officer, who slapped him and put him in a carriage
in which were two men, each armed with a container of dirty water and
pieces of old shoe soles. The carriage took him along the streets of Damascus,

including to the entrance to the Suq al-Hamadiyya quarter, Bab Tuma, and other areas. The two men made periodic stops during which they slapped Mutran with the shoe soles and shouted at him, "The people curse you, o traitor." On its way back to the government building, the carriage went by the palace, where Jamal Pasha stayed when in Damascus. Jamal Pasha came out rolling a cigarette and looking very happy with what he saw. In the government building the prisoner was put in a dark basement room with a small chair, and was given bread and water. After twenty-five days, his relatives were allowed to see him from a distance and then he was put on a train to Aleppo. His final destination seems to have been Anatolia: an eyewitness cited by Yammin saw him on the train to Urfa, and Ajay wrote that Mutran was banished to the town of Diyarbakır.[108]

The details surrounding Mutran's death are murky. Jamal Pasha tells us that he tried to escape one night during the journey and that "he was found dead [the] next day by the guards."[109] According to Nicholas Ajay, who analyzed these events: "The circumstances of his death were never explained, but there was little or no doubt among some Lebanese that he had been the victim of political assassination."[110] The rest of his family was later deported, and his death was followed by the hanging of a Maronite priest by the name of Yusuf Hayik from Sinn al-Fil in March 1915.

Salim Ali Salam's memoir, written after 1929 (he died in 1938), confirms the growing alienation of notables. It covers the period from 1908 to 1918, when he was one of the most established Sunni Muslim notables in Beirut; his career included serving on the city's commercial court, on its municipal and administrative councils, and as a deputy for the province of Beirut in the Ottoman parliament. He was forty years old when the Young Turks came to power and, like many others, he saw their rise as an opportunity to rejuvenate the Ottoman Empire.

He supported the Ottoman Empire, but was not blind to its shortcomings. On one occasion he wrote that "it was surprising to see that the Turks were against any constructive endeavor even if that was not going to cost a cent to the treasury and to the contrary would be beneficial to it. I did not see among their people who came to us anyone who was interested in development except for two of them: Midhat Pasha and Azmi Bey."[111] Salim Ali Salam was cautious about the nationalist aspirations of Arab friends around him, but he sympathized with them and, in the words of the historian Kamal Salibi, in effect became the middleman between Arab nationalists and the Ottoman authorities. In this way, after the Italian invasion of Libya in 1911–1912 and the Balkan Wars of 1912–1913, when the empire seemed to be losing strength, he urged the local Ottoman representatives to consent to the founding of a reform society committed to decentralization; they did so at first but turned against reform by 1913. By this time, he and other Beiruti notables had gone to attend the Paris conference and an Arab congress that called for full political rights to Arabs within the Ottoman Empire on the basis of decentralization. The following year, as deputy in the Ottoman parliament, he supported the formation of an Arab bloc, and in the last session of parliament just before World War I called for public education in the Arab provinces.

After the Ottomans entered the war and Jamal Pasha was sent to Syria, Salim Ali Salam met him in Damascus and pleaded for mercy for two men who had been arrested for planning to annex areas of the Syrian districts to Mount Lebanon. The pasha reacted badly. Salim Ali Salam decided to stay out of his way and keep a low profile, despite pressure to do otherwise from some of his Arab activist friends. When several of them were arrested by Jamal Pasha and the military court was set up in Alay in 1915, Salim Ali Salam was brought there; officially he was to present testimony at the trials, but in reality he was under guard and felt like a prisoner. The pasha and the military court could find no fault with him and released him a few days before several of his Arab nationalist associates were either hanged for high treason or exiled to Anatolia. Thereafter Salim Ali Salam spent much of the war years in Istanbul as a parliamentary deputy.

Kamal Salibi takes the view that Salam was a loyal Ottoman citizen who until 1916 thought that Ottomanism and Arabism were reconcilable, at which point his alienation from the empire became more evident; at least his anger at Jamal Pasha did. Referring to the resumption of trials in Alay in 1916, he wrote that Jamal Pasha had resumed his campaign of vengeance; when summoned to meet him in Damascus and finding out that the whole train was reserved for prisoners on their way to Damascus, he wrote that when he saw them, he realized that they were going to be put to death: "I said to myself: how shall I be able to meet this butcher on the day on which he will be slaughtering the notables of the country? And how will I be able to converse with him?"[112] When reasonable and moderate politicians like Salim Ali Salam were alienated from the government, there is little doubt that a course of separation between Arabs and Turks was well under way.

Among the Christians of Greater Syria, criticism of the Ottomans was prevalent by the late years of the war if not earlier. We have as witness Bishara al-Buwari. His memoir is invaluable for the account of his service alongside the French forces and the French navy during the four years of the Great War and for the situation in Lebanon and other parts of Greater Syria. It is full of stories of Maronites as well as Muslims who chose to work for the French during the war. It is unclear how many preferred the French to the Ottomans as clearly as Buwari did, but by 1917 he felt secure enough at one point to tell the notables of Arwad Island—where he spent much time working for the French—that they should help move flour from the customs warehouse so it would not get hit by bombing, adding, "I told them how the French and the Turks differed, in that the former would compensate them and the latter would confiscate everything, and had mistreated everybody, even the women."[113]

Because soldiers were often conscripts and not volunteers, how they felt about the Ottoman government was likely to influence their political feelings and identities after the war. There is much less information about how common soldiers from the Ottoman world felt than about how German soldiers in Europe felt. However, through desertion numbers, memoirs, and reports, it is possible to infer that the Ottoman government, responsible for keeping soldiers on duty for years and years, gave cause to soldiers' complaints. Nicola Ziadeh tells us that when the Ottomans lost the war they had no time to demobilize the troops, so conscripts from Nazareth, Jenin, Damascus, and elsewhere began to return home in small groups. They "were left with their lives and had to work their way back home from Anatolia," adding that it took them about four months to reach Jenin.[114] The voice of the Turkish soldier remained "largely unheard," noted Erik Zürcher, but he added, "the one authentic expression on the part of the soldiers we do have, is contained in songs." Although some of the songs originated in earlier times and previous wars, new lyrics were added about the 1914–1918 years, mostly expressing feelings of despair. The best known of these was "Dardanelles Song," which spoke of being dumped alive in a grave.[115] More generally, "the prevailing sentiment in the lyrics of the songs is therefore nearly always that those who went on campaign had no chance of returning and that they would die in some far off desert."[116] Typical of these feelings of a wasted life and of the depth of dissatisfaction with the war were the "Yemen songs"—at least a dozen—that were popular among Ottoman troops in Syria, Palestine and Iraq.[117] Stanzas of the Yemen songs include: "Here in Yemen the waters never flow; / No surgeon comes to look after the sick; / Who falls ill there will without question die. / In Yemen I stay behind and cry." They also include criticism of the government: "Merciless rulers let their soldiers stand / For ten years in the Hejaz's sand; / Those who go will stay there till the end."[118]

So immense was the trauma of the Great War that it was bound to transform political identities after the war. Noting the tremendous numbers of people lost and dislocated during the war, Zürcher claims that the Ottoman population suffered more than the peoples of Western and Central Europe, however tragic that experience was. In his opinion: "For the Ottoman population the war experience was fundamentally different from that of the European peoples. It was part of a decade of war and the end of a process of disintegration and communal violence going on for a century. After ten years of almost continuous warfare what remained of the country was depopulated, impoverished and in ruins to a degree almost unparalleled in modern history."[119]

For much of the population, there was no glorious cause to die for, no nationalism to believe in or jingoism to mask the dislocation, mutilation, and loss inherent in war. As a result, many questioned whether the Great War was worth the suffering. Even for those elites who then or later claimed to have been politically conscious and to have favored independence from the start, the price of war was too high. Buwari's reflections on the cost of the Great War are emblematic. Thinking back on 1914 when the Ottoman government began to make every effort to enlist men, close some newspapers, and prepare for war entry, he wrote: "I concluded from all this that the [Ottomans] would enter the war on the side of Germany and that gave me hope for my country, thinking that liberation from the [Ottomans] would be one of the consequences of the war. However, at the time, I was ignorant of the number of lives that would be lost in the process. If I had been asked whether I would have accepted to see all these victims in order to achieve the liberation of my country, I would have hesitated greatly and maybe even refused to find salvation in this exorbitant price."[120]

In 1918–1919, with battlefield wounds still fresh, the Frenchman Abel Gance directed a silent film, *J'accuse*. In the climactic scene, filmed on a southern French battlefield, two thousand French soldiers on leave from the front act out the "return of the dead" in which the fallen rise from their graves, return home, and confront the living with their sacrifice. These war dead symbolized that poignant question of all wars—in this instance, the Great War: "Was it worth it?" This scene is evoked by the historian Jay Winter in his sensitive study of mourning in post–World War I Europe. He describes the scene as one of the most powerful and haunting visions of the war, and writes: "At the very end of the 1914–18 conflict, Gance's film brought to the cinema a vision of war in which the dead were the central figures. This is what turned it from a celebration of patriotic certainties into the exploration of eternal themes of love, death, and redemption."[121]

There is no equivalent cinematic production that wrestles with the impact of the war in the Ottoman territories so grippingly, but it is reasonable to extrapolate Winter's analysis to the Middle East. It was hardship that defined the Ottoman soldier's service; that and the long shadow of death obscured any ideological motivators in most soldiers' thinking about the war. Indeed, the Great War earned its name because of the unprecedented scale of destruction it wrought, and not because it served any overarching ideological purpose. In addition, the fact that the rulers were distant if not foreign (many accepted the Ottoman sultan but not his unionist war government) and disinclined to treat all equally only made it easier for people to dissociate themselves from their rulers in times of extreme duress. Referring to the end of the Ottoman era, Rashid Khalidi speaks of "the intense Arab-Turkish mistrust and ill-feeling which accompanied and followed it."[122]

Egypt was different because it faced a unique set of political circumstances. Focused on their immediate antagonist in Britain, Egyptians were less inclined to criticize the Ottomans.[123] Furthermore, once war was declared, Egyptians paid even less attention to the plight of Ottoman Arabs, since the Egyptian press was unable to report from enemy territory. Reliant on sporadic anecdotes and challenged by difficult communications, but also focused on the immediacy of British rule—at the height of its power and very much in charge of the country—Egyptians were barely affected by the Syrian hangings. Syrian refugees flooded Egypt during the war and constituted a major source of information, but local concern and criticism remained trained on Britain. Nonetheless, despite the different priorities of populations living under different foreign rule, the peoples of Egypt, Syria, and Iraq, and for that matter the rest of North Africa, had in common that the war increased tensions between them and their rulers and heightened their sensitivity to national aspirations and craving for sovereignty.

As the war progressed, British policies alienated Egyptians and strengthened Egyptian nationalism. The British had feared that their war enemies would provoke an uprising in Egypt, but nationalist anger did not surface during the war, despite much dissatisfaction among the population. There had long been nationalist sentiment in Egypt, and in the years leading up to the war it had coalesced around political parties that the British tolerated after 1906 and until 1914. However, with Egypt being the headquarters of the British war effort in the Middle East, major battles being fought on Egyptian territory, the economy in decline, and war measures exasperating the Egyptians—who had to put up with the arrests of nationalists, the outlawing of a number of political parties and newspapers, and the effective control of much of Egyptian life—feelings of resentment surged. Despite repeated prewar declarations by the British about leaving Egypt as soon as possible and despite British assurances that Egyptians would be spared front-line action, Egyptians performed corvée labor in the Egyptian Labour and Camel Transport Corps, undertaking the backbreaking, laborious tasks of constructing roads and digging trenches and thereby paving the way for the British thrust into Palestine.[124] As soon as the war ended, a national movement of new and unprecedented proportions surfaced throughout the country.

Everywhere else, national subgroups that had become more conscious of their separate identities before the war but had generally remained loyal to the Ottoman Empire changed positions during the course of the war; in postwar Syria, Palestine, and Iraq, where the political structure that had been in place for centuries collapsed and was replaced by European colonialism, nationalist sentiment mixed with other aspirations or objectives exploded onto the scene. Hopes of self-determination fueled by President Woodrow Wilson's Fourteen Points and European promises also contributed to new expectations among some of the politically conscious, who hoped for a world redrawn on the basis of national aspirations; in the case of Palestinians, expectations were raised by the 1919 King-Crane Commission to Syria, which reported that most people wanted independence.

In reality, such dreams were smashed by secret war agreements and postwar peace treaties, as well as by the reality of military occupation at the end of the war by mostly French and British colonial powers who took over much of the region. While some among the politically aware nationalists of the higher strata of Arab society felt betrayed, tribal, rural, and urban groups frustrated by the war years and the postwar foreign occupation grew restless and organized themselves. That movement was made possible by the war experience and by the enormity of its transformative effects on the Middle East. In the end, they would have to fight long and hard for decades to achieve real independence.

After the war, colonial rule was so blatant and so pervasive that opposition to it and nationalism increasingly became one and the same sentiment, superimposed on regional and other separate identities in areas where diversity and compartmentalization had dominated or been reinforced by the war years.[125] That was particularly true for the parts of the Arab world directly under colonial rule—whether relatively homogeneous populations such as in Egypt or more varied and compartmentalized such as in Syria and Iraq. But it was also true for areas not directly under Western hegemony, since Western power and influence affected policies and outcomes everywhere in the Middle East in the interwar period and helped shape the political responses and choices of Arab populations from North Africa to Mesopotamia to Arabia. As Nadine Méouchy writes, with so many actors and interests in the field, the end of the Ottoman Empire launched a period of military engagements, rebel activities, insecurity, and intense political turbulence.[126]

The colonial stronghold propelled the rise of nationalism and was felt everywhere to one degree or another and in one form or another. In Algeria calls for Muslims to be represented in the French parliament without having to give up Islamic laws of personal status were suppressed. In northern Morocco an armed resistance to French and Spanish rule was defeated in 1926; French rule in Morocco and Italian rule over Libya were extended. In the Sudan an opposition movement in the army was defeated. In Egypt British refusal to allow nationalist leaders to make a case for Egyptian independence at the peace conference ignited a general national uprising in spring 1919, the scale and likes of which had never been seen before; although it was defeated, it helped shape and articulate the nationalist agenda of the interwar years.

The unrest represented a mix of nationalistic, religious, and class concerns. It began in Cairo with student demonstrations that involved al-

Azhar, spreading to the urban poor from new slums in Cairo and spilling over to the towns of Alexandria and Tanta—where students, civil servants, and artisans led the demonstrations, although most of the damage was done by the urban poor; then Cairo's railway workers from working-class quarters went on strike. Just as the urban unrest began to settle down, rural disturbances by local and provincial notables, government employees, and peasants took place, different from place to place and with different agendas; sometimes, too, they simply amounted to pillaging of settled areas by tribal groups; some regions were more violent than others, such as the area around Minya and Asyut in upper Egypt. Farther south, other patterns of revolt and alliances emerged that differed depending on the variety of political, economic, or religious local concerns and grievances of notables, bureaucrats, or peasants.

In the regions of the former Syrian and Iraqi provinces, now divided into several states under French and British mandates—Great Britain had Transjordan, Palestine, and Iraq, while France had Syria and Lebanon—various uprisings took place. In Syria bands of irregulars raided areas controlled by the French and fighting erupted between French and Arab forces in northern Syria. This agitation was tied to the upheavals that preceded the war, for even before the war settlements, unrest had spread in many places. The historian Keith Watenpaugh shows how the urban unrest generated by the transformations of the first two decades of the twentieth century extended to the end of the war and into the interwar period, including exceptional violence near Aleppo after the Armistice of October 1918. He confirms that although the Armistice ended the war in the Middle East, civil and communal conflict persisted throughout Anatolia and northern Syria.[127] Unrest also extended to the countryside southwest of Aleppo starting in the fall of 1919.[128]

On March 7, 1920, the General Syrian Congress, dominated by Damascene notables, offered the throne of Greater Syria to Sharif Husayn's son, Faysal, and a new United Kingdom of Syria was proclaimed the next day. However, neither the British nor the French had approved of the new kingdom. Assigned the Syrian Mandate at the San Remo Conference in northwest Italy, France sprang into action. In July 1920, French General Henri Gouraud drew up an ultimatum to Faysal, who accepted its fundamental terms. Unsatisfied, General Gouraud marched on Damascus, and on July 24, 1920, met the Syrian army just west of Damascus at Maysalun. The quintessential moment in which the aspirations of an entire people were shattered by an act of colonialism occurred at that narrow mountain passage near Maysalun.

In his book *The Arabs,* the historian Eugene Rogan describes the defeat of the lightly armed Arab Muslim irregulars at the hands of a well-equipped French colonial army. Rogan brings to life the intense emotions of Maysalun by quoting from the memoirs of Sati al-Husri, the social philosopher, political activist, and pioneer theorist of Arab nationalism, then a Syrian provisional government member: "By 10 o'clock . . . we received word that the army had been defeated and the front shattered. Yusuf al-Azmah [the minister of war and commander of the armed forces] was reported to have been killed. I said no—he committed suicide at Maysalun, a true martyr!"[129]

The French proceeded to occupy Damascus, dissolve the Syrian Arab Kingdom, and evict King Faysal from the country. Headquartered in Beirut, and administered by the French High Commissioner, the French Mandate proceeded to carve out a state of Lebanon from the state of Syria. This new political constellation was firmly established by 1925, after the French defeated a rebellion in the Syrian Druze region.[130] Thereafter, despite the valiant efforts of that initial resistance force at Maysalun, Syria and Lebanon faced elements of foreign interference while managing their pluralistic societies during a century of modernization. The story of that century is a familiar one, playing out on the front pages even today, but the historical preconditions that account for that journey have been less frequently discussed.

In Palestine, under the British Mandate, special circumstances pitted the Arab and Jewish communities against one another during the interwar period and since. There, escalating Arab and Jewish protests were tied not only to British policies and local reactions but also to the stipulations of the Balfour Declaration of 1917, which famously stated: "His Majesty's Government view with favour the establishment in Palestine of a national home for the Jewish people, and will use their best endeavours to facilitate the achievement of this object, it being clearly understood that nothing shall be done which may prejudice the civil and religious rights of existing non-Jewish communities in Palestine, or the rights and political status enjoyed by Jews in any other country."[131]

In the region east of the Jordan river, from territory that also had been part of the Ottoman Syrian provinces and had witnessed most of the fighting of the Arab revolt against Ottoman rule, a newly created principality of Transjordan was set up. Officially under the British Mandate for Palestine, Transjordan had a fully autonomous governing system under the general oversight of Prince Abdallah, another of Sharif Husayn's sons. In Iraq, revolts combining tribalism, religion, and nationalism lasted from July until the end of October 1920 and were a turning point in the history of Iraq. The revolts were ultimately suppressed by the British, who decided to step back from direct administration and create a monarchy to head Iraq while they maintained the mandate. Faysal, who had been ousted from Syria, was crowned king on August 23, 1921.

In western Arabia, nationalism was practically insignificant as an ideology compared to religious identity, despite the fact that the Arab Revolt was led by Sharif Husayn ibn Ali, amir of Mecca between 1916 and 1918. During the war both Sharif Husayn and his CUP rivals sought legitimacy for their opposite sides by appealing to Islam. Although Sharif Husayn's sons were attracted to nationalist ideology, few from the Hijaz were. European influence was limited in the area and the great numbers of Muslims who came to the Hijaz from around the world for pilgrimage, learning, or business had religion in common, not ethnicity.[132] When the Arab Revolt was launched on June 10, 1916, most people supported the Sharif and his family more out of concern about Ottoman leadership and its willingness or ability to protect western Arabia than out of commitment to national ideas. Even after the war, clashes in the region were of a different nature than they were in areas where Europe was strong or nationalism challenged foreign occupation. When the war ended, Sharif Husayn proclaimed himself king for a few years until he was ousted by a rival amir, Abd al-Aziz Ibn Saud, who founded the kingdom of Saudi Arabia. Yet although the Arabian peninsula was the only part of the Arab world free from European colonialism, Britain preferred Ibn Saud to Sharif Husayn and succeeded in excluding other great powers from the peninsula. Outside of the area that became Saudi Arabia, British influence was also felt in the Gulf states and in Aden.[133]

In India, Muslims had identified with the Ottoman sultan even before the Great War and worried about Ottoman defeats in the Balkans. Until 1857 Indians had regarded the Mughal emperor as the ultimate symbol of sovereignty. The trial and deportation to Burma of the last Mughal emperor in 1858 triggered the search for an alternative locus of sovereignty among many Indian Muslims. The proclamation of Queen Victoria as Empress of India in 1877 accelerated that trend. By the turn of the twentieth century the Ottoman Sultan-Khalifa had emerged as a significant repository of temporal and spiritual sovereignty for those Muslim subjects uncomfortable with the British raj. In this period Indian pan-Islamic sentiment was such that "the mass of the Indian Muslims were worked up to a pitch of emotion and frenzy. Turkey's defeat was the defeat of Islam; its humiliation, the shame of every Muslim."[134] The Khilafat movement of 1919–1924, a pan-Islamic political protest campaign launched by Muslims to influence the British government and to protect the Ottoman Empire during the aftermath of World War I, gave focus to this sentiment. Although mainly a Muslim religious movement, this campaign became a part of the wider Indian independence movement. As Ayesha Jalal has shown, there was no necessary contradiction in the immediate aftermath of World War I between territorial Indian nationalism and extraterritorial Islamic universalism.[135] Both the Gandhian charkha (spinning wheel) and the Islamic crescent became symbols of the anticolonial mass movement that raged in India from 1919 to 1922.

The Ottoman sultan was the most important religious Muslim symbol worldwide, and many assumed that his call for jihad against the Triple Entente on November 11, 1914, was meant to make it harder for the French, British, or Russians to control their provinces with large Muslim populations. Others understood the call for jihad not as a way to agitate Muslims universally but to garner support within the Ottoman Empire for the sultan's war effort and to undermine any effort by the Entente powers to enlist support for their cause.[136] Still, the call was heard by Muslim supporters outside the empire.

Indian Muslims followed the onslaughts on Ottoman power during the Italian (1911) and Balkan Wars (1912–1913) and knew of the Ottoman defeats in World War I. With the signing of a pact on October 30, 1918, between the Ottoman Empire and Great Britain (representing the Allied powers) at the port of Mudros on the Aegean island of Lemnos, and the signing of the Treaty of Versailles on June 28, 1919, by Germany and the Allied forces, concerns mounted in India about the survival of the Ottoman caliphate. The Khilafat movement picked up steam after the Allies and the Ottoman Empire signed the Treaty of Sèvres on August 10, 1920, which downsized and divided the empire, allowing Greeks and other non-Muslim powers to acquire some of its central lands. A campaign in defense of the sultan was launched by the brothers Muhammad and Shawkat Ali, who joined forces with Mahatma Gandhi's noncooperation movement for Indian freedom, promising nonviolence in return for his support. Gandhi was willing to espouse Khilafat because he saw it primarily as an anti-British movement that provided a way to win over Muslims to the nationalist movement and to strengthen his drive to expand the Congress into a mass movement. However, the Khilafat movement suffered setbacks due to the flight of thousands of Muslim peasants from India to Afghanistan in 1920 and to the riots and a bloody outbreak among the Muslim population in south India (Malabar) in 1921, eventually collapsing when the Turkish national movement regained territory and asserted itself against Greece in 1922. The Turkish nationalists secured formal recognition of Turkey's independence and new borders in the peace treaty of Lausanne on July 23, 1923. The new Turkish National Assembly abolished the sultanate on November 4, 1922, and the caliphate on March 3, 1924, sending the last Ottoman sultan Abdulmajid II (reigned November 19, 1922–March 3, 1924) into exile along with the remaining members of the Ottoman dynasty. This marked the formal end of the Ottoman caliphate.[137] Younger Indian nationalists like Jawaharlal Nehru and Subhas Chandra Bose became great admirers of Kemal Atatürk.

Muslim Indians had demonstrated their disapproval of the Arab Revolt as soon as they heard about it. Although some historians question the military significance of a revolt of Bedouin irregulars and their supporters in a world war that involved international regular armies, others consider the Arab Revolt to have played a pivotal role in helping defeat the Ottomans in key theaters of World War I in the Middle East. There is agreement that the symbolic meaning of an Arab army led by the Protector of the Holy Places against the Ottoman sultan helped delegitimize his call for jihad. The British and the French who later ruled over large numbers of Muslim subjects in their colonies and spheres of influence understood that and valued the moral significance of the revolt.[138]

Indian Muslims also understood the danger that the revolt presented to the Ottomans. Islam was their "common denominator" and to them Islamic solidarity meant supporting the Ottoman ruler and categorically denying the Arab Revolt any legitimacy.[139] They considered the revolt an attack on Islam, particularly as they were weary of British designs on Arabia and also concerned about the safety of the holy places in western Arabia. They criticized Sharif Husayn openly at public meetings in India as early as the end of June 1916, and their hostility to him persisted such that after the war they called for keeping the sultan of Turkey as the only recognized head of the Muslim community. They were unhappy with stories of profiteering and of mistreatment of pilgrims to the holy places, and the Sharif had done nothing to reassure them.[140] By 1919, when the Khilafat movement was at its height, Indian Muslims were upset that Istanbul had been invaded by Allied forces, worried about the future of the Holy Places of Mecca and Medina, and opposed to the transfer of Palestine to Jews. They also complained that the British government of India had forced Muslims to fight the Ottomans and, in so doing, had turned Muslims into infidels; furthermore, they supported the idea that the Indian Muslims should back the Ottoman government.[141] In a letter to the *Times,* it was stated that Indian Muslims did not recognize the rulers of Hijaz as servants of God and that Indian Muslims considered the Ottoman Empire as the keystone of the Islamic world.[142] Gandhi condemned the British for breaking their pledge to respect the immunity of the holy places in Arabia and Mesopotamia and of Jeddah, and not to deprive Turkey of its capital or of its lands in Asia Minor and Thrace. In his view a British nominee had been set up in the Hijaz under the protection of British guns.[143]

When soon after the abolition of the caliphate in Turkey the Sharif accepted to be named caliph by Muslims in the Arab lands without any evident consideration for the opinion of Muslims elsewhere, this incensed Indian Muslims greatly.[144] The Sharif was unfairly accused of putting his interests above those of Islam. However, as George Antonius notes, "His acceptance of the caliphate, although hesitant and half-hearted, gave an appearance of reality to the charge and wrought havoc with his name."[145] The uproar became irrelevant as the Sharif was defeated by Ibn Saud and his Wahhabi forces and ultimately died powerless near his sons in Amman.[146]

While Indians were in the Middle East in very large numbers mostly as soldiers in the British military, Arabs were in India in much smaller numbers, primarily as prisoners of war in British camps. Hundreds among them were then recruited into the Arab Revolt, but others refused to join the revolt out of caution, loyalty to the Ottoman state, or other personal reasons.[147] There is a dearth of information on the Arab side regarding the

Indian Muslim presence in Arab lands where they served as soldiers, nurses, and in other capacities in the British war effort. This seems to be true, too, for the numbers of Arabs taken as prisoners in India and Egypt. The few memoirs and the British sources tell us little about what Arabs thought about Indians, either as fellow Muslims (when applicable) or as sympathizers with the Ottoman sultan.[148] In contrast, especially after the start of the Arab Revolt, Indians wrote extensively about Arab betrayal of the Muslim Ottoman state and at the end of the war voiced their views most forcefully through the Khilafat movement.

The variety of political scenarios that emerged at the end of the Great War suggests that the war was transformative in paradoxical ways. On the one hand, the war altered political affiliations; during the rule of the relatively unpopular Young Turks, the war detached the population from those in power, and in so doing prepared people for a world without Ottomans; at the end of the war, it closed off the option of loyalty to the Ottoman family. The war also eliminated loyalty to particular local families or clans either no longer in existence or with diminished influence, and generated or strengthened national and subnational ideologies, particularly in areas where foreign rulers ruled directly. These changes sharpened political sentiment and also focused it on the common goal of getting rid of the outsiders.

On the other hand, localism was reinforced during the war, which had long-term repercussions when new states came into being in the postwar decades. Difficulties of travel and other restrictions of war isolated subregions, forced them to be self-reliant, and strengthened their local sense of identity.[149] However, the war also made many move around, as conscripts or refugees—individuals or whole families in search of a livelihood or security, displaced often more than once for long and hard periods. They were brought face-to-face with inhabitants from other regions, and although much was similar in their social traditions, much also was different, depending on their communities (rural, urban, or tribal), ethnic groups, and social classes. In addition, the dislocations created by the war led many to yearn for their places of origin and for what set them apart from everyone else. In the short run, separatism was sharpened; in the long run, broader ideologies emerged that more or less transcended older loyalties and affiliations and invited more cohesion. There were as many scenarios as there were regions and types of rule in the Middle East.

Even when ties between regions existed, they did not result in more co-hesion in the post–world war world. The encounter of Arabs and Indians did not have any effect in the Middle East politically, although their eco-nomic, cultural, and intellectual exchanges were very important, both be-fore and after their close encounters in World War I. As C. A. Bayly has written, for centuries the Indian and the Middle Eastern worlds had been connected "by trade, faith, legends, and imaginings," so much so that "inter-regional connections may have reached their peak in the eighteenth and nine-teenth centuries, before they were fragmented as the political control of the nation-state asserted itself so strongly in the twentieth century."[150] In addi-tion, there was just too much variation in national and subnational agendas between the regions, and too wide a spectrum of traditional ethnic, social, and religious ties.

Nationalism became the dominant ideology of the next century, but it did not eradicate older ties. Where homogeneity existed before the Great War, there was a better chance to fight the colonial intruders, but where pluralism dominated, internal squabbles and divisions simmered under the surface, ready to explode. Much also depended on the quality of local leader-ship, the degree to which the colonial powers cared about particular regions, and how much these powers were willing to endure or sacrifice to continue controlling them directly. In many places, what characterized politics was less shared ideologies than what Bayly has referred to as "the explosion of ethnic nationalism and religious reaction" that thrust aside democratic liber-alism after 1916.[151]

In this way, Bedouins joined Sharif Husayn's Arab Revolt out of tribal loyalty or out of concern over local issues with the rule of the Young Turks, while supporters in the Syrian and Iraqi cities saw the revolt as a means to achieve some degree of pan-Arab independence. After the war, nationalism went its separate ways in the Arabian peninsula with Sharif Husayn's de-feat, the creation of Saudi Arabia, and the maintenance of separate princi-palities and governments.

Elsewhere, the postwar decision to divide the Ottoman territories into separate states eventually led to separate national causes.[152] The inability of those with reservations about colonial powers to unite in common causes also prepared the way to a divided century. Every effort to create pan-Arab national causes failed, because although incumbents pretended to favor pan-Arabism and manipulated pan-Arab popular sentiment among their citizens to claim regional leadership, in reality they saw calls for pan-Arabism as a threat to their power. They feared and acted on the assumption that pan-Arabism, which denied the legitimacy of artificially drawn postwar national borders, gave rival neighboring powers the right to interfere in their affairs. Internal opposition to their rule could combine with external opposition to topple them from power. These incumbent leaders' interests and the interests of the separate states created after World War I took precedence over the interests of Arabs as a whole. While the Great War helped unleash national sentiment, the postwar settlements helped defeat it, turning it into a series of separate national agendas used and manipulated by Arab leaders everywhere.

No wonder, then, that cynicism was one outcome of the Great War. The promises by the Allies to respect and support national aspirations took second place to realpolitik, and the peoples of the Middle East learned the hard way not to trust any ruler's promises. Cynicism in small doses can be useful in politics, but the massive disappointment felt after the outcome of World War I led to a depth of distrust in government that did not bode well for the rest of the century. The dominant popular attitude to politicians—foreign or local—has been one of general weariness and suspicion. There are few heroes among Arab leaders, at least none for whom there is unanimity. Coupled with an increasingly dictatorial set of what is often aptly referred to as "militarized parties and politicized armies," this skeptical attitude has made people choose to avoid political participation or to expect little from politicians other than corruption and self-serving behavior. As a result, many citizens have turned inward, accepting that they can make a difference only on the small scale of family, clan, or locality. Things have come full circle since the Great War, which created a window of opportunity for a new participatory type of politics.

Another outcome of the Great War, brought on by the final settlements, was competing claims on territory—primarily, and for the longest time, over the land of Palestine, but more recently over contested territory elsewhere. This pitted states, or groups within states, against one another. More often than not, disputes have been over competing claims of regional hegemony. Practically not one state in the Middle East comes out looking clean. The failure to resolve regional territorial claims and counterclaims as well as the continued involvement of Western powers in the disputes of the region have also undercut groups, undermined governments, and slowed down progress toward inclusive politics. Generally speaking, ethnic and religious relations have deteriorated and become more enmeshed in regional and international agendas.

The Great War was the turning point from a stable politics to a tumultuous future, and remains a dominant memory in the region even a century later. That memory, however, has evolved substantially. The historical reality of the Great War merged with subsequent political and social developments in the region—and shifting methods of commemoration—to yield a dynamic, living memory of the war.

Epilogue

War Memory

THE GREAT WAR ended in 1918 but left a complex and lasting legacy in the Middle East, quite as much as in Europe. The defeat of the last surviving precolonial empire, that of the Ottomans, did not herald the victory of nationalism, Arab or any other ilk. Vast tracts of erstwhile Ottoman Syrian provinces were carved up into mandated territories to be ruled by colonial empires, the British and the French. The forces of anticolonial nationalism would have many more battles to fight before they could be free from imperial domination. In addition to redrawing the political map of the Middle East, World War I bequeathed inheritance of the quotidian kind. It had altered the everyday lives of the people of the region.

Mariam Cortas explained this changing world in simple terms to her grandchildren: "We lived on *khubz marquq,* also known as *khubz al-saj* (thin, flat bread baked at home on a metal dome [*saj*] heated over an open flame). Later, bakeries were established, to which you could take your homemade *talami* dough (for thick, regular bread) and bake it there in wood ovens. The baker would take as his price one of each six baked loaves, and would sell them to those who needed a small amount and did not prepare the dough at home." The system was more efficient than *marquq*-making, hence the saying: "Give your bread to be baked by the baker even if he eats half of it." The word for baker was *ekmekji* (*ekmek* means "bread" in Turkish), and the baked *talami*, in contrast to *khubz marquq*, was called *khubz kmeji*. That was the term used in Mount Lebanon, subsequently replaced by *khubz arabi* (also known as pita). After World War I, large-scale dough-making tools were introduced, and bakeries started making the dough themselves, selling the bread either directly to customers or through shops. Large commercial bakeries took over from smaller neighborhood bakeries. The healthier *khubz marquq* almost vanished, found only in some of the mountain villages. In time, the commercial bakeries offered a large variety of breads with recipes mainly from France and eastern Europe. Similar European influences emerged in other skilled trades as well, such as carpentry and blacksmithing.[1]

Wadad Makdisi Cortas remembered similar everyday transformations brought about by World War I to the life she knew in Beirut. A passage of her memoir, translated into English by her daughter, reads as follows: "We would not have thought it then, but the war brought the twentieth century to Beirut. Those who gave a certain rhythm to our daily life—the potters propelling their wheels by foot amid the fragrance of wet clay; the neighborhood blacksmith and his two boys, deaf from typhus, who helped in the shop but whose great talent was kite-making; the baker, who didn't make and sell bread at all but rather baked the prepared dough that the people, without ovens, brought him; the blind man who roamed the streets singing for alms until he learned to mend chairs, at which point he had two occupations—all of those people belonged to another time."[2]

This passage captures the changes that took place in day-to-day life and society and more generally delineates how the Great War is remembered. It also provides clues to the present in the Middle East. On the political level, there is nostalgia for the bygone days of a multinational, multireligious, and multiethnic Ottoman Empire that, despite its many limitations, offered far more geographical fluidity and population mobility than is possible in today's world of guarded national borders. Precolonial empires were better able to negotiate cultural differences and multiple identities than colonial empires and their successor nation-states. Also, people knew their conventional places in society. Although this meant that they had little chance of social mobility, it also made for a world with lower expectations and fewer confrontations.

The effects of the war brought people together while also dividing them. Youssef Mouawad has observed that because famine hit Christians disproportionately, it was described from varying perspectives by authors of different religious communities. In contrast, the Ottoman executions of alleged activists by hanging in Martyrs' Square crossed religious and cultural boundaries and attained the status of a national remembrance. Similarly, the cross-sectarian criticism of Jamal Pasha acted as a unifier of society.[3]

Mostly, however, there has been sadness and bitterness about the Great War. The estimates of human loss caused by the war vary widely, but that the losses were enormous is uncontested.[4] In Greater Syria alone, perhaps half a million people died. Linda Schatkowski Schilcher has analyzed various estimates and suggests that this figure might be conservative. She also points out that George Antonius concluded in the 1930s that the "countries of the Middle East probably made the greatest proportional sacrifice of any of the belligerents in World War I."[5]

The large number of dead may have lost some of its shocking effect because of the violence that followed during the remainder of the twentieth century. Wars all over the globe, including in the Middle East, encompassed serial intraregional and interregional conflicts that have dulled people's remembrance of the Great War. Jay Winter and Antoine Prost described this process in another context: "Public expectations and preoccupations have changed; the questions posed about the First World War have been transformed by the Second World War, by the wars in Algeria and Vietnam. For our generation, attitudes to tolerable levels of violence, and to the body, patterns of consumption, and modes of living are radically different from those of a century ago."[6]

But for many in the Middle East who survived the Great War, what made it worse was that all the sacrifices were in vain. In the peace treaties that settled World War I, the victorious colonial powers divided up the region in ways that ignored natural divisions in favor of artificial borders that still cause resentment or conflict. In her classic article on Ottoman Syria during the Great War, Najwa al-Qattan wrote that in the region the war "cast a long shadow" and that its memory had "an enduring effect on the construction of identity."[7] One reason why the war had such a lasting impact was the political divisions and repercussions it created for decades to come.

At the same time, the war did not necessarily transform society; at times it reinforced the status quo. Elizabeth Thompson points out that the very horrors of war worked in favor of a reaffirmation of the values of the old social order, which were seen by some as preferable to the moral and social wreckage brought on by war. She gives examples of how women were considered to fare better when men were able to protect them, and how the continued separation of people along sectarian lines was reinforced by narratives that framed very different experiences and perceptions of the war—for example, "Christian suffering and Muslim profiteering." However, for others, as she shows, the war discredited the old social order and opened up other political options.[8]

Postwar governments were quick to take advantage of the collective war memory to produce patriotic occasions that would create or reinforce nationalist sentiment. As Winter and Prost noted with regard to Europe, in the interwar years commemorative practices became common—notably by political leaders who were "always ready to conjure up the spectre of those who died for 'us.'"[9] The authors found that while those who lived through the war were at the center of its remembrance in a period broadly defined from 1918 to 1970, in the last decades of the twentieth century people experienced commemoration as "both subject and object, both a matter of participation and of contemplation."[10] In the first period, those who had fought in the war and those who were in power during the war dominated the discourse of remembrance. They were sometimes also instrumental in how the war was depicted in textbooks, which became a source of transmission of accounts of the war, as did publications for pilgrims and tourists, paintings, and photography. Letters and cards that were written during the war sometimes ended up in print, and war poetry came to the fore, as in Britain.[11]

In the 1960s and 1970s, with the passing of the survivors and the commemoration of some major landmarks of the war, a sea change[12] took place in the study of the memory of the war in Britain, the Commonwealth states, and to some extent in France.[13] Archives were opened, collections of memoirs and other sources were published, and television series about the war were broadcast, helping to bridge the "gap between memory and history."[14] A "commemorative industry" had developed, institutionalized in school and university curricula.[15] The revival of war literature by means of novels and films in the 1980s and 1990s made the Great War "iconic, a symbol of the catastrophic character of the twentieth century as a whole." War museums, war novels, and war films all added to the legacy of remembrance.[16] Indeed, "collective remembrance is public recollection. It is the act of gathering bits and pieces of the past, and joining them together in public."[17] Significant differences do exist among countries in how they relive the past: "Since the 1970s 'memory' has been configured in a host of ways, but among them, the word connotes stories, myths, and legends ordinary people tell about the past, usually their past, but sometimes about the abstract national past. Thus the 'memory of the Great War' is the sum total of stories told about it. Now those tales are told by those without direct experience of the war or even contact with the survivors. The stories have become iconic."[18]

Both of these processes of memory—the reliving and the commemoration of the Great War—have already begun in the Middle East, but it is still a young industry. James Gelvin has shown the various ways that the short-lived Syrian kingdom of Faysal I mobilized society after the war through symbolic tributes to the war effort. It used the military, guilds, schools, and the press to celebrate war heroes or create remembrances of war ordeals and triumphs. Such celebrations served the government's national agenda as well as its search for legitimacy, but they also encouraged literary and artistic productions that created collective remembrances of the war.[19] Plays, poems, public readings, and other expressions of the arts celebrated the heroism of the population, deplored the famine and other war ordeals endured by the people, and condemned the evil acts of those like Jamal Pasha who contributed to the suffering.[20]

In the decades that followed, the remembrance of the Great War continued to find expression, including in movies. Najwa al-Qattan's scholarship includes studies of poems, novels, and other creative outputs that were inspired by or included the Great War:

> Over the course of the twentieth century, a large number of Syrian men and women and their descendants (Syrian, Lebanese, and Palestinian) committed their remembrances of the war to paper. They wrote a variety of texts—newspaper and magazine articles, histories, textbooks, memoirs, poems, popular poetry (zajal), plays, and novels. In the early 1960s, Safarbarlik, a popular motion picture on the war, opened in Beirut, and as recently as the 1990s, several Syrian works of fiction set in the war made their appearance. Although few of these works are on a literary par with more recent English-language war novels, their publication is in itself evidence of the enduring memory of the war in official as well as popular culture.[21]

As recently as 2013, Nayla Aoun Chkaiban published a novel on the hardship endured during the war in Bayt Kassine, a village in the Shuf southern district of Mount Lebanon. She tells the story of what daily life was like for people like her grandmother Marie. As Chkaiban comments, she uses the literary form of the novel to highlight Lebanon's memory of the years between 1910 and 1920, a period remembered as one of the most stressful in Lebanese history. The novel commemorates the darkening of the sky when a swarm of locusts descended on the village, foreshadowing famine, and recounts Ottoman wartime administration, how Jamal Pasha imposed himself on local government, and how much adversity the villagers—standing in for all Lebanese—endured.[22]

In *A Turkish View of Gallipoli: Çanakkale,* the authors offer a window into the experiences of soldiers.[23] At the end of the book, they quote from two different sources to show the suffering endured by soldiers at the battle of Gallipoli in May 1915. Nazim Hikmet (died 1963), described as Turkey's most famous modern poet, wrote a historical poetic saga of over seventeen thousand lines ("Human Landscapes from My Country") in the early 1940s, which "tells the stories not of prominent figures in recent Turkish history, but of many ordinary men and women."[24] The passage from Hikmet is in the voice of a Turkish war veteran who describes how he was wounded in eight places, crawled to his trench, was thrown onto a horse cart where the wounded were piled on top of each other, taken to a tent on the pier, laid on the beach with maybe a thousand other wounded, and finally loaded onto a ship bound for Istanbul and hospital.[25] The other passage is from the song "And the Band Played Waltzing Matilda," written in 1971 by Eric Bogle, a Scottish-born Australian folk singer, in which he details the gruesome ordeal of the ANZAC at Gallipoli ("the armless, the legless, the blind and insane"). The song "contains many historical inaccuracies, but nevertheless captures the barbarity and futility of war."[26]

Elizabeth Thompson brings a new dimension to the reading of the way war is remembered. The two Martyrs' Squares in central Beirut and Damascus were renamed for men, while women are practically forgotten in public memorials.[27] Men are described as heroes, while women are remembered as going crazy from hunger and misery, turning to prostitution and even, in rare and surely apocryphal cases, eating their own children to survive.[28] Yet, as Thompson points out, the private memory of the war, in which women made a tangible and courageous difference, is very different from the public one.[29] As in other wars, women stepped into roles and tasks usually filled by men while continuing to perform traditional roles and tasks. Women became heads of household and did whatever it took to keep their families fed and functioning—working in the fields and in home industries and factories.[30] Women also helped with relief efforts and other social services. Sometimes they wrote about their charitable activities during the war years. Some described how they tried in small ways from their homes to help the poor on the streets nearby; others talked about their role or their mothers' roles in relief activities; while yet others recalled their education and personal growth. Some like Mariam Cortas were very active in relief work.

The fact is that even before the war women of social standing were active outside the home, knew about the achievements of women in the rest of the Middle East and beyond, and took part more and more visibly in literate discussions and activities in public spaces.[31] In his study of Lebanon between 1870 and 1920, Akram Khater summed up the development: "Charity work, social visits, presence at public ceremonies and in public rituals were the means through which many more women—consciously or unwittingly—kept overstepping and moving the drawn lines of 'family' life and perforating the shell of domesticity."[32]

This is vividly delineated in *Qissat Asmahan,* the story of Amal al-Atrash, a singer and actress from the notable Atrash family of Jabal al-Druze who became renowned in the late 1930s and early 1940s but died young. In this book, women at the turn of the century are portrayed as feisty and standing up to authority. One of Amal's two brothers, Fuad al-Atrash (the other was the famous singer Farid al-Atrash), describes how their mother left Lebanon for Egypt, where little Amal became the famed Asmahan and her brother made a career in music. Another example of women's bravery is how during the reign of Abdulhamid II village women insisted that their men protect a woman who was in danger of being taken by Ottoman soldiers to the house of the town governor.[33]

Men are remembered mostly for their endurance or martyrdom during war, or bravery in battle.[34] However, when acts of heroism are associated with battle, it is hard to know who is a hero and who is not, because defining a hero can be very hard at times of conflict.[35] To Jamal Pasha, the men he hanged were traitors; to the families of those men, they were heroes unjustly accused of treason. To supporters of the Ottoman government during the war, those who fought in the Arab Revolt were traitors. To the Arabs who took part in the revolt, they were brave men who risked everything. To someone like Bishara Buwari, spying for the French required courage and principles; to his Ottoman overlords, he was a war criminal. To Sarkis Torossian, changing sides during the war was an act of courage in support of his family and other people who suffered at the hands of the Ottomans. To the Ottomans and their war partners, he and other deserters were wrong. Every case was singular, based on personal decisions and individual acts, yet every case was also larger than the individual involved, taking on an archetypal significance in the collective war memory. It was a window into how one lived the war and gave it meaning, while also giving it meaning to those who would remember it and interpret it for the following century.

Monuments arose, as they do after every war. Work on the remembrance of war in U.S. history has shown us how it takes time to learn from wars— how to remember them, institutionalize their legacy, and make the experience of war meaningful for future generations. Jay Winter's work on sites of memory in Europe after the Great War—on how the war was made a central and valuable part of the collective remembrance for those who lived it and remembered it, on the culture of commemoration, and on the ways in which communities find collective comfort after such a tragedy—is highly instructive. Drew Gilpin Faust's analysis of how the American Civil War caused institutions to evolve to deal with the realities of death—for example, the logistics of counting and memorializing the dead—demonstrates how war transforms the ways in which people deal with their losses. For the survivors, as Gilpin Faust so succinctly states, "death had redefined what life might be."[36]

There is some of this transformative process of remembrance for the Middle East in the Great War. Various scholars have done excellent work on how novelists, poets, playwrights, even film makers kept *safarbarlik* alive in people's memory. There is also evidence that villages created lists of the war dead; a rare insight into efforts to generate remembrance at the most local level.[37]

Youssef Mouawad thoughtfully traces how the meaning of remembrance sites has evolved for Beirut's Martyrs' Square, showing how government and opposition groups have interpreted and used the symbolism associated with the site.[38] As early as October 1918, a committee for the commemoration of martyrs of the Great War requested from the new French Mandatory government that May 6 be dedicated as the official holiday. However, the High Commissioner refused to give his consent. The matter was then brought to the Chamber of Deputies where the French had more influence and the date was designated as September 2, one day after the day chosen to celebrate independence of the new state of Greater Lebanon. "May 6 or September 2," wrote Mouawad, "each side had selected its camp"—those who wanted Greater Syria united versus those who wanted a separate Lebanon, mostly Sunnis of Beirut confronting the French Mandatory regime versus the majority of Christians in favor of it.[39]

The result was that under the French Mandate in Lebanon and Syria, there were two celebrations for the martyrs of World War I—an official celebration on September 2 and a popular celebration on May 6, the latter attracting supporters from various opposition groups to the Mandate from the hinterland to the coast.[40] The first popular celebration took place on May 6, 1925, with mostly Beiruti Muslims and others from Damascus and elsewhere. Christians also participated but it was understood to be a protest against the Mandate. This went on for about ten years, with two celebrations taking place yearly. However by 1937, and again in 1938, only May 6 remained as the official and popular celebration of Martyrs' Day. As Mouawad points out, this change was a precursor of the national pact of 1943, which brought together Sunni and Maronite notables and others. By 1944, the commemoration of May 6 was used to unite all communities and reinforce national unity. On May 6, 1960, under Lebanese president Fuad Shihab, a new monument known as Martyrs' Square was inaugurated with great pomp, as a way to unite the Lebanese divided by the 1958 crisis. Speakers emphasized the sacrifices of all the martyrs for the glory of Lebanon, without drawing attention to their sects. Over time, a succession of changes had transformed the event from a celebration that caused division to one that affirmed unity. As Mouawad notes, "the golden legend of the martyrs was the counterweight to the black legend of Jamal Pasha."[41]

The historian Albert Hourani points out that the transformations the Middle East has seen since World War I could be assessed from the change in vocabulary in the last century.[42] The world of 1914 was made of empires and their provinces. The world today is made up of nation-states and interstate unions. Sultans have been replaced by presidents of republics, imperial edicts have been replaced by referenda, the ruling class by elected officials, and advisory councils by houses of representatives and parliaments.

Yet perhaps nothing has changed more clearly in the last hundred years than the trenches of World War I, replaced by the drones of 2014. The modern Middle East is so challenging that despite considerable progress in health, education, science, and technology, the world of 1900 has its appeals, the greatest of which is that people of the region then still had hope. In the concluding stanza of his poem "Dead Are My People," Khalil Gibran acknowledges the horrendous suffering of the war, but appeals to the compassion of his people to build a more promising future:

> My People and your people, my Syrian
> Brother, are dead. . . . What can be
> Done for those who are dying? Our
> Lamentations will not satisfy their
> Hunger, and our tears will not quench
> Their thirst; what can we do to save
> Them from between the iron paws of
> Hunger? My brother, the kindness
> Which compels you to give a part of
> Your life to any human who is in the
> Shadow of losing his life is the only
> Virtue which makes you worthy of the
> Light of day and the peace of the
> Night. . . . Remember, my brother,
> That the coin which you drop into
> The withered hand stretching toward
> You is the only golden chain that
> Binds your rich heart to the
> Loving heart of God.[43]

That promising future seems very elusive; yet woven inextricably into any "golden legend" will always be the plain, yet poignant, narrative threads of people's stories. The use of the past to help shed light on the present and to shape the future will endure. What is beyond doubt is that unnamed heroes did what they could to survive difficult times and that their legacy will continue. Historians just need to be attentive to their sometimes muffled voices and, in this way, ensure that they can still be heard, not entirely silenced by the drumbeats of war.

NOTES

ACKNOWLEDGMENTS

INDEX

Notes

ANZAC   Australian and New Zealand Army Corps

CUP   Committee of Union and Progress

EEF   Egyptian Expeditionary Force

FO   United Kingdom, National Archives, London, Foreign Office

KCO   King's Commissioned Officer

MEF   Mediterranean Expeditionary Force

NCO   Non-Commissioned Officer

NWFP   North West Frontier Province

POW   Prisoner of War

VCO   Viceroy's Commissioned Officer

WO   United Kingdom, National Archives, London, War Office

INTRODUCTION

1. Wadad al-Maqdisi Qurṭas, *Dhikrayāt, 1917–1977* [Reminiscences, 1917–1977] (Beirut: Mu'assasat al-Abhath al-'Arabiyya, 1982), 21–22.

2. Ibid., 22.

3. For King Faysal's address, see Abu Khaldun Sati' al-Husri, *The Day of Maysalun: A Page from the Modern History of the Arabs* (Washington, DC: Middle East Institute, 1966), 112–114. The sentence is: "We Arabs are bound together in life, separated only in death. There is no division among us except when we are buried." A little later, he added: "I hope that every Syrian is an Arab before anything else. And I hope that everyone who speaks Arabic feels the way I do." I am grateful to Abdul-Karim Rafeq and Salim Tamari for their input.

4. For postwar politics, see Michael Provence, *The Great Syrian Revolt and the Rise of Arab Nationalism* (Austin: University of Texas Press, 2005); Elizabeth F. Thompson, *Colonial Citizens: Republican Rights, Paternal Privilege, and Gender in French Syria and Lebanon* (New York: Columbia University Press, 2000), 43–50; James L. Gelvin, *Divided Loyalties: Nationalism and Mass Politics in Syria at the Close of Empire* (Berkeley: University of California Press, 1998), 251; Adeed Dawisha, *Arab Nationalism in the Twentieth Century: From Triumph to Despair* (Princeton, NJ: Princeton University Press, 2003), 42; Keith David Watenpaugh, *Being Modern in the Middle East: Revolution, Nationalism, Colonialism, and the Arab Middle Class* (Princeton, NJ: Princeton University Press, 2006), 155.

I. A CHANGING MIDDLE EAST

1. *A League of Nations: Volume 1, 1917–1918* (pamphlet no. 4, April 1918), 173 (Boston: World Peace Foundation), http://books.google.com.

2. Andrew James McGregor, *A Military History of Modern Egypt: From the Ottoman Conquest to the Ramadan War* (Portsmouth, NH: Greenwood Publishing Group, 2006), 166. See also http://www.nationalarchives.gov.uk/battles/egypt/.

3. Albert Hourani, *A History of the Arab Peoples* (Cambridge, MA: Harvard University Press, 1991), chaps. 13–17. The Ottoman Citizenship Law of 1869 did establish the "Ottoman citizen." See Johann Büssow, *Hamidian Palestine: Politics and Society in the District of Jerusalem 1872–1908* (Leiden: Brill, 2011), 62, citing Cihan Osmanağaoğlu, *Tanzimat dönemi itibariyla omanli tabiiyyetinin (vatandaşliğinin) gelişimi* [The development of Ottoman citizenship since the Tanzimat period] (Istanbul: Legal, 2004).

4. M. E. Yapp, *The Making of the Modern Near East, 1792–1923* (London: Longman, 1987), 29–31; Charles Issawi, ed., *The Economic History of the Middle East, 1800–1914: A Book of Readings* (Chicago: University of Chicago Press, 1966), 416–429. For the growing imports of grain in the last quarter of the nineteenth and the early twentieth century (in 1910–1911, Ottomans imported twice as much cereal in value as was exported) and how this dependence had important effects during the famine of World War I, see Yapp, *Modern Near East,* 17. For a sampling of the European ports that received Egyptian cotton, see George Robins

Gliddon, *A Memoir on the Cotton of Egypt* (London: J. Madden & Co., 1841) 45–58.

5. Issawi, *Economic History*, 506. See also Abdul-Karim Rafeq, "A Different Balance of Power: Europe and the Middle East in the Eighteenth and Nineteenth Centuries," in *A Companion to the History of the Middle East*, ed. Y. Choueiri (Malden, MA: Blackwell, 2005), 229–247; Yapp, *Modern Near East*, 31–36. The best and the worst from Europe is vividly portrayed in the case of Egypt by David Landes, *Bankers and Pashas: International Finance and Economic Imperialism in Egypt* (Cambridge, MA: Harvard University Press, 1979), chaps. 3–6.

6. Issawi, *Economic History*, 506.

7. Although the name of the capital city was not officially changed from Constantinople to Istanbul until 1930, I will mostly use Istanbul as the more familiar appellation.

8. Yapp, *Modern Near East*, 25–28.

9. Ibid., 34–35. For cholera in Baghdad in 1889, see Paul Dumont, "Les Juifs, les arabes et le choléra," in *Villes ottomanes à la fin de l'Empire*, ed. P. Dumont and F. Georgeon (Paris: L'Harmattan, 1992), 153–170.

10. Yapp, *Modern Near East*, 27; Hourani, *History of the Arab Peoples*, 296; Jens Hanssen, *Fin de siècle Beirut: The Making of an Ottoman Provincial Capital* (New York: Oxford University Press, 2005), 9, et passim; Hala Fattah, "Islamic Universalism and the Construction of Regional Identity in Turn-of-the-Century Basra: Sheikh Ibrahim al-Haidari's Book Revisited," in *Modernity and Culture: From the Mediterranean to the Indian Ocean*, ed. L. Fawaz and C. A. Bayly (New York: Columbia University Press, 2002), 112–116.

11. Robert Ilbert, "Egypte 1900, habitat populaire, société coloniale," in *Etat, ville et mouvements sociaux au Maghreb et au Moyen-Orient: Actes du colloque C.N.R.S.—E.S.R.C., Paris, 23–27 mai 1986*, ed. K. Brown et al. (Paris: L'Harmattan, 1989), 271; Aïda K. Boudjikanian, "Les rôles socio-économiques et politiques des Arméniens d'Égypte au XIXe siècle," *Economie et sociétés dans l'empire ottoman (fin du XVIIIe–début du XXe siècle): Actes du colloque de Strasbourg (1er–5 juillet 1980)*, ed. J.-L. Bacqué-Grammont and P. Dumont (Paris: Centre National de la Recherche Scientifique, 1983), 441–448; Jacques Besançon, "Une banlieue du Caire: Héliopolis," *Revue de géographie de Lyon*, 33, 2 (1958): 119–151.

12. Robin Ostle, "Alexandria: A Mediterranean Cosmopolitan Center of Cultural Production," in *Modernity and Culture*, 314–329.

13. Aïda K. Boudjikanian, "Un people en exil: La nouvelle Diaspora (XIXe–XXe siècle)," *Histoire des Arméniens*, ed. Gérard Dédéyan (Toulouse: Privat, 1982), 601–670; Boudjikanian, "Les rôles socio-économiques"; Robert Ilbert, "Qui est Grec? La nationalité comme enjeu en Egypte (1830–1930)," *Relations Internationales* 54 (1988): 139–160.

14. Landes, *Bankers and Pashas,* 69. See also Robert Ilbert, "Alexandrie, cosmopolite?" in *Villes ottomanes à la fin de l'Empire,* ed. P. Dumont and F. Georgeon (Paris: L'Harmattan, 1992), 171–185; Robert Ilbert, *Alexandrie, 1830–1930: Histoire d'une communauté citadine* (Cairo: Institut Français d'Archéologie Orientale, 1996); Michael J. Reimer, "Colonial Bridgehead: Social and Spatial Change in Alexandria, 1850–1882," *International Journal of Middle East Studies* 20 (1988): 531–553; Reimer, *Colonial Bridgehead: Government and Society in Alexandria, 1807–1882* (Boulder, CO: Westview, 1997); Ostle, "Alexandria," 314–329; Reşat Kasaba, "Izmir 1922: A Port City Unravels," in *Modernity and Culture,* 209–211; Hourani, *A History of the Arab Peoples,* chap. 16; Will Hanley, "Foreignness and Localness in Alexandria, 1880–1914," Ph.D. diss., Princeton University, 2007, chaps. 1, 5–7.

15. Hanssen, *Fin de siècle Beirut;* Leila Fawaz, *Merchants and Migrants in Nineteenth-Century Beirut* (Cambridge, MA: Harvard University Press, 1983); Engin Deniz Akarli, *The Long Peace: Ottoman Lebanon, 1861–1929* (Berkeley: University of California Press, 1993).

16. Reşat Kasaba, *The Ottoman Empire and the World Economy: The Nineteenth Century* (Albany: State University of New York Press, 1988), 210; Elena Frangakis-Syrett, *The Commerce of Smyrna in the Eighteenth Century: 1700–1820* (Athens: Centre for Asia Minor Studies, 1992); Kasaba, "Izmir 1922." See also Richard G. Hovannisian, "Armenian Smyrna/Izmir," in *Armenian Smyrna / Izmir: The Aegean Communities,* ed. Richard G. Hovannisian (Costa Mesa, CA: Mazda, 2012), 1–38.

17. Kasaba, *Ottoman Empire and World Economy,* 210; Frangakis-Syrett, *Commerce of Smyrna;* Kasaba, "Izmir 1922."

18. D. K. Fieldhouse, *Western Imperialism in the Middle East 1914–1958* (New York: Oxford University Press, 2006), 9: "There evolved a new class of substantial land-owners, often closely associated with urban commerce and the professions, who became the dominant ruling class in many parts of the empire, particularly in the Arabian territories."

19. Hourani, *History of the Arab Peoples,* 295.

20. Halidé Edib, *Memoirs* (London: John Murray, 1926), 450, noted that around 1917 "there were the rich Lebanon and Beirut Christian nobility, an Arab imitation of the Parisian world; the dresses, the manners, the general bearing were of French importation." In "The First World War as a Time of Moral Failure: Its Reflections in Turkish Novels," in *The First World War as Remembered in the Countries of the Eastern Mediterranean,* ed. Olaf Farschid, Manfred Kropp, and Stephen Dähne (Beirut: Orient-Institut, 2006), 321–328, Christoph Neumann comments on the postwar corruption of *riche* elites of Istanbul and the young Turkish elite.

21. See Charles Issawi, *The Fertile Crescent, 1800–1914: A Documentary Economic History* (New York: Oxford University Press, 1988), 219; Hourani, *History*

of the Arab Peoples, 295–298, 337; Kasaba, "Izmir 1922," 211. For the first motorcar in Aleppo, see Issawi, *Economic History*, 275, who also tells us that by 1939 there were 9,000 trucks, buses, and passenger cars in Palestine, 6,300 in Lebanon, 4,100 in Syria, and 600 in Transjordan, a total of 20,000.

22. Janet L. Abu-Lughod, *Cairo: 1001 Years of the City Victorious* (Princeton, NJ: Princeton University Press, 1971).

23. Johann Strauss, "The Disintegration of Ottoman Rule in the Syrian Provinces as Viewed by German Observers," in *The Syrian Land: Processes of Integration and Fragmentation: Bilad al-Sham from the 18th to the 20th Century*, ed. T. Philipp and B. Schaebler (Stuttgart, Germany: F. Steiner, 1998), 307–329 (how German observers viewed the Syrian provinces during the Great War), especially 315 (how the Levantine element was abhorred by most Germans); Hanssen, *Fin de siècle Beirut*, 131; Neumann, "The First World War as a Time of Moral Failure," 324–326.

24. Hanssen, *Fin de siècle Beirut*, 134–135; Eugene Rogan, "Madness and Marginality: The Advent of the Psychiatric Asylum in Egypt and Lebanon," in *Outside In: On the Margins of the Modern Near East*, ed. E. Rogan (London: I. B. Tauris, 2002), 104–125; Hoda El-Saadi, "Changing Attitudes Towards Women's Madness in Nineteenth-Century Egypt," *Hawwa* 3, 3 (2005): 293–308.

25. Fieldhouse, *Western Imperialism in the Middle East 1914–1958*, 9.

26. Kamal S. Salibi, *Maronite Historians of Medieval Lebanon* (Beirut: American University of Beirut, 1959).

27. Hourani, *History of the Arab Peoples*, 339.

28. The activities of the Islamic Society for Good Causes in Beirut (Jam'iyyat al-Maqasid al-Khayriyya al-Islamiyya fi Bayrut) were expanded over time: they arranged funerals for all Muslims in Beirut (free for poor families) and gave grants to institutions, such as orphanages and the boy scouts, and to individuals. Linda Schatkowski, "The Islamic Maqased of Beirut: A Case Study of Modernization in Lebanon," M.A. thesis, American University of Beirut, Lebanon, 1969.

29. Hasan Kayali, "Wartime Regional and Imperial Integration of Greater Syria during World War I," in *The Syrian Land*, 302–303.

30. Ibid.

31. See "Encyclopedia of the Middle East: Ottoman Empire," available at http://www.mideastweb.org/Middle-East-Encyclopedia/ottoman.htm. Jewish refugees from the Spanish Inquisition established a Hebrew printing press about 1494. Armenians had a press in 1567, and Greeks in 1627. These presses were not allowed to print in Ottoman Turkish or in Arabic script, owing to objections from the religious authorities. One result of this delay was to give Greeks, Armenians, and Jews an advantage in literacy, and therefore an advantage in commerce and in having a means to preserve and propagate their culture, which was denied to Turks and Arabs. The major result was to retard the development of modern literate society,

commerce, and industry. The first Turkish printing press in the Ottoman Empire was not established until 1729. It was closed in 1742 and reopened in 1784. The press operated under heavy censorship throughout most of the Ottoman era. Elections were unknown, of course, though government decisions were usually reached by consultation of the government, provincial chiefs, and religious authorities.

32. Rashid Khalidi, "Arab Nationalism in Syria: The Formative Years, 1908–1914," in *Nationalism in a Non-National State: The Dissolution of the Ottoman Empire,* ed. W. W. Haddad and W. Ochsenwald (Columbus: Ohio State University Press, 1977), 208, 212, 234 and n. 3.

33. Hourani, *History of the Arab Peoples,* 303–304, 338; Yapp, *Modern Near East,* 203, 219–220, 236; Fruma Zachs, *The Making of Syrian Identity: Intellectuals and Merchants in Nineteenth Century Beirut* (Leiden: Brill, 2005), 154–212; Ilham Khuri-Makdisi, *The Eastern Mediterranean and the Making of Global Radicalism, 1860–1914* (Berkeley: University of California Press, 2010), chaps. 2 and 3.

34. Hasan Kayali, *Arabs and Young Turks: Ottomanism, Arabism, and Islamism in the Ottoman Empire, 1908–1918* (Berkeley: University of California Press, 1997), 44–45.

35. Ibid., chap. 1.

36. Akarli, "The Tangled Ends of an Empire and Its Sultan," in *Modernity and Culture,* 261–280; Yapp, *Modern Near East,* 134, et passim.

37. Yapp, *Modern Near East,* p. 119; Akarli, "The Tangled Ends of an Empire and Its Sultan," 158–203.

38. Akarli, "The Tangled Ends of an Empire and Its Sultan," 273, et passim; Yapp, *Modern Near East,* 134.

39. Feroz Ahmad, *The Young Turks, the Committee of Union and Progress in Turkish Politics, 1908–1914* (Oxford: Clarendon, 1969), 14. See also Kayali, *Arabs and Young Turks,* 4, et passim; Mustafa Aksakal, *The Ottoman Road to War in 1914: The Ottoman Empire and the First World War* (Cambridge: Cambridge University Press, 2008), 1–41. Yapp also points out that the Tanzimat was not a liberal movement but a bureaucratic one, with a group of bureaucrats interested in protecting their position and the empire (*Modern Near East,* 119). He notes, "In all essential lines of policy the Hamidian era was a continuation of the Tanzimat; the differences are those of emphasis, presentation and style" (179).

40. Yapp, *Modern Near East,* 192.

41. Ahmad, *The Young Turks,* 141. Ahmad notes that between the loss of Libya and of the former Balkan provinces, the Ottomans had lost about 424,000 square miles out of a total area of about 1,153,000 square miles and approximately 5 million out of a total population of about 24 million. Ibid., 152. For an analysis of the impact of the Balkan wars on Ottoman thinking and of the reasons for the Ottoman entry into the First World War, see Aksakal, *Ottoman Road to War.*

42. Ahmad, *The Young Turks*, 143. See also Kayali, *Arabs and Young Turks,* 82–96, et passim.

43. Yapp, *Modern Near East,* 210.

44. Ahmad, *The Young Turks,* 124–125; Kayali, *Arabs and Young Turks,* 93–94; Mahmoud Haddad, "West and East as Analysed by a Disappointed Arab Officer and First World War Veteran," in *The First World War as Remembered in the Countries of the Eastern Mediterranean,* 345–362.

45. Kayali, *Arabs and Young Turks,* 117, 119–122.

46. Ibid., 3–4, 113–114; Thomas Philipp, *The Syrians in Egypt, 1725–1975* (Stuttgart, Germany: Steiner, 1985), 115.

47. Ahmad, *The Young Turks,* 134–135.

48. Ibid., 135.

49. Ibid., 93.

50. Kayali, *Arabs and Young Turks,* 107–108.

51. Italians militarily supported the revolt of Idrisi of Asir in 1911. Sharif Husayn led the Ottoman expedition that stopped Ibn Sa'ud from expanding in the Arabian interior in 1910; see ibid., 108–112, chap. 5.

52. Ibid., 123–134.

53. Ibid., 131.

54. Kayali, "Wartime Regional and Imperial Integration," 295–306, quote on 302.

55. Yapp, *Modern Near East,* 208, 212; Ahmad, *The Young Turks,* 127.

56. Kayali, *Arabs and Young Turks,* 135–138.

57. Ahmad, *The Young Turks,* 126, et passim; Habib Jamaty, "Al-Qadiyyat al-arabiyya fi khamsin sana" [The Arab cause—Fifty years], published in the commemorative edition of the Egyptian-based magazine *al-Hilal* on the occasion of its fiftieth anniversary, *Golden Book of al-Hilal (1892–1942),* 115–120.

58. Kayali, *Arabs and Young Turks,* 135–138, nn. 60, 61.

59. Yapp, *Modern Near East,* 209.

60. Ahmed Emin Yalman, *Turkey in the World War* (New Haven, CT: Yale University Press, 1930), 200.

61. Kayali, *Arabs and Young Turks,* 138–142. Kayali shows that Beirut Muslims of note were eager to assert their loyalty to the Ottomans. He mentions that Salim Ali Salam, Ahmad Mukhtar Bayhum, and Ahmad Tabbara of the Beirut delegation to the Arab Congress visited Istanbul on their return from the congress and declared their loyalty to the Ottoman state and caliphate. This is particularly interesting as they, too, had grievances with the government—Salim Ali Salam, for example, who had served as vice president of the Beirut commercial court and president of the municipal council, resigned his position in the provincial administrative council when the CUP rejected the Beirut reform proposal early in 1913; see 132. See also Hanssen, *Fin de siècle Beirut,* 73–79.

62. Hourani, *History of the Arab Peoples,* 295–298, 337; Kasaba, "Izmir 1922," 211. On the religiously conservative opposition in 1910, see Ahmad, *The Young Turks,* 23.

63. Kayali, *Arabs and Young Turks,* 174.

64. Ilbert, "Egypte 1900, habitat populaire, société coloniale," 268.

65. Ibid., 270.

66. Issawi, *Economic History,* 226–247; Yapp, *Modern Near East,* 34–35. See also Akram Fouad Khater, *Inventing Home: Emigration, Gender, and the Middle Class in Lebanon, 1870–1920* (Berkeley: University of California Press, 2001).

67. Joel Beinin, *Workers and Peasants in the Modern Middle East* (New York: Cambridge University Press, 2001), 63–64.

68. Jean Vallet, *Contribution à l'étude de la condition des ouvriers de la grande industrie au Caire* (Valence, France: Imprimerie Valentinoise, 1911), 101–102.

69. Ilbert, "Egypte 1900, habitat populaire, société coloniale," 267, citing Vallet, *Contribution à l'étude,* and defining local population as applying not only to Egyptians but to other local Ottoman subjects.

70. Beinin, *Workers and Peasants,* 78 (see his masterly coverage of urban workers and the Young Turk revolution, 77–80); Khuri-Makdisi, *The Eastern Mediterranean,* chap. 5.

71. See Vallet, *Contribution à l'étude;* Khuri-Makdisi, *The Eastern Mediterranean,* 124, 134–135, et passim.

72. Edmund Burke III, "Towards a History of Urban Collective Action in the Middle East: Continuities and Change 1750–1980," in *Etat, ville et mouvements sociaux au Maghreb et au Moyen-Orient,* ed. K. Brown et al. (Paris: L'Harmattan, 1989), 47. Burke understands the action as the crowds being less motivated by the price of bread than by the weight of fiscal exactions and the usurious business dealings of certain merchants over the preceding decade.

73. Beinin, *Workers and Peasants,* 78–79; Joel Beinin and Zachary Lockman, *Workers on the Nile: Nationalism, Communism, Islam, and the Egyptian Working Class, 1882–1954* (Princeton, NJ: Princeton University Press, 1987), 48–82. Kayali (*Arabs and Young Turks,* 120) mentions that the boycott of Austrian goods in 1908 was orchestrated by an agitator with close relations to the CUP. See also Khuri-Makdisi, *The Eastern Mediterranean,* 136–146, 155–159.

74. See the insightful points made by Farhad Kazemi on the deterrents to peasant revolts in "Peasant Uprisings in Twentieth-Century Iran, Iraq, and Turkey," in *Peasants and Politics in the Modern Middle East,* ed. F. Kazemi and J. Waterbury (Miami, FL: International University Press, 1991), 100–104; see Donald Quataert, "Rural Unrest in the Ottoman Empire," in ibid., 43–44.

75. Quataert, "Rural Unrest in the Ottoman Empire," 45–46.

76. Linda Schatkowski Schilcher, "Violence in Rural Syria in the 1880s and 1890s: State Centralization, Rural Integration, and the World Market," in *Peasants and Politics,* 50–84; Khuri-Makdisi, *The Eastern Mediterranean,* 4 and n. 4.

77. Khuri-Makdisi, *The Eastern Mediterranean,* 4.

78. Hanssen, *Fin de siècle Beirut,* 268.

79. Albert Hourani, "Introduction," in *The Lebanese in the World: A Century of Emigration,* ed. A. Hourani and N. Shehadi (London: Centre for Lebanese Studies in association with I. B. Tauris, 1992), 5.

80. Issawi, *Economic History,* 271; Carole Hakim, "Shifting Identities and Representations of the Nation among the Maronite Secular Elite in the Late Ottoman Period," in *From the Syrian Land to the States of Syria and Lebanon,* ed. T. Philipp and C. Schumann (Beirut: Orient-Institut, 2004), 242–243.

81. Issawi, *Economic History,* 270. See also Andrew Arsan, " 'This Age Is the Age of Associations': Committees, Petitions, and the Roots of Interwar Middle Eastern Internationalism," *Journal of Global History* 7, 2 (2012): 166–188.

82. Beinin, *Workers and Peasants,* 64.

83. The following discussion of religion in the Middle East is taken from Leila Fawaz, *An Occasion for War: Civil Conflict in Lebanon and Damascus in 1860* (Berkeley: University of California Press, 1995), 10–13. See also Albert Hourani, "Religions," in *The Cambridge Encyclopedia of the Middle East and North Africa,* ed. Trevor Mostyn and Albert Hourani (Cambridge: Cambridge University Press, 1988), 32–37; Hourani, *Minorities in the Arab World* (Oxford: Oxford University Press, 1947), 3–6; Kamal S. Salibi, *A House of Many Mansions: The History of Lebanon Reconsidered* (London: I. B. Tauris, 1988), 5–6, chaps. 4 and 5; Fawaz, *Merchants and Migrants,* 15–16.

84. Hourani, *History of the Arab Peoples,* 242, et passim; Salibi, *Maronite Historians of Medieval Lebanon.*

85. Abdul-Karim Rafeq, "The Social and Economic Structure of Bab al-Musalla (al-Midan), Damascus, 1825–1875," in *Arab Civilization: Challenges and Responses, Studies in Honor of Constantine K. Zurayk,* ed. G. N. Atiyeh and I. M. Oweiss (Albany: State University of New York Press, 1988), 272–311; Rafeq, "The Impact of Europe on a Traditional Economy: The Case of Damascus, 1840–1870," in *Economie et société dans l'empire ottoman,* 419–432. See also Rafeq, "Arabism, Society, and Economy in Syria, 1918–1920," in *State and Society in Syria and Lebanon,* ed. Y. M. Choueiri (Exeter, UK: University of Exeter Press, 1993), 1–26; Rafeq, "Coexistence and Integration among the Religious Communities in Ottoman Syria," in *Islam in the Middle Eastern Studies: Muslims and Minorities,* ed. A. Usuki and H. Kato (Osaka: Japan Center for Area Studies, National Museum of Ethnology, 2003), 97–131.

86. Bruce Masters, "The 1850 Events in Aleppo: An Aftershock of Syria's Incorporation into the Capitalist World System," *International Journal of Middle East Studies* 22, 1 (1990): 3–20; Masters, *The Origins of Western Economic Dominance in the Middle East: Mercantilism and the Islamic Economy in Aleppo, 1600–1750* (New York: New York University Press, 1980); Moshe Ma'oz, *Ottoman Reform in Syria and Palestine, 1840–1861: The Impact of the Tanzimat on Politics and Society* (Oxford: Clarendon, 1968), 50 (noting that military expeditions were sent from time to time to curb rebellions in Iraq); Sarah Shields, *Mosul before Iraq* (Albany:

State University of New York Press, 2000), 58, 87–88; Orlando Figes, *The Crimean War: A History* (New York: Metropolitan, 2010), 429–430.

87. Akarli, *The Long Peace,* 82–84; Ussama Samir Makdisi, *The Culture of Sectarianism: Community, History, and Violence in Nineteenth-Century Ottoman Lebanon* (Berkeley: University of California Press, 2000).

88. Beinin, *Workers and Peasants,* 48–49; Ilbert, "Egypte 1900, habitat populaire, société coloniale," 269; Ilbert, *Alexandrie, 1830–1930,* vol. 2, 631.

89. Akarli, *The Long Peace,* 184–185.

90. Ahmad, *The Young Turks,* 50, 60, and other references to the "Lynch Affair"; Kayali, *Arabs and Young Turks,* 100–102.

91. Fawaz, *Merchants and Migrants,* chap. 8. Kayali (*Arabs and Young Turks,* 129) notes that the Beirut Reform Committee had two presidents: Muhammad Bayhum (Sunni Muslim) and Yusuf Sursock (Greek Orthodox Christian). In the Korkor memoir, there is mention of tensions between sects in Beirut in 1909 after the deposition of Sultan Abdulhamid II. The information pertaining to George Korkor comes from his handwritten unpublished memoir in Arabic (private collection); no title, unpaginated. Some pages are loose, and from interviews with three of his four daughters and some of their own children. I am grateful to the Tarazi and Badran families for a copy of the memoir. I am particularly grateful to Randa Baroody Tarazi for her insights and for her work on the memoir.

92. Kayali, *Arabs and Young Turks,* 174–181.

2. THE EMPIRE AT WAR

1. Hew Strachan, *The First World War: To Arms* (New York: Oxford University Press, 2001), 648; see also Dan Van der Vat, *The Ship That Changed the World: The Escape of the Goeben to the Dardanelles in 1914* (London: Hodder and Stoughton, 1985), 39–40, 95–120.

2. Strachan, *First World War,* 646; Victor Rudenno, *Gallipoli: Attack from the Sea* (New Haven, CT: Yale University Press, 2008), 6; Van der Vat, *Ship That Changed the World,* 95–97.

3. Strachan, *First World War,* 645–648; Rudenno, *Gallipoli,* 6; Van der Vat, *Ship That Changed the World,* 75–102.

4. Thomas R. Frame and Greg J. Swinden, *First In, Last Out: The Navy at Gallipoli* (Kenthurst, Australia: Kangaroo Press, 1990), 54; Van der Vat, *Ship That Changed the World,* 183–232.

5. Strachan, *First World War,* 677–678; Rudenno, *Gallipoli,* 8; Van der Vat, *Ship That Changed the World,* 118–119.

6. Peter Hart, *Gallipoli* (New York: Oxford University Press, 2011), 12–13.

7. Strachan, *First World War,* 680; Hart, *Gallipoli,* 12.

8. Feroz Ahmad, "The Late Ottoman Empire," in *The Great Powers and the End of the Ottoman Empire,* ed. M. Kent (London: George Allen and Unwin,

1984), 15–16; Mohammad Gholi Majd, *Persia in World War I and Its Conquest by Great Britain* (Lanham, MD: University Press of America, 2003), 72–74.

9. Mustafa Aksakal, *The Ottoman Road to War in 1914: The Ottoman Empire and the First World War* (Cambridge: Cambridge University Press, 2008), 103–104.

10. Ibid., 42, 4–5, 19–41 (the quote is from 42); see also Ahmad, "The Late Ottoman Empire," 15.

11. Feroz Ahmad, *The Young Turks* (Oxford: Clarendon, 1969), 123.

12. Strachan, *First World War*, 668; Aksakal, *Ottoman Road to War*, 43.

13. Strachan, *First World War*, 662; see the excellent analysis by Aksakal, *Ottoman Road to War*, 42–56.

14. Ahmad, "The Late Ottoman Empire," 14–15; Aksakal, *Ottoman Road to War*, 59–61.

15. Strachan, *First World War*, 668.

16. Justin McCarthy, *The Ottoman Peoples and the End of Empire* (London: Arnold, 2001), 95.

17. Strachan, *First World War*, 663–664.

18. Ibid., 668.

19. Ibid., 667.

20. Ibid., 651; Aksakal, *Ottoman Road to War*, 65–66.

21. Ahmad, "The Late Ottoman Empire," 16.

22. Strachan, *First World War*, 670.

23. Ibid.

24. Ahmad, "The Late Ottoman Empire," 16.

25. Strachan, *First World War*, 670.

26. B. H. Liddell Hart, *Lawrence of Arabia* (New York: Da Capo, 1989), 27. Aksakal, *Ottoman Road to War*, 109, tells us that the British confiscated the ships on August 1.

27. Liddell Hart, *Lawrence of Arabia*, 28.

28. Orhan Koloşlu, *1918, aydınlarımızın bunalım yılı: Zaferi nihai'den tam teslimiyete* [1918, the year of depression for our intellectuals: From ultimate victory to total surrender] (Istanbul: Boyut Kitapları, 2000), 15. I am grateful to Şakir Dinçşahin for the translation.

29. Strachan, *First World War*, 723.

30. Ibid., 722.

31. Ibid., 718–719.

32. Justin McCarthy, *The Ottoman Turks* (London: Addison Wesley Longman, 1997), 359.

33. Strachan, *First World War*, 723; Michael A. Reynolds, *Shattering Empires: The Clash and Collapse of the Ottoman and Russian Empires, 1908–1918* (Cambridge: Cambridge University Press, 2011), 124–127.

34. McCarthy, *Ottoman Turks*, 359.

35. Strachan, *First World War*, 724; Reynolds, *Shattering Empires*, 125.

36. McCarthy, *Ottoman Turks,* 359; see also Reynolds, *Shattering Empires,* 125.

37. Strachan, *First World War,* 723.

38. Ibid.

39. Ibid., 724.

40. Ibid.

41. Ibid., 725.

42. Ibid.

43. Ibid., 726.

44. Ibid.

45. Ibid., 728.

46. Ibid.; McCarthy, *Ottoman Turks,* 359.

47. Imanuel Geiss, "The Civilian Dimension of the War," in *Facing Armageddon: The First World War Experienced,* ed. H. Cecil and P. H. Liddle (London: Cooper, 1996), 10; McCarthy, *Ottoman Turks,* 364.

48. William Cleveland and Martin Bunton, *A History of the Modern Middle East* (Boulder, CO: Westview, 2009), 162; Majd, *Persia in World War I,* 151–152; Ronald Grigor Suny, "Writing Genocide: The Fate of the Ottoman Armenians," in *A Question of Genocide: Armenians and Turks at the End of the Ottoman Empire,* ed. R. Suny, F. Goçek, and N. Naimark (Oxford: Oxford University Press, 2011), 15–41; Taner Akçam, *The Young Turks' Crime against Humanity: The Armenian Genocide and Ethnic Cleansing in the Ottoman Empire* (Princeton, NJ: Princeton University Press, 2012); Donald Bloxham, *The Final Solution: A Genocide* (Oxford: Oxford University Press, 2009).

49. Feroz Ahmad, *Turkey: The Quest for Identity* (Oxford: Oneworld, 2003), 66.

50. Michael Hickey, *Gallipoli* (London: J. Murray, 1995), 42; Hart, *Gallipoli,* 14.

51. Roger Ford, *Eden to Armageddon* (London: Weidenfeld and Nicolson, 2009), 205.

52. Ibid. McCarthy (*Ottoman Peoples,* 99) also points to "the two forces behind the British invasion of the Gallipoli peninsula—the needs of the Russians and Winston Churchill."

53. Rudenno, *Gallipoli,* 14; Ahmad, *Turkey,* 66.

54. Hart, *Gallipoli,* 2–3, 16; Ford, *Eden to Armageddon,* 206.

55. Graham Clews, *Churchill's Dilemma* (Santa Barbara, CA: Praeger, 2010), 133–148.

56. Under the supervision of the German coastal defense specialist, the Prussian admiral Guido von Usedom, eighty-two batteries were linked to a series of fortifications on the European and Asiatic coasts overlooking the Dardanelles. These guns protected a heavy mining program higher up in the strait, featuring ten to eleven spaced lines of tethered mines. Ford, *Eden to Armageddon,* 207–208; Rudenno, *Gallipoli,* 26–27.

57. Hart, *Gallipoli,* 23–32; Rudenno, *Gallipoli,* 33–40. The *Queen Elizabeth* did not enter the strait until March 8, although she was in action well before then. Rudenno, *Gallipoli,* 45.

58. Sarkis Torossian, *From Dardanelles to Palestine: A True Story of Five Battle Fronts of Turkey and Her Allies and a Harem Romance* (Boston: Meador, 1947), 36.

59. Ibid., 43.

60. Ibid., 44.

61. Rudenno, *Gallipoli,* 43–44, 49.

62. There is still an ongoing debate as to how successful the fleet was in damaging the Ottoman defenses. Peter Hart (*Gallipoli,* 43) suggests that the forts were battered but still standing and sufficiently supplied. He also notes that the main minefield had not been reached, let alone breached, and howitzers were still firing. As a last reserve, *Goeben* waited for any ship that might have made the passage.

63. Harry Stürmer, *Two War Years in Constantinople* (New York: George H. Doran, 1917), 78.

64. Rudenno, *Gallipoli,* 55; Clews, *Churchill's Dilemma,* 275–281.

65. Martin Gilbert, *Churchill: A Life* (London: Heinemann, 1991), 306.

66. Hickey, *Gallipoli,* 101; Fewster, Vicihi Başarın, and Hatice Hürmüz Başarın, *A Turkish View of Gallipoli: Çanakkale* (Richmond, Australia: Hodja, 1985), 52.

67. Rudenno, *Gallipoli,* 68.

68. Ibid.

69. Hart, *Gallipoli,* 58.

70. Hickey, *Gallipoli,* 101; Fewster, Başarın, and Başarın, *Turkish View of Gallipoli,* 54; Rudenno, *Gallipoli,* 71; Hart, *Gallipoli,* 60–61.

71. Fewster, Başarın, and Başarın, *Turkish View of Gallipoli,* 55; see also L. A. Carlyon, *Gallipoli* (Sydney: Pan Macmillan Australia, 2001), 85.

72. Ford, *Eden to Armageddon,* 216–217.

73. Rudenno, *Gallipoli,* 69.

74. Hickey, *Gallipoli,* 20.

75. Rudenno, *Gallipoli,* 69; Hart, *Gallipoli,* 121.

76. Rudenno, *Gallipoli,* 74–76.

77. Ford, *Eden to Armageddon,* 215.

78. M. Şükrü Hanioğlu, *Atatürk: An Intellectual Biography* (Princeton, NJ: Princeton University Press, 2011), 17.

79. For quotation and mention of the type of school, see ibid., 8–23, 25. For more extensive detail of Kemal's primary school, see Vamik D. Volkan and Norman Itzkowitz, *The Immortal Atatürk: A Psychobiography* (Chicago: University of Chicago Press, 1984), 29–32. "Fully half the city's 70,000 inhabitants at the time of Ataturk's birth were Jews. Turks, numbering about 15,000, made up the second largest group, with the Greeks in third place." Volkan and Itzkowitz, *Immortal Atatürk,* 13.

80. Hanioğlu, *Atatürk,* 48–67.

81. This sentiment pervades studies of Mustafa Kemal. One example of many indicative of this attitude comes from Hanioğlu (*Atatürk,* 70–71): "As [Kemal]

once expressed it in a personal letter to a female friend, he had 'grand desires' to render extraordinary services to his homeland."

82. Patrick Kinross, *Ataturk, the Rebirth of a Nation* (Nicosia, Northern Cyprus: K. Rustem, 1981), 25.

83. Niyazi Berkes, *The Development of Secularism in Turkey* (London: Hurst, 1998), 435.

84. Kinross, *Ataturk,* 89.

85. Ibid., 90.

86. Ibid.

87. Carlyon, *Gallipoli,* 158.

88. Salim Tamari, *Year of the Locust: A Soldier's Diary and the Erasure of Palestine's Ottoman Past* (Berkeley: University of California Press, 2011), 13.

89. Carlyon, *Gallipoli,* 158.

90. Hart, *Gallipoli,* 121–122.

91. Ibid.

92. Ibid., 123.

93. Hans Kannengiesser, *The Campaign in Gallipoli* (London: Hutchinson and Co., 1927), 106.

94. Hart, *Gallipoli,* 126; Kannengiesser, *Campaign in Gallipoli,* 106–107.

95. Rudenno, *Gallipoli,* 107.

96. Hart, *Gallipoli,* 132–133, 139–141; Hickey, *Gallipoli,* 126.

97. Hart, *Gallipoli,* 132; Hickey, *Gallipoli,* 127.

98. Kannengiesser, *Campaign in Gallipoli,* 102.

99. Hart, *Gallipoli,* 133–134; Rudenno, *Gallipoli,* 80.

100. Rudenno, *Gallipoli,* 80.

101. Hickey, *Gallipoli,* 127.

102. Kannengiesser, *Campaign in Gallipoli,* 156.

103. Carlyon, *Gallipoli,* 200.

104. Andrew Mango, *Atatürk* (London: John Murray, 1999), 143.

105. Rudenno, *Gallipoli,* 81.

106. Hart, *Gallipoli,* 139.

107. Ibid., 160, 166–167; Rudenno, *Gallipoli,* 105.

108. Rudenno, *Gallipoli,* 105.

109. Ibid., 108; Carlyon, *Gallipoli,* 225–226; Hickey, *Gallipoli,* 145; Hart, *Gallipoli,* 208.

110. McCarthy, *Ottoman Peoples,* 102.

111. Hart, *Gallipoli,* 194.

112. Ibid., 195.

113. Carlyon, *Gallipoli,* 288.

114. Ibid., 260.

115. Hart, *Gallipoli,* 193.

116. Rudenno, *Gallipoli*, 153, citing C. F. Aspinall-Oglander, *Military Operations Gallipoli* (London: Imperial War Museum, 1992) (original publication, 1929).

117. Ibid.

118. Winston Churchill, *The World Crisis* (New York: Simon and Schuster, 2005), 477.

119. Rudenno, *Gallipoli*, 192–193.

120. Ibid., 193.

121. Ibid., 194.

122. Ibid., 194–195.

123. Hart, *Gallipoli*, 282.

124. Kinross, *Ataturk*, 95–96.

125. Rudenno, *Gallipoli*, 195.

126. Kinross, *Ataturk*, 102.

127. Ibid.

128. Ibid.

129. Ibid., 105–106.

130. Mango, *Atatürk*, 152.

131. Kinross, *Ataturk*, 111.

132. Ibid.

133. Rudenno, *Gallipoli*, 204.

134. Mango, *Atatürk*, 152.

135. Kinross, *Ataturk*, 106.

136. Ibid., 109; Carlyon, *Gallipoli*, 462–465.

137. Kinross, *Ataturk*, 109; Carlyon, *Gallipoli*, 465.

138. Carlyon, *Gallipoli*, 465.

139. Torossian, *Dardanelles to Palestine*, 81.

140. Rudenno, *Gallipoli*, 204.

141. Ibid., 271.

142. McCarthy, *Ottoman Peoples*, 102; McCarthy, *Ottoman Turks*, 360.

143. Torossian (*Dardanelles to Palestine*, 82) described one battle in the Dardanelles in terms that could be applied to the entire Gallipoli campaign: "Neither side had gained ground and death had the victory."

144. Stürmer, *Two War Years in Constantinople*, 78–79.

145. Ahmad, *Turkey*, 68.

146. Peter Hopkirk, *The Great Game: On Secret Service in High Asia* (Oxford: Oxford University Press, 2001), 123.

147. Ibid., 1–2.

148. Cleveland and Bunton, *Modern Middle East*, 162; Majd, *Persia in World War I*, 53–54.

149. Steven R. Ward, *Immortal: A Military History of Iran and Its Armed Forces* (Washington, DC: Georgetown University Press, 2009), 110.

150. Much of the war's chronology in the Persian theater is taken from Majd's *Persia in World War I;* in this instance, 37–38.

151. Major Roger Evans, *A Brief Outline of the Campaign in Mesopotamia* (London: Sifton, Praed and Co., 1926), 3.

152. Majd, *Persia in World War I*, 12.

153. Ward, *Immortal,* 109; Majd, *Persia in World War I,* 24–25.

154. Majd, *Persia in World War I,* 38–44.

155. Ibid., 32–36.

156. Ibid., 35–36.

157. Ibid., 58.

158. Ibid., 59.

159. Ibid., 72–74. This "emigration" is expertly described in Mansoureh Ette-hadiyyeh, "The Iranian Provisional Government," in *Iran and the First World War: Battleground of the Great Powers,* ed. T. Atabaki (London: I. B. Tauris, 2006), 9–27.

160. Majd, *Persia in World War I,* 45–47.

161. Ibid., 191.

162. A. J. Barker, *The First Iraq War, 1914–1918: Britain's Mesopotamian Campaign* (New York: Enigma, 2009), 9–10.

163. Majd, *Persia in World War I,* 60.

164. Ibid., 63–65.

165. Donald McKale, *War by Revolution: Germany and Great Britain in the Middle East in the Era of World War I* (Kent, OH: Kent State University Press, 1998), 138.

166. Ibid., 129.

167. Majd, *Persia in World War I,* 71–75.

168. Ibid., 77–81.

169. Ibid., 75.

170. Ibid.

171. Ibid., 106–115.

172. Ibid., 81–83.

173. Ibid., 87.

174. Ibid., 91–93.

175. Ibid., 95–96.

176. Ibid., 118–120, 125, 128–130, 189–216, 226–230; Ward, *Immortal,* 111.

177. Majd, *Persia in World War I,* 7, 154–156.

178. Ibid., 189, 194, 215.

179. Ibid., 2.

180. Ward, *Immortal,* 123.

181. Evans, *Brief Outline,* 4.

182. Ibid., 5.

183. Kristian Coates Ulrichsen, *The Logistics and Politics of the British Campaigns in the Middle East, 1914–22* (Basingstoke, UK: Palgrave Macmillan, 2011), 24.

184. Barker, *The First Iraq War*, 11.

185. Evans, *Brief Outline*, 6.

186. Ibid., 6–7.

187. Ibid., 7.

188. Ibid., 8–9.

189. Ibid., 7.

190. Ibid.

191. Russell Braddon, *The Siege* (London: Cape, 1969), 17.

192. J. D. Crowdy to Nora Crowdy, January 9, 1916, No. 1. Major J. D. Crowdy Collection: United Kingdom, St. Antony's College, Middle East Center Archive (hereafter Crowdy Collection).

193. J. D. Crowdy to Nora Crowdy, January 9, 1916, Basrah. Crowdy Collection.

194. Evans, *Brief Outline*, 8.

195. Ibid., 24.

196. Ibid., 13.

197. Ibid., 17.

198. Ibid.

199. Barker, *The First Iraq War*, 34–35.

200. Ibid., 34.

201. Ibid., 36–39, 50; Evans, *Brief Outline*, 24.

202. Barker, *The First Iraq War*, 49–51.

203. Youssef H. Aboul-Enein, *Iraq in Turmoil: Historical Perspectives of Dr. Ali al-Wardi, from the Ottoman Empire to King Feisal* (Annapolis, MD: Naval Institute Press, 2012), 73.

204. Barker, *The First Iraq War*, 67–68.

205. Evans, *Brief Outline*, 26–27, 35.

206. Barker, *The First Iraq War*, 81.

207. Ibid., 76.

208. Martin Swayne, *In Mesopotamia* (London: Hodder and Stoughton, 1917), 51. Martin Swayne was the pseudonym of Maurice Nicoll (1884–1953).

209. J. D. Crowdy to Nora Crowdy, September 15, 1917, Samarra. Crowdy Collection.

210. Evans, *Brief Outline*, 33, 36.

211. Ibid., 36–37; Barker, *The First Iraq War*, 85–90.

212. Barker, *The First Iraq War*, 90.

213. George Buchanan, *The Tragedy of Mesopotamia* (Edinburgh: William Blackwood and Sons, 1938), 28, 60.

214. Ibid., 27.

215. Evans, *Brief Outline*, 49.

216. Ibid., 48; Barker, *The First Iraq War*, 101–102; Braddon, *Siege*, 91.

217. Evans, *Brief Outline*, 48–49; Buchanan, *Tragedy of Mesopotamia*, 28.

218. Evans, *Brief Outline,* 49–50.

219. Buchanan, *Tragedy of Mesopotamia,* 29.

220. Barker, *The First Iraq War,* 104.

221. Evans, *Brief Outline,* 50.

222. Barker, *The First Iraq War,* 110–112.

223. Ibid., 107.

224. J. D. Crowdy to Nora Crowdy, January 9, 1916, No. 1. Crowdy Collection.

225. Barker, *The First Iraq War,* 115.

226. Ibid., 115–116.

227. Evans, *Brief Outline,* 53.

228. Barker, *The First Iraq War,* 152.

229. Ibid.

230. Ibid., 153.

231. Ibid., 154. Other units would be formed as the battle progressed, but the Seventh set out under General Youngblood and the others followed later. See ibid., 177, for an account of the Fifth Division.

232. Ibid., 156–168, 171.

233. Ibid., 207.

234. J. D. Crowdy to Nora Crowdy, January 19, 1916, Camp near Orah. Crowdy Collection.

235. Swayne, *In Mesopotamia,* 40.

236. J. D. Crowdy to Nora Crowdy, September 11, 1916, Sannaiyat Trenches. Crowdy Collection.

237. Barker, *The First Iraq War,* 213.

238. Ibid., 225.

239. Braddon, *Siege,* 220.

240. Barker, *The First Iraq War,* 235.

241. Braddon, *Siege,* 149.

242. Ibid., 255.

243. Ibid., 258.

244. Barker, *The First Iraq War,* 242.

245. Evans, *Brief Outline,* 71.

246. Buchanan, *Tragedy of Mesopotamia,* 107.

247. Evans, *Brief Outline,* 75.

248. Ibid.

249. J. D. Crowdy to Nora Crowdy, May 20, 1917, Muscat. Crowdy Collection. In 1917 Crowdy also reported that "there is now a . . . Central Power Station in Basra, which provides light for all the 'suburbs' as well as for the city itself." J. D. Crowdy to Nora Crowdy, July 15/17, 1917, Samarra. Crowdy Collection.

250. J. D. Crowdy to Nora Crowdy, April 8, 1917, Amara. Crowdy Collection.

251. Evans, *Brief Outline,* 88–89, 93, 103; Barker, *The First Iraq War,* 277–278.

252. Evans, *Brief Outline*, 115–118.

253. Barker, *The First Iraq War*, 315, 325.

254. J. D. Crowdy to Nora Crowdy, March 12, 1917, Baghdad. Crowdy Collection.

255. Barker, *The First Iraq War*, 274.

256. A. P. Wavell, *The Palestine Campaigns* (London: Constable, 1929), 26–27.

257. Ibid., 27.

258. David Nicolle, *Lawrence and the Arab Revolts* (London: Osprey, 1989), 4.

259. Jamal Pasha, *Memories of a Turkish Statesman* (New York: George H. Doran, 1922), 154.

260. Cleveland and Bunton, *Modern Middle East*, 152.

261. Wavell, *Palestine Campaigns*, 29.

262. Otto Liman von Sanders, *Five Years in Turkey* (Annapolis, MD: United States Naval Institute, 1927), 44.

263. Wavell, *Palestine Campaigns*, 31.

264. Nicolle, *Lawrence*, 6.

265. For firsthand battle descriptions and reorganization of the Sanusi tribes, see *A Soldier's Story: From Ottoman Rule to Independent Iraq; The Memoirs of Jafar Pasha Al-Askari (1885–1936)*, trans. M. Tariq al-Askari (London: Arabian, 2003), 56–60, 65, 74–77, 80–93; Ahmad, "The Late Ottoman Empire," 15–16.

266. McCarthy, *Ottoman Turks*, 359.

267. Wavell, *Palestine Campaigns*, 39–40.

268. Ibid., 43.

269. Ibid., 44–45, 47.

270. Ibid., 48–49.

271. Liddell Hart, *Lawrence of Arabia*, 42–51; Cleveland and Bunton, *Modern Middle East*, 157–160; George Antonius, *The Arab Awakening* (New York: Capricorn, 1965), 164–183.

272. Cleveland and Bunton, *Modern Middle East*, 158.

273. For action in Medina, see Antonius, *Arab Awakening*, 195–200 (quoting *al-Qibla*, the newspaper in Mecca).

274. Liddell Hart, *Lawrence of Arabia*, 65.

275. Torossian, *Dardanelles to Palestine*, 197.

276. Suleiman Mousa, *T. E. Lawrence: An Arab View*, trans. A. Butros (Oxford: Oxford University Press, 1966), 34, 41–42.

277. Ibid., 42.

278. Antonius, *Arab Awakening*, 217.

279. Wavell, *Palestine Campaigns*, 55.

280. Ibid.

281. Mousa, *T. E. Lawrence*, 22, 32, 43, 51.

282. Ibid., 61, 72.

283. Askari, *A Soldier's Story,* 121–122.

284. Ibid., 156.

285. Ibid., 157.

286. Wavell, *Palestine Campaigns,* 59–61.

287. Ulrichsen, *Logistics and Politics,* 115. "The CTC peaked in size in June 1917 when it comprised 33,584 camels and 19,886 Egyptian personnel." Ibid., 148. The contributions of the Donkey Transport Corps should also be acknowledged. Ibid., 44.

288. Ibid., 115.

289. Wavell, *Palestine Campaigns,* 67–68.

290. Ibid., 73.

291. Ibid., 84–85.

292. Ibid., 85–87.

293. Ibid., 97.

294. Ulrichsen, *Logistics and Politics,* 118.

295. Wavell, *Palestine Campaigns,* 96–97.

296. Ibid., 97–108.

297. Ulrichsen, *Logistics and Politics,* 8.

298. Wavell, *Palestine Campaigns,* 112–115.

299. Ibid., 116.

300. Ibid., 128–129.

301. Ibid., 136–137.

302. Ibid., 155–156.

303. Although dominated by the British, the campaign for Jerusalem was international in nature. For example, as Comte Roger de Gontaut-Biro points out, the French government dispatched "a small expeditionary force made principally of two battalions of Algerian tirailleurs, and of one battalion of the 115th territorial infantry. . . . After the takeover of Jerusalem, one of these companies was called to provide the guard of the Saint-Sepulcre." *Comment la France s'est installée en Syrie 1918–1919,* 2nd ed. (Paris: Plon, 1923), 39.

304. Hagop Arsenian and Arda Arsenian Ekmekji, "Surviving Massacre: Hagop Arsenian's Armenian Journey to Jerusalem, 1915–1916," *Jerusalem Quarterly* 49 (2012): 34.

305. Antonius, *Arab Awakening,* 229.

306. Wavell, *Palestine Campaigns,* 177–178.

307. Liddell Hart, *Lawrence of Arabia,* 210.

308. Ibid., 207.

309. Wavell, *Palestine Campaigns,* 195.

310. Ibid., 195–200.

311. Ibid., 211.

312. Ibid., 220–221.

313. Antonius, *Arab Awakening,* 238.

314. Wavell, *Palestine Campaigns,* 230; Antonius, *Arab Awakening,* 238.

315. Cleveland and Bunton, *Modern Middle East,* 153; Antonius, *Arab Awakening,* 240.

316. Wavell, *Palestine Campaigns,* 230–233.

317. Hasan Kayali, *Arabs and Young Turks: Ottomanism, Arabism, and Islamism in the Ottoman Empire, 1908–1918* (Berkeley: University of California Press, 1997), 202.

318. Ulrichsen, *Logistics and Politics,* 14.

319. Ibid.

320. Van der Vat, *Ship That Changed the World,* 220–227.

3. LIVING THE GREAT WAR

1. Nadiya al-Ghazzi, *Shirwal Barhum: Ayyam min safarbarlik* (Damascus: al-Shadi li-l-Nashr wa-l-Tawziʻ, 1993), 9. Although no date is mentioned, the visit must have occurred sometime in the second half of the century.

2. Ibid., 9–10.

3. Halidé Edib, *Memoirs of Halidé Edib* (London: John Murray, 1926), 398.

4. Ibid., 399. Edib commented somewhat surprisingly: "No woman can wring her hands like an Arab woman; there is the same life and beauty in it which one sees in the inspired art of days gone by."

5. Ibid., 392.

6. Sarkis Torossian, *From Dardanelles to Palestine: A True Story of Five Battle Fronts of Turkey and Her Allies and a Harem Romance* (Boston: Meador, 1947), 82.

7. Edib, *Memoirs,* 375.

8. Jirjis al-Khuri Maqdisi (d. 1943), *Aʻzam harb fi l-tarikh wa-kayfa marrat ayyamuha* [The greatest war in history and its events] (Beirut: al-Matbaʻa al-ʻIlmiyya, 1927), tabʻah 2, 28.

9. George Korkor (unpublished memoir), 1914. Private collection. Access provided by the Tarazi family.

10. Jaʻfar Muhsin al-Amin, *Sira wa-ʻamaliyyat* (Beirut: Dar al-Farabi, 2004), 22–23; Mohamad Rihan, "An Intimate Account of a Shiʻi Family during the Formation of Modern Lebanon: The Story of Jaʻfar al-Amin," paper presented at a conference on "The Local Histories of Lebanon Revisited," Orient-Institut, Beirut, October 18–19, 2012, 2, 4. I am grateful to Mohamad Rihan for drawing my attention to this source and making his unpublished article available to me.

11. Hasan Kayali, *Arabs and Young Turks: Ottomanism, Arabism, and Islamism in the Ottoman Empire, 1908–1918* (Berkeley: University of California Press, 1997), 131.

12. An official proclamation issued by the "Selimeh Recruiting Bureau," which included Constantinople and Scutari, in War Office (London, hereafter WO) 157/695, Secret, Military Intelligence Office, War Office, Cairo, 2nd September 1915 [A. Clark], Lieut-Col A/Dir of (Military) Intelligence, extracts from MEDFORCE BULLETIN 24/8/15.

13. Ibid.

14. Ahmad Djemal Pasha, *Memories of a Turkish Statesman—1913–1919* (London: Hutchinson and Co., 1922), 116; *Handbook of the Turkish Army (1916)* (Skokie, IL: Imperial War Museum in association with the Battery Press—Nashville and Articles of War, Ltd., 1996), 5, 31; Nadine Méouchy, "From the Great War to the Syrian Armed Resistance Movement (1919–1921): The Military and the *Mujahidin* in Action," in *The World in World Wars: Experiences, Perceptions and Perspectives from Africa and Asia,* ed. H. Liebau et al. (Leiden: Brill, 2010), 501 and nn. 7–9; Najwa al-Qattan, "Safarbarlik: Ottoman Syria and the Great War," in *From the Syrian Land to the States of Syria and Lebanon,* ed. T. Philipp and C. Schumann (Beirut: Orient-Institut, 2004), 164 n. 4; Erik Jan Zürcher, "Between Death and Desertion: The Ottoman Empire Experience in World War I," *Turcica* 28 (1996), 235–258; Leila Fawaz, "The Soldiers in World War I in the Middle East," in *Histoire, archéologie, littérature du monde musulman: Mélanges en l'honneur d'André Raymond,* ed. G. Alleaume, S. Denoix, and M. Tuchscherer (Cairo: Institut Français d'Archéologie Orientale, 2009), 205–219. See also Erik Jan Zürcher, "The Ottoman Conscription System in Theory and Practice, 1844–1918," *International Review of Social History* 43 (1998): 437–449. For Mount Lebanon regulations between 1861 and 1930, see Engin Deniz Akarli, *The Long Peace: Ottoman Lebanon, 1861–1929* (Berkeley: University of California Press, 1993), on the Lebanon militia: "This militia force is not liable for service outside its own district, where its duties are chiefly those of police. It consists of two battalions of infantry (each of four companies), one squadron of cavalry and a band" (55).

15. Al-Amin, *Sira wa-'amaliyyat,* 26.

16. Ibid.

17. Khairia Kasmieh, "The First World War as Represented in Autobiographies in Contemporary Damascus," in *The First World War as Remembered in the Countries of the Eastern Mediterranean,* ed. O. Farschid, M. Kropp, and S. Dähne (Beirut: Orient-Institut, 2006), 279, quoting Khalid 'Azm, *Mudhakkirat* [Memoirs], vol. 1 (Beirut: al-Dar al-Muttahida li-l-Nashr, 1972), 75 (italics mine).

18. Abdallah Hanna, "The First World War According to the Memories of 'Commoners' in the Bilad al-Sham," in *The World in World Wars,* 300, 305–307.

19. "Christian Military Recruits in Syria," *al-Ahram* (Cairo), March 17, 1916, 4.

20. Hanna, "First World War," 303–304.

21. Paul Huvelin, "Que vaut la Syrie?" in *Chambre de Commerce de Marseille, Congrès français de la Syrie, Marseille, 3, 4, and 5 January 1919, fascicule 1,* 24 and n. 2.

22. Akram Fouad Khater estimated that, between 1899 and 1914, 47 percent of the total number of Lebanese immigrants to the United States were women, and that women also left for Australia, Argentina, and Brazil. About half were married

and the other half single or widowed. "'House' to 'Goddess of the House': Gender, Class, and Silk in 19th-Century Mount Lebanon," *International Journal of Middle East Studies* 28 (1996): 337.

23. *L'Asie française* no. 198 (January 1922): 17. See also the interesting articles in *The Lebanese in the World: A Century of Emigration,* ed. A. Hourani and N. Shehadi (London: Center for Lebanese Studies and I. B. Tauris, 1992).

24. "News from Syria is still confirming that the Ottoman government is still preventing traveling from the Syrian lands. A Greek ship arrived to Alexandria from Beirut transporting a number of Syrian immigrants from America. The military authorities allowed them to descend in Egypt." "Alexandria Every Day: The Situation in Syria and Lebanon and the Statements of the Immigrants," *al-Ahram* (Cairo), April 8, 1915, 4.

25. Henry Morgenthau, *Ambassador Morgenthau's Story* (London: Sterndale Classics, 2003), 114.

26. Ibid., 115–116.

27. Ibid., 116. See also 120, when Morgenthau returned to the railroad station where he had arranged for another train for the removal of foreign residents. There he found that "a mass of distracted people filled the enclosure; the women were weeping, and the children were screaming."

28. Edib, *Memoirs,* 392–393.

29. Halidé Edib Adıvar, *The Turkish Ordeal: Being the Further Memoirs of Halidé Edib* (Westport, CT: Hyperion, 1981), 6.

30. WO 157/695, Censored telegram to Reuter, Cairo, September 6, 1915.

31. Foreign Office (London, hereafter FO) 141/461, "S.N.O" Suez to High Commissioner for Egypt, telegram dated/dispatched June 1, 1916: "Following recd from HMS Fox, RIMS Harding report from Jeddah."

32. FO 141/461, A. Henry McMahon to Edward Grey, with enclosures from Sharif Husayn of Mecca, May 10, 1916.

33. FO 371/2668, Commander-in-Chief, Egyptian Expeditionary Force, to Secretary of War Office, London, General Headquarters, October 5, 1916 (italics mine).

34. Salim Tamari, *Year of the Locust: A Soldier's Diary and the Erasure of Palestine's Ottoman Past* (Berkeley: University of California Press, 2011), 51.

35. Antun Yammin, *Lubnan fi l-harb: Aw-dhikra al-hawadith wa al-mazalim fi Lubnan fi l-harb al-'umumiyya, 1914–1919* [Lebanon in war: Remembrance of the events and the oppression in the world war, 1914–1919], vol. 1 (Beirut: al-Matba'a al-Adabiyya, 1919–1920), 98–99.

36. Kayali, *Arabs and Young Turks,* 131–132.

37. Djemal Pasha, *Memories of a Turkish Statesman,* 170. Ma'an was a Transjordanian district of Vilayet Dimashq (Province of Syria).

38. Tamari, *Year of the Locust,* 51.

39. François Georgeon, "Au bord du rire et des larmes: Les Turcs d'Istanbul pendant la guerre et l'occupation (1914–1923)," in *Des Ottomans aux Turcs: Naissance d'une nation* (Istanbul: Les Editions Isis, 1995), 338. See also Feroz Ahmad, *Turkey: The Quest for Identity* (Oxford: Oneworld, 2003), 71.

40. Hanna, "First World War," 304–305. The poem by Sa'id Jawmar is quoted on 305.

41. Yammin, *Lubnan fi l-harb,* vol. 1, 98–99.

42. Erik Zürcher, "Little Mehmet in the Desert: The Ottoman Soldier's Experience," in *Facing Armageddon: The First World War Experienced,* ed. H. Cecil and P. H. Liddle (London: Leo Cooper, 1996), 234. For lack of transport, see Henry John Turtle, *Quaker Service in the Middle East with a History of Brummana High School 1876–1975* (London: Headley Brothers, 1975), 78–79: "It was in the first days of January 1919, that Dr. Tanius with three others got back to Brummana. They had to take the three hours' walk from Beirut on foot, as there were no carriage horses and, as yet, no motor cars."

43. Tamari, *Year of the Locust,* 9.

44. Ibid., 9, and nn. 7 and 8, citing Salah Isa.

45. In 1915 one Indian soldier wrote to another stationed in Egypt: "My friends, dates are not produced in this country. They grow in Arabia, Persia, and Egypt. Here, however, we have an abundance of royal apples and pears." Ram Singh, Rouen France, to Sirdar Khundan Singh, Egypt, November 13, 1915. British Library, India Office Records, Military Dept., Censor of Indian Mail 1915–1916, L/MIL/5/825, PT8, 1276. #31 Sikh.

46. WO 157/695, Secret, Military Intelligence Office, War Office, Cairo, September 1, 1915, Red Sea, Nn Patrol [Signed Newcombe, Major RE Dir of Military Intelligence].

47. "The official daily rations of an Ottoman soldier consisted of: 900 grams of bread, 600 grams of biscuit, 250 grams of meat, 150 grams of bulgur (broken wheat), 20 grams of butter, and 20 grams of salt." PRO/WO 157/735 (May 29, 1915), quoted in Erik Zürcher, *The Young Turk Legacy and Nation Building: From the Ottoman Empire to Atatürk's Turkey* (London: I. B. Tauris, 2010), 179.

48. Zürcher, *Young Turk Legacy,* 179.

49. Ibid., and the rest of chapter 13; Kristian Coates Ulrichsen, *The Logistics and Politics of the British Campaigns in the Middle East, 1914–22* (Basingstoke, UK: Palgrave Macmillan, 2011), 145, 175.

50. Ahmed Emin Yalman, *Turkey in the World War* (New Haven, CT: Yale University Press, 1930), 251. Perhaps it was the same soup the novelist Hanna Mina's uncle complained about.

51. WO 157/695, Secret, Military Intelligence Office, War Office, Cairo, September 2, 1915 [A. Clark], Lieut-Col A/Dir of (Military) Intelligence, CAUCASUS—LONDON 31/8/15.

52. Zürcher, *Young Turk Legacy*, 178.

53. Ibid., 180 and nn. 72, 73.

54. Mark Harrison, "The Fight against Disease in the Mesopotamia Campaign," in *Facing Armageddon*, 476–478. On 479, Harrison cites T. J. B. Williams, "Report on Scurvy," May 16, 1916, Wilcox Papers, Library of the International Institute of Human Nutrition.

55. David Omissi, *Indian Voices of the Great War: Soldiers' Letters, 1914–1918* (New York: St. Martin's, 1999), Letter No. 298, 178, Gunga Singh to Dafadar Jaswant Singh, April 21, 1916.

56. Djemal Pasha, *Memories of a Turkish Statesman*, 149.

57. Ibid., 153–154.

58. 'Ali al-Wardi, *Lamahat ijtima'iyya min tarikh al-'Iraq al-hadith* [Social aspects of Iraqi modern history], vol. 4: *min 'am 1914 ila 'am 1918* [From 1914 to 1918] (Baghdad: Matba'at al-Sha'ab, 1974), 34–35.

59. Yalman, *Turkey in the World War*, 231, quoting General Hussein Hüsni Emir, who was with the Yildirim army during 1917 and 1918.

60. Ibid., 251, quoting General Emir on the eve of the third battle of Gaza.

61. WO 158/634, Bassett (Wejh) to Arbur (Cairo), telegram, September 9, 1917.

62. FO 141/461, Telegram, No. 39, Abdalla to unknown, March 31. Enclosure 4, copy of original; "Sheikh of Sheikhs" of Beni Selman Refada Arabs to Abdalla, letter, March 2.

63. Linda Schatkowski Schilcher, "The Famine of 1915–1918 in Greater Syria," in *Problems of the Modern Middle East in Historical Perspective: Essays in Honor of Albert Hourani*, ed. J. P. Spagnolo (Reading, UK: Ithaca, 1992), 230 n. 8.

64. Zürcher, *Young Turk Legacy*, 177–181; Zürcher, "Little Mehmet in the Desert," 234. Already before the Great War it was well known to local notables and others that the soldiers were badly paid, if at all, and rumors circulated that the government let soldiers know that salaries were paid to them only because of the goodwill and kindness of the sultan, so that they had no right to complain about delays in payment. Salim 'Ali Salam, *Mudhakkirat Salim 'Ali Salam* [Memoirs] (Beirut: al-Dar al-Jami'iyya, 1982), 108.

65. See Johann Strauss, "The Disintegration of Ottoman Rule in the Syrian Provinces as Viewed by German Observers," in *The Syrian Land: Processes of Integration and Fragmentation: Bilād al-Shām from the 18th to the 20th Century*, ed. T. Philipp and B. Schaebler (Stuttgart, Germany: F. Steiner, 1998), 326.

66. Zürcher, *Young Turk Legacy*, 181.

67. Tamari, *Year of the Locust*, 52 (citing Muhammad 'Izzat Darwaza's memoir), 177 n. 28.

68. Turjman's diary was discovered by the Haganah in 1948. It has been in the Hebrew University National Library since then. The first person to use it was Adel Mana, a Palestinian historian. It was mentioned and used by several scholars since

then, including Abigail Jacobson and Khader Salameh among others. Salim Tamari was the first person to edit it and publish it. I am grateful to Salim Tamari for this information.

69. Tamari, *Year of the Locust*, 93–94. See also Abigail Jacobson, "Negotiating Ottomanism in Times of War: Jerusalem during World War I through the Eyes of a Local Muslim Resident," *International Journal of Middle East Studies* 40 (2008): 69–88.

70. Korkor unpublished memoir, 1908.

71. I am grateful to Randa Baroody Tarazi for this reminiscence of her father, who used to tell her that people would go to the fields or send the kids to hit tin cans in the hope that that would scare the locusts away, and for giving me access to the unpublished memoir of Bechara Baroody.

72. Yammin, *Lubnan fi l-harb*, vol. 1, 102–103; Elizabeth Thompson, *Colonial Citizens: Republican Rights, Paternal Privilege, and Gender in French Syria and Lebanon* (New York: Columbia University Press, 2000), 19 and the rest of her excellent chap. 1.

73. *Al-Ahram* (Cairo), April 8, 1915.

74. "Locusts," *al-Muqattam* (Cairo), May 15, 1915, 5.

75. "Locusts," ibid., July 2, 1915, 6.

76. "News from Sudan," ibid., July 13, 1915, 5.

77. "News from Syria," ibid., April 30, 1915, 5; Yammin, *Lubnan fi l-harb*, vol. 1, 102, reported on locusts in Jaffa.

78. http://www.loc.gov/exhibits/americancolony/amcolony-locust.html.

79. Ibid.

80. Yammin, *Lubnan fi l-harb*, vol. 1, 103.

81. Ibid.

82. "News from Syria and Lebanon," *al-Ahram* (Cairo), March 17, 1916, 4.

83. "Famine in Lebanon," ibid., March 9, 1916, 4.

84. Jean Touma (unpublished diary). Private collection. I am grateful to Lena and Naji Touma, who gave me access to the diary. August 28 and 29, 1915, and April 13, 1915.

85. Ibid., April 13, 1915. One *oqqa* is equivalent to 1.2828 kilos. Jirji Zaydan, *The Autobiography of Jurji Zaidan, Including Four Letters to His Son*, trans. T. Philipp (Washington, DC: Three Continents, 1990), 95 n. 14.

86. Touma, unpublished diary, March 10, 1916.

87. Torossian, *Dardanelles to Palestine*, 132.

88. Tawfiq Yusuf 'Awwad, *al-Raghif* (Beirut: Maktabat al-Madrasa wa-Dar al-Kitab al-Lubnani li l-Tiba'a wa-l-Nashr, 1964); see Amaya Martin Fernandez, "National, Linguistic, and Religious Identity of Lebanese Maronite Christians through their Arabic Fictional Texts during the Period of the French Mandate in Lebanon," Ph.D. diss., Georgetown University (2009), 86.

89. Schilcher, "Famine of 1915–1918," 230–231.

90. Al-Ghazzi, *Shirwal Barhum*, 94.

91. Mohammad Gholi Majd, *Iraq in World War I: From Ottoman Rule to British Conquest* (Lanham, MD: University Press of America, 2006), 400; Dina Rizk Khoury, "Ambiguities of the Modern: The Great War in the Memoirs and Poetry of the Iraqis," in *The World in World Wars*, 313–314.

92. Thompson, *Colonial Citizens*, 23 and n. 22, citing Ahmad al-Jundi, *Lahw al-ayyam: mudhakkirat: Sanawat al-mut'a wa-l tarab wa-l thaqafa* (London: Riad El-Rayyes, 1991), 16–25.

93. Djemal Pasha, *Memories of a Turkish Statesman*, 203.

94. Halidé Edib Adıvar, *House with Wisteria: Memoirs of Halidé Edib* (Charlottesville, VA: Leopolis, 2003), 321. On 335–336 Edib gives examples of the Pasha's benevolence and even popularity, while noting that the "Armenian world seemed to consider Djamal Pasha a godsend."

95. Al-Amin, *Sira wa-'amaliyyat*, 25.

96. Georgeon, "Au bord du rire et des larmes," 336.

97. Torossian, *Dardanelles to Palestine*, 94.

98. Kayali, *Arabs and Young Turks*, 131.

99. Yalman, *Turkey in the World War*, 147, 111.

100. Tamari, *Year of the Locust*, 51.

101. Georgeon, "Au bord du rire et des larmes," 335.

102. Schilcher, "Famine of 1915–1918," 238.

103. Mary Bliss Dale, Journal, June 19, 1916 (unpublished manuscript). Private collection. I am grateful to William A. Rugh for his help and to Jane Rugh and Kathy Dorman Wright who made the 1916 and 1918 journals of Mary Bliss Dale available to me.

104. Bechara Baroody, unpublished memoir. Private collection, 39.

105. On the absence of sugar in the Arab provinces, see Private Turjman's diary entry for April 23, 1915, which mentions that people were deprived of sugar, kerosene, and rice, as well as of what he considered hardest, tobacco. Cited in Tamari, *Year of the Locust*, 52–53. See also Yammin, *Lubnan fi l-harb*, vol. 1, 94–95, which mentions shortages of gas, rice, sugar, corn, wheat, barley, lentils, beans, and other grains.

106. Tamari, *Year of the Locust*, 141.

107. Georgeon, "Au bord du rire et des larmes," 334–335, quoting Zafer Toprak, *Türkiye'de "Millî İktisat" (1908–1918)* (Ankara, 1982). Georgeon (334) writes that a kilo of sugar went from 3 to 250 piasters from July 1914 to the end of the war.

108. Baroody, unpublished memoir, 21.

109. Al-Wardi, *Lamahat ijtima'iyya min tarikh al-'Iraq al-hadith*, vol. 4, 29.

110. "La Rescision des ventes de guerre au Liban," *L'Asie française* no. 198 (January 1922): 17.

111. Al-Wardi, *Lamahat ijtima'iyya min tarikh al-'Iraq al-hadith*, vol. 4, 29.

112. Tarif Khalidi, "The Arab World," in *The Great World War, 1914–1945*, vol. 2: *The Peoples' Experience*, ed. J. Bourne, P. Liddle, and I. Whitehead (London:

HarperCollins, 2001), 292; Rashid Khalidi, "Shaykh Ahmad 'Arif al-Zayn and al-'Irfan," in *Intellectual Life in the Arab East, 1890–1939,* ed. M. R. Buheiry (Beirut: Center for Arab and Middle East Studies, American University of Beirut, 1981), 110–124.

113. Harry Stürmer, *Two War Years in Constantinople: Sketches of German and Young Turkish Ethics and Politics,* trans. E. Allen (New York: George H. Doran, 1917), 118.

114. "Famine and Misrule in Syria," *The Times* (London), April 5, 1916.

115. Ibid.

116. Schilcher, "Famine of 1915–1918," 230, 238–239.

117. Nazik Ali Jawdat, "Pictures from the Past," in *Remembering Childhood in the Middle East: Memoirs from a Century of Change,* ed. E. Warnock Fernea (Austin: University of Texas Press, 2002), 29.

118. Hew Strachan, *The First World War: A New Illustrated History* (London: Simon and Schuster, 2003), 112. Thompson (*Colonial Citizens,* 21) mentions that contemporary attempts to quantify the loss of life varied widely; Schilcher ("Famine of 1915–1918," 229) draws on German sources and supports the higher estimates of about five hundred thousand for those who died "from starvation or starvation-related diseases." Schilcher points out that "visibly starving pilgrims returning from Mecca, and Armenian refugees from regions further north, were not counted in the sources" (ibid.). What seems certain is that hundreds of thousands of people died (ibid., 231 and n. 13, where she calls George Antonius's total of about five hundred thousand civilian and military losses in Ottoman Syria "a conservative estimate"). Guido Steinberg ("The Commemoration of the 'Spanish Flu' of 1918–1919 in the Arab East," in *The First World War as Remembered in the Countries of the Eastern Mediterranean,* 151–162) mentions that a large number of those who died probably succumbed to the Spanish flu that struck in Syria. The Spanish flu is rarely mentioned by writers of the period. According to Paul Huvelin ("Que vaut la Syrie?" 17), "Malgré les épidémies et la famine, qui ont fait disparaître 160.000 Libanais entre 1915 et 1918, le Liban est la seule partie du pays qui ait gravement souffert entre 1914 et 1918." Adib Pacha noted that since the Ottoman Empire entered the war, there had been no confirmed news from Lebanon, and all that was known was that the unfortunate population was dying "by the tens of thousands from hunger and deprivation. *Le Liban après la guerre* (Paris: E. Leroux, 1919), 63. The numbers vary but there is no question that the damage was immense.

119. Baroody, unpublished memoir, 38.

120. WO 157/695, Censored telegram. Private telegram. SOFIA. September 1, 1915.

121. FO 141/461, Telegram. From High Commissioner for Egypt, Cairo, to F.O. (related to India). No. 322, my tel No. 312 of April 30; WO 157/695, Secret,

Military Intelligence Office, War Office, Cairo, 3d September 1915, A. C. Parker, Lieut-Col, A/Dir of (Milit) Intelligence, Armenia, Censored Telegram 3/9/15.

122. WO 157/695, T. E. Lawrence, Lieut-Col, A/Dir of (Military) Intelligence, Secret, Military Intelligence Office, War Office, Cairo, September 7, 1915, Mesopotamia, Sir Mark Sykes reports from India, September 4; WO 157/695, T. E. Lawrence, Lieut-Col, A/Dir (Milit) Intelligence, Secret, Military Intelligence Office, War Office, Cairo, September 7, 1915. Censored Telegram to "Mokattam," Cairo, September 7, 1915.

123. Ibid.

124. FO 141/468, Thomas K. Mergeditchian, Intelligence Office, to Major W. H. Deeds, D.S.O., General Staff, Intelligence Section, Cairo, January 18, 1917.

125. WO 158/634, T. E. Lawrence to General Clayton (Tafileh), January 22, 1918.

126. WO 157/695, T. E. Lawrence, Lieut-Col, A/Dir of (Military) Intelligence, Secret, Military Intelligence Office, War Office, Cairo, September 7, 1915, Mesopotamia, Sir Mark Sykes reports from India, on 4th Sept; Leslie Davis, American consul in Erzurum, reporting from Kharput, the principal transit point, in July 1915, as cited in Strachan, *First World War,* 54.

127. One powerful account of the odyssey of one family is by Joyce Barsam, available at http://farescenter.tufts.edu/events/roundtables/2012Apr12Video.asp. I am grateful to Dr. Barsam for making this account available to me.

128. Strachan, *First World War,* 112.

129. Al-Amin, *Sira wa-'amaliyyat,* 25.

130. Anis Furayha, *Qabla an ansa: Tatimmat isma' ya rida!* [Before I forget: I continue: Listen o Rida!] (Beirut: Dar al-Nahar li-l-Nashr, 1979), 42.

131. Ibid., 47.

132. Arsun is a typical traditional Lebanese village of the upper Matn. For the Quaker High School at Brumana and its role during the war, see Turtle, *Quaker Service.*

133. Muhammad 'Izzat Darwaza, *Mudhakkirat* [Memoirs], vol. 1 (Beirut: Dar al-Gharb al-Islami, 1993), 288.

134. Stürmer, *Two War Years in Constantinople,* 118.

135. Darwaza, *Mudhakkirat,* vol. 1, 288–289.

136. 'Anbara Salam Khalidi, *Jawla fi l-dhikrayat bayna Lubnan wa-Filastin* (Beirut: Dar al-Nahar li-l-Nashr, 1978), 106. See also Christoph Schumann, "Individual and Collective Memories of the First World War," in *From the Syrian Land,* 261.

137. Bishara al-Buwari, *Arba' sinin al-harb* [Four years of the war] (New York: al-Huda, 1926), 400.

138. Kasmieh, "The First World War," 281.

139. Edib, *Memoirs,* 390.

140. Al-Wardi, *Lamahat ijtima'iyya min tarikh al-'Iraq al-hadith,* vol. 4, 32.

141. Mary Bliss Dale, Journal, unpublished manuscript, February 28, 1916.

142. Ibid., February 29, 1916.

143. Ibid., May 2, 1916.

144. Thompson, *Colonial Citizens,* 20. Schilcher, "Famine of 1915–1918," 230 n. 6, references a "clipping from *The Near East,* Cairo, April 3, 1916, enclosed in F.O. 371/2777" that essentially makes the same observation for the areas outside Beirut: "An eyewitness reported that 'between Beirut and the mountains one meets crowds of starving men, women and children, many of whom die on the roadside.'"

145. Ibrahim Kan'an, *Lubnan fi l-harb al-kubra, 1914–1918* [Lebanon in the Great War] (Beirut: Mu'assasat 'Asi, 1974), 139.

146. Turtle, *Quaker Service,* 159. Appendix C, "The Brummana Soup-Kitchen: 1916–1918," derives from information supplied by Emile Cortas. I am grateful to Nadim Cortas for information about the Cortas relief efforts during the World War I.

147. Turtle, *Quaker Service,* 63.

148. Ibid., 159; Nicholas Z. Ajay, "Mount Lebanon and the Wilayah of Beirut, 1914–1918: The War Years," Ph.D. diss., Georgetown University (1973): Appendix VII, "The Private Papers of Bayard Dodge," 292–311; Section B of Appendix VII, Report on Relief Work in Syria during the Period of the War, 297–299, citing Bayard Dodge (Beirut) to C. H. Dodge (New York City), "Brief Account of Relief Work in Syria during the Period of the War." See also Margaret McGilvary, *The Dawn of a New Era in Syria* (New York: Fleming H. Revell, 1920), 216–219. McGilvary, who was an outside observer more than a participant, assumed that the initiative was Dray's. She recognized that Mrs. Cortas "held the keys" to the stores department and "had assisted Dray from the very beginning," but she gave him most of the credit. McGilvary wrote about Mrs. Cortas: "As a matter of fact, although she and her husband had now several hundred employees under them, the entire management of the plant was in their hands—*of course under the supervision of Dr. and Mrs. Dray.*" Ibid., 224 (italics mine). However, it was local women and men who had created and maintained the soup kitchen. For local sources, as one person put it privately to me, "then as it is now, the contribution of foreigners hijacks, through prolific writings, such successful endeavors and usually those that started and did most of the work become marginal or totally ignored."

149. Al-Wardi, *Lamahat ijtima'iyya min tarikh al-'Iraq al-hadith,* vol. 4, 31. Jirjis (George) Khuri Maqdisi was Anis Makdisi's elder brother by seventeen years, with whom he founded the journal *al-Mawrid al-Safi.* See also Maqdisi, *A'zam harb fi l-tarikh,* 68–70.

150. Schilcher, "Famine of 1915–1918," 230 n. 6.

151. Edib, *Memoirs,* 442.

152. Quoted by Strauss, "The Disintegration of Ottoman Rule," 318.

153. Thompson, *Colonial Citizens,* 21.

154. Touma, unpublished diary, December 20, 1916.

155. Darwaza, *Mudhakkirat,* vol. 1, 289.

156. Al-Wardi, *Lamahat ijtima'iyya min tarikh al-'Iraq al-hadith,* vol. 4, 32.

157. Yammin, *Lubnan fi l-harb,* vol. 2, 5–14, et passim.

158. Ibid., vol. 1, 158.

159. Ibid., 157.

160. Nicola Ziadeh, "A First-Person Account of the First World War in Greater Syria," in *The First World War as Remembered in the Countries of the Eastern Mediterranean,* 269.

161. Ibid., 266.

162. Ibid., 269. *Araq* is the local ouzo.

163. Ibid., 267.

164. Ibid., 268–269. "Now in Damascus in that time, and perhaps in Aleppo as well, the best way to keep *kusa*—squash—for stuffing during the winter was to keep them in salt water. And during the winter, men would sell them on the street saying '*Asharat bi-asharat ya kusa!*' Ten for ten, ten squashes for ten *baras.* The *bara* was 1/40th of a Turkish piaster." Ibid., 269.

165. Tamari, *Year of the Locust,* 174 n. 2; Kasmieh, "The First World War," 281.

166. Kasmieh, "The First World War," 281, citing Khalil al-Sakakini, *Kadha ana ya dunya* [Such am I, o'world] (Jerusalem: N.p., 1955), 138.

167. Al-Wardi, *Lamahat ijtima'iyya min tarikh al-'Iraq al-hadith,* vol. 4, 32.

168. Walter Armbrust, *Mass Culture and Modernism in Egypt* (Cambridge: Cambridge University Press, 1996), describes Masabni as "the leading dancer of the time and famous as a night club proprietress" (77). Roberta L. Dougherty, "Badi'a Masabni, Artiste and Modernist: The Egyptian Print Media's Carnival of National Identity," in *Mass Mediations: New Approaches to Popular Culture in the Middle East and Beyond,* ed. Walter Armbrust (Berkeley: University of California Press, 2000), describes Masabni as "an impresario responsible for promoting the careers of many Egyptian artists and an actress, singer, and dancer famous in her own right" (246). See also *Mudhakkirat Badi'ah Maṣābinī, bi-qalam Nāzik Bāsīlā* (Beirut: Dār Maktabat al-Ḥayāh, n.d.).

169. Al-Wardi, *Lamahat ijtima'iyya min tarikh al-'Iraq al-hadith,* vol. 4, 33, citing Nazik Basila, *Mudhakkirat Badi'a Masabni* [Memoirs of Badi'a Masabni] (Beirut: N.p., n.d.), 166.

170. Hanna Mina, *Fragments of Memory: A Story of a Syrian Family,* trans. O. Kenny and L. Kenny (Austin: Center for Middle Eastern Studies at the University of Texas, 1993), xiii.

171. Ibid., vii.

172. Ibid., 4.

173. Ibid., 5; see also chap. 1.

174. For a thorough analysis of the term *safarbarlik,* see al-Qattan, "Safarbarlik: Ottoman Syria and the Great War," 163–173.

175. Mina, *Fragments of Memory,* biographical information based on the introduction by Khaldoun Shamaa, ix–xiv.

176. Ibid., 5–6. The town of "Baleemadak" is probably near Mersin, which saw lots of refugees going by; cf. Sean McMeekin, *The Baghdad-Berlin Express: The Ottoman Empire and Germany's Bid for World Power* (Cambridge, MA: Harvard University Press, 2010), 252.

177. Al-Ghazzi, *Shirwal Barhum,* 42.

178. Ibid., 45–46.

179. Ibid., 42–48.

180. Ibid., 99–100.

181. Ibid., 49–50.

182. Asuman Tezcan, "Savas yillarinda Istanbul ve Anadolu'da verem" [Tuberculosis in Istanbul and Anatolia during the war years], *Bilgi ve Bellek* 5 (2006): 105–123.

183. "Typhoid Fever," *al-Muqattam* (Cairo), April 24, 1915, 1.

184. "Plague in Fayoum," ibid., April 27, 1915, 6.

185. "Typhoid Fever in the Capital," ibid., May 1, 1915, 4. Prior to that, infections had reached sixty per day and on the day before twenty-eight became sick.

186. "Typhoid Fever," ibid., May 29, 1915, no. 7962, 5.

187. "Typhoid Fever in Egypt," ibid., July 24, 1915, 5.

188. Ahmad Kamel Fayez, "Save the Nation from the Epidemic," ibid., May 5, 1915, 2.

189. Ibid.

190. "Typhoid and Typhus: People's Complaints and the Government's Duty," ibid., June 7, 1915, 1.

191. "Typhus in Egypt: Its Prevention," *al-Ahram* (Cairo), March 30, 1916, 6.

192. Robert Ilbert, *Alexandrie, 1830–1930: Histoire d'une communauté citadine* (Cairo: Institut Français d'Archéologie Orientale, 1996), vol. 1, 380.

193. "Fever in Egypt," *al-Muqattam* (Cairo), April 27, 1915, 5.

194. Ilbert, *Alexandrie, 1830–1930,* vol. 1, 380: "La peste, la typhoïde, le typhus et surtout la tuberculose trouvaient là un terrain de choix."

195. Majd, *Iraq in World War I,* 401, 403, 407.

196. "News from Syria and Lebanon," *al-Ahram* (Cairo), March 17, 1916, 4. *Al-Ahram* also reported that Jewish charitable organizations in the United States petitioned the American secretary of state to secure permission from the Porte to allow a ship carrying wheat and flour to reach fellow Jews suffering from famine in Syria.

197. Huvelin, "Que vaut la Syrie?" 26. He mentions that the mission was initiated by the chambers of commerce of Lyon and of Marseille, 12.

198. Thompson, *Colonial Citizens*, 20. See also James L. Gelvin, *Divided Loyalties: Nationalism and Mass Politics in Syria at the Close of Empire* (Berkeley: University of California Press, 1998), 22–23.

199. Ziadeh, "A First-Person Account," 269.

200. "The food of the Ottoman army: boiled water with a few grains of lentils in it. Father says that a diver was the only one who could get a grain of it." Mina, *Fragments of Memory*, 7.

201. Ibid.

202. Morgenthau, *Ambassador Morgenthau's Story*, 157.

203. "Familiar Mediterranean Fever and Dairy Products," *al-Ahram* (Cairo), March 29, 1916, 4.

204. Georgeon, "Au bord du rire et des larmes," 335, citing *Karagöz*, no. 979, July 1917.

205. Torossian, *Dardanelles to Palestine*, 93–94.

206. WO 158/634, T. E. Lawrence to General Clayton (Tafileh), January 22, 1918.

207. Georgeon, "Au bord du rire et des larmes," 338–339.

208. Yalman, *Turkey in the World War*, 241.

209. Ibid. One illicit trade the author mentions as an example is the smuggling of gold from Germany and Austria.

210. "Bad News from Syria," *al-Muqattam* (Cairo), August 3, 1915, 5.

211. Darwaza, *Mudhakkirat*, vol. 1, 289; Najwa al-Qattan, "Everything but the Plague: Telling Tales of Another War in Lebanon," paper presented at Tufts University workshop on "The Middle East in the Two World Wars," held at Harvard and at Tufts, May 10–12, 2002; Thompson, *Colonial Citizens*, 26; Schilcher, "Famine of 1915–1918," 232. See also Mina, *Fragments of Memory*, 173.

212. Yammin, *Lubnan fi l-harb*, vol. 1, 158–159.

213. Ibid., 159.

214. Al-Wardi, *Lamahat ijtima'iyya min tarikh al-'Iraq al-hadith*, vol. 4, 35.

215. Ibid.

216. Schilcher, "Famine of 1915–1918," 231.

217. George Antonius, *The Arab Awakening* (New York: Capricorn, 1965), 204.

218. Al-Wardi, *Lamahat ijtima'iyya min tarikh al-'Iraq al-hadith*, vol. 4, 35.

219. FO 371/2669, Captain Gwatkin-Williams, H.M.S. "Tara." Further Extracts from Report. General Headquarters (Cairo), Egyptian Expeditionary Force, April 24, 1916.

220. Major J. D. Crowdy bemoaned General Townshend's poor accounting of foods inside Kut: "General Townshend's share of the responsibility for this hurried advance, which has already cost the relieving force over 8,500 men in a fortnight,

must not be forgotten. Not till after the battle of HANNAH had been fought, did he take stock of the foodstuffs available in KUT, to find that he can hold out up till the beginning of April, instead of only up to the end of January. Had he only done this earlier, Aylmer would have been able to concentrate at AMARAH, instead of at ALI GHARBI, right under the enemy's nose." J. D. Crowdy to Nora Crowdy, January 29, 1916. Major J. D. Crowdy Collection: United Kingdom, St. Antony's College, Middle East Center Archive (hereafter cited as Crowdy Collection).

221. Maqdisi, *A'zam harb fi l-tarikh,* 63–67.

222. WO 158/634, T. E. Lawrence to General Clayton, January 22, 1918.

223. Edib, *Memoirs,* 443.

224. Ibid.

225. Tamari, *Year of the Locust,* 52.

226. Suzanne Brugger, *Australians and Egypt: 1914–1919* (Carlton, Australia: Melbourne University Press, 1980), 57, plate 380.

227. "Famine and Misrule in Syria," *The Times* (London), April 5, 1916.

228. Al-Wardi, *Lamahat ijtima'iyya min tarikh al-'Iraq al-hadith,* vol. 4, 34.

229. Ibid., 34–35, citing Munir al-Rayyis, *al-Kitab al-dhahabi li l-thawrat al-wataniyya fi l-mashriq al-'arabi* [The golden book of national revolts in the Arab East] (Beirut: Dar al-Tali'a li l-Tiba'a wa-l-Nashr, 1969), 51–52.

230. Kasmieh, "The First World War," 281, citing Khalil al-Sakakini, *Kadha ana ya dunya,* 138.

231. Kasmieh, "The First World War," 281, citing Badr al-Din al-Shallah, *Li l-tarikh wa l-dhikra* [For history and remembrance] (Damascus, 1990), 13–14.

232. Yalman, *Turkey in the World War,* 246–247.

233. Ibid.

234. Djemal Pasha, *Memories of a Turkish Statesman,* 17.

235. Yalman, *Turkey in the World War,* 244–246. See also Khaled Fahmy, "Prostitution in Egypt in the Nineteenth Century," in *Outside In: On the Margins of the Middle East,* ed. E. Rogan (London: I. B. Tauris, 2002), 77–103.

236. Yalman, *Turkey in the World War,* 246.

237. Ibid., 242.

238. That war freed people from traditional restrictions illustrates this comment by an Indian soldier stationed in France, although what he says could apply to different areas: "The ladies (mémán) are very nice and bestow their favors upon us freely. But contrary to the custom in our country they do not put their legs over the shoulders when they go with a man (Deleted) [*sic*]." Balwant Singh to Pandit Chet Ram, October 24, 1915. British Library, India Office, Military Department, Censor of Indian Mails 1915–1916, L/MIL/285/Part P. 1151, no. 50, Sikh.

239. Tamari, *Year of the Locust,* 7.

240. See the very informative article by Jacobson, "Negotiating Ottomanism in Times of War," 76–77.

241. Jens Hanssen, "Public Morality and Marginality in Fin-de-Siècle Beirut," in *Outside In,* 184, 195–197, 200; Hanssen, *Fin de siècle Beirut: The Making of an Ottoman Provincial Capital* (New York: Oxford University Press), 128, 193, 209–211. Akram Fouad Khater, in *Inventing Home: Emigration, Gender, and the Middle Class in Lebanon, 1870–1920* (Berkeley: University of California Press, 2001), shows how women and girls who worked away from home in the silk factories of Mount Lebanon to sustain their families' honor were considered to be involved in immoral work (235–248), and Jens Hanssen (*Fin de siècle Beirut,* 210–211) elaborates on this, pointing out that the word for female workers became synonymous with "brothels" in Lebanon. For prostitution under the French Mandate, see Thompson, *Colonial Citizens,* 86–87; for prostitution in more modern times, see Samir Khalaf, *Prostitution in a Changing Society: A Sociological Survey of Legal Prostitution in Beirut* (Beirut: Khayats, 1965).

242. Al-Wardi, *Lamahat ijtima'iyya min tarikh al-'Iraq al-hadith,* vol. 4, 30.

243. 'Awwad, *al-Raghif,* 26; it is implied in other places that the stepmother wants Zayna to sell her favors to the men there. For example, there is mention of cows being hungry and unable to find food but the soil is bare. Ibid., 32.

244. Yammin, *Lubnan fi l-harb,* vol. 1, 160–163. Najwa al-Qattan first brought attention to this reference in "Everything but the Plague." For Bishara 'Abdallah Khuri, see Maysa Abu-Youssef, "Symbolic and Intersubjective Representations in Arab Environmental Writing," in *Literature of Nature: An International Sourcebook,* ed. P. D. Murphy (Chicago: Fitzroy Dearborn, 1998), 352; "Introduction," in *Beyond the Dunes: An Anthology of Modern Saudi Literature,* ed. M. I. al-Hazimi et al. (London: I. B. Tauris, 2006), 14.

245. Isa Salah, *Rijal Rayya wa-Sakina: Sira ijtima'iyya wa-siyasiyya* (Cairo: Dar al-Ahmadi li-l Nashr, 2002). This book also has information on the houses of prostitution and how they were regulated.

246. Beth Baron, *Egypt as a Woman: Nationalism, Gender, and Politics* (Berkeley: University of California Press, 2005), 52.

247. Peter Englund, *The Beauty and the Sorrow: An Intimate History of the First World War,* trans. P. Graves (London: Profile, 2011), 109 (Friday, 16 April, 1915 "William Henry Dawkins writes to his mother from the harbor on Lemnos").

248. Ibid., 70 (Saturday, 26 December, 1914 "William Henry Dawkins is sitting by the Pyramids, writing to his mother").

249. J. G. Fuller, *Troop Morale and Popular Culture in the British and Dominion Armies 1914–1918* (Oxford: Clarendon, 1991), 170.

250. Suzanne Welborn, *Lords of Death: A People, a Place, a Legend* (Fremantle, Australia: Fremantle Arts Centre Press, 1982), 63. The author quotes officers who defended the behavior of the soldiers, including a young driver named D. Barrett-Lennard, a winegrower from Guildford, Western Australia (now a suburb of Perth), who wrote in 1915 from Mena camp that there "certainly had been cases of disorderly conduct—drunkenness and a fair amount of diseases but this can only

be expected from 40,000 troops who don't care a damn now that they are going to the War, time enough to pull yourself in they say on the way home if you are lucky enough to escape." Ibid., 62.

251. Englund, *The Beauty and the Sorrow*, 109 (Friday, 16 April, 1915 "William Henry Dawkins writes to his mother from the harbor on Lemnos").

252. Welborn, *Lords of Death*, 62.

253. Ibid., 63.

254. Ibid. According to a popular and perhaps inexact author, John Costello, "In World War I the venereal infection rates of the British army in general were seven times higher than the Germans, principally because national prudery prevented the British high command from acknowledging that there was any problem at all until 1915, when the Canadian and New Zealand prime ministers forced the chiefs of staff to issue free contraceptives to the troops." *Love, Sex and War: Changing Values, 1939–45* (London: Collins, 1985), 289.

255. Welborn, *Lords of Death*, 63.

256. Isa, *Rijal Rayya wa-Sakina*, 41–44.

257. Ibid.

258. "The Women Killers," *al-Ahram Weekly Online*, http://weekly.ahram.org.eg /1999/434/chrncls.htm.

4. ENTREPRENEURS AND PROFITEERS

1. Ali al-Wardi, *Lamahat ijtima'iyya min tarikh al-'Iraq al-hadith* [Social aspects of Iraqi modern history], vol. 4: *Min 'am 1914 ila 'am 1918* [From 1914 to 1918] (Baghdad: Matba'at al-Sha'ab, 1974), 33. Translated by Youssef H. Aboul-Enein as *Iraq in Turmoil: Historical Perspectives of Dr. Ali al-Wardi, from the Ottoman Empire to King Feisal* (Annapolis, MD: Naval Institute Press, 2012).

2. Quoted by Ahmed Emin Yalman, *Turkey in the World War* (New Haven, CT: Yale University Press, 1930), 240. For the uneven distribution of wealth already obvious in the years before the war, see Samir Seikaly, "Shukri al-'Asali: A Case Study of a Political Activist," in *The Origins of Arab Nationalism*, ed. R. Khalidi et al. (New York: Columbia University Press, 1991), 78–79.

3. Yalman, *Turkey in the World War*, 240.

4. Ibid., 240–241.

5. Abdallah Hanna, "The First World War According to the Memories of 'Commoners' in the Bilad al-Sham," in *The World in World Wars: Experiences, Perceptions and Perspectives from Africa and Asia*, ed. H. Liebau et al. (Leiden: Brill, 2010), 308; Khairia Kasmieh, "The First World War as Represented in Autobiographies in Contemporary Damascus," in *The First World War as Remembered in the Countries of the Eastern Mediterranean*, ed. O. Farschid, M. Kropp, and S. Dähne (Beirut: Orient-Institut, 2006), 282, citing Faris al-Khuri, *Awraq* (Damascus:

Talas, 1989), vol. 1, 169, and Muhammad Kurd Ali, the journalist and man of letters (*al-Mudhakkirat*, 72–73).

6. Yalman, *Turkey in the World War*, 251.

7. For more information on Michel Sursock and the Sursock family, see Lorenzo Trombetta, "The Private Archive of the Sursuqs, a Beirut Family of Christian Notables: An Early Investigation," *Rivista Studi Orientali* (Pisa-Rome), 2009, 205 and n. 47. I am grateful to the author for making his findings available to me before they were published and for his help thereafter. I am grateful to Carole Corm for working with me on the Sursock family history and on other topics related to this project, to Yvonne Lady Cochrane for making the Sursock family papers available to me when I worked on Beiruti families, and to Alfred Sursock Cochrane for his helpful information on the family.

8. I thank Sursock family members for this anecdote. Reportedly Jamal Pasha was visibly saddened whenever he ordered the execution of Lebanese patriots.

9. Faris al-Khuri, *Awraq*, vol. 1, 169–170.

10. Elizabeth F. Thompson, *Colonial Citizens: Republican Rights, Paternal Privilege, and Gender in French Syria and Lebanon* (New York: Columbia University Press, 2000), 28.

11. Linda Schatkowski Schilcher, "The Famine of 1915–1918 in Greater Syria," in *Problems of the Modern Middle East in Historical Perspective: Essays in Honor of Albert Hourani*, ed. John P. Spagnolo (Reading, UK: Ithaca, 1992), 249.

12. Michel Sursock later became Linda Sursock's husband. I thank Sursock family members for their information on Michel Sursock.

13. Jirjis al-Khuri Maqdisi, *A'zam harb fi l-tarikh wa-kayfa marrat ayyamuha* [The greatest war in history and its events] (Beirut: al-Matba'a al-'Ilmiyya, 1927), 66.

14. An example of give and take between notables and the Ottoman authorities is given in Salim 'Ali Salam, *Mudhakkirat Salim 'Ali Salam* [Memoirs] (Beirut: al-Dar al-Jami'iyya, 1982), 189. During the war, Michel Ibrahim Sursock, Omar Bayhum, and Salim Ali Salam presented a proposal to develop land in Hula in Syria to the Ottoman governor of Beirut. The project met with opposition from rival parties and the governor used their request to make them compromise on some of the reform agenda in which they were interested.

15. "The Situation in Beirut and Syria (2)," *al-Muqattam* (Cairo), June 10, 1915, 5. See also Antun Yammin, *Lubnan fi l-harb: aw-dhikra al-hawādith wa-al-mazalim fi Lubnan fi l-harb al-'umumiyya, 1914–1919*, vol. 1 (Beirut: al-Matba'a al-Adabiyya, 1919–1920), 94–95.

16. *Le Soir*, September 9, 1918. I am grateful to Feroz Ahmad for information on this press clipping, most likely derived from Turkish papers like *Yeni Gün*, *Tanin*, or *İkdam* that also gave the news. See also Eliezer Tauber, *The Arab Movements in World War I* (London: Frank Cass, 1993), 37, 265 n. 4, which refers

to FO 371/4210: t30, Gilbert Clayton (Cairo), February 7, 1919, regarding Salim Ali Salam being suspected of profiting from food products, along with several other notables.

17. Al-Wardi, *Lamahat ijtima'iyya min tarikh al-'Iraq al-hadith,* vol. 4, 33–34.

18. Yammin, *Lubnan fi l-harb,* vol. 2, 16.

19. Ibid., 17.

20. Kasmieh, "First World War," 279, 282 citing Khalid al-Azm, *Mudhakkirat* [Memoirs] (Beirut, 1972), vol. 1, 72–73.

21. Alfred Musa Sursock was involved with the development of the Beirut hippodrome. I am grateful to Nabil Nasrallah, Director of the Hippodrome of Beirut, for the information below and to Carole Corm for putting me in touch with him. The race track at Beirut and its records were destroyed after the Israeli bombings in 1982. Some information is available, however, about the beginnings of horse racing in Beirut and the building of the city's hippodrome. Horse racing was started in 1883 at Bir Hassan, which was then on the western outskirts of Beirut, but it was during World War I that the Beirut hippodrome got under way. On June 28, 1915, 'Azmi Bey, Ottoman governor of Beirut during the World War I, suggested the creation of a club with social and sport activities in the Pine Forest. By December 5, the municipality of Beirut signed an agreement with Alfred Sursock for the development of the six hundred thousand square meters of pine forest with social activities, horse racing, and a casino, with protection for trees. A year later, the Public Garden was opened and by 1917, the "Residence des Pins" was completed. In September 1918, the governor placed the undertaking under Omar Daouk, president of the municipality of Beirut. The "Grand Liban" was proclaimed September 1, 1920, but the records remain incomplete. The year 1923 was often mentioned as the year when the grandstands of the hippodrome were built by an engineer named Bahjat Abdel-Nour, and the first horse-racing records of the Hippodrome go back to 1927. For information about 'Azmi Bey, see Hanssen, *Fin de siècle Beirut: The Making of an Ottoman Provincial Capital* (New York: Oxford University Press, 2005), 80.

22. Trombetta, "The Private Archive of the Sursuqs," 204–205, 220; Hanssen, *Fin de siècle Beirut,* 122; Thompson, *Colonial Citizens,* 99. Emilie Khalil Sursock is also identified as cofounder of the Saint George Hospital, built in the late 1880s and early 1890s (Trombetta, "The Private Archive of the Sursuqs," 204–205 n. 44).

23. Charles Corm, unpublished curriculum vitae, 1948, Charles Corm archives, Beirut, Lebanon; interviews with Carole Corm. I am also grateful to George Ellmore for the information he provided. Corm's initiative was so successful that in 1918–1919 the French made him director of Beirut's food supplies ("Ravitaillement general civil de Beyrouth"). The French also offered Corm the Legion of Honor for his role—which he refused. Later they offered him the job of director of the department of public instruction in the new government created by General

Gouraud, but he refused again, as he did not want to be too close to the French Mandate.

24. "Bhib kun hsan 'and bayt Sursock tay ta'muni fustok wa-bundok." The translation into English does not capture the rhyme in Arabic. I am grateful to Carole Corm and to Alfred Sursock Cochrane for their help.

25. Kamal S. Salibi, "Beirut under the Young Turks: As Depicted in the Political Memoirs of Salim Ali Salam (1868–1938)," in *Les Arabes par leurs archives: XVIe–XXe siècles,* ed. J. Berque and D. Chevallier (Paris: Centre National de la Recherche Scientifique, 1976), 196.

26. Ibid., 193.

27. Salim 'Ali Salam, *Mudhakkirat,* 123–124. The principal, Julia Tohme, later caused a minor scandal by getting involved with a member of the society, the married man Badr Efendi Dimashkiyya (Demichkieh), who also had three children. Salam wrote that he regretted Julia Tohme leaving the school before the end of the war and marrying the then-divorced Badr. As a result, Salam decided to resign from the society, transferring the presidency to Omar Beik Daouk.

28. Salibi, "Beirut under the Young Turks," 193–194.

29. "Guerre Mondiale/ Pour être Représentée / Au profit des malheureux pendards/ Qui souffrent de la Guerre /Au léger détriment des heureux de Sofar/ Qui ne s'en soucient guère," Charles Corm, "La vérité toute nue" (Sofar, 1914). Charles Corm archives. I am grateful to Carole Corm for providing access to this source.

30. Maqdisi, *A'zam harb fi l-tarikh,* 70.

31. Johann Strauss, "The Disintegration of Ottoman Rule in the Syrian Provinces as Viewed by German Observers," in *The Syrian Land: Processes of Integration and Fragmentation; Bilad al-Sham from the 18th to the 20th Century,* ed. T. Philipp and B. Schaebler (Stuttgart, Germany: F. Steiner, 1998), 314.

32. Halidé Edib Adıvar, *House with Wisteria: Memoirs of Halidé Edib* (Charlottesville, VA: Leopolis, 2003), 331.

33. Ibid., 336.

34. Ibid., 336–338.

35. Al-Wardi, *Lamahat ijtima'iyya min tarikh al-'Iraq al-hadith,* vol. 4, 33.

36. Strauss, "The Disintegration of Ottoman Rule," 320.

37. Khairia Kasmieh, "The First World War as Represented in Autobiographies in Contemporary Damascus," in *The First World War as Remembered in the Countries of the Eastern Mediterranean,* 99, 133, 142, 145, 147, 149, 150–151.

38. Ibid., 282.

39. Qattan, "Safarbarlik: Ottoman Syria and the Great War," in *From the Syrian Land to the States of Syria and Lebanon,* ed. T. Philipp and C. Schumann (Beirut: Orient-Institut, 2004), 163–173, quote on 168.

40. Muhammad Kurd 'Ali, *al-Mudhakkirat* (Damascus: Matba'at al-Taraqqi, 1948–[2008]), 172.

41. Ibid. See also Kasmieh, "The First World War," 282.

42. Kurd 'Ali, *al-Mudhakkirat,* 173.

43. Ibid.

44. "The Situation in Beirut and Syria (2)," *al-Muqattam* (Cairo), June 10, 1915, 5.

45. Adib Pacha, *Le Liban après la guerre* (Paris: Ernest Leroux, 1918), 60.

46. Strauss, "The Disintegration of Ottoman Rule," 320.

47. Yammin, *Lubnan fi l-harb,* vol. 2, 16.

48. Ibid., vol. 2, 8–14, quote on 14.

49. Ibid., vol. 2, 15, 18.

50. Ibid., vol. 2, 18–19.

51. Wadad al-Maqdisi Qurṭas, *Dhikrāyat, 1917–1977* (Beirut: Mu'assassat al-Abhath al-'Arabiyya, 1982), 34; Christoph Schumann, "Individual and Collective Memories of the First World War," in *The First World War as Remembered in the Countries of the Eastern Mediterranean,* 259. Many of the families of Zahlé came from the villages at the foot of Mount Sannin, such as Baskinta, Ayn al-Abu, and Kfar A'qab. The inhabitants would divide up the proximal Biqa' areas, plant them, and then retreat to their mountain villages; when the crops needed to be harvested, they would return to reap them. They would take what they did not sell back to their villages to store. The Cortases (from Baskinta), Maaloufs (from Kfar A'qab and Ayn al-Abu), Abu Haydars, and Hrawis were among the many families who came from these villages. The Ottomans would take the *jizya*—a tax, a portion of the crop—they received from non-Muslim *(dhimmi)* residents. To avoid the *jizya,* the villagers would harvest some crops earlier if possible. The farmers were given the right to own the land if they stayed and lived in the valley, that is, Zahlé and vicinity. Many Cortases did, where a large number still live. I am grateful to Nadim Cortas for the information provided here.

52. François Georgeon, "Au bord du rire et des larmes: Les Turcs d'Istanbul pendant la guerre et l'occupation (1914–1923)," in *Des Ottomans aux Turcs: Naissance d'une nation* (Istanbul: Les Editions Isis, 1995), 336.

53. Ibid., citing Şerif Mardin, "Super Westernization in Urban Life in the Ottoman Empire in the Last Quarter of the Nineteenth Century," in *Turkey: Geographic and Social Perspectives,* ed. P. Benedict and T. Tümertekin (Leiden: Brill, 1974).

54. See the instructive article by Christoph K. Neumann, "The First World War as a Time of Moral Failure: Its Reflections in Turkish Novels," in *The First World War as Remembered in the Countries of the Eastern Mediterranean,* 322–328.

55. Yalman, *Turkey in the World War,* 239.

56. Georgeon, "Au bord du rire et des larmes," 334 (my loose translation).

57. James L. Gelvin, *Divided Loyalties: Nationalism and Mass Politics in Syria at the Close of Empire* (Berkeley: University of California Press, 1998), 24.

58. Georgeon, "Au bord du rire et des larmes," 337.

59. T. E. Lawrence, *Seven Pillars of Wisdom: A Triumph* (London: Penguin, 2000), 163.

60. George Korkor (unpublished memoir), approx. 1892–1915. Private collection. Access provided by the Tarazi family.

61. Ibid.

62. Ibid. Saydnaya is a city located in the mountains north of Damascus. It is famous for its convent, Our Lady of Saydnaya, with an icon of the Virgin Mary in the main church. Long a center of pilgrimage, it is considered a place of spiritual renewal and healing.

63. Ibid.

64. Yalman, *Turkey in the World War,* 144.

65. Ajay, "Mount Lebanon and the Wilayah of Beirut, 1914–1918: The War Years," Ph.D. diss., Georgetown University (1973), 305–309; Isma'il Haqqi, *Lubnan: Mabahith 'ilmiyya wa-ijtima'iyya,* ed. F. I. al-Bustani, 2 vols. (Beirut: al-Matba'a al-Kathulikiyya, 1969–1970), 305–307.

66. Ajay, "Mount Lebanon," 311.

67. Ibid., 297–208 and n. 734.

68. Maqdisi, *A'zam harb fi l-tarikh,* 27.

69. Ibid., 27–28.

70. Ibid.

71. Ajay, "Mount Lebanon," 456.

72. Maqdisi, *A'zam harb fi l-tarikh,* 28.

73. Yalman, *Turkey in the World War,* 144; Darwaza, *Mudhakkirat* [Memoirs], vol. 1 (Beirut: Dar al-Gharb al-Islami, 1993), 187–288.

74. Ajay, "Mount Lebanon," 314–328.

75. Yalman, *Turkey in the World War,* 145–146.

76. Ibid., 241.

77. Edib, *House with Wisteria,* 432–433.

78. Ajay, "Mount Lebanon," 323, and Appendix 1, 28.

79. Ibid., Appendix 1, 27–28.

80. Ibid., 323 and n. 799; Mary Dale Dorman, Journal, March 22, 1916 (unpublished manuscript). Private collection. I am grateful to William A. Rugh for his help and to June Rugh and Kathy Dorman Wright who made the 1915–1918 journals of Mary Dale Dorman available to me.

81. Bishara al-Buwari, *Arba' sinin al-harb* [Four years of the war] (New York: al-Huda, 1926), 187–188.

82. Yalman, *Turkey in the World War,* 110. For currency rates in this period, consult "Note on Exchange Rates" in this book; see also Şevket Pamuk, "The

Ottoman Economy in World War I," in *The Economics of World War I,* ed. Stephen Broadberry and Mark Harrison (New York: Cambridge University Press, 2005), 112–136; Abdul-Karim Rafeq, "Arabism, Society, and Economy in Syria, 1918–1920," in *State and Society in Syria and Lebanon,* ed. Y. M. Choueiri (Exeter, UK: University of Exeter Press, 1993), 20, 22. I am grateful to Feroz Ahmad, Hasan Kayali, and Abdul-Karim Rafeq for information about currency rates.

83. Maqdisi, *A'zam harb fi l-tarikh,* 74. Ajay, "Mount Lebanon," 324, also quotes from an anonymous interviewer who told him that the Ottomans "circulated paper money at the rate of one paper pound per one gold pound. The price of the paper fluctuated such that my father would give the people one gold pound for ten paper pounds whereas the going rate in Beirut was ten paper pounds for two gold pounds."

84. Yalman, *Turkey in the World War,* 139.

85. Ibid., 139–141.

86. Ibid., 136–138.

87. Bechara Baroody, unpublished memoir. Private collection, 16.

88. Ibrahim Kan'an, *Lubnan fi l-harb al-kubra, 1914–1918* [Lebanon in the Great War, 1914–1918] (Beirut[?]: Mu'assasat 'Asi, 1974[?]), 355.

89. Ibid., 40.

90. Nadim Baroody, welcoming speech given at the centennial celebration of the Baroody company, Hilton Hotel at Sin al-Fil, Beirut, Lebanon, October 4, 2012. I am grateful to Randa Baroody Tarazi for information she provided about the Baroody family, including the memoir that she gathered from Nadim Baroody and from Raja Baroody (the son of Benjamin) and others. Note that Benjamin Baroody is mentioned in the memoir of Wadad Cortas, who wrote about her brother-in-law's (Benjamin Baroody) entrepreneurial spirit, describing him as a model of energy and vitality. Al-Maqdisi Qurṭas, *Dhikrayāt,* 34.

91. Muhammad Kurd 'Ali, *Khitat al-Sham* (Beirut: Dar al-'Ilm li l-Malayin, 1969–1971), vol. 4, 230–233; Muhammad Kurd 'Ali, in *al-Muqtabas,* vol. 7, 57.

92. Kurd 'Ali, *Khitat al-Sham,* vol. 4, 230.

93. Elias Khoury, *Little Mountain,* trans. M. Tabet (New York: Picador, 2007), 8–9. Kurd 'Ali wrote that he visited the factory in 1912 and that it belonged to Ilyas Jirji Sioufi. *Khitat al-Sham,* vol. 4, 230–233.

94. Khoury, *Little Mountain,* 8.

95. Ibid., 9. Abu George mentioned that there might have been another reason for the bankruptcy: "People who knew Nkoula Sioufi—who had become an 'errand-runner' at the Ministry of Finance—said the reason was that he drank and gambled and associated with foreigners. God only knows, Abu George would say. But the decline set in with the beginning of this new-style thieving."

96. Keith David Watenpaugh, *Being Modern in the Middle East: Revolution, Nationalism, Colonialism, and the Arab Middle Class* (Princeton, NJ: Princeton University Press, 2006), section I, 55–120.

97. Ibid., xvii–xix; see also Claude Mutafian, "Les princesses arméniennes et le Liban latin (XIIe–XIIIe siècle)," in *Armenians of Lebanon: From Past Princesses and Refugees to Present-Day Community,* ed. A. Boudjikanian (Beirut: Haigazian University; Belmont, MA: Armenian Heritage Press, 2009), 3–28.

98. R. G. Hovannisian, "The Ebb and Flow of the Armenian Minority in the Arab Middle East," *Middle East Journal* 28 (1974): 22.

99. Ibid., 20; Vahé Tachjian, "L'établissement definitive des réfugiés arméniens au Liban dans les années 1920 et 1930," in *Armenians of Lebanon,* 56–76. I am also grateful to Dr. Dickran Kouymjian for information he provided me concerning Armenian migration.

100. Scholars have looked into the numbers of Armenians who lived in Anatolia or left it around World War I and after. For one discussion of the numbers of refugees, see Nicola Migliorino, *(Re)constructing Armenia in Lebanon and Syria: Ethno-Cultural Diversity and the State in the Aftermath of a Refugee Crisis* (New York: Berghahn, 2008), 30–43. Migliorino points out that estimates of the Armenians who were victims of the genocide of 1915–1916 vary widely; the most quoted figures range from 600,000 to 1.5 million. Estimates of the Armenian population that lived in Turkey before the war range from less than 1 million to over 2 million. He reports that by 1927 Armenians were reduced to less than 1 percent of the total population. The difficulties of estimating the population stem in part from the fact that displacements took place not only in 1915–1916 but continued through the period of the two world wars and after, so that there are four major waves of Armenian refugees: (1) after 1918 when the British and French armies took control of Cilicia; (2) in 1921 when France gave up control of Cilicia and signed an accord with the Turkish government allowing it to reoccupy the country; (3) between 1929 and 1930, when more Armenians left under government pressure; and (4) in 1939–1940 at the end of the French Mandate over the sanjak of Alexandretta, which was returned to Turkey. Relying on research by Richard Hovannisian and others, Migliorino concludes that with the exception of a few areas such as Aleppo, the sanjak of Alexandretta, and Latakia, where Armenians were already settled before 1914, "most of the Armenian communities of Lebanon and Syria were formed as a direct consequence of the inflow of refugees." Ibid., 34. Relying on Hovannisian's estimate, he suggests that in 1925 "well over 200,000 exiles had been received into the Arab lands under French or British mandate." Their breakdown in the countries of the Middle East in 1925 came to 100,000 in Syria, 50,000 in Lebanon, 10,000 in Palestine and Jordan, 40,000 in Egypt, 25,000 in Iraq, and 50,000 in Iran. Ibid., 34.

101. Watenpaugh, *Being Modern,* 32.

102. Ibid., 124.

103. Hovannisian, "Ebb and Flow," 26.

104. Darwaza, *Mudhakkirat,* vol. 1, 253–254; Q. B. Khuwayri, *al-Rihla al-suriyya fi l-harb al-ʿumumiyya 1916: Akhtar wa-ahwal wa-ʿajaʾib* [The Syrian journey in the

Great War, 1916: Perils, horrors, and marvels], ed. Y. Tuma al-Bustani (Cairo: al-Matba'a al-Yusufiyya, 1921), 76, quoting a French commander at sea to the Allies; Nicholas Z. Ajay, "Political Intrigue and Suppression in Lebanon during World War I," *International Journal of Middle East Studies* 5 (1974): 145.

105. Iskenderun, formerly Alexandretta, is in the south of Turkey, on the Gulf of Alexandretta, an inlet of the Mediterranean Sea. The principal Turkish port on the Mediterranean, it was founded by Alexander the Great to commemorate his victory over the Persians at Issus in 333 B.C., then conquered in A.D. 1515 by the Ottoman sultan Selim I; it was transferred in 1920 to the French Mandate as part of the sanjak of Alexandretta. It was ceded by the French to Turkey in 1939.

106. I am grateful to Aïda K. Boudjikanian for information on Anjar. Boudjikanian, "Success Stories Libano-Arméniennes," *Le commerce du Levant,* no. 5633 (October 2012): 66, reported that the last great exodus of Armenians came in the 1940s after Iskenderun was ceded to Turkey and that the majority of these refugees settled in Anjar where they concentrated on agriculture.

107. In 2012, the number of Lebanese-Armenians was about 150,000, settled mostly in Beirut, Burj Hammud, and Anjar ("Success Stories Libano-Arméniennes," 66). For the Armenians of Beirut, see Aïda K. Boudjikanian, "Les Arméniens de l'agglomération de Beyrouth: Étude humaine et économique. Première partie," *HASSK* (revue arménologique) (1981–1982): 401–440; Boudjikanian, "Les Arméniens de l'agglomération de Beyrouth: Étude humaine et économique. Deuxième partie," *HASSK* (1983–1984): 383–415.

108. Hovannisian, "Ebb and Flow," 25.

109. Hagop Arsenian, *Towards Golgotha: The Memoirs of Hagop Arsenian, a Genocide Survivor,* trans. and annot. Arda Arsenian Ekmekji (Beirut: Haigazian University Press, 2011), xiv–xv, 25–141. The journey in 1915–1916 was excerpted from Arsenian's diary and recently published: Hagop Arsenian and Arda Arsenian Ekmekji, "Surviving Massacre: Hagop Arsenian's Armenian Journey to Jerusalem, 1915–1916," *Jerusalem Quarterly* 49 (2012): 2–42.

110. Arsenian and Arsenian Ekmekji, "Surviving Massacre," 36–40.

111. Arsenian, *Towards Golgotha,* 131; Arsenian and Arsenian Ekmekji, "Surviving Massacre," 31–34.

112. Margaret McGilvary, *The Dawn of a New Era in Syria* (New York: Fleming H. Revell, 1920), 226, 231. McGilvary pointed out that Dr. Arthur Dray, a member of the faculty of the Syrian Protestant College and its dental department, was enthusiastic in praise of his management of the medical department. Thanks to Aïda K. Boudjikanian for drawing my attention to the five-volume study of Armenians by Sissag Hagop Varjabedian, *Hayere Lipanani Metch* [Armenians in Lebanon: Encyclopedia of the Armenian community in Lebanon], 5 vols. (Beirut: N.p., 1951–1983). In the first volume of the series, two Utudjian are mentioned: Wahram A. Utudjian graduated in 1910 with a bachelor of arts from the Syrian

Protestant College, and Dikran Utudjian graduated in 1911 with a bachelor of arts in business administration. This book has numerous lists of the Syrian Protestant graduates of the nineteenth century in different disciplines, including medicine, but no Dikran Utudjian.

113. "Success Stories Libano-Arméniennes," 84. I am grateful to Aïda Boudjikanian for pointing me to this case.

114. Sami Toubia, *Sarrafian Liban 1900–1930* (Mansourieh, Lebanon: ALEPH, 2008), 9–10; *A Brief History of the Postcard*, "Early Postcards of the Lebanon," http://www.libanpostcard.com/postcard_history.html.

115. I am grateful to Aïda Boudjikanian for this point as well and for her work on the Armenians, including letting me know of a paper she presented in Jerusalem in 2010 on this topic.

116. Toubia, *Sarrafian Liban 1900–1930*, 13–16.

117. One Fine Art, "The Sarrafian Brothers," http://onefineart.com/en/artists /sarrafian_brothers/.

118. See the detailed and very useful information on intelligence provided by Ajay, "Political Intrigue," 142–144; Yammin, *Lubnan fi l-harb*, vol. 2, 158–160, 184–185, 195; Lewen Francis Barrington Weldon, *"Hard Lying": Eastern Mediterranean, 1914–1919* (London: Herbert Jenkins, 1925), which are the diaries kept by Captain Weldon for 1914–1919. Weldon explains that hard lying is "a term applied to a special allowance granted to men serving in small crafts, such as destroyers, torpedo-boats, trawlers, etc.," vi. See also Kristian Coates Ulrichsen, *The Logistics and Politics of the British Campaigns in the Middle East, 1914–22* (Basingstoke, UK: Palgrave Macmillan, 2011), 6, 35.

119. Weldon, *"Hard Lying,"* 9.

120. Ibid., 184, 210.

121. Ibid., 186.

122. Ajay, "Political Intrigue," 143.

123. Weldon, *"Hard Lying,"* 195; Ajay, "Political Intrigue," 143.

124. 'Aziz Bek, *Suriya wa-Lubnan fi l-harb al-'alamiyya: al-Istikhbarat wa-l-jasusiyya fi l-dawla l-'uthmaniyya* (Beirut, 1933), 308 and the rest of chap. 23. 'Aziz Bek specifically wrote that the Lebanese inhabitants were against us and did not hesitate at all to spy on behalf of the enemy because they thought that we were fierce enemies as they saw the French as their friends and protectors in this part of this Ottoman land.

125. Ajay, "Political Intrigue," 146, n. 1.

126. Weldon, *"Hard Lying,"* 210–211.

127. Ajay, "Political Intrigue," 146, n. 1.

128. Weldon, *"Hard Lying,"* 195.

129. Ibid., 188.

130. 'Aziz Bek, *Suriya wa-Lubnan*, 102–104; Khuwayri, *al-Rihla*, 8–9.

131. Khuwayri, *al-Rihla,* 10.

132. ʿAziz Bek, *Suriya wa-Lubnan,* 103–105.

133. Ibid., 105.

134. Ibid., 304.

135. Ibid., 301–302. "At first on May 7, 1915, the Ottoman General Command issued a secret order to the police and heads of the seaside guards that whoever was able to apprehend Bechara Buwari and send him to the General Command would receive a prize of 200 liras with immediate promotion of rank. This did not work as Buwari circulated easily, so on May 20, 1915, the prize was doubled to 500 liras. In a secret order proclaimed by ʿAziz Bek on June 18, 1915, the bounty was increased to 1,000 Turkish liras for whoever would catch Buwari alive; if dead, 500 liras. On August 3, 1915, a military tribunal sentenced Buwari to death in absentia and the confiscation of all his money and property. He was also given ten days to surrender."

136. Ibid., 308–309.

137. Yammin, *Lubnan fi l-harb,* vol. 2, 203.

138. Ajay, "Political Intrigue," 145–146; Khuwayri, *al-Rihla,* 5–6, 9–11, 16–18, 38–41, et passim.

139. Al-Buwari, *Arbaʿ sinin al-harb,* 9, mentions that Buwari received a permit from the French on which he was described as a Lebanese from a French protectorate and a businessman; ibid., 147, clarifies that he is from Jounieh.

140. Ibid., 16.

141. Ibid., 17.

142. Ibid., 18.

143. Ibid., 248–252.

144. Sometimes spelled Rouad by the French and Ruad by the British.

145. Al-Buwari, *Arbaʿ sinin al-harb,* 371, tells us that he received the Medal of War, probably sometime in 1917.

146. Ibid., 79.

147. Ibid., 100–103.

148. Ibid., 105.

149. Ibid. Trabaud is mentioned on several occasions including at 100, 133, 153, 160, 201, and 381; Ajay ("Political Intrigue," 143–144) mentions the French occupation of Arwad and its use during the war, where he also describes the *D'Estrées* (which he spells *Destri*) as a destroyer. See also Khuwayri, *al-Rihla,* 72–73 and notes.

150. Al-Buwari, *Arbaʿ sinin al-harb,* 154.

151. Ibid., 119.

152. Ibid., 118–119.

153. Ibid., 41.

154. Ibid., 132.

155. Ibid., 380.

156. Ibid., 397–405.

157. Ibid., 355–358; the quote is from 357.

158. Ibid., 160–164. This example is about a Father Butrus who had to be picked up from Jubayl under dangerous circumstances. There are many examples of these perilous activities in which local people worked with the French and their collaborators.

159. Ibid., 279.

160. Ibid., 30.

161. Al Okeibeh is a quarter in Damascus. I am grateful to Abdul-Karim Rafeq for information on this quarter. See also Brigitte Marino, *Le Faubourg du Midan à Damas à l'Epoque Ottomane* (Damascus: Institut Français de Damas, 1997), 64: "Selon J. Sauvaget, c'est surtout à partir du XIIIe siècle que commencent à se développer des faubourgs hors des murs de Damas, notamment ceux de 'Ukayba."

162. Al-Buwari, *Arba' sinin al-harb*, 30–37.

163. Ibid., 72.

164. Ibid., 358–359.

165. Ibid., 74.

166. Ibid.

167. Ibid., 74–75.

168. Ibid., 389–390.

169. Ibid., 388–390.

170. Ibid., 106.

171. Ibid., 109.

172. Ibid., 111–112.

173. Ibid., 123–124.

174. Ibid., 146–153.

175. Ibid., 153.

176. Ibid., 315.

177. Ibid., 315–316.

178. Ibid.

179. Ibid., 317–318.

5. THE SOLDIERING EXPERIENCE

1. Mapaseka Mogotsi, "Tibetan City to Open Doors," *The Star* (South Africa), April 3, 2008.

2. "Yakup Satar," *The Times* (London), April 8, 2008; "Turkey's Last Veteran of World War I Dies," *BBC Monitoring European*, April 3, 2008.

3. Erik J. Zürcher, "Between Death and Desertion: The Ottoman Empire Experience in World War I," *Turcica* 28 (1996): 236.

4. Ibid., 235–236.

5. Hans Kannengiesser, *The Campaign in Gallipoli* (London: Hutchinson & Co., 1927), 157.

6. Zürcher, "Between Death and Desertion," 240; Zürcher, *Arming the State: Military Conscription in the Middle East and Central Asia, 1775–1925* (London: I. B. Tauris, 1999), 85.

7. Zürcher, *Arming the State*, 85.

8. Ibid., 91.

9. Ibid., 85; Mehmet Beşikçi, *The Ottoman Mobilization of Manpower in the First World War: Between Voluntarism and Resistance* (Leiden: Brill, 2012), chaps. 1 and 2; Yücel Yanikdağ, *Healing the Nation: Prisoners of War, Medicine and Nationalism in Turkey, 1914–1939* (Edinburgh: Edinburgh University Press, 2013), 14–15.

10. In this context, Zürcher has speculated that "the army generally performed far better when it defended than when it attacked . . . due mainly to the lack of experienced non-commissioned officers (NCOs) who could lead and inspire the units. Too many of these had died in the Balkan War of 1912–1913" ("Between Death and Desertion," 239).

11. The Janissary Corps is a famous exception. See Zürcher, *Arming the State*, 87–88. For estimates of the Ottoman population during the Great War, including estimates of war casualties and war prisoners, see Yanikdağ, *Healing the Nation*, 16–18, and elsewhere. See also Beşikçi, *Ottoman Mobilization*, 139–149, on the problems of exemptions.

12. Ibid., 86.

13. Ibid.

14. Ibid. 87–90.

15. Ibid., 86.

16. Ibid.

17. Ibid. "Most Ottoman Christians were equally unenthusiastic. By and large they felt themselves to be subjects of the Ottoman state, not members of an Ottoman nation" (ibid., 88–89).

18. Ibid., 87–90; Zürcher, "Between Death and Desertion," 240.

19. Zürcher, *Arming the State*, 87.

20. Ibid., 91.

21. Najwa al-Qattan, "Safarbarlik: Ottoman Syria and the Great War," in *From the Syrian Land to the States of Syria and Lebanon,* ed. T. Philipp and C. Schumann (Beirut: Orient-Institut, 2004), 164.

22. *Records of Iraq 1914–1918, vol. 1,* ed. A. de L. Rush and J. Priestland (Chippenham, UK: Antony Rowe, 2001), 157.

23. Erik J. Zürcher, *Savaş, devrim ve uluslaşma: Türkiye tarihinde geçiş dönemi, 1908–1928* [The war, the revolution and Turkey in the process of becoming a nation, 1908–1928] (Istanbul: Bilgi University Publication, 2005).

24. Ziya Yergök, *Tuğgeneral Ziya Yergök'ün anıları: Sarikamis'tan esarete, 1915–1920* [Memoirs of brigadier general Ziya Yergök: From Sarikamis to captivity], ed. S. Onal (Istanbul: Remzi Kitabevi, 2006), 23.

25. Ibid.

26. "Diaries of a Christian Ottoman Soldier (Bassili 'Abdini)," *al-Muqattam* (Cairo), October 8, 1915, 2.

27. Ibid.

28. Salim Tamari, *Year of the Locust: A Soldier's Diary and the Erasure of Palestine's Ottoman Past* (Berkeley: University of California Press, 2011), 11.

29. Otto Liman von Sanders, *Five Years in Turkey*, trans. Carl Reichmann (Annapolis, MD: United States Naval Institute, 1927), 191.

30. *Al-Ahram* (Cairo), July 31, 1914.

31. "Military Recruitments of the Head of Families," *al-Muqattam* (Cairo), July 16, 1914, 4.

32. Ibid.

33. *Handbook of the Turkish Army (1916)* (Skokie, IL: Imperial War Museum in association with the Battery Press—Nashville and Articles of War, Ltd., 1996), Intelligence Section–Cairo, 5.

34. *Records of Iraq*, 158.

35. Tarif Khalidi, "The Arab World," in *The Great World War, 1914–1945*, vol. 2: *The Peoples' Experience*, ed. P. Liddle, J. Bourne, and I. Whitehead (London: HarperCollins, 2001), 293.

36. Ibid.

37. Abigail Jacobson, "Negotiating Ottomanism in Times of War: Jerusalem during World War I through the Eyes of a Local Muslim Resident," *International Journal of Middle East Studies* 40, 1 (2008): 74.

38. Ibid.

39. Ibid.

40. Abdallah Hanna, "The First World War According to the Memories of 'Commoners' in the Bilad al-Sham," in *The World in World Wars: Experiences, Perceptions and Perspectives from Africa and Asia,* ed. H. Liebau et al. (Leiden: Brill, 2010), 304.

41. Zürcher, *Arming the State*, 85–86.

42. Hanna Mina, *Fragments of Memory: A Story of a Syrian Family*, trans. Olive Kenny and Lorne Kenny (Austin: Center for Middle Eastern Studies, University of Texas, 1993).

43. Jacobson, "Negotiating Ottomanism," 74.

44. Ibid.

45. Zürcher, *Arming the State*, 86.

46. "News from Jaffa," *al-Muqattam* (Cairo), July 24, 1914, 3.

47. Ibid.

48. Al-Qattan, "Safarbarlik," 166; See also Bruce Masters, *The Arabs of the Ottoman Empire, 1516–1918: A Social and Cultural History* (New York: Cambridge University Press, 2013), 217.

49. Al-Qattan, "Safarbarlik," 164.

50. Ibid., 171. See also Nadiya al-Ghazzi, *Shirwal Barhum: Ayyam min safarbarlik* (Damascus: al-Shadi li l-Nashr wa-l-Tawzi', 1993), 35, 50, 60, et passim.

51. Hanna, "First World War," 299.

52. Al-Qattan, "Safarbarlik," 166.

53. Ibid.

54. WO 157/695, A. C. Parker, A/Dir of (Military) Intelligence, September 11, 1915.

55. Zürcher, *Arming the State,* 91.

56. "Military Recruitment in Syria," *al-Muqattam* (Cairo), September 30, 1914, 5.

57. Jacobson, "Negotiating Ottomanism," 74; "News from Beirut," *al-Muqattam* (Cairo), September 29, 1914, 2–3; "News from Syria: Military Recruitment and Financial Affairs," ibid., August 18, 1914, 3.

58. *Al-Muqattam* reported on men attempting to evade service by boarding an Italian ship at Jounieh. "News from Beirut," September 29, 1914, 2–3. The *vilayet* of Beirut was alerted and sent thirty armed men to arrest them. Consequently, the boat was obliged to leave Beirut for Alexandria.

59. 'Abd al-Fattah Rawwas Qal'aji, *'Urs halabi wa-hikayat min safar barlik: Thulathiyya masrahiyya al-khutuba, al-'urs, al-ahzan* (Damascus: Manshurat Wizarat al-Thaqafah, 1984), 37–38, 142–143.

60. Ibid.

61. Jacobson, "Negotiating Ottomanism," 73–74.

62. Zürcher, "Between Death and Desertion," 242.

63. Ibid.

64. Translation of an official proclamation, issued by the "Selimeh Recruiting Bureau," which included Constantinople and Scutari, in WO 157/695, Secret, Military Intelligence Office, War Office, Cairo, September 2, 1915 [A. Clark], Lieut-Col A/Dir of (Military) Intelligence, extracts from MEDFORCE BULLE-TIN, August 24, 1915.

65. "The True Situation in Syria and Lebanon. Written by a British Citizen," *al-Muqattam* (Cairo), July 29, 1915, 5–6; "Military Aid in Lebanon," ibid., July 30, 1915, 5; "Military Recruitment in Syria," ibid., December 17, 1915, 5. According to Zürcher, "in the course of mobilization males between the ages of 19 and 45 were called up. By 1916, however, the age limits had been extended to 15 and 55 respectively and, according to British reports by mid-1917, 12% of the total were between the ages of 16 and 19" ("Between Death and Desertion," 242).

66. "Military Recruitment in Syria," *al-Muqattam* (Cairo), December 17, 1915, 5.

67. "In Syria and Lebanon," *al-Ahram* (Cairo), January 6, 1915, 5; idem., February 3, 1915, no. 11265, "Alexandria Every Day: News and Ideas," 5.

68. Ahmed Emin Yalman, *Turkey in the World War* (New Haven, CT: Yale University Press, 1930), 248–253.

69. "Alexandria Every Day: News and Ideas," *al-Ahram* (Cairo), February 3, 1915, 5.

70. For the Lebanon militia, see *Handbook of the Turkish Army (1916)*, 55; for Mount Lebanon regulations between 1861 and 1930, see Engin Deniz Akarli, *The Long Peace: Ottoman Lebanon, 1861–1920* (Berkeley: University of California Press, 1993).

71. "The Situation in Syria and Lebanon," *al-Muqattam* (Cairo), December 18, 1915, 5; "Military Recruitment in Syria," ibid., December 17, 1915, 5.

72. Zürcher, *Arming the State,* 90.

73. Sarkis Torossian, *From Dardanelles to Palestine: A True Story of Five Battle Fronts of Turkey and Her Allies and a Harem Romance* (Boston: Meador, 1947), 132–133.

74. Tamari, *Year of the Locust,* 10.

75. *Handbook of the Turkish Army (1916)*, 3. For example, on March 17, 1916, *al-Ahram* reported on ten thousand young Christians, recruited into the army, who were ordered to work the railway between Damascus and Palestine. "Christian Military Recruits in Syria," 4.

76. Tamari, *Year of the Locust,* 9.

77. Zürcher, "Between Death and Desertion," 240.

78. Tamari, *Year of the Locust,* 9.

79. Elizabeth F. Thompson, *Colonial Citizens: Republican Rights, Paternal Privilege, and Gender in French Syria and Lebanon* (New York: Columbia University Press, 2000), 22.

80. Ibid.

81. "Syria and Its Government: When Will They Lose Patience?" *al-Muqattam* (Cairo), July 1, 1915, 1. Khalid al-Azm, son of a prominent family of Damascus, "includes in his memoirs news of the war as his family was told by visiting guests, or as it was published in the only official newspaper in Damascene, *Al-Sharq*. . . . 'By the order of Military Headquarters, Syrian soldiers were taken to faraway fronts such as Sinai, the Dardanelles or the Caucasus. Many of these young men lost their lives, were wounded or sent to captivity. The number of those who went into hiding to avoid service outnumbered those who joined the military service.'" Khairia Kasmieh, "The First World War as Represented in Autobiographies in Contemporary Damascus," in *The First World War as Remembered in the Countries of the Eastern Mediterranean*, ed. O. Farschid, M. Kropp, and S. Dähne (Beirut: Orient-Institut, 2006), 279. See also "The Situation in Syria and Lebanon," *al-Muqattam* (Cairo), December 18, 1915, 5: "The government sent the Arab soldiers to Armenia and the Dardanelles. The government was trying to get them away from Syria

because it feared a rebellion. If there are any Arab soldiers left in Syria or Egypt, I can assure you that these soldiers are waiting for their first chance to escape the army and surrender to the allies."

82. Liman von Sanders, *Five Years,* 264–265.

83. Torossian, *Dardanelles to Palestine,* 51.

84. Liman von Sanders, *Five Years,* 264.

85. Eliezer Tauber, *The Arab Movements in World War I* (London: Frank Cass, 1993), 111.

86. Ibid., 110.

87. Zürcher, "Between Death and Desertion," 246.

88. Yalman, *Turkey in the World War,* 262.

89. Bishara al-Buwari, *Arba' sinin al-harb* [Four years of the war] (New York: al-Huda, 1926), 75–76.

90. Ibid., 175. The young man was named Gilles Dargham.

91. Torossian describes the *Legion d'Orient* in one engagement "conducting a united attack along the whole front, resulting in less than an hour in complete disaster to the Turks who became panic-stricken and rushed in the direction of headquarters in extreme disorder." *Dardanelles to Palestine,* 187–188.

92. Ibid., 186.

93. Thompson, *Colonial Citizens,* 23; Kasmieh, "First World War," 279, citing Khalid 'Azm, *Mudhakkirat* [Memoirs], vol. 1 (Beirut: al-Dar al-Muttahida li-l-Nashr, 1972), 75.

94. George Antonius, *The Arab Awakening* (New York: Capricorn, 1965), 188.

95. "Military Recruitment in Syria," *al-Ahram* (Cairo), March 10, 1916, 4.

96. "News from Syria and Lebanon," *al-Ahram* (Cairo), June 19, 1916, 4.

97. Liman von Sanders, *Five Years,* 265.

98. Zürcher, "Between Death and Desertion," 246.

99. Rafael de Nogales Méndez, *Four Years beneath the Crescent* (London: Taderon, 2003), 253.

100. Liman von Sanders, *Five Years,* 263.

101. Nogales Méndez, *Four Years,* 222.

102. Ibid., 222–223.

103. Zürcher, "Between Death and Desertion," 246.

104. "Beirut and Syria and Lebanon," *al-Muqattam* (Cairo), October 29, 1914. There were six reports that five hundred deserters were arrested and sent to jail in Damascus, Homs, Hama, and Aleppo and were still waiting for the verdict of the military court. They might escape execution and be sentenced to jail with hard labor.

105. Ibid.; "Famine and Misrule in Syria," *The Times* (London), April 5, 1916.

106. WO 157/695, Secret, Military Intelligence Office, War Office, Cairo, September 2, 1915 [A. Clark], Lieut-Col A/Dir of (Military) Intelligence, June 21.

107. WO 157/695, "Desertion," A. Clark, Lieut-Col A/Dir of (Military) Intelligence, September 2, 1915.

108. Alfred Chevallier Parker, *The Diaries of Parker Pasha: War in the Desert, 1914–18* (London: Quartet, 1983), 84.

109. Yalman, *Turkey in the World War,* 177.

110. P. G. Elgood, *Egypt and the Army* (Oxford: Oxford University Press, 1924), 238–239.

111. Ibid., 239.

112. Ibid., 315.

113. FO 141/469, Archibald Murray, May 22, 1917.

114. A. P. Wavell, *The Palestine Campaigns,* 2nd ed. (London: Constable, 1929), 63.

115. David Woodward, *Hell in the Holy Land* (Lexington: University Press of Kentucky, 2006), 36.

116. Ibid.

117. Ibid.

118. Ibid., 40.

119. Ibid., 42.

120. Elgood, *Egypt and the Army,* 311–312.

121. Ibid., 330.

122. Liman von Sanders, *Five Years,* 243–244.

123. Fawzi Qawuqji, *Mudhakkirat 1912–1932* [Memoirs] (Beirut: Dar al-Quds, 1975), 43.

124. Zürcher, "Between Death and Desertion," 246.

125. Yalman, *Turkey in the World War,* 264.

126. Ibid.

127. Tamari, *Year of the Locust,* 56.

128. Zürcher, "Between Death and Desertion," 245.

129. Tauber, *Arab Movements,* 111.

130. Feroz Ahmad, "The Dilemmas of Young Turk Policy during the Great War 1914–1918," paper presented at Tufts University workshop on "The Middle East in the Two World Wars," held at Harvard and at Tufts, May 10–12, 2002, citing the Mecilis-I Mebusan [Chamber of Deputies] debates for October 10 and 16, 1918. I am grateful to Feroz Ahmad for giving me permission to quote from his paper.

131. Woodward, *Hell in the Holy Land,* 1.

132. Wavell, *Palestine Campaigns,* 22.

133. Kress von Kressenstein, *Zwischen Kaukasus und Sinai: Jahrbuch des Bundes der Asienkämpfer* (Berlin: Mulzer and Cleemann, 1921), 37–38.

134. Trevor Wilson, *The Myriad Faces of War: Britain and the Great War, 1914–1918* (New York: Blackwell, 1986), 269.

135. Wavell, *Palestine Campaigns,* 21.

136. Ibid., 50.

137. Woodward, *Hell in the Holy Land,* 3.

138. Justin McCarthy, *The Ottoman Turks* (London: Longman, 1997), 362.

139. Kannengiesser, *Campaign in Gallipoli,* 159.

140. Nogales Méndez, *Four Years,* 259; Liman von Sanders, *Five Years,* 112.

141. Liman von Sanders, *Five Years,* 20.

142. Ibid., 30.

143. Wavell, *Palestine Campaigns,* 21.

144. Woodward, *Hell in the Holy Land,* 88.

145. J. D. Crowdy to Nora Crowdy, October 28, 1917, Samarra. Major J. D. Crowdy Collection: United Kingdom, St. Antony's College, Middle East Center Archive (hereafter cited as Crowdy Collection).

146. Ibid.

147. Edward Woodfin, *Camp and Combat on the Sinai and Palestine Front* (New York: Palgrave Macmillan, 2012), 131.

148. Kannengiesser, *Campaign in Gallipoli,* 154.

149. Ibid., 155.

150. Kermit Roosevelt, *War in the Garden of Eden* (New York: C. Scribner's Sons, 1919), 113.

151. Harry Stürmer, *Two War Years in Constantinople: Sketches of German and Young Turkish Ethics and Politics,* trans. E. Allen (New York: George H. Doran, 1917), 95–96.

152. WO 158/634, Bassett to Arbur, telegram, September 9, 1917.

153. Roosevelt, *Garden of Eden,* 113.

154. "Ottoman Prisoners," *al-Ahram* (Cairo), July 23, 1915, 5; "Ottoman Detainees in Tora," *al-Muqattam* (Cairo), June 12, 1915, 5.

155. WO 157/695, A. C. Parker to "Al Ahram, Cairo," cablegram, September 4, 1915.

156. Hikmet Özdemir, *The Ottoman Army 1914–1918: Disease and Death on the Battlefield* (Salt Lake City: University of Utah Press, 2008), 88–89: The notorious death marches were the subject of animated discussion. Enfeebled soldiers died during their forced marches, sometimes stretching hundreds of miles long, into captivity.

157. Yanikdağ, *Healing the Nation,* 14–118.

158. Salim Tamari, "With God's Camel in Siberia: The Russian Exile of an Ottoman Officer from Jerusalem," *Jerusalem Quarterly* 35 (2008): 39.

159. Ibid., 38.

160. Ibid., 39.

161. Ibid.

162. T. Khalidi, "The Arab World," 294: "Many Muslims were later to question the legitimacy of a call to Jihad against some Christian powers (Russia, France and Britain) while allied to others (Austria and Germany). Meanwhile, an Arab nationalist man of letters in Jerusalem, a Christian, recorded in his diary that the call to *Jihad*

was a throw-back to the dark ages of bigotry. It was clearly not an empire whose citizens, in any significant proportion, had any deep or sincere or even jingoistic desire to die in its defence."

163. Hasan Kayali, *Arabs and Young Turks: Ottomanism, Arabism, and Islamism in the Ottoman Empire, 1908–1918* (Berkeley: University of California Press, 1997), 187.

164. Tamari, "God's Camel," 40.

165. Ibid., 45–56.

166. Tamari, *Year of the Locust,* 68–69.

167. Walid Khalidi, "Aref al Aref, al Nakbah and Paradise Lost," *Review of Palestinian Studies* (2012): 54; 'Arif al-'Arif, *Ru'yay* [My dreams] (Jerusalem: Matba'at al-Aba' al-Fransin, 1934), 2.

168. Tamari, "God's Camels," 46.

169. Ja'far al-'Askari, *A Soldier's Story: From Ottoman Rule to Independent Iraq. The Memoirs of Jafar Pasha Al-Askari (1885–1936),* trans. Mustafa Tariq al-Askari, ed. William Facey and Najdat Fathi Safwat (London: Arabian, 2003). The Arabic edition is *Mudhakkirat Ja'far al-'Askari,* ed. Najdat Fathi Safwat (London: Dar al-Lam, 1988), 97–98.

170. Ibid., 104.

171. Ibid., 105.

172. Ibid., 110.

173. Ibid., 110–111.

174. Tauber, *Arab Movements,* 102.

175. Ibid., 110.

176. Zürcher, "Between Death and Desertion," 240.

177. Ibid.

178. Tauber, *Arab Movements,* 59.

179. Zürcher, "Between Death and Desertion," 240–241.

180. Ibid., 241.

181. Tamari, *Year of the Locust,* 13.

182. Zürcher, "Between Death and Desertion," 241.

183. Ronald Millar, *Kut: The Death of an Army* (London: Secker & Warburg, 1969), 275.

184. C. C. R. Murphy, *Soldiers of the Prophet* (London: John Hogg, 1921), 95.

185. Roosevelt, *Garden of Eden,* 47.

186. Ibid., 47.

187. Nogales Méndez, *Four Years,* 230.

188. Murphy, *Soldiers of the Prophet,* 103.

189. Reliant on Arab forces, Ottoman Colonel Suleiman al-'Askari attacked Nasiriyya in July 1915 and was decisively defeated. Despondent at his defeat after his tribal allies abandoned him, Askari committed suicide. Ibid., 112–113.

190. Ibid., 71.

191. Liman von Sanders, *Five Years,* 219.

192. Roosevelt, *Garden of Eden,* 47–48.

193. Woodfin, *Camp and Combat,* 131.

194. Roosevelt, *Garden of Eden,* 43.

195. Ibid., 139.

196. Hanna, "First World War," 305.

197. Liman von Sanders, *Five Years,* 235.

198. Roosevelt, *Garden of Eden,* 94–95.

199. Kasmieh, "First World War," 280.

200. Ibid., 285.

201. Ibid., 279, 285.

202. Ahmad Djemal Pasha, *Memories of a Turkish Statesman—1913–1919* (London: Hutchinson and Co., 1922), 153.

203. Jacobson, "Negotiating Ottomanism," 71.

204. Ibid., 69.

205. Ibid., 75.

206. Ibid.

207. Ibid., 75–77; Tamari, *Year of the Locust,* 53.

208. Jacobson, "Negotiating Ottomanism," 79.

209. Ibid. 80.

210. Qawuqji, *Mudhakkirat,* 37.

211. Ibid., 13.

212. Tauber, *Arab Movements,* 78.

213. Ibid., 67.

214. Liman von Sanders, *Five Years,* 50.

215. Ibid., 51.

216. Ibid.

217. Özdemir, *Ottoman Army,* 30.

218. Zürcher, "Between Death and Desertion," 250.

219. Liman von Sanders, *Five Years,* 28–29.

220. Zürcher conveys the importance of uninterrupted supply from Germany: "The armament was improved when the Germans started equipping the Ottomans with rifles taken from the Belgians after the occupation of Belgium and from the Russians after the German victories at the Mazurian lakes in Eastern Prussia. The only problem was the lack of ammunition, especially for the artillery, as most of this had to be imported from Germany and Austria." "Between Death and Desertion," 247.

221. Liman von Sanders, *Five Years,* 28–29; Zürcher, "Between Death and Desertion," 250–251; Özdemir, *Ottoman Army,* 29.

222. Liman von Sanders, *Five Years,* 28–29; Zürcher, "Between Death and Desertion," 251–252; Özdemir, *Ottoman Army,* 29.

223. Zürcher, "Between Death and Desertion," 252.

224. Waldemar Frey, *Kut El-Amara* (Berlin: Brunnen Verlag, 1932), 250–253, 263.

225. Ibid., 263–265.

226. Ibid., 266.

227. Zürcher, "Between Death and Desertion," 252.

228. Ibid., 251.

229. Ibid., 252.

230. Ibid., 253.

231. Ibid., 254.

232. Liman von Sanders, *Five Years*, 114.

233. Ibid., 231.

234. Roosevelt, *Garden of Eden*, 73.

235. Ibid., 172

236. Millar, *Kut*, 274.

237. C. A. Bayly, "Distorted Development: The Ottoman Empire and British India," *Comparative Studies of South Asia, Africa and the Middle East* 27, 2 (2007): 343.

238. Roosevelt, *Garden of Eden*, 56; Frey, *Kut El-Amara*, 365–381.

239. J. D. Crowdy to Nora Crowdy, September 15, 1917, Samarra. Crowdy Collection.

240. Yergök, *Tuğgeneral Ziya Yergök'ün anıları*, 26.

241. Ibid.

242. Zürcher, "Between Death and Desertion," 252.

243. Ibid., 252–253.

244. Ibid., 253.

245. Kress von Kressenstein, *Zwischen Kaukasus und Sinai*, 34.

246. Zürcher, "Between Death and Desertion," 247.

247. For the first quote, Woodward, *Hell in the Holy Land*, 189; for the second, Liman von Sanders, *Five Years*, 9–10.

248. Liman von Sanders, *Five Years*, 253.

249. Özdemir, *Ottoman Army*, 86.

250. Liman von Sanders, *Five Years*, 74.

251. Yalman, *Turkey in the World War*, 251.

252. Nogales Méndez, *Four Years*, 44.

253. Ibid.

254. Özdemir, *Ottoman Army*, 35.

255. Ibid.

256. Ölçen, Mehmet Arif, *Vetluga Memoir: A Turkish Prisoner of War in Russia, 1916–1918*, trans. G. Leiser (Gainesville: University Press of Florida, 1995).

257. Azade-Ayse Rorlich, review of Ölçen, *Vetluga Memoir*, *International Journal of Middle East Studies* 29 (1997): 458.

258. Zürcher, "Between Death and Desertion," 247; Özdemir, *Ottoman Army,* 35, 43.

259. Özdemir, *Ottoman Army,* 36.

260. Liman von Sanders, *Five Years,* 131

261. Ibid.

262. Kannengiesser, *Campaign in Gallipoli,* 157.

263. Zürcher, "Between Death and Desertion," 248.

264. Liman von Sanders, *Five Years,* 259–260.

265. Millar, *Kut,* 279–280.

266. Liman von Sanders, *Five Years,* 103.

267. Ibid., 103.

268. Ibid., 266.

269. Özdemir, *Ottoman Army,* 38–39.

270. Woodfin, *Camp and Combat,* 98–99.

271. Thompson, *Colonial Citizens,* 26.

272. Zürcher, "Between Death and Desertion," 248.

273. Ibid.

274. Ibid.

275. Ibid., 249.

276. "News from Beirut," *al-Muqattam* (Cairo), October 23, 1914, 2.

277. Ibid.

278. Zürcher, "Between Death and Desertion," 249.

279. Kannengiesser, *Campaign in Gallipoli,* 148–149.

280. Ibid., 149.

281. Özdemir, *Ottoman Army,* 39.

282. Zürcher, "Between Death and Desertion," 249–250.

283. Ibid.

284. Özdemir, *Ottoman Army,* 40.

285. Yalman, *Turkey in the World War,* 251.

286. Ibid.

287. Nogales Méndez, *Four Years,* 17.

288. Kannengiesser, *Campaign in Gallipoli,* 149.

289. Torossian, *Dardanelles to Palestine,* 103–104.

290. Yergök, *Tuğgeneral Ziya Yergök'ün anıları,* 79.

291. Qawuqji, *Mudhakkirat,* 41.

292. Yalman, *Turkey in the World War,* 251.

293. Tamari, *Year of the Locust,* 52.

294. Kannengiesser, *Campaign in Gallipoli,* 152–153.

295. Millar, *Kut,* 50.

296. Ibid., 147.

297. Zürcher, "Between Death and Desertion," 254.

298. Ibid., 255.

299. Ibid., 256.

300. Eran Dolev, *Allenby's Military Medicine* (London: I. B. Tauris, 2007), 101.

301. Özdemir, *Ottoman Army*, 7; Edward J. Erickson, *Ordered to Die: A History of the Ottoman Army in the First World War* (Westport, CT: Greenwood, 2001), 208.

302. Erickson, *Ordered to Die*, 210.

303. Ibid., 208.

304. Zürcher, "Between Death and Desertion," 256–257.

305. Ibid., 256–258.

306. Erickson, *Ordered to Die*, 208–211.

307. Özdemir, *Ottoman Army*, 9.

308. Zürcher, "Between Death and Desertion," 244–245.

309. Ibid.

310. Ibid.

311. Al-Qattan, "Safarbarlik," 169.

312. Özdemir reports that the "biggest problem bedeviling the cities of Baghdad and Mosul in 1916–1917 was amoebic dysentery." *Ottoman Army*, 90.

313. Ibid., 36–37.

314. Ibid., 28, 54.

315. Ibid., 36.

316. Liman von Sanders, *Five Years*, 156.

317. Ibid., 49–50.

318. Ibid., 132.

319. Yergök, *Tuğgeneral Ziya Yergök'ün anıları*, 76.

320. Özdemir, *Ottoman Army*, 69.

321. Ibid., 74.

322. Ibid., 69.

323. Ibid., 82–83.

324. *A Soldier's Story*, 119.

325. Ibid., 126.

326. Frey, *Kut El-Amara*, 396.

327. Özdemir, *Ottoman Army*, 34.

328. Ibid., 37.

329. Zürcher, "Between Death and Desertion," 245.

330. Frey, *Kut El-Amara*, 269.

331. Özdemir, *Ottoman Army*, 43.

332. T. Khalidi, "The Arab World," 301.

333. Özdemir, *Ottoman Army*, 33.

334. Ibid., 41.

335. Liman von Sanders, *Five Years*, 11–12.

336. Ibid.

337. Halidé Edib, *Memoirs of Halidé Edib* (London: John Murray, 1926), 420.

338. Liman von Sanders, *Five Years,* 11.

339. Dolev, *Allenby's Military Medicine,* 162.

340. Ibid., 162.

341. Ibid.

342. McCarthy, *Ottoman Turks,* 362.

343. Tamari, *Year of the Locust,* 57.

344. Ibid., 58.

345. Ibid.

6. SOUTH ASIANS IN THE WAR

1. "The Basra Memorial," *Commonwealth War Graves Commission: Forever India,* http://www.cwgc.org/foreverindia/memorials/basra-memorial.php, accessed July 26, 2013; Fergal Keane, "Basra's 'Lost' Imperial War Grave," http://news.bbc.co .uk/2/hi/middle_east/3124828.stm, accessed July 26, 2013.

2. Santanu Das, "Ardour and Anxiety: Politics and Literature in the Indian Homefront," in *The World in World Wars: Experiences, Perceptions, and Perspectives from Africa and Asia,* ed. H. Liebau et al. (Leiden: Brill, 2010), 341; Sugata Bose, *A Hundred Horizons: The Indian Ocean in the Age of Global Empire* (Cambridge, MA: Harvard University Press, 2006), 122.

3. See Leila Fawaz and C. A. Bayly, eds., *Modernity and Culture: From the Mediterranean to the Indian Ocean* (New York: Columbia University Press, 2002).

4. Kaushik Roy, "The Army in India in Mesopotamia from 1916–1918: Tactics, Technology and Logistics Reconsidered," in *1917: Beyond the Western Front,* ed. I. F. W. Beckett (Leiden: Brill, 2009), 133; Tan Tai-Yong, "An Imperial Home Front: Punjab and the First World War," *Journal of Military History* 64 (2000): 375.

5. Roy, "Army in India," 133. See also David Omissi, *Indian Voices of the Great War: Soldiers' Letters, 1914–1918* (New York: St. Martin's, 1999), 1–2.

6. Roy, "Army in India," 131; Omissi, *Indian Voices,* 2.

7. Omissi, *Indian Voices,* 4.

8. Stephen P. Cohen, "The Military Enters Indian Thought," in *War and Society in Colonial India, 1807–1945,* ed. K. Roy (Oxford: Oxford University Press, 2006), 172; Omissi, *Indian Voices,* 4.

9. Bose, *Hundred Horizons,* 59.

10. Ibid., 122–123.

11. Tai Yong Tan, "Imperial Home Front," 372.

12. Nikolas Gardner, "Morale of the Indian Army in the Mesopotamian Campaign," in *The Indian Army in the Two World Wars,* ed. K. Roy (Leiden: Brill. 2011), 395.

13. Omissi, *Indian Voices*, 2; David Omissi, *The Sepoy and the Raj: The Indian Army, 1860–1940* (Basingstoke, UK: Macmillan, 1994); Jeffrey Greenhut, "Sahib and Sepoy: An Inquiry into the Relationship between the British Officers and Native Soldiers of the British Indian Army," *Military Affairs* 48 (1984): 15–16.

14. Gardner, "Morale of the Indian Army," 395.

15. Ibid.

16. Ibid., 396.

17. Tai Yong Tan, "Imperial Home Front," 381–382.

18. Omissi, *Indian Voices*, 16.

19. Mario Ruiz, "Manly Spectacles and Imperial Soldiers in Wartime Egypt, 1914–1919," *Middle Eastern Studies* 45, 3 (2009): 355.

20. Edmund Candler, *The Sepoy* (London: J. Murray, 1919), 217.

21. J. D. Crowdy to Nora Crowdy, July 15–17, 1917, Samarra. Major J. D. Crowdy Collection: United Kingdom, St. Antony's College, Middle East Center Archive (hereafter Crowdy Collection).

22. Bose, *Hundred Horizons*, 125; Tai Yong Tan, "Imperial Home Front," 374.

23. Cohen, "Military Enters Indian Thought," 172–174.

24. Bose, *Hundred Horizons*, 125.

25. Omissi, *Indian Voices*, 19.

26. Omissi, *Sepoy and the Raj*, 82.

27. *47th Sikhs War Record: The Great War, 1914–1918* (Chippenham, UK: Picton, 1992), 1–2.

28. Philip Mason, *A Matter of Honour: An Account of the Indian Army, Its Officers and Men* (London: Cape, 1974), 440–441.

29. Ibid.

30. Y. D. Prasad, *Indian Muslims* (New Delhi: Janaki Prakashan, 1985), 43.

31. Ibid., 48–49.

32. Sunampadu Arumugam, *The Golden Key to World Power and the War* (London: Longmans, Green and Co., 1915), 36.

33. Ruiz, "Manly Spectacles," 354.

34. James E. Kitchen, "The Indianization of the Egyptian Expeditionary Force: Palestine 1918," in *The Indian Army in the Two World Wars*, 175.

35. Ibid.

36. Ibid., 176.

37. Ibid.

38. Ibid., 176–177.

39. Ibid., 177.

40. Das, "Ardour and Anxiety," 350.

41. Kitchen, "Egyptian Expeditionary Force: Palestine 1918," 177.

42. Mason, *Matter of Honour*, 439.

43. Ibid.

44. Omissi, *Indian Voices,* 286.

45. "The Battlefield in the Arab Lands," *al-Ahram,* November 10, 1914, 5.

46. Ayesha Jalal, *Partisans of Allah: Jihad in South Asia* (Cambridge, MA: Harvard University Press, 2008), 178.

47. Omissi, *Indian Voices,* 25.

48. Ibid., 175.

49. *47th Sikhs War Record,* 236.

50. Gardner, "Morale of the Indian Army," 399–400; after a spell of heavy trench warfare, the Sikhs eventually donned helmets for protection. *47th Sikhs War Record,* 236.

51. Richard J. Popplewell, *Intelligence and Imperial Defence: British Intelligence and the Defence of the Indian Empire, 1904–1924* (Portland, OR: Frank Cass, 1995), 181–182.

52. Ibid., 176.

53. Azmi Özcan, *Pan-Islamism: Indian Muslims, the Ottomans and Britain, 1877–1924* (Leiden: Brill, 1997), 168–171.

54. Ibid., 170–171.

55. While in the Hijaz, one revolutionary persuaded the visiting Enver and Jamal to sign documents in Arabic, Persian, and Turkish that sympathized with Indian demands for independence. These documents were concealed in silk garments and sent to India so that photographed copies could be distributed among Muslims. Sayyid 'Abid Husain, *The Destiny of Indian Muslims* (Lahore: Qadiria Book Traders, 1983), 76–77.

56. Records of Department of State relating to internal affairs of Turkey, 1910–1929. Microform. Washington, DC: National Archives and Records Service, General Services Administration, 1961.

57. Jalal, *Partisans of Allah,* 176–238.

58. Popplewell, *Intelligence and Imperial Defence,* 181–182.

59. Ibid., 182.

60. Prasad, *Indian Muslims,* 53.

61. Ibid., 55.

62. Prasad, *Indian Muslims,* 54–55.

63. Popplewell, *Intelligence and Imperial Defense,* 179–180.

64. Prasad, *Indian Muslims,* 63–80.

65. Ibid., 63–87.

66. Ibid., 45–46; Popplewell, *Intelligence and Imperial Defense,* 179.

67. Prasad, *Indian Muslims,* 56–57.

68. Popplewell, *Intelligence and Imperial Defense,* 166.

69. Tai Yong Tan, "Imperial Home Front," 382–383; Ravi Ahuja, "The Corrosiveness of Comparison," in *The World in World Wars,* 141.

70. Ahuja, "The Corrosiveness of Comparison," 142.

71. Mason, *Matter of Honour,* 422; Gardner, "Morale of the Indian Army," 394–395.

72. Gardner, "Morale of the Indian Army," 403.

73. Omissi, *Sepoy and the Raj,* 79.

74. Omissi, *Indian Voices,* 243.

75. Prasad, *Indian Muslims,* 105–107.

76. Ibid., 110.

77. Ibid., 108–110.

78. Omissi, *Indian Voices,* 204.

79. Ibid., 15.

80. Ibid., 169.

81. Gardner, "Morale of the Indian Army," 402.

82. Bose, *Hundred Horizons,* 126.

83. Ibid., 130. A British officer in Mesopotamia is quoted as saying that 48 percent of gunshot wounds suffered during the relief of Kut were in the hand or the foot and likely self-inflicted. Charles Trench, *The Indian Army and the King's Enemies, 1900–1947* (London: Thames and Hudson, 1988), 79.

84. Bose, *Hundred Horizons,* 130; Omissi, *Indian Voices,* 25.

85. Omissi, *Indian Voices,* 25; Gardner, "Morale of the Indian Army."

86. Ahuja, "The Corrosiveness of Comparison," 142.

87. Omissi, *Indian Voices,* 15

88. Ibid., 187–188.

89. Ibid., 187–188, 186.

90. Ibid., 186.

91. Ibid., 199. One member of the Fifteenth Lancers wrote: "We received good rations and good food. We were blameless, and so Government showed us mercy. May God give our noble King and our illustrious Government victory for having treated us with such clemency." Ibid., 323.

92. Greenhut, "Sahib and Sepoy," 16.

93. Ibid.

94. Ibid.

95. Gardner, "Morale of the Indian Army," 398.

96. Ibid., 400–401.

97. However, Townshend wrote disparagingly that he would not have suffered the debacle at Kut had he had only British soldiers.

98. *Valour Enshrined: A History of the Maratha Light Infantry* (Bombay: Orient Longman, 1971–1980), 157–158.

99. Ibid., 159.

100. Ibid., 189.

101. Ibid., 189–191.

102. Trench, *Indian Army and the King's Enemies,* 83.

103. Ibid.

104. Mason, *Matter of Honour.*

105. Ibid., 437.

106. "An Indian Champion," *al-Ahram* (Cairo), March 20, 1915, 5.

107. Ibid.

108. Das, "Ardour and Anxiety," 345.

109. Mason, *Matter of Honour,* 438–439.

110. "The Indian Force in Egypt," *al-Ahram* (Cairo), August 23, 1914.

111. "The Army Coming from India," *al-Ahram,* (Cairo), August 21, 1914.

112. Ruiz, "Manly Spectacles," 354.

113. "The Indian Soldiers' Display in Egypt," *al-Ahram* (Cairo), September 17, 1914.

114. Kitchen, "Egyptian Expeditionary Force: Palestine 1918," 165.

115. Omissi, *Indian Voices,* 226–227.

116. Ibid.

117. Ruiz, "Manly Spectacles," 356.

118. Australians and New Zealanders accounted for nearly half of the eighty-four thousand troops stationed in Egypt in 1915. This influx created a growing market for alcohol, narcotics, and prostitution. Ruiz, "Manly Spectacles," 357.

119. Ibid., 356.

120. Dineśa Candra Varmā, *Indian Armed Forces in Egypt and Palestine, 1914–1818* (New Delhi: Rajesh, 2004), 19.

121. Ibid.

122. Ibid., 37.

123. Ibid., 35–39.

124. Mason, *Matter of Honour,* 428, 430.

125. Dennis Showalter, "The Indianization of the Egyptian Expeditionary Force, 1917–18: An Imperial Turning Point," in *The Indian Army in the Two World Wars,* 147–151.

126. Ibid., 153.

127. Kitchen, "Egyptian Expeditionary Force: Palestine 1918," 189.

128. Ibid., 187–188.

129. Ibid., 175.

130. Showalter, "Indianization of the Egyptian Expeditionary Force," 145–147.

131. Kitchen, "Egyptian Expeditionary Force: Palestine 1918," 172.

132. Showalter, "Indianization of the Egyptian Expeditionary Force," 147.

133. Ibid., 150–163.

134. Trench, *Indian Army and the King's Enemies,* 91.

135. Ibid.

136. Showalter, "Indianization of the Egyptian Expeditionary Force," 150–151.

137. W. T. Massey, "Gen. Von Sanders Abandoned Army," *New York Times,* September 24, 1918.

138. Ibid.

139. Trench, *Indian Army and the King's Enemies,* 99–100.

140. Ibid., 100.

141. Kitchen, "Egyptian Expeditionary Force: Palestine 1918," 177.

142. "The camps were pitched in the desert; the surrounding country was deep sand and the going was difficult. . . . The men did not take kindly to bathing in salt water, it was supposed by them to have a bad effect on the hair." *47th Sikhs War Record,* 252–253; see David Woodward, *Hell in the Holy Land* (Lexington: University Press of Kentucky, 2006), x.

143. Roy, "Army in India," 135.

144. Ibid., 134.

145. Ibid., 135.

146. Mason, *Matter of Honour,* 430.

147. Bose, *Hundred Horizons,* 60.

148. Mason, *Matter of Honour,* 431.

149. Popplewell, *Intelligence and Imperial Defense,* 188.

150. Andrew Syk, "Command in the Indian Expeditionary Force D: In Mesopotamia," in *The Indian Army in the Two World Wars,* 65.

151. Ibid., 70–71, 96–97.

152. Ibid., 76–77.

153. Bose, *Hundred Horizons,* 60.

154. Ibid., 61; Ross Anderson, "Logistics of the Indian Expeditionary Force D in Mesopotamia: 1914–18," in *The Indian Army in the Two World Wars,* 106.

155. Bose, *Hundred Horizons,* 125.

156. Syk, "Command in the Indian Expeditionary Force D," 98.

157. Gardner, "Morale of the Indian Army," 410.

158. Ibid., 417.

159. Trench, *Indian Army and the King's Enemies,* 80.

160. Gardner, "Morale of the Indian Army," 410–411.

161. Trench, *Indian Army and the King's Enemies;* Gardner, "Morale of the Indian Army," 410–411.

162. Gardner, "Morale of the Indian Army," 411.

163. Ibid.

164. Bose, *Hundred Horizons,* 62; Gardner, "Morale of the Indian Army," 410–411.

165. Gardner, "Morale of the Indian Army," 411.

166. Mason, *Matter of Honour,* 435.

167. Gardner, "Morale of the Indian Army," 412.

168. Trench, *Indian Army and the King's Enemies,* 80; Gardner, "Morale of the Indian Army," 411–412.

169. Gardner, "Morale of the Indian Army," 413–414; Mason, *Matter of Honour,* 435.

170. Ronald Millar, *Kut: The Death of an Army* (London: Secker and Warburg, 1969), 228–229; *Middle East Online, Series 2: Iraq 1914–1974,* online archive accessible at www.gale.com; WO 32/5113, *Report on State of Nutrition at Kut-al-Amarah Garrison for Period 11th to 18th April 1916.* October 23, 1916.

171. Edward Opotiki Mousley, *The Secrets of a Kuttite* (London: John Lane, 1921), 151.

172. Gardner, "Morale of the Indian Army," 412–413.

173. Mason, *Matter of Honour,* 435–436.

174. George Buchanan, *The Tragedy of Mesopotamia* (Edinburgh: William Blackwood and Sons, 1938), 94.

175. Frederick James Moberly, *The Campaign in Mesopotamia 1914–1918* (London: H. M. Stationery Office, 1924), vol. 2, 534.

176. Trench, *Indian Army and the King's Enemies,* 79.

177. Gardner, "Morale of the Indian Army," 397.

178. Crowdy to Nora Crowdy, January 29, 1916, Camp Wadi. Crowdy Collection.

179. Gardner, "Morale of the Indian Army," 397.

180. Omissi, *Indian Voices,* 144.

181. Buchanan, *Tragedy of Mesopotamia,* 65–66.

182. Omissi, *Indian Voices,* 165.

183. *47th Sikhs War Record,* 121, 188.

184. Ibid., 179.

185. Ibid.

186. Mason, *Matter of Honour,* 436–437

187. Ibid., 437.

188. Gardner, "Morale of the Indian Army," 393.

189. Omissi, *Indian Voices,* 95.

190. Trench, *Indian Army and the King's Enemies,* 50.

191. Mason, *Matter of Honour,* 428.

192. Trench, *Indian Army and the King's Enemies,* 51.

193. Ibid.

194. Ibid.

195. Ibid., 56.

196. Ibid., 68.

197. Ibid.

198. Ruiz, "Manly Spectacles," 355.

199. W. T. Massey, "Liberation of Syria," *The Times* (London), October 23, 1918.

200. "The Indian Soldiers during War," *al-Ahram* (Cairo), November 3, 1914, 3.

201. Crowdy to Nora Crowdy, November 9, 1917, Tikrit. Crowdy Collection.

202. Crowdy to Nora Crowdy, September 15, 1917, Samarra. Crowdy Collection.

203. Dina Rizk Khoury, "Between Empire and Nation: Remembrance of the Great War and Iraqi National Identity" (unpublished manuscript). I thank the author for giving me access to this paper.

204. Ibid.

205. Ibid.

206. Ibid.

7. COOPERATION AND DISAFFECTION

1. Nadiya al-Ghazzi, *Shirwal Barhum: Ayyam min safarbarlik* (Damascus: al-Shadi li-l-Nashr wa-l-Tawzi', 1993), 138–140. The quote in translation appears on 140.

2. Hanna Mina, *Fragments of Memory: A Story of a Syrian Family*, trans. O. Kenny and L. Kenny (Austin: Center for Middle Eastern Studies at the University of Texas, 1993), 7.

3. Klaus Kreiser, "War Memorials and Cemeteries in Turkey," in *The First World War as Remembered in the Countries of the Eastern Mediterranean*, ed. O. Farschid, M. Kropp, and S. Dähne (Beirut: Orient-Institut, 2006), 183.

4. Erik Zürcher, "Little Mehmet in the Desert: The Ottoman Soldier's Experience," in *Facing Armageddon: The First World War Experienced*, ed. H. Cecil and P. H. Liddle (London: Leo Cooper, 1996), 237, where the years of almost continuous warfare (1912 to 1922) are slightly different from Kreiser, "War Memorials," who puts the starting point at 1911.

5. *An Introduction to Khalil Gibran*, ed. S. B. Bushrui (Beirut: Dar al-Mashreq, 1970), 48.

6. *Modern Arabic Poetry: An Anthology with English Verse Translations*, ed. and trans. Arthur J. Arberry (Cambridge: Cambridge University Press, 1967), 65–66. For the Arabic text, see Mikha'il Nu'ayma, *Hams al-jufun* (Beirut: Dar Sadir, 1968), 14–15. I am grateful to Robin Ostle for his insights into the works of Nu'ayma and to Najwa al-Qattan for the reference to the poet in her unpublished paper, "Everything but the Plague." See also Linda Schatkowski Schilcher, "The Famine of 1915–1918 in Greater Syria," in *Problems of the Modern Middle East in Historical Perspective: Essays in Honor of Albert Hourani*, ed. J. P. Spagnolo (Reading, UK: Ithaca, 1992), 231 n. 14.

7. Christof Schumann, "Individual and Collective Memories of the First World War," in *The First World War as Remembered in the Countries of the Eastern Mediterranean*, 247–263.

8. Ibid., 253.

9. Ibid., 257–259; George Korkor (unpublished memoir), approx. 1892–1914. Private collection. Access provided by the Tarazi family; Salim 'Ali Salam,

Mudhakkirat Salim ʿAli Salam [Memoirs] (Beirut: al-Dar al-Jamiʿiyya, 1982);
Wadad al-Maqdisi Qurṭas, *Dhikrayāt, 1917–1977* [Reminiscences, 1917–1977]
(Beirut: Muʾassasat al-Abhath al-ʿArabiyya, 1982), 21–24.

10. Fuad I. Khuri, *From Village to Suburb: Order and Change in Greater Beirut*
(Chicago: University of Chicago Press, 1975).

11. Bishara al-Buwari relates an anecdote about visiting a French encampment
in Alexandria in April 1915 with a French lady. Together they went to meet with
Senegalese soldiers. When they reached the barracks of the black soldiers, they
found that guards were posted around it in order to prevent the soldiers from
communicating with people from the outside. This was because some passersby had
tried to dissuade them from fighting the Turks, people of the same religion. *Arbaʿ
sinin al-harb* [Four years of the war] (New York: al-Huda, 1926), 12.

12. François Georgeon, "Kémalisme et monde musulman (1919–1938):
Quelques points de repère," in Georgeon, *Des Ottomans aux Turcs: Naissance d'une
nation* (Istanbul: Les Editions Isis, 1995), 443–449.

13. W. Knott, *Diary,* Imperial War Museum, MSS P 305, entry October 31, 1917.

14. *Egyptian Delegation to the Peace Conference*, a collection of official correspondence from November 11, 1918, to July 14, 1919: twelve appendices containing
verbatim transcriptions of official Egyptian reports, correspondence, depositions
of victims and eyewitnesses, and photographs of atrocities committed by British
troops in Egypt (Paris: Delegation, 1919), 86–87, quoting Miss Durham, *Daily
News,* April 2, 1919. Although numerous firsthand accounts of mistreatment, even
atrocities, are available in a collection of official correspondence put together by the
Egyptian Delegation to the Peace Conference, it is impossible to verify any of the
claims; however, it is worth noting that one author suggests that many of the
claims, against the Australians at least, were exaggerated.

15. Oral history gives us this example: Many of the families of Zahle came
from the mountain villages at the foot of Sannine, such as Baskinta, Ayn al-Abou,
and Kfar Aʿqab. The inhabitants used to divide the proximal Biqaʿ areas, plant them
and go up for safety into their mountain villages, coming back to reap the crops.
What they did not sell then, they took up for storage in their mountain villages.
The Cortases, Maaloufs, AbuHaydar, and Hrawi, among many other families,
come from these villages. The Cortases came from Baskinta, the Maaloufs from
Kfar Aʿqab and Ayn al-Abou. The Ottomans used to take a poll tax from families
such as the Freij, the Sursoks, and the Bustros, among others in Beirut. The
villagers used to collect some crops earlier than their time if they could, to avoid the
tax. The Ottomans gave the farmers the right to own the land if they stayed and
lived in the Valley, that is, Zahleh. Many Cortases did, and there are more Cortases
now in Zahleh than in Baskinta. Adil Cortas was minister of agriculture several
times. Many of the Zahleh Cortases live in Maalaqa. Those that did not accept the
government's offer, perhaps as a matter of principle, were said ultimately to have to

abandon their rights to their plantations. There is an area in the Biqa' called Dwar Cortas, which was given to the Freij family. It still exists today as part of the property of Marquis de Freij (the Freij became Marquis de Freij under the French).

16. Mohammad Gholi Majd, *Iraq in World War I: From Ottoman Rule to British Conquest* (Lanham, MD: University Press of America, 2006), 175.

17. Dina Rizk Khoury, "Ambiguities of the Modern: The Great War in the Memoirs and Poetry of the Iraqis," in *The World in World Wars: Experiences, Perceptions and Perspectives from Africa and Asia,* ed. H. Liebau et al. (Leiden: Brill, 2010), 333–334.

18. Her mother was from the "Sbhai family," which probably should be read as "Sbahi," a well-known family name in Aleppo, probably derived from the Ottoman *sipahi,* "feudal soldier." Nazik Ali Jawdat, "Pictures from the Past," in *Remembering Childhood in the Middle East: Memoirs from a Century of Change,* ed. E. Warnock Fernea (Austin: University of Texas Press, 2002), 19.

19. Jawdat, "Pictures from the Past," 27.

20. Johann Strauss, "The Disintegration of Ottoman Rule in the Syrian Provinces as Viewed by German Observers," in *The Syrian Land: Processes of Integration and Fragmentation; Bilad al-Sham from the 18th to the 20th Century,* ed. T. Philipp and B. Schaebler (Stuttgart, Germany: F. Steiner, 1998), 321.

21. For a thoughtful analysis of "Turkification" and how it is understood, see Hasan Kayali, *Arabs and Young Turks: Ottomanism, Arabism, and Islamism in the Ottoman Empire, 1908–1918* (Berkeley: University of California Press, 1997), 82–96.

22. Jawdat, "Pictures from the Past," 28–29.

23. Ibid., 29.

24. Ibid., 29–30.

25. T. E. Lawrence, *Seven Pillars of Wisdom: A Triumph* (London: Penguin, 2000), 50; see also Hasan Kayali, "Wartime Regional and Imperial Integration of Greater Syria during World War I," in *The Syrian Land,* 295.

26. Mas'ud Dahir, *Tarikh Lubnan al-ijtima'i, 1914–1926* (Beirut: Dar al-Farabi, 1974), 26.

27. Youssef Mouawad, "Jamal Pacha, en une version libanaise: l'Usage positif d'une légende noire," in *The First World War as Remembered in the Countries of the Eastern Mediterranean,* 425.

28. 'Aziz Bek, *Suriya wa-Lubnan fi l-harb al-'alamiyya: al-Istikhbarat wa-l-jasusiyya fi l-dawla l-'uthmaniyya* (Beirut, 1933), 237; Eliezer Tauber, *The Arab Movements in World War I* (London: Frank Cass, 1993), 38. I am grateful to Abdul-Karim Rafeq for his help.

29. Margaret McGilvary, *The Dawn of a New Era in Syria* (New York: Fleming H. Revell, 1920), 210. The whole story is at ibid., 209–212.

30. Ibid., 212.

31. Ibid., 227.

32. I am grateful to Walid Khalidi, who shared with me this experience he and his family had. There are other versions of the story than the one the villagers gave in the 1950s to the present renters of the house.

According to Nadim Cortas, who heard this from his grandparents, Arthur Dray came with a group of missionaries and foreign families in the 1870s to Brumana. He initially lived with Thomas and Wega Little at the Hotel Cedarhurst (originally "Sallmuller," Wega Little's maiden name), which adjoined the Cortas home in Brumana. (Thomas Little built the first tennis court in Lebanon.) Dray later moved to the house referred to as Bayt al-Muna. In this version, Jamal Pasha was shot in one eye and feared the autoimmune loss of the other eye. Dray enucleated his injured eye and saved the good eye. To reward him, Jamal Pasha gave him food rations to distribute to the starving natives of Brumana and the neighboring villages. Members of the Lebanese Cortas family, Tanios and Maryam, had started a food distribution process from their home in Brumana. The Cortases suggested that a kitchen be built and cooked food be distributed on regular basis to the suffering population. The kitchen was built in a house facing the Cortas house that belonged to a certain Umm Bishara. The Cortases were responsible for food storage; the food was kept in the cellar of their house and in Dray's house, where it was also dispatched by Jamal Pasha, hence the house's name. Dray had an Armenian maid whose fiancé used to visit on certain nights, covering himself with white sheets and running away when he suspected that someone noticed him. The house was therefore thought to be haunted. The fiancé suspected that Dray was having an affair with his bride-to-be and in a psychotic fit barged into Dray's dental practice in Beirut one day and slaughtered him with a butcher's knife. The fiancé ended up in the Asfuriyya jail and died sometime in the late 1990s. I thank Nadim Cortas for this oral history.

33. Anis Furayha, *Qabla an ansa: Tatimmat isma' ya rida!* [Before I forget: I continue: Listen o Rida!] (Beirut: Dar al-Nahar li-l-Nashr, 1979), 49.

34. Kayali, "Wartime Regional and Imperial Integration," 295; Ahmad Djemal Pasha, *Memories of a Turkish Statesman—1913–1919* (London: Hutchinson and Co., 1922), 144. His appointment dated back to November 1914, according to Tauber, *Arab Movements,* 35; and Mouawad tells us that the pasha left Syria in January 1918. "Jamāl Pacha, en une version libanaise," 425. His replacement in command of the Fourth Army was Muhammad Jamal Pasha, " 'the lesser.' " Tauber, *Arab Movements,* 133, 154.

35. Hasan Kayali, "Ottoman Policy in Syria during World War I and the German Alliance" (unpublished paper delivered at Sarajevo, May 2012).

36. Zeine N. Zeine, *Arab-Turkish Relations and the Emergence of Arab Nationalism* (Beirut: Khayat's, 1958), 102; Tauber, *Arab Movements,* 10–36; James L. Gelvin, *Divided Loyalties: Nationalism and Mass Politics in Syria at the Close of*

Empire (Berkeley: University of California Press, 1998), 67; Nadine Méouchy, "From the Great War to the Syrian Armed Resistance Movement (1919–1921): The Military and the *Mujahidin* in Action," in *The World in World Wars*, 503.

37. Tauber, *Arab Movements*, 37.

38. Elizabeth Thompson, *Colonial Citizens: Republican Rights, Paternal Privilege, and Gender in French Syria and Lebanon* (New York: Columbia University Press, 2000), 28.

39. Philip Graves, *Palestine, the Land of Three Faiths* (New York: George H. Doran, 1924), 38.

40. Axel Havemann, "The Impact of the First World War on Lebanon's History and Memory: The Case of Shakib Arslan (1869–1946)," in *The First World War as Remembered in the Countries of the Eastern Mediterranean*, 217.

41. Antun Yammin, *Lubnan fi l-harb: Aw-dhikra al-hawadith wa al-mazalim fi Lubnan fi l-harb al-'umumiyya, 1914–1919* [Lebanon in war: Remembrance of the events and the oppression in the the world war, 1914–1919], vol. 1 (Beirut: al-Matba'a al-Adabiyya, 1919–1920), 88.

42. George Antonius, *The Arab Awakening* (New York: Capricorn, 1965), 186–187. According to Antonius, these executions took place on August 21, but other sources record the date as August 20, a Friday. See, for example, Nicholas Z. Ajay, "Political Intrigue and Suppression in Lebanon during World War I," *International Journal of Middle East Studies*, 5, 2 (1974): 154.

43. Rashid Khalidi, "Shaykh Ahmad 'Arif al-Zayn and al-'Irfan," in *Intellectual Life in the Arab East, 1890–1939*, ed. M. R. Buheiry (Beirut: Center for Arab and Middle East Studies, American University of Beirut, 1981), 113.

44. Antonius, *The Arab Awakening*, 189–190, quotation at 190; Ajay, "Political Intrigue," 151, 157; see also Bruce Masters, *The Arabs of the Ottoman Empire, 1516–1918: A Social and Cultural History* (New York: Cambridge University Press, 2013), 220.

45. Ajay, "Political Intrigue," 157.

46. Zeine, *Arab-Turkish Relations*, 103–104; Ajay, "Political Intrigue," 102; Rashid Khalidi, "The Arab Experience of the War," in *Facing Armageddon*, 645–646, who also notes that one source put the total of those exiled from Syria during the war at fifty thousand. Eliezer Tauber writes: "The authorities did not always take the trouble to put the suspects on trial. In many cases they deported whole families to Anatolia without trial. The number of deported families is estimated at 300, and they include several of the most eminent families in the Levant. . . . The number of the deportees during the war is estimated at 50,000." *Arab Movements*, 38.

47. Nicholas Ajay, "Mount Lebanon and the Wilayah of Beirut, 1914–1918: The War Years," Ph.D. diss., Georgetown University (1973), 283; Ajay, "Political Intrigue," 156–157; McGilvary, *Dawn of a New Era*, 143–144; Tauber, *Arab Movements*, 39–41.

48. Commandement de la IVème Armée, *La vérité sur la question syrienne* (Istanbul: Imprimerie Tanine, 1916); Ajay, "Political Intrigue," 156–158.

49. Korkor, unpublished memoir, 1909, referring to the hanging of Mahmud Bashir al-Mitwali, an Imami Shiʻi.

50. Ajay, "Political Intrigue," 153–155. Yammin (*Lubnan fi l-harb*, vol. 1) describes the condemned and their alleged crimes (48–64) and their last words and moments (64–87). The nationalists hanged in Beirut on May 6, 1916, at Cannon Square were Saʻid Akl, Father Yusuf Hayik, Abdul Karim al-Khalil, Abdelwahhab al-Inglizi, Yusuf Bishara Hani, Muhammad Mahmasani, Mahmud Mahmasani, Omar Hamad, Filip al-Khazin, Farid al-Khazin, and Shaykh Ahmad Tabbara. Those among the nationalists executed in Damascus on May 6, 1916, at Marja Square are given in Korkor's unpublished memoir.

51. Antonius, *The Arab Awakening*, 187. Among those who were executed in 1915 and 1916 were deputies to the Ottoman parliament such as Shafiq al-Muʻayyad, Abd al-Hamid Zahrawi, Shukri al-Asali, Rushdi al-Shamʻa, and Hafiz al-Saʻid: see Rashid Khalidi, "ʻAbd al-Ghani al-ʻUraisi al-Mufid: The Press and Arab Nationalism before 1914," in *Intellectual Life in the Arab East*, 40.

52. Ajay, "Political Intrigue," 155; the interviewee is Dr. Raʼif Abi l-Lamaʻ.

53. Tauber, *Arab Movements*, 50.

54. Abigail Jacobson, "Negotiating Ottomanism in Times of War: Jerusalem during World War I through the Eyes of a Local Muslim Resident," *International Journal of Middle East Studies* 40, 1 (2008): 79.

55. WO 157/695, Notes from an American, Military Intelligence Office, War Office, Cairo, September 8, 1915.

56. Martyrs' Square in Beirut acquired a new memory site on top of the original one from World War I after the popular protest known as the Cedar Revolution, which followed the assassination of former Prime Minister Rafiq Hariri in 2005.

57. Ajay, "Political Intrigue," 160.

58. Zeine, *Arab-Turkish Relations*, 103–104; Ajay, "Political Intrigue," 160.

59. Tarif Khalidi, "The Arab World," *The Great World War, 1914–1945*, vol. 2: *The Peoples' Experience*, ed. J. Bourne, P. Liddle and I. Whitehead et al. (London: HarperCollins, 2001), 298.

60. Kayali, "Ottoman Policy in Syria."

61. Mumtaz Ayoub Fargo, "Arab-Turkish Relations from the Emergence of Arab Nationalism to the Arab Revolt, 1848–1916," Ph.D. diss., University of Utah (1969), 239.

62. R. Khalidi, "The Arab Experience of the War," 648.

63. Ami Ayalon, *The Press in the Arab Middle East: A History* (New York: Oxford University Press, 1995), 69–71, 82; ibid., 65, mentions that the journalistic reaction to the 1908 revolution "was immediate and powerful, like the rush of a great river

upon the collapse of a great dam." Ayalon also notes that before the year was over, no fewer than forty-four new Arabic papers had appeared in Lebanon, Syria, Palestine, and Iraq, as well as in Istanbul and that "in the Ottoman capital alone, some twenty-seven newspapers and journals were launched in "six feverish years." Ibid., 65. See also Filib Di Tarrazi, *Tarikh al-sihafa l-'arabiyya*, vol. 1 (Beirut: al-Matba'a l-Adabiyya, 1913–1933); Rashid Khalidi, "Arab Nationalism in Syria: The Formative Years, 1908–1914," in *Nationalism in a Non-National State: The Dissolution of the Ottoman Empire*, ed. W. W. Haddad and W. Ochsenwald (Columbus: Ohio State University Press, 1977), 208, mentions the figures that are cited in the text for the growth of the press.

64. Kayali, *Arabs and Young Turks*, 198. For Jamal Pasha's governorship in Syria, see especially ibid., 192–196.

65. Djemal Pasha, *Memories of a Turkish Statesman*, 217–222 and other sections of chapter 8, "The Arab Rebellion."

66. Kayali mentions that in Syria Jamal Pasha's entourage of writers included the prominent novelists Falih Rifki and Ahmed Rasim, and that both the Turkish feminist Halidé Edib and the Islamist-modernist Mehmed Akif spent time in Syria during his governorship. "Ottoman Policy in Syria."

67. Djemal Pasha, *Memories of a Turkish Statesman*, 199–201; Zeine, *Arab-Turkish Relations*, 103–104; Ajay, "Political Intrigue," 101.

68. Fa'iz al-Ghusayn, *Mudhakkirati 'an al-thawra al-'arabiyya* (Damascus: Matba'at al-Taraqqi, 1956), 26–33.

69. Halidé Edib, *Memoirs* (London: John Murray, 1926), 390.

70. 'Aziz Bek, *Suriya wa-Lubnan*, 237; Tauber, *Arab Movements*, 38, including n. 7. The list of pejorative names is given above.

71. Kasmieh, "The First World War as Represented in Autobiographies in Contemporary Damascus," in *The First World War as Remembered in the Countries of the Eastern Mediterranean*, 283–284. Kasmieh points out that although Kurd Ali's loyalty was not without reservation, he defended the Ottoman Empire, expressed disapproval of the leaders of the Arab nationalist movement, and opposed them for seeking an alliance with the British "whom he suspected of having no good intentions toward the Arabs in general, and Syria in particular." Ibid., 284.

72. Strauss, "The Disintegration of Ottoman Rule," 307–329.

73. Ibid., 319.

74. Ibid., 321.

75. Ajay, "Political Intrigue," 155–156.

76. This is based on C. A. Bayly, "Distorted Development: The Ottoman Empire and British India, circa 1780–1916," *Comparative Studies of South Asia, Africa and the Middle East*, 27, 2 (2007): 334, citing Reşat Kasaba, *The Ottoman Empire and the World Economy: The Nineteenth Century* (Albany: State University of New York

Press, 1988), and Feroz Ahmad, *The Young Turks: The Committee of Union and Progress in Turkish Politics, 1908–1914* (Oxford: Clarendon, 1969). See also Kayali, *Arabs and Young Turks,* 90, 170–171; Engin Akarli, *The Long Peace: Ottoman Lebanon, 1861–1920* (Berkeley: University of California Press, 1993); Kasaba, *The Ottoman Empire.*

77. Bayly, "Distorted Development," 334.

78. Points also well made by Hasan Kayali, "The Long War, the Arab Provinces, and the Rump Ottoman Empire," paper presented at Tufts University workshop on "The Middle East in the Two World Wars," held at Harvard and at Tufts on May 10–12, 2002.

79. On Jamal Pasha's complex legacy in Syria, see for example Kayali, "Wartime Regional and Imperial Integration," 295–306; Kayali, "Ottoman Policy in Syria."

80. Kayali, "Ottoman Policy in Syria."

81. Samir Seikaly, "Damascene Intellectual Life in the Opening Years of the 20th Century: Muhammad Kurd'Ali and al-Muqtabas," in *Intellectual Life in the Arab East,* 131; Kayali, *Arabs and Young Turks,* 176–177, et passim; M. E. Yapp, *The Making of the Modern Near East, 1792–1923* (London: Longman, 1987), 324.

82. Georgeon, "Kémalisme et monde musulman (1919–1938)," 448.

83. Albert Hourani, "Middle Eastern Nationalism Yesterday and Today," in *The Emergence of the Modern Middle East* (London: Macmillan, 1981), 186.

84. Ibid., 309.

85. Bayly, "Distorted Development," 336.

86. M. Şükrü Hanioğlu, "The Young Turks and the Arabs before the Revolution of 1908," in *The Origins of Arab Nationalism,* ed. R. Khalidi et al. (New York: Columbia University Press, 1991), 32, 43 (where Hanioğlu reinforces the point, noting that in the eyes of the Young Turks "the Arabs were not only betraying the empire by establishing separatist organizations, they were also innately inferior"). See also Hanioğlu, *The Young Turks in Opposition* (New York: Oxford University Press, 1995).

87. C. Ernest Dawn, *From Ottomanism to Arabism; Essays on the Origins of Arab Nationalism* (Urbana: University of Illinois Press, 1973); Tauber, *Arab Movements,* 2; R. Khalidi, "Arab Nationalism in Syria," 206–237.

88. Mahmoud Haddad, "West and East as Analysed by a Disappointed Arab Officer and First World War Veteran," in *The First World War as Remembered in the Countries of the Eastern Mediterranean,* 345.

89. Ibid.

90. Kayali, *Arabs and Young Turks,* 108–112.

91. Seikaly, "Damascene Intellectual Life," 126.

92. Ibid.

93. R. Khalidi, "Arab Nationalism in Syria," 217.

94. See, for example, Hakim, "Shifting Identities and Representations of the Nation among the Maronite Secular Elite in the Late Ottoman Period," in *From the Syrian Land to the States of Syria and Lebanon*, ed. T. Philipp and C. Schumann (Beirut: Orient-Institut, 2004), 239–253.

95. R. Khalidi, "Arab Nationalism in Syria," 223.

96. Ibid.

97. Rashid Khalidi, "Ottomanism and Arabism in Syria before 1914: A Reassessment," in *The Origins of Arab Nationalism*, 59.

98. In his memoir Muhammad Kurd 'Ali claimed that he was the son of a Kurdish father and a Circassian mother, but Samir Seikaly points out that Kurd 'Ali was born in 1876 into a family that had long lived in Damascus. "Damascene Intellectual Life," 141. See also ibid., 131, on Turkish cultural shortcomings. On Kurd 'Ali's comments on the positive sides of Jamal Pasha and the Ottomans, see Kasmieh, "First World War," 283–284.

99. Kasmieh, "First World War," 280, 284.

100. Samir Seikaly, "Shukri al-'Asali: A Case Study of a Political Activist," in *The Origins of Arab Nationalism*, 73–96; R. Khalidi, "Arab Nationalism in Syria," 217–222. See also Kayali, *Arabs and Young Turks*, 176–179.

101. William L. Cleveland, *Islam against the West: Shakib Arslan and the Campaign for Islamic Nationalism* (Austin: University of Texas Press, 1985); Havemann, "Impact of the First World War," 213–221; 'Aziz Bek, *Suriya wa-Lubnan fi l-harb al-'alamiyya*, 283–287.

102. Kayali, *Arabs and Young Turks*, 113.

103. R. Khalidi, "Arab Nationalism in Syria," 215–216.

104. The *falaqa*, an apparatus such as a plank used for immobilizing the feet so as to whip them, was applied as a method of torture (by the Turks) or as punishment in school (in North Africa). G. Lecomte, "Falaka," in *Encyclopaedia of Islam*, vol. 2, ed. B. Lewis et al. (Leiden: E. J. Brill, 1983), 763.

105. Tauber, *Arab Movements*, 37–38; al-Ghusayn, *Mudhakkirati 'an al-thawra al-'arabiyya*, 49.

106. Ajay, "Political Intrigue," 153; Yammin, *Lubnan fi l-harb*, vol. 2, 129–130.

107. Djemal Pasha, *Memories of a Turkish Statesman*, 198.

108. Yammin, *Lubnan fi l-harb*, vol. 2, 129–133; Ajay, "Political Intrigue," 153. Hasan Kayali mentions that one of the earlier and better-known deportees to Anatolia was Nakhla Mutran, *Arabs and Young Turks*, 193.

109. Djemal Pasha, *Memories of a Turkish Statesman*, 198.

110. Ajay, "Political Intrigue," 153. See also Yammin, *Lubnan fi l-harb*, vol. 2, 133; Tauber, *Arab Movements*, 45.

111. Salam, *Mudhakkirat*, 117.

112. Salibi, "Beirut under the Young Turks: As Depicted in the Political Memoirs of Salim Ali Salam (1868–1938)," in *Les Arabes par leurs archives: XVIe–XXe siècles,* ed. J. Berque and D. Chevallier (Paris: Centre National de la Recherche Scientifique, 1976), 193–215, quote on 214.

113. Al-Buwari, *Arba' sinin al-harb,* 368.

114. Nicola Ziadeh, "A First-Person Account of the First World War in Greater Syria," in *The First World War as Remembered in the Countries of the Eastern Mediterranean,* 272.

115. Zürcher, "Little Mehmet in the Desert," 235.

116. Ibid., 236.

117. Ibid., 236–237.

118. Ibid., 237.

119. Ibid., 238.

120. Al-Buwari, *Arba' sinin al-harb,* 9.

121. Jay Winter, *Sites of Memory, Sites of Mourning: The Great War in European Cultural History* (Cambridge: Cambridge University Press, 1995), 17 and other passages of chap. 1.

122. R. Khalidi, "The Arab Experience of the War," 643.

123. T. Khalidi, "The Arab World," 299.

124. R. Khalidi, "The Arab Experience of the War," 649–650.

125. This whole section relies heavily on Hourani, *History of the Arab Peoples,* 315–319, and on Yapp, *Modern Near East,* 301–345.

126. Méouchy, "From the Great War to the Syrian Armed Resistance Movement," 500.

127. Keith David Watenpaugh, *Being Modern in the Middle East: Revolution, Nationalism, Colonialism, and the Arab Middle Class* (Princeton, NJ: Princeton University Press, 2006), 62, 161, and sections I and II.

128. Nadine Méouchy, "Le movement des 'isabat en Syrie du Nord à travers le témoignage du chaykh Youssef Saadoun (1919–1921)," in *The British and French Mandates in Comparative Perspectives,* ed. Nadine Méouchy and Peter Sluglett (Leiden: Brill, 2004), 649–671. See also Abdul-Karim Rafeq, "Arabism, Society and Economy in Syria 1918–1920," in *State and Society in Syria and Lebanon,* ed. Youssef M. Choueiri (Exeter, UK: University of Exeter Press, 1993), 1–26; Gelvin, *Divided Loyalties,* 85; Fred H. Lawson, "The Northern Syrian Revolts of 1919–1921 and the Sharifian Regime: Congruence or Conflict of Interests and Ideologies?" in *From the Syrian Land,* 257–274; Méouchy, "Rural Resistance and the Introduction of Modern Forms of Consciousness in the Syrian Countryside," in *The World in World Wars,* 275–289.

129. Eugene L. Rogan, *The Arabs: A History* (New York: Basic, 2009), 163.

130. Michael Provence, *The Great Syrian Revolt and the Rise of Arab Nationalism* (Austin: University of Texas Press, 2005); idem, "A Nationalist Rebellion without Nationalists? Popular Mobilizations in Mandatory Syria 1925–1926," in *The British*

and French Mandates in Comparative Perspectives, 673–692; Gérard D. Khoury, *La France et l'Orient arabe: Naissance du Liban moderne, 1914–1920* (Paris: A. Colin, 1993).

131. The Balfour Declaration, Arthur James Balfour to Lionel Walter Rothschild, November 2, 1917. Available online at http://wwi.lib.byu.edu/index.php/The _Balfour_Declaration.

132. William Ochsenwald, "Ironic Origins: Arab Nationalism in the Hijaz, 1882–1914," in *The Origins of Arab Nationalism,* 189–203; C. Ernest Dawn, "The Origins of Arab Nationalism," in ibid., 19–30; William L. Cleveland, "The Role of Islam as Political Ideology in the First World War," in *National and International Politics in the Middle East: Essays in Honour of Elie Kedourie,* ed. E. Ingram (London: F. Cass, 1986).

133. Hourani, *History of the Arab Peoples,* 318–319; Kayali, *Arabs and Young Turks,* chap. 5.

134. S. T. Wasti, "The Circles of Maulana Mohamed Ali," *Middle Eastern Studies* 38, 4 (2002): 52–53.

135. Ayesha Jalal, *Partisans of Allah: Jihad in South Asia* (Cambridge, MA: Harvard University Press, 2008), 176–238.

136. Antonius, *The Arab Awakening,* 135–136; Kayali, *Arabs and Young Turks,* 187–188.

137. Gail Minault, *The Khilafat Movement: Religious Symbolism and Political Mobilization in India* (New York: Columbia University Press, 1982); Jalal, *Partisans of Allah.*

138. Bernard Lewis, *The Middle East: A Brief History of the Last 2,000 Years* (New York: Scribner, 1995), 341.

139. Minault, *The Khilafat Movement,* 57.

140. Antonius, *The Arab Awakening,* 205, 327, et passim.

141. *İslam Mecmuası,* no. 3, 30–31.

142. *Sebilürreşad,* vol. 18, no. 455, 23 Rebiülahir 1338 (January 15, 1920), 156.

143. Sugata Bose, "Nation, Reason and Religion: India's Independence in International Perspective," *Economic and Political Weekly,* August 1–8, 1998.

144. Jalal, *Partisans of Allah,* 210–213; *Sebilürreşad,* vol. 18, no. 455, 23 Rebiülahir 1338 (January 15, 1920), p. 156, A Reply by His Highness Sayyid [Seyid] Amr [Emir] Ali; Antonius, *The Arab Awakening,* p. 335. On Indian Muslims and the Caliphate see also *Sebilürreşad,* vol. 9/2, no. 212/30, 15 Şevval 1330 (September 27, 1912), p. 79; *Sebilürreşad,* vol. 10, no. 236, 12 Rebiülahir 1331 (March 21, 1913), pp. 51–53; *Sebilürreşad,* vol. 10, no. 237, 19 Rebiülahir 1331 (March 28, 1913), pp. 51–53; *Sebilürreşad,* vol. 10, no. 239, 4 Cemaziyelevvel 1331 (April 11, 1913); *Sebilürreşad,* vol. 11, no. 262, 18 Zilhicce 1331 (November 18, 1913), pp. 25–26; *Sebilürreşad,* vol. 11, no. 272, 27 Zilhicce 1331 (November 27, 1913), p. 191; *Sebilürreşad,* vol. 11, no. 279, 17 Safer 1332 (January 15, 1914), p. 304; *Sebilürreşad,* vol. 12, no. 292, 20 Cemazeyilevvel 1332 (April 16, 1914), pp. 105–111; *Sebilürreşad,*

vol. 12, no. 294, 4 Cemazeyilahir 1332 (April 30, 1914), pp. 140–142; *Sebilürreşad*, vol.12, no. 295, 11 Cemazeyilahir 1332 (May 7, 1914), p. 167; *Sebilürreşad*, vol. 12, no. 297, 25 Cemazeyilahir 1332 (May 21, 1914); *Sebilürreşad*, vol. 12, no. 299, 10 Recep 1332 (June 4, 1914); *Sebilürreşad*, vol. 12, no. 309, 11 Şevval 1332 (September 2, 1914); *Sebilürreşad*, vol. 12, no. 311, 25 Şevval 1332 (September 16, 1914), p. 436; *Sebilürreşad*, vol. 12, no. 312, 9 Zilhicce 1332 (October 29, 1914), p. 447; *Sebilürreşad*, vol. 13, no. 315, 7 Muharrem 1333 (November 25, 1914), p. 24; *Sebilürreşad*, vol. 15, no. 316, 15 Zilkade 1336 (August 22, 1918), pp. 31–32; *Sebilürreşad*, vol. 15, no. 376, 24 Muharrem 1337 (October 30, 1918), pp. 225–226; *Sebilürreşad*, vol. 15, no. 399, 4 Cemaziyelevvel 1337 (February 5, 1919); *Sebilürreşad*, vol. 16, no. 406, 16 Recep 1337 (April 17, 1919), pp. 159–160; *Sebilürreşad*, vol. 18, no. 455, 23 Rebiülahir 1338 (January 15, 1920), p. 156; *Sebilürreşad*, vol. 18, no. 458, 21 Cemaziyelevvel 1338 (February 11, 1920); *İslam Mecmuası*, no. 3: 30-1; no. 4, pp. 127–128; no. 5, p. 160; no. 7, p. 223.

145. Antonius, *The Arab Awakening*, 335.

146. Ibid., 337.

147. Tauber, *Arab Movements*, chap. 5.

148. For example, most of the prisoners who joined the revolt were Iraqis, including Ja'far al-Askari, whose memoir has little on Indians.

149. T. Khalidi, "The Arab World," 291–292.

150. Bayly, "Distorted Development," 343. See also *Modernity and Culture from the Mediterranean to the Indian Ocean, 1890–1920*, ed. L. Fawaz and C.A. Bayly (New York: Columbia University Press, 2002).

151. Bayly, "Distorted Development," 343.

152. For a cautionary reflection on not reducing Arab nationalism to a coherent homogeneous movement, see Gelvin, *Divided Loyalties*, 1–50.

EPILOGUE

1. I am grateful to Nadim Cortas, one of Mariam Cortas's grandchildren, for relating the story to me.

2. Wadad Maqdisi Cortas, *A World I Loved: The Story of an Arab Woman* (New York: Nation, 2009), 3–4. This quote is not found in the Arabic edition of the memoir used throughout this book. Mariam Cortas Said, who published *A World I Loved*, maintains that the quote is based on an earlier out-of-print edition of her mother's memoir. I thank her for the explanation she provided.

3. Youssef Mouawad, "Jamal Pacha, en une version libanaise: L'Usage positif d'une légende noire," in *The First World War as Remembered in the Countries of the Eastern Mediterranean*, ed. O. Farschid et al. (Beirut: Orient-Institut, 2006), 440, 444; Youssef Mouawad, "Grande guerre et grande famine," *Lebanus* (special ed. *Histoire*) 2004: 12–13.

4. Orhan Koloğlu repeats the claim that the Ottoman state mobilized 3 million to 4 million people during the war; at least 600,000 died while fighting or in prison, 120,000 had to stay in other countries as war prisoners, and 800,000 became disabled by the end of the war. In the eastern provinces 800,000 Armenians, 500,000 Muslim Turks, and 200,000 Christians (*rum,* Greeks of Anatolia) died from various reasons related to the war in this period. Armenian sources, in contrast, estimate that between 1 and 1.5 million died from war-related causes and squarely put the blame on the Ottoman government's policies for their losses, whereas Koloğlu cites civil war, migration, and starvation. *1918, aydinlarimizin bunalim yili: Zaferi nihai'den tam teslimiyete* [1918, the Year of Depression for Our Intellectuals: From Ultimate Victory to Total Surrender] (Istanbul: Boyut Yayınları, 2000), 18. Justin McCarthy has written that "it should be considered that the Ottoman Arab provinces suffered worse mortality than any European country in World War 1 except Russia. (Anatolian loss was much worse than that of Russia)." *The Ottoman Turks* (London: Longman, 1997), 165. See also chap. 5, nn. 301–306, for additional estimates.

5. Linda Schatkowski Schilcher, "The Famine of 1915–1918 in Greater Syria," in *Problems of the Modern Middle East in Historical Perspective: Essays in Honor of Albert Hourani,* ed. John P. Spagnolo. (Reading, UK: Ithaca, 1992), 231. See also Elizabeth F. Thompson, *Colonial Citizens: Republican Rights, Paternal Privilege, and Gender in French Syria and Lebanon* (New York: Columbia University Press, 2000), 20–21.

6. Jay Winter and Antoine Prost, *The Great War in History: Debates and Controversies, 1914 to the Present* (New York: Cambridge University Press, 2005), 3.

7. Najwa al-Qattan, "Safarbarlik: Ottoman Syria and the Great War," in *From the Syrian Land to the States of Syria and Lebanon,* ed. T. Philipp and C. Schumann (Beirut: Orient-Institut, 2004), 163.

8. Thompson, *Colonial Citizens,* 30.

9. Winter and Prost, *Great War in History,* 173.

10. Ibid., 174. More generally, see 173–191.

11. Ibid., 174–178.

12. Ibid., 179.

13. Ibid., 178–179.

14. Ibid., 179.

15. Ibid.

16. Ibid., 188.

17. Jay Winter and Emmanuel Sivan, "Setting the Framework," in *War and Remembrance in the Twentieth Century,* ed. J. Winter and E. Sivan (Cambridge: Cambridge University Press, 1999), 6.

18. Winter and Prost, *Great War in History,* 190; see also 174–186.

19. James L. Gelvin, *Divided Loyalties: Nationalism and Mass Politics in Syria at the Close of Empire* (Berkeley: University of California Press, 1998), 241, et passim.

20. Ibid., 252–259.

21. Al-Qattan, "Safarbarlik," 163.

22. Nayla Aoun Chkaiban, *Celle que tu es devenue, 1910–1920: Un destin libanais* (Beirut: Tamyras, 2013). I am grateful to Lena Khouri Touma for making this novel available to me.

23. Kevin Fewster, Vicihi Başarın, and Hatice Hürmüz Başarın, *A Turkish View of Gallipoli: Çanakkale* (Richmond, Australia: Hodja, 1985).

24. Ibid., 124.

25. Ibid., 127–129.

26. Ibid., 124.

27. Thompson, *Colonial Citizens,* 25.

28. Ibid.

29. Ibid.

30. Ibid., 26; Abdallah Hanna, "The First World War According to the Memories of 'Commoners' in the Bilad al-Sham," in *The World in World Wars: Experiences, Perceptions and Perspectives from Africa and Asia,* ed. H. Liebau et al. (Leiden: Brill, 2010), 304–305.

31. See for example the useful information offered by Akram Fouad Khater, *Inventing Home: Emigration, Gender, and the Middle Class in Lebanon, 1870–1920* (Berkeley: University of California Press, 2001), 146–178.

32. Ibid., 147.

33. Fu'ad Yusuf Atrash, *Qissat Asmahan* (Beirut, 1962), 11–13. On Asmahan and how her first film was banned by the French Mandatory authorities, see Thompson, *Colonial Citizens,* 209, 240; Sherifa Zuhur, *Asmahan's Secrets: Woman, War, and Song* (Austin: Center for Middle Eastern Studies, University of Texas at Austin, 2000); Ghada El Atrache, "Hassan El Atrache raconté par sa fille," *Le Bulletin* (Rotary Club of Beirut), vol. 82, no. 48 (2012–2013): 9–10. I am also grateful to Ghada El Atrache for information on Asmahan.

34. Thompson, *Colonial Citizens,* 26.

35. I am grateful to Salim Tamari for the comment during a conversation.

36. Drew Gilpin Faust, *This Republic of Suffering: Death and the American Civil War* (New York: Vintage, 2009), 267.

37. Mouawad, "Grande guerre," 12–18, 26–29.

38. Mouawad, "Jamal Pacha," 441–444.

39. Ibid., 441, citing *Lisan al-hal,* September 2, 1924, May 5, 1922, May 6, 1922.

40. Ibid.

41. Ibid., 444.

42. Hourani made these points in class lectures as well as in *A History of the Arab Peoples* (Cambridge, MA: Harvard University Press, 1991), 295–298; see also other parts of chapter 17 and part 4.

43. *An Introduction to Kahlil Gibran,* ed. Suheil B. Bushrui (Beirut: Dar al-Mashreq, 1970), 52.

Acknowledgments

I would like to begin by thanking All Souls College, Oxford, and the Carnegie Corporation of New York, as well as the Fletcher School and the School of Arts and Sciences, both at Tufts University, for facilitating this project. Without their generous financial support and encouragement, this project would not have come to fruition. Larry Bacow, Jamshed Bharucha, Stephen Bosworth, and Peggy Newell were members of the Tufts University leadership team when I launched this project, and I am indebted to them for their support. Their successors at the university, including James Stavridis and Ian Johnstone, have continued that tradition. Jeswald Salacuse, a former dean and current professor at the Fletcher School, has been a source of inspiration straddling both eras.

I am privileged to teach at such an outstanding university as Tufts, and I would like to thank my colleagues for making the experience so rewarding. As any professor will attest, however, such a university requires an equally dedicated staff. I have profited from the excellent support of several Tufts centers and departments, and thank Don Button, Omar Dauhajre, Paulette Folkins, Lupita Freire, Annette Lazzara, Dan Modini, Diane Tan, and Christopher Zymaris for their professionalism.

This book rests on a wide array of resources, and I am thankful to all those who helped me gather these materials. I am grateful to the staff of Harvard's Widener

Library Access Services, most of all to Francesca Giacchino and to the staff of its Phillips room: Eugenia Dimant, Ellen Harris, Cynthia Hinds, and Neiel Israel. I also thank Michael Hopper and the librarians of the Harvard Middle Eastern Division, the Government Documents Unit, Andras Riedlmayer at the Harvard Fine Arts Library, and the staff at Imaging Services and at Library Privileges.

For facilitating requests for copyrights, I thank the publisher Dar el-Machreq as well as Mona Nsouli and the Institute for Palestine Studies in Beirut; the Middle East Centre Archive at St Antony's College, Oxford; and Cambridge University Press.

In France, I would like to thank the Archives nationales d'outre-mer, the Service des archives du port autonome de Marseille, and the Médiathèque de la maison méditerranéenne des sciences de l'homme (MMSH) at Aix-Marseille Université for opening their doors to me. Robert Ilbert and Brigitte Marin, past and current directors of MMSH, respectively, deserve special thanks. In Great Britain, I would like to acknowledge the staffs of Oxford University's Bodleian Library and All Souls College's Carrington Library, the British Library, and the National Archives. Debbie Usher assisted me at the Middle East Centre Archive at St Antony's College, Oxford. In Lebanon, I am grateful to Abdul-Rahim Abu-Husayn and the American University of Beirut's History Department, Carla Chalhoub and the Jafet Library; the Near East School of Theology; and the German Orient-Institut. At my home institution, Miriam Seltzer and her colleagues at the Ginn and Tisch Libraries proved efficient, helpful, and knowledgeable. I benefited from the research skills of Ricardo Borgesdecastro, Natalie Bowlus, Amelia Cook, Lauren Dorgan, Abeer Kazimi, Alex Nisetich, Lata Parwani, Julie Younes, and especially Joelle Boutros, Şakir Dinçşahin, Nicholas Kenney, Randa Baroody Tarazi, and Matteo Tomasini. Carole Corm has been a constant source of information, analysis, and research. I also thank the many students, former and present, who helped refine my thinking in the course of seminars probing the historical effects of wars on societies.

I am fortunate to know many scholars, colleagues, former students, and friends who contributed to my project in different ways. A big thanks, therefore, to Andrew Arsan, Christine Assaf, Alexandra Asseily, Ghada El Atrache, Nadim Baroody, Joyce Barsam, Aïda K. Boudjikanian, Asdghik Cortas, Leon Dermenjian, George Ellmore, Dalia Mroue Fateh, William Granara, Christophe Guilhou, Aida Hawila, Maha Kaddoura, Abbas Kelidar, Samir Khalaf, Rashid Khalidi, Youssef Khlat, Dickran Kouymjian, Nabil Nasrallah, Robin Ostle, Makram Rabah, Candice Raymond, Mohamad Rihan, Gary Roberts, Wilfrid J. Rollman, Salah and Wadad Salman, Camille Sawaya, Cyrus Schayegh, Joe Soussou, Camille Tarazi, Wheeler Thackston, Lorenzo Trombetta, and Andrei and Eugenia Vandoros.

Moreover, Alfred Sursock Cochrane, Yvonne Lady Cochrane, Carole Corm, Nadim Cortas, Ibrahim Najjar, June Rugh, William and Andrea Rugh, Randa

Baroody Tarazi, Lena and Naji Touma, Lorenzo Trombetta, June Rugh, and Kathy Dorman Wright granted me access to unpublished personal papers or facilitated access to private archives, recordings, illustrations, or contacts. Many of them answered multiple queries about sources, and offered helpful feedback. I am particularly grateful to Nadim Cortas for his valuable input and for bringing back to life a bygone era in Mount Lebanon.

I also am in debt to the readers selected by Harvard University Press for their endorsements. Their comments complemented the feedback I received from Feroz Ahmad, Sugata Bose, Aïda K. Boudjikanian, Nadim Cortas, Stephen Guerra, and Randa Baroody Tarazi, who graciously agreed to read some or all of the manuscript. I thank them all for their suggestions, attention to detail, and judicious judgment.

Peri Bearman edited the manuscript and I have depended on her professional support; I would also like to thank June Rugh, James Cappio, and Christine Dahlin for their additional editing. Nadim Shehadi assisted me with innumerable sources, contacts, archives, and illustrations. He is an authority on collections of visual materials for the Middle East, among other things, and his generosity has always been accompanied by good humor and cheer. Most of the photos used in this book are the product of his efforts and those of Carole Corm. Also helpful in locating and identifying photos were Christine Lindner, Maurice Missak Kelechian, Salim Tamari, Melanie Tanielian, Kamal Abu Husayn, Joelle Boutros, and Makram Rabah. For maps, I am in debt to the cartographer Isabelle Lewis, whom I had the good fortune of meeting through Harvard University Press. Together with Randa Baroody Tarazi and Joelle Boutros, I am responsible for translations from Arabic and French, except for sources that have already been published in English. In such cases, I have consulted the originals but most often I have quoted from the existing translations. I thank Şakir Dinçşahin for locating, translating, and analyzing essential primary and secondary sources from Turkish, and for his excellent assistance and ideas.

At Harvard University Press, Kathleen McDermott has been a joy to work with; I thank her for her knowledge, advice, and general support, and Andrew John Kinney for his effectiveness and responsiveness. Marc Goodheart, Sandra Spanier, Susan Kearney, and their colleagues at Harvard University's Loeb House eased my work. More generally, my affiliation with Harvard University has made for an exciting journey stretching over decades now. I am thankful for the many colleagues and friends who have enriched my life over the years.

Among the pioneers of research on Greater Syria during World War I are Najwa al-Qattan and Linda Schatkowski, and their work is central to mine. I thank them, as well as Feroz Ahmad, Hasan Kayali, Dina Rizk Khouri, Mohamad Rihan, and Lorenzo Trombetta for making their unpublished articles available to me. Gérard

D. Khoury also offered information and assistance on several occasions. Salim Tamari's innovative research on Palestine during World War I was immensely helpful; his generosity in sharing unpublished primary sources, secondary works and illustrations, and his vast information are humbling. I cannot think of many other scholars so willing to share their findings, and his research constitutes the starting point of much of what will be written on Ottoman Palestine and the rest of Ottoman Syria in World War I.

I am also grateful to a generation of historians that inspired and prepared me. Abdul-Karim Rafeq, our *ustadh* (teacher) par excellence, is a model of passion for knowledge, generosity, and modesty, who put up with numberless queries on the history of *bilad al-Sham*. Similarly, Feroz Ahmad, Abdul-Rahim Abu-Husayn, Nelly Hanna, Walid Khalidi, and, before them, Albert Hourani, David Landes, Kamal Salibi, and André Raymond have inspired generations of researchers; in my case, the debt also extends to educators in Lebanon. C. A. Bayly and Hew Strachan assisted me in their areas of historical expertise, and their own works remain standards in the field. I am privileged to have learned from them, and to have interacted with John Davies and the rest of the fellows and visiting fellows while on leave at All Souls College.

I have also found it rewarding and inspiring to become familiar with a new generation of exciting and brilliant young historians on whom we now depend for our work. This includes a groundbreaking initiative for the study of World War I in the Middle East and North Africa, led by Mustafa Aksakal and Elizabeth Thompson.

At the Carnegie Corporation, I am very thankful to Vartan Gregorian, who has gone out of his way at pivotal points in my career to offer his wise counsel. He is an inspiration.

Over the years, I have built a circle of advisers and friends on whose counsel and friendship I depend. I thank Abdul-Rahim Abu-Husayn, Ina Baghdiantz McCabe, Ali Banuazizi, Anne Betteridge, Sugata Bose, Selma Botman, Jeffrey Cox, John L. Esposito, William Graham, Ayesha Jalal, Joel Migdal, Malik Mufti, Richard Augustus Norton, Jeanne Penvenne, Mark Tessler, John O. Voll, and Ibrahim Warde for sharing their knowledge and talents, and Vali Nasr for his continued wise counsel. My greatest debt of all, however, goes to Peter Rough. As a brilliant student at the Fletcher School, it was self-evident that I would ask him to work as my research assistant on this book. Once committed to this project, he immersed himself in World War I and turned down a number of other professional opportunities. For fifteen months, we worked next to each other in Widener Library, and I gained lasting respect for his depth, breadth, attention to detail, tenacity, and grasp of the broad implications of the transformative effects of war. Although he began by focusing on particular aspects of the book, he quickly mastered all its themes and was invaluable in helping to shape and in editing the initial draft of the manuscript. I am grateful to Peter and all those listed above for their contributions, and for saving me from many errors. For any remaining mistakes, I alone am responsible.

My final debt is to my family. Hoda Saddi, Joumana Saddi Chaya, Dimitri Saddi, Nakhle, Randa, Carine, and Najeeb Tarazi, Leila Adib Fawaz, Rashid and Marcia Fawwaz, and our extended families are at the centers of my life. Towering as my central source of vitality and joy is my husband, Karim. In his youth, when he was a Davis Cup player and Lebanon's tennis champion for ten years, I was his most devoted fan. I still am, decades later, dazzled and enchanted to have had such a long and joyous journey next to him. I hope he views this book as partially his own, because I surely dedicate it to him.

Index